WALTER HILTON

THE SCALE OF PERFECTION

BOOK II

EARLY ENGLISH TEXT SOCIETY

O.S. 348

2017 for 2016

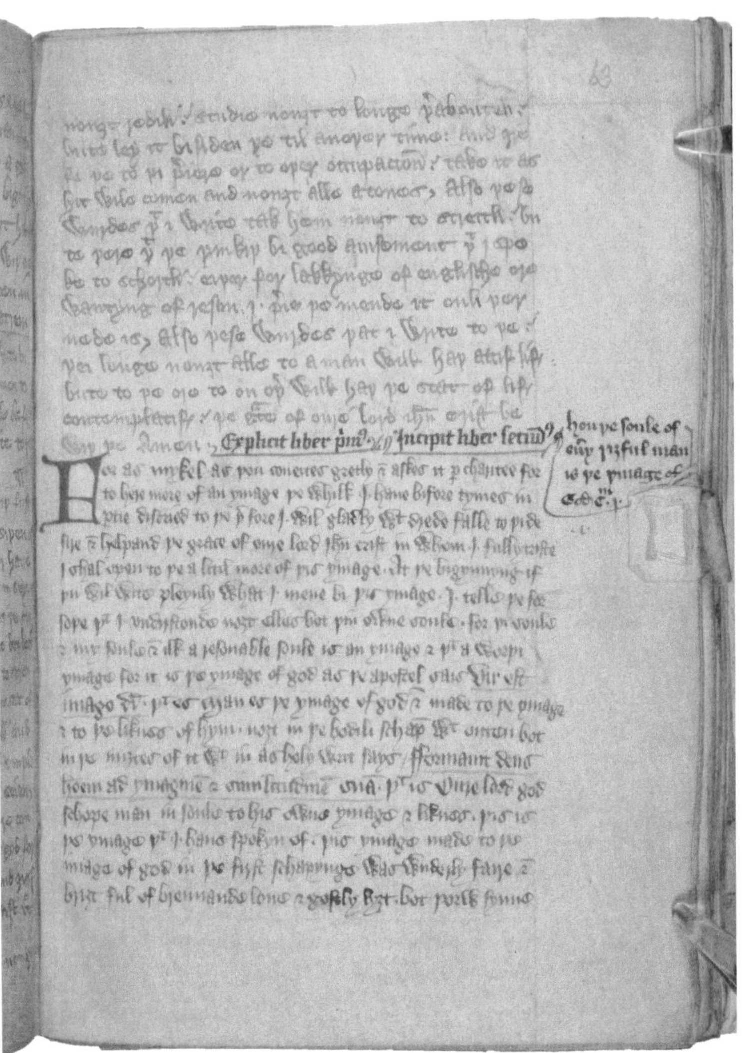

British Library MS Harley 6579, f. 63r. © The British Library Board

WALTER HILTON
THE SCALE OF PERFECTION
BOOK II

AN EDITION
BASED ON BRITISH LIBRARY MSS HARLEY
6573 AND 6579

BEGUN BY

S. S. HUSSEY

COMPLETED BY

MICHAEL G. SARGENT

Published for
THE EARLY ENGLISH TEXT SOCIETY
by the
OXFORD UNIVERSITY PRESS
2017 for 2016

OXFORD
UNIVERSITY PRESS

Great Clarendon Street, Oxford, OX2 6DP,
United Kingdom

Oxford University Press is a department of the University of Oxford. It furthers the University's objective of excellence in research, scholarship, and education by publishing worldwide. Oxford is a registered trade mark of Oxford University Press in the UK and in certain other countries

First edition published in 2017
Impression: 1

British Library Cataloguing in Publication Data
Data available

ISBN 9780198789093

Typeset by Alan Bennett, Oxford
Printed in Great Britain
on acid-free paper by
TJ International Ltd, Padstow, Cornwall

FOREWORD: S. S. HUSSEY (1925–2004)

At the time of Stan Hussey's death in 2004, the Council of the Early English Text Society committed itself to shepherding through the press his edition of the second book of *The Scale of Perfection*, a project on which he had worked for over forty years, and to which he continued to devote himself in the last months of his life. The Society now offers it in his memory, and in grateful acknowledgement of a life energetically well spent in the service of the subject he loved.

S. S. Hussey, universally known as Stan, was an enthusiastic, gifted, and humane scholar of medieval literature, Shakespeare, and the history of the English language. He was also a dedicated university teacher and an academic leader and administrator of great skill, perseverance, and versatility. His energy, humour, and warmth made him one of the most loved and respected of his generation of medieval English scholars. Physically and intellectually, Stan was a large presence in English medieval studies for over half a century. Tall and imposing, but with a persistent twinkle of kindness and amusement in his eyes, Stan was an ideal Head of Department, a kind but demanding external examiner, an acute assessor for appointments, and a trusted chairman of potentially troublesome committees. Calm, meticulously well prepared, clear about his strategic aims, and lacking in personal grandeur or professional egotism, he was a reassuring presence in any academic milieu, and a reliable and heavyweight contributor to any academic publication. Though much of his long career was spent nurturing English studies at the new University of Lancaster, he was a widely respected, quietly effective, and unfailingly influential figure in the development of the discipline nationally and internationally. His plain dealing, common sense, and obvious dedication to scholarship and intellectual integrity won him the lasting affection and professional admiration of his colleagues.

Stanley Stewart Hussey was born in Trowbridge, Wiltshire, on 14 May 1925, and was educated at Trowbridge High School. On leaving school in 1943, he joined the RAF, serving in Egypt and Cyprus. (It was typical of his personal modesty that, like many of his generation, he never talked about his military service.) After demobilization in

1947, Stan entered University College London to read English. Already revealing his legendary appetite for heavy workloads, he completed the three-subject 'Inter' year (compulsory for ex-servicemen) and the subsequent English Honours course in three years rather than the more usual four. He graduated with First Class Honours in 1950 and was rewarded with a two-year Assistantship in the UCL English department. In 1952 he completed his MA (awarded 'with mark of distinction') on 'Eighty Years of *Piers Plowman* Scholarship: A Study of Critical Methods'. Typically, Stan had chosen to study one of the major keystones of Middle English literature. *Piers Plowman* was then, and remains now, a text marked by ferocious textual difficulties, challenging editorial problems, and embedded and pugnaciously defended critical views. Described by one of the poem's finest recent scholars, Anne Middleton, as 'unequalled in the published literature', Stan's dissertation marked the beginning of a long scholarly association with Langland, resulting in his 1969 volume *Piers Plowman: Critical Approaches*, a book which continues to offer succour and comfort to struggling undergraduates.

From 1952 until 1966, Stan was first Assistant Lecturer and then Lecturer in English at the then Queen Mary College, London (now Queen Mary, University of London), and during this time he completed his doctoral thesis (1962), an edition of Book II of Walter Hilton's *Scale of Perfection.* Stan's work on the *Scale* became the silken thread that held together his diverse and catholic intellectual tastes. Hilton (d. 1396), a Cambridge canon lawyer, eschewed a potentially glamorous career in episcopal service, eventually and finally to become an Augustinian canon at the order's house in Thurgarton, Notts. Unlike more contemplative monastic orders, Augustinian canons followed a mixed life of pastoral service and ruminative scholarship, and that same mixture of vocations characterized Stan's own career, in which he balanced often thankless but necessary and valuable public service in various branches of university administration against refreshing spells of research, scholarship, and editorial work on the *Scale*, with the bridge between both lives being his dedicated and enthusiastic work as a modestly understated but very effective lecturer and teacher.

In 1966, Stan, his wife Joyce (whom he had met when they were both English students at UCL), and their young son David moved to the new University of Lancaster, where he was successively Senior

Lecturer (1966–8), Reader (1968–74), and then Professor from 1974 until his nominal retirement in 1991. During these years, Stan was heavily involved in building (sometimes literally) a new academic community, and in influencing, shaping, and often leading the development of English studies to occupy a leading role in the life of the new institution. Widely recognized by his colleagues as a gifted committee-man and an effective Chairman, Stan served during these years on most of the key planning and policy committees of the University, and sought to inscribe his strongly held but mildly expressed intellectual and cultural values into the University's policies. At the same time, he published lively, scholarly, and accessible books on *Chaucer* (1971) and *The Literary Language of Shakespeare* (1982). Both books later received revised second editions, a clear token of their success in meeting the needs of their readership and in shaping contemporary critical views. After his retirement, he published *The English Language: Structure and Development* (1995), a clear and accessible synthesis of his years of study and teaching the subject. Alongside the books, a steady series of important articles ranged across most of the major texts of Middle English literature. Through his publications, Stan was able to open up challenging and complex authors for many generations of undergraduates, graduates, and scholars.

Middle English devotional and contemplative writing occupied a special place in Stan Hussey's scholarly affections. He and Joyce participated energetically in a series of conferences on Carthusian spirituality organized in Austria by James Hogg in the early 1980s, and they were both a source of great encouragement and support to several generations of new scholars beginning to work on the English mystics. His published work on the writings of the medieval English mystical tradition, and above all on the works of Walter Hilton, helped to prepare the way for the remarkable efflorescence since 1980 of scholarship and editorial activity in this now vibrant area of English studies. As early as 1956, he had published an article on 'Langland, Hilton and the Three Lives' in *RES*, NS 7, followed by an important investigation of 'The Text of *The Scale of Perfection*, Book II' in *Neuphilologische Mitteilungen*, 65 (1964), and a thoughtful and perceptive analysis of 'Latin and English in *The Scale of Perfection*' in *Mediæval Studies*, 35 (1973). In 1989, he contributed a typically wide-ranging and wise account of 'The Audience for the Middle English Mystics' to Michael Sargent's collection of essays *De Cella in*

Seculum: Religious and Secular Life and Devotion in Late Medieval England. His ongoing work on the many manuscripts of both books of Hilton's *Scale* gave him an unequalled vantage point to survey the audience for English contemplative writing, and the ways in which these texts circulated in later medieval England.

Like the man himself, Stan's writings were notable for the patient clarity of their exposition, the completeness of their address to the topic under discussion, and the patent humanity, critical even-handedness, and intellectual fair-mindedness of their attention to the subject under discussion. It was entirely fitting, therefore, that Stan gave the opening paper at the first symposium on *The Medieval Mystical Tradition in England* in Exeter in 1980, for his own work had done much to prepare the ground for the revival of interest in and scholarly attention to such texts. His title that day, 'Walter Hilton: Traditionalist?', may have had a touch of autobiography in it, for Stan was not much taken with the waves of literary and cultural theory then beginning to sweep through British universities. But his active participation in each of the following meetings of the *Mystical Tradition* symposium established him as the paterfamilias of UK mystical studies. At the meeting in July 2004, shortly before his death in October that year, Stan presided over the opening session with characteristic geniality, wickedly impish humour, and genuine affection for a group of scholars and authors whom he had grown to love. His affection was generously returned, even by contributors who had not been born at the time of that first meeting in 1980.

Over many decades, Stan discussed and debated the production, dissemination, and reception of Hilton's *Scale* with Professor Alan Bliss, who was engaged in editing the first book of the *Scale*. The different textual histories of the two books led Bliss and Hussey to develop somewhat different opinions about the relative authority and priority of particular copies, and Stan's natural courtesy and gentleness sometimes found it hard to sustain his own views in the face of Bliss's more trenchantly and emphatically expressed opinions. These exchanges, conducted privately and in print, led to both editors repeatedly revisiting their collations and stemmata, and often tweaking their edited texts. For both editors and for their families, Hilton became a powerful if often elusive and enigmatic presence in their lives for many decades, and at their deaths they both left behind them a dizzying paper trail of versions, recensions, and variants, reflecting the complexity and the profound intellectual challenges of editing such a work.

A few years after Alan Bliss's death in 1985, and with the Bliss family's consent and cooperation, Michael Sargent was invited by Council to complete Bliss's editorial work on *Scale* I. Stan Hussey later began extensive and lively discussions of Hilton's text with Sargent, drawing on his expertise in editing another complex large-corpus text, Nicholas Love's *Mirror of the Blessed Life of Jesus Christ*, a work closely contemporary with the *Scale*. So, when Hussey died, it was agreed to ask Sargent to take on the very significant additional burden of completing *Scale* II. The Council of the Society is profoundly indebted to Michael Sargent for his willingness to reconstruct, reassess, and see through to press the editorial work of both these scholars. This hugely challenging and demanding process has been helped by his clear and subtle grasp of the textual complications attending the transmission of both parts of the *Scale*. In publishing the present volume, Council is especially grateful for his meticulous and sensitive work on the text of *Scale* II, and for the skill, thoroughness, and sympathy with which he has revisited, refreshed, and re-presented Stan Hussey's life's work, using his own exceptional theoretical and practical understanding of complex textual traditions.

Vincent Gillespie, Honorary Director

PREFACE

The present edition stems from the scholarly consensus of the mid-twentieth century that the differences in textual history of the two books of *The Scale of Perfection* were great enough to justify their separation into two distinct editorial projects, each of which was to be undertaken for the EETS. At the suggestion of Helen Gardner, Rosemary Birts (later Dorward) produced a specimen edition of a central section of the text of *Scale* I. This project was eventually taken up by T. P. Dunning and A. J. Bliss. At Bliss's death, Michael Sargent undertook, at the request of EETS Council and with the kind permission of the Bliss family, to complete his unfinished edition, work on which continues actively at this point. Stan Hussey produced a recensionist edition of *Scale* II for his doctoral thesis in 1962. Hussey continued to work on *Scale* II for another forty years, producing an edition in which he argued for a bifurcate stemma, one branch of which (**x**) was based on BL MS Harley 6579, and the other (**y**) on Lambeth Palace Library MS 472. He further argued that the **y** form of the text was an expanded version of **x**, and was itself further expanded in Fishlake's Latin version. This edition was returned to him with the observation that he had demonstrated the difference, but not the derivation, of **y** from **x**, and the recommendation that he produce a two-text edition. Hussey produced this edition months before his death in 2004, and it was accepted subject to final revisions. Since I had been working on the textual history of the *Scale* since the 1970s, and on the revision of the Bliss edition of *Scale* I since the 1990s, I offered to undertake the revision of Hussey's edition for publication, with the approval of EETS Council and the permission of Joyce Hussey.

The status of the edition proved, however, to be more complex than appeared on the surface. In part, this was a difficulty of the times in which the editorial work was done: both Bliss's and Hussey's recensionist editions were produced before the publication of George Kane and Talbot Donaldson's Athlone edition of the B-Text of *Piers Plowman*. Hussey responded in a short article to the shift in editorial theory advanced by that edition, but it must be recognized that an argument for genealogical relations among manuscript versions of a text that was put forward in the mid- to late-twentieth century would not have been seen at the time to need the support of the amount of evidence that must be mustered today. Neither Bliss's nor Hussey's editions provided this level of evidence. The second problem with Hussey's textual argument is one familiar to any editor of a text that has been revised by its author: parts of Hussey's final edition that were retained from his original version either duplicate or contradict parts that have been revised. This was particularly a problem with the argument for the internal relations of the manuscripts of **x** and **y**, and the relation of the two to each other. The only way to sort this out was to return to the original collations and compile the evidence anew; but the original collations no longer exist. It remained for me to collate the manuscripts and compile the evidence again.

In the article that I contributed to the volume *Probable Truth*, I explained what I had discovered at the point that I had collated all of the manuscripts of Hussey's **x** tradition, but only two of **y** (for comparison). This collation demonstrated the fundamental soundness of Hussey's description of the internal relations of the **x** manuscript group. When I had completed the collation and the compilation of results for Hussey's **y** group, however, I found that the manuscripts that did not agree with **x** do not constitute a single group: they agree only in that they are not **x** texts. This required a complete reconceptualization of the editorial project. The Lambeth Palace manuscript, I found, was representative only of a small group of surviving manuscripts circulating in London in the fifteenth century. The other manuscripts of Hussey's **y** group had other group affiliations, or none at all. Noting that Bodleian MS Rawlinson C.285 represents an equally large cluster of manuscripts, I briefly considered whether the best solution might be a pair of volumes presenting four different manuscripts of the text, but was quickly and firmly dissuaded by Ralph Hanna and Nicholas Watson. Because Harley 6573 presents the closest to a normative text among the surviving manuscripts, I have chosen it as the base text of a two-text edition. Stan Hussey's text, based on Harley 6579——but lacking the **y**-based 'corrections' that a recensionist construction of the ideal text had required——is presented on the facing page.

Hussey's editorial practice and mine vary slightly. I tend to be more sceptical of the idea that an overstroke represents a suspended nasal letter, but I have changed his text only in cases that appear to be etymologically and phonologically improbable (e.g. 'Johun' for

'John', 'borun' for 'born', and initial 'coun-' and 'coum-' for 'con-' and 'com-'). Hussey's sense of punctuation and of sentence and paragraph boundaries and mine differ (even taking into account my tendency to North American practice). In some cases I have yielded to his reading of the text; in others I have allowed the difference between his text and mine to stand. A number of these differences, of course, derive from differences in wording in the two manuscripts on which our texts are based.

The critical apparatus, representing all readings of all manuscripts, has been completely reconstructed on the basis of Harley 6573, although its original skeleton is that of Hussey's edition. Elements of his brief manuscript descriptions have been incorporated into the more extensive descriptions of the present edition. The same is true of the Explanatory Notes. Hussey had originally produced separate sets of textual and explanatory notes; these, upon advice, have been combined into a single series and expanded considerably. The Glossary, likewise, is a revised and expanded version of what he originally produced. Hussey also produced a critical edition Book II of Thomas Fishlake's Latin version of the *Scale*. When they offer evidence of the English text on which it was based, readings from this text are included in the critical apparatus; these readings and others that demonstrate Fishlake's revision of the text of the *Scale* into something more devotional and Christocentric are discussed in the Explanatory Notes.

As Stan Hussey noted in his final version of the edition of *Scale* II, an edition which has been so long in the making as this one has must inevitably be indebted to the support of many scholars, only a few of whom can be thanked here. Both he and I owe an enormous debt to our mentors and graduate supervisors, Phyllis Hodgson and Edmund Colledge, and to the examiners of our doctoral dissertations, George Kane for Stan Hussey, and Stan Hussey for me. We also acknowledge, with thanks, help from the libraries whose collections include the manuscripts of *Scale* II, and especially the British Library, for permission to quote and reproduce plates from the base manuscripts. We are grateful, he to Helen Gardner and to Joy Russell-Smith for the gift of microfilm and to the universities of London and Lancaster for support in the form of study leave; and I to Wilma Fitzgerald of the Pontifical Institute of Mediaeval Studies and Monique Prince of the Library of Baruch College, CUNY, for assistance with provision of and access to microfilms. I am also thankful to the Research

Foundation of the Professional Staff Congress of the City University of New York for funding a series of research trips to examine the manuscripts of *Scale* II in seven different countries on three continents, to correct transcripts and collations made from microfilm copies by comparison with the originals. Finally, this edition would not have taken the form it has, nor been completed as soon, had it not been for a year's research leave from Queens College, CUNY in 2012–13, a fellowship from the American Council of Learned Societies in support of that leave, and a Visiting Fellowship at Magdalen College, Oxford that enabled me to get the necessary work done.

Stan Hussey and I share a number of debts of gratitude: to Ian Doyle, of whom Hussey noted that, 'like so many others, [we] have profited from his unrivalled knowledge in this field'. John Clark's publications, culminating in the Introduction and Notes to the Paulist Press modernization by Rosemary Dorward and himself, have many times put us right about the theological background. Great thanks also to Anne Hudson and Ralph Hanna, who spent much time on the drafts of this edition and are responsible for considerable improvements to it; and to Roger Ellis, Vincent Gillespie, Malcolm Godden, and James Hogg. I would also add a note of thanks to Stephen Kelly and Ryan Perry, and my colleagues in New York, Valerie Allen, Jennifer Brown, Glenn Burger, Matthew Goldie, Steven Kruger, Marlene Hennessey, and Nicole Rice, for useful conversations on textual-critical theory. Special thanks must go to Helen Spencer, Editorial Secretary of EETS, for her skill, patience, and encouragement, and to Bonnie Blackburn for turning our text into something that works (beautifully) on a printed page. As Hussey notes, 'the contributions of all the above have made this edition much better than it would otherwise have been, but if the editor's decision is final so must be his responsibility'.

In all of this, it is my hope that the end product represents the addition of strength to strength, and not of weakness to weakness. My intention has been to bring Stan Hussey's edition forward in a way that responds to critical issues and approaches with which he did not engage because they were not present, or were not yet as prominent, as they are now. For the final form of the edition, I must take responsibility. The credit for editing *Scale* II is something that I am pleased and honoured to share with him; I hope that he would also have been pleased to share it with me.

Stan's last thanks go to his wife Joyce, 'who can probably no longer contemplate a life without the ghostly presence of Walter Hilton'; mine go to my wife, Ann Day, who looks forward to the day when *Scale* II is off my desk at last.

M.G.S.

Queens College of the City University of New York

CONTENTS

LIST OF ILLUSTRATIONS

PLATES

FIGURE

SIGLA OF MANUSCRIPTS AND EARLY PRINTS

A	London, British Library Additional MS 11748 (*Scale* I and II: English)
Ad	London, British Library Additional MS 37049 (*Scale* I and II: extracts in English)
Ad_2	London, British Library Additional MS 37790 (*Scale* I and II: extracts in English)
As	Oxford, All Souls College MS 25 (*Scale* I and II: English)
B	Oxford, Bodleian Library MS Bodley 100 (*Scale* I and II: English)
B_2	Oxford, Bodleian Library MS Bodley 584 (*Scale* II: Latin)
B_3	Oxford, Bodleian Library MS Bodley 592 (*Scale* I and II: English)
B_4	Oxford, Bodleian Library MS Lat. theol. e. 26 (*Scale* I and II: Latin)
Bn	Paris, Bibliothèque nationale de France, MS latin 3610 (*Scale* I and II: Latin)
Br	Brussels, Bibliothèque royale de Belgique MS 2544–5 (*Scale* I and II: English)
C	Cambridge, University Library MS Additional 6686 (*Scale* I: English)
Cc	Cambridge, Corpus Christi College MS R.5 (James 268) (*Scale* I and II: English)
Ch	Chatsworth (*Scale* I and II: English)
D	Cambridge, University Library MS Dd.v.55 (*Scale* I: English)
E	Cambridge, University Library MS Ee.iv.30 (*Scale* I and II: English)
Ed	Edinburgh Fragments (present location unknown) (*Scale* I: English)
Es	Modena, Biblioteca Estense Universitaria MS Lat. 999 (*Scale* I and II: Latin)
F	Cambridge, University Library MS Ff.v.40 (*Scale* I: English)

H	London, British Library MS Harley 6579 (*Scale* I and II: English)
H_2	London, British Library MS Harley 330 (*Scale* I: English; *Scale* II: Latin)
H_3	London, British Library MS Harley 1022 (*Scale* I: English)
H_4	London, British Library MS Harley 1035 (*Scale* I: English)
H_5	London, British Library MS Harley 2387 (*Scale* I and II: English)
H_6	London, British Library MS Harley 2397 (*Scale* II: English)
H_7	London, British Library MS Harley 6573 (*Scale* I and II: English)
H_8	London, British Library MS Harley 6576 (*Scale* I and II: Latin)
H_9	London, British Library MS Harley 6615 (*Scale* I: extract in English)
He	New Haven, Yale University, Beinecke Library, Prof. T. Takamiya's MS (*olim* Heneage 3083) (*Scale* I and II: Latin)
Hu	San Marino, Calif., Huntington Library MS HM 112 (*Scale* I: English)
Hu_2	San Marino, Calif., Huntington Library MS HM 266 (*Scale* I and II: English)
J	Cambridge, St John's College MS G.35 (James 202) (*Scale* I: English)
Jo	Oxford, St John's College MS 77 (*Scale* II: extract in Latin)
L	London, Lambeth Palace Library MS 472 (*Scale* I and II: English)
Ld	Oxford, Bodleian Library MS Laud misc. 602 (*Scale* I and II: English)
Ln	London, British Library Lansdowne MS 362 (*Scale* I: English)
Lt	Longleat House Library MS 298 (*Scale* I: English)
Lw	New Haven, Yale University, Beinecke Library, Prof. T. Takamiya's MS 3 (*olim* Luttrell Wynne) (*Scale* I and II: English)

M	Cambridge, Magdalene College MS F.4.17 (*Scale* II: English)
Ma	Marseilles, Bibliothèque municipale MS 729 (*Scale* I and II: Latin)
Mo	Oxford, Magdalen College MS 141 (*Scale* I: Latin)
N	Edinburgh, National Library of Scotland MS 6126 (*Scale* I: English)
Na	Naples, Biblioteca nazionale MS VII.G.31 (*Scale* I: Latin)
No	Julian Notary, 1507 (*STC* 14043) (*Scale* I and II: English)
P	London, Inner Temple Library MS Petyt 524 (*Scale* I and II: English)
Pl	New York, Columbia University Library Plimpton MS 257 (*Scale* I and II: English)
Pn	Philadelphia, University of Pennsylvania Library MS Codex 1559 (*olim* New York: Hispanic Society of America) (*Scale* I and II: Latin)
Pr	Princeton, Princeton University Library Taylor MS 22 (*olim* John Shirwood) (*Scale* I and II: Latin)
R	Oxford, Bodleian Library MS Rawlinson C.285 (*Scale* I and II: English)
R_2	Oxford, Bodleian Library MS Rawlinson C.397 (*Scale* I and II: Latin)
R_3	Oxford, Bodleian Library MS Rawlinson C.894 (*Scale* I: extracts in English)
Ri	Ripon Cathedral fragment (*Scale* II)
Ro	London, British Library MS Royal 17 C XVIII (*Scale* I: extracts in English)
Ry	Liverpool University Library MS Rylands F.4.10 (*Scale* I: English)
S	London, British Library Additional MS 22283 (Simeon) (*Scale* I: English)
Sr	Philadelphia, University of Pennsylvania Library MS Codex 218 (*olim* Stonor) (*Scale* I and II: English)
St	Stonyhurst College MS A.vi.24 (*Scale* I: English)
T	Cambridge, Trinity College MS B.15.18 (James 354) (*Scale* I and II: English)
T_2	Cambridge, Trinity College MS O.7.47 (James 1375) (*Scale* I: English)

Td	Dublin, Trinity College MS A.5.7 (122) (*Scale* II: extracts in English)
Td_2	Dublin, Trinity College MS C.5.20 (352) (*Scale* I and II: extracts in English)
T^G	Corrections by James Grenehalgh in T
Th	Lincoln Cathedral Chapter Library MS 91 (A.5.2.: Thornton) (*Scale* I: extract in English
U	Oxford, University College MS 28 (*Scale* I: English)
Up	Uppsala, Universitetsbibliotek MS C.159 (*Scale* I and II: Latin)
Up_2	Uppsala, Universitetsbibliotek MS C.618 (*Scale* I and II: Latin)
Ut	Utrecht, Universiteitsbibliotheek MS 5.F.34 (*Scale* I and II: Latin)
V	Oxford, Bodleian Library MS Eng. poet. a.1 (Vernon) (*Scale* I: English)
W	Wynkyn de Worde, 1494 (*STC* 14042) (*Scale* I and II: English)
W_2	Wynkyn de Worde, 1519 (*STC* 14043.5) (*Scale* I and II: English)
W_3	Wynkyn de Worde, 1525 (*STC* 14044) (*Scale* I and II: English)
W_4	Wynkyn de Worde, 1533 (*STC* 14045) (*Scale* I and II: English)
Wc	London, Westminster Cathedral Treasury MS 4 (*Scale* I and II: extracts in English)
W^G	Corrections by James Grenehalgh in the Rosenbach copy of W
Wo	Worcester Cathedral Chapter Library MS F.172 (*Scale* I: English)
Ws	London, Westminster School MS 4 (*Scale* I and II: English)
Y	York, Dean and Chapter Library MS xvi.K.5 (*Scale* I and II: Latin)

ABBREVIATIONS

Anselm, *Opera*	*Sancti Anselmi Cantuariensis archiepiscopi Opera Omnia*, ed. F. S. Schmidt, ii (Edinburgh, 1946)
Aquinas, *ST*	Thomas Aquinas, *Summa Theologiae*, ed. J.-P. Migne, 4 vols. (Paris, 1860)
Augustine, *Civ. Dei*	Augustine, *De Civitate Dei*, CCSL 47–8 (Turnhout, 1955); *PL* 41
Conf.	Augustine, *Confessionum libri XI*, CCSL 27 (Turnhout, 1981); *PL* 32: 659–867
De Doct. christ.	Augustine, *De Doctrina christiana*, CCSL 32 (Turnhout, 1962), 1–167; *PL* 34: 15–122
De Quanti. anim.	Augustine, *De Quantitate animae*, *PL* 32: 1035–80
De Trin.	Augustine, *De Trinitate*, CCSL 50–50A (Turnhout, 1968); *PL* 42: 819–1098
Enar. in Psalm.	Augustine, *Enarrationes in Psalmos*, CCSL 38–40 (Turnhout, 1956); *PL* 36–7
Serm.	Augustine, *Sermones*, CCSL 41 (Turnhout, 1961–); *PL* 38–9
Tract. in Ep. Ioan.	Augustine, *Tractatus in Epistolam Ioanni ad Parthos*; *PL* 35: 1977–2062
Bernard, *Opera*	*Sancti Bernardi Opera Omnia*, ed. Jean Leclercq, Henri Rochais, and C. H. Talbot (Rome, 1957–98)
De Dilig. Deo	Bernard, *De Diligendo Deo*, in *Opera*, iii (1963), 109–54; *PL* 182: 971–1000
De Grad. Hum.	Bernard, *De Gradibus humilitatis et superbiae*, in *Opera*, iii. 1–59; *PL* 182: 939–72
Qui Hab.	Bernard, *Sermones in Psalmo 'Qui habitat'*, in *Opera*, iv (1966), 383–492; *PL* 183: 185–254
Serm. in Quad.	Bernard, *Sermones in Quadragesima*, in *Opera*, iv. 353–80; *PL* 183: 173–86
Sermon. super Cant.	Bernard, *Sermones super Canticum*, *Opera*, i–ii (1957–8); *PL* 183: 785–1198
Birgitta of Sweden, *Rev.*	*Sancta Birgitta: Revelaciones*, 12 vols. (Uppsala, 1956–2002)

Bonaventure, *Opera*	S. *Bonaventuræ Opera* (Quaracchi, 1882–1902)
In Sent.	Bonaventure, *Commentaria in quatuor libros sententiarum*, *Opera*, x (1902)
Med. vitae	Bonaventure, *Meditationes vitae Christi*, ed. A. C. Peltier, *S. Bonaventuræ Opera Omnia*, xii (Paris, 1868)
CCSL	Corpus Christianorum Series Latina
de Ricci, *Census*	Seymour de Ricci and W. J. Wilson, *Census of Medieval and Renaissance Manuscripts in the United States and Canada*, 2 vols. (New York, 1935–40)
DIMEV	*Digital Index of Middle English Verse* website: www.dimev.net
DR	*Downside Review*
Emden, *BRUO*	A. B. Emden, *A Biographical Register of the University of Oxford to A.D. 1500* (Oxford, 1958)
EW	*English Writing of Richard Rolle, Hermit of Hampole*, ed. Hope Emily Allen (Oxford, 1931)
Gregory, *Hom. in Ezech.*	Gregory the Great, *Homilia in Ezekielem*, CCSL 142 (Turnhout, 1971); *PL* 76: 785–1072
Hanna, *EMRR*	Hanna, Ralph, *The English Manuscripts of Richard Rolle: A Descriptive Catalogue* (Exeter, 2010)
Hilton, *Ad Quemdam*	Walter Hilton, *Ad Quemdam seculo renunciare volentem*, in *LW*, ii. 245–98
An Exposition	*An Exposition of Qui Habitat and Bonum Est in English*, ed. Björn Wallner, Lund Studies in English, 23 (Lund, 1954)
Angels' Song	*Of Angels' Song*, cited from *English Mystics*, ed. Windeatt, 131–6; see also *Two Minor Works* and *YW*, i. 175–82
Bonum est	*An Exposition of . . . 'Bonum Est'*, in Wallner, *Exposition*, 51–92
De Ador. imag.	*De Adoracione Imaginum*, *LW*, i. 175–214
De Imag. pec.	*De Imagine peccati*, in *LW*, i. 69–102

De Lecc.	*Epistola de Leccione, Intencione, Oracione, Meditacione et aliis*, in *LW*, ii. 215–43
De Util.	*De Utilitate et prerogativis religionis*, in *LW*, i. 103–73
Eight Chapters	*Eight Chapters on Perfection*, cited from *English Mystics*, ed. Windeatt, 137–48; see also *Two Minor Works*
Epist. ad Quem.	*Epistola ad Quemdam seculo renunciare volentem*, in *LW*, ii. 245–98
Minor Works	See *Minor Works*, ed. Jones
Mixed Life	*Epistle on Mixed Life*, cited from *English Mystics*, ed. Windeatt, 108–30; see also *Walter Hilton's Mixed Life, Edited from Lambeth Palace MS 472*, ed. S. J. Ogilvie-Thomson, Salzburg Studies in English Literature: Elizabethan & Renaissance Studies, 92:15 (Salzburg, 1986)
Qui habitat	*An Exposition of 'Qui Habitat'*, in *An Exposition*, ed. Wallner, 1–50; extracts in *English Mystics*, ed. Windeatt
Two Minor Works	*Two Minor Works of Walter Hilton: The Inner Temple MS of Walter Hilton's 'Eight Chapters on Perfection' and 'Of Angels' Song'*, ed. Fumio Kuriyagawa and Toshiyuki Takamiya (Tokyo, 1980)
IMEP	*Index of Middle English Prose*, Handlist series, 22 vols. Cambridge, 1984–
IMEV	*The Index of Middle English Verse*, by Carleton Brown and Rossel Hope Robbins (New York, 1943); see also *DIMEV*
Ker, *MLGB*	Ker, N. R., *Medieval Libraries of Great Britain: A List of Surviving Books*, 2nd edn. (London, 1964)
LALME	*A Linguistic Atlas of Later Middle English*, ed. A. McIntosh, M. L. Samuels, and M. Benskin, with M. Laing and K. Williamson, 4 vols. (Aberdeen,1986), www.lel.ed.ac.uk/ihd/elalme/elalme.html
MÆ	*Medium Ævum*

MED	*Middle English Dictionary*, ed. Hans Kurath and Sherman Kuhn (Ann Arbor, 1952–2001), www.quod.lib.umich.edu/m/med/
MMTE	*The Medieval Mystical Tradition in England*, ed. Marion Glasscoe (vols. 1–2: Exeter, 1980–2; vols. 3–6: Cambridge, 1984–99) and E. A. Jones (vols. 7–8: Cambridge, 2004–13)
PL	*Patrologiæ Latinæ Cursus Completus*, ed. J.-P. Migne
Peter Lombard, *Sent.*	Peter Lombard, *Sententiarum libri quatuor*, *PL* 192: 519–964
Priv. Couns.	*The Book of Privy Counselling*, in *Cloud*, 135–72
SC	*Summary Catalogue of Western Manuscripts in the Bodleian Library at Oxford* (7 vols.; Oxford, 1895–1953)
STC	A *Short-Title Catalogue of Books Printed in England, Scotland, and Ireland, and of English Books Printed Abroad, 1475–1640*, ed. A. W. Pollard and G. R. Redgrave, 2nd edn., completed by Katharine F. Pantzer (London, 1976–86)
YW	*Yorkshire Writers: Richard Rolle and his Followers*, ed. C. Horstmann, 2 vols. (London, 1895–6; repr. in 1 vol. with a new preface by Anne Clark Bartlett (Woodbridge, Suffolk, 1999)

INTRODUCTION

Over the course of a writing career spanning most of the last three decades of the fourteenth century, Walter Hilton wrote several works of spiritual guidance in response to requests from a variety of people who had asked him to provide them with advice on how to live a more perfect Christian life. To fellow clerics, he wrote Latin letters on the rejection of secular life and on the superiority of the religious orders; to a well-to-do layman who wished to take up the contemplative life in the midst of his worldly obligations, he wrote his famous English letter *On Mixed Life*. To a woman who had recently been enclosed as an anchoress, he wrote the most prominent of these responses, the two-part work known as *The Scale of Perfection*. The first book of the *Scale* is closely directed to his interlocutor's need for guidance in introspective meditation since, as Hilton notes, she was not capable of the traditional monastic exercise of reading the Latin text of Scripture, and meditation and prayer based on that reading. The second book of the *Scale*, written perhaps ten years later, offers no less than a complete textbook on the theology of salvation and spiritual progress from the 'reformation in faith' of the deformed image of God in the sinful human soul to the 'reformation in faith and in feeling' that is the contemplative life.

Scale I circulated widely across England and survives without the second book in nineteen complete or originally complete manuscripts, to two of which the second book was added by different hands. The two books of the *Scale* survive together in twenty-one originally complete manuscripts; the second book alone in two (see Table 1). In one manuscript, an English copy of *Scale* I is followed by a Latin copy of *Scale* II. The two-book *Scale* is particularly prominent among the copies belonging to the monks and nuns of the Carthusian and Brigittine orders, and to London book owners. Hilton's *Scale of Perfection* and, probably, the *Mixed Life* were read and referred to by Nicholas Love and Margery Kempe.

The *Scale* continued to be influential into the sixteenth century and beyond: it was printed by Wynkyn de Worde in 1494, together with the *Mixed Life*, at the request of Lady Margaret Beaufort; it was recommended to the pious faithful by Thomas More; and it was printed another four times before the Reformation in England. The

TABLE 1. Manuscript distribution of the texts of *Scale* I and *Scale* II in English and Latin

Of the seventy manuscripts of Hilton's *Scale of Perfection* fifty-two are in English, seventeen in Latin, and one combines the two languages.

Language	Manuscripts
English	
Scale I only	C, D, F, H_3, H_4, Hu, J, Ln, Lt, N, Ry, S, St, T_2, U, V, Wo + H, R (*Scale* II added in other hands)
Scale I + Latin *Scale* II	H_2
Scale I and II	A, As, B, B_3, Br, Cc, Ch, E, H, H_5, H_7, Hu_2, L, Ld, Lw, P, R, Pl, Sr, T, Ws
Scale II only	H_6, M
Scale I fragments or extracts	Ed, H_9, R_3, Ro, Th
Scale II fragments or extracts	Ri, Td
Scale I and II fragments or extracts	Td_2, Wc, Ad_4, Ad_7
Latin	
Scale I and II	B_4, Bn, Es, H_8, He, Ma, Pn, Pr, R_2, Up, Up_2, Ut, Y
Scale I	Mo, Na
Scale II	B_2+H_2
Scale II extract	Jo+

later incunable editions of the *Scale* were all based on the Wynkyn de Worde *editio princeps*, and one seventeenth-century manuscript and a modernized seventeenth-century edition were based on these. This was further modernized, and the text much altered, by the seventeenth-century English Benedictine Serenus Cressy; the Cressy version was published in the nineteenth century, as was an English modernization based on the Wynkyn de Worde text. A French translation based on the de Worde text and an English modernization by Evelyn Underhill based on an examination of ten manuscripts were both published in 1923.

1. DESCRIPTION OF THE MANUSCRIPTS AND EARLY PRINTS

Only manuscripts comprising English *Scale* II are described here; manuscripts comprising *Scale* I alone will be described in the edition of *Scale* I.[1]

[1] I wish to thank Ian Doyle and Ralph Hanna for their assistance in compiling the following descriptions.

Complete or Originally Complete Manuscripts of *Scale* II in English

A: London, British Library Add. MS 11748 s. xv$^{1-2}$

Parchment. 145 ff. (numbered 1–147 in pencil, counting two modern flyleaves).[2] 195 × 135 mm (140 × 85 mm);[3] the final two gatherings are trimmed at the bottom by approximately 10 mm. Frame and lines ruled in drypoint; prickings in the margins. The Hilton material, ff. 1–138^{v}, is written in gothic formata, in a single column at 30 lines per page. A second, cursive Anglicana hand begins on the final folio of the penultimate gathering (f. 138^{v}), and continues through ff. 140–144^{v} in a single column, 33 lines per page. The final item is written in another Anglicana hand, with Latin subtitles formata, at 36 lines per page.

CONTENTS

1. Ff. 3^{r}–59^{r}: Walter Hilton, *Scale* I, with the *explicit* 'Explicit liber primus Magistri Walteri Hilton, decretorum inceptoris, de vita contemplativa.'

2. Ff. 59^{r}–138^{v}: Walter Hilton, *Scale* II with the extended ending;[4] with the *incipit* 'Incipit liber secundus unde prius' and *explicit* 'Explicit liber Magistri Walteri Hilton de vita contemplativa.'

3. Ff. 138^{v}–139^{r}: A Latin version of the 'Vision of St John on the Sorrows of the Virgin' that names only the five sorrows, and does not include the benefits of meditation on each that normally follows.[5]

4. Ff. 140^{r}–143^{r}: Richard Rolle's *Oleum effusum* in English:[6] Hope Emily Allen, *Writings Ascribed to Richard Rolle, Hermit of Hampole, and Materials for his Bibliography* (New York, 1927; repr. New York, 1966); *IPMEP* 506 (this copy not noted).

[2] The page count and collation of the manuscripts include only medieval and early modern materials, including parchment flyleaves in 16th- or early 17th-c. bindings. Paper flyleaves in more recent bindings are excluded. Pen-trials and flyleaf notes of later than the16th c. are not recorded.

[3] In this and the following descriptions, the dimensions of the written space are given in parentheses following those of the folios.

[4] i.e. the material following the phrase 'þis is þe voyce of Jesu', 46/74. (All chapter and line references will take this form.)

[5] Elizabeth May Towl, 'An Edition of Marian Devotional Texts Extant in English Manuscripts of the Fifteenth and Early-Sixteenth Centuries' (Ph.D. thesis, Otago, 2010), notes two Latin and three Middle English versions of this text, none of which seems to be derived from any of the others.

[6] *YW*, i. 186–91.

5. Ff. 143^{r}–144^{v}: *The Rule of the Life of Our Lady*:[7] *IPMEP* 22 (this copy not noted).[8]

6. Ff. 144^{v}–147^{r}: Middle English *Arma Christi*: *IMEV* 2577; *DIMEV* 4083.

COLLATION: 1^{12}–11^{12}, 12^{4} + 1 + 13^{8}. The verso of the final leaf has glue residue around the marks of binding strips.

DECORATION: Four-line illuminated initial with demi-vinet on f. 3^{r}, at the head of *Scale* I; three-line lombard initial to *Scale* II; two-line lombard chapter initials throughout. Frequent grey penwork floral decoration of uncertain date in the margins and unfilled line-endings, surrounding catchwords, and descenders.

BINDING: Modern.

DIALECT: In private correspondence with A. J. Bliss *c.*1964, Angus McIntosh described the dialect of the text of the *Scale* as 'Dorset overlaying some kind of Midland English, but also with signs of some more southerly overlay'.[9] *LALME*, i. 239, describes the language of ff. 140^{r}–142^{r} (item 4 above) as possibly from northern Staffordshire, or the Cheshire/Derbyshire border, mixed with a more northerly element. The language of ff. 144^{v}–147^{r} (item 6 above) is LP 5340, Grid 386 122 (Dorset).

PROVENANCE: F. 1^{r}, in a hand not occurring elsewhere in the manuscript: 'Hunc librum et librum vocatum Gracia Dei qui est in custodia Willelmi Carente habeant abbatissa et conventus Shaftoniensis [*over erasure*: in succursum anime Johannis Horder].' F. 138^{v}, in the same hand as the text of the *Scale*: 'Iste liber constat Willelmo Smyth sacerdoti cuius anime propicietur Jesus. Quem post obitum suum [*another hand, engrossed*: Johannes Horder emebat].' The physical and dialectal makeup of this manuscript suggests that the text of the *Scale* may have been copied by a Dorset scribe from a Midland exemplar, but the *ex libris* notes at the beginning and end have been altered to reflect its purchase by John Horder, from whom it passed to the Benedictine nuns of Shaftesbury Abbey. William Carent, a prominent landholder in Somerset and Dorset, was at one

[7] *YW*, i. 158–61.

[8] The English version of Rolle's *Oleum effusum* and *The Rule of the Life of our Lady* also occur together in Booklet 3 of Manuscript 2 (ff. 62–5) of *Scale* I MS H_3, written s. xiv *ex.* or xv *in.* in the central West Riding of Yorkshire. See Hanna, *EMRR*, 94–7.

[9] Bliss and McIntosh corresponded often about the dialectal character of the manuscripts of *Scale* I. McIntosh's initial characterizations are included here for the reader's information, but should be considered as superseded by the eventual *LALME* descriptions for those parts of the manuscripts that *LALME* surveys.

point steward of Shaftesbury (where his first wife's aunt, Margaret Stourton, was abbess from 1423 to 1441); Carent died in 1476. Item 3 begins below the *ex libris* at the end of *Scale* II, and extends onto a separate, additional folio. Items 4 (West Midlands) through 6 (Dorset) have been added in a further gathering that reflects the manuscript's southward travels.

LITERATURE: Ker, *MLGB*, 177, 304 (Johannes Horder erroneously listed under Sempringham); David N. Bell, *What Nuns Read: Books and Libraries in Medieval English Nunneries* (Kalamazoo, 1995), 164–5; Peter Brown and Elton D. Higgs, *IMEP Handlist V: British Library, Additional MSS 10001–14000* (Cambridge, 1988), 39–41; *MWM* (accessed 29 June 2016).

As: Oxford, All Souls College MS 25 s. xv^{1}

Parchment. Ff. 134. 227 × 170 mm (180–95 × 115–25 mm). Written in Bastard Anglicana in a single column, 30–7 lines per page. Pricked in outer, upper, and lower margins; frame ruled in crayon.

CONTENTS:

1. Ff. 1^{r}–55^{r}. Walter Hilton, *Scale* I, with title: 'This tretys ys called Scala Perfeccionis.'

2. Ff. 55^{v}–134^{r}: Walter Hilton, *Scale* II without the extended ending, but with an *explicit* that includes the *incipit* of *The Abbey of the Holy Ghost* (*IPMEP* 39): 'þys is þe abbaye of þe Holi Gost þat is founded in a place þat is cleped þe conscience. ¶ Explicit Scala Perfeccionis.' There is no following copy of the *Abbey*. There are a number of textual displacements in Chapters 35–6 and 41–3 of *Scale* II (occurring at mid-page, mid-line, and mid-sentence) that seem to result from disordering of the folios of an examplar of As—a disordering that the scribe of As either did not notice or was not in a position to repair. These displacements are noted in the critical apparatus and Explanatory Notes.

COLLATION: 1^{8}–12^{8}, 13^{7} (wants 5, with no loss of text), 14^{8}–15^{8}, 16^{10}, 17^{5} (ff. 130/133 and 131/132 are conjoint pairs; f. 134, which seems originally to have been a paste-down, with considerable paste residue remaining on the verso side, does not match either f. 129 or f. 130). The first sixteen folios all have catchwords; thereafter only the final folios of the gatherings; gathering 12 has no catchword.

DECORATION: Three-line lombard capital to the title on f. 1^{r}; four-line lombard capital to the opening of the text of *Scale* I; three-line lombard capitals to the openings of all chapters thereafter. The title of the volume and chapter titles are rubricated in the scribal hand, as are Latin scriptural quotations. Alternating red and blue paragraph signs at the beginning of each sentence through f. 88^{r}; thereafter only blue, immediately preceding and following all Latin quotations. The opening of *Scale* II has the remainder of a trimmed header: 'Capitulum primum'.

BINDING: Seventeenth-century blind-tooled calf, rebacked.

DIALECT: In private correspondence with A. J. Bliss, Angus McIntosh reported a dialectal location in 'northern Essex, although not entirely homogeneous; some forms suggest an intermediate Norfolk copying, though they might be explained as northern Midland'.

PROVENANCE: F. 55^{v} (fully legible only in ultraviolet light): '⟨Rose Pac⟩het professyd in Syon.' Pachet is recorded as a nun in the Brigittine abbey of Syon in 1518, after the dissolution in 1539, and in 1557, during the Marian re-establishment.

DESCRIBED IN: Andrew G. Watson, *A Descriptive Catalogue of the Medieval Manuscripts of All Souls College Oxford* (Oxford, 1997), 51–2.

LITERATURE: G. J. Aungier, *The History and Antiquities of Syon Monastery* (London, 1840), 82, 89, 97; Ker, *MLGB*, 309; Christopher de Hamel, *The Library of the Bridgettine Nuns and their Peregrinations after the Reformation* (London, 1991), no. 28; Bell, *What Nuns Read*, 196; S. J. Ogilvie-Thomson, *IMEP Handlist VIII: Manuscripts in Oxford College Libraries* (Cambridge, 1991), 2.

B: Oxford, Bodleian Library MS Bodley 100 s. xv in.

Parchment. Ff. ii + 172 + i. 215 × 147 mm (160 × 107–8 mm). Ruling of the writing-block is purple, and remains quite clear through the first two gatherings, but fades increasingly through the book. Written in Anglicana Formata, in two columns, at 29 lines per page.

CONTENTS:

i. On the recto of the first front flyleaf (s. xvi/xvii): 'Vita contemplatiua'; slightly below (s. xvi): '. . . contemplatiffe'; at bottom (s. xv): 'þu ssalt abugge herefore anoþer day ful sore . . .'.

ii. On the verso of the same leaf, in the hand of the main text, a collection of Latin and English proverbs and scriptural quotations, beginning: 'Omnis Christi accio fuit nostra instruccio', and including 'On the Evils of the Time' (*IMEV* 1138).

iii. On the second front flyleaf, in the same hand, more compressed (f. ii$^{r–v}$), 30 lines of French verse, *incipit*: 'Pur veyr nul homme per ira'; *explicit*: 'Et moy amenez a saluacioun. Amen.' Seven further lines of French verse follow, *incipit*: 'Quant le cheytif pecchour'; *explicit*: 'Et de ces pecchez auera remissioun. Amen.'

iv. Continuing on the verso, in the same hand, several Latin notes on indulgences and prayers, *incipit*: 'Nota quod Johannes papa xxij^{us} concessit.'[10]

1. Ff. 1ra–70vb. Walter Hilton, *Scale* I. The first gathering lacks its first three leaves, which may have comprised a Table of Chapters, and the text ends on the verso of the singleton added after gathering 9.

2. Ff. 71ra–172vb. Walter Hilton, *Scale* II without the extended ending, preceded by a Table of Chapters.

COLLATION: ii + 1^5 (first three ff. missing), 2^8–9^8 + 1 + 10^8–21^8 + 22^6 (plus two stubs) + i. Catchwords throughout.

DECORATION: Three-line gold initial with multicoloured (blue, red, green, purple, orange) floral top-and-side border illumination to *Scale* I; four-line initial, the same, to the Table of Chapters; and two-line Lombard capital to *Scale* II; (usually) two-line chapter initials, alternating red with purple penwork and blue with red, to chapters throughout. The illumination is not metropolitan. Chapter titles in red, underlined in black, with blue paragraph signs throughout *Scale* I; Latin scriptural quotations are engrossed, underlined in red, with blue paragraph signs throughout. *Scale* II lacks chapter titles; chapter numbers are in red. The scriptural texts are identified in marginal notes. Other paragraph signs throughout, at a rate of *c.* eight per opening, in red. Small capitals highlighted with yellow. Each gathering of *Scale* I has a blue 'I' in the upper margin; *Scale* II 'II'. In a (s. xv) Formata hand, at the top left and right corners of f. 73^r, the opening of *Scale* II, are 'Jesus' and 'In nomine Jesu'. Catchwords throughout in ornate scrolls, touched in red. In the empty space of the right-hand column of f. 72^v is a pen sketch of a half-naked penitent with a staff, and one of a black-shaded, shackled human figure, with a tormenting devil holding his neck-shackle; these are labelled in a (s. xv) Formata hand, 'ymago penitenti' and 'Anima captiua'. There is a (s. xv/xvi) cipher at the bottom of f. 172^v.

[10] These indulgenced prayers are mentioned by R. N. Swanson in ch. 6, 'Indulgences Debated', in *Indulgences in Late Medieval England: Passports to Paradise* (Cambridge, 2011), 224–77.

BINDING: Parchment, with a post-medieval shelfmark on the spine: [..]h / 4° A / 20, below which is the Bodleian shelfmark.

DIALECT: Southwestern, perhaps Gloucestershire.

PROVENANCE: According to the Bodleian *SC*, presented by Dr William Cotton, bishop of Exeter, in 1605.

B_3: Oxford, Bodleian Library MS Bodley 592 s. xv^{1}

Parchment. Ff. 186. 203 × 135 mm (147 × 95 mm). 26 lines per page; lines and pricking are still visible. Written in Textura, in single columns.

CONTENTS:

1. Ff. 1^r–80^r: Walter Hilton, *Scale* I, preceded by a Table of Chapters. The rubric of the Table has the title 'Scala perfeccionis'.

2. Ff. 80^r–185^r: Walter Hilton, *Scale* II with the extended ending, preceded by a Table of Chapters. The rubric after the Table refers to this as 'þe secunde partie of þe book'.

COLLATION: iii + 1^8–8^8, 9^6, 10^8–23^8, 24^4 (missing the middle two bifolia). Catchwords throughout, some signatures visible.

DECORATION: Two-line lombard capitals on ff. 4^r and 83^r, at the beginnings of *Scale* I and II. Chapter titles are in red with a blue paragraph sign, chapter initials in blue, and marginal chapter numbers in red with blue paragraph signs, throughout. In the Tables of Chapters to *Scale* I and II, paragraph signs are alternately red and blue. Latin scriptural quotations are underlined in red. There are headers throughout, in red with blue paragraph signs, at the outside and inside margins of the verso and folio, reading across each opening: f. 1^r: Incipit tabula; ff. 1^v–2^r: tabula – pri || me – partis; ff. 4^v–5^r to 79^v–80^r: pri – ma || pars – libri; ff. 80^v–81^r and 81^v–82^r: tabula – partis || secun – de; ff. 83^v–84^r to the end) secun – da || pars – libri. The disposition of the headers is virtually identical to that in MS L.

BINDING: Early modern.

DIALECT: Central Midlands Standard, according to M. L. Samuels.[11]

PROVENANCE: In both script and dialect, this manuscript is a completely standardized production, and thus difficult to localize.

[11] M. L. Samuels, 'Some Applications of Middle English Dialectology', in Margaret Laing (ed.), *Middle English Dialectology: Essays on Some Principles and Problems* (Aberdeen, 1989), 64–80 at 79 n. 5.

On the first parchment flyleaf (numbered iv) is a copy of an agreement by Isabella Edrygge of Lyme Regis, 1515, 'per me fratrem Thomam Sutton Glastonie cellerium forinsicum'; on the second flyleaf is an acknowledgement of a debt by Thomas Bragg of Thornecombe in Devonshire, in Latin, 16th c.; and on f. 185^{v} a copy of a letter from Nicholas Webber, of Lyme Regis, 16th c. There is scribbling on ff. iii, v, 186. 'John Deare', 1583 (f. iii); 'John Peache', early 17th c. (f. 186^{v}). Presented by Joseph Maynard, late fellow of Exeter College, Oxford, on 8 May 1662, having been bought by him at Dorchester on 22 Nov. 1660.

Br: Brussels, Bibliothèque royale de Belgique, MS 2544–45 1608

Paper. Ff. 153; those of the text of the *Scale* (excluding the Table of Chapters of *Scale* I) and *Mixed Life* are numbered 1–146 in modern ink. 200 × 155 mm (*c.*158 × 125 mm). More than one stock, that in the earlier part of the manuscript being slightly lighter. The watermark on the second-outermost bifolium of the last gathering (f. 140 and its unnumbered conjoint leaf) appears to be a form of Bricquet's 'Griffon',[12] but does not resemble any example closely enough for identification. Written in an Italian humanist 'Roman' hand, dry-ruled at 31–3 lines per page. Probably copied from a print subsequent to that of Notary, 1507 (*STC* 14043).

CONTENTS:

1. Ff. [4][13] –56^{r}: Walter Hilton, *Scale* I, preceded by a Table of Chapters.

2. Ff. 56^{v}–133^{r}: Walter Hilton, *Scale* II with the extended ending, followed by a Table of Chapters.

3. Ff. 133^{v}–146^{v}: Walter Hilton, *Mixed Life*, preceded by a Table of Chapters.

COLLATION: iii + 1^{8}–19^{8} (the last is the rear paste-down).

DECORATION: All chapters are provided with penwork initials in four- to six-line squares or rectangles with dotted and flourished, textile-like, decoration; the decoration of a number of initials, up to

[12] C. M. Bricquet, *Les Filigranes: Dictionnaire historique des marques du paper dès leur apparition vers 1282 jusqu'en 1600 . . . A Facsimile of the 1907 Edition with Supplementary Material Contributed by a Number of Scholars*, ed. Allan Stevenson (Amsterdam, 1968). Note that Bricquet's catalogue ends several years before this manuscript was written.

[13] This folio is unnumbered in the manuscript; the following folio, the first of the text of *Scale* I, bears the number 1. All further folio references to this manuscript will use the ink numbering present there.

Scale I, Chapter 49, is either partially or entirely in red. The remainder of the first word of most chapters is in engrossed red capitals, and the initials of chapter titles, both within the text and in the Tables of Chapters of each book, are in red, as are the initial letters of the book and chapter headers throughout. Chapter titles and Latin scriptural quotations in the text are written in a humanist cursive ('italic') hand. Latin scriptural quotations in the text are identified in cursive marginal notes. A woodblock print of Christ on a lignum-vitae cross has been pasted on the title page in the same position as the woodblock on the title page of printed versions of the *Scale*. Above, in red: 'Scala Perfectionis'; below, with red capitals: 'The greatest Comfort in Temptacyon / Is the remembraunce of Crystes passyon.'

PROVENANCE: The Charterhouse of Sheen Anglorum in Mechelen, Belgium. On f. 1^{r}: 'This book belonghet to the English Cartusians in Mechlin. Anno Domini 1615.' In the hand of the scribe at the end of *Scale* I on f. 56^{r}, following the final 'Amen' of the text, but preceding the *explicit*, is: 'Anno Domini 1608, xvj° Iunii.' Below the *explicit* is: 'Orate pro me Fratre Abrahamo Conuerso Carthusiensi.' At the end of the text of Scale II on f. 133^{r}, in the same hand, is the *explicit*: 'Finis. Anno Domini 1608. Orate pro me Fratre Abrahamo Conuerso Carthusiensi.' On f. 146^{v}, in the same hand as the *ex libris* on f. 1: 'Orate pro Fratre Abrahamo, libri huius Scriptore. Frater Abrahamus, conversus Domus Sheen de Bethlehem in Anglia.' These refer to Abraham Ellis, a converse brother in the first half of the seventeenth century.

BINDING: Original parchment with the stubs of thongs at front and back. The title on the binding reads: 'Hiltons Scale of Perfection written by Br. Abraham Ellis.' There is slight water damage to the upper outer corners in the latter half of the book, and apparent mildew damage to the back cover.

DESCRIBED IN: J. Van den Gheyn, *Catalogue des manuscrits de la Bibliothèque Royale de Belgique*, iii: *Théologie* (1903), no. 2478, pp. 506–7.

Cc: Cambridge, Corpus Christi College MS R.5 (268)
s. xv med.

Parchment. Ff. ii (the first of which is paper pasted to parchment, the second parchment) + 169 + ii (paper). 265 × 180 mm (187 × 125 mm). Written in Anglicana in a single column, at 33–8 lines per page.

CONTENTS:

i. On the verso of the first front end-sheet (s. xv Textura): 'Vnto euery man or woman þat seyth þis prayere folowyng, "Benedictum sit dulce nomen Domini nostri Jesu Christi & gloriosissime virginis Marie matris eius in eternum & vltra. Amen. Nos cum prole pia, benedicat virgo Maria. Amen." ar grantyd iij yer of pardon, tociens quociens, of pope Clement þe fourthe atte þe requeste of seynt Lowys Kyng of France.'

ii. On the facing recto, the first words are repeated as a pen-trial (s. xv, formal secretary), below which is a crude sketch of a four-decade set of rosary beads. At the top right is the Corpus Christi College Library shelfmark: R 5, above and to the right of which is a penned (former folio?) number: 1^{v} (the '1' corrected to 'i').

iii. On the verso of the second front end-sheet, in the same hand, is the *incipit* of the following text, done as a pen-trial: 'Sine fide Im- . . .'

At top of f. 1^{r}, in a humanist hand: 'Liber contemplationum Walteri Hilton', and a shelfmark: C 32. The title refers to the main contents of the book, which begin on f. 10^{r}, and not to the present text.

1. Ff. 1^{r}– 9^{v}: 'A confortable tretyes to strengthyn and confortyn creaturys in the feyth specialy hem that arn symple and disposyd to fallyn in desperacyon.' P. S. Jolliffe, *Check-List of Middle English Prose Writings of Spiritual Guidance* (Toronto, 1974), K.13.

2. Ff. 10^{r}–54^{r}: Walter Hilton, *Scale* I, followed by a Table of Chapters; both Table and text refer to it as 'the fryst book of Maister Walter Hylton'.

3. Ff. 54^{r}–97^{r}: *The Seven Points of True Love and Everlasting Wisdom*, preceded by a Table of Chapters (*IPMEP* 465). F. 97^{v} is blank, which suggests that the following text of *Scale* II was not to hand when the book was completed to this point.

4. Ff. 98^{r}–169^{v}: Walter Hilton, *Scale* II with the extended ending, followed by a Table of Chapters; both Table and text refer to it as 'the secunde boke of Maister Waltyr Hylton'. Below, in a more cursive hand, 'Explicit liber 2^{dus} M Walteri Hylton / Nunc scripsi totum pro Christo da mihi potum. Nunc finem feci da mihi quod merui.'

COLLATION: 1^{8} + 1 + binding stub + 2^{8}–21^{8}; boxed catchwords throughout. Items 1, 2, and 4 all begin new gatherings.

DECORATION: Three-line blue and red lombard initials at opening of each text; two-line lombard initials to each chapter of each book of the *Scale*. Chapter titles throughout in red; Latin scriptural quotations underlined in red; small initials highlighted in red. Headers giving chapter number for items 2–4. On fore-edge of the book is the name 'Elisabeth Wyllughby', with red initial 'E' and 'W'.

BINDING: Modern.

DIALECT. *LALME* LP 8390, Grid 638 265: Suffolk.

PROVENANCE: On f. 169^{v}, in a hand other than that of the main scribe, 'Memorandum that I Elizabeth Wylby [*read by A. I. Doyle by ultraviolet light*: Nonne of campessey] Gyffe thys boke . . .'. The lower 54 mm or so of the page have been cut away. Elizabeth Wilby (or Willowby) was recorded as a nun of the Augustinian priory of Campsey, Suffolk, in 1514 and 1526. She is also recorded as giving a printed copy of *The Chastising of God's Children* to Catherine Symond of the same house.[14] The *Scale* manuscript was given to Corpus Christi College by Archbishop Parker.

DESCRIBED IN: M. R. James, *A Descriptive Catalogue of the Manuscripts in the Library of Corpus Christi College, Cambridge* (Cambridge, 1912), 24–5.

LITERATURE: Ker, *MLGB*, 28; Bell, *What Nuns Read*, 123; Kari Anne Rand, *IMEV Handlist XX: Corpus Christi College, Cambridge* (Cambridge, 2009), 34–37.

Ch: Chatsworth House, Derbyshire, uncatalogued manuscript s. xv^{1-2}

Parchment. Ff. 93. 235 × 145 mm (165 × 97 mm). Written in Anglicana Formata in a single column, at 29 lines per page. Ruling in drypoint; brown crayon occasionally visible.

CONTENTS:

1. Ff. 1^{r}–62^{v}: Walter Hilton, *Scale* I, entitled at top of first page, 'Speculum contemplacionis. M. W. Hylton. Canonicus.'

2. Ff. 63^{r}–92^{v}: Walter Hilton, *Scale* II, atelous, ending at 24/39 'grace'. Also lacks material from 8/46 to 10/10, and from 20/94 to 21/69.

COLLATION: 1^{12} (f. 9 a stub) – 6^{12}, 7^{10}, 8^{11}. Catchwords in cartouches, some signatures visible.

DECORATION: five-line red initial with blue penwork infill and red

[14] Mary C. Erler, *Women Reading, and Piety in Late Medieval England* (Cambridge, 2002), 125.

and blue border decoration for *Scale* I; four-line initial, the same, for *Scale* II; two- and three-line lombard chapter initials throughout; Latin quotations in textura, underlined in red.

BINDING: s. xv white parchment on boards. The boss and clasp are not original. There appears to have been nothing lost at the end of the volume after binding, thus that the latter part of the text of *Scale* II was not present when the volume was bound.

DIALECT: *LALME* LP 65, Grid 423 276: Warwickshire.

PROVENANCE: A small number of non-textual annotations by James Grenehalgh, Carthusian of Sheen (fl. 1500), then of Coventry (1508); †1529 at Hull. Because he did not collate this manuscript with those that he did at Sheen, he probably came upon it later in his career. From dialectal evidence, this was probably at Coventry Charterhouse.

LITERATURE: Sargent, *James Grenehalgh*, ii. 492–3; *MWM*.

E: Cambridge University Library MS Ee.iv.30

s. xv^{3-4}

Parchment. Ff. 139 (numbered 1–136 in pencil, not counting the missing leaf at the end of the eighteenth gathering and two ruled leaves at the end). 265 × 185 mm (185 × 125 mm); ruled, with prickings 5 mm from the outside edge of the page. Written in a Textura hand, at 31 lines per page.

CONTENTS:

1. Ff. 1^r–62^v: Walter Hilton, *Scale* I, preceded by a Table of Chapters. Both Table and text refer to themselves as 'the firste parti of þis booke, þe whiche is cleped Scala Perfeccionis'. F. 3^v, following the Table of Chapters, is blank, as are the lower twenty-five lines of f. 62^v.

2. Ff. 63^r–135^r: Walter Hilton, *Scale* II with the extended ending, preceded by a Table of Chapters. Both Table and text refer to themselves as 'þe secunde party of þe foreseide boke, Scala Perfeccionis'. Followed by the *explicit*, 'Explicit libellus Magistri Walteri Hilton, canonici de Thurgarton qui obijt Anno Domini Millesimo CCC° nonagesimo, quinto decimo kalendas Aprilis, circa solis occasum.' Two lines down, 'Nunc finem feci, penitet me si male scripsi.' The lower twenty-two lines of f. 65^v, following the Table of Chapters, are blank, as are the last five lines of f. 135^r and all of f. 135^v, following the text. The final leaf of the gathering was cut out.

COLLATION: i (Parchment) + 1^8–16^8, 17^7 (missing its last leaf), 18^2 + i (Parchment).

DECORATION: A six-line gold initial, with left-side floral border work in gold, green, blue, pink, and mauve, on ff. 4^{r}, 66^{r}, at the head of each book of the *Scale*; three-line lombard capitals at the beginning of each chapter; smaller capitals throughout the text are highlighted in yellow. Chapter titles in the text are in red, with a blue initial; chapter numbers are in red, Roman in the text, Arabic in the margin, apparently by same hand. The *explicit* of each book is in an engrossed hand; that of *Scale* I with an elaborate penwork initial, touched in yellow. Latin scriptural quotations (preceded by identification of the text cited) throughout the text are underlined in red, with a blue paragraph sign preceding.

BINDING: Modern, incorporating what may be the front and back of an earlier leather binding, with holes and impressions of a pair of clasps on front and back. The parchment flyleaf at the end has sixteenth- and seventeenth-century notes in Latin and Italian.

DIALECT: *LALME* LP 6450, Grid 505 175: Middlesex.

PROVENANCE: London Charterhouse. Beginning at f. 4^{r}, and extending to f. 62^{r} (thus for the entirety of the text of *Scale* I), in neatly written capitals, one letter at foot of each recto page, in the same hand and ink as the text itself, is the *ex libris* inscription: 'Liber Domus Salutacionis Matris Dei Ordinis Cartusiensis prope London.' Later *probationies pennae*, possibly marks of ownership, occur on the two-leaf gathering at the end (ruled precisely the same as the remainder of the volume): f. 137^{v}: This byll mayde the xvjth day off May, in the yere of the Rengne off (oure most dredd . . .) ; f. 138^{v}: Thys ys mayster Asshes boke of Petar howsse. And wittenes her of ys John Sutton and John Bregge. [*in margin, in the same hand*: per me Johannem Sutton seruientem Georgij Colte armigeri manentem apud Bury sancti Edmundi in Com. Suff]. These leaves are otherwise blank.

LITERATURE: Ker, *MLGB*, 122; Margaret Connolly, *IMEP Handlist XIX: Manuscripts in the University Library, Cambridge (Dd–Oo)* (Cambridge, 2009), 114–15.

H: London, British Library MS Harley 6579 s. xiv ex.

Parchment. Ff. 143 + 2 (paper). 205 × 140 mm (170 × 100 mm). 26–30 lines per page. Written in several Anglicana hands, ranging from the end of the fourteenth century through the mid-fifteenth, in single columns.

CONTENTS:

1. Ff. 1^{v}–63^{r}: Walter Hilton, *Scale* I. At head, in a Textura hand: 'Magister Walterus Hylton Canonicus de Thurgarton qui fuit homo

venerabilis sciencia et vite sanctitate, composuit hunc librum plenum catholica doctrina et edificatione.' The *explicit* refers to this as 'liber primus'.

2. Ff. 63^r–140^r: Walter Hilton, *Scale* II, with the extended ending added in another hand (f. 140^r).

3. Ff. 141^r–142^v: Walter Hilton, *Scale* I and II, Table of Chapters, added in another hand.

i. Ff. 144^r–145^r (paper): Fifty-five verse couplets in a sixteenth-century hand, *inc.*: 'No wight in this world', printed by John Herforde in 1545, together with Surrey's *Excellent Epitaph of Sir Thomas Wyatt* (*STC* 2760).[15]

COLLATION: i + 1^8–3^8, 4^{12} (includes an extra bifolium tipped in between the second and third leaves), 5^8, 6^2, 7^9 (includes an extra half-folio sewn to the outer edge of the third folio, f. 48), 8^{10} (*Scale* I ends and *Scale* II begins on the second-last recto—f. 63—which has a parchment tab sewn at its edge), 9^{14}, 10^{16}–12^{16} + 2 singletons (ff. 127, 128; f. 127^r written in a different hand) + 13^{12} (end of *Scale* II) + 2 ff. (Tables of Chapters on ff. 142^r–143^v, in another hand, at 44–39–39 lines per page) + 2 ff. (paper). Catchwords on every folio of *Scale* I; catchwords on the last folio of each gathering for *Scale* II. The catchword on f. 27 refers to f. 30 (that is, the bifolium added to gathering 4 had not been added at that point).

DECORATION (*Scale* II): A parchment tab is sewn to the outer edge of f. 63, on which *Scale* II begins. Most chapter initials have two-line red ink initials. Occasional red paragraph signs. Chapters have Arabic numbers in the margin; that for chapter 35 reads '55'. Chapters 1–9, 20–2, 31, 34 have titles added in pen, interlinear or in the margins; 24 and 42–6 in pencil; 30 rubric. F. 102^r, on which chapter 30 begins, also has a thread bookmark sewn into its lower border.[16]

BINDING: Modern.

DIALECT: *LALME*, i. 113, describes five hands. Hand A is ff. 2^r–63^r, line 13 (*Scale* I), except ff. 28–9 (Hand B: the 'Holy Name

[15] See Hyder E. Rollins, 'No Wight in this World that Wealth Can Attain', *RES* 5 (1929), 56–79.

[16] On the use of tabs and thread place-markers, see Daniel Sawyer, 'Navigation by Tab and Thread: Place-Markers and Readers' Movement in Books', in Flannery and Griffin (eds.), *Spaces for Reading*, 99–114; Lois Swales and Heather Blatt, 'Tiny Textiles Hidden in Books: Toward a Categorization of Multiple-Stand Bookmarkers', in Robin Netherton and Gale R. Owen-Crocker (eds.), *Medieval Clothing and Textiles*, 3 (2007), 145–79.

passage'). Hand C is ff. 63^{r}, line 14 to the end (*Scale* II), except for f. 127 (Hand D) and ff. 141^{r}–143 (Hand E: Table of Chapters). 'Hands A to D all have characteristics suggesting origins in Ely or extreme southern Lincolnshire'; Hand E is LP 753, Grid 501 288: extreme eastern Northamptonshire.

PROVENANCE: At the foot of f. 2^{r} is an *ex libris* in a fifteenth-century Anglicana hand: 'Liber Domus Matris Dei Ordinis Cartusiensis prope London'.

LITERATURE: *The Scale of Perfection by Walter Hilton, Canon of Thurgarton, Newly Edited from MS. Sources with an Introduction*, ed. Evelyn Underhill (London, 1923), pp. xlv–xlvii, lii–liii; Ker, *MLGB*, 122; Michael G. Sargent, 'The Transmission by the English Carthusians of Some Late Medieval Spiritual Writings', *Journal of Ecclesiastical History*, 27 (1976), 225–40 at 235–7; Sargent, 'Walter Hilton's *Scale of Perfection*: The London Manuscript Group Reconsidered', *MÆ* 52 (1983), 189–216.

H_5: London, British Library MS Harley 2387 s. xv^{1}

Parchment. Ff. 134 (modern numbering begins on f. 4, so totals 130). 210 × 145 mm (147 × 95 mm). 30–6 lines per page. Written in an Anglicana hand, in a single column.

CONTENTS:

1. Ff. 1^{r}–53^{r}: Walter Hilton, *Scale* I, entitled 'þe boke þat is iclepyde *Scala Perfeccionis*, and it haþ twey partyes'.

2. Ff. 54^{r}–129^{v}: Walter Hilton, *Scale* II without the extended ending, with the *incipit* and *explicit* 'secunda pars'.

COLLATION: 1^{12}–4^{12}, 5^{10} (two missing between f. 53 and f. 54, before the last two folios of the gathering, i.e. just before the opening of *Scale* II), 6^{12}–11^{12}, 12^{3}.

DECORATION: Illuminated initials, in gold, blue, mauve, and white, with demi-vinets at the openings of *Scale* I and *Scale* II. The style of the illumination is early fifteenth century. Lombard chapter initials, 2–5 lines (usually three-line) throughout. The titles of *Scale* I are engrossed Textura rubric; *Scale* II chapters do not have titles, but chapter numbers, in Textura rubric, are given in the text-block. Latin biblical quotations are engrossed, preceded by a paragraph sign, and underlined in red. Red and blue paragraph signs throughout, at a rate of approximately four to five per page.

BINDING: Modern.

DIALECT: *LALME* LP 6380, Grid 543 177: London.

PROVENANCE: Syon, Brigittine Abbey, by the bequest of Margery Pensax, according to a note on f. 130^{v}: 'Istum librum legauit domina Margeria Pensax dudum inclusa apud Bysshoppisgate monasterio sancti Saluatoris de Syon iuxta Schene.' Pensax is recorded as an anchoress at Bishopsgate in 1399 and 1413, before the foundation of Syon. The incipit of the *Scale*, which addresses itself to a 'Ghostly brother . . .', might indicate that this copy was not originally made for her, although the form of address might equally represent that of its exemplar.

LITERATURE: Ker, *MLGB*, 185; Bell, *What Nuns Read*, 149 (assigned to Aldgate); Erler, *Women*, 59.

H_6: London, British Library MS Harley 2397 s. xv med.

Parchment. Ff. 102 (Numbered 1*–4*, 1–98). 215 × 153 mm (140 × 100 mm). The outer two gatherings, of four leaves each, are from a liturgical manuscript, and are written in a Textura hand, in a single column at 20 lines per page, with musical notation. The Hilton material, ff. 1–94, is written in Textualis, in a single column at 29 lines per page.

CONTENTS:

i. Ff. 1^{*r}–4^{*v}: The service for the dead, with masculine forms (e.g. 'famuli tui' in the 'Obsecramus' with which this fragment closes).

1. Ff. 1^{r}–72^{r}: Walter Hilton, *Scale* II with the extended ending, entitled 'þe secunde \`part´ of þe reformyng of mannys soule drawyn of Maistir Watir Hiltone hermyte'. F. 73^{v} is blank.

2. Ff. 73^{r}–85^{r}: Walter Hilton, *Mixed Life*.

3. Ff. 85^{v}–94^{r}: Walter Hilton, *Bonum est*.

ii. Ff. 95^{r}–98^{v}: The service for the dead, from the same manuscript as i, above.

COLLATION: 4 + 1^{8}–11^{8}, + 4 12^{6} (signatures and catchwords present: a–j for *Scale* II; a, 2, 3 for *Mixed Life* and *Bonum Est*; the signature of f. 91, the innermost bifolium of the last gathering, is 'ȝiij non plus').

DECORATION (Hilton manuscript only): Three-line blue initial to text of the *Scale*; two-line blue chapter-initials throughout, as also for the titles and section divisions of the *Mixed Life*, and for the title of *Bonum est*. The titles of the *Scale* and all of its chapters, and of the *Mixed Life*, are in red; the chapter title rubrics in the *Scale* are preceded by blue paragraph signs. Latin scriptural quotations in the *Scale* and the *Mixed Life* are underlined in red. Latin quotations in *Bonum est* have a slightly more Textura aspect, and have a blue initial; the direct translations into English that follow immediately upon the Latin in the psalm commentary have a red paragraph sign and are underlined in red.

BINDING: Modern. The two outer gatherings seem to have been bound as endleaves to the Hilton manuscript at some later date (having perhaps originally formed part of its medieval binding). The two outer leaves are covered with a paste residue; they were probably glued to the inside of a cover.

PROVENANCE: A note of bequest on f. 94^{v}, apparently the original end-leaf of the Hilton manuscript: 'Dame Elyzabeth Horwode, Abbas of the Menoresse off London to here gostle comforthe bowȝth thys boke, hyt to remayne to the vse off þe sayde place, to pray for þe yeuere and ffor þe sowles off hyre Fader and here Modere, Thomas Horwode and Beatryxe, and þe sowle of Maister [Th *canc.*] Robert Alderton.' Elizabeth Horwood is recorded as Abbess of the house of Franciscan nuns ('Poor Clares' or 'Minoresses') in the time of Edward IV, between Christine St Nicholas (†1455/6) and Joan Barton (fl. 1481). Her father, probably Thomas Horwood, goldsmith of London, is associated with Robert Allerton in a document of 1431; Robert Allerton, LLB, bequeathed 20 shillings to Elizabeth Horwood and the same amount to the house of minoresses in his will of 1437.[17]

LITERATURE: Ker, *MLGB*, 123; *Minor Works of Walter Hilton*, ed. Dorothy Jones (London, 1929), p. xx; *An Exposition of Qui Habitat and Bonum Est, Edited from the Manuscripts with Introduction, Notes and Glossary*, ed. Björn Wallner (Lund, 1954), pp. xx–xxi; *Walter Hilton's Mixed Life, Edited from Lambeth Palace MS 472*, ed. S. J. Ogilvie-Thomson, Salzburg Studies in English Literature, Elizabethan & Renaissance Studies, 92:15 (Salzburg, 1986), pp. xv–xvi; Erler, *Women*, 158.

H_7: London, British Library MS Harley 6573 s. xv in.

Parchment. Ff. 116. 245 × 160 mm (188 × 120 mm). Foliation is provided in ink in a large contemporary hand, beginning with the opening of the text of *Scale* I; the two preceding folios, comprising the Table of Chapters of *Scale* I, are unnumbered. The ink foliation skips from f. 35 to f. 44, where an original gathering has been lost. The manuscript was re-foliated in modern pencil; this foliation

[17] Reported by Erler, *Women*, 158 n. 1, from A. I. Doyle.

counts the first two folios as 1*, 2*, and does not count the missing gathering.[18] Written in several Anglicana hands of *c.*1400, in single columns, at 28–32 lines per page. The ruling, and occasionally the pricking, is visible throughout. Changes of hand are discernable at the gathering break between ff. 11^{v} and 12; at f. 29^{r}, line 5; at f. 32^{r}, line 29; at the beginning of *Scale* I, Chapter 72 (old f. 44^{r}, not numbered in the modern sequence); at the beginning of *Scale* I, Chapter 79 (old f. 45^{v}); and at the gathering break between modern ff. 43^{v} and 44^{r} (old ff. 51^{v} and 52^{r}), just after the opening lines of *Scale* II (see Pl. 1). It is also possible that the hand changes at the gathering break between modern ff. 58^{v} and 59^{r}.[19] The text at the foot of f. 11^{v} has been compressed in order to fit two more lines into the writing space, which would indicate that this was a production copy, on the second gathering of which a second scribe was already at work before the first scribe was finished with the first gathering. Except for its first sentence, the extended ending of the text (f. 114$^{r–v}$, from 46/76 'schewe . . .'), is added in another hand with Secretary characteristics. Chapter titles are added in red in a hand contemporary with that of the scribe, with the exception of that of *Scale* II, Chapter 21 (f. 65^{r}), which seems to be an educated guess at the title, added in a later hand in a space large enough to have accommodated the actual chapter title.

CONTENTS:

1. Ff. 1*^{r}–1^{r}: The Table of Chapters of *Scale* I, with the initial rubric, 'þis is a tretes drawyn of two lyues actyfe and contemplatyfe and þe werkis of hem, deuised in two parties.' The last three words of the title of the penultimate chapter of the table are written at the top of f. 3^{r} with space for a chapter number that is not provided, followed by the title of the final chapter, with 'Cap.^{m} j.^{m}' in the margin as if it were the title of the first chapter, which follows immediately. The first sentence of the second chapter, 'On is clepid actife, þe toþer contemplatyf', is written as a rubric, with 'Cap.^{m} ii.^{m}' in the margin. The scribe seems to have been uncertain of the title and text boundaries; the text of *Scale* I is in fact not provided with chapter titles in this manuscript.

2. Ff. 1^{r}–43^{v}: Walter Hilton, *Scale* I.

3. Ff. 43^{v}–114^{v}: Walter Hilton, *Scale* II with the extended ending,

[18] This numeration, rather than the contemporary ink numeration, which counts a gathering no longer present in the manuscript, will be used throughout.

[19] Information from Ralph Hanna by private correspondence, 29 Nov. 2013.

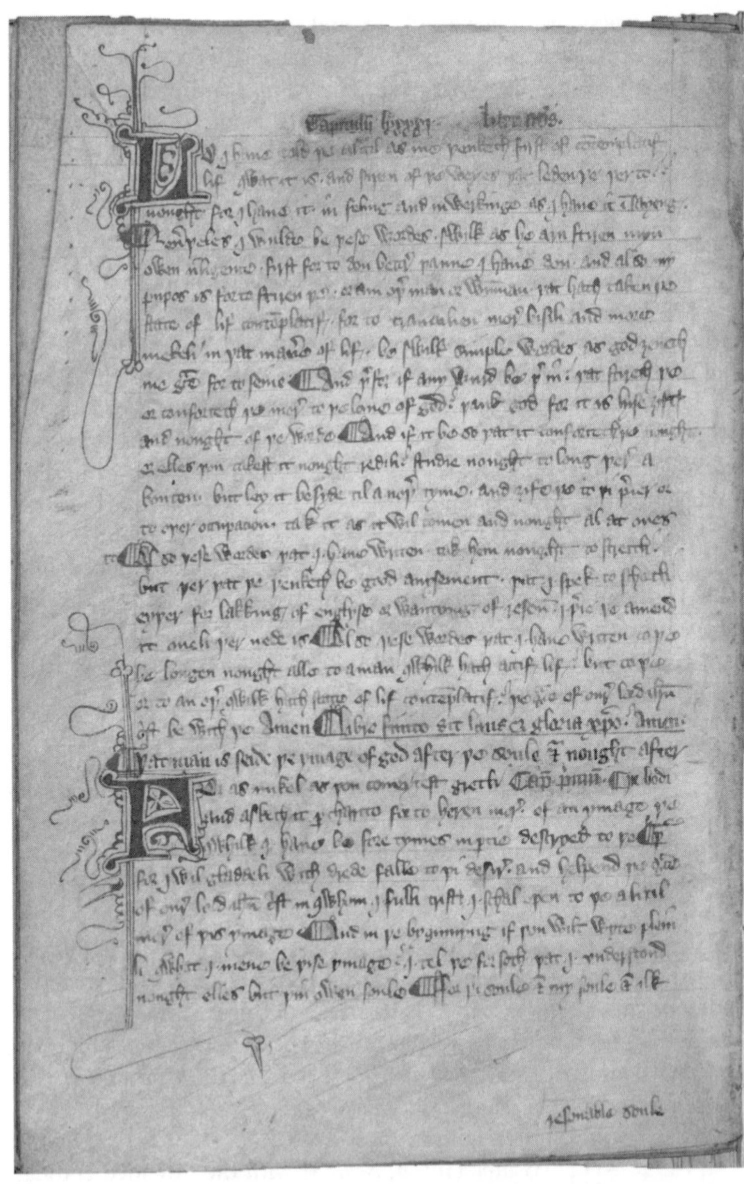

Pl. 1a. British Library MS Harley 6573, f. 43[v] (orig. 51[v]). © The British Library Board

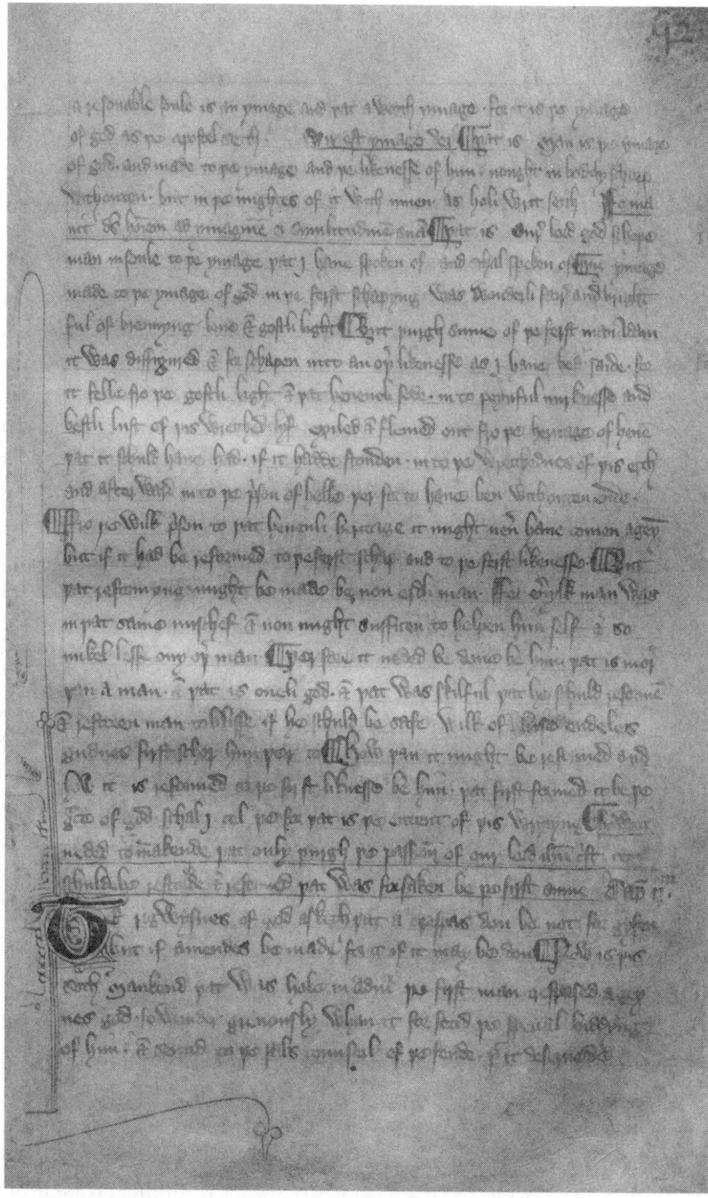

Pl. 1b. British Library MS Harley 6573, f. 44r (orig. 52r). © The British Library Board

all but the first sentence of which (i.e. from 46/76 'schewe') is in another hand.

COLLATION: ii (parchment) + 1^8 + 1 (attached to the following gathering) 2^4, 3^8–6^8, 7^6 + 1 (attached to the following gathering) + 8^8–15^8 + i (parchment). Catchwords, some signatures remain. The original sixth gathering is missing following f. 35.

DECORATION: Two-line lombard capitals throughout; capitalized second letters of chapter initials are touched in red. The title of the volume, and chapter numbers throughout, are in red; Latin scriptural quotations are underlined in red. The titles in the Table of Chapters of *Scale* I are provided with blue paragraph signs. Sentence initials are marked with red paragraph signs (particularly frequently in *Scale* II) and touched in colour, with varying frequency in the different scribal stints: most commonly with yellow in *Scale* I, and with red in *Scale* II. Chapter titles in *Scale* II are engrossed, but in the same Anglicana hand of the text itself; the chapter numbers are in red, usually in the text block, but occasionally in the margin.

BINDING: Modern; the gatherings are all mounted separately.

DIALECT: *LALME* describes the first two hands. Hand A, ff. 1^r–11^v, is LP 49, Grid 539 305: Ely (a little south-west of Wisbech). Hand B, ff. 12^r–29^r, is LP 634, Grid 597 323: Norfolk (a little south of Fakenham). The conjunction of 'ilk' for PDE 'each', 'hwilk' (also 'qhwilk', sporadically in the first third of the text) for 'which', 'werd' for 'world', 'hey-' for 'high-', forms of 'enough' with 'o' + consonant ('inogh', 'inogw'), 'eye/eyes' with medial '-gh-' ('eyghe'), 'luf-' for 'love', third person singular present verb forms in '-eþ' or '-eth', and present plural verb forms in '-en' (*LALME* features 12, 11, 49, 168, 125, 127, 196, 61, and 62 respectively) would place the scribal dialectal profile of *Scale* II in extreme western Norfolk or the adjacent area of Ely.

Hu$_2$: San Marino, Huntington Library MS HM 266

s. xv med.

Parchment. Ff. 84. 219 × 150 mm (148 × 100 mm). The remains of a manuscript originally comprising 159–61 folios, with an earlier limp parchment cover, now bound in complete disorder. Written in an Anglicana hand with some Secretary forms, in a single column of 26–30 lines per page (f. 1^r, exceptionally, has 23); biblical quotations in Textura. Frame-ruled in ink. Corrections to the text occasionally extend into the margin.

CONTENTS:

1. Ff. 1^r–84^v: Walter Hilton's *Scale of Perfection* I and II, disordered. The text of *Scale* II occupies present ff. 30–6 (Chapters 1–7.4 lost), ff. 43–84 (15/8 lyen – 33/65 þat), ff. 37–8 (33/65 nedeþ – 34/51 we), f. 41 (34/51 now – 93 of), ff. 7–8 (34/93 lufe – 35/38 soule), f. 42 (35/38 and – 76 be-), ff. 39–40 (35/76 -fore – 36/81 vertus), ff. 11–12 (39/127 so – 40/87 creatures), f. 15 (43/9 in – 44 heuenly), ff. 5–6 (44/8 lufely – 45/15 of^2), and ff. 9–10 (45/15 reson – 46/16 presence), i.e. approximately two-thirds of the text.

COLLATION: As reconstructed by Hanna, the original manuscript comprised twenty quires of eight, plus a single folio added into the fifth gathering, preceded and followed by the separated sheets of an earlier limp parchment cover. What survives is: i parchment leaf from a former cover + 2 stubs + c^2 (original ff. 3 and 6 of the gathering; present ff. 13–14 of the manuscript) + e^1 (present f. 3) + f^7 + 1 (original ff. 2–8 of the gathering, plus a single folio of text apparently omitted in the original copying, to be inserted after 2; present ff. 1–2, 4, 16–20) + g^8-h^8 (complete; present ff. 21–36) + k^2 (original ff. 5–6 of the gathering; present ff. 43–4) + l^8-q^8 (complete; present ff. 45–84) + s^2 (two consecutive leaves; present ff. 11–12 + t^1 (present f. 15) + $v^{6?}$ (original ff. 1–4 of the gathering; present leaves 5–6, 9–10) + i parchment leaf from a former cover + 1 stub. The final gathering might have been of six folios rather than eight like the others, as the text could have been completed within this space.

DECORATION: Two- and three-line chapter initials and paragraph signs are in red. Longer chapters are divided into smaller sections by marginal Textura letters A–E, anywhere from fifteen to thirty lines apart (probably marks for reading units). Scriptural references and chapter numbers are given in the margin; there are no chapter titles. Headers placed flush left and right of each opening identify book and chapter (occasionally in *Scale* I, always in *Scale* II). A tab is pasted to the outer edge of f. 30, at the beginning of *Scale* II.[20]

BINDING: Modern; front and back sheets of an earlier limp parchment binding are bound in before and after the text. This cover (unless trimmed at the binding edge) probably did not originally belong to this manuscript, since it lacks the binding perforations found on the inner edge of all folios of the manuscript itself.

[20] See Sawyer, 'Navigation', 105.

DIALECT: *LALME* LP 4683, Grid 428 257: Warwickshire, with a note that the language changes very slightly at the top of f. 14ʳ.

PROVENANCE: A. I. Doyle has identified the scribal hand as that of John Clerk of Hinton Charterhouse (†1472), who also wrote Cambridge, St John's College Library MS E.22, a theological miscellany (*MLGB*). There are fifteenth-century annotations in other hands.

DESCRIBED IN: Ralph Hanna III, 'The Archaeology of a Manuscript: Huntington Library HM 266', *Scriptorium*, 36 (1982), 99–102; *Guide to Medieval and Renaissance Manuscripts in the Huntington Library*, ed. C. W. Dutschke (San Marino, 1989), i. 229–30.

LITERATURE: de Ricci, *Census*, 65; Doyle, 'Book Production'; Ralph Hanna, *IMEP Handlist I: Manuscripts in the Henry E. Huntington Library* (Cambridge, 1984), 25.

L: London, Lambeth Palace Library MS 472

s. xvᴵ (after 1416)

Parchment. Ff. 262 + iv (parchment). 203 × 145 mm (104 × 148 mm). Written in an Anglicana hand, in a single column at 26 lines per page; ruling and pricking are visible throughout.

CONTENTS:

1. Ff. 1ʳ–83³: Walter Hilton, *Scale* I with preceding Table of Chapters, the rubric of which entitles the 'Scala Perfeccionis' and notes that 'it haþ twey parties'. The *explicit* notes: 'Here endeþ þe firste partye and aftir sueþ þe table of þe secund party'.

2. Ff. 83ʳ–192ᵛ: Walter Hilton, *Scale* II with extended ending, and preceding Table of Chapters. The last five lines of f. 192ᵛ are blank.

3. Ff. 193ʳ–213ʳ: Walter Hilton, *Mixed Life* with expanded opening and conclusion, and preceding Table of Chapters. The last nine lines of f. 213ʳ are blank.

4. Ff. 213ᵛ–223ᵛ: Walter Hilton, *Eight Chapters on Perfection* with preceding Table of Chapters, followed by four blank lines.

5. Ff. 223ᵛ–239ᵛ: Walter Hilton, *Qui habitat*.

6. Ff. 239ᵛ–252ʳ: Walter Hilton, *Bonum est*.

7. Ff. 252ᵛ–259ᵛ: Walter Hilton, *Benedictus*. The last nine lines of f. 259ᵛ are blank.

COLLATION: 4 + $1^8 - 32^8$, 33^6 + 4. Signatures and catchwords remain: the (apparently) original red signatures in the right lower margin run '+', 'a'–'dd'; later black-ink signatures at the centre of the lower margin of the first folio of each gathering run 'a'–'k'.

DECORATION: Two-line lombard initials at the head of each item;

one-line lombard at the head of the Table of Chapters of *Scale* I. Chapter titles throughout are in red, preceded by a blue paragraph sign, with the initial of the following text in blue. Paragraph signs preceding the titles in the Tables of Chapters alternate in red and blue; the chapter numbers, which are given in the margin both of the Tables of Chapters and in the text, are red. Latin scriptural quotations in the text are underlined in red; the scribe has written the source for each quotation in the margin, also underlined in red. There are headers throughout, in red, at the outside and inside margins of the verso and folio, reading across each opening: f. 1^{r}: Incipit tabula; ff. 1^{v}–3^{r}: tabula – pri || me – partis; f. 3^{v}: tabula – prime – partis; ff. 4^{r}–83^{r}: pri – ma || pars – libri; ff. 83^{v}–86^{r}: Tabula – partis || secun – de; ff. 86^{v}–192^{r}: secun – da || pars – libri; 193^{r-v}: Tabula vite mixte; ff. 194^{r}–213^{r}: vita – mixta || vita – mixta; ff. 213^{v}–223^{r}: octo – capitula || perfec – torum; ff. 223^{v}–239^{r}: qui – ha || bi – tat; ff. 239^{v}–252^{r}: Bonum – est || Bonum – est; ff. 252^{v}–259^{v}: be – ne || dic – tus. The disposition of the headers is thus virtually identical to that in MS B_3. There are numerous thread bookmarks sewn into the outer margins of the folios.[21]

BINDING: Modern, incorporating older leather panels front and back: the parchment end-leaves, with their inscription by John Graunt, dated 1493, probably belonged to the binding from which the older materials of the present binding derived.

DIALECT: *LALME* LP 672, Grid 542 271: just east of Willingham, Cambridgeshire.

PROVENANCE/OWNERSHIP: On f. 260^{r}, in a Textura hand of the first quarter of the fifteenth century, underlined in red: 'This booke was maad of þe goodis of Jon Killum for a comyne profite / That þat persoone þat haþ þis booke committed to him of þe persoone þat haþ power to committe it haue þe vse þerof þe teerme of his lijf, preiyng for þe soule of þe same Jon. And þat he þat haþ þe forseid vse of commissioun, whanne he occupieþ it not, leene it for a tyme to sum oþer persoone. Also þat persoone to whom it was committid for þe teerme of lijf vndir þe forseid condicions delyuere it to a noþer persoone þe teerme of his lijf / And so be it delyuerid & committid fro persoone to persoone man or womman as longe as þe booke enduriþ.' The 'Common Profit' inscription of John Killum.

On f. 262^{v}: (a note at the lower outer corner): vi^{c} l xxiii.

21 See Sawyer, 'Navigation', Swales and Blatt, 'Tiny Textiles'.

On the recto of the third parchment flyleaf at the end (in accordance with the inscription on the first parchment flyleaf at the beginning), 'Memorandum: þat þis boke be deliuered to Richard Colop, Parchmanere of London, after my discesse. And in caas he die or I, þen I wol it be take to som deuowte persone to haue it vnder þe forme and condicion wretyn in þe ende of þis book heere tofore. Mordon [signed with what appears to be a scrivener's flourish].' Then 'Per me, Dominum Johannem Graunt, in nomine Domini nostri Jhesu Christi. God graunt grace omnibus nobis. 1493.' Followed by pen-trials: 'God graunt grace omnibus nobis / In nomine Domini nostri Jhesu Christi / Dominum Somme in mondo . . .'.

The will of John Killum, a grocer of London, is recorded in 1416. Since the book was 'made of his goods', it was presumably (although not necessarily) copied after his death. It belonged, after Killum, to Richard Colop, a London stationer at least by 1472 (†1476).[22] The 'Mordon' who was to convey the book to Colop is recorded as a London attorney and notary in the second quarter of the fifteenth century. At the end of the fifteenth century, the manuscript was in the possession of John Graunt.

LITERATURE: Montague Rhodes James, *A Descriptive Catalogue of the Manuscripts in the Library of Lambeth Palace: Medieval Manuscripts* (Cambridge, 1932), 648–50; Hilton, *Minor Works*, ed. Jones, pp. xi–xvi; Sargent, 'Walter Hilton's *Scale of Perfection*: The London Manuscript Group', 205–6; Wendy Scase, 'Reginald Pecock, John Carpenter and John Colop's "Common-Profit" Books: Aspects of Book Ownership and Circulation in Fifteenth-Century London', *MÆ* 61 (1992), 263–74; O. S. Pickering and V. M. O'Mara, *IMEP Handlist XIII: Manuscripts in Lambeth Palace Library* (Cambridge, 1999), 36–8. Mishtooni Bose, 'Reginald Pecock's Vernacular Voice', in Fiona Somerset, Jill C. Havens, and Derrick G. Pitard (eds.), *Lollards and their Influence in Late Medieval England* (Woodbridge, Suffolk, 2003), 217–36 at 230–1.

Ld: Oxford, Bodleian Library MS Laud misc. 602 s. xv^{3}

Parchment. Ff. i + 74 + i. 295 × 200 mm (220 × 153 mm). Writing-space ruled in two columns for 220 × 147 mm, but the writing of the second column usually exceeds the width of the ruled space; 43 lines

[22] C. P. Christianson, *A Directory of London Stationers and Book Artisans* (New York, 1990), 91–3.

per page; pricking in outer margins. Written in several late fifteenth-century Secretary hands interchanging with each other throughout (similar in some forms to the hand of William Ebesham, according to A. I. Doyle).[23]

CONTENTS:

i. On the front paste-down is a (s. xiv ex.) fragment of a Latin legal text.

ii. On the recto of the front end-leaf, mounted sideways (top end out), '. . . vitellares aut Officiales seu Ministros nostros . . . duximus durature. Teste me ipso apud Westmonasterio vicesimo sexto die Octobris Anno regni nostro secundo. / per ipsum Dominum Regem & de data predicta Auctoritate parliamenti.' A fragment of a grant by King Edward IV to Syon Abbey, dated to 1462.

1. Ff. 1ra–31rb: Walter Hilton, *Scale* I with preceding Table of Chapters, which has the *incipit* 'Here begynneþ þe vij partie of þys boke maad of Rycharde Hampole heremyte to an Ankeresse'. The text has the *explicit* 'Here endiþe þe first partie of þe vij partie of þis booke maad of Richard Hampole Heremite to an Ankeresse. And begynneþ þe secunde.' What the preceding six parts of the book attributed to Rolle may have been is unknown.

2. Ff. 31va–74vb: Walter Hilton, *Scale* II without the extended ending, with preceding Table of Chapters.

One line blank, then: 'Raynes: Ihesus est amor meus.'

iii. On the rear paste-down is a fragment of a (s. xiv) philosophical treatise.

COLLATION: i + 1^3, 2^{12}–6^{12}, 7^{11}. NB: gathering 2 has '. . . q. 19' on bottom verso of the first six folios; gathering 3 has '. . . q. 20'; and so on through the gatherings . In fullest form (e.g. f. 43^v) the signature reads: 'fo 4. q. 22'. This would indicate that there were eighteen preceding gatherings in the original manuscript, which would have comprised (if the *incipit* of item 1 is correct), six other works attributed to Richard Rolle. On the other hand, ff. 43^r and 44^r (i.e. the fourth and fifth of gathering 5 of the manuscript as presently constituted) are signed 'b iiij' and 'b v'; and f. 67^r (the fourth of gathering 7) is signed 'c iiij'.

DECORATION: Three-line gold initial on a blue background, with floral partial border decoration, to *Scale* I; four-line blue initial with

[23] See A. I. Doyle, 'The Work of a Late Fifteenth-Century English Scribe, William Ebesham', *Bulletin of the John Rylands Library*, 39 (1957), 298–325.

red penwork decoration to *Scale* II; two-line chapter initials, the same, throughout. The two Tables of Chapters have alternating blue and red paragraph signs and decoration at the line-ends of the chapter titles. The first two gatherings (ff. 1^r–15^v) have a header that reads across the opening: '7^a / pars'. Chapter titles and Latin scriptural quotations (preceded in each case by the identification of the text) are engrossed, and underlined in red through the first five gatherings (up to f. 51^v), at which point the underlining ceases. Alternating blue and red paragraph signs (approximately ten per opening) throughout; initials in the text are touched in red.

BINDING: The covers are medieval, leather on boards, wheel-stamped. Nail holes for decorative mounts and clasps are still visible. The binding edge is a modern brown leather replacement.

DIALECT: *LALME*, i. 177, describes the language of the main hand as the same as that of MS L (although the hand is not the same). Thus LP 672, Grid 542 271: Cambridgeshire.

PROVENANCE/OWNERSHIP: The fragment of a grant to Syon Abbey by Edward IV, dated 26 October of his second regnal year (i.e. 1462) preserved in the medieval binding of this manuscript argues that it was there after this time. The 'Raynes' whose name occurs in the colophon on f. 74vb may be identifiable as W. Reydnes, a Syon monk (†1483).[24]

At the outer edge of f. 1^r: 'Robert Hedrington his Bookes. 1577.' At the foot of the page: 'Liber Guilielmi Laud Archiepiscopi Cantuariensis et Cancellarij Vniuersitatis Oxonie. 1633.' Owned by Robert Hare.

DISCUSSED IN: Bodleian *SC* 1499; Ogilvie-Thomson, *IMEP Handlist XVI*, 75.

Lw: Yale University, Beinecke Library, Prof. T. Takamiya's MS 3 (*olim* Luttrell Wynne) early s. xv

Parchment. Ff. ii + 174 + i. 172 × 146 mm (135 × 90 mm). Written in a Secretary hand, in a single column at 29–30 lines per page. Notes throughout in a more formal Secretary (probably the same hand) correcting a large number of omissions and dittographies. Since the corrections generally register omission and dittography

[24] S. S. Hussey, 'The Text of *The Scale of Perfection*, Book II', *Neuphilologische Mitteilungen*, 65 (1964), 75–92 at 81; information from A. I. Doyle.

rather than any other kind of variation, they were presumably by comparison with the exemplar, perhaps during or soon after copying.

CONTENTS:

1. Ff. 1^r–68^v: Walter Hilton, *Scale* I with preceding Table of Chapters. The *explicit* identifies the text as 'primus liber Magistri Walteri Hylton'.

2. Ff. 69^r–169^v: Walter Hilton, *Scale* II with the extended ending, with preceding Table of Chapters. The *explicit* identifes the text as 'liber 2us Magistri Walteri Hylton quondam canonici de Thurgarton, et hic liber vocatur Scala Perfectionis, anglice The Ladder of Perfection'.

3. Ff. 170^r–174^r: Walter Hilton, *Angels' Song*.

At the top of f. 174^v is a line from *Scale* II 43/32–3, 'to þe castel of Emaus brennyng in desyre and'.

COLLATION: 1^{12}–13^{12}, 14^{14} (an extra bifolium—ff. 160–1—added between the third and fourth leaves, containing material omitted by the original scribe) + two singletons + 15^2.

DECORATION: Three-line lombard initials throughout. No chapter headings. Scriptural quotations are underlined in red.

BINDING: Contemporary white tawed leather over wooden boards, now stained.

DIALECT: Probably East Berkshire.

PROVENANCE: Unknown. The hand has been misidentified as the same as that of *Scale* MS T.[25]

DESCRIBED IN: Toshiyuki Takamiya, 'A Hilton Manuscript Once in the Possession of Luttrell Wynne', *The Book Collector* (Special Number for the 150th Anniversary of Bernard Quaritch, 1997), repr. in *The Pleasures of Bibliophyly: Fifty Years of the Book Collector, An Anthology* (London, 2003), 305–10.

LITERATURE: Toshiyuki Takamiya, 'A Handlist of Western Medieval Manuscripts in the Takamiya Collection', in James H. Marrow, Richard A. Linenthal, and William Noel (eds.), *The Medieval Book: Glosses from Friends and Colleagues of Christopher de Hamel* (Houten, 2010), 421–40 at 422.

[25] Michael G. Sargent, *James Grenehalgh as Textual Critic*, Analecta Cartusiana, 85 (Salzburg, 1984), 44–5, repeated by Kathryn Kerby-Fultin, Maidie Hilmo, and Linda Olson, *Opening Up Middle English Manuscripts: Literary and Visual Approaches* (Ithaca, NY, 2012), 330.

M: Cambridge, Magdalene College, Old Library MS fo.4.17 s. xv med.

Parchment. Ff. 117 (paginated 1–334). 235 × 155 mm (150 × 95 mm). Written in two Bastard Anglicana hands (*LALME* Hand A, with more of a Secretary *ductus* and occasional strapwork ascenders in the top line, ends at p. 150 (f. 75^{v}); Hand B has a more Quadrata aspect), at 28–9 lines per page, in a single column. Ruling is in ink, and still visible where not water damaged. The manuscript is badly water damaged, particularly at the front, and at the bottom and binding edges; overwritten in places.

CONTENTS:

1. Ff. 1^{r}–4^{v}: Walter Hilton, *Scale* II, Table of Chapters with the title 'the book of reformynge of manes soule. Wheche book a religious man made, holy in leuynge, heylyche visited, connynge of clergie, and taught of the holy goost fully gostleche felyng; wheche man was named Maister Watier Hylton, comensour of degrees and Chanon of Thurgarton'.

2. Ff. 5^{r}–117^{v}: Walter Hilton, *Scale* II, *incipit* 'This book þat folweth may skilfully be cleped the Scole of Perfeccion. For who so wole rede besily and vnderstonde spedfully the matier that here folweth may haue ful techyng how he shal mowe comen to gostly felyng and to swetnesse of contemplacion ȝif his wille be stable and feruent to conne loue our lord Crist Jesu. For wheche loue alle men and wemmen nyght and day shuld trauayle, and namelych religious, wheche be wordus of profession haue forsake all þe world, and outward beth clothed with a dedly habite þat semyth contemplatyf or ful of perfeccion.' Walter Hilton, *Scale* II, with the extended ending.

3. f. 118^{r-v}: (in a s. xvi hand) How the soule of man is ordayned . . . which is Jesus Christe our Lord and savyour.

COLLATION: 1^{8}–9^{8}, 10^{14} (the last three of which are cut away, with no loss of text), 11^{8}–14^{8}, 15^{6} (the last three of which are cut away). Catchwords throughout.

DECORATION: Sporadic strapwork ascenders to the top line of text throughout. Four-line blue initials to the rubrics at the head of items 1 and 2, and to the text of item 2; two- and three-line blue chapter initials throughout. Chapter titles, marginal chapter numbers, and Latin scriptural quotations in text in red.

BINDING: Modern.

DIALECT: *LALME*, i. 63, describes Hand A as mixed, Warwickshire with NE Midland components, and localizes Hand B to Ely.

PROVENANCE: Cancelled catalogue numbers 'G.6.28' on front paper end-leaf, 'L.5.10' above the Magdalene College bookplate on the front parchment end-leaf. James notes that this manuscript is not included in Gustav Haenel's *Catalogi librorum manuscriptorum* (Leipzig, 1830).

DESCRIBED IN: M. R. James, *A Descriptive Catalogue of the Manuscripts in the College Libary of Magdalene College* (Cambridge, 1909), 44–5.

P: London, Inner Temple Library MS Petyt 524 s. xv med.

Parchment. iv (parchment) + 146 (numbered in pencil, modern, 4–149). 290 × 205 mm (171 × 127 mm). Written in a Secretary hand of the mid-fifteenth century in a single column, at 31–2 lines per page. The front parchment flyleaf is taken from a different manuscript, written in an Anglicana hand, also of the mid-fifteenth century, in two columns of 41–2 lines, trimmed at the top, with some loss of text.

CONTENTS:

i. (unnumbered parchment flyleaf): Lydgate, *Siege of Thebes* Prologue, ll. 109–50, 160–200, 10–50, and 59–100. *DIMEV* 3995, record 19.

1. f. 4^{r}: Walter Hilton, *Mixed Life*, acephalous (comprising only the final 151 words). Followed by one blank line.

2. Ff. 4^{r}–11^{r}: Walter Hilton, *Eight Chapters on Perfection*, preceded by a Table of Chapters.

3. Ff. 11^{v}–70^{v}: Walter Hilton, *Scale* I with preceding Table of Chapters, *incipit* 'Here begynneth the boke that is cleped Scala Perfeccionis, and it hath two parties, wherof heere sueth the table of þe first partie'; *explicit* 'Heere endeth the first partie, and after sueth the table of the seconde partie.'

4. Ff. 70^{v}–147^{v}: Walter Hilton, *Scale* II with the extended ending, preceded by a Table of Chapters, which refers to the text as 'the seconde partie of the boke'.

COLLATION: iii (paper) + iii (parchment) + 1^{4} (missing first four leaves) + 2^{8}–17^{8}. No signatures; the gatherings comprising *Scale* II (9–17) have catchwords.

DECORATION: Full border decoration, in blue, green, mauve, and white with gold, at the openings of *Scale* I and *Scale* II (ff. 14^{r} and

73^{r}); half borders at the Table of Chapters of each (ff. 11^{v} and 70^{v}); two-line gold initials (initial 'I' often extending six lines), champed, with vinet flourishing, for all chapters. The paragraph signs introducing the chapter titles in the tables, sentence initials throughout, and at each of the marginal notes (both those identifying scriptural quotations and reader's 'notae'—both of which are virually identical to those of MS L) alternate between gold-on-blue and blue-on-red. Scriptual quotations, usually rubricated or underlined in manuscripts of the *Scale*, are not marked in this manuscript.

BINDING: Modern.

DIALECT: In private correspondence with A. J. Bliss, Angus McIntosh reports a dialectal location 'in the southern part of present Greater London, just north of the junction of northeastern Surrey and northwestern Kent'.

PROVENANCE: F. 149^{v}, in various hands: [at top] 'Hospicij rector sit letus semper vt Hector / Vt Job sit pasiens atque sibilla sciens.' [below] 'be me Hari Langeforde / and Jane his wife and Jane Cox and William Folle and Bes Foll and gret Bes more folle.' [below] 'I loueid a litill preti flax wife / dwellin in Hollborne. [the same hand?, cursive] I lowyd her so longe / Tyll she tyed me in a thonge.' [below] 'Hospicij rector sit letus semper vt Hector / Vt Job sit pasiens atque sibilla sciens.' [below, in a numerical cipher] 'This is Henri Langefordes boke organemaker of Lundone and warden of the same sienes.'[26] London. Belonged to Henry Langford, organmaker, dwelling in the Minories.

DESCRIBED IN: J. Conway Davies, *Catalogue of Manuscripts in the Library of the Honourable Society of the Inner Temple* (Oxford, 1972), i. 324–5.

Pl: New York, Columbia University Library, Plimpton MS 257 s. xv$^{3/4}$

Parchment. Ff. 241 (The numeration by Samuel Ives, the Plimpton librarian in the 1930s, counts a number of stubs that are conjugate with single leaves as full folios, for a total of 250; an earlier system of numeration counted only every tenth page, starting with 'p. 21' on f. 1). 170 × 110 mm (120 × 85 mm). The writing space is roughly

[26] The same cipher is used in Langford's *ex libris* in British Library MS Royal 18 A XIII (f. 113^{v}) of Walton's *Boethius*, 'Be me Henri Langeforde organmaker of London duellinge bi the Minores'. See A. S. G. Edwards, 'Reading John Walton's Boethius in the Fifteenth and Sixteenth Centuries', in Flannery and Griffin (eds.), *Spaces*, 35–49.

ruled in plummet, but no line ruling is apparent. Written in two similar Secretary hands (ff. 1–226 and 227–43), at 21–7 lines per page.

Pl originally formed a single codex with Plimpton MS 271, from which it was separated, probably in the nineteenth century. Both were sold by Sotheby's in 1929 and by Tregaskis in 1930 (the latter in two different sales); both were purchased from the latter by George A. Plimpton, whence they came together to Columbia. Plimpton 271, which continues the work of the second scribe of Pl, comprises 22 folios. The whole was reconstructed by A. J. Bliss.

CONTENTS:

Plimpton MS 257:

1. Ff. 1^r–104^v: Walter Hilton, *Scale* I.

2. Ff. 105^r–250^v: Walter Hilton, *Scale* II with the extended ending. The lower half of f. 250^v is blank.

Plimpton MS 271:

3. Ff. 1^r–22^r: Walter Hilton, *Mixed Life*.

COLLATION (MS 257): 1^{10}–3^{10}, 4^{8}, 5^{10}–6^{10}, 7^{9}, 8^{12}, 9^{10}–10^{10}, 11^{11}, 12^{10}–14^{10}, 15–16^{8}, 17^{10}, 18^{11}, 19^{16}, 20–22^{12}, 23^{10}, 24^{2} (MS 277) 1^{8}, 2^{2}, 3^{12}. The last gathering of Plimpton MS 257 and the first two of Pl were originally a single gathering of twelve. Bliss notes the singletons bound into gatherings 7, 11, 12, 16, 18, and 20. Catchwords throughout. The numbering 'p. 21' in the upper right corner of Pl, f. 1^r (a numbering that is repeated in tens for every five folios throughout both manuscripts) suggests that the first gathering was originally preceded by another gathering of ten. Bliss suggests, on the basis of the greater textual similarity of Pl with S than V of its two congeners for *Scale* I, that this gathering may have comprised a copy of Rolle's *Ego dormio*, which precedes *Scale* I in S, rather than Hilton's *Qui habitat* and *Bonum est*, which precede it in V. *Scale* II does not occur in V or S.

DECORATION: Three-line red initials to *Scale* I, *Scale* II, and the *Mixed Life*; two-line chapter initials throughout. Chapter titles are in red. Scriptural quotations are in an engrossed version of the second scribal hand, underlined in red.

BINDING: Modern.

DIALECT: *LALME* LP 5620, Grid 499 169: Surrey, about 10 miles south of Windsor.

DESCRIBED IN: A. J. Bliss, 'Two Hilton Manuscripts in Columbia University Library', *MÆ* 38 (1969), 157–63.

LITERATURE: de Ricci, *Census*, 1799–1800; Hilton, *Mixed Life*, ed. Ogilvie-Thomson, p. xvii.

R: Oxford, Bodleian Library MS Rawlinson C.285 s. xv in.

Parchment. Ff. iii (all stubs) + 118 + iii (all stubs). 220 × 160 mm. Comprises four booklets in different hands, with variations in layout. Booklets 1–3 are parallel in contents to *Scale* I MSS D and F, of which Ralph Hanna has demonstrated that R is the original;[27] Booklet 4 is a later, but still early fifteenth-century, addition. For the description of Booklets 1–3, see Hanna, *EMRR* no. 94, pp. 174–5.

Booklet 4: Writing area 180–5 × 115–25 mm. Written in a Bastard Anglicana hand of s. xv^{1} (Scribe 4: begins as Textura, but lapses into a more informal script with both Anglicana and Secretary forms of 'a'), in a single column of 38–40 lines per page.

CONTENTS:

1. Ff. 74^{r}–118^{v}: Walter Hilton, *Scale* II, with the extended ending. Several leaves are missing in the last gatherings, comprising text for 40/33 creature – 106 mykel and 41/70 chaungeablyte – 45/5 Neuerþeles.

COLLATION: 1^{10}–3^{10}, 4^{6}. Calculating by the amount of text lacking in the final chapters, it seems that the original final gatherings comprised a conjoint pair and a gathering of ten like those preceding, of which the first leaf of the pair and the middle three conjoint leaves of the final gathering of ten are now lacking. The first three gatherings have catchwords and are signed 'a'–'c'.

DECORATION: As for each booklet of this manuscript, there is a gold initial at the opening of the text, f. 74^{r}, with violet penwork decoration in the lower margin added in a modern hand. All other chapters have two-line red initials; chapter-titles in red; Latin scriptural quotations are underlined in red; occasional initials and ascenders in the top line of text are touched in red.

DIALECT: Booklets 1–3 are described by *LALME*, LP 22, as Northern, probably Yorkshire. The dialect of booklet 4 is not described in *LALME*. Hanna describes the language as 'probably southwest of the Wash, perhaps the Ely–Norfolk border'. Note that 3rd singular verbs end in '-eth' (rarely '-is'); 3rd plural verbs in '-en'; present participles in '-and/-end'; 3rd plural personal pronoun forms

[27] Hanna, *EMRR* nos. 12 and 15, pp. 24–5, 28–30.

'þai/þei', 'þair/þeire/here/her/hir', 'hem'; 'whilk/qwilk'; 'kirke/chirche'; 'þorw/þorow/thorow/thorew'; 'ageyn/aȝeyn/aȝeyns'; 'sithen' 'ȷnow'; 'mekil'; 'als . . . as'; 'euer ilk'; PDE 'though' is 'thow/þoȝw/þoȝu'.

PROVENANCE: On f. 1^{v}: '[O]biit dominus Johannes Marschal.' As Lewis and McIntosh note, this is 'a common name among secular priests in Yorkshire in the 15th c.' *Scale* I MS D, which Hanna argues was copied from R before the addition of Booklet 4, is dialectally localizable to northern Yorkshire; *LALME* localizes MS F, copied like D from R, to north-eastern Norfolk; MS H_3, which is cognate with RDF for *Scale* I and comprises a similar selection of Rolleana,[28] is localized by *LALME* to the West Riding, as is MS U, also cognate for *Scale* I. The first three booklets of R would appear to have been written in the North, but the manuscript was brought south to East Anglia, where both the text of *Scale* I in F and that of *Scale* II in R were copied.

BINDING: A brown leather chemise, s. xv, sewn on six staggered thongs; a piece of the upper board leather cut for use as a strap, with no sign of a corresponding lower board attachment; in addition, there are stubs of two leather straps, and intact staple-like clasps along the leading edge of the lower board.

DESCRIBED IN: Hanna, *EMRR*, no. 9, pp. 174–6.

LITERATURE: Robert E. Lewis and Angus McIntosh, *A Descriptive Guide to the Manuscripts of the* Prick of Conscience, *Medium Ævum* monographs, NS 12 (Oxford, 1982), no. E 8, 157; Vincent Gillespie, 'Vernacular Books of Religion', in Jeremy Griffiths and Derek Pearsall (eds.), *Book Production and Publishing in Britain 1375–1475* (Cambridge, 1989), 317–44 at 328–9; *Richard Rolle: Uncollected Prose and Verse with Related Northern Texts*, ed. Ralph Hanna, EETS OS 329 (2007), pp. xlviii–l; Ralph Hanna, 'The History of a Book: Bodleian Library, MS Rawlinson C.285', in *Introducing English Medieval Book History: Manuscripts, their Producers, and their Readers* (Liverpool, 2013), 59–95.

Sr: Philadelphia, University of Pennsylvania Library codex 218 (*olim* Stonor; *olim* University of Pennsylvania Library MS English 8) xv^{I}

Parchment. Ff. 159 + i. 385 mm × 255 mm (283 mm × 180 mm).

[28] *EMRR* no. 48, pp. 94–7.

Ink ruling throughout, including double-ruled top and bottom lines and 12 mm space between columns. Written in two sections (ff. 1–146 and ff. 147–59) in an Anglicana hand of the early fifteenth century, 41–2 lines per page, in two columns. Writing from beginning through f. 22^{r} is 41 lines per page (bottom line blank); 42 lines per page from f. 22^{v} through f. 151^{v}; 45 lines from f. 152^{r} to the end. Contents (1, 4, 5, 6 below) are numbered 1–4, with appropriate chapter numbers, in the upper right-hand corner of each recto. This section ends on f. 146va (the second folio of gathering 't') with one and a half columns blank. Section 2 (ff. 147–59) leaves space for chapter initials, but without guide-letters, and there is no rubrication at all. The top line of writing is above the top line of the ruled text box. Because the verse text of the *Prick of Conscience* that this section comprises allows for a different spread of the hand than the prose texts preceding, it has a different appearance, and has been identified as a second hand in previous literature; but the letter-forms in both the Anglicana text and the Formata of Latin quotations appear to be the same for both sections of the manuscript.

CONTENTS:

1. Ff. 1ra–28ra: Walter Hilton, *Scale* I, acephalous (beginning in ch. 19). The *explicit* refers to the text as 'primus liber'.

2. F. 28^{ra-b}: Qui timetis deum . . . þat is Holy Chirche. Walter Hilton, *Scale* II, 10/61–90. The scribe omits this passage in its proper place (f. 35rb), referring the reader 'ut supra'.

3. Ff. 28rb–77vb [four lines from the bottom]: Walter Hilton, *Scale* II with extended ending only as far as the quotation of Psalm 28:9, with preceding Table of Chapters.

4. Ff. 77vb–127va: *The Prickynge of Love* preceded by a Table of Chapters, with an ascription to Walter Hilton: 'Iste liber sequens primo fuit compositus in latino sermone per quemdam fratrem minorem Cardinalem nobilem doctorem Bonauenturam nomine; postea translatus est in linguam anglicanam pro minoribus latinum non intelligentibus per quemdam canonicum Walterum Hilton nomine in amore Dei valde deuotum.'

5. Ff. 127va–145vb [top two lines]: *Contemplations of the Dread and Love of God* (*IPMEP* 362).[29]

6. Ff. 145vb–146va [continuing straight on from the former]:

[29] *Contemplations of the Dread and Love of God*, ed. Margaret Connolly, EETS os 303 (1993).

'Meditation on the Five Wits' (*IPMEP 192*).[30] The lower half of this column and the adjacent column are blank.

7. Ff. 147ra–159vb: *The Prick of Conscience*, imperfect, Prologue–III:157b.[31]

COLLATION: 1^{8}–18^{8}, 19^{6+1}, 20^{8}. Signatures in a contemporary Textura, gatherings a–c; catchwords throughout items 1–6.

DECORATION: Space is left for chapter capitals throughout, with guide-letters, but none are supplied. Chapter titles in the text and chapter numbers in the Table of Chapters of each of the constituent works are in red; sentence capitals throughout the text are touched in red; Latin scriptural quotations in the text are in an engrossed Formata, underlined in red.

DIALECT: The language of the *Scale* is *LALME* LP 559, Grid 541 282: Ely. According to Lewis and McIntosh, the language of the *Prick of Conscience* is of South-east Lincolnshire.

BINDING: Late fifteenth-century blind-stamped binding, by the 'Virgin and Child' binder, active in the Winchester area.

DESCRIBED IN: Norman Zacour and Rudolph Hirsch, *Catalogue of Manuscripts in the Libraries of the University of Pennsylvania to 1800* (Philadelphia, Pa., 1965), 50.

LITERATURE: Allen, *Writings Ascribed to Richard Rolle*, 373 n. 1, 539–40; Krochalis, '*Contemplations*'; Lewis and McIntosh, *Descriptive Guide*.

T: Cambridge, Trinity College MS B.15.18 (354) s. xv^{4}

Parchment. Ff. 120. 275 × 190 mm (173 × 120 mm). Written in the Secretary hand of Robert Benet, Procurator of Sheen Charterhouse, at the end of the fifteenth century, in a single column, 36–41 lines per page. Annotations by James Grenehalgh of Sheen throughout, dated 1499 at the end.

CONTENTS:

Fo. 1 blank.

1. Ff. 2^{r}–52^{v}: Walter Hilton, *Scale* I with preceding Table of Chapters. The *incipits* of both the table and text refer to it as the 'firste boke'; the table adds 'of Walter Hilton, þe which is callid Scala perfeccionis, þat is to sey þe ladder of perfeccion'.

[30] Jeanne Elizabeth Krochalis, '*Contemplations of the Dread and Love of God*: Two Newly Identified Pennsylvania Manuscripts', *Library Chronicle*, 42 (1977), 3–22.

[31] Lewis and McIntosh, *A Descriptive Guide to the Manuscripts of the* Prick of Conscience, 124–5.

2. Ff. 52^{v}–119^{r}: Walter Hilton, *Scale* II with preceding Table of Chapters. The *incipits* of both the table and text refer to it as the 'secunde booke'. The extended ending has been added by the annotator, James Grenehalgh.

Ff. 119–20 are blank except for s. xvi pen-trials at the foot of f. 119^{v} and various unsigned *loci communes*, one dated 1595, on f. 120^{r-v}, with the offset of some other (no longer facing) text in the middle of f. 120^{v}.

COLLATION: 1^{8}–2^{8}, 3^{10}, 4^{8}–5^{8}, 6^{10}–7^{10}, 8^{8}–14^{8}, 15^{2}. The signatures 'f 2' and 'o 2', and the catchwords of gatherings 9–13 survive.

DECORATION: Eight-line lombard initials to *Scale* I and II; three- and four-line lombards for all chapters. Chapter titles are in red, slightly engrossed; Latin quotations in the text are underlined in red.

BINDING: Modern.

DIALECT: *LALME* LP 5750, Grid 514 167: Surrey, approximately 10 miles south of Richmond.

PROVENANCE: On f. 119^{r}, Grenehalgh has added: 'et sic finitur liber venerabilis Walteri Hylton summi contemplatiui, cuius foelicissimus obitus fuit in vigilia intemerate Assumptionis intemerate Virginis Dei genitricis Marie Anno Domini M. CCC. lxxxxv. Scriptus quidem est hoc opus per Benet quondam procuratorem in Carthusia de Schen super Tamisiam. Quod Grenehalgh, eiusdem domus professus indigna manu sua. In festo Relliquiarum fe. 6^{a}. sero. 1499. [JA.G monogram].'[32] The *obit* of Robert Benet, former procurator of Sheen Charterhouse, is recorded in 1518; James Grenehalgh, who corrected this manuscript thoroughly against the Rosenbach Library copy of W and MS H_8 of the Latin translation of the *Scale*, was removed for disciplinary reasons from Sheen to Coventry Charterhouse by 1508, and died a guest in Hull Charterhouse in 1529.

DESCRIBED IN: Montague Rhodes James, *The Western Manuscripts in the Library of Trinity College, Cambridge: A Descriptive Catalogue*, i (Cambridge, 1900), 481–2.

LITERATURE: Ker, *MLGB*, 178; Sargent, *James Grenehalgh*, 487–91;

[32] Grenehalgh provides the same information in a note at the end of the Rosenbach copy of W. The dating of Hilton's death is incorrect: it was the vigil of the Annunciation, not the Assumption. The same mistake occurs in the colophon of MS B_4 of the Latin *Scale*, written by John Feriby of Sheen (†1445). See Joy Russell-Smith, 'Walter Hilton and a Tract in Defence of the Veneration of Images', *Dominican Studies*, 7 (1954), 180–214 at 210–11. The Carthusian Fest of Relics was 8 November.

Linne R. Mooney, *IMEP Handlist XI: Manuscripts in the Library of Trinity College, Cambridge* (Cambridge, 1995), 18.

Ws: London, Westminster School, MS 4 **s. xv^{1}**

Parchment. Ff. 92, numbered in pencil in the lower right corner of each recto. 202 × 137 mm (163 × 102 mm); written in an Anglicana Formata hand in two columns, at 31–7 lines per page. Text space is outlined in crayon.

CONTENTS:

1. Ff. 1^{r}–49^{r}: Walter Hilton, *Scale* I with preceding Table of Chapters. The *incipit* refers to the text as 'Scala Perfectionis'; the *explicit* refers to the 'prima pars libri qui dicitur Scala Perfeccionis'. The lower six lines of f. 49^{v} are blank.

2. Ff. 49^{v}–91^{v}: Walter Hilton, *Scale* II without the extended ending. The preceding Table of Chapters is atelous, ending in Chapter 37. The *explicit* refers to the text as 'secunda pars huius operis'.

COLLATION: 1^{8}–5^{8}, 6^{10}, 7^{8}–11^{8}, 12^{2}. There are perhaps two folios missing following gathering 6 that would have comprised the remainder of the Table of Chapters of *Scale* II, and a gathering missing between 8 and 9 that would have comprised text from 20/13 As – 30/79 hem.

DECORATION: Four-line lombard capitals at the head of each book; three-line lombard chapter initials; occasional sentence initials touched in blue. The chapter titles in the Table of Chapters of *Scale* I have blue paragraph signs; those of *Scale* II are red. Chapter titles in the text of *Scale* I are engrossed and underlined in red, as are all scriptural quotations; there are no chapter titles in *Scale* II.

BINDING: Modern.

DIALECT: According to *LALME*, i. 137, Ely.

PROVENANCE: There are several s. xvi *probationes pennae* on f. 91^{v}, including 'Nouerint vniuersi per presentes me Ihone Farryn de'; 'Ihon Stonbanckes of Fylgrave'; 'Master Frauncis Tyrryngham'. Ker notes that Filgrave is a hamlet of Tyringham in north Buckinghamshire. There is also a note on the recto of the first flyleaf, in the hand of Richard Busby (†1695), headmaster of Westminster School for most of the latter half of the seventeenth century.

DESCRIBED IN: Ker, *MMBL*, i: *London*, 425.

Early Printed Editions

W: Wynkyn de Worde, *editio princeps* of 1494 (*STC* 14042)
No: Julian Notary, 1507 (*STC* 14043)
W_2: Wynkyn de Worde, 1519 (*STC* 14043.5)
W_3: Wynkyn de Worde, 1525 (*STC* 14044)
W_4: Wynkyn de Worde, 1533 (*STC* 14045)

Fragment of an Originally Complete Manuscript

Ri: Ripon Cathedral binding fragment 63 (on deposit at Leeds University Brotherton Library)

A parchment fragment, 174 × 30 mm, from the binding of a copy of Dudley Fenner's *Defence of the Godlie Ministers* (*STC* 10771: Middleburgh: Schilders, 1587). The fragment comprises approximately four lines in two columns per side: *Scale* II, 43/21 vp – abo- (l. 23); 38 openeth – vnsought (l. 40); 58 vos – thynges (l. 60); and 74 synne — withouten (l. 75).

Extracts

Ad: London, British Library, Add. MS 37049 s. xv²

Paper. Ff. 96. 267 × 185 mm (225–37 × 150–60 mm). An illustrated anthology of devotional prose and verse, comprising 101 separate items.[33] Written in three Anglicana hands, at 40–5 lines per page. The dialectal characteristics of the pieces vary. The tract *Of Actyfe lyfe and contemplatyfe declaracion* (*IPMEP* 319, ff. 87ᵛ–89ᵛ),[34] item 92 in Brantley's list, is one of the majority of the texts whose dialectal profiles locate them in Nottinghamshire.

The tract comprises extracts from *The Cloud of Unknowing* and several works of the *Cloud* corpus, Rolle's *Form of Living*, an English version of Hugh of Balma's *Mystica Theologia*, and both books of Hilton's *Scale of Perfection* in answer to the question, 'I beseke þe reuerent doctour to informe me þe way of goode lyfyng, and how I sal dispose me to cum to euerlastyng lyfe, þe whilk is ordand for þaim þat here dewly lufs and serfys almyghty God.' There are six

[33] Listed in Jessica Brantley, *Reading in the Wilderness: Private Devotion and Public Performance in Late Medieval England* (Chicago, 2007), 307–25.

[34] P. S. Jolliffe, 'Two Middle English Tracts on the Contemplative Life', *Mediæval Studies*, 37 (1975), 85–121. See Brantley, *Reading in the Wilderness*, 232–4.

brief extracts from *Scale* II, Chapters 21 and 22 in the tract, in the order 21/43 For – pees (l. 44); 21/50 for – weye (l. 54); 21/55 þe – Jesu (l. 61); 21/96 And – boght (l. 99); 22/26 Also – God; and 22/29 trow – it^{1} (l. 30).

COLLATION: Not feasible.

BINDING: Modern.

DIALECT: *LALME* describes three hands: Hand A, ff. 2^{v}–45^{v} (with the exception of 26^{v}–27^{r}) and 67^{v}–96^{v}, is LP 225, Grid 482 370: on the Nottinghamshire/Lincolnshire border, about 10 miles north of Newark on Trent; Hand B, ff. 26^{v}–27^{r}, is north-west Lincolnshire; Hand D, ff. 46^{v}–66^{v}, is LP 410, Grid 439 440: West Riding of Yorkshire, about 10 miles north-east of Leeds.

PROVENANCE: The illustrations of monks in distinctive Carthusian habit and a number of pieces of specifically Carthusian interest indicate a Carthusian provenance. A. I. Doyle suggests that the most probable locations are Axeholme or Beauvale Charterhouse, in Lincolnshire and Nottinghamshire respectively.[35]

DESCRIBED IN: Hanna, *EMRR*, no. 41, pp. 78–80.

LITERATURE: Brantley, *Reading in the Wilderness.*

Ad$_2$: London, British Library, Add. MS Add 37790

s. xv med.

Parchment. Ff. 237 + i (the last two are stubs) + i (f. 238, a medieval flyleaf). Written in a single Anglicana Formata hand in three booklets of different sizes. The third booklet, in which the Hilton material occurs, measures 178–83 × 110 mm (185 × 120 mm), athough the filler material at the end of each booklet is irregular, and larger in size.[36] Each booklet begins a new gathering with one or two major prose pieces, and is followed by several lesser pieces. The text is written in a single column, but the number of lines per page varies from 27 to 45 depending on the need for space to fit the minor pieces into the last folios of each booklet. The major works in Booklet 1 are:

[35] A. I. Doyle, 'English Carthusian Books not yet Linked with a Charterhouse', in Toby Barnard, Dáibhí Ó Cróinín, and Katharine Simms (eds.), '*A Miracle of Learning*': *Studies in Manuscripts and Irish Learning. Essays in Honour of William O'Sullivan* (Aldershot, 1998), 122–36 at 128; Doyle, 'Book Production by the Monastic Orders in England', in Linda Brownrigg (ed.), *Medieval Book Production: Assessing the Evidence* (Los Altos Hills, Calif., 1990), 1–19 at 14.

[36] The same hand is responsible for Cambridge, St John's College MS G.21 (*The Pilgrimage of the Life of the Soul*) and British Library, Egerton MS 2006 (Mechtild of Hackeborn's *Revelations*).

Richard Misyn's English version of Richard Rolle's *Emendatio vitae* and *Incendium amoris* (ff. 1^{r}–95^{v}: *IPMEP* 652 and 92 respectively).[37] In Booklet 2: the Short Text of the *Showings* of Julian of Norwich (ff. 97^{r}–115^{r}: *IPMEP* 321),[38] and *The Treatise of Perfection of the Sons of God*, the English translation of Jan van Ruusbroec's tract *Van den blinckenden Steen* (ff. 115^{r}–130^{r}: *IPMEP* 846).[39] In Booklet 3: the translation by 'M.N.' of Marguerite Porete's *Mirouer des simples âmes anienties* (ff. 137^{3}–225^{r}: *IPMEP* 732). The short tract *Via ad contemplacionem* (*IPMEP* 784), which is closely related to the tract *Of Actyfe lyfe and contemplatyfe declaracion* in Ad, occurs among the materials at the end of Booklet 3, on ff. 234^{r}–236^{r}. The *Via* has ten extracts from *Scale* II, in the order 21/43 For – pees (l. 44); 21/50 for – weye (l. 54); 21/55 þe – Jesu (l. 61); 21/96 And – boght (l. 99); 22/6 Now^{2} – moun (l. 7); 22/16 what-so – Jesu (l. 18); 22/26 Also – God; 22/29 trow – it^{1} (l. 30); 22/29 trow – it^{1} (l. 30); 22/33 And – to; and 23/9 kepe – abaysshed (l. 10). Six of these extracts also occur in Ad.

COLLATION: Booklet 1: 1^{8}–12^{8}; Booklet 2: 13^{8}–17^{8}; Booklet 3: 18^{8}–29^{8}; 30 (probably also originally a gathering of 8, of which the stubs of ff. 5—numbered 237—and 6 remain).

DECORATION: Headings are in red; four- and five-line lombard initials to each of the major pieces; three-line lombards to chapter initials. Scriptural quotations and chapter titles are in red.

BINDING: Modern.

DIALECT: *LALME*, i. 214, locates the scribal dialect in Lincolnshire, but various pieces have more central, eastern, or western Lincolnshire characteristics, and some Northern forms. The dialect of Booklet 3, including the *Via ad contemplacionem*, is southern Lincolnshire mixed with central eastern Worcestershire.

PROVENANCE: The monogram of the Carthusian monk James Grenehalgh occurs on ff. 23 and 37. Annotations in his hand refer to London and Mount Grace (although the notes may not have been

[37] *The Fire of Love and The Mending of Life or The Rule of Living*, ed. Ralph Harvey, EETS OS 106 (1896).

[38] *Julian of Norwich's Revelations of Divine Love: The Shorter Version*, ed. Frances Beer, Middle English Texts, 8 (Heidelberg, 1978); *A Book of Showings to the Anchoress Julian of Norwich*, ed. Edmund Colledge and James Walsh (Toronto, 1978); *The Writings of Julian of Norwich*, ed. Nicholas Watson and Jacqueline Jenkins (University Park, Pa., 2006).

[39] *The Chastising of God's Children and The Treatise of Perfection of the Sons of God*, ed. Joyce Bazire and Eric Colledge (Oxford, 1957), 229–58; Colledge, '*The Treatise of Perfection of the Sons of God*: A Fifteenth-Century English Ruysbroec Translation', *English Studies*, 33 (1952), 49–66.

made in those houses).[40] Considering the dialectal character of Ad and Ad_2, it is possible that he encountered this manuscript in one of the more northerly Carthusian houses: Beauvale, Axeholme, or Hull.[41]

DESCRIBED IN: Hanna, *EMRR*, no. 42, pp. 80–2.

LITERATURE: Marleen Cré, *Vernacular Mysticism in the Charterhouse: A Study of London, British Library, MS Additional 37790*, The Medieval Translator/Traduire au moyen age, 9 (Turnhout, 2006), esp. 239–45.

Td: Dublin, Trinity College Library, MS A.5.7 (122) *c.*1500

Paper. Ff. 116. Badly worn: *c.*215–25 × 140–45/50 mm (*c.*160 × 110 mm). Comprises three books written on different stocks of paper in four roughly contemporary hands of the late fifteenth or early sixteenth century.

BOOK 1: Ff. 1–102. The contents are divided into two booklets written on different stocks of paper.[42] Written space 160 mm × 110 mm. ff. $1–73^v$ and 76^v are written in a Bastard Anglicana hand; ff. $74^{r–v}$ and $77–102^r$ are written in a smaller, contemporary hand. Written at 27 lines per page.

Booklet 1:

CONTENTS:

1. Ff. 1^r –74^v: *The Cloud of Unknowing* (*IPMEP* 320).

Ff. $74–76^r$ are blank.

2. F. 76^v: Extracts from Chapters 57 and 62 of *The Cloud of Unknowing*.

DECORATION: Two- and occasionally three-line chapter initials, occasionally lightly outlined, overwritten, or touched in red in the first two gatherings, some underlining in red. Some marginal chapter numbers in red throughout.

COLLATION: $1^{12}–4^{12}$, $5^{14}–6^{14}$.

Booklet 2:

CONTENTS:

2. Ff. $77^r–102^r$: *The Book of Privy Counselling* (*IPMEP* 251).

Ff. $102^v–103^r$ are blank.

3. F. 103^v: A five-line fragment of a letter: 'My hert is ful heuy to

[40] See Sargent, *James Grenehalgh*, i. 144–6, 161.

[41] Doyle, 'English Carthusian Books', 126–7.

[42] The different paper stocks are discussed in the Scattergood notes mentioned below.

send ȝow þis boke for I supposid þat ȝe suld hafe commen home, þat we myght hafe comond togedir þerof. Send me word how it is and þat þat I may do for ȝow I wil with alle my hert if it lyke ȝow to lat me wytt [*add*: why ȝe come not]. Ora pro me.'

DECORATION: Two-line chapter initials.

COLLATION: 7^{12}–8^{14} (the latter a gathering of eight with a gathering of six tipped in).

BOOK 2: Ff. 104^r–116^r. Written space 165 mm × 120 mm. 31–2 lines per page. Written in a Bastard Anglicana hand at 31–2 lines per page.

CONTENTS:

1. Ff. 104^r–116^r: *Scale* II, extracts from Chapters 21–5 and 41–6, in the following order: 24/35 þou – lytel² (l. 25/21); 41/149 common – herte (l. 43/ 13); 43/122 Jesu – wil (l. 144); 44/61 þe¹ – messangers (l. 46/59; 46/4 þan – soule (l. 24); and 21/3 for¹ – tyme (l. 23/56).

Ff. 116^v–118 are blank.

DECORATION: Each extract has a two-line red initial. Minor initials on ff. 104^r–106^6 and 110^v–112^r are touched in red, with infrequent red underining.

COLLATION: 1^8–2^8.

BINDING: Modern.

DESCRIBED IN: *Cloud*, ed. Hodgson, p. xvii. There is a draft catalogue entry by John Scattergood, dated January 1996, kept with the manuscript.

Td$_2$: Dublin, Trinity College Library, MS C.5.20 (352)

s. xvi$^{1-2}$

Paper. 291 leaves. 148 × 89 mm. An English and Latin theological commonplace book with recusant sympathies, in several hands. There are quotations from Scripture, from Chrysostom, Augustine, Henry VIII against Luther, Erasmus, More, and others. On ff. 227–35 a section is added in a later hand, defending the Roman Catholic doctrine on the Sacrament of the Altar. There are also sections written in a form of shorthand. The material on ff. 1^r–226^r is written in the same hand as the name 'Edmond Horde' at the top of f. 1^r. The material from the *Scale* occurs on ff. 106^r–112^v, and comprises extracts, varying in length from two to twelve lines, from both books. Specific extracts from *Scale* II that can be identified include (f. 108^r, ll. 8–10): 2/4– 5; (f. 108^r, ll. 11–17): 21/64–8; 'A notable sayinge', ff. 108^r, l. 18–108^v, l. 8): 21/103–5 and 22/68–72; (f. 108^v, ll. 9–15):

27/48–51; (f. 108v, ll. 16–22): 27/152–56; (f. 111v, ll. 1–12): 28/48–50 and 45–8; and (f. 111v, l. 18–112v, l. 25): 26/28–62. The text has been altered, and did not prove useful for collation.

PROVENANCE: An Edmund Horde was fellow of All Souls Oxford 1504, DCL 1510, procurator of London Charterhouse, then prior of Hinton (1529–39), which he surrendered to the commissioners of King Henry VIII; he later joined the Marian re-foundation of Sheen, and was exiled with that community to Louvain, where he died in 1578.[43]

DESCRIBED IN: Marvin L. Colker, *Trinity College Library Dublin: Descriptive Catalogue of the Medieval and Renaissance Manuscripts*, i (Aldershot, 1991), 750–1.

Wc: Westminster Cathedral Archives MS 4 s. xvi *in.*

Parchment. Ff. 112. 157 × 100 mm (113 × 73 mm). Ruled for 17 lines per page; written in a Bastard Secretary hand.

CONTENTS:

1. Ff. 1r–25r: Extracts from Walter Hilton, *Qui habitat.*
2. Ff. 25r–35v: Extracts from Walter Hilton (?), *Bonum est.*
3. Ff. 35v–72r: Extracts from Walter Hilton, *Scale* I and II. The *Scale* II extracts are from Chapters 27–8, 30, 32–9, and 41–6, in the following order:[44] ll. 459–61: Chapter 30/7 It – itself² (l. 8); [five extracts from *Scale* I interpose at this point]; ll. 510–14: 30/22 þan – þiself (l. 29); 30/30 þe¹ – þiself (l. 33); ll. 519–22: 30/36 God – itself (l. 41); ll. 523–47: 32/5 A – felynge (l. 30); ll. 547–56: 30/48 a – it (l. 61); ll. 558–68: 30/68 Neuerþeles – wrytynge (l. 81); ll. 569–71: 33/4 What – God (l. 8); ll. 571–5: 34/9 þe – soule (l. 13); ll. 575–80: 34/16 þerfor – it (l. 20); ll. 581–3: 34/22 þer – Gost (l. 24); ll. 583–5: 34/39 he² – him² (l. 41); ll. 585–93: 34/46 And – saluacion (l. 57); ll. 594–5 [echoes 34/57 For – none (l. 61)]; ll. 595–613: 34/62 þerfore – soule (l. 83); ll. 613–19: 34/97 for – synne (l. 104); ll. 620–33: 34/107 Al – he (l. 124); ll. 635–41: 35/20 For – lufe (l. 27); ll. 642–53: 34/32 by – him (l. 46); ll. 655–9: 36/80 a – soule¹ (l. 86); ll. 659–60: 37/31 Parfyte – Jesu (l. 32); ll. 660–6: 37/35 it¹ – þe (l. 43); l. 667–

[43] *The Heads of Religious Houses: England and Wales*, iii: *1377–1540*, ed. David M. Smith (Cambridge, 2008), 358–59; Emden, *BRUO*, ii. 961–2; David Knowles, *The Religious Orders in England*, iii:, *The Tudor Age* (Cambridge, repr. with corrections, 1971), 238.

[44] Line references are to Marleen Cré, 'London, Westminster Cathedral Treasury, MS 4: An Edition of the Westminster Compilation', *Journal of Medieval Religious Cultures*, 37 (2011), 1–59.

72: 38/33 And – allone (l. 39); ll.673–6: 27/52 yre – man² (l. 56); 679–91: 39/103 it – him (l. 118); ll. 692–712: 30/162 maner – wylle (l. 188); ll. 713–27: 42/6 The – lufe (l. 26); ll. 728–38: 41/161 þe – itself (l. 173); ll. 739–63: 41/5 Schew – absence (l. 37); ll. 764–72: 28/49 dredys – þerin (l. 61); [five extracts from *Scale* I interpose at this point]; ll. 811–37: 42/104 þe² – ende (l. 137); ll. 838–42: 43/5 When – herte (l. 11); ll. 842–53: 43/17 þan – made (l. 31); ll. 856–66: 43/122 a – Jesu (l. 134); ll. 868–74: 44/61 þe¹ – seyde (l. 69); ll. 874–910: 45/5 Neuerþeles – malice (l. 79); ll. 910–17: 45/81 Mykel – dredyth (l. 60); l. 917: 45/63 riȝtfully – deserued; ll. 918–21: 45/66 Bretheren – Jesu (l. 71); ll. 922–7: 46/4 þan – cessyng (l. 10); ll. 927–31: 46/13 þan – soule (l. 17); and ll. 931–46: 46/21 For – openly (l. 40).

The extracts from *Qui habitat*, *Bonum est*, and the *Scale* are treated as a single sequence.

4. Ff. 72ᵛ–112ᵛ: Extracts from the Long Text of the *Showings* of Julian of Norwich.

COLLATION: 1^8–14^8.

DECORATION: Two-line lombard capitals at 18 points: the beginning of the series of extracts from *Qui habitat*, *Bonum est*, the *Scale*, and the *Revelations*, and sporadically at fourteen other beginnings of extracts within the series. The Latin scriptural quotations among the *Scale* extracts are in red.

BINDING: Modern.

DESCRIBED IN: Ker, *MMBL*, i: London, 418–19.

LITERATURE: *Book of Showings to the Anchoress Julian of Norwich*, ed. College and Walsh, 9–10; Cré, 'London, Westminster Cathedral Treasury, MS 4'.

Appendix: Thomas Fishlake's Latin Translation

Y: York Minster, Dean and Chapter Library MS xvi.K.5 s. xiv *ex*.

Parchment. Ff. 193. 218 × 160 mm (175 × 118 mm), in a single column throughout. Trimmed very close at the top. Comprises three originally independent books, each in a different hand, but of the same period.

BOOK 1. Ff. 1–97. Comprises two booklets, written in a Textura hand (with the exception of ff. 1–2, which are Bastard Anglicana), at

36 lines per page. Two-line lombard initials, capitals touched in yellow.

Booklet 1. Ff. 1–37.

CONTENTS:

1. Ff. 1^{r}–36^{r}: Walter Hilton, *Scale* I, in the Latin translation of Thomas Fishlake. The *explicit* describes the book as 'libellus Magistri Valteri Hilton canonici de Thurgarton, qui obiit Anno Domini M° XXX° lxxix. v. in vigilia Annunciacionis. Quem libellum transtulit de Anglico in Latinum Magister & frater Thomas Fislake Ordinis Beate Marie genitricis Dei de Monte Carmeli & constat Magistro fratri Johanni Pole eiusdem ordinis quem fecerat scribi ex elemosinis amicorum suorum, quorum omnium animabus propicietur Deus amen.

Ff. 36^{v}–37^{v} are blank.

COLLATION: 1^{8}–4^{8}, 5^{5}. No signatures or catchwords.

Booklet 2. Ff. 38–97.

CONTENTS:

2. Ff. 38^{r}–95^{r}: Walter Hilton, *Scale* II, in the Latin translation of Thomas Fishlake, with preceding Table of Chapters.

3. F. 95^{r-v}: The Latin 'Summary' of *Scale* II,[45] followed by the *explicit*, 'Explicit libellus Magistri Walteri Hilton canonici de Thurgarton, qui obiit anno domini M° CCCC° lxxxxv in uigilia Annunciacionis. Quem libellum transtulit de anglico in latinum frater & magister Thomas Fyslake Ordinis Beate Marie de Monte Carmeli.'

COLLATION: 6^{8}–12^{8}, 13^{4}.

BOOK 2: Ff. 98–117. Written in an Anglicana hand at 32 lines per page. No signatures or catchwords.Three-line blue or red initials.

CONTENTS:

1. Ff. 98^{r}–113^{v}: Guigo II Carthusiensis, *Scala Claustralium*,[46] attributed to St Bernard.

2. Ff. 113^{v}–117^{v}: Non in aduersitate seu prosperitate . . . et non te excruciet. On the virtue of patience.

COLLATION: 14^{8}–15^{8}, 16^{4}. Signatures aj, bj, bij, and part of biij visible.

[45] See critical apparatus; S. S. Hussey, 'Latin and English in *The Scale of Perfection*', *Mediæval Studies*, 35 (1973), 456–76 at 458–9.

[46] Guigues II le Chartreux, *Lettre sur la vie contemplative (L'échelle des moines), Douze meditacions*, ed. Edmund Colledge and James Walsh, Sources Chrétiennes, 163 (Paris, 1970).

BOOK 3: Ff. 118–93. Written in a Textura hand, at 34–6 lines per page (with the exception of the last two folios, in Anglicana Formata, at 42 lines). Four-line blue initial at f. 123^{r}; capitals touched in red.

CONTENTS:

1. Ff. 118^{r}–119^{r}: An alphabetical index to item 3 below.
2. Ff. 119^{r}–123^{r}: A versified Table of Chapters to item 3 below.
3. Ff. 123^{r}–193^{r}: *Speculum humanae salvationis*.[47]

F. 193^{v} is blank.

COLLATION: 17^{8}–24^{8}, 25^{10}, 26^{2}. No catchwords or signatures.

DECORATION: Item 3 (f. 123), has a four-line blue capital. No paragraph signs.

BINDING: Modern, parchment.

PROVENANCE: An *ex libris* at the end of *Scale* II (f. 95^{v}) states that this book 'constat Magistro fratri Johanni Pole, quem fecerat scribi ex elemosinis amicorum suorum quorum animabus propicietur Deus. Amen.' Emden, *BRUC*, 456, notes that John Pole is recorded at the Cambridge convent. Ker, *MLGB*, 24, assigns Y to the Carmelite convent at Cambridge; Ker and Piper, *MMBL*, suggest that it was more probably given by Pole to the convent at Coventry, as was Berlin, MS Hamilton 503.

DESCRIBED IN: Ker and Piper, *MMBL*, iv. 725–7.

2. THE PLACE OF *SCALE* II IN HILTON'S OPUS

The interrelations demonstrable among Walter Hilton's works indicate that he wrote *Scale* II during the last decade of his life, between the mid-1380s, when he wrote the Latin letter *De Utilitate et prerogativis religionis* (hereafter *De Util.*), and his death in the house of Augustinian canons at Thurgarton in Nottinghamshire on the eve of the Feast of the Annunciation (i.e. 24 March), 1395/96.

There are few ascertainable facts about Hilton's career.[48] His name

[47] F. Stegmüller, *Repertorium biblicum medii aevi*, I–II (Madrid, 1950–80), no. 11765, mentions this copy.

[48] The details of Hilton's academic career are discussed in Russell-Smith, 'Walter Hilton and a Tract in Defence', 180–7; J. P. H. Clark, 'Walter Hilton in Defence of the Religious Life and of the Veneration of Images', *DR* 103 (1985), 1–25 at 1–2; and *Walter Hilton: The Scale of Perfection*, ed. and trans. John P. H. Clark and Rosemary Dorward (Mahwah, NJ[o], 1991), 13–19. Note that the vigil of the Annunciation is the last day of the year according to the medieval ecclesiastical calendar; he died in 1396 according to modern dating.

occurs only twice in the documentary record: once, in a papal mandate to the Official of the diocese of Ely, dated 28 January 1371, petitioning for the reservation for 'Walterum Hilton, clericum Lincolniensis diocesis, Bacallarium in legibus apud vos', of the canonry and prebend of Abergwili, near Carmarthen in Wales. Second, the Ely Consistory Register records him there in 1375, witnessing, together with Thomas Gloucester (the bishop's official), to the settling of the accounts of the vacant parish of Willingham, 'Presentibus Magistris Thoma Gloucestre & Waltero Hilton Baculario in legibus Lincolniensis Diocesis testibus & rogatis'.[49]

According to the normal practice of clerical incardination, it is probable that Walter Hilton was born in the Huntingdonshire village of Hilton, about 15 miles north-west of Cambridge, the only place of that name recorded in the fourteenth-century diocese of Lincoln. If Hilton, as is probable, had attained the MA before proceeding to the study of law and was BCL by 1371, then he would probably have been born by 1343 at the latest.

Hilton is described in the explicit of *Scale* MS A, which contains a complete copy of both books written in a hand of the first half of the fifteenth century, as 'decretorum inceptor', and in the incipit of MS M, which contains the second book of the *Scale* with a unique opening that adapts the text to stand without the preceding *Scale* I, written in a mid-to-late fifteenth-century hand, as 'comensour of decrees'. If these two references are correct,[50] then Hilton would have continued at Cambridge until the early 1380s and passed his examinations for a mastership, but—apparently—did not complete the necessary regency for the degree. As a BCL in 1371 and 1375, he would probably have been in his late twenties or early thirties; if he continued work without interruption towards the DCL, he could have been ready to incept by 1381–2.

What is not known is when Hilton gave up his legal career and withdrew from the world, but he left an acerbic note on the venality of ecclesiastical courts in the *Epistola ad Quemdam seculo renunciare volentem* (hereafter *Epist. ad Quem.*), describing those who once told

[49] Emden, *BRUC*, 305–6. See Clark, 'Walter Hilton in Defence', 18–19 n. 8 for clarification. Ely Consistory Court met in All Saints parish church in Cambridge through Nov. of 1375, and in St Michael's church in December. See Margaret Aston, *Thomas Arundel: A Study of Church Life in the Reign of Richard II* (Oxford, 1967), 397–400.

[50] As we shall see below, pp. cxv–cxvii, A and M share a degree of textual relation, and their testimony could possibly represent a single line of evidence.

him, 'With your knowledge and intelligence, how well you would do in court cases and lawsuits and suchlike! . . . "Come with us, let us" go to the Roman Curia. . . . "We will find" fat benefices [Prov. 1:10].'[51]

Further evidence concerning Hilton's career is to be found in *De Util.*, written to Adam Horsley, a prominent secular cleric, an officer of the King's Exchequer (appointed Controller of the Great Roll in 1375), who felt a calling to the Carthusian Order. This letter provides another of the dates around which the chronology of Hilton's works can be organized, for Horsley resigned the benefice that he had held from 1369 (when he appears to have entered the king's service) at the end of 1385, and the prior of Beauvale Charterhouse was granted permission by the Carthusian General Chapter of May 1386 to receive 'Domnum Adam, clericum Regis Angliae' into the order.[52]

De Util. is a defence of the religious life on several fronts, including Wycliffite criticism of 'private religion' and various personal considerations. Hilton's first major argument, however, was not directed either against detractors of the religious vocation or his at own personal impediments: rather, he expounds the argument from canon law that the dignity of the religious vocation is such that, according to Pope Urban II (in a passage cited both in the *Decretals* and in Thomas Aquinas's *Summa Theologica*), a secular cleric feeling himself called to the religious life cannot be impeded in his vocation even by his bishop.[53] This argument would be unexceptional were it not for the fact that the prior of Beauvale had felt it necessary to obtain permission from the General Chapter for the order to receive Adam Horsley. This apparent act of scrupulosity might well have been occasioned by an actual refusal of Horsley's superiors, whether ecclesiastical or civil, to release him from his secular clerical duties (and thus his bureaucratic position) to follow his religious vocation.

The second aim of Hilton's defence is to answer Wycliffite objections to the religious life. He begins this section of *De Util.*, as he does in defending orthodox doctrine elsewhere (such as the

[51] 'O quantis prodesse poteris per scienciam tuam et per concilium tuum in causis et in litibus et in ceteris consimilibus . . . "Veni nobiscum et" eamus ad curiam Romanam. . . . Pinguia beneficia "optinebimus".' *LW*, ii. 262.

[52] Sargent, *James Grenehalgh*, ii. 580–1, referring to Grande Chartreuse MS 1 Cart 43, 56. Horsley's *obit* is recorded in the *carta* of the General Chapter in 1424.

[53] *LW*, i. 123–4, ll. 80–93 and notes.

defence of the veneration of images in churches in *De Adoracione imaginum*),[54] by arguing from the difference between the spiritual needs of the early Christian community, who had known Jesus and heard his message personally, and those of the present age. Finally, Hilton deals with the specific doubts and scruples that appear to have held Horsley back personally from fulfilling his intention to enter religion—impediments ranging from embarrassment over his inability to sing to fear that he will be unable to fulfil his religious vows because of the weakness of the flesh.

Addressing himself to the spiritual benefits of the religious vocation, Hilton refers to Horsley's intention to enter the Carthusian order in particular primarily in the section dealing with personal doubts and impediments,[55] but refers only once to the specific details of life in a Carthusian house, when he mentions the utility of the division of time between silence alone in one's cell and communal prayer in the chapel.[56] Although he praises the religious life in this letter, however, Hilton describes himself in it with remarkable diffidence, for he does not—or at least not yet—feel himself drawn to the same vocation:[57]

[54] *LW*, i. 187–8; Clark, 'Walter Hilton in Defence'.

[55] Specific references to the Carthusian Order are made at *De Util.*, ll. 32, 532, 555, 561, 572, 734, and 862–4; *LW*, i. 120, 149, 151–2, 161, and 169.

[56] *De Util.*, ll. 734–6, *LW*, i. 161. Hilton also mentions 'ceremonial observances like silence, prostration on the ground, bowing, and such like'; *LW*, i. 153, ll. 596–7. Although these are practices common to the religious orders generally, Hilton may be referring more particularly to the strictness of Carthusian observation.

[57] 'Parce michi misero, queso, frater karissime, ignosce insipiencie mee, quod ego arrogauerim michi ad presens comendacionem religionis; certissime scio quia non eget commendacione mea. . . . Set forsan cogitacio tua dicit tibiipsi mirando forsan, cur alios tam instanter ad religionem prouocem, eamque religionem commendem ut sanctam, et tamen eiusdem religionis habitum me suscipere minime dispono. . . . Fateor me miserum illud spirituale et feruens desiderium ad ingressum religionis ex diuina gracia inspiratum minime sentire sicut sentiri necesse est ab eo qui zelo deuocionis et puro mentis affectu religionem ingredi disponit. Tu vero desiderium religionis gracia Dei semitum in corde tuo concepisti, ideoque tibi expedit tanquam specialiter a Deo ad hanc vocato istud desiderium nutrire, vt prodeat in maturam spicam realis execucionis. . . . Verumptamen recognosco me indignum et opto me esse seruum eciam minimi religiosi in ecclesia Dei, et spero per Dei graciam me eorum fore participem. . . . Item econuerso, si Deus ordinauerit michi misero et abiecto, sic vocaueritque per graciam suam ut *solitarius sedeam* [Lam. 3: 28, 'sedebit solitarius'] seruiamque ei taliter prout ipse michi donare dignatur, quare non in hac vocacione perseuerabo? . . . Scio quia non omnibus conuenit solitudo, ac eciam scio quod aliquibus non expedit congregacio, et ideo paratus sis tu et quilibet alius obedire diuine vocacioni. Si enim et ego, omnibus consideratis, tue conuersacioni que iam est similis existerem, et tale desiderium religionis haberem sicut tu, procul dubio ad effectum perduceretur per religionis ingressum.' *De Util.*, ll. 450–514; *LW*, i. 145–8.

Forgive me, brother, I beg you, wretch that I am, ignore my foolishness in arrogating to myself the commendation of the religious life; I certainly know that it does not need my commendation . . . But perhaps it occurs to you—perhaps even with wonder—why I exhort others so urgently to the religious life and commend the holiness of that life, and yet I have not taken up the religious habit myself. . . . I confess that, wretch that I am, I have never felt that burning spiritual desire, inspired by divine grace, to the extent that someone who disposes himself in zeal of devotion and pure feeling of mind to enter a religious order must feel it. You, on the one hand, have conceived the desire planted in your heart by the grace of God to enter religion, and it is thus appropriate to you to nourish this desire as someone especially called by God, so that it may ripen to a mature harvest. . . . I, on the other hand, recognize my own unworthiness, and choose rather to be the servant of the least member of a religious order in the church of God, and hope by the grace of God to be a sharer with them. . . . But if God has ordained for me, caitiff wretch that I am, and called me by his grace that I should 'sit solitary' [Lam. 3:28], and serve him as he has deigned to grant me to do, why should I not persevere in that vocation? . . . I know that solitude is not fitting for all, just as I know that community is not convenient for some, and thus you and everyone else should be prepared to obey his divine calling. If I, too, all things considered, felt a calling like yours, and had such a desire to enter religion as you have, doubtless it would bring me to enter a religious order.

Hilton's description of his vocation here as 'sitting solitary' in 'solitude' implies that after leaving his secular profession but before becoming a canon regular, he lived for some time as a solitary—perhaps trying his vocation as a hermit after the model of Richard Rolle. But at this point in his life, he does not feel that his calling is to enter a religious order. Another reference to his eremitic, but not religious, vocation is to be seen in the letter *De Imagine peccati*, written, it appears, for someone who, like him, had left the world of secular occupation but not joined a religious order. Here he traces, probably for the first time, the outlines of the introspective meditation on the disfigured image of the Trinity in the fallen soul that would form an important part of the first book of *The Scale of Perfection*.[58] In writing of the 'lower members' of the image of sin—the tendency to carnal temptation—he describes his and his reader's spiritual condition as having rejected the worldly life, but not

[58] *LW*, i. 73–4, ll. 14–19. See Nicholas Watson, '"Et que est huius ydoli materia? Tuipse": Idols and Images in Walter Hilton', in Jeremy Dimmick, James Simpson, and Nicolette Zeeman (eds.), *Images, Idolatry, and Iconoclasm in Late Medieval England* (Oxford, 2002), 95–111.

undertaken anything more positive. He compares the two of them to those in the parable of the workers in the vineyard who have been idling in the marketplace all day:[59]

What then do you and I do, and others like us, useless, lazy men 'standing the whole day idle' [Matt. 20:3]? We do not labour in the Lord's vineyard ministering the sacraments, nor running from parish to parish preaching the word of the Lord, nor do we perform any other works of mercy, nor do we willingly submit ourselves to the yoke of obedience like 'Ephraim the heifer taught to love to tread out corn' [Hos. 10:11]. We never occupy the place even of the lowest minister in the church, but like free men left to our own devices and our own will, we are as it were in no order at all. We should fear lest we be cast out where 'no order, but everlasting horror dwelleth' [Job 10:22].

To which he adds:

I do not say this to confuse, but to humble us both, not to blame but to instruct, for we have the consolation that even though we are little occupied in outward ministry, we believe firmly that by the inner keeping of the mind we belong to that body of Christ which is the church.

Hilton also alludes to 'Ephraim the heifer taught to love to tread out corn' in *De Util.* to refer to a member of a religious order who has learned to master self-will by subjecting himself to the will of his superiors—one of the benefits of the religious life.[60]

In fact, it is one of the characteristics of Hilton's writing that he works out his thought in terms of biblical allegories and striking, often quite physical imagery: the corrupted image of the Trinity in the fallen soul as an image of Satan, an idol, or as a stinking, putrid well that cannot be capped off, but must be dug up and cleaned out in *Scale* I; the reformation of the soul as a danger-filled journey to

[59] *LW*, i. 90–1: 'Quid ergo facimus tu et ego, nostrique similes, homines pigri et inutiles, "tota die stantes ociosi?"' Non laboramus in vinea Domini sacramenta ecclesiastica ministrando, nec discurrimus per parochias verbum Domini predicando, nec cetera misericordie opera exhibemus spiritualiter, neque iugum obediencie sub alterius imperio tanquam "vitula Effrahim docta diligere trituram" voluntarie portamus, nusquam occupamus locum alicuius ministri eciam minimi in ecclesia ordinati, sed quasi liberi, relicti nostro sensui nostreque voluntati, quasi in nullo ordine sumus. Timendum est nobis ne proiciamur vbi "nullus est ordo, sed sempiternus orror". Verumtamen non ad confusionem nostram hec dico, sed ad humiliacionem, non ad exprobacionem sed ad instruccionem, quia hec fiducia consolacionis nobis tribuitur, quod licet exterioribus ministeriis minime fuerimus ocupati, firmiter tamen credimus per interiorem mentis custodiam ad corpus Christi misticum quod est ecclesia nos pertinere.'

[60] *LW*, i. 156.

Jerusalem, or as a comparison of the relative abilities of a blind man, a man with his eyes shut, and a man with open eyes to see the sun in *Scale* II; the comparison of the wealthy man who wants to live a contemplative life but cannot leave his worldly responsibilities to Jacob, who must serve each of his wives in turn, in the *Mixed Life*. And we may use some of these repeated themes, images, and allegorizations in Hilton's writings as an aid in fleshing out the details of his career.

It was certainly during Hilton's time at Cambridge and Ely that Thomas Arundel, the 20-year-old brother of Richard FitzAlan, Lord Arundel, was ordained priest and consecrated bishop of Ely in 1374; he was promoted to the see of York in 1388. In *Pastors and Visionaries*, his study of the interrelationships of northern English families and officialdom and the circulation of the texts of the literature of vernacular spirituality in the later fourteenth and fifteenth centuries, Jonathan Hughes surmised that Hilton was one of the talented young administrators who followed Arundel to York.[61] In fact, Hilton seems to have tired of the blandishments of secular life late in the 1370s or early in the 1380s, and retired to consider his vocation.

It is interesting to note that several manuscripts of the earliest version of the text of *Scale* I,[62] usually accompanied by the *Mixed Life*, survive in two clusters connected with the west and north-west of England. The first of these comprises the Vernon and Simeon manuscripts (V and S), as well as Pl, a later copy dialectally localized to Surrey, comprising *Scale* II as well. Of R and its congeners D and F, H_3 and U, four (R, D, H_3, and U) are all dialectally localized to western or north-western Yorkshire; F is eastern Norfolk and the added text of *Scale* II in R is far-western Norfolk. R, D, and U do not have the *Mixed Life*; R, D, and F have *Angels' Song*.[63] If Hilton

[61] Jonathan Hughes, *Pastors and Visionaries: Religious and Secular Life in Late Medieval Yorkshire* (Woodbridge, 1988), 179–85.

[62] The discussion of the relationship of the various manuscript versions of *Scale* I is partly conjectural at this point, based on the agreement of my own observations of the state of the text of *Scale* II and A. J. Bliss's draft discussions of the text of *Scale* I.

[63] On the connection of R, D, and F, see Hanna, *EMRR*, 174–6, 47–50, 28–30, items 94, 25, and 15; on H_3, see 94–7, item 48. On the relation of R, D, F, H_3, and U, see below, pp. cxiv–cxv. See also Michael G. Sargent, 'Walter Hilton's *Scale of Perfection* in Devotional Compilations', in Marleen Cré, Diana Dinessen, and Denis Renevey (eds.), *This Tretice, by me Compiled: Late Medieval Devotional Compilations in England* (Turnhout, in press).

did not go north with Arundel's court, certainly some early copies of his works did.[64]

To sum up: in the time between his appearance in Ely Consistory Court as a BCL and his letter to Adam Horsley *De Util.*—roughly the years from the mid-1370s to the mid-1380s—Hilton may have continued in the study of law up to the point where he was entitled to become a master, but he did not undertake the necessary regency. He appears rather to have given up his legal career and tried his vocation as a hermit. At some time while he was considering his retirement from the legal profession or soon after, Hilton probably wrote *De Imag. pec.* and the first book of the *Scale*. *Scale* I, it should be noted, was perhaps originally the record of a series of colloquies with an actual interlocutor, which might explain the relatively disorganized way that it shifts from topic to topic, and the fact that there are two quite divergent sets of chapter divisions extant in the manuscript tradition.[65] The discussion of the active and contemplative lives in the opening chapters of *Scale* I is also quite close to the treatment of the same theme in the *Mixed Life*, and it is possible that it was written in the same period. Thus the letter *De Imag. pec.*, the *Mixed Life*, and *Scale* I in its earliest version would have been written between Hilton's retirement from his worldly career and the composition of the letter *De Util.* for Adam Horsley around the year 1385/86. At some point after this Hilton revised *Scale* I and wrote *Scale* II. It would also have been in the period after 1385/86 that he entered the house of Augustinian canons at Thurgarton.

Whenever it was that he entered Thurgarton, Hilton did remain in contact with Cambridge, or with people whom he had known at Cambridge, for some time, as is shown by his connections there with the Carmelites Thomas Fishlake and John Pole and the Franciscan Lluis de Font.[66] Fishlake, who is described as 'Magister' in the colophons of six manuscripts of his Latin translation of Hilton's *Scale*,[67] is recorded as a Bachelor of Theology in the Cambridge

[64] I am not convinced that Hilton's eremitic vocation—such as it was—took him north to Yorkshire: see Sargent, 'Bishops, Patrons, Mystics, and Manuscripts: Walter Hilton, Nicholas Love, and the Arundel and Holland Connections', in Simon Horobin and Linne R. Mooney (eds.), *Middle English Texts in Transition: A Festschrift Dedicated to Toshiyuki Takamiya on his 70th Birthday* (York, 2014), 159–76.

[65] See Sargent, 'The Organization of *The Scale of Perfection*', in *MMTE* ii. 231–61.

[66] See Emden, *BRUC*, 231, 456, and 236 respectively.

[67] *Scale* MSS Y, B_2, B_4, H_2, H_8, and He. These manuscripts represent two separate affiliational groups in the textual tradition of the Latin *Scale*, and thus most probably two separate lines of attestation.

Carmelite convent *c.*1375; on 25 May 1377 he was appointed by Bishop Arundel to preach at the Ely diocesan synod.[68] York Minster Library MS xvi.K.5, a first-generation copy of Fishlake's translation, probably made *c.*1400, belonged, according to its colophon, to 'Magistro Fratri Johanni Pole eiusdem ordinis [Beate Marie genitricis Dei de Monte Carmeli], quem fecerat scribi ex elemosinis amicorum, quorum omnium animabus propicietur Deus'. Pole, who was originally from the diocese of Coventry and Lichfield, is described in Bishop Arundel's register at Ely as STD in 1376, when he was attached to the Carmelite convent at Cambridge; he was named prior of that convent in 1381, and is recorded later as having died in Coventry.[69]

Lluis de Font was an Aragonese Franciscan who was sent by the general chapter of his order to Cambridge to read the *Sentences* in 1383. According to the incipits of four of the seven surviving complete manuscripts of the *Eight Chapters* and the colophon of one other,[70] Hilton translated this work from a Latin original 'found in Master Lluis de Font's book at Cambridge'. If the degree is not a scribal honorific (not rare in manuscript attributions of authorship), and if the academic career of Lluis de Font followed the usual course for the time, then as John Clark has noted, his regency as Master could not have been before 1391–2.[71] If he left Cambridge after this, then Hilton's translation would date from some point in the last five years of his life, although it should be noted that the ascription of the *Eight Chapters* does not necessarily imply that Font had left Cambridge before Hilton translated it.[72]

[68] Aston, *Thomas Arundel*, 74 n. 3, 75; Emden, *BRUC*, 231.

[69] Pole was ordained acolyte in Dec. 1366 (Lambeth registers: Archbishop Langham), subdeacon on 13 Mar. 1366/67 (London registers: Bishop Sudbury), and priest on 17 Apr. 1367; Bishop Arundel's register records his licence to preach and hear confessions in 1376—the first time that Arundel is recorded as being resident in the diocese of Ely. See Helen Gardner, 'The Text of "The Scale of Perfection"', *MÆ* 5 (1936), 11–30 at 22; J. P. H. Clark, 'Thomas Maldon O.Carm., a Cambridge Theologian of the Fourteenth Century', in Patrick Fitzgerald-Lombard O.Carm. (ed.), *Carmel in Britain: Essays on the Medieval English Carmelite Province*, ii: *Writings and Theology* (Rome: Institutum Carmelitanum, 1992), 125–67 at 126 n. 9.

[70] The incipits of the *Eight Chapters* in *Scale* MSS L and P, and British Library MSS Harley 993 and Additional 10053; and the colophon of Paris, Bibliothèque nationale de France, fonds anglais MS 41. See *Walter Hilton's Eight Chapters on Perfection, Edited from All the Known Medieval Manuscripts*, ed. Fumio Kuriyagawa (Tokyo, 1967), 35–6.

[71] Clark, in Hilton, *Scale*, ed. Clark and Dorward, 17.

[72] Clark suggests, 'Walter Hilton in Defence', 2: 'Presumably the book was "found" after Luis left the University, and passed to Hilton at Thurgarton by a Cambridge friend.'

There are several examples of parallelism of thought and expression between the *Eight Chapters* and *Scale* II,[73] all in the latter half of the text. As Clark notes, Hilton seems to be working out ideas and phrases in his translation of the *Eight Chapters* that he expounds at greater length in *Scale* II. The similarity in treatment of scrupulous doubts about faulty confession in the first half of *Scale* II and the *Epist. ad Quem.* also suggests an earlier version of ideas that will occur in fuller form in the first half of *Scale* II.[74]

The greatest number of parallelisms of thought and expression to *Scale* II, however, is to be found in Hilton's commentary on Psalm 90, 'Qui habitat'. There we find explications of the 'midday fiend', of the 'terror in the night' and the 'arrow that flies by day', of Jesus' humanity as a shield with which he 'tempers' his divinity and overshadows us for our protection from enemies on all sides, and of the ministry of the angels, which he will expand upon in a more systematic way at various points, particularly in the latter half of *Scale* II.[75] These parallelisms suggest that the *Eight Chapters*, the letter *Epist. ad Quem.*, and the *Qui habitat* commentary were written soon before, or during, the period that Hilton was writing *Scale* II—that is, probably, between the mid-1380s and his death in 1396. There do not appear to be any apposite parallelisms of thought or expression between these works and the English translation of the *Stimulus amoris* that is attributed to Hilton in four manuscripts.[76] If this translation is by Hilton, then the marked difference in subject matter—the *Stimulus amoris* is an extended meditation on the passion—may have left little to carry over from one work to the other.

Where Hilton's entry into the house of Augustinian canons fits into this chronology is not discernible. It should be noted that the

[73] See Explanatory Notes to 26/18, 26/61–2, 27/65, 27/120–1, 28/35, 28/48, and 39/28–35.

[74] See Explanatory Notes to 6/18, 7/15–19, 7/44–50, 11/122, 14/42, and 22/20.

[75] See Clark, 'Walter Hilton and the Psalm Commentary *Qui habitat*', *DR* 100 (1982), 235–62; and Explanatory Notes to 21/8, 22/36, 22/40, 26/4, 26/46–56, 26/49, 26/61–2, 28/48–57, 30/105–28, 34/46–7, 34/118, 37/103-104, 37/115, 38/21, 38/71, 40/95, 40/144, 43/120–1, 43/124–5, 44 Headnote, and 46/13.

[76] *Scale* MS Sr and Durham University Library, Cosin MS v.III.8 have closely affiliated texts of the *Prickynge of Love* with identical ascriptions of the text to Hilton, as do Heneage MS 3084 (now Yale University, Osborn MS fa 46) and the set of extracts in Cambridge University Library MS Hh.1.12. See Michael G. Sargent, 'A New Manuscript of *The Chastising of God's Children* with an Ascription to Walter Hilton', *MÆ* 46 (1977), 49–65; *The Prickynge of Love*, ed. Harold Kane, Salzburg Studies in English Literature: Elizabethan & Renaissance Studies, 92:10 (Salzburg, 1983), pp. xxii–xxiv; J. P. H. Clark, 'Walter Hilton and the *Stimulus Amoris*', *DR* 102 (1984), 79–118.

pattern of production of manuscripts of *Scale* II, which will be discussed below,[77] seems to demonstrate lines of transmission outward from the area of Cambridge, Ely, southern Lincolnshire, and western Norfolk, with specific groups of manuscripts associated with the Carthusian and Brigittine orders and the city of London (the earliest of which, in either case, is dialectally localizable to Cambridge). Unlike *Scale* I, *Scale* II does not demonstrate any pattern of dissemination in the west or north of England, nor from the area of Nottinghamshire in which Thurgarton is situated. Wherever he may have been when he decided to expand upon and clarify the themes of *Scale* I in a second book, and wherever he may have been when he finished, the diffusion of copies of *The Scale of Perfection* comprising *Scale* II seems to have been from East Anglia outward.

Hilton begins the second book of the *Scale* by linking it back to the first: he says that his reader has requested a clarification of the idea of the reformation of the soul to the image of God that underlies most of the latter half of *Scale* I. He begins the discussion of reformation with an extended discourse on the theology of justification: the necessary reformation in faith that precedes the reformation in faith and in feeling. In this section, Hilton draws upon Anselm of Canterbury's *Cur Deus homo* to argue the necessity of the sacrifice of the innocent God-man Jesus in atonement for the sin of Adam and Eve, and concentrates on the need for the sacraments of baptism and penance to restore the human soul to the image of God in faith. Hilton alludes to the twofold reformation of the soul in Chapters 5 and 13. In the latter, he distinguishes between reason and sensuality, and—drawing upon William of St-Thierry's *Lettre d'or* (the letter to the Carthusians of Mont-Dieu)—he distinguishes among animal, rational, and perfect souls.[78] For William, what distinguishes the perfectly reformed souls is that they are drawn to love of God 'per affectum' of the Holy Spirit. This is, I believe, the source of Hilton's conceptualization of reformation 'in faith *and in feeling*', which will dominate the discussion of the contemplative life in the latter part of *Scale* II.[79]

Chapters 14 through 20 are occupied with the description of the spiritual state of those who are reformed in faith, but not yet in

[77] See below, pp. civ–cxviii..
[78] See Explanatory Note to 13/23–38.
[79] See Sargent, 'Walter Hilton's *Scale of Perfection* in Devotional Compilations'.

feeling. The discussion of the latter reformation begins with the parable of the pilgrim to Jerusalem in Chapter 21, but Hilton does not continue with his use of this parable in any consistent way. Drawing on St Bernard's exposition of Psalm 90, 'Qui habitat', particularly as he has reworked it in his own exposition, he deploys the image of the 'lyȝt mirknes' of desire for God, particularly in Chapter 22, but also throughout the remainder of the text. As has been pointed out elsewhere, this 'mirkness' is not the apophatic darkness of *The Cloud of Unknowing* and other works of the tradition of the pseudo-Dionysus,[80] which *is* God insofar as the human mind can comprehend him, but a stage through which the contemplative must pass in order to arrive at 'reformation in faith and in feeling'.

In Chapter 31, Hilton defends his conceptualization of 'reformation in faith and in feeling' on the basis of a number of Pauline texts, most importantly Rom. 12:2, 'Et nolite conformari huic saeculo, sed reformamini in novitate sensus vestri': 'And be not conformed to this world; but be reformed in the newness of your mind'—which Hilton translates as 'Ȝe þat are þurgh grace reformed in feith, conforme ȝow not henforward to maners of þe werd, in pride, in coueytyse, and oþer synnes, bot be ȝe reformed in newhed of felynge.' Hilton emphasizes the suppport that he finds in this text: 'Lo, here þou maight se þat Seyn Poule spekeþ of reformynge in felynge, and what þat new felynge is he expouneþ in anoþer place [Col. 1:9] þus: . . . We preye God þat ȝe moun be fulfilled in knowynge of Goddis wille, in al vndirstondynge and in al maner gostly wysdom. Þis is reformynge in felynge.' The next five chapters form the theological core of *Scale* II: Hilton's discussion of grace, love, and light. Chapters 37 to 39 recapitulate the teaching of *Scale* I on the eradication of the vices in the soul in terms of contemplative grace by which Christ accomplishes within the soul the work of which the soul itself is incapable. This is summed up in Chapters 40 and 41, in which Hilton lists the attributes of contemplative grace according to tradition:[81]

> [P]urete and pouerte of spirit, gostly reste, inward silence and pees in conscience, heyghnes of thoght, onlynes and pryuete of herte, waker slepe of þe spouse, þat hath lost lykyng and ioyes of þis werd, taken with delyte of

[80] J. P. H. Clark, 'The "Lightsome Darkness"—Aspects of Walter Hilton's Theological Background', *DR* 95 (1977), 95–109; Clark, 'The "Cloud of Unknowing", Walter Hilton and St John of the Cross: A Comparison', *DR* 96 (1978), 281–98.

[81] See 41/8–16.

heuenly sauour, ay threstende and softly syghende þe blissed presence of Jesu. And I dar hardily pronownce þat þis soule brenneth al in lufe and schyneth in gostly lyght, wurthi for to come to þe name and to þe wurschepe of þe spowse, for it is reformed in felyng, made able and redy to contemplacyon. Þese are þe toknes of inspiracyon in openynge of þe gostly eye.

The remainder of *Scale* II is occupied with the discussion of the effects of the reformation in faith and in feeling in the soul: the destruction of sin (Chapter 42), the understanding of Scripture (Chapter 43), the sounding of 'the voice of Jesus' (Chapter 44), the ability to see God in the nature and actions of all beings, including the church in the world and the angels, both the bad (Chapter 45) and the good (Chapter 46), and to glimpse the Trinity insofar as it can be seen in this life. From Chapter 40 onwards, Hilton alludes repetitively to 'the voice of Jesus', the last repetition occurring in Chapter 46, at what may have been the original conclusion of the text:[82]

[I]lk a gracyous knowyng of sothfastnes, felt with inly sauour and gostly delyte, is a pryuey rownynge of Jesu in þe ere of a clene soule. Him nedeth for to haue mykel clennes in soule, in mekenes and in oþer vertus, and to ben halfe defe to noyse of werdly iangelyng, þat schuld wysely parceyuen þese swete gostly rownyngges. Þis is þe voyce of Jesu.

All seven non-atelous manuscripts of what will be identified below as the Carthusian/Brigittine group (HBH$_5$AsWsLdT) originally ended at this point; those that do continue (H, B, and T) are completed in other hands. H$_7$RLB$_3$SrLwAEPH$_6$CcMPl and the print W continue, noting that David spoke of this voice in the Psalter, 'Vox Domini preparantis ceruos, et reuelabit condensa' [Psal. 28:9]: 'The voice of the Lord prepareth the stag, and he will discover the thick woods.' H$_7$ and Sr end at this point (Sr after providing the second half of the Psalm text, 'and in his temple all shall speak his glory'). H$_7$ continues in another hand. (See Pls. 2 and 3.)

What follows in `H$_7$´RLB$_3$SrLwAEPH$_6$CcMPlW is an allegorical reading of this verse, followed, a hundred words later, by the observation that:

Þese arn goostly thyngys þat I spak of beforn, and þe mow be kallyd newe gracyous felyngys, and I do but touche hem a lytel for wyssyng of þe soule.

82 46/69–74; the other occurrences are at 40/49–51, 41/167, 44/1, 44/55, and 46/56.

For a soule þat ys clene, styred be grace to vse of thys werkyng, may se more in an hour of swych goostly mater þan myht ben wryten in a gret bok.

In neither case has the text of *Scale* II come to a satisfying conclusion.

Hilton appears to have ended his book with a final reference to 'the voice of Jesus', then to have reopened it with a reference to a Psalm that provides a sixfold repetition of the phrase 'vox Domini'. The verse cited is the last of these and the explication of it is brief—almost truncated—the text of *Scale* II at that point appears less to be concluded than shut off. If this final paragraph is in fact Hilton's work, and not that of an unknown 'continuator of the school of Walter Hilton', it would appear to mark the end of his career as a writer, and a final descent, perhaps, into illness and death.

3. EDITING *SCALE* II

This edition is based upon a complete examination and analysis of the surviving manuscript evidence for the text of *Scale* II, evidence that demonstrates several discrete lines of transmission among twenty-three surviving originally complete manuscipts (plus one fragment), five early prints, one manuscript copied from a print, and five sets of extracts. One line of transmission, the Carthusian/Brigittine group, comprises eleven manuscripts, of which seven were made or owned by monks of the English Charterhouses or the Brigittines of Syon abbey, as well as the incunable prints, all of which derive from the Wynkyn de Worde *editio princeps* of 1494. Another line of transmission, the London group, comprises five manuscripts, of which four have demonstrable connections to Londoners of the early to mid-fifteenth century. A third group of four manuscripts shares a tendency to Theocentric readings ('God' rather than 'Jesus'). One of the above-mentioned manuscripts is a demonstrable conflation of the Carthusian/Brigittine and the London groups; another changes allegiance halfway through the text from the Theocentric to the Carthusian/Brigittine group. Two other manuscripts have large numbers of isolative variants, but also other readings that show possible influence from Thomas Fishlake's contemporary Latin translation of the *Scale*. Another two show no signs of affiliation with any of the above-mentioned groups not because they are idiosyncratic, but because they deviate from the

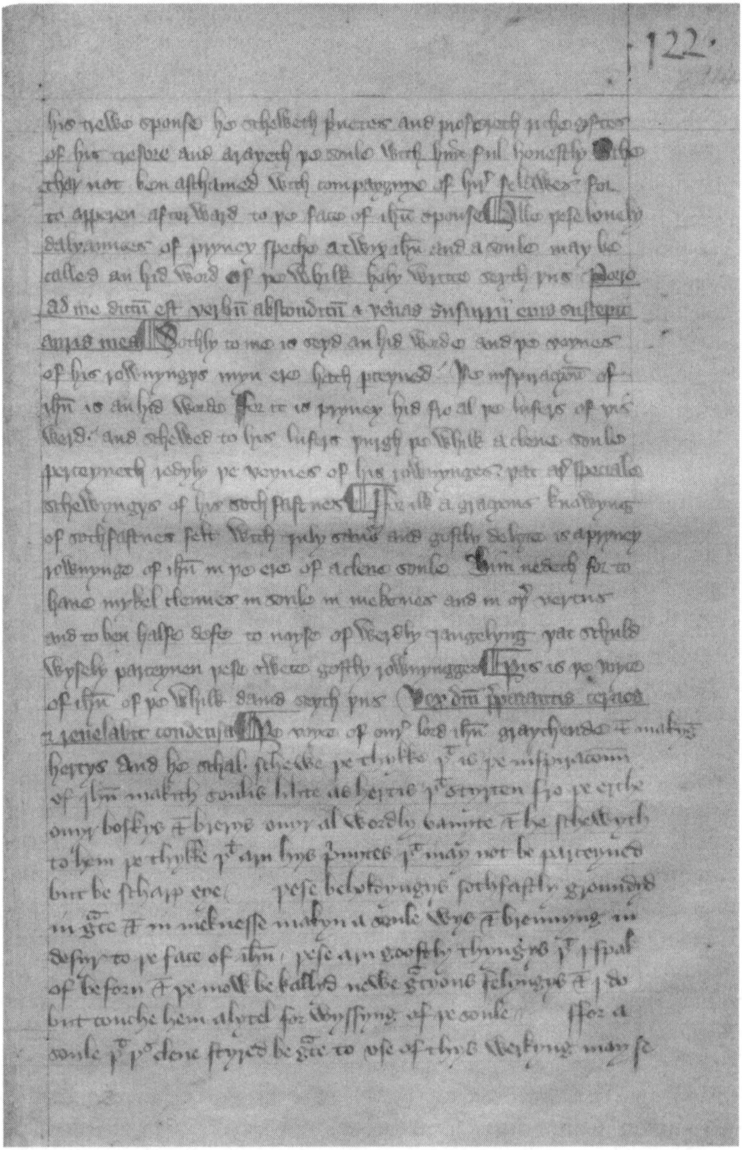

Pl. 2. British Library MS Harley 6573, f. 114r (orig. 122r). © The British Library Board

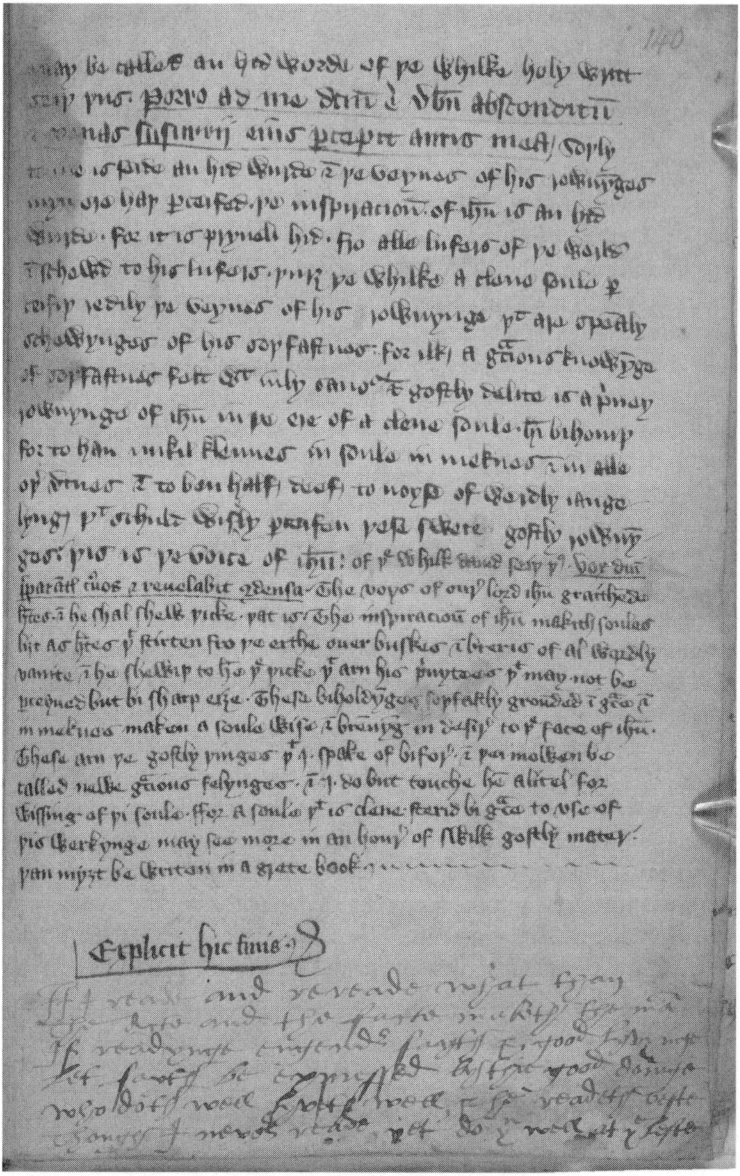

PL. 3. British Library MS Harley 6579, f. 140r. © The British Library Board

consensus of readings of all manuscripts less often than any others. It should also be noted that the Latin translation does not agree with any of the English manuscripts or manuscript groups; the exemplar upon which it was based was an independent (and occasionally faulty) copy.

All of these separate lines of textual evidence are equally representative of an original text that shows signs of possible authorial revision during the process of composition. Because of the complexity of the surviving evidence, and because of the known methodological inadequacies of modern critical reconstructions of an 'authoritative' text,[83] no such editorial construct is attempted here. The aim is to produce the edition of record, but because there has been no previous examination of the textual evidence, it is incumbent that this edition furnish that record. This is provided through a facing-page edition of the texts of British Library MS Harley 6573 (H_7) and British Library MS Harley 6579 (H), supported by a critical apparatus that reports all variant readings of all manuscripts.[84] These texts have not been editorially 'improved', with the exception of the correction, in square brackets, of clearly erroneous readings. Even when the editor believes some other reading to be more cogent (which will be discussed on a case-by-case basis in the Explanatory Notes), the readings of the manuscripts will stand.

I have argued elsewhere that complicated textual relationships like those of *The Scale of Perfection* should be conceived of rhizomorphically, rather than stemmatically.[85] To do so is not to eschew the discussion of genetic relationships, for the surviving manuscripts of the text are indeed related. All manuscripts have been copied from other manuscripts, but the hierarchy of descent is not the best way to conceptualize the relationship. The schematic representation of the relations of the manuscripts presented in Fig. 1 thus shows seven

[83] See Sargent, 'Organic and Cybernetic Metaphors for Manuscript Relations: Stemma — Cladogram — Rhizome — Cloud', in Ian Johnson and Alan F. Westphall (eds.), *The Pseudo-Bonaventuran Lives of Christ: Exploring the Middle English Tradition* (Turnhout, 2013), 197–255; 'Editing Walter Hilton's *Scale of Perfection*', in Gillespie and Hudson (eds.), *Probable Truth*, 509–34; and for a case similar in complexity to that of the *Scale*, the 'Textual Introduction' of *Ancrene Wisse: A Corrected Edition of the Text in Cambridge, Corpus Christi College, MS 402, with Variants from Other Manuscripts*, ed. Bella Millett, i, EETS OS 325 (2005), pp. xi–lxvi.

[84] The reasons for this choice of base manuscripts are discussed below, pp. cxxxviii–cxl.

[85] Sargent, 'Organic and Cybernetic Metaphors for Manuscript Relations' and 'Editing Walter Hilton's *Scale of Perfection*'.

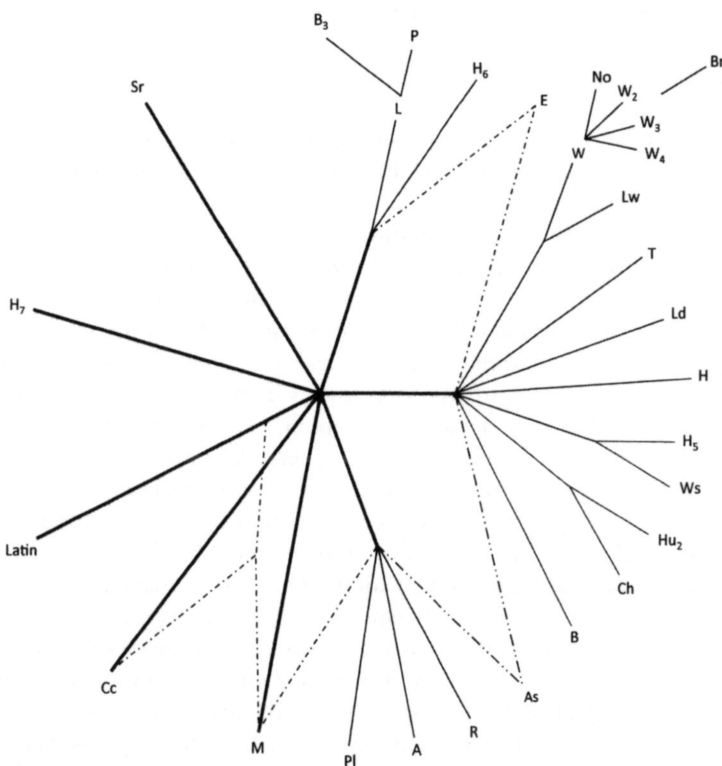

FIG. 1. Affiliations of the manuscripts and early prints of *Scale* II. Lines of double width designate separate lines of transmission. Double-dotted broken lines designate a text of mixed allegiance. Single-dotted broken lines designate lines of probably conflation.

lines of dissemination from what may well have been an unstable centre point, a text possibly revised in the process of composition. Two of these lines are realized in a single surviving manuscript (H_7 and Sr); three in groups of related manuscripts (H, B, Ch, Hu_2, H_5, Ws, Ld, T, Lw, W and the copies dependent on W; L, B_3, P, and H_6; and R, A, and Pl); and one in the Latin text (Lat.). There are also two manuscripts related to two groups each (As and E), and two manuscripts that appear to have been influenced by the Latin text (Cc and M).

Modern critical discussion of the text of the *Scale of Perfection* began with the introduction to Evelyn Underhill's modernization (1923), which was based on H, compared with nine other manuscripts.[86] Underhill's observations focused on the additions and corrections made by several mid-fifteenth-century hands to the text of *Scale* I in H, which was written in a hand of the end of the fourteenth century.[87] These corrections included an additional page of text on devotion to the Holy Name of Jesus added at one point, and a series of minor textual variations and substitutions throughout the text—notably, in a number of cases, 'Christocentric' substitution of the name of 'Jesus' where the underlying text had read 'God'. Underhill conjectured that these corrections and additions represented probable authorial revisions of the text of *Scale* I. She noted that *Scale* II, which is also corrected by the same hands, but does not have the multiple addition of varying chapter titles and divisions that *Scale* I has, 'seems never to have been revised. The text is practically identical in all the MSS. that I have examined.'

Underhill's observations were extended and given more precision by Helen Gardner, whose 1936 study of the manuscripts noted that the text of *Scale* II ended a paragraph early in seven of the thirty manuscripts that she examined;[88] in two of these seven, the fuller ending is added in other hands. This, she observed, 'does not appear to be significant and is probably due to the loss of a final leaf in a parent manuscript.' The 'considerable body of variant readings' observable elsewhere 'may be classified under the headings of eye-

[86] *Scale*, ed. Underhill, pp. xliii–l (the quotation below is at p. xlv). By her own account, Underhill compared H with H_5, H_7, S, J, Cc, T_2, T, L, and V, and checked the text closely with H_5 and L. S, J, T_2, and V comprise *Scale* I only.

[87] All of the hands in this manuscript are dialectally localized to Ely or extreme southern Lincolnshire; it belonged to London Charterhouse in the 15th c.

[88] Gardner, 'Text' (quotations below from pp. 16, 15).

slips, inversions, alterations in syntax, sometimes due to the desire to expand elliptical constructions, additions of adjectives to make a phrase more pointed and substitutions either of different forms of the same word or of other words.' Gardner's general impression was the same as that of Underhill, that the 'textual problems' of *Scale* II appeared 'much simpler' than those of *Scale* I—on which Gardner, too, focused the majority of her attention.

In his 2000 TEAMS edition of the *Scale* from MS L (compared with B), Thomas Bestul repeated Underhill's and Gardner's observations in simplified form: '[t]he textual situation of Book II is less complicated. There are many fewer manuscripts, and the textual variations, though considerable, are less substantial.'[89] Bestul cited S. S. Hussey's discussion of the state of the text of *Scale* II in a way that implied concurrence in Underhill's and Gardner's observations, although Hussey's position was in fact one of polite deference rather than full agreement.

In 1962, Hussey produced the draft edition of *Scale* II for his University of London doctoral thesis that is the basis of the present edition, and published a survey of his textual-critical observations in 1964.[90] With regard to the lack of 'extensive omissions or additions' to the text of *Scale* II comparable to the 'Holy Name' passage that Underhill and Gardner had noted in *Scale* I, Hussey observed that the 'only comparable feature' of *Scale* II was the truncation of the end of the text that Gardner had dismissed as a possible result of the loss of a final folio.[91] With respect to the 'additions', 'Christocentric' or otherwise, Hussey was to note that

> In both books of Harley 6579 (H) a number of interpolations are insertd by a later hand (or hands) between the lines and in the margins. . . . The demonstrable 'Christo-centric' additions in Book II are fewer (although there are more in Book II's Latin) than in Book I. . . . [B]ut is it important

[89] Walter Hilton, *The Scale of Perfection*, ed. Thomas H. Bestul, TEAMS Middle English Texts Series (Kalamazoo, 2000); d.lib.rochester.edu/teams/publication/bestul-hilton-scale-of-perfection, 10, citing S. S. Hussey, 'Editing *The Scale of Perfection*: Return to Recension', in A. J. Minnis and Charlotte Brewer (eds.), *Crux and Controversy in Middle English Textual Criticism* (Cambridge, 1992), 97–107 at 103, and Hussey, 'The Text of *The Scale of Perfection*, Book II', 85–6.

[90] S. S. Hussey, 'An Edition from the Manuscripts of Book 2 of Walter Hilton's *Scale of Perfection*' (Ph.D. thesis, London, 1962); and 'Editing *The Scale of Perfection*'.

[91] Gardner also suggests that this was the cause of the omission of the 'Holy Name' passage in those manuscripts that lack it. See 'The Text', 29.

to realise that the variants in Book II, although individually they are usually less dramatic, are very considerable in number.[92]

In fact, as we shall see, there are some 22,000 points of variation in the 56,000 words of the text of *Scale* II. Although the final demonstration must await the publication of the edition of *Scale* I, it is hard at this point to escape the impression that the difference in textual complexity observed by Underhill and Gardner between the two books has more to do with the relative prominence of the additions and corrections in H than with the degree of variation among the manuscripts of the texts themselves.

In his analysis of the text of *Scale* II, Hussey considered the variations that he had noted among the manuscripts in three ways. First, he considered the traditional forms of unconscious scribal variation noted by Gardner.[93] Second, he observed the occurrence of the various forms of scribal error described by George Kane in the Athlone edition of the A-Text of *Piers Plowman*.[94] Third, in support of an edition that he was later to characterize as a 'return to recension',[95] he described the relations among the manuscripts of the English text, setting out what he saw as five persistent textual groupings among the twenty-two manuscripts that could usefully be collated:[96]

(1) H, H_5, and Ws;
(2) Br and the 1494 Wynkyn de Worde *editio princeps*, W;
(3) B, Ld, and Hu_2;
(4) P, L, H_6, and B_3; and
(5) A, R, Pl, and M.

The first three of these groups, Hussey noted, together with T and Lw, combine to form a larger group, which he designated **x** (later **χ**); the latter two groups, together with H_7, Cc, and the extracts in Td, combine to form a second larger group designated **y** (later **υ**). As, E, and Ws could not be placed precisely in this schema: Hussey noted

92 Hussey, 'Editing *The Scale of Perfection*', 102–3.

93 Hussey, The Text of *The Scale of Perfection*', 82–5, citing Gardner, 'The Text', 15.

94 Hussey, 'The Text of *The Scale of Perfection*', 89–91, referring to *Piers Plowman: The A Version*, ed. George Kane (London, 1960), 115–46.

95 Hussey, 'Editing *The Scale of Perfection*', 106, states his position succinctly: 'I believe recension to be the most valuable editorial technique I have, although of course no one nowadays would seek to devise a stemma for other than very simple textual relationships.'

96 I am here using the sigla for the manuscripts that were later to be worked out between Hussey and A. J. Bliss, which differ from those that Hussey used in his earlier work.

that As and E most probably represent the conflation of different forms of **χ** and **υ**, and found the evidence of Ws intractable.

In constructing his textual groupings, Hussey employed a method developed from the form of *eliminatio codicorum descriptorum* developed by Phyllis Hodgson for her edition of the works of the *Cloud*-corpus.[97] Manuscripts of the *Cloud* that could be grouped by their agreement in common readings were examined to determine which of them might have served as the source for the others; once one manuscript was identified as the most 'authoritative' of a given group, the others were dismissed as derivative. They did not need to be collated further, and their readings did not need to be reported in a confusing 'cloud of variants' that 'would certainly not justify the great amount of space it would occupy'.[98] In Hussey's final analysis, the best representative manuscript of each textual group of *Scale* manuscripts was similarly treated as if it were equivalent to the hyparchetype from which its group derived.[99] In this way, H was not merely the best representative, but treated as the possible source of the **χ** subgroups H_5Ws, BLdHu_2, WBrLw, T and Ch; L was not merely the best representative, but treated as the possible source of the **υ** subgroups PLB_3H_6 (and possibly E), ARMPl, the loosely associated Cc, Sr, H_7, and As, and the extracts in Td.

Following Underhill and Gardner in characterizing the corrections and additions to the text by the annotators of H as expansions to the underlying text and noting that a number of these 'expansions' were to be found among the manuscripts of the **υ** textual tradition, Hussey observed a tendency to incremental expansion of the text of *Scale* II (although nothing as marked as the 'Christo-centric additions' to the text of *Scale* I) that made the 'unexpanded' **χ** text the basis of the 'expanded' **υ**. In a later study, Hussey argued that Thomas Fishlake's Latin translation of the *Scale* was representative of the **υ** form of the English text, probably most closely related to the form of the text found in L; and that 'the Latin translation carries further the treatment of the [**χ**] group of English manuscripts by the [**υ**] adaptor whose text Fishlake clearly used'.[100] Hussey's provisional edition of

[97] *The Cloud of Unknowing and The Book of Privy Counselling*, ed. Phyllis Hodgson, EETS OS 218 (1944); *Deonise Hid Diuinite and Other Treatises on Contemplative Prayer Related to The Cloud of Unknowing*, ed. Phyllis Hodgson, EETS OS 231 (1955).

[98] *Cloud of Unknowing*, ed. Hodgson, p. xxiv.

[99] The following paragraphs summarize part of the argument of Sargent, 'Editing *The Scale of Perfection*'.

[100] Hussey, 'Latin and English', 475.

Scale II was based on H, corrected by recension to reflect the hypothetical archetype of the entire manuscript tradition.

This recensionist narrative of the expansion of the text from **χ** to **υ**, which was then further expanded in Fishlake's Latin version, was questioned by readers of Hussey's draft edition, however, who accepted his observation of the degree of variation between the two forms of the English text, but not his derivation of **υ** from **χ**. It was suggested that he make a facing-page edition of the two versions. This he provided in a final submission: a facing-page edition of a critical edition of **χ** based on H and a critical edition of **υ** based on L, each with its own apparatus. Unfortunately, at the time of Hussey's death in November 2004, the work was not complete. Parts of the introductory discussion still reflected the earlier stage of his formulation of the textual relations, in which **υ** was derived from **χ**, and thus contradicted other parts of the same discussion that presented those same relations according to the later conceptualization of **χ** and **υ** as parallel. Further, the critical apparatus supporting the two forms of the text proved impossible to disentangle: the lemmata of each form of the text often occurred amongst the variant readings of the other form; and some variants were recorded amongst the manuscripts of both forms of the text, which created duplication between the two apparatus. Hussey's original collations, which might have provided the evidence to sort things out, were no longer available. At this point, it became necessary to collate the manuscripts anew; and the results of a full collation, from which no manuscript evidence was precluded, proved to provide different results than the selective collation undertaken before.

Tabulation of the Results of Collation of the English Text

A full collation of the twenty-two surviving originally complete manuscripts and the Wynkyn de Worde *editio princeps* of 1494 reveals the following: for a text of approximately 56,000 words, there are approximately 22,000 variant readings, distributed across approximately 16,000 lemmata.[101]

[101] The raw count of variations in the following discussion provides a close, but not an absolute measure of the actual degree of variation among the various manuscripts. A strict statistical analysis would depend on the weighting of variants according to Damerau-Levenshtein distance—the measure of variation between two finite strings of symbols (e.g. letters or words) according to the number of insertions, deletions, substitutions, or transpositions required to turn one string into the other. Because computational linguistics

Approximately 12,600 readings present isolative variants:[102] H_7 has 387, H has 154, R 213, B 475, H_5 302, L 409, B_3 234, As 1,824, Sr 655, Ws 96, Ch 103, Lw 244, A 779, Hu_2 451, E 456, P 31, H_6 592, Cc 1,630, M 1,474, Ld 663, Pl 687, T 683, and W 312. The average number of isolative variants per manuscript is 548. The manuscripts with the smallest numbers of such variants, P, Ws, and Ch, are all—as we shall see below—close congeners of other manuscripts with which they share high numbers of common variants. A number of manuscripts with low numbers of isolative variants are also members of larger groups identifiable by common shared variants. Four manuscripts have lost substantial portions of the text: at present, Ch comprises approximately three-eighths of the text; Hu_2 a little less than two-thirds; R approximately seven-eighths; and Ws approximately nine-tenths. If the missing portions of these manuscripts had the same textual profile as those that survive, then Ch would have 275 isolative variants, Hu_2 would have 680, R 240, and Ws 120. Three manuscripts are markedly idiosyncratic: M has 1,474 isolative variants, Cc has 1,630, and As has 1,824.

A further 2,586 readings present pairs of manuscripts agreeing in a unique variant. The number of possible pairings among the twenty-three surviving originally complete manuscripts of *Scale* II (including the Wynkyn de Worde *editio princeps*) is 253; in fact, 191 pairings occur. These range from twenty-six pairings occurring once each through BLd, which agree in a unique variant forty-four times; TW, which agree in a unique variant forty-seven times (almost entirely in

has not yet worked out the appropriate weightings for an analysis of Levenshtein distances for Middle English texts (for both lexical and syntactic reasons), and because the texts of the manuscripts of *Scale* II are not available in machine-readable form in any case, a strict statistical analysis of the degree of variation among the manuscripts is not possible at this time. The difficulty is compounded in the not-uncommon case of variation within variants (where, e.g., eight manuscripts agree in a variant phrase, but two of the eight have a one- or two-word variation on that variant). In such cases, rather than registering a single variant more than once (as a two-, a six-, and an eight-manuscript variant), I have usually reported the smaller variational groupings, with the result that the largest variational groups are somewhat underreported in the discussion below.

[102] The citation order of the manuscripts in the present discussion is based on that of the critical apparatus, which reflects approximately the dating of the various manuscripts and prints: $H_7H[H^{\circ}]RBH_5LB_3AsSrWsChLw[H^{c}]AHu_2EPH_6CcMLdPlTW$. The one exception to this is that the original readings and the corrections in H, which date to the end of the 14th and the middle of the 15th c. respectively, distinguished as H° and H^{c} in the critical apparatus, will be discussed separately below (pp. cxii–cxiv), as will the corrections made to T and W at the end of the 15th c., which are distinguished in the apparatus as T^{G} and W^{G} (pp. cxiv–cxv).

chapter titles); RM, which agree in a unique variant sixty-one times; RAs, which agree in a unique variant sixty-eight times; LdT, which agree in a unique variant ninety-one times; CcM, which agree in a unique variant 118 times; H_5Ws, which agree in a unique variant 341 times (although Ws lacks approximately one-tenth of the text); and LwW, which agree in a unique variant 397 times.

The agreements between Lw and W represent 90 per cent of all two-manuscript variants that include Lw and 75 per cent of all that include W. The 342 agreements between H_5 and Ws represent 90 per cent of all two-manuscript variants that include Ws and 80 per cent of the total for H_5. The difference in the figures for the latter pair of manuscripts is probably attributable to the fact that for the one-tenth of the text missing in Ws, H_5 has a larger number of isolative variants; if Ws were complete and its textual profile were the same in the now-missing section as in the rest, their agreement would account for more than 90 per cent of all two-manuscript agreements for both manuscripts. The thirty-three agreements between the incomplete texts of Ch and Hu_2 are probably also to be taken as evidence that they are genetically related: they overlap for only approximately one-fifth of the text, and each agrees with other manuscripts for sections of text that do not survive in the other of the pair. Even so, their agreements represent 70 per cent of all two-manuscript variants that include Ch, although only 30 per cent of the total for Hu_2 (like H_5, the member of the pair of which considerably more survives). The twenty-eight agreements of L and P, representing 75 per cent of all two-manuscript variants that include L and 55 per cent of the total for P, are also notable; they will be discussed further below. We shall also return later to the discussion of the text of Cc and M (two manuscripts whose large numbers of isolative variants we have already noted), whose 118 agreements represent just under 30 per cent of all two-manuscript variants that include either manuscript.

It should also be noted that L and P are among the manuscripts that occur least often among pairings in unique readings: L occurs only in thirty-seven pairs, paired with a total of six different manuscripts (twenty-eight times with P, as noted above), H in fifty pairs, paired with fifteen different manuscripts, P in forty-nine pairs, paired with six different manuscripts (including L), B_3 in sixty-eight pairs, paired with eighteen different manuscripts, and H_7 in ninety-three pairings, paired with eighteen different manuscripts (with none more than thirteen times). At the opposite end of the scale, W occurs in 526 pairings, paired with seventeen different manuscripts (although 397 times with Lw, as noted above), Lw in 440 pairings, paired with fifteen different manuscripts (including W), H_5 in 427 pairings, paired with twenty different manuscripts (although 341 times with Ws, as noted above), M in 425 pairings, paired with nineteen different manuscripts, Cc in 409 different pairings, paired with twenty-one different manuscripts, Ws in 370 pairings, paired with thirteen different manuscripts (including H_5), and As in 325 pairings, paired with twenty-one different manuscripts. The three manuscripts with the largest numbers of isolative variants (M, Cc, and As) are thus also among those with the largest numbers of apparently random agreements in pairs.[103]

There are 1,130 occurrences of groups of three manuscripts agreeing in a unique variant. The number of possible combinations of three witnesses among the twenty-three manuscripts and early prints of *Scale* II is 1,771; 336 of these combinations occur. These range from 193 groups of three manuscripts occuring once each through RAPl, which agree with each other in eighty unique variants, and LB_3P, which agree with each other in 150 unique variants. This latter group amounts to 85 per cent of all three-manuscript variants that include L, 80 per cent of those that include B_3, and 80 per cent of those that include P. It should also be recalled here that the twenty-eight two-manuscript agreements of LP represent a significant number of the two-manuscript variants including either of those manuscripts. The three agreements of LB_3 and the fifteen of B_3P are not remarkable in themselves. The thirteen three-manuscript agreements of LPH_6, most of which occur at a point in the text where B_3 is lacking, should also be noted. Groups of three manuscripts in agreement in variation also support the pairings observed above. The pair LwW is supported by 135 groups of three. On the other hand, either Lw or W alone occurs in a group of three a total of seventy-eight times (primarily in groupings occurring once each). The pair H_5Ws is supported by 144 groups of three. On the other hand, either H_5 or Ws alone occurs in a group of three a total of fifty-seven times (primarily in groups occurring once

[103] 'Random' in the sense that the pairings in which Cc, M, and As occur do not seem to fit into any overall genetic pattern, as do those of Lw and W, H_5 and Ws, L and P, and probably Ch and Hu_2—although, as we shall see below, there are definite local patterns that do involve Cc, M, and As.

each). Again here, the differential between H_5 and Ws (forty-two against fifteen) is notable, and probably attributable to the loss of text in Ws.

There are 893 occurrences of groups of four manuscripts agreeing in a unique variant. There are 8,855 possible combinations of four witnesses among the twenty-three manuscripts and early prints of *Scale* II; in fact, 352 groups of four occur. These range from 140 groups occurring once each through LB_3PH_6, which agree 150 times in a unique variant. BHu_2LdT and SrALdT agree seven times each: these are all examples of the probably coincidental substitution of normative 'alwey' for dialectal 'ay' or 'euer' in other manuscripts. AsH_6LdT agree twelve times, primarily in the substitution of forms of 'clep-' for the Northern form 'call-'. ALdTW agree twenty-two times, in variants all but two of which occur in chapter titles.

Four groups of four manuscripts cluster themselves around two of the groups of three manuscripts noted above. Around RAPl (which, as we have seen, agree with each other eighty times) are clustered, from Chapter 27 onward (with two exceptions), RAMPl, which agree seventy-eight times in a unique variant, and in the first twenty-six chapters of *Scale* II (with one exception), RAsAPl, agreeing ninety-four times in a unique variant. The combination RAPl thus accounts for 75 per cent of all four-manuscript variants that include R, 65 per cent of those that include A, and 75 per cent of those that include Pl. The combination RAsAPl accounts for 65 per cent of all four-manuscript groups that include As. The combination RAMPl accounts for 55 per cent of those that include M. As will be noted below, As is affiliated with a different group of manuscripts in the latter part of the text. The agreement of M with RAPl coincides with the change of hand and dialect at f. 75^v. Around LB_3P, which agree with each other 150 times, are clustered LB_3EP, which agree forty-two times in a unique variant, and LB_3PH_6, which agree 151 times in a unique variant. The combination LB_3P thus accounts for 90 per cent of all four-manuscript variants that include L, 90 per cent of those that include B_3, and 85 per cent of those that include P. The combination LB_3PH_6 accounts for 70 per cent of all four-manuscript groups that include H_6; and the combination LB_3EP accounts for 35 per cent of those that include E.

There are 550 occurrences of groups of five manuscripts agreeing in a unique variant, representing 292 combinations. These range from 240 groups of five that occur once each through LB_3EPH_6, which agree eighty-four times. RAsAMPl agree fifty-three times in a unique variant. This group of five manuscripts reinforces the four-manuscript groupings RAsAPl and RAMPl, overlapping at the point where the agreement of As with RAPl leaves off and the agreement of M with RAPl begins. LB_3EPH_6 reinforces the four-manuscript groupings LB_3EP and LB_3PH_6 that, as we have seen, cluster around the three-manuscript group LB_3P.

There are 418 occurrences of groups of six manuscripts agreeing in a unique variant, representing 294 combinations. These range from 247 groups of six that occur once each through $HH_5WsLwTW$, which agree sixteen times. Eleven groups, totalling nineteen occurrences, share the feature that they identify Hilton's Latin quotations from Scripture either in the text or the margin. These groups, comprising manuscripts B, L, Hu_2, E, P, Ld, T, and W in varying combinations, vary in form, occasionally disagree on the identification of the text cited, and probably represent independent attempts to provide Hilton's text with an apparatus of scriptural citations. Sixty-seven groups of six manuscripts, representing 118 readings, support the group LB_3P and twenty-seven groups, representing thirty-one readings, support RAPl.

There are 415 occurrences of groups of seven manuscripts agreeing in a unique variant, representing 278 combinations. These range from 222 groups of seven that occur once each through BLEPLdTW, which agree twenty-seven times in the provision of identification of scriptural quotations. There are 390 occurrences of groups of eight manuscripts agreeing in a unique variant, representing 254 combinations. Of these groups, 216 occur once each. $BLHu_2$-EPLdTW agree twenty-seven times in the identification of scriptural quotations. The three eight-manuscript groups $HBH_5WsLwLdTW$, $HBH_5ChLwLdTW$, and HBH_5LwHu_2LdTW, which occur a total of forty-seven times, represent the same group of ten manuscripts, $HBH_5WsChLwHu_2LdTW$, allowing for the loss of portions of the text in Ws, Ch, and Hu_2.

There are 509 occurrences of groups of nine manuscripts agreeing in a unique variant, representing 242 combinations. Of these groups, 212 occur once each. $H_7HRLSrPCcMPl$ agree twenty-seven times in reading forms of 'mirk-', 'myrk-' rather than 'dark-', 'derk-'. HBH_5-$LwHu_2ELdTW$ agree with each other in twenty-three variants, and $HBH_5WsChLwLdTW$ in fifty-eight variants in the quarter of the text that survives in both Ws and Ch; and $HBH_5AsWsLwLdTW$

agree with each other in seventy-nine variants. The coincidence of As with HBH$_5$WsLwLdTW, which occurs primarily in the latter half of the text, has been noted before; it should also be kept in mind that As shares a large number of readings with RAPl in the first half of the text, and that it also has the largest number of isolative variants of any surviving manuscript.

There are 528 occurrences of groups of ten manuscripts agreeing in a unique variant, representing 245 combinations. Of these groups, 195 occur once each. H$_7$HRLAsSrPCcMPl agree twenty-seven times in 'mirk-' readings. HBH$_5$AsWsLwELdTW agree with each other twenty times; and HBH$_5$AsWsLwHu$_2$LdTW twenty-eight times. HBH$_5$WsChLwHu$_2$LdTW agree with each other thirty times in the 15 per cent of the text that survives in all copies: the total number of unique variants in which all surviving manuscripts of this group agree is 160.

There are 472 occurrences of groups of eleven manuscripts agreeing in a unique variant, representing 233 combinations. Of these groups, 193 occur once each. BH$_5$B$_3$LwAHu$_2$EH$_6$LdTW agree with each other twenty-five times in readings representing the substitution of forms of 'dark-' for forms of 'mirk-'. HBH$_5$As-WsLwHu$_2$ELdTW agree with each other twenty-eight times: this grouping represents the absence of Ch from the ten-manuscript group HBH$_5$WsChLwHu$_2$LdTW plus the addition of the probably conflated E and As in the latter half of the text. The total of readings in which HBH$_5$AsWsChLwHu$_2$ELdTW agree, taking into account the losses to Ws, Ch, and Hu$_2$, and the addition of As and E, is 406.

H$_7$RLB$_3$SrAPH$_6$CcMPl agree in a single variant sixty-nine times; H$_7$LB$_3$SrAEPH$_6$CcMPl twenty-eight times; H$_7$RLB$_3$AsAEPH$_6$CcPl nine times; and H$_7$RLB$_3$SrAEPH$_6$CcPl nine times, for a total of 114 readings. These are readings in which all other manuscripts agree in a single variant against the various combinations of HBH$_5$-WsChLwHu$_2$LdTW with As and E.

There are 438 occurrences of groups of twelve manuscripts agreeing in a unique variant, representing 219 combinations. Of these groups, 190 occur once each. BH$_5$B$_3$AsLwAHu$_2$EH$_6$LdTW agree with each other twenty-two times in reading forms of 'dark-' for forms of 'mirk-'. H$_7$RLB$_3$AsSrAEPH$_6$CcPl agree in a single variant twelve times, H$_7$RLB$_3$AsSrAPH$_6$CcMPl thirty-four times, H$_7$RLB$_3$AsAEPH$_6$-CcMPl twenty times, and H$_7$RLB$_3$SrAEPH$_6$CcMPl ninety-five times. These groups present readings in which all other manuscripts agree in a single variant against HBH$_5$WsChLwHu$_2$LdTW plus As and E. There are 303 occurrences of groups of thirteen manuscripts agreeing in a unique variant, representing 190 combinations. Of these groups, 177 occur once each. H$_7$RLB$_3$AsSrAEPH$_6$CcMPl occurs ninety-two times; this group presents readings in which all other manuscripts agree in a single variant against the various combinations of HBH$_5$WsChLwHu$_2$LdTW.[104]

In sum, the vast majority of groupings of manuscripts in shared readings occur very seldom. Of a total of approximately 22,000 variants, nearly 15,500 represent manuscript groupings that occur only once (approximately 12,600 are isolative variants); 332 are groupings of manuscripts that occur twice each; 108 are groupings that occur thrice each; seventy-seven groupings occur four times each, and fifty-one groupings occur five times each. There is only one grouping of ten manuscripts that occurs more than ten times; there are thirteen groupings—one of six manuscripts, one of three, and four of one each—that occur a total of thirteen times. There are only two groupings of more than thirteen manuscripts that occur more than once: one pair of manuscripts and one group of three each occurs thirty-three times, and two pairs of manuscripts each occur forty-four times.

Finally, there are a small number of manuscript groups that agree in large numbers of readings: LdT agree in unique variants ninety-one times; CcM agree 118 times; H$_5$Ws agree 341 times; and LwW agree in unique variants 397 times. LB$_3$P agree with each other in 151 unique variants; LB$_3$PH$_6$ agree 150 times; LB$_3$EP agree forty times; and LB$_3$EPH$_6$ agree eighty-four times. RAPl agree with each other in eighty unique variants, although R lacks approximately one-eighth of the text; RAMPl agree seventy-eight times; RAsAPl agree ninety-four times; and RAsAMPl agree fifty-three times. HBH$_5$WsChLwHu$_2$LdTW agree with each other thirty times in the 15 per cent of the text that survives coincidently in all copies. The total number of unique variants in which all surviving manuscripts of this group agree (taking acount of the loss of text in Ws, Ch, and Hu$_2$) is 160. As agrees with this group (again, taking account of missing text in Ws, Ch, and Hu$_2$) 124 times; E agrees forty-seven

[104] The majority of variants supported by more than thirteen manuscripts (out of twenty-three substantially complete surviving independent copies) are perforce a mirror-image of variants already listed above.

times. As and E together agree with this group seventy-five times. The total number of readings in which $HBH_5AsWsChLw$-Hu_2ELdTW agree, taking into account the losses to Ws, Ch, and Hu_2, and adding As and E, is 406.[105]

The agreeement of manuscripts in such large numbers of unique readings throughout the entire text may be taken as *prima facie* evidence of genetic relationship; cases of coincidence and conflation, which have their own patterns of occurrence, will be discussed below. The probable affiliational groups of surviving manuscripts of *Scale* II that this analysis demonstrates are: $HBH_5WsChLwHu_2LdTW$, also agreeing with As in the latter half of the text (Hussey's textual group **χ**), and with E. Subgroups of this affiliational group are: LwW, H_5Ws, LdT, and Ch Hu_2. LB_3PH_6 is a second probable affiliational group, also agreeing with E, and with the subgroup LB_3P. RAPl is a third probable affiliational group, not as strongly attested, also agreeing with As and M. CcM may also be taken as related, although the nature of their relationship, which seems to depend in part on agreement with the Latin text, is unclear.

The existence of Hussey's textual group **υ** cannot be demonstrated; it is the reflex of **χ**, the product of the binary tendency of recension, according to which all that is not **χ** must be **υ**. Further, there is no evidence that any of the affiliational groups demonstrated above derived from any other: they all represent separate lines of derivation. No more than one or two examples of any combination of HBH_5(As)$WsChLwHu_2$(E)LdTW, LB_3(E)PH_6, and R(As)A(M)Pl occur in the entire text. Nor can the variations among **χ** and the other affiliational groups, or between the English and the Latin text, be characterized simply as 'expansions', as will be seen in detail below.

Thomas Fishlake's Latin Version of *Scale* II

Thomas Fishlake's Latin version provides a separate line of evidence concerning the text of *Scale* II.[106] The translation is very early:

[105] It should be kept in mind that only the core readings of each group have been tabulated; readings in which even one manuscript is lacking (except for loss of text), or one manuscript outside the group is added, and readings in which the group is divided between two variants (no matter how close in wording) have not been counted.

[106] See Hussey, 'Latin and English'. Hussey produced a critical text of Fishlake's Latin *Scale* II based on Y, together with a critical apparatus of the readings of all other surviving manuscripts, with the exception of the more recently discovered 16th-c. Italian manuscripts. It was originally planned that this text would be published as part of the present

Fishlake probably knew Hilton in Cambridge and Ely, and because York Minster MS xvi.K.5 of Fishlake's version was written for his Cambridge Carmelite confrère John Pole and dates from *c.*1400, the English manuscript upon which it was based would have pre-dated virtually all that now survive. The translation is very close to the English text upon which it is based, for the most part 'worde for worde, and actif for actif, and passif for passif, arewe right as thei stondeth, without chaunging of the ordre of wordes', as John Trevisa has it.[107]

A complete collation of the Latin and English texts discovers approximately 1,700 points at which they diverge.[108] Of these, some 615 are isolative variants. For the most part, these reflect normal textual variation: thirty-eight, for example, represent doublets (often explanatory) in the Latin text, like 'cooperante et laborante' for 'werkynge', or 'pena et penitencia' for 'pyne'. Omissions of words and phrases, like that of 'þogh it be contrarie to þe biddyng of God' (15/25), account for fifty-three variants. More significant is a tendency to Christocentric devotion characteristic of the Latin version of the text. This includes 124 cases of substitution or expansion of phrases like 'Jesus Christus' or 'Dominus noster Jesus Christus' for 'God' or 'Jesus' in the English text; these overlap with thirty-five Christocentric devotional expansions of the text, such as 'visionem Jesu Christi, ad considerandum intime humilitatem humanitatis sue et ad gustandum modicum de bonitate deitatis sue', for the English text's 'syght of sothfastnesse, how Jesu is alle and þat he doth al' (37/33–4). It is probably in the light of this emphasis on Christocentric devotion that we are to understand Fishlake's omission of several passages in Chapter 30 dealing with the limitations of imaginative meditation, such as:

For wyte þou wel, fele a soule neuer so mikel feruour, so mikel þat him þenkeþ þe body may not bere it, or þogh he melte al into wepynge, as longe

edition. The editor hopes to be able to publish this text together with A. J. Bliss's critical text of Fishlake's Latin *Scale* I in a single volume in the near future.

[107] Trevisa, 'Epistle to Thomas, Lord Berkeley, on the Translation of Higden's Polychronicon', cited from *The Idea of the Vernacular: An Anthology of Middle English Literary Theory, 1280–1520*, ed. Jocelyn Wogan-Browne, Nicholas Watson, Andrew Taylor, and Ruth Evans (University Park, Pa., 1999), 134–35. For the theory of translation underlying this issue, see Roger Ellis, 'The Choices of the Translator in the Late Middle English Period', in *MMTE* ii, 18–46.

[108] The present discussion offers revisions and corrections to John P. H. Clark, 'English and Latin'.

as his þynkynge and his beholdynge of God is al in ymagynacyon and not in vnderstondynge, he come not ȝit to perfyte lufe ne to contemplacyon. (30/53–7)

The Latin version also omits references to Hilton's key concept of the 'mirkness' in which the soul toils towards the gift of contemplation, substituting more devotional terms, and weakens his statements on the limitations of imaginative devotion. As a result, Fishlake's version presents a more devotional, Christocentric spirituality than does Hilton's original text.[109]

A larger change made by Fishlake is the omission of a passage in Hilton's defence of the necessity of oral confession where he points out that one of the utilitites of confession is that some sinners do not feel compunction before they are actually confessing to a priest, and concedes, ironically, that if people were more morally self-aware, the Church might not have needed to require annual confession. Since, however, the majority of people are not morally self-aware, the Church does require confession (7/63–71). This passage is omitted from Fishlake's translation: it is possible that he did not see the fitness of the ironic argument.

One other change in the Latin version is that it ends with a 250-word summary of the text of *Scale* II written in the first person: 'Ecce declaraui tibi secundum scienciam meam simplicem . . .'.[110] According to this summary, the work is divided in four parts, of which the first is an essay on the theology of salvation addressed beginners, dealing with the reformation of the soul to the image of God in faith alone and the eradication of sin through baptism and confession. The second, addressed to the proficient, deals with the progress, the exercises, and the temptations of those who wish to advance to reformation in feeling. The third, addressed to those who are reformed in feeling, deals with the effects of that reformation in the soul. The fourth treats of a yet higher level of spiritual experiences and revelations. A note following this summary in

[109] In current critical discourse, Christocentric, imaginative devotion is usually treated as characteristically vernacular; I hope to explore Fishlake's inversion of this 'vernacularizing' tendency at some later point when I can deal with his treatment of *Scale* I as well.

[110] See below, 46/86; Hussey, 'Latin and English', 458–9. Only two of sixteen surviving copies of the Latin *Scale* II (Oxford, St John's College MS 77, a three-chapter extract, and Uppsala, Universitetsbibliotek MS C.618 (an eight-chapter extract from *Scale* II accompanying a complete copy of *Scale* I) lack the summary. Note that there is no comparable summary of the Latin text of *Scale* I.

several manuscripts alots the chapters of the Latin *Scale* to the four parts just described.[111] Hussey noted that Joy Russell-Smith thought that the first-person address of the summary demonstrates that it is authorial.[112] He added that it resembles Hilton's English writing stylistically, but that 'neither point is conclusive'. Certainly the Latin voice of the summary is consonant with that of Fishlake's translation of Hilton's English text; further, it refers to 'reformation in faith and in feeling' using the word 'sensacio', Fishlake's characteristic translation of Hilton's 'feeling'.[113] The summary reads like an *envoie* to *Scale* II, and its address, first person singular to second person singular, appears to imply that Hilton is directing this work to Fishlake.[114] On the other hand, the opening of *Scale* II addresses it nominally to the recipient of *Scale* I, a woman recently enclosed as an anchoress; and there is no evidence of the summary in the English textual tradition. The final chapter of *Scale* I briefly summarizes that work, and the summary is translated by Fishlake; but it is by no means parallel to the latin summary of *Scale* II.

Collation of approximately 600 readings where it is possible to identify variants in the English text that agree with the Latin demonstrates no consistent pattern of agreement of the Latin version with any of the textual groups of English manuscripts identified above. The pattern for individual manuscripts is as follows: the text in Hu_2 agrees with the Latin version in ninety readings; W in 121 readings; H in 125 readings;[115] H_5 in 125 readings; B in 146 readings; T in 146 readings; Ld in 158 readings; Lw in 192 readings; As in 216 readings; E in 291 readings; B_3 in 333 readings; A in 336 readings; M in 343 readings; L in 349 readings; P in 350 readings; Pl in 355 readings; H_6 in 354 readings; Sr in 364 readings; Cc in 378 readings; and H_7 in 390 readings. The partial

[111] According to the chapter division of the Latin text, Chapters 1–16, 17–31, 32–41, and 42–7; i.e. Chapters 1–16, 17–30, 31–9, and 40–6 of the English. Latin *Scale* MSS Y, B_2, Bn, H_2, Ma, Up and Es have this note.

[112] Russell-Smith, 'Walter Hilton and a Tract in Defence', 207.

[113] As I have argued elsewhere, Fishlake is translating what Hilton probably intended as 'affectus' with a term more appropriate to the spirituality of Richard Rolle or of Nicholas Love. See Sargent, 'Walter Hilton's Affective Turn', paper presented at the conference '"This Tretice, by me compiled": Late Medieval Devotional Compilations in England', Université de Lausanne, Switzerland, 31 Mar.–2 Apr. 2016, to be published in the proceedings.

[114] It is also possible that Fishlake has become so familiar with Hilton's 'voice' that he feels comfortable ventriloquizing.

[115] Counting the readings of thirty corrections in H.

text in Ch agrees with the Latin in fifty-six readings; that in Ws in eighty-three readings; and that in R in 309 readings.[116]

Collation of 706 readings where it is possible to identify variants in the English text that disagree with the Latin text equally demonstrates no consistent pattern of agreement with the various textual groups. The pattern for individual manuscripts is as follows: the text in H_5 disagrees with the Latin in 408 readings; that in H 393 times;[117] that in Lw 392 times; that in T 381 times; that in Ld 372 times; that in B 365 times; that in W 359 times; that in As 319 times that in E 240 times; that in Hu_2 229 times; that in P 222 times; that in L 209 times; that in B_3 207 times; that in H_6 194 times; that in M 192 times; that in A 179 times; that in Cc 164 times; that in Sr 160 times; that in H_7 155 times; and that Pl 153 times. The partial text in Ws agrees with the Latin version 284 times; the partial text in R 153 times; and the partial text in Ch 100 times.[118]

As noted above, the Latin version of *Scale* II does not agree with any identifiable group of manuscripts in any consistent way, but agrees sporadically with single manuscripts and small, shifting groups of manuscripts. The three complete English manuscripts that agree with the text of the Latin version most often are thus Sr, Cc, and H_7; the four that disagree with the Latin least often are Cc, Sr, H_7, and Pl. The three manuscripts that agree with the Latin version least often are W, H, and H_5; the three manuscripts that disagree with the Latin most often are H, W, and T. The Latin version thus agrees least often with manuscripts of Hussey's **χ** group, and most often with manuscripts of the notional **υ** (i.e. non-**χ**) group; but the Latin text cannot be derived from its varying agreements with various manuscripts whose only textual unity lies in that they do not belong to the affiliational group **χ**.

Chapter Titles

The titles of the chapters of *Scale* II, both within the text itself and in tables of chapters preceding or following the text, present a

[116] If these three copies were complete and their textual complexion had remained the same, Ch would agree with the Latin version in 149 readings, Ws in 124 readings, and R in 353 readings.

[117] Including thirty-one disagreements between the original text of H and the Latin version, and eleven disagreements between the corrections in H and the Latin.

[118] If these three copies were complete and their textual complexion had remained the same, Ws would disagree with the Latin version 426 times, Ch 267 times, and R 245 times.

different set of patterns of variation that reinforces, at least in part, the textual groups $HBH_5WsChLwHu_2LdTW$ (Hussey's χ), LB_3PH_6, and RAPl. Seven χ manuscripts, $HBH_5WsChLwHu_2$, and Cc, originally had no chapter titles in the text. H was later supplied with a set of idiosyncratic titles for Chapters 1–8, 10, 20–2, 24, 30–1, 34, 42–6, in several different hands. Most of these appear in each case to reflect a cursory reading of the first sentence of the text of the chapter. In one case, Chapter 21, a corrector has inserted the title that occurs in L, B_3, As, and P. It should also be noted that B numbers the second chapter as 'Capitulum primum' and the twenty-fourth chapter as 'Capitulum idem', and thus presents itself as having only forty-four chapters.

For the first twelve chapters of *Scale* II, all but H of the witnesses that have chapter titles in the text, $H_7RLB_3AsSrAEPH_6MLdPlTW$, present only minor variants on the same titles. At Chapter 12/47, however, SrCcM have a chapter break unmarked in other manuscripts: Sr has the title here that occurs in other manuscripts at Chapter 13; M has a unique chapter title; and Cc has no chapter title. CcM number Chapter 13 as Chapter 14, which adds one to the total count of chapters in these two manuscripts. Sr has no chapter break where the others have Chapter 13 (CcM 14), so that its total remains forty-six chapters.[119]

At Chapter 21, which begins a new section of the text of *Scale* II (with a chapter title *incipit* 'An Entre'—'Introductio' in the Latin version—and a text *incipit* that echoes the opening of *Scale* II), the chapter titles diverge. H_7 has an abbreviated form of the title of Chapter 21 that occurs in $RSrAEPH_6MLdPlTW$; the chapter title in the Latin version corresponds to this latter form, with the exception of the final words.[120] LB_3AsP, however, as well as a correcting hand in H, have a different title.

The title of Chapter 22 in the Latin version corresponds to that in the text of RSrALdPlTW. In place of this, $H_7LB_3EPH_6$ have the title of the following chapter in RSrALdPlTW. As and H^c have a unique title for Chapter 22 that is quite similar to the title of Chapter 21 in the idiosyncratic Table of Chapters in B. From this point onwards, the chapter titles in As are the same as those of the Table of Chapters in B.

119 The result is thus that Sr has moved the break for Chapter 13 forward by thirty-five lines, while CcM have inserted an extra chapter break.

120 Interestingly, Ld omits this phrase.

The title of Chapter 23 in H_7 is the same as the title of Chapter 24 in RSrALdPlTW, and corresponds to the title of the same chapter in the Latin version. E has a version of the same title, with an additional phrase at the end. The title of Chapter 24 in $H_7LB_3PH_6M$ is the same as the title of Chapter 25 in R and Pl, and it occurs as the title of a chapter break occurring at 24/57 in the Latin version. This title also occurs in M as the title at 24/62, an otherwise unique chapter break in Cc and M; Cc has no chapter titles, but both manuscripts add one to their count of chapters at this point. An annotator has added a unique title for Chapter 24 in H, which has been almost completely erased. $H_7LB_3SrAEPH_6MLdTW$ have the same title for Chapter 25; RPl, as noted above, have the title of Chapter 24 in $H_7B_3PH_6M$ at this point. The titles of the chapters in Pl continue to be behind by one from here through Chapter 33; at Chapter 34, it rejoins the consensus.

As noted above, LB_3P have a variant title for Chapter 21, although it touches on the same theme as that of the other manuscripts: the pilgrimage to Jerusalem. This title also occurs in As, and has been added in by a corrector in H. $H_7LB_3EPH_6$ have a different title for Chapter 22 than RALdPlTW, although it also touches on the same theme: hindrances placed by man's enemies, the world, the flesh, and the devil, on the way to the heavenly Jerusalem. This occurs as the title of Chapter 23 in RASrLdPlTW. The wording of the title of Chapter 21 in $RSrAEPH_6MLdPlTW$, and of Chapter 22 in RSrALdPTW, is closer to the Latin version than that of LB_3AsH^cP in the former case, and of $H_7LB_3EPH_6$ in the latter. LB_3AsEP have a title for Chapter 23 that is similar to the unique title of Chapter 22 in As and H^c. LB_3PH_6 agree with H_7 and M in the title of Chapter 24, and with $H_7SrAEMLdTW$ in Chapter 25; with the exception of the unique titles of As and the one-chapter lag in the titles of Pl, there are no more than minor variations in the titles of chapters in the text from that point onward.

Thirteen manuscripts have tables of chapters preceding the text of *Scale* II: $BLB_3SrWsLwEPCcMLdTW$. H has tables for both books of the *Scale*, in a hand that occurs nowhere else in the manuscript, appended at the end. For the first twenty chapters and the last twenty-two, no manuscripts with Tables of Chapters, with the exception of B, and SrM, show more than minor variation. At the mid-point, however, a set of variations similar to those that occur in the chapter titles in the text also occurs in the Tables of Chapters:

LB_3 have the same variant titles for Chapters 21 through 24 in the table as LB_3AsH^cP did in the text. The title of Chapter 22 in the text of $H_7LB_3EPH_6$ is thus also the title of Chapter 22 in LB_3E in the Table of Chapters and of Chapter 23 in the text of RASrLdPlTW; and the title of Chapter 23 in the text in H_7 is thus also the title of Chapter 24 in RSrAELdPlTW, of the extra chapter division at 24/62 in M, and of Chapter 24 in the Table of Chapters in HSrWsLwELdTW. In E, the title of Chapter 21 in the Table of Chapters agrees with HWsLdLwTW and Sr, but adds an extra phrase that echoes the final words of the title in LB_3; and the title of Chapter 24 in the Table of Chapters in E adds an extra phrase that echoes the final phrase of the title in LB_3Cc.

The titles of the chapters in the table in B are unique, corresponding only to those in the text of As, from Chapter 21 to the end. The first chapter title in the table in B, although numbered 'Ca^{m}. 1^{m}', appears to refer to the text of Chapter 2. This would correspond with the numbering of the chapters in this manuscript, which begins with the second chapter of the text. The Tables of Chapters in Cc and M also have the same additional chapter titles that occur in M at the extra chapter breaks at 13/47 and 24/62 in Cc and M.

The Latin version has the same title for Chapter 21 as $RSrAEH_6MLdPlTW$; a much-abbreviated version of this title has been added into H_7 in a different hand than that of the text. As noted above, LB_3AsP have a variant title, which has also been added into H by a different hand. The title of Chapter 22 in the Latin version is the same as that in RALdPlTW; H_7 agrees here with the variant title of LB_3EPH_6 (this variant title being the same as that of Chapter 23 in RASrLdPlTW). The title of Chapter 23 in the Latin version is the same as that in RASrLdPlTW; LB_3EPH_6 have a variant title. The variant title of Chapter 23 in H_7 is the same as the title of Chapter 24 in the Latin version and E, as well as of an extra chapter division at Chapter 24/62 in M. The title of Chapter 24 in the Latin version is the same as that in E. At Chapter 24/57, the Latin version has an extra chapter division with the title halfway through this chapter, which is the same as the title of Chapter 24 in $H_7LB_3PH_6M$; it also occurs as the title of Chapter 25 in RPl. The Latin version returns to consensus with the chapter titles of $H_7RLB_3SrAEPH_6MLdTW$ for the remainder of the text; it thus has forty-seven chapters, rather than the forty-six of the English text.

The fact that two of the three earliest manuscripts of *Scale* II, manuscripts that do not appear from the collation of the text to be closely related to each other, and the Latin version of the *Scale* as well, all have chapter titles suggests that in at least some form, these titles are original. The exception to this is that the Carthusian/ Brigittine group of manuscripts does not appear originally to have had either chapter titles in the text or a Table of Chapters. A set of idiosyncratic titles has been added in the text of H; a different set of idiosyncratic titles has been added in a Table of Chapters in B (half of which are reflected in the titles in the latter portion of the text of As, which varies with the Carthusian/Brigittine group); and a standard set of titles is given in a Table of Chapters added at the end of H. Five manuscripts of the Carthusian/Brigittine group, H_5WsChLwHu$_2$, lack chapter titles entirely. H_7 and the 'Theocentric' manuscript group, RAsAPm, as well as H_6, have titles in the text, but not tables of chapters. The disruption of chapter titles in H_7 from Chapter 21 through Chapter 26, the shifting and variation in titles within the English manuscript tradition and between the English and Latin versions, suggests a process of revision, possibly authorial. The variant placement of chapter divisions in Sr, Cc and M suggests possible influence from the Latin version, or from the English manuscripts on which it was based.

Correction and Conflation

Three manuscripts of the English text of *Scale* II, one manuscript of the Latin text, and one copy of the 1494 Wynkyn de Worde *editio princeps* have been extensively corrected in hands other than those of the original scribes, by comparison with other copies.[121] These corrections are also a source of textual evidence.

Leaving aside corrections of spelling (particularly the insertion of medial 'h' in forms of the word 'flesch-' dozens of times throughout the text), and simple cases of deletion (which were possibly made by the scribe in the initial process of copying of the text), there are 256 corrections made to the text of *Scale* II in H that provide textual-critical evidence. Although it is not always clear (particularly in the case of corrections made over erasure) what the original reading was, it is possible in 191 cases to identify at least the most probable form

[121] Lw is also extensively corrected by the scribe himself, apparently repairing his own dittographies and omissions during the process of writing; these corrections do not provide textual-critical evidence, and will not be discussed here.

of the corrected original text and to note its agreement with other manuscripts.

Twenty-six of the original readings in H that have been corrected are isolative variants. In sixty-five cases, the original text of H agrees, or probably agreed,[122] with a variant recorded in other manuscripts, ranging from five manuscripts that agree with the original text of H in a single reading each to H_5, which agrees nine times. Ten pairs of manuscripts occur in agreement with the original text of H, of which H_5Ws agree most often, twenty times. Sixteen groups of three manuscripts occur in agreement with the original text of H, of which H_5AsWs occur most often, fourteen times.

The manuscripts that agree most often with the text of H before correction are H_5 and Ws: both of these agree together with H in twenty otherwise unique variants; and H_5 alone agrees with H in another nine variants, primarily where the text of Ws is lacking. Counting examples where other manuscripts of the group BH_5WsChLwHu_2LdTW are also present, both H_5 and Ws occur in a total of eighty-eight variants in agreement with the original text in H, and H_5 alone in another thirty-six. Readings agreeing with the corrections made to H can be identified 125 times. Four single manuscripts agree with corrections in H. Three of them, E, M, and T, agree once each; another, Lw, agrees four times. Four pairs of manuscripts agree with corrections in H, BLw, LwCc, LwM, and LwW—the latter six times. Ten groups of three manuscripts agree with corrections in H, of which LwTW agrees twice and LwEW three times. There is also one group of fifteen manuscripts, H_7RLB_3AsSrLwAEPH_6CcMPlW, that agrees with corrections in H ten times.

The manuscripts that agree most often with corrections in H are LwW: these two manuscripts agree together with corrections in H in six isolative variants; and Lw alone agrees with H in another four variants. Lw and Ws occur together in agreement with corrections in H in a total of eighty-three variants, Lw in eleven and H_5 in another three. It should also be noted that among the corrections that agree

[122] Agreement is deemed probable in cases of deletion where the original reading cannot be recovered but appears (based on, e.g., the number of letters that seem to have been deleted), to have been identical to a variant recorded in other manuscripts. Usually, this occurs in cases where only one other variant is recorded, or where only one surviving variant would fit the space occupied by the deletion; but the variant must also appear to be a reasonable possibility in its own right.

with the largest numbers of manuscripts, the original text usually agrees with $BH_5ChLwHu_2LdTW$ and As, or with BH_5ChHu_2LdT and As, while the correction usually agrees with LwW—both the corrected readings and the corrections being thus representative of the affiliational group $HB(As)H_5ChLwHu_2LdTW$.

Leaving aside corrections of spelling and simple cases of deletion where it is impossible to tell the hand or source of the deletion, we may note that there are 290 corrections made to the text of *Scale* II in L that provide textual-critical evidence. As noted above in the treatment of corrections made to the text of *Scale* II in H, it is not always clear, particularly in the case of corrections made over erasure, what the original reading of the text was; but in 221 cases, it is possible to identify at least the most probable form of the corrected original text and to note its agreement with other manuscripts. 168 of the original readings in L that have been corrected are isolative variants. In forty-five cases, the original text of L agrees, or probably agreed, with a variant recorded in other manuscripts, ranging from eighteen cases in which the original text of L agreed with a variant recorded in one other manuscript to thirteen readings where L agrees, or probably originally agreed, with a variant recorded in B_3. Four of the corrections to L result in isolative variants. Corrections to L can be identified in agreement with other manuscripts ninety-eight times. Those that occur most commonly are: nine corrections in L that agree with the reading of P alone; twenty-six corrections that agree with the readings of B_3P; seven with the readings of B_3EP; and four with B_3EPH_6. Corrections in L agree with H_6 twenty times; with E forty-two times; with B_3 sixty-nine times; and with P ninety-one times.

James Grenehalgh of Sheen Charterhouse is known to have compared three surviving copies of the *Scale*: MSS T of the English text, H_8 of Fishlake's Latin version, and the Rosenbach copy of the Wynkyn de Worde print, W. Grenehalgh's nine hundred textual notes in these three copies demonstrate his comparison of each of them with the other two, as well as with one or two other manuscripts.[123] Grenehalgh made approximately 300 textual-critical annotations to W and T; 203 to W, which seems to have been his

[123] The count of Grenehalgh's annotations to *Scale* II here differs from that in Sargent, *James Grenehalgh*, 382–95, 434–72 because only readings illustrative of the English text are cited here.

working copy; fifty-one to T, and forty-four corrections to the same lemma in both copies. Forty annotations in W correct isolative variants in its text of *Scale* II. Of the annotations for which manuscripts or groups of manuscripts agreeing with the underlying text of W can be identified, 106 agree with its close congener Lw. In thirty-five readings LwW are in unique agreement. The other manuscripts agreeing with the uncorrected text of W are all from the group $HBH_5AsWsChLwHu_2LdTW$. T agrees with the uncorrected text of W most often, forty-seven times. H agrees forty-four times, H_5 forty-two, Ld thirty-five, As thirty-two, B thirty, Ws twenty-five, the fragmentary text in Hu_2 twenty-four times, and E twenty-three times. Eighteen of Grenehalgh's annotations in T correct isolative variants.

The majority of Grenehalgh's annotations to the text of *Scale* II in T and W correct readings common to small groups of manuscripts to bring them into agreement with all, or at least the majority, of other manuscripts. There is a slight predominance of readings of manuscripts of the group $HBH_5WsChLwHu_2LdTW$ among the readings corrected, and a slight predominance of readings of manuscripts outside of that group among the corrections, but the primary pattern observable is that although all of Grenehalgh's corrections in T can be derived from W (including corrections presumably made by him to W previously), 127 of the corrections made to W do not derive from T. The manuscript with which the Grenehalgh annotations in W that do not derive from T most often agree is E (84 times), followed closely by Ld (79 times), Hu_2 and H_6 (74 times each), Cc (72 times), and H_7 (70 times). There are six minor readings in which a Grenehalgh annotation agrees with E alone. It is certain that Grenehalgh corrected W against some other manuscript before T, and that some of his annotations in T carry these corrections over from W; but it is not apparent what the affiliation of that manuscript was. It should also be noted that although the readings offered by Grenehalgh's annotations usually agree with readings of English manuscripts, he also compared the text in W with the Latin manuscript H_8, in which he has made numerous annotations that either agree with the text of W, or offer his own alternative Latin translations of the English text.[124]

[124] See Sargent, *James Grenehalgh*, 331–40.

Extracts

Five manuscripts, Wc, Td, Td_2, Ad, and Ad_2, contain extracts from *Scale* II. The first of these is MS Wc, comprising the three-part 'Westminster Compilation' of approximately 21,000 words on the contemplative life. Each section of the compilation is made up of extracts from a different source text: the first, of approximately 6,600 words, comprises thirty-nine extracts from Hilton's commentaries on the psalms 'Qui habitat' and 'Bonum est'; the second, of some 7,000 words, derives from *The Scale of Perfection*; the third, of approximately 7,600 words, comprises forty-nine extracts from the long text of the *Revelations* of Julian of Norwich. Most Julian-centred scholarship has tended to treat the three parts of the compilation as separate works, although Marleen Cré has argued that it should be considered rather as a single composition.[125] Structurally and stylistically, the 'Qui habitat' and 'Bonum est' sections and the Julian section are similar, each following the order of its original, and altering only by excision. The *Scale* section, on the other hand, is a much more sophisticated production, weaving back and forth among the nineteen chapters of the latter half of *Scale* II and five chapters from two points in the middle of *Scale* I to stitch together forty-four extracts into a piece that a sixteenth-century hand entitled, in the top margin of its first page (f. 35^v), as 'Of the Knowledge of Oureselves and of God'.[126] There are also a large number of minor variations of phrasing in the adaptation of the text of the *Scale* to the Westminster Compilation. Isolative variants have not been recorded here, but there are also some 190 variants that agree with readings of various manuscripts and manuscript groups observed above. The evidence argues that the section of the 'Westminster Compilation' drawn from *Scale* II was based on a manuscript of the HBH_5AsWsChL-wHu_2ELdTW textual group.[127]

The extracts from *Scale* II in Td comprise a straightforward collection of passages from Chapters 21–5 and 41–6, added in a two-gathering booklet at the end of a manuscript of *The Cloud of Unknowing* and *The Book of Privy Counselling* copied *c.*1500.[128]

[125] See Cré, 'London: Westminster Cathedral Treasury, MS 4'.

[126] For the order of the extracts, see above, pp. lxii–iii.

[127] Wc shows no agreement with Ch because it is drawn from the latter half of the text of *Scale* II, which is lacking in Ch.

[128] For the order of the extracts, see above, p. lxx.

The first of the extracts, of some 2,000 words from Chapters 24 and 25, has 110 isolative variants, and fifty-one variants that agree with other manuscripts. Seventeen of these agreements are with the idiosyncratic texts of M and Cc; the other variants in the first extract show no persistent pattern of agreement with other manuscripts of the text of *Scale* II. A few readings in the second through the fifth extracts suggest affiliation with the manuscript group HBH_5AsWsLwELdTW. On the other hand, several readings in the sixth extract suggest some relationship with Fishlake's Latin version. The most prominent of these occurs at 21/61, where Td adds

þat is to sey, mekenes seys þus: I am vnmyȝty, vnwytty and vnwylly, full of syn and wrecchidnes, and fully I vntryste and despeir of my self. Luf seis: I trist fully in Jhesu Crist. Sett all þi þoȝt and þi desyre in beholding of hym as he hang on þe cros for þe. For he is myȝty and witty and wylly to helpe þe,

which seems to reflect an addition in the Latin text:

Intellectus horum verborum est iste: Inpotens sum et insipiens et involuntarius, plenus peccato et miseria, et ideo totaliter diffido et despero de meipso. Set amor dicit: Confide in Jesu Christo, et ideo statuere volo totam cogitacionem meam et desiderium meum in consideracione ipsius.

It seems possible that this extract derives from an English manuscript that has been corrected to reflect the Latin. Because the first extract in Td, drawn from *Scale* II, Chapters 24 and 25, seems to be affiliated with CcM (and more closely with M), the second through the fifth extracts, drawn from *Scale* II, Chapters 41 to 46, possibly with HBH_5AsWsLwELdTW, and the sixth extract, drawn from *Scale* II, Chapters 21 to 23, with a copy corrected against the Latin text, it seems probable that these extracts were drawn from different copies of *Scale* II.

The extracts from *Scale* II in Td_2 comprise a set of quotations and paraphrases on ff. 108^r–112^v, drawn perhaps from a printed copy, as is much of the other material in this manuscript.[129] The rendering of the text of the *Scale* in these extracts is not exact enough to provide useful evidence of the textual affiliation of the compiler's source.

The related compilations 'Of Actyfe lyfe and contemplatyfe declaracion' and 'Via ad contemplacionem', in Ad and Ad_2 respec-

[129] For the order of the extracts, see above, p. lxii.

tively, comprise extracts from *The Cloud of Unknowing* and two other works of the *Cloud*-corpus, the *Benjamin Minor* and the *Pistle of Discrecioun of Stirings*, Hugh of Balma's *Mystica theologia*, Rolle's *Form of Living*, and both books of *The Scale of Perfection*.[130] The 300-word section of the tract in Ad_2 comprising material from *Scale* II consists of ten discrete extracts taken in order from Chapters 21 to 23. In the version in Ad (the longer compilation overall) one of these ten extracts is altered and four are lacking.[131] There are two readings in agreement with Td, two with H_6, one with BW, one with HBH_5Hu_2, one with $HBH_5ChLwHu_2CcLdTWTd$, and one with $HBH_5LB_3SrLwHu_2EPCcMLdTW$; but although these suggest affiliation with $HBH_5WsChLwHu_2LdTW$ plus Td, there is not enough evidence to demonstrate a genetic connection.

Patterns of Convergence and Patterns of Affiliation

Certain categories of the textual agreements listed above point to convergent variation, rather than to genetic relationship. The first of these, already mentioned above,[132] is the identification of Hilton's Latin quotations from Scripture in $BLHu_2EPLdTW$. The primary evidence that these agreements are the result of convergent variation is that this particular group of manuscripts agrees in little other than the identification of Hilton's sciptural sources. Nor are the identifications uniformly handled textually: in B, they occur as interlinear or marginal notes in another hand immediately preceding the quotation; in LHu_2PTW, they are provided in the margin; in E, they are in the text, preceded by a paragraph sign as part of the rubricated citation; in Ld they also precede the quotations. Finally, it should be noted that the identifications do not always agree. In sum, the identifications of scriptural texts in the surviving manuscripts of *Scale* II most probably represent coincident, independent work by various scribes.

Similarly, there are a number of dialectal or obsolescent expressions found in the earliest manuscripts (particularly H_7, H, and R) that are variously replaced with more current standard expressions in later manuscripts,[133] such as forms using 'ay' (including 'aylastande')

[130] Jolliffe, 'Two Middle English Tracts', 101–4.

[131] For the order of the extracts in these two tracts, see above, pp. lxvii–lxviii.

[132] See above, pp. c–ci.

[133] It should be noted that the Table of Chapters in H is to be numbered among the later manuscript witnesses on this point.

vs forms using 'euere' or 'alwey'; forms of 'call-' vs forms of 'clep-'; 'forþi' vs 'þerfore'; 'il' vs 'euel' or 'wykede'; forms of 'ilk' and 'ilk a' vs 'each' and 'euery'; forms of 'irk' vs forms of 'wery'; forms of 'ken-' vs forms of 'tech-', and forms of 'ler-' vs forms of 'lern-'; forms using 'mirk-' vs forms of 'derk-'; forms of 'sere' vs forms of 'diuerse'; 'spered' vs 'closed', 'shut', or 'stopped'; 'as tyte' vs 'anon' or 'as sone'; forms of 'trow-', including 'troth' vs forms of 'beleue-', 'leue-', 'belefe', or 'feyth'; and 'weyke' vs 'feble' or 'liþi'. These variations occasionally do coincide with other affiliational groupings that appear to be genetic, but not with any regularity.

Affiliation among surviving manuscript witnesses of a text can be demonstrated through four kinds of evidence, particularly when they concur. The first of these is a persistent pattern of agreement in unique readings representing known types of scribal variation throughout the text. This we have seen above in the textual groups HBH_5(As)WsChLwHu_2(E)LdTW and LB_3(E)PLH_6, and, more weakly, in R(As)A(M)Pl. A second kind of evidence is codicological, and consists in details such as similarity in contents, *ordinatio*, mise-en-page, and decoration. This is true of all three of the above-listed groups, but again, more weakly in R(As)A(M)Pl. A third kind of evidence is found in production and ownership of a textually affiliated group of manuscripts among members of a distinct social group, or in a particular location or region. This is true of HBH_5(As)WsChLwHu_2(E)LdTW and LB_3(E)PLH_6, and perhaps in R(As)A(M)Pl. A fourth kind of evidence lies in congruence in outlook or expression in the variations present in an affiliated group of manuscripts. This is true of R(As)A(M)Pl in particular.

The largest affiliational group of surviving manuscripts of *Scale* II comprises ten manuscripts, HBH_5WsChLwHu_2LdTW, presenting 160 unique readings throughout the entire text and As in another 100 readings in the latter half of the text.[134] This group is identical with Hussey's χ group. Of these manuscripts, five are connected with monasteries of the Carthusian order:[135] Although its scribal dialectal

[134] Note that this figure takes account of the missing portions of Ws, Ch, and Hu_2. It should also be noted that this is the count only of the core readings of χ—those readings in which all members of the group, and no others, agree. The text of As will be further discussed below, pp. cxiv–cxv, and that of E below, pp. cvii, cxii.

[135] For details, see the descriptions of the manuscripts and early prints above, and Sargent, 'Affective Reading and Walter Hilton's *Scale of Perfection* at Syon', paper presented at the conference 'Reading and Writing in City, Court, and Cloister', Fordham University, 7 Mar. 2015; to be published in the proceedings. The first full description of

profile places it in Ely or extreme southern Lincolnshire, H belonged to London Charterhouse by the mid-fifteenth century; Ch was probably annotated by James Grenehalgh (†1529, originally of Sheen Charterhouse) during his time in the house at Coventry *c.*1508; Hu_2 was written by John Clerk, a monk of Hinton Charterhouse (†1472); and T was written by Robert Benet, proctor of Sheen Charterhouse (†1518) and annotated there by Grenehalgh in 1500. Another three of this group of manuscripts have connections to Syon Abbey: H_5 was bequeathed to Syon by Margery Pensax, recluse at Bishopsgate; As, which shares the readings of this group of manuscripts in the latter half of the text, belonged to Rose Pachet, a nun of the Syon community from before the Henrician dissolution through the Marian restoration; and Ld has among its binding materials the fragments of a deed to Syon from the time of King Edward IV. The Rosenbach copy of W belonged to James Grenehalgh and was dedicated by him to Joanna Sewell of Syon; and the Cambridge University Library copy was in the gift of Katherine Palmer of Syon. One further manuscript, Br, was copied in 1608 by Abraham Ellis, a lay brother in the exiled Carthusian community of Sheen Anglorum, from an incunable print subsequent to No.[136]

The variants in which this group manifests itself do not seem to be driven by any theological issues or ideological concerns, but by a variety of conscious and unconscious scribal *usus*. These include substitution of synonyms, such as: 'confession' for Σ 'schrifte' (7/56–8);[137] 'wiþ' for Σ 'ageyns' (11/43); 'liknes' for Σ 'ymage' (13/27); 'hee most' for Σ 'him behoueth' (17/20); 'sobirte' for Σ 'sobernesse' (36/64); 'to' for Σ 'anemptis' (38/11); 'penaunce' for Σ 'peyn' (38/45); 'werdly' for Σ 'erthly' (39/94); and 'list' for Σ 'wil' (42/143).

the textual relations of the English Carthusian houses, and of those (particularly Sheen Charterhouse) with Syon Abbey, is A. I. Doyle, 'A Survey of the Origins and Circulation of Theological Writings in English in the Fourteenth, Fifteenth and Early Sixteenth Centuries, with Special Consideration of the Part of the Clergy therein' (Ph.D. thesis, University of Cambridge, 1953); see also Sargent, 'The Transmission'. Vincent Gillespie has added some refinements to this, particularly with regard to transmission of texts to lay readers by way of Syon Abbey, rather than by the Carthusians: see 'The Haunted Text: Ghostly Reflections in *A Mirror to Devout People*', in Jill Mann and Maura Nolan (eds.), *The Text in the Community: Essays on Medieval Works, Manuscripts, Authors, and Readers* (South Bend, Ind., 2006), 129–72.

136 Because it was copied directly from a print, Br has been excluded from the collation and tabulations above as *descriptus*.

137 In the following discussion, as in the critical apparatus, the sigil Σ is used to designate all other manuscripts but those under discussion.

Other verbal substitutions include a number cases of probable mistranscription of orthographic similars, such as 'lifen' for Σ 'lesten' (10/17), but also 'and' for Σ 'or' (10/18); 'fallyþ' for Σ 'fareþ' (27/157); 'lifynge' for Σ 'felynge' (28/66); 'gode' for 'of God' (35/73); 'open to' for Σ 'opon' (37/98); 'holdiþ' for Σ 'beholdeþ' (37/101); and 'of' for Σ 'on' (43/16); or theological equivalents: 'God' for Σ 'Jesu' (39/57, 42/93); 'Jesu' for Σ 'him' (36/34); and 'God' for Σ 'him' (42/93).

There are changes of number, such as: 'synnes' for Σ 'synne' (11/97); 'þei moste' for Σ 'hem behoueth' (15/14); 'mens soules' for Σ 'mans soule' (20/29); 'fantasies' for Σ 'fantasye' (22/52); 'þinge' for Σ 'þynges' (22/65); 'soule' for Σ 'soules' (34/98); 'stirynges' for Σ 'sterynge' (35/45); 'miȝt' for Σ 'myghtes' (36/77); 'affeccioun' for Σ 'affeccyons' (40/32); 'counseylle' for Σ 'counseyls' (43/15); and 'rownynge' for Σ 'rownynges (46/68).

Change of determiner, such as: 'þe' for Σ 'his' (27/72).

Reinforcement of negation, such as: 'coueite not no' for Σ 'coueyte no' (27/75).

Variant wording of comparable phrases, such as: 'his owne ymage and liknes', for Σ 'þe ymage and þe likenesse of him' (1/16); 'of lustly stirynges' for Σ 'steryng of lust' (8/45); 'his mercy' for Σ 'þe mercy of God' (10/32); 'generally or specially' for Σ 'of þese in general or in special' (11/104); 'by a man þat', for Σ 'if a man' (18/38); 'of þe yuel dede of þat oþer man' for Σ 'þurgh his euel dede' (38/80); 'Goddis lufe' for Σ 'þe loue of Jesu' (39/36); 'for to þinken on' for Σ 'fro thenkyng of' (39/104); and 'þe presence of him' for Σ 'his presence' (43/21).

There are also transpositions, such as: 'þorw Jesu / is made' (2/79); 'leue þeire own / and / take it' (3/43); 'better for vs', where Σ reads 'for vs mikel better' (4/56); 'not agaynstandand þat felyng if he wilfully assente not þerto, he may', where Σ reads 'he may nought ageynstondene al þat felinge if he wifully assent not þerto' (5/12–13); 'fro synne / to God' (10/42); 'or not / in þe tyme of temptacion' (11/78–9); 'steris and techeþ' (20/36–7); 'bodily and gostly / as mikel' (20/51); 'fasten or waken' (20/106–07); 'venym / to drynke' (23/17); 'werkynge of / most' (34/94); 'schewed owtward' (35/35); 'for þe tyme / in a soule' (35/78); 'mikel / . . . / gretly' (36/15); 'harde and a grete maistrie' for Σ 'maystrie and grete hardnes' (38/8–9); 'schewed and feled' (40/147); 'gostly and godly' (42/122); 'more and more / in þe' (42/129); and 'stable and hole' (44/36).

Addition of words or phrases, such as: 'no`i´þer' (14/32); 'hafe' (25/11); 'ony' (27/60); 'neuere' (39/96 *bis*); and 'and þerfore' (46/35).

Omissions, such as: 'only' (8/29, 33/74, 36/47, 36/75, 39/114, 40/100); 'it so be þat' (10/12), 'and þat he felyth no more of it' (11/88); 'byddende' (20/100); 'and þat þou dost' (22/57); 'ypocryses ne' (26/116); 'priuey' (33/43); 'schewyng of' (35/31); 'ay' (35/44, 41/89); 'gostly' (37/82); 'of God' (37/104); 'and passen' (39/10); 'kendly' (40/9); 'or depnes' (40/17); 'frely' (40/85); 'felably' (41/64); 'brennende' (41/65); 'oure Lord' (42/55); 'and seeth' (42/111); 'and seen' (42/115); and 'in a soule' (43/7); and textual abbreviations, such as: 'þat' for Σ 'onlynes of body' (40/120).

Within the Carthusian/Brigittine group, we may also note two demonstrably affiliated pairs of manuscripts: LwW and H_5Ws, as well as (probably) $ChHu_2$. As noted above, LwW agree in unique variants 397 times, and H_5Ws agree 341 times.[138] Ch and Hu_2 agree only thirty-one times, but they coincide for only one-fifth of the text, and it is possible that when complete, they agreed in as many as 150 unique variant readings. We should also note that BLd share forty-four unique readings; TW share forty-seven unique variant readings, almost all of which are in chapter titles; and LdT share ninety-one unique variant readings. These may also be taken as probable evidence of affiliation, either by genetic relationship or by conflation among χ manuscripts. Further, the majority of the English manuscripts that identify Hilton as a canon of Thurgarton—H, Ch, Lw, and E—belong to the Carthusian group.[139]

E also varies with the Carthusian group forty-seven times; as we shall see, E seems to represent a complete conflation of this group with the London group, LB_3PH_6.[140] E is also found in agreement with the Carthusian group and As seventy-five times, for a total of 122 readings: they thus represent a total of 406 readings. As noted above,[141] these are the 'core' readings, in which all surviving manuscripts of the group, and no others, agree. Hussey's recensionist calculation of all readings that could plausibly be attributed to the hyparchetype of the Carthusian group of manuscripts claims some 1,100 readings.[142] A particularly notable addition occurs in the

[138] See above, p. ciii.

[139] M does as well. The copy of *The Prickynge of Love* in Sr is attributed to Hilton, but not the *Scale*.

[140] See below, p. cxxviii.

[141] See above, n. 105.

[142] This is useful as a measure of the total degree of divergence between the χ manuscript group and Σ, and not just the 'core' readings.

description of the ministry of the angels in the final chapter of *Scale* II.[143] All other manuscripts read:

þei are ful tendre and ful besy abowte swilk a soule for to helpe it, þei are meystres for to kenne it, and oft þurgh here gostly presence and touchyng of here lyght dryuen out fantoms fro þe soule and mynystren to it al þat it nedeth.

This reading is supported by the Latin text:

Et valde soliciti sunt circa talem animam ad auxiliandum ei, ipsi sunt magistri ad informandum illam, et frequenter per presenciam suam spiritualem et per tactum luminis sui expellunt ab anima fantasias, et ministrant ei quicquid est necessarium.

Before the final phrase, 'and mynystren to it al þat it nedeth', however, the Carthusian group, inlcuding As and E, adds the following:

And þei illuminen þe soule graciously, þei confort þe soule by swete wordes sodenly sowned in a clene hert, and if ony disese falle gostly, þei seruen þe soule.

The addition is not inappropriate to Hilton in either doctrine or phrasing, but lacks the support of the rest of the manuscript tradition in both English and Latin.

Other notable textual variations characteristic of the Carthusian group include the omission of the final 161 words of the text, 'of þe whilk . . . gret bok' (46/74–86). HBH_5WsLdT all originally ended with the words 'þis is þe voyce of Jesu'. ($ChHu_2$ both lack this part of the text); As ends 'þys is þe Abbaye of þe Holigost þat is founded in a place þat is cleped þe conscience. Explicit Scala Perfeccionis' (although no copy of *The Abbey of the Holy Ghost* follows here). The omitted passage has been added in later hands in HBT. Of all the witnesses to the Carthusian group, only W has this final passage; and it was probably added to the print edition by comparison with some other manuscript copy.

Similarly, it is probable that the original form of this group lacked chapter titles throughout the text: they did not originally occur in H,[144] or in $BH_5ChLwHu_2$; and the titles added by a corrector in H are, with one exception, otherwise unique. As has chapter titles, but those from Chapter 21 onwards are the same as those in the unique

[143] See below, 46/14–17.

[144] Space has been left for chapter titles in H, and later hands have supplied a set of idiosyncratic titles that, as noted above, appear to have suggested themselves from a cursory reading of the first sentence or two of each chapter.

Table of Chapters in B. The title of Chapter 22 that has been added by a corrector in H is the same as that in As and in the Table of Chapters in B. Only the three latest witnesses to χ, LdTW, have titles throughout, as does E. It is possible that the Carthusian group originally had a Table of Chapters. Such tables occur once more often among manuscripts of this group (HBWsLwLdTW) than outside it (LB_3SrEPCc); although we should note that the Table in H is a later addition, and B has a variant set of titles that, as noted above, agrees only with the titles of the chapters in the text of As from Chapter 21 onwards.

The degree of textual contamination by 'correction' of copies of the Carthusian group against other manuscripts and prints of the same textual group is also noteworthy. The corrections of H are one of the characteristics of this text that have been most often noted by modern critics: in fact, it is because of its presumed authority as a corrected copy of the *Scale* belonging to London Charterhouse that it has held a predominant place in the discussion of the text ever since its provenance was first noted by Evelyn Underhill.[145] As we have seen above, the original text of H agrees most often with WsH_5, and the corrected text most often with LwW. James Grenehalgh corrected the Rosenbach copy of W and T against each other, and against the Latin text of H_8; W was also probably corrected against some other, unidentifiable manuscript. Lw was corrected, but apparently against its own exemplar over the course of a very inaccurate (perhaps hasty) job of copying. Finally, as we shall see below, E is the product of a conflation of the Carthusian and London groups. It appears that a number of the Carthusian owners of copies of *Scale* II were interested in producing, if not the most accurate, then at least the most full copies of the text available, but primarily by comparison of their copies with other Carthusian copies. It should also be noted that the incorrect variant dating of Hilton's death to the Vigil of the Assumption rather than the Vigil of the Annunciation occurs only in the Latin *Scale* manuscript B_4 and the Grenehalgh annotations in T and W.

[145] According to Underhill, '*Scale*', pp. xlvi–xlvii, 'This MS. has therefore a special importance, as coming from the library of the London charterhouse: for the Carthusians, the most learned of the contemplative orders, had always shown a peculiar devotion to Hilton's work, and may be expected to have taken some care to secure a correct text of the "Scale".' She goes on to praise the sanctity of the Carthusian martyrs, and of Thomas More, when they were put to death under Henry VIII, which is not exactly a germane argument for textual authority.

It should also be noted that all manuscripts of this group comprise both books of *The Scale of Perfection*, and only Lw contains anything else—a copy of *Angels' Song*. Hilton's *Mixed Life* was added later as a 'Third Book' to the first printing of W, and—from a different exemplar—to No and all subsequent incunable editions.

Although the readings characteristic of these manuscripts do not demonstrate any unity of ideology or theological or ecclesiological outlook (like, for example, the Lollard versions of various late medieval English religious texts), the manuscripts themselves do share a certain unity of provenance: five out of ten manuscripts are connected with various houses of the Carthusian order, and three with Syon Abbey. Considering that there were only nine Carthusian houses in England in the fifteenth century, with a total of some 175 choir monks, and a further sixty nuns and twenty-five priests and brothers in Syon, the Carthusian/Brigittine textual group may well represent a disproportionately high rate of survival of what was originally a relatively small number of manuscripts. This rate of survival, like the prominence in twentieth-century scholarship of the London Carthusian manuscript H and the textual-critical work of James Grenehalgh of Sheen, may have been driven by considerations of piety and historical tradition rather than textual authority.[146]

The affiliational group LB_3PH_6 sometimes varies with E. LB_3P agree in a unique variant 151 times, LB_3PH_6 150 times, LB_3EP forty times, and LB_3EPH_6 eighty-four times, for a total of 325. Four manuscripts of this group have London connections: L was the 'Common Profit' book made in the first quarter of the fifteenth century from the goods of the grocer John Killum; P belonged to Henry Langford, organmaker, living in the Minories, and H_6 was purchased late in the fifteenth century by Elizabeth Horwood, abbess of the convent of Franciscan nuns (i.e. 'the Minories') to remain there for the use of the community; and E belonged to London Charterhouse.

The LB_3P variants include substitution of synonyms, such as: 'pur' for H_7HSrChLw 'per', RBAsAPlH_5WsLdH$u_2$$H_6$TW 'for' (1/3), 'vnwilled' for H_7RAsSrAPlM 'myswilled', HBH_5Ws-ChLwECcLdTW 'yuel willed' (14/41), 'myȝti' for Σ 'syker' (44/15); or theological equivalents, such as: 'Jesu Crist' for Σ 'Jesu' (27/179).

[146] Nicholas Watson, 'The Middle English Mystics', in David Wallace (ed.), *The Cambridge History of Medieval English Literature* (Cambridge, 1999), 539–65 at 543, suggests that, 'because mystics scholarship has never adequately distinguished itself from religious practice, the field's priorities tend to be devotional, not historical'.

Other verbal substitutions include a number of cases of probable mistranscription of orthographic similars, such as: 'and' for 'in' (20/26), 'receyue vp hem' for H_7RSrH^{c}AECcMPl 'reysen hem vp', LwW 'areyse hem', H°BH_5AsHu_2LdT 'rysen vp', H_6 'receyue hem vp' (28/80), 'partie' for 'perfyte' (31/57), 'briȝt' for Σ 'be it' (33/53), 'symple' for Σ 'synful' (34/19), 'hiȝest' for Σ 'heght' (38/68), 'feelinge' for Σ 'fleynge' (41/36), and 'fleschflie' for Σ 'fleschly' (42/50).

There are variations of morphology, syntax, or semantics, such as: 'wiþ' for Σ 'be' (17/21), 'and' for Σ 'or' (22/64), 'flaterie' for Σ 'flaterynge' (23/10), 'or' for Σ 'and' (23/54), 'of' for Σ 'in' (24/38), 'in' for Σ 'of' (25/40), 'þanne' for Σ 'þat' (27/79), 'was' for Σ 'were' (28/62), 'schewid' for Σ 'shew' (29/56), 'strengthed' for Σ 'strengtheþ' (30/112), 'worþiere' for Σ 'wurthines' (33/14), 'stireþ' for Σ 'wuld stere' (42/89), 'mai' for Σ 'myght' (43/148). A few variants alter the sense of the text: 'þouȝt' for Σ 'southe' (25/39), 'he is' for 'as' (27/114), 'sauourly' for Σ 'vnsauourly' (32/17).

There are changes of number, such as: 'venyal' for Σ 'venials' (11/96), 'synne' for Σ 'synnes' (12/71), 'weiken . . . smyten' for Σ 'weykeþ . . . smyteth' (15/28–9), 'pilgrymages' for Σ 'pilgrymage' (21/36), 'his dedis' for 'dede' Σ (27/82), 'synnes' for Σ 'synne' (34/104), 'stiringe' for Σ 'sterenges' (40/168), 'mennys' for Σ 'manes' (43/42), 'hem' for Σ 'him' (43/143).

Change of determiner, such as: 'þis' for Σ 'þe' (26/19).

There are also transpositions, such as: 'not / in . . . is' (3/47), 'þat is wilfully don / sinne' (6/6), 'hem inowȝ' for Σ 'inogh to hem' (18/14), 'þese . . . are / þurgh grace' (31/38), 'ȝifere / . . . / ȝifte' (34/40), 'vs most' (34/55), 'frely be' (39/24).

Additions, such as: 'ryȝt' (20/109) and 'hem' (32/77).

Omissions, such as: 'þat is' (11/123), 'wel' (17/21), 'ay' (21/20, 41/64), 'alle' (25/54), 'moun' (27/11), 'þat a man' (27/75), 'grete' (29/24), 'speken' (33/68), 'in knowynge and' (34/12), 'ne han not' (35/19), 'and man' (36/40), 'þe^{I} . . . grace^{I}' (41/74), 'in . . . grace' (42/112–13), and 'þu come to' (42/137).

Further, twenty-six unique LB_3P variants represent corrections made in L,[147] including additions such as: 'seruio' (11/50), 'and reformyd' (17/31, over erasure in L), 'him and' (22/45), 'oonly' (22/

[147] See above, p. cxiv.

70), 'grace and' (26/35), 'before' (26/106), now (31/42), 'alle' (32/56: part of a larger correction over erasure in L).

Substitution of synonyms, such as: 'fleischli' for Σ 'bodily' (24/69, over erasure in L).

Or theological equivalents, such as: 'Jesu' for Σ 'him' (35/82: over erasure in L).

Substitution of orthographic similars such as: 'feeliþ' over erasure in L, B_3P 'feliþ', for Σ 'fleth' (12/62), 'l⌜o⌝ueþ \not/' in L, B_3P 'loueþ not', for Σ 'leueth' (14/12), 'þe fendes' for Σ 'feyned' (26/75, over erasure in L).

Other verbal substitutions, such as: 'knowynge' for Σ 'lykynge' (24/46, over erasure in L).

Change in number, such as: 'maneres' for Σ 'maner' (34/22: over erasure in L).

Variations of morphology, syntax, and semantics, such as: 'coueityng' for Σ 'coueyten' (22/45: partially over erasure in L).

Additions, such as: 'ferforþ' for Σ 'fer' (42/74).

Cancellation and omission, such as: 'and' (27/163: cancelled in L, omitted in B_3P).

Another nine corrections in L present readings shared uniquely with P, such as: '\vn/de⌜ynte⌝' L, 'deynte' B_3, 'vndeynte' P, for Σ dedeyne (40/91: L marginal note 'quere'), 'maki⌜þ him parfite bygynnyng and⌝' L, 'maketh hym parfite begynnyng and' P, for Σ 'maketh him also perfyte, and' (40/152–3), or 'loned' L (L marginal note 'quere: loned or lened'), 'loned or lened' P (marginal note: 'quere'), lenedest B_3, 'lenest' H_7CcLd, 'lenethe' M, 'lenid' HBH_5Sr-WsLwAH_6PlTW, 'lendist' E (42/131).

In fact, it appears from the pattern of agreement of B_3P with corrections in L that the two latter manuscripts derive from the corrected text of L; that P does so has been noted before.[148] Although the scribal dialect has been translated in P, the text in these two manuscripts is otherwise virtually identical; and all of the annotations in L, whether corrections (in more than one hand) or readers' remarks and guides (including marginal notes, manicula, and bracketing), have been copied in by the scribe of P. Even the note 'From þis to the ende of this chapitill is more þan oþere bookys haue', written by an annotator against the 'Holy Name Passage' at the end of Chapter 44 of *Scale* I has been written in the margin

[148] Sargent, 'London Group', 196.

adjacent to the same point in the text by the scribe in P; and as we have just seen, two marginal notes in L querying alternative forms ('quere: bi or be', and 'quere: loned or lened') have been copied in by the scribe in P, with the alternative forms entered into the text ('bi or be', 'loned or lened'), and the word 'quere' alone left in the margin.[149] B_3, on the other hand, does not reflect the corrections in L quite as closely as does P; B_3 appears to have been copied (or to descend from a copy made) after some of the corrections had been entered in the margins of L, but before others. Finally, it should be noted that the London group of manuscripts all have the final 161 words of the text, 'of þe whilk . . . gret bok' (46/74–86).

A fourth manuscript, H_6, joins LB_3P in 150 unique readings. E, which agrees with the Carthusian group in fifty-two otherwise-unique readings and with that group and As in seventy-two readings,[150] also agrees with LB_3P in forty unique readings, and with LB_3PH_6 in eighty-four readings. All of the manuscripts of this group have chapter titles through the text that diverge from those of other manuscripts for Chapters 21 to 24. LB_3EP have tables of chapters; H_6 does not. L and B_3 also share a page-header format that is unique among *Scale* manuscripts.[151]

An interesting characteristic of the London group of manuscripts is that the majority of them comprise collections of Hilton's works:[152] besides the *Scale*, L has the *Mixed Life*, the *Eight Chapters*, and the commentaries on 'Qui habitat', 'Bonum est', and the 'Benedictus'; P has the *Mixed Life* and the *Eight Chapters* preceding the text of the *Scale*; H_6, which contains *Scale* II without *Scale* I (but with an *incipit* that refers to the former book), has the *Mixed Life* and 'Bonum est' in a set of gatherings added at the end.

The association of the 'Common Profit' manuscripts and the London group of manuscripts of *The Scale of Perfection* is interesting; both represent patterns of circulation of works of spiritual profit among the relatively well-to-do pious laity in fifteenth-century London. H_6 is an exception in that it was bequeathed by the abbess of the Poor Clares to that house; but even its provision

[149] Note that the observation that the text and notes in P derive from those in L does not depend on these two instances, but on the regular agreement of P with L, in both its original text and its corrections and marginal notes. These are merely the most remarkable examples.

[150] See above, p. cxxii.

[151] See above, pp. xxxiv, li.

[152] See Sargent, 'Walter Hilton's *Scale of Perfection* in Devotional Compilations'.

retains some of the forms of private donation, use, and compensatory prayers for the dead apparent in the 'Common Profit' manuscripts. Further, the geographic juxtaposition of P and H_6 in the Minories is in itself notable. Wendy Scase has suggested that the patterns of provision and circulation of the 'Common profit' manuscripts may be related to Bishop Reginald Pecock's ideas about the free provision of appropriate reading material for the poor laity and unbeneficed clergy;[153] but the textual and codicological details of this group of manuscripts lends little support to this hypothesis. It should also be noted that, like the Carthusian/Brigittine group, the London group of manuscripts of *Scale* II may be an example of a disproportionately high rate of survival among what was originally a relatively small number of manuscripts.

The 'Theocentric' group, RAPl, shares seventy-three unique variations. All but four of the agreements of these manuscripts occur in eight chapters in the middle third of the text (Chapters 27, 29–30, and 32–6). Twenty-four of these readings represent the substitution of 'God' for Σ 'Jesu'; and one the substitution of 'loue' for 'Jesu'; another eight represent the omission of the name 'Jesu', or of phrases in which the name occurs; and two represent the addition of 'of God' and 'þe godhede'. There are also a number of omissions, such as: 'and grete synne' (27/68), 'and to a meke felynge' (27/107), 'þat is . . . þat he may' (27.107), and 'þy lyȝt . . . schul seen' (33/57), and additions such as: 'þat he wele forgiuen hem here trespas' (30/78), and 'and of ȝoure owen manly wirkyng also' (36/39).

It should be remembered that R is lacking approximately 15 per cent of the text in the later chapters of *Scale* II. RA also agree eleven times in unique variants, RPl eighteen times, and APl twenty-seven times. As, which agrees with the Carthusian group 100 times, also shares ninety-five readings with RAPl, almost all of which occur in the first half of the text (Chapters 1 to 28). These include fifteen occurrences of the substitution of 'God' for 'Jesu', and three of 'God' for 'him', and the omissions, once each, of the name 'Jesu', the phrase 'and þat is only Jesu', and the phrase 'of God'.

There is also substitution of other synonyms, such as: 'knowyng' for 'connynge' (10/59) and 'Take' for 'Preent' (21/103).

Other verbal substitutions include a number cases of probable mistranscription of orthographic similars, such as: 'þorew . . . þat is'

[153] Scase, 'Reginald Pecock'.

for Σ 'þogh . . . be' (9.11), 'loueþ hem nouȝt' for Σ 'lotheth hem' (12/61), 'leeuen' for Σ 'lese' (18/35), and 'schynith' for Σ 'scheweþ him' (26/17).

There are changes of number, such as: 'affeccions' for Σ 'affeccion' (11/26).

There are also transpositions, such as: 'clere . . . clene' (4/6), 'þe fende of helle for þei arn liȝk vnto beestis, ȝa, and wers þan beestis' for Σ 'beestis . . . fend of helle' (14/59–60), and 'how . . . ende / and / how . . . punysched' (14/75–7).

Addition of words or phrases, such as: 'only hym to wetyn' (14/9), 'þat þei hauen no grace for' (15/10), 'and þerfore it nedith hym þat he be ay besy' (18/38), and 'and sey I couete nouȝt but for to loue God' (22/17).

Omissions, such as: 'And þis is on skil why þat confession is nedful' (7/43), 'and kan not helpen itself' (11/92), 'is a mans soule' (12/5), 'arn son . . . if þei' (14/45), 'of þe wurthynes' (21/67–8), 'dynne of . . . werdly' (24/77), 'and vnclennes of þiself' (24/104), and 'with a gostly beholdynge of him' (24/156–7).

M agrees with RAPl in seventy-nine variant readings of much the same type, primarily in the latter half of the text. These include twelve readings substituting 'God' for Σ 'Jesu'; three substituting 'loue' for 'Jesu'; one substituting 'God' for 'him', and 'of God' for 'his'; two omissions of 'Jesu'; and seven omissions of phrases containing 'Jesu'.There are also other omissions, such as: 'and to al vertus' (27/70), 'as are religyouse and seculers' (27/104), 'and seen himself' (27/110), 'þan gyfeþ he himself to vs, and' (34/68), 'it so be þat' (34/90), 'and makeþ oure wil . . . alle synnes' (34/101), 'in alle vertus' (34/103), 'It is frely had . . . before' (35/9–10), 'him in his' (35/82), 'ne gode thoght felt in ȝow' (36/43), 'lufe, myghtyly, wittyly, and' (36/44), 'lokeþ on me and' (36/52), 'and are not . . . biddyng of reson' (36/71–2), 'And also . . . synnes' (37/16).

Additions, such as: 'þe most þat miȝt be schewid in manhode' (34/66), 'of God' (36/30), 'nouȝt by hymselue but' (37/29), 'or of ony of þe bodily witte or of' (39/121).

The transposition 'by . . . hemself / þurgh . . . God' (35/47–8).

As and M agree together with RAPl in fifty-three unique readings, most of which occur between Chapters 20 and 26. These include fifteen occurrences of the substitution of 'God' for 'Jesu'; one of 'him' for 'Jesu', and of the phrase 'forsaken hem alle and forgetyn hem' for Σ 'aretten hem al to Jesu' (20/92); the addition of the phrase, 'of God', three cases of the omission of the name 'Jesu'; and four cases of omission of phrases including the name 'Jesu'. R(As)A(M)Pl thus agree in a total of 221 unique variants; it should also be noted that RM agree in sixty-one unique variants, and RAs in sixty-eight.

Reference to 'God' rather than 'Jesu' in the Theocentric group of manuscripts, and the large number of omissions that are not the result of eye-skip (the largest single source of omission as a form of textual variation) together constitute the inverse of the phenomenon characterized by Underhill and Gardner as 'Christocentric additions' (found as additions in H) in manuscripts of *Scale* I.[154] That is, the text of *Scale* II in the Theocentric group lacks readings of precisely the kind that is described as 'Christocentric additions' when they occur in other manuscripts of *Scale* I. A direct comparison of the text of the two books in these manuscripts will have to await the complete collation of manuscripts of *Scale* I: unfortunately, Gardner did not notice that R comprises a copy of *Scale* II; As has the 'Christocentric additions' in *Scale* I but not in the first half of *Scale* II, where it is a member of the Theocentric group; A and Pl were not available for examination at the time; and M does not include *Scale* I.

Although the present discussion has (for the sake of clarity) treated reference to 'God' rather than 'Jesu' as a matter of 'substitution', the possibility must be kept in mind that it may just as well be a recessive representative of an early, Theocentric form of the text of *Scale* II, a form that has been largely superseded among the surviving manuscripts. If this be the case, the omissions referred to above may equally be considered as evidence of authorial expansion of the text during the writing process. On the other hand, it is also possible that the use of 'God' rather than 'Jesu' in RAPl at least is the result of conscious alteration by scribes who wanted to make the diction of *Scale* II more congruent with that of the Theocentric text of *Scale* I that their manuscripts already included.

The manuscripts of *Scale* I most closely affiliated with the Theocentric group of *Scale* II have geographical connections with the North, the West, and the South of England, although the texts of *Scale* II themselves have more central and East Anglian localizations.

[154] *Scale*, ed. Underhill, pp. xliv–xlv.

The manuscripts of *Scale* I to which the Theocentric group are related also often comprise collections of writings by Hilton (particularly the *Mixed Life*), Richard Rolle (particularly *The Form of Living*, *The Commandment*, and an English version of the *Oleum effusum*) and others. R comprises a collection of Rolleana that it shares (along with 'Theocentric' texts of *Scale* I) with two other manuscripts, *Scale* MSS D and F. In R and D, the text of *Scale* I and the other materials have dialectal profiles localizable to northern and north-western Yorkshire; the dialectal profile of F is localizable to north-eastern Norfolk; *Scale* II is added in R in a dialect localizable to the Norfolk/Ely border area. The 'Theocentric' text of *Scale* I in Pl is closely affiliated with that in the famous west Midland compilations Vernon and Simeon, but Pl, which also originally (like V and S) comprised Hilton's *Mixed Life*, was written in the later fifteenth century in a dialect localizable to Surrey. A, which is dialectally localizable to the Staffordshire/Cheshire/Derbyshire border area, with an admixture of more southerly forms, was in Dorset at the beginning of the fifteenth century, where it was donated to Shaftesbury abbey; it also comprises a collection of Rolleana similar to that in R. This collection also occurs with a 'Theocentric' copy of *Scale* I in H_3, which is localizable to north-west Yorkshire. M, which, like As, presents a highly idiosyncratic text of *Scale* II, does not contain *Scale* I, but begins with a paragraph that adapts the opening of *Scale* II as if it were a free-standing work. It has no other contents, and is dialectally localizable to southern Lincolnshire.

It is not certain for whom these copies of the *Scale* were made. V and S were most probably addressed to communities of nuns, but *Scale* I in VS and Pl addresses itself to a 'Ghostly brother or sister in Jesus Christ'. As belonged to Rose Pachet of Syon Abbey, but addresses itself to a 'Ghostly brother'. A, written in the first quarter of the fifteenth century, belonged to the Benedictine nuns of Shaftesbury by mid-century. M adapts the beginning of *Scale* II so that it may stand independent of the preceding book. At several points, manuscripts of the Theocentric text of *Scale* II omit references to the difference in clerical or lay status among the readers, or to the advice of religious superior,[155] which suggests adaptation for secular clerical, lay, or anchoritic (i.e. non-religious)

[155] See Explanatory Notes to 19/42, 21/115–16, 21/136, 22/57, 23/53, 27/29, and 27/106.

readers, although the fact that they do not occur uniformly through all manuscripts of the group suggests that these may have been independent alterations of the text. It should also be noted that the unique opening of M directs the text particularly to 'religious, wheche be wordus of profession haue forsake all þe world, and outward beth clothed with a dedly habite þat semyth contemplatyf or ful of perfeccion'.[156]

The Theocentric manuscripts thus share early connections with the North and West of England, but later broad geographic dispersal, and represent some degree of adaptation of the text to a non-religious audience. It should also be kept in mind that these manuscripts may well represent the broader circulation of the text of *Scale* II throughout England, rather than in the hands of members of the Carthusian order and Brigittine nuns, or the pious bourgeoisie of fifteenth-century London and their beneficiaries.[157]

M shares some 118 otherwise unique readings with Cc, inlcuding a number of verbal additions in the middle third of the text, such as: 'And that thyng is nout ellys but Jesu, God and man, for to lovyn hym and sen hym in gostly felynge thurgh grace here in partie and afftirward fully in ioye' (23/27), 'And puttyn the from bodily and gostly exercise' (23/33), 'And go thanne forth to thyn werk' (23/38), 'and Jesu hymself' (23/41), 'For Jesu shewith nout his gostly face to þe soule restfully' (24/131), 'for to han be the gracious onseable presens of Jesu' (24/132), 'thrugh his graceful onseable presens' (25/9), 'For Jesu shewyd hym nout fullyȝet as he myth' (25/33), 'þat is Jesu' (25/36), 'for to sekyn Jesu' (27/163), 'thurgh a gracious shadwyng of Jesu' (27/179), 'and beholdyn hym with reverence' (27/182), 'This payne felith the soule whanne Jesu withdrawith a lytil his gostly presens and suffryth the soule to fallyn in the self' (28/55), 'and þe sith of Jesu' (30/44), 'of þe manhod' (30/125), 'of Jesu, if he myth come therto' (30/127), 'Jesu nout only as man be ymaginacyon, but he seth hym God in man' (32/11). CcM also share the additions 'and that tyme may it only and frely and devoutly beholdyn Jesu whethir it wyl prey or thynk' (24/124), and 'If it be paynful þan' (24/128) with LwW and Td.

The character of the variations in which CcM are united, and

[156] See above, p. lvi.

[157] This consideration represents an application of the traditional geographical criterion of textual criticism to circulation, rather than authenticity.

particularly the large proportion of them represented by the additions in Chapters 23 to 32, as well as the addition of the chapter breaks and titles in Chapters 12 and 24 in CcM, Sr, and the Latin version, suggests that they are related by conflation, rather than genetic affiliation.

Sr has the extra chapter division occurring in Chapter 12 in CcM and the Latin version, but otherwise shows no pattern of affiliation with any other surviving manuscripts. Likewise, H_7 shows no tendency to affiliation with any other manuscripts, but differs from the consensus of readings of surviving manuscripts less often than any other.

The Fishlake translation of *Scale* II does not agree to any significant extent with any of the surviving manuscripts or manuscript groups: it appears to have been made from an unaffiliated English exemplar—although not from the authorial original, since there are readings in the Latin text that can only have derived from faulty readings in the English manuscript on which it was based.

In sum: there are three demonstrable affiliational groups among the surviving manuscripts of the second book of Walter Hilton's *Scale of Perfection*: the Carthusian/Brigittine group, HBH_5-$WsChLwHu_2LdTW$ plus As for the latter part of the text, conflated with E throughout; the London group, LB_3PH_6, also conflated with E; and the Theocentric group, RAPl plus As in the earlier part of the text, and conflated with M. Cc and M may be related by conflation, perhaps with the Latin translation. Sr and H_7, the dialectal profiles of which place them in south-east Lincolnshire and far-western Norfolk, are independent of any of these affiliational groups.

None of the surviving manuscript witnesses, nor any hypothetical hyparchetype of any group, is Hilton's original copy of *The Scale of Perfection*—even assuming that there was a single original copy, and not a text constantly evolving even in the author's hands. The relationship of the manuscripts is thus not stemmatic, but, as I have described it elsewhere, rhizomorphic.[158] Every manuscript and every printed copy is ultimately a witness to itself and to its textual group, not to some hypothetical original. In this context, it is useful here to extend the idea of isolative variants discussed above,[159] to speak more inclusively of the degree of deviation of each manuscript

[158] Sargent, 'Editing Walter Hilton's *Scale of Perfection*'.
[159] See above, p. xcvii.

from the consensus of the textual tradition, measured as the sum of its isolative variants plus the sum of the readings characteristic of the variational groups with which it is affiliated. In these terms, H_7 diverges from the consensus of the English manuscripts least often: 387 times; H diverges second least often: 439 times; P 486 times; E 607 times; Sr 655 times; B_3 654 times; B 760 times; H_6 826 times; L 867 times; H_5 928 times; Pl 992 times; Lw 993 times; W 994 times; Ld 1,039 times; T 1,079 times; A 1,084 times; M 1,623 times; Cc 1,748 times; and As 2,050 times. The defective manuscript Ch (which represents approximately three-eighths of the text) deviates 172 times; R (which represents approximately seven-eighths of the text) deviates 518 times; Hu_2 (which represents a little less than two-thirds of the text) deviates 567 times; and Ws (which represents approximately nine-tenths of the text) deviates 722 times.[160] Further, not only does H_7 deviate from the consensus of surviving English manuscripts least often; it also agrees most often with Fishlake's Latin *Scale*.[161]

Conclusion: A Postmodern Critical Edition of *Scale* II

The modern critical edition, whether produced by recension or by modernist-aestheticist analysis,[162] will always function in the realm of

[160] If these three manuscripts were complete and their textual complexion had remained the same, Ch would deviate from the consensus 459 times, R 583 times, and Hu_2 850 times.

[161] See above, pp. cvii–cviii.

[162] Traditionally, the phrase 'critical edition' refers only to editions produced by recension; it should apply rather to any edition based on a complete analysis of the surviving manuscript evidence, no matter what the method of analysis, and will be used here with that meaning. By 'modernist-aestheticist' I mean particularly editions done in the tradition of the Athlone *Piers Plowman*, which is grounded in both a modernist, 'New-Critical' focus on close reading and an aesthetic judgement of textual authority aptly described by Lee Patterson as 'The Way of Genius'. See Patterson, 'The Logic of Textual Criticism and the Way of Genius: The Kane-Donaldson *Piers Plowman* in Historical Perspective', in Jerome McGann (ed.), *Textual Criticism and Literary Interpretation* (Chicago, 1985), 55–91; repr. in *Negotiating the Past: The Historical Understanding of Medieval Literature* (Madison, Wis., 1987), 77–113. See also George Kane, 'Conjectural Emendation', in Christopher Kleinhenz (ed.), *Medieval Manuscripts and Textual Criticism* (Chapel Hill, NC, 1976), 211–26; Ralph Hanna III, 'Producing Manuscripts and Editions', in A. J. Minnis and Charlotte Brewer (eds.), *Crux and Controversy in Middle English Textual Criticism* (Cambridge, 1992), 109–30; Hanna, 'George Kane and the Invention of Textual Thought: Retrospect and Prospect', *Yearbook of Langland Studies*, 24 (2010), 1–20. The ideas of textuality expressed here are explored in Sargent, 'Organic and Cybernetic'; I hope to be able to return to them in fuller form elsewhere. I wish also to thank Stephen Kelly, Ryan Perry, and the CUNY medieval discussion group (Glenn

representation: it seeks to reconstitute an ideal text by eliminating the difference among the particular instantiations, the manuscript repetitions, of that text.[163] Both my recensionist edition of Nicholas Love's *Mirror of the Blessed Life of Jesus Christ*, for example, and the Athlone B-Text of *Piers Plowman* 'restored' to the 'authoritative' text some three hundred readings that are not to be found in the actual manuscripts.[164] At this point, I (at least) will admit that in doing so, I created a text of which the author may well have approved, but which may not have existed in his day. This is the nature of the modern critical edition: it is a chimera, a uniform, authorized text, a construct of the collusion of the editor and the printer.[165] The more perfect it is, the more fully it counterfeits the manuscript evidence upon which it is based. In Deleuzean terms, it exists as a form of generalization, and obfuscates the traces of the difference between repetitions that constitutes the actual manuscript history of the text.

A postmodern critical edition is not the representation of an idealized text that has been abstracted from the surviving manuscripts by either a genetic or an aesthetic process of generalization, but the record of the difference of the surviving manuscripts, recorded as variance. The critical apparatus of such an edition is not simply a list of the readings that can be safely ignored once the critical text has been constructed from them, but an integral part of the text itself. The critical text is the text; the critical apparatus is also the text. The postmodern editor puts into play a text that is different from all other forms of the text, but which has been

Burger, Steven Kruger, Matthew Goldie, Jennifer Brown, and Valerie Allen) for helping me to conceptualize the argument presented here.

[163] I am drawing here on the concepts of repetition, difference, and representation as articulated in Gilles Deleuze, *Difference and Repetition*, trans. Paul Patton (London and New York, 1994), originally published as *Différance et répétition* (Paris, 1968).

[164] Nicholas Love, *The Mirror of the Blessed Life of Jesus Christ: A Full Critical Edition, Based on Cambridge University Library Additional MSS 6578 and 6686, with Introduction, Notes and Glossary*, ed. Michael G. Sargent (Exeter, 2005); *Piers Plowman: The B Version. Will's Visions of Piers Plowman, Do-Well, Do-Better and Do-Best. An Edition in the Form of Trinity College Cambridge MS B.15.17, Corrected and Restored from the Known Evidence, with Variant Readings*, ed. George Kane and E. Talbot Donaldson (London, 1975). The source of the 'restored' readings in the **α** text of Love's *Mirror* is the agreement of the **β** and **γ** texts with the underlying Latin *Meditationes vitae Christi*; the source of the 'restored' readings in the B-Text of *Piers Plowman* is editorial conjecture based on the readings of the A- and C-Texts.

[165] The role of the printer in the spread of the modern conceptualization of the univocal authorized text cannot be ignored.

constructed on the basis of the differences of all of them each from each. It is not a generalization abstracted from differences but the presentation of all differences: the pleroma that is the text.

Ideally, such a rhizomorphic edition should be achievable through electronic media.[166] In an electronic edition a transcript of each manuscript could be linked on a page-by-page, line-by-line, or word-by-word basis to every page, line, and word of a transcript of every other manuscript, and further, to images of the manuscript pages themselves. Yet even an electronic edition, no matter how equipollent the linking of the text of the various manuscripts and versions, will open up to a default text.[167] It is at this point that the editor will always be active and engaged, not as a 'mere stage-hand', but as the producer who brings the show to the stage and the director who gives it coherence.

As noted above, the relations of the surviving manuscripts of *Scale* II are not stemmatic but rhizomorphic. That is, each affiliational group of manuscripts and each of the manuscripts that does not belong to a group derives independently from a no-longer-extant 'original' that was possibly in the dynamic process of revision during the time that copies were being made, and each manuscript of each group is defined textually by agreement in unique readings that they produce in common (as well as other, non-textual factors). A postmodern edition of the kind envisaged here will recognize the genetic relationship of all of the surviving manuscripts and the affiliational groups in which most of them are associated, but without recourse to the construction of an idealized archetype from which each descends.

An alternative to the production of a modern critical edition, particularly common since the disruption of the recensionist tradition by the Athlone *Piers Plowman*, is the best-text edition. Such an edition eschews the process of generalization necessary to produce a stemma from the difference among the instantiations, the repetitions of the text among the surviving manuscripts. But it differentiates by

[166] For the relationship between electronic media and the kind of postmodern critical text that I envisage, see Jerome McGann, 'The Rationale of HyperText', www2.iath.virginia.edu/public/jjm2f/rationale.html, accessed 28 Nov. 2015, and *A New Republic of Letters: Memory and Scholarship in the Age of Digital Reproduction* (Cambridge, Mass., 2014).

[167] Similarly, despite the publication of the various manuscripts of Chaucer's *Canterbury Tales* by the Chaucer Society, critical work to this day depends primarily on the six (or eight) texts privilegd by Furnivall's original publication.

means of a survey of what the editor sees as the most salient textual differences and other, non-textual factors, and elects one instantiation of the text to stand in place of all. Difference itself has been suppressed as not worth the readers' time and effort.

Because there are seven rhizomorphic lines of testimony to the English text of *Scale* II, a postmodern critical edition should attempt to present all seven lines of evidence as fully as possible. One way to maximize the presentation of the difference of the manuscript tradition is the publication of a multiple-text edition, like the Chaucer Society's *Six-* (later *Eight-*) *Text* version of Chaucer's *Canterbury Tales*, or the Early English Text Society's series of diplomatic editions of the manuscripts of *Ancrene Wisse*.[168] Such editions provide an alternative to the 'grand narrative' of the critical edition: a set of local narratives of the textuality of a given work.[169] They function as multiple best-text editions, with minimal presentation in each volume of the variant readings of other manuscripts. At the same time, however, they also consume immense publication resources. Within a single-volume printed edition, the presentation of textual difference can be accomplished most fully by presenting two texts, each representative of one line of testimony,[170] in facing-page format, together with a critical apparatus comprising all of the evidence of the other English manuscripts, and the Latin version as well, whenever it gives evidence of the underlying English text. The question is which two forms of the text it would be best to present.

The best representatives of the seven lines of transmission of the English text of *Scale* II are H_7, Sr, H, L, R, Cc, and M. Although H_7 is an early manuscript, the dialectal profile of which places it just south-west of the Wash, on the border between Norfolk and Ely (near the epicentre of the circulation of copies of *Scale* II), it has not been considered heretofore as important to textual-critical analysis of

[168] It should be noted that the culmination of this latter series, *Ancrene Wisse: A Corrected Edition of the Text in Cambridge, Corpus Christi College, MS 402, with Variants from Other Manuscripts*, ed. Bella Millett and Richard Dance, EETS OS 325–6 (2005–6) comes closest to expressing the ideal towards which the present edition aims.

[169] The use of the terms 'grand narrative' and 'local narratives' reflects the ideas of Jean-François Lyotard, *The Postmodern Condition: A Report on Knowledge*, trans. Geoff Bennington and Brian Massumi (Minneapolis, 1984; originally published as *La Condition postmoderne: Rapport sur le savoir* (Paris, 1979).

[170] 'Representative' in the sense that it is the form of the text to which the editor would draw the reader's attention first and foremost; not in the sense that it somehow includes and subsumes the difference of the other instantiations of the text.

Scale II. Because it does not have the readings characteristic of either the London or the Theocentric manuscript groups, Hussey dismissed it as an idiosyncratic copy of his **v** textual group. Not belonging to any of the identifiable textual groups, however, H_7 distinguishes itself as both the single manuscript that deviates least often from the consensus of the English textual tradition, and agrees most often with the English text from which Fishlake made his translation. Although the agreement of large numbers, or even the majority, of manuscripts in a given reading is no guarantee of textual authority, the general consensus of manuscripts in thousands of readings throughout the text (given a sufficiently large corpus) may be taken as a very strong indicator both of the form of the text that the author wrote, and that the fifteenth-century readers read. I will not argue that the manuscript that deviates least from the consensus is thus 'authoritative', certainly not in particular readings, but I will say that it is the text that we should read first.

Like H_7, Sr is an early manuscript that does not agree in any of the readings characteristic of the identifiable manuscript groups. Its scribal dialectal profile places it in Ely. It also comprises a copy of the *Prickyng of Love* attributed to Walter Hilton. There is no notable degree of agreement between Sr and H_7;[171] they are coincidently independent. Sr is not notably more in agreement with the consensus of the English manuscript tradition than any others.

H is the earliest representative of the Carthusian/Brigittine manuscript group, and is one of the two manuscripts that deviates least from the consensus of the English manuscript tradition. Its scribal dialect is of Ely or extreme southern Lincolnshire. On the other hand, like other manuscripts of the Carthusian/Brigittine group, it is not closely affiliated with the text upon which Fishlake's Latin translation was based. The predominance of the Carthusian/Brigittine group among the surviving manuscripts may not reflect textual predominance among the fifteenth-century readers of *Scale* II, because the manuscripts of this group may be disproportionately often preserved; but the incunable printings of *Scale* II belong to this group, and this was probably the form of the text most often read in the late fifteenth and sixteenth centuries.

L is the earliest representative of the London manuscript group, the source of one other, and probably of two. It scribal dialectal

[171] The textual pairing H_7Sr occurs only twelve times.

profile places it near Willingham in Cambridgeshire; it probably reflects Hilton's own usage quite closely. The London group is not, as we have seen above, the source of the Latin version, which was made from an independent manuscript. Further, it probably represents an even more restricted circulation among fifteenth-century readers than the Carthusian/Brigittine group.

R is the earliest representative of the Theocentric manuscript group, which is worth consideration because it possibly represents—like the Theocentric manuscripts of *Scale* I—an early version of *Scale* II. Unfortunately, this issue canot be decided until the edition of *Scale* I is complete. All that can be said at this point is that this group varies from the others in reading 'God' where others read 'Jesus'. The scribal dialect of R appears to localize it, like H_7, just south-west of the Wash, on the border between Norfolk and Ely. Unfortunately, R is lacking approximately one-eighth of the text, which disqualifies it from consideration as a base text of the edition.

Cc and M, both quite idiosyncratic in text, and possibly conflated with the Latin version, would each have a claim to presentation in a multiple-text edition, but need not be considered here.

The two manuscripts that have the strongest claim to presentation in this edition are H_7 and H: the former, as the best representative of the textual tradition as a whole, and the latter as the best representative of the form of the text that achieved widest readership. Sr presents similar claims to those of H_7, but not as strong. L, like H, represents an important form of the text, but more narrowly localized—and it is already available in both print and electronic forms. R presents a strong claim on our attention, but the strength of its claim is as not yet completely determined, and it is an imperfect copy. H_7 is the base-text of this edition, and the critical apparatus is keyed to its readings; H is presented on the facing (right-hand) page.

The text of these two manuscripts is not copied blindly here: they are not without errors, and not all of their readings are the most cogent. Where their readings are visibly erroneous, they have been corrected; where they are not strictly in error, but their readings appear to be less cogent than the readings of other manuscripts, I have not corrected the reading of H_7 or H (which tend to cancel out each other's deficiencies, at any rate), but have discussed the cogency of the variants in the Explanatory Notes. Cases where I think that the cogency of the variants is debatable, or where I think that the H_7 variant is more cogent, even when it occurs in isolation, are also discussed in the Explanatory Notes. All judgements of error or relative cogency have been made on a reading-by-reading basis and are discussed in the Explanatory Notes. In either case, the intention is to let the witnesses speak in their own voice(s).

It should also be noted here that the purpose of the critical apparatus in what has been conceived as a postmodern critical edition is not entirely the same as that of a modern (recensionist or modernist-aesthetic) critical edition: it is not there to support the decisions of the editor in constructing an authoritative text. For this reason, the presentation of the evidence of the manuscripts has not been reduced to the reporting of the variants of selected representative manuscripts, nor is the reader expected to pay little or no attention to the apparatus except as evidence for the authority of the critical text it supports. All variant readings of all manuscripts are presented in the apparatus as part of this edition's goal of presenting the pleroma of the text of *Scale* II with as little reduction or representation as possible. The reader is not just encouraged, but required (so far as an editor may require of a reader) to follow the text in its apparatus. It is not ballast: it is the cargo.

4. EDITORIAL CONVENTIONS

The Text

The text of this edition conforms, with some variance, to the usual protocols for editions of Middle English texts of the period. Capitalization has been modernized: specifically, capital second letters following coloured initials have been transcribed in lower case, and proper names, including the nomina sacra and forms for 'Holy Church', 'Holy Writ', and 'Gospel', have been capitalized. All chapter titles are in a slightly larger font than the body of the chapters; direct citations of Scripture in Latin are italicized.

Hussey has expanded the forms 'ihu' and 'irlm' (and variants thereof) in the H text to 'Ihesu', 'Iherusalem'; I have expanded in the H_7 text to 'Jesu' and 'Jerusalem'. The word 'þou' is spelled three ways: without suspension, either 'þou' or 'þu'; with suspension, 'þ^{u}' is transcribed 'þou'. Compound words are written as single words if they are so in *OED*, otherwise, they have been hyphenated. For example, 'noþyng' is written as one word except where it is necessary (because of, e.g., grammatical parallelism) to write it as 'no þyng'; 'as tytte' is written as two words; 'what-so' and 'what-so-euer' as hyphenated words. All suspensions, including the ampersand, are expanded silently, according to the scribe's usage when spelling out in full.

Treatment of overstroking as a marker of a suspended nasal letter is complex, but attempts to reflect in a consistently rationalized manner the spelling of words without suspension. Because final '-on' occurs without suspension, but final '-oun' does not, overstroking of final '-on' will be taken as otiose. Other cases of overstroking are generally governed by the same rules of etymology and syllable closure (and thus the marking of length of a preceding vowel) as is reflected in Present-day English forms: 'John', not 'Johun'; 'born', not 'borun'; 'con-' and 'com-', not 'coun-' and 'coum-'; 'woman', not 'womman'; 'comen', not 'commen'; 'synne', not 'syne'; 'done', not 'doune' for Present-day 'done'; and 'doun', not 'don' for Present-day 'down'.

The question of whether a final downstroke on the final consonant of a word (particularly '-g', '-t', or '-k') is otiose, or whether it represents a final '-e' in suspension is equally problematic. The guiding principle here is that a suspended final '-e' is more likely when it might represent the reflex of a former grammatical ending, but the graphic prominence of the ductus itself (varying from a hairline to a minim's width) has also been taken into account as a sign that the scribe may have intended it to be taken as a mark of suspension.

The question of punctuation is more difficult: the clauses of Hilton's prose tend to run on, either by coordination ('and', 'but', 'also', 'neuerþeles') or by subordination ('while', 'for', 'þerfore'), as well as the frequent disruption of his prose by interjection and parenthesis ('Ʒe', 'Lo', 'þe qwhilk I haue before seid', 'namely . . .'). These tendencies are characteristic of his prose style, and are reflected in the relative paucity of punctuation of the text as compared to modern usage. Complete accuracy to the manuscript tradition would lead the editor to punctuate the edition to reflect Hilton's text as it was copied and read by his contemporaries: to transcribe the simple punctus as a full stop or a comma, depending on whether it is followed by a capital, and the punctus elevatus as a semicolon or a query, depending on sense. For the sake of clarity for a modern reader, however, the editors have chosen to impose modern punctuation on the text.

2. Critical Apparatus

The citation order, which reflects approximately the order in which the various textual witnesses were produced, including fragments, extracts, and textual corrections in H, T, and W, is: $H_7HRBH_5LB_3AsSrWsChLwH^cAHu_2EPH_6CcMLdPlTWT^GW^GTd$-WcAl. The sigil Σ is used to designate all manuscripts but those already cited in any particular case.

When any two variant readings are witnessed by more than five manuscripts each, the full record of manuscript attestation for all variants is given in the critical apparatus. Lexical and syntactic variation is registered in the apparatus, but phonological variation usually is not; in particular, dialectal variant forms (which are registered in the scribal profiles of the various manuscripts in LALME) are not usually recorded. The following are especially common:

PDE 'against': – aȝens – aȝen – anemptes;
'alike': ilyk – ylyke – alike;
'as': as – als – also (particularly not as the first element of an 'as . . . as' comparison);
'at': at – atte (but 'atte' as a variant for 'at þe' will be noted);
'betwix' – betwixte (but 'atwix' and 'betwene' will be noted);
'either': eyþer – ouþer – oyþer – oþer (but 'or' will be noted);
'each': ilk – ech (but 'ilk a' – 'ech a' will be noted);
'-end(e)' (participial suffix): end(e) – yng(e) (but the French form '-a(u)nt' is noted);
'every': euerilk – eueriche – euery (but 'euerilk a' will be noted);
'evil': euel – yuel (but 'ill' forms will be noted);
'from': from – fro;
'-y' (adjectival suffix); -y – i – e;
'-ly' (adverbial suffix): -ly – -le;
'may': may – maist (but clearly subjunctive forms like 'might' will be noted);
'might': maist – maight – maiȝt (but clearly indicative forms like 'may' will be noted);
'much': mikel – miche;
'near': nigh – niȝ – ner (but not 'nerer', or 'neer', 'nerre' when taken to be comparative forms);
'nearer': nerre – neere – nerere (but not 'nigh', 'ner', or 'nerre' when taken to be positive forms);

'nor': ne – nor (but forms of 'neither' will be noted);
'often': oft(e) – often;
'or': or – oþer;
'saw': seyen – seyȝen – sawe – seen (when the latter is not clearly a present-tense form);
'shall': schal – ssal – schul;
'since': syþen – sethen – seþþe – syn – sen (but variants of the form 'syþen þat' – 'syn þat' will be noted);
'these': þise – þese (but variants of the form 'þose' will be noted).

Superscript numbers in the lemmata relate to the occurrence of the word indicated within the line. For the sake of clarity, variations in capitalization (e.g. 'The' as the first word of a sentence, or 'the' as a succeeding word) are counted as repeated occurrences of the same word; varying spellings of the same word in a given line (e.g. 'eiþer' – 'eyther') are counted as separate words.

Variants are listed in the order of their level of difference from the lemma (e.g. 'invisible' before 'unseeable', 'unseeable' before 'unable to be seen'). Latin variants are listed last. Verbal variations are listed before additions, additions before the lemma (*prec.*) are listed before those after (*add.*), and additions and variations before omissions. When there are variations both to a phrase and to individual words within the phrase, the full-phrase variations are listed before the word variants.

Additions to the base manuscripts are marked `addition´ in the text, and corrections over erasure ⌜correction⌝; the precise nature of these emendations, and of cancellations in the base manuscripts (whether by expunction, erasure, or striking-out) are noted in the critical apparatus. Additions, corrections over erasure, and cancellations in other manuscripts are noted in the apparatus in the same way, but without specifying whether they are expunctions, erasures, etc. When an addition or correction in a manuscript is identical to the reading of the critical text, the lemma is marked so (e.g. ` . . . ´, ⌜. . .⌝) in the apparatus. When a variant addition or correction is made to the reading of the text, but is not considered to be the authoritative reading of the text, the variant is marked (as, e.g., when the word 'of' is added to 'maner' in one manuscript or more: maner] `of´ *add.* MS X). In similar cases where a variant reading is an addition or correction in one manuscript, but other readings have that variant as well, it is the sigil of the manuscript in the list of those supporting that variant that is marked (as: maner] of *add.* MS_1`MS_2´MS_3).

Additions and corrections marked *s.h.* (same hand), particularly in H, designate corrections clearly made in the hand of the primary scribe, rather than a later corrector. All corrections made in H that cannot be clearly identified as by the scribe will be identified simply as H^c. Because of the large number of omissions, additions, and corrections made by the original scribe in MS Lw, alterations to its text are not be noted.

Variations in the spelling or location (textual, interlinear, or marginal) of the scriptural citations given in MSS B, L, Hu_2, E, P, Ld, and T, and the printed edition W are not noted.

Variations of the Latin text of *Scale* II from the English critical text are noted in the critical apparatus; when they give evidence of the possible agreement of the English text from which the Latin translation was made with textual variants among the English manuscripts, they are discussed in the Explanatory Notes as well. Variations of the Latin text from the English textual tradition that appear to demonstrate revision of Hilton's text by the translator are discussed in the Explanatory Notes, but not necessarily registered in the apparatus. Generally, minor verbal variations are registered in the apparatus, and more extensive variations are discussed in the Explanatory Notes.

The following conventions have been used:

]	a single square bracket separates the lemma from the variants
,	a comma separates variants to the same lemma
add.	added
back	the end of a long omission (e.g. missing folios) in a given manuscript
canc.	cancelled, either by subpunction or by crossing through
canc. seq.	cancellation following
corr.	corrected
corr. fr.	corrected from
d.h.	different hand
eras.	erased
gl.	glossed

Lat.	The reading of Fishlake's Latin version of *Scale* II
marked for rev.	the words are written in order stated but marked for reversal
om.	omitted
rev.	the word order is reversed
s.h.	same hand
`. . .´	insertion above the line or in the margin
⟨. . .⟩	letters or words cropped or otherwise illegible and restored editorially on the basis of other manuscripts
[. . .]	editorial alteration to the base text
/	separates elements reversed in a variant reading

BIBLIOGRAPHY

EDITIONS OF *THE SCALE OF PERFECTION*

The Scale of Perfection by Walter Hilton, Canon of Thurgarton, Newly Edited from MS. Sources with an Introduction, ed. Evelyn Underhill (London, 1923).

'The Scale of Perfection by Walter Hilton, Canon at the Augustinian Priory of Thurgarton: Book I, Chapters 38–52', ed. Rosemary Birts [Dorward] (M.Litt. thesis, Oxford, 1951).

'An Edition from the Manuscripts of Book 2 of Walter Hilton's *Scale of Perfection*', ed. S. S. Hussey (Ph.D. thesis, London, 1962).

Walter Hilton: The Scale of Perfection, ed. and trans. John P. H. Clark and Rosemary Dorward (Mahwah, NJ, 1991).

Walter Hilton The Scale of Perfection, ed. Thomas H. Bestul, TEAMS Middle English Texts (Kalamazoo, 2000), http://d.lib.rochester.edu/teams/publication/bestul-hilton-scale-of-perfection.

EDITIONS OF OTHER WORKS BY WALTER HILTON (INCLUDING *SPURIA*)

A Commentary on the 'Benedictus', Edited from the Two Extant Middle English Manuscripts with Introduction, Notes, and Glossary, ed. Björn Wallner (Lund, 1957).

English Mystics of the Middle Ages, ed. Barry Windeatt (Cambridge, 1994).

An Exposition of Qui Habitat and Bonum Est, Edited from the Manuscripts with Introduction, Notes and Glossary, ed. Björn Wallner (Lund, 1954).

Minor Works of Walter Hilton, ed. Dorothy Jones (London, 1929).

The Prickynge of Love, ed. Harold Kane, Salzburg Studies in English Literature, Elizabethan & Renaissance Studies, 92:10 (Salzburg, 1983).

Two Minor Works of Walter Hilton: Eight Chapters on Perfection and Of Angels' Song, ed. Fumio Kuriyagawa and Toshiyuki Takamiya (Tokyo, 1980).

Walter Hilton's Eight Chapters on Perfection, Edited from All the Known Medieval Manuscripts, ed. Fumio Kuriyagawa (Tokyo, 1967).

Walter Hilton's Latin Writings, ed. John P. H. Clark ad Cheryl Taylor, 2 vols., Analecta Cartusiana, 124 (Salzburg, 1987).

Walter Hilton's Mixed Life, Edited from Lambeth Palace MS 472, ed. S. J.

Ogilvie-Thomson, Salzburg Studies in English Literature, Elizabethan & Renaissance Studies, 92:15 (Salzburg, 1986).

Yorkshire Writers: Richard Rolle and his Followers, ed. C. Horstmann, 2 vols. (London, 1895–6), i. 175–82 (*Angels' Song*); 264–92 (*Mixed Life*); repr. in 1 vol. with a new preface by Anne Clark Bartlett (Woodbridge, 1999).

PRIMARY SOURCES

Ancrene Wisse: A Corrected Edition of the Text in Cambridge, Corpus Christi College, MS 402, with Variants from Other Manuscripts, ed. Bella Millett and Richard Dance EETS OS 325–6 (2005–6).

Aquinas, Thomas, *Super Boethium de Trinitate*, in *Opera Omnia*, 50 (Rome, 1992).

The Book of Margery Kempe, ed. by Sanford Brown Meech and Hope Emily Allen, EETS OS 212 (1940).

The Chastising of God's Children and The Treatise of Perfection of the Sons of God, ed. Joyce Bazire and Eric Colledge (Oxford, 1957).

The Cloud of Unknowing and The Book of Privy Counselling, ed. Phyllis Hodgson, EETS OS 218 (1944).

Contemplations of the Dread and Love of God, ed. Margaret Connolly, EETS OS 303 (1993).

Deonise Hid Diuinite, and other Treatises on Contemplative Prayer Related to The Cloud of Unknowing, ed. Phyllis Hodgson, EETS OS 231 (1955).

English Mystics of the Middle Ages, ed. Barry Windeatt (Cambridge, 1994; repr. with corr. 1997).

The Fire of Love and The Mending of Life or The Rule of Living, ed. Ralph Harvey, EETS OS 106 (1896).

Flete, William, *De Remediis contra temptaciones*: Edmund Colledge and Noel Chadwick, '"Remedies over Temptations": The Third English Version of William Flete', *Archivio italiano per la storia della pietà*, 5 (Rome, 1968), 202–40; *YW*, ii. 106–23.

Guigues II le Chartreux, *Lettre sur la vie contemplative (L'échelle des moines), Douze meditacions*, ed. Edmund Colledge and James Walsh, Sources Chrétiennes, 163 (Paris, 1970).

The Holy Bible, Containing the Old and New Testaments, with the Apocryphal Books, in the Earliest English Versions, made from the Latin Vulgate by John Wycliffe and His Followers, ed. J. Forshall and F. Madden, 4 vols. (Oxford, 1850; repr. New York, 1982).

The Idea of the Vernacular: An Anthology of Middle English Literary Theory, 1280–1520, ed. Jocelyn Wogan-Browne, Nicholas Watson, Andrew Taylor, and Ruth Evans (University Park, Pa., 1999).

Iohannis de Caulibus Meditationes vitae Christi, olim S. Bonaventuro attributae, ed. M. Stallings-Taney (Turnhout, 1997).

Ives: Épitre à Severin sur la charité, Richard de Saint-Victor: Les quatres degrés de la violent charité, ed. Gervais Dumeige (Paris, 1955).

Julian of Norwich, *A Book of Showings to the Anchoress Julian of Norwich*, ed. Edmund Colledge and James Walsh (Toronto, 1978).

——— *Julian of Norwich's Revelations of Divine Love: The Shorter Version*, ed. Frances Beer, Middle English Texts, 8 (Heidelberg, 1978).

——— *The Writings of Julian of Norwich: A Vision Showed to a Devout Woman and A Revelation of Love*, ed. Nicholas Watson and Jacqueline Jenkins (University Park, Pa., 2006).

Love, Nicholas, *The Mirror of the Blessed Life of Jesus Christ: A Full Critical Edition, Based on Cambridge University Library Additional MSS 6578 and 6686 with Introduction, Notes and Glossary*, ed. Michael G. Sargent (Exeter, 2005).

The Macro Plays, ed. Mark Eccles, EETS OS 262 (1969).

Meister Eckhart: Die deutschen und lateinischen Werke, ed. J. Quint, ii (Stuttgart, 1970).

Misyn, Richard, *The Fire of Love and The Mending of Life or The Rule of Living*, ed. Ralph Harvey, EETS OS 106 (1896).

'*My Compleinte' and Other Poems*, ed. Roger Ellis (Exeter, 2001).

Piers Plowman: The A Version, ed. George Kane (London, 1960).

Piers Plowman: The B Version. Will's Visions of Piers Plowman, Do-Well, Do-Better and Do-Best. An Edition in the Form of Trinity College Cambridge MS B.15.17, Corrected and Restored from the Known Evidence, with Variant Readings, ed. George Kane and E. Talbot Donaldson (London, 1975).

Richard Rolle, *Biblical Commentaries*, trans. Robert Boenig, Salzburg Studies in English Literature: Elizabethan & Renaissance Studies, 92:13 (Salzburg, 1984).

——— *De Emendatione vitae: Eine kritische Ausgabe des lateinischen Textes von Richard Rolle, mit einer Übersetzung ins Deutsche und Untersuchungen zu den lateinischen und englischen Handschriften*, ed. Rüdiger Spahl (Bonn, 2009).

——— *Form of Living*, in *English Writings of Richard Rolle, Hermit of Hampole*, ed. Hope Emily Allen (Oxford, 1931).

——— *Prose and Verse, Edited from MS Longleat 29 and Related Manuscripts*, ed. S. J. Ogilvie-Thomson, EETS OS 293 (1988).

——— *Uncollected Prose and Verse with Related Northern Texts*, ed. Ralph Hanna, EETS OS 329 (2007).

Richard of St-Victor, *Benjamin Major*, *PL* 196: 63–202.

——— *Benjamin Minor*, *PL* 196: 1–94. For the Middle English version in the *Cloud*-corpus, see *Deonise*, 12–46.

——— *De Quatuor gradibus violentae charitatis*, in *Ives: Épitre à Severin sur la charité, Richard de Saint-Victor: Les quatres degrés de la violent charité*, ed. Gervais Dumeige (Paris, 1955); *PL* 196: 1211.

William of Saint-Thierry, *Lettre aux frères du Mont-Dieu* (*Lettre d'or*), ed. Jean Déchanet, OSB, Sources Chrétiennes, 223 (Paris, 1975).

Women's Writing in Middle English, ed. Alexandra Barratt (London, 1992).

SECONDARY LITERATURE

Allen, Hope Emily, *Writings Ascribed to Richard Rolle, Hermit of Hampole, and Materials for his Bibliography* (New York, 1927; repr. New York, 1966).

Arbesmann, Rudolph, 'The Concept of "Christus Medicus" in St. Augustine', *Traditio*, 10 (1954), 1–28.

Aston, Margaret, *Thomas Arundel: A Study of Church Life in the Reign of Richard II* (Oxford, 1967).

Aungier, G. J., *The History and Antiquities of Syon Monastery* (London, 1840).

Bell, David N., *What Nuns Read: Books and Libraries in Medieval English Nunneries* (Kalamazoo, 1995).

Bliss, A. J., 'Two Hilton Manuscripts in Columbia University Library', *MÆ* 38 (1969), 157–63.

Bloomfield, M. W., *The Seven Deadly Sins: An Introduction to the History of a Religious Concept, with Special Reference to Medieval English Literature* (East Lansing, Mich., 1952).

Bose, Mishtooni, 'Reginald Pecock's Vernacular Voice', in Fiona Somerset, Jill C. Havens, and Derrick G. Pitard (eds.), *Lollards and their Influence in Late Medieval England* (Woodbridge, Suffolk, 2003), 217–36.

Brantley, Jessica, *Reading in the Wilderness: Private Devotion and Public Performance in Late Medieval England* (Chicago, 2007).

Bricquet, C. M., *Les Filigranes: Dictionnaire historique des marques du paper dès leur apparition vers 1282 jusqu'en 1600 . . . A Facsimile of the 1907 Edition with Supplementary Material Contributed by a Number of Scholars*, ed. Allan Stevenson (Amsterdam, 1968).

Brown, Peter, and Higgs, Elton D., *IMEP Handlist V: British Library, Additional MSS 10001–14000* (Cambridge, 1988), 39–41; *MWM* (accessed 29 June 2016).

Butler, Cuthbert, *Western Mysticism: The Teaching of SS. Augustine, Gregory, and Bernard on Contemplation and the Contemplative Life*, 2nd edn. (London, 1926).

Chodorow, Stanley, *Christian Political Theory and Church Politics in the Mid-Twelfth Century: The Ecclesiology of Gratian's "Decretum"* (Berkeley, 1972).

Christianson, C. P., *A Directory of London Stationers and Book Artisans* (New York, 1990), 91–3.

Clark, J. P. H., 'Action and Contemplation in Walter Hilton', *DR* 97 (1979), 258–74.

——— 'Augustine, Anselm, and Walter Hilton', in *MMTE* ii (Exeter, 1982), 102–26.

——— 'The "Cloud" and Walter Hilton', in *The Cloud of Unknowing: An Introduction*, 3 vols., Analecta Cartusiana, 119:4 (Salzburg, 1995), i. 86–92.

——— 'The "Cloud of Unknowing", Walter Hilton and St John of the Cross: A Comparison', *DR* 96 (1978), 281–98.

——— 'English and Latin in "The Scale of Perfection": Theological Considerations', in James Hogg (ed.), *Spiritualität Heute und Gestern*, i, Analecta Cartusiana, 35:1 (Salzburg, 1982), 167–212.

——— 'Image and Likeness in Walter Hilton', *DR* 97 (1979), 204–20.

——— 'Intention in Walter Hilton', *DR* 97 (1979), 69–80.

——— 'Late Fourteenth-Century Cambridge Theology and the English Contemplative Tradition', in *MMTE* v (Exeter, 1992), 1–16.

——— 'The "Lightsome Darkness"——Aspects of Walter Hilton's Theological Background', *DR* 95 (1977), 95–109.

——— 'Notes', in Walter *Hilton: The Scale of Perfection*, trans. John P. H. Clark and Rosemary Dorward (New York, 1991), 303–28.

——— 'The Problem of Walter Hilton's Authorship: *Bonum est*, *Benedictus* and *Of Angels' Song*', *DR* 101 (1983), 15–29.

——— 'Some Monastic Elements in Walter Hilton and in the "Cloud" Corpus', in James Hogg (ed.), *Die Kartäuser und die Reformation*, i, Analecta Cartusiana 108:1 (Salzburg, 1983), 237–57.

——— 'Thomas Maldon O.Carm., a Cambridge Theologian of the Fourteenth Century', in Patrick Fitzgerald-Lombard O.Carm. (ed.), *Carmel in Britain: Essays on the Medieval English Carmelite Province*, ii: *Writings and Theology* (Rome: Institutum Carmelitanum, 1992), 125–67.

——— 'The Trinitarian Theology of Walter Hilton's *Scale of Perfection. Book Two*', in Helen Phillips (ed.), *Langland, the Mystics and the Medieval English Religious Tradition: Essays in Honour of S. S. Hussey* (Cambridge, 1990), 125–40.

——— 'Walter Hilton in Defence of the Religious Life and of the Veneration of Images', *DR* 103 (1985), 1–25.

——— 'Walter Hilton and "Liberty of Spirit"', *DR* 96 (1978), 61–78.

——— 'Walter Hilton and the Psalm Commentary *Qui habitat*', *DR* 100 (1982), 235–62.

——— 'Walter Hilton and the *Stimulus Amoris*', *DR* 102 (1984), 79–118.

Clark, Patrick M., '"Feeling" in Walter Hilton's *Scale of Perfection*', *DR* 127 (2009), 23–48.

Colker, Marvin L., *Trinity College Library Dublin: Descriptive Catalogue of the Medieval and Renaissance Manuscripts*, i (Aldershot, 1991).

Colledge, Eric, '*The Treatise of Perfection of the Sons of God*: A Fifteenth-Century English Ruysbroec Translation', *English Studies*, 33 (1952), 49–66.

——— and Marler, J. C., '"Poverty of the Will": Ruusbroec, Eckhart and *The Mirror of Simple Souls*', in P. Mommaers and N. de Paepe (eds.), *Jan van Rusbroec: The Sources, Content and Sequels of his Mysticism* (Leuven, 1984), 14–47.

Connolly, Margaret, *IMEP Handlist XIX: Manuscripts in the University Library, Cambridge (Dd–Oo)* (Cambridge, 2009).

Copeland, Rita, *Pedagogy, Intellectuals, and Dissent in the Later Middle Ages: Lollardy and Ideas of Learning* (Cambridge, 2001).

Cré, Marleen, 'London: Westminster Cathedral Treasury, MS 4: An Edition of the Westminster Compilation', *Journal of Medieval Religious Cultures*, 37 (2011), 1–59.

——— *Vernacular Mysticism in the Charterhouse: A Study of London, British Library, MS Additional 37790*, The Medieval Translator/Traduire au moyen age, 9 (Turnhout, 2006).

Davies, J. Conway, *Catalogue of Manuscripts in the Library of the Honourable Society of the Inner Temple* (Oxford, 1972).

de Hamel, Christopher, *The Library of the Bridgettine Nuns and their Peregrinations after the Reformation* (London, 1991).

Deleuze, Gilles, *Difference and Repetition*, trans. Paul Patton (London and New York, 1994); originally published as *Différance et répétition* (Paris, 1968).

Dietz, Maribel, *Wandering Monks, Virgins, and Pilgrims* (College Park, Pa., 2005).

Doiron, Marilyn, 'Marguerite Porete: "The Mirror of Simple Souls", a Middle English Translation', *Archivio italiano per la storia della pietà* 5 (Rome, 1968), 241–355.

Doyle, A. I., 'Book Production by the Monastic Orders in England', in Linda Brownrigg (ed.), *Medieval Book Production: Assessing the Evidence* (Los Altos Hills, Calif., 1990), 1–19.

——— 'English Carthusian Books not yet Linked with a Charterhouse', in Toby Barnard, Dáibhí Ó Cróinín, and Katharine Simms (eds.), *'A Miracle of Learning': Studies in Manuscripts and Irish Learning. Essays in Honour of William O'Sullivan* (Aldershot, 1998), 122–36.

——— 'A Survey of the Origins and Circulation of Theological Writings in English in the Fourteenth, Fifteenth and Early Sixteenth Centuries, with Special Consideration of the Part of the Clergy therein' (Ph.D. thesis, University of Cambridge, 1953).

——— 'The Work of a Late Fifteenth-Century English Scribe, William Ebesham', *Bulletin of the John Rylands Library*, 39 (1957), 298–325.

Edwards, A. S. G., 'Reading John Walton's Boethius in the Fifteenth and Sixteenth Centuries', in Flannery and Griffin (eds.), *Spaces*, 35–49.

Eisermann, Falk, *Stimulus Amoris: Inhalt, lateinische Überlieferung, deutsche Übersetzungen, Rezeption* (Tübingen, 2001).

Ellis, Roger, 'The Choices of the Translator in the Late Middle English Period', in *MMTE* ii. 18–46.

Erler, Mary C., *Women, Reading, and Piety in Late Medieval England* (Cambridge, 2002).

Fanous, Samuel, and Vincent Gillespie (eds.), *The Cambridge Companion to Medieval English Mysticism* (Cambridge, 2011).

Gardner, Helen, 'The Text of "The Scale of Perfection"', *MÆ* 5 (1936), 11–30.

——— 'Walter Hilton and the Authorship of "The Cloud of Unknowing"', *Review of English Studies*, 3 (1933), 129–47.

Gillespie, Vincent, 'The Haunted Text: Ghostly Reflections in *A Mirror to Devout People*', in Jill Mann and Maura Nolan (eds.), *The Text in the Community: Essays on Medieval Works, Manuscripts, Authors, and Readers* (South Bend, Ind., 2006), 129–72.

——— 'Hilton at Syon Abbey', in James Hogg (ed.) '*Stand up to Godwards': Essays in Mystical and Monastic Theology in Honour of the Reverend John Clark on his Sixty-Fifth Birthday*, Analecta Cartusiana, 204 (Salzburg, 2002).

——— *Looking in Holy Books: Essays on Late Medieval Religious Writing in England* (Turnhout, 2011).

——— 'Vernacular Books of Religion', in Jeremy Griffiths and Derek Pearsall (eds.), *Book Production and Publishing in Britain 1375–1475* (Cambridge, 1989), 317–44.

——— and Anne Hudson (eds.), *Probable Truth: Editing Medieval Texts from Britain in the Twenty-First Century* (Turnhout, 2013).

Grady, Frank, *Representing Righteous Heathens in Late Medieval England* (New York, 2005).

Guide to Medieval and Renaissance Manuscripts in the Huntington Library, ed. C. W. Dutschke (San Marino, 1989).

Haenel, Gustav, *Catalogi librorum manuscriptorum* (Leipzig, 1830).

Hanna III, Ralph, 'The Archaeology of a Manuscript: Huntington Library HM 266', *Scriptorium*, 36 (1982), 99–102.

——— 'George Kane and the Invention of Textual Thought: Retrospect and Prospect', *Yearbook of Langland Studies*, 24 (2010), 1–20.

——— 'The History of a Book: Bodleian Library, MS Rawlinson C.285', in *Introducing English Medieval Book History: Manuscripts, their Producers, and their Readers* (Liverpool, 2013), 59–95.

——— *IMEP Handlist I: Manuscripts in the Henry E. Huntington Library* (Cambridge, 1984).

——— 'Producing Manuscripts and Editions', in A. J. Minnis and Charlotte Brewer (eds.), *Crux and Controversy in Middle English Textual Criticism* (Cambridge, 1992), 109–30.

The Heads of Religious Houses: England and Wales, iii: *1377–1540*, ed. David M. Smith (Cambridge, 2008).

Horstmann, Karl, '*Orologium Sapientiae*, or *The Seven Poyntes of Trewe Wisdom* aus MS Douce 114', *Anglia*, 10 [1888], 323–89.

Hudson, Anne, *The Premature Reformation: Wycliffite Texts and Lollard History* (Oxford, 1988).

Hughes, Jonathan, *Pastors and Visionaries: Religious and Secular Life in Late Medieval Yorkshire* (Woodbridge, 1988).

Hussey, S. S., 'The Audience for the Middle English Mystics', in Michael G. Sargent (ed.), *De Cella in Seculum: Religious and Secular Life and Devotion in Late Medieval England* (Cambridge, 1989), 109–22.

——— 'Blind Trust, Naked Truth and Bare Necessities: Walter Hilton and the Author of *The Cloud of Unknowing*', in James Hogg (ed.) '*Stand up to Godwards': Essays in Mystical and Monastic Theology in Honour of the Reverend John Clark on his Sixty-Fifth Birthday*, Analecta Cartusiana, 204 (Salzburg, 2002), 1–8.

——— 'Editing the Middle English Mystics', in James Hogg (ed.), *Spiritualität Heute und Gestern*, ii, Analecta Cartusiana, 35:2 (Salzburg, 1983), 160–73.

——— 'Editing *The Scale of Perfection*: Return to Recension', in A. J. Minnis and Charlotte Brewer (eds.), *Crux and Controversy in Middle English Textual Criticism* (Cambridge, 1992), 97–107.

——— 'From *Scale* I to *Scale* II', in James Hogg (ed.), *The Mystical Tradition and the Carthusians*, iv, Analecta Cartusiana, 130:4 (Salzburg, 1995), 46–67.

——— 'Latin and English in *The Scale of Perfection*', *Mediæval Studies*, 35 (1973), 456–76.

——— 'The Text of *The Scale of Perfection*, Book II', *Neuphilologische Mitteilungen*, 65 (1964), 75–92.

——— 'Walter Hilton, Traditionalist?', in *MMTE* i (1980), 1–16.

James, M. R., *A Descriptive Catalogue of the Manuscripts in the College Libary of Magdalene College* (Cambridge, 1909).

——— *A Descriptive Catalogue of the Manuscripts in the Library of Corpus Christi College, Cambridge* (Cambridge, 1912).

——— *A Descriptive Catalogue of the Manuscripts in the Library of Lambeth Palace: Medieval Manuscripts* (Cambridge, 1932).

——— *The Western Manuscripts in the Library of Trinity College, Cambridge: A Descriptive Catalogue*, i (Cambridge, 1900).

Johnson, Ian, *The Middle English Life of Christ: Academic Discourse, Translation, and Vernacular Theology* (Turnhout, 2013).

Jolliffe, P. S., *A Check-List of Middle English Prose Writings of Spiritual Guidance* (Toronto, 1974).

——— 'Two Middle English Tracts on the Contemplative Life', *Mediæval Studies*, 37 (1975), 85–121.

Kane, George, 'Conjectural Emendation', in Christopher Kleinhenz (ed.), *Medieval Manuscripts and Textual Criticism* (Chapel Hill, NC, 1976), 211–26.

Karnes, Michelle, *Imagination, Meditation and Cognition in the Middle Ages* (Chicago, 2011).

Kerby-Fultin, Kathryn, *Books under Suspicion: Censorship and Tolerance of Revelatory Writing in Late Medieval England* (Notre Dame, Ind., 2006).

——— Hilmo, Maidie, and Olson, Linda, *Opening Up Middle English Manuscripts: Literary and Visual Approaches* (Ithaca, NY, 2012).

Knowles, David, *The Religious Orders in England*, iii: *The Tudor Age* (Cambridge, repr. with corrections, 1971).

Krochalis, Jeanne Elizabeth, '*Contemplations of the Dread and Love of God*: Two Newly Identified Pennsylvania Manuscripts', *Library Chronicle*, 42 (1977), 3–22.

Lacey, Helen, *The Royal Pardon: Access to Mercy in Fourteenth-Century England* (Woodbridge, 2009).

Lerner, Robert, *The Heresy of the Free Spirit in the Later Middle Ages* (Notre Dame, Ind., 1972).

Lewis, Robert E., and McIntosh, Angus, *A Descriptive Guide to the Manuscripts of the* Prick of Conscience, *Medium Ævum* Monographs, NS 12 (Oxford, 1982).

Lovatt, Roger, 'Henry Suso and the Medieval Mystical Tradition in England', *MMTE* 2 (1982), 47–62.

Lubac, Henri de, *Medieval Exegesis: The Four Senses of Scripture*, trans. Marc Sebanc and E. M. Macierowski (Grand Rapids, Mich., 1998–2009; originally published as *Exégèse médiévale: Les quatre sens de l'écriture* (Paris, 1959–69)).

Lyotard, Jean-François, *The Postmodern Condition: A Report on Knowledge*, trans. Geoff Bennington and Brian Massumi (Minneapolis, 1984; originally published as *La Condition postmoderne: Rapport sur le savoir* (Paris, 1979).

McGann, Jerome, *A New Republic of Letters: Memory and Scholarship in the Age of Digital Reproduction* (Cambridge, Mass., 2014).

——— 'The Rationale of HyperText', www2.iath.virginia.edu/public/jjm2f/rationale.html, accessed 28 Nov. 2015.

McGinn, Bernard, 'Introduction: The Ordering of Charity', in *The Presence of God: A History of Western Christian Mysticism*, ii: *The Growth of*

Mysticism: Gregory the Great through the 12th Century (New York, 1996), 149–57.

—— *The Varieties of Vernacular Mysticism, 1350–1550*, The Presence of God: A History of Western Christian Mysticism, 5 (New York, 2012).

McGrath, Alister E., *Iustitia Dei: A History of the Christian Doctrine of Justification*, 3rd edn. (Cambridge, 2005).

Marchand, James W., 'An Unidentified Latin Quote in *Piers Plowman*', *Modern Philology*, 88 (1991), 398–400.

Minnis, Alastair, 'Affection and Imagination in "The Cloud of Unknowing" and Hilton's "Scale of Perfection"', *Traditio*. 39 (1983), 323–66.

—— '*The Cloud of Unknowing* and Walter Hilton's *Scale of Perfection*', in A. S. G. Edwards (ed.), *Middle English Prose: A Critical Guide to Major Authors and Genres* (New York, 1984), 61–81.

Mooney, Linne R., *IMEP Handlist XI: Manuscripts in the Library of Trinity College, Cambridge* (Cambridge, 1995).

Mulligan, R., '"Ratio Superior and Ratio Inferior": The Historical Background', *New Scholasticism*, 29 (1955), 1–32.

Ogilvie-Thomson, S. J., *IMEP Handlist VIII: Manuscripts in Oxford College Libraries* (Cambridge, 1991).

Patterson, Lee, 'The Logic of Textual Criticism and the Way of Genius: The Kane-Donaldson *Piers Plowman* in Historical Perspective', in Jerome McGann (ed.), *Textual Criticism and Literary Interpretation* (Chicago, 1985), 55-91; repr. in *Negotiating the Past: The Historical Understanding of Medieval Literature* (Madison, Wis., 1987), 77–113.

Pickering, O. S., and O'Mara, V. M., *IMEP Handlist XIII: Manuscripts in Lambeth Palace Library* (Cambridge, 1999).

Rahner, Karl, 'Some Implications of the Scholastic Concept of Uncreated Grace', *Theological Investigations*, 1 (London, 1961), 319–46.

Rand, Kari Anne, *IMEV Handlist XX: Corpus Christi College, Cambridge* (Cambridge, 2009).

Rice, Nicole, *Lay Piety and Religious Discourse in Middle English Literature* (Cambridge, 2008).

Rollins, Hyder E., 'No Wight in this World that Wealth Can Attain', *RES* 5 (1929), 56–79.

Ross, Ellen M., 'Ethical Mysticism: Walter Hilton and the *Scale of Perfection*', *Studia Mystica*, 17 (1996), 160–83.

—— 'Submission or Fidelity? The Unity of the Church and Mysticism in Walter Hilton's *Scale of Perfection*', *DR* 106 (1988), 134–44.

—— 'The Use of Scripture and the Spiritual Journey in Walter Hilton's *Scale of Perfection*', *Augustiniana*, 89 (1989), 80–9.

Russell-Smith, Joy, 'Walter Hilton and a Tract in Defence of the Veneration of Images', *Dominican Studies*, 7 (1954), 180–214.

Samuels, M. L., 'Some Applications of Middle English Dialectology', in

Margaret Laing (ed.), *Middle English Dialectology: Essays on Some Principles and Problems* (Aberdeen, 1989), 64–80.

Sargent, Michael G., 'Affective Reading and Walter Hilton's *Scale of Perfection* at Syon', paper presented at the conference 'Reading and Writing in City, Court, and Cloister', Fordham University, 7 March 2015; to be published in the proceedings.

——— 'Bishops, Patrons, Mystics, and Manuscripts: Walter Hilton, Nicholas Love, and the Arundel and Holland Connections', in Simon Horobin and Linne R. Mooney (eds.), *Middle English Texts in Transition: A Festschrift Dedicated to Toshiyuki Takamiya on his 70th Birthday* (York, 2014), 159–76.

——— 'Editing Walter Hilton's *Scale of Perfection*', in Gillespie and Hudson (eds.), *Probable Truth*, 509–34.

——— *James Grenehalgh as Textual Critic*, 2 vols., Analecta Cartusiana, 85 (Salzburg, 1984).

——— 'Marguerite Porete', in Alastair Minnis and Rosalynn Voaden (eds.), *Medieval Holy Women in the Christian Tradition, c. 1100–c.1500* (Turnhout, 2010), 291–309.

——— 'A New Manuscript of *The Chastising of God's Children* with an Ascription to Walter Hilton', *MÆ* 46 (1977), 49–65.

——— 'Organic and Cybernetic Metaphors for Manuscript Relations: Stemma — Cladogram — Rhizome — Cloud', in Ian Johnson and Alan F. Westphall (eds.), *The Pseudo-Bonaventuran Lives of Christ: Exploring the Middle English Tradition* (Turnhout, 2013), 197–255.

——— 'The Organization of *The Scale of Perfection*', in *MMTE* ii (Exeter, 1982), 231–61.

——— 'Thomas Fishlake's *Scala Perfectionis*: The Agenda of the Translator', paper presented at the conference 'Origins of the Vernacular Mode: The XI Cardiff Conference on the Theory and Practice of Translation in the Middle Ages', Universität Wien, 15–18 Mar. 2017.

——— 'The Transmission by the English Carthusians of Some Late Medieval Spiritual Writings', *Journal of Ecclesiastical History*, 27 (1976), 225–40.

——— 'Walter Hilton on the Gift of Interpretation of Scripture', in *MMTE* viii (Woodbridge, 2013), 51–8.

——— 'Walter Hilton's Affective Turn', paper presented at the conference '"This Tretice, by me compiled": Late Medieval Devotional Compilations in England', Université de Lausanne, Switzerland, 31 Mar.–2 Apr. 2016.

——— 'Walter Hilton's *Scale of Perfection* in Continental Europe in the Fifteenth and Sixteenth Centuries', *Textus: English Studies in Italy*, 24 (2011), 463–76.

——— 'Walter Hilton's *Scale of Perfection* in Devotional Compilations', in Marleen Cré, Diana Dinessen, and Denis Renevey (eds.), *This Tretice, by me Compiled: Late Medieval Devotional Compilations in England* (Turnhout, in press).

——— 'Walter Hilton's *Scale of Perfection*: The London Manuscript Group Reconsidered', *MÆ* 52 (1983), 189–216.

Sawyer, Daniel, 'Navigation by Tab and Thread: Place-Markers and Readers' Movement in Books', in Flannery and Griffin (eds.), *Spaces for Reading*, 99–114.

Scase, Wendy, 'Reginald Pecock, John Carpenter and John Colop's "Common-Profit" Books: Aspects of Book Ownership and Circulation in Fifteenth-Century London', *MÆ* 61 (1992), 263–74.

Somerset, Fiona, *Feeling like Saints: Lollard Writings after Wyclif* (Ithaca, NY, 2015).

——— 'Wycliffite Spirituality', in Helen Barr and Ann M. Hutchison (eds.), *Text and Controversy from Wyclif to Bale: Essays in Honour of Anne Hudson* (Turnhout, 2005), 375–86.

Southern, R. W., *Saint Anselm and his Biographer: A Study of Monastic Life and Thought, 1059–c. 1130* (Cambridge, 1963).

Stegmüller, F., *Repertorium biblicum medii aevi*, 1–11 (Madrid, 1950–80).

Swales, Lois, and Blatt, Heather, 'Tiny Textiles Hidden in Books: Toward a Categorization of Multiple-Stand Bookmarkers', in Robin Netherton and Gale R. Owen-Crocker (eds.), *Medieval Clothing and Textiles*, 3 (2007), 145–79.

Swanson, R. N. *Indulgences in Late Medieval England: Passports to Paradise* (Cambridge, 2011).

Takamiya, Toshiyuki, 'A Handlist of Western Medieval Manuscripts in the Takamiya Collection', in James H. Marrow, Richard A. Linenthal, and William Noel (eds.), *The Medieval Book: Glosses from Friends and Colleagues of Christopher de Hamel* (Houten, 2010), 421–40.

——— 'A Hilton Manuscript Once in the Possession of Luttrell Wynne', *The Book Collector* (Special Number for the 150th Anniversary of Bernard Quaritch, 1997), repr. in *The Pleasures of Bibliophyly: Fifty Years of the Book Collector, An Anthology* (London, 2003), 305–10.

Walther, Hans, *Lateinische Sprichwörter und Sentenzen des Mittelalters in alphabetischer Anordnung*, 6 vols. (Göttingen: Vandenhoeck and Ruprecht, 1963–9).

Watson, Andrew G., *A Descriptive Catalogue of the Medieval Manuscripts of All Souls College Oxford* (Oxford, 1997).

Watson, Nicholas, '"Et que est huius ydoli materia? Tuipse": Idols and Images in Walter Hilton', in Jeremy Dimmick, James Simpson, and Nicolette Zeeman (eds.), *Images, Idolatry, and Iconoclasm in Late Medieval England* (Oxford, 2005), 95–111.

——— 'The Middle English Mystics', in David Wallace (ed.), *The*

Cambridge History of Medieval English Literature (Cambridge, 1999), 539–65.

——— *Richard Rolle and the Invention of Authority* (Cambridge, 1991).

——— 'Visions of Inclusion: Universal Salvation and Vernacular Theology in Pre-Reformation England', *Journal of Medieval and Early Modern Studies*, 27 (1997), 145–87.

Yoshikawa, Naoë Kukita, *Margery Kempe's Meditations: The Context of Medieval Devotional Literature, Liturgy and Iconography* (Cardiff, 2007).

Zacour, Norman, and Hirsch, Rudolph, *Catalogue of Manuscripts in the Libraries of the University of Pennsylvania to 1800* (Philadelphia, 1965).

THE SCALE OF PERFECTION
BOOK II

f. 43v þat man is seide þe ymage of God after þe soule and nought after ⌜þe⌝ bodi. ⌜Capitulum primum⌝

For as mikel as þou coueytest gretli and aske[st] it per charite for to heren more of an ymage þe whilk I haue before-tymes in partie descry[u]ed to þe, þerfor I wil gladdeli with drede falle to þi desire and, helpend þe grace of oure Lord Jesu Crist in qwhom I fulli trist, I schal open to þe a litil more of þis ymage. And in þe byginnyng, if þou wilt wyte pleinli qwhat I mene be þise ymage, I tel þe forsoth þat I vnderstond nought elles but þin owen soule. For þi soule and my
f. 44r soule and ilk | a resonable soule is an ymage, and þat a worth[i] ymage, for it is þe ymage of God as þe Apostel seith: *Vir est ymago Dei*. þat is: Man is þe ymage of God and made to þe ymage and þe likenesse of him; nought in bodily schapp withouten but in þe mightes of it withinnen, as Holy Writ seith: *Formauit Deus hominem ad ymaginem et similitudinem suam*. þat is: Oure Lord God schope man in soule to [þe ymage and þe likenesse of him. þis is] þe ymage þat I haue spoken of and schal speken of.

þis ymage made to þe ymage of God in þe ferst schapyng was wonderli faire and bright, ful of brennyng loue and gostli light, but þurgh sinne of þe ferst man Adam it was disfigured and forschapen into anoþer likenesse, as I haue before saide. For it felle fro þe gostli

title/rubric: *No title* H$_7$H$^{\circ}$RBLB$_3$AsSrChLwAEPH$_6$CcLdPl Incipit secunda pars H$_5$ Incipit secunda pars libri qui vocatur Scala Perfectionis Ws Incipit liber secundus H^c Here byginnyþ þe secunde parte Hu$_2$ This book þat folweth may skilfully be cleped the scole of perfeccion. For who-so wele rede besily and vnderstonde spedfully the matier that here folweth may haue ful techyng how he shal mowe comen to gostly felyng and to swetnesse of contemplacion, ȝif his wille be stable and feruent to conne loue our Lord Crist Jesu. For wheche loue alle men and wemmen nyght and day shuld trauayle, and namelych religious wheche be wordus of profession haue forsake all þe world and outward beth clothed with a dedly habq ite þat semyth contemplatyf or ful of perfeccion M Here bigynnith þe secunde booke of Maister Walter Hilton T Here after folowyth the seconde boke of mayster Walter Hylton W

Chapter 1 *title*: H$_7$RLB$_3$AsSr`H^{c}´AEPH$_6$CcMLdPlTW *om.* H$^{\circ}$BH$_5$WsChLwHu$_2$ 1 þat] þis chapitle schewiþ *prec.* LB$_3$SrP, The firste chapitule schewiþ *prec.* H$_6$, Hou H^{c}M man] H$_7$SrH$_6$M, a *prec.* H$_5$WsHu$_2$LdTW, þe soule of euery ryȝful man H^c seide] made M, *om.* H^{c}LdTW þe[1]] *om.* RM after[1] . . . bodi] *om.* H^c þe[2]] his RSrAsMPl and . . . bodi] *om.* H$_6$ 2 þe] his SrM 3 þou . . . to þe (l. 5)] many men for ful knowyng desire to here of this glorious ymge M askest] asketh H$_7$ per] H$_7$HSrChLw, pur LB$_3$P, for RBAsAPlH$_5$WsLdHu$_2$H$_6$TW for] *om.* H$_6$ 4 an] þat T before-tymes] bifortime AH$_6$ in partie] in alio libro in parte Lat. 5 þerfor] to the worship of God *add.* M I wil/gladdeli] *rev.* M with drede] *om.* M þi] hure M 6 and . . . þe] be helping and M and] with Cc helpend] wiþ þe help and H$_6$ of] God *add.* T Lord] *om.* R in . . .

3r ⌜INCIPIT LIBER SECUNDUS⌝

[CHAPTER I]

For as mykel as þou coueites gretly and askes it per charitee for to here more of an ymage þe whilk I haue bifore tymes in partie discried to þe, þerfore I wil gladly with drede falle to þi desire, and helpand þe grace of oure Lord Ihesu Crist in whom I fully triste, I shal open to þe a litil more of þis ymage. At þe bigynnyng, if þu wil wite pleynly what I mene bi þis ymage, I telle þe for soþe þat I vndirstonde noȝt elles bot þin owne soule. For þi soule and my soule and ilk a resonable soule is an ymage, and þat a worþi ymage, for it is þe ymage of God as þe apostel sais: *Vir est imago Dei*. Þat es: Man es þe ymage of God and made to þe ymage and to þe liknes of hym. Noȝt in þe bodili schape withouten bot in þe miȝtes of it within, as Holy Writ says: *Formauit Deus hominem ad ymaginem et similitudinem suam*. Þat is: Oure Lord God schope man in soule to his owne ymage and liknes. Þis is þe ymage þat I haue spokyn of.

Þis ymage made to þe image of God in þe first schapynge was wnderly faire and briȝt, ful of brennande loue and gostly liȝt, bot þorw
3v synne | of þe first man Adam it was disfigured and forschapyn into anoþer liknes, as I haue bifore said. For it fel fro þat goostly liȝt and þat heuenly fode into pynful mirknes and lust of þis wrecchid liif,

trist] *om.* T   in qwhom] þat *add.* Sr   7 þe[1] . . . ymage] hem fully as I fele of this matier M   And in . . . ymage (l. 8)] *om.* A   And in] H$_7$RLB$_3$AsSrPH$_6$MPl, At HBH$_5$WsChLwHu$_2$ECcLdTW, Et in Lat.   byginnyng] be thow man be thow woman, in what maner degree *add.* M   8 pleinli/qwhat I mene] *rev.* H$_6$ \`þe´ *marg.* R   9 þin owen] *om.* T   10 ilk a] eueri LB$_3$PH$_6$MPl, ech a As   and[2] . . . ymage[1] (l. 11)] *om.* BLd   a worthi ymage[1] (l. 11)] worthy Cc   worthi] worth H$_7$ 11 for . . . ymage[2]] *om.* T   seith] 1 Cor. 11 *add.* Hu$_2$ 12 is[1]] *om.* A, to saye *add.* H$_5$WsW   Man] A *prec.* RAsLwAW   ymage and þe] *om.* H$_6$ and þe] H$_7$RH$_5$WsAPlT, and AsM, and to þe HBLB$_3$SrChLwHu$_2$EPCcLdW   13 in[1]] þe *add.* HBChHu$_2$ELwW   withouten] outewarde E   14 of it] *above line* Pl   withinnen] *om.* T   seith] techeth and *prec.* M, Ge. 2° *add.* LHu$_2$ELdT   15 ymaginem et] *om.* LB$_3$PH$_6$Cc   et] ad *add.* Ld   þat] This T   is] to say *add.* H$_5$WsE   schope] formed T   man/in soule] *rev.* LB$_3$PH$_6$ man] a *prec.* SrM   16 in] his *add.* W   þe ymage . . . is] *om.* H$_7$ þe ymage . . . of him] RLB$_3$AsSrAPH$_6$CcMPl, his owne ymge and liknes HBH$_5$WsChLwHu$_2$LdTW   and þe] and to þe add. B$_3$SrM, and E   þis is . . . speken of (l. 17)] *om.* T   þis] þat ChHu$_2$ 17 and schal speken of] H$_7$LB$_3$SrPH$_6$M, *om.* HBH$_5$AsWsChLwHu$_2$ECcLdW, et de qua adhuc dicere plus intendo Lat.   18 ymage[1]] is *add.* T   ymage[2]] liknesse LB$_3$PH$_6$M\`W^{G}´   was] it *prec.* ChHu$_2$ 19 wonderli] wondirful H$_5$B$_3$Ws, wondur M   20 it] is Ws   21 before saide] *rev.* H$_6$ þe] H$_7$RAsSrLwACcPl, þat HBH$_5$LB$_3$WsChHu$_2$EPH$_6$MLdTW light and þat heuenli fode into peynful mirknesse and bestli lust of þis wrecchede lyf, exiled and flemed out fro þe heritage of heuen þat it schuld haue had if it hadde stonden, into þe wrecchednes of þis erth and afterward into þe prison of helle, þer for to haue ben withouten ende; fro þe wilk prison to þat heuenli heritage it might neuer haue comen ageyn but if it had be reformed to þe ferst schap and to þe ferst likenesse. But þat reformyng might be made be non erdli man, for euerylk man was in þat same mischef, and non might sufficen to helpen himself, and so mikel lesse ony oþer man. Þerfore it neded be done be him þat is more þan a man, and þat is oneli God. And þat was skilful þat he schuld reformen and restoren man to blisse if he schuld be safe, wilk of ⌜hise⌝ endeles gudnes first schop him þerto. How þan it might be reformed, and how it is reformed to þe first liknesse be him þat first formed it, be þe grace of God schal I tel þe, for þat is þe entent of þis writyng.

How it neded to mankende þat only þurgh þe passion of our Lord Jesu Crist it schulde be restor`e´de and reformed þat was forsaken be þe first sinne. Capitulum ii^{m}

T[h]e rig[ht]wysnes of God asketh þat a trespas don be not forgyfen but if amendes be made for it if it may be don. Now is þis soth, mankend, þat was hole in Adam þe first man, trespased ageynes God so wonder greuously whan it forfetid þe special biddynge of him and
f. 44^{v} sentid to þe fals counseil of þe fende, þat it deseruede | rightfulli for

22 and[1]] in Sr, *om.* T þat] *om.* B into] þe *add.* REH$_6$Cc, þat *add.* LB$_3$P peynful] of *add.*, *canc.* As mirknesse] H$_7$HRAsSrChHu$_2$CcMPl, derknesse BH$_5$B$_3$WsLwAELdTW bestli] H$_7$RLB$_3$AsSrAPH$_6$CcM, *om.* HBH$_5$WsChLwHu$_2$LdTW, bestialem Lat. 23 lyf] love Lw fro þe] of A heritage] habitage Sr 24 had] *om.* A stonden] stille *add.* Lw`H$^{c}$´ETW [*one-word canc. seq.* H], and not fallen *add.* T, but it fel *add.* M þis] þe H$_5$Ws 25 þe] *om.* Lw for] H$_7$RBAsSrChAHu$_2$MLdPl, *om.* HH$_5$LB$_3$Ws-LwEPH$_6$CcLdTW `haue´ Pl 26 fro] for H$_5$ þe wilk] this wikkyd Cc to þat . . . heritage] *om.* Ws þat] þe E 27 if] *om.* Ld reformed] aȝeyn *add.* H$_5$Ws þe ferst[1]] *om.* Cc to þe[2]] H$_7$LB$_3$PH$_6$, þe Σ, *om.* E 28 might] H$_7$RAsSrH$_6$M, not *add.* HBH$_5$LB$_3$WsChLwAHu$_2$EPCcLdPlTW, *canc.* Pl made] had LB$_3$PH$_6$Cc, had nor made Hu$_2$, fieri non poterit Lat. non] other *add.* M 29 þat] H$_7$RAsSrPl, þe HBH$_5$LB$_3$WsChLwHu$_2$PH$_6$CcLdTW 30 helpen] oþer *add.* T, liberare . . . uel iuuare Lat. so mikel lesse] muche lesse þanne H$_5$Ws mikel] þe *add.* A ony oþer] anoþer TW neded] nedeth H$_5$ChLwHu$_2$W be] H$_7$HBLB$_3$SrChHu$_2$EP, to be RH$_5$AsWsLwAH$_6$CcMLdPlTW 31 a man] any man erþlyche H$_5$Ws a] *om.* LwCcLdW and[1]] *om.* W 32 þat] *om.* B$_3$H$_6$Cc blisse] þe *prec.* Pl 33 be safe] sauyn hym Sr wilk] þat SrM hise] þis Ch first] *om.* LB$_3$APH$_6$W þan/it might be] *rev.* As þan] þat M, *om.* H$_6$ 34 might] *om.* Sr and . . . reformed] *om.* AM first] *om.* W 35 þe] *om.* B God] oure Lord *prec.* Hu$_2$ schal I] *rev.*

exiled and flemed oute fro þe heritage of heuen þat it schuld haue had if it had stonden, into þe wrecchednesse of þis erþe and afterward into þe prisoun of helle, þer to haue ben wiþouten ende; fro þe whilk prisoun to þat heuenly heritage it miȝt neuer haue comen agayn bot if it had ben reformed to þe first schap and þe first liknes. Bot þat reformyng miȝt not be mad bi none erþely man, for euerilke man was in þe same meschief, and non miȝt suffice to help hymself, and so mikel lesse ony oþer man. Þerfore it nedid be don bi hym þat is more þen a man, and þat is only God. And þat was skilful þat he schuld reforme and restore man to blis if he schuld be sauf, whilk of his eendles goodnes first schope hym þerto. How þan it miȝt be reformed, and how it is reformid to þe first liknes bi hym þat first formed it, bi þe grace of God schal I telle þee, for þat is þe entent of þis writynge.

[CHAPTER 2]

Þe riȝtwisnes of God askes þat a trespas don be not forgifen bot if amendes be maad for it if it may be don. Now is it soþe, mankynde, þat was hol in Adam þe first man, trespassid agayns God so wonder greuously whan it forfetid þe special biddyng of hym and sentid to þe fals conseil of þe fend, þat it deseruid riȝtfully for to haue ben departid fro hym and dampned to helle wiþouten ende, so fer forþe

H_5WsLwHu$_2$$H_6$CcMW for . . . writynge (l. 36)] *om.* Sr þat[2]] it As 36 writyng] at this tyme *add.* Cc

Chapter 2 *title*: H_7RLB_3AsSrAEPH_6CcMLdPlTW ˋHou þe riȝtwisnes of God wole not þat a trespas be forȝouen but if ame[n]dis be made.ˊ H^c *om.* H°BH_5WsChLwHu$_2$ 1 it[1]] *om.* R, is *add.*, *del.* Pl neded] nedeþ AsCcMLd ˋþatˊ E þe] *om.* Pl our Lord Jesu Crist] H_7SrCcM, Christ RAsAELdPlTW, oure Lord LB_3PH_6 2 ˋitˊ L, *om.* LdT restored and reformed] *rev.* H_6 3 forsaken] H_7LB_3SrPH_6, forschapen RAsAELdPlTW, transformata Lat. sinne] of Adam *add.* Cc ii[m]] Capitulum primum B, *and so one number off for the remainder of the text* 4 The] Te H_7, *om.* A, ˋNow schal I telle þe howˊ *prec.* H^c rightwisnes] rigwisnes H_7, ryȝtfulnesse Ld of God] *om.* RAsAPl 5 if[1]] *om.* H_5SrWs made] had Ld if it may be don] *om.* H_5Ws is þis soth] soth hit is A is þis] H_7 it is, BChHu$_2$CcMLdW, is it Σ soth] so Sr, þat *add.* As 6 hole] et incorrupta *add.* Lat. man] *om.* B, þat *add.* As 7 wonder] *om.* Cc greuously] grymly M whan] þat Ws it] H_7HBH_5WsLwCcMLdTW, he RLB_3AsSrChAHu$_2$EPH_6Pl him] God LB_3PH_6, eius Lat. 8 sentid] H_7HRBAsLwPl, asentyde H_5WsAHu$_2$CcMLdTW, consentide LB_3PH_6, ˋconˊsentid Ch to . . . of] *om.* Lat. þat] so þat H_5Ws it] he ChHu$_2$Cc rightfulli] riȝtwisli LB_3PH_6, be ryght M for to haue] to H_5Ws, for to MT, to haue H_6

to haue ben departid fro him and dampned to helle withouten ende, so ferforth þat, standend þe rightwysnesse of God, þe trespas might nought be forgyfen but if amendes and ful satisfaccion wer first mad þerfore.

But þis amendes might no man make þat was man only and come out of Adam be kendly generacioun, for þis skil: for þe trespas and þe vnwirschepe was endles grete, and þerfore it passed mannes might for to make amendes for it. And also for þis skil: he þat trespast and schal make amendes, him behoueth gyf to him þat he trespast vnto al þat he oweth þow he had nought trespast, and also ouer þat him behoueth gyfe sumqwat þat he owe not, but only for þat he trespast. Bot mankende had nought qwerewith [þat] he might payen God for hise trespas ouer þat he awght him, for qwhate gode dede þat man might don in bodi or in soule, it was bot his dette. For euerilk man oweth, as þe Gospel seith, for to loue God with al hise herte and al his soule and al his mightes, and bettre might he not don þan þis. And neuerþeles þis dede sufficed nought to þe reformynge of mankynde, ne þis might he not don bot if he had ben first reformed.

þan nedid þat if man[nys] soule schulde be reformed and þe trespase mad good, þat oure Lord God himself schuld reforme þis ymage and make amendis for þis trespase, syþen þat no man might. Bot þat might he nought don in his godhede, for he might nought ne awght nought make amendis be suffryng of pyne in his owen kynde. þerfor it nedid þat he schuld take þe same mankynde þat had trespast and become man; and þat might he nought be commine lawe of kendli generacion, for it was inpossible Goddis sone to be born of a touched

10 þe trespas] H_7RLB_3AsSrPH_6Cc, it HBH_5WsChLwAHu_2EPlTW, delictum illud Lat. 11 amendes] were *add.*, *canc.* L and . . . satisfaccion/wer . . . mad] *rev.* LwW ful] *om.* Lat. first mad] *rev.* B_3AsLd first] *om.* AM 13 was man/only] *rev.* H_5Ws, was [`man´ Hu_2] only ChHu_2 and] was *add.* T come] cam M 14 of] *rep.* L skil] reson Hu_2 for] *om.* Hu_2, bothe *add.* Cc and þe vnwirschepe] *canc.* Cc þe[2]] H_7RBLB_3AsSrAPH_6CcPl, *om.* HH_5WsChLwHu_2MLdTW 15 mannes] *rep.*, *canc.* L 16 it] þat Sr And] *om.* T skil] reson Hu_2 trespast] H_7, haþ *prec.* Σ, deliquit Lat. 17 hym behoueth gyf] by oure gifte Lw gyf] to yife Hu_2ECcT, `to´ gyfe Ch, for to yeue W to] *om.* Sr trespast] H_7LB_3AsSrAPH_6Pl, has trespasid HRBH_5WsChLwHu_2ELdCcTW, deliquit Lat. vnto] to SrMLdPl, *om.* A 18 oweth] of duyte or dette *add.* B þow] þouȝ þat LB_3SrEPCcM ouer þat] *om.* Pl him behoueth] he moste Hu_2, to *add.* CcMT 19 gyfe] him *add.* LAsPCc owe] H^7, ow`g´ $H^c$, how R, oweþ Σ, tenebatur Lat. but only] *om.* Cc but] *om.* $Hu_2$ he trespast] trespas M, propter delictum quod comisit Lat. Bot] oonli `L´B_3PH_6, now A 20 had] haþ H_5WsChHu_2CcW qwerewith] whereof H_5Ws þat] *om.* H_7LB_3PH_6Cc 21 awght] oweth RAsPl, owed AM, in quo sibi tenebatur Lat. `man´ Sr 22 or in] and M or] oþer H_5 was] *rep.* A, nas M his] *om.* Hu_2 23 seith] Luc. 10 *add.* Hu_2 and[1]] wiþ B_3M and al his mightes] *om.* Cc 24 al] *om.* B

þat, standand þe riȝtwisnes of God, it miȝt not be forgyuen bot if amendis and ful satisfaccioun were first maad þerfore.

Bot þis amendes miȝt no man make þat was man only and com oute 64r of Adam by kyndly generacioun, for þis skil. For þe trespas and | vnworschip was endles gret, and þerfore it passed mannes miȝt for to make amendes for it. And also for þis skil: he þat has trespassid and shal make amendes, hym bihoueþ gif to hym þat he has trespasid vnto, al þat he oweþ þauȝ he had not trespasid, and also ouer þat, hym behouys gif sumwhat þat he ow`g´ not, bot only for þat he trespasid. Bot mankynde had not wherewith þat he miȝt pai God for his trespasse ouer þat he auȝt him, for what good dede þat man miȝt do, in bodi or in soule, it was bot is dette. For euerilk man awȝt, as þe Gospel sais, for to lufe God wiþ alle his herte and al his soule and alle his miȝtes, and better miȝt he not do þen þis. And neuerþeles þis dede sufficid not to þe reformyng of mankynd, ne þis miȝt he not do bot if he ⸢had⸣ ben first reformid.

þan nedid `it´ þat if mannes soule schuld be reformid and þe trespas mad good, þat oure Lord God himself schuld reforme þis ymage and make amendis for þis trespas, siþyn þat no man miȝt. Bot þat miȝt he not do in his godhed, for he miȝt not ne aȝt not to make amendis bi suffryng of pyne in his awn kynde. þerfor it nedid þat he schuld take þe same mankynde þat had trespasid and become man; and þat miȝt he not do bi þe comoun lawe of generacioun, for it was impossible Godis son to be born of a touchid womman. þerfore hym

mightes] myȝt H$_5$Ws   might . . . don/þan þis] *rev.* H$_6$ he/not] *rev.* Pl   he . . . don] be . . . done R   þis] þus B   25 dede sufficed] deþ suffiseþ B   sufficed] sufficeþ SrCc þe] *om.* H$_6$Cc   mankynde] mannys kynderne Hu$_2$ ne] nor M   26 he/not] *rev.* H$_5$Ws, be not Ld, noȝt `be´ L, not be EPH$_6$Cc, no be B$_3$, non poterat Lat.   if] *om.* Ld   ⸢had⸣ H$^c$ ben/first] *rev.* LB$_3$AsAPH$_6$ [`be´ H$_6$]   27 nedid þat] H$_7$H°BChHu$_2$LdM, nedid `it´ þat H$^c$, nedid it `þat´ L, nedid it þat RH$_5$B$_3$AsSrWsLwEPPlW, nedid it AH$_6$, it nedid T, nedith Cc   if] a *add.* AHu2   mannys] man H$_7$Pl   and] in Lw   þe] þat M   28 `God´ Pl þis] his Hu$_2$ 29 syþen þat no] for as myche Hu$_2$ þat] *om.* SrM   might] not *add.* ChHu$_2$, potens ad hoc fuerat vel sufficiens Lat.   30 might/he] *rev.* Cc   for . . . his (l. 31)] *om.* Lat.   ne] nor M   31 awght] owed AM   make] H$_7$RLB$_3$AsSrPH$_6$Pl, to make HBH$_5$WsChLwHu$_2$ECcMLdTW, forto make A   his] þis Ld   owen kynde] natura propria deitatis Lat.   32 nedid] nedyþ Ld   þe] þat RAsPl   mankynde] mannys kynde Hu$_2$ trespast] trespas H$_5$ 33 he/nought] *rev.* AsM   nought] H$_7$RLB$_3$AsSrAEPH$_6$CcMPl, do *add.* HBH$_5$WsChLwHu$_2$LdTW, facere *add.* Lat. commine] H$_7$, þe *prec.* Σ   kendli generacion] Pl *marked for rev.*   kendli] H$_7$RLB$_3$AsSrAEPH$_6$CcMPl, *om.* HBH$_5$WsChLwHu$_2$LdTW, naturalis Lat. 34 was] `is´ Cc   inpossible] vnpossible H$_6$, to *add.* T   to be born/of a touched wumman] *rev.* B   touched] a viro cognita seu corrupta Lat.

wumman. þerfor he most become man þurgh a graciouse generacion be þe werkyng of þe Holy God of a clene graciouse mayden, oure Ladi Seynt Marie. And so was it don. For oure Lord Jesu, Goddis Son, become man, and þurgh his preciouse dede þat he suffred mad amendis to þe Fader of heuene for mannys gilt; and þat might he wel do for he was God and he awght nought for himself, bot in as
f. 45^{r} mikel as he was man, born | of þe same kend þat Adam was þat ferst trespast. And so, þow he awght \`it´ nought for hise owen persone, for himself might nought sinnen, neuerþeles he awght it of his owen fre wil for þe trespas of mankynde, [þe qwhilk kynde] he toke for saluacion of man of his endles mercy. For soth it is, þer was neuer man þat might ȝeld to God ony þinge of his owen þat he awght nought, but oneli þis blissed man, Jesu. For he might payen on þing þat awght not as for himself, and þat was nought bot on þinge: and þat was for to gyfen his precious lyfe be wilful takyng of ded for loue of sothfastnesse. þis awght he nought. As mikel good as he might don to þe wurchip of God in hise lyfe was al bot dette. But for to taken ded for loue of ryghtwysnesse, he was nought bounden þerto.

He was bounden to þe loue of rightwisnes bot he was not bounden to dien, for ded is only a peyn ordeynd of God to man for his owen sinne. Bot oure Lord Jesu sinned neuere, ne he might [not] sinnen, and þerfore awght he not to dyen. þan syþen þat he awght not for to dyen, and ȝet wilfully he dyed, þan payed he to God more þan he awght. And syþen þat was þe best mans dede and þe most wurthi þat euer was don, þerfore was it resonable þat þe sinne of mankynde

35 he most] H$_7$BLB$_3$Hu$_2$PH$_6$CcMLd, hym most HRH$_5$AsSrWsChLwEPlTW, him bihouid A become] ben Sr þurgh . . . generacion be] be generacyon thurgh Cc þurgh] bi A 36 þe^{1}] H$_7$HRBH$_5$AsWsChLwHu$_2$CcLdPlTW, *om.* LB$_3$SrAEPH$_6$M God] H$_7$, Gost Σ of^{2}] on H$_6$ mayden] maide A, þat was *add.* Cc oure Ladi Seynt] *om.* Lat. oure] on þe blissed Hu$_2$ 37 so] *rep.* A was/it] rev. CcLd was] is *add.* H$_5$ For . . . do (l. 40)] *om.* A Jesu/Goddis sone] *rev.* H$_5$ Jesu] H$_7$HRBH$_5$AsSrWsChLw-Hu$_2$LdPlTW, Christ *add.* LB$_3$AEPH$_6$CcM, Christus Lat. Goddis Son] *om.* Lat. Son] of heuene *add.* M 38 his] þe H$_6$ 39 gilt] gyltes Ld might . . . do] merueilous dede he wolde for loue of man kiend and he myȝt wel Hu$_2$ might/he] *rev.* Cc 40 in] for in T, for LB$_3$PH$_6$M, be Cc 41 man] *om.* B$_3$ of] in M 42 awght] owed A it nought] not þis T, þat *add.* Ld \`it´ H$_7$, *om.* LB$_3$PH$_6$ persone] trespasse T 43 himself] he Hu$_2$ awght] owed A owen] H$_7$MT, *om.* Σ 44 wil] and gentilnesse *add.* Hu$_2$ þe qwhilk kynde] *om.* H$_7$ kynde] *om.* H$_6$, mankynd LwW 45 saluacion] þe *prec.* H$_5$WsLwLdW of man] *om.* M of^{2}] on A For] *om.* BH$_5$Ws is] that *add.* Cc 47 oneli] *om.* ChHu$_2$ man] H$_7$RLB$_3$AsSrAEPH$_6$Cc, *om.* HBH$_5$WsChLwHu$_2$LdPlTW, homine Lat. Jesu] H$_7$HRBH$_5$AsSrWsChLwAHu$_2$MLdPlTW, Christ *add.* LB$_3$EPH$_6$Cc, Christo Lat. payen] H$_7$LB$_3$PH$_6$Cc, God *add.* HRBH$_5$AsSrWsChLwAHu$_2$EMLdPlTW, soluere Lat. on þing] þinges LB$_3$PH$_6$, aliquid Lat. 48 þat^{1}] H$_7$, he *add.* Σ as] *om.*

most bycome man þorw a graciouse generacioun bi þe wirkyng of þe Holy Gost of a clene graciouse mayden, oure Lady Seynt Marye. And so was it don. For oure Lord Ihesu, Godis sone, bicome man, and þorw his precious deeþ þat he suffrid mad amendis to þe Fader of Heuen for mans gilt; and þat miȝt he wel do for he was God, and he awȝt not for himself bot in als mikil as he was man born of þe same kynde þat Adam was þat first trespast. And so, þowȝ he awȝt it nouȝt for his owne persone, for hymself miȝt not synne, neuerþeles he awȝt
54v it of his fre wil for þe trespas of mankynde, | þe whilke kynde he toke for saluacioun of man of his endeles mercy. For soþ it is, þer was neuer man þat miȝt ȝeld to God ony þing of his owen þat he awȝt not, bot only þis blissid Ihesu. For he miȝt pay God on þing þat he awȝt not as for hymself, and þat was noȝt bot on þinge: þat was for to gif his precious lif be wilful takynge of ded for luf of soþfastnes. Þis auȝt he nouȝt. Als mikil good as he miȝt do to þe worschipe of God in his liif, al was bot dette. Bot for to take ded for lufe of riȝtwisnes, he was not bounden þerto.

He was bounden to riȝtwisnes bot he was not bounden to dey, for ded is only a peyn ordeynyd to man for his owne synne. Bot oure Lord Ihesu synned neuer, ne he miȝt not synne, and þerfore he aȝt not for to deye. Þen siþin he aȝt not for to deye, and ȝit wilfully he deyed, þen paied he to God more þen he auȝt. And sen þat was þe best mans ded and most worþi þat euer was don, þerfor was it resonable þat þe syn of mankynd schuld be forgyuen in als mikel als mankynd had founden a

SrA   was nought] ne was A   nought bot on] no thing but Cc   nought] *om.* WsLd   bot] for *add.* As   and[2]] H_7RLB_3AsSrAEPH_6MPl, *om.* HBH_5WsChLwHu_2LdTW   49 for to gyfen] to forȝiue *prec.*, *canc.* B_3 for] *om.* LwW   lyfe] deeþ *prec.*, *canc.* L   50 sothfastnesse] iusticie Lat.   þis] þat Pl   awght] owed A   As] as so B   to . . . God/in hise lyfe] *rev.* M   51 þe] *om.* M   hise] this W   was/al] H_7RB_3AsSrAH_6CcMPl [Cc *marked for trsp.*], *rev.* HBH_5LWsChLwHu_2EPLdTW [L *marked for trsp.*]   was] were W   taken ded] make him deed $B_3$$H_6$Cc, mori Lat.   taken] him *add.*, *canc.* L   52 ryghtwysnesse] ryȝtfulnesse Ld, but *add.* $B_3$$H_6$ 53 `He . . . bot´ *d.h.* L, *om.* $B_3$   þe loue of] $H_7$RAsSrA$H_6$CcPl, loue of M, *om.* HB$H_5$`L´WsChLwHu_2EPLdTW, diligere Lat.   rightwisnes] riȝtfulnesse LPMLd, but *add.* Cc   54 dien] deþ BWsT, mori Lat.   only/a peyn] *rev.* H_5Ws   of God] H_7BLB_3SrChHu_2EPH_6CcMLd, *om.* HRH_5AsWsLw-APlTW, a Deo Lat.   owen] *om.* Ld   55 Jesu] Crist *add.* Cc, he *add.* H_5Ws   ne] for Cc   not] *om.* H_7 56 awght he] H_7, *rev.* Σ   `not´[1] R   to[1]] $H_7$$H_5$Ws, for to Σ   þan . . . dyen] *om.* L$B_3$AP$H_6$Ld, Quia ergo mori non tenebatur Lat.   þat] $H_7$, *om.* Σ   for to dyen] *om.* M   for to] to $H_5$Ws   57 wilfully] `wil-´ Cc   he[1]] *om.* As   to God/more] *rev.* M   to] onto Cc   58 awght] owed A   syþen . . . þerfor (l. 59)] so that oure Lord Jesu Cryst God and man willfully deied Cc   þat[1]] it *add.* H_5Ws   mans] maner LB_3PH_6, hominis Lat.   dede] opus Lat.   þe[2]] H_7Sr, *om.* Σ   59 don] *om.* A   was/it] *rev.* CcLd schuld be forgyfen, in als mikel as mankynde had founden a man of þe same kynde withouten wemme of sinne—þat is Jesu—þat might make amendis for þe trespas don and might paye oure Lord God al þat he awght, and ouermore þat he awght nought. Þanne syþen oure Lord Jesu, God and man, dyed þus for saluacion of mannis soule, it was rightful þat sinne schuld be forgyfen, and mans soule þat was his ymage schulde moun ben reformed and restored to þe first liknesse and to þe blisse of heuene.

Þis passion of oure Lord and þis precious ded is þe grounde of al þe reformynge of mans soule, withouten qwhilk might neuer mans soule haue ben reformed to þe liknesse of him ne come to þe blisse of heuene. Bot blissed mote he be in al his werkyng, now is it so þat
f. 45^v þurgh þe vertu of hise passion þe brynnyng swerde | of cherubyn þat drofe Adam out of Paradys is now put away and þe endles gates of heuene arn opned to ilk man þat wil entren in þerto. For þe persone of Jesu is boþe God and kyng, euene in þe blisse to þe Fader, and as man he is porter atte þe gate redy to resceyue ilk a soule þat wil be reformed [here in þis lyfe to his liknesse. For now may ilk a soule, if þat he wil, be reformed] to þe liknesse of God, syn þat þe trespase is forgyfen and þe amendis is made þurgh Jesu for þe first gilt. Neuerþeles, þogh þis be soth, al soules han not þe profyt ne þe froyte of þis preciouse passion, ne arn reformed to þe liknesse of him.

60 als] also B mankynde . . . man] vnus homo repertus fuit Lat. 61 wemme] ony spotte Hu$_2$ is] was Cc Jesu] swete Jesu H$_5$Ws \`make′ Pl 62 God] *om.* A \`þat . . . ouermore′ H^c, *om.* H°H$_5$WsCc, quicquid sibi debuit, et aliquid plus ultra Lat. 63 syþen] H$_7$RLB$_3$AsSrWsAEPH$_6$CcMLdPlT, þat *add.* HBH$_5$ChLwHu$_2$W \`Lord′ H^c, *om.* H°B 61 Jesu, God] swete Jesu verray God H$_5$Ws Jesu] Crist *add.* M dyed] did RA, dede As, dide Pl, moriebatur Lat. þus] þis Pl 65 þat^1] þe *add.* A be] ful *add.* H$_5$Ws 66 moun] *om.* A reformed and] *om.* BLd; ad primam similitudinem reformi et Lat. 68 þis] blissid *add.* Ld and] *om.* Lw ded] mors Lat. grounde] causa . . . et origo Lat. of^2] *rep.* W þe^2] *om.* SrChHu$_2$ 69 qwhilk] þe *prec.* RAsM might neuer/mans soule] *rev.* H$_6$ 70 haue ben] be Hu$_2$ ne] nor M to] vnto T 71 he] euer *add.* T \`be′ *d.h.* L his] þis Ld werkyng] werkis CcM now] But now Pl is/it] *rev.* H$_5$B$_3$AsWsChHu$_2$EH$_6$CcT [B$_3$ *marked for trsp.*] 72 þurgh] bi A þe$^1$] *om.* LB$_3$SrAPH$_6$Cc \`vertu of′ Cc hise] þis HLwHu$_2$, istius Lat. passion] preciouse *prec.* HBChLwHu$_2$LdTW, so precious *add.* H$_5$Ws, passionis Lat. 73 Adam/out] *rev.* Sr is/now] *rev.* M now] *om.* Pl þe] *om.* B 74 opned] H$_7$RLB$_3$AsSrEPH$_6$Pl, open HBH$_5$WsChLwAHu$_2$CcMLdTW, patefacte sunt Lat. ilk] H$_7$HRLChP, ilk a As, ech a B$_3$, ech H$_6$M, euery BH$_5$SrWsLwAHu$_2$ECcLdPlTW þat] there *add.* Cc in] *om.* A

man of þe same kynde withouten wemme of synne—þat is, Ihesu—þat miȝt make amendes for þe trespas don and miȝt paie oure Lord God al `þat he auȝt, and ouermore´ þat he auȝt not. Þan sen þat oure `Lord´ Ihesu, God and man, died þus for saluacioun of mans saule, it was riȝtful þat synne schuld be forgifen, and mannus soule þat was his ymage schuld mowe be reformed and restored to þe first liknes and to þe blis of heuen.

Þis passioun of oure Lord and þis precious ded is þe ground of alle þe reformyng of mannus soule, withouten whilk miȝt neuer mannus saule haue ben reformed to þe liknes of hym ne come to þe blis of heuen. Bot blissid mot he be in alle his wirkyng. Now is it so þat þorw þe vertue of þis preciouse passioun þe brynnand swerd of cherubyn þat drof Adam out of paradis is now put awey, and þe endles gates of heuen are open to ilk man þat wil entre in þerto. For þe person of Ihesu is boþe God and kyng, euen in þe blis ⌜to⌝ þe Fader, and as a
65r man he is | porter at þe ȝate redy to receyue ilk a saule þat wil be reformed here in þis lif to his liknes. For now may euerilk a saule, if þat he wil, be reformid to þe liknes of God, sen þat þe trespas is forgifen and þe amendes þorw Ihesu is maade for þe first gilte. Neuerþeles, þouȝ þis be soþ, alle soules has not þe profit ne þe frut of þis preciouse passioun, ne are not reformid to þe liknes of hym.

þerto] *om.* Cc   þe] blissid *add.* Hu$_2$ 75 Jesu] goode *prec.* H$_5$Ws   God] and man *add.* Hu$_2$ euene] of heuen RAsSr, `of heuen´ H^c, of heuen euen Lw, in heuen, euen E, *om.* W, equalis Lat.   þe[1]] *om.* LB$_3$EPH$_6$CcM   to] H$_7$LB$_3$Lw⌜H^c⌝AEPH$_6$CcPlW, of RBH$_5$AsSrWsChHu$_2$LdT, with M, Deo Patri Lat.   and as] H$_7$RB$_3$AsSrLAPH$_6$CcMW, and as a HBH$_5$WsChLwHu$_2$LdTW, as a As   76 atte þe gate/redy] *rev.* H$_5$Ws   atte] of Ld, to H$_6$ gate] ȝatys B   to] for to H$_7$AsSrAPl   ilk a] H$_7$HRLAsChAM, ech a B$_3$, eche BH$_6$Ld, euery H$_5$SrWsLwHu$_2$EPCcLdPlTW   soule] *om.* Ws   77 here . . . reformed (l. 77)] *om.* H$_7$M, in vita ista ad eius similitudinem voluerit reformati. Iam enim potest quilibet anima, si voluerit, ad Dei similitudinem reformari Lat.   to] vnto T   his liknesse] þe lycknes of hym Ld   ilk a] H$_7$HLChAPM, ech a B$_3$, eche BH$_6$Ld, euer R, euery H$_5$SrWsLwHu$_2$ECcLdPlTW, euere eche a As   78 þat] *om.* Hu$_2$ 79 amendis] mendes B   is made/þurgh Jesu] H$_7$RLB$_3$AsSrAEPH$_6$CcMPl, *rev.* HBH$_5$WsChLwHu$_2$LdTW   is] be LB$_3$EP, *om.* A   Jesu] blissid *prec.* Hu$_2$ 80 Neuerþeles] ȝet Cc, þat *add.* As   al . . . not] not al þe soules haue Ld   ne] and H$_5$WsLd   þe[2]] *om.* Ld   froyte] fructum vel effectum Lat.   81 þis] his LB$_3$EPH$_6$Cc, the M, huius Lat.   arn] H$_7$LB$_3$SrPH$_6$CcM, not *add.* HRBH$_5$AsWsChLwAHu$_2$LdPlTW

þat Jewes and paynemys and also fals cristen men are not reformed effectuly þourgh vertue of þis passion for here owen defaute. Capitulum iii^m

Two maner of men are not reformed be vertue of þis passion. On is of hem þat trow it not; anoþer is of hem þat lufen it nought. Jewes and paynemys han not þe benefice of þis passion for þey trowen it not. Jewes trowen not þat Jesu man, þe son of virgine Marie, is Goddis Son of heuene. Also paynemys trowen not þat þe souereyne wysdom of God wold become son of man and in manhede suffre þe peyns of ded. And þerfor Jewes helden þe prechynge of þe croys and of þe passion of Crist not bot sclaundere and blasfeme, and þe paynemys helden it not but fantum and folie. But trew cristen men helden it þe souereyn wysdom of God and his grete might. þus Seynt Poule seith: *Predicamus vobis Christum crucifixum, Iudeis quidem scandalum, gentibus autem stulticiam. Ipsis autem vocatis Iudeis et Grecis Christum Dei virtutem.* þat is: We preche to ȝow þat ȝe trowen þat Jesu Crist crucified, þe son of Marie, is Goddis Son, souereyn vertu and wysdom of God, þe qwhilk Jesu to þe Jewes and to þe paynemys þat trowe not in him is but sclaundre and folie.

And þerfore þese men be þeyre vntrowthe putten hemself fro þe reformynge of here owen soule and, standende here vntrowthe, schal þey neuere be saufe ne come to þe blisse of heuene. For soth it is, fro þe bygynnynge of þe werld vnto [þe] last ende was þere neuer man

Chapter 3 *title*: H_7RLB_3AsSrAEPH_6CcMLdPlTW ˋHou þer ben two maner of men þat wole not be reformid be þe vertue of þis precious passion of oure Lord Jesu Crist.ˊ H^c *om.* H°BH_5WsChLwHu_2 1 þat] How M also] *om.* CcPl 2 þorugh . . . for] be Cc þourgh] the *add.* SrW ˋþisˊ W^G, þe SrELdW, his M ˋpassionˊ *d.h.* L, of Cryst *add.* SrT here] he As owen] *om.* Sr 3 defaute] proper desyre and euel leuyng M 4 Two] Tho H_5 ˋofadd., *canc.* H^c are not reformed] minime reformantur Lat. vertue] the *prec.* LwEW þis] hys BLB_3EPH_6, holy *add.* Hu_2, istius Lat. is/of hem] *rev.* Hu_2Cc 5 hem] him Ch trow] leeueþ BHu_2, bileuith A, or bileven *add.* T it/not] *rev.* Ld ˋitˊ R not] and *add.* M anoþer . . . nought] as Cc anoþer] And oþir E is/of hem] *rev.* Hu_2 is] *om.* Sr hem²] hym BCh lufen] leuen Pl 6 han . . . it not] for they beleue it nout Cc benefice] benefetis LB_3EP, benefices H_6, beneficium Lat. þis] holy *add.* Hu_2 trowen] leeuen BLd, bileue A 7 trowen] leeueþ BA, bileuen T Jesu] oure blissid Lord *prec.* Hu_2 man] H_7RBLB_3AsSrChAHu_2EPH_6MLdPl, *om.* HH_5WsLwCcTW, *om.* Lat. þe] *om.* H_7RAsSrA 8 heuene] *overwritten d.h.* L Also] And also H_5Ws paynemys] pay⌜nems⌝ H, þe *prec.* HBH_5WsChLwHu_2TW trowen] byleueþ B, leuith A 9 God] Dei patris Lat. son] H_7HH_5LB_3WsChHu_2PLdT, þe *prec.* BSrLwEH_6CcMTW son of] a RAs, om. A ˋofˊ Pl in] his *add.* ChHu_2 suffre] wolde *prec.* W 10 And²] *corr. from* yf B Jewes] H_7RAsSrACcMPl, þe *prec.* HBH_5LB_3WsChLwHu_2EPH_6LdTW helden] H_7HChLdW, hoelde Lw, holden RBH_5LB_3AsSrWsAHu_2EPH_6CcMPlT ˋþe²ˊ Cc and . . . passion] *om.*

[CHAPTER 3]

Two maner of men are not reformed be vertue of þis passioun. One is of þem þat trow it not; anoþer is of þem þat loue it not. Iewes and pay⌜nems⌝ has not þe benefice of þis passioun, for þei trowe it not. Iewes trowes not þat Ihesu þe son of þe Virgyn Marye is Godis Sone of heuyn. Also þe pay⌜nems⌝ trow not þat þe souereyne wisdom of God wald bicome sone of man and in manhed suffre þe payns of ded. And þerfore þe Iewes heldyn þe prechyng of þe cros and of þe passioun of Crist not bot sclaundre and blaspheme, and þe paynems ald it not bot fantum and foly. Bot trew cristen men held it þe soueren wisdom of God and his grete miȝt. Þus saide Seint Poule: *Predicamus vobis Christum crucifixum, Iudeis quidem scandalum, gentibus autem stulticiam. Ipsis autem vocatis Iudeis et Grecis Christum Dei virtutem, etcetera*. Þat is: We preche to ȝow þat ȝe trow þat Ihesu Crist crucified, þe sone of Marye, is Godis Son, soueren vertue and wisdom of God, þe whilk Ihesu to Iues and paynems þat trow not in hym is bot sclaunder and foly.

And þerfor þis`e´ men be þeire vntrowþ puttes þemself fro þe reformyng of þeire owne sowle, and standand þeire vntrowþ schal þei neuer be sauf ne come to þe blis of heuen. For soþ it is, fro þe bigynnynge of þe world vnto þe last ende, was þer neuer man saf, ne

A `and´ E, *om.* LB$_3$PH$_6$ 11 not] *om.* A 12 helden] HLwW, ald H, holden RBH$_5$LB$_3$AsSrWsChAHu$_2$EPH$_6$CcMLdPlT it] *om.* Cc not] *om.* LB$_3$PH$_6$CcM fantum and folie] vanitatem . . . et stulticiam Lat. fantum and] *om.* Cc fantum] fantezi E, `-sy´ *add.* Lw But] *overwritten* H helden] H$_7$HLwW, holdeþ B, holden RBH$_5$LB$_3$AsSrWsChAHu$_2$EPH$_6$CcMLdPlT 13 Seynt Poule/seith] H$_7$RLB$_3$AsSr-APMPl *rev.* HBH$_5$WsChLwHu$_2$EH$_6$CcLdTW seith] i° Cor. i° *add.* BLHu$_2$PLdTW, i° ad Cor. 4° *add.* E seith] H$_7$, saide Σ, dicit Lat. 14 quidem] qui As 15 autem^{1}] *om.* B et] atque LB$_3$EPH$_6$ Christum] *om.* As 16 virtutem] H$_7$RLB$_3$AsSrPH$_6$CcMPl, etcetera *add.* HBH$_5$WsChLwHu$_2$, et Dei sapienciam *add.* ALdTW, atque Dei sapientiam *add.* E, et Dei sapientiam Lat. þat] and þat T is] to say *add.* AsPlT We/preche] *rev.* ChHu$_2$ ȝe] þe *prec.* H, we LB$_3$EPH$_6$Cc, credatis Lat. trowen] bylyue ALd þat^{3}] *om.* M 17 Marie] þe *prec.* Hu$_2$ Goddis Son] þe Sone of God Hu$_2$ 18 to þe^{1}] H$_7$A, to Σ to þe^{2}] H$_7$Cc, to RLB$_3$AsSrEPH$_6$CcPl, *om.* HBH$_5$WsChLwAHu$_2$MLdTW 19 trowe] leueþ B, bileueth A in] on B but] a *add.* As 20 vntrowthe] vnbyleeue BA, and vnbyleue Ld, vntrowyng T putten] away *add.* Pl þe reformynge] reformacion M 21 soule] soulis H$_6$ standende] standen in Pl, in *add.* H$_6$ vntrowthe] vnbyleue B 22 be saufe ne] *om.* T saufe] saued Sr ne] and H$_5$Ws þe blisse of heuene] gloriam sempiternam Lat. þe] *om.* LB$_3$P soth/it is] *rev.* Hu$_2$, *om.* Lat. 23 þe^{2}] this M vnto] til to Ld, intoSrA þe^{3}] *om.* H$_7$ ende] endyng LwW þere] *om.* H$_6$

f. 46r saufe, ne schal be saufe, | bot if he had or haue trouth general or special in Jesu Crist, ouþer comende or comen. For right as al chosen soules þat weren befor þe incarnacion vnder þe Eld Testament hadden trouth in Crist, þat he schuld come and reforme mans soule, ouþer openli as patriarkes and prophetes and oþer holi men hadden, or elles prueli and generali as children and oþer simple and inperfyte soules hadden þat knewen not speciali þe priuetes of þe incarnacion; ryght so al þe chosen soules vnder þe New Testament han trouthe in Crist þat he is comen, ouþer openli and felendli as gostli men and wys men han, or elles generaly as children þat dyen cristned and oþer symple and lewed soules han þat arn norysede in þe bosum of Holi Kirk.

Syþen þis is soth, þan þenketh me þat þese men gretly and greuous[ly] erren þat seyn þat Jewes and Saraceyns, by kepyng of here owen lawe, moun be made saufe þow þey trowen nought in Jesu Crist as Holi Kirk troweth—in als mikel as þey wene þat here owen trouthe is good and sikire and suffisande to here saluacion, and in þat trouthe þey don as it semyth many gode dedes of rightwysnesse, and perauenture, if þey knewen þat cristen feyth were bettre þan here is, þey wolden taken it and leuen þer owen—þat þey þerfore schulde be saufe. Nay it is not inow so. For Crist God and man is boþe weye and ende, and he is mediatour atwixen God and man, and withouten him may no soule be reconsiled ne come to þe blis of heuene. And þerfore þey þat trowen not in him, þat he is boþe God and man, moun neuere be sauf ne come to blisse.

24 saufe^{1}] sauyd Hu$_2$Ld `ne . . . saufe$^{2}$´ Pl, *om.* A saufe$^{2}$] sauyd Hu$_2$, *om.* Ld if] *om.* B had] haue T or haue] H$_7$RLB$_3$AsPH$_6$CcM, and haue Sr, `or hath´ W^{G}, *om.* HBH$_5$WsChLwAHu$_2$ELdPlTW, vel habuerit Lat. trouth] byleeue BALd, þe *prec.* HBH$_5$WsChLwHu$_2$Ld 25 special] implicitam seu explicitam *add.* Lat. ouþer . . . comen] *om.* Cc ouþer] H$_7$RLB$_3$AsSrAEPH$_6$MPl, *om.* HBH$_5$WsChLwHu$_2$LdTW, `in´ *add.* E `comende´ W^{G}, to comyng Ld, to come LwW, as in þe olde lawe *add.* B comen] as now *add.* B al] *om.* Hu$_2$, *canc.* Ch chosen] þe *prec.* Sr 26 befor] aforn M 27 trouth in Crist] *om.* A trouth] byleeue BLd 28 patriarkes] þe *prec.* E and^{1}] or M 29 elles] *om.* RSrM and^{1}] or AsM simple and] *om.* M 30 inperfyte] vnperfite Pl knewen] knowen LB$_3$PM, cognouerunt Lat. þe priuetes of] *om.* B þe priuetes] *om.* H$_5$Ws priuetes] H$_7$RLB$_3$AsSrAEPH$_6$CcMPl, pryuyte HChLwHu$_2$LdTW, sacramenta Lat. 31 al] as H$_5$Ws þe^{2}] H$_7$RLB$_3$AsSrAEPH$_6$CcPl, *om.* HBH$_5$WsChLwHu$_2$-MLdTW vnder] of Ws 32 han] had H$_5$Ws trouthe] H$_7$HRH$_5$AsSrWsChLw-Hu$_2$MPlTW, byleue BALd, trowid LB$_3$EPH$_6$Cc, fidem Lat. in Crist] *om.* Hu$_2$ Crist] Jesu *prec.* M openli and felendli] explicite et in speciali Lat. and] or M `as´ W^{G}, and W 33 and wys men] *om.* APl elles] *om.* Ld generaly] implicite seu in generali Lat. children] hath *add.* LwW dyen cristned] deieden vncristened As 34 and lewed] *om.*

schal be saf, bot if he had þe trowþ general or special in Ihesu Crist, comand or comen. For riȝt as alle chosen soules þat were bifore þe incarnacioun vndir þe Old Testament had trowþ in Crist, þat he schuld come and reforme mannus soule, ouþer openly as patriarkes and prophetes and oþer holy men hadden, or ellis priuely and generally as children and oþer symple and inperfite saules had þat knew not specially þe pryuyte of þe incarnacioun, riȝt so alle chosen f. 65^{v} soules vnder þe New Testament has | trouþ in Crist þat he is comen, ouþer openly and felandly, as gostly men and wise men has, or elles generally as childre þat dees cristned and oþer symple and lewd soules has þat ar norschid in þe bosom of Haly Kirke. Sen þis is soþ, þen þink me þat þ⌜ese⌝ men gretly and greuously erre þat saien þat Iewes and Sarezeins, bi keping of þeir own law, moun be mad saf þawȝ þei trowe not in Ihesu Crist als Haly Kirke trowes; in als mikel as þei wene þat þeir owne trowþ is good and siker and suffisaunt to þair saluacioun, and in þat trouþ þei doo as it semes many gode dedes of riȝtwisnes, and perauenture, if þei knewe þat cristen feiþ ware better þen þaires is, þei would leue þeire own and take it þat þei þerfore schuld be saf. Nai it is not inowȝ so. For Crist God and man is boþ wei and ende, and he is mediatour bitwix God and man, and wiþouten hym may no soule be reconsilid ne come to þe blis of heuen. And þerfor þei þat trow not in hym, þat he is boþ God and man, moun neuer be saf ne come to blis.

Ld 35 of] all *add.* M 36 Syþen] and *prec.* M þis] it SrM þan] þat Ld and greuously] *om.* RAsAPl, grauiter multum Lat. 37 greuously] greuous H$_7$ Jewes] þe *prec.* H$_5$Ws Saraceyns] and paynemes *add.* LB$_3$SrEPH$_6$Cc kepyng] knowynge B 38 þow] if RAsPl trowen] byleeue B Jesu] *om.* Sr 39 `Crist´ Pl `as Holi Kirk´ L troweth] byleeues BALd, doþ SrM, and as cristen men don *add.* LB$_3$EPH$_6$Cc `in . . . trouthe´ R in] And Ld as] þat B wene] trowen RAsA owen] *om.* RAsAPl 40 trouthe] byleeue BALd and^{1}] *om.* A here] *om.* M 41 trouthe] byleeue BLd, faith A of] or Lw rightwysnesse] riȝtfulnesse Ld 42 if] and E knewen] knowen R here] heres M, her owne W is] *om.* LwLd 43 taken it and leuen her owen] H$_7$RLB$_3$AsSrAEPH$_6$CcMPl, *rev.* HBH$_5$WsChLwHu$_2$LdTW, eam recipere et propriam dimittere Lat. þat þey/þerfore] *rev.* LwW 44 saufe] saued H$_5$Ws inow] *om.* A Crist] boþe *add.* A 45 atwixen] H$_7$RLP, bitwix HBB$_3$AsSrChPlW, betwen H$_5$WsLwHu$_2$EPH$_6$CcMLdT withouten] by þowte B 46 no] non Pl `ne´ Sr, nor M, and R þe blis of heuene] eternam beatitudinem Lat. þe] *om.* LB$_3$P And . . . blisse (l. 48)] *om.* H$_5$Ws 47 þey . . . trowen] he . . . troweþ Sr trowen] leeuen BM, bileuene A not/in . . . is] *rev.* LB$_3$P in] on BLd `he´ W^{G}, *om.* W boþe] *om.* Ld moun] may he Sr 48 sauf] saued CcLd ne . . . blisse] eternaliter Lat. ne] nor M to] þe *add.* BLw

Oþer men also, þat louen not Crist ne his passion, arn not reformed in here soule to þe liknes of him. And þese men arn fals cristene men, þe qwilk arn out of charite and lyuen and dyen in dedli sinne. Þese men trowen wel, as it semeth, þat Jesu is Goddis Son and þat his passion sufficeth to saluacion of mannis soule, and þe trowen also alle f. 46v þe articles of þe feith. But it is an vnschapli trouþe and a ded, for | þey loue him not, ne þey chese not þe froyte of his passion, but þey ligge stil in here sinne and in here fals loue of þis werd vnto her last ende. And so be þey not reformed to þe liknes of God, but gon to þe peynes of helle endlesly, as Jewes and Saracenys don, and into mikel more peyne þan þey, in as mikel as þei hadden þe trouth and keped it not, for þat was more trespase þan if þey had neuere had it.

Þan if þou wilt wyte whilk soules arn reformed here in þis life to þe ymage of God þurgh vertue of his passion, sothli only þo þat trowen in him and louen him. In þe qwhilk soules þe ymage of God, þat was þurgh sinne forschapen as it were into a foule bestes liknes, is restored and reformed to þe first schap and to þe wurthinesse and wurchip þat it had in þe bygynnyng, withouten qwilk reformyng schal neuer soule be sauf ne come to blis. Soth it is, bot if he haue noght þat reformyng in þis lyf, it may haue it qwhen it is purged of sinne in purgatorie. And atte þe hardest, withouten þat clensyng and þat last reformyng schal neuer soule be saufe ne haue þe blis of heuene.

Of two maner reformyng of þis ymage, on in fulnes and anoþer in partye. Capitulum iiii^m^

Now seist þou: Hou may þis be soth þat þe ymage of God, þe qwilk is

49 louen] levyn Cc   ne] nor M, neyþer H_5 50 here] the MT   men] *om.* Ws 51 þe] *om.* E   out of] nought in AsSr   dyen in] *rep.* B   52 men] *om.* Sr   trowen] byleeueþ BHu_2, and belyuen *add.* Ld   wel] *om.* Hu_2 þat[1]] *om.* A   53 sufficeth] sufficyd H_5WsEPl, suffice ChHu_2 to] þe *add.* H_5Ws   trowen] byleeueþ BAHu_2Ld   alle þe] *om.* Cc   alle] *om.* As   54 articles] H_7RLB_3AsSrAEPH_6MPl, oþer *prec.* HBH_5-WsChLwHu_2CcLdTW, alios articulos Lat.   ˋBut . . . God (l. 57)ˊ H^c, *om.* H°H_5WsT, Set fides eorum mortua est et informis, quia non diligent eum, nec querunt seu eligunt fructum passionis sue, sed iacent in peccatis et falsa dileccione huius mundi vsque in finem vite. Et non reformantur ad Dei similitudinem. Lat.   But it is] Alle þis is but Hu_2 trouþe] byleeue BA, feiþ Ld   55 ne] nor M   chese not] settyn be Cc, nec querunt seu eligunt Lat.   þe froyte of] *om.* A   þey] þere As   56 ligge] lyue Cc   stil] styllyche B   here[1]] the M   in[2]] *om.* As   here[2]] H_7LB_3SrEPH_6Cc, þe RBAsSrLwH^cALdPlW, *om.* ChHu_2M, *om.* Lat.   vnto] and to B, til Ld, to A, in to As, on to Lw   her] þe B   57 be/þey] *rev.* W   gon] þei go H_5Ws   þe[2]] H_7HBH_5SrWsChLwHu_2ECcLdTW, *om.* RLB_3AsPH_6MPl 58 peynes] peyn A   endlesly] endeles M   and] *om.* Lw   into] þe *add.* M   59 more] gretter *add.* W   þe] *om.* A   trouth] feyþ B, bileue A, oþer byleue *add.* Ld   keped] kepuþ Ch, keep As, secundum illam non vixerunt Lat.   60 ˋifˊ W^G, þat LwW   had[1] . . . it]

Oþer men also þat luf not Crist nor his passioun er not reformid in þare soule to þe liknes of hym, and þes men are fals cristen men, þe whilk are out of charitee and lifes and dies in dedly synne. Þese men trow wel as it semys þat Ihesu is Godis son and þat his passioun suffisiþ to sauacioun of mannus soule, and þei trowe als so al þe oþer articles of þe fa[i]þ. `But it is an vnshapli trouþ and a ded, for þei louen him noȝt, ne þei chese not þe frute of his passioun, but þei lige stille in her syn and in þe fals loue of þis world vnto þeir last end. And so be þei not reformyd to þe liknes of God´ bot go to þe paynes of helle endlesly, as Iewes and Sarecens doos, and into mikil more payne þen þei, in als mikil as þei had þe trowþ and kepid it not, for þat was more trespas þen if þei ad neuer had it.

Þan ȝif þou wilt wite whilk soules are reformed here in þis liif to þe ymage of God þorw vertue of his passioun, soþly only þo þat trowes in hym and loues hym. In þe whilk soules þe ymage of God, þat was þorw synne forschapyn as it were into a foule bestes liknes, is restored and reformed to þe first schape and to þe worþines and þe worschip þat it had in þe bigynnyng, withouten whilk restoryng and reformyng schal neuer saule be saf ne come to blis.

[CHAPTER 4]

Now saist þou, how may þis be soþ þat þe ymage of God, þe whilk is

nunquam fuissent in fidei articula informati Lat. had/neuer] *rev.* LB$_3$SrEPH$_6$M [haddyn *rep.* Sr], neuer Cc it] non RAsAPl 61 wilt/wyte] *rev.* Ld wilt] wold BLd, wit H$_6$ whilk] what RAsAPl `soules´ L here] *om.* Cc 62 þurgh] the *add.* LwW his] blissed *add.* Hu$_2$ `þo´ L, þilke Ld, those W, þai RAsAPl trowen] byleeueþ BAHu$_2$Ld, louen M 63 in] on BH$_5$Ws louen] leuen on M þe] *om.* W soules] of *add.* As of God] *om.* B 64 bestes liknes] bestlinesse A 65 to[1]] H$_7$HBH$_5$WsLwALdMTW, vnto RLB$_3$AsChAHu$_2$EPH$_6$Pl, into SrCc to[2]] H$_7$RAs`Sr´AH$_6$CcMPl, `in´to LH$_6$, into B$_3$P, *om.* HBH$_5$WsChLwHu$_2$LdTW wurchip] H$_7$RLB$_3$AsSrAEPH$_6$CcPlW, þe *prec.* HBH$_5$WsChLwHu$_2$MLdT 66 reformyng] H$_7$RAsSrACcMPl, restoryng and *prec.* HBH$_5$WsChLwHu$_2$ELdTW, reformyng in feiþ LB$_3$PH$_6$Cc, reformacione per fidem Lat. soule] man A 67 to] þe *add.* BLd blis] of heuen *add.* ALd, endelees *add.* M Soth . . . heuen (l. 70)] H$_7$, *om.* Σ

Chapter 4 *title*: H$_7$RLB$_3$AsSrAEPH$_6$CcMLdPlTW `Hou þe ymage of God þe whiche is mannis soule may be reformid in þis lif to his liknes.´ H[c] *om.* H°BH$_5$WsChLwHu$_2$ 1 þis] þe Sr `and´ T[G], H$_7$RAsSrAMLd, *om.* LB$_3$EPH$_6$CcLdTW `partye´ T[G]W[G], feith ALdTW, parte Lat. 3 soth] sithen H$_5$Ws þe qwilk] whilk RAsEMLd, þat H$_5$Ws `is´ L

mans soule, might be reformed here in þis life to his liknes in ony creature? It semeth nay, it myght nought be. For if it were reformed, þan schuld it haue stable mende, and clere syght, and clene brennynge loue in God and in gostli þynges aylastendli as it had in þe bygynnynge. But þat is in no creature as þou trowest lifend in þis lyfe. For as anemptis þiself þou canst wel say þe þinkest þe ful fer þerfro; þi mende and þi reson and þe loue of þi soule arn so mikel sette in beholdyng and in lofe of erdli þinges, þat of gostli þinges þou felest ryght litel. þou felest no reformyng in þeself, bot art so vmbylapped with þis blak ymage of sinne for owt þat þou mayght
f. 47r don, þat vpon what syde þou turnest þe þou | felest þiself diffouled and spotted with fleschli steringes of þis foule ymage. Oþer chaungynge felyst þou non fro fleschlihed into gostlines, neiþer in þe priue myghtes of þi soule withinnen ne in bodily felynge withouten. Wherefore þou þynkest þat it myght not be þat þis ymage myght be reformed, or elles if it myght be reformed þan askest þou how it myght be reformed.

To þis I answere and sey þus: þer is two maner of reformynge of þe ymage of God þe qwilk is mans soule. One is in fulnes, anoþer is in partye. Reformynge in fulnesse may nought ben had in þis life, but it is delayde aftere þis lyfe to þe blisse of heuene qwere mans soule schal fully be reformed, note to þat state þat it had at þe first begynnynge be kynde, or myght haue had þurgh grace if it had standen hol; bot it schal be restorid to mikel more blisse and mikel heyere ioye þurgh þe mikel mercy and endeles goodnes of God þan it schuld haue had if it

4 reformed . . . be (l. 5)] *rep.*, *canc.* H, *rep.* H$_5$WsT   life] *om.* As   ony] H$_7$RLB$_3$AsSr`H^c′AEPH$_6$CcMPlTW, *om.* H°BH$_5$WsChLwHu$_2$Ld   5 semeth] well *add.* T (*2nd iteration*)   myght] may T (*2nd iteration*)   be] so *add.* TW   6 and[1]] H$_7$, *om.* Σ   clere/. . ./clene] *rev.* RAsAPl   syght] cognicionem Lat.   clene brennynge] ardentem Lat.   clene] clere W   brennynge] *om.* SrM   7 `and′ Pl   in[1]] H$_7$RLB$_3$AsSrAEPH$_6$CcMPlT, *om.* HBH$_5$WsChLwHu$_2$LdW   þynges] as it *add*, *canc.* B$_3$   aylastendli] H$_7$HRBH$_5$LWsChAHu$_2$PH$_6$, euerlastyngli B$_3$AsLwECcMPlW, alweie lestyngli SrLdT   8 is] est . . . taliter reformata Lat.   `in′ W^G, *om.* LwW   no] non B   trowest] suppose Hu$_2$ lifend] H$_7$RLB$_3$AsSrAEPH$_6$CcMPl, here *add.* HBH$_5$WsChLwHu$_2$LdTW, in vita ista Lat.   þis] þe As   9 For as anemptis] As for Hu$_2$ as] *om.* AsSrWsEM   `anemptis′ *d.h.* Pl   wel] *om.* AHu$_2$ þe þinkest . . . and[1] (l. 10)] thow Cc   þe þinkest] H$_7$, þe þinke HRChLwLdW, þe þenkeþ BAsSrHu$_2$M, þat þe þenkith T, þou þenkist H$_5$LB$_3$WsAEPH$_6$, nay, þan þinkest þou Pl, iudicas Lat.   þe ful . . . and[1]] *om.* W   þe ful] þi self H$_5$Ws, þat þu art ful Hu$_2$, þe wol Sr, þou ful Pl   10 and[1]] H$_7$RLB$_3$AsSrAEPH$_6$MPl, *om.* HBH$_5$WsChLwHu$_2$LdT   þe] H$_7$RBLB$_3$AsSrLwAEPH$_6$MTW, þ⌜e⌝ H^c, þi H°H$_5$WsChHu$_2$CcLd   loue] life T   so . . . sette] ita occupantur et firmantur Lat.   11 in[1]] þe *add.* RAsA   in[2]] þe *add.* R`L′APH$_6$CcPl   þinges[1]] þing Sr   þinges[2]] þing SrM   12 ryght] ful H$_5$Ws, but Cc   no] non As   art] H$_7$RH$_5$LAsSrWsAEPCcMPl, þu *prec.* HBB$_3$ChLwHu$_2$H$_6$LdTW   so] *om.* BLd

mannes saule, miȝt be reformid here in þis liif to his liknes in
66^{r} creature? It semys nay it miȝt not be. | For if it ware reformid, þan schuld it haue stabil mynde, clere siȝt, and clene brennand luf in God and goostly þinges aylastandly als it had in þe bigynnyng. Bot þat is in no creature as þu trowes lifand here in þis liif. For als anente þiself þou can wel say þe þinke þe ful ferre þerfro; þi mynde, þi resoun, and þ⌜e⌝ luf of þi soule are so mikel sette in bihaldyng and in luf of erþly þinges, þat of gostly þinges þu felis riȝt litel. Þu felis no reformyng in þiself, bot þu art so vmbilappid wiþ þis blak ymage of synne for oȝt þat þou may do, þat vpon what syde þu turnes þee þou felis þiself defoulid and spotted wiþ flescly styrynges of þis foule ymage. Oþer chaungyng felis þou none fro fleschlynes into gostlynes, nouþer in þe priue miȝtes of þi soule wiþinne ne in bodily feling wiþouten. Wherfore þe þinkiþ þat it miȝt not be þat þis ymage miȝt be reformed, or elles if it miȝt be reformid þan askes þou how it miȝt be reformid.

To þis I answere and say þus. Þer is two maner of reformyng of þe ymage of God whilk is mannus soule. On is in fulnes, anoþer is in partie. Reformyng in fulnes mai not ben had in þis liif, bot it is delaied after þis lif to þe blis of heuen where mannus soule shal fulli be reformid; not to þat stat þat it had at þe first bigynnynge by kynde, or miȝt haue had þorw grace if it had stonden hool, bot it schal be restored to mikil more blis and mikil hiȝere ioye þorw þe mikil mercy and þe endeles goodnes of God þan it schuld haue had if it had neuer

13 vmbylapped] vmlapped As, bilapped AH$_6$, al aboute belappyd H$_5$Ws, onstabil and belappyd Cc, wrapped aboute M þis] þat Ld, þe Sr owt] withoutyn Sr, quocunque Lat. mayght] may RMPl 14 vpon] on M syde] euer *add.* T `turnest þe´ W$^{G}$, *rev.* LwW diffouled and spotted] maculari Lat. 15 fleschli] flesc`h´ly H^{c}. *This correction is made throughout the text, and will not be noted further* þis] þe Sr 16 fleschlihed] H$_7$RLB$_3$SrAEPH$_6$CcMPl, fleischlynes HBAsWsChLwHu$_2$LdTW, flesschely lyues H$_5$ gostlines] gostly lyues H$_5$, gostlyhed AsSr þe] þi ELd, *om.* B$_3$SrLwW priue myghtes] potenciis Lat. 17 myghtes] myȝt H$_5$Ws ne] neyþer H$_5$, nor WsM in] þe A, thys *add.* Cc, thi *add.* M 18 þou þynkest] H$_7$RLB$_3$AsEPH$_6$CcMPl, þe þinkiþ HBH$_5$SrWsChLwAHu$_2$LdTW, apparet tibi Lat. myght] may CcM 19 or . . . reformed^{2}] *om.* H$_5$AsWsChHu$_2$, *om.* Lat. or . . . reformed (l. 20)] *om.* Cc or elles] And T it^{2}] he BLdT 20 myght] *om.* Ld reformed] *om.* M 21 To] Tho Ld, Vnto SrCcM I . . . and] answere I M sey] *om.* Lw is] ben H$_5$Ws maner] maneres BEM 22 þe] H$_7$RLB$_3$AsAPH$_6$CcMPl, *om.* HBH$_5$SrWsChLwHu$_2$ELdTW in^{1}] of H$_5$Ws anoþer] And anoþer RAsCc, And þat oþer E is^{3}] *rep.* L, *om.* A in^{2}] of R, þe *add.* M 23 life] *om.* As 24 delayde] til *add.* H$_5$Ws 25 fully/be] *rev.* ELd fully] *om.* Cc reformed] restored and *prec.* T þat^{1}] þe RAsAE þat^{2}] *om.* B `þe´ L, his A first/begynnynge] *rev.* Cc first] *om.* T 26 þurgh] bi APl had^{2}] þo *add.* M 27 schal] ssulde B restorid] reformyd CcM, in *add.* A and . . . ioye] *om.* M mikel^{2}] *om.* Cc, more *add.* LB$_3$EP 28 mikel] endless SrCcM, grete Hu$_2$EW and] H$_7$H$_5$LB$_3$WsPH$_6$; þe *add.* HRBAsSrChLwAHu$_2$ECcMLdPlTW endeles] *om.* SrCcM

had neuere fallen. For þan schal þe soule resceyuen þe hol and þe fulfillinge of God in al þe myghtes of it, withouten medelure of ony oþer affeccion, and it schal seen mankende in þe persone of Jesu abouen þe kynde of angeles, oned to þe godhede. For þan schal Jesu boþe God and man be al in al, and only he, and non oþer þan he, as þe prophete seyth: *Dominus solus exaltabitur in die illa*. Þat is: Oure Lord Jesu in þat day, þat is þe aylastend day, schal be heghed only, and non bote he. And also þe bodi of man schal þan be glorifyed, for it schal resceyue fully þe riche dowarye of vndedlynes with al þat longeth þerto. Þis schal a soule han with þe bodi, and mikel more þan I kan seyn, but þat schal be in þe blisse of heuene and nought in þis lyfe.

For þow it be so þat þe passion of oure Lord be cause of þis ful reformynge of mans soule, neuerþeles it was nought his wil for to graunte þis ful reformynge as tyte aftere his passion to alle chosen soules þat weren lyuend in þe tyme of his passion; but he delayed it
f. 47^{v} vnto þe last day, and þat for | þis skil. Soth it is þat oure Lord Jesu of his mercy hath ordeyned a certeyn nombre of soules to saluacion, þe qwilk nombre was not fulfilled in þe tym of his passion. And þerfore it nedid þat be lengthe of tyme þurgh kendly generacion of men it schuld be fulfilled. Þan if it had so ben þat, as tyte after þe deth of oure Lord, euerilk a soule þat wuld haue trowed in him schuld anon sodeynli ha ben blissed and be ful reformed withouten any oþer abydyng, þer wuld no creature þat liued þan þat he ne wld han resceyued þe feith fore to ha ben made blissed; and þan schuld

29 had/neuer] *rev.* LB$_3$P   fallen] cecidisset in peccatum Lat.   soule] *om.* B$_3$ hol] holynesse A, oyle M, feling *add.* T   ⌜and . . . myghtes (l. 30)⌝ L   þe^{3}] *om.* SrWs   30 fulfillinge] fullyng M, full felynge W   þe] H$_7$RBAsSrAECcMPlT, `þe´ H$_6$, *om.* HH$_5$LB$_3$WsChLwHu$_2$PLdW   myghtes] viribus et potenciis Lat.   wiþouten] *rep.*, *canc.* Pl   medelure] medlynge BAsLwAH$_6$TW   31 and] þat RAs   Jesu] oure blissed Lord *prec.* Hu$_2$   32 oned] vnyed E, ioyned M   33 boþe God] Deus Lat. [Deus *om.* Y]   `only´ Pl   and^{3} . . . he^{2}] *om.* Lat.   and^{3}] in H$_5$Ws   þan] H$_7$RLB$_3$AsAPH$_6$, bot HBH$_5$SrWsChLwHu$_2$ECcMLdPlTW   34 seyth] Ysa. 2° *add.* BLHu$_2$EPLdTW   die illa] H$_7$RLB$_3$AsSrAEPH$_6$CcMPl, *rev.* HBH$_5$WsChLwHu$_2$LdTW, die illa Lat.   þat is] *om.* A   35 Jesu] *om.* As   þat is þe . . . day^{2}] *om.* M   is] in *add.* A   þe] H$_7$RBLB$_3$AsSrAPH$_6$Pl, *om.* HH$_5$WsChLwHu$_2$ELdCcTW   aylastend] H$_7$HRLAPCcMPl, euerelastynge BH$_5$B$_3$AsSrWsChLwHu$_2$EH$_6$LdTW   day] *om.* Cc   heghed] heyued Sr   only] *om.* A   non] oþir *add.* A   36 And] *om.* SrLd   þan] *om.* Cc   37 resceyue fully] *rev.* E   of] and Cc   vndedlynes] vndedly lyues B   with] *om.* Pl   38 a] the M   soule] doo *add.*, *canc.* L   kan seyn] scio exprimere vel sufficio Lat.   39 `þat´ Sr, þis H$_5$Ws   schal] he *add.* BH$_5$   þe blisse of heuene] regno celorum Lat.   lyfe] vita misera et mortali Lat.   40 be cause] was because Sr   be] bi L [*marg*: quere bi or be], bi or be P [bi or *canc.*, *marg.*: quere]   ful] H$_7$R`L´B$_3$AsSr`H$^{c}$´AEPH$_6$CcMPlW, *om.* H°BH$_5$WsChHu$_2$LdT, plene Lat.   41 `of . . . reformynge (l. 42)´ H^{c}, *om.* H°H$_5$Ws, anime humane, non tamen voluit concedere hanc plenam reformacionem Lat.   neuerþeles]

fallen. For þan schal þe saule resaiue þe hole and þe fulfillyng of God in alle miȝtes of it, wiþoutyn meduleure of ony oþer affeccioun, and it schal see mankynde in þe persoun of Ihesu abouen þe kynde of aungels, aned to þe godhed. For þan schal Ihesu boþ God and man be al in al, and anly he, and none oþer bot he, as þe prophet saiþ: *Dominus*
66v *solus exaltabitur in illa die.* | þat is: Oure Lord Ihesu in þat day, þat is aylastand day, sal be heiȝed only, and non bot he. And also þe body of man schal þan be glorified, for it sal resaiue fully þe riche dowary of vndedlynes with alle þat longes þerto. þis shal a soule haue with þe body, and mikel more þen I can sey, bot þat schal be in þe blis of heuen and not in þis liif.

For þawȝ it be so þat þe passioun of oure Lord be cause of þis reformyng \`of mannes soule, neuerþeles it was ⌜not⌝ his wille for to grant þis ful reformyng′ als tite after his passioun to alle chosen saules þat were lifand in tyme of his passioun; bot he delayed it vnto þe last day, and þat for þis skil. Soþ it is þat oure Lorde Ihesu of his mercy has ordeyned a certeyn noumbre of saules to saluacioun, whilk noumbre was not fulfillid in þe tyme of his passioun. And þerfore it nedid þat bi lengþe of tyme þorw kyndly generacioun of men it suld be fulfillid. þan if it had so ben þat, as tit aftir þe ded of oure Lord, euerilk a saule þat wald haue trowed in hym sulde belyue haue ben blessed and ful reformed wiþouten ony oþer abydynge, þer wald no creature þat lyued þan ha ben þat he ne wald haue receyuide þe feyþe for to ha ben blessid; and þan suld generacioun ha sesid, and so suld

ȝit Cc nought] ⌜not⌝ H^c for] *om.* E 42 \`ful′ R, *om.* As reformynge] fully *add.* As, of mannes soule *add.* E as tyte] H$_7$HRChLwHu$_2$LdT, anon H$_5$LB$_3$WsAECcMPl, as anon B, as soone As, as swithe Sr, ryght anone W his] þe T \`to . . . passion′ (l. 43) L, *om.* RAsSrCc, omnibus electis animabus que tunc erant Lat. 43 þe] H$_7$, þat A, *om.* Σ his] holy *add.* Hu$_2$ but] *om.* H$_5$Ws 44 vnto] into BAsAE, til to Ld þat] *om.* LB$_3$EPH$_6$CcM, is *add.* Ch, was *add.* W skil] reson Hu$_2$ Jesu] *om.* SrCcM, Cryste *add.* W 45 his] grete *add.* H$_5$WsHu$_2$ þe] H$_7$RLB$_3$AsSrAPH$_6$CcMPl, *om.* HBH$_5$WsChLwHu$_2$ELdTW 46 þe] *om.* LB$_3$SrAPH$_6$ And] *om.* ACcM it] *om.* As 47 nedid] nedeth M be] *om.* Cc, in þe H$_5$Ws, þe *add.* LB$_3$EPH$_6$ lengthe] longitudine et processu Lat. 48 so ben] *rev.* ELd so] *om.* M as tyte] H$_7$HRLChLw, anon BH$_5$B$_3$WsAHu$_2$EH$_6$MLd, as sone AsSrPCcTW, *om.* Pl after . . . Lord] as the passion of oure Lord was don Cc þe deth] passion A 49 Lord] Jesu *add.* H$_5$Ws euerilk a] H$_7$HR, euerilk Ch, eueryche a BH$_5$Ws, eueryche As, euery LB$_3$SrAHu$_2$EPH$_6$CcMLdPlTW euery a Lw þat . . . him] *om.* M trowed] troweþ As, leued B, belyued AHu$_2$ELd anon sodeynli] H$_7$LB$_3$PH$_6$, anon RAsSrAHu$_2$ECcMLdPlT, belyue H, by lyfe BCh, by hys lyf LwW, be bileue H$_5$Ws 50 ben] sauyd and *prec.* H$_5$Ws be] H$_7$RLB$_3$AsSrLwAEPCcPl, *om.* HBH$_5$WsChHu$_2$MLdTW, haue be H$_6$ ful] fully RAsT 51 no] non Cc liued] lyuys Ld þan] H$_7$RLB$_3$AsSrLwAEPH$_6$CcMPl, ha ben *add.* HBH$_5$WsChHu$_2$LdTW þat^2 . . . wld] but M 52 made] H$_7$RLB$_3$AsSrLwAEPH$_6$CcMPl, *om.* HBH$_5$WsChHu$_2$LdT þan . . . and (l. 53)] *om.* M \`schuld′ L

generacion han sesid, and so schuld we þat arn now lyuend chosen soules, and oþer soules þat comen after vs, not ha ben born, and so schuld oure Lord ha failed of his nombre. But þat may not be. And þerfor oure Lord purueyd for vs mikel bettre, in þat þat he delayed þe ful reformynge of mans saule `vn´to þe last end. As Seynt Poule seith: *Deo pro nobis melius prouidente ne sine nobis consummarentur*. Þat is: Oure Lord purueyd bettre for vs in delayinge of þe ful reformynge þan if he had graunted it þanne, for þis skil: þat þe chosen soules herebeforn schuld not make a ful end withouten vs þat comen after.

Anoþer skil is þis. For syn þat a man in hise first formynge of God was sette in his fre wil and had fre chesyng wheyþer he wuld hafe fully God or non, it was þerfor resonable þat, syn he wulde not chesen God þanne bote wrecchedly fel fro him, if he schuld afterward be reformed þat he schuld ben sette ageyn in þe same fre chesynge þat he was first in, wheþer he wuld haue þe profyte of his reformynge or non. And þis may ben a skil qwhi mans soule was not fully reformed anon aftere þe passion of oure Lord Jesu Crist.

Þat reformynge in partie is on two maneris: on in feith; anoþer is in feith and in felynge. Capitulum v^{m}

Anoþer reformynge of þis ymage `is´ in partye, and þis reformynge may ben had in þis lyfe; and but if it be had in þis lyfe, it schal neuer ben had, ne þe soule schal neuer be saufe. But þis reformynge [is] on
f. 48^{r} þis two maneris: on is in feith only, anoþer is in feith and in felynge. | þe ferst, þat is reformynge in feith, suffyceth to saluacion; þe secound

53 han] ha`ue´ H$^{c}$ so] *om.* P lyuend/chosen soules] *rev.* LwW 54 and . . . soules$^{2}$] *rep.* M, *om.* P and] or H$_{6}$ soules$^{2}$] *om.* Sr þat comen] *rep.* Sr þat] whiche E comen] schulle *add.* H$_{5}$Ws 55 ha] *om.* H$_{5}$Ws nombre] numerus electorum . . . eternaliter ordinatus Lat. `be´ R `And´ Pl 56 oure] blissed *add.* Hu$_{2}$ for vs/mikel better] H$_{7}$RLB$_{3}$AsSrAEPH$_{6}$CcMPl, *rev.* HBH$_{5}$WsChLwHu$_{2}$LdTW bettre] bet H$_{5}$Ws `he´ L 57 of] in H$_{5}$Ws `vn´to] H$_{7}$, to AH$_{6}$, til H$_{5}$Ws, and to B, til to Ld, into Sr end] diem Lat. As] And M seith] ad Hebr. xi° *add.* LHu$_{2}$EPLd, Eze. 11° *add.* B 58 melius prouidente] *rev.* Cc melius] *om.* Ld ne sine] sine fine Ch 59 purueyd bettre] *rev.* Cc purueyd] purueyeth W delayinge] the delaye W þe] our W ful] H$_{7}$RLB$_{3}$AsSrAEPH$_{6}$CcMPl, *om.* HBH$_{5}$WsChLwHu$_{2}$LdTW, plene Lat. 60 `he´ Pl `it´ H^{c}, *om.* H°BChHu$_{2}$Ld þanne] hem M, peracta passione Lat. skil] reson Hu$_{2}$ 61 herebeforn] here ben forn Cc `make´ Cc a ful] an LB$_{3}$EPH$_{6}$CcM, plenarie Lat. þat] whiche E 62 Anoþer] And *prec.* LB$_{3}$EPH$_{6}$ skil] reson Hu$_{2}$ For] that Cc þat] *om.* CcM a] H$_{7}$RLB$_{3}$AsAEPH$_{6}$CcMPl, *om.* HBH$_{5}$SrWsChLwHu$_{2}$LdTW first formynge] *rev., marked for trsp.* Cc formynge] reforming A 63 chesyng] choys AHu$_{2}$ hafe fully] *rev.* EM, fallyn to Cc 64 non] no H$_{5}$ALwEW, nout Cc it was/þerfor] *rev.* EH$_{6}$ þat] for þat H$_{6}$, and Pl syn] þat *add.* H$_{5}$LWsPH$_{6}$ 65 þanne] *om.* A wrecchedly] voluntarie Lat. fel] ful B, fle LB$_{3}$EP, tho went M, cecidit Lat. schuld] wold

we þat are now lifand chosen soules, and oþer soules þat come after vs, not ha ben born, and so suld oure Lord ha failed of his numbre. But þat may not be. And þerfor oure Lord purueid mikel better for vs, in þat þat he delaied þe ful reformyng of mannus saule vnto þe last ende. As Saint Poul seis: *Deo pro nobis melius prouidente ne sine nobis consummarentur*. Þat is: Oure Lord purueid better for vs in delayng of þe reformyng þan if he had granted \`it´ þanne, for þis skil: þat þe chosen soules herbeforn suld not make a ful ende wiþouten vs þat come aftir.

Anoþer skil is þis. For sen þat man in his first fourmyng of God was set in his fre wil and had fre chesyng wheþer he wald haue fully God or non, it was þerfore resonable þat, sen he wald not chese God þan bot wrecchidly fel fro hym, if he schuld aftirward be reformid þat
67^r | he suld be set agayn in þe same fre chesyng þat he was first in, wheþer he wald haue þe prophet of his reformyng or non. And þis may be a skil whi mannus soule was not reformid fulli als fast aftir þe passioun of oure Lord Ihesu Crist.

[CHAPTER 5]

Anoþer reformyng of þis ymage is in partie, and þis reformyng may ben had in þis liif; and bot it be had in þis lif it may neuer be had, ne þe soule neuer sal be saf. Bot þis reformyng is on two maners. On is in faiþ only, anoþer is in faiþ and in felyng. Þe first, þat is reformyng in faiþ only, sufficeþ to saluacioun; þe second is worþi to haue passand

CcM be] han ben Cc 66 schuld ben] *om.* A sette] *om.* Sr in] and put to M same] *om.* Cc fre] wil and *add.* Hu$_2$ chesynge] choys A first in] *rev.* E 67 þe] *om.* ALw, ff- *add.*, *canc.* E his] þys BLd non] no H$_5$LB$_3$APLdW 68 a] oon M skil] reson Hu$_2$ anon] als fast HChLwW, as swiþe Ld, as sone T \`aftere´ L 69 oure Lord] *om.* LwCcW Jesu Crist] *om.* SrM

Chapter 5 *title*: H$_7$RLB$_3$AsSr\`H^c´AEPH$_6$MLdPlTW *om.* H°BH$_5$WsChLwHu$_2$Cc 1 þat . . . on^1] Hou mannis soule may be reformid to þe liknes of Crist in H^c þat] þe Pl, þe *add.* LB$_3$EPH$_6$ on^1] in AMLdPl on^2] þat is H^c, is *add.* E feith^1] and *add.* EMLdW anoþer . . . in^2 (l. 2)] *om.* H^c anoþer] þat oþer E, is *add.* EPl 2 \`feiþ and in´ T$^G$W$^G$, *om.* TW in$^2$] *om.* AH$_6$M 3 \`is´ *interl.* H$_7$ 4 \`if´ Sr, *om.* HH$_5$WsLwH$_6$CcMT schal] H$_7$RLB$_3$AsSrAEPH$_6$CcMPl, may HBH$_5$WsChLwHu$_2$LdTW, habebitur Lat. 5 had] *om.* SrM schal neuer] H$_7$RLB$_3$AsSrLwEPH$_6$CcMPlT, *rev.* HBH$_5$WsChHu$_2$Ld, maye neuer W schal] *om.* A neuer] *om.* Cc, nec unquam . . . post hanc vitam Lat. saufe] sauyd Hu$_2$CcLdPl is] *om.* H$_7$ on] H$_7$HRLB$_3$AsSrLwAPH$_6$CcTW, in BH$_5$WsAHu$_2$EMT, vnto Ch 6 þis] H$_7$, *om.* Σ maneris] manere P in^1] the *add.* P anoþer] and *prec.* M, and þat oþer E in^3] *om.* M 7 þat is] *om.* LwW, which is E reformynge] reformed Pl, þe *prec.* LEP feith] H$_7$RLB$_3$AsSrAPH$_6$MPl, only *add.* HBH$_5$WsChLwHu$_2$ECcLdTW, fide Lat. suffyceth] suffice Ch

is wurthi to haue passend mede in þe blis of heuene. þe first may be had lyghtly and in schort tyme; þe secounde may not so, bot þurgh length of tyme and mikel gostli trauaille. þe first may ben had with þe felynge of þe ymage of sinne, for þow a man fele noþyng in himself bot alle sterynges of sinne and fleschly desyres, he may nought ageynstondene al þat felinge if he wilfully assent [not] þerto, reformed in feith to þe liknes of God. But þe seconde reformynge putteth oute þe lykinge and þe felynge of fleschli sterynges and werdly desires, and suffreth non swilk spottes abyden in þis ymage. þe first reformyng is only of begynnynge and protyfend soules and of [actyf men]; þe secunde is of perfyt soules and of men contemplatyfe. For by þe first reformynge þe ymage of sinne is not destroied, but it is lefte as it were al hol in felyng. Bot þe seconde reformynge destroieth þe old felynges of þis ymage of sinne, and bryngeth into þe soule newe graciouse felyngis þurgh werkyng of þe Holi Gost. þe first is good, þe seconde is bettre, bot þe þridde, þat is in þe blisse of heuene, þat is alderbest. First begyn we [to] speke of þat on, and siþen of þat oþer, and so schal we comen to þe þredde.

þat þurgh þe sacrament of baptem, þat is grounded in þe passion of Crist, þis ymage is reformed fro þe original sinne. Capitulum vi^{m}

Two maner of sinne maken a soule to lesen þe schap and þe lyknes of God. þat on is kalled original, þat is þe ferst sinne; þat oþer is called

8 to] for to Sr be had/lyghtly] *rev.* Sr 9 `in′ H$^c$, *om.* H°BChHu$_2$ not] be *add.* RAsPl þurgh length] by processe B 10 length of] long RAsHu$_2$ `of′ Sr tyme] the *prec.* M mikel] grete Hu$_2$ may] nouȝth *add.* As with] þourȝe Pl 11 þe] *om.* CcPl þow] þat *add.* E man] wil *add.* H^c noþyng] nout CcM 12 sterynges] steryng SrWs sinne] synnys CcM he may/nought . . . þerto (l. 11)] H$_7$RLB$_3$AsSrAEPH$_6$CcMPl, *rev.* HBH$_5$WsChLwHu$_2$LdTW 13 ageynstondene] H$_7$RAsAMPl, ageynstondend HBH$_5$WsChLwLdTW, wiþstondynge LB$_3$SrHu$_2$EPH$_6$ [synne *add.*, *canc.* L], withstondyn the felyngis Cc al] And *prec.* M þat felinge] tho felyngis Cc þat] þe Pl if] but if Sr wilfully/assente not þerto] *rev.* T wilfully] wil fully Cc not] *om.* H$_7$ þerto] H$_7$, be *add.* HBH5LB$_3$WsChLwAHu$_2$EPH$_6$LdPlTW, he schal be *add.* RAsSr, is *add.* M, ne he hath delectacyon therinne, thanne is he *add.* Cc, nec in ea delectetur Lat. 14 in feiþ] *om.* M oute/þe . . . sterynges (l. 15)] *rev.* Cc 15 þe^1] *om.* HH$_5$LwT and þe felynge] *om.* M and þe] in þe Lw, in W felynge of] *om.* Cc of] þe *add.* M fleschli] flesch by Lw sterynges] likyngis ChHu$_2$ and . . . desires] *om.* CcM 16 non] no H$_5$WsELdW, noȝt A spottes] spott H$_5$Ws þis] the Cc is only] *om.* As 17 `and$^2$′ H$_6$, *om.* Cc actyfe men] atycement H$_7$ 18 of perfyt . . . contemplatyfe] homines perfectos contemplatiuos Lat. of$^2$] perfite *add.* H$_5$Ws men contemplatyfe] H$_7$RAsSrCcMPl, *rev.* HBH$_5$LB$_3$Ws-ChLwAHu$_2$EPH$_6$LdTW by] *om.* Cc 19 `were′ L 20 in] as in E þe^2] þis H$_5$Ws, al A, *om.* LB$_3$PH$_6$ felynges] felynge H$_5$Ws 21 þis] þe Cc into] in Ch þe]

mede in þe blis of heuen. þe first may be had liȝtly and `in´ schort tyme; þe seconde may not so, bot þorw lengþe of tyme and mikil gostly trauail. þe first may ben had wiþ þe felyng of þe ymage of synne, for þawȝ a man fele noþing in hymself bot alle stirynges of synne and flescly desires, not agaynstandand þat felyng if he wilfully assente not þerto, he may be reformid in feiþ to þe liknes of God. Bot þe secunde reformyng puttes out likyng and þe felyng of fleschly stirynges and wordly desires, and suffres non swilk spottes abide in þis ymage. þe first reformyng is only of bigynnand and profitand soules and of actiue men; þe seconde is of perfite soules and of contemplatif men. For by þe first reformyng þe ymage of synne is not distroed, bot it is left as it were al hole in felyng. Bot þe second reformyng distroyes þe olde felynges of þis ymage of synne, and brynges into þe soule new gracious felynges þorw wirkyng of þe Holy Goost. þe first is gode, þe seconde is better, bot þe þridde þat is in þe blis of heuen is alþerbest. First bigyn we to speke of þe ton, and siþen of þe toþer, and so sal we come to þe þridde.

[CHAPTER 6]

67^v Two maners of syn makes a soule to lese þe schape and þe | liknes of God. þat on is cald original, þat is þe first synne; þat oþer is callid

om. As 22 felyngis] felynge H_5Cc, of thys ymage *add.* Lw þurgh] be Cc werkyng] þe *prec.* RAsHu_2ECcW, werkes Pl Holi] *om.* Pl good] and *add.*, *canc.*, *canc. erased* L, and *add.* B_3EP, but Sr 23 bot] *om.* Cc þat[1]] which E þat[2]] H_7RH_5LB_3AsWsAPH_6MPl, *om.* HBSrChLwHu_2ECcLdTW `is´ L alderbest] best of alle AHu_2, al þe best E, moos best W, optima . . . et perfectissima Lat. 24 begyn we to] lett vs LwW to] forto T, *om.* H_7 of[2]] on M so] at þe laste *add.* H_5Ws schal we] *rev.* H_5WsLwW schal] schuld Cc 25 to] that other, that is *add.* M þredde] aftyr þat we arn passed out of this world *add.* Cc

Chapter 6 *title*: H_7RLB_3AsSrAEPH_6MLdPlTW `Hou a soule may lese his shap and his reformyng þoruȝgh two maner of synnes: on is original, an oþer is actuel.´ $H^c$ *om.* $H^\circ$B$H_5$WsChLw$Hu_2$Cc 1 þe[1]] *om.* A sacrament] uirtutem Lat. þat is grounded] que fundatur et constitit Lat. 2 `ymage´ T^GW^G þe[3]] *om.* AsLdTW original] generall T 4 Two] THo H_5, Hwoo E maner] maners HBE, genera Lat. sinne] H_7H°BH_5LB_3WsChAEPH_6, synnes RAsSrLw`H^c´Hu_2CcMLdPlTW, peccatorum Lat. a] þe BH_6LdW soule] man H_5Ws to] forto SrM þe schap and þe lyknes] similitudinem Lat. and] of Cc þe[2]] worschip *add.*, *canc.* L 5 kalled original] *rev.* ChHu_2 kalled] clepid H_6Ld þat[2] . . . sinne] *om.* A þat[2] . . . ferst] *om.* Cc þat[3]] the Cc called] clepid H_6Ld

actuel, þat is wilfully don sinne. Þese two sinnes putten a soule fro þe blisse of heuene and dampne it to þe endles peyn of hell bot if it be by grace of God reformed to his liknes or it passe hennis out of þis lyfe.

Neuerþeles two remedies þer arn ageynes þese two sinnes, by þe qwhilk a forschapen soule may be restored ageyn. On is þe sacrament of baptem ageyns þe original sinne; anoþer is sacrament of penance ageyns actuel sinne. A soule of a child þat is born and is vncristened f. 48v bycause of þe original | sinne hath no lykenes of God; he is nought but an ymage of þe fende and a bronde of helle. But as son as it is cristned it is reformed to þe ymage of God, and þurgh vertu of feith of Holi Kirke sodeynli is turned fro þe liknes of þe fend and made like to an angle of heuene. Also þe same falleth in a Jewe or in a Saraceyne, þe qwilk er þay ben cristened arn nought but manciples of helle. Bot qwen þey forsaken þer errour and fallen mekly to þe trowth in Crist, and resceyuen þe baptem of water in þe Holi Gost, sothli withouten any more taryenge þey arn reformed to þe liknes of God so fully, as Holi Kirke troweth, þat if þey myghten als swyþe after baptem passen out of þis werld þei schulden streight flyen into heuene withouten any more lettynge, had þey don neuer so mikel sinne beforn in tyme of her vntrowth, and neuer schulde þe felen þe peyn of helle ne of purgatorie; and þat priuylege schulde þei haue be þe merite of þe passion of Crist.

6 þat is wilfully don/sinne] *rev.* LB$_3$P, þat is synne wilfully don EH$_6$, Original synne is the first synne. Actual synne is wilfully don Cc þat is] *om.* RAs wilfully] wilful H$_5$Ws sinne] *om.* Ld putten] away *add.* LwPlW 7 to] into Cc þe] H$_7$RLB$_3$AsSrLwAEPH$_6$CcMLdPlW, *om.* HBH$_5$WsChLwHu$_2$T peyn] peynes B$_3$ of hell] *om.* SrCcM if] *om.* Hu$_2$ by] H$_7$, þorw Σ, per Lat. 8 grace] H$_7$RLB$_3$AsSrAPCcMPl, þe *prec.* HBH$_5$WsChLwHu$_2$EH$_6$LdTW passe] passeth RAs hennis] *om.* SrHu$_2$H$_6$CcMLd lyfe] werld Cc 9 two remedies/þer arn] *rev.* H$_6$ þer arn] H$_7$RBH$_5$LB$_3$AsSrWsAHu$_2$EPH$_6$MPl, *rev.* HChLwCcTW, ben Ld þese] þe AsAM 10 þe] *om.* RAMPl 11 þe] H$_7$RLB$_3$AsSrAEPH$_6$CcMPl, *om.* HBH$_5$WsChLw-Hu$_2$LdTW original . . . is] *om.* P \`anoþer . . . sinne′ (l. 12) R  anoþer] The toþer E, The secunde Hu$_2$  sacrament] H$_7$H°RBChAPM, þe *prec.* H$_5$LB$_3$AsSrWs-Lw\`H^c′Hu$_2$EH$_6$CcLdPlTW 12 actuel] H$_7$HBH$_5$WsChLwHu$_2$CcMLdTW, þe *prec.* RLB$_3$AsSrAEPH$_6$Pl A] Also of *prec.* A, þe LB$_3$EPH$_6$M is[2]] *om.* AM vncristened] nouȝt cristened H$_5$WsECcM, as *add.* M 13 bycause] as *prec.* M þe] H$_7$RLB$_3$AsSrAEPH$_6$CcMPl, *om.* HBH$_5$WsChLwHu$_2$LdTW hath . . . God] non reformatur ad Dei similitudinem Lat. no] non As nought] *om.* Cc, ellis *add.* E 14 as] also AsM it] he B$_3$ 15 to þe ymage] *om.* M vertu] the *prec.* AsSrLwEMW feith] H$_7$HBH$_5$LB$_3$ChLwHu$_2$PH$_6$CcLdW, þe *prec.* RAsSrWsAEMPlT 16 is] it is

actuel, þat is wilfully don syn. þese two synnes puttes a saule fro þe blis of heuen and dampnes it to endeles peyne of helle, bot if it be þorw þe grace of God reformed to his liknes or it passe heyn out of þis lif.

Nerþeles two remedies ar þer agayns þis two synnes, be þe whilk a forschapyn soule may be restored agayn. On is þe sacrement of bapteme agayn original synne; anoþer is `þe´ sacrament of penaunce agayns actuel synne. A soule of a child þat is borne and is vncristned because of original synne has no liknes of God; he is not bot an ymage of þe fende and a brand of helle. Bot als sone as it is cristned it is reformid to þe ymage of God, and þorw vertue of faiþ of Holy Kirke sodenly is turned fro þe liknes of þe fende and made like to an aungel of heuen. Also þe same fa⌜lliþ⌝ in a Iewe or in a Sarecene, þe whilk are þei be cristned ar nouȝt bot manciples of helle. Bot when þei forsake þere errour and falles mekely to þe trowþ in Crist, and receyue þe bapteme of watir in þe Holy Gost, soþly wiþouten ony more tarynge þei are reformed to þe liknes of God, so fully as Holy Kirke trowes, þat if þei miȝt as swiþ after baptem passe out of þis world þei suld strey`ȝ´t flye to heuen withoutyn ony more lettyng, had þei doun neuer so mikel syn bifore in þe tyme of þeire vntrouþ, and neuer suld þei fele þe peyn of helle ne of purgatorie; and þat priuilege suld þei haue bi þe merite of þe passioun of Crist.

AsCcW þe[1]] *om.* H_5Ws liknes of þe] *rep.* B to] vnto Sr 17 an angle] aungeles M falleth in] H_7RAsLwAEPlCcW, fa⌜lliþ⌝ in H^c, falleþ into Sr, falle in M, falleþ to LB_3PH_6, faiþ in BH_5WsChHu_2LdT, accidit de Lat. in] to W, *om.* H_6CcM 18 þe] *om.* LB_3EP er] til H_5Ws nought bot] *om.* Cc nought] *om.* Hu_2 manciples] and brondys *add.* Cc 19 errour] errourys As to] vnto T trowþ] feyþ BA in] of CcLd 20 and] *om.* A þe] to R, *om.* Cc of] þe *add.* ChHu_2 `water in´ L sothli] anon *add.* M 21 more] *om.* LB_3PH_6, absque mora Lat. so fully] *om.* Cc 22 troweth] leeueþ BM, bileuiþ AHu_2Ld myghten . . . werld (l. 23)] deyid forthwith aftyr here baptem Cc als swyþe] anon BH_5WsHu_2, as soone W 23 of] *om.* Pl þei] the M streight flyen] *rev.* H_5Ws, gon streyt Cc into] H_7Sr, to Σ, ad Lat. 24 more] *om.* CcM þey] he H_5 don neuer] *rev.* H_6Ld in] *om.* A tyme] H_7RLB_3ChAHu_2EPH_6CcMLdPl, þe *prec.* HBH_5AsSrWsLwTW 25 vntrowþ] vnfeiþfulnes Ld, of byleeue *add.* B neuer schulde/þe] *rev.* H_5Ws, þei schulde neuere H_6Cc felen] of *add.* LB_3EPH_6, fyndyn Cc þe[2]] *om.* SrCcM peyn] peyns Hu_2 of[1]] in Cc ne of purgatorie] vel purgatorii Lat [*canc.* YHe] ne of] ner in Cc 26 schulde] H_7HBH_5SrWsChLwAHu_2CcMLdTW, schuln RLB_3AsEPH_6Pl, haberent Lat. þe] *om.* M merite] myȝt Lw þe passion of Crist] Cristus passion LwACcW 27 Crist] Jesu Ld, oure blissed Lord Jesu Hu_2, oure Lord Jesu Crist M, Jesu Christi Lat.

þat þurgh þe sacrament of penance, þat stondes in contricion, and in confession, and in satisfaccion, þis ymage is reformed fro actuel sinnes. Capitulum vii^{m}

Also qwat cristen man or wumman þat hath lost þe liknes of God þurgh dedli sinne, brekend Godis comandementz, if he þurgh touchynge of grace sothfastli forsake his synne with sorowe and contricion of herte, and be in ful wil for to amende him and turne him to God and to gode lyuynge, and in þis he resceyueth þe sacrament of penance if þat he may, or elles if þat he may not he is in ful wil þerto; sothly I seye þat þis mans soule or wummans þat was forschapen ferst to þe ymage of þe deuel þurgh dedly synne, is now be þe sacrament of penance restorid and schapen ageyn to þe ymage of oure Lord God. þis is a grete curteysye of oure Lord and an endles mercy, þat so lightly forgyfeth al maner synne and so sodeynly gyfeth plente of grace to a synful soule þat asketh mercy of him. He abydeth no grete penance doynge ne pynful fleschli sufferyng or he forgyfe it,
f. 49^{r} bot he asketh a loþing of synne and a ful forsakynge of it in wil of þe | soule for loue of him, and a tornyng of þe herte to him. þis asketh he, for þis gifeth he.

And þan whan he seeth þis, withouten any delayenge he forgefeth þe sinne and reformeth þe soule to his liknes. þe synne is forgifen þat þe soule schal not be dampned. Neuerþeles þe pyn dettid for þe synne is not ȝete fully forgifen, bot if contricion and loue be þe more. And þerfore schal he gon and schewen him and schryuen him to his gostli fadere, and resceyuen penance enioyned for his trespase and gladli

Chapter 7 *title*: H$_7$RLB$_3$AsSrAEPH$_6$MLdPlTW `Hou a soule þat haþ lost þe liknes of Crist þorow dedly synne, yet þorow þe sacrament of penaunce wilfully taken he may be restorid to þe ymage and to þe ful liknes of Crist Jesu.´ H$^{c}$ *om.* H°BH$_5$WsChLwHu$_2$Cc 1 `þurgh´ L 2 and in^{1}] *om.* EH$_6$ and^{1}] H$_7$LB$_3$PTW, *om.* RAsSrAMPl in^{2}] *om.* AH$_6$M 3 sinnes] H$_7$SrM, synne Σ (*from* R), peccatis actualibus Lat. 4 cristen man or wumman] christianus Lat. þat] *om.* Cc lost . . . lyen (l. 15/8)] *om.* Hu$_2$ *(fourteen ff. missing)* þe] *rep.* A 5 þurgh^{1}] with Cc, a *add.* LwW comandementz] comaundement BChLd þurgh^{2}] H$_7$HH$_5$SrWsLwH$_6$MLdTW, þe *add.* RBLB$_3$As-ChAEPCcPl 6 grace] God`us´ *prec.* A synne] brekynge *add.* H$_5$Ws, *canc.* H and] in H$_5$Ws 7 `ful´ L for] *om.* B 8 to God and] *om.* LwW and to] be Cc and^{1}] *om.* A to^{1}] *om.* Ld in . . . resceyueth] receiue Cc þis] H$_7$, wil *add.* Σ [forsayd wylle *add.* W], voluntate Lat. he resceyueth] resceyue M he] *om.* W 9 þat] H$_7$RLB$_3$AsSrAEPH$_6$MPl, *om.* HBH$_5$WsChLwCcLdTW elles] H$_7$RLB$_3$AsSrAEPH$_6$Pl, *om.* HBH$_5$WsChLwCcMLdTW if . . . not/he/is . . . wil] *rev.* Cc þat] H$_7$RLB$_3$AsSrAEPMPlW, *om.* HBH$_5$WsChLwH$_6$CcLdT he^{3}] *om.* Cc is] be Cc 10 ful] H$_7$RBLB$_3$AsSrChAEPH$_6$CcMLdPl, *om.* HH$_5$WsLwTW, plenam Lat. þerto] *om.* Cc þis mans] his Cc mans] *om.* A or wummanns] *om.* ACc, illius Lat. þat] which E

[CHAPTER 7]

Also what cristen man or womman þat has lost þe liknes of God, þorw dedly syn brekand Godis comandementes, if he þorwȝ touchyng of grace soþfastly forsake his synne with sorw and contricioun of hert, and be in ful wil for to amende hym and turne hym to God and to goode lifyng, and in þis wil he ressayues þe sacrament of penaunce if he may, or if he may not he is in wil þerto; soþly I say þat þis mannus soule or wommannus þat was forschapyn first to þe liknes of þe deuil
68r þorw dedly syn, is now be þe sacrament | of penaunce restored and schapen agayn to þe ymage of oure Lord God. þis is a gret curtesie of oure Lord and an endeles mercy, þat so liȝtly forgifes al maner of syn and so sodenly gifes plente of grace to a synful soule þat askis mercy of hym. He abides not gret penaunce doyng ne pynful flescly suffryng or he forgife it, bot he askes a loþing of synne and a ful forsa[k]yng in wil of þe soule for þe luf of hym, and a turnyng of þe herte to hym. þis askes he, for þis gifes he.

And þan when he sees þis, wiþoutyn ony delayng he forgifes þe syn and reformes þe soule to his liknes. þe syn is forgifen þat þe saul sal not be dampned. Neuerþeles þe payn dettid for þe syn is not ȝit fully forgifen, bot if contricioun and luf be þe more. And þerfore schal he go and schewe hym and schryfe hym to his gostly fadir, and resayue penaunce enioyned for his ⌜tres⌝pas and gladly fulfille it, so þat boþ þe

was] þis *add.* Ld 11 forschapen] forshaped T ymage] H_7, liknes Σ be] in T 12 to] vnto T 13 Lord[2]] God *add.* RAsSr and . . . mercy] *om.* Cc `and an´ L an] *om.* H_6 14 lightly] sone Cc maner] $H_7RLB_3AsAPH_6Cc$, of *add.* $HBH_5SrWsCh$-LwELdPlMTW gyfeth] ȝif M 15 of[1]] et R þat] which E He] and M 16 no] $H_7RLB_3SrAEPH_6CcMPl$, not $HBH_5WsChLwLdTW$, non As, Non expectat Lat. ne . . . sufferyng] *om.* Cc 17 a[2]] *om.* T forsakynge] forsasyng H of it in wil of] $H_7RLB_3AsAEPH_6MPl$, þerof in wille of Sr, in wil of HBChLwLdTW, of wil in H_5Ws, of it Cc, et illud relinquat voluntarie Lat. wil] þe *prec.* E 18 loue] $H_7RH_5LB_3As$-SrWsAEPH_6Pl, þe *prec.* HBChLwCcMLdTW and . . . he (l. 19)] *om.* Cc and a tornyng] et per conuersionem Lat. 19 for . . . he] quia istud ex gracia sua donat et concedit Lat. þis] H_7HRH_5AsSrWsChLwAMLdPlTW, þus LB_3EPH_6Cc he] hem H_5Ws 20 þan] *om.* Cc þis] þus Ld delayenge] delay SrCcM 21 reformeth] reformed M 22 Neuerþeles] But Cc, But *prec.* M dettid] dew AMLd, *om.* Cc þe[3]] *om.* H_6 23 ȝete] *om.* RCcM forgifen] put awey Cc and loue] *om.* RAsLd, seu dileccio Lat. 24 schal he] *rev.* AsH_6CcM gon . . . to] be shrevyn of Cc and[1]] *om.* SrM schewen . . . him[2]] confessionem facere Lat. schewen him and] *om.* RAsAPl schewen/. . . /schryuen] *rev.* Ld and schryuen hym] *om.* MT to] at As, the prest *add.* M 25 enioyned] enened M, *om.* Cc

fulfille it, so þat boþe þe sinne and þe peyne may be don away or he passe hens. And þat is þe skilful ordinance of Holi Kirke for grete profyte of mans soule: þat þogh þe synne be forgifen þurgh verrey contricion, neuerþeles in fulfillyng of meknes and for to make hol satisfaccion, he schal if þat he may schewe to his prest plener confession, for þat is his tokne and his waraunt of forgifnes ageyns al his enemys, and þat is nedful for to haue. For if a man had forfetyd his lyfe ageyns a kynge of þis erth, it were nought inogh to him as ful sykernes for to haue only forgyfnes of þe kynge, but if he haue a chartre þe whilk may be his tokne and his waraunt ageyns al oþer men. Ryght so it may be seide gostli: if a man haue forfetyd ageyns þe kynge of heuene his lyfe þurgh dedly synne, it is nought inogh to him to ful sykernes for to haue forgyfnes of God only betwix God and him, bot if he haue a chartre made be Holy Kirke, if he may come þerto, and þat is þe sacrament of penaunce, þe qwhilk is his chartre and his tokne of forgifnes. For syþen þat he forfetid boþen ageyns God and Holy Kirke, it is skilful þat he haue forgyfnes for þe ton and a waraunt for þe toþer. And þis is on skil why þat confession is nedful.

Anoþer skil is þis: for syþen þis reformynge of þe soule stondeth in þe feith only, not in felynge, þerfore a fleschli man þat is rude and boystous and kan nought demen lyghtly bot outwarde of bodili þinges, schuld not moun han trowed þat his synnes had ben forgyfen but if he had sum bodily tokne, and þat is confession, þurgh þe whilk f. 49v tokne | he is made siker of forgifnes if he do þat is in him. Þis is þe trouþe of Holy Kirke, as I vnderstonde.

Also anoþer skil is þis: þogh þe grounde of forgifnes stonde not

26 so þat] and so Cc 27 hens] away *add.* Pl, ex hac vita Lat. `is þe´ L, *om.* B_3, is H_6 Kirke] is *add.* B_3 28 verrey] $H_7RLB_3AsSrPH_6CcMPl$, vertue of $HBH_5WsChELdT$, the wertue of Lw, per veram Lat. 29 neuerþeles] ȝet Cc meknes] and obedience *add.* B for to make] for to takyn SrCc, in makinge LB_3P, plenam satisfaccionem peragendam Lat. 30 if] as sone as Cc `þat´ W^G, *om.* $H_5LB_3PH_6Cc$ schewe] it *add.* Cc, hym *add.* M to] *rep.*, *canc.* Sr his] thys Lw prest] gostly fader Cc plener] be pleyn Cc 31 tokne . . . waraunt] signum . . . et securitas Lat. his[2]] *om.* H_6 ageyns . . . enemys] *om.* Lat. 32 for[1]] *om.* T had] have Cc 33 erth] werld Cc `nought´ $H^c$ to] for M as] $H_7RLB_3AsAPH_6CcM$, for a *add.* HBChLwECcTW, for `a´ *add.* H_5, for *add.* WsLd, to *add.* Sr, pro Lat. 34 for . . . kynge] of þe kyng only to haue forȝifnes H_5Ws of þe kynge] *om.* A haue] hadde Cc 35 chartre] tokne H_5Ws þe whilk] which H_5Ws, þat H_6 may] shuld Cc tokne and . . . waraunt] signum . . . et defensio Lat. tokne and his] *om.* CcM 36 it may] H_7CcM, *rev.* Σ haue] ouȝt *add.* M forfetyd] forfended B 37 of] *om.* Ch his lyfe] *om.* SrCcM þurgh] be Cc `nought´ As to him] *om.* SrM 38 to[1]] of Cc ful] *om.* A, haue As `for´ Sr, *om.* Cc `of God´ L only] H_7, by contricion *add.* Σ [oonli *further add.*, *canc.* B_3], per solam cordis contricionem Lat. betwix] bitwen AEH_6CcM, atwix L 39 be] of Cc 40 and[1] . . .

syn and þe payn may be don awey or he passe heþen. And þat is þe skilful ordinaunce of Holy Kirke for gret profit of mannus soule: þat þowȝ þe syn be forgifen þorw vertue of contricioun, neuerþeles, in fulfillyng of meknesse and for to make hole satisfaccioun, he schal if þat he may schew to his prest plener confessioun, for þat is his tokne and his warant of forgifnes ageyns alle his enemise, and þat is nedful for to haue. For if a man had forfetid his liif ageyn a kyng of þis erþ, it were \`not´ inow to hym as for a ful sikernes for to haue only forgifnes of þe kyng, bot if he haue a chartre þe whilk may be is tokne and his warant agayns alle oþer men. Riȝt so may it be said gostly: if a man haue forfetid agayn þe kyng of heuen his lif þorw dedly syn, it is not inow\`ȝ´ to hym to ful sikernes for to haue forgifnes of God only by contricioun bitwix God and hym, bot if he haue a chartre mad by Holy Kirke, if he may come þerto, and þat is þe sacrement of penaunce, þe whik is his chartre and his token of forgifnes. For sen þat he forfetid boþ agayn God and Holy Kirke, it is skilful þat he haue forgifnes for þe ton and warant for þe toþer.

8v And þis is o skil whi þat confessioun |is nedful. Anoþer skil is þis: for sen þis reformyng of þe saule standes in fayþ only and not in felyng, þerfor a flescly man þat is rude and boistus and can not deme liȝtly bot outward of bodili þinges, sold not mow haue trowed þat his synnes had be forgifen him bot if he had som bodily tokne, and þat is confessioun, þorw þe whilk tokne he is made a⌜s⌝ siker of forgifnes if þat he do þat in hym is. Þis is þe trouþ of Holy Kirke, as I vndirstande. Also anoþer skil is þis: þawȝ þe ground of forgifnes

chartre] et certe sacramentum penitencie est carta sua Lat.   þe[2]] *om.* E   41 syþen þat] siþþe LB$_3$P, siþe he þat [he *canc.*] E   forfetid] forfeteþ LB$_3$PH$_6$, forisfecit et deliquit Lat. 42 skilful] skyl Sr   a waraunt] H$_7$BLB$_3$ALdEPH$_6$W, waraunt HRH$_5$AsSrWsChLwMPlT, \`a´ warnyng Cc, securitatem defensinam Lat.   43 toþer] oþer Lw   And . . . nedful] *om.* RAsAPl, Et hec est vna causa quare confessio expediens est et necessaria Lat.   þis] that Cc   is[1]] *om.* SrW   on] the Cc   þat] *om.* CcM   is[2]] was and is H$_5$Ws   44 Anoþer] And *prec.* M   for syþen þis] þat siþen þe LB$_3$PH$_6$ reformynge of þe soule] de qua nunc loquor *add.* Lat.   in þe feith/only] *rev.* Cc   45 þe] H$_7$, *om.* Σ   not] H$_7$RLB$_3$AsSrAEPH$_6$CcPl, and *prec.* HBH$_5$WsChLwMLdTW   in] of As   \`man´ *d.h.* H$_5$, lyuer Ws   rude and] stiborne M, *om.* Cc   and boystous] *om.* Sr   46 and] that M   kan nought demen] not demyth Cc   nought] *om.* T   lyghtly] *om.* M   47 schul\`d´ Sr   moun han] *rev.* M   moun] *om.* A   trowed] byleeued B   synnes] synne R   forgyfen] H$_7$RLB$_3$AsSrAPH$_6$CcMPl, him *add.* HBH$_5$WsChLwELdTW, remitti Lat.   48 tokne] tokening A, signe M   is] verrey *add.* M   þe] *om.* ECc   49 siker] H$_7$SrACcM, al *prec.* RLwW, as *prec.* ⌜H⌝BH$_5$LB$_3$AsWsChEPH$_6$LdPlT, assecuratur Lat.   if] so be T, þat *add.* HBChLwTW   is/in him] H$_7$, *rev.* Σ   þis is] *om.* M   50 trouþe] leeue B, bileue ALd   of Holy Kirke] *rep.*, *canc.* Sr   Kirke] and þe feyþ *add.* B   vnderstonde] ytt *add.* LwW   51 Also] And *prec.* As, *om.* Cc   not] only and *add.* M princypally in confession bot in contricion of herte and forþenkynge of sinne, neuerþeles I hope þat þer is many a soule þat schuld neuer han feled verrey contricion ne had ful forsakynge of sinne if confession had not ben. For it falleth ofte-syþes þat in tyme of schrifte grace of compunccion cometh to a soule þat beforn neuer feled grace, bot ay was colde and drye and fer fro felynge of grace. And forþi, syþen schrifte was so profytable to þe more part of cristene men, [Holi Kirke ordayned for more sykernes generally to al cristene men], þat euerilk man and wumman schuld ones in þe ȝere atte leste be schryuen of al here synnes þat comen to þer mende to here gostli fadere, þogh þei haue had neuer so mykel contricion befor tyme.

Neuerþeles, I hope wel þat if al men had ben as besy aboute þe kepyng of hemself in fleyng of alle maner sinne and had come to as grete knowyng and felyng of God as sum man is, þat Holy Kirke schuld neuere haue ordeynd þe tokne of confession as for a nedeful bonde, for it had not nedid. Bot for al men arn not so perfyte, and perauenture mikel of þe more partye of cristen men is vnperfyte, þerfore Holy Kirke ordeynd confession be weye of general bonde to al cristen men þat wilen knowen Holy Kirke as her modere and wil ben buxum to hire biddyng. If þis be soth, as I hope it is, þan erreth he gretly þat generaly seith þat confession of synnes for to schewe to a prest is neyþere nedful to a synnere ne behofely, and þat no man is bounden þerto. For by þat þat I haue seid, it is boþe nedful and spedful to alle soules þat in þis wrecched lyf arn diffouled þurgh

52 herte] H$_7$RH$_5$LB$_3$AsSrWsChAEPH$_6$CcMPl, þe *add.* HBLwLdTW and] H$_7$RLB$_3$AsSrAEPH$_6$CcMPl, in *add.* HBH$_5$WsChLwLdTW forþenkynge] forsakyng Ld, ovirthynkyng Cc 53 sinne] þe *prec.* T hope] trow AH$_6$ þat^1] *om.* Cc soule] man AM 54 ne] noþer B, neiþer T had] *om.* Cc if . . . not (l. 55)] ne had confession H$_5$Ws 55 ofte-syþes] oftyn Sr, oft tyme AH$_6$, oftyn tymes CcW^G in] the *add.* W 56 schrifte] H$_7$RLB$_3$AsSrAEPH$_6$CcMPl, confession HBH$_5$WsChLwLdTW \`cometh´ Cc þat] which E neuer feled] *rev.* As 57 bot . . . grace] *om.* P ay] H$_7$HRLAsChPCc, euere BH$_5$B$_3$WsLwAEH$_6$MPlTW, alwey SrLd fer] ferder W felynge] visitacione Lat. 58 forþi] H$_7$HRLB$_3$AsChPH$_6$MPlT, for þe Ld, þerfore BH$_5$SrWsLwAEW, *om.* Cc syþen] þat *add.* H$_5$Ws schrifte] H$_7$RLB$_3$AsSrAEPH$_6$CcMPl, confession HBH$_5$WsChLwLdTW to] for H$_5$Ws 59 Holi . . . men (l. 60)] Σ, *om.* H$_7$, ideo Ecclesia pro maiori securitate ordinauit generaliter pro omnibus christianis Lat. ordayned] it *add.* LB$_3$PH$_6$ for] þe *add.* LwW to] for B \`al´ L, *om.* H$_6$ cristene men] *rev.*, *marked for trsp.* Pl 60 euerilk] ech H$_6$ man and wumman] vtriusque sexus Lat. man] cristene *prec.* MLd and] H$_7$HBSrWsChLwAECcMLdPlTW, or RH$_5$LB$_3$AsPH$_6$ atte leste] *om.* Sr 61 \`al´ L þat . . . fadere] *om.* Lat. þat] whiche E comen] *rep.*, *canc.* Cc 62 haue] *om.* RAsLwACcMPlW mykel] gret Cc tyme] þe *prec.* As, tymys SrM 63 Neuerþeles . . . biddyng (l. 71)] *om.* Lat. Neuerþeles] But ȝit Cc 64 hemself] himself H$_5$, hem Cc fleyng H$_7$Ws-

stonde not principally in confessioun bot in contricioun of þe hert and in forþinkyng of syn, neuerþeles I hope þat þer is many a saule þat suld neuer haue felid verrey contricioun nor had ful forsakyng of syn if confessioun had not ben. For it fallis oft-siþis þat in tyme of confessioun grace of conpunccioun comes to a soule þat before neuer felid grace, bot ay was coold and drye and ferre fro felyng of grace.

And forþi sen confessioun was so profitable to þe more partie of cristen men, Holy Kirke ordaynd for more sikernes generally to alle cristen men, þat euerilk man and womman sulde ones in þe ȝere at þe lest be schryuen of alle þaire synnes þat come to þaire mynde to þare gostly fader, þawȝ þei haue had neuer so mikil contricioun before tyme. Nerþeles I hope wel þat if al men had ben als bisy aboute þe kepyng of þamself in ⌜fle⌝yng of al maner of syn, and had comen to als grete knowyng and felyng of God as sum man ⌜haþ⌝, þat Holy Kirke suld not haue ordeynd þe tokne of confessioun as for nedful bonde, for it had not nedid. Bot for alle men are not so perfite, and perauenture mikil of þe more partie of cristen men is vnperfite, þerfore Holy Kirke ordaynd confessioun bi way of general bond to alle cristen men þat wil knowe Holy Kirke as þaire modir and wil be buxum to here biddyng. If þis be soþ, as I hope it is, þen erres he gretly þat generally says þat confessioun of synnes for to schewe a prest is nouþer nedful to a synner ne behofle, and þat no man is
69r bounden | þerto. For bi þat þat I haue seid, it is boþ nedful and spedful to alle soules þat in þis wrecchid lif er defouled þorw synne,

ChLwECcMLdW^{G}, ⌜fle⌝yng H^{c}, eschewynge W, felyng RBH$_5$LB$_3$AsSrAPH$_6$PlT `of^{1}' E maner] H$_7$RH$_5$LB$_3$SrWsChAPH$_6$CcMLdPlT, of *add.* HBAsLwECcW sinne] synnes M as] a Ld, moche *add.* W 65 grete] good A and felyng] *om.* BSrLd of God] *om.* H$_6$ sum man] synne M man] men RB is] H$_7$BH$_5$LB$_3$WsChPMT, hath RAsSrLw⌜H^{c}⌝A-ECcPlW, doþ H$_6$, *om.* Ld 66 neuere] H$_7$LB$_3$SrPH$_6$CcM, not HRBH$_5$AsWs-ChLwAELdPlTW haue] had *add.*, *canc.* L for] to A a] H$_7$RBLB$_3$AsSr-AEPH$_6$CcMLdPl, *om.* HH$_5$WsChLwTW 67 bonde] bon Ch for] be as moche as Cc 68 mikel of] for Cc, *om.* SrM of^{1}] or Ws partye] peple H$_5$Ws is] ben A, are H$_6$CcM vnperfyte] inperfiȝt B$_3$M 69 ordeynd] ordeyneþ B$_3$As confession] confessions B, schrifte SrCcM be] in LB$_3$EP of] a *add.* SrCcM 70 men] *om.* BT þat] whiche E wilen] *om.* SrPl as] as for ET wil] *om.* Cc ben] *om.* M 71 hire] þer B biddyng] heest Ld it is] *om.* Cc erreth he . . . seith (l. 72)] errant qui dicunt Lat. 72 generaly seith] *rev.* H$_5$Ws þat . . . nedful/to a synnere (l. 73)] *rev.* Sr þat confession] *rep.*, *canc.* Sr synnes] synne LB$_3$EP for to] to H$_6$ to^{2}] H$_7$H$_5$LB$_3$AsWsEPH$_6$CcTW^{G}, hit M, *om.* HRBSrChLwALdPlW a] þe B 73 behofely] H$_7$HBSrWsChCcPl, behoueful RH$_5$LB$_3$AsLwAEPH$_6$LdTW, spedeful WsM þat^{1}] *om.* LB$_3$PH$_6$ 74 þerto] ad confessionem huius modi Lat. `þat^{2}' L, whiche E, *om.* H$_6$M it] talis confessio Lat. 75 alle] þe *add.* As þat] whiche E

sinne, and nameli to þo þat arn þurgh dedli synne forschapen fro þe liknes of God, þe whilk moun not be reformyd to his liknes bot by þe sacrament of penance þat principally stondeth in contricion and sorwe of herte, and secundarylye in schrifte of mouth folwende after if it mow ben had. Vpon þis maner, be þe sacrament of penaunce is a
f. 50^{r} synful soule reformyd to þe ymage of God and to his | lyknes.

How in þe sacrament of baptem and of penance, þurgh a preuey vnperceyueable werkyng of þe Holi Gost, þis ymage is reformed, þogh it be not seen ne feled. Capitulum viii^{m}

Bot þis reformynge stondeth in feyth and not in felyng. For ryght as þe properte of feith is to trowen þat þu seest not, ryght so it is to trowe þat þou felest not. But he þat is reformed in his soule be þe sacrament of penaunce to þe ymage of God, he felith no chaungynge in himself, neyþer in his bodily kende withouten ne in þe priuey substaunce of his soule withinnen, oþer þan he dyd. For he is as he was vnto his felynge, and he feleth þe same sterynges of synne and þe same corrupcion of his flesch in passions and werdli desyres risend in hise herte as he dyd beforne. And ȝete neuerþeles schal he trowe þat he is þurgh grace reformed to þe liknes of God, þogh he neyþer fele it ne see it. He may fele wel sorwe for his synne and a turnynge of his wil fro synne to clennesse of lyuynge, if þat he haue grace and take good kepe of himself, bot he may neþer seen ne felen þe reformynge of his soule, how it is wunderly and vnperceyuably chaunged fro filthe of þe fende to þe fayrhed of an angel þurgh a priuey ⟨gracyous⟩ werkynge of oure Lord God. Þat may he not seen, but he schal trowe it; and if he trowe it, þan is his soule reformed in feith.

76 þo] those W, þilke Ld, hem A þat] þe whiche E þurgh] be Cc 77 þe whilk] whyche LwEW to] vnto T `bot´ L 78 and] in *add.*, *canc.* Sr 79 and] may be had *add.* As secundarylye] $H_7RLB_3AsSrLw$⌜H^c⌝$AEPH_6MPl$, þe secunde $BH_5WsChLd$, secundary CcTW 80 Vpon] On H_6 þe] thys LwW penaunce] þat principally stondeþ in contricion and sorowe of herte *add.* AsCc 81 synful] *om.* Cc soule] man H_5 reformyd] þat is synful *add.* Cc to²] vnto M lyknes] blysful *prec.* Cc

Chapter 8 *title*: $H_7RLB_3AsSrAEPH_6MLdPlTW$ `Hou a soule þat is reformid þorow þe sacrament of penaunce muste stonde stabelly in þe feiþ of Holy Chirche.´ H^c *om.* $H^{\circ}BH_5WsChLwCc$ 1 in] þoru H_6 þe sacrament] sacramentys Sr of¹] penance *add.* A þurgh] *rep.* A 2 Gost] is *add.* Ld 4 For] *om.* As ryght] *om.* SrE 5 properte] profite T feith] the *prec.* LwCcW to¹] H_7Cc, for to Σ trowen] byleeue BALd þat] þyngis þat *add.* Ld not] *om.* Ch to²] H_7ACc, for to Σ trowe] byleeue BALd, leue M 6 `he´ Pl þat] whiche E `is´ Pl 7 in] of H_5Ws 8 neyþer] ne E, nor M ne] neyþer H_5, nor Ws þe] *om.* CcT 9 his] the LwW dyd] before *add.* T is] still *add.* T vnto] as to ALd, to E 10 felynge] of himself *add.* A sterynges] styrynge H_5WsCcM, felyngis and *prec.* As 11 corrupcion] corrupcions B_3 in¹] his *add.* As passions] passion M desyres] desiryngs

and namly to þoo þat are þorw dedly synne forschapyn fro þe liknes of God, þe whilk may not be reformed to his liknes bot be þe sacrament of penaunce þat principally stondis in contricioun and sorow of hert, and ⌜secundarily in⌝ shrift of mouþ folwand after if it may be had. Vpon þis maner, bi þe sacrement of penaunce, is a synful soule reformed to þe ymage of God and to his liknes.

[CHAPTER 8]

Bot þis reformyng stondiþ in faiþ and not in felyng. For riȝt as þe proprete of faiþ is for to trow þat þou sees not, riȝt so it is for to trow þat þou felis not. Bot he þat is reformid in his soule bi þe sacrament of penaunce to þe ymage of God, he felis no chaungyng in hymself, neþer in his bodily kynde wiþouten ne in þe priue substaunce of his soule within, oþer þan he did; for he is as he was vnto his felyng, and he felis þe same stirynges of syn and þe same corupcioun of his flesche in passions and werdly desyres risand in his hert as he did bifore. And nerþeles schal he trowe þat he is þorw grace reformid to þe liknes of God, þawȝ he neiþer fele it ne se it. He may wel fele so`r´w for syn and a turnyng of his wil fro syn to clennesse of lifyng, if þat he haue grace and take gode kepe of hymself, bot he may noþer see ne fele `þe´ reformyng of his soule, how it is wonderly and vnperceyuablely chaunged fro þe filþ of a fende to þe fairhed of an aungel, þorw a priue graciouse wirkyng of oure Lord God. Þat may he not see, bot he sal trowe it; and if he trowe it, þan is his soule reformid in trouþ.

M, *om.* LwW 12 And ȝete] H_7RLB_3AsSrAEPH_6CcPl, And HBH_5WsChLwLdTW, As M neuerþeles] *om.* Cc schal he] *rev.* MW trowe] byleeue B 13 neyþer] neuere B 14 `ne´ L  fele wel] $H_7$RL$B_3$AsSrAEPCcMPl, *rev.* HB$H_5$WsChLw$H_6$LdTW  for] of Ch  his[1]] $H_7$RL$B_3$AsSrLw`H^c´AEPH_6CcMPlW, *om.* H°BH_5WsChLdT, suis Lat. synne] peccatis suis Lat. and . . . synne] *om.* M 15 to] into Cc clennesse of] clensynges in M lyuynge] feelynge B haue] H_7HBH_5AsWsChLwECcMLdPlTW, haþ RLB_3SrAPH_6 take . . . of[1] (l. 16)] inspiciat diligenter Lat. 16 kepe] help B of[1]] to AsCcMT neþer] neuere Sr, nout Cc `þe´ H reformynge] reformacyon Cc 17 wunderly] H_7HRBH_5AsSrWsChLwAECcLdTW, wondirfully LB_3PH_6M vnperceyuably] is *add.* Sr filthe] H_7RLB_3SrAEPH_6CcMPl, þe *prec.* HH_5AsWsChLwLdTW, þe foulhede B þe] H_7RLB_3AsSrLwAEPH_6CcMPlW, þis Ld, *om.* HBH_5WsChT 18 to] vnto LwTW fayrhed] fairnes WsLwTW an] *om.* E gracyous] grace/cyous H_7 [*at line end*] 19 oure Lord God] the Holy Ghost LwCcMW [Lw *text* oure Lord Gode *canc.*, the Holy Gost *part of an addition of missing text*], Domini Dei nostri Lat. þat . . . seen] *om.* Lat. þat] whiche E may he] *rev.* E he not] be not *marked for rev.* R trowe] two in R, byleeue BA, leue M and . . . it] *om.* SrCc 20 trowe] byleue BALd, leue M is his soule] schal his soule be H_6 `his soule´ Pl, in anima sua Lat. his] the Cc feith] H_7RBLB_3AsSrAEPH_6CcMLdPl, trouþ HH_5WsChLwTW, per fidem ad Dei similitudinem Lat.

For ryght as Holy Kirke troweth be þe sacrament of þe baptem sothfastly resceyued a Jewe or a Saraceyn or a child born is reformed in soule to þe lykenes of God þurgh a priuey vnperceyuable wirkyng of þe Holy Gost—not ageynstondende al þe fleschly sterynges of his bodi of sinne, þe whilk he schal felen after his baptem as wel as he dyd before—ryght so be þe sacrament of penaunce mekly and trewly resceyuede a fals cristen man þat hath ben encumbred with dedly synne al his lyf tyme is reformed in his soule withinne vnperceyuably, outtakyn only a turnyng of his wil þurgh a priuey myght and a gracious werkyng of þe Holi Gost þat sodeynly wirketh and in tyme of
f. 50^v a moment or a | twynkelynge of an eye, ryghtith a f[ro]ward soule and turneth it fro gostly filth to fayrnes vnseable, and of a seruaunt of þe fende maketh a son of ioye, and of þe prisoner of helle maketh a percenere of heuenly heritage, not ageynstondend al þe fleschly felyng of þis synful ymage, þat is þe bodily kende. For þou schalt vnderstonden þat þe sacrament of baptem or of penaunce is not of þat vertu for to letten and destroien vtterly al þe steryngis of fleschly lustes and pynful passions, þat a man schuld neuer felen no maner rysyng ne sterynge of hem no tyme. For if it were so, þan were a soule fully reformed here to þe wurchipe of þe ferst makynge; but þat may not be fully in þis lyfe. Bot it is of þat vertu þat it clenseth þe soule fro al þe synnes before don, and if it be departed fro þe body saueth it fro dampnacion, and if it dwelle in þe body it gyfeth þe soule grace for to ageynstonden þe sterynges of synne. And it kepeth it in grace also, þat no maner steryng of lust or of passiouns þat it felith in þe flesch, be it neuer so greuous, schal deren it ne departen it fro God, as long as it wilfully senteth not þerto. þus Seynt Poul mened when he seyd þus:

21 troweth] byleeueþ BLd, leueth M, that *add.* CcM þe²] H_7, *om.* Σ 22 resceyued] and *add.* Ld a²] *om.* Ld born] *om.* A 24 ageynstondende] withstanding ACcE sterynges] steryng Cc of² . . . sinne] *om.* Lat. 25 of] to Ld þe] *om.* E 26 before] afore H_6 be] lo Ch 27 with] in HH_5WsT 29 only] H_7RLB_3AsSrAEPH_6CcMPl, *om.* HBH_5WsChLwLdTW myght] *om.* Cc 30 þat] whiche E in] þe *add.* M 31 a moment or] *om.* Ld \`a¹´ Cc ryghtith] rightneth M a²] in T froward] Σ, forward H_7M, distortam Lat. 32 it] him B_3, *om.* H_6 filth] foulehed B to] and M vnseable] inuisible A, vnceyuable Pl, vnperceyuable M, þat is gostly and invisible B, þat may nat be seyn H_6 a] the Cc of²] *om.* Sr 33 son . . . a²] *om.* As son] soule ECc of²] *om.* HBChLd 34 percenere . . . heritage] heredem celestis regni Lat. percenere] H_7HRAsSrChAMPl, pertynere BH_5LB_3WsLwEPH_6LdT, perceyuer W, pursuere Cc ageynstondend] withstanding AE al] of Ld felyng] felyngis AsPl 35 þat] whiche E \`is´ Cc 37 and] or H_5Ws, to *add.* M steryngis] steryng H_6 38 passions] so *add.* H_6 man . . . felen] H_7RLB_3AsSrAPH_6CcMPl, mans saule . . . felid HBH_5WsChLd, mannys sowle . . . fele LwETW, homo . . . senciet Lat. no . . .

For riȝt as Holy Kirk trowes, by þe sacrament of bapteme soþfastly
resceyued, a Iewe or a Sarecene or a child born is reformed in soule to
þe liknes of God, þorw a priue vnperceuable wirkyng of þe Holy
Gost, not agaynstandand alle þe flescly stirynges of his body of synne,
þe whilk he sal fele aftir his bapteme als wele als he did bifore; riȝt so
bi þe sacrement of penaunce, mekly and trewly rescayued, a fals
9v cristen man þat has ben encumbred in dedly synne alle | his lif tyme is
reformid in his saule wiþinne vnperceyuably, outtakyn a turnyng of
his wille, þorw a priue miȝt and a gracious wirkyng of þe Haly Gast,
þat sodanly wirkes and in tyme of a moment or a twynkelyng of an yȝe
riȝtes a fraward saule and turnes it fra gastly filþ to fairnes vnseable,
and of a seruant of þe feende makes a sone of ioy, and þe prisoner of
helle makes a percener of heuenly heritage, not agaynstandand alle þe
flescly felyng of þis synful ymage, þat is þe bodily kynd. For þu sal
vndirstande þat þe sacrament of bapteme or of penaunce is not of þat
vertu for to let and distroie vtterly alle þe stirynges of flescly lustes
and paynful passions þat a mans saule neuer felid no maner risyng ne
stiryngis of þam no tyme. For if it were so, þan were a soule fully
reformed here to þe worscipe of þe first makyng; bot þat may not be
fully in þis lif. Bot it is of þat vertu þat it clensiþ þe soule fro alle þe
synnes before done, and if it be departid fro þe body saues it fro
dampnacioun, and if it dwelle in þe body it gifes þe soule grace to
agaynstand þe steryng of syn. And it kepis it in grace also, þat no
maner of lustly stirynges or of passiouns þat it felis in þe flesch, be it
neuer so greuous, sal dere it ne depart it fro God, as longe as it wilfully
sentis not þerto. Þus Seynt Poul menyd when he seid þus: *Nichil*

sterynge (l. 39)] tales motus Lat. maner] of *add.* ACc 39 ne] and Cc sterynge] stiryngis HLwTW \`hem' L  \`it' H$_6$Pl were/a soule] *rev.* M 41 lyfe] here *add.* H$_5$Ws þat it] *om.* Lw \`þe' Pl  42 þe synnes] synnes M, synne Cc  body] it *add.* RAsAECcMPlW$^G$, he *add.* Sr  43 \`it' L þe soule] þe only H$_5$Ws, \`soule' *d.h.*H$_5$, it oonly T, also *add.* E, illi Lat. þe^2] *om.* Pl for to] H$_7$RLB$_3$AsSrAPCcMPl, to HBH$_5$WsChLwEH$_6$LdTW 44 ageynstonden] withstand AE. sterynges] H$_7$LB$_3$SrWsEPH$_6$CcMPlW, steryng HRBH$_5$AsChLwALdT, motibus Lat. it^2] *om.* Cc also] And also Cc, *om.* E 45 steryng of lust] H$_7$LB$_3$SrEPH$_6$CcMPl, of stirynge of lust RAsA, of lustly stirynges HBH$_5$WsChLwLdTW [lusty T], motus voluptatum Lat. passiouns] passioun LB$_3$EP, compassiones M, passionum Lat. it felith] it felid Ch, *om.* Cc 46 schal] nat *add.* H$_6$ deren . . . heued (l. 10/10)] *om.* Ch deren] greue Pl, oþer anoye *add.* Ld ne] or H$_5$Ws departen] parten RAsH$_6$ 47 wilfully . . . not] wole fully nout consentyn Cc senteth not] *rev.* M senteth] H$_7$HLB$_3$LwPH$_6$CcPlTW, assentiþ RBH$_5$AsSrWsALdM, consentiþe E þus] þis As Seynt Poul/mened] *rev.* H$_6$ mened] menyþ H$_5$WsCcM seyd] seyþ H$_5$WsCc þus] þis wordus M, Ro. 4° *add.* B, ad Ro. 8° *add.* LEPLd

Nichil dampnacionis est hiis qui sunt in Christo, qui non secundum carnem ambulant, etc. þat is: þese soules þat arn reformed to þe ymage of God in feith þurgh þe sacrament of baptem or of penaunce, schul not be dampned for felynges of þis ymage of synne, if it so be þat þei go not after þe sterynges of þe flesch be fulfyllyng of dede.

þat we schul trowen stedfastly reformyng of þis ymage if oure conscience witnesse vs a ful forsakyng of synne and a trew turnynge to God of oure will to gode lyuynge. Capitulum ix^m

Of þis reformynge in feith speketh Seynt Poul þus: *Iustus autem ex fide viuit.* þe ryghtwys man lyueth in feith; þat is, he þat is made ryghtful be baptem or penaunce he lyueth in feith, þe qwilk sufficeth vnto f. 51r saluacion and to | heuenly pes, as Seynt Poul seith: *Iustificati ex fide pacem habemus ad Deum.* þat is: We þat arn ryghtyd and reformed þurgh feith in Crist han pes and acorde made betwixen God and vs, not ageynstondende þe viciouse felynges of oure bodi of synne.

For þogh þis reformynge be priuey and may not wel be feled here in þis lyfe, neuerþeles whoso trow it stedfastly and chape his werkes bisily for to acorde to his trowþe, and þat he turne not ageyn to dedly sinne, sothly whan þe howre of deth cometh and þe soule is departyd fro þis bodily lyfe, þan schal he fynd it soth þat I seye now. þus Seyn John seyd in comfort of chosen soules þat lyuen here in feith vnder þe felyng of þis pynful ymage: *Karissimi, et nunc sumus filii Dei, sed non apperuit quid erimus; scimus autem quoniam cum apperuerit, tunc*

48 est] in Lw, in *add.* E sunt/in Christo] *rev.* Pl in Christo qui] *om.* LwW Christo] Jesu *add.* A 49 etc.] H$_7$HH$_5$LB$_3$WsPT, *om.* RBAsSrLwAEH$_6$CcMLdPlW þat is] to seye *add.* As, *om.* T, Quasi diceret Lat. þese] þe H$_5$WsMT, Here Cc þat] þe whiche E 50 þe sacrament of] *om.* SrCcM þe] *om.* A or of penaunce] *om.* R `or´ L of^2] *om.* SrH$_6$CcM schul] shulde T 51 felynges] H$_7$HRLB$_3$AsLwAEPH$_6$PlTW, felyng BH$_5$SrWsCcMLd, sensacionibus Lat. þis] þat RAsAPl of synne] om. Sr so be] *rev.* H$_6$ 52 sterynges] stirynge H$_5$Ws, and the onclene mevyngis *add.* Cc þe/flesch be] *rev.* H$_5$Ws fulfillyng of dede] deed doyng LwW of] in BAsE, of þe T, that in *add.* Cc dede] `in ful concert´ *add. d.h.* L

Chapter 9 *title*: H$_7$RLB$_3$AsSrAEPH$_6$MLdPlTW *om.* HBH$_5$WsLwCc 1 schul] sholde BTW trowen] bileue ALd, leue M stedfastly] þe *add.* T þis] þe Ld if] of AsLd 2 witnesse] to *add.* LdTW and] `after´ *add. d.h.* L, aftir *add.* E 3 to God] H$_7$, *om.* Σ, to^2 . . . lyuynge] *om.* Sr 4 Of] Ef M in feith] *om.* CcM feith] H$_7$RLB$_3$AsSrLwAEPH$_6$CcMPlW, þe *prec.*, *canc.* H, *prec.* BH$_5$WsLdT þus] Hebr. 10° *add.* BELdTW autem] H$_7$RLB$_3$SrAEPH$_6$CcMPl, *om.* HBH$_5$AsWsLwLdTW 5 viuit] þat is*add.* EH$_6$M ryghtwys] ryghtful SrE is^1] *om.* As ryghtful] riȝwis A, a rythwysman Cc 6 or] and As penaunce] H$_7$RLB$_3$AsAPH$_6$CcMPl, be *add.* HBH$_5$SrWsLwELdTW þe] *om.* EW vnto] H$_7$HRBH$_5$AsWsLwAEPlW, to LB$_3$SrPH$_6$CcMLdT 7 seith] *om.* B$_3$, Ro. 5° *add.* BLEPLdTW, alibi *add.* Lat. 8 þat] þis LB$_3$PM ryghtyd] justefied B `and reformed´ Pl 9 þurgh feith/in Crist]

dampnacionis est hiis qui sunt in Christo qui non secundum carnem ambulant, etcetera. Þat is: þase saules þat are reformid to þe ymage of God in faiþ þorw þe sacrament of baptem or of penaunce, schal not be dampned for felynges of þis ymage of synne, if it so be þat þai go not aftir þe stirynges of þe flesche by fulfillyng of dede.

[CHAPTER 9]

Of þis reformyng in [þe] faiþ spekis Seynt Poul þus: *Iustus ex fide viuit*: þe riȝtwis man lifes in faiþ; þat is, he þat is mad riȝtful be baptem or be penaunce he lifes in faiþ, þe whilk sufficeþ vnto
70r sauacioun and to heuenly pees, | as Seynt Poul says: *Iustificati ex fide pacem habemus ad Deum*. Þat is: We þat ar riȝtid and reformed þorw faiþ in Crist has pees and acorde made bitwix God and vs, not agaynstandand þe vicious felynges of oure body of syn.

For þawȝ þis reformyng be priue and may not wel be felid here in þis liif, nerþeles whoso trowes it stedfastly and schape his werkes besily for to acorde to his trowþ, and þat he turne not agayn to dedly synne, soþly when þe oure of ded comeþ and þe soule is departid fro þis bodily ⌜lyfe⌝, þan schal he fynde it soþ þat I say now. Þus saide Seint Johan, in conforþ of chosen soules þat lifen here in faiþ vnder þe felyng of þis peynful ymage: *Karissimi, et nunc sumus filii Dei, sed nondum apparuit quid erimus. Scimus quoniam cum Christus a⌜ppa⌝-ru`er´it, tunc apparebimus cum eo, similes ei in gloria*. Þat is: My dere

rev. CcM made] *om.* Cc betwixen] H$_7$HRB$_3$AsSrLwPlW, bytwyxte B, bytwene H$_5$WsAEH$_6$CcLdT, atwixe LP, atwene M 10 not ageynstondende] And thus mow we aȝenstondyn Cc ageynstondende] withstanding AEH$_6$ felynges] felynge H$_5$WsH$_6$CcT, motibus vel sensacionibus Lat. bodi] bodies Cc 11 þogh . . . be] þorew . . . þat is RAsAPl, quamuis . . . sit Lat. 12 neuerþeles] ȝet Cc trow] H$_7$H$_5$, trowes HRLB$_3$AsSrWsLwAEPH$_6$CcMPlTW, byleeueþ BLd, credit Lat. it] it not *add.*, *canc.* L chape] H$_7$HBLSrAEPH$_6$T, schapiþ RH$_5$B$_3$AsWsLwCcMLdPlW, conformat Lat. his] our A 13 to^2] with CcM his] this Cc, our A trowþe] feyþ BLd, bileue A 14 sothly] *om.* Lat. deth] oure *prec.* B 15 þis] H$_7$HRBH$_5$LAsWsLwEPH$_6$LdTW, þe B$_3$SrACcMPl bodily lyfe] bodily ⌜lyfe⌝ H^c, bodylych werk BH$_5$WsLdT, body M, a corpore Lat. he] we A it] *om.* EH$_6$Cc þat . . . now] *om.* A Seyn John/seyd] H$_7$RLB$_3$AsSrEPCcMPl, *rev.* HBH$_5$WsLwAH$_6$LdTW 16 John] Jerom RAs seyd] seith A, dicit Lat. here] þe sones of God *add.* M in^2] *rep.* Sr þe] *om.* SrCcM 17 ymage] 1° Io. 3° *add.* BLEPLdTW et] *om.* SrWsECc `nunc´ Cc  non] H$_7$RLB$_3$AsSrAEPH$_6$CcMPl, nondum HBH$_5$WsLwLdTW, nondum Lat.  18 autem] *om.* HBAsLdT, autem Lat.  quoniam] quod SrAE  cum] H$_7$LB$_3$PH$_6$Ld, *om.* Pl, Christus *add.* HRBH$_5$AsSrWsLwAECcMPlTW, cum Christus Lat.  apperuerit] a⌜ppa⌝ru`er´it H^c, apparuit H°BW *apperebimus cum eo, similes ei in gloria*. Þat is: Mi dere frendes, we arn ryght now, whyles þat we lyuen here þe sones of God, for we arn reformed be feith in Crist to his likenes. But it scheweth not ȝit what we arn, bot it is priuey. Neuerþeles we knowe wel þat whan oure Lord schal schewen him atte last day, þan schal we aperen with him lyke vnto him in endles ioye. If þou wilt wyte þan if þi soule be reformed to þe ymage of God or non, by þat I haue seide þou mayght haue entre. Ransake þin owen conscience and loke what þi wil is, for þerin stondeth al. If it be turned fro al dedly sinne þat þou wuldest for no þyng wytendly and wilfully breke þe comaundement of God, and for þat þat þou hast mysdone here beforn ageyns his byddynge þou hast schriuen þe mekly, with ful herte to lef⟨e it⟩ and with sorwe þat þou dedist it: I seye þan sikirly þat þi soule is reformed in feith to þe lyknes of God.

Þat alle þe soules þat lyuen mekly in þe trouthe of Holi Kirke and han her trouthe quikned with loue and charite are reformed be þe sacrament, þogh it be so þat þei moun not felen þe special ȝifte of deuocion or of gostli felynge. Capitulum x^{m}

f. 51^{v} In this reformyng þat is only in feith þe most part of chosen soules | leden here lyfe, þat setten here wil stedfast for to fleen al maner dedly synnes, and for to kepen hem in loue and charite to her euene-cristen, and for to kepen þe comaundementz of God after here connynge; and whan it so is þat wikked sterynges and euel willes rysen in her hertis of

19 eo] illo E `is´ Cc Mi] *om.* M we arn] *rev.* Sr 20 ryght] *om.* BLwH_6W þat] *om.* LwW here] *om.* Sr 21 be] H_7RLB$_3$AsSrLw⌜H^c⌝EPH_6CcLdPlW, in BH_5WsMLdT, per Lat. in Crist] *om.* R in] be Sr scheweth] schewed As 22 arn] shul ben Ws bot] for RAsAPl priuey] H_7Ld, al priue Σ, totaliter . . . occultum Lat. Neuerþeles] but ȝet Cc wel] *om.* Ld 23 schewen him] apper A with him] *om.* Cc with] to A 24 vnto] H_7HRBAsSrLwPlTW, to H_5LB$_3$WsAEPH_6CcMLd ioye] blysse CcM, gloria Lat. 25 non] H_7HRBH_5AsSrWsCcMT, no LB$_3$LwEPLdW, noȝt AH_6Pl þat] H_7HRBH_5SrWsLwH_6LdPlTW, þat þat LB$_3$SrWsEPCcM seide] þat *add.* As mayght] maye AsLwMW entre] H_7HRH_5AsSrWsLwACcMLdPlTW, an *prec.* BLB$_3$EPH_6, introitum ad hoc sciendum Lat. 26 þin owen] *rep.*, *canc.* L owen] *om.* LwW, ⌜oon⌝ Cc `þi wil´ *d.h.* H_5, þerinne H_5Ws 27 al[1]] euerydel T it] þou T al[2]] H_7LB$_3$SrPH_6CcM, maner of *add.* HRBH_5AsWsLwELdPlW, maner A, *om.* T, omni Lat. sinne] and *add.* H_6, in all wyse *add.* T no] maner *add.* T, nullo modo pro aliqua re mundi Lat. 28 þyng] þyngis Ld comaundement] commaundementis AsSrECc, mandatum Lat. of God] *om.* A 29 þat þat] H_7RBAECcMPl, þat HH_5LB$_3$Sr-WsLwPH_6LdTW, þat þou seist þat As mysdone here] *rev.* H_6 mysdone] don mys Sr, done amys Pl here] *om.* A 30 schriuen þe] H_7RAsSrM, be schreven LB$_3$PH_6, þerof *add.* HBH_5WsLwAECcLdPlTW, es confessa Lat. ful] a *prec.* Sr herte] hauyng ful desyre *add.* H_5Ws lefe it] Σ, *corr. to* lef⌜en⌝ *d.h.* H_7 with sorwe] sory E, `arte´ sory Lw,

frendis, we arne riȝt now while þat we lif here þe sones of God, for we are reformid [in] faiþ in Crist to his liknes. Bot it schewþ not ȝit what we arne, bot it is al priue. Neuerþeles we knowe wel þat when oure Lord schal schewe hym at þe last day, þan schul we apperen with hym like vnto hym in endles ioye. If þou wilt wite þan if þi soule be reformed to þe ymage of God or non, by þat I haue saide þu maiȝt haue entre. Ransake þin own conscience and loke what þi wil is, for þarin stondeþ al. If it be turnyd fro alle maner of dedly syn þat þou woldest for no þing wityngly and wilfully breke þe comaundement of God, and for þat þu has misdon here biforn agayn his biddyng þou ast schryuen þe þerof mekely, with ful herte to lefe it and with sorw þat þu dedist it: I say þan sikerly þat þi soule is reformid in faiþ to þe liknes of God.

[CHAPTER 10]

In þis reformyng, þat is only in faiþ, þe most part of chosyn soules ledyn here lif, þat setten here wil stedfast`li´ for to fleen al maner of dedly syn, and for to kepyn hem in luf and charite to here euen-cristen, and for to kepe þe comaundementes of God vp her cunnyng; and whan it so is þat wicked stirynges and ille willes rise in her hertes

arte sory W, hast sorwe H_6Cc þat] *rep.*, *canc.* L 31 seye] þe *add.* As, to the *add.* Cc sikirly] soþly H_5Ws feith] trouthe T to] onto Cc þe] *om.* M 32 God] oure Lord Jesu Cryst Cc

Chapter 10 *title*: H_7RLB_3AsSrAEPH_6MLdPlTW `Hou a soule þat is fulli reformid to þe ymage of God sekiþ al þat he may to fle al maner synne and to kepyn hym in perfit charite of þe loue of God and of his euen-cristen.´ H^c *om.* H°BH_5WsLwCc 1 alle] *om.* PlT þe[1]] *om.* As þe[2]] *om.* B_3 trouthe] feith ALdTW of Holi Kirke] *om.* As 2 trouthe] feith ALdTW, trewe Pl 3 þe[1]] H_7RB_3AsSrH_6PlTM, þis AEPLdW, ⸢þis⸣ L, `þis´ T sacrament] sacramentys Sr, of penaunce *add.* M, sacramenta Lat. be so] $H_7$Pl, *rev.* Σ 4 or] eiþer Ld 5 `I´N Sr this] *rep.* A part] H_7HRLB_3AsLwAEPH_6-CcPlW, partye BH_5WsMLdT, *om.* Sr 6 here wil/stedfast] *rev.* H_6 here[2]] the M wil] lyf H_5Ws stedfast] H_7H°H_5LB_3SrWsAPCcPl, stedfastly RBAsLw`$H^{c}$´-E$H_6$MLdPlTW, constanter Lat. maner] $H_7$RL$B_3$AsSrEPM, of *add.* HB$H_5$WsLw-A$H_6$CcLdPlTW 7 synnes] $H_7$RL$B_3$AsAEP$H_6$MPl, syn HB$H_5$SrWsLwCcLdTW, peccata Lat. hem] him A, hem`silf´ L, hemsilf B_3EP and[2]] in *add.* SrPl her euene-cristen] oþer cristen men M 8 and[1]] *om.* A comaundementz] comaundement BLB_3P, mandata Lat. after] vp HBH_5T, vpon Ws, wiþ Ld connynge] L *corr. fr.* vnkunnynge 9 so is] H_7HBLB_3SrPH_6CcMPlW, *rev.* RH_5AsWsLwAELdT euel] ille H hertis] hert H_5

pride or enuye, of yre or licherie, or of ony oþer heued synne, þei ageynstonden hem and stryuen ageyn hem be displesyng of wil, so þat þey folwen not in dede þese wikked willes. And neuerþeles if it so be þat þei fallen lyghtly as it were ageyns here wil þurgh frelte or vnkunnynge, as tyte here conscience greueth hem and pyneth hem so greuousely þat þei moun haue no rest til þei be schryuen and may haue forgifnes. Sothly al þe soules þat þus lyuen, as I hope arn reformed in feith to þe ymage of God. And if þei lesten in þis reformynge or ben founden þerin in þe houre of here ded, þei schul be safe and come to þe ful reformyng in þe blisse of heuene, þogh it be so þat þei neuer myght haue gostli felynge ne inly sauour ne special grace of deuocion in al her lyfe tyme. For ellis if þou say þat no soule schal be saufe but if it were reformed into gostli felynge, þat it myght felen deuocion and gostli sauour in God, as sum soules done þurgh speciale grace, þan schuld few soules be sauf in þe rewarde of þe multitude of oþer.

Nay it is not likly for to trowen þat, þat for þo soules þat arn only deuoute and by grace comen to gostli felynge, and for no mo, oure Lord Jesu schuld haue taken mankynde and suffred þe hard passion of dede. It had ben bot a lytil purchace to him for to ha come fro so ferre to so nere and fro so heygh to so lowe for so fewe soules. Nay his mercy \`is´ spred larger þan so. Neuerþeles, on þe contrarye wise, if þou trowe þat þe passion of oure Lord is so preciouse and þe mercy of God is so mikel þat þer schal no soule be dampned, and namly of no cristene man do he neuer so ille, as sum foles wenen, sothly þou errest

10 or^1] H$_7$RBALdPl, or of HH$_5$LB$_3$WsLwEPH$_6$W, and of AsT, of SrM, *om.* Cc of^1] or of H$_5$Ws, or LdPl, *om.* CcM yre] wreþþe BAEH$_6$LdPl or^2] H$_7$H$_5$WsLwMW, or of HRBLB$_3$AsSrAEPH$_6$CcLdPlT, and of As licherie, or of] *om.* Cc or of] oþer for As heued] Ch *back* synne] synnys Cc þei] doo *add.* E 11 ageynstonden] withstondyn CcT stryuen . . . þey] *om.* Cc be] *rep., canc.* H of] his *add.* Ch 12 folwen] foule As in] wille and *add.* As þese] here Cc willes] steryngis Cc, and steryngis rysen in here hertys *add.* As, voluntates Lat. neuerþeles] ȝet thow Cc it . . . þat] H$_7$RLB$_3$AsSrAEPH$_6$CcMPl, *om.* HBH$_5$WsChLwLdTW, contingat quod Lat. so be] *rev.* AH$_6$ 13 \`þei´ E or] of B$_3$SrE, and Cc 14 as tyte] H$_7$HRLB$_3$ChLwP, anon BH$_5$AsWsAEH$_6$CcLdPl, as sone TW, as swithe as Sr, *om.* M greueth . . . pyneth] *rev.* A and pyneth hem] *om.* AsWs hem^2] *om.* Cc 15 greuousely] bitterly A haue no] not C, haue non As 16 þe] H$_7$Cc, þes Σ soules] homines Lat. as] H$_7$RLB$_3$AsSrAEPH$_6$CcMPl\`T$^G$W$^G$´, *om.* HBH$_5$WsChLwLdTW, vt estimo Lat. ⌜I hope . . . lesten (l. 17)⌝ W$^G$, *om.* LwW 17 lesten] H$_7$RLB$_3$AsSrAPH$_6$CcMPl, lifen HBH$_5$WsChLwLdTW, abiden E\`W^G´, þei *add.* T, *canc.* T^G, uiuant Lat. 18 or] H$_7$RLB$_3$AsSrAEPH$_6$CcMPl, and HBH$_5$WsChLwLdTW, atque Lat. þerin in] þer in HBChA. here] H$_7$HRBH$_5$AsSrWsChACcLdPlT, *om.* LB$_3$LwEPH$_6$MW ded] de⌜þ⌝ *corr. fr.* ded H^c þei schul] ȝet schul þei Sr be] deed *add., canc.* L 20 neuer myght] H$_7$HRBLB$_3$AsChLwPH$_6$LdPlT, *rev.* H$_5$SrWsAECcMW \`haue´ H$_6$, felyn Cc felynge] reformyng Cc ne^1] *om.* Pl inly] inwarde LwH$_6$TW, have

of pride or of enuye, of ire or of leccherye, or of ony oþer hed syn, þei
70v agenstonden hem and stryfen ageyns hem | bi displesyng of wiþ so
þat þei folwe not in dede þese wicked willes. And nerþeles if þei fallen liȝtly as it were ageyn here wille þorwe frelte or vnkunnyng, as tite here conscience greuiþ hem and pynyþ hem so greuously þat þei mowen haue no reste til þei be schrifen and may haue forgifnes. Soþly alle þes soules þat þus lifen, I hope are reformid in faiþ to þe ymage of God. And if þei lifen in þis reformyng and be founden þer in þe houre of þeir de⌜þ⌝, þei schul be sauf and come to þe ful reformyng in þe blis of heuen, þawȝ it be so þat þei neuer miȝt haue gostly felyng ne inly sauour ne special grace of deuocioun in al her lif tyme. For elles if þu saie þat no soul schal be saf bot if it were ⌜reformed⌝ into gostly felyng, þat it miȝt felen deuocioun and gostly sauour in God, as summe soules don þorw special grace, þen schuld few soules be sauf in reward of multitude of oþer.

Nay it is not for to trowe þat, þat for þoo soules þat only ern deuoute and by grace come to gostly felyng, and for no moo, oure Lord Ihesu schuld haue taken mankynde and suffred þo hard passioun of ded. It had ben a litil purchace to hym for to ha come fro so ferre to so ner and fro so hiȝe to so lowe for so fewe sowles. Nay his mercy is sprad larger þen so. Nerþeles, on þe contrarie wise, if þou trow þat þe passioun of oure Lord is so precious and his mercy is so mikel þat þer schal no soule be dampned, and namly of no cristen man do he neuer so hille, as summe foles wenen, soþly þu erres gretly. Þerfor go in þe

gostly Cc 22 saufe] saued Ld if] om. SrLwLdW it] he H$_5$WsCcT were reformed] *rev., marked for trsp.* Sr ⌜reformed⌝ H[c] *over erasure of a shorter word*, ronnen H$_5$Ws, oned T, reformata Lat. into] H$_7$HRBH$_5$LB$_3$SrWsChAPH$_6$LdPlT, in AsLwECcMW 23 and] in BH$_5$ChT 24 grace] ȝifte Ld schuld] schal A few] þynges *add.*, *canc.* L þe[1]] H$_7$, *om.* Σ þe[2]] H$_7$RLB$_3$AsSrWsAEPH$_6$CcMLdPl, *om.* HBH$_5$ChLwTW 26 not] but As likly] H$_7$RLB$_3$AsSrAEPH$_6$Pl, lythly Cc, like M, *om.* HBH$_5$WsChLwLdTW, verisimile Lat. for[1]] *om.* Cc trowen] beleue M þat[1]] it Ld, *om.* CcM for[2]] if *add.* Cc þo] þe RLwCcMW þat arn only] H$_7$RLB$_3$AsSrEPH$_6$CcMPl, þat only ern HBH$_5$WsChLwLdTW, onli þat ben A 27 gostli] lyvyng and gostly *add.* Cc 28 Jesu] *om.* WsACc haue] *om.* Cc taken] of *add.* As suffred] suffre BACc, a suffrid H$_6$ þe] þo HCh, that LwCcW, *om.* LB$_3$EPLd hard] *om.* Cc of] his *add.* H$_6$ 29 bot] H$_7$RLB$_3$AsSrAEPH$_6$MPl, put Cc, *om.* HBH$_5$Ws-ChLwLdTW for] *om.* H$_6$ 30 to so nere] *om.* Cc nere] nyȝe BAT 31 is] *add. interl.* H$_7$ on . . . wise/if þou trowe] *rev.* T, if þow trowe on þe contrarie wise, as if þou trowe HH$_5$Ws [if þow trowe[1] *canc.* H] 32 trowe] byleeue B of oure Lord] *om.* Cc and] wiþ B$_3$ þe mercy of God] H$_7$RLB$_3$AsSrAEPH$_6$CcMPl, his mercy HBH$_5$WsChLwLdTW `þe[2]´ Pl 33 is] *om.* LwW so] *om.* Cc þer] neuer As no] non As no cristene man . . . he (l. 34)] cristen men . . . they Cc no] non As 34 do] vixerit Lat. ille] H$_7$HRLChEP, euyll BH$_5$B$_3$AsSrWsLwAPH$_6$CcMLdlTW sothly] For soþe H$_6$ þou errest] þei erren LB$_3$PH$_6$, erras Lat.

gretly. Þerfore go in þe mene and held þe in þe myddes, and trowe as Holy Kirke troweth: and þat is þat þe most synful man | f. 52r þat lyueth in erthe, if he turne his wil þurgh grace fro dedly synne, with sothfast repentaunce to þe seruise of God, he is reformed in his soule, and if he dey in þat state he schal be saufe. Þus behyght oure Lord be his prophete, seyende þus: *In quacumque hora conuersus fuerit peccator et ingemuerit, vita viuet et non morietur*. Þat is: In what tyme þat it be þat þe synful man is turned fro synne to God and he haue sorwe þerfore, he schal lyuen and he schal not dyen endlesly.

Also on þat oþer syde, who so lyth in dedly sinne and wil not leuen it ne amende him þerof, ne resceyfe þe sacrament of penaunce, or elles if he resceyfe it he taketh it not sothfastly for lufe of God, þat is for loue of vertu and clennes, bot only for drede or schame of þe werd, or elles for drede only of þe pyn of helle: he is not reformed to þe liknesse of God. And if he deye in þat plight he schal not be saufe, his trowth schal not saufen him; for þis trowth is a dede trouthe and lakketh lufe, and þerfore it serueth him nought. Bot þey þat han trowthe quykned with loue and charite arn reformed to þe lyknesse of God, þogh it be bote þe lest degre of charite, as arn simple soules, þe qwhilke felen not þe gifte of speciale deuocion ne gostli knowyng of God as sum gostly men don, bot trowen generally as Holi Kirke troweth, and wyten not fully what þat is—for it nedeth not to hem—and in þat trowthe þey kepen hem in lufe and charite to hire euene-cristen as mykel as þey moun, and fleen al dedly synnes after here connynge, and done þe dedes of mercy to here euene-cristen, al þese longen to þe blis of heuene.

35 go/. . ./held þe] *rev.* H$_6$ go] þou *add.* Cc myddes] middist R, myddil H$_6$ trowe] leue BAM, bileue Ld 36 troweth] byleeues BALd, leueþ M, doþe Pl þat lyueth] *om.* Cc þat] *om.* Sr lyueth] lyuen Ch in] on þe M 37 erthe] levende *add.* Cc wil] herte H$_5$Ws þurgh grace/fro dedly synne] *rev.* H$_5$Ws 39 dey] deyde SrW state] estate LB$_3$P þus] þis Ws behyght] hyȝt H$_6$ be[2] to As 40 þus[2]] *om.* Cc, Eze. 18° *add.* BLEPLdTW fuerit] *om.* H 41 ingemuerit] gemuerit M vita] *rep.* A þat[1]] þis SrPl þat[2]] euere *add.* T it be þat] *om.* Cc 42 þe] a M fro synne/to God] H$_7$RLB$_3$AsSrAEPH$_6$CcMPl, *rev.* HBH$_5$WsChLwLdTW fro] his *add.* A 44 Also] And MW, Also *corr. to.* And Lw, *as part of a larger correction* lyth] lyueþe LwW, leve Cc, leues M, dwelliþ H$_6$, iacet Lat. 45 ne] noþer M amende] it *add.*, *canc.* L þerof] þerfore of it RAsPl, *om.* A resceyfe] þerfor *add.* A of] *rep.* H$_6$ or elles if] and þouȝ LB$_3$PH$_6$Cc 46 if he] *rev.* R he taketh it] And Cc he[2]] and RAsAPl taketh] take RAs it not] *rev.* Pl for[1]] H$_7$HRBAsChLdPlT, þe *add.* H$_5$LB$_3$SrWsLwAEPH$_6$CcMW for[2]] the *add.* W 47 vertu] vertuys Sr [-ys *canc.*] and] or H$_5$Ws or] H$_7$HRBAsSrChLwACcPlTW, þe *add.* Ld, of H$_5$LB$_3$WsEPH$_6$M, vel Lat. 48 elles] *om.* LwW for drede/only] *rev.* SrH$_6$ drede] dredes E only] *om.* Cc þe[1]] H$_7$RBLB$_3$AsSrAEPH$_6$CcMPlT, *om.* HH$_5$WsChLwLdW he] þis *add.* H$_6$ is] *om.* As

mene and hald þe in þe middes, and trowe as Holy Kirke troweþ: and þat is þat þe most synful man þat lifiþ in erþe, if he turne his wille þorw grace ⌜fro⌝ dedly syn, wiþ soþfast repentance to þe seruice of God, he is reformid in his soule, and if he dey in þat stat he schal be saf. Þus beheiȝte oure Lord be his prophete, seynde þus: *In quacumque hora conuersus [fuerit] peccator et ingemuerit, vita viuet et mon morietur*. Þat is: In what tyme þat it be þat þe synful man is turned to God fro syn and he haue sorwe þerfore, he schal lifen and he schal not dye endelesly.

71r Also on þat oþer side, whoso liþ in | dedly syn and wil not lef it ne amende hym þerof, ne reseyue þe sacrament of penaunce, or elles if he reseyue it he takiþ it not soþfastly for luf of God, þat is for luf of vertue and clennesse, bot oonly for drede or shame of þe warld, or elles for drede only of peyns of helle: he is not reformed to þe liknes of God. And if he dey in þat pliȝt he schal not be sauf, his trowþ schal not sauen hym; for his trouþ is a ded trouþ and lackeþ luf, and þerfor it seruiþ hym noȝt. Bot þei þat han trouþ quyckynd wiþ luf and charyte arne reformed to þe liknes of God, þawȝ it be þe lest degre of charyte, as arne symple soules, þe whilk felen not þe gift of special deuocioun ne gostly knowyng of God as summe gostly men don, but trowen generally as Holy Kirke troweþ, and witen not fully what þat is for it nediþ not to hem. And in þat trouþ þei kepen hem in luf and charite to her euen-cristen as mikel as þei mowen, and fleen alle dedly synnes after her kunnyng, and don þe dedis of mercy to here euen-cristen. Alle þis longen to þe blis of heuen. For it is writen in þe Apocalips þus: *Qui timetis Deum pusilli et magni laudate eum*. Þis is: Ȝe þat dredyn God, boþ smale and gret, þankeþ hym.

49 deye] deyede BChLd his . . . nought (l. 51)] *om.* APl 50 trowth[1]] byleeue B, feiþ Ld for] fro Lw þis] H_7, his Σ, sua Lat. trowth[2]] byleeue B, feiþ Ld a dede trouthe] dede LwLdW trouthe] byleue B 51 serueth him] H_7HBH_5WsChLwW, saueþ him LdT, of *add.* R⌜L⌝B_3AsSrEPH_6CcM, sibi prodest Lat. 52 trowthe] byleue B, feiþ ALd quykned] quyckyde H_5Ws, qwyknynge B `of God´ L 53 bote] $H_7$RL$B_3$As-SrAE$H_6$CcMPl, *om.* HB$H_5$WsChLwPLdTW simple] simplices . . . et inperfecte Lat. þe qwhilke] that CcM þe[2]] *om.* E 54 `not´ As ne] of *add.* As 55 gostly] *rep.* A `men´ $H_6$ don] *om.* B trowen] byleeuen BLd, bileuith A 56 troweth] byleeueþ BLd, bileuith A `wyten´/not] *rev.* Cc wyten] knowyth W þat] hit BB_3Ch, is A, it *add.* SrCc hem] hym Ch 57 trowthe] leue or feyþ B, belyue Ld, feith A hem] hym Ch and[2]] in *add.* AsELd`T´ 58 as[1]] in als RAs mykel as] *om.* W fleen] fro *add.* Sr synnes] synne LwW after] vp Ld 59 connynge] knowing RAsAPl done . . . cristen] subueniunt proximis Lat. dedes] werkys Ld here euene-cristen] oþer cristene men M euene-cristen] power and konyng Cc þese] þis HLw, those R, tho Cc, isti Lat.

For it is writen in þe Apocalips þus: *Qui timetis Deum, pusilli et magni, laudate eum*. Þat is: Ʒe þat dreden God, bothe grete and smale, þankeþ him. By grete arn vnderstonden soules þat arn profytend in grace, or elles perfyte in loue of God, þe qwhilk arn reformed in gostli felynge. Be smale arn vnderstonden soules vnperfyte of werdly men and wummen, and oþer þat han bot a childes knowyng of God and ful f. 52v lytil felyng of him, bot arn broght forth in þe bosum of Holy Kirke | and norisched with þe sacramentys as children arn fed with melke. Al þes schal lofe God and thank him for saluacion of here soules by his endles goodnesse. For Holy Kirke, þat is modere of al þese and hath tendre loue to all here children gostly, preyeth and asketh for hem al tenderly of here spouse, þat is Jesu, and geteth hem hele of soule þurgh vertu of his passion; and namly for hem þat kun not speke hemselfe by gostly prayere for here owen nede. Þus I fynd in þe Gospel þat þe wumman of Chanane asked of oure Lord hele to here doghtere þat was trauayled with a fend. And oure Lord made ferst daungere bycause þat sche was an alyen. Neuerþeles sche sesseid not for to cryen til oure Lord had graunted to hire hire askynge, and seyd to hire þus: A, wumman, mykil is þi trouthe, be it to þe ryght as þou wilt. And in þe same houre was hir doghtire made hole. Þis womman betokeneth Holy Kyrke þat asketh help of oure Lord for symple vnkunnende soules þat arn trauayled with temptacion of þe werd and kun not speken perfitely to God be feruour of deuocion ne brennend loue in contemplacion. And þogh it were þat oure Lord make daunger

61 it is writen/in þe Apocalips] *rev.* H$_6$ þus] Apo. 19° *add.* BLEPLdTW pusilli] vt supra *add.* Sr. *This passage, from* Qui timetis *through the end of this chapter, is written at the head of the text of Scale II in* Sr, *on f. 28*^{ra} 62 eum] Deum M þat] þis HH$_5$WsLwCc Ʒe] þe M bothe] *om.* B grete and smale] H$_7$LB$_3$AEP, *rev.* HRBH$_5$AsSrWsChLwH$_6$CcLdPlTW, symple and grete M 63 þankeþ] ȝe oþer herie ȝe *add.* Ld, preisiþ T By] þe Pl, þe *add.* E vnderstonden] vndurstondynge Lw profytend] perfite M 64 elles perfyte] *om.* Cc elles] *om.* RAsWs perfyte/in loue] *rev., marked for trsp.* L perfyte in] *rev.* E perfyte] H$_7$HBLB$_3$ChLwAEPH$_6$TW, profeten RH$_5$AsSrWsLd, pertifite M, perfecte Lat. in] H$_7$RLB$_3$AsEPH$_6$Pl, þe *add.* HBH$_5$SrWsChLwACcMLdTW loue of] louyng As þe] *om.* EPl 65 Be] *om.* Pl smale] H$_7$HRBAsSrChLwAH$_6$CcLdTW, þe *prec.* H$_5$LB$_3$WsEPMPl soules] *om.* T vnperfyte] imperfit AsA of] and H$_5$Ws, ⌜as⌝ Cc, or M men . . . þat] hominum qui Lat. 66 and[1]] or M wummen] womman A and[2]] or M han . . . childes] arn as childryn of gostly Cc childes] childisch LB$_3$EPH$_6$, childeþ B, puerilem Lat. of God] *om.* Cc 67 of him] *om.* B of] in E him] hem Ch, God Cc bot] þey *add.* H$_5$WsCc forth] *om.* A 68 and] *om.* Sr norisched . . . Al] *om.* M sacramentys] H$_7$HRAsSrAECcMLdPlT, sacrament BH$_5$LB$_3$WsChLwPH$_6$W, sacramentis Lat. Al] Also B 69 þes] þose R schal] scholde H$_5$WsW lofe . . ./. . . thank] H$_7$HRBH$_5$AsWsChLwACcMLdPlTW *rev.* LB$_3$SrEPH$_6$ lofe] herie Ld, preyse A for] þe *add.* Sr 70 goodnesse] H$_7$RAsSrACcMPl, mercy and *prec.* HBH$_5$WsChLwELdTW, mercy

By grete are vnderstonden soules þat are profitand in grace, or elles
perfit in þe luf of God, þe whilk arn reformed in gostly felyng. Be
smale are vndirstondyn soules vnperfite of worldly men and wymmen,
and oþer þat haþ bot a childes knowyng of God and ful litel felyng of
hym, bot arne broȝt forþ in þe bosum of Holy Kirke and norisched
wiþ þe sacramentz, as children are fed wiþ milk. Alle ⌜þese⌝ schul loue
God and þanken hym for saluacioun of here soules by his endles
mercy and godnes. For Holy Kirke, þat is modir of alle þeese and haþ
tendre luf to alle here children gostly, preieþ and askeþ for hem alle
tendrely of her spouse, þat is Ihesu, and geteþ hem hele of soule þorw
vertu of his passioun. And namely for hem þat kun not speken for
hemself bi gostly preier for here own nede. Þus I fynde in þe Gospel
71^v þat þe womman of Canane asked of oure Lord hele to here | douȝter
þat was trauailed wiþ a fende. And oure Lord made first daunger
bycause þat sche was an alien. Nerþeles sche sesed not for to crien til
oure ˋLordˊ had graunted hir hire askynge, and saide to hir þus: A
womman, mikel is þi trowþ, be it to þe riȝt as þu wilt; and in þe same
houre was her doȝter hool. Þis womman bitokneþ Holy Kirke þat
askiþ helpe of oure Lord for simple vnkunnand saules þat arn
trauailed wiþ temptacioun of þe werld and kun not spekyn perfitely
to God bi feruour of deuocioun ne brynnande luf in contemplacioun.
And þawȝ it seme þat oure Lord make daunger first bicause þat þei

LB$_3$PH$_6$, bonitate Lat. al þese] hem Cc þese] þose R 71 children gostly] *rev.* SrE gostly preyeth] in gostly prayere H$_5$Ws hem al] *rev.* H$_5$ al] as A 72 of[1]] to H$_6$ þat is] *om.* Ws hem] hym BCh hele] helthe CcLd ˋof[2] . . . hem (l. 73)ˊ R 73 þurgh] heele *add.*, *canc.* L, *two-letter canc.* P 74 hemselfe] H$_7$RLB$_3$AsSrAPH$_6$M, for *prec.* HBH$_5$WsChLwECcLdPlTW, qui loqui nesciunt Lat. owen] *om.* LwW nede] indigencia releuanda Lat. 75 Gospel] M^t 15° *add.* LEPLd þat] of Cc Chanane] shee *add.* B, þat *add.* Cc hele] helthe CcLd 76 was] *om.* H$_6$ trauayled] trauelynge E, of *add.*, *canc.* Cc fend] deuel Ld ˋAndˊ *d.h.*, of *add.* Lw made ferst daungere] ei primo reddidit se extraneum Lat. ferst] *om.* LB$_3$P 77 þat] H$_7$HRBH$_5$AsSrWsChACcMLdPlW^G, *om.* LB$_3$LwEPH$_6$TW an] *om.* M Neuerþeles] But Cc, But *prec.* Pl 78 had] til he *prec.* PCc to hire/hire askynge] *rev.* H$_5$Ws to] *om.* HLwTW hire[2]] H$_7$HRBH$_5$LSrWsChAEPH$_6$CcLdPl, *om.* B$_3$AsLwMTW and] he *add.* H$_6$Cc 79 to hire] *om.* H$_5$Ws trouthe] H$_7$HH$_5$B$_3$AsSrWsChLwEPMPlTW, trouþe *corr. fr.* feiþ L, feiþ RBAH$_6$CcLd it] doon *add.* BLH$_6$Ld ryght] *om.* P 80 And] *om.* AW þe] that Cc was/hir doghtire] *rev.* Cc made] H$_7$RLB$_3$AsSrEPH$_6$CcMPl, *om.* HBH$_5$Ws-ChLwALdTW, sanata Lat. womman] *om.* H$_5$ 81 betokeneth] toknith R Lord] þat askeþ oure Lord *add.*, *canc.* H symple] and *add.* Cc 82 vnkunnende] vnknowyng M temptacion] H$_7$HBH$_5$LB$_3$SrChLwAEPMLdPlT, temptations RAsWsH$_6$CcW, temptacionibus Lat. þe] thys Cc 83 kun] can AsAEPl to] vnto T ne brennend] and brennyng of Sr ne] ne *prec.*, *canc.* E, be *add.* CcW^G 84 ˋwereˊ Cc make daunger] se reddat extraneum seu difficilem Lat.

first bicause þat þei arn as it were alyens fro him, neuerþeles, for þe grete trouthe and þe desert of Holy Kirke, he graunteth hir al þat sche wil. And so arn þese simple soules þat trowen stedfastly as Holy Kirke troweth, and putten hem fully in þe mercy of God, and meken hem vnder þe sacramentes and lawes of Holi Kyrke, made saufe þurgh þe preiere and þe trowth of here gostly modere, þat is Holy Kirke.

þat soules reformed neden ay for to feghten and stryuen ageyns sterynges of synne whyles þei lyuen here, and how a soule may wyten whanne he assenteth to ille sterynges and whan note. Capitulum xi^{m}

This reformynge in feith may lightly be getyn, bot it may note so lygthly ben holden. And þerfor what man or | [f. 53r] wumman þat is reformed to þe liknes of God in trowthe, mykel trauail and besynes hem behoueth to haue if he wil kepe þis ymage hole and clene, þat it fal not doun ageyn þurgh weyknes of wille to þe ymage of synne. He may not ben ydel ne rykles, for þe ymage of synne is so nere fastned to him and so continuely preseth vpon him by dyuers sterynges of synne, þat bot if he \`be´ ryght ware he schal ful lygthly þurgh assent fallen ageyn þerto. And þerfore it nedeth him ay be st[r]yuende and fyghtende ageyns wykked sterynges of þis ymage of synne, and þat he make non acorde þerwith, ne take no frenchipe with it for to be buxum to his vnskilful byddynges; for if he do he bygyleth himself. Bot sothly, if he stryue with hem, him nedeth not mikel to dreden of

85 alyens] H$_7$RH$_5$LB$_3$AsSrWsAEPH$_6$CcMPl, alien Ch, aliend HBLwLdTW, alieni Lat. neuerþeles] but ȝet Cc 86 trouthe] byleeue B, feith AH$_6$Ld þe desert] H$_7$RBLB$_3$AsSrAPMPl, desert HH$_5$WsW, þe desyre B, deseir ChLd, dysterte LwT hir] H$_7$RLB$_3$AsSrAPH$_6$CcMPl, to *prec.* HBH$_5$WsChLwELdTW 87 wil] wilneth M þese] þe BSr simple soules] *rev.* AT (*marked for trsp.* A) ⸢simple⸣ L soules] *om.* SrPl trowen] byleeuen BALd, leuen M 88 troweth] byleeueþ BALd, leueþ M 89 sacrament\`es´ *d.h.* L, sacrament BH$_5$B$_3$H$_6$W, sacramentis Lat. and] of M lawes] H$_7$RBLB$_3$AsPH$_6$CcLdPlW, þe *prec.* HH$_5$SrWsChLwAEMT Holi Kyrke] *om.* A made] and be mad H$_6$, arn mad Cc þe] H$_7$RLB$_3$AsSrAEPH$_6$CcMPl, *om.* HBH$_5$WsChLwLdTW 90 preiere . . . trowth] feith . . . praier A, fide . . . precibus Lat. preiere] beleue M, grace *prec.*, *canc.* L þe] H$_7$RLB$_3$AsSrAEPH$_6$MPl, *om.* HBH$_5$WsChLwCcLdTW trowth] byleeue B, feiþ Ld here] the Cc, our M gostly] holy M, *om.* AsLwW þat] H$_7$RH$_5$LB$_3$AsSrWsAPH$_6$CcMPl, whilk HBChELdT, *om.* LwW

Chapter 11 *title*: H$_7$RLB$_3$AsSrAEPH$_6$MLdPlTW *om.* HBH$_5$WsChLwCc 1 soules . . . neden] a soule . . . nedeþ M ay] euer B$_3$AEH$_6$M, alwey Sr for to] *rep.*, *canc.* Sr, for As feghten and stryuen] stryuen RAs, fiȝt Pl 2 sterynges] þe sturinge T, stirynge W synne] synnes M whyles . . . note] *om.* Pl þei lyuen] hit leueþ M 3 whanne] þat *add.* E he] hit AMLdTW assenteth] assent R ille] yuel B$_3$SrEH$_6$M, alle As, *om.* ATW sterynges] þe sturinge TW 5 may[1]] H$_7$RBLB$_3$As-SrChAEPH$_6$CcMLdPl, is HH$_5$WsLwTW, potest Lat. be getyn] be ygete BLdCh, to be

arn as it were aliend fro him, nerþeles, for þe gret trouþ and desert of Holy Kirke, he grauntiþ to her al þat sche wile. And so arn þese simple soules þat trowen stidefastly as Holy Kirke trowes, and putten hem fully in þe mercy of God, and meken hem vndre þe sacramentz and þe laghes of Holi Kirk, mad sauf þorw praier and trowþ of her gostly modir whilk is Holi Kirk.

[CHAPTER II]

þis reformyng in faiþ is liȝtly begeten, bot it may not so liȝtly ben holden. And þerfore what man or womman þat is reformed to þe liknes of God in trouþ, mikil trauail and bisynes most þei haue if þei wil kepe þis ymage hool and clene þat it fal not doun agayn þorw weiknes of wil to þe ymage of syn. He may `not´ be ydel ne rekles, for þe ymage of syn is ⌜so n⌝ere festned to hym and so contynuely preceþ vpon hym bi diuers styrynges of syn, þat bot if he be riȝt war he schal ful liȝtly þorw assent fallen agayn þerto. And þerfore hym nediþ ay be stryfand and feiȝtande agayn wicked styrynges of þis ymage of synne, and þat he make non acord þerwiþ, ne take no frenschep wiþ it for to be buxum to his vnskilful biddyngges; for if he do he bigileþ hymself. Bot soþly if he stryfe with h⌜e⌝m, `him´ nediþ not mikil drede of

getyne H_5Ws, goten LwW, to begoten T, adquiri Lat. may[2]] is Ws, *om.* H_5 6 ben holden] to be holden Ws, beeholde LwW what] whan T þat] *om.* RAs 7 to] in RAsAPl in] *om.* As trowthe] byleeue BLd, feith A trauail/. . ./besynes] *rev.* H_5Ws 8 hem behoueth] H_7RLB_3AsSrAEPH_6CcMPl, most þei HBChLwLdW, moste he H_5Ws, muste he, *corr. to* muste `þei´ T, oportet eum Lat. to] for to R he] H_7H_5WsCcM, þei HRBLB_3AsSrChLwAEPH_6LdPlTW hole and clene] *rev.* H_5Ws 9 ⌜doun⌝ L weyknes] fybelnesse BH_5Ws, wykkedenesse AsCc, feyntise A, leþynesse Ld 10 ne] and Cc so nere] H_7LB_3SrLwEPH_6W, ⌜so n⌝ere H^c, so ney ACcM, sonere RAs, sone Ws, sore H_5PlT, so BLd, swere Ch, tam propinqua Lat. 11 him] hem R sterynges] *om.* Pl of] *rep., canc.* H. 12 þat bot if] bute B, but if Ld if] *om.* SrECcM `he´ Pl `be´ *marg., d.h.*H_7, `be´ Cc ryght] wele *add.* WsW, `wele´ *add.* Lw þurgh assent] *om.* Ld þurgh] be Cc 13 it nedeth him] H_7, hym nediþ Σ ay] H_7HRLAsChPH_6Cc, euer LwAEMPlW, alway H_5SrWsLdT, *om.* BB_3 be stryuende] to stryue M be] to be T stryuende and] *rep., canc.* Ch stryuende] styuende H_7 14 fyghtende] chydynge B wykked] swilk *prec.* RAs sterynges] steryng Cc of synne] *om.* Sr 15 no] non Cc with it] þerwiþ Sr with] to W it] hym Cc for to be buxum] nec obedire Lat. 16 to] vnto E byddyngges] byddynge H_5Ws `if´ Cc, þou *add., canc.* L do] do so T himself] hemself Lw, fro þis image þat it schulde *add., canc.* L 17 h⌜e⌝m $H^c$, him B$H_5$WsChLd, *om.* T him nedeth] he þar SrCcM `him´ H^c, it H_5Ws, he T mikel to] *om.* M to] H_7RLB_3AsSrWsAEPH_6CcPl, forto T, *om.* HBH_5ChLwLdW

assentynge, for stryf breketh [pees and fals acord. It is good þat a man haue pees] with al þynge, outtaken with þe fend and þis ymage of synne, for ageyns hem him nedeth ay fyghten in his þought and in his werke vntil he haue geten of hem þe maystrie, and þat schal neuer ben fully in þis lyfe as long as he bereth and feleth þis ymage. I say not bot þat a soule may þurgh grace han þe heygher hand ouer þis ymage, so ferforth þat it schal not folwen ne assenten to þe vnskilful sterynges of it. Bot for to ben so clene deluyered fro þis ymage þat it schulde felen no suggestion ne ianglynge of no fleischly affeccion ne of veyn thowght no tyme, may no man haue in þis lyfe.

I hope þat a soule þat is reformed in felyng be a ravischynge of loue into contemplacion of God may be so ferre fro þe sensualite and fro veyn ymaginacion, and so ferre drawen out and departed fro þe fleschly felyng for a tyme, þat it schal not felen bot God. Bot þat lasteþ not alwey. And þerfore sey I þat ilk man behoueth stryuen ageyns þis ymage of synne, and namly he þat is only reformed in feith, þat so lightly may be disseyued þerwith. In þe person of þe whilk men [Seynt Poule seyth þus]: *Caro concupiscit aduersus spiritum, et spiritus aduersus carnem.* Þat is: A soule reformed to þe liknes of God feyghteth ageyns þe fleschly sterynges of þis ymage of synne, and f. 53[v] also þis ymage of synne stryfeth | ageyns þe wil of þe spirit. Þis maner fyghtyng in þis duble ymage Seynt Poule knew wele whan he seyd þus: *Inueni legem in membris meis, repugnantem legi mentis mee et captiuum me ducentem in legem peccati.* Þat is: I hafe founden two lawes in myself, on lawe in my soule withinnen, and anoþer laghe in

18 stryf] H_7RLB_3AsSrLwAEPH_6CcMPlW, ⌜strife⌝ H[c], Crist BH_5WsChLdT, contencio Lat. pees . . . pees] al þese H_7, vnpees H_5Ws, feyned pees Ld 19 þynge] þynges BChLdPl, -s *canc.* T, saf wiþ alle þing *add.*, *canc.* H outtaken] H_7RLB_3AsSrAEPH_6CcMPl, sauf HBH_5WsChLwLdTW and] H_7RAsSrACcMPl, wiþ *add.* HBH_5LB_3WsChLwEPH_6LdTW, et Lat. 20 him] it B_3EH_6, *om.* LP ay] H_7HRH_5LAsSrWsChW, euere BLB_3LwAEH_6CcMLdPlT, alwey Sr fyghten] to *prec.* SrAECcM, forto *prec.* T, fiȝtyng Ch, be fiȝtand Pl in] *rep.* B_3 his[1]] þis Pl þought] *rep.*, *canc.* E 21 werke] werkis Cc vntil] H_7HRBH_5LSrWsChEPPl, til LwAH_6CcMLdW, vnto B_3, into þe tyme As, vnto tyme þat T ⌜haþ geten ouer hem⌝ L haue] haþ LB_3SrPCc of hem/þe maystrie] *rev.* H_6T of] H_7AsSrACc, ouer HRBH_5LB_3WsChEPH_6MLdPlT, on LwW, de Lat. hem] him Pl ben] *om.* Ld 22 fully/in þis lyfe] *rev.* EH_6 bereth] heriþ H_5Pl 23 þat] *om.* Ch þurgh grace/han . . . hand] *rev.* M han . . . hand] preuelare Lat. ouer] of AsCh 24 \`it′ L, he Cc folwen ne] *om.* M folwen] fulle Pl ne] neyþer H_5, nor Ws assenten] H_7RBAsSrWsAH_6CcMLd, senten HH_5LB_3ChLwPTW, consente E to] *om.* Cc of it] þerof Sr 25 for] *om.* E it[2]] he WsW, he *corr. from* it Lw schulde] shul Cc 26 no[1]] non As suggestion] suggion Cc no[2]] none As, *om.* W affeccion] affeccions RAsAPl veyn] no *prec.* M 27 þowght] thoȝtis RBAsAPl ⌜may . . . lyfe⌝ L may] þat *prec.* Sr, þere *add.* T lyfe] tyme H_6 28 þat] *om.* M \`is′ Cc of loue/into

assentynge, for ⌜strife⌝ brekiþ pees and fals acorde. It is good þat a 72r man haue pees with al þinge | sauf wyþ þe fende and wiþ þis ymage of syn, for agayns hem hym nediþ ay fiȝten in his þouȝt and in his dede vntil he haue geten ouer hem þe maistrye, and þat schal neuer ben fully in þis lif as longe as he bereþ and feliþ þis ymage. I say not bot þat a soule may þorw grace haue þe hiȝere hande ouer þis ymage, so fer forþ þat it schal not foluen ne senten to þe vnskilful stirynges of it. Bot for to ben so clene diliuered fro þis ymage þat it schuld fele no suggestioun ne iangelyng of no flescly affeccioun ne of veyn þouȝt no tyme, may no man haue in þis lif.

I hope þat a soule þat is reformed in felyng bi rauischyng of luf into contemplacioun of God, may be so f⌜erre⌝ fro þe sensualite and fro vayn ymaginacioun, and so ferre drawen owt and departid fro þe flescly felyng for a tyme, þat it schal not felen bot god`e´. Bot ⌜þat⌝ lasteþ not ay. And þerfor say I þat ilk man behouiþ strife agayn þis ymage of syn, and namely he þat is only `reformed´ in faiþ, þat so liȝtly may be deseyued þerwiþ. In þe person of whilk men Seynt Poul seiþ þus: *Caro concupiscit aduersus spiritum et spiritus aduersus carnem*, þat is: A soule reformed to þe liknes of God feȝtes ageyn þe flescly styrynges of þis ymage of syn, and also þis ymage of syn stryfeþ agayn þe wil of þe spirit. Þis maner of feȝtyng of þis double ymage Seynt Poul knew when he saide þus: *Inueni legem in membris meis, repugnantem legi mentis mee et captiuum me ducentem in legem peccati*, þat is: I haue founden two lawes in myself, on laghe in my soule wiþinne, and

contemplacion] *rev., marked for trsp.* Sr 29 into] in SrW God] *om.* M ferre] H$_7$LB$_3$AsLw⌜H^c⌝EPH$_6$CcMPlW, fre RBH$_5$SrWsChALdT, libera Lat. `þe´ L `and´ L 30 veyn] `þe´ *prec.* L, þe *prec.* B$_3$P ferre] free B drawen] drawyng H$_5$Ws 31 felen] *om.* As God] H$_7$RHBH$_5$AsSrWsChLwLdPlTW, god`e´ H^c, good LB$_3$APH$_6$CcM, Deum Lat. þat[2]] hit BChLd 32 alwey] H$_7$RLB$_3$AsSrAEPH$_6$CcMLdPlT, ay HH$_5$WsCh, euere BLwW sey I] *rev.* H$_6$CcM ilk] H$_7$HRAsCh, euery BH$_5$LB$_3$SrWsLwAEPH$_6$PlTW, yche CcMLd behoueth] to *add.* EH$_6$CcM 33 is] *om.* P only/reformed in feith] *rev.* LwW only reformed] *rev.* M only] *om.* Cc `reformed´ H^c, *om.* H°BChLdT 34 þat] et Lat. þe whilk] such A þe[2]] H$_7$RLB$_3$AsSrAEPCc, *om.* HBH$_5$WsChLwH$_6$MLdPlTW men] *om.* Sr 35 Seynt Poule seyth þus] *om.* H$_7$, seyth Seynt Powle LwW, Gal. 5° *add.* BLEPLdTW concupiscit] concupiscet A et spiritus] spiritus autem A 36 þat is] *om.* H$_5$Ws 37 of synne] *om.* Pl 38 also] þese flesshely steringes of *add.* T þis[1]] þe As of synne] *om.* SrCc stryfeth] *corr. fr.* stryfen H þe[1]] *om.* H$_6$Pl þe[2]] *om.* Pl maner] H$_7$RAsLdPl, of *add.* HBH$_5$LB$_3$SrWsChLwAEPH$_6$CcMTW 39 fyghtyng] fiȝteþ Ld in] H$_7$RLB$_3$AsSrAEPH$_6$CcMPl, of HBH$_5$WsChLwTW, *om.* Ld, in Lat. ymage] as *add.* Ld wele] H$_7$RBLB$_3$AsSrChAEPH$_6$CcMLdPl, *om.* HH$_5$WsLwTW, bene Lat. 40 þus] Ro. 7° *add.* BLEPLdTW meis] *om.* As 41 captiuum me ducentem] captiuantem A legem] lege H$_5$SrWsA `is´ Pl 42 in[1]] myn flysch and in *add.* Cc lawe] is *add., canc.* L and] *om.* H$_5$B$_3$Ws laghe] H$_7$RLB$_3$AsSrAEPH$_6$CcMPl, *om.* HBH$_5$WsChLwLdTW, is *add.* B$_3$

my fleschly lymes withouten fightende ageyns it, þat often ledeth me as a wrecched prisonere into þe laghe of synne.

Be þese two laghes in a soule I vnderstonde þis double ymage. Be þe laghe of þe spirit I vnderstonde þe reson of þe soule whanne it is reformed to þe ymage of God; be þe laghe of þe flesch I vnderstonde þe sensualite whilk I calle þe ymage of synne. In þese two laghes a soule reformed ledeth his lyfe, as Seynt Poule seyth þus: *Mente enim seruio legi Dei; carne vero legi peccati*. In my soule, þat is in my wil and in my reson, I serue to þe laghe of God, bot in my flesch, þat is in felynge of my fleschly appetyte, I serue to þe laghe of synne. Neuerþeles þat a soule reformed schulde not desperen, þogh he serue \`to′ þe laghe of synne by felynge of þe vicious sensualite ageyns þe wil of þe spirit bycause of corrupcion of his bodily kend, Seynt Poule excuseth it, seyende þus of his owen persone: *Non enim quod volo bonum hoc ago, sed malum quod odi, hoc facio. Sed autem malum quod odi facio, iam non ego operor illud, sed quod habitat in me, pecatum*. I do not þat good þat I wulde don; þat is, I wulde felen no fleschly sterynge, and þat do I not; but I do þat iuel þat I hate; þat is, þe synful sterynges of my flesche I hate and ȝete I fele hem. Neuerþeles syn it is so þat I hate wykked sterynges of my flesch, and ȝete I fele hem and often delyte in hem ageyns my wil, þei schul not ben aretted ageyns me for dampnacion as if I had don hem. And why? For þe corrupcion of þis ymage of synne doth hem, and not I.

Lo here Seynt Poule in his owen persone comforteth al soules þat
f. 54r arn þurgh grace reformed in feith, þat þei | schuld not to mikel dreden þe birthen of þis ymage with þe vnskilful sterynges þerof, be

43 lymes] membris Ld ageyns] H$_7$RLB$_3$AsSrAEPH$_6$CcMPl, wiþ HBH$_5$Ws-ChLwLdTW it] þat SrCc 44 a] *om.* Lw into] H$_7$RBLB$_3$AsSrChEPH$_6$Cc-MLdPl, to HH$_5$WsLwTW 45 þese] þe H$_5$Ws þis double ymage] duas has ymagines Lat. double] dedly B 46 þe$^{1, 2}$] þis Ld þe^3] *om.* Ld þe^4] þis Ch 47 \`of God′ H$^c$, *om.* H°Ch \`þe laghe′ Pl \`þe^3′ L flesch] body M 48 þe^1] *om.* Ch sensualite] sensualytees LwTW whilk] þat H$_5$WsCcM calle] clepe Ld 49 soule] soulis B$_3$ þus] H$_7$RAsSrAMPl, *om.* HBH$_5$LB$_3$WsChLwEPH$_6$MLdTW, sic Lat, Ro. 5° *add.* BLEPTW, Ro. 7° *add.* Ld 50 vero] H$_7$LB$_3$SrEPH$_6$CcM, enim HRBH$_5$AsWsCh-LwALdPlTW, seruio *add.* \`L′B$_3$P, uero Lat. In] H$_7$RLB$_3$AsSrAPH$_6$MPl, That is *prec.* HBH$_5$WsChLwECcLdTW my$^1$] *om.* RAsAPl þat] þer H$_5$Ws in$^2$] H$_7$RLB$_3$AsSrLw\`H^c′AEPH$_6$CcMPlTW, *om.* H°BH$_5$WsChLd and in my reson] *om.* M 51 in^1] *om.* AH$_6$ to] *om.* M God] go *prec., canc.* Sr in^2] *om.* RH$_5$WsPl flesch . . . my] *om.* M 52 felynge of] H$_7$Sr, my feeling of RAsAPl, þe felinge of LB$_3$P, *om.* HBH$_5$WsChLwLdTW, sensacione Lat. my] *om.* A to] *om.* M 53 þat] for M a . . . schulde/not] *rev.* Cc schulde] H$_7$RLB$_3$AsSrAEPH$_6$CcMPl, schal HBH$_5$Ws-ChLwLdTW \`not′ H$_6$ 54 \`to′ *interl.* H$_7$ þe^1] *om.* H$_6$Cc felynge] appetitum Lat. þe^2] *om.* SrA 55 of^2] the *add.* M his] H$_7$RLB$_3$AsSrAEPH$_6$CcMPl, þe HBH$_5$-

anoþer in my flescly lymes wiþouten feȝtand wiþ it, þat oft lediþ me as a wrecched prisoner to þe laghe of syn.

Be þese two laghes in a soule I vndirstonde þis double ymage. Be þe lagh of þe spirit I vndirstonde þe resoun of þe soule whan it is reformed to þe ymage `of God´; be þe laghe of þe flesch I vndirstonde þe sensualite whilk I calle þe ymage of syn. In þese two laghes a soule
72^{v} reformid lediþ his lif, as Seynt | Poul seiþ: *Mente enim seruio legi Dei carne enim legi peccati.* In my soule, þat is `in´ my wil and in my resoun, `I serue´ to þe laghe of God, bot in my flesch, þat is in my flescly appetite, I serue to þe laghe of syn. Nerþeles þat a soule reformed schal not dispeiren, þowȝ he serue to þe laghe of syn be felyng of þe vicious sensualite agayn þe wil of þe spirit bicause of corupcioun of þe bodily kynde, Seynt Poul excusiþ it, saiand þus of his owne person: *Non enim quod volo bonum hoc ago, sed malum quod odi hoc facio. Si autem malum quod odi hoc facio, non ego operor illud, sed quod habitat in me, peccatum.* I do not þat good þat I wold do, þat is, I wolde fele no flescly stiryng, and þat do I not; bot I do þat yuel þat I hate, þat is þe synful stirynges of my flesche: I hat and ȝit I fele hem. Nerþeles siþen it is so þat I hate þe wikkid stirynges of my flesch, and ȝit I fele hem and often delite in hem ageyn my wille, þei schul not ben aretted ageyn me for dampnacioun as if I had don hem. And whi? for þe corupcioun of þis ymage of syn doþ hem, and not I.

Loo here Seynt Poul in his own person conforteþ alle soules þat þurwȝ grace arn reformed in faiþ, þat þei suld not to mikel drede þe birþen of þis ymage with þe vnskil[ful] stirynges þerof, ⌜if it⌝ so `be´

WsChLwLdTW, *om.* Lat. bodily kend] kynde of þe bodi Ld 56 of] in A persone] Ro. 7° *add.* BLEPLdTW 57 ago] facio vel *prec.* Lw `hoc´ L Sed . . . iam (l. 58)] *om.* RAsAE Sed . . . facio (l. 58)] `Si . . . facio´ L, *om.* Ld, Sed autem] H_7, Sed B_3SrCc, Si autem HBH_5`L´WsChLwP$H_6$LdTW, Si Pl, Si autem Lat. 58 facio] $H_7$L$B_3$SrP$H_6$CcMPl, hoc *prec.* HB$H_5$WsChLwLdTW, hoc *prec.* Lat. iam] $H_7$L$B_3$SrP$H_6$CcM, *om.* HB$H_5$WsChLwLdPlTW, iam Lat. non ego] enim ego `non´ Lw non] enim *add.* A, *om.* M habitat] habitet M I] He seiþ *prec.* H_6, That is *prec.* Cc 59 I wulde^{1}] wold `I´ Pl felen] *om.* Ws no] noon L$B_3$AsSrP fleschly] þinge *add.*, *canc.* L 60 sterynge] styrynges BChLdPl, felynges M, carnales motus Lat. do I] *rev.* As þat$^{2}$] $H_7$HB$H_5$WsLwLdTW, þe RBL$B_3$AsSrChAEP$H_6$CcM, `þen´ Pl is] *om.* Ld 61 Neuerþeles . . . hem (l. 63)] *om.* SrCc syn] þat *add.* H_5Ws 62 hate] haue LwW wykked] H_7RLB_3AsAEPH_6MPl, þe *prec.* HBH_5WsChLwLdTW and^{2} . . . hem] *om.* M `and$^{2}$´ Sr 63 delyte] I *prec.* T wil] but ȝet *add.* Cc schul] schuld Lw aretted ageyns] accounted to M aretted] reherced W 64 for] `no´ *add.* H_6 if] þouȝ Ld, *om.* SrCcM `why´ Pl 66 here] *om.* LwW owen] *om.* W soules] personys Cc 67 arn/þurgh grace] H_7RLB_3AsSrAEPH_6CcMPl, *rev.* HBH_5WsChLwLdTW grace] þe *prec.* Lw schuld] schul H_5WsA to mikel/dreden] *rev.* Ld 68 vnskilful] vnskil H þerof] of it H_5WsE be so] H_7LB_3SrAPH_6CcMPl, bote so BH_5WsChLd, if it be so RE, if it so be Lw⌜H^{c}⌝W, be it so T, dummodo Lat.

so þat þei sente not wilfully þerto. Neuerþeles in þis poynt many soules þat arn reformed in trouthe arn ofte-sythes mikel turmentyde and trubled in veyn. As þus: whan þei han felyd fleschly sterynges of pride, of enuye, of coueytyse, or of licherie or of ony oþer heued synne, þei wyten not sumtyme whethire þei sentyden to hem or non. And þat is no grete wondre, for in tyme of temptacion a frele mans þoght is so trubled and so ouerleyd þat he hath no clere syght ne fredom of himself, bot is taken often with lykyng vnwarly and goth forth with it a grete whyle or þan he perceyfeth it. And þerfor fallen sum of hem oftyn in doute and in were wheþer þei synneden or not in þe tyme of temptacion.

As anemptes þis poynt I sey as me þenketh, þat a soule may hafe assayenge on þis maner wheþer he sentyd or non: if it so be þat a man be stired to ony maner of synne, and þe lykynge is so grete in his fleschly felynge þat it trubleth his reson and as it were þurgh maistrye occupieth þe affeccion of þe soule, neuerþeles he kepeth him þat he folweth not in dede ne he wulde not þogh he myght, bot it is rather to him pynful for to felen þe lykynge of þat sinne and fayn he wulde putten it away if þat he myght, an þan whan þe sterynge is ouerpassed he is glad and wel payed þat he is delyfered of it and þat he felyth no more of it. By þis assay may he wyten þat, were þe lykyng neuer so grete in þe fleschly felynge, þat he asentid not ne synned not, namly dedlyche. Neuerþeles, a remedy þer is þat is siker and certeyn to swilk a simple soule þat is merryd in itself and kan not helpen itself: þat he

69 þat] *om.* LwW sente] H$_7$HBH$_5$LB$_3$ChLwPPlW, assent RAsSrWsAH$_6$CcMLdT, consenten E `not´ Cc wilfully þerto] *rev.* Ld in þis poynt/many soules] *rev.* T 70 trouthe] feyþ BALd sythes mikel] *om.* A sythes] tymys SrPlW, tyme H$_6$ turmentyde and trubled] *rev.* Sr 71 and trubled] *om.* A As] and ChM sterynges] steryng Cc 72 of[1]] or MW, or *prec.* SrCc of[2]] or SrCcM or of[3]] or ChW, of B$_3$T, other M or] oþer As 73 not] neuer A sentyden] H$_7$BLB$_3$SrPPl, sentid H, senten H$_5$ChLwW, assentid RAsAH$_6$CcMT, assenten Ws, consentiden ELd to hem] þerto SrW non] H$_7$HRBSrWsChAEPH$_6$CcPlT, noo H$_5$LB$_3$AsLwPLdW, not M 74 þat] hit Pl no] noon Ch 75 þoght] wit B he] *rep.*, *canc.* Cc no] non As syght] liȝt LB$_3$PH$_6$, cognicionem Lat. 76 fredom] iudicium Lat. bot] he *add.* Cc taken often] *rev.* H$_6$ often] tyme *add.* T with lykyng] *om.* Lat. goth forth] retinet et continuat Lat. 77 with it] H$_7$RLB$_3$AEPH$_6$Pl, withal SrM, therwith Cc, with As, *om.* HBH$_5$WsChLwLdTW, eam Lat. or] and T þan] H$_7$HLB$_3$ChLwPH$_6$CcMTW, þat RBH$_5$AsWsALdPl, whan Sr, *om.* E perceyfeth] H$_7$RPl, perceyfe Σ fallen/sum of hem] *rev.* H$_6$ 78 of hem oftyn] H$_7$RAsAECcPl`T$^G$W$^G$´, of hem LB$_3$SrPH$_6$, *om.* HBH$_5$WsChLwLdTW, tales frequenter Lat. and in were] *om.* Cc and] or M were] H$_7$H°BH$_5$SrWsChAMPl, a wheer Ld, dwere RLB$_3$Lw`H^c´PH$_6$W, diswere As, as yt were T, `hesitacioun´ W^G or not/in . . . temptacion] H$_7$RLB$_3$AsSrAEPH$_6$CcMPl, *rev.* HBH$_5$WsChLwLdTW not] H$_7$RLB$_3$AsWsAEPH$_6$Pl, non HBChT, no H$_5$SrLwCcMLdW 79 þe] H$_7$RLB$_3$AsSrAEPH$_6$CcMPl, *om.* HBH$_5$WsChLwLdTW 80 anemptes] to E þis] *rep.*, *canc.* Sr 81 assayenge] assay SrCcM, knowyng *marg.* Cc on] H$_7$RLB$_3$SrAEPH$_6$CcMPl, in HBH$_5$WsChLwLdTW, of As

þat þei sent not wilfully þerto. Neuerþeles in þis poynte many soules þat er reformed in trowþ arn oft-siþes mikel turmentid and troubled in vayne. As þus: whan þei han felid flescly sterynges of pride, of enuie, of coueitise, or of leccherie or of ony oþer heued syn, þei witen not sumtyme wheþer þei sentid to hem or non. And þat is no grete wonder, for in tyme of temptacioun a freel mannus þouȝt is so trowbled and so ouerlaide þat he haþ no clere siȝt ne fredom of hymself, bot is taken often with likyng vnwarly and goþ forþ a gret while er þan he perceyue it. And þerfor fallen sum in doute and in were wheþer þey synned in tyme of temptacioun or non.

As anentis þis poynt I say as me þinkes, þat a soule may haue
73^r assaying in þis maner wheþer þat he assentid or non: | if ˋitˊ so be þat a man is stirid to any maner of syn, and þe likyng is so grete in his flescly felyng þat it trobleþ his ⌜resoun and⌝ as it were wiþ maistrie ocupiiþ þe affeccioun of þe soule, nerþeles he kepiþ hym þat he folweþ it not in dede ne he wald not if he miȝte, bot is raþer to hym peynful for to felen þe likyng of þat syn and fayn he wold put it awey if he miȝte; and þan whan þe stiryng is ouerpassed he is glad and wele paied þat he is deliuered of it. Bi þis assay may he witen þat were þe likyng neuer so gret in þe fleschly felyngis, þat he assentid not namely dedliche. Nerþeles a remedie þer is þat is sikir to swilk a simple soule þat is marred in itself and kan not helpen itself: þat he be not to bold

wheþer] H$_7$RLB$_3$AsSrAPH$_6$CcMPlT, þat *add.* HBH$_5$WsChLwLdW sentyd] H$_7$SrCc, assentid HRBH$_5$AsWsChAELdPlT, assentiþ LB$_3$P, assente LwH$_6$W, synned M non] H$_7$HRBAsSrWsChH$_6$MCcT, no H$_5$LB$_3$LwEPLdW, noȝt APl ˋitˊ H^c, *om.* H°BChMLd so be] *rev.* SrAW 82 of] *om.* A 83 felynge] liking Ch trubleth] toubled As þurgh] H$_7$RLB$_3$AsSrAEPH$_6$CcPl, wiþ HBH$_5$WsChLwMLdTW 84 ocupieth] occupied AsCh him] hem Ch 85 not] H$_7$RLB$_3$AsSrLwAEPH$_6$CcMPlW, it *prec.* HBH$_5$WsChTW^G, it *add.* Ld þogh] H$_7$RBLB$_3$AsSrAEPH$_6$CcMLdPlˋT^{G}W^{G}ˊ, if HH$_5$WsChLwTW, ˋþatˊ *add.* T^G it] *om.* HBChLwW rather/to him] *rev.* B rather] *om.* H$_6$ to him/pynful] *rev.* LwH$_6$W 86 for] *om.* H$_6$ þe] that Cc fayn] gladly T he] *om.* Sr 87 it] þat Sr þat] H$_7$AsSrAEPlˋT^{G}W^{G}ˊ, *om.* HRBH$_5$LB$_3$WsChLwPH$_6$CcMLdTW ouerpassed] passed M 88 glad and] *om.* Cc wel payed] appayd As þat^1 . . . and^2] *om.* Lat. of it] þerof As, þerfro SrCcM and^2 . . . it (l. 89)] H$_7$RLB$_3$AsSrAEPH$_6$CcMPl, *om.* HBH$_5$WsChLwLdTW, quod plus de hac non sentit Lat. 89 of it] þerof SrH$_6$ By] But *prec.* As assay] I say Pl may he] *rev.* Pl were þe lykyng] if þe likynge were E; thow the lykyng were Cc þe] þat As 90 felynge] felyngis H assentid] assentith Cc, consentid E ne synned not] H$_7$RLB$_3$AsSrLwˋH^{c}ˊAEPH$_6$CcMPlW, *om.* H°BH$_5$ChLdT, nec in hoc peccauit Lat. ne] nor E, he Cc synned] synnyth Cc 91 a] on M þat is siker] *om.* RAs þat is] *om.* LwAPlW and certeyn] H$_7$RLB$_3$AsSrAEPH$_6$CcMPl, *om.* HBH$_5$WsChLwLdTW, securum Lat. 92 a . . . soule] soules B$_3$ soule] *om.* Pl merryd] þus marred or destroubled T, marrid eiþer astonyed Ld, greued M itself^1] H$_7$HRB$_3$AsChLwEPH$_6$CcMPlTW, it hit silf [hit *canc.*] L, hymself BH$_5$SrWsALd, *om.* Cc and . . . itself^2] *om.* RAsAPlT helpen] kepe M itself^2] hymself BSrPCcLd, it LwW þat . . . himself (l. 93)] *om.* M þat] and þat is *prec.* H$_6$

be not to bold in himself, vtterly wenend þat swilk fleschly sterynges with lykynge arn no synnes, for he myght so fallen into reklesnes and into fals sykirnes; ne also þat he be not to dredful ne to simple in witte for to demen hem alle as dedly synnes or elles | f. 54v | as grete venials, for neyþer is soth; bot þat he halde hem al as synne and wrecchednes of himself and þat he hafe sorwe for hem, and þat he be not to besy for to demen þem neyþer dedly ne venial. Bot if his conscience be gretly greued, þat he hastily go and schew it to his confessour in general or in specyal swilk sterynges—and namly þat ilk sterynge þat bygynneth fasten rote in þe herte and most often occupyeth it for to drawen it doun to synne and werdly vanite—and whan he is þus schryuen of þese in general or in special, trow þan stedfastly þat þei arn forgyfen, [and dispute no more aboute hem þat arn passed and forgyfen] wheþer þei were dedly or venial; bot þat he be more besy for to kepen him bettre ageyn hem þat arn comende. And if he do þus þan may he come to rest in conscience.

Bot þan sum arn so fleschly and so vnkonende þat þei wulden felyn or seen or heren þe forgyfnes of hire synnes as openly as þei moun felen or seen in bodily þynges; and for as mikel as þei felen it not so þei fallen oftyn in swilk weris and doutes of hemself and neuer moun come to rest. And in þat ben þey not wyse, for feith goth byfor felynge. Oure Lord seid to a man þat was in þe palasie whan he heled him þus: *Confide fili remittuntur tibi peccata tua*. Þat is: Sone, trowe

93 be not to bold] presume nouȝt RAsAEMPl, non sit nimis audax Lat. to bold/in himself] *rev.* SrCc in himself/vtterly] *rev.* RAs in] of RAsAE, on Pl fleschly] felynges and *add.* M sterynges] stiryng W 94 lykynge] likynges LB$_3$EPH$_6$ no] none M, not Pl synnes] synne RSrACc he myght/so] *rev.* H$_6$ reklesnes] recleshed SrCcM 95 into] a *add.* LB$_3$PH$_6$ sykirnes] and ben deceyued *add.* Cc, securitatem de seipsam Lat. ne] neiþer Ld, *om.* SrCc also] he must takyn heed *add.* Cc þat he be] be he M 96 hem] hym Ch or elles] H$_7$RLB$_3$AsSrAPH$_6$CcMPl, nor HWsChLwW, noþer BH$_5$ELdT, uel Lat. as] al *prec.* RAs, *om.* Pl venials] venyal LB$_3$P, venyal synnes H$_6$Cc, peccata venialia Lat. 97 as] *om.* SrA synne] H$_7$RLB$_3$AsAEPH$_6$CcMPl, synnes HBH$_5$SrWsChLwLdTW, peccata Lat. wrecchednes] wrechidnessis Ld, miserias Lat. 98 þat] *om.* RAs sorwe] no *prec.* B þat he[2]] H$_7$LB$_3$SrAEPH$_6$CcMPl, he RAs, *om.* HBH$_5$WsChLwLdTW for[2]] *om.* CcM 99 þem] alle *add.* Ld neyþer] ne T venial] gret *prec.* Cc, venially SrM 100 greued] agreued Cc, greueþ, *corr. d.h.* Ch þat . . . go] þan go he hastely T he] þanne *add.* Sr, *om.* B hastily go] *rev.* H$_6$ it] H$_7$H$_5$SrWsCcM, *om.* HRBLB$_3$AsChLwAEPH$_6$LdPlTW in[1] . . . specyal/swilk sterynges] *rev.* H$_6$ 101 namly] of *add.* M þat ilk sterynge] the steryngis Cc þat[1]] þe BH$_5$Ws, *om.* LwW ilk] H$_7$LB$_3$PCcLd, same H$_5$Ws, ille HRAsCh, euele BAMPlT, euery LwEW, wicked Sr, *om.* H$_6$, malum Lat. sterynge þat bygynneth] stirynggis þat bygynnyn H$_5$Ws bygynneth] H$_7$LB$_3$PH$_6$Cc, to *add.* HRBH$_5$AsSrWsChLwEMLdPlTW, forto *add.* A 102 fasten] fast AM, his *add.* M rote] ony rote LwW, and rotyn Sr þe] his H$_6$ most] *om.* Cc often] H$_7$RLB$_3$AsSrEPH$_6$CcPl, oftest M, *om.* HBH$_5$WsChLwALdTW,

in hymself, vtterly wenend þat swilk fleschly stirynges wiþ likyng arne no synnes, for he miȝte so falle into reklesnes and into fals sikernes. Ne also þat he be not to dredful ne to simple in witte for to demen hem alle as dedliche synnes nor as grete venials, for ne`i´þer is soþ. Bot þat he holde hem alle as synnes and wrecchednes of hymself, and þat he haue sorwe for hem, and be not to bisy for to deme hem neiþer dedly ne venial. Bot if his conscience be gretly greued þat he hastly go and schewe to his confessour in general or in special swilk stirynges, and namely þat ille styrynge þat bigynneþ to festen rote in þe hert and most ocupieþ it for to drawen it doun to syn and werdly vanytee. And whan he is þus schrifen generally or specially, trow stidefastly þat þei arn forgifen, and dispute no more aboute þeim þat are passed and forgifen wheþer þei were dedly or veniale, bot þat he be more bisy for to kepyn hym better ageyn þem þat are comand. And if he do þus þan may he come to reste in conscience.

Bot summe are þan so flescly and so vnkunnand þat þei wald felen or heren or seen þe forgifnes of þaire synnes as openly as þei mowen felen or seen a bodily þing; and for as mikel as þei felen not so þei
73^v fallen often in swilk weeres and doutes of hemself and neuer mowen | come to reste. And in þat are þei not wise, for faiþ goþ bifore felyng. Oure Lord saide to a man þat was in parlsy when he helid hym þus: *Confide fili remittuntur tibi peccata tua*, þat is: Sone, trow stedfastly þi

frequencius Lat. ocupyeth] occupie Ws 103 and^1] to *add.* SrECcM and^2] thenne *add.* LwW of . . . special (l. 104)] H$_7$RLB$_3$AsSrAEPH$_6$CcMPl, generally or specially HBH$_5$WsChLwLdTW, de eis in generali vel in speciali Lat. 104 þese] this Cc trow] by leeue BLwMLdW þan] H$_7$RLB$_3$AsSrLwAEPH$_6$W, þou CcMPl, *om.* HBH$_5$WsChLdT, *om.* Lat. þei] þer sennes Ch 105 `and . . . forgyfen´ Pl, *om.* H$_7$ 106 wheþer] þat *add.* H$_6$ þei] þer B dedly or venial] *rev.* Cc be] no *add.*, *canc.* R, þe *add.* E for] *om.* LwCcW to . . . him/bettre (l. 107)] *rev.* Lw `hem´ B$_3$, tales motus Lat. comende] to-comyng Ld if he] þou H$_6$ 107 he] þou H$_6$ rest] þe *prec.* Cc in] of H$_5$WsCc, his *add.* M 109 þan sum arn] H$_7$RB$_3$AsSrLwAH$_6$CcMW, summe are þan HBH$_5$WsChLdT, þanne are some LEP, sume men are Pl so^2] *om.* A þei] *om.* R felyn or seen or heren] here or se or fele M felyn or] *om.* Cc 110 seen or heren] H$_7$RLB$_3$AsSrLwAEPH$_6$PlTW, *rev.* HBH$_5$WsChCcMLd þe] her LwW moun] myȝt LwMW, *om.* T 111 felen or seen] *rev.* LwECcM or] and LwCcW bodily þynges] H$_7$, a bodily þing Σ, rem aliquem Lat. þynges] as *add.*, *canc.* L as] a As it] H$_7$RLB$_3$AsSrLwAEPH$_6$CcMPlW, *om.* HBH$_5$WsChLdT so] se Sr 112 þei] H$_7$HBH$_5$LB$_3$WsChPH$_6$LdT, þerfore *prec.* RAsSrLwAECcMPlW, ideo Lat. oftyn] oft-tyme RAsA, ofte-tymes ECcT in] into CcT weris and doutes] dowtis and dredys Cc weris] H$_7$HBH$_5$SrWsChLwEMLdPlW, dweris RLB$_3$APH$_6$T, diwseres As and^2] þat þei H$_6$ 113 to] vnto T, non *add.* As rest] quietem consciencie Lat. `in´ Pl not wyse] vnwise LwW byfor] afore H$_6$Cc 114 felynge] felynges BLd, þe *prec.* T, sensacionem corporalem þe] *om.* HB$_3$ChT 115 þus] in þis wise T, Mt. 9° *add.* BLEPTW fili] et *add.* M Sone] *om.* Pl trowe] by leeue BLd, leue M, þou *add.* CcT

stedfastly þi synnes arn forgyfen þe. He seid not to him, se or fele how þi synnes arn forgyfen þe—[for] forgyfnes of synnes is don gostly and vnseably þurgh grace of þe Holy Gost—bot trow it. Ryght vpon þe same wyse, ilk man þat wil come to rest in conscience, him behoueth first, if he do þat in him is, trowen withouten gostly felynge forgifnes of his synnes; and if he first trowe it, he may afterward þurgh grace felyn it, and vnderstonden it, þat it is so. þus seith þe Apostel: *Nisi credideritis, non intelligetis*. þat is: Bot if ȝe first trowen, ȝe moun not vnderstonden. Trowth goth before and vnderstondynge cometh after, þe qwhilk vnderstondynge, þat I calle þe syght of God, if it be graciouse, a soule may not hafe bot þurgh grete clennes, as oure Lord seyth: *Beati mundo corde, quoniam ipsi Deum videbunt*. Blissed be clene of hert, for þei schul se God. þat is: þei schul se God, not with here
f. 55r fleschly eyghe bot [with] þe innere eyghe, þat is | vnderstondynge clensed and illumyned þurgh grace of þe Holy Gost for to seen sothfastnes. þe wilk clennes a soule may not felen bot if it hafe stable trowþe goende beforn, as þe Apostel seith: *Fide mundans corda eorum*. þat is: Oure Lord clenseth þe hertys of his chosen þurgh feith. þerfor it is nedful þat a soule trowe first þe reformynge of his soule made þurgh þe sacrament of penaunce, þogh he se it not, and þat he dispose him fully for to lyfen ryghtwysly and vertuously as his trouþe asketh, so þat he may aftere þat come to þe syght and to þe reformynge in felynge.

116 He] Lo *prec.* M `to him´ L se or fele] *rev.* T or] and M fele] here Cc how] *om.* RAsACcPl, qualiter Lat. 117 for] HRBH_5AsWsChLwAECcPlTW, forwhi Sr, *om.* H_7LB_3PH_6MLd, þe *add.* W, quia Lat. synnes] H_7RAsAMPlW, syn HBH_5-LB_3SrWsChLwEPH_6Cc, peccatorum Lat. is] beth A don] *om.* Cc and vnseably] *om.* A, and onseable bot Cc 118 þurgh] by As grace] H_7RLB_3AsSrAEPH_6CcMPl, þe *prec.* HBH_5WsChLwLdTW bot] and þerfore Sr, he said *add.* RAsAEPl`$T^G W^G$´ trow it] confide quod remittuntur peccata tua Lat. trow] trist A, ⌜bileue⌝ L, bileue EPLd, leue M it] wel *add.* M Ryght] wel *add.* Cc, *om.* T vpon] H_7RLB_3AsEPMPlT, on HBH_5SrWsChLwAH_6CcLdW 119 ilk] H_7R, ilke a HAsCh, euery BLB_3SrWs-AEPH_6MPlTW, eueryche H_5, euery a Lw, eche CcLd rest] þe *prec.* As in] of Cc 120 if] þat *prec.* Pl, þat *add.* CcM do] doth RAs in him/is] *rev.* Ld is] þis Lw trowen] leuen BM, belyue Ld withouten] *corr. from*in Cc, wiþ Sr, by-þowten B forgifnes] ful *prec.* H_5Ws 121 his] *om.* A trowe] byleeue BLd, leue M may] H_7RLB_3AsSrAEPH_6CcMPl, schal HBH_5WsChLwLdTW afterward/þurgh grace] *rev.* B 122 seith] H_7Ch, saide Σ, dicit Lat. þe Apostel] *canc.* W, our Lord H_6, þe prophete Ld, Ysa. 7° *add.* BLEPLdTW 123 credideritis] H_7HRBH_5AsSrWsLwAEMLdT, cred⌜i⌝de´ritis Ch, crederitis LB_3PH_6CcPlW, credideritis Lat. þat is] þis is Pl, *om.* LB_3P if] *om.* RLd ⌜ȝe⌝ (*bis*)] H, he Ch trowen] H_7RLB_3AsSrChPH_6, trowe HH_5WsLwAECcPlTW, byleeuen BLd, leue M moun] H_7RLB_3SrCc, mowe AsP, may HBH_5WsChLwAEH_6MLdPlTW 124 vnderstonden] it, that it is so. For *add.* M Trowth] trowyng H_6Cc, byleeue BA, Feiþ Ld before] afore H_6 cometh] come L 125 calle] clepe Ld syght] lyght W if it be gracious] H_7RLB_3AsSrLw`H^c´EPH_6CcMW,

synnes are forgifen þe. He said not to hym, see or fele how þi synnes are forgifen þee, for forgifnes of syn is don gostly and vnseablely þurwȝ þe grace of þe Holy Gost, bot trow it. Riȝt on þe same wise, ilke a man þat wil come to reste in conscience, hym behouiþ first, if he do þat in hym is, trowen withouten gostly felyng forgifnes of his synnes; and if he first trowe it, he schal aftirward þurwȝ grace felen it, and vndirstonden it, þat it is so. Þus saide þe Apostle: *Nisi credideritis, non intelligetis*, þat is: Bot if ⌜ȝ⌝e first trowe, ⌜ȝ⌝e may not vndirstonde. Trowþ gooþ bifore and vndirstondyng comeþ after, þe whilk vndirstondyng, þat I calle þe siȝt of God, a soule may not haue bot þorwȝ grete clennes, as oure Lord saiþ: *Beati mundo corde quoniam ipsi Deum videbunt*. Blessud be clene of herte, for þei schul see God. Þat is: þei schul see God, not with þeire flescly hiȝe bot with þe innere `hiȝe´, þat is vndirstondyng clensid and illumined þu`r´w grace of þe Holy Gost for to seen soþfastnes. Þe whilk clennes a soule may not felen bot if he haue stable trouþ goand bifore, as þe Apostle saiþ: *Fide mundans corda eorum*, þat is: Oure Lord clensiþ þe hertes of his chosen þorwȝ faiþ. Þerfor it is nedful þat a soule trowe first þe reformyng of hymself made þurwȝe þe sacrament of penaunce, þaw he see it not, and þat he dispose hymselfe fully for to lif riȝtwisly and vertuosly as his trouþ askiþ, so þat he may after come to þe siȝt and to þe reformyng in felyng.

om. H°BH$_5$WsChALdPlT, si sit graciosa Lat.   126 may] m *prec.*, *canc.* Sr   hafe] it *add.* SrCc   grete] grace and Cc, grace of Pl   as] and H$_5$Ws   127 seyth] Mat. 5° *add.* BLEPLdTW   mundo] mundi R   Blissed] H$_7$HRBLB$_3$AsSrChLwPLdPlTW, þat is *prec.* H$_5$WsEH$_6$CcM   `be´ Pl   clene] þe *prec.* WsCcMLd   128 þat is . . . God[2]] H$_7$HRBH$_5$AsSrWsChAEMLdPl`T^{G}W^{G}´, *om.* LB$_3$LwPH$_6$CcTW, Id est, Deum videbunt Lat.   here] þe A   129 eyghe[1]] eyȝen MT   bot . . . eyghe[2]] *om.* M   with] *om.* H$_7$ þe innere] here preueye As, here inly Cc   þe] her T   vnderstondynge] but with here ynner eyen *add.* M   130 clensed] clensyng Cc, *om.* As   illumyned] illumynyng Cc, liȝtned Ld, lyghted W   þurgh grace] *rep.*, *canc.* Sr   grace] þe *prec.* H$_6$ þe] *om.* H$_6$ 131 wilk] synne *add.*, *canc.* L   clennes a] a clensed Cc   clennes] clensith APl   a] of M   soule] þat *add.* APl   not felen] *rev.*, *marked for trsp.* B$_3$ felen] it *add.* Sr   if] H$_7$HRBH$_5$AsChLwAEMLdPlTW, *om.* LB$_3$SrWsPH$_6$Cc   it hafe] be H$_5$Ws   it] H$_7$RLB$_3$AsSrAEPH$_6$CcM`W$^{G}$´, he HBChLwLdPlTW   132 trowþe] feyþ BAPl, beleue MLd   goende] *om.* Ld   seith] Act. 15° *add.* BLdTW, Act. 5° LEP   133 is] to seye *add.* As   þe . . . chosen] `her hertys´ Cc   134 soule] man H$_6$ trowe] byleeue BAMLd   þe] his A   his soule] H$_7$RB$_3$AsSrAEPH$_6$CcMPl, hymselfe HBH$_5$⌜L⌝Ws-ChLwLdTW, anime sue Lat.   135 þurgh] bi *prec.*, *canc.* E   136 him] H$_7$RBLB$_3$As-SrChAEPH$_6$CcMLdPl, hymselfe HH$_5$WsLwTW, mad *add.* HH$_5$Ws, mad, *canc.* H   for] *om.* RH$_5$WsACc   ryghtwysly] rightfully SrLwEH$_6$W   trouþe] byleeue BALd   asketh] *one-word canc. seq.* L   137 þat[2]] *om.* Pl   come] bi grace of oure lord Jesu Crist *add.* Ld   þe[1]] *om.* W   to þe[2]] in to þe Lw, *om.* Ld

þat þis ymage is boþe faire and foule whyls it is in þis life, þof-all it be reformed, and of diuerste of felinge priuely had atwyx þese soules þat are reformed and oþer þat are not reformed. Capitulum xii^{m}

Fayre is a mans soule, and foule is a mans soule. Faire in as mikel as it is reformed in trouthe to þe lykenes of God. Bot it is foul in as mikel as it is ȝet medled with fleschly felynges and vnskilful sterynges of þis ymage of synne. Foul withouten as it were a best, fayre withinne lyke to an aungel. Foul in felynge of þe sensualite, fayre in trowþe of þe reson. Foul for þe fleschly appetyte, fayre for þe good wille. Þus fayre and þus foul is a chosen soule, sayende Holy Wrytte þus: *Nigra sum sed formosa filie Jerusalem sicut tabernacula Cedar et sicut pelle*[*s*] *Salomonis*. I am blak bot I am fayre and schaply, ȝe doghters of Jerusalem, as þe tabernacles of Cedar and as þe skynnes of Salomon. Þat is: [Ȝ]e aungels of heuene þat arn doghters of þe heyghe Jerusalem, wondreth not on me ne despise me not for my blak sch`a´dwe, for þogh I be blak withouten bycause of my fleschly kynde, as is a tabernacle of Cedar, neuerþeles I am ful fayre withinne, as is þe skyn of Salomon, for I am reformed to þe liknes of God.

Be Cedar is vnderstonded mirknes, and þat is þe deuel. Be a tabernacle of Cedar is vnderstondyn a reproued soule, þe whilk is a tabernakle of þe deuel. Be Salomon, [þat] betokneþ pesible, is vnderstondyn oure Lord, for he is pees and pesible. Be þe skynne
f. 55v of Salomon is vndirstondyn a blissed aungel, in whom | oure Lord woneth and is hid, as lyfe is hid within þe skyn of a quik body, and

Chapter 12 *title*: H$_7$RLB$_3$AsSrAEPH$_6$MLdPlTW *om.* HBH$_5$WsChLwCc 1 life] here *add.* TW þof-all] H$_7$RAsAPl, alþow Sr, þouȝ LB$_3$EPH$_6$MLdTW 2 and . . . reformed^{2} (l. 3)] *om.* Pl and of] in M diuerste of] diuerse AsSr felinge] felinges T atwyx] H$_7$LSrEP, atwen H$_6$, betwix RB$_3$AM, betwene AsLdTW 3 reformed^{2}] H$_7$RLB$_3$AsEPM, *om.* SrAH$_6$LdTW 4 xii^{m}] P *omits from count; Chapter 13 is numbered 12* 5 Fayre] and louely *add.* H$_5$Ws is^{1}] H$_7$LB$_3$LwPH$_6$W, is þan HRBH$_5$AsSrWsChAECcMT, þan is Ld, ergo est Lat. a mans soule^{1}] a soule of a man M a^{1}] *om.* LB$_3$LwPH$_6$W and . . . soule^{2}] *om.* Ch is^{2} . . . soule^{2}] *om.* RAsAPl a^{2}] *om.* M 6 trouthe] H$_7$RLB$_3$AsSrEPH$_6$CcMPl, faiþ HBH$_5$WsChLwALdTW in as] *om.* Ch 7 ȝet] *om.* W fleschly] *om.* Pl felynges] felyng Cc vnskilful] vnskilfully M sterynges] steryng Cc þis] H$_7$RLB$_3$AsAEPH$_6$M, þe SrCc, his Pl, foul *add.* HBH$_5$Ws-ChLwLdTW 8 Foul] Turpis est Lat. lyke to] as it were SrCcM 9 to] vnto ET an] *om.* H$_5$ þe^{1}] *om.* BLd trowþe] byleeue B þe^{2}] *om.* AMLd 10 for^{1}] in Ws, to Cc for^{2}] to Cc 11 `a´ H$_6$ sayende/Holy Wrytte] *rev.* Cc sayende] For þus seiþ H$_6$, in *add.* Sr þus] *om.* H$_6$, Cant. i° *add.* BLEPLdTW 12 filie Ierusalem] *rev.* Ch filie] fili⌜e⌝ H, filiae Ws, filia BLdPl sicut] *om.* H°H$_5$Ws pelles] LB$_3$Sr`Lw´AEPH$_6$CcMPl, pelle H$_7$, pellis HRBH$_5$AsWsChLdTW, pelles Lat. 13 Salomonis] H$_7$RLB$_3$AsSrAPMPl, þat is *add.* HBH$_5$WsChLwEH$_6$CcLdTW and

[CHAPTER 12]

Faier is þan a mannus soule, and foule is a mannus soule. Faire in als mikel as it is reformed in faiþ to þe liknes of God. Bot it is foule in als mikel as it is ȝit medlid with flescly felynges and vnskilful stirynges of þis foul ymage of synne. Foul withouten as it were a beste, faire withinne like to an aungel. Foul in felyng of þe sensualite, faire in
74r trouþ of | þe reson. Foul for þe flescly appetite, faire for þe good wil. Þus faire and þus foule is a chosen soule, seiende Holy Writ þus: *Nigra sum sed formosa fili*⌜e⌝ Jerusalem sicut tabernacula Cedar et `*sicut*′ *pellis Salamonis*, þat is: I am blak bot I am faire and schaply, ȝe doȝters of Ierusalem, as þe tabernacles of Cedar, as þe skynne of Salamon. Þat is: Ȝe aungels of heuen þat arn doȝters of þe heiȝe Ierusalem, wondreþ not on me ne despice me not for my blake shadwe, for þa`ȝ′k I be blak withouten because of my flescly kynde, as is a tabernacle of Cedar, nerþeles I am ful faire withinne as þe skynne of Salamon, for I am reformed to þe liknes of God.

Be Cedar is vondirstonden mirknes, and þat is þe deuel. By a tabernacle of Cedar is vnderstanden a reproued soule, þe whilk is a tabernacle of þe deuil. Be Salamon þat betokneþ pesible is `vnderstondyn oure Lord Ihesu, for he is pees and pesible. Bi þe skyn of Salomon is′ vndirstonden a blissid aungel, in whom oure Lord woneþ and is hid, `as lif is′ hid within þe skyn of a qwyk body, and þerfore is

schaply] *om.* Sr ȝe] þe M, þe *add.* RAsPl doghters] doughter W of] *om.* R 14 þe[1]] *om.* M tabernacles] tabernacle RAsSr and] H_7RLB_3AsSrWsAEPH_6CcMPl, *om.* HBH_5ChLwLdTW as[2]] of Cc, *om.* Ws skynnes] H_7LB_3SrAEPH_6CcMPl, skynne HRBH_5AsWsChLwLdTW 15 is] for to seye SrCcM Ȝe] þe H_7H_5AsMLd, That Cc, vos Lat. doghters] þe *prec.* SrECcMPl þe] *om.* H_5WsE heyghe] *om.* Cc 16 wondreth] wondyr Sr, ȝe *add.* SrLdT on] of Sr for] *om.* RAs 17 withouten] forþe *add.* Ld 18 is] *om.* AH_6 a] þe As neuerþeles] ȝet Cc 19 is] H_7RLB_3AsSrEPH_6CcMPl, *om.* HBH_5WsChLwALdTW, *om.* Lat. 20 vnderstonded] H_7, vondirstonden Σ `mirknes . . . vnderstondyn (l. 20)′ $W^G$, *om.* LwW mirknes] $H_7$HRLAsSrChPCcMPl, derknesse B$H_5B_3$WsAE$H_6$LdT$W^G$ and] *om.* M is] in *add.* A `þe′ Cc Be] And *prec.* Cc a] *canc.* L, the PCc 21 þe whilk] wiche B; þat H_5Ws 22 `þat betokneþ pesible′ $W^G$, *om.* LwTW þat] is $H_7$, *om.* $H_6$ is] and *prec.* $H_6$ 23 `vnderstondyn . . . is (l. 24)′ H^c, *om.* $H^o H_5$Ws Lord] H_7BLB_3SrChPH_6CcMLd, Jesu *add.* RAsLwH^cAEPlTW, Deus Lat. is] *om.* Cc pees and pesible] *rev.* Sr 24 vndirstondyn] to vnderstonde E blissed] blysful H_5Ws aungel] soule H_6 25 woneþ] dwellith AW `is′[1] L as . . . hid] as lyfe hydde is $W^G$ `as lyfe is′ H^cW^G, as ys lyfe LwT, as is the lyfe W, *om.* H^oH_5WsM, sicut vita Lat. within] in LwW and . . . skyn (l. 26)] *om.* Lat.

þerfore is an aungel likned to a skyn. þan may a chosen soule with meke trist in God and gladnesse of herte sey þus: þogh I be blak bycause of my body of synne, as is a reproued soule þat is one of þe tabernacles of þe fende, neuerþeles I am withinne wel fayre þurgh trowþe and good wille, lyke to an aungel of heuene. For so seith he in anoþer place: *Nolite considerare me quod fusca sum, quoniam decolorauit me sol.* þat is: Beholdeþ me not for þat I am swart, for þe sunne hath defaded me. þe sunne maketh a skyn swart only withouten and not withinne, and it betokneth þis werdly lyfe. þerfor seith a chosen soule þus: Reproue me not for I am swart, for þe swartnesse þat I haue is al withouten, of touchynge and of berynge of þis ymage of synne. Bot it is noþyng withinne. And þerfore sothly, þogh it be so þat a chosen soule reformed in feith dwelle in þis bodi of synne, and fele þe same fleschly sterynges and vse þe self bodily werkes as doth a tabernacle of Cedar, so fereforth þat in mans dome þer schuld no difference be bytwyx þat on and þat oþer, neuerþeles withinne in here soules is þere ful grete dyuerste and in þe syght of God is þer ful mikel twynnynge. Bot þe knowyng of þis, whilk is on and whilk is oþer, is only kept to God, for it passeth mans dome and mans felynge, and þerfor we schul no man demen as ille for þat þynge þat may be vsed boþe iuele and wel.

A soule þat is not reformed is taken so fully with þe loue of þis werld, and so mikel ouerleyd with þe lykyng of his flesch in al his sensualyte, þat he cheseth it as a ful rest of his herte, and in his priuey menynge he wulde not elles haue bot þat he myght ay be sekyr þerof.

26 is an aungel] his aungel is As an aungel] a soule H_6 27 meke] moche H_6, mekenes M and] wiþ *add.* M gladnesse] clennesse Cc of] \`in´ L, in $B_3$SrEP þogh] þou\`ȝ´ L 28 as] *om.* Ld is[1] . . . soule] an As is[1]] *om.* LwW one of þe tabernacles] H_7RAsSrLwACcMPlW, \`one´ H[c], of þe tabernacles H°BH_5WsChLd, of þe tabernacle T, on tabernacle H_6, on *canc.* L, þe tabernacle LB_3EP, tabernaculum Lat. 29 wel] ful WsLwW 30 trowþe] feyþe B; belyue Ld to] vnto T he] Holy Writ H_5Ws 31 place] Cant. i° *add.* BELPLdTW me] *om.* SrLw quod] quia LB_3PH_6MLd fusca] fuscus R quoniam] quia Cc decolorauit] decorauit M 32 þat is] *om.* Sr þat] This P for þat] H_7AsSrCc, for RLB_3EPH_6M, þat HBH_5WsChLwLdTW swart] broun ACcM for[2] . . . swart (l. 33)] *om.* M 33 defaded] H_7RLB_3AsLwAPPlW, defaced HBH_5WsChELdTW, descolorid H_6, wanheewed or defated Sr, defated Cc swart only] *rev.* Cc swart] broun ACc withouten] wiþoutforþe Ld 34 it] þat SrT þis] þe RAsSrAT werdly] H_7, fleschly Σ (fleschly lyfe *rev.* M) carnalem Lat. \`lyfe´. And] *add.* Cc 35 swart] broun ACcM þe] þat Sr swartnesse] brounnesse A, blaknesse CcM al] *om.* $H_5$Ws 36 withouten] wiþoutforþ Ld of touchynge and of berynge] tactu et onere Lat. of[1, 2]] þe *add.* (*bis*) Cc of[2]] *om.* Pl þis] \`is an´ As 37 noþyng] \`so´ *add.* Cc 38 dwelle] dwellyth CcM fele] felyth Cc of[3]] H_7HBW_5WsChLwECcLdTW, *om.* RLB_3AsSrAPH_6MPl 39 vse] vsiþ ECc self] H_7RAsSrAPl, same HBH_5LB_3WsChLwEPH_6CcMLdTW 40 ⌜mans . . . and (l. 41)⌝ L no difference/be] *rev.* M no] non As be] est Lat. 41 bytwyx]

an aungel likned to a skyn. Þan may a chosen soule with meke trost in God and gladnes of herte sai þus: Þawȝ I be blak bicause of my body of syn, as is a reproued soule þat is of þe tabernacles of þe fende, nerþeles I am withinne wel faire þorw trou⌜þ⌝ and good wiþ like to an aungel of heuen. For so saiþ he in anoþer place: *Nolite considerare me quod fusca sum, quoniam decolorauit me sol*, þat is: Behold me not þat I am swart, for þe sonne haþ defaced me. Þe sonne makiþ a skyn swart only withouten and not withinne, and it betokneþ þis fleschly lif. Þerfore saiþ a chosen soule þus: Reproue me not for I am swart, for þe swartnes þat I haue is al withouten, of touchyng and of beryng of þis ymage of synne. Bot it is noþing withinne. And þerfore soþly, þawȝ it be so þat a chosen soule reformed in faiþ dwelle in þis body of syn, and fele þe same flescly styrynges and vse þe same bodily werkes as doþ a tabernacle of Cedar, so fer forþ þat in mannus dome þer schuld no difference be bitwix þe ton and þe toþer, nerþeles withinne in þaire
4^{v} soules | þer is ful grete diuersite and in siȝt of God þer is ful mikil twynnyng. Bot þe knowyng of þis, whilk is on whilk is oþer, is only kept to God, for it passiþ mannus dome ⌜and mannus felyng, and þerfore we schul no man⌝ demen as ille for þat þing þat may be vsed boþ yuel and wel.

For a soule þat is not reformid is taken so fully with þe luf of þe werld, and so mikel ouerlaide with þe likyng of his flesch in al his sensualite, þat he chesiþ it as ful reste of his hert, and \`in´ his pryue menyng he wld not elles haue bot þat he miȝt ay be siker þerof. He

H$_7$RLB$_3$SrLwAEPCcLdPlW, bytwene HBH$_5$AsWsH$_6$MT, twex Ch   þat (*bis*)] the Cc   neuerþeles] ȝet Cc   in] *om.* ET   here] þe M   soules] soule MLd   is þere] H$_7$RLB$_3$AsSrAEPM, *rev.* HBH$_5$WsChLwLdTW, is H$_6$CcPl   42 þe] H$_7$RBLB$_3$As-SrEPH$_6$CcMLdPlW, *om.* HH$_5$WsChLwT   is þer] H$_7$RLB$_3$AsSrAPCcPl, *rev.* HBH$_5$WsChLwLdTW, is EH$_6$M   mikel] grete LB$_3$PH$_6$ twynnynge] partyng H$_6$ 43 and] *om.* HBChLd   oþer] anoþer AsCc   45 no man/demen] H$_7$HH$_5$LB$_3$Sr-WsChLwAEPMLdPlW, *rev.* RBAsH$_6$CcT   ille] H$_7$HH$_5$LChP, iuel RBB$_3$AsSrWs-LwAECcMLdPlTW, wikke H$_6$ iuele and wel] *rev.* M   47 *Chapter-break and initial here* SrCcM; Of þre maner of men, of þe whiche summe arn not reformed and summe arn reformed, and summe arn reformed only in feiþ and summe in feiþ and felyng. Capitulum 13 Sr (*see below, Chapter 13 title, where no break occurs in* Sr); That a soule before hit be reformed is born of þis ymage of synne as a sike man is of a liter, and also sone as he is reformed hit is born of hym. Capitulum terciodecimum incipit. M   *No chapter title* Cc   A soule] H$_7$LB$_3$SrLwPH$_6$CcMW For *prec.* HRBH$_5$AsWsChAELdPlT, Anima Lat.   þe] *om.* T   þis] H$_7$RLB$_3$AsAEPH$_6$CcMPl, þe HBH$_5$SrWsChLwLdTW   49 sensualyte] sensualitees M   it] huiusmodi dileccionem et delectacionem Lat.   a] H$_7$\`L´B$_3$LwEPMW, *om.* HRBH$_5$AsSrWsChAH$_6$CcLdPlT   rest of his] *rep.*, *canc.* Cc   and] *om.* T   his . . . menynge] priueye menynge of hym self B   his] cordis sui Lat.   50 þat] if *add.* Sr   ay/be sekyr] *rev.* Sr   ay] H$_7$HRBH$_5$LAsWsChLwPCcLdTW, euere B$_3$AEH$_6$MPl, alwey Sr   þerof] de huiusmodi delectacione Lat.

He feleth no lycour of grace sterende him for to loþe þis fleschly lyfe ne for to desyren heuenly blis. And þerfor I may seyn þat he bereth not þis ymage of synne, bot he is born of it; as a man þat were seek and
f. 56r so | weyk þat he myght not bere himself, and þerfor is leyd in a bed and born in a liter. Ryght so swilk a synful soule is so weyk and so vnmyghty for lakkynge of grace þat it may neyþer steren hand ne fote for to don any gode dede, ne for to ageynstonden by displesyng of wil þe lest sterynge of synne whan it cometh, bot it falleth doun þerto as doth a best vpon karion.

Bot a soule þat is þurgh grace reformed, þogh he vse his fleschly wyttes and fele fleschly likynges, neuerþeles he lotheth hem in his herte, for he wulde for no þyng fully resten in hem. Bot he fleth þe reste as þe bytynge of an neddere, and had lefere han his rest and þe lufe of his hert in God if þat he kowthe, and sumtyme desyreth þerto, and often yrketh of þe likynge of þis lyfe for lufe of þe lyfe aylastende. Þis soule is not born in þis ymage of synne as a seek man, þogh he fele it, bot he bereth it. For þurgh grace he is made myghty and stronge for to suffren and beren his body with alle ille sterynges of it, withouten hurtynge or diffoulynge of himself; and þat is in als mikel as he loueth hem not ne folweth hem not ne senteth not to hem þe whilk arn dedly synnes, as anoþer doth.

Þis was bodily fulfilled in þe Gospel of a man þat was in þe palasye and was so feble þat he myght not gon; þerfore was he born and leyd in a litere and broght to oure Lorde. And whan oure Lord sey him in

51 He . . . seyn (l. 52)] *om.* APl for] *om.* LB$_3$APH$_6$ loþe] letyn Cc þis] his LwCcW 52 þat he] this man RAsAPl 53 it] þat Sr þat] *om.* Sr were] so *add.* AsM 54 so weyk þat] debilis Lat. weyk] febil APl, leþy Ld he] it T is] H$_7$RLB$_3$SrAEP, he is HBH$_5$WsChLwLdTWH$_6$CcMLdTW, he `is´ Pl leyd/. . ./born (l. 55)] *rev.* Ws 55 swilk] *om.* P synful] mannes Ws, mannus *add.* H$_5$ weyk] feble B, leþy Ld and so vnmyghty] *om.* Cc 56 lakkynge] lak Cc, wantyng H$_6$ it] H$_7$RLB$_3$AsSrAEPH$_6$CcMPl, he HBH$_5$WsChLwLdTW neyþer steren] *rev.* H$_5$Ws steren] H$_7$RH$_5$LB$_3$AsSrWs-AEPH$_6$CcMPl, mefe HBWsChLwLdTW 57 don] *om.* M for[2]] *om.* H$_6$ to] *om.* LP ageynstonden] ayenstondynge PCc, wiþstonde E by] þe H$_5$Ws 58 lest] lusty B whan it cometh] *om.* Lat. bot] *om.* M it] *om.* Cc falleth doun] decidit et quiescit Lat. doun] *om.* CcM 59 doth/a best] *rev.* Pl doth] it were LwW karion] H$_7$SrChLwH$_6$PlW, a *prec.* HRBH$_5$LB$_3$AsWsAEPCcMLd, þe *prec.* T 60 is] *om.* As þurgh grace] H$_7$RLB$_3$AsSrAEPH$_6$CcMPl, *om.* HBH$_5$WsChLwLdTW, per graciam Lat. fleschly] lustes and *add.* M 61 and . . . likynges] *om.* M fleschly] þe *prec.* B likynges] H$_7$LB$_3$SrEPH$_6$Cc, stirynges HRBH$_5$AsWsChLwALdPlTW, delectaciones Lat. neuerþeles] ȝet Cc lotheth hem] loueþ hem nouȝt RAsAPl 62 for[1]] ne A, et Lat. wulde] H$_7$HRBAsChLwMLdPlTW, wol A, wolde nouȝt H$_5$Ws, nolde LB$_3$SrEPH$_6$Cc fully] *om.* SrAECc fleth] ⌜feeliþ⌝ L, feliþ B$_3$P, fugit et declinat Lat. 63 reste] restyng Sr, in hem *add.* LB$_3$EPH$_6$, quietem in eis Lat. þe[1]] H$_7$RLB$_3$AsLwAEPH$_6$CcW, a Pl, *om.* HBH$_5$SrWsChMLdT an neddere] H$_7$As, an addere BH$_5$LB$_3$SrWsLwEPH$_6$CcMLdTW,

feliþ no likour of grace stirand hym for to loþ þis fleschly lif ne for to desiren heuenly blys. And þerfore I may seien þat he beriþ not þis ymage of synne, bot he is born of it; as a man þat were seke and so waike þat he miȝt not beren hymself, and þerfore he is laide in a bedde and born in a litere. Riȝt so swilk a synful soule is so waike and so vnmiȝty for lackyng of grace þat he may neiþer mefe hand ne foot for to do ony gode dede, ne for to agaynstonde be displesyng of wille þe leste stirynge of synne whan it comeþ, bot it falliþ doun þerto as doþ a beste vpon a carioun.

Bot a soule þat is reformid, þof he vse his flescly wittes and fele flescly stirynges, nerþeles he loþeþ hem in his hert, for he wulde for no þing fully reste in hem. Bot hee fleeþ þe reste as bityng of a ⌜neddre⌝, and had leuer han his rest and þe luf of his herte in God, if þat he koude, and sumtyme desireþ þerto, and often irkeþ of þe likyng of þis liif for lufe of þe liif aylastande. þis soule is not born in þis ymage of syn as a seke man, þawȝ he fele it, bot he beriþ it. For þurw grace he is made miȝty and stronge for to suffren and beryn his body with alle þe ille stirynges of it, withouten hurtyng or defoulynge of hymself; and þat is in as mikel as he lufeþ hem not, ne folweþ hem not, `ne´ senteþ not to hem, þe whilk arn dedliche synnes, as anoþer doþ.

þis was bodilich fulfillid in þe Gospel of a man þat was in þe parlsy
75r and was so feble þat he miȝt not | gon, and þerfore was he leid and born in a liter and brouȝt to oure Lord. `And when our Lord´ sawȝ

a neddre RChPl, a ⌜neddre⌝ H^c had] H_7HRBH_5AsWsChLwACcMLdPlTW, he had LB_3SrEPH_6 rest/. . ./lufe] *rev.* SrM and] in RAs, to A þe lufe of his hert] his loue H_5WsCc 64 his hert/in/God] *rev.* As þat] *om.* E and . . . þerto] *om.* Lat. desyreth] he *prec.* H_6 65 often] oftyme As, oftyn tyme Cc, he *add.* H_6 yrketh] H_7HRLB_3SrChLwAPH_6CcPlT, weryeþ BAsLd, is wery H_5WsM, rekiþ E, grutcheth W, tediosa est ei Lat. likynge] felyng Pl, leuyng M þis] his M, the Cc lufe] the *prec.* CcT aylastende] H_7HRLAsSrChPCc, euerelastynge B$H_5$$B_3$WsLwAE$H_6$MLdPlW, alway lastinge T 66 in] of ChLdT þis] þe As of synne] *om.* Pl synne as a] *om.* A as] but *prec.* As 67 bereth] bere As For] but Sr 68 and beren] *om.* T beren] to *prec.* M with] of Cc alle] H_7, þe *add.* Σ ille] H_7HRChPl, euele BAsLwAH_6CcMLdTW, wyckede H_5SrWs, *om.* LB_3EP of it] þerof Cc 69 or] oþer A, of BCh and þat is] þat Pl, *om.* RAsA `is´ L 70 hem] hym Ch, *om.* Pl ne . . . not/ne . . . hem] *rev.* As not[1]] *om.* CcM `ne´[2] *interl.* H senteth] H_7HBH_5LB_3ChLwEPPlW, assenteth RAsSrWsAH_6CcMLdT synnes] synne LB_3P, peccata Lat. 72 was bodily] *rev.* As was[1]] is Sr bodily] boldelyche As fulfilled] forth-filled M was in] had Cc 73 `not´ Cc þerfore] $H_7$, and *prec.* $\Sigma$ was he] *rev.* CcM born and leyd] $H_7$, *rev.* $\Sigma$ leyd] in a bed *add.* $H_5$Ws 74 in] vpon M to] so to T `And . . . Lord´ H^c whan] *om.* T Lord] God *add.* Ws, God God *add.* H_5 in] atte T, þe *add.* Ch, his *add.* H_6, this *add.* M, moche *add.*, *canc.* L

meschef, of his goodnesse he seyd to him þus: *Surge et tolle grabatum tuum et vade in domum tuam*. Þat is: Ryse vp and take þi bed and go into þin house. And so he dyd, and was hole. And sothly ryght as þis man bare vpon his bak whan he was made hole þe bed þat beforn bare him, ryght so it may be seyd gostly, þat a soule reformed in feith bereth þis ymage of synne þe whilk he was born inne beforn. And þerfore be not adred to mikel of þi blaknes þat þou hast of beryng of þis ymage of synne, bot aȝeyns þe schame and þe discomfort þat þou
f. 56v hast of | þe beholdynge of it, and also aȝens þe vpbraydyng þat þou felest in þin herte of þin gostly enemys, whan þei sey to þe þus: Where is þi Lord Jesu? What sekest þou? Where is þi fayrhed þat þou spekest of? What feles þou oght bot blyndenes of synne? Where is þat ymage of God þat þou saist is reformed in þe? Comfort þe þan by trouþe stifly, as I haue beforn seyd, and if þou do so þou schalt be þis trouthe destruyen alle þe temptacions of þin enemys. Þus seyth þe Apostel Paul: *Accipe scutum fidei, in quo tela hostis nequissima poteris extinguere*. Þat is: Take to þe a scheld of stedfast trouþe þurgh þe whilk þou schalt moun qwenchen al þe brennende dartis of þin enemy.

Of þ[r]e maner of men, of þe qwilk sum arn not reformed and sum arn reformed only in feith, and sum in feith and in felynge. Capitulum xiii^{m}

Be þis þat I haue beforn sayd may þou seen þat aftere dyuers partyes of þe soule arn dyuers statys of men. Sum arn noght reformed to þe

75 of his goodnesse/he] *rev*. Cc his] grete *add*. T to hym/þus] *rev*. H$_5$Ws þus] *om*. LwCcW, Mar. 2°, *add*. BLEPLdW, Joh. 5° T et] *om*. B$_3$E 76 vade] ambula Sr þat] þis Pl 77 into] into into into As, in A he] *om*. M hole] totaliter sanus Lat. sothly ryght] ryth so sothly Cc 78 vpon] on Cc bak] his bedde *add*. Cc `was′ H$_6$ þe] his M, suum Lat. þat . . . him] in quo prius portabatur Lat. þat] whiche Sr, þe wheche M 79 gostly] *om*. Sr reformed in feith] perfecte reformata Lat. 80 þis] þe SrCc þe . . . beforn] *om*. Lat. þe] in *prec*. `L′B$_3$EPCc he . . . inne] H$_7$RLB$_3$AsSrEPH$_6$CcMPl, bare hym HBH$_5$WsChLwALdTW beforn] aforn M 81 adred to mikel] to muchil agast H$_5$Ws þat] *om*. B of^2 . . . hast (l. 83)] *om*. Lat. of^2] þe *add*. Sr beryng of þis] þe M 82 bot] H$_7$RH$_5$LB$_3$AsSrWsAEPH$_6$CcMPl, as *add*. HBChLwLdTW, et eciam Lat. þe^2] *om*. RBAsT 83 of þe] in Ws þe^2] H$_7$RBLB$_3$AsSrChAEPH$_6$CcMLdPl, *om*. HH$_5$WsLwTW 84 felest] hast and *prec*. Pl to þe/þus] *rev*. Cc 85 What] Where Sr sekest] felist LB$_3$PT, sais M Where . . . synne (l. 86)] *rep*., *canc*. Cc þi^2] H$_7$HH$_5$AsWsH$_6$MT, þe RBLB$_3$SrChLwAEPCcLdPlW fayrhed] H$_7$RLB$_3$As-AEPH$_6$CcMPl, fayrnes HBH$_5$SrWsChLwLdTW 86 spekest of] speke As feles] sekist E of^2] H$_7$BLB$_3$APH$_6$CcMLdW, and HRH$_5$AsSrWsChLwEPlT, peccati Lat. þat] þe LB$_3$P 87 þat] *om*. Pl Comfort þe/þan] *rev*. H$_6$ þe] H$_7$RLB$_3$As-SrAPH$_6$CcMPl, þiself HBH$_5$WsChLwELdTW `þan by trouþe′ W^G, and be faythfull

hym in meschief, of his goodnes he sayde to hym þus: *Surge et tolle grabatum tuum, et vade in domum tuam*, þat is: Rise vp and take þi bed and go into þi hous. And so he dide, and was hool. And soþly riȝt as þis man bar vpon his bak whan he was made hool þe bed þat biforen bar hym, riȝt so it may be seyde gostly, þat a soule reformid in faiþ beriþ þis ymage of syn þe whilk bare hym biforn. And þerfore be not adred to mikil of þi blaknes þat þu hast of berynge of þis ymage of synne, bot as agayn þe shame and þe disconfort þat þu hast of þe beholdyng of it, and also agayn vpbraydyng þat þu felist in þi hert of þi gostly enemys, whan þei say to þe þus: Where is þi Lord Ihesu? What sekes þu? Where is þi fairnes þat þu spekis of? What felis þu oȝt bot blyndnes and syn? Where is þat ymage of God þat þu seist is reformed in þe? Conforte þiself þan bi trouþ stifly, as I haue biforne seide, and if þu do so þu schalt bi þis trouþ distroien al þe temptacions of þin enemis. Þus seide þe apostle Poul: *Accipe scutum fidei, in quo tela hostis nequissima poteris extinguere*. Þat is: Take to þe a scheld of stedfast trouþ þorwȝ þe whilk þu maiȝt quenchen al þe brennand dartes of þin enemy.

[CHAPTER 13]

By þis þat I haue bifore sayde may þou seen þat after diuerse parties of þe soule arn diuerse states of men. Sum men arn not reformed to þe

LwW, *om.* H_5Ws 88 trouþe] feyþ BALd, Domini nostri Jesu Cristi *add.* Lat. stifly] stilly H_5WsH_6, fully B_3, *om.* SrM, fortiter Lat. beforn seyd] *rev.* Ld 89 trouthe] feyþ BALd þe^1] *om.* LB_3P of þin enemys] inimici Lat. of] þe fende and *add.* T þus] for *prec.* H_6 seyth] H_7RLB_3AsSrAPH_6CcMPl, seide HBH_5WsChLwELdTW, teste . . . sic dicente Lat. þe Apostel] Seynt CcM 90 Paul] *om.* LB_3EP, Eph. 6° *add.* LEPTW, Eph. 5° *add.* B in] *om.* M tela] omnia *prec.* W tela . . . poteris] possitis omnia tela nequissimi ignea Ld, tela hostis nequissimi ignea poteris Lat. nequissima] nequissimi M poteris] possis A 91 þat] þis RAPl to] *om.* As a] þe As trouþe] by leeue þat is trewe feyþ B, bileue AM, feiþ H_6Ld, in Domino Jesu Christo *add.* Lat. 92 schalt moun] H_7RLB_3AsAEPH_6CcMPl, schalt Sr, maiȝt HBH_5WsChLwLdTW 93 enemy] þe devil *add.* Cc

Chapter 13 *title*: H_7RLB_3AsAEPH_6MLdPlTW *om.* HBH_5SrWsChLwCc *No chapter-break* Sr; *this title occurs at 12/47 in* Sr 1 þre] þe H_7, tribus Lat. þe] *om.* R ˋand . . . reformed (l. 2)ˊ *d.h.* L, *rep.* SrM 2 reformed only] *rev.* E only . . . felynge] *om.* Pl in^3] *om.* Sr 3 xiii^m] 14^m CcM, *and so hereafter* 4 Be] But B_3 beforn] toforn As, *om.* LwW 5 Sum] H_7RLB_3AsSrAEPH_6CcMLdPl, men *add.* HBH_5Ch-LwTW to . . . reformed (l. 6)] *rep.* LwW þe] *om.* H_6

lyknes of God, and sum arn reformed only in feyth, and sum arn reformed in feith and in felyng.

For þou schalt vnderstondyn þat a soule hath two partyes. Þat on is kalled þe sensualite, þat is þe fleschly felynge be þe fyue owtward wyttes, þe whilk is common to man and to best. Of þe whilk sensualite, whan it is vnskilfully and vnordinatly rewlyd, is made þe ymage of synne, as I hafe beforn seyd, for þan is þe sensualite synne whan it is not rewled after reson. Þat oþer partye is kalled reson and þat is departed in two: in þe ouer partye and in þe nether partye. Þe over is likned to man, for it schuld be maistre and soueraygne, and þat is properly þe ymage of God for by þat only þe soule knoweth God and loueth him. An þe neþer is likned to wumman, for it schuld be buxum to þe ouere partye of reson as wumman is buxum to man; and þat lythe in knowyng and rewlyng of erthly þynges, for to vsen hem discretly after nede and for to refusen hem whan it is no nede, and for to ay hafe with it þyn eye vpward to þe ouer partye of reson with
f. 57[r] drede | and with reuerence for to folwe it.

Now may I seyn þat a soule þat lyfeth after lykyngis and lustes of þe flesch, as it were an vnskilful best, and neuer hath knowyng of God ne desyre to vertus ne to good lyfynge, bot is al blynded in pride, freten in enneuy, ouerleyd with coueytyse and diffouled with licherye and oþer grete synnes, is not reformed to þe ymage of God. For it lyth and resteþ fully in þe ymage of synne, þat is sensualite. Anoþer soule þat dredeth God and geynstondeþ dedly sterynges of þe sensualite and

6 reformed only] *rev.* E only/in feyth] *rev.* Ld in] þe *add.* R sum[2]] men *add.* HBT 8 two] þre A þat on] þe oone Lw, on Cc 9 kalled] clepud BH$_6$Ld þe[1]] H$_7$HH$_5$LB$_3$SrWsChAPCcMLdT, *om.* RAsLwEH$_6$PlW þat] and *prec.* W þe[2]] *om.* RAsLwLdW owtward] *om.* A 10 is] arn Cc man] a man H$_5$Ws to[2]] *om.* Cc best] a best H$_5$WsA Of] Vp LB$_3$P, vpon E, and M 11 sensualite] essensualite M it is/vnskilfully and vnordinatly] *rev.* H$_5$Ws \`it´ Cc vnskilfully and vnordinatly] indebite Lat. vnskilfully and] *om.* T and vnordinatly/rewlyd] *rev.* Sr vnordinatly] vnor⌜dinatly⌝ H[c], vnordeynely H$_5$WsCh rewlyd . . . rewled (l. 13)] regulatur . . . regitur Lat. rewlyd] it *add.* Cc is made þe] *rep.*, *canc.* H 12 as . . . seyd] *om.* LwW for . . . synne/when . . . reson (l. 13)] *rev.* LwW \`is[1]´ R  þe] *om.* Ld  13 whan] is *add.*, *canc.* L  reson] þe *prec.* RAs  þat . . . reson[2]] *om.* H$_6$  þat] The Cc  is kalled] icallid A  kalled] clepid Ld  14 \`is´ Pl in[1]] on LB$_3$P two] tweyn H$_6$Cc, that is into *add.* Cc in[2]] *om.* LB$_3$P þe] *om.* Pl ouer] oþer Ch, *corr. to* vppur in[3]] into Cc, *om.* LB$_3$APPl partye[2]] *om.* LwW, *om.* Lat. 15 over] H$_7$LB$_3$PH$_6$CcM, \`vppur´ Ch, partye *add.* HRBH$_5$AsSrWsChLwAELdPlTW, 'superior pars' Lat. likned] likneþ Ch to] *om.* Ld man] H$_7$Ld, a man Σ maistre and soueraygne] magistra Lat. 16 by þat/only] *rev.* H$_6$ 17 him] God LB$_3$PH$_6$ neþer] nedrer Lw, partye *add.* H$_5$WsPCc wumman] H$_7$RSr, a woman Σ 18 \`of reson´ L wumman is] *rev.* H$_5$Ws wumman] H$_7$HRAsSrChLwAMTW, a *prec.* BH$_5$LB$_3$WsEPH$_6$CcLdPl is] shulde be M man] H$_7$HRH$_5$AsSrWsLwATW a *prec.* BLB$_3$ChEPH$_6$CcMLdPl 19 þat] *om.* RAs and] in

liknes of God, and summe arn reformed only in faiþ, and sum men are reformed in faiþ and in felyng.

For þou schalt vndirstandyn þat a soule haþ two parties. Þe ton is callid þe sensualite, þat is þe flescly felyng be þe fife outward wittes, þe whilk is comoun to man and to best. Of þe whilk sensualite, whan it
5v is vnskilfully and vnor⌜dinatly⌝ rewled, is made þe | ymage of syn, as I haue bifore seid, for þan is þe sensualite syn when it is not rewlid after resoun. Þat oþer party is called resoun and þat is departed in two: in þe ouer party and in þe neþer party. Þe ouer party is likned to a man, for it schuld be maister and souerayn, and þat is proprely þe ymage of God for bi þat only þe soule knowiþ God and lufiþ hym. And þe neþer is likned to a woman, for it schuld be buxum to þe ouer partie of resoun a`s´ womman is buxum to man; and þat liþ in knowyng and reulynge of erþly þinges, for to vse hem discretly after nede and for to refuse hem whan it is no ned, and for to haue ay with it an iȝe vpward to þe ouer party of reson with drede and with reuerence for to folwe it. Now may I seien þat a soule þat lifiþ after þe likynges and þe lustes of his flesch, as it were an vnskilful beste, and neþer haþ knowyng of God ne desire to vertues ne to gode lifynge, bot is a`l´ blynded in pryde, freten in enuye, ouerleide with coueitise and defoulid with leccherye and oþer grete synnes, is not reformed to þe liknes of God. For it liþ and restiþ fully in þe ymage of synne, þat is þe sensualite. Anoþer soule þat drediþ God and agaynstondeþ dedly stirynge of þe

add. R   for to vsen] ut homo . . . vtatur Lat.   vsen] rule H_6 20 after . . . nede[2]] prout exigit necessitas et non aliter Lat.   for[1]] *om.* H_5WsCh   `no´ Sr, non As, *om.* ChH_6M   and] *om.* LwW   21 ay . . . eye] haue euere an eie wiþall M   ay . . . it] haue with hit euer A   ay hafe] H_7RChPl, *rev.* HH_5Ws, euere haue BB_3EH_6Pl; haue alweie LdT; haue euer LwW, haue SrCc   with it] therwith Cc   þyn eye] *om.* Pl   þyn H_7LB_3EPH_6M, an HRBH_5AsSrWsChLwACcLdPlTW   eye] iȝen B_3, alwey *add.* Sr   22 drede . . . reuerence] *rev.* Lat.   with] *om.* AsW   for . . . it] vt eius imperium impleat et sequatur Lat. 23 lykyngis and lustes] *rev* Pl   lykyngis] H_7RLB_3AsSrLwAEPH_6MPlW, likyng Cc, þe *prec.* HBH_5WsChLdT   lustes] H_7RLB_3AsSrAEPH_6MLdPl, lust Cc, þe *prec.* HBH_5WsChLwTW   þe] his HH_5WsLwW   24 an] *om.* Lw   vnskilful] vnresonable A   neuer] H_7H_5Ws, neþer Σ, nec Lat.   25 desyre] ne *add.* As   to[1]] of Sr   vertus] vertu Cc   ne] noo *add* Sr   to[2]] H_7HBH_5WsChLwEMLdPlTW, *om.* RLB_3AsSrAPH_6Cc   lyfynge] lyuyngis Pl   is] *om.* A   al blynded] H_7LB_3LwAPLdW, a`l´ blynded $H^c$, ablynded H°$H_5$, al y blyndyd B, `al´ blyndede Pl, as blindid Ch, blynded SrWsT, blynd RAsEH_6CcM, totaliter . . . excecata Lat.   in] H_7HBH_5LB_3SrWsChEPH_6CcMLdT, with RAsLwAPlW   pride . . . with (l. 26)] *om.* As   26 in] with RA   and[1]] *om.* LwW 27 is] H_7HRBH_5AsWsLwAELdPlTW, it is LB_3SrPH_6M, and *prec.* Cc, *om.* Ch   ymage] H_7RLB_3AsSrAEPH_6CcMPl, liknes HBH_5WsChLwLdTW, ymaginem Lat.   28 is] appellatur Lat.   sensualite] H_7W, þe *prec.* Σ, `þe´ *prec.* W^G Anoþer] But a Cc 29 geynstondeþ] withstondiþ ECc   dedly] flesshly M, carnalibus Lat.   sterynges] stirynge HBChLw, motibus Lat.   of þe sensualite] *om.* A

folweth hem not, bot lyfeth resonably in rewlynge and gouernaunce of werdly þynges and sette[th] his entent and his will for to plese God be his owtward werkes, is reformed to þe lyknes of God in feith; and þogh he fele þe same sterynges of synne as þat oþer dyde it schal not deren him, for he resteþ not in hem as þat oþer doth. Bot anoþer soule þat fleeth þorgh grace alle dedly sterynges of þe sensualite and venials also, so ferforth þat he feleth hem not, it is reformed in felynge. For he folweth þe ouer partye of reson in beholdyng of God and of heuenly þynges, as I schal telle þe after.

How men þurgh synne forschapen hemself into sere bestis liknes, and þese are called þe louers of þis werd. Capitulum xiiii^m

A wrecched man is he þan þat knoweth not þe wurthynes of his soule, ne wil not knowe it: how it is þe most wurthy creature þat euer God made owttakyn an aungel whom it is lykned to, heyghe abouen al oþer bodyly kynde, to þe qwhilk nothynge may suffycen as ful rest bot only God; and þerfor he schuld noþynge louen ne lyken bot only hym, ne coueytin ne seken bot how he might be reformed to his lyknes. Bot for he knoweth not þis, þerfore he seketh and coueytez his rest and his lykyng outward in bodily creatures werse þan himself is. Vnkyndly he doþ and vnresonabely he werketh, þat leueth þe souereyn good and aylastend lyf þat is God vnsought and vnloued, vnknowen and vnwurchipd, and cheseth his rest and his blis in a passand delyte of an erdly þinge. Neuerþeles, þus don al þe louers of þis werd þat han f. 57v here blis and here ioye in þis wrecched lyf. | Sum han it in pride and

30 rewlynge and gouernaunce] *rev.* M rewlynge] rewle CcLd 31 setteth] sette H_7 his[2]] *om.* ECc for] *om.* H_5Ws 32 his] þese H_5WsT owtward] oute Pl is] he *prec.* Sr to . . . God/in feith] *rev.* M feith] byleue Ld 33 as] *om.* H_5Ws þat . . . as (l. 34)] *om.* Lw þat oþer[1]] alia anima non reformata Lat. dyde] doth T 34 deren] dysease W, or hurte *add.* T þat oþer doth] oþer don H_5Ws þat] þe HChLw doth] dede H_6Cc anoþer soule] anima Lat. `soule´ Pl 35 fleeth] feleþ B alle] þe *add.* $H_6$ dedly sterynges] deed⌜li steringes⌝ L sterynges] sterynge M þe] *om.* L$B_3$P venials] venyal Sr$H_6$Cc 36 also] *om.* Ws `so´ $H^c T^G W^G$, *om.* $H^\circ H_5$TW it] H_7RLB_3AsSrPMPl, he AH_6Cc, *om.* HBH_5WsChLwLdTW 37 he] it RAM of[1]] *rep.* H; þe *add.* H_5Ws in] þe *add.* MPl God] Jesu M of heuenly] H_7RLB_3AsSrAEPH_6CcMPl, gostly HBH_5WsChLwLdTW, celestium Lat. 38 `I´ R þe] *om.* Cc after] afterward BMTW, ⌜afterward⌝ Lw

Chapter 14 *title*: H_7RLB_3AsSrAEPH_6MLdPlTW *om.* HBH_5WsChLwCc 1 þurgh] þat ben yn LdTW hemself] hem B_3 sere] H_7RLAsSrPMPl, diuerse B_3AEH_6LdTW, sundry AsSr 2 þese] þo A, þei LdTW, þose Pl called] clepid Ld þe] *om.* RAsPl þis] H_7LB_3AsEPMLdPl, þe RSrAH_6TW 4 his] owne *add.* B_3 5 wil] wolde Ld not] *om.* Cc þe] *om.* LwCcW 6 an aungel] natura angelica Lat. an] *om.* B_3SrAH_6Cc whom] ⌜to whom⌝ Cc lykned] H_7, lyke Σ to] *om.* H_6CcT

sensualite and folwþ hem not, bot lifeþ resonably in reulyng and gouernance of ⸢werldly þinges⸣ and settes his entente and his wil for to plese God bi his outward werkes, is reformed to þe liknes of God in faiþ; and þof he fele þe same stirynges of syn as þat oþer did it schal not dere hym, for he resteþ not in hem as þe oþer doþ. Bot anoþer soule þat fleeþ þurw grace alle dedly stirynges of þe sensualite and venials also, \`so´ fer forþ þat he feliþ hem not, is reformed in felynge. For he folweþ þe ouer party of resoun in beholdyng of God and gostly þinges, as I schal telle þe after.

[CHAPTER 14]

A wrecched man is he þan þat knoweþ not þe worþines of his soule, ne wil not knowe it: how it is þe most worþi creature þat euer God
6r mad outakyn an aungel whom | it is like to, heiȝe abouen alle oþer bodyly kynde, to þe whilk noþing may sufficen as ful rest bot only God; and þerfore he schude noþing luf ne liken bot hym only, ne coueiten ne seken bot how he miȝt be reformed to his liknes. Bot for he knowþ not þis, þerfore he sekiþ and coueitiþ his reste and his likyng outward in bodily creatures wers þen hymself his. Vnkyndely he doþ and vnresonablely he wirkiþ, þat lefiþ þe souerayn gode and aylastande lif þat is God vnsoȝt and vnlofed, vnknowen and vnworscipid, and chesiþ his reste and his blis in a passand delit of an erþly þinge. Nerþeles þus don alle þe louers of þis werlde þat han her ioy and here blys in þis wrecched lif. Sum han \`it´ in pride and

heyghe] hire Sr oþer] *om.* H_5WsCc 7 bodyly kynde] *rev.* LwW kynde] kendis Cc þe] *om.* A as] for *add.* Cc 8 and] *om.* RAs þerfor] for Pl schuld] schu\`l´de H[c] louen ne lyken] diligere Lat. ne[1]] and L$B_3$P$H_6$ lyken] eþir plese *add.* Ld only hym] $H_7$RAsAECcPl, *rev.* HB$H_5$WsChLwLdTW, oonly God L$B_3$P$H_6$, hym SrM 9 bot] only hym to wetyn *add.* RAsAPl his lyknes] þe lyknes of him $H_5$Ws for] *om.* A 10 \`not´ L þis] his worthynesse Cc ⸢þerfore⸣ L rest . . . lykyng] delectacionem Lat. his[2]] *om.* Pl 11 Vnkyndly/he doþ] *rev.* Cc he doþ] *rev.* As 12 leueth] l⸢o⸣ueþ \`not´ L, loueþ not B_3P good] goodnesse Cc and aylastend lyf] euerelastyng M 13 aylastend] H_7HRLChPM, euerlastyng B$H_5$$B_3$AsWsLwAE$H_6$CcLdTW, alwey lestyng Sr, all lastand Pl vnsought . . . vnwurchipd] nec eum querit, honorat, diligit vel cognoscit Lat. and[1]] *om.* WsCc vnloued] vnfelede Pl vnknowen] *om.* H_5Ws 14 cheseth] chesid Ch, statuit Lat. and his blis] *om.* Sr his[2]] in T passand] passaunt M, schort and *prec.* B delyte] dedlyte H_7, -d- *canc.* of an] and of Ch of] and RAsA an . . . þinge] terrenorum Lat. an] any H_5Ws, in A 15 þinge] creature E Neuerþeles] *om.* Cc þus don] *om.* Ch \`þus´ Sr, þis E ⸢al . . . blis⸣ L þis] þe BM 16 blis/. . ./ioye] $H_7$RL$B_3$AsSrAP$H_6$CcMPl, *rev.* HB$H_5$WsChLwELdTW Sum] men *add.* $H_5$Ws \`it´ H[c], her delite H_5Ws, *om.* T, gloriam suam Lat. and[2]] in *add.* SrALd veyn-glorie of hemself, þat whan þey han lost þe drede of God þey trauailen and studien niȝt and day how þei moghte come to wurchip and preysynge of þe werd, and make no force how, be so þey mighten come þerto and ouerpassen al oþer men ouþer in clergie or in crafte, in name or in fame, in richesse and in reuerences, in souereynte and maysterschipe, in heyghe state and in lordschipe. Sum men han here delyt and here rest in richesse and in owtraious auere of erthly good, and setten here hertes so fully for to geten it þat þei seken not elles bot how þey mighten come þerto. Sum haue here lykyng in fleschly lust of glotonie and licherye and oþer bodily vnclennes, and sum in o þing and sum in anoþer. And þus wrecchedly þese þat don þus forschapen hemself fro þe wurthines of man and turnen hem into dyuers bestis liknes.

Þe proud man is turned into a lyon for pride, for he wuld be dred and wurchepd of alle men, and þat no man aȝenstode þe fulfillynge of his fleschly wil in worde ne in dede; and if any man wil letten his mysproud wille he waxeþ fel and wroth, and wil be wroken of him as a lyon wreketh him on a litel best. Þis man þat doþ þus is now no man, for he doth vnresonabely aȝens þe kynd of man, and so is he turned and transformed into a lion. Enuyous and angry men arn turned into houndes þurgh wretth and enuye, þat berken aȝens here euene-cristen and byten hem by wykked and malicious wordes, and greuen hem þat not trespast with wrongful dedes, harmend hem in bodi and in soule

17 þat] is *add.* B$_3$ of^2] in Sr trauailen and studien] *rev.* SrE 18 moghte] mow LwW, *om.* M wurchip and preysynge] preysynge and worschipynge H$_5$Ws 19 þe] þis H$_6$ and . . . þerto (l. 20)] *om.* Lat. and] þei *add.* H$_6$ \`no´ H$_6$, non As how] H$_7$LB$_3$SrPH$_6$CcM, it *add.* HRBH$_5$AsWsChLwAELdPlTW \`be´ L so] H$_7$LB$_3$PH$_6$CcPl, þat *add.* HRBH$_5$AsSrWsChLwAEMLdTW mighten] may M 20 and] how þey myȝt *add.* Ld men] man LP, *om.* A ouþer] or BCh; eiþir B$_3$SrETW, *om.* P or] ouþur A 21 in^1] or *prec.*, *canc.* L, or incresse of Cc or in^2] and Cc in^3] or *prec.* Cc richesse] riches SrLwH$_6$PlW and^1] H$_7$HRBH$_5$SrWsChH$_6$MLdPl, or LB$_3$AsLwEPCcTW, oþer A, vel Lat. reuerences] H$_7$, reuerence Σ, honoribus Lat. in^5] or in Cc souereynte] souerayncе Pl and^2] H$_7$HBH$_5$WsChLwLdTW, in *add.* RLB$_3$AsSrAEPH$_6$CcMPl, or in ACc, et Lat. 22 state] H$_7$HRBH$_5$AsSrWsChLwALdPlTW, estate LB$_3$EPH$_6$CcM and] *om.* Cc in^2] H$_7$RLB$_3$AsSrAEPH$_6$CcMPl, *om.* HBH$_5$WsChLwLdTW men] *om.* AsSrCcPl 23 delyt and here] *om.* LwW here] *om.* Ch richesse] H$_7$RBH$_5$LB$_3$AsWsChEPH$_6$MLdT, riches HSrLwAPlCcW and^2] or Cc \`in^2´ H^c, on H$_5$Ws, *om.* H°BChE owtra⌜gious⌝ H, gret H$_5$Ws auere] hauing A erthly] worldly SrAM good] goodis LB$_3$PM 24 for] *om.* H$_5$Ws it] diuicias Lat. 25 þerto] illas Lat. Sum] men *add.* M lykyng/. . ./lust] *rev.* A lust] H$_7$HRBH$_5$AsSrWsChLw-ACcLdPlT, lustes LB$_3$EPH$_6$MW, voluptate Lat. 26 and^2] H$_7$RLB$_3$AsSr-APH$_6$CcMLdPl, in *add.* HBH$_5$WsChLwETW vnclennes] vnclennesses M and^3] *om.* SrCcM 27 anoþer] þyng *add.* Ch þus] *om.* RAs þese] þai RAsCc don þus] *rev.* Ld 28 hemself] hem Ld hem] H$_7$HRBLB$_3$AsChLwAEPH$_6$PlTW, hemself H$_5$WsCcLd, hymself M, *om.* Sr 29 liknes] lyknesses As, *om.* Ch 30 man] *om.*

vayn-glorie of hemself, þat whan þei han lost þe drede of God þei trauailen and studyen nyȝt and day how þei moȝt come to worschipe and preysyng of þe world, and make no force how it be, so þat þei miȝten come þerto and ouerpassen alle men ouþer in clergie or in craft, in name or in fame, in richesse and in reuerence, in soueraynte and maistersch\`i´pe, in hiȝe state and lordschipe. Sum men han here delite and here reste in riches and \`in´ outra⌜gious⌝ auere of erþly gode, and setten her hertes so fully for to geten it þat þei seken not elles bot how þei miȝte come þerto. Summe han here likynge in fleschly luste of glotenye and leccherye, and in oþer bodily vnclennesse, and summe in oo þing and summe in anoþer. And þus wrecchedly þese þat don þus forschapen hemself fro þe worþines of man and turnen hem into diuerse bestes liknes.

þe proude man is turned into a lyon for pryde, for he wold be dred and worschepid of alle men, and ⌜þat⌝ no man agaynstode þe fulfillyngge of his fleschly wil no\`i´þer in worde ne in dede; and ȝif ony man wulde letten his mysproude wil he waxiþ felle and wroþ, and wil be wroken of hym as a lyoun wrekiþ hym on a littel beste. þis man þat doþ þus is no man, for he doþ vnresonably agayn þe kynde of man, and so is he turned and transformed into a lyon. Enuyous and
76v angry men are turned into houndus | þurwȝ wreþþe and enyue, þat berken aȝen here euen-cristen and biten hem by wickid and malicious wordes, and greuen hem þat not haue trespassid with wrongful dedis, harmend hem in body and in soule aȝens Goddis biddyng. Summe

RAsAPlCc is turned] *om.* Ld, conuertitur et mutatur Lat. for pride] *om.* ECc for] þorw SrM 31 wurchepd] worschype Ld \`þat´ $H^{c}B_3$ aȝenstode] $H_7$HR$H_5$AsWsChAMPl, aȝeynstonde BL$B_3$LwEP$H_6$LdTW, schulde ayenstondyn Sr, ageyn seyn Cc, resisteret Lat. fulfillynge] forthfullyng M 32 fleschly] *om.* A wil[1]] $H_7$RL$B_3$AsSrAEP$H_6$CcMPl, no\`i´þer *add.* HBH_5WsChLwLdTW in[2]] *om.* LB_3P wil[2]] H_7RLB_3AsSrAEPH_6Cc, wulde HBH_5WsChLwMLdPlTW, voluerit Lat. letten . . . waxeþ (l. 33)] he þat is mysproude and As 33 mysproud] proud LB_3SrPH_6 waxeþ] þan *add.* T fel] sterne Ld wroth] angri A wil] wold BLd wroken] venged LB_3EPT, avengid H_6 of] H_7HBLB_3SrChLwPCcLdW, on RH_5AsWsAEH_6MPlT \`as´ Pl 34 wreketh] H_7HRBH_5AsSrWsChLwACcMPlW, awrekiþ Ld, vengeþ LB_3EPH_6T, appetit vindicari Lat. him] himself Cc on] opon A þis man] He Cc now] H_7RBLB_3AsSrChAEPH_6MLdPl, *om.* HH_5WsLwTW, iam Lat. 35 aȝens] et contra Lat. man] a *prec.* LwW is he] H_7HRBH_5AsSrWsChLwACcMPlT, *rev.* LB_3EPH_6LdW turned and transformed] *rev.* RAs 36 transformed] transfygured B Enuyous] þe *prec.* H_5Ws and angry/men] *rev.* AsCc into] in Pl 37 wretth] wrecchydnes As, that he hath *add.* Cc þat] þe whic H_6 berken] breken As 38 greuen . . . trespast/with . . . dedes (l. 39)] *rev.* H_6 39 not] haue *prec.* H_5WsChLd, haue *add.* HBLwTW trespast] H_7RLB_3AEPMPl, trespacen AsSrH_6, trespacen aȝens \`hem´ Cc, deliquerunt Lat. with . . . dedes] *om.* Lat. dedes] wordis and *prec.* Cc harmend] harmen H_5WsChLd in[2]] *om.* H_5WsECcM

ageyns Goddys byddynge. Sum men arn forschapen into aschis, þat arn slowe to þe seruice of God and myswilled for to don ony good dede to here euene-cristen. þei arn redy inogw for to renne to Rome for werdly profyt or for erthly wurchepe or for plesaunce of an erdly man. Bot for gostly mede, for help of here owen soules or for wurchep of God, þei arn son irke. þei wil not þerof, and if þei oght don þei gon bote a passe, and ȝit with a froward wil. Sum men arn turned into swyn, for þei arn so blynd in witte and so bestly in maners þat þei han
f. 58[r] no drede of God, bot folwen | only þe lustes and þe likynges of here flesch, and haue no rewarde to þe honeste of man for to rewlen hemself aftere þe byddyng of reson for to restreyn þe vnskilful sterynges of þe fleschly kynde; bot as sone as ony fleschli sterynge of synne comeþ þei arn redy for to fallen þerto, and folweth it as swyn doth. Sum men arn turned into wulfes þat lyuen be raueyn as a fals coueytous man doþ, þat þurgh maistrie and ouerledyng robbeþ his euene-cristen of here werdly godes. Sum into foxes, as fals men and dissayuable þat lyuen in treccheri and gyle.

Al þese, and many oþer mo þat lyuen not in drede of God bot breken his comaundementz, forschapen hemself fro þe liknes of God, and make hem lyke vnto bestis. Ȝa, and wers þan bestys, for þei arn lyke vnto þe fend of helle. And þerfor sothly, þese þat lyuen þus, if þei be not reformed whan þe houre of deth comeþ and þe soules of

40 Goddys byddynge] the biddyng of God H_6 Goddys] wille *add.*, *canc.* L byddynge] biddingis Ch men] *om.* H_6Cc forschapen/into aschis] *rev.* Sr into] to SrM 41 arn] þo þat be H_6 to[1]] H_7BH_5LB_3SrWsChEPH_6CcLdW, in RAsLw⌜H^c⌝AMPl, into T þe . . . God] Goddus seruis A ⌜þe⌝ H^c, *om.* H°ChLd myswilled] H_7RAsSrAMPl, yuel willed HBH_5WsChLwECcLdTW, vnwilled LB_3P, vnwilli H_6, nec volunt Lat. for] H_7HRBH_5LB_3AsChLwAEPMLdPlW, *om.* SrWsH_6CcMT 42 here] his M for] *om.* SrWsMT to Rome] *om.* LwW 43 for[1]] *om.* H_5Ws werdly] worldes Pl profyt] prosperite B_3 or[1]] H_7RLB_3AsSrEPCcMPl, oþer A, and HH_5WsChLwLdTW, et Lat. for erthly] *om.* Cc for[2]] *om.* H_5WsH_6 wurchepe] worche Cc or for[2]] and for þe T an] any H_5Ws, *om.* Cc 44 man] men Cc mede] or *add.* BWsCc for[2]] *om.* BH_6 help . . . soules] helthe of soule Cc soules] soule Ld wurschep] the *prec.* LwW 45 arn . . . þei[2] (l. 47)] *om.* RAsAPl arn] ful *add.* Cc irke] H_7HRLB_3AsSrChLwAEPCcPlTW, wery BH_5WsH_6MLd, reke *prec.*, *canc.* E, fastidiunt Lat. and] *om.* M 46 ȝit] H_7RLB_3AsSrAEPH_6CcMPl, *om.* HBH_5WsChLwLdTW a[2]] *om.* LwW men] H_7Cc, *om.* Σ 47 swyn] a *prec.* Pl, hoggis H_6 blynd] blont B witte] wiþ Pl so[2]] *om.* M in maners] *om.* Cc 48 no] noon As of[1]] in LdPl folwen] sapiunt Lat. only þe] *om.* M lustes] likyng Sr þe[2]] H_7RBLB_3SrAPH_6CcPl, *om.* HH_5AsWsChLwEMLdTW likynges] lykyng Cc, lust Sr 49 flesch] flesshes As and haue no] ne han Cc þe] *om.* LB_3PCc honeste . . . reson (l. 50)] honestatem nature humane Lat. honeste of man] honeste manhood Cc for] ne *prec.* LwW, *om.* Cc 50 hemself] H_7LB_3PH_6M, hem HRBAsWsLwALdPlTW, him H_5Ch, himself Sr for] H_7LB_3PH_6Cc, ne *prec.* HRBH_5AsSrWsChLwAEMLdTW, vel Lat. restreyn] refreyne H_5Ws, refrenandum Lat. þe[2]] wil *add.*, *canc.* A 51 sterynges]

men are forschapen into assis, þat arne slow ⌜in þe⌝ seruice of God and yuel willed for to done ony gode dede to here euen-cristen. Þei arn redy inow for to renne to Rome for werdly profite and for erþly worschipe or for plesaunce of an erdly man. Bot for gostly mede, for help of þeire owne soules or for wurschip of God, þei are sone irke. Þei wil not þerof, and if þei ouȝt don þei goon bot a paas and with a frawarde wil. Summe are turned into swyne, for þei arn so blynde in wit and so bestly in maners þat þei han no drede of God, bot folwen oonly þe lustes and likynges of þaire flesche, and han no reward to þe honeste of man for to reulen hem after þe biddyng of resoun, ne for to restreyn þe vnskilful stirynges of þe flescly kynde; bot als sone as a flescly stiryng of syn comeþ þei arn redy for to falle þerto, and folwe it as swyne doþ. Summe men arn turned into wulfes þat lifen by rauyn als fals coueitous man doþ, þat þu`r´we maistrie and ouerledyng robbeþ here euen-cristen of her werldly godes. Summe men `arn turned´ into foxes, as fals men and disseyuable þat lifen in trecherye and in gyle.

Alle þese, and many oþer mo þat lifen `noȝt´ in drede of God bot breken his comaundementes, forschapen hemself fro þe liknes of God and maken hem like to bestes. Ȝe, and werre þan bestes, for þei are like vnto þe fende of helle. And þerfore soþly, þese men þat lifen þus, if þei be not reformed whan þe houre of deþ comeþ and þe soules of

steryng Cc þe] *om.* B$_3$ kynde . . . fleschli] *om.* As as sone] all one W ony] H$_7$RH$_5$B$_3$AsSrWsAEPH$_6$CcMPl, ⌜ony⌝ L, a HBChLdTW, *om.* Lw sterynge] stiringis Ch 52 of synne/comeþ] *rev.* LwW for] H$_7$HBLB$_3$AsSrChLwAPMLdTW, *om.* RH$_5$WsEH$_6$CcPl and folweth it] *om.* Lat. folweth] H$_7$, folwe[n] Σ it] *om.* LwW swyn] H$_7$HBH$_5$WsLwEH$_6$TW, a *prec.* RLB$_3$As`Sr´ChAPCcMLdPl, porci Lat. 53 doth] don ETW men] *om.* AsSrPl turned] *rep.* A a] H$_7$RH$_5$LB$_3$AsWsAEPH$_6$Pl, þe T, *om.* HBSrChLwCcMLdW 54 man] H$_7$HRH$_5$LB$_3$AsWsLwAEPH$_6$PlT, men BSrChCcMLdW, auarus Lat. doþ] don SrM, *om.* ACc robbeþ] robbed As, robbyn CcM, als fals men *add.* Ch his euene-cristen] othyr men Cc his] H$_7$RLB$_3$AsSr-AEPH$_6$MPlW, here HBH$_5$WsChLwLdT 55 werldly] *om.* H$_5$Ws godes] good Sr, And *add.* Cc Sum] H$_7$LSrAPH$_6$CcMPl, men *add.* H°BH$_5$B$_3$WsLwTW, men be turned *add.* BChLd, `arn turned´ *add.* H$^{c}$, arn turned *add.* RAsE, Aliqui . . . transmutantur Lat. into] to Cc fals] deceyuable *add.* Sr and dissayuable] *om.* Sr 56 dissayuable] men *add.* LwW and] H$_7$RBAsSrAH$_6$CcLdPlTW, in *add.* HH$_5$LB$_3$WsChLwEPM 57 oþer mo] *rev.* A lyuen not in] leuyn þe H$_5$Ws `not´ H^{c}Cc drede] þe *prec.* SrAE bot] and H$_5$Ws 58 hemself] hem Cc 59 vnto] H$_7$HRBH$_5$LB$_3$As-SrWsChEPCcMT, to LwAH$_6$LdPlW bestis . . . helle (l. 60)] þe fende of helle for þei arn liȝk vnto beestis, ȝa, and wers þan beestis RAsAPl ȝa . . . bestys] *om.* Cc ȝa] *om.* A bestys] any *prec.* R, vnresonabil *prec.* H$_6$ 60 vnto] to AH$_6$Cc þe fend] feendes E sothly] *om.* A þese] H$_7$LEPPl, þose R, þei B$_3$SrAH$_6$M, þei þese As, men *add.* HBH$_5$WsChLwLdTW, *om.* Cc, hii Lat. þat . . . þus/if . . . reformed (l. 61)] *rev.* Cc if þei] *om.* M if] þat *add.* LB$_3$EPH$_6$ 61 þe`i´ Sr of^{1}] here *add.* Cc þe^{2} . . . hem] here soulys Cc soules] soule H$_5$A

hem arn departed fro þe bodies, þan schal here eyghe ben opned þat is now stopped with synne, and þan schal þei felyn and fyndyn þe pyne of here wikkednes þat þei lyfed here in. And for als mikel as þe ymage of God was not reformed þurgh þe sacrament of penaunce in hem, neyþer in feyth ne in felynge here in þis lyf, þei schul ben as cursed kest owt fro þe blissed face of oure Creatour, and þei schul be dampned with þe deuel into þe depnes of helle, þere for to ben ay wythouten ende. Þus seyth Seyn John in þe Apocalyps: *Tumidis et incredulis, excec[r]atis et homicidis, fornicatoribus, veneficis et ydolatris, et omnibus mendacibus: pars illorum erit in stangno ardenti igne et sulphure.* Þat is: To proud men and mystrowend, to cursed and to mansleers, to liccherous and to coueytous, to poysunners, and to alle fals lyghers, dole schal ben with þe deuel in þe pyt of helle, brennend with fere and brenstone. If þe louers of þis werd wolden often þenken of þis, how þis werd schal passen and draw to an ende, and how al wykked loue schal ben hard punysched, þei schuld withinne a schort tyme loþen al werdly lust þat þei now most lyken, and þei schuld lyfte vp here herte
f. 58v for to loue God, and besyly seken and | trauayllen how þei mighten be reformed to his lyknes or þei passed hens.

How louers of þis werd vnablen hemself on sere wyse to þe reformynge of here owen soules. Capitulum xv[m]

Bot now seyn sum of hem þus: I wold fayn lofe God and ben a good man and forsake þe lufe of þe werd if þat I myght, but I haue no grace

62 þe] here E bodies] body SrA eyghe] H$_7$HRB$_3$AsSrChLwAMPlW y3ene BH$_5$LWsEPH$_6$CcLdT, oculus Lat. is now] *rev.* SrCc, are nou WsECcT, nowe ben Ld 63 stopped] spered Pl schal þei] *rev.* Sr felyn and fyndyn] *rev.* Sr `pyne of here´ Pl 64 wikkednes] wretchydnes W here in] H$_7$RAsSrPl, *rev.* HBH$_5$LWsChLw-EPH$_6$CcMLdTW, in B$_3$AM als . . . as] *om.* Cc 65 þurgh . . . penaunce/in hem] *rev.* Sr in] hem *add.*, *canc.* L 66 feyth ne in felynge] *rev.* T ne] neiþer H$_5$ ben/as cursed] *rev.* CcM as cursed] H$_7$HRBH$_5$SrWsChLwACcMPlTW, acursid LB$_3$AsEPH$_6$, a`s´cursde Ld, tanquam excommunicati Lat. 67 blissed] blis⸢sed⸣ H[c], blisful H$_5$Ws face] place Sr oure Creatour] God Cc þei schul] *om.* Cc 68 into þe depnes] *om.* Cc into] in Ch þe[2]] *om.* Ld þere . . . ende] eternaliter Lat. for] *om.* CcM ay] H$_7$HRH$_5$LAsWsChLwPH$_6$, euer BB$_3$AELdPlT, euere mor SrM, om. CcW 69 Seyn] *om.* H Apocalyps] Apo. 22° *add.* B, Apo. 21 *add.* LEPLdTW 70 execratis] excecratis HH$_5$Ws, excecatis H$_7$RAsAPl, et excecatis B et[1]] *om.* H$_5$WsLd fornicatoribus] fornicatoriis H$_5$, fornicatore Ws veneficis] et *prec.* RH$_5$WsA 71 illorum erit] *rev.* Cc erit] est M stangno] H$_7$BL, stagno Σ ardenti] ardente ACc 72 To] þat Pl and[1]] to *add.* M mystrowend] misbileuynge B$_3$, men *add.* LwCcMW to[2]] *om.* M mansleers] men sleers W 73 liccherous] H$_7$HRAsSrChLwAEH$_6$CcMLdPlTW, lechours BH$_5$LB$_3$WsP to[1]] *om.* HChLwTW to poysunners] to apoyseners B, and *add.* LwW, to *add.* E, *om.* Cc poysunners] H$_7$RB$_3$AsSrAMPl; wurchipers of maumetis *add.* HBH$_5$`L´WsChLwEPLdTW,

hem arn departid from þe bodies, þan schal here iȝe ben opunned þat is now stoppid with syn, and þan schul þei felen and fynden þe peyne of þeire wickednes þat þei lifed inne here. And for as mikel as þe ymage of God was not reformed þurwȝ þe sacrament of penaunce in hem, neiþer in faiþ ne in felynge here in þis lif, þei schul bene as
77r cursed, kest out fro þe blis`sed´ | face of oure Creatour, and þei schul be dampned with þe deuyl into þe depnes of helle, þer for to ben ay withouten ende. Þus saiþ Johan in þe Apocalipse: *Tumidis et incredulis, excecratis, et homicidis, fornicatoribus, veneficis et ydolatris et omnibus mendacibus: pars illorum erit in stagno ardenti igne et sulphure*. Þat is: To proude men and mistrowand, to cursid and to mansleers, to lecherous and coueitous, to poisonners, worschipers of maumetis, and to alle fals liers: here dole schal be with þe deuyl in þe put of helle, brennand with fure and bry⌜m⌝ston. If þe lufers of þis werld walden often þinke on þis, how alle þis werld schal passen and drawe to an ende, and how alle wikked luf schal ben hard punisched, þei schulde withinne schort tyme loþen alle wordly luste þat þei now most liken, and þei schulden liften vp þeire herte for to luf God, and þei wolden bisily seken and trauailen how þei miȝten be reformed to his liknes or þei passed hennus.

[CHAPTER 15]

Bot now saien summe of hem þus: I wold fayn luf God and be`n´ a gode man and forsake þe luf of þe werld if þat I miȝte, bot I haue no

and ydolatreris *add.* H$_6$, to ydolatrourys *add.* Cc to[3]] *om.* Cc fals lyghers] *om.* As lyghers] H$_7$RLB$_3$AsAP, here *add.* HB 74 dole] H$_7$RLAsChP, here dole HCh, here dele LwW, þis dole Pl, here part BH$_5$SrWsEH$_6$MLdT, part B$_3$A in þe pyt] *om.* Ld 75 `wolden´ Pl often þenken] *rev.* E, frequenter hoc attenderent et diligenter cogitarent Lat. often] tyme *add.* H$_5$Ws, tymes *add.* T of] H$_7$, vpon T, on Σ þis[2]] and *add.* M how . . . ende/and/how . . . punysched (l. 77)] *rev.* RAsAPl how] H$_7$, alle *add.* Σ 76 draw to] han Cc al] *om.* Cc wykked] malus et inordinatus Lat. loue] loues M 77 ben hard] *rev.* Cc schuld/withinne . . . tyme] *rev.* Cc withinne] in M a] H$_7$, *om.* Σ schort] *om.* Ld al] *om.* LB$_3$PH$_6$ 78 werdly lust] þe lustes of þe world M lust] lustes W now . . . lyken] han most lykyd in Cc now] mowen As, *om.* B$_3$ `and´ L lyfte] rere Ld herte] H$_7$HRBLB$_3$Ch-LwAEPH$_6$LdPlTW, hertis H$_5$AsSrWsCcM, corda Lat. 79 and[1]] H$_7$LB$_3$SrEPHrCcM, þei wolden *add.* HBH$_5$WsChLwLdTW, þei sholden *add.* RAsAPl seken and trauayllen] laboryn Cc, laborarent Lat. þei] þe R, that *prec.* Cc 80 passed] H$_7$HRBLB$_3$AsCh-AEPMLdW^G, passen H$_5$SrWsLwH$_6$CcTW hens] out of this lyfe *add.* Cc, ante eorum transitum ex hac vita Lat.

Chapter 15 *title*: H$_7$RLB$_3$AsSrAEPH$_6$MLdPlTW *om.* HBH$_5$WsChLwCc 1 hemself] hem ALdTW sere] H$_7$RLPPl, diuerse B$_3$AEH$_6$MLdTW, sundry AsSr wyse] wises RAs, maners ALdTW to . . . soules] *om.* Pl to] vnto Sr 2 soules] soule Sr 3 þus] *om.* A 4 þe lufe] þis lif Ch þe] this Cc no] non A þerto. If I had þe same grace þat a good man haþ, I schuld don as he doth, but I haue it not. þerfore I am not, and so it is not me to wyten, bot I am excused. Vnto þese men I sey þus: Sothe it is as þei seyn þat þei han no grace, and þerfore þei lyen stille in here synne and moun not rysen owt. Bot þat auayleþ hem ryght noght; it excuseþ hem not ageyns God, for it is here owen defaute. þei vnable hemself by dyuers wayes so mikel þat þe lyght of grace may not schyne to hem ne resten in here hertes. For sum arn so froward þat þei wilen no grace haue, ne þei wulden no gude men ben; for þei wyten wele, if þei schulden ben gude men hem behoueth nedes forberen and lefen þe grete lykyng and þe lust of þis werld þat þei han in erthly þynges. And þat wil þei not, for þei þenke it so swete þat þei wolde not forgon it. And also hem behoueth for to taken werkes of penaunce, as fastynge, wakynge, preynge and oþer good dedis doynge, in chastysynge of here flesch and in withdrawynge of here fleschly wil. And þat moun þei not don, for it is made so scharpe and so peynful to her thynkynge þat þei vggen and loþen for to þenken þer-vpon, and so cowardly and wrecchedly dwel þei stille in her synne.

Sum wolden haue grace as it semeth, and þei begynne for to ablen hem þerto. Bot here wil is wondere weyk, for as son as ony steryng of synne cometh, þogh it be contrarie to þe biddyng of God, þei fallen as tyte þerto, for þei arn so bounden þurgh custum be ofte fallynge and often assent[ynge] to synne before, þat hem þinkeþ it inpossible for to ageynstonde it, and so feyned hardnes of performynge weykeþ here

5 I schuld] þan schuld I Sr 6 but] H$_7$T, for *add.* Σ, quia Lat. haue it not] have no grace Cc, talem graciam non habeo Lat. it[1]] *om.* LB$_3$PH$_6$ I am] H$_7$, may I RAsSr, I may Σ and] *om.* H$_5$Ws me] to *prec.* W, to *add.*, *canc.* L to] for to Sr 7 þus] in this wise T as] þat H$_5$WsLd 8 no] non RAs lyen] ben As, Hu$_2$ *back* stille] *om.* M 9 owt] þerof *add.* T þat . . . it] ȝit this Cc ryght] H$_7$RLB$_3$AsSrAEPH$_6$CcMPl, *om.* HBH$_5$WsChLwHu$_2$LdTW, aliqualiter Lat. it . . . God] nec per hoc quoad Deum aliqualiter excusantur Lat. it . . . not] *om.* LwW it] H$_7$RLB$_3$AsSrAEPH$_6$CcMPl ne it H$_6$, ne HBH$_5$WsT, noþer Hu$_2$Ld, ner Ch not] *om.* Ld 10 defaute] þat þei hauen no grace for *add.* RAsAPl þei] for *prec.* Sr, that *prec.* Cc hemself] H$_7$RBLB$_3$AsSr-AEPH$_6$CcMPl, hem HH$_5$WsChLwHu$_2$LdTW 11 wayes] wyse in *add.* Cc þe] *rep.* B to] on B$_3$, in Sr 12 no] non LAsP 13 wulden] H$_7$RAsPl, wilen Σ no] *om.* Cc gude men/ben] *rev.* Cc wele] *om.* Ld if] if þat `H'Lw, þat if H$_5$WsTW 14 hem behoueth] H$_7$RLB$_3$AsSrAEPMPl, hem byhouid H$_6$, þei moste HBH$_5$WsChLwHu$_2$CcLdTW nedes] nede M, nedles Ch, nedlyng Hu2, *om.* Cc forberen and lefen] H$_7$RLB$_3$AsAEPH$_6$Pl, *rev.* SrCcM, forbere HBH$_5$WsChLwHu$_2$LdTW, abstinere Lat. forberen] to *prec.* H$_6$M lykyng] likingus A 15 þe] grete *add.* Ld, *om.* BChHu$_2$ lust] lustes A of þis werld] *om.* Lat. þis] þe M 16 for . . . not] *om.* ChHu$_2$ þei þenke] H$_7$RLB$_3$AsSrAEPH$_6$CcPl, þem þinkeþ HBH$_5$WsLwMLdT, hem thynken W it[1]] H$_7$RBLB$_3$AsSrAEPH$_6$CcMPl, is *add.* HH$_5$WsChLwHu$_2$LdTW wolde]

grace þerto. If I had þe same grace þat a good man haaþ, I schuld done as he dooþ; bot for I haue it not þerfore I may not, and so it is not me to witen, bot I am excused. Vnto þese men I say þus: Soþ it is as þei seyne þat þei han no grace, and þerfore þei lien stille in þeire syn and mowen not risen out. Bot þat aueiliþ hem not ne excuseþ hem not ageyn God, for it is here owne defaute. Þei vnable hem by dyuers waies so mikel þat þe liȝt of grace may not schyne to hem ne resten in here hertes. For summe arn so froward þat þei willen no grace han, ne þei willen no gode men ben; for þei witen wel `if´ þat þei schuld be gode men þei moste nedis forbere þe grete likyng and þe lust of þis
77v werld þat þei han in erþly | þinges. And þat wil þei not, for þem þinkeþ it is so swete þat þei wold not forgon it. And also þei most taken werkes of penaunce, as fastyng, wakyng, preyng, and oþer gode dedis doyng, in chastisyng of þeire flesche and in withdrawynge of here flescly wil. And þat moghen þei not don, for it is made so scharp and so dredful to here þinkyng þat þei vggen and loþen for to þinken þer vpon, and so cowardly and wrecchedly dwelle þei stille in þeire synne.

Summe wolden haue grace as it semiþ, and bigynnyn for to ablen hem þerto. Bot her wil is wondre waike, for as sone as ony stiryng of syn comeþ, þawȝ it be contrarie to þe biddyng of God, þei fallen as tite þerto, for þei are so bounden þurwȝ custom be often fallyng and often assentyng to syn before, þat hem þinke it impossible for to agaynstonden it, and so feyned hardnes of performyng waikeþ her wil

H_7HRH_5LB_3AsSrWsChLwAHu_2EPH_6Pl, wol BCcMLdTW   it[2]] *canc.* Ch, *om.* Hu_2 And] *om.* T   also] þanne *prec.* Sr   hem . . . to] H_7RB_3AsSrAH_6CcMPl, nedes *add.* W   17 for] *om.* M   as] as in W, of M   wakynge] and *add.* RAsM   18 oþer] many *prec.* W   doynge] *om.* Ch   flesch . . . here (l. 19)] *om.* T   flesch] for to take werkis of *add.* A   20 scharpe] harp Ch   and so peynful] *om.* Cc   peynful] H_7LB_3PH_6, dredful HBH_5WsChLwHu_2ELdTW, ferdful RAsPl, ferful SrAM, terribile Lat.   21 vggen and loþen] aren loth M, abhominantur Lat.   vggen] abhorreþ B; beþ aferd Hu_2Ld, grucchyn As, grise A   for] *om.* AsAE   þer-] þeron B_3, vpon it LwW   so] *om.* H_6 22 dwel þei] *rev.* H_6M, *rev., marked for trsp.* Sr   dwel] levyn Cc, by Hu_2 stille/in her synne] *rev.* Sr   synne] synnys AsM   23 semeth] besemeth M   þei] H_7RLB_3AsAEPH_6CcMPl, *om.* HBH_5SrWsChLwHu_2LdTW   for] *om.* SrLwEH_6W   ablen] dispose Hu_2 24 hem] hemself Cc   wondere] *om.* T   weyk] wicked Pl, febil A, liþie Ld   25 þogh . . . God] *om.* Lat.   þogh] þurgh As   as tyte] H_7HRLChLwEP, anon B$H_5$$B_3WsAHu_2$$H_6$CcMLdPlW, as sone T, as swiþe Sr, also anon As   26 þerto] þerfro B_3 so bounden] *rev.* P   þurgh] be Sr, wiþ vse and Hu_2 `be´ L, of $Hu_2$$H_6$, and Cc, in T, *om.* B_3 and] in Cc   27 often] *om.* Hu_2 assentynge] assenten H_7, consensum Lat.   hem þinkeþ] they thynk Cc   it] is *add.* Hu_2, *om.* H_5WsECcT   inpossible] vnpossible H_6Cc   28 it] hem M, huiusmodi motui seu instigacioni Lat.   so] wiþe *add.* E   feyned] faynhed As, feynen þei B_3 weykeþ] weiken LB_3P, febleþ BAPl, makeþ liþi Ld

wil and smyteth it doun ageyn. Sum also felen sterynge of grace, as whan þei han bytynge of conscience for here euel lyfynge and þat þei
f. 59[r] schulde lefe it. | But þat is so peynful to hem and so heuy þat þei wil not sufre it ne abyde with it, bote þei flee þerfro and forȝeten it if þei moun; so ferforth þat þei seken lykynge and comfort owtewarde in fleschly creatures, so þat þei schuld not felen þis bytyng of conscience withinne in here soule.

And ouermore sum men arn so blynde and so bestly þat þei wene þat þer is non oþer lyf bot þis, ne þat þer is no soule of man oþer þan is of a beste, bot þat þe soule of man dyeth with þe bodi as doth þe soule of a best. And þerfor þei seyn: Ete we and drynk we and make we merye here, for of þis be we syker; we sen non oþer heuene. Sothly swilk arn sum wrecches þat seyn þus in here herte, þogh þei seyn it not with here mouþe. Of þe whilk men þe prophete seyth þus: *Dixit insipiens in corde suo: Non est Deus.* Þat is: Þe vnwys man seyd in his hert, þer is no God. Þis vnwys man is euerilk wrecched man þat lyketh and loueth synne and cheseþ þe lust of þis werd as rest of his soule. He seyth þat þer is no God, not with his mouþe for he wil speken of him sumtyme whan he fareth wele fleschly, as it were in reuerence whan he seyth: Blissid be God! Sumtyme in despyte, whan he is angri ageyns God or his euene-cristen and swereth be his blissed body or ony of his membris. Bot he seyth in his þoght þat þer is no God, and þat is eyþer for he weneth þat þer is non oþer lyf þan þis. Or elles if he wene þat þer is anoþer lyf, neuerþeles he weneth þat God seeth not his synne or þat he wil not punysche it so hard as Holy

29 wil] willes M smyteth] smyten LB_3P it] hos Lat. sterynge] styrynges H_5SrWsM as] and M 30 euel] ille HCh þat] iste remorsus Lat. 31 so] *om.* LB_3LwPW to hem] *om.* Sr 32 it[1]] *om.* A with] *om.* LwW it[2]] þat Sr þerfro] from hit M 33 seken] see whan As 34 fleschly] liking *add.* Ch, lykyng of *add.* Hu_2 schuld] H_7RLB_3AsSrLwAEPH_6CcMPlW, `schuld´ H^c, wolden *canc.* H, wolden BH_5WsChHu_2LdT 35 in] H_7HRBH_5AsSrWsChLwAHu_2ECcLdT, *om.* LB_3PH_6-MPlW soule] soules M 36 And] also *add.* CcM ouermore] euermore B_3As, more ouer WsW, ȝit ouer þis H_6, ouer this more Cc men] *om.* H_5Ws blynde] blyndyd Cc þei] *om.* Sr 37 þat[1]] H_7RH_5LB_3AsSrWsEPH_6CcMPlT, *om.* HBChLwAHu_2LdW is[1]] H_7RLB_3AsAEPH_6CcMPlW, be HBH_5WsChLwHu_2LdT, were Sr is[2]] `is´ Cc, were Sr, habet Lat. of man] *om.* W `man´ Pl 38 is] H_7RH_6M, *om.* Σ of[1]] *om.* ChHu_2 a] an vnresonable H_5Ws, *om.* CcPlT bot . . . best (l. 39)] *om.* MLd, set consimiliter moritur vt anima besie siue bruti Lat. bot] and Hu_2W þat] *om.* As man] a *prec.* RSrLwA dyeth] vp *add.* H_5Ws doth] H_7RBLB_3AsSrAEPH_6CcMPl, *om.* HH_5WsChLwHu_2LdTW, *om.* Lat. 39 And[1]] *om.* A and[2]] H_7RBH_5LB_3AsSr-WsAEPH_6CcMPl, *om.* HChLwHu_2LdTW 40 we[1]] us *add.* B_3 þis] H_7RLB_3AsSr-APH_6CcMPl, life *add.* HBH_5WsChLwHu_2ELdTW, ista vita Lat. be we] *rev.* B_3CcTW sen] gete M 41 swilk/arn/sum] *rev.* LB_3EPH_6, þere be syche Hu_2, swiche arn synful Cc þat] *rep.* H_7 seyn] thenkyn Cc in . . . þus (l. 42)] *om.* As `here´ LPl, *om.* H_6

and smytiþ it doun agayn. Summe also felyn stiryng of grace, as whan þei han bityng of conscience for here ille lifyng and þat þei schuld leue it. Bot þat is so peynful to hem and so heuy þat þei wil not suffre it ne abide with it, bot þei fle þerfro and forȝeten it if þei mowen; so fer forþ þat þei seken likyng and conforþ outward in fleschly creatures, so þat þei wolden not felyn þis bytyng of conscience withinne in her soule.

And ouermore summe men are so blynde and so bestly þat þei wene þer be none oþer lif bot þis, ne þat þer is no soule of man oþer þan of a beste, bot þat þe soule of man di`e´þ with þe body as þe soule of a beste. And þerfor þei seien: Ete we, drynge we, and make we merye here, for of þis lif be we siker; we se none oþer heuene. Soþly swilke arne summe wrecches þat saien þus in her hertes, þawȝ þei sey it not with þaire mouþ. Of þe whilk men þe prophet saiþ þus: *Dixit insipiens in corde suo: Non est Deus*, þat is: Þe vnwise man seide in his herte, þer is no God. Þis vnwise man is euerilk wrecchid man þat liuyþ and lufþ synne and chesiþ þe luf of þis werld as reste of his soule. He saiþ þat
78r þer is no God, not with his mouþe | for he wil spekyn of hym summetyme when he fariþ wel flescly, as it were in reuerence whan he seiþ: Blessed be God; sumtyme in dispit, whan he is angri agayns God or his euen-cristen and sweriþ bi his blessud body or ony of his membres. Bot he saiþ in his þoȝt þat þer is no God, and þat is eiþer for þat he weneþ [þat þer is non oþer lyf þan þys, or elles ȝyf he wene þat þer ys anoþer lyf, nerþeles he weneþ] þat God seeþ not his synne,

herte H_7RSrAH_6CcM, hertes HBH_5LB_3AsWsChLwHu_2EPLdPlTW, cordibus Lat. it] *om.* SrPl 42 not] so *add.* Pl here] m *add.*, *canc.* Sr þe whilk men] swyche Cc þe prophete/seyth] *rev.* Cc þe] *om.* T þus] Psalmo 52° *add.* BLHu_2ETW, Ps. 13 *add.* Hu_2 43 seyd] seiþ H_5WsE 44 \`man^{1}´ Pl euerilk] H_7HRCh, eueryche BAs, euery H_5LB_3SrWsLwHu_2EPH_6CcMLdPlTW, man þat is *add.* As wrecched man] *rev.* B wrecched] widkede M man^{2}] *om.* As 45 lyketh and loueth] *rev.* Cc lyketh] H_7RBLB_3AsSrChHu_2PH_6LdPl, liken M, liuyþ HH_5WsLwTW, iacet in peccato Lat. loueth] louen M cheseþ þe] cheson M þis] þe ChHu_2 as] for *add.* Cc \`rest´ Pl 46 soule] for *add.* M þat] H_7HRBH_5AsSrWsChAHu_2CcMLdPlT, *om.* LB_3Lw-EPH_6W no] non As not] no Ld, but M 47 speken of him/sumtyme] *rev.* E fareth wele] delectabiliter viuit Lat. 48 Sumtyme] summe LB_3PH_6, And *prec.* Cc 49 his^{1}] *om.* Lw swereth] swere M 50 or . . . membris] *om.* SrM or] by *add.* T membris] lymus A 51 and þat is] *om.* Sr eyþer] ouþer A, oþer As, only M, *om.* H_6Cc for] H_7SrACcMPl, þat *add.* HRBH_5LB_3AsWsChLwHu_2EPH_6LdTW þer . . . þat^{2} (l. 52)] H_7RBLB_3SrChAHu_2EPH_6CcMLdPl, *om.* HH_5AsWsLwTW, et hoc ideo est vel quia credit quod nulla est vita alia quam ista, vel licet credat quod alia est vita, credit tamen Deum Lat. þan] bute BChHu_2CcLd 52 if . . . þat^{1}] he weneth then Cc wene] belyue Ld þat^{1}] *om.* M is] be CcM lyf] H_7RLB_3AEPH_6CcPl *om.* BSrChHu_2MLd, vita Lat. neuerþeles] ȝet Cc þat^{2}] *om.* B_3 53 seeth] sey Cc \`or . . . seyth´ (l. 54)] H^c, *om.* $H°H_5$Ws so hard] *om.* A

Writte seyth, or þat he wil forgyfe him his synne þogh þat he fele it not; or elles þat þer schal no Cristen man be dampned do he neuer so ille; or elles if he fast oure Lady fast, or seith ilk day a certeyn orison, or here ilk day two messis or þre, or do a certeyn bodily dede as it were in wirchepe of God, he schal neuer gon to helle, do he neuer so mikel synne, þogh he forsake it not. Þis man seith in his hert þat þer is no
f. 59^v God, bot he is vnwys, as þe prophete seith, for | he schal felen and fynden in pyne þat he is a God whom he forgate and sette noght [b]y in welth of þis werd, as þe prophete seyth, *Sola vexacio dabit intellectum*. Þat is: Only pyne schal gyf vnderstondynge; for he þat knoweth not þis here schal wele knowen it whan he is in pyne.

A lytel counseil how lofers of þis werd schul don if þei wil ben reformed in here soule beforn þei passen hens. Capitulum xvi^m

T[h]es men, þogh þei wyten wele þat þei ben out of grace and in dedly synne, þei han no kare ne sorwe ne þoght þerfor; bot þei maken fleschly myrthe and werdly solace as mikel as þei moun, and þe ferþer þat þei ben fro grace þe more myrthe þei maken. And perchaunce sum hold hem wel payde þat þei han no grace, so þat þei moun as it were þe more fully and frely folwe þe lykynge of fleschly lustes, as þogh God were oslepe and myght not seen hem. And þis is on of þe most defaute. And so by here owen frowardnes þei stoppe þe light of grace fro here owen soule þat it may not resten þerin; þe qwhilk grace, in as mykel as in it is, schyneth to al gostly creatures, redy for to entren in þer it is resceyued, as þe sonne schyneþ ouer al bodily

54 Writte] Chirche LwCc, \`wryt´ *corr.* Lw or] oþer A he[1]] God Ld him] *om.* RAsPl his] þat LwW synne] to hym *add.* RAsSrM þat[2]] H$_7$RLB$_3$SrAEPH$_6$MPl, *om.* HBH$_5$AsWsChLwHu$_2$CcLdTW fele] H$_7$H$_5$ChHu$_2$T, leue RBLB$_3$AsSr⌜H$^c$⌝AEPH$_6$LdPl, fle Ws, \`fle : lefe/T^{G}W^G, see LwW, relinquere non proponat Lat. 55 do . . . ille] quantumcunque vixerit viciose Lat. 56 ille] H$_7$RLChPPl, euele HBH$_5$B$_3$AsSrWsLwAHu$_2$EH$_6$CcMLdTW or elles] or E, *om.* Hu$_2$ Lady] H$_7$HBH$_5$LB$_3$WsChLwAHu$_2$EPH$_6$MLdW, Ladiis RAsSrCcPlT or[2]] if he *add.* Sr, elles *add.* T seith] H$_7$RAsAPl, seie Σ, dicat Lat. ilk] H$_7$Ch, ilk a HR, euery BH$_5$LB$_3$SrWsLwHu$_2$EPPlTW, eche AsH$_6$CcMLd 57 here] herith RAsA ilk] H$_7$RCh, ilk a H, euery BH$_5$LB$_3$SrWsLwHu$_2$EPPlTW, eche H$_6$CcMLd, eche a As 58 in] H$_7$HRBH$_5$AsWsChACcMLdPlTW, þe *add.* LB$_3$SrHu$_2$EPH$_6$, *om.* Lw 59 þat] H$_7$RH$_5$LB$_3$AsSrWsAPH$_6$CcMPlW, *om.* HBChLwHu$_2$ELdT \`is´ L 60 and] ek *add.* M 61 \`he´ Sr, ther Cc a] *om.* LB$_3$PH$_6$ forgate] forsak B by] vy H$_7$ 62 in] þe *add.* WsECc; but sette by the W welth] H$_7$LB$_3$SrAHu$_2$EPH$_6$CcMPlT, wele HRBH$_5$AsWsChLwLdW, prosperitate Lat. þis] the W seyth] Ysa. 28° BLHu$_2$EPLdTW 63 intellectum] H$_7$RLB$_3$AsSrAEPH$_6$CcMPl, auditui *add.* HBH$_5$WsChLwHu$_2$LdTW þat is] *om.* H$_5$Ws he] *om.* Ws 64 here] H$_7$RLB$_3$AsSrAEPH$_6$CcMPl, ne wil not knowen *add.* HH$_5$WsLwLdTW, nor while not knowen *add.* BChHu$_2$, ne woll not knowe it LdW, in presenti Lat. schal . . . it/whan . . . pyne] *rev.* B schal] he *prec.* B, he *add.* W wele] *om.* B

`or þat he wil not punisch it so harde as Holi Writ seiþ', or þat he wil forgife hym his syn þof he ⌜leue⌝ it not; or elles þat þer schal no cristen man be dampned doo he neuer so euele; or elles if he fast oure Lady fast, or say ilk a day a certayn orisoun, or here ilk a day two messes or þre, or do a certeyn bodily dede as it were in wurschip of God, he schal neuer gon to helle, do he neuer so mikel synne þawȝ he forsake it not. þis man saiþ in his herte þer is no God, bot he is vnwise, as þe prophet saiþ, for he schal felen and fynden in peyn þat he is a God whom he forgat and sett not by in wele of þis world, as þe prophet saiþ: *Sola vexacio dabit intellectum auditui.* þat is: Only peyn schal gifen vndirstondyng; for he þat knowiþ not þis here, ne wil not knowen, schal wel knowen it when he is in peyne.

[CHAPTER 16]

þese men, þawȝ `þei' witen wele þat þei arn owt of grace and in dedly synne, þei haue no kare ne sorwe ne þouȝt þerfore; bot þei maken flescly mirþ and wordly solace als mikel as þei mowen, and þe ferþer þat þei ben fro grace þe more mirþ þei maken. And perchaunce summe holden hem wel paied þat þei han `no' grace, þat þei mowen as it were þe more fully and frely folwe þe likyng of flescly lustes, as þawȝ God were on slepe and myȝt not seen hem. And þis is oon of þe most defaut. And so by here owne frowardnes þei stoppe þe liȝt of grace fro here owne soule þat it may not resten þerin; þe whilk grace, in as mikel as in it is, schyneþ to alle gostly creatures, redy for to entren in þere it is resceyued, as þe sone schynyþ ouer al bodily

Chapter 16 *title*: H$_7$RLB$_3$AsSrAEPH$_6$MLdPlTW *om.* HBH$_5$WsChLwHu$_2$Cc 1 schul] schulden SrH$_6$ 2 soule] soulis RLB$_3$P, animabus Lat. beforn] or *add.* E, þat *add.* LB$_3$SrPCcLd þei passen] þei parten Ld, her partinge TW hens] fro *prec.* Sr, ex hac vita Lat. 3 Thes] Tes H$_7$ þogh] þat *add.* LEP, *om.* H$_5$Ws `þei$^1$' *scr.* H 4 no] non As ne$^1$] *om.* T ne þoght] *om.* Cc þerfor] þerynne B 5 `fleschly' Pl and . . . solace] *om.* Sr þe ferþer þat] therfore Cc ferþer] ferre A, ferrer Pl 6 þat] *om.* LwW perchaunce] haply H$_6$ 7 sum] they Cc wel] right *prec.* T `no' H^c, *om.* H$^\circ$H$_5$Ws so/þat þei moun] *rev.* Sr so] H$_7$RLB$_3$AsSrAPH$_6$CcMPl, *om.* HBH$_5$Ws-ChLwHu$_2$ELdTW, vt sic Lat. as it were] *om.* LB$_3$PH$_6$, sic Lat. 8 þe^1] *om.* LB$_3$P lykynge] delectaciones Lat. of] þe *add.* RM, here *add.* Cc 9 hem] him H$_5$Ws And . . . so (l. 10)] Bot al þis is here owne defaute for Hu$_2$ `is' Cc on . . . defaute] defectus magnus Lat. 10 most] and grettist *add* T defaute] defautes CcPl, that maye be *add.* W And so] For thus Cc so] thus W by] for Hu$_2$ 11 resten] intrare Lat. 12 in it/is] *rev.* Cc in] *om.* M it] hym B, þat Sr is] *om.* As schyneth] it *prec.* Sr redy] *om.* Ws for] *om.* M 13 þer it is] if it be Sr þer] þeras E resceyued] recipitur et admittitur Lat. al] *om.* Ld bodily creatures] *rev.* W bodily] *om.* Lw creatures þere it is not lettid. þus seith Seynt John in þe Gospel: *Lux in tenebris lucet, et tenebre eam non comprehenderunt*. þat is: þe light of grace schyneþ in myrknes, þat is to mannys hertis þat arn myrk þurgh synne, bot þe myrknes takeþ it not; þat is, þe blynde hertys resceyuen not þat gracious light ne han no profyte of it. Bot right as a blynde man is al vmbilapped with light of þe sunne whan he stondeþ þerin, and ȝet seeþ he it not ne hath no profyte þerof for to gon þerby, right so gostly, a soule blynded with dedly synne is al vmbelapped with þis gostly light, and ȝet he is neuer þe bettre, for he is blynde and will not seen ne knowen his blyndenes. And þat is on of þe most lettynge of f. 60r grace, þat | a wrecched man wil not ben aknowe his owen blyndnes for pride of himself; or elles if he knowe it he chargeþ it not, bot makeþ mirthe and game as he were oueral syker.

þerfor vnto al þese men þat arn þus blynded and bounden with þe fals loue of þis werd and arn so foule forschapen fro þe fayrhed of man, I sey and counseil þat þei þenken on here soule and þat þei able hem to grace as mikel as þei moun. And þat moun þei don vpon þis wyse, if þat þei willen. Whan þat þei felen hemself out of grace and ouerleyd with dedly synne, þan þat þei þenke what myschief and what peryle is to hem for to ben out of grace and be departyd fro God as þei arn; for þer is noþyng þat holdeþ hem fro þe pitte of helle þat þei ne schulden as tytte fallen þerin bot on bare sengle þrede of þis bodily lyfe whoreby þei hangen, þat liȝtlyer may be lost þan a sengle þrede may be broken on two. For were þe breth stopped in þe body, and þat

14 þere] where Cc it . . . lettid] impedimentum non habeat vel obstaculum Lat. seith] seyd H_5Ws Gospel] Jo. primo *add.* BLHu$_2$EPLdTW 15 non] *om.* Lw 16 myrknes] H_7HRLAsSrChPMPl, derknes BH_5B_3WsLwAHu$_2$EH_6CcLdTW to] *om.* E mannys] mene M `hertis´ Sr myrk] $H_7$HRLAsSrChPMPl, derke B$B_3$ChLwAHu$_2$E$H_6$CcLdTW, wiþinne *add.* $H_5$Ws 17 myrknes takeþ] $H_7$RLAsPMPl, myrknesses taken HSrCh, derknes takiþ B$H_5B_3$WsLwAHu$_2$E$H_6$CcW, derkenesse taken Ld takeþ] receyvith Cc þe$^2$] $H_7$, þese Σ `hertys´ H^c, *om.* $H^{\circ}H_5$Ws 18 þat] þe RAECcW, this M ne] þei *add.* Sr no] H_7, not þe Σ, *om.* Cc of it] þerof B_3SrA right] *om.* RAsE 19 is] þat *prec.* Sr al vmbilapped] wrapped aboute M al] *om.* RLwPlW vmbilapped] aboute bewrappid H_5Ws, bylappid H_6, bigon A `with . . . vmbelapped (21)´ $H^c$, *om.* $H^{\circ}H_5$Ws with] $H_7$RL$B_3$AsSr$H^c$AEPPl, the *add.* BChLwHu$_2$CcMLdTW, in þe $H_6$ 20 seeþ he] *rev.* $H_6$CcM he] *om.* W no] noon P, *om.* Cc gon] `go´ H^c þerby] by H_6 21 gostly] H_7HRH_5LB_3AsWsLwAEPH_6CcPlTW, *om.* BSrChHu$_2$MLd, spiritualiter Lat. blynded with] blyndeþ with As, blynd by B al] *om.* E vmbelapped] bylappid BAH_6, wrapped aboute M with] in H_6 22 he is] H_7HRBH_5AsSrWsChLwHu$_2$MLdTW, he `is´ Cc, *rev.* LB_3AEPH_6, nys he B is^2] b- *add.*, *canc.* Sr blynde] blyndyd LwW will] may Cc 23 of . . . lettynge] de maximis impedimentis Lat. of] *om.* M 24 wrecched] wickid LB_3PH_6 wil] wold E ben aknowe] ben yknowen of B, be acnowe of ATW, knowe Hu$_2$, fateri Lat. blyndnes] wickednes and *add.* E 25 himself] hemself M or] oþer As if] þow B knowe] knoweþ HCh, beknowe M, fateatur seu recognoscat Lat. chargeþ] chaungeþ As, chaungeth

creatures þer it is not letted. þus saiþ Seynt Johan in þe Gospel: *Lux*
78v *in tenebris lucet, et tenebre eam non comprehen|derunt*. þat is: þe liȝt of
grace schyneþ in mirknes, þat is to mennus hertes þat arn mirk þurgh synne, bot þe mirknesses taken it not; þat is, þese blynde `hertes´ resceyue not þat gracious liȝt ne han not þe profet of it. Bot riȝt as a blynde man is al vmbilappid `wiþ liȝte of þe sonne when he stondiþ þerinne, and ȝet seeþ he it not ne haþ no profet þerof for to `go´ þerbi, riȝt so gostly, a soule blynded wiþ dedly synne is al vmbilappid´ with þis gostly liȝt, and ȝit he is neuer þe better, for he is blynde and wile not seen ne knowen his blyndnesse. And þat is on of þe moost lettyng of grace, þat a wrecched man wil not ben aknowen his owen blyndenes for pride of hymself; or elles if he knoweþ it he chargeþ it not, bot makiþ mirþ and gamen as he were oueral siker.

þerfore vnto alle þese men þat arn þus blynded and bounded with þe luf of þis world and arn so foule forschapen fro þe fairhed of man, I sey and conseile þat þei þinken on þeire soule and þat þei ablen hem to grace as mikel as þei mowen. And þat mowe þei don vpon þis wise, if þat þei wilen. When þei felen hemself out of grace and ouerleide with dedly synne, þan þat þei þinken what mischief and what peril it is to hem for to ben out of grace and departid fro God as þei ben; for þer is no þinge þat holdeþ hem fro þe pit of helle þat þei ne schuld as tite falle þerinne bot on bare sengle þrede `of þis bodily lyfe wherbi þei hangen. What liȝtlier may be loste þan a sengle þrede´ may be brokyn on two? For were þe breþ stopped in her body, and þat may

hit nor chargeth M it[2]] *om.* W not] neyþer settiþ þerbi *add.* Hu_2 26 as] þoȝ *add.* ALdT oueral] *om.* Hu_2 syker] ynooȝ *add.* Hu_2T 27 þese] þo Sr, þe Pl blynded] blynd ChHu_2 and . . . werd (l. 28)] *om.* As bounden] H_7RLB_3SrAEPH_6CcMPl, bounded HBH_5WsCh-LwHu_2LdTW, ligati Lat. 28 fals] H_7RLB_3SrAEPH_6CcMPl, *om.* HBH_5WsChLw-Hu_2LdTW, falso Lat. of[1]] in Lw so] *om.* LwW foule] folyly RAsPl, fouli A fayrhed] fayrnes SrWs 29 sey and] *om.* Cc counseil] hem Cc, hym M soule] soulys CcM 30 hem] hemself Cc to] vnto W moun þei] *rev.* E þei] be Cc vpon] H_7HBH_5LB_3Sr-WsLwPPlTW, on RAsChAHu_2EH_6CcM, in Ld 31 þat[1]] H_7HRBH_5AsWsChLw-AHu_2ECcMPlTW, *om.* LB_3SrPH_6Ld Whan þat] þan As Whan] han Sr þat[2]] H_7RLB_3AsSrAEPH_6W, `þat´ Pl, *om.* HBH_5WsChLwHu_2CcMLdT hemself] hem LB_3PH_6 32 þan þat þei] *om.* Cc what] *om.* LB_3PH_6 33 is] H_7RLB_3AsSrLwAPH_6Pl, it is HBH_5WsChHu_2ECcMLdTW for] *rep.* Pl, *om.* H_6M out] put *prec.* W grace] caritatem Lat. be] H_7RLB_3AsSrAEPCcMPl, to be H_6, *om.* HBH_5WsChLwHu_2LdTW 34 noþyng] non þynge As 35 as tytte] H_7HRLChLwP, anon B$H_5$$B_3$AsWsA$Hu_2$-$H_6$CcMLdPl, as soone E, þus sone T, right soone W, as swiþe Sr, *om.* Lat. on] oure Pl sengle þrede] *rev.* M `of . . . þrede (l. 36)´ $H^c$, þat lyȝtly $H_5$Ws, þat ful lightly T þis] $H_7$RL$B_3$AsSr$H^c$AEP$H_6$CcMPl, þat BChLw$Hu_2$LdW 36 `lyfe´ Pl þei hangen] he hangeþ Sr þat] H_7BLB_3SrChAHu_2EPH_6CcMLd, What RAsLw`$H^c$´PlW, que Lat. liȝtlyer] liȝter AM lost] lefte As 37 may be] *om.* M be broken] *om.* As on] in SrAMPl and þat] as Sr `þat´ R, *om.* T

may liȝtly falle, here soule schuld passen forth and on-one ben in helle withouten ende. And if þei wolden þenken þus, þei schuld quaken and schaken for drede of þe ryȝthwys domes of God and of þe hard punyschynges of synne, and þei schulden mornen and sorwen for here synne and for þei han no grace. And þan schuld þei cryen and prayen þat þei myghten haue grace, and if þei deden þus þan schuld grace fallen in hem and putten out myrknes and hardnes of herte and weyknes of wil, and ȝifen hem myght and strenght for to forsake þe fals loue of þis werd as mikel as is dedly synne. For þer is no soule so fer fro God þurgh wikkednes of wil in dedly synne—I outtake none þat lyfeþ in þis body of synne—þat he ne may þurgh grace be ryghted and reformed to clennes of good lyfynge if he wil bowen his will to God with mekenes for to amendyn his lyfe, and hertly asken grace and forgyfnes of him, and excusen oure Lord and fully accusen himself. For Holy Wrytte seyth: *Nolo mortem peccatoris, sed magis vt conuertatur et viuat*. Þat is, oure Lord seyth: I wil not þe dede of a synnere, bot I f. 60^{v} wil more þat he be turned to me and lyfe. For oure Lord | wil þat þe most froward man þat lyfeþ forschapen þurgh synne, if he turne his wil and asken grace, þat he be reformed to his lyknes.

Þat reformynge in feith and in feleng may not sodeynly be geten, bot þurgh grace and mikel bodili and gostly trauaille. Capitulum xvii^{m}

This reformyng `is´ in feith, as I haue beforn seyd, þat lightly may ben had. Bot after þis comeþ reformynge in feith and in felynge þat may not so lightly be geten bot þurgh long trauail and mekel besines. For reformyng in feith is common to alle chosen soules, þogh þei ben bot

38 schuld] schalle LwW 39 if] *om.* M þenken þus] *rev.* RAsAPl þus] þys B, on þis Hu$_2$, for sothe I trowe *add.* Cc quaken and schaken] *rev.* Sr 40 ryȝthwys domes] riȝtwisnese R, riȝt wisdome E riȝthwys] H$_7$LB$_3$AsAPH$_6$Pl, riȝtful HBH$_5$SrWsChLwHu$_2$CcMLdTW of[3]] for H$_6$ þe] his ChHu$_2$ 41 punyschynges] H$_7$Pl, punyschynge Σ, punicionem Lat. of] for Sr mornen and sorwen] H$_7$RLB$_3$AsAEPH$_6$CcLdPl, *rev.* HBH$_5$SrWsChLwHu$_2$MTW, dolorent Lat. sorwen] make sorow LwW 42 þei han no] H$_7$RLB$_3$AsSrAPH$_6$CcMPl, lakkynge of HBH$_5$WsChLwHu$_2$ELdTW, carencia Lat. And[2] . . . grace (l. 43)] *om.* Sr schuld] schul A, *om.* Pl 43 deden] don LB$_3$SrPH$_6$, facerint Lat. `schuld´ Sr, schol A 44 in] into Cc hem] *om.* LwW myrknes] H$_7$HRLAsSrChPCcMPl, derknesse BH$_5$B$_3$WsLwAHu$_2$EH$_6$LdTW 45 weyknes] febilnesse B, feyntnesse A, leþynesse Ld, wykkidnesse CcM, debilitatem Lat. hem] him H$_5$, to *add.* Sr for] *om.* H$_6$Pl 46 þis] þe Sr as[2]] *rep.* A, it *add.* ChHu$_2$, it *add.*, *canc.* T dedly synne] *om.* ChHu$_2$ þer] þis A 47 of wil] *om.* ACc none] nouȝt oon M 48 þat lyfeþ] *om.* LB$_3$PH$_6$ þis] *om.* A body of] bodily M þat] but *prec.* Pl ne] *om.* M þurgh . . . and] *om.* Lat. 49 to] þoruȝ B$_3$ good] H$_7$RLB$_3$AsSrAEPH$_6$CcMPl, *om.* HBH$_5$WsChLwHu$_2$LdTW, bone Lat. wil] wolde Ld

liȝtly falle, here soule schuld passe forþ and anon ben in helle withoutyn ende. And if þei wolden þinke þus, þei schulden qwakyn and schaken for drede of þe riȝtful domes of God and of þe harde punyschynge of synne, and þei schulde sorw and mornen for her synne and for lackynge of grace. And þan schude þei cryen and preien
79r þat þei miȝten haue | grace, and if þei deden þus þan schuld grace fallen in hem and putten out mirknes and hardnes of herte and waiknes of wil and gifen hem miȝt and strengþ for to forsakyn þe fals luf of þis world as mikel as is dedly synne. For þer is no soule so ferre fro God þurwȝ wickidnes of wil in dedly synne—I outake none þat lifiþ in þis body of syn—þat he ne may þurw grace be riȝted and reformed to clennes of lyuynge if he wil bowen his wille to God with meknes for to amenden his liif, and hertly asken grace and forgifnes of hym, and excusen oure Lord and fully accusen hymself. For Holy Writ saiþ: *Nolo mortem peccatoris, sed magis ut conuertatur et viuat*, þat is: Oure Lord saiþ: I wile not þe deþ of a synner, bot I wil more þat he be turned to me and lif. For oure Lord wile þat þe most fraward man þat lifiþ forschapen þurwȝ synne, if he turne his wille and aske grace þat he be reformed to his liknes.

[CHAPTER 17]

þis reformyng is in faiþ, as I haue before seide, þat liȝtly may ben had. Bot aftir þis comeþ reformyng in faiþ and in felyng þat may not so liȝtly be getyn bot þurwȝ longe trauaile and mikel bisynes. For reformyng in faiþ is comun to alle chosen soules, þawȝ þei ben bot

50 with] be Cc for] *om.* H_6 and[1]] *om.* RAsAPl hertly/asken grace] *rev.* Ld asken] asking A grace] mercy B, mercy and *prec.* Hu_2 51 him] hem Ch, his mysdedis Hu_2 Lord] þat he is so gracious and so good *add.* H_5Ws himself] hemself Ch, hym M 52 seyth] thus *add.* Cc, I [*following reference blank*] *add.* E, Ezec. 18 *add.* Hu_2T peccatoris] peccatorum Lw magis vt] *rev.* H_5Ws 53 viuat] etc. *add.* M a] þe B_3M 54 more] raþer A, *om.* Cc to me] *om.* SrCcM and] me *add.* Ld Lord] *om.* As `wil´ L 56 `be´ Cc

Chapter 17 *title*: H_7RLB_3AsSrAEPH_6MLdPlTW *om.* HBH_5WsChLwHu_2Cc 1 þat] *canc.* L feith . . . feleng] *rev.* RAsALdPl sodeynly be] *rev.* As 2 bot þurgh grace] *om.* W þurgh] by T mikel] grace *add.*, *canc.* L bodily and gostly/trauaille] *rev.* LB_3EPH_6 trauaille] H_7LB_3SrPH_6, in lengthyng of tyme *add.* RAsA, in lengþe of tyme *add.* ELdPlTW, and grete labour *add.* M, laborem Lat. 4 `is´ *interl.* $H_7$ 6 so] $H_7$HRB$H_5$AsSrWsChA$Hu_2$E$H_6$MLdPlT$W^G$, *om.* L$B_3$LwPCcW, ita Lat. be geten] begote W þurgh] wiþ As long] gret A mekel] gret $H_5$Ws For] þe *add.* $B_3$ 7 `bot´ W^G, not M, *om.* LwH_6W in þe lowest degre of charite. Bot reformynge in felynge is specially of þese soules þat moun comen to þe state of perfeccion, and þat may not sodeynly ben had, bot after grete plente of grace and mikel gostly trauail a soule may come þerto. And þat is whan it is first heled of his gostly sekenes, and whan al bitter passions and fleschly lustes and oþer old felyngis ar brent out of þe herte with feyre of desyre, and new gracious felynges arn broȝt in with brennend lofe and gostly lyght. Þan neggheth a soule to perfeccion and to reformynge in felyng.

For soth it is, right as a man þat is broght nere to þe dede þurgh bodili sekenes, þogh he resceyue a medycyne be þe whilk he is restored and syker of his lyfe, he may not for it as tytte rysen vp and gon to werke as an hole man may, for þe feblenes of his body holdeþ him doun þat him behoueth vmbyden a gode whyle, and kepen him wel with medycynes, and dyeten him be mesure after þe techynge of a leche til he may fully recoueren bodily hele; ryght so gostli, he þat is broght to gostly dede þurgh dedly synne, þogh he þurgh medycyne of þe sacrament of penaunce be restored to lyfe þat he schal not be dampned, neuerþeles he is not as tyte hole of alle his passions and of alle his fleschly desyres, ne able to contemplacion. Bot him behoueth abyden a grete whyle and taken gode kepe of himself, and rewlyn him so þat he might recoueren ful hele of soule, for he schal langoure a grete whyle or þan he be fully hole. Neuerþeles if þat he take
f. 61r medycynes of a gode leche and vse hem in tyme | with mesure and discrecion, he schal mikel þe sonnere be restored to his gostly strength and come to reformynge in felynge.

For þe reformynge in feith is þe lowest state of alle chosen soules, for beneþen þat might þei not wel ben; bot reformynge in felynge is

8 ˋof þeseˊ Pl   9 þese] þo WsA, þe Sr   soules] *om.* Cc   and þat] que perfeccio Lat. þat[2]] *om.* T   may not/sodeynly] *rev.* H_5Ws   10 mikel] grete Hu_2 11 And] *om.* Sr   it] $H_7RLB_3AsSrAPH_6CcMPl$, he $HBH_5WsChLwHu_2ELdTW$ first heled] *rev.* Sr   first] *om.* H_6 his] þys B, *om.* LB_3P 12 sekenes . . . bitter] *om.* M   and[2]] of B, whenne alle bitter passions and *add.* M   13 felyngis] felyng Cc   brent] brouȝt BH_5WsLd, consumuntur et . . . comburuntur Lat.   þe] þi A   feyre] þe *prec.* T   of[2]] and $AsHu_2Pl$ new] now Pl   14 felynges] felyng Cc   with] gostly *add.* H_5Ws 15 þan] þat As neggheth] right nyghe hygheth W   16 soth] þe *prec.* M   þat] $H_7RLB_3AsSrAEPH_6Cc$-$MLdPlW$, *om.* $HBH_5WsChLwHu_2T$ nere] $H_7HRBH_5SrWsChLwAPH_6CcLdPlT$, neiȝ LB_3AsHu_2MW, nyȝher E   þe] *om.* LwELdW   dede] bodely *prec.* T   17 þogh] ȝif A þe] *om.* Sr   18 ˋhisˊ H^c, *om.* $H^{\circ}BChHu_2LdT$ for it as tytte] H_7RLP, for it anoon B_3AsAH_6Pl, for it als swiþe Sr, þerfore as tite HChLw, for it as sone E, þerfore anon BH_5WsHu_2CcMW, anoon þerfor Ld, þerfore as sone T   19 to] his *add.* M   werke] worchyng Pl, trauaile A   man] *om.* W   20 him behoueth] $H_7RLB_3AsSRAEPH_6Cc$-MPl, hee most $HBH_5WsChLwHu_2LdTW$ vmbyden] to *prec.* LB_3PH_6M, for to *prec.* Cc 21 wel] a good while T, *om.* LB_3P ˋwithˊ Sr   dyeten] deyntes H_5Ws ˋhimˊ H^c, *om.* $H^{\circ}BH_5WsCh$ be] wiþ LB_3P a] þe H_6Cc 22 til] *om.* H_5Ws recoueren] coueren

in þe lowest degre of charite. Bot reformyng in felyng is specialy of þese soules þat mowen comen to þe stat of perfeccioun, and þat may not sodenly ben had, bot aftir gret plente of grace and mikel gostly trauail a soule may come þerto. And þat is when hee is first heeled of his gostly seknes, and whan alle bitter passions and flescly lustes and oþer elde felynges are brent out of þe herte with fiire of desire, and newe gracious felynges are brow3t in with brennand luf and gostly li3t. Þan ne3eþ a soule to perfeccioun and to reformyng in felyng.

For soþ it is, ri3t as a man is brou3t ner to þe ded þorw bodily
79^v seknes, | þaw3 he resceyue a medicine bi þe whilk he is restored and siker of `his´ lif, he may not þerfore as tite risen vp and gon to werk as an hol mon may, for þe febilnes of his body holdis hym doun þat hee most abide a goode while, and kepen hym wel with medicynes, and dieten `him´ be mesure aftir þe techyng of a leche til he may fully recoueren bodily hele; ri3t so gostly, he þat is bro3t to gostly ded þurw3 dedly synne, þaw he þorw medicyne of þe sacrament of penaunce be restored to lif þat he schal not be dampned, nerþeles he is not as tit hool of alle his passions and of alle his flescly desires, ne able to contemplacioun. Bot hym bihouiþ abiden a grete while and take gode kepe of hymself, and rewlen hym so þat he mi3t recoueren ful hele of soule, for he schal languren a grete while ar þan he be fully hool. Nerþeles if he take medicines of a gode leche and vse hem in tyme with mesure and discrecioun, he schal mikel þe sonner be restored to his gostly strengþe and come to reformyng in felyng.

For reformyng in faiþ is þe lowest state of alle chosen soules, for bineþ þat mi3t þei not wel ben; bot reformyng in felynge is þe hei3este

Hu$_2$, and han *add.* Cc hele] helthe CcMLd, sanitatem . . . et fortitudinem Lat. gostli] *om.* Pl, *om.* Lat. 23 to] vnto Sr dede] seknesse Cc þogh] 3if A 24 þe] *om.* Ch not] *om.* As 25 neuerþeles] yit *prec.* Hu$_2$, but 3et Cc as tyte hole] hool anoon B$_3$CcPl as tyte] H$_7$HRLChLwPM, anon BH$_5$LB$_3$AsWsAHu$_2$EH$_6$CcLdPlW, as swithe Sr, as sone T his] *om.* Cc and] ne Ld of^2] *om.* H$_5$Ws 26 alle] *om.* LB$_3$P desyres] desire Pl him behoueth] he most Hu$_2$, to *add.* T him] *om.* Cc 27 whyle] and þat he be fully hole *add.* As and^1] to *add.* E of] to MLd, on Pl 28 ful] fully B, goode As hele] helthe CcLd langoure] languische AT, be feble and syklich B, be feble Ld, be secke Hu$_2$ 29 þan] H$_7$HH$_5$LB$_3$SrWsLwHu$_2$EPH$_6$MT, þat RBAsChACcLdPlW, *om.* Ws Neuerþeles] 3it Cc þat] H$_7$RLB$_3$AsEPH$_6$W, *om.* HBH$_5$SrWsChLwAHu$_2$CcMLdPlT take] wold taken Cc 30 medycynes] medicyne M hem] *om.* Sr 31 mikel þe sonnere] muche sonnere come and H$_5$Ws, raþer a grete dele Hu$_2$ mikel þe] wel M restored] ⌜restorid and reformyd⌝ L, and reformed *add.* B$_3$P to] into E his] *om.* H$_5$Ws 32 reformynge] H$_7$HRBH$_5$AsSrWsLwAHu$_2$ECcMLdPlTW, þe *prec.* LB$_3$ChHu$_2$PH$_6$ 33 þe^1] H$_7$RH$_5$AsWsAPl, *om.* HBLB$_3$SrChLwHu$_2$EPH$_6$CcMLdTW state] in þis liif *add.* E 34 þat] `it´ *add.* Cc þei] he LB$_3$SrPH$_6$, *om.* Cc not wel] *rev.* ChHu$_2$ ben] esse vel saluari Lat.

þe heyest state of þis lyfe þat þe soule may come to. Bot fro þe logwest to þe heygest may not a soule sodeynly stirte, no more þan a man þat wil clymbe vpon an heygh leddre and setteth his foot vpon þe loghest stele may at þe nexte flyen vp to þe heyghest, bot him behoueth by processe gon one after anoþer til he may come to þe ouerest. Ryght so it is gostly: no man is mad sodeynly souereyn in grace, bot þurgh longe excersyse and sleygh werkynge a soule may come þerto, namely whan he helpeth and techeth a wrecched soule in whom al grace lygheþ. For withouten speciale help and inly techynge of hym may no soule come þerto.

On encheson why so few soules as in þe reward of þe multitude of oþer come to þis reformynge in feith and in felynge. Capitulum xviii^{m}

Bot now seist þou: Syn oure Lord is so curteys of his godenes and of his graciouse gyftes so fre, wonder it is þan þat so few soules as it semeth, in rewarde of þe multitude of oþer, moun come to þis reformynge in felynge. It semeth þat he were daungerouse, and þat is not soth, or þat he toke no reward at his creatures, þe whilk by takynge of feith arn become his seruauntes.

Vnto þis I may answere and seyn as me þenkeþ, þat on encheson is þis: Many men þat arn reformed in feith setten not here herte for to profyten in grace, ne for to seken none heyghere state of gode lyfynge þurgh besy trauail in preynge and þenkynge and oþer bodily and gostly werkynge; bot hem þenkeþ it inogh to hem for to kepe hem fro dedly synne, for to stande stil in þat plyte as þey arn in. For þei seyn

35 of] H_7M, in Σ, in Lat. þe^{2}] H_7HRBLB$_3$AsSrLwAEPH$_6$MPlTW, a H_5WsChHu$_2$CcLd come to] habere Lat. fro] *om.* Ld 36 to] vnto T `soule´ L sodeynly] redily Sr stirte] come to Hu$_2$ no] ne LP 37 vpon^{1}] on RAs heygh leddre] *rev.* LwW setteth] settyn RCc foot] fete As vpon^{2}] on SrH$_6$ loghest] *om.* As 38 stele] gree B, stake H$_6$, scale Pl, steppe Ld, or rounde *add.* T may] nat *add.* BELd at þe] atte ChT; at Hu$_2$M, laste *add.*, *canc.* L flyen] H_7HRAsSrChLwAEPl, flen BLB$_3$PH$_6$MLdTW, styȝen H_5Ws, goyng Hu$_2$, setten the othir fot Cc, attingere Lat. vp] *om.* M by processe/gon] H_7RLB$_3$AsAEPH$_6$CcPl, *rev.* HBH_5SrWsChLwHu$_2$MLdTW by processe] succesiue et per processum Lat. 39 gon] to *prec.* H_6M, for to *prec.* Hu$_2$, on *add.*, *canc.* L, *om.* Pl til] to Hu$_2$ ouerest] heyeste BHu$_2$CcM, ouermoste ALdT 40 souereyn] perfectus Lat. 41 excersyse] hauntyng H_6 sleygh] diligentem Lat. a] of a MW þerto] ad perfeccionem Lat. namely] And *prec.* H_6 42 helpeth and techeth] *rev.* H_5WsLd and techeth] *om.* Sr wrecched] *om.* Cc in . . . lygheþ] a quo datur et diffunditur omnis gracia Lat. 43 lygheþ] is Cc inly] H_7RLB$_3$AsSrAEPMPl, inward H_6Cc, inwardly HBH_5WsChLwHu$_2$LdTW 44 þerto] ad graciam Lat.

Chapter 18 *title*: H_7RLB$_3$AsSrAEPH$_6$MLdPlTW *om.* HBH_5WsChLwHu$_2$Cc 1 On encheson] On cause H_6, A cause Sr, þe cause LdTW as] H_7LB$_3$SrEPH$_6$M, *om.*

state in þis lif þat þe soule may come to. Bot fro þe lowest to þe heiȝest may not a soule sodeynly stirte, no more þan a man þat wil clymbe vpon an hiȝe laddre and settiþ his fot vpon þe lowest stele may at þe ne⌜ȝst⌝ flien vp to þe heiȝest, bot hym behouiþ gon by processe on aftir anoþer til he may come to þe ouerest. Riȝt so it is gostly: no man is made sodenly souerayn in grace, bot þurw longe exercise and sleiȝ wirkyng a soule may come þerto, namely whan he helpiþ and techiþ a wrecched soule in whom alle grace liþ. For wiþouten special helpe and inwardly techyng of him may no soule come þerto.

[CHAPTER 18]

80r Bot now says `þou´, siþen oure Lord is so curteys of his gode | nes and of his gracious giftes so fre, wondre it is þan þat so fewe soules as it semiþ in reward of þe multitude of oþer, mowen comen to þis reformyng in felyng. It semiþ þat he were daungerous, and þat [it] is not soþ or þat he toke no rewarde at his creatures, þe whilk be takyng of faiþ arn becomen `his´ seruauntes.

Vnto þis I may answeren and seien as me þinkeþ þat on enchesoun is þis. Manye men þat arn reformed in faiþ setten not þaire hertes for to profiten in grace, ne for to seken none heiȝere state of gode lifyng þurȝ bisy trauaile in prayng and þinkyng and oþer bodyly and gostly wirkyng; bot hem þinke it inowȝ to hem to kepe hemself oute of dedly syn, for to stonde stille in þat pliȝt as þei arn in. For þei seien þat is

RAsALdPlTW in] þe *add.* H_7 þe] *one-word canc. seq. in* H_7 2 þis] *om.* M 4 now seist þou] þow sayst þanne H_5WsT `þou´ $H^c$ his] *om.* Cc 5 it[1]] *om.* Sr þan] *om.* A þat] is *add.* Ld 6 moun] `not´ *add.* Cc þis] þe LB_3PH_6 7 in] faiþ and in *add.* H_5Ws þat[1]] as *add.* H_5Ws þat[2]] H_7RBLB_3AsSrLwA Hu_2EPH_6CcMPlTW, it *add.*, *canc.* H, it *add.* H_5WsChLd, quod Lat. 8 or] ouþer A, and H_6 at] H_7RH_5LAsSrWsChHu_2CcMLdPl, of BLB_3LwAEPH_6TW, to Ws by takynge] bitakyng RL, ben taken M 9 of] on M, þe *add.* RAsAPl 10 þat . . . þis] *om.* B_3 on] a A encheson] cause SrAH_6CcLd, resoun Hu_2 11 þis] *om.* Sr men] *canc.* Lw, *om.* W setten] sentten W herte] H_7RLB_3AsSrAEPH_6CcPl, hertes HBH_5WsChLwHu_2MLdTW, corda Lat. for] *om.* H_6Cc 12 ne] noþer Hu_2 seken] fele T none] no SrAE heyghere] grace nor *add.* M state] estate W of] in A lyfynge] likyng M, *om.* Cc 13 preynge] prayere RAsPl bodily] *one-letter canc. prec.* H_7 14 `it´ B_3 inogh to hem] hem inowȝ LB_3P to[1]] for As for] *om.* H_6 to kepe] *rep.*, *canc.* H hem fro] H_7RLB_3AsSrEPH_6CcMPl, hem out of A, hemself oute of HBH_5WsChLwHu_2LdTW 15 for[1]] $H_7RHBH_5LB_3$AsSrWsChLwAEPLdPl, and *prec.* Hu_2H_6CcMTW in[1]] on B plyte] degre and state Hu_2 as] þat H_5WsHu_2T in[2]] *om.* RAs For . . . þat] *om.* As

þat it is inogh for hem for to ben sauf and han þe lest degre in heuene; þei wil coueyten no more. þus perchaunce don sum of þe chosen soules þat leden in þe werd actyf lyfe; and þat is litel wondre of hem,
f. 61^{v} for þei arn so occupied with werdly | besynes þat neden to be don þat þei moun not fully setten her herte for to profyten in gostly werkynge. And neuerþeles it is perylous to hem, for þei fallen out and in alday, and arn now vp and now down, and moun not come to stablenes of gode lyfynge. Neuerþeles þei arn sumwhat excusable for here state of lyfynge. Bot oþer men and wummen þat arn fre fro werdly besynessis if þei willen and moun han here nedful sustenaunce withouten grete bodily besynes, as speciali religious men and wummen moun þat bynden hemself to þe state of perfeccion by takynge of religion, and oþer men also in seculere state þat han mikel reson and grete kyndly witte and mighten if þei wolden disposen hem þerto: þese men arn more for to blamen for þat þei standen stille as þei weren ydel, and wil not profyten in grace ne no ferther seken for to come to þe blisse and to þe knowynge of God.

For sothly it is perylous to a soule þat is reformed only in feith and wil no more seken ne profyten ne ȝife him besily to bodili and gostly trauaile; for he may so lyghtly lese þat he hath and fallen aȝeyn to dedly synne. For a soule may not standen stil alwey in on state whyl þat it is in þe flesch, for it is eyþer profytend in grace or elles payrend in synne. For it fareth be him as it doth if a man were drawen out of a foule pytte, and whan he were vp he wuld no ferþer gon þan þe pyttis brynke. Sothly he were a mykel fole, for a lytel puff of wynde or an

16 þat it] H$_7$H$_5$LB$_3$AsSrWsLwAPPlTW, that `it´ Cc, þat HBChHu$_2$, it REH$_6$MLd for] *om.* Pl sauf] saued Ld han] þay *prec.* RAs, to *prec.* H$_6$ degre] gre B in] of Ch heuene] for to ben saf *add.* Cc, and *add.* H$_6$ 17 more] maius premium Lat. perchaunce] perauenture M of þe] *om.* As þe] þes Ld, *om.* M chosen soules] *rev.* Ld 18 leden] lyuen BLB$_3$PH$_6$, ducunt Lat. þe] þis LB$_3$PH$_6$CcM, *om.* H$_5$ is] a *add.* ChHu$_2$ 19 werdly besynes] bisines of þe wordle H$_5$Ws werdly] *om.* B$_3$ besynes] bysenesses R neden] H$_7$RLB$_3$AsSrAPPl, nediþ HBH$_5$WsChLwHu$_2$EH$_6$CcMLdTW 20 herte] H$_7$RLB$_3$AsSrAEPH$_6$CcPl, hertes HBH$_5$WsChLwHu$_2$MLdTW, corda Lat. for to] to LB$_3$P 21 And neuerþeles] ȝet Cc perylous/to hem] *rev.* M out and in] *rev.* Sr, ofte and B$_3$H$_6$, often and LP and in/alday] *rev.* H$_5$Ws `and in´ W$^G$, *canc.* Lw, *om.* W 22 and[2]] *om.* R stablenes] þe *om.* LwLdW 23 Neuerþeles . . . lyfynge] *om.* ALd Neuerþeles] But As, And ȝet Cc sum`what´ Cc, sum del H$_5$Ws for] of LB$_3$PH$_6$ state] astate W 24 fre] fer AM besynessis] H$_7$, bisynes, solicitudinibus Lat. 25 þei] moun *add.*, *canc.* L willen] wolde Pl nedful] bodili Ld 26 as speciali] (as *canc.*) specyaly as Lw, *rev.* W, as arn specialy H$_5$Ws speciali] in *prec.* E and wummen] *om.* A moun] *om.* H$_5$Ws 27 religion] þe *prec.* RAs 28 also] and women *add.* Cc in] of T state] estate EM mikel] grete Hu$_2$ and] in LwW grete] *om.* M 29 if] and E ⌜þerto . . . standen (l. 30)⌝ L þerto] þer to `come to mikel grace´ H$^c$, þerto `and´ come to mych grace Lw, there to come to moche grace W, ad bonam vitam Lat. men] me A, and

inowȝ to hem for to be sauf and han þe leste degre in heuen; þei wile coueiten no more. Þus perchaunce don summe of þe chosen soules þat leden in þe werld actife lif; and þat is litil wonder of hem, for þei are so occupied with worldly bisynys þat nediþ for to be don þat þei mowen not fully setten here hertes for to profiten in gostly wirkyng. And nerþeles it is perilous to hem, for þei fallen out and in alday, and arn now vp and now doun, and mowen not come to stabilnes of gode lifyng. Nerþeles þei arn sumwhat excusable for here state of lifyng. Bot oþer men and wymmen þat arn fre fro worldly bisynes if þe `wilen´ and mowen haue here nedful sustenance withouten grete bodily bisynes, as specialy religious men and wymmen mowen þat bynden hemself to þe state of perfeccioun by takyng of religioun, and oþer men also in seculer state þat han mikel resoun and grete kyndely wit and miȝten if þei wolden disposyn hem þerto: þese men are more
80v for to blame for þat þei stonden stille as þei were ydel and wil `not´ | profiten in grace ne no ferþer seken for to come to þe luf and þe know`ynge´ of God.

For soþly it is perilous to a soule þat is reformed only in faiþ and wil no more seken ne profiten ne ȝifen hym bisyly to bodily and gostly trauaile; for he may so liȝtly lese þat he haþ and fallen agayn to dedly syn. For a soule may not stonde stille alwey in on stat while þat it is in þe flesche, for it is eiþer profitend in grace or peirynde in synne. For it fariþ by hym as it doþ by a man þat were drawen out of a pitt, and whan he were vp he w`o´lde no ferþer gon þan þe pyttes brynke. Soþly he were a mikel fool, for a litel puf of wynde or an vnwarly

women *add.* Cc 30 `for´ Sr, *om.* ACcPlW þat] *om.* AMPlW 31 profyten] *om.* Cc no ferther seken] in no ferthyr seekyng LwW ferther] fer A blisse] H_7, luf Σ, dileccionem Lat. 32 to þe] $H_7RLB_3AsPH_6CcPl$, þe $HBH_5WsChLwHu_2ELdW$, *om.* SrAMT God] oure lord *prec.* Hu_2 33 sothly] $H_7HBH_5B_3LwsChLwAEPH_6MLdW$, soth $RAsSrHu_2PlT$, truly Cc, absque dubio Lat. `it´ Cc and] si Lat. 34 ne[1]] *om.* LwW ne[2]] and A him besily] *om.* LB_3PH_6 him] hem As, *om.* H_5Ws bodili/and/gostly trauaile] *rev.* Sr bodily and] *om.* LwW 35 so] ful E lese] leeuen RAsAPl hath] was M aȝeyn] *om.* LB_3PH_6Pl to] vnto T 36 dedly] *om.* Lat. standen stil/alwey] *rev.* T alwey] alle Lw whyl þat] as long as Hu_2 37 it] H_7HRBH_5As-$SrWsChLwHu_2ECcLdPlTW$, he LB_3APH_6M in[1] . . . eyþer] *om.* Lw flesch] fleisshly body Hu_2 it is[2]/eyþer] *rev.* T or] oþer H_5, eiþer Sr elles] $H_7RLB_3AsAEPH_6CcMPl$, *om.* $HBH_5WsChLwHu_2LdTW$, eiþer Sr payrend] enpeyrend RAsPl, apeyrynge BAH_6Cc 38 synne] and þerfore it nedith hym þat he be ay [euer APl, *om.* As] besy *add.* RAsAPl, mortali culpa Lat. if a man] $H_7RLB_3AsSrAEPCcMPl$, by a man þat $HBH_5WsChLwHu_2LdTW$, by a man H_6, sicut de homine Lat. were] is M, *om.* Lat. drawen] drawande Pl 39 foule] $H_7RLB_3AsSrEPH_6CcMPl$, *om.* $HBH_5WsChLw$-AHu_2LdTW, turpi Lat. and whan he] qui Lat. wuld] wil H_5Ws þan þe pyttis brynke] set supra ipsam putei ripam stare Lat. 40 Sothly] truly Cc mykel] gret H_5WsAHu_2T, *om.* Cc for] Forwhi Sr an] *om.* Cc vnwarly sterynge of himself schuld kast him doun ageyn wers þan he was before. Neuerþeles if he fle fro þe brynke as fer as he may and go forth on þe erthe, þan þogh þer come a grete storme he is þe more syker, for he falleth not ageyn in þe pitte. Ryght so gostly, he þat is drawen out of þe pitte of synne þurgh reformynge of feith, and whan he is out of dedly synne he þenkeþ him syker inogh, and þerfor he wil not profyten bot wille halden him stil as he is by þe pittes brynke as nere as he may; sothly he is not wyse, for at þe lest temptacion of þe f. 62[r] enemy or | of his flesch he falleth into synne aȝeyn. Bot neuerþeles if he fle fro þe pitte, þat is if he sette his herte fully for to come to more grace and for to trauaile besily how he may come þerto, and gif him hertly to preyinge, þenkynge, and oþer gode werkes doynge, þan þogh grete temptacyons rysen ageyns him he falleth not lyghtly into dedly synne ageyn.

And sothly it is wundre to me þat siþen grace is so gode and so profytable, why a man whan he hath bot a lytel þerof, ȝa, so lytel þat he myght no lesse han, þat he wil seyn: Hoo! I wil no more of þis, for I hafe inogh, when I se a werdly man, þogh he haue of werdly gode mikel more þan him nedeþ, ȝet he wil neuer seyn: Hoo! I haue inogh, I wil no more of þis. Bot he wil ay coueyten more and more, and trauaile alle `his´ wyttes and al his myghtes, and neuer wil stynten of his coueytyse til he may haue more. Mikel more þan schuld a chosen soule coueyten gostly gode, for þat is aylastand and makeþ a soule blissed, and he neuer schuld sessen of his ȝernynge if he did wel, gete

41 vnwarly] vnwardly Ch, vnwardely Pl, vnware LB$_3$EPH$_6$ sterynge] meuyng Hu$_2$ schuld] H$_7$RLB$_3$AsSrAEPH$_6$MPl, myth Cc, sone *add.* HBH$_5$WsChLwHu$_2$ELdTW, posset . . . faciliter Lat. wers] happely *prec.* Hu$_2$, peius et profundius Lat. 42 þe] pittes *add.* T `as he´ Cc and . . . erthe (l. 43)] *om.* Lat. and] *rep.* A go] goþ H$_5$Ws 43 on] vpon T grete storme] magnus ventus et validus Lat. þe[2]] *om.* LB$_3$PM 44 for . . . not] that he shal nout fallyn Cc ageyn] H$_7$LB$_3$EPH$_6$Cc, *om.* HRBH$_5$AsSrWsChLwAHu$_2$MLdPlTW, iterum Lat. in] into T pitte] pyne M 45 of[1]] in ChHu$_2$CcLd, in Lat. 46 `is[2]´ Cc of] þe pyt of *add.* Cc he[2]] H$_7$HRBH$_5$AsSrWsChLwHu$_2$EH$_6$LdPlTW, him LB$_3$APCcM him] hem Ch, hymself W, *om.* M he wil] *rev.* A, hym willeþ M he[3]] *om.* RAs 47 not] to *add.* M bot] he *add.* ECc wille halden] holdeþ Sr wille] H$_7$RLB$_3$AsAEPH$_6$Cc, wold Pl, *om.* HBH$_5$SrWsChLwHu$_2$MLdTW `as he is´ B$_3$, *om.* SrA 48 as he may] *om.* Lat. sothly] But truly Cc `not´ Cc lest] laste M þe[2]] his W 49 his] the Cc falleth] may falle E into] in H$_6$ Bot] *om.* Cc 50 fle] wyl *prec.* Cc, fleeþ B sette] wole *prec.* Cc his herte/fully] *rev.* A, in corde suo plene Lat. more] *om.* Sr 51 for . . . gif] laboret . . . occupet Lat. for] þerfor Ld, *om.* E may] myth Cc 52 preyinge . . . doynge] orationibus, meditacionibus, et aliis bonis operibus Lat. preyinge] prayer Cc þenkynge] *om.* Cc and] or M werkes] dedis AMT doynge] worchynge Pl þan] H$_7$RBLB$_3$AsSrChAHu$_2$EPH$_6$CcMLdPl, And *prec.* M, *om.*

stiryng of hymself suld sone keste hym doun agayn wers þan he was bifore. Nerþeles if he fle fro þe brynke as fer as he may and go forþ on þe erþ, þan þawȝ þer come a grete storme he is þe more siker, for he fallიþ not in þe put. Riȝt so gostly, he þat is drawen out of þe pitt of synne þurwȝ reformyng of faiþ, and whan he is out of dedly syn he þinkiþ hym siker inowȝ, and þerfore he wil not profiten bot halden hym stylle as he is be þe pittes brynke, als nere as he may: soþly he is not wise, for at þe leste temptacioun of þe enemy or of his flesch he falliþ into syn agayn. Bot nerþeles if he flee fro þe put, þat is if he sette his herte fully for to come to more grace and for to trauaile bisily how he may come þerto, and gif him hertly to preynge, þinkynge, and oþer gode werkes doynge, þawȝ grete temptaciouns risen ageyns hym he falliþ not liȝtly to dedly synne ageyn.

And soþly it is wonndre to me þat seþen grace is so good and so
1r profitable, whi a man whan he haþ bot a litel þerof, | ȝe, so litel þat he miȝt no lesse han, þat he wil saien: Hoo! I wil no more of þis, for I haue inowȝ. Whan I see a werdly man, þawȝ he haue of werdly gode mikil more þan hym nediþ, ȝit he wil neuer saien Hoo! I haue inow, I wil [no] more of þis. Bot he wil ai coueiten more and more, and trauaillen alle his wittes and his miȝtes, and neuer wil stynten of his coueitise til he may haue more. Mikel more þan schude a chosen soule coueiten goostly goode þat is aylastand and makeþ a soule blissed, and he neuer schuld cesen of his coueitynge if he ded wel, gete what he

HH$_5$WsLwTW, tunc Lat. 53 rysen] arisen H$_5$WsT him] hem Cc into] H$_7$, vnto Sr, to HRBH$_5$LB$_3$AsWsChLwAHu$_2$EPH$_6$CcMLdPlTW, in graue peccatum . . . seu mortale Lat. 55 is[1]] no *add.*, *canc.* B$_3$ so[1]] *om.* B$_3$ gode and so] *om.* E 56 why] whyle Ch, whan Hu$_2$ \`whan he´ Ch, *om.* Hu$_2$ bot a] so Cc a] H$_7$HBH$_5$LB$_3$WsLwAPH$_6$CcLdPlTW, *om.* RAsSrChHu$_2$EM þerof] *om.* T so lytel] *om.* Cc 57 myght] auȝte Ld he[2]] *om.* Cc wil] wold Pl Hoo . . . þis/I . . . inogh] *rev.* Lat. for] *om.* E 58 I se] *om.* E of] þe *add.* H$_6$, *om.* T gode] godis H$_5$Ws 59 mikel] *om.* A he wil] *rev.* H$_6$ 60 no] *om.* H of þis] *om.* Cc Bot . . . more[2]] *om.* Lat. he wil/ay] *rev.* Hu$_2$ ay] H$_7$HRH$_5$LAsWsChLwPCcW, euere BB$_3$AHu$_2$EH$_6$MPl, euermore Ld, alwey SrT ay coueyten] *rev.* E and[2]] euere *add.* Ld 61 trauaile] labir Hu$_2$, þerfor *add.* H$_6$, with *add.* T \`his[1]´ *marg.*, *plummet* H$_7$ al] H$_7$B, *om.* Σ his[2]] *om.* E stynten] sese Hu$_2$ 62 til] whil ET, þat *add.* H$_5$Ws haue] no Cc, no *add.* H$_5$AsWsW more] and *add.* M Mikel . . . myght (l. 65)/For . . . gretely (l. 66)] *rev.* Lat. schuld/a . . . soule] *rev.* M a . . . soule] soulis Pl 63 for] H$_7$BChHu$_2$Ld, *om.* Σ \`is´ L aylastand] H$_7$HRH$_5$LAsWsChP, euerelastynge BLB$_3$LwAHu$_2$EH$_6$MLdPlTW, alwey lastynge Sr 64 he . . . ȝernynge/if . . . wel] *rev.* Hu$_2$ neuer schuld] H$_7$HRBH$_5$LWsChLwAHu$_2$EPMPlTW, *rev.* B$_3$AsSrH$_6$CcLd his] þis Hu$_2$ ȝernynge] H$_7$RLB$_3$PH$_6$Pl\`T^{G}W^G´, coueitynge HBH$_5$SrWsChLwEMLdTW, couettise As, gostly coueitise Hu$_2$, labour Cc gete] for to *prec.* H$_5$Ws, to *prec.* Cc

what he gete myght. For he þat most coueyteþ most schal haue; and sothly if he dyde þus he schuld profyten and wexen in grace gretely.

Anoþer encheson also of þe same, and how wilful bodily custumys vndiscretly rewarded and vsed sumtyme hyndren soules fro felynge of more grace. Capitulum xix[m]

Anoþer encheson is þis: sum men þat arn reformed in feith in þe bygynnynge of here turnynge to God setten hemself in a certeyn manere of doynge, wheþer it be bodily or gostly, and þenken for to kepyn ay þat maner of werkynge forth and not for to chaunge it for non oþer þat cometh þurgh grace, þogh it were bettre. For þe wenen þat þat doynge schuld be best for hem alwey for to holden; and þerfore þei resten hem þerin, and þurgh custome þei bynden hem so þerto þat whan þei han fulfilled it þei þenken hem wondere wel esed,
f. 62v for þei wene þat þei han don a grete | þyng to God. And perchaunce if it fal þat þei ben lettyd fro hire custome, þogh it be for a skilful cause, þei ben heuy and angry and han troblynge of conscience, as if þei had don a grete dedly synne. Þese men hyndren hemself sumwhat fro felynge of more grace, for þei setten here perfeccion in a bodily werk, and so þei make an ende in þe myddys of þe weye where non ende is.

For why, bodily customes þat men vsen ferst in here bygynnynge are gode, bot þei arn bot menes and weyes ledend a soule to perfeccion; and þerfore he þat setteþ his perfeccyon in bodily werke, or in ony gostly werke þat he feleth in þe bygynnynge of his turnynge to God, þat he wil no ferþer sekyn, bot ay resten þerin, he hyndreth himself gretely. For it is a simple crafte þat a prentys is ay

65 what] that Cc coueyteþ/. . ./schal haue] *rev.* Lat, *followed by* et ab huiusmodi desiderio non cessare, adquirat quod adquirere valeat (*see* 18/59–62 and trauaile . . . haue more) 66 sothly] sekir Cc he (*bis*)] þey H$_5$Ws dyde] do Cc wexen] encresyn Cc in grace/gretely] *rev.* H$_6$ in] into A gretely] *om.* SrCc

Chapter 19 *title*: H$_7$RLB$_3$AsSrAEPH$_6$MLdPlTW, *om.* HBH$_5$WsChLwHu$_2$Cc 1 Anoþer] And *prec.* M encheson] cause SrAH$_6$ also] H$_7$RAsAEMLdPlTW *om.* LB$_3$SrEPH$_6$ same] whi *add.* M wilful] wilfully M 2 custumys] custom LB$_3$EPH$_6$ hyndren] hyndriþ H$_6$ 3 more] *om.* M 4 encheson] cause SrAH$_6$, cause or enchesoun T; resoun Hu$_2$ is] þere *prec.* T þis] H$_7$RLB$_3$AsLw`H^c′AEPH$_6$CcMPlW, *om.* H°BH$_5$SrWsChHu$_2$LdT, ista Lat. sum] tyme *add.*, *canc.* L þat] *om.* Cc in[2]] at M 6 wheþer] were Ch þenken] purpose hem Hu$_2$ for to kepen/ay] H$_7$RBLB$_3$AsChA-Hu$_2$PCcLdPl, *rev.* HH$_5$SrWsLwEH$_6$TW, euyr for to kepe euer [euer[2] *canc.*] Lw for to kepen] *om.* CcM for] *om.* EH$_6$ 7 ay] H$_7$HRBH$_5$LAsWsLwHu$_2$PCcT, euere B$_3$ChAEH$_6$MPlW, alwey SrLd of werkynge] *om.* APl of] *om.* H$_5$SrWs werkynge forth] *rev.* LB$_3$EP, continue obseruare Lat. and . . . it] *om.* Hu$_2$ `it′ L 8 þat . . . grace] *om.* AMPl 9 þat þat] þat BLwE for hem/alwey] *rev.* B$_3$ for[1]] to H$_6$ alwey

gete miȝte. For he þat most coueitiþ most schal haue; and soþly if he did þus he schulde profiten and waxen in grace gretly.

[CHAPTER 19]

Anoþer enchesoun is: summe men þat arn reformed in faiþ in þe bygynnynge of her turnyng to God setten hemself in a certeyn maner of doyng, wheþer it be bodily or gostly, and þenken ay for to kepe þat maner of wirkyng forþ and not for to chaungen it for non oþer þat comiþ þurw grace, þaw⸢ȝ⸣ it were better. For þei wenen þat þat doyng schuld ben best for hem alwey for to holden; and þerfor þei resten hem þerin, and þorw custome þei bynden hem so þerto, þat whan þei haue fulfillid it þei þinken hem wondre wel esed, for þei wenen þat þei han don a grete þinke to God. And perchaunce if it falle þat þei be letted fro þaire custome, þaw⸢ȝ⸣ it be for a skilful cause, þei ben heuy and angry and han troblyng of conscience, as if þei had done a grete dedly synne. Þese men hyndren hemself sumwhat fro felyng of more grace, for þei setten here perfeccioun in a bodily werk, and so þei make an ende in þe middes of þe wey where none ende is.

1v For whi, bodily customus þat men vse in her | bigynnynge are gode, bot þei are bot menes and weies ledynde a soule to perfeccioun; and þerfor he þat settes his perfeccioun in a bodily werk, or in a gostly werk þat he feliþ in þe bygynnynge of his turnynge to God, and he wil no ferrer seken bot ay resten þerin, he hyndreþ hymself gretly. For it is a symple craft þat a prentise is ay ilike wise in, and þat kan on þe

. . . holden] continuare Lat. alwey] *om.* M for[2]] *om.* B_3 10 þei[1]] þei⸢y⸣ H_7 þei[2]] *om.* Cc hem[2]] hym Ch so þerto] *rev.* RAsCcM \`so´ A, *om.* Ld 11 þat] so *prec.* E þei[1]] þe Pl wondere wel] wondyrfull Lw, wondrely wele T, wonderly W esed] quietatos Lat. 12 þat] *om.* A don . . . þyng] obsequium perstitisse Lat. don] *om.* Pl 13 fal] befalle Sr hire] þe T a skilful] *rev.* Lw 14 and[1]] *om.* B_3 han] *om.* E if] þow BAM 15 dedly] *om.* T men] folk H_6 fro] þe *add.* Sr 16 felynge . . . grace] *om.* H_6 felynge] sensacione seu adquisicione Lat. þei . . . vsed (l. 35)] *om.* R þei setten here] he settith his AsAPl 17 þei make] *rev.* Cc, he maketh AsAPl ⸢ende⸣ L, heed B_3 þe[1]] *om.* H_6 non] no E 18 why] *om.* AsAMPl ferst] H_7\`L´$B_3$AsSrEP$H_6$CcMPl, *om.* HB$H_5$WsChLwA$Hu_2$LdTW here] þe Sr bygynnynge] of his turnynge to God *add.*, *canc.* H 19 gode . . . arn] *om.* AMPl þei . . . bot] *om.* Ch$Hu_2$ and weyes] *om.* A a] þe A 20 þerfore] *om.* A \`setteþ´ Sr, sayth W bodily] H_7, a *prec.* Σ 21 or . . . werke[2]] *om.* T ony] H_7LB_3SrEPH_6Cc, a HBH_5AsWsChLwAHu_2MLdPlW þat] and HAsLwW, et Lat. 22 no] not Ld ay] H_7HH_5LAsWsChPCc; euere BB_3LwAEH_6-MPlTW; alwey SrLd; stil Hu_2 23 þat] þere As a prentys] apprentise LCc ay] H_7HChCcM, euere BH_5AsWsLwA$Hu_2$$H_6$PlTW, alwei L$B_3$SrEPLd

ilyk wys in, and þat kan on þe ferst day as mikel of it as he kan twenty ȝere after; or elles if þe crafte be gode and sutyl, he is of a dul wytte or ellis of an ylle wil þat he profyteþ not þerin. Bot þan is it soþ þat of al craftes þat arn, þe seruice of God is most souereyn and þe most sotyl, þe heyghest and hardest for to come to þe perfeccion of it, and also it is most profytable and most of wynnynge to him þat may sothfastly performe it. And þerfore it semeþ þat þe prentys of it þat is ay ilyke ferforth in þe lerynge oþer is dul witted or ellys il willed.

I reproue not þese customs þat men vsen in þe state of begynnynge, wheþer þei ben bodily or gostly, for I sey þat þei arn ful gode and spedful to hem for to vsen. Bot I wold þat þei helden hem not bot as a weye and an entre toward gostly felynge, and þat þei vsed þem as a couenable mene vntil bettre come, and þat þei in vsynge of it coueyted aftere bettre. And þan if bettre come þat were more gostly and more drawend in þe þoght fro fleschlynes and fro þe sensualyte and veyn ymaginacions and þat schuld be lettyd because of þer wilful custome, þat þei lefe þan here custom whan it may be lefte withouten sklaundre or disese of oþer, and folwe þat þei felen; bot if neyþer lette oþer, þan
f. 63^r þat þei vse boþe if þat þei may. I mene not of customs nedful þurgh | bonde of laghe, or of rewle, or of penance, bot of oþer wilfully taken. þus techeþ þe prophete in þe Sautre sayend þus: *Etenim benediccionem*

24 ilyk H_7HWsPlT, ylyche BLd, eliche E, in lyche M, alike LAPCc, alich H_6, like ChLwHu$_2$W, lyche H_5B_3 wys] sapiens . . . vel sciens Lat. in and] *om.* A þat kan] in qua tam expertus est et sapiens Lat. þat] *om.* SrPl kan on] knowe Cc kan] kannyth Lw on . . . day/as mikel] *rev.* Sr on] *om.* Ld of it] þerof Sr of] on H_5 kan^2] schulde Cc twenty] thyrty W 25 ȝere] ȝeeres As, wynter M and sutyl] *om.* APl a] *om.* E 26 ylle] H_7Pl, yuel HRBH_5LB_3AsSrWsChLwAHu$_2$EPH_6CcMLdTW wil] wit M he] H_7H_6, *om.* Σ Bot] B- *prec.*, *canc.* Sr is it] H_7HBLB_3AsSrWsChLwAHu$_2$EPH_6M, *rev.* H_5CcLdPlTW þat^2] *om.* H_5WsChAHu$_2$ 27 þat arn] *om.* T þe^1] longing to *prec.* B_3 is] arn B_3 most] þe *prec.* AsACcPl souereyn] sotil *prec.*, *canc.* B_3 and] *corr. from* in Lw, *om.* M þe^2] H_7HBH_5AsSrWsChLwHu$_2$MLdPlTW, *om.* LB_3AEPH_6Cc 28 þe heyghest] *om.* Lat. þe] an M and^1] *om.* LB_3PH_6 hardest] H_7HBLwMPlW, þe *prec.* H_5LB_3AsSrWsChAHu$_2$EPH_6CcLdT, crafte is *add.* E for] *om.* Pl þe^2] *om.* H_5WsAH_6 of it] þerof Sr, *om.* BLd 29 is] *om.* W most^1 . . . it (l. 30)] maxime lucratiua et vtilis petenti in ea perfecte et veraciter laborare Lat. of] oft H, *om.* H_6 soþfastly] truly Hu$_2$ 30 it semiþ] *om.* Ws prentys] H_7H_5LB_3WsAEPH_6CcPl, apprentys As, prentises HBSrChLwHu$_2$MLdTW, apprehenticus Lat. of it þat] þerof Sr of it] þerof A is] H_7LB_3AsAEPH_6CcPl, arn HBH_5SrWsChLwHu$_2$MLdTW, proficit Lat. ay] H_7HH_5LWsChAsSrP, euere BB_3LwAHu$_2$EH_6CcMLdPlW, alwey SrT ilyke] H_7HBH_5SrWsLwAEPlW, iliche T, liche Ld, like LB_3AsChHu$_2$PM, alich H_6, alyke wys and alyke Cc 31 lerynge] H_7HH_5AsWs, lernynge BLB_3SrChLwAHu$_2$EPH_6CcMLdPlTW, of yt *add.* Cc oþer] or As is] H_7A, he is LB_3AsEPH_6Cc, *rev.* Pl, arn HBChLwHu$_2$MLdW, þey are H_5SrWs, are they T dul witted] of dul wit M witted] *om.* A ellys] *om.* M il] H_7LP, yuel HRBH_5B_3AsSrWsChLwAHu$_2$EH_6CcMLdPlTW 32 I] ne *add.* M þese] þe AsAPl, *om.* M þat men] of men þat þei *add.* As of] here *add.* AsT begynnynge] incipiencium Lat. 33 for] set Lat. I sey

first day as mikel of it as he kan twenti wyntur aftur; or elles if þe craft be gode and sotile he is of a dul wit or elles of an yuel wille þat profitiþ not þerin. Bot þan is it soþ þat of alle craftes þat are, þe seruice of God is most soueren and þe most sotiþ þe heiȝeste and hardist for to come to þe perfeccioun of it, and also it is most profitable and most oft wynnynge to hym þat may soþfastly performe it. And þerfore it semiþ þat þe prentises of it þat arn ay ilike fer forþ in leryng eiþer arn dul witted or elles yuel willed.

I reprofe not þese customes þat men vsen in þe stat of bygynnynge, wheþer þei be bodily or gostly, for I say þat þei arn ful gode and spedful for hem for to vsen. Bot I wolde þat þei helden hem not bot as a wey and an entre toward gostly felyng, and þat þei vsed hem as a couenable mene til better come, and þat þei in þe vsynge of hem coueitid after better. And þan if better come þat were more gostly and more drawend in þe þouȝt fro fleschlynes and fro þe sensualite and vayn ymaginacioun and þat schud be letted because of her customus, þat þei lefe þan here custome, when it may be left withouten sclaundre or disese of oþer and folo þat þei felen. Bot if neiþer lette oþer, þan þat þei vse boþ if þei may. I mene not of customes nedful þurȝ bonde of lawe, or of rewle, or of penaunce, bot of oþer wilfuly taken. þus techiþ vs þe prophet in þe Sauter saieng þus: *Etenim*

þat] *om.* E þat] *om.* M ful gode/and/spedful] *rev.* ChHu$_2$ ful] for þat tyme AsPl, for þe tyme AM, *om.* Ld 34 to^1] H$_7$H$_5$LB$_3$AsSrWsAEPH$_6$PlT, for HBChLwHu$_2$CcMLdW 35 vsed] H$_7$HRBLB$_3$SrLwEPH$_6$CcLdPlW, vse H$_5$AsWsChAHu$_2$MT, vterentur Lat, R *back.* as] *om.* L a] *om.* RAsAPl 36 couenable mene] mediis conuenientibus Lat. couenable] conuenient Cc mene] menus A, in conable tyme Cc vntil] H$_7$LSrEPH$_6$Cc, vnto RB$_3$AsPl, til HBH$_5$SrWsChLwAHu$_2$MLdTW, þat *add.* A bettre] a *prec.* H$_5$B$_3$LwEP and . . . come (l. 37)] *om.* Ld vsynge] H$_7$RH$_5$LB$_3$AsWsAEPH$_6$PlW, þe *prec.* HBSrChLwHu$_2$CcMT it] H$_7$RB$_3$AsAPH$_6$CcPl, hem HBH$_5$WsChLwHu$_2$EMTW, earum Lat. coueyted] coueite WsMT 37 And] *om.* M if] a *add.* LB$_3$EPH$_6$ þat] and A, *om.* M 38 fleschlynes] flesshsly lykyngis RAs, fleyshly lustis Cc fro^2] of Cc `þe' Lw, *om.* M and$^2$] of M 39 ymaginacions] H$_7$CcPl, ymaginacioun Σ, ymaginacione Lat. and þat] if they Cc and] yf LwMTW, ȝif *add.* H$_6$ þer] oþir LB$_3$PPl wilful] H$_7$RLB$_3$AsSrAEPH$_6$CcPl`T^{G}W^G', *om.* HBH$_5$WsChLwHu$_2$MLdTW, voluntarie Lat. custome] customys SrECcM, consuetudinis Lat. 40 þat þei] they shuld Cc lefe þan] *rev.* H$_6$ custom] customys SrCcM whan] cicius quam Lat. it] þei SrCcM lefte] best H$_6$ sklaundre] disclandir A 41 or disese] *om.* RAsAMPl, vel inquietacione Lat. folwe] fele H$_5$Ws þat þei] *om.* ACcMPl 42 vse] folwe M if] as Cc þat^2] H$_7$RBLB$_3$AsSrAPH$_6$CcMPl, *om.* HH$_5$WsChLwHu$_2$ELdTW þei^2] he APl, þou Cc `may' Lw I . . . taken (l. 43] *om.* AMPl customs] craftes B 43 `bonde' Cc `or^1' L oþer] *om.* H$_5$Ws wilfully] wilful H$_6$ taken] takynge H$_5$Ws 44 techeþ] H$_7$RLB$_3$AsEPH$_6$CcMPl, taȝt A, vs *add.* HBH$_5$SrWsChLwHu$_2$LdTW, docet Lat. in þe Sautre] *om.* Cc þus] Ps. 83° *add.* BLHu$_2$EPLdTW benediccionem] Dominus Cc *dabit legislator: ibunt de virtute in virtutem, et videbitur Deus deorum in Syon.* Sothly þe bryngere of þe laghe schal ȝife his blissynge; þei schal gon fro vertue to vertue, and God of goddys schal be seen in Syon. Þe bryngere of þe laghe; þat is, oure Lord Jesu Criste, schal gyfe his blissynge; þat is, he schal gyfe his gyftes of grace to his chosen soules, callend hem fro synne and ryghtende hem be gode werkys to his lyknes, þurgh whilk grace þei schul profyten and waxen fro vertu to vertu vntil þei come to Syon; þat is, vntil þei come to contemplacion, in þe whilk þei schul see [God of goddis; þat is, þei schul see] wel þat þer is not bot o God, and þei schul see þat þer is noght bot God.

How þat withouten mikel bodily and gostly besynes and wythouten mikel grace of meknes soules moun not be reformed in felynge ne be kept in it whan þei come þerto. Capitulum xx^{m}

Now seyst þou, syn it is so þat reformynge in feith is so logwe and so perylous for to resten in bycause of drede of fallynge ageyn to dedly synne, and reformynge in felynge is so heygh and so syker, whoso might come þerto: þan coueytes þu for to wyten what maner trauaile were most spedful for to vsen by þe whilk a man myght profyten in and come þerto, or if þer were ony certeyn trauelle or speciale dede by þe whilk a man might come to þat grace and to þat reformynge in felynge.

As vnto þis, I sey þus: þou wost wel what man or wumman wil disposen him for to come to clennes of herte and to felynge of grace, hem behoueth hafe mikel trauaile and grete feyghtynge in wil and in

45 et] H_7LB_3AsSrAEPH_6CcMPl, etc. R, *om.* HBH_5WsChLwLdTW videbitur . . . Syon] *om.* R videbitur] donec *prec.* Hu_2 deorum] eorum T 46 Sothly] H_7RLB_3AsSrAPPl, þat is *prec.* HBH_5WsChLwHu_2EH_6CcMLdTW his] H_7H°BLB_3SrChAHu_2EPH_6CcMLdT, *canc.* H, *om.* RH_5AsWsLwAPlW, þe *add.*, *canc.* L blissynge] blessyngis Ld 47 gon] *om.* Cc to] H_7RLB_3AsPH_6CcMPl, into HBH_5Sr-WsChLwAHu_2ELdTW ˋseenˊ Pl 48 þat] *om.* Ws oure Lord] *om.* Sr 49 he] *om.* LB_3P his gyftes of] of his Cc, his LwW soules] *rep.*, *canc.* Pl, and *add.* M 50 callend] clepyng MLd gode] Godis H_5 51 profyten] encrese T to^1] into LdT 52 vntil^1] H_7LEPH_6, til HBH_5SrWsChLwAHu_2CcMLdTW, vnto RB_3AsPl, to Hu_2 vntil þei come^2] *om.* Cc vntil^2] H_7RLEP, til HBH_5SrWsChLwAHu_2H_6MLdTW, vnto B_3AsPl, to E 53 God . . . see] *om.* H_7 God] good H ˋisˊ Pl see wel] *rev.* A 54 not . . . God^1] no God bot on B_3Hu_2 not] H_7HRBAsChLwCcLdˋTˊW, non LEP, *om.* H_5SrWsAH_6MPl and . . . God^2] in whom al goodnesse is inne Cc, *om.* LwTW, et quod ipse omnia est in omnibus Lat.

Chapter 20 *title*: H_7RLB_3AsSrAEPH_6MLdPlTW ˋHowe a man þat will come to perfeccioun moste haue mykyll trauaile and clennes ofe herte.ˊ H^c *om.* BH_5WsCh-LwHu_2Cc 1 mikel] *rep.*, *canc.* Sr 2 of] and TW meknes] of *add.*, *canc.* L

82r *benediccionem dabit legislator: ibunt de virtute in virtutem, vide | bitur Deus deorum in Syon*, þat is: Soþly þe brynger of þe laghe schal gif blessyng; þei schal go fro vertu into vertu, and God of goddis schal be seen in Syon. Þe brynger of þe lawe, þat is oure Lord Ihesu Crist, schal gif his blissynge, þat is, he schal gifen his giftes of grace to his chosen soules, callend hem fro syn and riȝtende hem by gode werkes to his liknes; þurw whilk grace þei schul profiten and waxen fro vertu to vertu til þei come to Syon, þat is til þei come to contemplacioun, in þe whilk þei scul see [God] of goddis; þat is þei schul see wel þat þer is not bot on God, and þei schul see þat þer is not bot God.

[CHAPTER 20]

Now sais þou, siþen it [is so] þat reformyng in faiþ is so lowe and so perilous for to resten in, bicause of dred of fallyng ageyn, and reformyng in felynge is so hiȝe and so siker, whoso miȝte come þerto: þan coueites þou for to witen what maner trauail were most spedful for to vsen be þe whilke a man miȝt profiten in and come þerto, or if þer were ony certen trauaile or speciale dede bi þe whilke a man miȝte come to þat grace and þat reformyng in felynge.

As vnto þis, I say þus: þu wost wel þat what man or womman wol dispose hym for to come to clennes of herte and to felynge of grace, hym bihouiþ haue mikel trauaile and grete feȝtyng in wil and in werke

3 ne . . . þerto] om. Pl be kept] kepe W be] *om* T in it] þerin A it] þat reformyng RAsSrM whan . . . þerto] *om.* As whan] aftir ET, þat *add.* R come] mai LB_3SrAP 5 Now] How Ld it . . . disposynges (l. 24)] *om.* R is so] *rev.* HB, is *canc.* so is Ch 6 for] *om.* H_6 to . . . synne] $H_7LB_3AsAEPH_6CcPl$, *om.* $HBH_5SrWsChLwHu_2MLdTW$, in peccatum mortale Lat. to] into Pl 7 reformynge] þe *prec.* Pl in] of Pl is] *om.* As so heygh] *rev., marked for trsp* . Cc and] *om.* M 8 come þerto] animo *add.* Lat. þan . . . to] I wold Cc þan] þat Pl for] *om.* M maner] $H_7HBH_5AsSrWsChLwACcMLdPlTW$, of *add.* $LB_3Hu_2EPH_6$ trauaile] *om.* As 9 þe] *om.* Pl myght] most *add.* M in] yt *add.* CcM, *om.* BALd 10 were] where Cc `ony´ Pl or] of Sr 11 might] profit and come þerto so þat he miȝt *add.* AsAPl þat[1]] special *add.* E grace . . . reformynge] graciam reformacionis Lat. to[1]] $H_7LB_3AsSrHu_2EPH_6CcMPl$, *om.* $HBH_5WsChLwLdTW$ þat[2]] the Cc 13 As . . . hem (30/79)] *om.* Ws [*one quire missing*] vnto] to ACc wel] $H_7LB_3AsEPH_6Pl$, þat *add.* $HBH_5SrChLwAHu_2CcMLdTW$, quod *add.* Lat. `what´ Cc wil] þat wolde H_5, þat wele H_6 14 him] hem A for] *om.* M to[1]] vnto T to[2]] *om.* Cc 15 hem] $H_7LB_3AsSrChAHu_2PH_6MPl$, him $HBH_5LwECcLdTW$, eum Lat. behoueth] $H_7HBLB_3AsChLwAPPlW$, to *add.* $H_5SrHu_2EH_6CcMLdT$ grete] grace M feyghtynge] felyng Pl in[1] . . . werk] *om.* Lat.

werk lastendly aȝens þe wikked sterynges of alle þe heued synnes. Not only ageyns pride or enuye, bot aȝens al oþer with alle þe spyces þat comen out of hem, as I hafe seyd here beforne in þe ferst partye of þis wrytynge. For why, passions and fleschly desyres letten þe clennes in herte and pees in conscience. And hem behoueth also trauailen for to geten al vertus, not only chastyte and abstenence, bot also pacience and myldnes, charite and meknes, and al þe oþer. And þis may not be f. 63v done | by o maner of werk, bot by diuers werkes and many, after dyuers disposynges of men: as now preyend, now thenkend, now werkend sum gode dede, now assayend hemself in dyuers wyse—in hungre, in þrest, in colde, in suffrynge of schame and despyt if nede be—and in oþer bodily deseses for lofe of vertu and sothfastnes. Þis knowest þu wel, for þis redest þou in euerilk boke þat techeth of gode lyfynge. Þus also seyþ ilk man þat wil stere mans soule to þe lofe of God. And so it semeþ þat þer is no speciale trauaile ne certeyn dede þurgh þe whilk only a soule might come to þat grace, bot principally þurgh grace of oure Lord Jesu and be many dedys and grete in al þat he may don, and ȝit alle is lytil inogh.

And o skil may be þis: for syn oure Lord Jesu himself is special maistre of þis crafte, and also he is special leche of gostly sekenes—for withouten him alle is noght—þerfor it is resonable þat after he steris and techeþ so a man folwe and werk. Bot he is a simple maystire þat kan not kenne his disciple whil he is in lerynge bot ay o lesson, and he is an vnwys leche þat by o medycyne wyl helen al sores. Þerfor oure

16 werk] werkes M lastendly] continually Hu$_2$ þe[1]] H$_7$LB$_3$AsAEPH$_6$CcLdPl, *om.* HBH$_5$SrChLwHu$_2$MTW þe[2]] *om.* As 17 al] H$_7$LB$_3$AsAPH$_6$CcMPl, þe *add.* HBH$_5$SrChLwHu$_2$ELdTW þe] *om.* LwLdW spyces] and braunches *add.* Cc, and circumstaunce *add.* T þat] *om.* H$_5$ 18 out] *rep.*, *canc.* E hafe] *om.* Hu$_2$ here] *om.* H$_6$ beforne] *om.* H$_5$ partye of þis] *om.* LwW 19 why] *om.* CcM and] of B in] of LwMW 20 herte] H$_7$LB$_3$AsSrAPH$_6$CcMPl, þe *add.* HBH$_5$ChLwHu$_2$ELdTW in] and H$_5$ And] thanne *add.* Cc hem behoueth/also] *rev.* H$_5$ hem behoueth] *rev.* SrCc hem] H$_7$LB$_3$AsAHu$_2$EPH$_6$MPl, him HBH$_5$SrChLwCcLdTW, eum Lat. trauailen] for to *prec.* LwW, to *prec.* CcM to geten] getyng of M 21 and] *om.* M 22 and meknes] *om.* As and[2]] also *add.* Ld, *om.* Cc not be done] he not do Ld 23 done by] *om.* Sr of] *om.* M by] *om.* H$_6$ 24 dyuers] H$_7$LB$_3$AsSrAHu$_2$EPH$_6$CcLdPl, sundry HBH$_5$ChLwMTW disposynges] H$_7$BLAsSrChAHu$_2$EPLdPl, disposyng H$_6$CcM, dispositions HH$_5$B$_3$LwTW, disposiciones Lat. of] R *back* preyend] and *add.* M 25 dede] H$_7$RLB$_3$AsAEPH$_6$CcMPl, werk HBH$_5$SrChLwHu$_2$LdTW[G], werkes W hemself] H$_7$HRLB$_3$AsSrChLwAEPH$_6$LdW, hem Cc, himself BH$_5$Hu$_2$MPlT wyse] H$_7$H$_5$LwH$_6$LdPlW, wises HRBChHu$_2$ECcMT, weies LB$_3$AsAP, vicys Sr, diuersimode Lat. in] as *prec.* H$_6$ 26 hungre] H$_7$HBH$_5$ChLwHu$_2$LdTW, and *add.* RLB$_3$AsSrAEPH$_6$CcPl þrest] ferst B, and *add.* H$_6$ in[3]] H$_7$HH$_5$SrChLwHu$_2$MLdTW, and in RAsECcPl, and LB$_3$P and] *om.* R 27 in] *om.* EH$_6$ deseses] H$_7$H$_5$LB$_3$SrEPH$_6$CcMLdT, dises HRBAsChLwAHu$_2$Pl, vexacionibus Lat. lofe] þe *prec.* T and[2]] of *add.* Pl 28 þis] þus BT redest þou] *rev.* AH$_6$ euerilk] ech H$_6$

lastandly agayn wickid stirynges of alle þe heed synnes. Not only ageyns pride or enuye, bot ageyns alle þe oþer with alle þe spices þat comen out of hem, as I haue seide bifore in þe first party of þis wrytyng. For whi, passions and flescly desires letten þe clennes in þe herte and pees in conscience. And hym bihouiþ also trauailen for to geten alle vertues, not only chastite and abstinence, bot also paciens and mildnes, charite and meknes, and alle þe oþer. And þis may not be don by o maner of werk, bot by diuers werkes and many, aftir
82v sundry | disposicions of men: as now preyand, now þinkand, now wirkand summe gode werk, now assaiand hemself in diuerse wises—in hungre, in þrest, in colde, in suffryng of shame and dispite if ned be—and in oþer bodily dises for luf of vertue and soþfastnes. þis knowis þu wel, for þis redis þu in euerilk boke þat techiþ of god lyuyng. þus also saiþ ilk man þat wil stire mens soules to þe luf of God. And so it semiþ þat þer is n[o] special trauail ne certeyn dede þurwȝ þe whilke only a soule miȝte come to þat grace, bot principally þurwȝ grace of oure Lord Ihesu and be many dedis and grete in al þat he may don, and ȝit al is litel inowȝ.

And o skil may be þis: for siþen oure Lord Ihesu himself is special maister of þis craft, and he is special leche of gostly seknes—for wiþouten him al is noȝt—þerfore it is resonable þat aftir þat he techiþ and stiriþ so a man folwe and wirke. Bot he is a symple maister þat can not teche his deciple whiles he is in leryng bot ay o lessoun, and he is an vnwise leche þat bi o medicyne wil hele alle sores. þerfore oure

29 þus also/seyþ] *rev.* Cc þus] And *prec.* H_6 also seyþ] H_7HRBH_5AsChAHu$_2$MLdPlT, *rev.* LB_3SrEPCc also] *om.* LwH_6W ilk] H_7H, ilke a Ch, euery RBH_5LB_3AsSrLwA-Hu$_2$EPH_6CcMPlTW, eche Ld wil] wolde Ld stere] stre R mans soule] H_7RLB_3AsSrAEPH_6CcMPl, mens soules HBH_5ChLwHu$_2$LdTW, animam hominis Lat. 30 it semeþ] *rev.* M no] ne H, non BAs 31 þe] *om.* LwCcW only/a . . . might (21)] *rev.* H_6 þat] *om.* H_6 32 of] or H_5 Jesu] H_7HBH_5SrChLwHu$_2$CcTW, God RAsAMPl, Crist LB_3EPH_6Ld, Jesu Lat. be] thorew RAsAPlW[G], good *add.* Cc, grete *add.* M and grete] *om.* M in] and SrE 33 alle is] it ys al Cc alle] thys *add.* LwW 34 may be] is B_3 syn] as myche as Hu$_2$, *om.* RAsAPl 'Lord' H_6, *om.* Lw Jesu] Crist *add.* B_3Hu$_2$Ld, *om.* BAsAPl 35 and] *rep.* L also] H_7RLB_3AsAEPH_6CcMPl, *om.* HBH_5SrChLwHu$_2$LdTW, eciam Lat. he is] *om.* LB_3EPCc 36 noght] right *prec.* T þerfor/it is] *rev.* LwW after] H_7RLB_3AsAEPH_6CcMPl, þat *add.* HBH_5SrChLwHu$_2$LdTW he] hit M steris and techeþ] H_7RLB_3AsSrAEPH_6CcMPl, *rev.* HBH_5ChLwHu$_2$LdTW 37 techeþ] þat *add.* E man] or a woman *add.* Cc folwe and werk] in opere prosequatur Lat. folwe] schold *prec.* H_5, to *prec.* RAsAMPl, aftir *add.* T and] in *add.* Ld werk] to *prec.* RAsAPl he] hit BM 38 kenne] H_7RLPH_6, knowe M, teche HB$H_5$$B_3$AsSrChLwAHu$_2$ECcLdPlTW his disciple] discipulos suos Lat. disciple] disciples A lerynge] H_7HRH_5AsCh, lernynge BH_5LB_3SrLwAHu$_2$EPH_6CcMLdPlTW, adiscendo Lat. ay] H_7HRLAsChPCc, alwey Sr, euer *rep.*, *canc.* B, euer $H_5$$B_3$LwAHu$_2EH_6$MLdPlTW 39 by] wiþ MT wyl] wenith to A al] maner *add.* H_5

Lord Jesu, þat is so wys and so good, for to schew his wysdom and his godenesse he techeþ sondry lessons to his disciples after þei profyten in here lerynge, and ȝefeþ to sondry soules sondri medicines after þe felynge of here sekenes. And also anoþer skil is þis: if þer were o certeyn dede by þe whilk a soule might come to perfyte lofe of God, þan schuld a man wene þat he might come þerto be his owen werke and þurgh his owen trauaile, as a marchaunt comeþ to his mede by his owen trauaile only and by his werke. Nay, it is not so gostly in þe lufe of God. For he þat wil serue God wysly and come to perfyte lufe of him, he schal coueyten for to hafe non oþer mede þan him only. Bot þan for to han him may no creatoure desserfen only þurgh his owen trauaile; for þogh a man might trauailen bodily and gostly as mikel as alle creatoures þat euer were myghten, he might not deseruen only be f. 64^r his werkes for to hafe | God for his mede. For he is souereyn blisse and endles goodnes, and passeth withouten comparison al mennes desertys; and þerfor he may not be geten be no mans special werke as bodily mede may. For he is fre, and gyfeþ himself where he wil and whan he wil, neyþer for þis werke ne for þat, ne þis tyme ne aftere þat tyme; for þogh a soule werke al þat he kan and may al his lyfe tyme, perfyte lufe of Jesu schal he neuer hafe til oure Lord Jesu wil frely gif it. Neuerþeles on þat oþer syde I sey also, þat I hope þat he ȝifeþ it not bot if a man werke and trauaile al þat he may and kan, ȝa, til him þenkeþ þat he may no more, or ellys be in ful wil þerto if þat he mighte.

And so it semeþ þat neyþer grace only withouten ful werkynge of a

40 Jesu] Cryste *add.* Ld, *om.* RAsAMPl wysdom] wisdomes B$_3$ 41 he] *om.* H$_5$ techeþ] sheweþ As sondry] H$_7$RLB$_3$AsSrAEPH$_6$CcMPl, diuerse BH$_5$B$_3$AHu$_2$MLdPlTW, sere HCh, sere *gl.* diuers Lw after] H$_7$RSrAMPl, þat *add.* HBH$_5$LB$_3$AsChLwHu$_2$EPH$_6$CcLdTW þei profyten] her profit A 42 in] *rep.*, *canc.* Sr lerynge] H$_7$HRH$_5$Ch, lernynge BSrLwAHu$_2$EH$_6$CcMLdTW, lyuynge LB$_3$AsPPl sondry] H$_7$HRBLAsSrChLwEPH$_6$CcM`T$^G$W$^G$´, diuerse H$_5$B$_3$AHu$_2$LdPlTW  sondri] H$_7$RLAsSrEPH$_6$CcM, sere HCh [*gl.* diuers Ch], sere and dyuers LwW, diuerse H$_5$B$_3$AHu$_2$LdPlT [`sere and´ *prec.* T^G] þe felynge] þei feelyn R, þat þei felen As 43 here sekenes] varias . . . infirmitates Lat. ⌜her⌝ H, þe H$_5$ And] *om.* LwW skil] resoun Hu$_2$ if] þat *add.* LB$_3$EPH$_6$ were] be Pl o] any AsW 44 þe] *om.* LB$_3$PH$_6$ to] H$_7$LB$_3$SrPH$_6$M, þe *add.* HRBH$_5$AsChLwAHu$_2$ECcLdTW perfyte] *om.* A God] Jesu M 45 wene] oþer suppose *add.* Ld werke] werkis AsPl 46 þurgh] by H$_5$B$_3$M comeþ] þat *prec.* Hu$_2$ mede] wynnyng Cc 47 owen] one Ld werke] H$_7$RLB$_3$AsSrAPH$_6$Pl, owen *prec.* HBH$_5$ChLwHu$_2$ECcMLdTW, laborem Lat. in] of LB$_3$EPH$_6$ 48 to] H$_7$RH$_5$LB$_3$AsSrLwAPH$_6$PlW, þe *add.* HBChHu$_2$ECcMLdT `lufe´ L 49 him] H$_7$RBLB$_3$AsSrChAHu$_2$EPH$_6$CcMLdPl, God HH$_5$LwTW for] H$_7$RBLB$_3$AsSrChAHu$_2$EPH$_6$CcMLdPl, *om.* HH$_5$LwTW þan H$_7$RLB$_3$AsSrAEPH$_6$CcMPl, bot HBH$_5$ChLwHu$_2$LdTW him only] *rev.* Hu$_2$ 50 him] ipsum in premium Lat. no] non As creatoure] man Cc þurgh] H$_7$RLB$_3$AsAEPH$_6$CcPl, bi

Lord Ihesu, þat is so wise and so gode, for to shewe his wisdome and his godnes he techiþ sere lessons to his disciples after þat þei profiten in here lerynge, and gifiþ to sundry soules sere medicynes after þe felynge of ⌜her⌝ seknes. And also anoþer skil is þis: if þere were o certene dede bi þe whilk a soule miȝt come to þe perfite luf of God, þan schude a man wene þat he miȝte come þerto bi his own werk and þurwȝ his owne trauail, as a marchant comeþ to his mede by his owne `trauail´ only and bi his owne werk. Nay, it is not so gostly in þe luf of
83r God. For | he þat wil serue God wisely and come to þe perfit luf of God, he schal coueite `to haue´ none oþer mede bot him only. Bot þan for to haue hym may no creature deserue only bi his owne trauail; for þawȝ a man miȝt trauailen als mikil bodily and gostly as alle creatures þat euer were miȝten, he miȝt not deserue only bi his werkes for to haue God for his mede. For he is soueren blis and eendeles godnes, and passeþ wiþoute comparisoun alle mennis desertes; and þerfore he may not be getyn be no mans special werk as bodily mede may. For he is free, and gifiþ himself where he wile and when he wil, neiþer for þis werk ne for þat, ne þis tyme ne after þat tyme; for þawȝ a soule wirke al þat he kan and may al his lif tyme, perfit luf of Ihesu schal he neuer haue til oure Lord Ihesu wil frely gife it. Nerþeles on þe toþer side I say also, þat I hope he ȝifiþ it not bot if a man wirke and trauaile al þat he kan and may, ȝe til him þinkiþ he may no more, or elles be in ful wil þerto ȝif he miȝte.

And so it semiþ þat neiþer grace only withouten ful wirkynge of a

HBH_5SrChLwHu_2MLdTW 51 bodily and gostly/as mikel] H_7RLB_3AsSrAEPH_6Cc-MPl, *rev.* HBH_5ChLwHu_2LdTW 52 alle] þe *add.* H_5Hu_2 myghten] *om.* RAsACc he might] ne shulde he M deseruen only] *rev.* H_6 53 mede] premium Lat. 55 desertys] deseruyngis Ch he may] *rev.* Pl mans] *om.* AT werke] werks ChLwHu_2MW 56 may] be *add.* As fre] and wil be fre *add.* AMPl gyfeþ] ȝeuon M himself] hemself Ch where] þat *add.* H_5, so *add.* Sr wil] wold Ld 57 wil] wold Ld, and *add.* M, and when best is *add.* H_6 werke] *om.* LwW þat[1]] þis Pl, werk *add.* Sr ne . . . tyme[1] (l. 58)] whethir it be bodily or gostly Cc `ne þis tyme´ Ld ne] in *add.* RAs`H[c]´AELdPl aftere] pro Lat. þat[2]] H_7HRAsSrChLwHu_2LdTW, þis H_5LB_3-AEPH_6CcMPl 58 werke] and labir *add.* Hu_2 þat] euer *add.* T 59 Jesu[1]] God RAsAMPl, Dei Lat. til] to E, for to Pl Jesu[2]] *om.* RAsAMPl 60 it[1]] hym *add.* H_6 þat[1]] þe LwCc þat I hope] and trowe *add.* A þat[2]] *om.* H_5W hope] trowe B, suppose Hu_2 þat[3]] H_7RLB_3AsSrAHu_2EPH_6CcPl, *om.* HBH_5ChLwLdTW 61 man] first RAsAMPl werke and trauaile] laboret Lat. and[1]] be M may and kan] H_7LB_3EPH_6, *rev.* HRBH_5AsSrChLwAHu_2CcMLdPlTW ȝa . . . more] *om.* Lat. ȝa] *om.* M til] to E him þenkeþ] he thynke M him] he Ld 62 þenkeþ] he can no more *add.* H_5 þat[1]] H_7RLB_3SrAEPH_6CcMPl, *om.* HBH_5AsChLwHu_2LdTW þerto] ad taliter laborandum Lat. þat[2]] H_7RLB_3SrAEPH_6CcMPl, *om.* HBH_5AsChLwHu_2LdTW 64 And] *om.* H_6 grace] *om.* A werkynge] wir- *prec.*, *canc.* L, cooperante et laborante Lat.

soule þat in it is, ne werkynge alon withouten grace, bryngeþ not a soule to reformynge in felynge, þe qwhilk reformynge standeþ in perfyte lofe and charite. Bot þat on ioyned to þat oþer, þat is, \`grace´ ioyned to werke, bryngeþ into a soule þe blissed felynge of perfyte lofe, þe whilk grace may not resten fully bot on a meke soule þat is ful of þe drede of God. Þerfore may I seyn þat he þat hath not mekenes ne doth not his besynes may not come to þis reformynge in felynge. He hath no ful meknes þat kan not felen of himself sothfastly as he is; as þus: he þat doth alle þe goode dedys þat he kan, as in fastynge, wakynge, werynge of þe hayre, and alle oþer suffrynge of bodily penaunce, or doth al þe owtward werkes of mercy to his euen-cristen, or ellys inward, as preyende, wepende, syghende, and þenkende; if he reste ay in hem, and lene so mikel to hem and reward hem so gretly in his owen syght þat he presumeth of his owen disertis, and þenkeþ himself ay riche and gode, and holy and vertuous: sothly, as long as he feleth þus, he is not meke inogh. Ne þogh he sey or þenke þat al þat he doth is of Goddis gifte and not of himself, he is not ȝet meke inogh, for he may not ȝet make himself | f. 64v naked fro alle his gode dedys, ne mak himself pore sothfastly in spirit, ne felen himself noght as he is. And sothly vntil a soule kan felabyly þurgh grace noghten himself, and baren himself fro al þe gode þat he doth þurgh byholdynge of sothfastnes of Jesu God, he is not perfytly meke.

For what is meknes bot sothfastnes? Sothly, not ellys. And þerfore he þat þurgh grace may seen Jesu, how he doth alle and himself doth

65 þat] as muche as H$_5$ in it/is] *rev.* AsCc, is þerynne Sr it] hym B alon] *om.* Cc \`withouten grace´ Cc bryngeþ] brynge M not] H$_7$RLB$_3$AsAEPH$_6$MPl, *om.* HBH$_5$SrChLwHu$_2$CcLdTW 66 to] þe *add.* H$_5$LwW \`in felynge´ Cc þe qwhilk reformynge] *om.* Cc, which T standeþ] standyng Cc 67 þat[1]] *om.* Hu$_2$ ioyned] ioyneth H$_5$ to] wiþ LB$_3$PH$_6$ \`grace´ *interl, s.h.* H$_7$ 68 ioyned] ioyneth H$_5$ to] the *add.* Cc werke] H$_7$RLB$_3$AsSrAPH$_6$CcMPl, wirkyng HBH$_5$ChLwHu$_2$ELdTW of] in Lw perfyte lofe] *rev.* RAsPl 69 lofe] deleccionis Lat. \`may´ L on] in M a meke soule] meeke sowlys LwW is] beth LwW 70 þe] H$_7$RH$_5$LwEH$_6$CcLd\`T´W, *om.* HBLB$_3$As-SrChAHu$_2$PMPl may] *om.* LB$_3$PH$_6$ þat[1]] *om.* LwW not] H$_7$HRBH$_5$LB$_3$AsCh-AHu$_2$PH$_6$CcLdT, noo SrLwEMPlW 71 ne . . . besynes] *om.* Lat. not[1]] *om.* SrLwCcW 72 no] H$_7$, not Σ not] deuote considerare humilitatem Domini nostri Ihsu Christi et *add.* Lat. himself] seipsum miserum esse sicut Lat. sothfastly] truly Hu$_2$, *om.* AMPl 73 in] *om.* RAsAPl 74 wakynge] werkyng *add.* M of[1]] *om.* Cc þe] *om.* LwM and] *om.* T oþer] *om.* Cc suffrynge] suffryngis H$_6$ 75 penaunce] peyne M doth] do Cc of] charitee and *add.* H$_5$ 76 inward] *om.* A as] or ellys As, *om.* Pl preyende . . . þenkende] H$_7$HRBCh, prayinge, wepynge, syȝynge and þenkynge H$_5$LB$_3$AsSrLwA-Hu$_2$EPH$_6$CcMLdPlTW, orationem, ploracionem, et meditacionem, et suspirium Lat. if he] of þe Pl 77 ay] H$_7$HRAsChAPCcM, euere BH$_5$B$_3$LwAEH$_6$PlTW, alwey SrHu$_2$Ld hem] hym Ch lene] lovith Cc to] into T hem[2]] hym Ch reward] rewardith Cc hem[3]] *om.* A 78 he] hym M presumeth . . . and] *om.* AMPl of] in LB$_3$EPH$_6$ disertis]

soule þat in hit is, ne wirkyng alone withouten grace, bryngiþ a soule to reformyng in felyng, þe whilke reformyng standiþ in perfite luf and charite. Bot þat on ioyned to þat oþer, þat is grace ioyned to wirkyng, bryngiþ into a soule þe blessed felyng of perfite luf, þe whilke grace may not resten fully bot on a mek soule þat is ful of drede of God. Þerfore may I seyen þat he þat haþ not meknes ne doþ not his bisynes may not come to þis reformynge in felynge. He haþ not ful meknes þat kan not felyn of hymself soþfastly as he is; as þus: he þat doþ alle þe gode dedis þat he kan, as in fastynge, wakynge, werynge of þe
83v heire, and al oþer suffrynge of bodily penaunce, or doþ alle þe | outward werkes of mercy to his euen-cristen, or elles inward, as preiende, wepende, seiȝend, and þinkand; if he reste ay in hem, and lene so mikel to hem and rewardeþ hem so gretly in his owne siȝte þat he presumiþ of his owne desertes, and þinkiþ himself ay riche and gode, holy and vertuous: soþly, as longe as he feliþ þus, he is not meke inowȝ. Ne þawȝ he say or þinke þat al þat he doþ is of Goddis gift and not of himself, he is not ȝit meke inowȝ, for he may not make himself ⌜ȝit⌝ nakid of alle his gode dedis, ne make himself pore soþfastly in spirit, ne felen himself noȝt as he is. And soþly vntil a soule kan felablely þurwȝ grace noȝten himself, and baren him fro alle þe gode dedis þat he doþ þurwȝ behaldyng of soþfastnes of Ihesu, he is noȝt perfitly meke.

For what is meknes bot soþfastnes? Soþly, noȝt elles. And þerfore he þat þurwȝ grace may see Ihesu, how þat he doþ al and himself doþ

deseruynge Hu$_2$ 79 ay riche] riche euere E ay] H$_7$HLChPCcM, euere B$_3$AsLwAHu$_2$EH$_6$PlTW, alweye SrLd, as R, om. BH$_5$ riche] ryȝtwise H$_5$ and[2]] H$_7$RLB$_3$AsEPPlT, *om.* HBH$_5$SrChLwAHu$_2$CcMLdW holy and vertuous] *rev.* RAs and[3]] in E vertuous] vertues BE 80 þus] þis ChHu$_2$, þ⌜u⌝s, *corr. fr.* þis B$_3$, himself *add.* H$_5$ is] `he´ *add.* Pl not] none Ld `Ne . . . inogh (l. 81)´ Pl `Ne´ A, And H$_5$, *om.* Cc þogh] ȝif A or] and R þat[1]] *om.* Sr he doth] *om.* Pl 81 of[1]] *om.* M gifte] yiftis T, grace LB$_3$PH$_6$ not[1]] n- *prec.*, *canc.* Sr he is not ȝet] ȝit is he not Pl 82 ȝet/make himself] H$_7$RH$_5$LB$_3$AsSrAEPH$_6$CcPl, *rev.* HBChLwHu$_2$MLdTW ȝet] *om.* Sr, sentire se miserum *add.* Lat. naked] nakeþ Ch fro] H$_7$RLB$_3$AsSrPH$_6$CcMPl, of HBH$_5$ChLw-AHu$_2$ELdTW ne] neiþer H$_5$ 83 himself[1]] hym LwW pore sothfastly] *rev.* H$_6$ pore] *om.* E `noght´ Pl, *om.* ACc 84 vntil] H$_7$HRBH$_5$LSrChLwHu$_2$PCcW, til AMLd, vnto B$_3$AsHu$_2$PlT, to E, vnto þe tyme þat H$_6$ felabyly] sensibelli A, ful ablye Pl þurgh grace] *om.* APl 85 and baren himself] *om.* H$_6$ himself] H$_7$RLB$_3$SrAEPH$_6$CcMPl, him HBH$_5$AsChLwHu$_2$LdTW þe] *om.* M gode] H$_7$RLB$_3$AsSrAPH$_6$Pl, dedis *add.* HBH$_5$ChLwHu$_2$ECcMLdTW, bonis operibus Lat. 86 Jesu God] H$_7$LB$_3$EPH$_6$, Jesu HBH$_5$SrChLwHu$_2$LdTW, God RAsACcMPl, Jesu Christi Lat. 87 For . . . meke (l. 90)] *om.* Lat. sothfastnes] soþfastne`sse´ L 88 þat . . . Jesu] seth God AMPl þurgh grace/may] *rev.* E how he] *om.* H$_6$ how] H$_7$RBLB$_3$AsSrChAHu$_2$EPH$_6$CcMPl, þat *add.* HH$_5$LwLdTW `he´ Pl

ryght noght but suffreth him werken in him what him lykeþ, he is meke. Bot þis is ful hard, and as it were inpossible and vnresonable to a man þat werkeþ al by mannys reson and seeþ no ferþer, for to don many gode dedys and þan for to aretten hem al to Jesu and setten himself at noght. Neuerþeles whoso might hafe `a´ gostly syght of sothfastnes, he schuld þenke it ful trew and ful resonable to don so. And sothly he þat hath þis syght, he schal neuer do þe lesse, bot he schal be steryd for to trauaile bodily and gostly mikel þe more and with mikel bettre wil. And þis may ben o cause why þat sum men perauenture swynken and sweten and pynen here wrecched body with owtragious penaunce al here lyf tyme, and arn ay seyend orisouns and sawters, byddende many oþer bedys, and ȝet moun þei not come to þat gostly felynge of þe lufe of God, as it semeþ þat sum men don in schorter tyme with lesse pyne, for þei kan not þat meknes þat I speke of.

Also on þat oþer syde, I sey he þat doþ noght his besynes may not come to þe felynge of grace. He doth not his besynes þat þenkeþ þus: Whareto schuld I trauailen? Wharto schuld I preyen or þenken, fasten or waken, or ony bodily penaunce don for to come to swilk grace, syn it may not be geten ne had bot only of þe free gyfte of Jesu? Þerfor I wil vmbyden in fleschlyhed as I am, and ryȝt not don of swilk werkys bodily ne gostly vntil he gyfe it, for if he wil gyf it he askeþ no werkynge of me; what-so þat I do, and how lytel þat I do, I schal hafe it. And if he wil not gyf it, trauayle I neuer so fast for it, I gete it neuer

89 suffreth] suffre H$_5$ him] H$_7$LB$_3$SrAPH$_6$Cc, Jesu HBH$_5$ChLwELdTW, oure Lord Jesu Hu$_2$, Jesu God As, God RAMPl, good As werken] to *prec.* Hu$_2$EH$_6$Cc, werkyng RAs in] on B lykeþ] list LB$_3$EPH$_6$ 90 is] *om.* As and[1]] *om.* MPl as] *om.* R it were] *om.* Cc and vnresonable] *om.* Cc 91 mannys] a *prec.* Ld seeþ] *om.* Sr no] not Pl ferþer] ferr Pl don] *om.* A 92 gode dedys] godedes L þan] þat ChHu$_2$, hem M for to] for Ch, to H$_6$M aretten . . . Jesu] forsakyn hem alle and forgetyn hem RAsAMPl (hem[1] *om.* M) aretten] recte B, ascribe Hu$_2$ hem] hym Ch, *om.* LwW 93 whoso] who þat H$_6$ `a´ *interl.* H$_7$, *om.* Pl syght] liȝt and a *prec.* M 94 he] hym Sr, hit M þenke it] thynken hym M [reso]-nable . . . and (21/69)] *om.* Ch (*folio missing* ) to] H$_7$LB$_3$EPH$_6$Cc, for *prec.* HRBH$_5$AsSrLwAHu$_2$MLdPlTW 95 `he[1]´ Cc `þat´ Pl þis] *om.* Ld syght he] *om.* M syght] humilitatem de qua dixi Lat. he[2]] *om.* Sr 96 bodily and gostly] *om.* RAsAMPl mikel] *om.* RLd þe] *om.* AT 97 mikel] H$_7$RSrAH$_6$CcM, þe HBH$_5$LwLdTW, þe *add.* LB$_3$AsEPPl, *om.* Hu$_2$, meliori Lat. why] which T þat] H$_7$LB$_3$SrAEPH$_6$CcMPl, *om.* HRH$_5$AsLwHu$_2$LdTW 98 perauenture] *om.* H$_6$ swynken] labir Hu$_2$ here] þe A body] bodies EM 99 owtragious] outrage H$_6$, contrarious Cc penaunce] penaunces M arn] *om.* Hu$_2$ ay] H$_7$HH$_5$LPCc, euere BB$_3$AsLwAHu$_2$EH$_6$MPlTW, alwey SrLd 100 sawters] H$_7$, and *add.* Σ byddende . . . bedys] et alias deuociones Lat. byddende] H$_7$RLB$_3$AsSrAEPH$_6$CcMPl, *om.* HBH$_5$LwHu$_2$LdTW bedys] dedes T ȝet] hytt Ld þei not] *rev.* Hu$_2$Ld come] for oȝt þat þey may do *add.* A, for ouȝte þat þei can do *add.* MPl 101 þat[1]] þe H$_5$LwH$_6$CcW þe] *om.* R þat[2]] as Cc, *om.* LB$_3$EPH$_6$ `men´ W^G, *om.* B$_3$W

riȝt noȝt bot suffreþ Ihesu wirken in him what him likiþ, he is meke. Bot þis is ful harde, and as it were impossible and vnresonable to a man þat wirkeþ al bi mannes resoun and seeþ no ferrer, for to done many gode dedis and þan for to arette hem alle to Ihesu and setten hymself at noȝt. Nerþeles whoso miȝte haue a gostly siȝt of soþfastnes, him schuld þinke it ful trew and ful resonable for to don so. And soþly he þat haþ þis siȝt schal neuer do þe lesse, bot he schal be stirid for to traueile bodily and gostly mikel þe more and with þe better wil. And þis may ben o cause whi summe men perauenture swinken and swetyn and pynen her wrecched body with outraious penaunce ale here lif tyme, and arn ay sayend orisouns and sawters and many oþer bedis, and ȝit mowen þei noȝt come to þat gostly felyng of þe luf of God, as
84r it semiþ þat sum men don in schort tyme with lesse peyn, | for þei han not þat meknes þat I speke of.

Also on þat oþer side, I sey he þat doþ not his bisynes may not come to þe felyng of grace. He doþ not his bisynes þat þinkeþ þus: Wha`r´to schud I trauailen? Wharto schude I preien or þinken, waken or fasten, or ony oþer bodily penaunce don for to come to swilk grace, siþen it may not be getyn ne had bot only of þe fre ȝifte of Ihesu? Þerfore I wil vmbiden in flesclynes as I am, and riȝt noȝt don of swilk werkes bodily ne gostly vntil he ȝife it, for if he wil ȝife it he askiþ no wirkyng of me; what-so þat I do, and how litel I do, I sal haue it. And if he wile not gif it, trauel I neuer so faste þerfore I gete it neuer þe

102 schorter] $H_7RLB_3AsAEPH_6CcMPl$, schort $HBH_5SrLwHu_2LdTW$, breuiori Lat. lesse] mikil *prec.* RAsAMPl pyne] penaunce B, þat is *add.* H_6, pena et penitencia Lat. speke] spake LwW 104 on] to H_6 þat oþer] anoþer H_5 þat[1]] the Cc syde] *om.* B_3H_6 I sey] *om.* Cc sey] seid Pl doþ noght] *rev.* Hu_2 his] *om.* Sr may . . . besynes (l. 105)] *om.* W 105 grace] this *prec.* RAsAPl He] For *prec.* Hu_2 106 Wharto[2] . . . I] *om.* Lat. schuld[2]] schule Ld preyen] prayer B þenken] or *add.* $AsHu_2$ fasten or waken] $H_7RLB_3AsSrAEPH_6CcMPl$, *rev.* HBH_5LwHu_2LdTW, ieiunare, vigilare Lat. 107 ony] $H_7RLB_3AsSrAPH_6CcMPl$, oþer *add.* HBH_5LwHu_2ELdTW, aliquam Lat. don] wirchen H_5 for] *om.* H_6 syn] so Pl, þat Cc 108 be] by H_5 bot only of] withoute A free] *om.* T Jesu] God RAsAPl, Domini Jesu Christi Lat. þerfor] And *prec.* H_6 109 vmbyden] H_7HRLB_3P, abyden $BH_5AsSrLwAHu_2EH_6CcMLdPlTW$, *corr. fr.* vmbyde Lw, and levyn *add.* Cc fleschlyhed] $H_7RLB_3AsSrEPH_6CcMPl$, flesclynes HBH_5LwAHu_2LdTW as I am] *om.* Cc as] riȝt *prec.* LB_3P `and´ Pl ryȝt] *om.* Cc werkys/bodily ne gostly] *rev.* Cc werkys] *om.* A 110 ne] or Cc vntil] til ALd, into $B_3AsCcPl$, vnto Hu2, vnto tyme T it[1]] me *add.* Cc, graciam Lat. for . . . it[2]] *om.* M wil] *om.* ACc it[2]] graciam Lat. he[3] . . . me (l. 111)] non exigit operacionem ex parte mea Lat. askeþ] it *add.*, *canc.* L no . . . me (l. 111)] nout werk Cc 111 me] *om.* B_3 þat[1]] *om.* BSrAM and . . . do[2]] *om.* Sr þat I do[2]] ȝit Cc þat[2]] $H_7RLB_3AsAEPH_6MPlW$, *om.* HBH_5LwHu_2LdT 112 it[1]] me *add.* A trauayle I] thou I traveyle Cc fast] sore Hu_2, miche T for it] $H_7RLB_3AsAEPH_6CcPl$, þerfore $HBH_5SrLwHu_2MLdTW$ gete] shal haue Hu_2

f. 65r þe more. He þat | seyth þus may not come to þis reformynge; for he draweth himself wylfully to ydelnes of fleschlyhed and vnableþ him to þe gyft of grace, in as mikel as he putteþ fro him boþe inward werkynge, þat standeþ in lastend desyre and in longynge to Jesu, and outward werkynge be trauayle of his bodi and gode outward dedys. So may he not hafe it. Þerfor I sey þat he þat hath not trew meknes ne ful hertly besynes may not come to þe reformynge in felynge. For withouten besynes, eyþer inward only by grete feruour and lastend desyre and besy preyere and þoght in God, or ellys boþe inward and outward, may he not come to þis gostly reformynge of þis ymage.

`An entre how þou schalt come to þis reformyng be exawmple of a pilgrym.´ Capitulum xxi[m]

Neuerþeles for þou coueytist for to han sum maner werkynge by þe whilk þou mightest þe raþer neyghen to þat reformynge, I schal sey þe as me þenkeþ by þe grace of oure Lord Jesu, þe schortest and þe redyest helpe þat I know in þis werkynge. And how þat schal be I schal telle þe by example of a gode pilgryme vpon þis wyse.

Þare was a man þat wolde gon to Jerusalem, and for he knew no`t´ þe weye he come to anoþer man þat he hoped kouþe þe weye þedir and asked, for he might not come to þat cyte. Þat oþer man seyd to him þat he might not come þedere withouten grete desese and grete trauaille, for þe weye is longe and peryles are grete of þefes [and]

113 more] H$_7$RBLB$_3$AsSrAEPH$_6$CcMLdPl, soner HH$_5$LwTW, raþir Hu$_2$, cicius Lat. come] *rep.*, *canc.* Cc to] til R 114 fleschlyhed] flessheed LwW, flesshelinesse T, flesshly lyuyng RAsE him] hymself Hu$_2$CcPl 115 gyft] ȝiftis RAsM inward] in þe wordilly M 116 desyre . . . longynge] consideracione . . . desiderio Lat. in²] *om.* RAsAH$_6$Pl longynge] lovyng and *prec.* Cc to] of Cc Jesu] God RAsAMPl, Jesu Christi Lat. and²] þe *add.* Sr 117 and] H$_7$, bi B$_3$, of Cc, in Σ, in Lat. gode] H$_7$RLB$_3$As-AEPH$_6$CcMPl, *om.* HBH$_5$SrLwHu$_2$LdTW, bonis Lat. outward dedys] *rev.* Cc So] and *prec.* H$_5$H$_6$Cc 118 may he] *rev.* Hu$_2$ he not] *rev.* Ld þerfor] And *prec.* Ld þat¹] *om.* W not²] no W 119 may . . . besines (l. 120)] *om.* HH$_5$LwTW þe] þis SrM 120 eyþer] outward or *add.* RAs 121 and¹] or outward be Sr preyere and] *om.* RAs-AMPl þoght] þenkynge SrCc in] into Ld, of H$_5$, on Sr boþe] be þe *add.* Sr and³] þe *add.* Sr 122 may he] *rev.* A þis¹] his T of . . . ymage] *om.* Cc þis²] H$_7$RLB$_3$AsAEPCcMPl, his HBH$_5$SrLwHu$_2$H$_6$LdTW, istius Lat.

Chapter 21 *title*: `An . . . pilgrym.´ *d.h.* H$_7$ An entre how a soule schal [schulde M] haue hym [her TW, it *canc.*, hir E] in menyng [monynge Ld] and in werkyng [and in in werkyng *om.* H$_6$] þat wil come to þis reformyng by exawmple of a pilgrym goend to Ierusalem, and of two maner [of *add.* Sr] meknes [and of bodii desessis and gostli. *add.* E] RSrAEH$_6$MLdPlTW [by . . . meknes *om.* Pl, and² . . . meknes *om.* Ld] þat a man þat wole come to Ierusalem, þat is [to *add.* As] vndirstonde to þe cite of pees, þe wich is contemplacioun, muste holde him lowe in meknesse and in [þe *add.* As] feiþ and suffre disese boþe bodili and goostly. LB$_3$As`H^c´P Introduccio qualiter anima habere se debeat

soner. He þat saiþ þus may not come to þis reformynge; for he drawiþ himself wilfully to ydelnes of fleschlyed and vnabliþ him to þe ȝifte of grace, in als mikel as he puttiþ fro him boþ inward wirkynge, þat stondiþ in lastende desire and in longynge to Ihesu, and outward wirkyng bi trauaile of his body in outward dedis. So may he not haue it. þerfor I say þat he þat haþ not trewe meknes ne ful hertly bisynes [may not come to þe reformynge in felynge. For withoute bisynes], eiþer inward only bi grete feruour and lastende desire and bisy prayere and þouȝt in God, or elles boþ inward and outward, may he not come to þis gostly reformyng of his ymage.

[CHAPTER 21]

Nerþeles for þou coueites for to haue sum maner wirkynge by þe whilke þu miȝtes þe raþer neiȝen to þat reformynge, I schal say þe as me þinkiþ bi þe grace of oure Lord Ihesu. And how þat schal be I schal telle þe by exaumple of a good pilgrym vpon þis wise.

þer was a man þat wold gon to Ierusalem, and for he knewe not þe weye he come to anoþer man þat he hopid knew þe wey þeder and asked wheþer he miȝte come to þat citee. þat oþer man seide to him þat he miȝte not come þeder withoute grete disese and mikil trauaile, for þe wey is longe and periles are grete of þefes and robbours, and

in intencione et operacione que ad reformacionem in sensacione voluerit peruenire, per exemplum de peregrino ad Ierusalem transeunte. Lat. *om.* BH$_5$LwHu$_2$Cc3 for[1]] þat *add.* Sr. *The sixth extract in* Td *starts here* for[2]] *om.* LB$_3$PH$_6$Cc maner] of *add.* H$_5$ALd 4 þe] *om.* SrTd. raþer] sonner A neyghen] come M to] *rep.*, *canc.* Td þ⌜at⌝] H^c, þe H$_5$EPl, *om.* Td reformynge] in feling *add.* Td `sey´ H$_6$, to *add.* AsCcM 5 þe[1]] *om.* W þe[2]] *om.* Cc oure Lord] *om.* Cc, *om.* Lat. Jesu] Crist *add.* MLd, Jesu Christi Lat. þe[3] . . . werkynge] H$_7$RLB$_3$AsSrLw`H^c´AEPH$_6$CcMPlW, *om.* H°BH$_5$Hu$_2$LdTTd, breuissimum auxilium et promptissimum quod cognosco in hac operacione Lat. 6 redyest] weye and *add.* M þat[2]] it As schal be] is M 7 telle] shewe M by] an *add.* SrCcW vpon] in ALd, on SrHu$_2$H$_6$Td 8 `was´ Cc gon] *om.* T for] þat *add.* `L´B$_3$AsEP knew] couþe B not] `t´ *above line* H$_7$ 9 þat] as *add.* T hoped] trowid A, supposid Hu$_2$ kouþe] H$_7$BLB$_3$APH$_6$, knew HRH$_5$AsSrLwHu$_2$ECcMLdPlTW weye] bettyr *add.* LwW 10 and] he *add.* Cc asked] him *add.* ECc, of hym *add.* RAs, ab eo Lat. for] H$_7$Sr, wheþer HH$_5$LB$_3$LwAHu$_2$EPLdTW, wher RBAsSrH$_6$Pl, if CcMTd, numquid Lat. not] H$_7$LB$_3$PH$_6$, *om.* Σ þat] And *prec.* H$_6$, The CcTd to . . . trauaille (l. 12)] Nay, withoutyn gret traveye or disese Cc 11 grete[2]] H$_7$RLB$_3$AsAHu$_2$EPH$_6$CcPl, mikil HBH$_5$SrLwMLdTW, magna vexacione et labore Lat. 12 is] so *add.* Pl and[1]] þe *add.* LB$_3$EP, nam Lat. peryles . . . grete] [þer Td] are grete periles MTd peryles] H$_7$HRBH$_5$LB$_3$SrAEPH$_6$CcMPlTTd`W$^G$´, perilous AsLwHu$_2$CcLdW`T^G´ are grete of] and full of grete LwTW, `ben grete of´ W$^G$, `ben grete´ T^G are] *rep.*, *canc.* L, and As grete] plente *add.* As of] H$_7$HRBH$_5$AsLwAHu$_2$EMLdPlTW, for LB$_3$PH$_6$Cc, *om.* Sr, nam Lat. and robbours] *om.* Cc and] *om.* H$_7$, of Pl

robbours, and many oþer lettynges þer ben þat fallen to a man in þe goynge. And also þere are many sondry weyes as it semeþ ledende þederward, bot men alday are slayne and spoyled and moun not come to þat place þat þei coueyten. Neuerþeles þer is o weye, þe whilk weye whoso wold take it and hold it he wolde vndertake þat he schuld come to þat cyte of Jerusalem, and he schulde neuer lesen his lyfe ne be slayne ne dyen for defaute. He schulde often be robbed and euel beten
f. 65v | and suffre mikel desese in þe goynge, bot he schuld ay han his lyf saufe.

þan seyth þe pilgrym: be so I may scape and hafe my lyf saufe and come to þat place þat I coueyte, I charge not what meschief I suffre in þe goynge; and þerfor sey me what þou wilt, and sothly I behete for to don after it. þat oþer man answereþ and seith þus: Lo, I sette þe in þe right weye; þis is þe weye, and þat þou kepe þis lerynge þat I kenne þe. What-so þou herest or seest or felest þat schul letten þe in þi weye, abyde not with it wilfully, tarye not for it restfully, behold it not, lyke it not, drede it not, bot ay go forth in þi weye, and þenke þat þou wuldest not ellys bot be at Jerusalem. For þat þou coueytest, þat þou desyrest, and not ellys bot þat. And if men robbe þe and spoyle þe, bete þe, scorne þe and despyse þe, stryfe not ageyn if þou wilt hafe þi lyfe; bot hold þe with þe harme þat þou hast and go forth as noght

13 lettynges/þer ben] Lw þer . . . fallen] occurrunt homini in eundo Lat. þer ben] *rev.* Hu$_2$ \`þer´ H^c, that Cc, *om.* H°BH$_5$SrLd þat . . . goynge] be the weye, the whiche fallyn oftyn tyme to hem that gon thedyr Cc a man] men Td 14 And] *om.* Td sondry] H$_7$RLB$_3$AsSrAEPH$_6$CcMPl, sere HLwHu$_2$MTWTd, diuerse BH$_5$B$_3$ALdPl as . . . ledende] *om.* Cc as . . . semeþ] *om.* Td, *om.* Lat. ledende] ledinges B$_3$ 15 bot] And oftyn tyme many Cc alday are] *rev.* RAsM alday] alwey M, *om.* Cc and] sum *add.* Td spoyled] H$_7$RBLB$_3$AsSrAHu$_2$EPH$_6$CcMLdPl, dispoiled HH$_5$LwHu$_2$TW, spoliantur Lat. \`not´ Cc 16 þat[1]] *om.* H$_5$ coueyten] wold go too Hu$_2$ Neuerþeles] Bot ȝet Cc þe whilk weye] that Cc, *om.* M weye[2]] H$_7$RLB$_3$AsAEPH$_6$CcMPl, *om.* HBH$_5$SrLw-Hu$_2$LdTWTd 17 wold take] H$_7$RLB$_3$AsEPH$_6$CcPl, wil take Hu$_2$, take Sr, takeþ HBH$_5$LwMLdTW, vellet arripere Lat. it[1]] *om.* H$_6$ hold it] *rev.* Cc hold] H$_7$RLB$_3$AsSrLwAHu$_2$EPH$_6$CcMPl, holdiþ HBH$_5$MLdTW, tenere Lat. it[2]] *om.* A he[1] . . . vndertake] *om.* Lat. he[1]] I SrCcLdPlTd wolde] wull LwMW vndertake] it *add.* Sr 18 to . . . Jerusalem] therto Cc þat] H$_7$RBAsSrLwAHu$_2$H$_6$Ld, þe HH$_5$LB$_3$EPMPlTW he] *om.* M neuer] noȝt ACc, neyþer H$_5$E ne . . . defaute (l. 19)] *om.* Cc 19 He] But *prec.* SrCcTd schulde often] *rev.* E often] oft tymes Hu$_2$, *om.* AM euel] ill Td 20 mikel] grete Hu$_2$, *om.* A desese] deseeses Ld, dispite Cc þe] his Cc \`he . . . saufe´ W$^G$, his lyfe scholde be saaf W he schuld/ay] *rev.* Hu$_2$ ay . . . saufe] nott care butt hys lyfe schuld be sauf Lw ay han] *rev.* SrE ay] H$_7$HRBH$_5$Ld, euer AsAHu$_2$H$_6$MPl\`W^G [*gl.* continue]´, alwey SrT, *om.* LB$_3$P, continue Lat. \`han´ T$^G$´, *om.* T his] \`him´ B$_3$ 22 \`seyth´ W^G, said Hu$_2$W þe] þis A pilgrym] toþer man Td, *om.* H$_5$ be so] so be þat Td be] H$_7$LB$_3$SrHu$_2$PH$_6$CcM, if it be HRH$_5$AsELdPlT, be hit BA, *om.* LwW so] H$_7$LB$_3$PH$_6$CcM, þat *add.* HRBH$_5$AsSrLwAHu$_2$ELdPlTW (*canc.* Sr) scape and] H$_7$RLB$_3$AsAEPH$_6$CcPl, *om.* HBH$_5$SrLwHu$_2$MLdTW my] *om.* Ld saufe] *om.* M 23 þat[1]] the Cc coueyte] to *add.* W charge] chargid H$_6$, rek Td \`what´ Pl meschief]

84^{v} many oþer | lettynges `þer′ ben þat fallen to a man in þe goyng. And also þer are mony sere weies as it semiþ ledand þederward, bot men alday are slayn and dispoiled and mown not comyn to þat place þat þei coueiten. Nerþeles þer is o wey, þe whilke whoso takiþ hit and holdiþ it he wolde vndirtake þat he schude come to þe cite of Ierusalem, and he schu`l′de neuer lese his lif ne be slayn ne dye for defaute. He sch`l′ude often be robbed and yuel betyn and suffren mikel disese in þe goynge, bot he schu`l′de ay han his lif safe.

þan saiþ þe pilgrym: if it be so þat I may haue my lif safe and come to þat place þat I coueite, I charge not what meschef I suffre in þe goynge; and þerfore say me what þu wilt, and soþly I bihote for to don aftir þe. þat oþer man answeres and says þus: Lo, I sette þe in þe riȝt wey; þis is þe wey, and þat þu kepe þe lerynge þat I kenne þe. What-so þou heres or sees or felis þat ⌜schulde⌝ lette þe in þi wey, abide not with it wilfully, tary not for it restfully, behold it not, like it not, drede it not, bot ay go forþ in þi wey, and þinke þat þu woldes be at Ierusalem. For þat þu coueites, þat þu desires, and noȝt elles bot þat. And if men robbe þe and dispoile þe, bete þe, scorne þe and dispise þe, strife not ageyn if þu wilt han þi lif; bot holde þe with þe harme þat þu has and go forþ as noȝt were, þat þu take no more harme. And

disese H$_6$, þat *add.* AsCc suffre] suffrid H$_6$ 24 þe] *om.* W and þerfor] *rep.*, *canc.* Cc me] *om.* Cc sothly] *om.* Cc behete for to] schal Td behete] H$_7$HBH$_5$LwHu$_2$LdT, þe *add.* RLB$_3$AsSrAEPH$_6$CcMPlW, promitto Lat. for] *om.* E 25 after it] H$_7$RAsMPl, þeraftir LB$_3$SrAEPH$_6$CcTd, aftir þe HBH$_5$LwHu$_2$LdTW, secundum consilium tuum Lat. þat] The Cc answereþ] answerd RAsSrCc, aȝen *add.* Cc `seith′ R, seyde AsSrCc þus] *om.* RAsAPl þe^2] *om.* M 26 right] H$_7$RLB$_3$AsSrEPH$_6$CcMPlW, *om.* HBH$_5$Lw-AHu$_2$LdT, recta Lat. þis . . . and] *om.* Cc þis . . . weye] *om.* Hu$_2$ weye^2] right *prec.* T, go foorth *add.* RAsAPl, þat þow be ay stedfaste *add.* H$_5$ and] look *add.* SrAH$_6$CcM, loke Td þat þou] *om.* RAPl þat] *om.* SrAM þou] lerne and *add.* Cc þis lerynge] *om.* Cc þis] H$_7$RLB$_3$AsAEPH$_6$CcPl, þe HBH$_5$SrLwHu$_2$MLdTW lerynge] H$_7$HR, lernynge BH$_5$LB$_3$AsSrLwAHu$_2$EPH$_6$CcMLdPlTW, leson Td, leccionem Lat. kenne] H$_7$HRH$_5$-LwHu$_2$EPCc, teche BB$_3$AH$_6$MLdPlTW, haue tauȝt As, tel Td 27 so] euer *add.* Hu$_2$T or^1] *om.* LwW schul] H$_7$, ⌜schuld⌝ H, schuld Σ þi] þe AsLwCcTW 28 abyde . . . wilfully/tarye . . . restfully] *rev.* Td with it] with þat Sr, þerwiþ Hu$_2$, þerfore Td wilfully] *om.* Td `tarye . . . restfully′ T$^G$ for it] þerwiþ Sr, with it A, to it M, þerfore Td, is *add.* Hu$_2$ restfully] ne reste Cc, *om.* Td behold] hold M `lyke . . . not^1′ (l. 19) T^G 29 not^2] ne love it nout ne *add.* Cc ay] H$_7$HRH$_5$LAsPCcM, euere BB$_3$Lw-AHu$_2$EH$_6$PlTW, alwey SrLd þi] þe M þenke] *om.* Cc `þou′ Td 30 not . . . bot] H$_7$RBLB$_3$AsSrAHu$_2$EPH$_6$CcMLdPl, *om.* HH$_5$LwLdTW, nichil aliud cogitando nisi Lat. be . . . bot (l. 31)] *om.* R `be′ H$_6$ coueytest/. . ./desyrest] *rev.* Hu$_2$ coueytest . . . þou^2] *om.* Cc coueytest] and *add.* SrH$_6$W þat þou desyrest] *om.* Td 31 bot þat] *om.* Hu^2 robbe] robbed As and^3] *om.* Sr spoyle] H$_7$RLB$_3$AsSrAPH$_6$CcPl, dispoile HBH$_5$LwHu$_2$EMLdTW 32 bete/. . ./scorne] *rev.* LB$_3$EPH$_6$ þe^1] and add. A and^1] or Pl, *om.* W stryfe] þu *add.* A ageyn] with hem Cc 33 hold] þou *add.* H$_5$ with] to T þe] þi Td þat þou hast] *om.* Td go forth] in thyn weye *add.* Cc, in via que procedas Lat. as] it *add.* AsPl were, þat þou take no more harme. And also if men wil tary þe with tales and fage [þe with] lesynges for to drawe þe to mirthes and to lefe þi pilgrymage, make defe ere and answere not ageyn, bot sey not ellys bot þat þou woldest ben at Jerusalem. And if men profer þe ȝiftes and wil make þe riche with werdly gode, tente not to hem; þenke ay of Jerusalem. And if þou wilt holden þis weye and don as I hafe seyd, I vndertake þi lyfe þat þou schalt not be slayne, bot þou schalt come to þat place þat þou coueytest.

Gostly to oure purpos: Jerusalem is as mikel to seyn as syght of pees, and it betokenes contemplacion in perfyte lufe of God. For contemplacyon is not ellys but a sight of Jesu, þe whilk is verrey pees. Þan if þou coueyte for to come to þis blissed sight of verrey pees and ben a trew pilgrym to Jerusalem-ward, þogh it be so þat I were neuer þere, neuerþeles as ferforth as I kan I schal sette þe in þe weye þederward. Þe bygynnynge of þe heygh weye in þe whilk þou schalt gon is reformynge in feith, groundede mekly in þe feith and in þe laghes of Holy Kirke, as I hafe seid before; for trust sikerly, þogh þou [f. 66^r] hafe synned here before, if þou be nowe | reformed be þe sacrament of penaunce after þe laghe of Holy Kirke, þat þou art in þe ryght weye.

Now þan, syn þou art in þe syker weye, if þou wilt spede in þi goynge and mak gode iornees, þe behoueth holden often þese two þynges in þi mende: meknes and lufe. Þat is, I am noght, I hafe noȝt, I coueyte noȝt bot on. Þou schalt hafe þe menynge of þese wurdes in

34 þat] lest Td take] katche Hu$_2$ no] *om.* Td harme] scathe Td also] *om.* Cc with] þe which A 35 tales] narracionibus seu fabulis Lat. and . . . with] fagis and Cc fage] H$_7$BH$_5$LB$_3$PCcMT, fawen Sr, f⌜ed⌝e H^c, fede RAsLwAEH$_6$PlW, flater Hu$_2$, glose Ld, adulari Lat. þe with] *rev.* H$_7$ \`þe´ *s.h.* H, and M mirthes] myrth Td and^2] H$_7$RLB$_3$AsSrAPH$_6$CcPl, for *add.* HBH$_5$LwHu$_2$EMLdTW to] make þe to *add.* M lefe] lesyn Sr 36 pilgrymage] pilgrymages LB$_3$P make] a *add.* AsLwHu$_2$TW, þou *add.* Cc, hem *add.* M bot] H$_7$RAsAPl, and HBH$_5$SrLwHu$_2$ECcLdTW, *om.* LB$_3$PH$_6$M, set Lat. sey . . . bot] *om.* Td 37 þat] *om.* RAsPl Jerusalem] and þat þou desirest gretly Ierusalem *add.* M 38 wil] wolde ECcM, *om.* AsSrA with] of A gode] H$_7$HRBH$_5$AsSrLwAHu$_2$MLdPlTW, goodis LB$_3$EPH$_6$Cc, bonis temporalibus Lat. tente not] take no hede Hu$_2$H$_6$Td, tak no kep Cc to hem] þerto A to] at Hu$_2$, of Cc hem] hym Lw, but *add.* Cc þenke ay of] bot sey þou wolde be at Td ay] H$_7$HRH$_5$LAsPCc, euere BB$_3$LwAEH$_6$MPlTW, alwey SrHu$_2$Ld of] of H$_7$RAsSr, on HBH$_5$LB$_3$LwAHu$_2$EPH$_6$CcMLdPlTW, de Lat. 39 if] *om.* Lw wilt] wile Sr, wit H$_6$ as] that W seyd] þe *add.* A 40 vndertake . . . slayne] manucapio vitam tuam et quod non occideris Lat. vndertake] for *add.* H$_5$ þat] and Pl, *om.* LB$_3$EPH$_6$ bot] þat Ld þou schalt] wel Cc 41 place] *om.* Cc þat] H$_7$HBH$_5$LwHu$_2$LdTW, þere RLB$_3$SrAPH$_6$MPl, þere þat AsCc, *om.* E, ad quem Lat. coueytest] to *add.* W, pergere concupiscis Lat. 42 Gostly] ostely [*space left for an initial not supplied*] Td, now *add.* H$_5$ \`mikel´ H$_6$ to] H$_7$RB$_3$AsAEH$_6$CcMPl, for *prec.* HBH$_5$\`L´SrLwHu$_2$PTW seyn] *om.* M syght]

also if men wil tary þe wiþ tales and f⌜ed⌝e `þe´ with lesynges, for to drawe þe to mirþes and for to lefe þi pilgrimage, make def ere and answer not ageyn, and sey not elles bot at þu wuldes be at Ierusalem. And if men profre þe ȝiftes and wil make þe riche with werdly gode, tente not to hem; þinke ay on Ierusalem. And if þu wil holde þis way and don as I hafe sayde, I vndirtake þi lif þat þu schal not be slayn, bot
85^{r} þou schal come to þat place þat | þu coueites.

Gostly to oure purpos; Ierusalem is as mikel for to seyen as siȝt of pes, and bitokneþ contemplacioun in perfit luf of God. For contemplacioun is not ellis bot a siȝt of Ihesu whilk is verrey pes. Þan if þu coueite for to come to þis blessid siȝt of verrey pees and ben a trew pilgrym to Ierusalem-ward, þawȝ it be so þat I were neuer þere, nerþeles as fer forþ as I kan I schal sette þe in þe weye þederward. Þe bygynnynge of þe hiȝe wey in þe whilk þu schalt gon is reformyng in faiþ, grounded mekly in þe feiþ and in þe lawes of Holy Kirke, as I hafe saide beforne; for trust sikirly, þawȝ þu haue synned here bifore, if þu be now reformed bi þe sacrament of penaunce aftir þe lawe of Holi Kirke, þat þu art in þe riȝt weie.

Now þan, siþen þu art in þe siker weye, if þu wile spedyn in þi goynge and make gode iurnaies, þe behouiþ to holden þese two þinges often in þi mynde: meknes and luf. Þat is, I am noȝt, I haue noȝt, I coueite noȝt bot on. Þou schalt hafe þe menynge of þese wordes in þin

a *prec.* LwHu$_2$W, a cyte Cc 43 it] H$_7$RH$_5$LB$_3$AsSrAEPH$_6$CcLdPl, *om.* HBLwHu$_2$MTWTd betokenes] as muche as *add.* Ld in] and E, of Ld For . . . pees (l. 44)] *This is the first extract in* AdAd$_2$ For] *om.* H$_5$ 44 Jesu] oure lord Jesu Hu$_2$, God RAsAMPlTTd, Jesu Christi Lat. þe] H$_7$RH$_5$LB$_3$AsSrAEPH$_6$CcMPlAlAdAd$_2$, *om.* HBLwHu$_2$LdTWTd 45 for . . . to^{2}] *om.* Td for] *om.* H$_6$ þis] þe AM blissed] blysful Cc, *om.* AM verrey] *om.* RAsAPl and] *om.* A 46 ben] to *prec.* H$_6$, wyl *prec.* Td -ward] *om.* Td be so] *rev.* RAsTd so] *om.* Lw were] was H$_5$SrAMLd, cam Cc neuer] `nat´ H$_6$ 47 neuerþeles] ȝit CcM ferforth as] *om.* Td 48 þederward] and telle [þe *add.* AM] þat most nedith þe for to know and kepe, and þe redist help in þi going *add.* RAsAMPl, [þat/. . ./þe *rev.* M], in via Lat. þe heygh] þi A þe^{2}] þis H$_5$ heygh] *om.* MTd þe^{3}] *om.* Cc whilk] þat *add.* As 49 in^{1}] of Td feith^{1}] after þe lawe of Holy Chirch *add.* RAs groundede . . . Kirke (l. 50)] *om.* AMPl groundede mekly] *rev.* H$_6$ þe^{1}] *om.* R 50 laghes] lawe Td I . . . before] *om.* Td before] aforn Cc for . . . weye (l. 54)] *This is the second extract in* AdAd$_2$ trust] þou *add.* T þogh] if M 51 here before] hertofore A here] *rep.* H nowe] *om.* Cc 52 after . . . Kirke] *om.* RAsAMPl þat] thanne Cc, *om.* AHu$_2$Pl ryght] sykir Td 54 Now . . . weye] and Ad Now] *om.* Cc þan] *om.* RH$_5$E syn . . . weye] *om.* Cc art] set *add.* RAsAPl þe] *om.* Lw syker] riȝt Hu$_2$H$_6$ 55 and . . . iournees] *om.* Td þe . . . Jesu (l. 61)] *This is the third extract in* AdAd$_2$ behoueth] H$_7$LB$_3$AsPM, behouen R, to *add.* HBH$_5$SrLwAHu$_2$EH$_6$CcLdPlTW holden] kepe Td often/þese two þynges] H$_7$RAsPl, *rev.* Σ often] *om.* ATd þese] *om.* Td two] *om.* Sr 56 þynges] *om.* Pl mende] þat is *add.* H$_6$AdAd$_2$, þat is to sey *add.* Td þat is] thinking þus Td, cogitando isto modo Lat. þat] and *prec.* LwW I hafe noȝt] *om.* T 57 noȝt] noþing H$_6$ þe menynge] thyn mende Cc þin entent and in habyte of þi soule lastendly, þogh þou hafe not speciali þese wurdes formed ay in þi þoght, for þat nedeþ not. Meknes seith: I am noȝt, I hafe noȝt; lufe seith: I coueyte noȝt bot one, þat is Jesu. Þese two strenges, wel festned wyth mende of Jesu, make gode acorde in þe harpe of þe soule whan þei ben craftily touched with þe fyngre of reson; for þe lowere þou smytest vpon þat on, þe heyghere sowneþ þat oþer. Þe lesse þou felest þat þou art or þat þou hast of þiself þurgh meknes, þe more þou coueytest for to han of Jesu in desyre of lufe. I mene not only of þat meknes þe whilk a soule feleth in sight of his owen synne or freltes or wrecchednes of þis lyfe or of þe wurthynes of his euene-cristen; for þogh þis meknes be sothfast and medycynable, neuerþeles it is boistous and fleschly as in regard, not clene, not softe ne lufly. Bot I mene also \`þis´ meknes þat þe soule feleth þurgh grace in sight and beholdynge of \`þe´ endles beynge and þe wunderful godenes of Jesu; and if þou moun not seen it ȝit with þi gostly eyge, þat þou trowe it. For þurgh sight of his beynge, eyþer in ful feith or in felynge, þou schalt holden þiself not only as þe most wrecche þat is bot also as noȝt in substaunce of þi soule, þogh þou haddest neuer don synne. And þat is lufly meknes, for in reward of Jesu þat is sothfastly al þou art right noght. And also þat þou þenke þat þou hast riȝt noȝt, bot art as a vessel þat standeþ ay tome or voide, as noȝt were þerin, as of þiself; for do þou neuer so many gode dedys

58 entent] herte Cc and . . . lastendly] *om.* Td in habyte of] inhabite hem in Cc habyte] a biȝt R lastendly] enduryngly Hu_2, stedfastly Cc hafe] þem *add.* Td not . . . formed] hem not euer specyally W 59 speciali/þese wurdes] *rev.* LB_3EPH_6 speciali] *om.* B þese . . . ay] *om.* Td formed . . . þoght] alwey in thyn thowt formyd Cc formed ay] H_7RLP, refourmed ay As, formed euer B_3AEH_6Pl, ay formed $HBH_5Hu_2AdAd_2$, euere formed T, euyr stormyd (stormyd *canc.*) Lw, alwey formed SrLd þoght] mouȝth Td 60 noȝt[1]] ne *add.* T noȝt[2]] And *add.* Ad lufe] *rep.*, *canc.* L seith[2]] seyȝe Ld noȝt[3]] noþing H_6 one] H_7RAsH_6Pl, and *add.* $HBH_5LB_3SrLwHu_2EPCcMLdTWAdAd_2$, solum Jesu Lat. \`is´ Cc 61 Jesu[1]] God RAsAMPl, þat is to sey, mekenes seys þus: I am vnmyȝty, vnwytty and vnwylly, full of syn and wrecchidnes, and fully I vntryste and despeir of my self. Luf seis: I trist fully in Jesu Crist. Sett all þi þoȝt and þi desyre in beholding of hym as he hang on þe cros for þe. For he is myȝty and witty and wylly to helpe þe *add.* Td, Intellectus horum verborum est iste: Inpotens sum et insipiens et involuntarius, plenus peccato et miseria, et ideo totaliter diffido et despero de meipso. Set amor dicit: Confide in Jesu Christo, et ideo statuere volo totam cogitacionem meam et desiderium meum in consideracione ipsius *add.* Lat. strenges] sterynges RLB_3PH_6M, corde Lat. wel . . . Jesu] *om.* AMPl wyth . . . acorde] *om.* Td mende] $H_7LB_3SrAPCcMPl$, þe *prec.* $HRBH_5AsLwHu_2EH_6LdTW$ gode] a swete Hu_2 62 þe[2]] þi LB_3EP ben] ch- *add.*, *canc.* L craftily] with mynde of Jesu *add.* Td þe[3]] *om.* Cc 63 fyngre] fyngres M lowere] $H_7HRBLB_3SrLwAHu_2PH_6MTW$, low þat H_5, þat *add.* AsECcLdPl vpon] on RAsAPl þat] *rep.* L 64 lesse] þat *add.* AE þat[2] . . . hast] *om.* Td þat[2] . . . or] *om.* RAsAMPl þat þou[2]] *om.* Sr of þiself] *om.* RAsAMPl 65 þurgh] be MT for . . . Jesu] *om.* RAsAMPl for] *om.* H_5Td Jesu] domino Jesu Christo Lat. 66 þe whilk]

entent and in habite of þi soule lastendly, þawȝ þu hafe noȝt specialy
þese wordes ay formed in þi þouȝte, for þat nediþ not. Meknes saiþ I
am noȝt, I hafe noȝt; lufe saiþ I coueite noȝt bot on, and þat is Ihesu.
þese two strenges, wel festned with þe mynde of Ihesu, makiþ gode
acorde in þe harpe of þe soule whan þei be craftly touchid with þe
fyngur of resoun; for þe lower þu smytes vpon þat on, þe hiȝer souniþ
þat oþer. þe lesse þou felist þat þu art or þat þu hast of þiself þurw
meknes, þe more þu coueites for to han of Ihesu in desire of luf. I
mene not only of þat meknes þat a soule feliþ in þe siȝt of his own syn
or freltees and wrecchednes of þis lif, or of þe worþines of his euen-
cristen; for þawȝ þis meknes be soþfast and medycynable, nerþeles it
85v is boistous and fleschly as in regarde, | not clene ne softe ne lufly. Bot
I mene also þis meknes þat þe soule feliþ þurwȝ grace, in siȝt and
beholdyng of þe endeles beynge and þe wndreful godnes of Ihesu; and
if þou mowe not seen it ȝit with þi gostly iȝe, þat þou trowe it. For
þurwȝ siȝt of his beynge, eiþer in ful feiþ or in felyng, þu scha[l]t
holden þiself not only as þe most wrecche þat is bot also as noȝt in
substaunce of þi soule, þawȝ þu haddist neuer don syn. And þat is
lufly meknes, for in reward of Ihesu þat is soþfastly al þu art riȝt noȝt.
And also þat þu þinke þat þu hast riȝt noȝt, bot art as a vessel þat
standiþ ay tome as noȝt were þerin, as of þiself; for doo þou neuer so

þat H_5Td in sight] *rep.* A in] H_7BLB$_3$SrAHu$_2$PH$_6$CPl, þe *add.* HRH$_5$AsLwECcLdTW 67 or[1]] of Sr, for LwW freltes] or freeltiez W^{G}, freelte CcLd, freelnes W or[2]] H_7RBH$_5$LB$_3$AsSrAEPH$_6$MPl, and HLwHu$_2$CcLdTW, et Lat. wrecchednes] wickidnes H_6 of[1] . . . wurthynes] *om.* RAsAPl þis] his Cc, his owne M or . . . cristen (l. 68)] *om.* Td þe wurthynes of] *om.* M 68 wurthynes] wurschepis Sr, wretchidnes LwW and] or Td 69 neuerþeles] yit Hu$_2$Cc fleschly] Ch *back* as in regard] *om.* AMPl as] *om.* H_5 regard] and *add.* E, of þe toþer *add.* E 70 not] H_7, ne Σ `þis´ *interl.* $H_7$ þe] a M 71 þurgh] be Cc and[1]] in *add.* ELd `þe´ *interl.* H_7, *om.* H_5 endles beynge] blyssed manhed Td, benedictam humanitatem Lat. beynge] of God *add.* RAsAMPl and[2] . . . Jesu (l. 72)] *om.* AMPl 72 godenes] mekenes and þe charite Td, humilitatem bonitatemque Lat. Jesu] Criste *add.* Td, Domini Jesu Christi Lat. and . . . it] *om.* Td, *om.* Lat. moun] H_7, mowen B, mowe HRLB$_3$AsLwPCcM, mow Ch, may H_5SrHu$_2$H$_6$W, miȝt A, maist ET ⌜ȝit⌝ H^{c}, riȝt H_5Ch, *om.* R 73 þat þou] *om.* Cc trowe] byleeue BAH$_6$MLd, trowe and bileue Hu$_2$ it] in *prec.* RAsMPl þurgh] þe Cc, in his RAs sight] grace and *prec.* Td his] þis Sr beynge] humilitatis et caritatis Lat. eyþer] or els Hu$_2$ 74 or] eiþer Ld schalt] not *add.* H_6 not . . . also (l. 75)] *om.* AMPlTd as] *om.* LwW 75 in . . . synne (l. 76)] *om.* Td, *om.* Lat. `þou´ Pl 76 neuer don] *rev., marked for trsp*. L lufly] goodly Cc 77 Jesu] hym RAsAMPl þat[1] . . . al] *om.* Td þat þou] þou `must´ H_6, *om.* Sr 78 bot art] ne þat þu art but Hu$_2$ art] stondest M as] *om.* CcLd ay . . . or] *om.* Pl ay] H_7HRLAsChPCcM, euere BB$_3$LwAHu$_2$EH$_6$TW, alway H_5SrLd tome] H_7RH$_5$LB$_3$AsLwEPMTW, tom⌜e⌝ H^{c}, tompe Ch, empty BSrAHu$_2$H$_6$Ld, *om.* Cc or . . . þerin] *om.* Td or voide] H_7RLB$_3$AsSrAEPCcMPl, and void H_6, *om.* HBH$_5$SrChLwHu$_2$MLdTW 79 as[1]] and Sr were] where Ld þerin] inne ChHu$_2$ as of þiself] *om.* ACcMPl as[2]] *om.* B$_3$ `gode´ L outward or inward, vntil þou hafe and fele þat þou hast þe lufe of Jesu þou hast right noght. For with `þat´ preciouse lyquour only may þi f. 66^v soule be fulfilled, and with non oþer. | And for as mikel as þat þinge allone is so preciouse and so wurthi, þerfore what þou hast or what þou dost, held it as noȝt to resten in withouten þe sight and þe lufe of Jesu. Keste it al behynd þe and forgete it, þat þou might hafe þat þat is best of alle.

Ryght as `a´ trew pilgryme goende to Jerusalem lefeþ byhynde him hous and londe, wyf and childe, and makeþ himself pore and bare fro al þat he hath, þat he might go lightly wythouten lettynge; right so if þou wilt be a gostly pilgrym, þou schalt make þiself naked fro alle þat þou haste, þat are boþe gode dedys and badde, and kasten hem alle behynde þe, þat þou be so pore in þyn owen felynge þat þer be nothynge of þyne owen werkynge þat þou wilt lene vpon restendly, bot ay desyrende more grace of lufe and ay sekende þe gostly presence of Jesu. And if þou do þus, þan schalt þu setten in þin herte fully þat þou woldest ben at Jerusalem and at non oþer place bot þere. And þat is, þou schalt setten in þin herte holly and fully þat þou woldest noþinge hafe bot þe lufe of Jesu and þe gostly sight of him as he wil schewe him; for to þat only þou art made and boght, and þat is þi bygynnynge and þin ende, þi ioye and þi blisse. And þerfor what-so-euer þat þou hafe, be þou neuer so riche in oþer dedys bodily and gostly, bot if þou hafe þat and knowe and fele þat þou hast it, helde þat þou hast riȝt noght. Preent wel þis reson in þe menynge of þin herte, and clefe sadly þerto, and it schal saufe þe fro alle peryles in þi goynge and þou schalt not peryschen. And it schal saufe þe fro þefes

80 vntil] H_7RLAEPCcMPl, vnto B_3As, til HBH_5B_3AsSrChLwHu$_2H_6$LdTW, bot if Td hafe . . . hast] senceas te habere Lat. þe lufe] *om.* Ld `of´ Ld Jesu] God RAsAMPl, Jesu Christi Lat. 81 `þat´ *interl.* H_7H^c, *om.* H°T preciouse lyquor] lufe Td 82 fulfilled] safe Td, oonli *add.*, *canc.* B_3 for] *one-letter canc. seq.* H_7 mikel as] *om.* M as^2] that Cc þat . . . allone] liquor iste Lat. 83 so] *om.* W what^2] whateuer T 84 it as] þat it is H_5 as] for E, of *add.* Cc noȝt] ryȝt *prec.* H_5LB_3EP to . . . in] *om.* Td to] H_7, as for to RLB_3AsSrAEPH_6CcPl, for to HBH_5ChLwHu$_2$MLdTW, as to Hu$_2$, quantum ad Lat. resten in] trust vpon Hu$_2$ withouten . . . Jesu] *om.* AMPl, si non habeas dileccionem Jesu Christi Lat. þe sight and] *om.* Td, *om.* Lat. and] of RLwW 85 Jesu] oure Lord *prec.* Hu$_2$ Keste] kestend RAs, Reste Pl it^1] *om.* Hu$_2$ might] *om.* Td þat^2] *om.* ACcTd 86 best] H_7RBLB_3SrAEPH_6CcMLdPl, þe *prec.* HH_5As-ChLwHu$_2$TW, scilicet dileccionem Dei *add.* Lat. 87 `as´ L, so as Cc, so T `a´ *interl.* H_7 trew pilgryme] *rev.* B_3 Jerusalem] Jerusalem-ward Sr him] his *add.* Hu$_2$, *om.* Ch 88 bare] goþ Sr fro] *om.* Td 89 al] thyng *add.* LwW þat he^1] þe H_5 might] may H_6Cc lettynge] any *prec.* H_5T 90 wilt] wolde B þiself] þe E naked] bare A 91 are] as to sey Td badde] yuel A hem] away Hu$_2$, *om.* LB_3APH_6 92 þe] *om.* Cc felynge . . . owen] *om.* As 93 lene] abyde B, þe *add.* A vpon] on H_6 restendly . . . Jesu (l.

many gode dedis outwarde or inwarde, til þu haue and fele þat þu hast þe luf of Ihesu þu hast riȝt noȝt. For with `þat´ precious licour only mai þi soule be fulfillid, and with none oþer. And for as mikel as þat þinge alone is so precious and so wurþi, þerfor what þu hast or what þu dost, holde it as noȝt for to resten in withoutyn þe siȝt and þe luf of Ihesu. Keste it al bihynde þe and forgete it, þat þu miȝte hafe þat þat is þe beste of alle.

Riȝt as a trewe pilgrym goende to Ierusalem lefiþ bihynde him hows and lande, wife and childe, and makiþ hymself pore and bare from al þat he haþ, þat he miȝt go liȝtly withouten lettynge: riȝt so if þu wil be a gostly pilgrym, þu schalt make þiself nakid fro al þat þu hast, þat are boþe gode dedis and badde, and kesten hem al bihynde þe, þat þou be so pore in þin owne felynge þat þer be noþinge of þin owne wirkynge þat þu wilt lene vpon restendly, bot ay desirend more grace of luf and ay sekend þe gostly presence of Ihesu. And if þu do þus, þan schalt þu setten in þi herte fully þat þu woldest be at
86r Ierusalem and at none oþer place | bot þere. And þat is, þu schalt setten in þin herte holly and fully þat þu woldest noþinge hafe bot þe luf of Ihesu, and þe gostly siȝt of hym as he wile schewe hym; for to þat only þu art made and boȝte, and þat is þi bigynnynge and þin ende, þi ioye and þi blisse. And þerfore what-so-euere þat þu hafe, be þu neuer so riche in oþer dedis bodily and gostly, bot if þu haue þat and knowe and fele þat þu hast it, halde þat þu hast riȝt noȝt. Preente wel þis resoun in þe menynge of þi herte, and clefe sadly þerto, and it schal safe þe fro alle periles in þi goynge þat þu schalt neuer perischen. And it schal saf þee fro þefes and robbours, þe whilk I

95)] *om.* RAsAMPl 94 ay[1]] H_7HLChPCc, euer B$H_5$$B_3LwEH_6$TW, euermore Hu_2, alwey SrLd of] and LwW ay[2]] H_7HLChPCc, euer B$H_5$$B_3LwEH_6$TW, euermore Hu_2, alwey SrLd sekende] on *add.* H_5 95 Jesu] Criste *add.* Td þan . . . þu] þou sal sone Td þu] *om.* B_3 ⌜in . . . woldest⌝ L fully] holly and *prec.*, *canc.* H, and hooly *add.* ⌜L⌝B_3EP, *om.* Td 96 And . . . boght (l. 99)] *This is the fourth extract in* AdAd_2 þat . . . þou] þus sal þou AdAd_2 97 is] þat *add.* As schalt] *om.* H_5 setten . . . fully] set fully in thy herte Ad_2 setten/in þin herte] *rev.* B_3 holly and fully] *rev.* LB_3EPH_6 holly and] *om.* TdAdAd_2 holly] holy R 98 bot] only M Jesu] God RAsAMPl, Criste *add.* Td gostly] *om.* RAsAMPl as . . . him] *om.* AMPl 99 to] vnto Ad_2 þou art] *rev.* BWAdAd_2 100 ende] endyng SrLwLdW so] som RAs, *om.* H_5 101 þat] *om.* RH_5AsACc and] or LwHu_2WTd 102 if] *om.* RAsELd it] þat M 103 þat] *om.* Pl hast] had`d´est Pl Preent] Prende Cc, Take RAsAPl þe menynge of] *om.* Td, *om.* Lat. þe] H_7HRH_5LB_3AsSrAEPH_6LdPlT, þi ChLwHu_2CcMW menynge] mynde AH_6Cc, begynnyng E of] in E, and in thyn Cc 104 sadly þerto] *rev.* Ld saufe þe fro] kepe þe in M 105 and[1]] H_7, þat Σ, ita quod Lat. not] H_7RLB_3AsAEPH_6CcM, neuer HBH_5SrChLwHu_2LdTWTd, `neuere´ Pl, non Lat. saufe] kepe M fro] the *add.* W þefes and] *om.* Ld and robbours, þe whilk I calle vnclene spyrytis, þat þogh þei spoiled þe and bete þe þurgh dyuers temptacions, þi lyfe schal ay be saufe. And schortly, if þou kepe it as I schal sey þe, þou schalt askape alle peryls and meschefes and come to þe cyte of Jerusalem within schorte tyme.

Now þou art in þe weye and knowest what þe place hight whedre þou schalt drawen to, begynne þan for to go forth in þi iurne. Þi forth goynge is not ellys bot gostly werkys, and bodily ⌜also⌝ whan þat it nedeþ, whilk þou schalt vsen by discrecyon vpon þis wyse. What werk
f. 67[r] þat | it be þat þou schuldest don aftere þe degre or state askeþ þat þou standest in bodily or gostly, if it helpe þis graciouse desyre þat þou hast for to lufe Jesu and mak it more hol and more esy, and more myȝthy to al vertus and to al godnes, þat wirk hold I best, be it preynge, be it þenkynge, be it redynge, be it werkynge; and as long as þat werke strengþes most þin herte and þi wil to þe lufe of Jesu, and ferþest draweth þin affeccion and þi þoght fro werdly vanite, it is gode for to vse it. And if it be so þat þurgh vse sauour of þat lesse and þe þenkeþ anoþer werke sauour þe more, and þou felest more grace in anoþer, take anoþer and lefe þat. For þogh þe desyre and þe ȝernynge of þin herte to Jesu schulde ay ben vnchaungeable, neuerþeles þi gostly werkes þat þou schalt vsen in preyinge oþer in þenkynge for to feden and norischen þis desire moun be dyuers, and moun wel be chaunged after þat þou felest þe disposed þurgh grace and applyenge of þin owen herte.

106 and] *om.* Lw þe] *om.* Td calle] clepe H$_6$LdT vnclene] wikkid Hu$_2$, ill Td \`þat′ L spoiled] H$_7$Pl, spoile Σ, spolient Lat. 107 and] or M temptacions] yit *add.* Hu$_2$Cc ay be] H$_7$HRH$_5$ChAsCc, *rev.* LP, euere be BSrLwAHu$_2$EMPlTW, be euer B$_3$H$_6$, be alweie Ld 108 as] *om.* M sey] to *add.* Cc 109 peryls and] *om.* RAsAPl and meschefes] *om.* Td schorte] a *prec.* RAsAPl 111 þe[1]] ryȝte *add.* Ld knowest] *om.* Td whedre] H$_7$HBH$_5$SrChAHu$_2$CcMLdPlT, that CcTd, and *add.* RLB$_3$AsLwEPW, ad quem Lat. 112 drawen to] go A þan] nowe Td, *om.* Lw for] *om.* As forth[1]] *om.* LwW in] on M forth goynge] *rev.* T, processus . . . seu progressio Lat. 113 werkys] H$_7$RLB$_3$As-AEPH$_6$CcPl, werkyng HBH$_5$SrChLwHu$_2$MLdTW, opera Lat. bodily also] *rev.* Td bodily] *initial* b- *corr. fr.* d- H$_7$ þat] H$_7$RLB$_3$SrA\`E′PH$_6$CcMPl, *om.* HBH$_5$AsChLwHu$_2$LdTW it nedeþ] H$_7$RLB$_3$AsAPH$_6$Pl, is nedith Cc, nede is HBH$_5$SrChLwHu$_2$EMLdTWTd 114 whilk] þe *prec.* Hu$_2$H$_6$ by] d- *prec.*, *canc.* H$_7$, wiþ LB$_3$Hu$_2$EPH$_6$ vpon] on H$_6$CcTd, in Ld What] *om.* Pl 115 þat[1]] euere *add.* T þat[2]] *om.* H$_5$ schuldest] schalt H$_5$LwW, schal Td aftere . . . in] *om.* AMPl þe] þy BLd, þat þi E, *om.* As or] H$_7$RLB$_3$AsEPH$_6$Cc, and HBH$_5$SrChLwHu$_2$LdTWTd, et Lat. state] H$_7$RBLB$_3$AsEPH$_6$Cc, þe *prec.* HH$_5$SrChLwHu$_2$LdTW askeþ] H$_7$RLB$_3$AsSrEPH$_6$Cc, *om.* HBH$_5$ChLwHu$_2$LdTWTd, *om.* Lat. 116 bodily or gostly] *om.*Sr þis] þin Cc graciouse] *om.* RAsACcMPl 117 for to] to Td, to the Cc, þe M Jesu] God RAsAMPl, of God Cc, dominum Jesum Christum Lat. mak] makith T and[2]] *om.* Td more[2]] *om.* A 118 to[1] . . . godnes] *om.* AMPl to al[2]] al Sr, *om.* RBAsChHu$_2$ \`hold′ L best] to þe *add.* Sr

calle vnclene spirites, þat þawȝ þei spoile þee and bete þe þurwȝ diuers temptaciouns, þi lif schal ay be safe. And schortly, if þu kepe it as I schal say þe, þu schalt askape alle periles and meschiefs and come to þe citee of Ierusalem within schort tyme.

Now þou art in þe wey and knowest what þe place hiȝte wheder þu schalt drawe to, bygynne þen for to gon forþ in þi iurney. Þi forþ goynge is noȝt elles bot gostly wirkynge, and bodily also whan nede is, whilk þu schalt vsen bi discrecioun vpon þis wise. What werk þat it be þat þu schulde don after þe degre and þe state þat þu standis in bodily or gostly, if it helpe þis gracious desire þat þu haste for to lufe Ihesu and make it more hol, more esy, and more miȝty to alle vertues and to alle goodnes, þat werke hald I beste, be it prechynge, be it þinkynge, be it redyng, be it wirkynge; and as longe as þat werke strengþeþ most þin hert and þi wil to þe luf of Ihesu, and ferrest drawiþ þin affeccioun and þi þoȝte fro werdly vanytee, it is gode for to vsen it. And if it be so þat þurwȝ vse sauour of þat lesseþ and þe þinkiþ anoþer werk sauoriþ þe more, and þu felist more grace in anoþer, take anoþer and lefe þat. For þawȝ þi desire and þe ȝerynge of þin herte to
86v Ihesu schuld | be ay vnchaungable, nerþeles þi gostly werkes þat þu schalt vsen in praynge or þinkynge for to feden and norischen þi desire may be dyuers, and may wel be chaunged aftir þat þu felis þe disposed þurw grace in appliynge of þin own hert.

119 preynge] prechynge HH$_5$LwWTd, be hit seiynge *add.* M, oracio Lat. be it werkynge] vel alia operacio qualisqunque Lat. and] *om.* H$_6$ 120 þat] þi Sr werke strengþes] werkith strength Ld most] *one-word erasure seq.* (in?) H$_7$, þe A þi] þe LPH$_6$ wil/. . ./lufe] *rev.* Ld of] *om.* B Jesu] God RAsAMPl, Jesu Christi Lat. 121 ferþest] ferþere RAs vanite] vanitees M, vanitatibus Lat. 122 for] *om.* Td if] *om.* Lw vse[2]] þe T, þe *add.* M sauour of þat] of that thyn savour Cc sauour] fauour Sr lesse] H$_7$Sr, is *prec.* RAsAPl, lesseþ HBH$_5$LB$_3$ChLwHu$_2$EPH$_6$CcMLdTWTd, minuatur Lat. þe . . . grace (l. 123)] þou fyndist more savour Cc þe þenkeþ] þou þenkiste H$_5$ þe] þou H$_6$ 123 þenkeþ] þenke H$_6$M, þinke þar Sr anoþer] oþur A sauour] H$_7$, fauour Sr, sauoriþ HRBH$_5$LB$_3$AsChLw-Hu$_2$EPH$_6$MLdPlTWTd, sapiat Lat. 124 anoþer[1]] þat oþer Hu$_2$ take anoþer/and/lefe þat] *rev.* Cc anoþer[2]] þat oþer ECc þe[1]] H$_7$RLB$_3$AsSrChAHu$_2$EPH$_6$CMPl, þi HBH$_5$LwLdTW, *om.* Td desyre/. . ./ȝernynge] *rev.* Hu$_2$ and þe ȝernynge/of þin herte] *rev.* Sr and þe ȝernynge] *om.* CcTd and[2]] to RAsAPl ȝernynge] longing A, couyttyng Ld 125 Jesu] God RAsAMPl, Jesu Christo Lat. ay ben] H$_7$RLAsPCcM, be ay HCh, euere be B$_3$EH$_6$Pl, be euere BLwAHu$_2$TW, be euere more H$_5$, be alwey Sr, be Ld vnchaungeable] vnchangeably Pl neuerþeles] ȝet Cc þi] þei Sr, in H$_5$ 126 gostly] corporalia et spiritualia Lat. werkes] werke is As schalt] scholdiste H$_5$ in[1]] as *prec.* E oþer in] H$_7$RH$_5$LB$_3$AsSrAEPH$_6$CcLdPl, oþer of M, oþer HBChLwHu$_2$TW, in Td 127 and[1]] or M, to *add.* E þis] H$_7$RBLB$_3$ChAEPH$_6$LdPl, þat þis As, þi HH$_5$SrLwCcMTWTd, illud Lat. and . . . chaunged] *om.* Lat. wel be] H$_7$HRBAsSrChLwAHu$_2$H$_6$CcMPlTW, *rev.* H$_5$LB$_3$EPLd 128 grace] *om.* Lw and . . . of] *om.* Cc and] in HH$_5$LwTWTd 129 owen] *om.* Td

For it fareth by werkes and by desyre as it doth by stykkes and by fyre; for þe mo stikkes are leyd to þe fyre, þe gretter is þe flawme and þe hattere is þe fyre. Ryght so þe more `diuers´ gostly werkynge þat a man hath in his þoght for to kepe hol his desyre, þe myghtyere and þe more brennende schal ben his desyre to God. And þerfore loke wysly what werk þou kanst best don, and þat most helpeþ þe for to saufen hol þis desyr to Jesu, if þou be fre and art not bounden bot vnder þe common laghe, and þat do. Bynde þe not to wilful customs vnchaungeably, þat schuld lette þe fredom of þin herte for to lufe Jesu if grace wulde vysyte þe specialy. For I schal tel þe whilk customs are ay gode and nedful to be kept. [Lo], swilk a custom is ay gode for to holden þat standeþ in getynge of vertu and lettynge of synne, and þat custom schulde neuer be lefte; for þou schalt ay be meke and pacient, sobre and chaste, if þou wel do, and so of alle oþer vertus. Bot þe custom of anoþer þynge þat letteth a bett⌜r⌝e is for to lefen whan tyme is, þer a man may. As þus: if a man hafe in custom for to seyn þus many bedys, or for to þenk only þis maner þoght and þus longe tyme, or for to waken or knelen þus longe, or ony oþer swilk bodily dede; þis custom is for to lefen sumtyme whan resonable cause letteþ
f. 67^v or ellys | if more grace come in oþer syde.

130 werkes] þe werk M by^2] *om.* Td desyre] þe *prec.* M, desires RAs by stykkes] de lignis accedit Lat. 131 fyre] H_7RAsH_6CcM, a *prec.* HBH_5LB_3SrChLwA-Hu_2EPLdPlTWTd for . . . fyre] *om.* As are] þat *prec.* RHu_2M to] on Cc gretter] more M flawme . . . þe^2 (l. 132)] H_7RLB_3AsAEPH_6CcPl, *om.* HBH_5Sr-ChLwHu_2MLdTWTd, maior est flamma, ignisque callidior Lat. 132 `diuers´ *marg., s.h.* H_7 gostly] *om.* LdPl werkynge] wyrkynges RAsSrPl, operaciones Lat. 133 þoght] herte H_5 for] *om.* H_6 his^2] þe Ld myghtyere] stranger Td þe] *om.* BWTd 134 brennende] brennandere B schal ben/his desyre] H_7RLB_3As-AEPH_6CcLdPl, *rev.* H_5, schal his desire be HBSrChLwHu_2MTW wysly] *om.* A 135 werk] þat *add.* As best don] *rev.* E don] *om.* Cc `and´ Td, in M `þat´ Pl helpeþ] likith RAsAMPl þe] *om.* LwW 136 þis] þi Td Jesu] God *prec., canc.* E, God RAsAMPl, dominum Jesum Christum Lat. if . . . laghe (l. 136)] *om.* AM and] *rep.* H_5 bot] and Ld 137 `and´ L, *om.* B_3H_6 þat do] *rev.* H_6, þat þou do H_5, do þou that Cc þe not] *rev.* Ld wilful customs] blynde custumes and *add.* M 138 vnchaungeably] vnchaungeable EM for] *om.* Td 139 Jesu] God RAsACcMPl, Jesu Christi Lat. wulde] wole LB_3PH_6, voluerit Lat. specialy] *om.* RAsAMPl þe^2] *om.*

For it fariþ bi werkes and bi desire as it doþ bi stikkes and bi a fiire; for þe mo stikkes arn leide to þe fiire, þe gretter is þe fire. Riȝt so þe more diuers gostly wirkynge þat a man haþ in his þoȝt for to kepe hol his disire, þe miȝtier and þe more brennand schal his desire be to God. And þerfore loke wisely what werke þu kannist best don, and þat most helpiþ þe for to safen hole þis desire to Ihesu, if þou be free and art not boundene bot vndir þe comen lawe, and þat do. Bynde þe not to wilful customes vnchaungebly, þat sculden let þe fredom of þin hert for to luf Ihesu if grace wolde visite þe specialy. For I schal telle þe whilke customes are ay gode and nedful to be kepte. Lo, swilke custome is ay gode for to holden þat stondiþ in getynge of vertue and lettynge of syn, and þat custome schuld neuer be lefte; for þu schalt ay be meke and paciente, sobre and chaste, if þu wel do, and so of alle oþer vertues. Bot þe custome of anoþer þinge þat lettiþ a better is for to lefen when tyme is, þer a man may. As þus: if a man hafe in custome for to say þus many bedis, or for to þinken þis maner of þoȝt þus longe tyme, or for to waken or knelen þus longe, or any oþer swilk bodily dede; þis custome is for to lefen sumtyme whan resonable cause lettiþ or elles if more grace come in oþer side.

AsPl 140 ay] H$_7$HH$_5$LAsChPCc, euere BB$_3$LwAHu$_2$EH$_6$MPlW, alwey SrLdT kept] and whilk nouȝt *add.* RAsAMPl Lo] Be H$_7$, *om.* Cc swilk] which MPl a] H$_7$RLB$_3$AsSrAEPH$_6$MPl, *om.* HBH$_5$ChLwHu$_2$CcLdTWTd custom is] customes arn H$_5$Cc, customs is Td ay] H$_7$HRH$_5$LAsChPCc, euere BB$_3$LwAHu$_2$EH$_6$MPlW, alwey SrLdT for] *om.* B$_3$H$_6$MW 141 holden] H$_7$HRH$_5$SrChLwAHu$_2$LdPlTW, ben *prec.* LB$_3$AsEPH$_6$Cc, be kept and *prec.* M, obseruare Lat. in] þe *add.* Ld vertu] vertues H$_5$T 142 þat] iche *add.* M schulde] schal Ld ay] H$_7$HH$_5$LAsChPCc, euere BB$_3$Lw-AHu$_2$EH$_6$MPlTW, alwey SrLd and] *om.* AW 143 wel] wyl Cc of] *om.* Cc oþer] *om.* As 144 bettre] operacionem meliorem Lat. is] as *prec.* B, \`is goode´ Lw, good *add.* W for] *om.* Ld 145 þer] as *add.* T a man hafe] habeas Lat. in] RH$_6$ 146 bedys] þus many psautirs *add.* Td to] *om.* Cc only] H$_7$LB$_3$SrEPH$_6$CcM, *om.* HRH$_5$AsChLwAHu$_2$LdPlTWTd, solum Lat. maner] H$_7$RLB$_3$AsSrAEPH$_6$CcMPlT, of *add.* HBH$_5$ChLwHu$_2$LdW and] H$_7$RLB$_3$AsSrAEPH$_6$MPl, or Cc, *om.* HBH$_5$Ch-LwHu$_2$LdTWTd, et Lat. þus longe tyme] tanto tempore vel tanto Lat. þus] þys Ld 147 \`or[1] . . . longe´ Pl for to] *om.* Td waken/or/knelen] *rev.* Td þus] þys Ld ony oþer] ouȝt M oþer swilk] *rev.* ELd oþer] *om.* RAsCh swilk] *om.* LB$_3$PH$_6$ 148 dede] dedus M, werk A lefen] ⌜leeue⌝ L, loue B$_3$, ben left Cc resonable] a *prec.* H$_6$ letteþ] not *add.* B$_3$ 149 if] *om.* Td \`grace´ B$_3$, *om.* Td come] cometh Ld in] H$_7$HRBH$_5$AsSrChAHu$_2$H$_6$LdPlT, on LB$_3$LwEPCcMW oþer syde] anodyr syde Ld, oþur sidis AM, otherwyse LwW

Of generale remedie ageyns wikked sterynges and pynful tarienges þat fallen in here hertes of þe flesch, of þe werd and of þe fende, and how a stedfast desyre to Jesu meyntened and strengthed with deuoute preyenge and besy þenkeng on him [is] a souereyn remedye. Capitulum xxii^{m}

Now art þou in þe weye, and þow wost how þou schalt gon. Now be ware of enemys þat wilen be besy for to lette þe if þei moun. For alle here entent is for to putten owt of þin herte þat desyre and þat longynge þat þou hast to þe lufe of Jesu, and for to dryfe þe home aȝen to lufe of werdli vanite, for þer is nothynge þat greueth hem so mikel. Þese enemys are princypaly fleschly desyres and veyn d[r]edys þat rysen out of þin herte þurgh corrupcion of þi fleschly kynde and wold lette þe desyre of þe lufe of Jesu þat þei myght fully and restfully occupien þin herte. Þese are þi nest enemys. Also oþer enemys þer are, as vnclene spyrites þat are besy with sleyghttes and wyles for to desceyue þe. Bot o remedie schalt þou hafe þat I seide before: what-so it be þat þei seyn, trowe hem not, bot hold forth þi weye and only desyre þe lufe of Jesu. Answere ay þus: I am noȝt, I haue noȝt, I coueyte noȝt, bot only for to lufe Jesu.

If þin enemys seyn to þe firste þus be sterynges in þin herte, þat þou art not schryuen aryȝt, or þer is sum old synne hyd in þin herte þat þou knowest not ne were not schryuen of, and þerfor þe most

Chapter 22 *title*: H$_7$LB$_3$EPH$_6$ Of [How Sr] taryengys and of temptacions þat soules [*om.* R] schuln [*om.* TW] feelyn by here gostly enemiis in þeire gostly goyng [knowinge and *prec.* TW] to heuenly [*om.* TW] Ierusalem, and of remediis ageyns hem [and^2 . . . hem *om.* Pl] RSrALdPlTW How a man þat is in þis weye shal haue enemyes to dryue him aȝene, and how he shal ouercome hem by þe knowynge of oure Lord Jesu and shrifte of mouth and contricion of hert and satisfaccion in dede. AsH^c De impedimentis et temptacionibus et obieccionibus peccatorum suorum per spirtuales inimicos excitatis quas sencient anime in eundo versus celestum ierusalem, et de remediis contra eas. Lat. *om.* BH$_5$LwHu$_2$CcMTd. M *has no chapter-division at this point* 1 Of] a *add.* LEPH$_6$ 2 of^2] H$_7$EH$_6$, *om.* Σ 3 of] H$_7$E, *om.* Σ 4 preyenge] preir LB$_3$EPH$_6$ is] as H$_7$ 5 a^2] *om.* E 6 þow] H$_7$RLB$_3$SrAEPH$_6$CcMPl, *om.* HH$_5$AsChLwHu$_2$LdTWTd Now^2 . . . moun (l. 7)] *This is the fifth extract in* Ad$_2$, And if it hapyn be þine enmys gostly or bodely to be sayd vnto þe in þi þoght or oþerways Ad Now^2] se and *add.* B$_3$H$_6$ 7 of] with þine Ad$_2$ enemys] þin *prec.* E þat] þey Ld for] *om.* H$_6$MTd `þe´ Pl alle] H$_7$RLB$_3$AsSrAEPH$_6$CcMPl, *om.* HBH$_5$ChLwHu$_2$LdTWTd, tota Lat. 8 here] other M for] *om.* T `owt´ Pl þat^1] þe As 9 hast] to haf *add.*, *canc.* Cc `þe^1´ RCc Jesu] God RAsAMPl, Jesu Christi (*bis.*) Lat. 10 lufe] H$_7$HRBLB$_3$AsChLwAHu$_2$PCcMPl, þe *prec.* H$_5$SrEH$_6$LdTW of] a B, þe As, þe *add.* CcLd vanite] vanyteys SrMTd, vanitates Lat. for] þerfore As nothynge] non þyng As hem] him H$_5$, hem *corr. fr.*hym Ch, *om.* Pl 11 princypaly] *om.* Td fleschly] flesch Ld dredys] dedys H$_7$, timores Lat. 12 corrupcion] cor- *prec.*, *canc.* L

[CHAPTER 22]

Now art þu in þe wey and wost how þu schalt gon. Now bewar of enmys þat wilen be bisy for to lette þe if þei mown. For here entente is
37r for to putten owt of þin herte þat desire | and þat longynge þat þu haste to þe luf of Ihesu, and for to drife þe hom ageyn to luf of wordly vanyte, for þer is noþinge þat grefiþ hem so mikel. Þese enmys arn principally flescly desires and vayne dredis þat risen out of þin hert þurwʒ corupcioun of þi flescly kynde and wolden let þi desire of þe luf of God þat þei miʒten fully and restfully occupien þin hert. Þese arn þi next enmys. Also oþer enmys þer are, as vnclene spirites þat are bisy with sleʒtes and wiles for to descayue þe. Bot o remedie schalt þu hafe þat I saide beforne: what-so it be þat þei saien, trowe hem not, bot holde forþ þi wey and only desire þe luf of Ihesu. Answere ay þus: I am noʒt, I hafe noʒt, I coueite noʒt, bot only þe luf of Ihesu.

If þin enmys seyen to þe first þus, bi stirynges in þin herte, þat þou `art not shryuen ariʒt, or þer is summe old synne hid in þi hert þat þou′ knowis not ne were neuer schrifen of, and þerfore þe most turne

wold] wolle T 13 þe[1]] H$_7$RLB$_3$AsSrChAHu$_2$EPMPl, þi HBH$_5$LwH$_6$CcLdTWTd, *om.* Lat. of[1]] fro BT Jesu] H$_7$LB$_3$EPH$_6$Cc, God HRBH$_5$AsSrChLwAHu$_2$MLdPlTWTd, Jesu Christi Lat. and restfully] *om.* Cc restfully] restingly Td 14 enemys[1]] And *add.* M Also . . . enemys[2]] *om.* As þer] þat RAs 15 vnclene spyrites] *rev.* M for] *om.* Ld 16 o] oon SrM schalt þou] *rev.* M þat . . . before] *om.* Td what-so . . . Jesu (l. 18)] *This is the sixth extract in* Ad$_2$ what-so] euer *add.* SrT 17 it be þat] *om.* TdAd$_2$ it be] *om.* Sr seyn] to þe *add.* T trowe] leeue BAM, beleue Ad$_2$ not] and [bot A] sey I couete nouʒt but for to loue God *add.* RAsAPl þi weye] *om.* Ad$_2$ only] *om.* Ad$_2$ 18 þe lufe] *rep.* A Jesu] God RAsAMPl, Jesu Christi Lat. Answere ay] *rev.* H$_6$, And *prec.* H$_6$MAd$_2$, and answere þem noʒt bot þink Td, Semperque respondeas Lat. ay] H$_7$HRBH$_5$LChPCc, euere B$_3$AsLwAHu$_2$EH$_6$MPlW, alwey SrLd, þou as T 19 coueyte noʒt] *om.* Sr only/for . . . Jesu] *rev.* Ld only] *om.* RAPl for to lufe H$_7$RLB$_3$AsSrAEPH$_6$MPl, þe luf of HBH$_5$ChLwHu$_2$CcLdTWTdAd$_2$, diligere Lat. Jesu] our lorde *prec.* LwW, God RAsAMPl, Jesum Christum Lat.20 If] þat *add.* Sr þin[1]] eny AM to . . . þus] þus to þe M sterynges] steryng CcMLd in] of TTd þin[2]] *om.* LwW 21 `art . . . þou (l. 22)′ H^c, *om.* H$^\circ$H$_5$ schryuen aryʒt] *rev.* Pl, wele schriuen Td aryʒt] riʒt APl or . . . of (l. 22)] *om.* Td þer] *rep.*, *canc.* L synne] þat is *add.* H$_6$ hyd/in þin herte] *rev.* M 22 ne] and Sr, þou *add.* Cc were not] neuer were W not] H$_7$RLB$_3$AsSrAEPH$_6$CcMPl, neuer HBH$_5$ChLwHu$_2$LdTW, non Lat. of] þerof Hu$_2$CcPl, þerof ariʒt AsT, aryʒt LwW and] *om.* ChHu$_2$ þe most] motest þou B, *om.* Td þe] H$_7$HChAPl, þou RBH$_5$LB$_3$AsSrLwHu$_2$EPH$_6$MLdPlTW most] motest LB$_3$, bihouith A

turne home aȝen and lefe þi desyre and go home and schryfe þe better: trow not þis seynge for it is fals; for þou art schryfen. Trust sykerly þat þou art in þe weye, and þe nedeþ no more ransakynge of schryfte for þat þat is passed; hold forth þi weye and þenke on Jerusalem. Also if þei seyn þat þou art not wurthy for to hafe þe lufe of God, whareto schalt þou coueyte þat þou maight not han ne art not wurthi þerto, trow hem not, bot go forth and sey þus: Not for I am wurthi, bot for I am vnwurthi, þerfore wold I lufe God; for if I hadde it, þat schuld f. 68r make me wurthi. And syn I was made þerto, þogh I schuld | neuer hafe it, ȝet wil I coueyte it, and þerfore wil I preyen and þenken, þat I might gete it. And þan if þin enemys seen þat þou bygynnest to waxen bolde and wel willed to þi werk, þei bygynne to wexen aferd of þe.

Neuerþeles þei wil not cessen of taryinge whan þei moun as longe as þou art goende in þe weye, what with drede and manassynge on þat o syde, what with flaterynge and fals plesynge on þat oþer syde, for to do þe breke þi purpose and turne home aȝen. Þei wil seye þus: If þou hold forth þis desyre to Jesu, so fully trauailende as þou begynnest, þou schalt fallen in sekenes, or in fantasyes, or into frenesyes, as þou seest oþer men don, or þou schalt falle in pouerte and bodily myschef, and no man schal wil helpe þe; or þou maight falle into priue temptacions of þe fende þat þou schalt not kun helpe þiself in. For it is wonder perylous ony man to ȝif him fully to þe lufe of God and lefen al þe werld, and noþinge coueyten bot only þe lufe of him, for so

23 home and] H_7, first and LB$_3$AsEPH$_6$CcMPl, first RA, *om.* HBH$_5$SrChLwHu$_2$LdTW schryfe] to *prec.* H_5 24 trow] leeue BM, bileue Hu$_2$, triste As, þou *add.* Cc not] to *add.* As seynge] seiengis E is] vtterli *add.* H_6 for[2] . . . schryfen] *om.* RAsAMPlTd. *om.* Lat. for[2]] whan *add.* H_6 schryfen] and *add.* Cc Trust] trowe RAsAPl, for *prec.* Td, þou *add.* H_5 sykerly] fulli E, and *add.* W 25 þat] *om.* H_6 in þe weye] schriuen Td of schryfte] *om.* RAsAPl 26 þat þat] þat ChHu$_2$LdTd, þat `þat´ Lw passed] ouerpassid A þi] þe R Jerusalem] Domino Jesu Christo Lat. Also . . . God (l. 27)] *This is the fifth extract in* Ad, *the seventh in* Ad$_2$ 27 þat] *om.* RAsSr art] nart B for to hafe] *om.* Cc for] $H_7$RBLB$_3$AsSrChHu$_2$AEPH$_6$CcMLd, *om.* HH$_5$LwPlTWAdAd$_2$ `þe´ Pl God] Jesu Td 28 þat] þat þat LdT maight] may R not[2]] *om.* Hu$_2$Ld 29 trow . . . it (l. 30)] *This is the sixth extract in* Ad, *the eighth in* Ad$_2$ trow] leue BA go] hold AdAd$_2$ forth] nott wyþ foote but wyth desyre *add.* Ld for[1]] þat *add.* T 30 wold I] *rev.* ChHu$_2$MLd lufe] han the love of Cc God] Jesu Td, Dominum Jesum Christum Lat. for] And Hu$_2$ it þat] hym he Cc, his luf it Td, it it AdAd$_2$, dileccionem eius Lat. 31 me wurthi] *rev., marked for trsp.* L syn] þat *add.* H$_5$E, for as mych as Hu$_2$ was] wite Ld 32 it[1]] hym Sr wil I[1]] *rev.* CcLd it[2]] hym Sr þerfore wil I] *om.* Hu$_2$ and þenken] *om.* Td I[3]] *om.* B_3 33 gete] haue Hu$_2$Ld it] hym Sr And . . . to] *This is the ninth extract in* Ad$_2$ þan if þin] *om.* H_5 þan if] eftyr this when Ad$_2$ bygynnest . . . and] ert so Ad$_2$ to] for *prec.* Sr 34 wel] *rep.* Pl þi] þis M bygynne] wile begynnyn Sr, schuld *prec.* H$_6$Cc 35 cessen] to *prec.* Ld taryinge] taryingis Td, þe *add.* LwW, and lettyng *add.* Hu$_2$ whan] whiles M 36 goende in] *rev.* A þe] þi SrA drede and manassynge/. . ./flaterynge . . . plesynge (l. 37)] *rev.* Ld drede and

hom ageyn and lefe þi desire and go schrife þe better: trowe not þis seiynge, for it is fals, for þu art schrifen. Trost sikirly þat þu art in þe wey, and þe nediþ no more ransakynge of schrifte for þat þat is passid; holde forþ þi wey and þenk on Ierusalem. Also if þei sey þat þu art not worþi to hafe þe luf of God, wharto schalt þu coueite þat þu maiȝte not hafe ne art not worþi þerto, trowe hem not, bot go forþ and say þus: Not for I am worþi, bot for I am vnworþi, þerfore wolde I luf God; for if I had it, þat schulde make me worþi. And siþen I was made þerto, þawȝ I schuld neuer hafe it, ȝit wil I coueite it, and þerfore wile I preien and þenken þat I miȝte geten it. And þan if þin enmys seeþ þat þu bigynnist to wexen bolde and wel willed to þi werk, þei bigynne to wexen aferde of þe.

Nerþeles þei wil not cesyn of taryynge whan þei mowen as longe as
7v þu art goende in þe wey, what wiþ | drede and manasynge on þat o side, what wiþ flaterynge and fals plesynge on þat oþer side, for to make þe breke þi purpos and turne home ageyn. Þei wil sey þus: If þu holde forþ þi desire to Ihesu, so fully trauailende as þu bigynnest, þu schalt falle into seknes, or into fantasies, or into frenesies, as þu seest þat som don, or þu schalt falle into pouerte and bodily meschief, and no man schal wil helpe þee; or þou miȝt falle into pryue temptaciouns of þe feende þat þu schalt not kun help þi selfyn. For it is wonder perilous to any man for to gif him fully to þe luf of God, and lefen alle þe werld and noþinge coueiten bot only þe luf of him, for so many

manassynge] thretyng Cc   manassynge] threting Td, þreetyngis Hu$_2$ 37 syde] and *add.* M   what . . . syde/for . . . purpose (l. 38)] *rev.* Td   and] wiþ *add.* B$_3$ on] in Ld   þat] the Cc   to] *om.* Ld   38 do] H$_7$RLB$_3$AsSrPH$_6$CcM, make HBH$_5$ChLwAHu$_2$ELdPlW, *om.* T   and] to Td   þei] Also *prec.* H$_6$ 39 þis] H$_7$RLB$_3$AsEPH$_6$MPl, thus Cc, þi HBH$_5$SrChLwAHu$_2$LdTWTd, istud Lat.   Jesu] God RAsAMPl   trauailende] and feruently Hu$_2$, *om.* RAsAMPl, laborandum Lat. 40 in[1]] H$_7$RLB$_3$AsAPH$_6$CcPl, into HBH$_5$SrChLwHu$_2$LdTWTd, to EM   in[2]] H$_7$RLB$_3$AsAPH$_6$Pl, into HBH$_5$SrChLwHu$_2$CcMLdTWTd, to E   or into frenesyes] *om.* A   into] *om.* Td   frenesyes] a frenesye As, frenesy E   41 oþer men] H$_7$, þat som HRBH$_5$B$_3$AsSrChLwHu$_2$EH$_6$MLdTWTd, þat sum men LAPCcPl, summe H$_6$LdTd, alios Lat.   in] H$_7$RLAsAPH$_6$M, into HBH$_5$B$_3$SrChLwHu$_2$ECcLdPlTWTd   pouerte . . . into (l. 42)] *om.* ChHu$_2$ 42 and . . . þe] *om.* Ld   and] þat *add.* A   wil] wel BLwW, to *add.* EH$_6$, *om.* M   maight] may As, schalt Ld   into] in RAsAPl, onto Cc   43 temptacions] temptacyon Cc   kun] *om.* LwW   þiself in] þi selfyn HHu$_2$, þiself H$_5$LwCcTWTd, in quibus nescies te iuuare Lat.   44 is] *om.* M   wonder perylous] perilous wonderly Hu$_2$, perilous Td   ony] H$_7$RLB$_3$AsSrAEPH$_6$MPl, to *prec.* HBH$_5$ChLwHu$_2$CcLdTW, to a Td, alicui homini Lat.   man] fulli *add.*, *canc.* L   to[1]] H$_7$RLB$_3$AsSrEPH$_6$CcMPl, for *prec.* HBH$_5$ChLwAHu$_2$LdTWTd   him] hymself Hu$_2$, hem Ch   45 lefen] to *prec.* H$_6$, lese M   al þe werld] delectacionem mundi Lat.   \`and´ B$_3$    noþinge coueyten] *rev.* Td    coueyten] coueit⸢yng⸣ L, coueitinge B$_3$P    only] him and *add.* \`L´B$_3$P, *om.* A   þe lufe of] *om.* H$_6$ him] Jesu Td, domini Jesu Christi Lat.   so] myȝt *add.* Td many peryles moun fallen þat a man knoweþ not of. And þerfor turne home aȝen and lefe þis desyr, for þou schalt neuer brynge it to an ende, and do as oþer werdly men don.

þus seyn þin enemys, bot trowe hem not, bot hold ay forth þi desyre, and say not ellys bot þat þu wuldest hafe Jesu and be at Jerusalem. And if þei perceyue þan þi wil so strengthed þat þou wil not spare for synne ne for sekenes, for fantasye ne frenesye, for dowtes ne for dredys of gostly temptacyons, for mischef ne for pouerte, for lyfe ne for dede; bot ay forth þou wilt with o þynge, and noþynge bot on, and makes defe ere to hem, what-so-euer þei seyn, as þogh þou herd hem not, and holdest þe forth styfly in þi preyers and in þin oþer gostly werkes withouten styntynge, and þat þou dost with discrecyon after counseil of þi souereyn or þi gostly fadere: þan bygynne þei for to [be wroth and to gon a litil nerre þe. þei bygynne for to] robbe þe and bete þe and do þe al þe schame þat þei moun. And þat is whan þei make þat al þi dedys þat þou dost, be þei neuer so wele don, are
f. 68v demed of oþer men as il and turnd into þe werse partye. | And what-so-euer it be þat þou wuldest hafe don in helpe of þi body or of þi soule, it schal be lettede or hyndred by oþer men, so þat þou schalt be putte fro þi wil in al þynges þat þou skilfully coueytest. And al þis þei don þat þou schuldest be styred to yre or malencolie or euel wil aȝens þin euen-cristen.

Bot aȝens al þese desesys and al oþer þat moun fallen, vse þis remedye. Tak Jesu in þi mynde and angre þe not with hem, tary not

46 many . . . fallen] may 'falle' many perlis H$_6$ moun] *om.* Td And] *om.* Pl 47 þis] þi A neuer brynge it] nouȝt brynge it neuer H$_5$ it] *om.* ATd to] vnto Sr an] H$_7$RAsACcMPl, þe HBH$_5$SrChLwHu$_2$LdTW, a good LB$_3$PH$_6$, *om.* Td 48 do] þerfore *prec.* Td, þou *add.* T werdly men] men of þe world M 49 trowe hem] leeue hym B, leeue hem AM, beleue hem Ld, trust hem Hu$_2$, trowe hym Ch bot[2]] And Cc ay forth] *rev.* Cc ay] H$_7$RLAsSrPCc, euere B$_3$AEH$_6$Pl, *om.* HBH$_5$SrChLwHu$_2$MLdTWTd, semper Lat. þi] weie and þi *add.* Hu$_2$ 50 þat þu] *om.* T þat] *om.* HChLwHu$_2$W 'þu' H$_6$T hafe Jesu and] *om.* RAsAMPl, Jesum habere velles Lat. 51 if . . . perceyve/þan] *rev.* Td if] *om.* H$_5$ þi wil] that thyn will is Cc strengthed] H$_7$RBLB$_3$As-SrChPH$_6$MLdPl, strong HH$_5$LwAHu$_2$ETWTd, gret and Cc, and so feruent *add.* Hu$_2$, roboratam Lat. þou] ne *add.* M 52 synne ne for] *om.* Ld ne for] nor SrCcTd fantasye] H$_7$RLB$_3$AsSrAEPH$_6$CcMPl, fantasies HBH$_5$ChLwHu$_2$LdTW, fantasia Lat. ne frenesye] *om.* A ne[2]] H$_7$HRLB$_3$SrChAHu$_2$PH$_6$LdPlT, for *add.* H$_5$AsLwECcMW frenesye] freenesys LwW dowtes] defautis Ld 53 for[1]] H$_7$RLB$_3$AsSr-AEPH$_6$CcMPlW, *om.* HBH$_5$ChLwHu$_2$LdTTd. of] ne for LB$_3$P, pro terroribus temptacionum spiritualium Lat. temptacyons] temptacioun B for[3]] of BLd for[4]] off Ld, *om.* Ch 54 ay] H$_7$HH$_5$LChP, euere BB$_3$LwEH$_6$MTW, alwey SrHu$_2$Ld, *om.* RAsAPl, semper Lat. forth/þou wilt] *rev.* H$_6$M wilt] wold B with o] and thinkest of non Cc and noþynge] *om.* Cc noþynge] no þyngis B 55 makes] make Sr hem] hym Ch what . . . seyn] H$_7$RLB$_3$AsAEPH$_6$CcPl, *om.* HBH$_5$SrChLwHu$_2$MLdTWTd, quicquid tibi

periles mown falle þat a man knowiþ not of. And þerfore turne hom ageyn and lefe þis desire, for þu schalt neuer brynge it to þe ende, and do as oþer werldly men don.

þus seien þin enmys, bot trow hem not, bot holde forþ þi desire, and sey not elles bot þu woldest han Ihesu and ben at Ierusalem. And if þei perceife þen þi wil so strong þat þu wil not spare for syn ne for seknes, for fantasies ne frenesy, for doutes ne dredis of gostly temptaciouns, for meschief ne for pouerte, for lif ne for dede; bot ay forþ þu wilt with o þinge, and noþinge bot on, and makes def ere to hem as þawȝ þu herd hem not, and holdest þe forþ stifly in þi preyers and in þin oþer gostly werkes withoutyn styntynge, with discrecioun aftir conseile of þi soueren or of þi gostly fader: þan bigynne þei for to be wroþ and to gon a litel nerre þe. þei bigynne for to robbe þe and bete þe and do þe al þe schame þat þei kan. And þat is whan þei make þat alle þe dedis þat þu dost, be þei neuer so wel don, are demed of oþer men als ille and turned into þe wers party. And what-so-euer it
8r be þat þu woldest haue don in helpe of þi body or of | þi soule, it schal be letted or hindred by oþer men, so þat þu schalt be put fro þi wil in al þinge þat þu skilfully coueites. And al þis þei don þat þu schuldest be stirid to ire or malencoly or yuel wil ageyne þin euen-cristen.

Bot ageyn alle þese diseses and alle oþer þat mown falle, vse þis remedie. Take Ihesu in þi mynde and angre þe not with hem, tary not

dixerint Lat. what-so-euer] what-so RAs, what-euer E þogh] *om.* ACc 56 hem] *om.* M þe] *om.* LB$_3$PH$_6$, te Lat. styfly] stilly LB$_3$PH$_6$Td, stilly and stifly Hu$_2$, constanter Lat. þi] purpos in þi RAs preyers] prayour LwW, purpos B þin] *om.* H$_5$As oþer] *om.* Cc 57 styntynge] restyng Hu$_2$, distyng Ld and . . . fadere (l. 58)] *om.* AMPl, et quod cum discrecione agis secundum consilium superioris vel patris spiritualis Lat. and . . . dost] H$_7$RLB$_3$AsSrEPH$_6$Cc, *om.* HBH$_5$ChLwHu$_2$LdTWTd þat] *om.* LB$_3$P dost] do it Cc with] be Td 58 or] H$_7$RLB$_3$AsAEPH$_6$CcMPl, of *add.* HBH$_5$ChLw-Hu$_2$LdTWTd, and of Sr for] *om.* B 59 be . . . to[3]] *om.* H$_7$, irasci incipiunt et plus tibi approximare. Tunc enim incipiunt Lat. to[2]] *om.* BLd nerre] ner BTd, to *add.* Sr þe[1]] *om.* Ld þei] þan *prec.* TW, and SrM for] *om.* AE 60 and bete þe] *om.* LB$_3$Ld, verberare Lat. and[1]] to E, for to M and[2]] to AsE moun] H$_7$RLB$_3$AsAPH$_6$CcPl, kan HBH$_5$SrChLwHu$_2$EMLdTWTd And] *rep.* Cc whan] it so is whan *add.* H$_5$ 61 þat[1]] *om.* H$_5$As þi] H$_7$RLB$_3$AsAEPH$_6$Pl, þe HBH$_5$SrChLwHu$_2$CcMTW 62 demed] denyed W il] H$_7$HRLChLwPMPl, euele BB$_3$SrAHu$_2$EH$_6$CcLdTW, wyckede H$_5$As, peruersa Lat. into] in Lw, to E þe] *om.* LB$_3$P werse] worste T 63 þou] *om.* B or] and T, ellis *add.* M 64 or] and LB$_3$P, vel Lat. by] of Sr 65 þynges] H$_7$RLB$_3$AsSrAEPH$_6$CcMPl, þinge HBH$_5$ChLwHu$_2$LdTWTd, omnibus Lat. skilfully] skilful R þis] is *add.*, *canc.* L 66 þat . . . styred] for to stere þe Td be styred] falle H$_6$ yre] wreþþe BAH$_6$Ld or[1]] to *add.* Hu$_2$CcTd 68 desesys] desees Ld al[2]] *om.* A moun fallen] thou maye fele W 69 Tak . . . mynde] *om.* AMPl and] H$_7$HBH$_5$SrCh-LwHu$_2$ECc, *om.* RLB$_3$AsAPH$_6$MPl, nec Lat. hem] hym Ch tary . . . hem] *om.* SrChHu$_2$MT, malencolica efficiaris Lat.

with hem, bot þenk on þi lesson—þat þou art noȝt, þou hast noȝt, þou maight noȝt lesen of erthly gode, þou coueytest noȝt bot þe lufe of Jesu—and hold forth þi weye to Jerusalem with þin occupacion. And nerþeles if þou be taried sumtyme þurgh frelte of þiself with swilk desesis þat fallen to þi bodily lyf þurgh euel wil of man or malyce of þe fende, as son as þou maight come aȝen to þiself and lefe of þe þenkynge of þat disese and go forth to þi werk; abyde not to longe with hem for drede of þin enemye.

Of an il day and of a gode nyȝt, what it meneth; and how þe lufe of þe werd is likned to an ille day and þe lufe of God is called a gode day. Capitulum xxiii^{m}

And after þis whan þin enemys seen þat þou art so wel willed þat þou art not angry ne heuy ne wrothe, ne mikel sterid aȝens no creature for oght þat þei moun don or speken aȝens þe, bot settest þin herte fully for to suffren al þat may fallen—ese and vnese, preysynge and lakkynge—and þat þou wilt charge noþinge with-þi þat þou might kepe þi þoȝt and þi desyre hol to þe lufe of God: þan are þei mikel abayssched. Bot þan wil þei assaye þe with flaterynge and veyn plesynge, and þat is whan þei brynge to þe sight of þi soule al þi gode dedys and þi vertus, and beren vpon [þe] þat al men preysen þe and speken of þin holynes and how al men lufen þe and wurchipe þe for þin holy lyfynge. Þis don þin enemys, þat þou schuldest þenke

70 þenk] oonly *add.* `L′B$_3$P on] vpon Sr þi] þe Pl þat . . . þou (l. 71)] *om.* Td `þat . . . lesen (l. 71)′ H^c, *om.* H°H$_5$T þat] is *add.* `L′B$_3$P noȝt$^1$] þat *add.* M `þou hast noȝt′ L `þou^2′ Lw, *om.* W þou maight] þy myȝt B 71 maight] may H^{c}Lw of^1] or Lw, and of none H$_5$ gode] thyng M, *om.* Pl þou] and *prec.* RAsLwH^{c}EPl, for *prec.* H$_5$ 72 Jesu] God RAsACcMPl, Jesu Christi Lat. with . . . occupacioun] *om.* RAsAMPl 73 nerþeles] *om.* Hu$_2$ if] þow B sumtyme/þurgh frelte] *rev.* Sr swilk] *om.* Td 74 desesis . . . fallen] disese . . . fallith A desesis] H$_7$RLB$_3$AsSrAEPH$_6$CcMPl, disese A, vneses HBH$_5$Sr-ChLwHu$_2$MW, besynysse Ld, euels T, molestibus Lat. þe] *om.* M 75 come] comen M and] H$_7$H°BLB$_3$ChAHu$_2$PH$_6$MLdPlT, *canc.* H, *om.* RH$_5$AsSrLwECcW of] *om.* Td þe] þi Pl, þat H$_5$ 76 þat] thy LwCcMW disese] wise H$_5$ to^1] ouer A, *om.* CcW 77 enemye] H$_7$RAsSrAMPl, enemys HBH$_5$LB$_3$ChLwHu$_2$EPH$_6$CcLdTWTd, inimici [gen. sg.) Lat.

Chapter 23 *title*: H$_7$ Of [a *add.* Σ, `a^1′ Pl, *om.* H$_7$] generale remedie ageyns wikked sterynges [stering Td] and pynful tarienges þat fallen in [to ALdT] here [*om.* R] hertes [and^1 . . . hertes] *om.* Td] of þe flesch, of [and *prec.* RW, or *prec.* Sr, *om.* H$_7$] þe werd and [or Sr] of þe fend, and how [*om.* H$_6$] a stedfast desyre to [of M] Jesu meyntened and strengthed [meyntenyng and strengþing H$_6$] with [be M] deuoute preyenge [preyer H$_6$] and [as M] besy þenkeng on [of H$_6$M] him [and^5 . . . him *om.* Sr] [is] [as H$_7$] a souereyn remedye [and^3 . . . remedye *om.* ALdPlTWTd] RASrH$_6$MLdPlTWTd, H$_7$ Chapter 22, *whence it is cited here* How þou þat art þus in þis weie and wolt not be put out bi no disesis, þine enemyes wolen þanne forgen þee and sette bifor þee [bifor þee *rev.*, *marked for trsp.* L] alle þi good dedis and

with hem, bot þinke on þi lessoun—\`þat þou art noȝt, þou hast noȝt, þou may noȝt lese´ of erþly goode, þu coueites noȝt bot þe luf of Ihesu—and holde forþ þi wey to Ierusalem with þin occupacioun. And nerþeles if þu be taried sumtyme þurgh frelte of þiself, with swilke vneses þat fallen to þi bodily lif þurgh yuel wil of man or malice of þe feende, as sone as þu maiȝt come ageyn to þiself [and] lefe of þe þinkynge of þat disese and go forþ to þi werk; abide not to longe with hem for drede of þin enemys.

[CHAPTER 23]

And after þis whan þin enmys seen þat þu art so wel willed, þat þu art not angry nor heuy ne wroþ, ne mikel stired ageyns no creature for owȝt þat þei mown don or spekyn ageyns þe, bot settes þi herte fully for to suffre al þat may falle—ese and vnese, preisynge or lackynge—and þat þu wilt charge noþinge with-þi þat þu miȝt kepe þi þouȝte and þi desire hol to þe luf of God: \`þan´ are þei mikel abasched. Bot þan wile þei assay þe with flaterynge and veyn plesynge, and þat is when þei brynge to þe siȝt of þi soule alle þi gode dedis and þi vertues, and beren vpon þe þat alle men preise þe and spekyn of þin holynes and how alle men lufe þe and wurschip þe for þin holy lyuynge. þis

commende þee of hem, and hou þou þanne [þou þanne *rev., marked for trsp.* L, *rev.* E] schalt [\`L´] putte hem awai. LB$_3$AsEP De generali remedio contra prauos motus et penales fatigaciones incidentes in corde homini carnis, mundi et diaboli, roboratum deuota oratione et diligenti meditacione de Jesu, summum est remedium. Lat. *om.* HBH$_5$LwHu$_2$CcM 1 þis] *om.* Sr þin] this Cc seen] fel Pl so . . . art] *om.* M 2 art] nart B ne^1] noþer B, neiþer T wrothe ne] *om.* A mikel] gretely Hu$_2$ sterid] derid RAs, meuid A no] ony RAsAMPl for . . . moun] what so þei Td 6 moun] m- *prec., canc.* Sr, kan Hu$_2$ speken] sey Td þe] him *prec., canc.* B$_3$ bot] þou B$_3$ 7 and^1] H$_7$HBH$_5$LB$_3$SrChLwA-Hu$_2$EPLdPlT, or RAsH$_6$CcMW, vel Lat. and^2] H$_7$H$_5$SrALdPl, or HRLB$_3$AsChLw-Hu$_2$EPH$_6$CcMTW, *om.* B, vel Lat. 8 lakkynge] blamyng Ld and . . . with-þi] so Td þat^1] *om.* Pl with-þi] H$_7$HBLB$_3$ChPl, with þe EM, with-whi RAs, with LwPLdTW, wiþ þine herte Hu$_2$, so H$_5$SrAH$_6$, *om.* Cc þou^2] þat Td 9 kepe . . . abaysshed (l. 10)] *This is the tenth extract in* Ad$_2$, *om.* Ad kepe\`þi´ þoȝt] *rev.* Td  þoȝt . . . God] desyre and thy lufe hole to God Ad$_2$  hol] holy Td  God] Jesu MTd, dominum Jesum Christum Lat.  \`þan´ *scr., interl.* H \`þei´ H$_6$ mikel] gretly Hu$_2$ECc 10 abaysscheḍ] scumfet Td, Via vnitiua. The Oned Waye *add.* Ad$_2$, territi . . . et turbati Lat. þe] *om.* RAsA flaterynge] flaterie LB$_3$P veyn] *om.* LB$_3$PH$_6$ 11 plesynge] preysing and *prec.* Cc brynge] wil *prec.* Hu$_2$ to] þe *add., canc.* H, þe *add.* H$_5$ þe . . . al] þi mynde Td þe] þy ChM, þe *add., canc.* H°, þe *add.* H$_5$ sight] cognicionem et memoriam Lat. þi^2] þe Ch 12 þi] H$_7$HRBLB$_3$AsSrChAHu$_2$PMPlT, *om.* LwEH$_6$CcLdW beren vpon þe] make þe to þinke Td vp\`on´ L  \`þe^1´ Cc, *om.* H$_7$, tibi Lat. þat] stifly *prec.* M preysen] prysyn Cc 13 spekyn] gode *add.* W, gode of þe and *add.* Hu$_2$ holynes/. . ./holy lyfynge (l. 14)] *rev.* Hu$_2$ þe^1] *om.* Ld 14 for] of RAsAPl þis] þus SrLwCcTW don] dicunt Lat. þat] for *prec.* H$_5$Sr schuldest þenke] þink Hu$_2$

here seyenge soth and han delyt in þis veyn ioye and resten þe þerin. Bot if þou do wel, þou schalt holden al swilke veyn ianglynge as falshed and flaterye of þin enemy ⸢þat proferth⸣ þe venym to drynke f. 69r tempred with hony. And þerfore refuse it and sey þou wilt | noȝt þerof, bot þou woldest ben at Jerusalem.

Swilk lettynges þou schalt felen, or ellys oþer lyke—what of þi flesch, what of þe werd, what of þe fend—mo þan I may rehersen now. For a man, as longe as he suffreth his þoght wilfully rennen al abowte þe werd in byholdynge of sundry þinges, he perceyueþ few lettynges. Bot as son as he dragheþ al his þoght and his ȝernynge vnto o þynge only, for to hafe þat, for to see þat, and for to knowe þat and lufe þat, and þat is only Jesu; þan schal he wel fele many peynful lettynges. For ilk a þoght þat he feleþ and is not þat þat he coueyteþ is lettynge to him. Þerfor I hafe tolde þe of sum specialy as for example, and ouermore I sey generaly þat what sterynge þat þou felest of þi flesch or of þe fend—plesaunt or pyneful, bittere or swete, lykend or dredful, gladsum or sorowful—þat wold draghen doun þi þoght and þi desire fro þe lufe of Jesu to werdly vanite and lette vtterly þi gostly coueytyse þat þou hast to þe lufe of him, and þat þin herte schuld be occupyed with þat sterynge restendly, sette it at no͡ȝt, receyfe it not wilfully, tarye not with it to longe.

Bot ˋifˊ it be of a werdly þinge þat behoueth nede to be don vnto þiself or to þin euen-cristen, ⸢spede þe⸣ son of it and brynge it to an

15 han] to *prec.* E, a *add.* H_6Cc delyt . . . ioye] vayn glorie in þise dedis Hu_2 þe] *om.* H_5EH_6Pl þerin] in þeme Hu_2 16 þou^1] *om.* B do] wille *prec.* M holden] þi waie and take *add.* Hu_2 ˋalˊ R, *om.* Td veyn] *om.* W ianglynge] gilyng RAs, flateryng Hu_2 as] H_7RLB_3AsAEPH_6CcMPl, *om.* HBH_5SrChLwHu_2LdTWTd 17 falshed] falsnes E, fals Td flaterye] H_7LB_3SrEP, flateryng HRBH_5AsChLwAH_6CcMLdTWTd, deceite Hu_2, adulacionem Lat. enemy] enemyes Pl þat proferth] *over erasure* H_7 venym/to drynke] H_7RLB_3AsSrAEPH_6CcMPl, *rev.* HBH_5ChLwHu_2LdTWTd (þe to *rev.* T) to] for *prec.* M 18 with] *om.* Td And] *om.* LEP þerfore] be wel ware and *add.* Hu_2 wilt no͡ȝt] nolle . . . recipere vel gustare Lat. 19 bot] that *add.* Cc þou . . . at] take Jesu in þi mynde and holde forþ þi weye to M 20 lettynges] lettes B or . . . lyke/what . . . fend (14)] *rev.* H_5 or] oþer As lyke] sych Ld, hem *add.* H_5 21 what^1] and Sr what^2] and Cc, and *prec.* SrM mo] ȝhe *prec.* H_6 may] kan Cc 22 now] *om.* Td a man/as longe as] *rev.* H_6 he] *om.* H_6 his þoght/wilfully] *rev.* E wilfully] to *add.* RAsCcTd, *om.* M al] H_7HBH_5LB_3SrChAHu_2EPH_6MLdT, *om.* RAsLwCcPlW 23 in] þe *add.* ChHu_2 sundry] diuers B_3ALdPlTd, diuers and many Hu_2 few] but *prec.* Hu_2Cc 24 þoght] þouȝtis Td and his ȝernynge] *om.* H_5Cc ȝernynge] desyre AH_6Ld, desires Td, wil Hu_2 vnto] into Ld, to HH_5LwTWTd 25 for^1] *om.* Sr þat^1] *om.* M for^2 . . . þat^1 (l. 26)] *om.* T, ad habendum ipsum, et ad videndum et cognoscendum et diligendum ipsum Lat. for^2 . . . þat^3] *om.* H_6 for^2 . . . þat^2] *om.* LwW for^2] *om.* Td and^1 . . . þat^3] *om.* RAsACcMPl and for] *om.* Td and^1] H_7RLB_3As-AEPH_6CcMPl, *om.* HBH_5SrChLwHu_2LdTW and^2] to Td, *om.* LwW 26 lufe] H_7RLB_3AsAPH_6CcMPl, forto *prec.* HBH_5SrChLwHu_2LdTW, to *prec.* E and^1 . . . Jesu]

don þin enmys, þat þu schuldes þinken here seying soþ and han delit
88v in þis veyn ioy and resten þe þerin. Bot | if þu do wel, þu schalt holden al swilke veyn iangelynge falshede and flateryng of þin enmy þat profreþ þe to drynke venym tempred with hony. And þerfore refuse it and sey þu wilt not þerof, bot þu wolde be at Ierusalem.

Swilke lettynges þu schalt felen, or elles oþer like—what of þi flesch, what of þe werld, what of þe fende—mo þan I may reherse now. For a man, as longe as he suffreþ his þouȝte wilfully ren al aboute þe werld in beholdynge of sundry þinges, he perceyfeþ few lettynges. Bot als sone as he drawiþ al his þouȝte and his ȝernyng to on þinge only, for to hafe þat, for to see þat, for to knowe þat, and for to luf þat, and þat is only Ihesu: þan schal he wel fele many peynful lettynges. For ilk a þinge þat he feliþ and is not þat þat he coueitiþ is lettynge to hym. Þerfore I hafe told þe of sum specially, as for example, and ouermore I say generally þat what stirynge þat þou felis of þi flesch or of þe fende—plesant or peynful, bitter or swete, likend or dredful, gladsum or sorwful—þat wolde drawe doun þi þouȝt and þi desire fro þe luf of Ihesu to werdly vanyte and let vtterly þi gostly coueitise þat þu haste to þe luf of him, and þat þi herte schude be occupied with þat stirynge restyndly: sett it at noȝt, resceyue it not wilfully, tary not þerwiþ to longe.

Bot if it be of werdly þinge þat behouiþ nedis to be don to þiself or to þin euen-cristen, spede þe sone of it and brynge it to an ende þat it

And that [on *add.* M] thyng is nout ellys but Jesu, God and man, for to lovyn hym and sen hym [and han hym *om.* M] in gostly felynge thurgh grace here in partie and afftirward fully in ioye *add.* CcM, *om.* RAsAPl `schal′ Cc wel] *om.* AM many] ful *prec.* Hu$_2$ 27 ilk a] H$_7$HRCh, ilche a M, eche a As, euery BH$_5$LB$_3$SrAHu$_2$EPH$_6$CcLdPlTW, euery a Lw þoght] H$_7$RLB$_3$AsSrAEPH$_6$CcPl, þinge HBH$_5$LwHu$_2$MLdTWTd, *om.* Ch, cogitacio Lat. feleþ] or euery thyng that he felyth *add.* Cc and is] if it be Td and] þat Sr, þe which Hu$_2$, *om.* Ch þat[1]] thing *add.* Cc þat[2]] *om.* AH$_6$Td he[2]] feleþ and *add.* As, feeleþ *add.*, *canc.* L is] it *prec.* Td, peynful *add.* CcM 28 for] an M 29 ouermore] moreouer Pl, ouer þat A, euermore EH$_6$M, euyr LwLd, *om.* Td sey] þe *add.* Td sterynge] stiringus A þi . . . or[2] (l. 30)] *om.* M 30 flesch] of the werld *add.* Cc fend] or of þe warld *add.* Td plesaunt] plesend RTd, plesing AsA 31 gladsum or sorwful] *om.* AsT 32 Jesu] God RAsAPl vtterly] *om.* Td 33 coueytyse] vanite and *prec.* As þou] *om.* Td to] for *prec.*, *canc.* L him] God RAsAPl, Jesu LdTd, Jesu *canc.* M, Jesu Christi Lat. and . . . restendly (l. 34)] *om.* Td and] And puttyn the from bodily and gostly exercise *prec.* CcM, *om.* Sr 34 þat[1]] þe ALd at] as Ld, *om.* A 35 with it/to longe] *rev.* H$_6$ with it] H$_7$RAsACcPl, þerwith HBH$_5$LB$_3$SrChLwHu$_2$EPH$_6$MLdTWTd, wiþalle M to] *om.* Ld 36 `if′ *interl.* H$_7$ a] H$_7$RLB$_3$AsSrAEPH$_6$MPl, *om.* HBH$_5$ChLwHu$_2$CcLdTWTd behoueth] þe *prec.* LwE nede] needly T be] *om.* E vnto] H$_7$RLB$_3$AsEPCcMPl, to HBH$_5$SrChLwAHu$_2$H$_6$LdTWTd 37 cristen] bot *add.* Td ⌜spede þe⌝ *over erasure* H$_7$ spede] þen *prec.* Hu$_2$ þe] *om.* B$_3$ it[1]] þat Sr

ende þat it hange not on ⌜þin herte.⌝ If it be of anoþer þinge þat nedeþ noȝt, or ellys it towcheþ not þe, drede it not, lyke it not, bot smyte it owt of þin herte redily; and sey þus: I am noȝt, I hafe noȝt, noȝt I seke ne coueyte bot þe lufe of Jesu. Knyt þi þoght to þis desyre, and strengthe it with preyere and with oþer gostly werke þat þou forgete it not, and it schal lede þe in þe ryȝt weye and saufe þe fro al peryles, þat þogh þou fele hem þou schalt not peryschen, and I hope þat it schal brynge þe to perfyte lufe of oure Lord Jesu.

Nerþeles on þat oþer syde I sey also, what werk or what sterynge it be þat may help þi desyre, strengthen it and norisschen it, and make þi þoght ferthest fro lufe and mende of þe werd, more hol and more brennende to þe lufe of Jesu, wheþer it be preynge or thenkynge, f. 69v stilnes or spekynge, redynge | or herynge, onlynesse or commonynge, goynge or sittynge; kepe it for þe tyme and werk þerin as longe as sauour lasteþ, be so þat þou take þerwith mete and drynke and slepe as a pilgrym doth, and kepe discrecyon in þi werkynge after counseil and ordinaunce of þi souereyne. For hafe he neuer so grete haste in his goynge, ȝet he wil in tyme eten and drynken and slepen. Do þou so; for þogh it lette þe o tyme, it schal forþen þe anoþer tyme.

38 it[1]] to longe *add.* M not] to longe *add.* Cc on] in ACcMTd ⌜þin herte⌝ *over erasure* H_7 herte] And go thanne forth to thyn werk *add.* CcM of] H_7RSrACcPl, *om.* HBH_5LB_3AsChLwHu$_2$EPH_6MLdTW anoþer] ony oþer Sr 39 or] oþer H_5 it[1] . . . not[2]] þat longis not to þe medil not þerwith Td it[1]] þat *prec.* Cc, *om.* M þe] þi M, to *prec.* A, to *prec.*, *canc.* B_3 drede it not] $H_7LB_3PH_6$ charge it not iangle not þerwiþ ne angre þe not *prec.* HBH_5ChLwLdTWSrM (it not] ȝet, þerwiþ] wiþalle, not[2]] wiþal *add.* M), take no hede þerof iangle not þerwiþ ne angre þe not *prec.* Hu$_2$, charge yt nout ne angre the nout therwith *prec.* Cc, charge it nouȝt RAsAPl, non cures de illo, non garules cum illo, nec molesteris, ne timeas illum Lat. not[2]] ne *add.* CcMLd lyke] loke R bot] as sone as þou may *add.* Td it[3]] doun *add.* RAs, *om.* W 40 redily] smartli A, anoon Hu$_2$, *om.* Td noȝt I seke ne] I Td noȝt/I seke] *rev.* ACc noȝt[3]] *om.* H_5M seke] iangle noght with it ne angre þe nouȝt drede it nouȝt nouȝt I seke *add.* RAsPl, noȝt Td 41 ne coueyte] nouȝte I coueite Pl, I coueyte nout Cc, *om.* A ne] \`y' *add.* Ld þe lufe of] to loue A Jesu] God RAsAPl, God *prec.* H_5, and Jesu hymself *add.* CcM, iangil noȝt þerwith ne angre þe noȝt dred hit noȝt noȝt I sek ne coueite but þe loue of God *add.* A, domini Jesu Christi Lat. Knyt] Lrnyghte W þis] þi H_6 and . . . werke (l. 42)] *om.* RAsAMPl 42 it[1]] $H_7LB_3EPH_6$Cc, and maynteyne it *add.* HBH_5SrChLwHu$_2$LdTW with[2]] *om.* SrH_6 werke] werkis H_7EWTd, operacione Lat. 43 schal] wol B \`þe in' H^c in] *om.* TTd þe[2]] thy LwW 44 þogh] *om.* Cc fele hem þou] *om.* Cc peryschen] perich- *prec.*, *canc.* E and] *om.* RAsAPl þat] *om.* H_5E 45 þe] *om.* B_3As to] H_7HRH_5AsSr-LwAHu$_2$TW, þe *add.* BLB_3EPH_6CcMLdPlTd of] God *add.* M oure Lord Jesu] Jesu

hange not on þin herte. If it be anoþer þinge þat nediþ not, or elles it touchiþ not þe, charge it not, iangle not þerwiþ, ne angre þe not, drede it not, like it not, bot smyte it oute of þin herte redily; and sei þus: I am noȝt, I haf noȝt, nouȝt I seke ne coueite bot þe luf of Ihesu. Knyt þi þoȝt to þis desire, and strenþe it and maynteyne it with preiere and with oþer gostly werke þat þou forgete it noȝt, and it schal
39r lede `þe in´ þe riȝt | wey and saufe þe fro alle periles, þat þawȝ þu fele hem þu schalt not perische, and I hope þat it schal brynge þe to perfit luf of oure Lord Ihesu.

Nerþeles on þat oþer syde I say also, what werk or what stirynge it be þat may helpen þi desire, strengþe it and norische it, and make þi þoȝt ferreste fro luste and mende of þe werld, more hole and more brennande to þe luf of God, wheþer it be preyinge or þinkynge, stilnes or spekynge, redynge or herynge, onlynes or comunynge, goynge or sittynge; kepe it for þe tyme and wirk þerin as longe as sauour lesteþ, if it be so þat þu take þerwith met and drynk and slepe as a pilgrym doþ, and kepe discrecioun in þi wirkynge after consel and ordinance of [þi] souerayn. For haf he neuer so grete hast in his goynge, ȝit he wil in tyme eten and drynken and slepen. Do þu so als; for þawȝ it let þe o tyme, it schal forþeren þe anoþer tyme.

Criste Td, Jesu Christi Lat. Jesu] Cryst Sr, *om.* Cc 46 I sey] `I seide´ L, I seide B_3EPH_6 also] þat *add.* H_6M or] *om.* $ChHu_2$ 47 strengthen . . . it^{2}] *om.* Td it^{1}] *om.* A 48 þi . . . werd] it Td ferthest] ferþer As, ferrest ChAM, and thyn hert *add.* Cc lufe] $H_7RBAsSrChHu_2MLdPl$, þe *prec.* LB_3APH_6Cc, luste HH_5LwTW, þe lust E mende] þe *prec.* AH_6Cc more^{1}] and *prec.* H_5E, yn *prec.* A and] *om.* B 49 to] in RAsACcPl Jesu] $H_7LB_3EPH_6CcM$, God $HRBH_5AsSrChLwAHu_2CcLdPlTW$, `do þat´ *add.* $Hu_2$, Jesu Christi Lat. wheþer] were Ld preynge] prechynge $H_5$ `or´ *om.* M 50 onlynesse] soleynnesse As, of lyuys Sr `or$^{3}$´ Ch commonynge] with company Td 51 goynge . . . lasteþ (l. 52)] *om.* $ChHu_2$ `or´ E 52 be] $H_7RBLB_3AsSrChAHu_2$-EPH_6CcMPl, if it *prec.* $HH_5LwTWTd$, if it *prec.*, *canc.* Ld, *om.* A þat] *om.* H_6 take] *om.* Td þerwith] þat with Lw, wiþal M, 53 and . . . souereyne (l. 54)] *om.* RAsAMPl et obserues discrecionem in operando secundum consilium et ordinacionem superioris tui Lat. after] or ord- *add.*,*canc.* B_3 54 and] or LB_3P `þi´ W^G, þe HLwW hafe he] haue a pylgryme H_5Ld, þouȝ a pilgrym haue Hu_2 he] þou Td grete] muche H_5 haste] hate B his] þi Td, *om.* AE 55 goynge] of his pilgrimage *add.* E he . . . tyme] þou muste Td in tyme] *om.* LwW eten] *om.* E and^{1}] *om.* Cc and slepen] et cum aliis loqui temporibus oportunis Lat. Do þou so] *om.* Td so] $H_7RLB_3AsSrAPH_6CcMPl$, so als HChLwT`W^{G}´ [*corr. fr.* so also T], also BELd, also in þe same maner H_5, on þe same wise Hu_2, lyke wyse W, consimiliter Lat. 56 þogh] if H_5A it^{1}] þese Td þe^{1}] $H_7HBH_5ChLwHu_2Cc$-LdPlTW, *om.* $RLB_3AsSrAPH_6M$ it^{2}] þei Td forþen] H_7, forþeren Σ þe^{2}] *om.* RAsA, wel more *add.* Cc tyme] *The sixth extract in* Td *ends here*

How a soule, whan it is hyd þurgh grace fro þe vyle noye and besines of þe werd, is in a gode nyȝt and in a lyghty myrkenes, for þan may it frely preyen and thenken on Jesu. Capitulum xxiiii^{m}

If þou wilt wyten þan what þis desyre is, sothly it is Jesu. For he makeþ þis desyre in þe and he ȝifeþ þe it, he it is þat desyreþ in þe and he it is þat is desyred. He is al and he doth al, if þou might seen him. Þou dost noȝt bot suffrest him werkyn in þi soule and assentest to him with grete gladnes of hert þat he vowcheþ-saufe for to do so in þe. Þou art not ellys bot a resonable instrument wherein þat he werkeþ. And þerfor whan þou felist þi þoght by towchynge of his grace be taken vp with þis desire to Jesu, with a myghty and devout wil for to plesen him and lufen him, þenk þan þat þou hast Jesu; for he it is þat desyreþ. Behold him wel: he goth befor þe, not in bodily lyknes bot vnseably, by priue presence of his gostly myght. Þerfor se him gostly if þou may, or elles trow him and folwe him whederso he goth; for he schal lede þe in þe ryȝt weye to Jerusalem, þat is þe syght of pees in contemplacyon. Þus preyed þe prophete to þe Fadere of heuene, sayend þus: *Emitte lucem tuam et veritatem tuam; ipsa me deduxerunt et adduxerunt in montem sanctum tuum et in tabernacula tua*. Þat is: Fader of heuene, send owt þi lyght and þi sothfastnes, þat is þi sone Jesu, and he schal leden me be desyre in me into þin holy hil and into þi

Chapter 24 *title*: H$_7$LB$_3$PH$_6$M, *used as title of* Chapter 25 RPl. *Fishlake's Latin translation has a version of this chapter title below, at line 57*: þan   Of an il [euyl SrAMLdPlTW] day and of [*om*. EMTW] a gode nyȝt, what it meneth; and how þe lufe of þe werd is likned to an ille [euyl SrAMLdPlTW] day and þe lufe of God is called [is callid RSr, to LdTW, is ylikned to M] a gode day [RSrAMLdPl, nyȝt TW] [*cited from* H$_7$, Chapter 23] RSrAMLdPl, nyȝt TW   RSrALdPlTW, *add. below, at line 57*: þis M   Of an yuel day and a good nyȝt, what it meneþ, and howȝ þe loue of þe worlde is likened to an yuel day and þe loue of God to a goode nyȝt, and when a soule may freli preie and þinke on Jesu. E   `How a soule þat is formed to þe lyknesse of Jesu desireþ no þyng bot Jesu and how he makeþ þis desire in þe soule. And he it is þat desires þy soule.' *almost completely canc.* H   De die mala et nocte bona, quid designant; et qualiter amor mundi comperatur diei male et amor Dei dies bona merito nominatur. Lat.   *om*. BH$_5$AsChLwHu$_2$Cc   1 vyle] foule M   and besines] *om*. M   2 werd] and þe blyndnesse *add*. M   in (*bis*)] *om*. LB$_3$PH$_6$ lyghty] lyght RMPl   myrkenes] derknesse B$_3$H$_6$ 3 for . . . Jesu] *om*. Pl   5 If . . . wyten/þan] *rev*. H$_6$ þan] þat ChHu$_2$, *om*. H$_5$EM   þis^{1}] þyn BLd, *corr. fr.* is þi B$_3$ 6 and . . . þe^{3}] *om*. Cc   he^{1}] *om*. RAsLwW   ȝifeþ/þe it] *rev*. ChHu$_2$ þe it] H$_7$RLB$_3$AsEPMPl, *rev*. HBH$_5$SrLwALdTW, it to þee H$_6$ he^{2}] H$_7$RLB$_3$AsAEPH$_6$CcPl, and *prec*. HBH$_5$SrChLwHu$_2$MLdTW   desyreþ . . . þat^{2}] *om*. T   desyreþ] þou desirist H$_5$ and^{2} . . . desyred] *om*. RAsAMPl   7 is^{1}] *rep*., *canc*. L   desyred] of þe *add*. Ld, and desiryth *add*. Cc   He] For *prec*. Hu$_2$ and . . . al^{2}] *om*. T   doth] makith Cc   if] and *prec*. ChHu$_2$ 8 þou dost noȝt] Videres teipsam nichil facere Lat.   suffrest] H$_7$RLB$_3$AsSr`H^{c}'AEPH$_6$CcMPlW, suffres H$_5$, suffre H$^{\circ}$BChLwHu$_2$LdT, quod permittis Lat.   werkyn] werkynge B   þi] þe T   9 hert] ⌜-te⌝ *added in plummet* H$_7$

[CHAPTER 24]

If þu wilt witen þen what þis desire is, soþly it is Ihesu. For he makiþ þis desire in þe and he gifiþ it þe, and he it is þat desiriþ in þe and he it is þat is desired. He is al and he doþ al, if þu mi3te seen him. Þou dost no3t bot suffre him wirke in þi soule and assentes to him with grete gladnes of herte þat he fouchiþsaufe for to do so in þe. Þou art not elles bot a resonable instrument wherin þat he wirkiþ. And þerfor whan þu felist þi þou3t by touchynge of his grace taken vp wiþ desire to Ihesu, with a mi3ti deuoute wil for to plesen hym and lufen him, þinke þan þat þu hast Ihesu; for he it is þat ⌜þou desirist⌝. Biholde him wel, for he goþ beforn þe, not in bodily liknes bot vnseablely, bi priue presence of his mi3te. Þerfore see him gostly if þu mai3t, or elles trowe him and folwe him whederso he goþ; for he schal lede þe in þe
89[v] ri3t wey to Ierusalem þat is | þe si3t of pees in contemplacioun. Þus preid þe prophet to þe Fader of Heuen, seiend þus: *Emitte lucem tuam et veritatem tuam; ipsa `me´ deduxerunt et adduxerunt in montem sanctum tuum et in tabernacula tua*. Þat is: Fader of Heuen, sende out þi li3t and þi soþfastnes, þat is þi sone Ihesu, and he schal lede me bi desire in me

he] *om.* A vowcheþ] wolde voche Cc for] *om.* BB_3H_6M to] wirke and to *add.* E þou art] þan arte þou Pl 10 þat] *om.* AT 11 by towchynge] be touched Sr, towchyd Cc, tangi Lat. be taken] H_7LB_3EPCc, to be take H_6, and be taken Cc, bytakyn Sr, taken $HRBH_5AsChLwAHu_2EMLdPlTW$, eleuari Lat. 12 with[1]] bi T þis] $H_7RLB_3AsAEPH_6CcMPl$, *om.* $HBH_5SrChLwHu_2LdTW$, illo Lat. Jesu] God RAsAPl with[2] . . . him[2] (l. 13)] *om.* RAsAMPl and] H_7Hu_2, *om.* Σ 13 þenk þan] *rev.* LwW 14 desyreþ] $H_7BLB_3ChHu_2PH_6LdT$, desyreþ þe H_5, ⌜þou desirist. Bi-⌝ [þe *canc.*] H^c, þou desirist RAsSrLwAEPlMW, and is desiryd *add.* Cc, and he it is þat is desired *add.* M, ipse est hoc desiderium Lat. he] $H_7RLB_3AsSrAPH_6CcMPl$, for *prec.* $HBH_5ChLwHu_2ELdTW$, ipse Lat. in . . . vnseably] bodily but gostly M in] þe *add.*, *canc.* H, *add.* H_5T lyknes] as a man *add.* RAsAPl 15 vnseably] vnseable Pl, vnsehilly A, invisibleli H_6, vnsenseably LwW, onsaciabily Cc by] a *add.* E, *om.* Cc priue] hid *add.* LB_3EPH_6 gostly[1]] $H_7RLB_3AsSrAEPH_6CcMPl$, vnseable and *prec.* M, *om.* $HBH_5ChLwHu_2LdTW$, *om.* Lat. `þerfor . . . may´ L him] himselfe T 16 may] $H_7RAsSrLwHu_2CcMPlW$, my3t $HBH_5LB_3ChEPH_6LdT$, potes Lat. or . . . him[1]] and fastyn all þi thow3t and þin affeccion to [in M] hym `Lw´MW or] and Cc trow] lefe B, byleue Ld, trust in him louely and feruently Hu_2 and . . . him[2]] *rep.* B whederso] wheresoo W, wheþersoeuere *add.* T `he[1]´ $H_6$ 17 in[1]] to As, *om.* AW þe[3]] thy Lw in contemplacyon] For he is pees and Ierusalem hymself *add.* M, *om.* Sr in] and LwW 18 preyed] preyeþ Sr of] in M 19 sayend] and seiþ right M þus] Ps. 42° *add.* $BLHu_2EPLdTW$ tuam] *om.* As `me´ *interl.* H^c, Domine *add.* M et adduxerunt . . . tua] etc. Ld et adduxerunt] *om.* Lw 20 þat] þis Pl Fader] þe *prec.* Ld 21 lyght] sy3t Ld 22 me[1]] þee B_3 `be desyre´ Pl in me] *om.* CcPl, in firma consideracione ipsius Lat. into[2]] to AsSrLwW `þin´ W^G, þe W holy . . . þi] *om.* BLd

tabernacles, þat is to þe felynge of perfyte lufe and heyght in contemplacion.

f. 70r Of þis desyre spekeþ þe prophete þus: | *Memoriale tuum Domine in desiderio anime mee. Anima mea desiderauit te in nocte, sed et spiritus meus in precordiis meis.* Þat is: Lord Jesu, þe mynde of þe is prented in desyre of my soule, for my soule haþ desyred þe in þe nyȝt and my spirit haþ coueyted þe in alle my thenkynges. And why þe prophete seyþ þat he desyreth God in al þe night, and what he meneþ þerby, I schal telle þe. Þou wost wel þat þe nyght is a tymeful space bytwix two dayes, for whan o day is endid, anoþer comeþ not as tyte, bot first comeþ þe nyght and departeþ þe dayes, sumtyme longe and sumtyme schort, and þan aftere þat comeþ anoþer day. Þe prophete mened not only of þis maner nyȝt, bot he mened of gostly nyȝt. Þou schalt vnderstonden þat þer ben two dayes or two lyȝtes; þe first is a fals lyȝt, þe second is a trew lyȝt. Þe fals liȝt is þe lufe of þis werd þat a man hath in himself of corrupcion of his flesch; þe trew liȝt is þe perfyte lufe of Jesu feled þurgh grace in a mans soule. Þe lufe of þe werd is a fals liȝt, for it passeþ away and lasteþ not, and so it performeth not þat it beheteth. Þis liȝt behyght þe fend to Adam whan he sterid him to synne, and seyd þus: *Aperientur oculi vestri et eritis sicut dii.* Þat is: Ȝowre eygne schul be opned and ȝe schul ben as goddys. And he seyd soth þer, for whan Adam had synned onon his inner eygh was sperred and gostly liȝt withdrawen, and þe vttere eygh were opned, and he felt and seye a new liȝt of fleschly lykynge and werdly lufe þat he seygh

23 tabernacles] tabernacle H_6 to] into RAsSrCc of] thyn *add.* Cc and heyght] *om.* RAsAPl heyght] heigh SrEM, þe *prec.* T in contemplacion] contemplacionis Lat. in] *om.* M 25 þe] a Cc þus] Ysa. 26° *add.* BLHu$_2$EPLdTW Memoriale] Memoria As Domine] *om.* LwW 26 mee] H$_7$LB$_3$LwAEPH$_6$CcMW, *canc.* Pl, *om.* HRBH$_5$AsSr-ChLwHu$_2$LdTW, mee Lat. Anima] quia *prec.* H_5 desider`auit´ L in nocte] *om.* As sed] *om.* Ch et] *om.* BCcLd 27 Lord] *rep.*, *canc.* L, oure *prec.* P Jesu] *om.* RAsAMPl `mynde´ Pl, desir M in] þe *add.* AECc 28 þe[2]] *corr. fr.*me Lw my] *canc.* Lw, *om.* MW 29 thenkynges] `kyng´ *interl.*, *s.h.* H, þenkinge LB$_3$EP, thyngis CcM why] for *add.* Sr þe prophet/seyþ] *rev.* Hu$_2$ 30 seyþ] sayde $H_5$ þat he] *rev.* Pl þat] H$_7$H$_5$LB$_3$AHu$_2$EPH$_6$CcMPl, *om.* HRBAsSrChLwLdTW desyreth H$_7$SrACcPl, desyred H°BH$_5$LB$_3$ChHu$_2$PH$_6$MLdT, hath desired RAsLw`H^c´EW, desiderasse Lat. in al] H$_7$A, *rev.* Σ and . . . nyght (l. 31)] *om.* LwW and . . . þerby] *om.* H_6 I schal] H$_7$HBH$_5$ChLwHu$_2$H$_6$CcLdTW, *rev.* RLB$_3$AsSrAEPMPl 31 is] as LwW tymeful space] tempus et plenum spacium Lat. tymeful] tyme of ful As, tyme and a Cc space] *om.* Sr bytwix] H$_7$HBB$_3$LwELdPlW, atwix RLAsSrChP, bitwene H$_5$AHu$_2$H$_6$CcMT 32 two dayes] *rev.* LwW whan] *om.* H_6 `day´ Ch endid] and *add.* As as tyte] H$_7$HLChLwP, anon BH$_5$B$_3$AHu$_2$EH$_6$CcMLdPlW, as swithe Sr, also sone As, as sone T 33 þe[1]] H$_7$H$_6$Cc, *om.* Σ þe[2]] þese A longe] lenger A and[2]] *om.* H$_6$M 34 schort] schorter A þat] *om.* LwW mened] menyþ H$_5$AsCcM `not´ H_6 35 only] *om.* SrT maner] of *add.* HBH$_5$ChLwHu$_2$TW, materiall Ld mened] meneþ AsCcMLd of[2]] *om.*

into þin holy hille and into þi tabernacles, þat is to þe felynge of perfite luf and heiȝte in contemplacioun.

Of þis desire spekiþ þe prophet þus: *Memoriale tuum Domine in desiderio anime. Anima mea desiderauit te in nocte, sed et spiritus meus in precordiis meis*. Þat is: Lord Ihesu, þe mynde of þe is preentid in desire of my soule, for my soule haþ desirid þe in þe niȝt and my spirit haþ coueitid þe in alle my þin`kyng´ges. And whi þe prophet seiþ he desired God al in þe niȝt, and what he menyþ þerby, I schal telle þe. Þou wost wel þat þe niȝt is a tymeful space bitwix two daies, for whan o day is endid anoþer comeþ not as tit, bot first comeþ niȝt and departiþ þe dayes, sumtyme longe and sumtyme short, and þan after þat comiþ anoþer day. Þe prophet menyd not only of þis maner of niȝt, bot he menid of a gostly niȝt. Þu schalt vndirstande þat þer ben two daies or two liȝtes; þe first is a fals liȝte, þe secunde is a trewe liȝt. Þe fals liȝt is þe luf of þis world, þat a man haþ in himself of corrupcioun of his flesch; þe trewe liȝt is þe perfit luf of Ihesu feld þurwȝ grace in a mans soule. Þe luf of þe werld is a fals liȝt, for it passiþ awey and it lasteþ not, and so it performiþ not þat þat it behotiþ. þis liȝt bihiȝt þe fende to Adam when he stirid hym to syn, and seid þus: *Aperientur oculi vestri, et eritis sicut dii*. Þat is: Ȝoure iȝen schul ben opned and ȝe schul ben as goddis. And he said soþ þere, for whan Adam had synned anon his inner eiȝe was sperid and gostly liȝt
90^r withdrawen, and his vtter `eiȝen´ | were opuned, and he feld and saw a new liȝt of flescly likynge and werdly luf þat he sawȝ not bifore. And

LwW gostly] H$_7$, þe *prec.* HBH$_5$LB$_3$ChLwHu$_2$EPLdTW, a *prec.* RAsSrAH$_6$CcMPl þou] For *prec.* Cc. *The first extract in* Td *starts here* schalt] wele *add.* Td 36 two^1] maner *add.* RAsAPl two^2] maner *add.* As first] light *add.* Td a] *om.* LB$_3$P 37 þe second is] and þat oþer M second] liȝt *add.* Td is] *om.* P trew lyȝt] gode light and trewe M þe^3] off þys Ld, *om.* LwM þis] H$_7$HRBH$_5$LB$_3$AsLwAEPH$_6$CcLdTW, þe H$_5$SrChHu$_2$MPl þat . . . flesch (l. 38)] *om.* Cc 38 in] of LB$_3$P, to Td of^1] or H$_6$, þorow MTd his] þe H$_6$ 39 Jesu] God RAsAPl, Jesu Christi Lat. feled . . . grace] *catchword* Ch, *which ends here* þurgh] be Td a^2] *om.* AsM 40 `and^1´ Sr lasteþ] it abidiþ Hu$_2$, it *prec.* HBH$_5$LwETW^G and so] for Td it performeth] [it *canc.*] perfourmyth it Ld performeth] fulfillis Td þat] H$_7$RLB$_3$AsSrAEPH$_6$CcMPlT, þat þat HBH$_5$LwHu$_2$LdTW, þyng þat *add.* Td 41 beheteth] behotid Hu$_2$, hiȝte LB$_3$PH$_6$M, hestis Td, promittit Lat. beheyght] behotid Hu$_2$Cc, behettes M, promisit Lat. 42 þus] Gen. 3° *add.* BLHu$_2$EPLdTW Aperientur] Aparientur Lw oculi] tui *add.*, *canc.* L dii] scientes &c. *add.* M 43 `be´ L goddys] goodes Pl 44 soth] *om.* E, aliqualiter verum Lat. whan] as sone as Td eygh was] eyȝen were H$_5$Td eygh] that *add.* M sperred] closed B, schit Ld 45 and] his *add.* Hu$_2$Td withdrawen] was *prec.* SrCc, subtractum erat Lat. þe] H$_7$RLB$_3$AsSrAEPH$_6$CcMPl, his HBH$_5$LwHu$_2$LdTW eygh were] eye was AM `eygh´ H^c, *om.* H°H$_5$M felt and seye] vidit Lat. 46 lykynge] knowynge ⌜L⌝B$_3$P, delectacionis Lat. þat] whilk Td

not before. And so seygh he a new day, bot þis was an ill day, for þis day was it þat Iob weryed whan he seyd þus: *Pereat dies in qua natus sum*. þat is: Peryssche mote þat day in þe whilk I was born. He weryed not þe day rennende in þe ȝere þat God made, bot he weryed þis day þat man made, þat is þe concupysc[ence] and þe lufe of þe werd in þe whilk he was borne, þogh he felt it not þan. þis day and þis liȝt is
f. 70v asked of God þat it schulde | perysche and no lengere lest.

Bot þe lufe of Jesu is a blissed liȝt and a trew day. For God is boþe lufe and lyȝt, and he is aylastende, and þerfor he þat lufeþ him, he is in liȝt aylastende. þus Seyn John seyth: *Qui diligit Deum manet in lumine*. þat is: He þat lufeþ God dwelleth in liȝt. þan what man þat perseyfeþ and seeþ þe lufe of þis werd fals and faylend, and forþi he wil forsake it and seke þe lufe of God: he may not as tyte fele þe lufe of him, bot him behoueth a whyle abyden in þe nyȝt, for he may not sodeynly come fro þat o liȝt to þat oþer, þat is fro þe lufe of þe werd to þe perfyte lufe of God. þis nyȝt is not elles bot a forberynge and a withdrawynge of þe perfeccion and þe þoght of þe soule fro erthly þinges, by grete desyre and ȝernynge for to seen and felen and lufen Jesu and gostly þinges. þis is þe nyȝt; for ryȝt as þe nyȝt is myrk and an hydynge of al bodily creatures and restynge of al bodily dedys, ryȝt so a man þat setteþ him fully for to þenken on Jesu and desyreth only

47 before] afore H_6 And . . . day[1]] *om.* A seygh he] *rev.* B_3H_6 bot . . . day[2]] *om.* Lat. þis] day *add.* Sr `was' Cc ill] $H_7HRH_5LPPl$, euele $BB_3AsSrLwHu_2EH_6CcMLdTW$ day[2]] $H_7LB_3SrEPH_6M$, *om.* $HRBH_5AsLwAHu_2CcLdPlTW$, dies Lat. 48 was it] *rev.* A `it' H^c, þe day Sr, *om.* $H^{\circ}H_5T$ weryed] curside B_3AHu_2Ld þus] Iob 3° *add.* $BLHu_2EPLdTW$ Pereat] Periat H_6 49 þat is] *om.* T mote/þat day] *rev.* Hu_2 mote] *om.* Lw þat[2]] $H_7RAsSrHu_2CcPl$, þe $HBH_5LB_3LwAEPH_6MLdTW$ þe] $H_7HRBH_5AsSrLwHu_2EMLdTW$, *om.* LB_3APH_6CcPl He] ne *add.* M weryed] curside B_3Hu_2Ld 50 þe[1]] þat SrCcPl rennende] þat renneþ M `bot' H^c, *om.* $H^{\circ}T$ he weryed] *rev.* Pl weryed] kurside H_5B_3Ld 51 þe[1]] *om.* Pl concupyscence] concupysche H_7, coueityse Pl, lust A and þe lufe] *om.* Pl þe[2]] *om.* B_3 þe[3]] $H_7RLB_3AsEPH_6CcPl$, þis $HBH_5SrLwAHu_2MLdTW$ þe[4]] *om.* B_3 52 borne] in *add.* Cc þogh] *om.* As `it' H^cH_5, *om.* $H^{\circ}BHu_2Ld$ þis[2]] *om.* Lw is] he Σ 54 lufe] aylastand *prec.* HH_5E, euerelastynge *prec.* $BSrLwHu_2LdTW$, amor Lat. a blissed liȝt/and/a trew day] H_7, *rev.* Σ For . . . lyȝt] *om.* H_5 God] Jesu CcM, Christus Lat. boþe] bettur Pl 55 aylastende] $H_7HRLPCcM$, euerlastinge $BH_5B_3AsLwAHu_2EH_6LdPlTW$, lestynge Sr and þerfor . . . aylastende (l. 56)] $H_7HBH_5Hu_2PCcPl$, *om.* $RLB_3AsSrLwAEH_6MLdTW$, et ideo qui eum diligit est in lumine eternaliter permanente Lat. he[2]] H_7BHu_2, *om.* Σ 56 liȝt aylastende] *rev.* Hu_2 aylastende] H_7HH_5LP, euerelastynge BHu_2CcPl þus] $H_7RLB_3AsSrAEPH_6CcMPl$, as HBH_5LwHu_2LdTW Seyn John/seyth] *rev.* H_6CcTd seyth] 1°. Io. 10 2° *add.* BLd, 1° Io. 2° *add.* LTW, Io. *add.* Hu_2 57 lumine] luce As þat is] *om.* $HH_5LwLdTTd$ dwelleth] H_7H_6, al *add.* Σ in] the *add.* LwW þan] *Chapter-break, numbered Capitulum 25[tm], with the usual initial and the title* Qualiter anima, quando per graciam a strepitu et mundi solicitudine occultatur, est in nocte bona et in caligine luminosa, quia tunc libere orare potest et de Jesu cordialiter cogitare Lat. þat[3]] $H_7LB_3SrAEPH_6CcPl$, *om.* $HRBH_5AsLwHu_2MLdTW$

so saw3e he a new day, bot þis was an ille day, for þis was `it´ þat Job waried whan he seide þus: *Pereat dies in qua natus sum*. Þat is: Perische mote þe day in þe whilk I was borne. He waried not þe day rennande in þe 3ere þat God made, `bot´ he waried þis day þat man maad, þat is þe concupiscence and þe luf of þis werld in þe whilk he was borne, þaw3 he feld `it´ not. Þan bis day and þis li3t he asked of God þat it schuld perisch and no lengir last.

Bot þe aylastand luf of Ihesu is a trew day and a blissed li3t. For God is boþe luf and li3t, and he is aylastande, and þerfore he þat lufiþ him is in li3t aylastand, as Seynt Þohan seiþ: *Qui diligit Deum manet in lumine*. He þat lufiþ God dwelliþ al in li3t. Þan what man perceifiþ and seeþ þe luf of þis werld fals and failand, and forþi he wil forsake it and seke þe luf of God: he may not as tit fele þe luf of him, bot he most abide a while in þe ni3t, for he may not sodeynly come fro þat o li3t to þat oþer, þat is fro þe luf of þe werld to perfit luf of God. Þis ni3t is not elles bot a forberynge and a withdrawyng of þe þou3t of þe soule fro erþly þinges, by grete desire and 3ernynge for to luf and seen and felen Ihesu and gostly þinges. Þis is þe ni3t; for ri3te as þe ni3t is mirk and `an´ hidynge for alle bodily creatures and a restynge of alle bodily dedis, ri3t so a man þat settiþ him fully for to þinken on Ihesu

58 and seeþ] *om.* M þe] þis Pl lufe] li3t RAsAPl werd] that it is *add.* Cc forþi he] *om.* Cc forþi] H$_7$HRLB$_3$AsSrPCcMPlT, þerfore BH$_5$AHu$_2$EH$_6$Ld, for that LwW 59 God] Jesu LwMW he . . . him[1] (l. 60)] `he may not anoon fele þe loue of God´ Ld, *om.* T as tyte] H$_7$HRLAPPl, anon BH$_5$B$_3$AsHu$_2$EH$_6$CcMLd, as sone LwW, as swithe Sr fele] and fynde *add.* Cc þe[2] . . . him[1] (l. 60)] it M `þe lufe[2]´ L 60 him behoueth] H$_7$RLB$_3$AsSrAEPH$_6$CcMPl, he most HBH$_5$LwHu$_2$LdTW `behoueth´ H$_6$ a whyle/abyden] H$_7$RAsLB$_3$AEPCcMPl, *rev.* HBH$_5$LwHu$_2$H$_6$LdTW a whyle] *om.* Sr þe] þis M 61 þat[1]] þe E, *om.* Cc þat[2]] an Cc oþer] light *add.* M þe[1]] *om.* H$_5$Ld 62 þe] H$_7$LB$_3$SrHu$_2$EPH$_6$CcMPl, *om.* HRBH$_5$AsLwALdTWTd God] *corr. fr.* good R, Domini Jesu Christi Lat. þis] *Chapter-break, numbered Capitulum xxvi^m, with the usual illuminated initial* CcM. M *inserts here the* RSrAH$_6$LdPlTW *title of Chapter 24* and] with As 63 perfeccion . . . þoght] [a]ffeccionis Lat. perfeccion and þe] H$_7$, affeccion and the RLB$_3$AsAEPH$_6$CcMPl, *om.* HBH$_5$SrLwHu$_2$LdTW and] of *add.* E þoght] and *add.* Lw þe[3]] a A 64 desyre] desires RAs, desyryng Cc and 3ernynge] *om.* Cc and[1]] in H$_5$ 3ernynge] 3ernyngis RAs, longing A, coueityng Ld, spede Hu$_2$ for] *om.* M seen and felen/and/lufen] H$_7$RLB$_3$AsSrAEPH$_6$CcMPl, *rev.* HBH$_5$LwHu$_2$TW, videndi, senciendi et diligendi Lat. and lufen] *om.* Ld, `of´ *add.* Td 65 Jesu] God RAsAPl, Dominum Jesum Christum Lat. myrk] H$_7$HRLAsSrPCcMPl, derk BH$_5$LwHu$_2$LdTW 66 `an´ H^c, euer LwW, *om.* SrCcPlTd of[1]] H$_7$LB$_3$SrAEPH$_6$MPl, for HBH$_5$LwHu$_2$LdTW, fro RAs, *om.* Cc, omnium creaturarum corporalium Lat. creatures] creature W and] H$_7$Sr, a *add.* Σ restynge] restynges W, tempus quietis Lat. dedys] trauayle A, dedin M 67 him] himsilf B$_3$ fully/for to þenken] *rev.* M on] of RPl Jesu] Jesu Christo Lat. desyreth] H$_7$SrH$_6$CcPl, desiren RLB$_3$AsAPM, for to desiren HBH$_5$LwHu$_2$ELdTW, desiderat Lat.

þe lufe of him is besy for to hyden his þoȝt fro veyn beholdynge and his affeccion fro fleschly lykynge of al bodily creatures, so þat his þoght be mad fre not ficched, ne his affeccion bounden ne pyned ne trobled in noþinge logwere or wers þan himself is. And if he may do so, þan is it nyȝt with him, for þan is he in myrkenes.

Bot þis is a gode nyȝt and a lyȝt mirknes, for it is a stoppynge owt of þe fals lofe of þe werd, and it is a neyghynge to þe trewe day. And sothly þe myrker þat þis nyȝt is, þe nerre is þe trew lyȝt of þe lufe of Jesu; for þe more þat þe soule may þurgh longynge to God ben hyd fro noyse and dynne of fleschly affeccyons, werdly desyres and vnclene þoghtes, þe nerre is it for to felen þe lyȝt of þe lufe of him, for it is euen at it. Þus semeþ þat þe prophete mened whan he seyd þus: *Cum in tenebris sedeo, Dominus lux mea est*. Þat is: Whan I sitte in
f. 71r myrknes oure Lord is my lyght; | þat is, whan my soule is hyd fro al sterynges of synne, as it were in slepe, þan is oure Lord my lyȝt, for þan negheth he of his grace for to schew me of his lyȝt.

Nerþeles þis nyȝt is sumtyme pynful [and sumtyme it is esy and confortable. It is pynful] first whan a man is mikel foule and is not þurgh grace vsed for to ben often in þis mirknes bot wuld fayn hafe it, and þerfor he setteþ his þoght and his desyre to God-ward as mikel as he may, þat he wuld not felen ne þenken bot only him. And because þat he may not lyȝtly hafe it, þerfor it is pynful, for þe custom and þe

68 lufe] blissid *prec.* Hu$_2$, diligere sibique placere Lat. beholdynge] byholdynges BLd; and perceyuynge *add.* W 69 his^1] *om.* Cc lykynge] lykynges BLdTd, and louynge *add.* W bodily creatures] creatures fleischli B$_3$ bodily] fleischli ⌜L⌝B$_3$P 70 be . . . ficched/ne his affeccion] *rev.* MTd be] may *prec.* W mad fre] *om.* RAsAPl mad] *om.* MTd fre] and *add.* W not ficched ne] and stable Hu$_2$ \`ficched´ W$^G$, subgett LwTW ne$^1$] and Td bounden ne pyned] noȝt fyched ne bounden Td, not *prec.* M bounden] \`is´ not *prec.* Hu$_2$, ne *prec.* Td pyned ne] *om.* LB$_3$PH$_6$ 71 or wers] *om.* Td or] ne LB$_3$PH$_6$Cc is] his Cc, *om.* LB$_3$PH$_6$W 72 is it] *rev.* W \`it´ LdTd him] himself Cc is he] *rev.* W myrkenes] H$_7$HRLAsSrPCcMPl, derknesse BH$_5$B$_3$LwHu$_2$AEH$_6$LdTW 73 Bot . . . mirknes] *om.* RAsAH$_6$MPl nyȝt and] *om.* Td mirknes] H$_7$HRLAsSrPCcMPl, derknesse BH$_5$B$_3$LwHu$_2$ELdTW 74 þe^1] *om.* LB$_3$PH$_6$Cc þe^2] H$_7$RLB$_3$AsSrAEPH$_6$CcMPl, þis HBH$_5$B$_3$LwHu$_2$LdTW to] of BW day] that Jesu *add.* Cc, þat is Jesu *add.* MTd 75 þe^1] *om.* Td myrker] H$_7$HRLAsSrPCcMPl, derkere BH$_5$B$_3$LwHu$_2$AEH$_6$LdTW þis niȝt/is] *rev.* Hu$_2$ þis] H$_7$HRBH$_5$AsSrLwAHu$_2$H$_6$LdTW, þe LB$_3$EPCcMPl nerre] ner AH$_6$ is^2] it is RAsM þe^2] to þe AsPl lyȝt] H$_7$RLB$_3$AsSrAPH$_6$CcMPl, day HBH$_5$LwHu$_2$ELdTW, lux Lat. of þe] and M of^2 . . . him (l. 78)] *om.* M \`of^2´ L 76 Jesu] God RAsAPl, Jesu Christi Lat. þe^2] H$_7$HRBH$_5$AsSrHu$_2$CcMTW, a LB$_3$AEPH$_6$LdPl may] is or may be As God] Jesu Td, Jesu et per deuotas preces ad ipsum fusas Lat. 77 and dynne] *om.* Hu$_2$ and^1] of Td dynne . . . werdly] *om.* RAsAPl affeccyons] affeccion Td, in *add.* Cc werdly desyres] H$_7$LB$_3$EPH$_6$CcM, dissesis R, desires AsAPl, *om.* HBH$_5$SrLwHu$_2$LdTWTd, et desideriorum mundialium Lat. 78 nerre] ner A is it] H$_7$HBH$_5$LB$_3$LwAHu$_2$PH$_6$MLdPlW, *rev.* RAsSrECcT it] he Ld þe^2 . . . him]

and for to desiren only þe luf of him, is bisy for to hiden his þouȝt fro veyn beholdyng and his affeccioun fro fleschly likynge of alle bodily creatures, so þat his þouȝt be made free not ficched, ne his affeccioun bounden ne pyned ne trobled in noþing lower or wers þan himself is. And if he may do so, þan is it niȝt with him, for þan is he in mirknes.

f. 90^{v} Bot þis is a gode niȝt and a liȝty mirknes, for it is a stoppynge out | of þe fals luf of þis werld, and it is a neiȝeng to þe trewe day. And soþly þe mirker þat þis niȝt is, þe nerre is þe trewe day of þe luf of Ihesu; for þe more þat þe soule may þorw longyng to God ben hid fro noise and dynne of flescly affeccliouns and vnclene þoȝtes, þe nerre is it for to felen þe liȝt of þe luf of hym, for it is euen at it. Þus semiþ it þe prophet mened whan he seide þus: *Cum in tenebris sedeo, Dominus lux mea est*. Þat is: Whan I sitte in þe mirkenes oure Lord is mi liȝt; `þat is, when mi soule is hid fro alle steringes of synne, as it were in slepe, þen is oure Lord my liȝt', for þen neiȝeþ he of his grace for to schewe me of his liȝt.

Nerþeles þis niȝt is sumtyme pyneful and sumtyme it is esy and confortable. It is pynful first whan a man is mikil foule and is noȝt þurwȝ grace vsed to ben often in þis mirknes bot wold fayn haf it, and þerfore he settiþ his þouȝte and his desire to God-ward as mikel as he may, þat he wold not felen ne þinken bot only of him. And bycause þat he may not liȝtly haf `it', þerfore it is pynful, for þe custome and

hym þat is both lyȝt and loue Td him] God RAsAPl 79 for . . . it^{2}] *om*. Lat. it^{2}] þat Sr þus] Thys Ld semeþ þat] H$_7$LB$_3$SrPH$_6$, semiþ it HLwMTW, it semith RH$_5$AsCc, semeþ hit þat BHu$_2$, it semes þat Td, semeþ me Pl, semeþ E, semid A mened] menyth Cc, menyng Pl 80 þus] Mich. 7° *add*. BLHu$_2$EPLdT sedeo] sedero A lux mea] *rev*. LB$_3$EPH$_6$ þat is] H$_7$HBSrLwHu$_2$EH$_6$CcMLdTW, *om*. RH$_5$LB$_3$AsAPPl 81 myrknes] H$_7$HRLAsSrPCcMPl, þe mirkenes HTd, derknesse B$_3$AEH$_6$W, þe derknesse BH$_5$LwHu$_2$LdT `þat . . . lyȝt (l. 82)' *marg*. H^{c} þat] And *prec*. T al] þe H$_5$, eny B 82 sterynges] prauis motibus Lat. synne] synnes Td in] nyȝt I H$_5$, nightes T þan . . . lyȝt] *om*. H$_5$T oure] mi A Lord] H$_7$RAsLwH^{c}APlW, Jesu *add*. BLB$_3$SrHu$_2$EP-H$_6$CcMLd, Dominus Jesus Lat. for] *om*. T 83 lyȝt] that is his blyssid gostly presence *add*. Cc, be his gostly presence MTd, graciam lucis sui Lat. 84 nyȝt] lyȝt ACc, lyȝt *canc*., nyȝt Lw sumtyme pynful] *rev*. Pl sumtyme^{1}] sumdel H$_5$ and . . . pynful (l. 85)] *om*. H$_7$LwW, et quandoque quieta et delectabilis. Penalis est Lat. 85 mikel foule] gretly fould Hu$_2$ `is^{2}' Td 86 for to ben/often] *rev*. M for] H$_7$RLB$_3$AsSrAEPH$_6$CcMPl, *om*. HBH$_5$LwHu$_2$LdTW þis] *om*. A mirknes] H$_7$HRLAsSrPCcMPl, derknesse BH$_5$B$_3$Lw-AHu$_2$EH$_6$LdTW, nocte Lat. bot] he *add*. Cc, for he *add*. MTd wuld] wol H$_5$ 87 and þerfor] *om*. Td þerfor] *om*. M setteþ] semith A to God-ward] to Jesu-ward M, toward God H$_5$, *om*. Lat. 88 may] and *add*. Sr þat] *om*. LwW not felen] *rev*. Td felen ne þenken] *rev*. Ld þenken] noþyng *add*. M only] H$_7$, of *add*. HBH$_5$SrLwHu$_2$MLdTW, on *add*. RLB$_3$AsAEPH$_6$CcPl, de Lat. him] Domino Jesu Christo Lat. 89 þat] *om*. H$_6$ not] *om*. Pl `it^{1}' H^{c}, þis H$_5$, him T, *om*. B$_3$, eius presenciam Lat. it^{2}] he Td for] forwhi MTd

homlynes þat he haþ had before with synnes of þe werd and fleschly affeccions and erthly þynges and his fleschly dedys pressen so vpon him, and ay smyten in by maistrie and drawe doun al þe soule to hem, þat he may not wel ben hyd fro hem as sone as he wold. And þerfor is þis mirkenes pyneful to him, and namly whan grace toucheth not haboundendly. Nerþeles if it be so with þe, be not to heuy ne stryfe not to mikel, as if þou wuldest þurgh maistrie putten hem out of þi þoght, for þou maight not do so. Bot abyde grace, suffre esyly, and breke not þiself to mikel; and sleyghly if þou maight dragwe þi desire and þi gostly beholdenge to Jesu, as if þou wuldest not chargen hem.

For wyte þou wel, whan þou woldest desyre Jesu and only þenken on him, and þou maight not frely for presynge in of swilk ⸢werdly⸣ þoghtes, soþly þou art owtward of þe fals day and þou art entred in þis mirkenes; bot þi mirknes is noȝt restful because of disvse and vnconnynge and vnclennes of þiself. And þerfor vse it often, and it schal by processe þurgh felynge of grace be more esy and more restful to þe. And þat is whan þi soule þurgh felynge of grace is made so fre and so mighty and so gadred into itself þat it lysteþ `to' þenk on ryȝt noȝt, and þat it may withouten lettyng of ony bodily þynge þenk of ryȝt noȝt; þan is it in a gode mirknes.

þis noght I mene þus: þat a soule may þurgh grace be gadred into f.71v itself, and stand stil in itself frely and holly, and not be | dryfen aȝens þe wille ne draghe doun be maistrie for to þenken or lyken or lufen

90 haþ had] H$_7$RLB$_3$AsSrLw`H$^{c}$'AEPH$_6$CcMPlW, had H°BH$_5$Hu$_2$LdT, habuerit Lat. before/with synnes] H$_7$HRLB$_3$AsSrAEPH$_6$CcMPl, *rev.* BH$_5$LwHu$_2$LdTW before] and *add.*, *canc.* H synnes] H$_7$RLB$_3$AsSrLw`H^{c}'AEPH$_6$CcMPl, synn H°BH$_5$Hu$_2$LdTW, peccatis Lat. of] þat is *prec.* H$_5$, what *prec.* T fleschly] H$_7$RLB$_3$AsSrAEPH$_6$CcMPl, of *prec.* HBH$_5$LwHu$_2$LdTW 91 affeccions] affeccion BLdT pressen] pursuen Pl so] euere *add.* H$_6$ 92 ay smyten] *rev.* B ay] H$_7$HRBH$_5$LPCc, euere B$_3$AsLwAHu$_2$EH$_6$MPlW, alwey SrLdT smyten] *om.* M and^{2} . . . maistrie (l. 96)] *om.* M `þe soule' L 93 wel . . . hem] felen reste ne savour in Jesu Cc wel/ben hyd] *rev.* RAsSrPlTd hem] ne he may not fele reste ne sauour in Jesu *add.* Td as] so A wold] ben *add.* `L'B$_3$EP And] *om.* LwW is/þis mirkenes] *rev.* LwW 94 mirkenes] H$_7$HRLAsSrPCcPl, derknes BH$_5$B$_3$LwAHu$_2$EH$_6$LdTW pyneful] as *prec.* BHu$_2$Ld toucheth] H$_7$HRBAsSrLwAHu$_2$CcLdPlTW, him *add.* H$_5$`L'B$_3$EPH$_6$Td, tangit eum Lat. 95 haboundendly] plenteuously CcLd, [or *canc.*] plenteuously *add.* B Nerþeles if] And thow Cc be so] *rev.* Hu$_2$ with þe] þat þou RAsAPl to] *om.* Cc 96 to] *om.* LwW mikel] with hem *add.* H$_5$, þerwith *add.* Td if] H$_7$RLB$_3$AsSrAEPH$_6$Pl, þawȝ HBH$_5$LwHu$_2$LdTW, *om.* Cc, quasi Lat. þurgh] by H$_6$CcTd hem] hym M out . . . þoght] awey A of] *om.* Cc 97 þoght] hert Cc for] nay Hu$_2$ maight] may RLPPlTd, poteris Lat. grace] and *add.* Cc suffre] þou *add.* E 98 sleyghly] esily T, draw *add.*, *canc.* L maight] may AsLwCcMWTd, potes Lat. desire] desyrys Sr 99 and . . . beholdenge] *om.* RAsAMPlTd, et spiritualem consideracionem tuam Lat. þi] *om.* Hu$_2$ Jesu] God RAsAPl if] þoȝ AH$_6$ chargen hem] compelle him Hu$_2$ chargen] off *add.* Ld 100 Jesu] God RAsAPl only/þenken on him] *rev.* Sr only] holly M

þe homlynes þat he had with synn bifore of þe werld and of flescly affecciouns and erþly þinges and his fleschly dedis presen so oppon him, and ay smyten in bi maistrie and draw doun alle þe soule to hem, þat he may not wel ben hid fro hem as sone as he wold. And þerfore is þis mirknes pynful to him, and namly whan grace touchiþ not abundandly. Nerþeles if it be so with þe, be not to heuy ne strife not to mikel, as þawȝ þu woldest þurwȝ maistrye put hem out of þi þouȝt, for þou maiȝt not don so. Bot abide grace, suffre esily, and breke not þiself to mikel; and slely if þu maiȝt drawe þi desire and þi gostly biholdyng to Ihesu, as if þu woldest not chargen hem.

For wite þu wel, when þu woldest desire Ihesu and only þinken on
91r him, and þu maiȝt not frely for presinge | in of swilke wordly þouȝtes,
soþly þu art outward of þe fals day and þu art entrynge into þis mirknes; bot þi mirknes is not restful bicause of disuse and vnkunnynge and vnclennesse of þiself. And þerfore vse it often, and it schal bi processe þurw felynge of grace be more esy and more restful to þe. And þat is whan þi soule þurwȝ grace is made so free and so miȝti and so gidrid into itself þat it lust not to þink on riȝt noȝt, and þat it may withouten lettyng of ony bodily þinge þinken of riȝt noȝt; þan is it in a gode mirknes.

Þis noȝt I mene þus: þat a soule may þurgh grace be gedrid into itself, and stande stille in itself frely and holy, and not be drifen ageyn þe wille ne `drawen´ downe bi maistrie for to þinken or liken or louen

101 `þou´ Pl maight] mai LLwPW, potes Lat. frely] *om.* RAsAMPlTd in] *om.* A werdly] *over the canc. of a shorter word* H$_7$ 102 þoughtes] þouȝte Pl entred] H$_7$RLB$_3$AsSrAPH$_6$CcMPl, entrynge HBH$_5$LwHu$_2$ELdTW, intrasti Lat. in] H$_7$RAH$_6$-CcPl, in`to´ L, into HBH$_5$B$_3$AsSrLwHu$_2$EPMLdTW 103 þis] þe M mirkenes] H$_7$HRLAsSrPCcMPl, derknesse BH$_5$B$_3$LwAHu$_2$EH$_6$LdTW mirknes] H$_7$HRLAsSr-PCcMPl, derknesse BH$_5$B$_3$LwAHu$_2$EH$_6$LdTW disvse] disese BW, diffuse Cc, þyn *prec.* As 104 and[1] . . . þiself] *om.* RAsAPl often] tymes *add.* Hu$_2$ 105 by . . . grace/be] *rev.* Sr processe] of tyme *add.* H$_5$CcTd, ex processu temporis Lat. more[2]] *om.* H$_5$ 106 felynge of] H$_7$RLB$_3$AsAEPCcPl`T$^G$W$^G$´, *om.* HBH$_5$SrLwMLdTWTd, sensacionem gracie Lat. `of grace´ Pl, *om.* RAs 107 mighty] and soo good *add.* LwW so[2]] *om.* T into] vnto M itself] hymself BM, thyn self Sr it lysteþ] *om.* H$_5$ `it´ R lysteþ] H$_7$RLB$_3$AsAEPH$_6$CcMPl, not *add.* HBH$_5$SrLwHu$_2$LdTW `to´ *interl.* H$_7$ on] of BHu$_2$Td 108 and . . . mirknes (l. 109)] *om.* AsSr, et sine impedimento alicuius rei corporalis potest de nichilo cogitare; tunc enim in bona nocte abscondita est seu in bona obscuritate Lat. and . . . noȝt (l. 109)] *om.* LwTW lettyng] *om.* Hu$_2$ ony] one Hu$_2$ of[2]] H$_7$HBH$_5$LwHu$_2$ELdPlTW, on RLB$_3$AsSrAPH$_6$CcM 109 þan . . . mirknes] *om.* H$_5$ is it] *rev.* Cc in] *om.* Td gode] *om.* Pl mirknes] H$_7$HRLAsSrPCcMPl, derknesse BH$_5$B$_3$LwAHu$_2$EH$_6$LdTW 110 into] to AMPl 111 itself] hymself BSrCcPl `and . . . itself´ Ld, *om.* LwW, *om.* Lat. itself] hymself BSrCcM 112 þe] H$_7$HRB-AsSrLwAHu$_2$CcTW, þy H$_5$Pl, his LB$_3$EPH$_6$MLd draghe] `drawen´ H^c, *om.* H°H$_5$ lyken or lufen] *rev.* Hu$_2$

with clefynge of affeccion ony synne or veynly ony erthly thinge. Þan þenkeþ þe soule noȝt; for þan þenkeþ it of non erthly þynge clefendly. Þis is a riche noght; and þis noȝt and þis nyght is a grete ese for a soule þat desyreþ þe lufe of Jesu. It is in ese as for þoght of erthly þinge, bot not as for Jesu; for þogh þe soule þenk not of ony erthly þinge, nerþeles it is ful besy for to þenke on him.

What þinge þan makeþ þis mirknes? Sothly not ellys bot a graciouse desyre for to hafe þe lufe of Jesu. For þat desyre and þat longynge þat he haþ þat tyme to þe lufe of Jesu, for to seen him and hafe him, dryfeþ out of þe herte al werdly vanites and fleschly affeccyons, and gedreþ þe soule into itself and occupyeþ it only for to þenken how it myȝt come to þe lufe of him, and so bryngeþ it into þis ryche noght. And sothly it is not al mirk ne noght whan it þenkeþ þus; for þogh it be mirk fro fals lyght it is not al mirk fro þe trewe. For Jesu, þat is bothe lufe and lyȝt, is in þis mirknes, wheþer it be pynful or restful. He is in þe soule as trauailende in desyre and longende to lyȝt, bot he is not ȝit as restende in lufe ne as schewende his lyȝt. And þerfor is it called nyght and mirknes, in as mikel as þe soule is hyd fro þe false lyȝt of þis werd and haþ not ȝete fully felynge of trewe lyȝt, bot is in abydynge of þe blissed lufe of God þat it desyreth.

Þan if þou wilt wyte whan þou art in þis syker mirknes and whan

113 clefynge] H$_7$HRBH$_5$AsSrLwAHu$_2$CcMLdPlTW, chesinge LB$_3$EPH$_6$, eleccione Lat. affeccion] H$_7$H°BH$_5$LB$_3$AsSrPH$_6$MLd, to *add.* RLw`H^c´AECcPlTW, on *add.* Hu$_2$ or/veynly] *rev.* E veynly/ony . . . thinge] *rev.* Hu$_2$, veyn þing or erþli H$_6$ ony] or H$_5$LB$_3$PH$_6$, to *prec.* EW 114 þe] H$_7$HRLB$_3$AsSrLwAEPH$_6$CcMPlW, þi BH$_5$LdHu$_2$T noȝt] H$_7$RLB$_3$AsSrLwAPH$_6$CcMPlW, riȝt *prec.* HBH$_5$Hu$_2$ELdT, nichil Lat. þenkeþ it] *rev.* H$_6$ of] H$_7$HBAsSrLwHu$_2$ECcLdW, on H$_5$LB$_3$APH$_6$MPlT non] no LEPPl, oo T, þe M `erþly´ H^c, *om.* H°H$_5$TTd 115 þis . . . noght] *om.* Lat. riche] ryȝte Ld noght] *rep.*, *canc.* Td and^1] H$_7$HBH$_5$LwHu$_2$ELdTW, *om.* RLB$_3$AsSrAPH$_6$CcMPlTd, *om.* Lat. noȝt/. . ./nyght] *rev.* M and þis nyght] *om.* Sr and^2] *corr. fr.* is E a^2] as Ld for a soule] *rep.*, *canc.* B$_3$ for] to RAsAPl a^3] H$_7$RLB$_3$AsSrAPH$_6$CcMPl, þe HBH$_5$LwHu$_2$ELdTW 116 þe lufe of] to loue H$_6$ Jesu] God RAsAPl, Jesu Christi Lat. It] for þan *prec.* RAsAPl þoght of] *om.* RAsAPlTd erthly] H$_7$RLB$_3$AsSrAPH$_6$CcMPl, ony *prec.* HBH$_5$LwHu$_2$ELdTW, alicuius *prec.* Lat. þinge] þinges H$_7$, terreni Lat. bot . . . þinge (l. 117)] *om.* SrAW 117 Jesu] God RAsPl of] on H$_6$Pl ony] *om.* RAsPl þinge] thynges M, terrenis Lat. 118 nerþeles] ne-(*canc.*)|uereþeles L, ȝet Cc for] *om.* M on him] on God AsAPl, of God R, on Jesu MTd, de Domino Jesu Lat. 119 mirknes] H$_7$HRLAsSrPCcMPl, derknesse BH$_5$B$_3$LwAHu$_2$EH$_6$LdTW, noctem vel obscuritatem Lat. a graciouse] *om.* RAsAMPlTd 120 for] *om.* MTd `þe´ Pl Jesu] God RAsAPl, God *add.* Td For . . . Jesu (l. 121)] `For . . . God´ H^c, *om.* H°H$_5$T 121 he] it Td to . . . him (l. 122)] *om.* Cc `Jesu´ W^G, God RAsH^{c}ALwPlWTd, Jesu cum constanti desideracione illius et firma adhesione eidem Lat. 122 hafe] to *prec.* EH$_6$T dryfeþ] and *prec.* H$_5$ 123 itself] hymself BM, þe self SrCc 124 it^1] he SrM myȝt] may T him] God RAsAPlTd, Jesu M, and that tyme maye it freely and deuoutly beholden Jesu wheder it woll pray er thinke *add.*

with clefyng of affeccioun ony synne or veynly ony erþly þinge. Þan þinkiþ þe soule riȝt noȝt; for þan þinkiþ it of none `erþly´ þinge clefendly. Þis is a riche noȝt. And þis noȝt and þis niȝt is a grete ese for þe soule þat desiriþ þe luf of Ihesu. It is in ese as for þoȝt of ony erþly þinge, bot not as for Ihesu; for þawȝ þe soule þink not of ony erþly þinge, nerþeles it is ful bisy for to þinke on him.

What þinge þan makiþ þis mirknes? Soþly not elles bot a gracious desire for to haue þe luf of Ihesu. `For þat desire and þat longing þat it haþ þat tyme to þe loue of God´, for to seen him and han him, drifeþ out of þe herte alle werdly vanitees and flescly affeccioun̄s, and gedriþ þe soule into itself and ocupieþ it only for to þinke how it miȝt come to þe luf of him, and so brynge`th´ it into þis riche noȝt. And soþly it is not al mirke ne noȝt whan it þinkiþ þus; for þawȝ it be mirk fro fals liȝt it is not al mirke fro þe trew luf. For Ihesu, þat is boþ luf and liȝt, is in þis mirknes, wheþer it be pinful or restful. He is in þe soule as trauailand in desire and longynde [f. 91^v| to liȝt, bot he is not ȝit as restend in luf and shewend his liȝt. And þerfor hit is callid niȝt and mirknes, in als mikel as þe soule is hid fro þe fals liȝt of þe werld and haþ not ȝit fully felyng of trewe liȝt, bot is in abidynge of þat blissed luf of God whilk it desiriþ.

Þan if þu wil wete whan þou art in þis siker mirknes and whan noȝt,

LwMWTd, and that tyme may it only and frely and devoutly beholdyn Jesu whethir it wyl prey or thynk *add.* Cc, ad eius dileccionem Lat. bryngeþ it] *rev.* LwW bryngeþ] brynge`th´ H$^c$, brynge H°H$_5$T it$^2$] him H$_5$, in Hu$_2$, *om.* LB$_3$P into] in Td 125 þis] þe Sr ryche] ryȝte LdW, *om.* Lat. `noght^1´ Cc, noctem seu obscuritatem Lat. mirk] H$_7$HRLAsSrPCcMPl, derk BH$_5$B$_3$LwAHu$_2$EH$_6$LdTW ne] neþer Ld, or M þenkeþ] semeþ H$_5$, is RAsAMPl 126 be] þus *add.* M mirk (*bis*)] H$_7$HRLAsSrPCcMPl, derk BH$_5$B$_3$LwAHu$_2$EH$_6$LdTW fro (*bis*)] for Cc it^2] yit *prec.* Hu$_2$ trewe] H$_7$RSrH$_6$, trouþe B$_3$As, lyght *add.* BLAHu$_2$EPCcMPlTW, luf *add.* H, lyȝt [*corr. fr.* love] *add.* Lw, loue of Jesu *add.* H$_5$, lumine vero Lat. 127 is^2] hud *add.* M mirknes] H$_7$HRLAsSrPCcMPl, derknesse BH$_5$B$_3$LwAHu$_2$EH$_6$LdTW wheþer] þat *add.* H$_5$ be] *om.* M 128 He is] If it be paynful þan *prec.* `Lw´W, If it be paynful thenne is he CcMTd `is´ L þe] þi H$_5$ as] a *add.* As and] in Ld 129 ne as] H$_7$RLB$_3$AsSrLwAEPH$_6$CcMPlW [*corr. fr.* and Lw], and HBH$_5$Hu$_2$LdT, et Lat. 130 is it] H$_7$Pl, *rev.* Σ called] clepid H$_6$Ld mirknes] H$_7$HRLAsSrPCcMPl, derknesse BH$_5$B$_3$LwAHu$_2$EH$_6$LdTW in] And Cc þe] *om.* H$_5$ 131 þis] H$_7$RLB$_3$AsAEPH$_6$CcMPl, þe HBH$_5$SrLwHu$_2$LdTW, huius Lat. ȝete] it Ld fully] the fulle M felynge] the *prec.* Cc trewe] þe *prec.* E lyȝt] for Jesu shewith nout his [blessede *om.* Cc] gostly face to þe soule restfully *add.* CcMTd, lucem dileccionis Jesu Christi Lat. 132 bot] it *add.* CcMTd abydynge] vnbidyng M þe] H$_7$RLAsSrAEPH$_6$CcMPl, þat HBH$_5$LwHu$_2$LdTW, *om.* B$_3$ blissed] blissful SrCc of God] of Jesu CcM, *om.* A, Jesu Christi Lat. þat] H$_7$RLB$_3$AsAPH$_6$Pl, whilk HBH$_5$SrLwEMLdTW, þe whiche Hu$_2$Cc it] he Td desyreth] for to han be the gracious onseable presens of Jesu CcMTd 133 mirknes] H$_7$HRLAsSrPCcMPl, derknesse BH$_5$B$_3$LwAHu$_2$EH$_6$LdTW

not, þou mayght assay þus and seke no ferþer bot þus: whan þou felest þin entent and þi wil fully sette for to desyren God and þenken only on him, þou maight as it were first aske þiself in þyn owen þoght wheþer þou coueyte for to hafe ony þinge of þis lyf for lufe of itself, or for to hafe þe vse of ony of þi bodily wittes in ony creature. And þan if þin eyge bygynne and answere þus, I wold seen ryȝt noȝt; and after
f. 72r þat þin ere, I wold here ryȝt noȝt; and þi mouth, | I wold sauour ryȝt noȝt; [I wolde speke ryȝt noȝt of erþly þinge; and þi nose, I wolde smelle ryȝt noȝt]; and þi body, I wold fele ryȝt noȝt; and aftere, þin herte seyþ I wold þenken ryȝt noȝt þat is of erthly þinges ne of bodily dede, ne I wold hafe affeccyon festned fleschly to no creature, bot only in God, and to God-ward if þat I cowthe. And whan þei answeren alle þus to þe, and þat is don ful redyly if grace touche þe, þan art þou entred sumwhat into þis mirknes. For þogh þou fele and perceyue glentynges and proferynges of veyn þoghtes and presynge in of fleschly affeccions, nerþeles þou art in þis profytable mirknes, be so þat þi þoght be not ficched on hem. For swilk veyn ymaginacyons þat fallen in þe herte vnavisyly troblen þis mirknes and pyne þe soule sumwhat, bycause þat it wolde be hyd fro hem and may not. Bot þei do not awey þe profyte of þe mirknes, for þe soule schal be þat weye come to restful mirknes. And þan is þis mirknes restful, whan þe soule is hyd for a tyme fro þe pyneful felynge of al swilk veyn þoghtes

134 mayght] may H_5LwW and . . . þus[2]] *om.* Cc ferþer] ferrer HHu_2 135 to] *om.* M desyren] þus *add.* `L´$B_3$EPM  God] Jesu Td, per orationem instanciam dileccionemque Jesu Christi Lat.  and] to *add.* $H_6$, *om.* Ld  þenken only] *rev.* Pl  þenken] þou thenkest Cc, to *prec.* Td  136 on] in Ld  maight] may LwWTd  as it were/first] *rev.* R  `were´ Pl first] *om.* AsA aske] examyne LB_3EP$H_6$$W^G$ owen] *om.* LB_3PH_6 137 coueyte] coueitist E for[1]] *om.* H_5 to hafe/ony þinge] *rev.* H_5 for[2]] þe *add.* M itself] þisilf Sr, þyn self AsCc or for] þerfore R, þerefore for As 138 þi] þe M ony[2]] a Ld 139 eyge bygynne] eyȝen bygynnen H_5 bygynne and] *om.* LwW and answere] to answeryn Cc answere] þee *add.* B_3LwMW ryȝt] *om.* Sr noȝt] of erthely þinge *add.* T and[2] . . . noȝt (l. 140)/and . . . noȝt[1] (l. 141)] *rev.* LwW and[2] . . . noȝt (l. 140)] *om.* Pl and[2]] After *prec.* As, þan *add.* H_5 after þat] afterward M 140 þat] *om.* RAsLwACcW and] than H_5Cc I wold[2]] and A I[2] . . . noȝt[1] (l. 141)] *om.* Hu_2 sauour . . . wolde[2] (l. 141)] *om.* Td 141 I wolde[1] . . . noȝt[1] (l. 142] *om.* H_7W I wolde[1] . . . noȝt] *om.* Lw þinge] þynges H_5Cc 142 and[1] . . . noȝt (l. 143)] *om.* As and[1] . . . and[2]] *om.* RA and[1] . . . noȝt[2]] *om.* PlTd and[1]] of erthlely þyng *prec.* Ld, thanne *add.* Cc I wold] wull Ld aftere] H_7, it *add.* HBH_5LwHu_2LdTW, if *add.* RLB_3Sr-AEPH_6CcMPl, þat if *add.* Td. postea Lat. 143 seyþ] H_7RLB_3SrEPH_6, sei HBH_5Lw-AHu_2CcMLdPlTW, dicat Lat. þat is] H_7RLB_3AsSrAEPH_6CcMPl, *om.* H$B_3$$H_5$Lw-$Hu_2$LdTW erthly] erly M þinges] H_7Td, þinge Σ, terrenis Lat. of] *om.* H_6 144 dede] deedis RAs, operibus Lat. ne I] neyþer I ne H_5 I] *om.* Ld wold] nouȝt *add.* H_5As hafe] myn *add.* ATd, none *add.* M festned] *om.* A to] H_7HBH_5LB_3Lw-Hu_2EPH_6LdTW, in RAsSrACcMPl, in Lat. 145 in] H_7HRBH_5AsSrLwA-

þu mai3t assaie þus and seke no ferrer bot þus. Whan þu felist þin entent and þi wil fully sette for to desire God and þenken only on him, þu mai3t as it were first ask þiself in þin owne þou3te wheþer þu coueite for to hafe ony þinge of þis lif for luf of itselfe, or for to hafe þe vse of ony of þi bodily wittes in ony creature. And þan if þin hi3e bigynne and answere þus, I wold see ri3t no3t; and after þat þin ere, I wold here ri3t no3t; and þi mouþ, I wold sauour ri3t nou3t, I wolde speke ri3t no3t of erþly þinge; and þi nese, I wolde smel ri3t not; and þi body, I wold fele ri3t not; and after it þin hert sei I wolde þinke ri3t nou3t of erþly þinge ne of bodily dede, ne I wold haf affeccioun festned flescly to no creature, bot only in God and to God-ward if þat I couþe: and when þei answeren alle þus to þe, and þat is done ful redily if grace touche þe, þan art þou entred sumwhat into þis mirknes. For þaw3 þu fele and perceife glentynges and proferynges of veyn þou3tes and presynge in of flescly affeciouns, nerþeles þu art in þis profitable mirknes, be so þat þi þou3te be no3t ficched in hem. For swilk veyn ymaginaciouns þat fallen in þe herte vnauisely troblen þis mirknes and pynen þe soule sumwhat, bicause þat it wold ben hid fro hem and may not. Bot þei do not awey þe profit of þis mirknes, for
92^r þe soule schal bi þat wey come to restful mirknes. And þan is | þis mirknes restful, whan þe soule is hid for a tyme fro þe pyneful felynge of alle swilk vayne þou3tis and only is restid in desire and longynge to

Hu$_2$CcMLdPlTW, to LB$_3$EPH$_6$, in Lat. God] Jesu CcMTd, Domino Jesu Christo Lat. and to God-ward] *om.* Lat. God-ward] hym-ward CcMTd þat] *om.* RH$_5$Td And] *om.* Hu$_2$ whan] thenne M þat *add.* BSrLd þei] þese A alle/þus to þe] *rev.* CcM alle þus] *rev.* T alle] *om.* Lat. 146 þat] thys Ld, it *add.* H$_5$ þe^2] For only grace and gladnes of þe soule gone togedere here *add.* MTd 147 entred sumwhat] *rev.* SrH$_6$MLdTTd into] in Lw þis] *om.* LB$_3$P mirknes] H$_7$HRAsSrPCcMPl, me`r´kenesse L, derknesse BH$_5$B$_3$LwAHu$_2$EH$_6$LdTW `þogh´ Pl 148 glentynges] glemerynges Sr proferynges] profires RAs, profering E presynge in] preisyng Cc, *om.* Lat. in] *om.* A 149 nerþeles] 3et Cc þou art] *rev.* Cc þis] þe M mirknes] H$_7$HRLAs-SrPCcMPl, derknesse BH$_5$B$_3$LwAHu$_2$EH$_6$LdTW, And þan is þis mirknes restful whan þe soule is hid for a tyme *add.*, *canc.* H be so] if it *prec.* H$_5$W, if it be Td, si Lat. be] it *add.* ET 150 þi] my3t *add.*, *canc.* L, þat *add.* Pl ficched] festned H$_6$ on hem] theron M swilk] þou3tis and *add.* Hu$_2$ veyn] *om.* Sr 151 þe^1] thi Ld vnavisyly] vnauysibly R, vnavisid H$_6$ troblen] trobleth M þis] thyn Cc mirknes] H$_7$HRLAsSrPCcMPl, derknesse BH$_5$B$_3$LwAHu$_2$EH$_6$LdTW pyne] peyneþ M 152 Bot] 3et *add.* Cc 153 `not´ L, *om.* B$_3$ þe^2 H$_7$, þis Σ mirknes] H$_7$HRLAsSrPCcMPl, derknesse BH$_5$B$_3$LwAHu$_2$EH$_6$LdTW schal/be þat weye] *rev.* As be] *om.* Td þat weye/come] *rev.* Td 154 to] þe *add.* CcPl mirknes^1] H$_7$HRLAsSrPCcMPlW, derknesse BH$_5$B$_3$-LwAHu$_2$EH$_6$LdT And . . . restful] *om.* Lat [et tunc est ista obscuritas quieta *add.* H$_8$UpB$_4$He] `þan´ Pl mirknes$^2$] H$_7$HRLAsSrPCcMPl, derknesse BH$_5$B$_3$Lw-AHu$_2$EH$_6$LdTW 155 hyd] his Ld a] þe LB$_3$PLd felynge] felyngis Sr `veyn´ Pl, *om.* T þoghtes] þinges P and only is rested in desyre and longynge to Jesu with a gostly beholdynge of him, as it schal be seyde aftere. Bot þat lasteþ bot a whyle hol; nerþeles, þogh it be bot a schort tyme, it is ful profytable.

How þat desyre of Jesu sothfastly feled in þis lyȝtly myrknes sleeth alle sterynges of synne and ableth þe soule for to perceyfen gostly lyghtenynges fro þe gostly Jerusalem þat is Jesu. Capitulum xxv^{m}

T[h]an syn þis mirknes and þis nyght is so gode and so restful, þogh it be schorte, þat standeþ only in desyre and longynge to þe lufe of Jesu with a blynd þenkynge of him; how gode þan and how blissed is it for to felen his lufe and for to be illumyned of his blissed vnseable lyght for to seen sothfastnes, þe whilk lyght a soule resceyfeþ whan þe nyȝt passeþ and þe day sprynggeþ. þis I hope was þe nyȝt þat þe prophete mened whan he seyde: Mi soule haþ desyred þe in þe nyȝt, as I befor seyde. It is mikel better for to ben hid in þis mirk nyȝt fro beholdynge of þe werd, þogh it were pyneful, þan for to ben owt in þe fals lykynge
f. 72^{v} of þis werd | þat semeþ so schynende and so confortable to hem þat are blynded in knowynge of gostly lyȝt. For whan þou art in þis mirknes þou art mikel nerre to Jerusalem þan whan þou art in myddys of þat fals lyȝt. þerfor applye þin herte fully to þe sterynge of grace, and vse þe for to wonen in þis mirknes, and by often assayenge to ben homly þerin, and it schal son be made restful to þe, and þe trew lyȝt of

156 and[1]] nanly *add., canc.* Td rested] reste Ld longynge . . . a] *om.* M longynge] gastly behaldyng Td to] in Hu$_2$ Jesu] God RAsAPl, Jesu Christi Lat. with . . . aftere (l. 157)] *om.* Td with . . . him] *om.* RAsAPl 157 him] Jesu MTd aftere] H$_7$RLB$_3$AsSrAEPH$_6$CcMPl, afterward HBH$_5$LwHu$_2$LdTW þat] it LB$_3$PH$_6$, hec consideracio Lat. 158 nerþeles] ȝet Cc be] so *add.* H$_5$ a] while and a *add.* As `ful´ Td, *om.* AsCcPl

Chapter 25 *title*: H$_7$LB$_3$SrAEPH$_6$MLdTW How a soule, whan it is hid thorew grace fro þe viȝl noyse and besynesse of þe werld, is in a good niȝt and in a liȝt mirknesse, for þan may it frely prayen and thynkyn on Jesu. RPl [*cf. above, Chapter 24 Title*] How goode and how blissful it is to þe fote to be liȝtned with þe liȝt of God in þyne derkenesse and in þyn desire. As *om.* HBH$_5$LwHu$_2$CcTd 1 desyre] the *prec.* LdTW of] in ALd sothfastly] *om.* ALdTW lyȝtly] liȝtsum ALdTW, liȝti B$_3$ myrknes] H$_7$LPH$_6$, derknesse B$_3$AELdTW 2 for] *om.* AEH$_6$LdTW 3 lyghtenynges] liȝtynges B$_3$, lettynges M fro] for LP, of H$_6$ gostly] heuenly LdTW 5 Than] Tan H$_7$ mirknes] H$_7$HRLAsSrPCcMPl, derknesse BH$_5$B$_3$LwAHu$_2$EH$_6$LdTW and þis nyght] *om.* H$_5$ so[1]] *om.* Pl 6 be] H$_7$RLB$_3$AsSr-LwAPH$_6$CcMPlW, bot *add.* HBH$_5$Hu$_2$ELdTWTd and longynge] *om.* Lat. to] vnto Ld Jesu] God RAsAPl, Jesu Christi 7 blynd] stable Cc, nuda Lat. of] H$_7$HBH$_5$LB$_3$As-SrHu$_2$PLdPlT, o⌜n⌝ H^{c}, on RLwAECcMW and how blissid/is it] *rev.* Ld how] *om.* Cc blissed] blisful Td is it] *rev.* RAsAM 8 felen] gustare Lat. `be´ Cc  illumyned] lyȝtened Ld  of] H$_7$RLB$_3$AsSrAPH$_6$MPl, with HBH$_5$LwHu$_2$ECcLdTW  blissed] blisful Td, *om.* Ld  vnseable] invisibile BA, present *add.* W, `presens/ *add.* Lw lyght . . .

Ihesu with a gostly biholdyng of him, as it schal be said afterward. Bot þat lasteþ bot a while hool; nerþeles, þawȝ it be bot a schort tyme, it is ful profitable.

[CHAPTER 25]

þan siþen þis mirknes and þis niȝt is so good and so restful, þawȝ it be bot schort, þat stondeþ only in desire and longynge to þe luf of Ihesu with a blynde þingynge o⌜n⌝ him; how gode þan and how blissid is it for to felen his luf and for to be illumined with his blissed vnseable liȝt for to seen soþfastnes, þe whilke liȝt a soule receyuyþ whan þe niȝt passiþ and þe day spryngiþ. þis I hope was þe niȝt þat þe prophet mened whan he saide: Mi soule haþ desired þe in þe niȝt, as I hafe bifore saide. It is mikil better to ben hid in þis mirke niȝt fro beholdyng of þe werld, þawȝ it were pyneful, þan for to ben out in fals likyng of þis werld þat semiþ so shynende and so confortable to hem þat are blynde in knowynge of gostly liȝt. For whan þu art in þis mirknes þou art mikel nerre Ierusalem þan whan þu art in middes of þat fals liȝt. þerfor applie þin hert fully to þe stirynge of grace, and vse for to wonen in þis mirknes, and be often assaynge to ben homly þerin, and it schal sone be made restful to þe, and þe trew liȝt of gostly

sothfastnes] presence Td lyght] syȝt Lw 9 sothfastnes] thrugh his graceful onseable presens *add.* CcM, de ueritate eius modicum uidere Lat. 10 and . . . seyde (l. 11)] *om.* Td hope] trow A, ut estimo Lat. 11 `mened´ Pl, meneþ As, spak offe M whan he seyde] *om.* B seyde] þus: Anima mea desiderauit te in nocte *add.* H$_5$, þus: Anima mea desiderauit te in nocte. That is *add.* E, þus *add.* Pl I] he R, *om.* As befor seyde] H$_7$RLB$_3$AsSrAEPH$_6$CcMPl, hafe *prec.* HBH$_5$LwHu$_2$LdTW, *rev.* Hu$_2$ 12 for] H$_7$RLAsSrAPCcPl, *om.* HBH$_5$B$_3$LwHu$_2$EH$_6$MLdTW þis] þe LB$_3$PM mirk] H$_7$HRLAsSrPCcMPl, derke BH$_5$B$_3$LwAHu$_2$EH$_6$LdTW, myrknes Td fro] þe *add.* B$_3$AsACc, by *add.* B 13 were] be SrM owt] *om.* SrCcM þe] H$_7$RLB$_3$AsSrAPH$_6$Cc, þis MPl, *om.* HBH$_5$LwHu$_2$ELdTW fals] lyȝt of *add.* Td 14 werd] *om.* RAs 15 `are´ Cc  blynded] H$_7$RLB$_3$AsSrAPH$_6$CcPl, blynde HBH$_5$LwHu$_2$EMLdTWTd, ceci Lat.  in[1]] þe *add.* H$_5$  For . . . lyȝt (l. 17)] *om.* Td  16 mirknes] H$_7$HRLAsSrPCcMPl, derknesse BH$_5$B$_3$LwAHu$_2$EH$_6$LdTW  nerre] ner AH$_6$M  to] H$_7$RBAsSrAHu$_2$ECcM`W^G´, *om.* HBH$_5$LB$_3$LwHu$_2$PH$_6$LdPlTW in myddys] amyddis M in] þe *add.* H$_5$LwCcLdW myddys of] *om.* T myddys] middel H$_5$ 17 þat] þe AsCcW þe] H$_7$RH$_5$LB$_3$AsSrAEPH$_6$CcMPl, *om.* HBLwHu$_2$LdTW 18 for] *om.* Hu$_2$ `to´ Cc wonen] dwelle AHu$_2$, abide E mirknes] H$_7$HRLAsSrAPCcMPl, derknesse BH$_5$B$_3$LwHu$_2$EH$_6$LdTW by] be HBSrLwECc often] H$_7$HBH$_5$LAsSrLwHu$_2$PH$_6$CcLdTW, oft RB$_3$AEMPl 19 and[1]] *om.* LB$_3$PH$_6$ son be] *rev.* W and[2]] For whanne þi conscience is purged and esed þorwe grace, thanne MTd þe[2]] *om.* T trew] *om.* As lyȝt] þat is trewe As gostly knowynge schal spryngen to þe; not al at ones, bot priuely by lytel and lytel, as þe prophete seith: *Habitantibus in regione vmbre mortis, lux orta est eis.* To þe wonende in þe contre of þe schadwe of ded, ly3t was sprongen. Þat is, ly3t of grace spronge and schal spryngen to hem þat kan wonen in þe schadwe of ded, þat is in þis mirknes þat is lyke to ded. For as ded sleth a lyfende body and al fleschly felynges of it, ry3t so desyre to lufe Jesu felt in þis mirknes sleþ al synnes, alle fleschly affeccions and vnclene þoghtes for þe tyme, and þan neghes þou fast to Jerusalem. Þou art not 3it at it, bot by smale sodeyn ly3tnynges þat glyderen out þurgh smale cranes fro þat cyte schalt þou moun see it fro ferre, or þat þou come þerto. For wyte þou wel, þogh þi soule be in þis restful mirknes withouten troblynge of werdly vanite, it is not 3et þer it schuld be, it is not 3it clothed al in ly3t ne turned al into [fyre] of lufe; bot it feleth wel þat þer is sumwhat abo[f]e itself þat it knoweþ not ne haþ not 3it, bot it wolde hafe it and brennendly 3erneth it. And þat is no3t ellys bot þe syght of Jerusalem withouteforth, þe whilk Jerusalem is lyke to a cyte þat þe prophete Ezechiel seygh in his visions.

He seyþ þat he sagw a cyte sette vpon an hille heldende to þe southe, þat to his syght whan it was meten was no more of lengthe and of brede þan a rede þat was sex cubytes and a palme of lengthe. Bot as son as he was broght into þe cyte and loked aboute him, þan þoght him þat it was wundere mikel, for he seygh many halles and

20 knowynge] leuyng M priuely/by . . . lytel^2 (l. 21)] *rev.* Hu$_2$ priuely] prinspaly Cc by] a *add.* As, *om.* H$_5$Sr 21 and] H$_7$RH$_5$LB$_3$AsSrAHu$_2$EPH$_6$CcMPl, by *add.* HBLwLdTW lytel^2] *The first extract in* Td *ends here* seith] Ysa. 9° *add.* LHu$_2$EPLdW Habitantibus . . . eis] *om.* As (*space left unfilled by the rubricator*) 22 eis] H$_7$RLB$_3$AsSrPH$_6$CcMPl, þat is *add.* HBH$_5$LwHu$_2$ELdTW To þe wonende] H$_7$RAs, `To the´ wonend H$^c$, wonend H°H$_5$T, To the wonyng SrMPl, To wonynge B, To wonyd Lw, To hem þat wonen LB$_3$PH$_6$, To hem wonyng A, To men dwellyng Hu$_2$Ld, To dwellynge W, To þe dwellers ECc contre] kyngdom M þe$^2$] H$_7$SrHu$_2$EPH$_6$CcLd, *om.* HRBH$_5$AsLwAMPlTW, `fals´ *add.*, *canc.* L, fals *add.* B$_3$ 23 was] is Hu$_2$H$_6$, `is´ Pl sprongen] spryngynge B spronge] spryngen B, `was´ sprongen L, was sprongen B$_3$EP, `was´ is sprongen Pl, is sprongen M 24 hem] all *prec.* LwW wonen] dwelle Hu$_2$E þis] þe H$_5$CcM, *om.* Lat. 25 mirknes] H$_7$HRLAsSrPCcMPl, derknesse BH$_5$B$_3$Lw-AHu$_2$EH$_6$LdTW lyke] liif B$_3$ to] vnto T as] a Cc a] þe H$_5$, eche Ld 26 felynges] felinge LB$_3$PH$_6$M, sencaciones Lat. of it] þerof Sr, *om.* M `so´ H$_6$ lufe] þe loue off LdTW, love of LwPl Jesu] God RAsAPl, and to seen hym *add.* M, Jesu Christi Lat. felt . . . mirknes] *om.* Lat. felt] *om.* A mirknes] H$_7$HRLAsSrHu$_2$PCcMPl, derknesse BH$_5$B$_3$LwAEH$_6$LdTW 27 synnes] synne M, flesshely *prec.* T fleschly] felyngis and *add.* As vnclene] H$_7$RLB$_3$AsSrAPH$_6$CcPl, alle *prec.* HBH$_5$LwHu$_2$LdTW, inmundas Lat. 28 and] *om.* RAsAPl `þou´ H$_6$, but *prec.* SrAH$_6$Ld 3it at it] þerat A, 3et þerat Sr, `þar´ yit Lw, there yet W 29 sodeyn] *om.* Hu$_2$ ly3tnynges] H$_7$RBH$_5$-LB$_3$AsSrAEPH$_6$CcMLdPl, li3tynges HLwHu$_2$PlTW glyderen] gleden ELd, glymer A, shyne Hu$_2$M þurgh] of LwW cranes] H$_7$RLB$_3$SrAPM, crenesse Pl, creves AsH$_6$Cc,

knowynge schal sprynge to þe; not al at ones, bot priuely by litel and
by litel, as þe prophet seiþ: *Habitantibus in regione vmbre mortis, lux
orta est eis*. Þat is: `To the´ wonend in þe contre of schadwe of dede,
liȝt was sprongen. Þat is, liȝt of grace spronge and schal sprynge to
hem þat can wonen in þe shadwe of ded, þat is in þis mirknes þat is
like to ded. For as ded sleeþ a lifend body and alle flescly felynges of
92v it, riȝt so desire to luf Ihesu | feled in þis mirknes sleeþ alle synnes,
alle flescly affeccions and alle vnclene þouȝtes for þe tyme, and þan
neiȝest þu fast to Ierusalem. Þou art not ȝit at it, bot bi smale sodeyn
liȝtynges þat glideren out þurgh smale caues fro þat citee schalt þu
mown seen it fro fer, or þat þu come þerto. For wete þu wele, þawȝ
þat þi soule be in þis restful mirknes withouten troblyng of werdly
vanitees, it is not ȝit þer it schuld be, it is not ȝit cloþed al in liȝt ne
turned al into fiire of luf; bot it feliþ wel þat þer is sumwhat aboue
itself þat it knowiþ not ne haþ not ȝit, bot it wolde hafe it and
brennandly ȝerniþ it. And þat is not elles bot þe siȝt of Ierusalem
withoutforþ, þe whilk is like to a citee þat þe prophet Ezechiel sawȝ in
his visions. He `saiþ þat he´ sawȝ a cite set vpon an hil heldand to þe
souþ, þat to his siȝt whan it was meten was no more of lengþe and of
brede þan a rode þat was sexe cubites and a palme on lengþe. Bot as
sone as he was broȝt into þe citee and loked aboute him, þan þouȝt
him þat it was wonder mikel, for he sawȝ many halles and chaumbres

caues HBH$_5$LwHu$_2$ELdTW, rimas Lat. 30 þat] þe LB$_3$PCcM cyte] anoon Pl moun] *om.* Sr it] to As ferre] afer T þat^2] H$_7$HRBH$_5$AsSrLwAHu$_2$ELdTW, *om.* LB$_3$PH$_6$CcMPl þerto] to it T 31 þogh] H$_7$RLB$_3$AsSrAPH$_6$CcMPl, þat *add.* HBH$_5$LwHu$_2$ELdTW in . . . mirknes] *om.* Lat. þis] *om.* Sr mirknes] H$_7$H-RLAsSrPCcMPl, derknesse BH$_5$B$_3$LwAHu$_2$EH$_6$LdTW 32 vanite] H$_7$RLB$_3$AsSr-APH$_6$CcMPl, vanitees HBH$_5$LwHu$_2$ELdTW, vanitatis Lat. it^1 . . . be] *om.* LwW it is not/ȝet] *rev.* Hu$_2$ is^2] *om.* H$_5$ 33 clothed] closyd CcPl into] to M fyre] HRBH$_5$SrLwAHu$_2$MLdPlTW, feyþ H$_7$, þe *prec.* LB$_3$AsEPH$_6$Cc lufe] For Jesu shewyd hym nout fully ȝet as he myth *add.* CcM bot it feleth] *canc.* Cc it] he M wel þat] *canc.* B 34 `is´ Cc abofe] aboþe H$_7$ itself] hymself B, yt Cc haþ] it *add.* Hu$_2$MT ȝit . . . noȝt (l. 35)] *om.* H$_5$ it^2] *om.* LwW 35 brennendly] interly Cc ȝerneth] H$_7$H-RH$_5$LSrLwPH$_6$MPlTW, desireþ B$_3$AsAHu$_2$ECcLd 36 syght] cite RAs, visio Lat. Jerusalem^1] þat is Jesu *add.* CcM withouteforth] without RAsAPl þe] *om.* AHu$_2$ Jerusalem^2] *om.* HH$_5$LwTW, *om.* Lat. 37 þat] þe whiche E, *om.* Pl seygh] seeþ B$_3$ 38 `seyþ . . . he^2´ *s.h.* H, *om.* Cc þat] *om.* AsA sagw] seiþ As sette] sytte As vpon] vp B heldende] beholdynge H$_5$Ld, holdend SrT, bowing A, lenynge *add.* As, vergentem Lat. to] into Pl 39 southe] þouȝt LB$_3$, ⌜s⌝outh P, quere *marg.* LP to] is M whan . . . meten/was no more] *rev.* LB$_3$PH$_6$ `it´ L meten] moten PlW, mensurata Lat. was] it *prec.* Cc of] on LB$_3$PH$_6$M and] ne E, nor M 40 of$^1$] in LB$_3$P, on H$_6$M a rede] a rode HHu$_2$PT, ⌜a rodde⌝ L, a r⌜odd⌝ Ld, a `roode´ W^G was] is LwW, of *add.* CcM of] H$_7$RAsSrAHu$_2$ECcMPlTW, on HH$_5$LB$_3$LwPLd, in B, in Lat. 41 into] RAs þe] þat LB$_3$PH$_6$ and] a R him] he Cc 42 þat it was] *om.* Ld was] *om.* B mikel] grete Hu$_2$ seygh] seeþ H$_6$, þere *add.* Hu$_2$, `boþe´ *add.* L

f. 73r chaumbres boþen open and pryuey; | he sagw gates and porches vtterwarde and innerwarde, and mikel more byggynge þan I sey now, on lenght and on brede many hundreþ cubytes. Þan was þis wonder to him how þis cyte within was so longe and so large, þat was so lytel to his syght whan he was withouten. Þis cyte betokeneþ þe perfyte lufe of God, sette in þe lyfe of contemplacyon, þe whilk, vnto þe eyghe of a soule þat is withouten þe felynge of it and trauaileþ in desyre toward it, semeþ sumwhat, bot it semeþ bot a lytel þynge, no more þan a rede þat is sex cubytz and a palme of length. Be sex cubytes is vnderstonden perfeccyon of mannys werke, be þe palme a lytel touchynge of contemplacion. He seeþ wel þat þer is swilk a thynge þat passeþ þe dissert of alle werkynge of man a lytel, as þe palme passeþ ouer þe sex cubites, bot he seeþ not within what þat is. Nerþeles if he may come withine þe cyte of contemplacyon, þan seeþ he mikel more þan he saw first.

How a soule may knowen fals illuminacions feyned be þe fend fro þe trewe lyght of knowynge þat comeþ oute of Jesu, and by what tokenes. Capitulum xxvi^m

Bot now beware of þe mydday fend, þat feyneþ liȝt as it come out of Jerusalem and it is not so. For þe fend seyþ þat oure Lord Jesu scheweth to his lufers lyȝt of sothfastnes; þerfore [in] dysceyuynge of hem þat arn vnwyse he scheweþ a lyȝt þat is not trewe vnder coloure of trew lyȝt, and so desceyfeþ hem. Nerþeles how a soule may know þe lyȝt of sothfastnes, whan it schyneþ fro God and whan it is feyned

44 vtterwarde . . . innerwarde] H$_7$HRBH$_5$LB$_3$AsSrAHu$_2$PMLdPl, outward . . . inward LwEH$_6$CcTW byggynge] bilding AMLdPlTW, beldenges B þan] þei RPl, þe As I sey now] he saw beforn Cc I] `he´ T$^G$ now on] before, what of Hu$_2$ 45 lenght/. . ./brede] *rev.* As lenght] high M and] *om.* H$_5$ on$^2$] in Ld, of Hu$_2$ brede] be *add.* Cc hundreþ] hundreþs of Hu$_2$ þis] þe B 46 within] *om.* T `so^1´ Cc, thus Lw long and so] *om.* H$_5$ was/so^3 . . . siȝt] *rev.* W 47 perfyte] of *add.* Lw 48 lyfe] H$_7$LB$_3$SrAPH$_6$, hill HRBH$_5$AsLwAHu$_2$ECcMLdPlTW, lyth vpon an hey *prec.* Cc, monte Lat. contemplacyon] or elles Jesu hymself, for all is one *add.* M vnto] to ALd, on`to´ Cc eyghe] H$_7$RLB$_3$AsSrAPH$_6$CcMPlW^G, siȝte HBH$_5$LwHu$_2$ELdTW, oculum Lat. 49 is] *om.* LwW withouten þe] wyth Ld þe] *om.* T of it] þerof Sr and] *om.* LwMW trauaileþ] haþ *prec.* As in] the *add.* LwW 50 it^1] H$_7$RLB$_3$AsSrAEPH$_6$CcPl, as it H$_5$, *om.* HBLwHu$_2$MLdTW, illam Lat. sumwhat . . . semeþ^2] *om.* BHu$_2$LdT bot it semeþ] *om.* H$_5$ bot] *om.* Cc rede] rod RLwCcPlT`W^G´, of *add.*, *canc.* E 51 is] was Cc, of *add.* E a] *om.* Pl of] H$_7$RAsHu$_2$AEMTW, on HBH$_5$LB$_3$SrLwPH$_6$CcLdPl is vnderstonden] I vnderstonde H$_5$ is] are LwW 52 perfeccyon] H$_7$RLB$_3$AsSrEPH$_6$CcMPl, þe *prec.* HBH$_5$LwAHu$_2$LdTW be] And *prec.* W þe] þis LB$_3$P, a Lw touchynge] degustacio Lat. 53 þat^1] *om.* LB$_3$PH$_6$ þe] þy H$_5$ 54 dissert] dissertys Cc, deseruynge E, merit A alle] the *add.* LwW, *om.* LB$_3$P

boþe open and pryue; he sawʒ gates and porches outerward and innerward, and mikel more biggynge þan I sey now, on lengþ and on brede many hundred cubites. Þan was þis wondir to him how þis citee within was so longe and so large, þat was so litle to his siʒt whan he was wiþouten. Þis cite bitokneþ þe perfit luf of God, sette in þe hille of contemplacioun, þe whilk, vnto þe siʒt of a soule þat is without þe felynge of it and traueiliþ in desire toward, semiþ sumwhat, bot it semiþ bot a litel þinge, no more þan a rede þat is sex cubites and a palme on lengþe. Bi sex cubites is vndirstonden þe perfeccioun of
93r mannes werke, bi þe palme a litil | touchyng of contemplacioun. He seeþ wel þat þer is swilk a þinge þat passiþ þe deserte of al wirkynge of man a litel, as þe palme passeþ þe sex cubites, bot he seeþ not withinne what þat is. Nerþeles if he may come within þe citee of contemplacioun, þan seeþ he mikel more þan he sawʒ first.

[CHAPTER 26]

Bot now bewar of þe midday feend, þat feynyþ liʒt as it come out of Ierusalem and is not. For þe feende seeþ þat oure Lord Ihesu schewiþ liʒt to his lufers of soþfastnes; þerfor in deceyuynge of hem þat are vnwise he schewiþ a liʒt þat is not trewe vnder colour of a trewe liʒt and desceyfiþ hem. Nerþeles how a soule may knowe þe liʒt of soþfastnes, whan it schyniþ fro God and whan it is feynid

werkynge] and of al worchynge *add.*, *canc.* H, *add.* H$_5$ þe[1]] *om.* T ouer] H$_7$RLB$_3$AsSr`H^c´AEPH$_6$CcPl, *canc.* Lw, *om.* H°BH$_5$Hu$_2$LdTW, vltra Lat. þe[2]] *om.* SrLd 55 seeþ] saw Cc what] ne *prec.* BLd þat] it SrLwEPl, þer A 56 seeþ he] schal he see H$_5$Cc 57 first] bifore Hu$_2$, radyr Ld

Chapter 26 *title*: H$_7$RLB$_3$SrAEPH$_6$MLdTW How þat desire of Jesu soþefastly feled in þis mirkenes sleeþ all stirynges of synne and ableþ þe soule for to perceyue goostly lyʒtenyngis. Pl [*cf. above, Chapter 25 title*] How þe fende wolde schewe to þe a feyned liʒt and how þou schalt be war of him and ouercome him. As *om.* HBH$_5$LwHu$_2$Cc 1 How] þat *add.* Sr `a soule´ L  soule] man ALdTW, anima Lat.  may] schal LdTW, schold A  2 oute] *om.* Ld  of] from M  3 tokenes] tokeningus ALdT, he schal knowe hem *add.* R  4 beware] be wel ware Hu$_2$  `as . . . lyʒt (l. 6)´ *d.h.* Ld as] thow *add.* CcLd `it´ H$_6$ of] *om.* H$_6$ 5 it] *om.* EMLd so] *om.* HH$_5$T seyþ H$_7$H$_5$, seeþ Σ, videt Lat. Jesu] *om.* RAsAPl 6 scheweth] hymself *add.* CcM lufers] that is the *add.* CcM of] his *add.* Pl in] *om.* H$_7$ dysceyuynge] disesyng R 7 coloure] þe *prec.* B 8 of] H$_7$RLB$_3$AsSrAPH$_6$CcMPl, a *add.* HBH$_5$LwHu$_2$ELdTW so] H$_7$RLB$_3$AsSrAPH$_6$CcMPl, *om.* HBH$_5$LwHu$_2$ELdTW desceyfeþ] he *prec.* A, he *add.* RAsPl 9 lyʒt . . . it] tru liʒt þat Hu$_2$ God] Jesu M

of þe enemye, schal I seye as me þenkeþ by an example of þe firmament.

Sumtyme in þe firmament scheweþ a ly3t fro þe sunne and semeþ þe sunne and is not, and sumtyme scheweþ þe trew sunne trewly. A knowynge of þat on fro þat oþer is þis: þe feyned sunne scheweþ him not bot atwyx two blake reyny clowdes; þan bycause þat þe sunne is nerre, þer schyneþ owt a ly3t fro þe clowdys as it were a sunne, and is
f. 73v non. Bot þe trewe | sunne scheweþ him whan þe firmament is clere or mikel clered fro blake clowdes. Now to owre purpose. Sum men as it semeþ forsaken þe lufe of þe werd and wulden come to þe lufe of God and to þe ly3t of vnderstondynge of him, bot þei wil not come þurgh þis mirknes þat I hafe spoken of byfore. Þei wil no3t know hemself trewly ne mekly what þei ha ben, ne what þei are 3et þurgh synne, ne how no3t þei are in here owen kynde anentys God. Þei are no3t besy for to entren into hemself, al oþer þynges outward lefte, and slen alle wycked sterynges of synne þat rysen in here hertes—of pride, of enuye, yre, and oþer synnes—þurgh lastende desyre to Jesu, in preynge and in þenkynge, in sylence and in wepynge, and in oþer bodily and gostly excersyce, as deuoute men and holy han don. Bot as tyte as þei han forsaken þe werd as it were outward in lyknes, or ellys son aftere, þei wenen þat þei arn holi and able for to hafe þe gostly vnderstondynge of þe Gospel in Holy Wrytte. And namly if þe moun fulfille letterly þe comandementys of God and kepe hem fro bodily synnes, þan þei wenen þat þei lufe God perfytly; and þerfor þei willen as tyte prechen and techen al oþer men as þogh þei had resceyfed

10 of] H_7RLB_3AsSrAEPH_6CcPl, þurw3 HBH_5LwHu_2LdTW, be M `þe$^{1}$′ L schal I] *rev.* $H_5$Cc seye] þe *add.* L`B_3′EPH_6 þenkeþ] semyþ Hu_2 an] *om.* LB_3PH_6LdT 12 in þe firmament/scheweþ . . . sunne] *rev.* M in] H_7RLB_3AsSrEPH_6CcMPl, *om.* HBH_5LwHu_2LdTW, in Lat. scheweþ] he *prec.* H_5 13 is] it B_3, it *prec.* Cc `not′ Cc, þe sunne *add.* Cc sumtyme] it *add.* H_6 trew] very Cc sunne] li3te Pl trewly] verreyli A A] In H_5 14 feyned] fictus et non verus Lat. him] *om.* M 15 not] comonly *add.* M atwyx] H_7HLSrLwPM, betwixin RBB_3AsLdPlW, bytwene H_5AHu_2EH_6CcT two] tweine LB_3P blake] *om.* M reyny] reyne T, *om.* RAsAPl þan . . . ly3t (l. 16] and þer it schewiþ H_6 þan] þat M `þat þe sunne′ R þat] *om.* LwECcMW þe sunne] verus sol Lat. 16 nerre þer] not þere hit M `nerre′ *corr. fr.* newe L, nerrer M, propinquus Lat. þ⌜er⌝ H^{c}, þat H_5 schyneþ] he *add.* Sr owt] *om.* T a ly3t/fro þe clowdys] H_7RLB_3AsSrAPH_6CcPl, *rev.* HBH_5LwHu_2EMLdTW ly3t] lite L, litel B_3P þe] þo H_6 clowdys] cloude B_3 a^{2}] þe LB_3PLd is non] hit is not M 17 scheweþ him] schynith RAsAPl him] hymself Hu_2 clere] dere Pl 18 mikel] mych dele Ld, gretely Hu_2 clered] voided A, clenside H_6 fro] H_7RLB_3AsSrAPH_6CcMPl, þe *add.* HBH_5LwHu_2ELdTW Now] þus H_6 19 `þe^{2}′ Pl, þis LB_3P wulden] seke Jesu and *add.* M þe^{3} . . . God] his loue M 20 of him] *om.* RAsAMPl him] Jesu H_5 wil] wolde H_6 come] *om.* B þurgh] to A 21 mirknes] H_7HRLAsSrPCcMPl, derknesse B$H_5$$B_3$LwAH$u_2EH_6$LdTW, noctem vel obscuritatem Lat. byfore] afore H_6, herebyfore H_5Pl, þat is to seyn Cc, that is for to sey M `no3t′ W^{G}, *om.* W

þurwȝ þe enemye, sal I sey as me þinkeþ bi an example of þe firmament.

Sumtyme þe firmament shewiþ a liȝt fro þe sonne and semiþ þe sunne and is not, and sumtyme schewiþ þe trew sunne treuly. A knowynge of þat on fro þat oþer is þis. Þe feyned sunne schewiþ him not bot atwix two blake reyny clowdis; þan bicause þat þe sunne is nere, þ⌜er⌝ schynyþ out fro þe clowdis a liȝt as it wer a sunne, and is none. Bot þe trewe sunne schewiþ him whan þe firmament is clere or mikel clered fro þe blake clowdis. Now to oure purpos. Sum men as it semiþ forsaken þe luf of þe werld and wolden come to þe luf of God and to þe liȝt of vndirstandynge of him, bot þei wil not come þurgh þis mirknes þat I hafe spoken of before. Þei wil not know hemself trewly ne mekely what þei haue ben bifore, ne what þei are ȝit þorw synne, ne how noȝt þei are in here owne kynde anentes God. Þei are not bisy for to entren into hemself, alle oþer þinges owtward left, and
93v sleien alle wicked | styrynges of synne þat risen in her hertes—of pride, enuye, ire, and oþer synnes—þurgh lastend desire to Ihesu, in preynge and in þinkynge, in silence and in wepynge, and in oþer bodily and gostly exercise, as deuoute men and holy men han don. Bot as tite as þei han forsaken þe werld as it were outward in liknes, or elles sone after, þei wenen þat þei are holy and able for to haf þe gostly vndirstondynge of þe Gospel and of Holy Writ. And namely if þei mown fulfille letterly þe comaundementis of God and kepen hem fro bodily synnes, þan þei wene þat þei lufe God perfitly; and þerfore þei wilen as tit prechen and techen alle oþer men as if þei had receyfed

22 ne[1]] and H$_6$ ben] H$_7$RLB$_3$AsSrAPH$_6$CcMPl, before *add.* HBLwHu$_2$ELdTW, byfore *prec.* H$_5$ what þei] *om.* RAs ne[3] . . . God (l. 23)] *om.* Lat. 23 noȝt/þei are] *rev.* H$_6$Cc noȝt[1]] *om.* Sr owen] -d *canc.* H$_7$ anentys] as *prec.* As God] Jesu CcM 24 hemself] hymself B al] *om.* Ld outward lefte] *rev.* Sr outward] *om.* LB$_3$PH$_6$ and] to *add.* EH$_6$Cc, for to *add.* H$_5$ slen] H$_7$HRH$_5$LB$_3$AsSrAPH$_6$CcMPl, fleen BLwHu$_2$ELdTW, destruere Lat. 25 wycked] vnkynd `or wykkid´ Ld of synne] *om.* LwW of[2]] as *prec.* H$_5$Cc of[3]] H$_7$RLB$_3$AsSrAPCcPl, *om.* HBH$_5$LwHu$_2$EH$_6$MLdTW 26 enuye yre] *rev.* M enuye] and *add.* H$_6$ yre] wrethe BAEH$_6$Ld, *om.* As and] or LwW to] of BSr Jesu] God RAsAPl, Dominum Jesum Christum Lat. 27 in[1]] *om.* RAsPl and[2]] *om.* BHu$_2$Ld in[3]] *om.* RAs in[4]] *om.* As oþer] maner *add.* M 28 bodily] exercise *add.*, *canc.* L exersyce] exercises E as . . . don] *om.* RAsAMPl men/and holy] *rev.* LB$_3$P holy] men *add.* HBH$_5$LwHu$_2$LdW as tyte] H$_7$HLLwPCc, also sone BAsSrECcMLdTW, anon H$_5$B$_3$AHu$_2$H$_6$Pl 29 han] *om.* R lyknes] signys Cc ellys] in habite *add.* H$_5$ 30 þei] *om.* A arn] weren Cc holi and] not M and] *om.* B þe] *om.* RAs 31 vnderstondynge] vndirstonde T `þe[1]/ L in] H$_7$, and of Σ Holy] þe *prec.* Lw 32 fulfille letterly] *rev.* M letterly] *om.* L 33 synnes] synne B þan] that W þei wenen] *rev.* H$_6$ þat] *om.* M 34 as tyte] H$_7$HLLwPW[G], anon BH$_5$B$_3$SrAHu$_2$H$_6$CcMLdPlW, as sone AsT, *om.* E and . . . al] *om.* A techen] anoon *add.* E al] *om.* H$_6$ þogh] H$_7$RBLB$_3$AsSrAEPH$_6$CcMPl, if HH$_5$LwHu$_2$LdTW þei] he RAs resceyfed] þorw *add.* M

grace of vndirstondynge and perfeccion of charite þurgh speciale ȝifte of þe Holy Gost. And also þei are mikel þe more steryd þerto, for as mikel as þei felen sumtyme mikel knowynge, as it were sodeynly gyfen to hem withouten grete studye beforegoende, and also mikel feruour of lufe, as it semeþ, for to prechen trewth and ryghtwysnesse to here euen-cristen. Þerfor þei hold it as a grace of God, þat vysyteþ hem with his blissed lyȝt befor oþer soules. Nerþeles if þei wil loke wel abowt hem, þei schul wel seen þat þis lyȝt of knowynge and þat hete þat þei felen comeþ not of þe trewe sunne, þat is oure Lord Jesu, bot f. 74^{r} it comeþ fro þe mydday fend þat | feyneþ lyȝt and lykneþ him to þe sunne; and þerfor schal he be knowen by þe example befor seyde.

Lyȝt of knowynge þat is feyned by þe fend to a mirke soule is ay schewed bytwix two blake reyne clowdys. Þe ouer clowde is presumpcion and an heyghynge of himself; þe neþer clowde is dounputtynge in alowynge of his euene-cristen. Þan what lyȝt of knowynge or of felynge of feruour þat it be þat schyneþ to a soule, with presumpcion and heyghynge of itself and dedyn of his euen-cristen þe self tyme felt, it is not þe lyght of grace gyfen of þe Holy Gost, þogh þe knowynge in itself were sothfast; bot it is eyþer of þe fend if it come sodeynly, or ellys [of] a mans owen wytte if it come þurgh studye. And so may it wel be knowen þat þis feyned lyȝt of knowynge is not þe lyȝt of þe trewe sunne.

For þei þat han þis knowynge on þis maner are ful of gostly pride and seen it not. Þei are so blent with þis feyned lyȝt þat þei holden þe heyghnes of here owen herte and vnbuxumnes to þe laghes of Holy Kirk as it were perfyte meknes to þe Gospel and to þe laghes of God.

35 and] in LwW speciale] grace and *add.* `L´B$_3$P ȝifte] ȝiftes M 36 þe[2]] H$_7$RLB$_3$AsSrAPH$_6$MPl, *om.* HBH$_5$LwHu$_2$ECcLdTW þerto] *om.* LwW 37 knowynge] cunnynge B `as it were´ B$_3$ sodeynly gyfen to] sodeyn ȝiftes vnto M 38 grete] mekyl Cc studye] studiyng M, labor and *prec.* Hu$_2$ beforegoende] H$_7$RLB$_3$AsSrAPH$_6$Pl`W^G´, beforhande HBLwHu$_2$MLdT, beforn ande Cc, before had H$_5$EW 39 lufe as] *om.* A trewth] þe *prec.* H$_5$Cc ryghtwysnesse] the *prec.* Cc to . . . cristen] aliis christianis Lat. 40 God] Jesu M þat] *om.* Pl vysyteþ] he *prec.* H$_5$ 41 his] a H$_5$ 42 schul] schulde H$_5$H$_6$ wel seen] fynde LwW þis] þe Ld knowynge] cognicionis et sciencie Lat. þat[2]] þe LB$_3$PH$_6$ hete] feruour M 43 þe] a M 44 lyȝt] *om.* Cc 45 be] *om.* RAs þe] *om.* HAsLwW befor] afore ECcM 46 Lyȝt of knowynge] *rev.* H$_6$ knowynge . . . feyned] kunnyd B knowynge] H$_7$RLB$_3$AsSrAEPH$_6$CcMPl, kunnynge HH$_5$LwHu$_2$LdTW, kunnyd B `fend´ R mirke] H$_7$HRLAsSrPCcMPl, derk BH$_5$B$_3$LwAHu$_2$EH$_6$LdTW ay] H$_7$HH$_5$LAsP, euere BB$_3$AHu$_2$EH$_6$CcT, alwey SrMLd, *om.* LwW 47 schewed] *om.* M bytwix] H$_7$RLAsSrPlW, atwix HBLwHu$_2$Ld, bytwene H$_5$B$_3$AEH$_6$CcMT blake reyne] *rev.* M reyne] reyn As 48 and] in LB$_3$PH$_6$ an heyghynge] enhyȝeng H$_6$ an] H$_7$LB$_3$SrEP, *om.* HRBH$_5$AsLwAHu$_2$CcMLdPlTW heyghynge] heynyng Cc, exaltyng E himself]

grace of vndirstondynge and perfeccioun of charitee þurwȝ special gifte of þe Holy Gost. And also þei are mikel more stirid þerto, for as mikel as þei felen sumtyme mikel knowyng, as it were sodeynly gifen to þem withouten grete studie beforhande, and also mikel feruour of luf, as it semiþ, for to preche trouþ and riȝtþwisnes to here euen-cristen. Þerfore þei holde it as a grace of God, þat visiteþ þem with his blissed liȝt before oþer soules. Nerþeles if þei wilen loke wel aboute hem, þei schul wel seen þat þis liȝt of knowyng and þat hete þat þei felen comiþ not of þe trewe sunne, þat is oure Lord Ihesu, bot it comiþ fro þe midday fende þat feyneþ liȝt and likneþ him to þe sunne; and þerfore schal he be knowen bi example bifore saide.

Liȝt of kunnynge þat is feyned bi þe fende to a mirke soule is ay schewd atwix two blake reyny cloudis. Þe ouer cloude is presumpcioun and heiȝenge of himself; þe neþer cloude is doune-puttinge and alowynge of his euen-cristen. Þan what liȝt of knowynge or felynge of feruour þat it be þat schineþ to a soule, with presumpcioun and hiȝeng of itself and dedeyn of his [euen-cristen] þe same tyme felid, is not liȝt of grace gifen of þe Holy Goste, þowȝ þe knowynge in itself
4r were soþfast; bot | it is ouþer of þe fende if it come sodeynly, or elles of mannes owne wit if it come bi studie. And so may it wel be knowen þat ⸢þis⸣ feyned liȝt of knowyng is not þe liȝt of þe trew sunne.

For þei þat han þis knowyng on þis maner are ful of gostly pride and seen it not. Þei are so blynded wiþ þis feyned liȝt þat þei holden þe heiȝenes of here owne hert vnbuxumnes to þe laghes of Holy Kirke as it were perfit meknes to þe Gospel and to þe laghes of God. Þei

hemself LwAH_6W þe . . . itself (l. 51)] *om.* A neþer] oþer M is] of *add.* Cc 49 in] H_7, and Σ alowynge] lowynge Cc of] to M þan . . . euen-cristen (l. 51)] *om.* Cc þan] þat BMLd of^2] or H_5M 50 or] oþer As, and Cc of^1] $H_7B_3H_6$Cc, *om.* Σ of^2] or M þat it be] *om.* RAsPl to] *rep.*, *canc.* Pl soule] betwene þuse two cloudus *add.* M 51 heyghynge] exaltinge E itself] hyt B dedyn] indeynyng E, a loþyng Hu_2 euen-cristen] euencristristen H 52 self] same AEH_6M `felt´ Pl it] $H_7RLB_3$SrLw-APCcMPlW, *om.* $HBH_5AsHu_2EH_6$LdT þe$^2$] $H_7RH_5LB_3$AsSrAP$H_6$CcMPl, *om.* HBLw$Hu_2$ELdTW gyfen] *om.* A 53 þogh] þorw $H_5$ itself] þe self M were sothfast] with soþfastnes $H_5$ were] be As, *om.* A sothfast] sooþ $B_3$ eyþer] nought but only M `it^2´ Pl 54 or] oþer B of] if H_7 a] H_7RLB_3AsSrAHu_2EPH_6CcMPlT, *om.* HBH_5LwLdW þurgh] H_7RLB_3AsSrPCcMPl, bi HBH_5LwAHu_2EH_6LdTW 55 so] also T may it] *rev.* EH_6CcW ⸢þis⸣ H^c, it is H_5T 56 is] and it is H_5, and T þe^2] *om.* M sunne] on þis maner *add.* T 57 For] þerfore LwW þis . . . maner] þis maner of knowynge T on] of H_5 58 so] *om.* H_6 blent] H_7LPCc, blynded $HRBH_5B_3Hu_2EH_6$T, bliȝnde RAsSrLwAPlW `blynde´ Ld, full of M, excecantur Lat. þis] þe A, om. $H_5$ holden] it *add.* Cc 59 `of here´ *rep.*, *canc.* Cc of] here owen of *add.*, *canc.* L and] H_7LB_3SrLwEPH_6CcMLdTW, *om.* HRH_5AsAHu_2Pl, þoruȝ B, the *add.* LwW, et Lat. to] of M 60 meknes] humiliacionem et submisisonem Lat. God] Jesu M

And þei wenen þat þe folwynge of here owen wil were fredam of spyryt, and þerfor þei bygynnen to reynen as blake clowdes water of errours and heresyes, for þe wordes þat þei reynen by prechynge sownen into bakbytynge, to stryfynge, and to discorde makynge, reprofynge of states and of persones; and ȝet þei seyn þat al þis is charite and zel of ryghtwysnes. Bot it is not soth, for Seyn Jem þe Apostel seyþ þus: *Vbi enim zelus et contencio, ibi inconstancia et omne opus prauum. Non est hec sapiencia desursum descendens a Patre luminum, sed terrena, animalis et diabolica.* Þat is: Whereso þat enuye is and flytynge, þer is vnstablenes and al euel werk. And þerfor þat knowynge þat bryngeþ forth swilk synnes comeþ not fro þe Fadere of Lyȝt, þat is God, bot it is erthly, bestly and fendly. And so be þese
f. 74v toknes, | þat are pride, presumpcyon, vnbuxumnes, indygnacion, bakbytynge and oþer swylk synnes—for þese folwen after—may þe feyned lyȝt be knowen fro þe trewe. For þe trewe sunne scheweþ him not be speciale visitacyon for to ȝif lyȝt of vnderstondynge or perfyt charite to a soule bot if þe firmament be first made bryȝt and clere fro blake clowdys, þat is bot if þe conscience be made clene þurgh fyre of brennend desyre to Jesu in þis mirknes, þe whilk fyre wasteþ and brenneþ al þe wykked sterynges of pride, veyn-glorie, yre, enuye, and al oþer synnes in þe soule, as þe prophete seyth: *Ignis ante ipsum precedet, et inflammabit in circuitu inimicos eius.* Fyre schal go befor him; þat is, desyre of lufe schal go befor Jesu in mans soule, and it schal brenne al his enemys; þat is, it schal wasten alle synnes.

For bo[t] if a soule be first smyten doun fro heyght of himself by

61 And] *om.* $\mathrm{HH_5T}$ wenen] also *add.* $\mathrm{H_5}$ 62 to reynen] reyne $\mathrm{BHu_2}$ blake] *om.* Pl, nigre et pluuiose Lat. clowdes] þat be blak *add.* Pl 63 errours and heresyes] *rev.* $\mathrm{Hu_2}$ reynen] $\mathrm{H_7BH_5LB_3SrHu_2LdPH_6CcMT}$, schewen RAsLw⌜H^c⌝AEPlW, seminant Lat. into] $\mathrm{H_7}$, to Sr, al to Σ, totaliter Lat. 64 bakbytynge] $\mathrm{H_7LB_3AsSrAPH_6CcMPl}$, and *add.* $\mathrm{HRBH_5LwHu_2ELdTW}$, detraccionem Lat. to[1]] *om.* RAsM stryfynge] stryuyngus A, flityng M to[2]] *om.* M makynge] and *add.* $\mathrm{H_5}$ 65 of[1]] þe $\mathrm{Hu_2}$ of[2]] *om.* T þei seyn] *rev.* LwW þat] *om.* A þis] *om.* T `is´ Pl, in *add.* M 66 zel] welle $\mathrm{H_5}$, loue BAs, doom Sr, cometh M it] þat $\mathrm{H_5}$, ȝit *prec.* Ld `is´ Sr for Seyn] Forwhi Sr þe Apostle] *om.* Ld 67 þus] *om.* Sr, Jac. 3° *add.* $\mathrm{BLHu_2ELdT}$ Vbi] Ibi M enim] est E, *om.* MLd 68 hec sapiencia] $\mathrm{H_7RLB_3AEPH_6CcMLdPl}$, *rev.* $\mathrm{HBH_5LwHu_2TW}$, hec sapiencia Lat. hec] *om.* AsSr sapiencia] nec *add.* As 69 sed] est *add* LwMW terrena . . . diabolica] terreno, animali et diabolico As terrena] et *add.*, *canc.* L `et´ Pl, *om.* A Whereso] wheresoeuere Cc, where Pl þat] $\mathrm{H_7RBLB_3AsAHu_2PH_6CcMLdPl}$, þer Sr, *om.* $\mathrm{HH_5LwETW}$ enuye is] *rev.* Sr, be enuy E and] in $\mathrm{H_5Ld}$ 70 flytynge] chydynge $\mathrm{BB_3Hu_2H_6Ld}$, fyghtyng Sr, stryfyng E, strif AsA al] an Sr, *om.* B þerfor] *om.* A þat] such B 71 knowynge] $\mathrm{H_7RLB_3AsSrAPH_6MPl}$, conyng $\mathrm{HBH_5LwHu_2ECcLdTW}$ swilk] thynges and *add.* M 72 Lyȝt] Liȝtes $\mathrm{LB_3PH_6}$ God] *corr. fr.* good L, Jesu M it] *om.* Ld þese] þis E, þose Pl 73 toknes] tokeningus A þat are] *om.* A are] is M pride] and *add.* Ld presumpcyon] and *add.* M indygnacion] and *add.* M, *om.* R 74 bakbytynge] bacbitynges H and . . .

wenen þat þe folwynge of here owne wil were fredam of spirit, and þerfor þei bigynnen to reynen as blake clowdes water of errours and heresies, for þe wurdes þat þei ⌜schewen⌝ bi prechyng souniþ al to bacbitynge and to strifynge, and to discorde makynge, reprofynge of states and of persones; and ȝit þei seien þat al þis is charite and zele of riȝtwisnes. Bot it is not soþ, for Seynt Jame þe Apostle seiþ þus: *Vbi enim zelus et contencio, ibi inconstancia et omne opus prauum. Non est sapientia haec desursum descendens a Patre luminum, sed terrena, animalis et diabolica*. Þat is: Wher-so enuye is and flytinge, þer is vnstabilnes and al yuel werk. And þerfor þat conyng þat bryngiþ forþ swilk synnes comiþ not fro þe Fader of Liȝt, þat is God, bot it is erþly, bestly and fendly. And so bi þes toknes, þat are pride, presumpcioun, vnbuxumnes, indignacioun, bacbitynges, and oþer swilke synnes, for þese folwen after, may þe feyned liȝt be know fro þe trewe. For þe trew sunne schewiþ him not bi special visitacioun for to gif liȝt of vndirstondyng or perfit charite to a soule bot if þe firmament be first made briȝt and cleer fro cloudes, þat is bot if þe conscience be made clene þurghe fire of brennande desire to Ihesu in þis mirknes, þe whilk wasteþ and brenniþ alle wicked styrynges of pryde, veynglorie, ire, enuye, and alle oþer synnes in þe soule, as þe prophet saiþ: *Ignis*
4v *ante ipsum procedet, et infllammabit in circuitu inimicos eius*. Fire | schal go bifore him; þat is, desire of luf schal go bifore Ihesu in a mans soule, and it schal brennen alle his enmys, þat is, it schal wasten alle synnes.

For bot if a soule be first smyten doun fro heiȝte of itself bi drede,

synnes] *om.* Lat. oþer] moo *add.* Pl for . . . after] *om.* H$_6$ for þese] þat H$_5$ for] fro Cc, where *add.* As folwen] folwyng Ld after] comynly *add.* B, ⌜þe fendis⌝ *add.* L, þe feend. þus *add.* B$_3$P, þe feendis. þus *add.* E 75 feyned] ⌜þe fendes⌝ L, fendis B$_3$P \`lyȝt´ L trewe[1]] liȝt *add.* B$_3$, sonne þat is Jesu M trewe[2]] lyȝt with þe *add.* H$_5$ sunne] schynyth and *add.* LwW scheweþ him] shynyth Cc 76 visitacyon] visitacions M of] lyȝt *add.* H$_5$ or] of RAsHu$_2$Cc, of *add.* T 77 if] *om.* LwW be first] *rev.* A first] fest B, But ȝif þe firmament *add.* As made . . . clowdys] *om.* As bryȝt and clere] *rev.* AM and clere] *om.* LB$_3$EPH$_6$ 78 blake] H$_7$LB$_3$AsSrAEPH$_6$CcPl\`W[G]´, *om.* HBH$_5$LwHu$_2$MLdTW, atris Lat. bot if þe] þyn As 79 Jesu] God RAPl, Jesu Christi et per consideracionem passionis sue Lat. mirknes] H$_7$HRLSrPCcMPl, derknes BH$_5$B$_3$AsLwAHu$_2$EH$_6$LdTW fyre] H$_7$BLB$_3$SrAHu$_2$PH$_6$CcMLd, *om.* HRH$_5$AsLwEPlTW, ignis Lat. 80 þe] H$_7$RA, *om.* Σ sterynges] of synne *add.* E pride] as *add.* As yre] wreþþe BEH$_6$Ld, *om.* As and] of *add.* E 81 seyth] Ps. 96° *add.* BLHu$_2$ELdTW 82 precedet] procedet H inflammabit] flammabit B inimicos] ig- *add.*, *canc.* Cc eius] þat is *add.* BHu$_2$EM, *om.* A 83 him . . . befor] *om.* As him] hem H$_5$, *om.* M befor] hym, þat is to say *add.* Pl mans] H$_7$LB$_3$SrLwPH$_6$CcMPlW, a *prec.* HRBH$_5$AsAHu$_2$ELdT soule] soulys Cc 84 \`is´ Pl schal] be *add.*, *canc.* L 85 \`bot´ Sr, bo H$_7$ if] *om.* LwAECc be first] firste \`be´ Pl heyght] H$_7$HRBSrLwAH$_6$PlTW, þe heiȝte H$_5$LB$_3$AsPCcM, hieȝnes Hu$_2$ELd himself] H$_7$BM, þe self Cc, itself Σ, in seipsa Lat. by] lastyng *add.* M

drede, and be wel examined and brent in þis fyre of desyre, as it were purifyed fro al gostly filthe by longe tyme in deuout prayers and oþer gostly excercises, it is not able to suffre þe schynynges of gostly lyȝt ne for to resceyuen þe precious lyquour of þe perfyte lufe of Jesu. Bot whan it is þus purifyed and made sotyl þurgh þis fyre, þan may it resceyfe þe graciouse lyȝt of vnderstondynge and þe perfeccyon of lufe, þat is þe trewe sunne. Þus seyth Holy Wrytte: *Vobis qui timetis Deum, orietur sol iusticie*. Þe trew sunne of ryȝtwysnes, þat is oure Lord Jesu, schal spryngen to ȝow þat dreden him; þat is, to meke soules þat meken hemself vndere here euen-cristen be knowynge of here wrecchednes and kasten hemself doun vndere God by noghttynge of hemself in here owen substaunce þurgh reuerent drede and gostly beholdynge of him lastendly, for þat is perfyte meknes.

Vnto þes soules þe trew sunne schal rysen, and illuminen þere reson in knowynge of sothfastnes and kyndel here affeccyon in brennynge of lufe, and þan schul þei boþe brennen and schynen. Þei schul þurgh vertu of þis heuenly sunne brennen in perfyte lufe f. 75r and schynen in knowynge | of God and gostly þynges, for þan be þay reformed in felynge. Þerfor he þat wil not be desceyfed, I hope it is gode to him to drawe doun himself and hyden him in mirknes first fro enteremetynge of oþer men, as I hafe seyd, and forȝete al þe werd if he may, and folwe Jesu with lastend desyre offred in preyere and þenkynge of him. And þan I trowe þat þe liȝt þat comeþ after þis mirkenes is syker and sothfast, and þat it schyneþ oute fro þe cyte of Jerusalem fro þe trew sunne to a soule þat trauaileþ in mirknes and cryeþ after lyȝt, for to wyssen it þe weye and confort it in trauaile. For

86 drede] and meknes *add.* LwCcMW, timorem Dei Lat. be wel] by wil B examined] wiþ þe fier of drede *add.*, *canc.* B_3 þis] þe SrACc as] H_7As, and *prec.* Σ 87 by] *rep.* A 88 exercises] exercise SrACcM, ocupacions H_6 suffre þe schynynges] shynyn [or to suffryn *canc.*] or to sufferen the shynyngis Cc shynynges] schynyng H_5 89 lyquor . . . perfyte] liȝt and As þe[2]] H_7RLB_3AsSrAEPH_6CcMPl, *om.* HBH_5LwHu_2LdTW Jesu] God RAPl, Domini Jesu Christi Lat. 90 \`is´ B_3 þus] *canc.* Lw, *om.* MW þis] his Sr, *om.* M 91 þe[1]] þys Ld vnderstondynge] H_7RLB_3AsSrAPH_6CcMPl, gostly knowynge HBH_5Lw-Hu_2ELdTW, intelligencie Lat. 92 þat . . . þus] as As þe] *om.* HLwEW, lyȝt of þe *add.* H_5 Holy Wrytte: Mal. 4° *add.* BLHu_2EPLdTW, Iob M 69 Vobis] *om.* M 93 sol] *om.* M iusticie] þat is *add.* BE 94 Jesu] Crist *add.* B_3, Jesus Christus Lat. him] God RAMLdPl to[2]] vnto T 95 hemself] hem\`self´ L, hymsylff Ld knowynge] of hemselfe and be knowynge *add.* As 96 here] H_7As, owne *add.* Σ kasten] castyng Hu_2 vndere God] sub pedibus Christi Lat. God] Jesu M noghttynge] lothyng Cc 97 of] *om.* Ld in] and M reuerent] reuerence As 98 lastendly] continually Hu_2 meknes] And holden forth þis same mekenesse continuelly in þe habit of þer soule, fele þei neuer so moche grace *add.* M 99 Vnto] To AH_6Ld þes soules] þys soule B þes] þ⸢ise⸣ L, þose Pl trew] *om.* H_6Pl sunne] of rithwisnes *add.* H_6 rysen] H_7RLB_3SrAPH_6CcPl, spryngen HBH_5As-LwHu_2EMLdTW illuminen] lyȝten Ld 100 reson] on *add.*, *canc.* B_3 and kyndel]

and be wel examined and brent in þis fiire of desire, and as it were purified fro al gostly filþ bi longe tyme in deuoute praiers and oþer gostly exercices, it is not able to suffren þe shynynges of gostly li3t ne for to receifen þe precious licour of perfit luf of Ihesu. Bot when it is þus purified and made sotile þurw3 þis fire, þan may it receif þe gracious li3t of gostly knowynge and þe perfeccioun of luf, þat is [þe] trewe sunne. Þus seiþ Holi Writ: *Vobis qui timetis Deum, orietur sol iusticie*. Þe trewe sunne of ri3twisnes, þat is oure Lord Ihesu, schal spryngen to 3ow þat dreden him; þat is, to meke soules þat meken hemself vndir here euen-cristen bi knowynge of here owne wrecchednes, and casten hemself doun vnder God bi no3tynge of hemself in here owne substaunce þurgh reuerent drede and gostly behaldynge of him lastandly, for þat is perfit meknes.

Vnto þise soules þe trewe sunne schal spryngen, and illumine here resoun in knowynge of soþfastnes and kyndelen here affeccioun in brennynge of luf, and þan schal þei boþ brennen and schynen. Þei schul þurw vertue of þis heuenly sunne bren in perfit luf and shynen in knowyng of God and gostly þinges, for þan be þei reformed in felynge. Þerfore he þat wil not be desceifed, I hope it is gode to him to drawe doun himself and hiden him in þis mirknes. First fro entermetynge of oþer men, as I hafe saide, and forgete al þe werld if he may, and folwe Ihesu with lastende desire offred in praiers and þenkynge on him. Þan I trowe þat þe li3t þat comiþ after þis mirknes
5[r] | is siker and soþfast, and þat it schinyþ of þe cite of Ierusalem fro þe trew sunne to a soule þat traueiliþ in mirknes and crieþ after li3t, for to wissen it þe wey and conforten it in traueil. For I hope after trew

studyenge As kyndel] kendeleth LwW, tend ALd, or tenden *add.* B 101 of] *om.* B$_3$H$_6$ 102 þurgh] þe *add.* As brennen] brennynge As 103 and[1]] to *add.* As God . . . þynges] Jesu gostli M and[2]] of *add.* As `þan´ Pl be þay] *rev.* LwPlW 104 I hope] in good hap H$_6$ is] be Ld, *om.* Lw 105 to[1]] for to BHu$_2$MLd hyden] to *prec.* AsE in] H$_7$, þis *add.* Σ mirknes] H$_7$HRLSrPCcMPl, derknesse BH$_5$B$_3$AsLwHu$_2$EH$_6$LdTW 106 entermetynge] entermetynges H$_7$, entermedlynge B of oþer men] *om.* A hafe] before *add.* `L´B$_3$P forȝete] to *prec.* H$_5$, for to geten AsM þe] *om.* Ld 107 with] in M, a *add.* Cc preyere] H$_7$RLB$_3$SrAPH$_6$CcMPl, praiers HBH$_5$AsLwHu$_2$ELdTW, oratione Lat. and] in *add.* As 108 of] H$_7$H$_5$LB$_3$AsPH$_6$, on HRBSrLwHu$_2$AECcMLdPlTW And] H$_7$RH$_5$LB$_3$AsSrAEPH$_6$CcMPl, *om.* HBLwHu$_2$LdTW, et Lat. þan] *om.* H$_5$ `þat[1]´ W[G], *om.* LwW þe] *om.* M after þis mirkenes] cum isto exercicio Lat. þis] þe M 109 mirkenes] H$_7$HRLSrAPCcMPl, derknesse BH$_5$B$_3$AsLwHu$_2$EH$_6$LdTW it] *om.* As oute] H$_7$RLB$_3$SrAEPH$_6$CcMPl`T[G]W[G]´, *om.* HBH$_5$AsLwHu$_2$LdTW fro] H$_7$, of Σ 110 sunne] þat is Jesu *add.* M to] of Ld mirknes] H$_7$HRLSrPCcMPl, derknesse BH$_5$B$_3$AsLwAHu$_2$EH$_6$LdTW, is syker *add.* As, tenebris huius vitae Lat. 111 ly3t] wyt As for] *om.* H$_5$ wyssen] teche Hu$_2$, oþer teche *add.* Ld confort] forte Ld, to *prec.* AsE

I hope after trew mirknes before comeþ neuer feyned lyȝt. Þat is, if a man trewly and fully sette him for to forsake þe lufe of þe werd, and may þurgh grace come to felynge and knowynge of himself, and holden him mekly in þat felynge, he schal not be desceyfed with none errours ne heresyes ne ypocrysyes ne fantasyes, for al þese come into a soule by þe gate of pride. Þan if pride be stopped owte þer schal non swilk resten in a soule, and þogh þei come and profer hem þei schul not entren. For grace þat þe soule feleþ in þis meke mirknes schal teche þe soule sothfastnes, and schew to it þat al swilk proferynges are of þe enemy.

How grete profyt is to a soule for to be broght þurgh grace into þis lyȝty mirknes, and how a man nedeth for to disposen him if he wil come þerto, and how it is only þe gate and þe entre of contemplacyon. Capitulum xxvii^{m}

T[h]er are many deuoute soules þat þurgh grace comen into þis mirknes and felen þe knowynge of hemself, and ȝet wyten þei not fully what it is, and þat vnconnynge in partye hindreþ hem. Þei fel wel often here þoght and here affeccion dragwen oute and departed fro þe mende of erthly þynges and broght into grete rest of delytable softnes withouten pyneful troblynge of veyn þoghtes or of bodily wyttes. And þei felen þat tyme so grete fredam of spirit þat þei moun þenken on Jesu pesybily, and offren here preyers and here psalmis myghtyly, sauourly and swetly to him as long as þe frelte of þe bodily

112 hope] trow A mirknes] H_7HRLSrPCcMPl, derknesse BH_5B_3AsLwAHu_2EH_6LdTW, obscuritatem Lat. 113 trewly and fully/sette him] *rev.* A for] *om.* H_6W 114 to] þe *add.* T, þat *add.* E knowynge] to *prec.* AsT himself] suiipsius proprias miseriasque Lat. 115 holden] holdyng Sr, to *prec.* As him mekly] hymself meek and low H_6 him] hem B, *om.* LB_3P þat] *om.* E felynge] knowyng and *prec.* Ld none] no ELd, *om.* Cc 116 errours ne] errour of M ne[1]] *om.* Lat. heresyes ne] *om.* Pl ne[2]] *om.* AM ypocrysyes ne] H_7RLB_3SrAEPH_6CcMPl, with As, *om.* HBH_5LwHu_2LdTW, ypocrisim Lat. ne fantasyes] *om.* E fantasyes] fantasie H_6, wyth *prec.* W, `nor ypocrisies´ *add.* $T^G W^G$ þese] those R `into a soule´ W^G, *om.* LwW into] H_7LB_3SrEPH_6CcM, in HBH_5AsHu_2LdT, vnto R, to APl a soule] H_7RLB_3AsSrAEPH_6CcMPl, *om.* HBH_5LwHu_2LdTW, animam Lat. 117 `þe´ BLd gate] grace Sr pride[2]] that pryde maye W þer] thenne *prec.* W non] not M 118 swilk] synne *add.* MW resten] rysen B þogh] that *add.* W hem] hemsylff Ld þei . . . þat] *om.* M 119 grace] þe *prec.* LB_3EPH_6 þis] þe M meke mirknes] derknesse meke B_3 mirknes] H_7HRLSrPCcMPl, derknesse BH_5B_3AsLwAHu_2EH_6LdTW, and þat grace *add.* M 120 teche] kenne HLwM sothfastnes] the *prec.* M it] him AM proferynges] proferis H_6

Chapter 27 *title*: H_7RLB_3SrAEPH_6MLdTW Quam vtile est anime adduci per graciam in hanc caliginem luminosam, et qualiter necesse est hominem se disponere si ad illam voluerit peruenire, et quomodo illa est sola via et introduccio ad contemplacionem. Lat. How a soule may know fals illuminacions feyned bi þe fende fro þe trewe liȝte of

mirknes before comiþ neuer feyned liȝt. þat is, if a man trewly and fully sette him for to forsake þe luf of þe werld, and may þurwȝ grace come to felynge and knowynge of himself, and holden him mekly in þat felynge, he schal not be disceifed with none errours ne heresies ne fantasies, for alle þese comen in bi þe gate of pride. þan if pride be stopped out þer schal none swilk resten in a soule, and þawȝ þei come and profren hem þai schal not entren. For grace þat þe soule feliþ in þis meke merknes schal kenne þe soule soþfastnes, and schew to it þat alle swilke proferynges are of þe enmy.

[CHAPTER 27]

þer are many deuoute soules þat þorw grace comen into þis mirknes and felen þe knowynge of hemself, and ȝit witen þai not fully what it is, and þat vnkunnynge in party hyndriþ hem. þei fele wel often here þouȝt and here affeccioun drawen out and departid fro þe mynde of erþly þinges and broȝt into grete reste of a delitable softnes withouten pyneful troblynge of veyn þoȝtis or of here bodily wittes. And þei felen þat tyme so gret fredam of spirit þat þei mowne þinken on Ihesu peisibly, and offren her preiers and here psalmes miȝtily, sauourly and swetly to him as longe as freelte of þe bodily kynde may suffre it. þei

knowynge þat comeþ oute of Jesu, and bi what tokens. Pl [*cf. above, Chapter 26 title*]   How deuout soulys comen into þis derkenes and weten nouȝt what it is, and how þei shullen knowe it and fele it in here affeccion. As   *om.* HBH_5LwHu_2Cc   1 is] H_7, it is Σ [*rev.* W]   to] *om.* A   a] þeTW, *om.* Ld   þurgh grace/into . . . mirknes] *rev.* M   2 þis] *om.* LdTW   `lyȝty´ $W^G$, liȝtsom LdTW   mirknes] $H_7$RLSrAPM, derknesse $B_3$E$H_6$LdTW   nedeth for to] schall LdTW   for] $H_7$RSrM, *om.* L$B_3$AEP$H_6$   `him´ H_6 3 and . . . contemplacyon] *om.* LdTW   `is´ H_6 only] *om.* R   þe[2]] *om.* A   5 Ther] Ter H_7 into] to SrAE   þis] þe M, *om.* Hu_2 6 mirknes] H_7HRLSrPCcMPl, derknesse B$H_5$$B_3$AsLwA$Hu_2EH_6$LdTW   þei not] *rev.* LdT   7 and . . . hem] *om.* Sr   vnconnynge] vnknowynge W   8 wel] ful H_5, *om.* H_6 here[2]] *om.* As   affeccion] affecciouns Hu_2 departed] departeþ As, departen M   9 grete] a *prec.* Pl, þe As, þe grettest M   of] H_7RLB_3AsSrAEPH_6CcMPl, and T, a *add.* HBH_5LwHu_2LdTW   delytable softnes] delectable thoutes and swetenesse Cc   delytable] delectable LwW   10 pyneful] and *add.* M   troblynge] trowyng As   `or´ E, *om.* AsACc   bodily] H_7, oþer *prec.* M, here *prec.* Σ, suorum Lat.   11 moun] may AsAEMPl, *om.* LB_3P   12 on] of RCc   Jesu] God RAPl, Domino Jesu Christo Lat.   pesybily] and restfully *add.* M   here[1]] *om.* Cc   preyers/. . ./psalmis] *rev.* W   preyers] prayour Lw   here[2]] *om.* EW   psalmis] salme M   13 `and´ L   þe[1]] H_7RSrACcMPl, *om.* HBH_5LB_3AsLwHu_2EPH_6LdTW   þe[2]] *om.* B_3LwLdTW

f. 75^{v} | kynde may suffre it. þei witen wel þat þis felynge is gode, bot þei witen not what it is. þerfor vnto al swilk soules I sey as me þenkeþ, þat þis maner of felynge, þogh it be bot schort and bot seldam, is sothfastly þis mirkenes þat I speke of. For it is a felynge of hemself [first and a rysynge abofe hemself] þurgh brennende desyre to þe syght of Jesu; or ellys if I schal sey mor soth, þis graciouse felynge is a gostly sight of Jesu. And if þei moun kepe hem in þat rest, and brynge it þurgh grace into custom so [þat] þei myghten ly3tly and frely hafe it whan hem list, and holden hem þerin, þei schuld neuer be ouercomen by temptacion of þe fende ne of þe flesch, ne be erroure ne heresye, for þei are sett in þe gate of contemplacyon, able and redy for to resceyfe þe perfyte lufe of Jesu. þerfor he þat haþ it, it is gode þat he knowe it mekly, kepe it tenderly, and pursue it feruently, þat no creature lette him vtterly fro it þat he ne folwe it whan he may; and þat he forgete and sett at no3t al þynge þat schuld put him fro þis, if he be fre of himself and may go where he wil withouten sklaundre or desese of his euene-cristen. For me þenkeþ þat he may not come to þis rest ly3tly bot if he hafe grete plente of grace and sett himself for to folwen aftere þe sterynge of grace, and þat oght he for to don. For grace wuld ay be fre, and namly fro synne and fro werdly besynes and fro al oþer þynges þat letten þe werkynge of it þogh þei ben no synne.

Nerþeles a`noþer´ soule þat haþ not 3et resceyfed þe fulnes of grace, if he desyre for to come to þis gostly knowynge of Jesu as mikel as in him is, him behoueth ablen himself to it and putten away alle lettynges þat stoppen grace as mikel as he may. Him behoueth leren

14 þei . . . is (l. 15)] *om.* As wel] *om.* Cc 15 witen not] noot LwW `not´ Cc þerfor] And *prec.* M vnto] H$_7$HRAsSrLwHu$_2$EMPlTW, to BH$_5$LB$_3$APH$_6$CcLd 16 þis] þer is som M `maner´ Pl bot[1]] *om.* T bot[2]] *om.* AsH$_6$Cc is] H$_7$RLB$_3$PH$_6$Pl, it *prec.* HBH$_5$AsSrLwAHu$_2$ECcMLdTW 17 sothfastly] douteles Hu$_2$ mirkenes] H$_7$HRLSrPCcMPl, meknes H$_6$, derknesse BH$_5$B$_3$AsLwAHu$_2$ELdTW felynge] cognicio Lat. hemself] himself H$_5$ 18 first . . . hemself] *om.* H$_7$ rysynge] restynge H$_5$T hemself] himself H$_5$ to] of Cc 19 syght] and þe felyng of *add.* M Jesu] God RAPl, Jesu Christi Lat. or . . . Jesu (l. 20)] *om.* RAMLdPl, vel vt magis verum fatear, hec sensacio graciosa est spiritualis visio Jesu Christi Lat. or] *om.* As soth] H$_7$RLB$_3$SrAPH$_6$CcMPl, soþly HBH$_5$AsLwHu$_2$ELdTW, magis verum Lat. 20 hem] hemself H$_5$ rest] restful traveyl CcM and[2]] H$_7$RLB$_3$SrAPH$_6$Pl, or HBH$_5$AsLwHu$_2$ECcMLdTW, et Lat. 21 it[1]] *om.* LB$_3$P into] a *add.* LwCcW þat] *om.* H$_7$ ly3tly and frely] *rev.* Sr 22 hem[1]] thei M þerin] H$_7$RLB$_3$SrAPH$_6$CcMPl, in it HBH$_5$LwHu$_2$ELdTW, in þat As schuld] shall T be] *om.* M 23 erroure] H$_7$RLB$_3$SrAPH$_6$CcMPl, errours HBH$_5$AsLwHu$_2$ELdTW, errorem Lat. ⌜ne[3]⌝ H^{c}, be *add.* AsSrCcLd heresye] H$_7$RLB$_3$SrAPH$_6$MPl, heresies HBH$_5$AsLwHu$_2$ECcLdTW, heresim Lat. 24 þei are] þanne ben þei As gate] grace M, stat R, gatys As, via Lat. for[2]] *om.* H$_5$ 25 perfyte] *om.* H$_6$ Jesu] God RAPl, Jesu Christi Lat. þerfor] and *prec.* H$_5$As gode] *om.* B 26 it[1]] and *add.* RH$_5$AsPl mekly] and *add.* H$_6$Cc it[2]] and *add.* H$_5$As 27 him] hem Lw vtterly] wyterly BLw, *om.* Lat. fro it] þerfro Sr

witen wel þat þis felynge is good, bot þei wite not what it is. Þerfore vnto alle swilke sowles I say as me þinkiþ, þat þis maner of felynge, þawȝ it be bot schort and bot seldom, it is soþfastly þis mirknes þat I speke of. For it is a felynge of hemself first and a risynge aboue hemself þurwȝ brennande desire to þe siȝt of Ihesu; or elles if I sal say
95v more soþly, þis gracious felynge | is a gostly siȝt of Ihesu. And if þei mown kepen hem in þat rest, or bryngen it þurwȝ grace into custome so þat þei miȝten liȝtly and frely han it when hem list, and holden hem in it, þei schuld neuer ben ouercomen bi temptacioun of þe fende ne of þe flesshe, ne bi errours ⸢ne⸣ heresies, for þei are set in þe gate of contemplacioun, able and redy for to receife þe perfit luf of Ihesu. Þerfore he þat haþ it, it is gode þat he knowe it mekely, kepe it tenderly, and pursue it feruently, þat no creature let him vtterly fro it þat he ne folwe it when he may; and þat he forgete and set at noȝt al þinge þat schuld put him fro þis, if he be fre of himself and may do what he wil withouten sclaundre or disese of his euen-cristen. For me þinkiþ þat he may not come to þis rest liȝtly bot if he hafe grete plente of grace and sette himself for to folwen after þe stirynge of grace, and þat ogwiþ he for to don. For grace wolde ay be free, namely fro syn and werdly bisynes and fro alle oþer þinges þat letten þe wirkynge of it þaw þei be no synne.

Nerþeles anoþer soule þat haþ not ȝit receifed þis fulnes of grace, if he desire for to come to þis gostly knowynge of Ihesu, as mikel as in him is, he most ablen himself to it and putten awey al lettynges þat stoppen grace as mikel as he may. He most leren for to dyen to þe

ne] *om.* Ld   it^2] not *add.* M   may] fele hit þorw grace *add.* M   28 þynge] þo þynges M   þis] And namly *add.* CcM   29 be . . . may] *om.* As   go where] $H_7RLB_3SrAPH_6CcMPl$, do what HBH_5LwHu_2ELdTW, do himselfe what As, ire possit quo voluerit Lat.   sklaundre] disclandir A   30 þat] $H_7HBH_5AsSrLWHu_2ECcMLdPlTW$, *om.* RLB_3APH_6Pl 31 if] *om.* BALd   `he´ LM   and . . . grace (l. 32)] *om.* As   32 sterynge] stiringes A, strengþe Pl   he] hym M   33 grace] *om.* H_5 wuld] wull LdTW   ay] H_7HRH_5LPM, euere $BB_3AsLwAHu_2EH_6CcPlTW$, alwey SrLd   fre] fro synne *add.* B_3 and^1] fro *add.* BHu_2Ld, *om.* EM   namly] *om.* B_3M fro^1] $H_7RBLB_3SrAHu_2PCcMLdPl$, *om.* $HH_5AsLwEH_6TW$ fro^2] *om.* As   34 oþer] outward M, worldly *add.* As   þynges] lettingus A   letten] lettes M   þe] þis H_5As, inward *add.* M   werkynge] *corr. fr.* werkyngis Sr   of it] þerof SrA   þei] it As   `no´ Cc   35 a`noþer´ *interl.* H_7 ȝet] it T, *om.* B_3 þe] H_7AsM, þis Σ, hanc Lat.   fulnes of] *om.* RAPl   36 if] *om.* As   desyre] desireþ As   for] *om.* LB_3PH_6 to^2 . . . Jesu] þerto M   gostly] *om.* Lat.   of Jesu] *om.* A   Jesu] God RPl   as] in *prec.* As   37 him behoueth] $H_7RLB_3SrAPH_6CcMPl$, he most $HBH_5AsLwHu_2ELdTW$ behoueth] to *add.* $LB_3AsEPCcM$ to it] þerto SrCc, *om.* As   38 stoppen] stoppeþ M   Him behoueth] $H_7RLB_3SrAPH_6CcMPl$, He most HBH_5LwHu_2ELdTW, and he muste As   leren] H_7HRPl, lerne $BH_5LB3AsSrLwAHu_2EPH_6CcMLdTW$, also to *prec.* Cc, to *prec.* M

for to dyen to þe werd and forsake þe lufe of it trewly. First pryde, bodily and gostly: þat he desyre after no wurchipe of þe werd ne preysynge, name ne fame, state ne degre, maistrie ne lordschip, werldly conynge ne werdly crafte, benefyce ne riches, precyouse f. 76^{r} cloþynge ne werdly aray, ne noþynge whereþurgh he schuld | be wurchiped afore oþer men. He schal coueyten none of al þis, bot if þei be put on him he schal taken hem with drede, so þat he be boþe pore owtward and inward or ellys fully inward in herte; and þat he coueyte for to be forȝeten of þe werd, þat men reward him no more, be he neuer so riche or so conende, þan þe porest man þat lyfeþ. Also þat he suffre not his herte resten in beholdynge of his owen gode dedys or of his vertus, wenende þat he doth better þan oþer for he forsakeþ þe werd and oþer don not so, and þerfor lete wel by himself.

Also him behoueth lefen al rysynges of herte and euel willes of yre and enuye aȝens his euene-cristen, and þat he desese no man ne angre hem vnskilfully in word ne in dede, ne ȝif any man matere wherþurgh he myȝt skilfully ben angred or stered, so þat he myȝt be fre fro euerilk man, þat no man hafe for to don with him ne he with ony man. And also þat he forsak coueytyse, þat he coueyte ryȝt noȝt of erdly gode, bot only aske his bodyly sustenaunce as him nedeþ and holde him payed whan God stereþ oþer men for to ȝif it him. And þat he put no maner troste in auere of erdly gode, ne in helpe or fauour of ony erdly frende, bot principally and fully in God; for if he do oþerwyse

39 for] fo H_5, *om.* H_6CcM dyen] as *add.* As and] to *add.* AsCc of it] þerof Sr trewly] vttirly Cc pryde] boþe H_6 40 ⌜þat . . . þe⌝] L after] H_7RLB_3SrAEPH_6CcMPl`W$^{G}$´, *om.* HB$H_5$AsLwHu$_2$LdTW `no´ L, non As, loue ne *add.* Hu$_2$ `of . . . lordschip (l. 41)´ W^{G}, *om.* LwW 41 state] ne estate As degre] ne *add.* As lordschip] ne *add.* AsT 42 werldly] clerklyche M benefyce] H_7H_5SrAECcLd, benefices HRBLB_3AsLwHu$_2$-PH_6MPlTW, beneficium Lat. riches] H_7HSrLwHu$_2$EH_6M, richesse RBH_5LB_3PLdTW, richesses Pl, riche As, diuicias Lat. 43 cloþynge] clothinges As ne^{1}] non *add.* As 44 afore] H_7, bifore B_3, abofe HRBH_5LAsSrLwAHu$_2$EPH_6CcMLdPlTW, pre Lat. men] nor *add.* M coueyten] coueitese T if] *om.* Pl 45 on] H_7LB_3SrAPCcM, opon HRBH_5AsLwHu$_2$EH_6LdPlTW him] þen *add.* Hu$_2$ he . . . hem] or taken him As he . . . taken] take he E he schal^{2}] H_7RLB_3SrAPH_6CcPl`W$^{G}$´, *om.* HB$H_5$LwHu$_2$MLdTW taken hem] *om.* Ld drede] degre Ld boþe pore] $H_7$RL$B_3$SrAP$H_6$CcPl, *rev.* HB$H_5$Lw-Hu$_2$ELdTW boþe] *om.* AsM pore] in spirit but *add.* As 46 or . . . inward$^{2}$] *om.* Hu$_2$Cc in herte] $H_7$RL$B_3$Sr`Lw´AEPH_6CcMPlW, *om.* HBH_5AsHu$_2$LdT, in corde Lat. in] his *add.* E 47 for] *om.* SrH_6 of] in M werd] And *add.* RAPl he] *om.* M 48 or] ne AsE, and A þan] þat he be as poure in spirit as As þat lyfeþ] leuynge As 49 resten] rysen B, to *prec.* H_6Cc gode] H_7RLB_3SrAPH_6CcPl, *om.* HBH_5AsLwHu$_2$EMLdTW, bonitatis Lat. or] as As of] H_7RLB_3SrAPH_6CcMPl, in HBH_5AsLwHu$_2$ELdTW 50 vertus] vertuouse As doth] do B_3AsCc oþer] H_7SrALd, anoþer HRBLB_3LwHu$_2$EPH_6Cc-MPlTW, any oþer H_5, any oþer man, oþer As, aliis Lat. for he] *corr. fr.* þat Pl for] þat *add.* H_5EPl 51 þerfor] so M, he *add.* Pl lete . . . by] H_7H$^{\circ}$BLB_3Hu$_2$PMLd, lete`þ´ H^{c}, leteþ

werld and forsake þe luf of it trewly. First pride, bodily and gostly: þat he desire no wurscipe of þe werld ne preisynge, name ne fame, state ne degre, maistrie ne lordschip, werdly kunnynge ne werdly craft, benefices ne riches, precious cloþinge ne werdly aray, ne noþinge wherþurgh he schuld be wurschiped abofe oþer men. He schal coueite none of alle þese, bot if þei be put opon him taken hem with drede, so þat he be pore boþe outward and inward or elles fully inward; and þat he coueite for to be forgeten of þe werld, þat men reward him no
96r more, be he neuer | so riche ne so conende, þan þe porest man þat lifiþ. Also þat he suffre not his herte resten in biholdynge of his owne dedis or in his vertues, wenende þat he doþ better þan anoþer for he forsakiþ þe werld and oþer do not so, and þerfor lete`þ´ wel bi himself.

Also he most lefen alle risynges of hert and yuel willes of ire and enuye ageyns his euen-cristen, and þat he disese no man ne angre him vnskilfully in wurde ne in dede, ne gif any man matere whereþurgh he miȝte skilfully be angred or stired, so þat he miȝt be fre fro euerilk man, þat no man hafe for to do with him ne he with ony man. And also þat he forsake coueitise, þat he coueite riȝt noȝt of erþly gode, bot only aske his bodily sustenaunce as him nediþ and hold him paied what God stiriþ oþer men for to gif him. And þat he put no maner of trost in hauere of ony werdly goode, ne in helpe or fauour of only werdly frende, bot principally and fully in God; for if he do oþerwise

RH_5AsSrCcPl, to lete H_6, he letith T, `letith or demyth´ W[G], set A, setteth W, leetheth Lw, demeþ E, iudicando Lat. wel] mich A 52 him behoueth] H_7RLB_3SrAPH_6CcMPl, he most HBH_5AsLwHu_2ELdTW lefen] bere doun M, to *prec.* CcMPl rysynges] rysyng W, ryches Ld, stirynges Hu_2 and] of *add.* H_6 willes] wylle LwELdW yre] wreþthe BALd 53 and[1]] *om.* As, of *add.* H_6Ld aȝens] of M and[2]] *om.* M desese . . . hem] ne angre nor disese no man M `ne´ Pl 54 hem] H_7LB_3PH_6CcMWc, him HRBH_5LwAHu_2LdPlTW, no man, ne himselfe As, no man E, *om.* Sr vnskilfully/in . . . dede] *rev.* Ld vnskilfully] vnresonable Hu_2 any] no H_6, to no E 55 myȝt] be *add.*, *canc.* H skilfully ben] *rev.* BH_5AsMLdWc ben] an *add.* As so] and As 56 euerilk] euerich a M þat . . . man[3]] *om.* AsLwW for] H_7HRBH_5SrLwAHu_2EPlTW, *om.* LB_3PH_6CcMLdWc ony] no AH_6CcM 57 And] *om.* LB_3PH_6Cc also] so As þat] as *prec.* As ryȝt] *om.* M 58 as] þat LwW and] þan to As holde] held Sr 59 payed] apayȝed H_5As, wel *prec.* Hu_2 whan] H_7RLB_3AsSrLwAPH_6MPlW, what HB$H_5$$Hu_2$ECcT, whatt so Ld, quando Lat. oþer] gode As it] H_7RSrMPl, to A, *om.* HBH_5LB_3AsLwHu_2EPH_6CcLdTW, illam Lat. him] *om.* Ld And . . . maner] *om.* As 60 maner] H_7RLB_3SrAPH_6MPl, of *add.* HBH_5LwHu_2ECcLdTW troste] in *prec.* As in[1]] of As auere] hauing AMT of[1]] H_7RLB_3SrAEPH_6CcMPl, ony *add.* HBH_5AsLwHu_2LdTW, alicuius Lat. erdly] H_7RLSrAPH_6CcMPl, werdly HB$H_5$$B_3$AsLw$Hu_2$ELdTW, terreni Lat. gode] godus M in[2]] *om.* H_6 or] ne AEH_6, nor M, of H_5As ony] only R 61 erdly H_7, werdly Σ (fleshly or *prec.* M), terreni Lat. frende] he byndeþ himsilf to þe world *add.*, *canc.* B_3 principally and fully] *rev.* M God] Jesu M do] doþ As oþerwyse] doutles *add.* Hu_2

he byndeþ himself to þe werd, and he may not þerfore be fre for to þenken on God. And also glotonye and liccherye and oþer fleschly vnclennes vtterly him behoueth lefen, þat þe affeccyon be not bounden to no woman by fleschly lufe or fleschly homlynes. For it is no dowte þat swilk blynd lufe þat is sumtyme atwix man and wuman, and semeþ gode and honest for as mikel as þei wuld not synnen in dede, in þe syȝt of God is ful vnclene and grete synne. For it is a grete synne þat a man schal suffre his affeccyon, þat schuld be festned to Jesu and to al vertus and to al gostly clennes, for to be bounden with ony fleschly lufe of ony creature wilfully; namly if it be f. 76[v] so mikel | þat it bereþ doun his þoght and makeþ it vnrestful þat he may no sauour han in God. Þus I hold it wilfully þat a man doþ it and seith it is no synne, or elles is so blent with it þat he wil not seen it. And also þat a man coueyte no delyces of metys and drynkes only for lust of his flesch, bot hold him payed with swilk mete as he may esyly hafe withouten grete besynes, namely—if he be hol—what mete it be þat wil don awey þe hungre and kepe þe body in common strength vnto þe seruice of God, and þat he grucche not, stryfe not, angre not for his mete, þogh he be not serued sumtyme as þe flesch wulde.

Al þese synnes and al oþer him behoueth forsaken vtterly in his wil and in dede whan he may, and al oþer þynges þat letten him, so þat he may disposen him for to þenken frely on Jesu. For as longe as þes

62 he[1]] be H$_5$ byndeþ] hyndrith Cc himself] him Ld he may not/þerfore] *rev.* H$_6$ þerfore/be fre] *rev.* Sr for to] and R 63 on] in As God] Jesu LwMW oþer] H$_7$RLB$_3$SrAPH$_6$CcMPl, al *prec.* HBH$_5$AsLwHu$_2$ELdTW, alias Lat. fleschly] synnys and *add.* Ld 64 vtterly/him . . . lefen] *rev.* H$_6$ vtterly/him behoueth] *rev.* M him behoueth] H$_7$RLB$_3$SrAPH$_6$CcMPl, he most HBH$_5$AsLwHu$_2$ELdTW lefen] H$_7$HRBH$_5$AsSrLwAHu$_2$ELdTW, to *prec.* `L′B$_3$PH$_6$CcMPl þe] his AsM not] H$_7$RLB$_3$SrAPH$_6$CcMPl, *om.* HBH$_5$AsLwHu$_2$ELdTW 65 lufe or fleschly] *om.* W or] elles be *add.* M 66 is[2]] smyten *add.*, *canc.* Pl sumtyme] *om.* M atwix] H$_7$HLLwPW, bytwix RBB$_3$AsSrELdPl, bytwene H$_5$AHu$_2$H$_6$CcMT. man . . . wuman] H$_7$RLB$_3$SrAHu$_2$EPH$_6$CcMPl, a *prec.* (*bis*) HBH$_5$AsLwLdTW 67 and[1]] þat Cc gode and honest] holinesse and gode M `þei′ H$_6$ wuld] nolde B, wul Ld 68 synnen] syn *add.*, *canc.* L God] Jesu M is] it *prec.* LB$_3$PH$_6$M and . . . synne (l. 69)] *om.* RAPl, *om.* Lat. and] H$_7$LB$_3$SrPH$_6$Cc, wel *add.* HBH$_5$AsLwELdW, ful *add.* Hu$_2$M, right *add.* T For . . . synn[e] (l. 69)] *om.* As 69 a[1]] so B$_3$, full M, *om.* RAPl suffre] þat *add.* Cc 70 Jesu] God RAPl, Deo Lat. and[1] . . . vertus] *om.* RAMPl and to al[2]] as into a M al[2]] *om.* R gostly] goodly Cc 71 with ony] in only *rep.* M of] to A it] he M 72 bereþ] bere H$_6$Cc his] H$_7$RLB$_3$SrAEPH$_6$CcMPl, þe HBH$_5$AsLwHu$_2$LdTW, suam Lat. makeþ] make H$_6$ 73 no . . . han] not haue no sauour Ld, saporem non potest penitus inuenire Lat. God] Jesu M, Deo Lat. it[2]] *om.* AsCc 74 seith] þat *add.* As `no′ W[G], *om.* AsLwW is] it *prec.* LB$_3$EP, it *prec.*, *canc.* Sr, he *prec.* M blent] H$_7$LB$_3$SrPH$_6$Cc, blynded HBH$_5$AsLwAHu$_2$EMLdTW, blynde RPl with it] þerwiþ Sr, wiþalle M þat . . . it[3]] *om.* As wil] may M 75 þat a man] þat he H$_6$, *om.* LB$_3$P

he bindiþ himself to þe werdle, and he may not þerfore be fre for to þinken on God. And also glotony and leccherye and al oþer flescly vnclennes vtterly he most lefen, þat þe affeccioun be bounden to no womman bi flescly luf or flescly homlynes. For it is no doute þat swilk blynde luf þat is sumtyme atwix a man and a woman, and semiþ gode and honeste for as mikel as þei wolden not syn in dede, in þe siȝt of God is ful vnclene and wel grete syn. For it is a grete synne þat a man schal suffre his affeccioun, þat schuld be festned to Ihesu and to alle vertues and to alle gostly clennes, for to ben bounden with ony flescly luf of ony creature wilfully; namely if it be so mikel þat it beriþ doun þe þouȝt and makiþ it vnrestful þat he may no sauour han in God. Þus I holde it wilfully þat a man doþ it and seiþ it is no synne, or elles is so blynded with it þat he wil not seen it. And also þat a man coueite not
96v no delices of metes and drynkes only for luste of his flesch, bot holde | him paied with swilke mete as he may esily hafe withouten grete bisynes, namely—if he be hol—what mete it be þat wil don awey hungre and kepe þe body in comune strengþe vnto þe seruice of God; and þat he grucche not ne strife not ne angre him not for his mete, þawȝ he be sumtyme not serued as þe flesche wold.

Alle þese synnes and alle oþer most be forsaken vtterly in his wil and in dede when he may, ⸢and oþer⸣ `þinges þat lettyn him so þat he may´ disposen him for to þinke frely on Ihesu. For as longe as þese

coueyte] H$_7$RLB$_3$SrAEPH$_6$CcMPl, not *add.* HBH$_5$AsLwHu$_2$LdTW no delyces of] ne delytith Cc no] neyþer H$_5$, none As, *om.* LwLdW delyces] delicious H$_6$, delite Pl of] *corr. to* in Cc metys and drynkes] mete nor of drynke M only] namly B for] of As 76 lust] lustys CcM his] *om.* As flesch] bodyly *prec.* Hu$_2$ `him´ Cc payed] apayd As, plesyd Ld, wel *prec.* E mete] and drynk *add.* Cc 77 mete] euer *add.* T 78 þe^1] H$_7$RBLB$_3$SrAHu$_2$EPH$_6$MLdPl, his Cc, *om.* HH$_5$AsLwTW kepe] to *prec.* As þe^2] þy H$_5$ in] into As strength] state T 79 vnto] to H$_5$SrA, and to B God] Jesu M þat] þanne LB$_3$P grucche] gruccheþ LB$_3$EP not^1] H$_7$RBLB$_3$SrAHu$_2$PH$_6$LdPl, ne *add.* HH$_5$LwECcMTW, ne besye nouȝt ne *add.* As stryfe not] *om.* Lat. not^2] ne H$_7$RLB$_3$APPl, *add.* HBH$_5$AsSrLwHu$_2$EH$_6$MLdTW, ne Cc angre] H$_7$RLB$_3$SrAPH$_6$Pl, angry B, him *add.* HBH$_5$AsLwHu$_2$ECcMLdTW 80 þogh] ȝif M not serued/sumtyme] H$_7$RH$_5$LB$_3$AsSrAEPH$_6$CcMPl, *rev.* HBLwHu$_2$LdTW serued sumtyme] *rev.* EM serued] wyþ hys mete *add.* Ld þe] his M wulde] wole Ld 81 Al] and *prec.* As þese] those R oþer] synnes *add.* As him behoueth] H$_7$RLB$_3$SrAPH$_6$CcM, most be HBH$_5$AsLwELdTW, most he Hu$_2$ forsaken] to *prec.* H$_6$M, for to *prec.* Cc vtterly] bitterly Ld 82 and in] an Cc and^1] *om.* M in dede/whan he may] *rev.* M dede] his *prec.* AsHu$_2$EH$_6$, his dedis LB$_3$P may] vtterly M and^2 . . . may (l. 83)] *om.* H$^{\circ}$H$_5$As, ⸢and oþer⸣ `þinges þat lettyn him so þat he may´ H$^c$ al] *om.* LwH$^c$EW him] ȝif he be in þat degre and in þat state þat he may done *add.* M `so´ Pl 83 may] H$_7$RLB$_3$SrLw-H^{c}AEPH$_6$CcMPlW, not *add.* BH$_5$Hu$_2$LdT frely/on Jesu] *rev.* Pl Jesu] God RAPl, and fully ȝeuen hym to his seruise *add.* M, Domino Jesu Christo Lat. þes] suche As lettynges and swilk oþer hangen vpon him he may not dyen to þe werd ne come into þis mirknes of knowynge of himself; and þerfor he þat myȝt come þerto, him behoueth for to don al þis as Seynt Poul dyde, seyend þus of himself: *Michi mundus crucifixus est, et ego mundo*. Þe werd is slayn and crucyfyed to me and I to þe werd. Þat is, he þat forsakeþ þe lufe of þe werd in wurschipes and rycches, and al oþer werdly þynges befor seyd, for þe lufe of God, and lufeþ it not ne desyreþ it not, ne pursueþ it not bot is wel payed þat he hath ryȝt noȝt of it, ne wuld hafe it þogh he myȝte; sothly to þe werd he is ded, for he haþ no sauour ne delyte þerin. Also if þe werd sett him at noȝt and haþ no reward to him, do him no fauour ne wurschip, setttеþ no prisse be him bot forȝeteþ him as a ded man, þan is he dede to þe werd. And in þis plyte was Seynt Poul sette perfytely, and so behoueth to anoþer man in partye þat wold folwen and come to þe perfyte lufe of God, for he may no[t] lyfen to God fully vntil he dye first to þe werd.

Þis deynge to þe werd is þis mirknes, and it is þe gate to contemplacyon and to reformynge in felynge, and non oþer þan þis.
f. 77^{r} | Þer moun ben many dyuers weyes and sere werkes ledende dyuers soules to contemplacyon; for after sundry disposynges of men and after sundry states—as are religyouse and seculers—þat þei are in arn dyuers exercices in werkynge. Nerþeles þer is no gate bot on. For what excercyse it be þat a soule hafe, bot if he may come by þat

84 hangen] *rep.*, *canc.* H, haue gone M he] ne *add.* M dyen] fully *add.* M 85 into] to AsAPl þis] thise R, þe LB$_3$EP, þat H$_6$, his Cc mirknes] H$_7$HRLSrPCcMPl, derknesse BH$_5$B$_3$LwAHu$_2$EH$_6$LdTW he þat] H$_7$SrHu$_2$, *rev.* HRBH$_5$LB$_3$AsWsLw-AEPH$_6$CcMLdTW, vt Lat. 86 him . . . to] H$_7$RLB$_3$SrAPH$_6$CcMPl, he most HBH$_5$AsLwHu$_2$ELdTW for] *om.* M þis] thyse LwW 87 of himself] H$_7$RLB$_3$Sr-AEPH$_6$CcMPl, *om.* HBH$_5$AsLwHu$_2$LdTW, de seipso Lat. himself] Ad Gal. 6° *add.* BLHu$_2$EPLdT, Gal. v. *add.* W mundo] þat is *add.* BEH$_6$ 88 þe] Thys LwW and crucyfyed] *om.* H$_6$ \`and^{2}′ Pl to^{2}] vnto As 89 forsakeþ] hath forsake LwW in] and H$_5$A and^{1}] *om.* M rycches] H$_7$HH$_5$SrLWHu$_2$H$_6$LdW, richesse BAsACcT, richesses RLB$_3$EPM, rychesesse Pl, diuicias Lat. and^{2}] *om.* LwW al oþer] *rev.* Cc al] H$_7$AH$_6$, in *prec.* Σ oþer] *om.* LB$_3$PH$_6$ 90 werdly] *om.* Ld befor] aforn Cc þe] H$_7$AsH$_6$Cc, þe *add.*, *canc.* Sr, *om.* HRBH$_5$LB$_3$WsLwAHu$_2$EPMLdTW God] Jesu M lufeþ it not] refuseþ it As it not] *rev.* W 91 desyreþ it not, ne] H$_7$BLB$_3$SrHu$_2$EPH$_6$CcMLd, *om.* HRH$_5$AsLwAHu$_2$PlTW it not^{2}] *rev.* W \`it$^{2}$′ L, *om.* B$_3$ not$^{2}$] *om.* Cc wel] riȝt *prec.* E payed] apayd As 92 of it] þerof SrM, *om.* Cc wuld] noȝt *add.* A it$^{2}$] H$_7$RLB$_3$Sr-APH$_6$CcMPl, *om.* HBH$_5$AsLwHu$_2$ELdTW þogh] if þat E þe werd he] H$_7$, him þe werld Σ, sibi mundus Lat. þe] to Pl \`is ded′ B$_3$ 93 no] non As ne] no H þerin] in hit M if] *om.* Hu$_2$ 94 to] vnto H$_5$As, at E do him no] of non As do him] *om.* LwW do] H$_7$Sr, to do RAPl, ne to do Cc, ne do H$_6$, doþ Σ, faciat Lat. no^{2}] ne W, *om.* RCc fauour] sauour Lw ne] no H wurschip] ne *add.* RAsAPlW, and *add.* Cc 95 forȝeteþ] forgeten As þan is he] þat is As is he] *rev.* Cc 96 \`so′ Pl, it *add.* Cc

lettynges and swilk oþer hangen vpon him he may not dyen to þe werld ne comen into þis mirknes of knowynge of himselfe; and þerfore þat he miȝt come þerto he most don al þis as Seynt Poul did, seiend þus: *Michi mundus crucifixus est et ego mundo*. Þe werld is slayn and crucified to me and I to þe werld. Þat is, he þat forsakiþ þe luf of þe werld in wurschipes and riches, and in alle oþer werdly þinges before saide, for lufe of God, and lufiþ it not ne pursueþ it not bot is wel payed þat he haþ riȝt not of it, ne wold haue þawȝ he miȝte: soþly to him þe werld is ded, for he haþ no sauour [ne] delit þerin. Also if þe werld settiþ him at nouȝt and haþ no reward to him, doþ him no fauour [ne] wurscipe, settiþ no prise bi him bot forgetiþ him as a dede man, þan is he dede to þe werld. And in þis plit was Seynt Þoul sette perfitly, and so most anoþer man in partie þat wolde folwen and comen to þe perfit luf of God, for he may not lifen to God fully bot if he dye first to þe werld.

Þis dyenge to þe werld is þis mirknes, and it is þe gate to contemplacioun and to reformyng in felynge and none oþer þen þis. Þer mown be mony sundry weies and sere werkes ledend sundry soules to contemplacioun; for after sundry disposynges of men and after sundry states, as are religious and seculers, þat þei are in ⌜are⌝ diuers exercices in wirkynge. Nerþeles þer is no gate bot on. For what exercice it be þat a soule haf, bot if he may come bi þat exercice to þis

97 behoueth to] H$_7$RLB$_3$SrAPH$_6$CcMPl, most HBH$_5$AsLwHu$_2$ELdTW to] *om.* M anoþer] any oþer M þat] ȝif þat he As folwen] hym *add.* M, *om.* Lat. 98 God] Jesu M not] no H$_7$ lyfen] loven Cc God] Jesu M vntil] H$_7$LSrPH$_6$Cc, til AM, vnto B$_3$Pl, but if HBH$_5$AsLwHu$_2$ELdTW, nisi Lat. 99 first] *om.* As to] vnto LP, `vn´to Sr 100 þis (*bis*)] maner *add.* M mirknes] H$_7$HRLSrPCcM, derknesse BH$_5$B$_3$AsLwAHu$_2$EH$_6$LdTW, that I spake offe *add.* M to^2] H$_7$HRSrCcMPl, of BH$_5$LB$_3$AsLwAHu$_2$EPH$_6$LdTW, ad Lat. 101 to] þe *add.* H$_5$, *om.* M in] to M and . . . þis] *om.* Lat. þan] but H$_6$ þis] þus B 102 moun] may AsH$_6$MW dyuers . . . ledende] *om.* As dyuers] H$_7$RLB$_3$SrAHu$_2$PH$_6$CcMLdPlT, sundry HBH$_5$LwEW`T$^G$´  and . . . werkes] *om.* Cc  and] of AMPl  sere] H$_7$HRLLwHu$_2$EPMPlW`T^G´, dyuerse BH$_5$B$_3$ALdT, sundry H$_6$, sekyr Sr `werkes´ T$^G$, werkynges H$_6$T  ledende] leden B, lettinge and *prec.* W, *canc.* W$^G$  dyuers$^2$] H$_7$RLB$_3$SrAHu$_2$EPH$_6$CcMLdPl`T^G´, sundry HBH$_5$AsLwTW 103 for after] And also Ld for] *om.* T sundry] H$_7$HRBLB$_3$AsSrEPH$_6$CcMPl, diuerse H$_5$LwAHu$_2$LdTW disposynges] dysposycyons Hu$_2$Ld, disposicion T 104 sundry] diuers Hu$_2$LdMT as . . . seculers/þat . . . in] *rev.* H$_6$Cc as . . . seculers] *om.* RAMPl are^1] *om.* H$_6$Cc þei] *om.* T ⌜are^2⌝ H^c, here H$_5$AsT, *om.* Cc 105 exercices] exercise A, hauntyngis H$_6$ in . . . exercyse (l. 106)] *om.* As in] and H$_5$, of H$_6$, *om.* T werkynge] For some aren in seculer state and some are in religious *add.* M Nerþeles] But ȝet Cc ⌜þer . . . on⌝ L no] non B gate] way BPl, state M, via Lat. 106 exercyse] exercyces LwW, þat *add.* ACc it be] *om.* M þat . . . hafe] to a soule whethir it be seculer or reguler Cc a soule] man M hafe] be hit seculer or religious *add.* M he] ytt Lw may] *om.* Ld by] grace and be *add.* CcM

excercyse to þis knowynge and to a meke felynge of himself—and þat is þat he be mortifyed and ded to þe werd as in lufe, and þat he may felen himself sette sumtyme in þis restful mirknes by whilk he may be hyd fro vanite of þe werd and seen himself what he is—sothly he is not ȝit come to þe reformynge in felynge ne he haþ not fully contemplacyon; he is ful fer þerfro. And if he wil come by ony oþer gate, he is bot a þefe and a breker of þe wal, and þerfor he schal ben as vnwurthi kasten owte. Bot he þat kan brynge himself first to noȝt þurgh grace of meknes and deyen on þis maner, he is in þe gate, for he is ded to þe werd and he lyfeþ to God. Of þe whilk Seynt Poul spekeþ þus: *Mortui enim estis, et vita vestra abscondita est cum Christo in Deo*. Ȝe are ded; þat is, ȝe þat for þe lufe of God forsaken al þe lufe of þe werd are ded to þe werd, bot ȝoure lyfe is hid with Crist in God; þat is, ȝe lyfe gostly in lufe of God, bot þat lyf is hid fro werdly men as Crist lyfeþ and is hyd in his godhede fro þe lufe and þe syȝt of fleschly lufers.

Þis gate oure Lord himself scheweþ in þe Gospel whan he seyþ þus: *Omnis qui reliquerit patrem aut matrem, fratrem aut sororem, propter me, centuplum accipiet, et vitam eternam possidebit*. Ilk man þat forsakeþ for my lufe fadere or moder, suster or broþer or ony erdly gode, he schal hafe an hundreþfold in þis lyf and afterward þe blisse of heuene. Þis hundreþfold þat a soule schal hafe if he forsake þe werd is not ellys bot þe profyte of þis lyȝty mirknes þat I calle þe gate of contemplacyon. For he þat is in þis mirknes and is hyd þurgh grace fro werdly vanite, he coueyteþ noȝt of werdly gode, he sekeþ it not, he is not

107 þis] þe H$_5$M, þat Cc and[1] . . . felynge] *om.* RAPl to a meke] gracious CcM a] *om.* E þat . . . may (l. 108)] *om.* RAPl 108 lufe] H$_7$M, his *prec.* HBH$_5$LB$_3$AsSrLwHu$_2$EPH$_6$CcMLdTW, of þe world *add.* M, amorem, per diligentem consideracionem Christi et humilitatis sue Lat. 109 felen] lesed from synne and *prec.* M himself] hym RAHu$_2$Pl sette sumtyme] *rev.* As sette] sytte B, *om.* LwW mirknes] H$_7$HRLSrPCcM, derknesse BH$_5$B$_3$AsLwAHu$_2$EH$_6$LdTW, derknes´nesse B$_3$ whilk] H$_7$H°BSrACc, *prec.* RH$_5$LB$_3$AsLw`H$^{c}$´Hu$_2$EPH$_6$MLdPlTW `be´ Pl 110 vanite of þe werd] wordly vanyte Ld vanite] vanitees M, þe *prec.* SrH$_6$ and . . . himself] to know himself and As, *om.* RAMPl and seen] as in hys love and þat he may feele LwW he[1]] it H$_5$As 111 ȝit] *om.* Ld þe] *om.* HT reformynge] formyng H$_5$Lw he] H$_7$RB$_3$AsSrCcMPl, *om.* HBH$_5$LLwAHu$_2$EPLdTW not] ȝit *add.* LB$_3$PH$_6$ 112 he[1]] for *prec.* H$_6$ wil] *om.* Cc ony oþer] anoþer A 113 `oþer´ W$^{G}$, *om.* W gate] grace B$_3$, way BPl is] ne *prec.* A bot] like Pl wal] wallis RAs he schal ben/as vnwurthi] H$_7$, *rev.* Σ 114 as] as an E, he as H$_6$, he is LB$_3$P `þat´ MPl kan] may M himself first] *rev.* T 115 of meknes] *om.* RAMPl þe] þis LB$_3$PLd gate] waye BPl 116 ded] as *add.* As he[2]] *om.* AsCc lyfeþ] loueþ M Seynt Poul/spekeþ] *rev.* A 117 þus] off Ld, Col. 3° *add.* BLHu$_2$ELdTW abscondita] *om.* H$_5$As in Deo] *om.* Cc, in Domino Pl 118 Deo] etc. *add.* M, þat is *add.* BE is] for soþe *add.* B þat[2]] for that *add.*, *canc.* Cc God] Jesu M 119 are] ȝe *prec.* H$_5$As bot . . . hid/with . . .

97r knowynge and to a meke felynge | of himself—and þat is þat he be mortified and ded to þe werld as in his lufe, and þat he may felen himself sette sumtyme in þis restful mirknes be `þe´ whilk he may be hid fro vanite of þe werld and seen himself what he is—soþly he is not ȝit come to reformynge in felynge ne haþ not fully contemplacioun; he is ful ferre þerfro. And if he wil come bi ony oþer gate, he is bot a þefe and a breker of þe wal, and þerfore as vnworþi he schal be kest out. Bot he þat can brynge himself first to noȝt þurwȝ grace of meknes and dien on þis maner, he is in þe gate, for he is dede to þe werld and he lifiþ to God. Of þe whilk Seint Poul spekiþ þus: *Mortui enim estis, et vita vestra abscondita est cum Christo in Deo*. Ȝe are dede, þat is, ȝe þat for þe luf of God forsaken alle þe luf of þe werld are ded to þe werld, bot ȝoure life is hid [with Crist in God, þat is, ȝe lyfe gostly in lufe of God. Bot þat lyf is hid] fro werdly men as Crist lifiþ and is hid in his godhed fro þe luf and þe siȝt of flescly lufers.

Þis gate oure Lord himself schewd in þe Gospel when he saide þus: *Omnis qui reliquerit patrem aut matrem, fratrem aut sororem, propter me, centuplum accipiet, et vitam eternam possidebit*. Ilk man þat forsakiþ for mi luf fader or moder, suster or broþer or ony erþly gode, he schal haue an hundreþfold in þis lif and afterward þe blisse of heuen. Þis hundredfold þat a soule schal haue if he forsake þe werld is not elles bot þe profet of þis liȝty mirknes, þe whilk I calle þe gate of contemplacioun. For he þat is in þis mirknes and is hid þurgh grace fro werdly vanite, he couetiþ not of werdly gode, he sekiþ it
97v not, he is not taried þerwith, he lokiþ not after it, he | lufiþ it not; and

God] *rev.* LwW hid] fro worldly men *add.* E with . . . hid (l. 120)] *om.* HH$_5$AsT with/ . . ./in] *rev.* Cc 120 ȝe lyfe] the liȝf R ȝe] þat *add.* B$_3$Hu$_2$EH$_6$ lyfe] loue Hu$_2$ God] Jesu LwW bot . . . hid] *om.* LwW lyf] loue B werdly] *rep.*, *canc.* Sr 121 Crist lyfeþ] Crystis lyf Cc and[1]] it *add.* RAPl his] þe A þe[2]] *om.* E of] þe *add.* Cc 122 lufers] loues H$_5$ 123 þis] manere *add.* Pl gate] *followed by erasure* H$_7$, way BAs Lord] God *add.* Cc himself schewed] *rev.* H$_6$ scheweþ] H$_7$, schewed Σ, suede As, demonstrauit Lat. seyþ] H$_7$, seyd Σ, dixit Lat. 124 þus] Mt. 19° *add.* BLHu$_2$TW, Mt. 9° *add.* E, Mt. 10 *add.* Ld Omnis] enim *add.* M reliquerit] relinquit H$_5$ fratrem] aut *prec.* H$_5$ 125 possidebit] That is *add.* B Ilk] H$_7$HRM, euery BH$_5$LB$_3$SrLwAHu$_2$EPCcLdPlTW, such a As forsakeþ/for my lufe] *rev.* Sr 126 or[1, 2]] and (*bis*) E suster or broþer] *rev.* Ld or[3]] oþer As erdly gode] *rev.* LwW128 is] it *prec.* RAsPl `ellys´ W[G], *om.* LwW 129 profyte . . . lyȝty] perfite liȝt of þis As liȝty] lyȝtly Lw, liȝtsum A, liȝt M, *om.* Cc mirknes] H$_7$HRLSrPCcMPl`W[G]´, derknesse BH$_5$B$_3$AsLwAHu$_2$EH$_6$LdTW þat] þe whiche AsEM I . . . þe] is R, is þe APl calle] clepe AsH$_6$ gate] yates M, way B 130 in þis mirknes and] *om.* Lat. þis] *om.* Hu$_2$ mirknes] H$_7$HRLSrPCcMPl, derknesse BH$_5$B$_3$AsLwAHu$_2$EH$_6$LdTW 131 vanite] vanytes H$_5$AsMT noȝt of] no Hu$_2$ noȝt] ne *add.* As he[2]] nor M it] *om.* As he[3] . . . þerafter (l. 132)] *om.* Lat.

f. 77v taryed withalle, | he lokeþ not þerafter, he lufeþ it not; and þerfor he haþ an hundreþfold more þan þe kynge haþ or he haþ þat most coueyteþ of erdly gode. For he þat noȝt coueyteþ bot Jesu haþ an hundreþfold, for he haþ more reste, more pees in hert, more verrey lufe and delyte in soule, in o daye þan he haþ þat most coueyteþ of þe werd and haþ þe welthe of it vnder his wil in al his lyf tyme.

Þis is þan a gode mirknes and a ryche noȝt þat bryngeþ a soule to so mikel gostly ese and so stille softenes. I trow þat þe prophete Dauid mened of þis niȝt whan he seyd þus: *Ad nichilum redactus sum, et nesciui*. Þat is: I was broȝt to noȝt and I ne wiste; þat is, þe grace of oure Lord Jesu sent into myn herte haþ slayn in me and brent to noȝt al þe lufe of þe werd, and I wist not how. For þurgh no werkynge of myself ne by myn owen witte I hafe it not, bot of þe grace of oure Lord Jesu. And þerfor me þenkeþ þat he þat wil hafe þe lyȝt of grace and fulsumly fele þe lufe of Jesu in his soule, him behoueth forsaken al þe fals lyȝt of þe werdly lufe and abyden in þis mirknes. And nerþeles if he be adred first for to wone þerin, turne not aȝen to lufe of þe werd, bot suffre a whyle and put alle his hope and his trist in Jesu, and he schal not longe be withouten sum gostly lyȝt. Þus biddeþ þe prophete: *Qui ambulat in tenebris, et non est lumen ei, speret in Domino, et innitatur super Deum suum*. Whoso goþ in mirknes and haþ no lyȝt; þat is, whoso wil hyden him fro þe lufe of þis werd and may not redily fele þe lyȝt of gostly lufe, despere not, turne not aȝen to þe werd, but hope

132 withalle] H$_7$RLB$_3$SrPH$_6$MPl, þerwith HBH$_5$AsLwAHu$_2$ECcLdTW þerafter] H$_7$RLB$_3$SrAPH$_6$Pl, after it HBH$_5$AsLwHu$_2$ECcMLdTW he[2]] and he ne As he haþ] H$_7$B$_3$H$_6$Pl, *rev.* Σ 133 þan] he þat haþ most *add.*, *canc.* H haþ[2]] H$_7$RBLB$_3$SrAHu$_2$EPH$_6$CcMLdPl, *om.* HH$_5$AsLwTW, habet Lat. or] oþere As he haþ] *rev.* H$_5$, *om.* T he] H$_7$, þan `he´ H^c, þan he Σ, quam Lat. most coueyteþ] *rev.* LwW 134 erdly] wordly M þat] hath M coueyteþ] coueited M Jesu] God RAPl haþ] he *prec.* RAMPlT 135 ⌜for . . . in⌝ L for he haþ] *om.* As reste] and *add.* Cc more pees] *om.* As 136 lufe and delyte] *rev.* R in[1]] his *add.* Hu$_2$ soule in] *om.* H$_6$ in[2]] on AsCc `he´ H haþ/þat . . . wil (l. 137)] H$_7$LB$_3$SrPH$_6$CcM, *rev.* HRBH$_5$AsLwAHu$_2$ELdPlTW haþ] *om.* H$_5$ þe] þis As 137 werd] wordly good M þe] H$_7$, al þe Σ, maxime Lat. `welthe´ W^G, helþe Ld, well W of it] *om.* M vnder] at M his[1]] *om.* Ld wil] welht W in] and As, *om.* H$_5$Pl al] in As, *om.* R 138 þis is þan] *rev.* H$_6$ mirknes] H$_7$HRLSrPCcMPl, derknesse BH$_5$B$_3$AsLwAHu$_2$EH$_6$LdTW, humilitas Lat. so] *om.* E 139 my`kil´ Cc gostly] *om.* Ld softenes] sothnesse Cc, and to grete clennesse in herte *add.* M þat þe prophete] H$_7$RLB$_3$SrAPH$_6$CcMPl, *om.* HBH$_5$AsLwHu$_2$ELdTW, propheta Lat. þat] *om.* H$_6$ Dauid] *om.* Pl 140 mened] menyth Cc niȝt] H$_7$H$^\circ$BHu$_2$LdT, noȝt H$_5$LB$_3$SrPH$_6$M, `or of þis noȝt´ *add.* H^c, niȝt or of þis nouȝt RLwECcPlW, noȝt or of þis niȝt A, miȝt As, adnichilacione Lat. þus] Ps. 72° *add.* BLHu$_2$EPLdTW 141 `I[1]´ R I[2]] *om.* M ne wiste] H$_7$HRBSrAELdPlT, ne wiste nouȝt H$_5$As, wiste not LB$_3$LwHu$_2$PH$_6$W, wiste hit not M, wost it nout how Cc 142 Jesu] God RAPl, Crist *add.* Hu$_2$ sent] set R herte] and *add.* E, he *add.* M

þerfore haþ he an hundredfolde more þan þe kynge or þan `he´ haþ þat most coueitiþ of erþly gode. For he þat nouȝt coueitiþ bot Ihesu haþ an hundredfolde, for he haþ more reste, more pees in hert, more verray lufe and delite in soule, in on day þan he þat most coueitiþ of þe werld and haþ alle þe welþe of it vnder his wil haþ in al his lif tyme.

þis is þan a good mirknes and a riche nouȝt þat bryngiþ a soule to so mikel gostly ese and so stille softnes. I trow Dauid mened of þis niȝt `or of þis noȝt´ whan he saide þus: *Ad nichilum redactus sum, et nesciui*. þat is: I was broȝt to noȝt and I ne wist; þat is, þe grace of oure Lord Ihesu sent into myn hert haþ slayn in me and broȝt to nouȝt alle þe luf of `þe´ werld, and I wist not how. For þurwȝ no wirkyng of myself ne bi myne owne wit I hafe it not, bot of þe grace of oure Lord Ihesu. And þerfor me þinkiþ, he þat wil hafe þe liȝt of grace and fulsumly fele þe luf of Ihesu in his soule, he most forsakyn al þe fals liȝt of werdly lufe and abiden in þis mirknes. And nerþeles if he be adred first for to wonen þerin, turne not ageyn to þe luf of þe werld, but suffre a while and putte al his hope and his trust in Ihesu, and he schal not longe be withouten sum gostly liȝt. þus bidiþ þe prophet: *Qui ambula*⌜t⌝ in tenebris, et non est lumen ei, speret in Domino, et innitatur super Deum suum. Whoso goþ in mirknes and haþ no liȝt, þat is, whoso wil hiden him fro þe luf of þe werld and may not redily fele liȝt of gostly luf, despere not, turne not ageyn to þe werld, bot

brent] H$_7$LB$_3$P, broȝt Σ, adnichilauit Lat. 143 `þe^{2}´ H^{c} wist not] ne wist H$_5$ 144 witte] ne *add.* M I hafe] I hadde B, *rev.* H$_6$Ld it not] *rev.* E þe] *om.* Ld oure . . . Jesu] God M, Jesu Christi Lat. oure] *rep.* Cc 145 Jesu] God RAPl, Crist *add.* LB$_3$PH$_6$ þerfor] the for Ld þat^{1}] H$_7$RB$_3$SrAH$_6$CcMPl, *canc.* L, *om.* HBH$_5$AsLwHu$_2$EPLdTW lyȝt] lyff Ld 146 fulsumly] fulli AsACcM þe lufe of] *om.* M Jesu] God RAPl him behoueth] H$_7$RLB$_3$SrAPH$_6$CcMPl, he most HBH$_5$AsLwHu$_2$ELdTW forsaken] to *prec.* H$_6$CcM 147 of] or Hu$_2$ þe] H$_7$, þis As, *om.* Σ mirknes] H$_7$HRLSrPCcMPl, derknesse BH$_5$B$_3$AsLwAHu$_2$EH$_6$LdTW And] *om.* H$_6$Cc 148 if] and M, licet Lat. adred first] *rev.* H$_6$ first] *om.* Ld wone] abide Hu$_2$ turne] and *prec.* Sr aȝen] þouh *add.* H$_6$ lufe] H$_7$RLB$_3$SrP, þe *prec.* HBH$_5$AsLwAEH$_6$CcMLdPlTW, þe fals *prec.* Hu$_2$ of] *om.* B$_3$ 149 his^{1}] help *add.*, *canc.* L and his] in þis As and^{2}] al *add.* SrM Jesu] God RAPl, Domino Jesu Christo Lat. 150 longe] *om.* H$_6$ be] abide Hu$_2$ sum] *om.* LB$_3$PH$_6$Ld lyȝt] *followed by erasure* H$_7$ þus . . . prophete] *om.* Cc prophete] Ysa. 50° *add.* BLHu$_2$EPLdTW 151 Qui] Quis M ambulat] ambula⌜t⌝, *one-letter canc. seq.* H, ambulauit B lumen ei] *rev.* CcM innitatur] imitatur H$_5$, mutabitur M 152 super] semper H$_5$, ad RAPl suum] That is *add.* ECc goþ] go H$_6$ mirknes] H$_7$HRLAsSrPCcMPl, derknesse BH$_5$B$_3$LwAHu$_2$EH$_6$LdTW no] non As, nat H$_6$ 153 þe] H$_7$HRBAsLwAHu$_2$ECcLdPlTW, *om.* H$_5$LB$_3$SrPH$_6$M lufe of þis] *om.* Ld þis] H$_7$, þe Σ redily] restfully M fele] Jesu þat is *add.* M 154 þe lyȝt] it As þe^{1}] H$_7$RLB$_3$SrAPH$_6$CcPl, *om.* HBH$_5$LwHu$_2$EMLdTW gostly] gosti As despere] he *add.* H$_5$Hu$_2$ not^{1}] ne *add.* LB$_3$PH$_6$ turne] come M hope] trust Hu$_2$

in oure Lord, and lene vpon him; þat is, trist in God and clefe sadly to him by desyre, and mekly abyde a whyle, and he schal hafe ly3t.

For it fareþ by it as it doþ be a man þat had ben in þe sunne a grete whyle and after þat comeþ sodeynly into a mirke hows þer no sunne f. 78r schyneþ. He schuld first be as he ware blynde | and seen ry3t no3t; bot if he wil abyden a whyle he schal moun son seen aboute him, first grete þynges and aftere smale, and syþen al þat is in þe hows. Ry3t so it is gostly: he þat forsakeþ þe lufe of þe werd and comeþ to himself into his owen conscience, it is first mirke sumwhat and blynde to his sy3t. Bot if he stonde stille and hold forth wyth besy prayere and often þenkynge þe same wil to þe lufe of Jesu, he schal moun seen afterward grete þynges and smale also þat he first knew not. Þus semeþ it þat þe prophete byhy3t, sayend þus: *Orietur in tenebris lux tua et tenebre tue erunt sicut meridies. Et requiem dabit tibi Dominus Deus tuus et implebit animam tuam splendoribus*. Ly3t schal spryngen to þe in mirknes; þat is, þou þat forsakest sothfastly þe ly3t of al werdly lufe and hydest þi þoght in þis mirknes, ly3t of blissed lufe and gostly knowynge of God schal springen to þe. And þi mirknes schal be as mydday; þat is, þi myrknes of trauellend desyre and þi blynd trust in God þat þu hast ferst schal turnen into clere knowynge and into sykernesse of lufe. And þi Lord God schal 3if rest to þe; þat is, þi fleschly desyres and þi pynful dredys and dowtys and wykked spirites þat han continuely befor trauayled þe, al þese schul weyken and lesen mikel of here my3t,

155 lene] leve Cc þat . . . him] *om.* As trist in God] Crist in Jesu M God] Jesu Cc sadly] H$_7$RLB$_3$AsSrAPH$_6$CcPl`W$^G$´, *om.* HBH$_5$LwHu$_2$EMLdTW, firmiter Lat. 156 by] love and *add.* Cc mekly] H$_7$RLB$_3$SrAPH$_6$CcPl, *om.* HBH$_5$AsLwHu$_2$EMLdTW, humiliter Lat. and[2]] *om.* BLd he] 3ou Cc 157 fareþ] H$_7$RLB$_3$AsSrAEPH$_6$CcMPl, `aliter fareþ´ W^G, fallyþ HBH$_5$LwHu$_2$LdTW, accidit Lat. by it] H$_7$RLB$_3$SrAPH$_6$CcMPl, þerby HBH$_5$AsLwHu$_2$ELdTW doþ] falleþ As be] H$_7$RLB$_3$AsSrAEPH$_6$CcPl, if HBH$_5$LwHu$_2$MLdTW, de Lat. þat] H$_7$RLB$_3$AsSrAEPH$_6$CcPl, *om.* HBH$_5$LwHu$_2$MLdTW, qui Lat. had] haþ As, haue M in þe sunne/a grete whyle] H$_7$RLB$_3$SrAPH$_6$CcMPl, *rev.* HBH$_5$AsLwHu$_2$ELdTW 158 þat] he *add.* Cc comeþ] H$_7$AsM, come HRBH$_5$LB$_3$SrLwAHu$_2$EPH$_6$CcLdPlT, came W, intrat Lat. into] to R mirke] H$_7$HRLSrPCcM, derke BH$_5$B$_3$AsLwAHu$_2$EH$_6$LdPlTW no] the Cc 159 schyneþ] nout *add.* Cc schuld] shul Hu$_2$ first be] *rev.* BELdPl first] *om.* LwW, primo quando intrat Lat. `as´ Pl he ware] *om.* Pl blynde] blinded T and] aftyr Pl seen ry3t no3t] my3t vneþe see Hu$_2$ 160 ⌜if . . . abyden⌝ L if] and M wil] while As a whyle] *om.* As moun son] *rev.* H$_6$ moun] *om.* Hu$_2$ son seen] H$_7$RBLB$_3$SrAPH$_6$CcMLdPlT, *rev.* HAsLwEW, sone sen BLdT son] *om.* H$_5$Hu$_2$ 161 þynges] þing H$_6$ aftere] H$_7$RAsSrLdPl, afterward LB$_3$Hu$_2$PH$_6$Cc, siþen HBH$_5$LwEMTW, sith A smale] modicas et subtiles Lat. and . . . hows] *om.* A syþen] after H$_5$ELd, after þat Hu$_2$ þat] H$_7$RLB$_3$SrAPH$_6$CcPl, euer *add.* HBH$_5$AsLwHu$_2$EMLdTW, omne quod est Lat. 162 it is] *om.* LB$_3$PH$_6$ 163 into] in Cc, to Ld his] wit and his *add.* M owen] *om.* AsLd conscience] for to sekyn Jesu *add.* CcM it] þatt LwLdW first mirke] *rev.*, *marked for trsp.* L first] *om.* As mirke sumwhat] *rev.* M mirke] H$_7$HRLSrPCcM,

hope in oure Lord and lene opon him, þat is, trost in God and clefe to
98r him bi desire, and abide a | while, and he schal haue liȝt.

For it fallyþ þerby as it doþ if a man had ben a grete while in þe sunne and after þat come sodeynly into a mirke hows þer no sunne schynyþ. He schuld first be as he were blynde and seen riȝt noȝt; bot if he wil abide a while he schal moune seen sone aboute him, first grete þinges and siþen smale, and siþen al þat euer is in þe hows. Riȝt so it is gostly: he þat forsakiþ þe luf of þe werld and comiþ to himself into his owne conscience, it is first mirk sumwhat and blynde to his siȝt. Bot if he stande stille and holde forþ with bisy prayynge and often þenkynge þe same wil to þe luf of Ihesu, he schal mown seen afterward grete þinges and smale þat he first knew nouȝt. þus semiþ it þat þe prophete behiȝt, saiend þus: *Orietur in tenebris lux tua, et tenebre tue erunt sicut meridies. Et requiem dabit tibi Dominus Deus tuus et implebit animam tuam splendoribus.* Liȝt schal spryngen to þe in mirknes; þat is, þou þat forsakist soþfastly þe liȝt of alle werldly luf and hidest þi þouȝt in þis mirknes, liȝt of blessud luf and gostly knowynge of God schal sprynge to þe. And þi mirknes schal be as midday; þat is, þi mirknes of traueilend desire and þi blynde trust in God þat þu hast first schal turne into clere knowynge and into sikirnes of luf. And þi Lord God schal gife rest to þe; þat is, þi flescly desires and þi pyneful dredis and doutes and wicked spirites þat han continuely beforhande traueiled þe, alle þese schul weiken and

derke $BH_5B_3AsLwAHu_2EH_6LdPlTW$ and] *canc.* L, *om.* B_3P 164 syȝt] liȝt As if he stonde] abide he Hu_2 and[1]] he *add.* Cc wyth] by BAs besy] bisyly Hu_2 prayere] $H_7RH_5LB_3SrAPH_6CcPl$, prayynge $HBAsLwHu_2EMLdTW$ often] oft tyme Hu_2 165 þenkynge] of *add.* LwH_6W, of *add.* M same] to þe *add.* As to . . . Jesu] of Jesu and to þe loue As Jesu] God RAPl, Jesu Christi Lat. schal] m- *add.*, *canc.* Sr moun] *om.* As seen afterward] *rev.* M 166 also] $H_7RLB_3SrAEPH_6CcPl$, *om.* $HBH_5AsLwHu_2MLdTW$ þus . . . þus (l. 167] *om.* As semeþ it] *rev.* E semeþ] semede B_3H_6 it] *om.* A þat] *om.* E þe Prophete/byhyȝt] *rev.* E 167 sayend þus] *rev.* LwW þus] Ysa. 58° *add.* LHu_2EPLd, Ysa. 57° *add.* B tue] *om.* As 168 Dominus] *corr. fr.* Deus L 169 splendoribus] þat is *add.* BEH_6 to þe] *om.* Cc in] *om.* $AsHu_2$ mirknes] $H_7HRLSrPCcMPl$, derknesse $BH_5B_3AsLwAHu_2EH_6LdTW$ 170 is] *om.* Pl forsakest] forsakeþ Pl sothfastly] *om.* T al] þe *add.* R lufe] likyng Pl 171 mirknes] $H_7HRLSrPCcMPl$, derknesse $BH_5B_3AsLwAHu_2EH_6LdTW$ lufe] *om.* R gostly knowynge] knowyngis gostely Pl God] Jesu M 172 mirknes] $H_7HRLSrPCcMPl$, derknesse $BH_5B_3AsLwAHu_2EH_6LdTW$ 173 myrknes] $H_7HRLSrPCcMPl$`W^{G}´, derknesse $BH_5B_3AsLwAHu_2EH_6LdTW$ blynd] blissed RAPl in God/þat . . . ferst] *rev.* Cc in God/þat þu hast] *rev.* B_3 hast] haddest BECcLd 174 ferst] it *add.* As, *om.* RAPl into[1]] þe *add.* As, a *add.* Cc clere] *om.* Ld into[2]] to þe As, *om.* H_5 175 God] Jesu Crist M, *om.* As to] vnto As is] *om.* As 177 befor] $H_7RLB_3SrAPH_6CcMPl$, beforhande $HBH_5AsLwHu_2LdTW$ trauayled] trobled M þese] þei Pl `weyken´ W^{G}, wax weike Hu_2H_6, wexe lythy Ld, wex febil APl, feblen B, worchen AsLwMW lesen] leuen As

and þou schalt be made so stronge þat þei schul not deren þe, for þou schalt be hyd in rest fro hem. And þan schal oure Lord Jesu fulfille þi soule with schynynges; þat is, whan þou art broȝt into þis gostly rest, þan schalt þou more esyly tente to God and noȝt ellys don but lufen him. And þan schal he with bemes of gostly lyȝt fulfille al þe myghtes of þi soule. Hafe þou no wundre þogh I kalle þe forsakynge of werdly lufe mirknes, for þe prophete calleþ it so, sayend to a soule þus: *Intra in tenebras tuas, filia Chaldeorum.* Go into þi mirknes þou doghtere of
f. 78v Chaldee; | þat is, þou soule, þat art as a doghter of Chaldee for lufe of þe werd, forsake it and go into þi myrknes.

þat in reformynge of a soule þe werkynge of oure Lord Jesu is departed in foure tymes, þat are callynge, ryghtyng, magnyfyenge and gloryfyenge. Capitulum xxviii[m]

Lo, I hafe seyd `þe´ a lytel, if þou coueyte for to be reformed in felynge, how þou schalt dispose þe toward in þi forth goynge. Nerþeles I say not þat þou mayght do þus of þiself, for I wote wel þat oure Lord Jesu bryngeþ al þis to þe ende whereso he wil. For he only þurgh his grace steryth a soule and bryngeþ it into his myrknes first and syþen into lyȝt, as þe prophete seyth: *Sicut tenebre eius, ita et lumen eius.* þat is: Ryȝt as þe lyȝt of knowynge and þe felynge of gostly lufe is of God, ryȝt so þe mirknes, þat is, þe forsakynge of werdly lufe, is of him. For he doþ alle: he formeþ and he reformeþ. He formeþ only by himself, bot he reformeþ vs with vs, for grace ȝefen and applyenge of oure wil to grace werkeþ al þis. And vpon what maner

178 and] þenne *add.* Hu$_2$ so] as M, *om.* AsLd deren] noye As, greue E, diseese Ld, or hurte *add.* T 179 in rest] thurgh a gracious shadwyng of Jesu CcM hem] him As Jesu] Crist *add.* LB$_3$P, *om.* RALdPlW 180 þat] and *prec.* H$_6$ broȝt into þis] sett in Ld into] to M þis] *om.* H$_5$As 181 ⌜þan . . . God⌝ L þan] `þou´ *add.* H$_6$ þou] *om.* H$_6$ more] þe *prec.* M tente] H$_7$HH$_5$LwHu$_2$PlTW, tend BLB$_3$AsSrACcMLd, take heed H$_6$ God] Jesu CcM 182 him] and beholdyn hym with reverence CcM schal he] *rev.* W with] bi LB$_3$PH$_6$ of] his *add.* B$_3$EH$_6$ lyȝt] miȝte M fulfille] fill Ld al] *om.* E þe] þi Sr 183 þi] þe Hu$_2$ soule] and *add.* As ⌜þou . . . þe⌝ L kalle] clepe AsLd forsakynge] forsakyn RM 184 mirknes] H$_7$HRLSrPCcMPl, derknesse BH$_5$B$_3$AsLwAHu$_2$EH$_6$LdTW calleþ] clepeþ AsH$_6$Ld so] *om.* B$_3$ to a soule/þus] H$_7$RLB$_3$SrAPH$_6$CcPl, *rev.* HBH$_5$LwHu$_2$TW to a soule] *om.* M þus] Ysa. 47° *add.* BLHu$_2$EPLdT, *om.* AsELd 185 in] *om.* R Chaldeorum] þat is *add.* EH$_6$, quasi diceret Lat. mirknes] H$_7$HRLSrPCcMPl, derknesse BH$_5$B$_3$AsLwAHu$_2$EH$_6$LdTW 186 Chaldee] Chaldes H$_5$ þat[2]] þou LB$_3$PH$_6$ art] calde *add.* As for] the Cc 187 it] *om.* Cc þi] *om.* Hu$_2$ mirknes] H$_7$HRLSrPCcMPl, derknesse BH$_5$B$_3$AsLwAHu$_2$EH$_6$LdTW, etc. *add.* Lw

Chapter 28 *title*: H$_7$RLB$_3$SrAEPH$_6$MLdTW How greet profite hit is to a soule for to be brouȝte þourȝe grace into þis liȝty mirkenes, and how a man nedeþ for to dispose him if he wol come þerto. Pl [*cf. above, Chapter 27 Title*] How a soule brouȝt þurgh grace into þis derknes shal afterward be brouȝt to liȝt of perfite knowyng. As Quod in reformacione

lesen mikel of her miȝt, and þu schalt be made so stronge þat þei schal not dere þe, for þu schalt be hid in rest fro hem. And þan schal oure Lord Ihesu fulfil þi soule with schynynges: þat is, whan þu art broȝt into þis gostly rest, þan schalt þu more esily tent to God and nouȝt elles do bot lufen him. And þan schal he with bemes of gostly liȝt fulfil
8v alle þe miȝtes of þi soule. Hafe þou no wonder þawȝ I calle | þe
forsakyng of werdly luf mirknes, for þe prophete calliþ it so, seiende þus to a soule: *Intra in tenebras tuas, filia Caldeorum.* Go into þi mirknes þou doghter of Chaldee; þat is, þou soule, þat art as a doghter of Chaldee for luf of þe werld, forsake it and go into þi mirknes.

[CHAPTER 28]

Lo, I hafe saide to þe a litel if þu coueite for to be reformed in felynge, how þu schalt dispose þe towarde in þi for`þ´ goynge. Nerþeles I say not þat þu maiȝte do þus of þiself, for I wote wel þat oure Lord Ihesu bryngeþ al þis to ende wherso he wil. For he only þurwȝ his grace stiriþ a soule and bryngiþ it into þis mirknes first and siþen into liȝt, as þe prophete seiþ: *Sicut tenebre eius, ita et lumen eius.* þat is: Riȝt as þe liȝt of knowynge and þe felynge of gostly lufe is of God, riȝt so þe mirknes, þat is þe forsakynge of werdly luf, is of him. For he doþ al; he formiþ and reformiþ. He formiþ only bi himself, bo`t´ he reformiþ vs with vs, for grace gifen and applynge of oure wil to grace wirkiþ al þis. And on what maner wise he doþ þat, Seint þoul reherciþ þus:

anime operacio Domini nostri Jesu Christi distinguitur in quatuor tempora, que sunt tempus vocacionis, tempus iustificacionis, tempus magnificacionis et tempus glorificacionis. Lat.   *om.* HBH$_5$LwHu$_2$Cc   *marg. note* Nota totum capitulum. H$_7$ 1 Jesu] *om.* LB$_3$PH$_6$ 2 þat] þe whilk R, which E   are] is AH$_6$LdTW   callynge] clepyng H$_6$Ld   4 þe] RSrACcMPl, `þe´ *d.h.* H$_7$, to þe HBLwHu$_2$LdTW, *om.* H$_5$LB$_3$PH$_6$, tibi Lat.    for] *om.* H$_6$Cc    `be´ H$_6$ 5 toward] *om.* RAsAPl   in] *om.* LB$_3$P   6 not/þat . . . mayght] *rev.* As   mayght] may LwLdW   þus] þis AsH$_6$ 7 Jesu] *om.* RAMPl, Dominus noster Jesu Lat.   þe] H$_7$RLB$_3$SrAPH$_6$CcPl, an As, *om.* HBH$_5$LwHu$_2$EMLdTW   `ende´ Cc, finem . . . et effectum Lat.    whereso] -`so´ Pl, wheresoeuere T   8 soule] for he steryþ a soule and *add.*, *canc.* Ld   into] to E   myrknes] H$_7$HRLSrPCcMPl, derknesse BH$_5$B$_3$As-LwAHu$_2$EH$_6$LdTW   9 syþen] after Ld, afterward Hu$_2$, thanne Cc   seyth] Ps 138° *add.* BLHu$_2$EPLdTW   10 þat is] *om.* H$_5$ þe^2] *om.* Pl   11 God] Jesu MW mirknes] H$_7$HRLSrPCcMPl, derknesse BH$_5$B$_3$AsLwAHu$_2$EH$_6$LdTW   þat is] and Sr þe^2] *om.* AEMT   12 `For he´ Cc    he$^1$] is al and he *add.* M    alle] for *add.* Cc    and . . . formeþ$^2$] *om.* As    he$^3$] H$_7$`L´B$_3$H$_5$SrAEPH$_6$CcLdPl, *om.* HRBLwHu$_2$MTW   He formeþ^2] *om.* Cc   13 bot] Boþe As   vs^1] *om.* Ld   with vs for] þurgh As   and] we *add.* Cc   14 applyenge] applyed H$_5$ of] grace *add.*, *canc.* B$_3$, *om.* Cc   grace werkeþ] gracious werchynge As   grace] God A   al] *om.* M   vpon] H$_7$LB$_3$AsSrPCcPl, on HRBH$_5$LwAHu$_2$EH$_6$MTW, in Ld, how and in As wyse he doþ þat, Seynt Poul reherseþ þus: *Quos Deus presciuit fieri conformes ymaginis Filii eius, hos vocauit; et quos vocauit hos iustificauit; et quos iustificauit hos magnificauit; et quos magnificauit hos glorificauit.* Þat is: þese þat God knew before þat schuld be made schapply to þe ymage of his Sone, þese he called, and þese he ryȝted, þese he magnyfyed, and þes he gloryfyed.

Þogh al þese wurdes moun be seyd of al chosen soules in þe logwest degre of charite þat are only reformed in feyth, nerþeles þei moun ben vnderstondyn more specially of þese soules þat are reformed in felynge, vnto þe whilk oure Lord Jesu scheweþ mykel plente of grace and doth mykel more besynes abowt hem. For þei are his owen sones specially þat beren þe ful schap and þe lyknes of his Sone Jesu. In þe whilk wurdes Seynt Poul departeþ þe werkynge of oure Lord f. 79^{r} into foure tymes. First is þe tyme | of callynge of a soule fro werdly vanite, and þat tyme is often esy and confortable. For in begynnynge of turnynge, swilk a man þat is disposed to mykel grace is so qwykly and so felendly inspyred and feleþ often so grete swetnes in deuocyon, and haþ so many terys in compunccyon, þat he þenkeþ him sumtyme as he were half in heuene. Bot þis softnes passeþ awey after for a whyle. And þan comeþ þe seconde tyme, þat is tyme of ryghtynge þat is trauauilous. For whan he bygynneþ for to go forth myghtyly in þe wey of ryȝtwysnes and setteþ his wil fully aȝen alle synnes withouten and wythinnen, and strekeþ oute his desyre to vertus and to þe lufe of Jesu, þan feleþ he mykel lettynge, boþe withinne himself of frowardnes and hardnes of his owen wil and fro withouten of tempta-

15 he doþ þat] *om.* As þat] it T reherseþ] seiþ As, and seiþ *add.* H$_6$ þus] Ro. 8° *add.* BLHu$_2$EPLdTW, *om.* As fieri conformes] *rev.* A 16 eius] sui A `et quos vocauit´ H$^{c}$, *om.* H°H$_5$AsH$_6$ hos$^{2}$] H$_7$HRBLB$_3$AsLwEPH$_6$CcMLdTW, et *add.* H$_5$SrAHu$_2$LdPl 17 et] *om.* LB$_3$PH$_6$ quos$^{1}$ . . . hos$^{2}$] *om.* As iustificauit] et *add.* H$_5$ hos$^{1}$ . . . magnificauit$^{2}$] *om.* RB$_3$ `et quos magnificauit´ H^{c}, *om.* H°H$_5$ hos^{2}] *om.* H$_5$ glorificauit] H$_7$RLB$_3$AsSrAEPH$_6$CcMPl, et *prec.* HBH$_5$LwHu$_2$LdTW, et *prec.* Lat. 18 þat is] H$_7$EH$_6$Cc, Ʒe seen As, *om.* HRBH$_5$LB$_3$SrLwAHu$_2$PMLdPlTW þese] Those R knew] knoweþ As þat] *om.* LwTW þe] *om.* B 19 ymage] liknesse M þese^{1}] þose RPl, hem Cc called] cleped AsH$_6$ and] H$_7$RLB$_3$SrAHu$_2$PH$_6$Pl, *om.* HBH$_5$AsLwELdTW þese^{2}] þose Pl, þeme Hu$_2$Cc þese^{3}] those RPl, þis A, hem Cc, whome Hu$_2$, and *prec.* RAHu$_2$Pl 20 þes] those RPl, þis A, thame Hu$_2$Cc 21 þogh al] H$_7$LB$_3$SrPH$_6$M, þawȝ HRBH$_5$SrLwAHu$_2$ECcLdPlTW moun] may Hu$_2$W 22 only reformed] *rev.* AsE moun] may AsHu$_2$W 23 ⌜þese soules þat are refor⌝med] L þese] those RPl, þe B$_3$, othir Cc `are´ Cc 24 vnto] to LwLdW Jesu] H$_7$LB$_3$PCc, Jesu Crist H$_6$, God HRBH$_5$AsSrLwAELdPlTW, *om.* M, Deus Lat. mykel] *one-letter eras. seq.* H$_7$ plente] *om.* Ld 25 abowt hem] *om.* As 26 sones] soulis Sr þat beren] þei ben As beren] beþ in H$_5$ ful] *om.* B$_3$MPl and þe lyknes] *om.* H$_5$ þe^{2}] *om.* E `Sone´ L Jesu] Christi *add.* Lat. 27 `Poul´ Cc 28 into] H$_7$RLB$_3$SrAEPH$_6$CcPl, in HBH$_5$AsLwHu$_2$MLdTW callynge]

Quos Deus presciuit fieri conformes ymaginis Filii eius, hos vocauit; `et quos vocauit´ hos iustificauit; et quos iustificauit hos magnificauit; `et quos magnificauit´ hos et glorificauit. Þese þat God knew bifore, þat schuld be made schaply to þe ymage of his Sone, þese he called, þese he riȝted, þese he magnified, and þese he glorified.

Þawȝ þese wurdes mowne be saide of al chosen soules in þe lowest degre of charite þat are reformid only in feiþ, nerþeles þei mown ben vndirstande more specially of þese soules þat are reformed in felynge, vnto þe whilk oure Lorde God schewiþ mikel plente of grace and doþ
99r mikel more bisynes aboute hem. For þei are his owne sones specially | þat beren þe ful schape and þe liknes of his Sone Ihesu. In þe whilke wordes Seynt Poul departiþ þe wirkynge of oure Lord in foure tymes. First is þe tyme of callynge of a soule fro werdly vanytee, and þat tyme is often esy and confortable. For in bygynnynge of turnynge, swilk a man þat is disposed to mikel grace is so qwikly and so felendly inspired and feliþ often so grete swetnes of deuocioun, and haþ so many teres in conpunccioun, þat he þinkiþ him sumtyme as he were half in heuen. Bot þis softnes passeþ awey after for a tyme. And þan comiþ þe secunde tyme, þat is tyme of riȝtynge þat is traueilous. For whan he bygynnyþ for to go forþ miȝtily in þe wey of riȝtwisnes and setten his wil fully agayne al synne withouten and within, and strecchiþ oute his desire to vertues and to þe luf of Ihesu, þan feliþ he mikel lettynge, boþ with[yn] himself of frowardnes and hardnes of his owne wil and fro withouten þurwȝ temptacioun of his enmy, þat

clepyng H$_6$Ld 29 vanite] vanites H$_5$AsMLd often] oft tymes Hu$_2$ esy] *om.* R in] H$_7$HRBLwHu$_2$ALdPlTW, þe *add.* H$_5$LB$_3$AsSrEPH$_6$CcMLd`W^{G}´ 30 to] of As qwykly] quykyde H$_5$ 31 felendly . . . feleþ] feruently inspyrynge and in felyng As feleþ] feelen R often] tymes *add.* Hu$_2$, þei han *add.* As in] H$_7$RBLB$_3$SrLwAHu$_2$EPH$_6$Cc-MLdPl, of HH$_5$AsLwTW, in Lat. 32 haþ] hauen As, he *prec.* LB$_3$PH$_6$ in] H$_7$HRLB$_3$-SrAHu$_2$EPH$_6$MPl, of BH$_5$AsLwCcLdTW, in Lat. compunccyon] contemplacion B he þenkeþ him] hym þenkiþ B him] *om.* RE 33 as] þat Sr softnes] sothfastnesse RPl, swetnesse Cc, aftirward *add.* H$_6$ awey] *om.* Lw after/for a whyle] *rev.* Pl after] sone *prec.* H$_5$, *om.* H$_6$ a] þe M 34 whyle] H$_7$RBLB$_3$SrAHu$_2$PH$_6$CcMLdPl, tyme HH$_5$As-LwETW tyme[2]] þe *prec.* AsW þat[2]] whiche H$_5$, and *prec.* CcM 35 bygynneþ] weneþ M for . . . forth/myghtyly] *rev.* A for] *om.* EM 36 ryȝtwysnes] ryȝtfulnysse Ld setteþ] setten HBAs, sett Ld, apponere Lat. fully/aȝen . . . synnes] *rev.* SrT fully] full W synnes] H$_7$RLB$_3$SrAPH$_6$CcMPl, synne HBH$_5$AsLwHu$_2$ELdW, manere synne T, peccatis Lat. 37 strekeþ] strenkith Cc, extendere Lat. oute/his desyre] *rev.* E oute his] forþe þe Ld and[3]] eke *add.* As to[2]] gode leuynge and gode werkes in *add.* M þe] *om.* AsPl of] *om.* As 38 boþe . . . frowardnes/and hardnes (l. 39)] *rev.* LB$_3$PH$_6$ withinne] -yn *canc.* H, with H$_5$LwW, of As, in *add.* Ld of] and LdPl, boþe *prec.* As 39 and[1]] of *add.* BAs ⌜and[2] . . . enemye⌝ (l. 40) Ld withouten] withoutforth TW of temptacyons] *om.* Cc of] H$_7$LB$_3$SrAsAPH$_6$, þurwȝ HRBH$_5$LwHu$_2$EMLdPlTW temptacyons] H$_7$RLB$_3$Sr-AEPH$_6$CcPl, temptacioun HBH$_5$AsLwHu$_2$MLdTW, temptacionibus Lat.

cyons of his enemye, þat he is often in ful grete turment. And þat is no wonder, for he haþ be so longe croked to þe fals lufe of þe werd þat he may not be made ryȝt and euene withouten grete beykynge and bowynge, ryȝt as a croked staf may not be made euene bot if it be kasten and beyked in þe fyre.

Þerfor oure Lord Jesu, seende wele what þynge is behouely to a froward soule, suffreþ it to be taryed and trauayled with sundry temptacyons, and for to ben wel examyned þurgh gostly tribulacyons, and til þat al þe rust of vnclennes myȝt be brent out of it. And þat schal be boþe withinne, of dredys and dowtes and [per]plexites, þat it schal nerhande fallen in despeyre, for it schal semen as it were forsaken of God and lefte al in þe handes of þe fende, owttaken a lytel priuey trust þat it schal hafe in þe godenes of God and in his mercy. For þat pryue trust oure Lord Jesu lefeþ in swylk a soule, go he neuer so fer fro it, be þe whilk þe soule is ay boren vp fro despeyre and safed fro gostly meschefes. And also withouten itself schal it be mortyfyed and pyned in þe sensualite, eyþer by dyuers seknes or by felable turmentynge of þe fend | (f. 79v) or ellys þurgh a priuey myȝt of God. Þe sely soule by felynge and berynge of þe wrecched body schal be so pyned, and it schal not wyten where ne how þat it schuld not moun suffren for to ben in þe body, ne [were þat] oure Lord Jesu kepeþ it þerin. And ȝete nerþeles had þe soule lefere for to ben in al þis pyne þan for to ben blended aȝen with þe fals lufe of þe werd, for þat were

40 ful] *om.* H$_5$AsPl þat] this Cc \`is´ Cc 41 for] þowȝ As haþ] haue As be/so longe] H$_7$RLB$_3$AsSrAHu$_2$PH$_6$CcMPlT, *rev.* HBH$_5$LwELdW þe$^2$] this RALdPl 42 ryȝt and] *om.* H$_6$ and euene] *om.* H$_5$LwLdW \`withouten . . . riȝt (l. 43)´ Ld, *om.* LwW grete] moche As beykynge and] *om.* As beykynge] beþynge BA, brekyng H$_5$ 43 bowynge] logwyng Pl, And *add.* As staf] stykke B \`not´ Pl euene] riȝt As bot if] *rev.* R bot] *om.* M it] he AsLwELdW 44 kasten and beyked] leyde As beyked] beþyd BALd, weykyd LwW 45 Jesu] *om.* Cc seende] sendeth LwW wele] H$_7$RBLB$_3$SrAHu$_2$PH$_6$CcLdPl, *om.* HH$_5$AsLwEMTW, bene Lat. þynge] *om.* M is behouely] behoueþ AsACc behouely] H$_7$HRSrHu$_2$Pl, behoful H$_5$LB$_3$LwPH$_6$LdTW, behouely and nedful B, nedeful M, spedful E, expediens and opportunum Lat. 46 suffreþ] he *prec.* Cc taryed and trauayled] H$_7$LB$_3$SrAPH$_6$Cc, *rev.* HRBH$_5$AsLwHu$_2$EMLdPlTW, vexari et turbari Lat. with] H$_7$LB$_3$SrHu$_2$PH$_6$Cc, bi HRBH$_5$AsLwAEMLdPlTW sundry] diuerse BB$_3$AHu$_2$Ld 47 and] *om.* M wel examyned] *rev.* M tribulacyons] temptacions As, temptacions and *prec.* H$_5$ 48 and til þat] H$_7$, til þat HRBSrLwEMLdPlT, til LB$_3$AsAPH$_6$Cc, and til H$_5$, to þe tyme þat Hu$_2$, þat LwW [til *canc.* Lw] þe] *om.* M brent] brouȝt B, euacuata et combusta Lat. 49 be] *canc.* Sr withinne of] with AsT dredys] H$_7$RH$_5$LB$_3$SrAEPH$_6$CcMLdPlW, drede HBAsLwHu$_2$LdTW, actus Lat. and^1] of As, of *add.* Pl dowtes] domes A perplexites] plexites H$_7$, perplexite As 50 nerhande fallen] *rev.* As nerhande] almost B in] H$_7$HRBH$_5$SrLwAHu$_2$EMLdPlTW, into LB$_3$AsPH$_6$Cc for . . . semen] ⌜and it shal seme⌝ H^c \`for´ W$^G$, and H$^c$LwEW schal semen] \`schal´ seme Sr, semeþ BH$_5$AsLwT 51 God]

he is often in ful grete turment. And þat is no wundre, for he haþ so longe bene croked to þe fals luf of þe werld þat he may not ben made riȝte and euen withoute grete beykynge and bowynge, riȝt as a croked staf may not be made euen bot if it be keste and beiked in þee fiire.

Þerfore oure Lord Ihesu, seend what þinge is behofely to a frawarde soule, suffreþ it to be traueiled and taried bi sundry temptaciouns, and for to ben wel examined þurgh gostly tribulaciouns til þat alle þe rust of vnclennes miȝt be brent out of it. And þat schal be boþ wiþin, of drede and doutes and perplexitees, þat it schal nerhand fallen in dispeire, ⌜and it shal seme⌝ as it were forsaken of God and left al in þe handes of þe fende, outaken a litel pryuey trust þat it `shal´ haue in þe godenes of God and in his mercy. For þat
99v pryuey | trist oure Lord Ihesu lefiþ in swilke a soule, go he neuer so ferre fro it, bi þe whilk þe soule is borne vp fro dispeire and saued fro gostly meschiefes. And also withouten itself it schal be mortified and pyned in þe sensualite, eiþer bi diuers seknes or bi felable turmentynge of þe fende or elles þurgh a pryuey miȝt of God. Þe sely soule bi felynge and berynge of þe wrecched body sal be so pyned, and it schal not witen where ne how þat it schuld not mown suffren for to ben in þe body, ne were þat oure Lord Ihesu kepiþ it þerin. And ȝit nerþeles had þe soule leuer for to ben in al þis pyne þen for to ben blynded with þe fals luf of þe werld. For þat were helle to swilk a soule; bot þe

Jesu M al] sumtyme M in] to A 52 trust] luste As þat] *om.* T it . . . trust (l. 53)] *om.* H_5As `schal´ H^{c} God] Jesu M in^{2}] H_7HRBSrLwHu$_2$EMLdTW, *om.* LB_3AsAPH_6CcPl 53 Lord] blissed *prec.* Hu$_2$ Jesu] *om.* LwMLdW in] to M swylk/a soule] *rev.* B_3Sr, *marked for trsp.*Sr go . . . ay (l. 54)] and þorugh þat is As 54 þe^{1}] a H_5 ay] H_7RLPCc, euer B_3AEH_6MPl, *om.* HBH_5SrLwHu$_2$LdTWWc, semper Lat. vp] alwey *add.* Sr 55 meschefes] H_7HRBH_5AsSrHu$_2$ECcMLdPlT, myschiefe LB_3LwAPH_6WWc, miseriis Lat. And] This payne felith the [a M] soule whanne Jesu withdrawith a lytil his gostly presens and suffryth the soule to fallyn in the self [to hitself M] *prec.* CcM also] so Cc itself] *om.* M schal it] H_7LB_3SrPCc, *rev.* HRBH_5AsLw-AHu$_2$EH_6MLdPlTW 56 pyned] pynese Ld, and *add.* Lw in] be As þe] *om.* LB_3AsEP, to *prec.* M eyþer] or A or] ouþer A 57 felable] fallable As, felably T, sensible A, oft H_5, cruel B, *om.* Cc turmentynge] tourmentyngis As, tourment W, turmentis LB_3PH_6 þe] *om.* Ld or] oþer As God] Jesu CcM 58 by felynge] *rep.* A and] or E be so] *rev.* LB_3PCc so] *om.* Hu$_2$ 59 and . . . how] `for . . . how´ L and] for `L´B_3EP where ne how] *rev.* Sr `where ne´ W$^{G}$, *om.* LwTW schuld] shall LwTW `not´ SrLwW^{G}, *om.* MW 60 for] *om.* AsH_6 were] where H_7M, nisi Lat. þat] *om.* H_7 `Lord´ Sr Jesu] God Wc, *om.* Sr$H_6$M kepeþ] kept $H_5$`Lw´W 61 þerin] inne Cc had/þe soule] *rev.* Cc þe soule] he H_6 for to] *om.* ACc for] *om.* H_6M þis] þat H_5 62 for^{1}] *om.* Cc aȝen] H_7RBLB_3SrAHu$_2$EPH_6CcMLdPl`W^{G}´, *om.* HH_5AsLw-TW with . . . lufe] in loue and synne M þe^{2}] H_7HRBH_5AsSrLwHu$_2$EH_6MLdTW, þis LB_3APCcPl were] was LB_3P, as it were *add.* Cc

helle to swilk a soule. Bot þe suffrynge of þis maner pyne is noȝt bot purgatorye, and þerfor he suffreþ it gladly and he wuld not put it awey þogh he myȝt, for it is profytable. Al þis doþ oure Lord in grete profyte of þe soule, for to dryfe it out fro þe rest [in] fleschly felynge and departen it fro þe lufe of þe sensualite, þat it myght resceyfe gostly lyȝt.

For after þis, whan þe soule is þus mortifyed and broght fro werdly lufe into þis mirknes, þat it haþ no more sauour ne delyte of werdly lykynge þan of a stre, bot he þynkeþ it bitter as wurmod; þan comeþ þe þridde tyme, of magnyfyen[g]e. And þat is whan þe soule is reformed in felynge in partye and resceyfeþ þe gifte of perfeccyon and þe grace of contemplacion, and þat is a tyme of grete rest. And aftere comeþ þe ferth tyme, of glorifyenge; þat is whan þe soule schal be fully reformed in þe blisse of heuene. For þese soules þat are þus called fro synne and þus ryȝted, or ellys on oþer maner lyke by dyuers assaynge boþe þurgh fire and water, and afterward are þus magnifyed, þei schul be glorifyed. For oure Lord schal ȝif hem þan fully þat þei here coueyted and more þan þei coude coueyten. For he schal reysen hem vp abouen al oþer chosen soules to þe euenhed of cherubin and seraphin, syn þei passed al oþer in knowynge and lufe of God here in þis lyfe.

þerfor he þat wil come to þis magnyfyenge, drede not þe ryȝtynge, for þat is þe weye. For oure Lord seith by his prophete a word of grete confort to al swilk soules þat are examined þurgh fire of tribulacyons
f. 80r þus: *Puer meus, noli* | *timere; si transieris per ignem, flamma non nocebit te*. þat is: My chyld, if þou passe þurgh fyre, drede not; for þe flawme

63 helle] hele As, supplicium infernale Lat. þe] þis H_6Ld, þat A þis] such MT maner] of *add.* AsLd noȝt] *om.* H_5M 64 purgatorye] a *prec.* Hu_2, quoddam purgatorium Lat. it[1]] *om.* AsSrCc gladly] *om.* M he[2]] *om.* As 65 þogh he] þurgh his As myȝt] til Jesu wole hymself *add.* M profytable] H_7, `so´ *prec.* $H_6$, so *prec.* Σ, tam vtilis Lat. Lord] Jesu *add.* Cc in] to B, for E, þe *add.* Ld 66 dryfe] and to drawe *add.* M out] *om.* M `fro . . . lufe (l. 67)´ W^G, *om.* LwW in] and H_7, of ET, in Lat. felynge] $H_7RLB_3AsSrAEPH_6CcMPl$`$T^G$´, lifynge $HBH_5LwHu_2LdTW^G$, sensacione Lat. 67 departen] departeþ $Hu_2$, departyng Cc, for to *prec.* E þe lufe] lust $LB_3PH_6$ þe[1]] *om.* M 69 fro] þe *add.* $H_5$AsM 70 `in´to] Pl mirknes] H_7HRLSrPCcMPl, derknesse $BH_5B_3AsLwAHu_2EH_6LdTW$ haþ] haue Cc, *om.* As more] loue *add.* As delyte] desyr Sr of] in no A 71 þan . . . stre] *om.* Cc of . . . þan] *om.* B_3 `a´ $W^G$, the LwW he] hym M, *om.* Cc 72 magnyfyenge] magnyfyende $H_7$ is] *om.* $Hu_2$ 73 and[2] . . . contemplacion (l. 74)] *om.* Cc 74 rest] `for þan is Jesu homly with a soule´ *add.* Lw, þanne is Jesu more homly wiþ a soule *add.* MW aftere] H_7, þat *add.* M, þis *add.* Σ 75 þat] þan T, and *prec.* Sr schal be] is As be fully] *rev.* AM 76 þese] those RPl, þe M are þus] *rev.* $AsHu_2$ þus] *om.* LB_3PH_6 77 called] ycleped As, clepid H_6 on oþer] anoþur AE on] in AsSrM oþer] anoþir CcT maner lyke] *rev.* Ld lyke by

suffrynge of þis maner pyne is nouȝt bot purgatorie, and þerfore he suffriþ it gladly and he wold not put it awey þawȝ he miȝte, for it is so profitable. Al þis doþ oure Lord in grete profit of þe soule, for to drife it oute fro þe reste in fleschly lifynge and departen it fro þe luf of þe sensualite, þat it miȝt receife gostly liȝt.

For after þis, whan þe soule is þus mortified and broȝt fro werdly luf into þis mirknes, þat it haþ no more sauour ne delite of werdly likynge þan of a stree bot he þinkeþ it bitter as wermode; þan comiþ þe þrid tyme, of magnifienge. And þat is whan þe soule is reformid in felynge in party and resceifiþ þe gift of perfeccioun and þe grace of contemplacioun, and þat is a tyme of grete rest. And after þis comiþ þe ferþe tyme of glorifiynge; þat is whan þe soule schal be fully reformed in þe blis of heuen. For þese soules þat are þus called fro synne and þus riȝted, or elles on oþer maner like be diuers assaiynge boþ þurgh fire and water, and afterward are þus magnified, þei schul
100r be glorified. For oure Lord schal þan gifen hem fully þat þei here | coueitid, and more þan þei couþe coueite. For he schal ⌜reysen hem vp⌝ abouen alle oþer chosen soules to þe euenhed of cherubyn and seraphyn, siþen þei passed alle oþer in knowynge and luf of God here in þis lif.

þerfore he þat wil come to þis magnifiynge, drede not þis riȝtinge, for þat is þe way. For oure Lorde saide be his prophete a worde of grete confort to alle swilk soules þat are examyned with fire of tribulacioun þus: *Puer meus, noli timere; si transieris per ignem, flamma non nocebit te.* þat is: My childe, if þu passe þurwȝ fire, drede not, for þe flaume schal not dere þe. It schal clense þe fro alle

dyuers] likli dyuersli LB$_3$PH$_6$ 78 assaynge] assailynges M þurgh] in A, *rep.*, *canc.* R and[1]] in *add.* A afterward] after M, þere *prec.* As magnifyed] in perfite loue of Jesu *add.* M 79 þei] þan *prec.* AsPl, þan schal *prec.* H$_6$, *om.* LB$_3$P schul] shulde W Lord] *om.* Ld schal] þan ferst *prec.* As ȝif hem/þan] H$_7$RAsACcMPlT, *rev.* HBH$_5$LwHu$_2$ELdW þan] *om.* LB$_3$AsPH$_6$ þan fully] *rev.* Sr 80 here coueyted] *rev.* Cc here] *om.* LB$_3$PH$_6$ and . . . coueyten] *om.* AsSr he] þei Hu$_2$T reysen hem vp] H$_7$⌜H^c⌝RSrAECcMPl, areyse hem LwW, rysen vp BH$_5$AsHu$_2$LdT, receyue vp hem LB$_3$P, receyue hem vp H$_6$, eleuabit eas Lat. 81 al] *om.* LB$_3$P oþer] *om.* A 82 syn] because Hu$_2$ passed] passe AsAM knowynge] alle oþer chosen soules to þe euenhed of cherubyn *add.*, *canc.* H and] of As lufe] louyng RCcMW of] *om.* Cc 84 come] here *add.* M to] vnto H$_5$ þe] H$_7$RLB$_3$APH$_6$CcMPl, þis HBH$_5$AsSrLwHu$_2$ELdTW 85 seith] H$_7$SrCcMW, saide HRBH$_5$LB$_3$AsLwAHu$_2$EPH$_6$LdPlT, dicit Lat. his] þe AsA 86 are] were B, þus *add.* H$_6$ þurgh] H$_7$LB$_3$SrPH$_6$Cc, with HRBH$_5$AsLwAHu$_2$EMLdTW, per Lat. fire] þe *prec.* MT tribulacyons] H$_7$LB$_3$SrAPH$_6$MPl, tribulacyon HRBH$_5$AsLwHu$_2$ECcLdTW, tribulacionis Lat. 87 þus] and it is *prec.* H$_6$, Ysa. 43° *add.* BHu$_2$ELdW 88 `te´ L, tibi Pl þat is] *om.* Cc fyre] þe *prec.* T drede . . . þe] *om.* B$_3$ drede] deed A, ne *prec.* As, þe *add.* H$_5$Cc, þu *add.* Ld schal not dere þe. It schal clense þe soule fro al werdly fylthe and mak it able for to resceyfe gostly fyre of þe luf of God. And þat nedeþ for to be don first, for, as I hafe before seyd, it may not ellys be reformed in felynge.

How it falleþ sumtyme þat soules begynnenge and profytende in grace han more feruour of lufe as by owteward toknes þan sum han þat are perfyte, and nerþeles ȝit it is not so. Capitulum xxix^{m}

Bot now seyst þou: How may þis be soth? For þer are many soules newly turned to God þat han many gostly felynges. Sum han grete compunccions for here synnes, and sum han grete deuocyons and feruours in preyers and han often sundri touchynges of gostly lyȝt in vnderstondynge, and sum han oþer maner felynges of confortable hete or grete swetnes; and nerþeles þese soules come neuer fully in þis restful myrknes þat I speke of, with feruent desyre and lastend þoght in God. Þan askest þou wheþer þese soules be reformed in felynge or noght: it semeþ ȝis, by as mykel as þei hafe swilk grete gostly felynges þat oþer men þat stonden only in feith felen not of.

Vnto þis I may seyn as me þenkeþ, þat þese gostly felynges, where þei standen in compunccyon or in deuocyon or in gostly ymaginacyon, are not þe gostly felynges whilk a soule schal hafe and fele in þe grace of contemplacyon. I sey not bot þat þei are sothfast and graciously ȝofen of God. Bot þese soules þat felen swilke are not ȝit reformed in felynge, ne þei kan not ȝit þe ȝifte of perfeccyon ne gostly

89 schal[1]] ne *prec.* As dere] noiȝe B$_3$T, anoye Ld, greue E, ne hurt *add.* Hu$_2$ þe[1]] but *add.* As schal[2]] not *add.*, *canc.* L þe soule] H$_7$LB$_3$SrPH$_6$, thi soule RACcMPl, þe HBH$_5$AsLwHu$_2$ELdTW, animam tuam Lat. al] *rep.* H$_6$ werdly] H$_7$, dedely As, bodily M, fleschly Σ, carnali Lat. fylthe] felthis M 90 it] þe E for] *om.* AsH$_6$LdW of[1]] and Ld God] Jesu M 91 for] *om.* Hu$_2$ before] aforn As 92 felynge] &c. *add.* Lw

Chapter 29 *title*: H$_7$RLB3SrAEPH$_6$MLdTW þat in þe reformynge of a soule þe worchyng of oure Lorde Jesu is departed in foure tymes, þat are callynge, riȝtynge, magnifiynge and gloryfiyng. Pl [*cf. above, Chapter 28 title*] þat certeyn soules þere ben þe whiche be grete trauaille omen into þis derkenes, and ȝit þei ben nouȝt reformed in felynge. As *om.* HBH$_5$LwHu$_2$Cc 1 How] þat *add.* Sr and] att W⌜T^{G}⌝ 2 grace] semen to *add.* ETW `feruour of´ T^{G}W^{G}, *om.* TW toknes] tokyngs Ld 3 sum] men *add.* LB$_3$P han] *om.* H$_6$ nerþeles] nouȝt forthy R it is] *rev.* H$_6$LdTW so] in soth withinne *add.* ALdTW, wiþinne *add.* E 5 be] *om.* As soth] *om.* T 6 newly] H$_7$LB$_3$AsSrPH$_6$CcMPl, new HRBH$_5$LwAHu$_2$ELdPlTW, nouiter Lat. to God] *om.* LB$_3$PH$_6$, to Jesu M þat] in hure begynnyng *add.* M Sum] men *add.* H$_5$As grete] manye M 7 conpunccions] H$_7$HRH$_5$LB$_3$AsAHu$_2$EPH$_6$MPl, conpunccioun BSrLwCcTW, contemplacyions Ld, compunccionem Lat. `for . . . deuocyons´ Pl for] of LB$_3$PH$_6$ deuocyons and feruours] deuocioun and feruent B and feruours] *om.* A 8 in]

fleschly filþ and make þe able for to resceife gostly fire of þe luf of God. And þat nediþ for to ben don first, for, as I hafe bifore saide, it may not elles be reformed in felynge.

[CHAPTER 29]

Bot now saist þow: How may þis be soþe? For þere are many soules new turned to God þat han mony gostly felynges. Summe han grete conpunccIouns for her synnes, and summe han grete deuocions and feruours in here praiers and often han sundry touchynges of gostly liȝt in vndirstandynge, and summe han oþer maner felynges of confortable hete and grete swetnes; and nerþeles þese soules come neuer fully in þis restful mirknes þat I speke of, with feruend desire and lastende þouȝt in God. Þan askes þu wheþer þese soules be reformed in felynge or nouȝt. It semiþ ȝis, in as mikel as þei haue swilke grete gostly felynges þat oþer men þat stande only in faiþ fele not of.

oo[v] Vnto þis I may say as me þenkiþ, | þat þese gostly felynges, wheþer þei standen in conpunccioun or in deuocioun or in gostly ymaginacioun, are nouȝt þe felynges whilk a soule schal han and felen in þe grace of contemplacioun. I say not bot þat þai are soþfast and graciously gifen of God. Bot þese soules þat felen swilk are not ȝit reformed in felynge, ne þei han not ȝit þe ȝift of perfeccioun ne gostly

H$_{7}$RLB$_{3}$SrAPH$_{6}$CcMPl, here *add.* HBH$_{5}$AsLwHu$_{2}$ELdTW, in Lat. preyers] preyer Cc and . . . han (l. 9)] *om.* Lw and] some *add.* M han often] H$_{7}$RLB$_{3}$SrAPH$_{6}$CcM, *rev.* HBH$_{5}$AsHu$_{2}$ELdTW often] ofte sithes M, *om.* Pl sundri] diuerse BB$_{3}$AHu$_{2}$T touchynges] techynges AsW 9 sum] men *add.* AsW han] manye *add.* M maner] *om.* M of] and As 10 or] H$_{7}$LB$_{3}$AsSrPH$_{6}$M, and HRBH$_{5}$LwAHu$_{2}$ELdPlTW, and of Cc, vel Lat. þese soules] þis soule LB$_{3}$PH$_{6}$, þuse M, they Cc come] came EH$_{6}$ fully in þis] to ful M 11 myrknes] H$_{7}$HRLSrPCcMPl, derknesse BH$_{5}$B$_{3}$AsLwAHu$_{2}$EH$_{6}$LdTW with . . . God] *om.* T þoght] love and *prec.* LwW 12 in God] *om.* As God] Jesu M, Domino Jesu Christo Lat. wheþer] where M þese] þose R, þo Pl 13 noght] non RBAT ȝis] þys Ld by] H$_{7}$, in Σ as mykel] *rep.* A as[2]] *om.* H$_{5}$ grete] *om.* M 14 þat[1] . . . felynges (l. 15)] *om.* Ld men] soules M of] *om.* B$_{3}$ 15 Vnto] To A seyn] þus *add.* H$_{5}$ þese] þis LB$_{3}$AsAP, those R, þoo Pl 16 in[1]] H$_{7}$HRBH$_{5}$AsSrAHu$_{2}$ECcMLdPlT, *om.* LB$_{3}$LwPH$_{6}$W 17 gostly felynges] *rev.*, *marked for trsp.* Pl gostly] H$_{7}$RLB$_{3}$SrAPH$_{6}$CcPl, *om.* HBH$_{5}$AsLwHu$_{2}$EMLdTW, spirituales Lat. whilk] þe *prec.* AsM schal] may M in] *om.* Pl 18 I . . . þat] *om.* M þat] *om.* LwW sothfast] good T 19 of] to Cc God] Jesu gracious M þese] those R, þe Pl ȝit] *om.* T 20 ne . . . of] *om.* Lat. kan] H$_{7}$, han Σ `ȝit´ Pl ȝifte] ȝiftes M ne] neþer As gostly þe] *rev.* Cc gostly] ne *add.* As

þe brennynge lufe in Jesu as þei may come to. And neuerþeles often it f. 80v semeþ oþerwyse, þat swilk soules felten more of þe lufe of God þan | oþer þat han þe ȝifte of perfeccyon; in as mikel as þe felynge scheweþ more owtward by grete feruour of bodily toknes, in wepynge and syghynge, preyenge, knelynge, and spekynge, and oþer bodily sterynge, so ferforth þat it semeþ to anoþer man þat þei were rauysched in lufe. And þogh me þenkyþ it not so, wel I wote þat þese maner felynges of deuocyon and compunccyon þat þese men felen are graciouse giftes of God, sent into chosen soules for to dragwen hem out fro werdly lufe and fleschly luste þat han longe tyme ben roted in here herte, fro þe whilk lufe þei schuld not be dragwen out bot by swilk felable sterynges of grete feruours.

Nerþeles þat þe feruour is so mikel in outward felynge is not only for mykelnes of lufe þat þei han, bot it is for lytilnes and weyknes of here soules þat moun not beren a lytel touchynge of God. For it is ȝit as it were fleschly, festned to here flesch, and neuer was ȝit departed fro it þurgh gostly mortyfyenge; and þerfore þe leste towchynge of lufe and þe lest sparcle of gostly lyȝt sent fro heuen into swilk a soule is so mykel, so confortable, so swete and so delytable, ouer al þe lykynge þat euer it felt before in fleschly lufe of erthly þynge, þat it is ouertaken with it. And also it is so new and so sodeyn and so vnkowþe þat it may not suffren for to beren it, bot it bresteþ and scheweþ it out be wepynge, sobbynge, and oþer bodily sterynge. Ryȝt as a costret þat is old and resceyfeþ new wyn þat is fresch and myȝty, þe costret

21 brennynge] perfite Ld   in Jesu] H$_7$HRH$_5$AsSrLwAHu$_2$CcLdPlTW, of Jesu LB$_3$EPH$_6$M, Dei Lat.   as . . . to] *om.* M   And] *om.* Cc   often] tymes add. Hu$_2$T 22 felten] H$_7$BLB$_3$Hu$_2$PH$_6$Pl, felen HRH$_5$AsSrLwAECcMLdTW, senciunt Lat.   þe] *om.* LB$_3$EPH$_6$ God] Jesu M   23 þat] þan B   ȝifte] ȝiftes M   \`scheweþ´ Cc 24 owtward] in hem *add.* RAPl   grete] *om.* LB$_3$P   feruour of] *om.* Hu$_2$   of] in A toknes] tokenyngis AsA   in] as in Hu$_2$   and syghynge] H$_7$RBLB$_3$SrHu$_2$PH$_6$CcMLdPl, \`siȝhyng´ T^{G}W^G, and singing A, *om.* HH$_5$AsLwETW, suspiriis Lat.   25 preyenge] *om.* Ld   and[1]] *om.* AM   sterynge] steryngis RH$_5$Sr, motibus Lat.   26 þat[1]] þeiȝe As þat[2]] *om.* Cc   were] H$_7$H$_6$, ay *add.* HBH$_5$LLwHu$_2$EPCcMLdTW, euer *add.* B$_3$AsAEPl, alwey *add.* Sr, semper Lat.   rauysched] restod M   27 þogh] ȝet B   it] H$_7$LB$_3$P, *rep.* Sr, it is H$_6$Cc, þat it is HRBH$_5$AsLwAHu$_2$LdPlTW   ⌜wel . . . and (l. 28)⌝ L   maner] of *add.* BH$_5$ 28 felynges] H$_7$, and feruour *add.* M, and feruours *add.* Σ, sensaciones et feruores Lat.   of] and H$_5$ compunccyon] causeth of hure synnes *add.* M   29 God] Jesu M   into] vnto M   chosen soules] gracious soules ychosen As   hem out] *rev.* As 30 fro . . . bot (l. 31)] *om.* Hu$_2$ fro] H$_7$RBSrAECcMLdPl\`W$^G$´, of HH$_5$LB$_3$AsLwAHu$_2$PH$_6$TW   and . . . luste] *om.* Lat.   luste] loue H$_5$   han/longe tyme] *rev.* H$_6$ han] hath CcM   longe tyme/ben] H$_7$RACcPl, *rev.* HBH$_5$LB$_3$AsSrLwEPMLdTW   ben] so SrM   31 schuld] schul Sr   out] *om.* Ld   32 \`felable´ W^G, feable W, sensible A sterynges] H$_7$RBLB$_3$AsSrAHu$_2$EPH$_6$CcMLdPl, stirynge HH$_5$LwTW, excitaciones Lat. 33 in] þe *add.* A, *om.* M   felynge H$_7$, schewynge Σ, ostensione Lat.   is[2]]

þe brennande luf in Ihesu as þei may come to. And nerþeles often it semiþ oþerwise, þat swilke soules felen more of þe luf of God þan oþer þat han þe ȝifte of perfeccioun; in as mikel as þe felynge shewþ more outwarde bi grete feruour of bodily toknes, in wepynge, preiynge, knelynge, and spekynge, and oþer bodily stirynge, so fer forþ þat it semiþ to anoþer man þat þei were ay rauisched in lufe. And þawȝ me þinkiþ þat it is not so, wel I wote þat þese manere felynges and feruours of deuocioun and conpunccioun þat þese men felen are gracious giftes of God, sent into chosen soules for to drawen hem out of werdly lufe and flescly lust þat han ben longe tyme roted in here herte, fro þe whilke luf þei schuld not ben drawen owt bot be swilke felable stirynge of grete feruours.

Nerþeles þat þe feruour is so mikel in owtwarde schewynge is not only for mikelnes of luf þat þei han, bot it is for litelnes and weiknes of here soule þat may not bere a litel touchynge of God. For it is ȝit as it were fleschly, festned to þe flesche, and neuer was ȝit departid fro it þurgh gostly mortifyinge; and þerfore þe leste touchynge of lufe and þe leste sperkle of gostly liȝt sent fro heuen into swilke a soule is so
1^r mikel and so | confortable, so swete and so delitable, ouer alle þe likynge þat euer it felt bifore in fleschly liif of erþly þinge, þat it is ouertaken with it. And also it is so newe and so sodeyn and so vncouþ þat it may not suffren for to beren it, bot bristiþ and schewiþ it out in wepynge, sobbynge, and oþer bodily stirynge. Riȝt as a costret þat is olde when it resceifiþ new wyne þat is fresch and miȝty, þe costret

H$_7$HRBH$_5$SrHu$_2$ECcMLd, nis As, it *prec.* LB$_3$LwAPH$_6$PlTW 34 mykelnes] gretnes Hu$_2$, excellence A for] *om.* Lw weyknes] wrecchednesse As, febilnesse APl 35 here] *rep.*, *canc.* E soules] soule RAsAEPl, animarum Lat. moun] H$_7$LB$_3$AEPH$_6$Cc, may HBH$_5$LwAsLdTW, þey may RMPl God] Jesu M 36 festned] festnynge As here] H$_7$, þe Σ neuer was] *rev.* H$_6$ 37 fro it] þerfro Sr þurgh] by LwW and] *om.* M 38 lufe] grace M sparcle] sparkelynge As, spark Hu$_2$ lyȝt] *om.* As into] to CcM 39 so mykel] *om.* Lat. mykel] grete Hu$_2$ so confortable] H$_7$LB$_3$SrPH$_6$Cc, and *prec.* HRBH$_5$AsLwAHu$_2$EMLdPlTW, tam confortabilis Lat. so swete] *om.* LwW delytable] delectable BLwHu$_2$W, delatable Ld 40 lykynge] likynges Hu$_2$ lufe of erthly] *rep.*, *canc.* L lufe of] or Cc, luste or Pl lufe] liif HE, of erþeli loue *add.*, *canc.* L þynge] þynges M it^2] *om.* Ld 41 with it] þerwiþ M, nec illum ferre potest vel sustinere *add.* Lat. it] his A, *om.* As so^1] *om.* LwW and^1] *om.* A 42 for] *om.* AsM it^3] H$_7$, *om.* Σ bresteþ] brekiþ B$_3$ ˋit^{2}ˊ W^G, *om.* LwW 43 be] H$_7$RLB$_3$Sr-APH$_6$CcMPl, in HBH$_5$LwHu$_2$ELdTW, of As, per Lat. sobbynge] and *prec.* B and . . . bodily] *rep.* As sterynge] sterynges BCcLd, motum corporalem Lat. ˋasˊ Cc a] the LwW costret] H$_7$HBH$_5$LB$_3$SrHu$_2$LdˋT^{G}W^{G}ˊ, costrel RAsLwAMPlTW, a flabette *add.* Hu$_2$ 44 old] yvsede As and^1] H$_7$RLB$_3$SrAPH$_6$CcMPl, whan it HBH$_5$AsLwHu$_2$-ELdTW þat] *om.* As costret] H$_7$HBH$_5$LB$_3$SrHu$_2$EPH$_6$CcLd, costrel RAsLwAMPlTW

bolneþ out and is in poynt for to klefen and bresten vntil þe wyn haþ boyled and spurged out al þe vnclennes; bot as son as þe wyn is fyned and clered, þan stondeþ it stille [and] þe costret hol. Ryȝt so a soule þat is old þurgh synne, whan it resceyfeþ a lytel of þe lufe of God, þat is so fresch and so myȝty þat þe body is in poynt for to clefen and to f. 81[r] bresten, ne were þat God kepeþ it hol; bot ȝit it | bresteþ out at þe eygne be wepynge, and at þe mouthe be spekynge, and þat is more for feblenes and weyknes of soule þan for mykelnes of lufe. For afterward, whan þe lufe haþ boyled out al þe vnclennes of þe soule by swilk grete feruours, þan is þe lufe clere and standeþ stille; and þan is boþe þe body and þe soule mykel more in pees, and ȝit haþ þe self soule mikel more lufe þan it had before, þogh it shew lesse outward. For it is now al hole in rest withinne, and not bot lytel in outward schewynge of feruour.

And þerfor I sey þat þese soules þat felen swilk grete bodily feruours, þogh þei ben in mikel grace, are not ȝit reformed in felynge, bot þei are gretly disposed toward. For I trow swilk a man, namly þat haþ ben gretly diffouled wiþ synne, schal not come to reformynge in felynge bot if he be brent first and puryfyed with swilk grete compunccyons goend before. Anoþer soule þat neuer was mykel diffouled with lufe of þe werd bot haþ ay ben kept fro grete synnes in innocence, may lyȝtlyere and more priuely, withouten grete feruour schewed outward, come to þis reformynge.

Þan is þis soth as I hope, þat swilk confortes and feruours þat a soule feleþ in þe state of begynnynge or of profytynge are as it were

45 bolneþ] borneþ Pl, swelleþ B out] *om.* Ld for] *om.* Ld to] *om.* Cc klefen and bresten] *rev.* R bresten] brekyn RB$_3$, to *prec.* As vntil] vnto B$_3$AsE, vnto þe tyme M, til AH$_6$Cc haþ] H$_7$LB$_3$SrHu$_2$PH$_6$CcPl, haue HRBH$_5$AsLwAEMLdTW, ebullieret Lat. 46 spurged] purged As out] *om.* Hu$_2$ þe[1]] H$_7$RLB$_3$SrAEPH$_6$CcMPl, *om.* HBH$_5$AsLwHu$_2$LdTW 47 þan] þat H$_5$ stondeþ it] *rev.* LwW and] in H$_7$R costret] H$_7$HRBH$_5$LB$_3$SrAHu$_2$EPH$_6$CcLd, costrel AsLwMPlTW hol] is *prec.* H$_5$ 48 old] wolde T whan] with As lufe] swete *prec.* Hu$_2$ God] Jesu M 49 so[1]] *om.* CcM so[2]] þe Ld `is´ B$_3$ clefen/. . ./bresten] H$_7$LSrPH$_6$CcM, *rev.* BHu$_2$Ld, cleue . . . breke HH$_5$B$_3$AsLwETW, breken . . . cleuen RAPl to[2]] H$_7$LwHu$_2$H$_6$CcW, for to HRBH$_5$AsAEMLdPlT, *om.* LB$_3$SrP 50 God] Jesu M, Jesu Christi Lat. kepeþ it] *rev.* Lw bresteþ] brekiþ B$_3$ 51 eygne] eye A be] þurgh As and[1]] *om.* M `þe´ Cc spekynge] preiynge M, and praying Cc is more] *corr. to.rev.* Pl 52 feblenes and weyknes] H$_7$, *rev.* Σ feblenes] feyntise A weyknes] lyþþernysse Ld soule] H$_7$LB$_3$SrPH$_6$Cc þe *prec.* HRBH$_5$AsLwAHu$_2$EMLdPlTW mykelnes] mekenesse As of[2]] *rep.* Ld, þe *add.* RMPl afterward] outwarde H$_5$ 53 þe[1]] H$_7$RLSrAPH$_6$CcMPl, *om.* HBH$_5$B$_3$AsLwHu$_2$ELdTW out/al þe vnclennes] *rev.* LwW out] of *add.*, *canc.* L 54 and[2]] *om.* As 55 boþe] *om.* AsPl þe[1,2]] H$_7$RLB$_3$AsSrLwAEPH$_6$CcMPlW, `þe´ H[c] *bis*, *om.* H°BH$_5$Hu$_2$LdT mykel more/in] *rev.* H$_5$Ld self] same A, *om.* LwH$_6$MTW

bolneþ out and is in poynt for to clefen and bresten vntil þe wyne haue boylid and spurged out al vnclennes; bot als sone as þe wyne is fyned and clered, þan standiþ it stil and þe costret hol. Riȝt so a soule þat is olde þurgh synne, when it resceifiþ a litel of þe luf of God, þat is so fresch and so miȝty þat þe body is in poynt for to clefen and for to breken, ne were þat God kepiþ it hole; bot ȝit it bresteþ out ate þe eiȝen by wepynge, and at þe mouþe bi spekynge, and þat is more for weiknes and feblenes of þe soule þan for mikelnes of luf. For afterward, whan luf haþ boiled out alle þe vnclennes of þe soule bi swilk grete feruours, þan is þe luf clere and standiþ stille; and þan is boþ body and soule mikel more in pees, and ȝit haþ þe self soule mikel more lufe þan it had bifore, þawȝ it schew lesse outwarde. For it is now al hole in reste within, and not bot litel in outward schewynge of feruour.

And þerfore I sei þat þese soules þat felen swilke grete bodily feruours, þawȝ þei ben in mikil grace are not ȝit reformed in felynge, bot þei are gretly disposid toward. For I trowe þat swilk a man, namely þat haþ ben gretly defoulid in synne, schal not be reformed in
1v felynge bot if he | be first brent and purified with swilk grete conpunccions goende bifore. Anoþer soule þat neuer was mikel defoulid with luf of þe world bot haþ ay be kepte fro grete synnes in innocence, may liȝtlier and more priuely, withouten grete feruour schewde outwarde, come to þis reformynge.

Þan is þis soþ as I hope, þat swilk confortes and feruours þat a soule feliþ in þe state of bigynnynge or of profitynge arn as it were his gostly

56 before] afore M shew] schewid LB_3P lesse] þe *prec.* As 57 ⌜is . . . in[1]⌝ L in[1]] þurgh As in outward/schewynge] *rev.* R in[2]] *om.* AHu_2 58 of] *om.* R 59 þese] þose RPl felen] *corr. fr.* han Cc bodily] *om.* AM 60 are] þei *add.* H_5AsSrHu_2 ȝit] *om.* Pl 61 are] ȝit *add.* As \`disposed′ Pl, ther *add.* Cc trow] $H_7$L$B_3$SrP$H_6$CcM, þat *add.* HRB$H_5$AsLwA$Hu_2$ELdPlTW namly þat] *rev.* As 62 wiþ] $H_7Hu_2$, in Σ come to reformynge] $H_7$RL$B_3$SrAP$H_6$CcMPl\`$T^G W^G$′, be reformed HBH_5AsWs-LwHu_2-ELdTW 63 ⌜bot . . . brent⌝ L if] *om.* H_5AsM be brent/first] *rev.* E brent first] H_7RBLB_3SrAHu_2PLdPl, browt first Cc, *rev.* HH_5AsLwH_6MTW, wiþ *add.*, *canc.* B_3, so *add.* Cc swilk] *om.* B_3 64 compunccyons] compunccion ACc, composicions As before] and *add.* AsCc Anoþer] And [-d *canc.*] oþer H neuer was] *rev.* EM neuer] *om.* T 65 diffouled] \`de′fouled Sr, foulede Pl lufe] þe *prec.* Cc haþ ay] *rev.* Cc ay ben] *rev.* Hu_2T ay] H_7HRH_5LPCc, euere BB_3AsLwAHu_2EH_6-MPlTW, alwey SrLd grete] *om.* As in] and E 66 innocence] innocensye B may] mowen As, be *add.* M priuely] priue M 67 schewed] shewyng M reformynge] in feling *add.* ECc 68 is þis] *rev.* Hu_2, it is Cc, is hit M hope] trowe A, trust Hu_2 þat[1]] quando Lat. [quod MaBnUt] feruours] brennyng M 69 þe] *om.* A of[1]] þe *add.* RAsPl or] oþer As of[2]] *om.* M

his gostly fode, sent fro heuene for to strengthe him in his trauelle. Ry3t as a pilgrym þat trauayleþ al day meteles and drynkles and is nerhand ouercomen with werynes falleþ at þe last to a gode in, and þer haþ he mete and drynke and is wel refresched for þat tyme; ry3t so gostly, a deuoute soule þat wil forsake þe lufe of þe werd, and wuld fayn lufe God and setteþ al his besynes þerto, prayeþ and trauaileþ al day bodily and gostly, and sumtyme feleþ no sauour ne confort in deuocyon. Þan oure Lord, hafend pyte ouer al his creatures, þat it schuld not peryschen for defaute ne turne into heuynes or grucchynge, sendeþ it amonge his gostly fode, and conforteþ it in deuocyon as he vowcheþ-sauf. And whan þe soule feleth ony gostly
f. 81^{v} confort, þan he holdeþ him wel payed | of al his trauaile and al his disese þat he had on þe day, whan it fareþ wel at euene by felynge of ony grace.

Þe self wyse falleþ it of oþer soules þat are profytende and ferforth in grace. Þei felen ofte-sythes gracyouse touchynges of þe Holy Gost in here soule, boþe in vnderstondynge and sy3t of gostly þynges and in affeccyon of lufe. Bot 3it ben þei not reformed in felynge ne þei are not 3it perfyte. For why, all swilk felynges comen to hem in þat state as it were vnwarly, for þei come or þei wyten it and gon fro hem or þei wyten it, and þei kan not come þerto a3en, ne þei know not where þei schuld seken it ne where þei schuld fynde it. For þei han 3it none homlynes with hem, bot sodeynly gone and sodeynly comen. Þei are not 3it made lordes of hemself be stablenes of þoght and lastende desyre in Jesu, ne þe eygh of here soule is not 3it opned to þe

70 his] *om.* H_6 sent] *om.* A him] ipsam animam Lat. 71 þat] H_7LB_3SrAEPH_6CcPl, *om.* HRBH_5AsLwHu_2MLdTW, laborans Lat. 72 nerhand] ne3e Hu_2, þan more As werynes] and *add.* As falleþ . . . last] at þe laste he falliþ H_6 þe] *om.* E 73 haþ he] *rev.* SrH_6Cc, haþ B_3 for] *om.* M þat] H_7RLSrPMPl, þe HBH_5B_3AsLwAHu_2EH_6CcLdTW ry3t] *om.* M 74 gostly] *om.* A deuoute] manes *add.* M wuld] wole M 75 lufe] serue T God] Jesu M prayeþ] he *prec.* H_5Cc, and *prec.* As 76 bodily and gostly] H_7RSrLwTW, *rev.* HBH_5LB_3AsAHu_2EPH_6CcMLdPl, corporaliter et spiritualiter Lat. no] non As, ne Cc sauour ne confort] H_7LB_3PH_6Cc, *rev.* HRBH_5LwAHu_2EMLdPlTW, feruoure As, saporem neque confortacionem Lat. 77 hafend] hadde As pyte] mynde M ouer] of BAHu_2MLd, on B_3 al] *om.* B creatures] creature B it] they Cc, talis anima Lat. 78 not] *om.* Pl ne] oþer As, ne H_6, nor M, to *add.* A 79 it²] among *add.* Cc 80 he vowcheþsauf] it plesiþ hym Hu_2 ˋgostlyˊ W^{G}, *om.* W 81 he holdeþ] H_7LB_3SrPH_6Cc, holdith R, *rev.* HBH_5AsLwAHu_2EMLdPlTW him] himself A payed] H_7HRBH_5SrLwHu_2ECcLdPlTW, apaied LB_3AsAPH_6M of . . . disese] de toto labore Lat. of] H_7RLB_3SrAEPH_6CcMPl, for HBH_5AsLwHu_2LdTW his¹] gostly *add.* Sr al²] *om.* As his²] H_7LB_3AsSrEPH_6Cc, þe HRBH_5LwAMLdPlTW *om.* Hu_2 82 he] H_7RLB_3SrAPH_6CcPl, it HBH_5AsLwHu_2EMLdTW had] haþ B day] wey A it] H_7HRBH_5SrLwAHu_2CcMLdPlTW, he LB_3AsEPH_6 83 grace] desuper sibi date *add.* Lat. 84 ˋþe

fode, sent fro heuen for to strengþ him in his trauaile. Riȝt as a pilgrym traueileþ alday metles and drynkles and is nerhande ouercomen with werynes falliþ at þe last to a gode in, and þer haþ he mete and drynke and is wel refresshed for þe tyme: riȝt so gostly, a deuoute soule þat wil forsake þe luf of þe werld, and wold fayn luf God and settiþ al his bisynes þerto, preieþ and traueiliþ alday gostly and bodily, and sumtyme feliþ no confort ne sauour in deuocioun. Þan oure Lord, hauend pite ouer alle his creatures, þat it schulde not perische for defaute ne turne into heuynes or grucchynge, sendiþ it amonge his gostly fode, and confortiþ it in deuocioun as he vouchiþsaue. And whan þe soule feliþ any gostly conforte, þan holdiþ he him wel paied for al his trauail and al þe disese þat it had on þe day, when it fariþ wel at euen by felynge of ony grace.

ʽThe selue wise falliþ it of oþer soules þat arne profitende and fer forþ in grace.ʼ Þei felen oft-siþes graciouse touchynges of þe Holy Gost in her soules, boþ in vndirstandynge and siȝt of gostly þinges and in affeccioun of lufe. Bot ȝit be þay not reformed in felynge ne þay
2r | are not ȝit perfit. For whi, alle swilke felynges come to hem in þat state as it were vnwarly, for þai comen or þei witen it and gos fro hem or þei witen it, and þai kun not come þerto agayn, ne witen not where þei schuld seken it ne where þei suld fynde it. For þei han not ȝit none homlynes with hem, bot sodeynly gon and sodeynly comen. Þai are not ȝit made lordes of hemself by stabilnes of þoȝt and lastande desire in Ihesu, ne þe iȝe of her soule is not ȝit opened to þe beholdynge of

. . . graceʼ H^{c}, *om.* H°H_{5}AsT þe] þese Ld, On *prec.* Hu_{2}Cc self] same AH_{6}Ld falleþ it of] yt fareth be Cc falleþ] faryþ BCcM ferforth] feruent Hu_{2} 85 ofte] off *prec.* Ld sythes] timus AHu_{2}TW, tyme H_{6} touchynges] touchynge H_{5} 86 in here soule] *om.* Lat. soule] H_{7}RB_{3}SrH_{6}Pl, soules HBH_{5}LAsLwAHu_{2}EPCcMLdT and[1]] in *add.* RH_{6} syȝt . . . þynges] þing of goostli siȝt B_{3}, gostly siȝttys As 87 in[1]] *om.* M affeccyon of lufe] affeccione per dileccionem Lat. ȝit] *om.* Cc ben þei] *rev.* SrCcPl þei not] *rev.* Hu_{2}Ld felynge . . . swilk (l. 88)] *om.* As felynge] fully *add.* RAPl, as muche as þey may be here *add.* M 88 ȝit] *om.* CcLd ⌜For . . . felynges⌝L why] *om.* M felynges] felyng Cc comen] comynge As in þat state] *om.* A 89 it[2]] *om.* T and . . . it (l. 90)] *om.* AsA and] þei *add.* R, also *add.* Cc gon] awey *add.* Sr fro hem] *om.* LdT or[2] . . . it (l. 90)] þei wete not how Sr 90 wyten] knowe Hu_{2} it] *om.* LdT þei[1]] *om.* H_{5} þerto aȝen] *rev.* H_{5} þei[2]] H_{7}RLB_{3}AsSrAEPH_{6}CcMPl, *om.* HBH_{5}LwHu_{2}LdTW know] H_{7}RLB_{3}SrAPH_{6}CcMPl, ʽwoten : knowenʼ W^{G}, witen HBH_{5}AsLwHu_{2}ELdTW 91 schuld[1]] H_{7}HBH_{5}AsLwHu_{2}ECcLdTW, schuln RLB_{3}-SrAPH_{6}MPl seken . . . schuld[2]] *om.* CcW schuld[2]] H_{7}HBH_{5}AsHu_{2}LdTW, schul RLB_{3}SrLwAEPH_{6}CcMPl þei[2]] *om.* As ȝit] H_{7}RBLB_{3}SrHu_{2}EPH_{6}CcMPl, it Ld, not *prec.* HLwATW, *om.* H_{5}As none] no E, *om.* LwAW 92 bot . . . stablenes (l. 93)] *om.* LwW gone and sodeynly] *om.* Cc 93 ȝit] *om.* MLd lastende] continual Hu_{2} 94 in Jesu] *om.* M in] to LB_{3}PH_{6}, off Ld, on E þe eygh] *om.* As soule] soulis Hu_{2}T not] *om.* LwCc ȝit] *om.* W þe[2]] *om.* LB_{3}P beholdynge of gostly þynges, bot þei neghen fast toward. And þerfor þei are not ʒit reformed in felynge ne þei han not ʒit þe ful ʒifte of contemplacyon.

On what manere a man schal han þe knowynge of his owen soule, and how a man schal setten his þoght and his lufe in Jesu God and man, o persone; and nerþeles ʒit is þe lufe þat is caused of beholdynge of him as God in man wurthyer and bettre þan þat þat is caused of him only as man. Capitulum xxx^{m}

It nedeþ to a soule þat wolde hafe knowynge of gostly þynges for to han þe knowynge first of itself. For it may not han knowynge first of a kynde abofe itself bot if it haue þe knowynge of itself. And þat is whan þe soule is so gedred into itself, and departed fro beholdynge of all erdly þynges and fro vse of þe bodily wyttes, þat it feleþ itself as it is in þe owen kynde withouten a body. Þan if þou coueyte for to knowen and seen þi soule what it is, þou schalt not turne þi þoght into þi body for to seken it and felen it, as it were hyd withinne in þi fleschly herte f. 82^{r} as þi herte is hyd and holden with|inne þi body. If þou seke so, þou schalt neuer fynde it [in itself; þe more þou sekest for to fynde and felen it] as þu woldest felen a bodily þynge, þe ferþer þou art þerfro. For þi soule is no body, bot a lyfe vnseable, not hyd and holden withinne þi body as a lesse þynge is hid and holden withinne a more, bot it is holdende and qwykende þi body, mikel more þan þe body is in myʒt and vertu.

95 gostly þynges] *om.* A neghen fast] neeʒ fasten Hu$_2$ toward] þere *prec.* As 96 þei are] *rev.* Hu$_2$ ʒit[1]] *om.* M not ʒit[2]] *om.* Cc ful ʒifte] fulfillynge As ful] loue H$_5$

Chapter 30 *title*: H$_7$RLB$_3$SrAEPH$_6$MLdTW How hit falleþ sumtyme þat soulis bigynnynge and profitynge in grace haue more feruoure of loue as bi outwarde tokenes þan sume haue þat are perfite, and ʒitt is hit not so. Pl [*cf. above, Chapter 29 title*] þat a soule muste ferst haue knowynge of himselfe beforn oþer þyngs absteyne him and withdrawen him fro þe vse of bodily wyttys, and how he shal fynde his myrrour in þe whiche ben besyde him. As 'How þou schalt se þyself.' H^{c} [*rubric, over plummet*], *om.* BH$_5$LwHu$_2$Cc 1 On . . . manere] How R þe] H$_7$RLB$_3$SrEPH$_6$M, *om.* ALdTW 2 þoght and his] owne E, *om.* LB$_3$PH$_6$TW 3 man] and *add.* ALd, in *add.* T and[2] . . . man (l. 4)] H$_7$RLB$_3$SrEPH$_6$M'T^{G}W^{G}', *om.* ALdTW[Pl Chapter30 Title] ʒit is] *om.* R is[1]] *om.* T^{G} þat is caused] *om.* R 4 in] H$_7$RSrM, and LB$_3$EPH$_6$T^{G}W^{G} man] is *add.* R wurthyer and] *om.* R 5 þat[2]] *om.* H$_6$ caused] *om.* R of him/only] *rev.* RM 7 to] *om.* HH$_5$AsLwW of] in M þynges] thyng Wc 8 þe] H$_7$, *om.* Σ knowynge first] H$_7$RSrACcMPl, *rev.* HBH$_5$LB$_3$AsLwHu$_2$EPH$_6$LdTWWc itself] himself H$_5$AsCcM For . . . itself (l. 9)] *om.* T knowynge[2]] a *prec.* R first[2]] H$_7$LB$_3$SrPH$_6$Cc, *om.* HRBH$_5$AsLwAHu$_2$EMLdPlTWWc, *om.* Lat. 9 kynde] knowyng Sr, thyng or of a *prec.* Cc abofe] *rep.*, *canc.* L itself[1]] it H$_5$, þe self Cc, *om.* As if] *om.* Sr it] he As þe] H$_7$RSrH$_6$CcPl, a LB$_3$P, *om.* HBH$_5$AsLwAHu$_2$EMLdTWWc itself[2]] the self Cc, first *add.* Wc þat] þis Pl 10 into] in As

gostly þinges, bot þei neiȝen fast towarde. And þerfore þei are not ȝit reformed in felynge ne þai han not ȝit þe ful ȝift of contemplacioun.

[CHAPTER 30]

It nediþ a soule þat wolde haue knowynge of gostly þinges for to haue first knowynge of itself. For it may not haue knowynge of a kynde aboue itself bot if it haf knowynge of itself. And þat is when þe soule is so gedred into itself, and departid fro beholdynge of alle erþly þinges and fro þe vse of bodily wittes, þat it feliþ itself as it is in þe owne kynde withouten a body. Þan if þu coueite for to knowen and seen þi soule what it is, þu schalt not turne þi þoȝt into þi body for to seken it and felen it, as it were hid within þin hert as þin hert is hid and holden within þi body. If þu seke so, þu schalt neuer fynde it in itself; þe more þu sekest for to fynde and felen it as þou woldest felen a bodyly þinge, þe ferrer þu art þerfro. For þi soule is no body, bot a lif vnseable, not hid and holden within þi body as a lesse þinge is hid and holden within a more, bot it is holdend and qwiknende þi body, mikel more þen þi body is in miȝt and in vertue.

itself] þe self Cc beholdynge of all] alle manere beholdynge of H_5 beholdynge] þe *prec.* AsCc all] *om.* M 11 vse of/þe] H_7RBSrAHu_2LdPlT, *rev.* HH_5AsLwEW, þe vse of þe LB_3PH_6Cc, þe vse of alle M feleþ] in *add.* As itself] the self CcM is] feleþ As 12 þe] his BH_5AsA kynde] *om.* E þan] *om.* As if] *om.* A for] *om.* M 13 seen] to *prec.* E þi soule] *om.* As soule] owne *prec.* M not] *om.* Cc þoght] with ymaginacion *add.* `Lw´MW (*canc.* $W^G$) into] to L$B_3$EP$H_6$ 14 it[1]] *om.* L$B_3$AsP$H_6$ felen] to *prec.* AsE as] þough *add.* T hyd] *om.* Pl in . . . withinne (l. 15)] *om.* M in þi fleschly] $H_7$L$B_3$P$H_6$CcM, þin HRB$H_5$AsLwAELdPlTW, `flesschly´ $T^G$$W^G$, þynne þyn B, þee in Hu_2, in carneo corde tuo Lat. 15 as þi herte] þat As hyd and holden] *rev.* E seke] hit *add.* MT 16 in . . . it (l. 17)] *om.* H_7 sekest] it *add.* RAPl fynde[2]] H_7HH_5LB_3AsSrLwEPH_6CcMTW, it *add.* RBA`Hu_2´LdPl 17 felen[1]] to *prec.* As it] *om.* M felen[2]] fynde M þynge] ymage H_5 þerfro] fro it RPl, ab eius cognicione Lat. 18 For] *om.* As is no] nys non As bot] hit is *add.* M vnseable] vnuisyble or *prec.* B and . . . holden (l. 19)] *om.* T and] ne LB_3EP holden] folden H_5 19 withinne] in `L´$B_3$P, *om.* $H_6$ þi] þe AsSr `as . . . more´ R þynge] ymage H_5 more] thyng *add.* Cc 20 `it´ Sr, *om.* Ld holdende] holden $Hu_2$ and] ys *add.* Ld qwykende] quykende $H_7$, quykneþ $Hu_2$, quykened withynne As, qwiknende Σ þi] of þe T mikel . . . is] *om.* As [*space left*] þe] $H_7$L$B_3$AsSrP$H_6$Cc, þi HRB$H_5$LwA$Hu_2$EMLdPlTW 21 in] of `L´B_3P vertu] H_7LB_3PH_6CcMPl, in *prec.* HRBH_5`As´SrLwAHu_2ELdTW þan if þou wilt fynde it, withdragwe þi þoght fro al bodyly þynge outward and fro mynde of þin owne body also and fro al þi fyfe wyttes, as mikel as þou mayght, and þenk of þe kynde of a resonable soule gostly, as þou woldest þenken for to knowen ony vertu, [as soþfastnes or meknes or ony oþer vertu]. Ryȝt so þenk þat a soule is a lyfe vndedly and vnseable, þat haþ myȝt in itself for to seen and knowen þe souereyn sothfastnes and for to lufen þe souereyn godenes þat is God. Whan þou sest þis, þan þou felest sumwhat of þiself. Seke þiself [in] non oþer place; bot þe more fully and þe more clerely þat þou mayȝt þenken on þe kynde and þe wurthynes of a resonable soule, what it is and what is þe kendly werkynge of it, þe better þou seest þiself. It is ful hard for a soule þat is rude and mykel in þe flesch for to han syȝt and knowynge of itself þus. For whan it wolde þenken of itself or of aungel or of God, it falleþ as tyt into ymaginacyon of bodily schap, and it weneþ by þat for to hafe þe syȝt of itself, and so of God and of oþer gostly þynges. And þat may not ben; for al gostly þynges are seen and knowen by vnderstondynge of þe soule, and not by ymaginacyon. Ryȝt as a soule seeþ by vnderstondynge þat þe vertu of ryȝtwysnes is for to ȝelden to ilk a þynge þat it oweþ for to han, riȝt so on swilk a maner by vnderstondynge may þe soule seen itself.

Nerþeles I sey not þat þi soule schal resten stille in þis knowynge, bot it schal by þis seken heyghere knowynge abofe itself, and þat is þe kynde of God. For þi soule is bot a myroure in þe whilk þou schal f. 82^{v} seen God gostly. And þerfor þou schalt first fynde þi | myrrour and

22 wilt] *one-word canc. seq.* H þoght] body B, selfe Wc þynge] þyngis AsCcMLdWc 23 also and] *rev.* As and^{2}] *om.* LwW fro al] þe vse of As 24 wyttes] also *add.* E as^{2}] euer *add.* T mayght] maye LwPlW þenk] þanne ȝif þou wole *add.* M of^{1}] H$_7$HRBH$_5$AsSrHu$_2$CcMLd, on LB$_3$LwAEPH$_6$PlTWWc þe] þy Ld a] þe H$_5$ 25 woldest] wolt M for] *om.* B$_3$ ony] euery As, oonly T as . . . vertu (l. 26)] *om.* H$_7$ 26 soþfastnes] soþfastnesses B or^{1}] oþer As, and R or^{2}] oþere As ony . . . vertu] such anoþer A oþer] HRBH$_5$AsLwHu$_2$EMLdPlTW, *om.* LB$_3$SrPH$_6$Cc 27 vndedly] vndely As and^{1}] *om.* RPl vnseable] vnseably W, inuisibele BA, vsable As þat] and HH$_5$AsLwW, que Lat. itself] hymself B, the self Cc for] *om.* H$_5$As 28 knowen] to *prec.* AsE souereyn sothfastnes] soþefast of souereingnys As soþfastnes . . . souereyn] *om.* Ld `and . . . souereyn´ L, *om.* M þe$^{2}$] *om.* E 29 God] Jesu CcM Whan] and *prec.* Sr þis] þus As þan] *om.* As þou felest] H$_7$LB$_3$AsSrPH$_6$Cc, *rev.* HRBH$_5$LwAHu$_2$ELdPlTWWc, seest þou M Seke þiself] *om.* As 30 in] and H$_7$ `non´ Sr 31 mayȝt] may H$_5$LwMTW on] H$_7$LB$_3$APH$_6$MT`W$^{G}$´, of HRBH$_5$AsSrLwHu$_2$ECcLdW. and] of AsCc, of *add.* H$_5$SrELd 32 what$^{2}$ . . . it$^{2}$] quid est [et que est *add.* R$_2$] eius operacio naturalis Lat. `is^{2}´ Cc þe . . . þiself] *om.* As þou seest] H$_7$LB$_3$SrPH$_6$Cc, *rev.* HRBH$_5$LwAHu$_2$EMLdPlTW 33 þiself] quantum ad naturam anime tue *add.* Lat. rude] boistus M þe] *om.* Hu$_2$ 34 itself] the self Cc, it LwW þus . . . itself (l. 36)] *om.* H°H$_5$As þus . . . itself (l. 35)] *om.* LwW whan] what E of^{2}] H$_7$RBSrHu$_2$LdPl, on

2^{v} þan if þu wilt fynde it, withdrawe þi þo3t fro alle bodily | þinge outwarde and fro mynde of þin owne body also and fro alle þi fife wittes, as mikil as þu mai3t, and þenke of þe kynde of a resonable soule gostly, as þu woldest þenken for to knowen ony vertue, as soþfastnes or meknes or ony oþer vertue. Ri3t so þinke þat a soule is a lif, vndedly and vnseable, and haþ mi3t in itself for to seen and knowen þe souereyn soþfastnes and for to lufen þe souereyn godnes þat is God. Whan þu seest þis, þan felist þu sumwhat of þiself. Seke þiself in none oþer place; bot þe more fully and þe more clerly þat þu mai3t þenken of þe kynde and þe worþines of a resonable soule, what it is and what is þe kyndly wirkynge of it, þe better seest þu þiself. It is ful harde for a soule þat is rude and mikil in þe flesche for to hafe si3t and knowynge of itself [þus. For whanne it wolde þenke of itsilf] `or of an aungel or of God, it falliþ as tite into ymaginacion of a bodily schappe, and it wenyth þerbi for to haue sy3t of itself', and so of God, and so of gostly þinges. And þat may not ben; for alle gostly þinges ere seen and knowen by vndirstandynge of þe soule, not bi ymaginacioun. Ri3t as a soule seeþ bi vndirstandenge þat þe vertue of ri3twisnes is for to 3elden to ilk a þinge þat it owiþ to haue, ri3t so on swilk a maner may þe soule see itself by vndirstandynge.

Nerþeles I sey not þat þi soule schal rest stil in þis knowynge, bot it schal bi þis seke hi3ere knowynge aboue itself, and þat is þe kynde of God. For þi soule is bot a mirrour in þe whilk þu schalt see God gostly. And þerfor þu schalt first fynde þi mirrour and kepen it bri3t

LB$_3$EPH$_6$CcMT, opon A 35 itself] hymself B, the self Cc `or . . . itself (l. 36)' H^c of^1] T aungel] H$_7$LB$_3$P, any *prec.* H$_6$M, an *prec.* Σ or^2] *om.* AM of^2] vpon T God] Jesu CcM it falleþ/as tyt] *rev.* H$_6$ as tyt] H$_7$RLAsSrLwH^{c}P, anon BB$_3$AHu$_2$H$_6$CcMPlW, alsone E bodily] H$_7$LwCcTW, a *prec.* Σ 36 by þat] H$_7$LB$_3$AsSrEPH$_6$`W^G', þerby RBLwH^{c}AHu$_2$CcMLdPlTW ⌜þe . . . oþer⌝ (l. 37) L þe] H$_7$RLB$_3$AsSrLw-H^{c}AEPH$_6$CcMPlW, *om.* BHu$_2$LdT itself] the self Cc God] Jesu M, et de seipsa *add.* Lat. 37 and] or APl of] H$_7$RAsSrAPCcMPl, so of HBH$_5$LwHu$_2$ELdTW, *om.* LB$_3$-PH$_6$, de Lat. oþer] H$_7$RBLB$_3$AsSrAHu$_2$PH$_6$CcMLdPlT`W$^G$', *om.* HH$_5$AsLwEW And$^2$ . . . þynges$^2$] *om.* As not] *om.* Pl þynges$^2$] *om.* B 38 and$^2$] *om.* RAsAMPl 39 `as' Cc a] *om.* T þat/þe . . . ry3twysnes] *rev.* Cc þe] sowle *add.* As 40 is] it *prec.* Cc for^1] *om.* ACc 3elden] eeld Ld, yeue LwW, yif and *prec.* Hu$_2$ to^2] *om.* As ilk a] H$_7$HRLAsP, euery BH$_5$B$_3$SrLwAHu$_2$EH$_6$MTW, yche a CcPl, eeche Ld for^2] H$_7$LB$_3$SrPH$_6$LdT, *om.* HRBH$_5$AsLwAHu$_2$ECcMPlW 41 on] *corr. fr.* and Lw, and *prec.* W, in ALd swilk a maner] þe same wise Hu$_2$, *om.* T swilk a] lyke Ld, the same Cc by vnderstondynge/may . . . itself] H$_7$RLB$_3$SrAPH$_6$CcMPl, *rev.* HBH$_5$AsLwHu$_2$ELdTWWc þe] a Pl itself] hymself B, the self Cc 42 schal] *om.* H$_6$ stille] *om.* AM þis] þyne As 43 seken] to *prec.* H$_6$ heyghere] her T itself] hymself B, the self Cc 44 kynde] cognicio Lat. of God] þat is Jesu M God] and þe sith of Jesu *add.* CcM þi] the W 45 God gostly] gostly good R, *rev.* Pl God] Jesu M first] *om.* E þi] þine owne As myrrour] and fynd yt *add.* Cc kepen it bryȝt and klene fro fleschly fylthe and werdly vanite, and holden it wel vp fro þe erthe, þat þou may seen it and oure Lord þerin also. For to þis ende trauailen al chosen soules in þis lyf in here menynge and in here entent, þogh þei hafe not specially þe felynge of þis. And for þat is it as I hafe seyde before, þat many soules bygynnend and profytend haue grete feruour and mikel swetnes in deuocyon and, as it semeþ, brennen al in lufe; and ȝit han þei not perfyte lufe ne gostly knowynge of God. For wyte þou wel, fele a soule neuer so mikel feruour, so mikel þat him þenkeþ þe body may not bere it, or þogh he melte al into wepynge, as longe as his þynkynge and his beholdynge of God is al in ymagynacyon and not in vnderstondynge, he come not ȝit to perfyte lufe ne to contemplacyon.

For þou schalt vnderstondyn þat þe lufe of God is on þre maner wyse. Al is gode, bot ilk better þan oþer. Þe first comeþ only þurgh feyþ, withouten gracyouse ymaginacyon or gostly knowynge of God. Þis lufe is in þe leste soule þat is reformed in feith, in þe logwest degre of charite, and it is gode for it suffyceþ to saluacyon. Þe secunde lufe is þat a soule feleþ þurgh feith and by ymaginacyon of Jesu in his manhed. Þis lufe is better þan þe first whan þe ymaginacyon is sterid be grace, and for why, þe gostly eyghe is opned in beholdynge of oure Lordes manhed. Þe þred lufe is þat þe soule feleth þurgh gostly syȝt of þe godhed in þe manhed, as it may be seen here; [þat] is best and most wurthy, and þat is perfyte lufe. Þis lufe a soule feleþ not til he be reformed in felynge. Soules bygynnende and profytende han not þis

46 it] þi mirrour M, *om.* As   47 holden] to *prec.* As   it wel] *rev.* Cc   vp] *om.* Pl   þe erthe] erþely As   may] mayst SrH$_6$Cc, mayȝt H$_5$Lw, miȝt A   þerin also] *rev.* EPl   48 to] vnto T, *om.* A   trauailen] *rep.*, *canc.* L   chosen] *om.* M   49 in] *om.* AsCc   `not´ H^c, *om.* H^{o}BH$_5$AsHu$_2$ specially þe] speciale As   50 þis] on [in M] this maner wyse *add.* CcM   for þat] þerfor HLwEW, for CcT   is it] H$_7$RBLB$_3$AsSrAHu$_2$PPlLd, *rev.* HLwEH$_6$CcMTW, is H$_5$ as I hafe] *om.* LwW   before] afore M   þat . . . soules] *om.* M   soules] *om.* As   51 bygynnend] in þe bygynnynge H$_5$Cc   and profytend] to profite T   grete] H$_7$RLB$_3$SrAPH$_6$CcMPl, many *prec.* HBH$_5$AsLwHu$_2$ELdTW, magnum Lat.   feruour] H$_7$RLB$_3$SrAPH$_6$CcPl, ferours HBH$_5$AsLwHu$_2$EMLdPlTW, feruorem Lat.   swetnes in] swete LwW   52 and[1]] *om.* As   brennen] brennynge AsLwAEW, þei ben T   þei not] *rev.* R   not] no B$_3$E   53 perfyte] perfiȝtly Hu$_2$W   God] Jesu M, in contemplacyon *add.* CcM   For . . . contemplacyon (l. 57)] *om.* Lat.   54 mikel[1]] grete H$_5$As, bodily *add.* M   feruour] bodily *add.* Cc   so mikel[2]] in *prec.* As, *om.* Ld   þenkeþ] H$_7$H$_5$LB$_3$AsSrPH$_6$CcM, þat *add.* HRBLwAHu$_2$ELdPlTW   55 `not´ L    he] it As    into] to H$_6$    wepynge] symtyme *add.* M    his þynkynge] hit þinkes M    56 his] *om.* As    of God is] `of God is most or´ H^c of God] of Jesu M, *om.* As   is] H$_7$H$_5$LB$_3$AsSrPH$_6$Cc moste or *add.* LwH^{c}Hu$_2$EPlTW, most *add.* RBAMLd   al] *om.* Ld   not] litel M   57 vnderstondynge] perfite *prec.* Pl   come] H$_7$HBLB$_3$SrLwHu$_2$PLdTW, comith RH$_5$AsACcMPl, cam EH$_6$ perfyte] þe *prec.* M   lufe] of God *add.* RAPl, of Jesu *add.* M   ne] no Lw   to[2]] vnto M   58 `of´ Cc   God] þis *prec.* Ld   on þre] þe heyȝer

and clene fro fleschly filþ and werdly vanitee, and holden it wel vp fro þe erþ, þat þu maiȝt seen it and oure Lorde þerin also. For to þis ende traueilen alle chosen soules in þis lif in here menynge and in here
03r entente, | þawȝ þei haue `not´ specially þe felynge of þis. And þerfor it is as I haue saide bifore, þat many soules bigynnande and profitande han many grete feruors and mikel swetnes in deuocioun and, as it semiþ, brennen al in luf; and ȝit han þei not perfit luf ne gostly knowynge of God. For wite þu wel, fel`e´ a soule neuer so mikel feruour, so mikel þat him þinkiþ þat þe body may not beren it, or þawȝ he melt al into wepynge, as longe as his þenkynge and his beholdynge `of God is moste or´ al in ymaginacioun and not in vndirstandynge, he come not ȝit to perfit luf ne to contemplacioun.

For þu schalt vndirstanden þat þe luf of God is on þre maner wise. Alle are gode, bot ilkon better þen oþer. Þe first comiþ oonly þurghe faiþ, withouten gracious ymaginacioun or gostly knowynge of God. Þis luf is in þe lest soule þat is reformid in feiþ, in þe lowest degree of charitee, and it is good for it sufficiþ to sauuacioun. Þe secunde luf is þat a soule feliþ þurgh faiþ and ymaginacioun of Ihesu in his manhede. Þis luf is better þen þe first when þe ymaginacioun is stirid bi grace, for whi, þe gostly eiȝe is opened in beholdynge of oure Lordes manhede. Þe þridde luf þat þe soule feliþ þurgh gostly siȝt of þe godhed in þe manhede, as it may be seen here, is best and most worþi and þat is perfit luf. Þis luf a soule feliþ not vntil he be reformid in felynge. Soules bigynnande and profitande haf not þis luf, for þei

As on] in MT maner] maneres H$_5$, of *add.* E 59 Al] H$_7$HRBSrLw-AHu$_2$EMLdTW, and *prec.* LB$_3$AsPH$_6$CcPl, þre *add.* H$_5$ is] H$_7$RLB$_3$SrAEPH$_6$MPl, are HBH$_5$AsLwHu$_2$CcLdTW, est Lat. gode] oo *prec.* H$_6$ ilk] H$_7$LAsP, ilkon HRLwM, ech B$_3$H$_6$Ld, ȝet eche Sr, iche one Hu$_2$W, eueryche H$_5$AET, eueryche on BPl, euery of hem Cc better] H$_7$HBSrHu$_2$PlT, is *prec.* RH$_5$LB$_3$AsLwAEPH$_6$CcMLdW, and worthier *add.* CcM, melior Lat. þe] For *prec.* Ld þurgh] wiþ LB$_3$PH$_6$, be Cc 60 ymaginacyon] ymacinacions BM God] Jesu M, Jesu Christo Lat. 61 is in] haþ M is[1]] only *add.* HH$_5$, *canc.* H soule] and þe lowest *add.* M in[2] . . . charite (l. 62)] *om.* M in[3]] and RACcPl 62 suffyceþ] hym *add.* M to] vnto R saluacyon] bi þe merci of God *add.* A lufe] *om.* T 63 feleþ] hit *add.* M and] strengþed and liȝtned M by] H$_7$LB$_3$Sr-PH$_6$CcM, in an As, *om.* HRBH$_5$LwAHu$_2$ELdPlTW, per Lat. Jesu] our Lord *prec.* M in] et Lat. 64 þis . . . manhed (l. 66)] *om.* A first] is *add.* M 65 and] H$_7$RLB$_3$Sr-AEPH$_6$MPl, *om.* HBH$_5$AsLwHu$_2$CcLdTW, *om.* Lat. for why] for Cc, *om.* M `is´ Pl  opned] open As  in] into louely M, þe *add.* As  oure Lordes] Domini Jesu Christi Lat.  66 is] H$_7$LB$_3$AsSrEPH$_6$PlT, *om.* HRBH$_5$LwAHu$_2$CcMLdW, est Lat.  þe] a LB$_3$APH$_6$  67 in] of As, and Sr  þat] RLw`H^c´AEPlW, þis LB$_3$SrPH$_6$, *om.* H$_7$H°BH$_5$As-Hu$_2$CcMLdT, hec Lat. is] it B best] þe *prec.* LB$_3$PH$_6$ 68 most] þe *prec.* LB$_3$PH$_6$ þat] *om.* M til] vntil HBLw, vnto AsEW, vnto þe tyme þat Hu$_2$, `bi´for Pl he] H$_7$HRH$_5$AsSrLwAHu$_2$EMLdPlT, it LB$_3$PH$_6$CcW be] clene from alle synnes and þat hit be *add.* M 69 felynge] and *add.* As þis] gostly *add.* M

lufe, for þei kun not þenken on Jesu ne lufen him godely, bot as it were al manly and fleschly aftere þe condicyons and þe lyknes of man. And vpon þat reward þei schapen alle here werkynge, in here þoghtes and in here affeccyons. þei dreden him as man, and wurchepyn and lufen him princypally in manly ymaginacion, and gon no ferþer, as f. 83r þus: if þei han don amys and trespast aȝens God, | þei þenkyn þan þat God is wroth with hem as a man schulde be if þei had trespast aȝens him, and þerfore þei falle doun as it were to þe foot of oure Lorde with sorwe of herte and cryen mercy. And whan þei han done þus, þei han a gode trust þat oure Lord of his mercy wil forgyfe hem here trespasse. þis maner of doynge is ryȝt gode, but it is not gostly as it myght ben. Also whan þei wil wurchipe God, þei presenten hemself in here þoght as it were in bodily ⌜lyknes⌝ befor þe face of oure Lord, and ymagynen a wondirful lyȝt þer oure Lord Jesu is; and þan þei reuerencen him, wurchepen him and dreden him, and fully putten hem in his mercy for to done with hem what he wille. And also whan þei wil lufen God, þei beholdyn him as a man, not ȝit as God in man, eyþer in his passion or in sum oþer þynge of his manhede; and in þat beholdynge þei felen here hertes mykel steryd to þe lufe of God.

þis maner of werkynge is gude and gracyouse, bot it is mykel lesse and logwere þan is þe werkynge of vnderstondynge; and þat is whan þe soule gracyously beholdeth God in man. For in oure Lord Jesu are two kyndes, þe manhed and þe godhed, oned togedre; for mankend was taken vp and in þe persone of Jesu is oned to þe godhed. þan ryȝt

70 kun] ne *prec.* As   not] non M   þenken on Jesu] þanken oure Lord R   þenken] *rep.*, *canc.* L   him] but *add.* R   `godely´ $\mathrm{W^G}$, God As, gostli $\mathrm{H_6}$, ne gostly *add.* Cc, and gostly add. M, goodly W   71 al] *om.* As   aftere] *rep.*, *canc.* L, only *prec.* M   þe[2]] $\mathrm{H_7HLB_3AsSrHu_2PH_6Pl}$, *om.* $\mathrm{RH_5ECcMLdTW}$ man] a *prec.* AsCc   72 vpon] on A   þat] þe $\mathrm{B_3}$ þei schapen] *rev.* M   þei] *om.* T   werkynge] wirchinges E   þoghtes] þo- *add.*, *canc.* Sr   73 here] alle *prec.* As   as] *om.* Pl   man] $\mathrm{H_7LB_3EPH_6CcLd}$, a *add.* $\mathrm{HRBH_5AsSrLwAHu_2MPlTW}$ and[2]] þei *add.* As   wurchepyn and lufen him] $\mathrm{H_7M}$, wurschipen him and luffen him $\mathrm{HRBH_5LB_3AsSrLwAHu_2ECcLdPlTW}$, honorant eum atque diligunt Lat.   wurchepyn and lufen] *rev.* T   74 manly] mannus AM   ymaginacion] of a man *add.* M   and . . . ferþer] *om.* M   as] but As, þan A   75 han . . . and] hadden M   han] hadde BLdT   trespast] trespasen As   God . . . aȝens (l. 76)] *om.* M   þenkyn] þenge B   76 hem] hym $\mathrm{Hu_2}$ a] *om.* H6   schulde] wold A   be] wiþ anoþir *add.*, *canc.* $\mathrm{B_3}$, *om.* W   77 þei] be $\mathrm{H_5}$ to] at Cc   foot] $\mathrm{H_7LB_3SrPH_6Cc}$, feet $\mathrm{HRBH_5AsLwAHu_2EMLdPlTW}$, pedes Lat.   78 sorwe] mekyl *prec.* Cc   cryen] cryinge $\mathrm{H_5Cc}$, [and Pl] þat he wele forgiuen hem here trespas *add.* RAPl   mercy] grace B, Jesu *add.* M   And[2] . . . trespasse (l. 80)] *om.* A   `han´ $\mathrm{W^G}$, *om.* RAsMPlW   þus] þanne *add.* M   79 gode] gret Cc   Lord] Jesu *add.* M   hem here] him al his As   here] Ws *back*   80 ryȝt] *om.* As   but] ȝet *add.* Cc   not] so good ne so *add.* CcM   81 ben] thurgh grace *add.* CcM   presenten] wilen *prec.* As   hemself] $\mathrm{H_7RLB_3SrAPH_6CcMPl}$, hem $\mathrm{HBH_5WsLwHu_2ELdTW}$, him As

kun not þenken on Ihesu ne lufen him godly, bot as it were al manly and flescly after þe condiciouns and þe liknes of man. And vpon þat
103v rewarde þei schapen al | here wirkynge, in here þouȝtes and in here affecciouns. Þei dreden him as a man, and wurschipen him and luffen him principally in manly ymaginacioun, and go no ferþer, as þus: if þei han don amys and trespast ageyn God, þei þinke þen þat God is wroþ with hem as a man schuld be if þei had trespast ageyn him, and þerfor þei falle doune as it were to þe feete of oure Lorde with sorwe of hert and cryen mercy. And when þei don þus, þei han a gode trist þat oure Lord of his mercy wile forgifen hem here trespas. Þis maner of doynge is ryȝt goode, bot it is not gostly as it miȝt ben. Also when þei wilen wurschipe God þei present hem in here þouȝt as it were bifore oure Lordes face in a bodily liknes, and ymaginen a wondirful liȝt þer oure Lord Ihesu is; and þan þei reuerencen him, wurscipen him and dreden him, and fully putten hem in his mercy for to don with hem what he wil. Also when þei wil luf God, þei beholdyn him, wurschipen him and dreden him as a man, not ȝit as God in man, eiþer in his passioun or in sum oþer þinge of his manhede; and in þat beholdynge þei felen here hertes mikel stirid to þe luf of God.

Þis maner of wirkynge is gode and gracious, bot it is mikel lesse and lowere þan is þe wirkynge of vndirstandynge, þat is whan þe soule graciously beholdiþ God in man. For in oure Lord Ihesu are two kyndes, þe manhede and þe godhede[, ooned togeder; for mankynde was takyn vp and in þe persone of Ihesu ooned to þe godhede]. Þan

82 it] they LwW in . . . lyknes/befor . . . Lord] H$_7$RLB$_3$SrAPH$_6$CcMPl, *rev.* HBH$_5$AsWsLwHu$_2$ELdTW, in corporali similitudine coram facie Domini nostri Jesu Christi Lat. ⌜lyknes⌝] *s.h.* H$_7$ þe face of oure Lord] H$_7$RLB$_3$SrAPH$_6$CcMPl, oure Lordes face HBH$_5$AsWsLwHu$_2$ELdTW þe] *rep.* A oure Lord] Domini nostri Jesu Christi Lat. 83 and[1]] þei *add.* H$_5$Ws a] off Ld wondirful] wonder As lyȝt] liȝ Pl Jesu] it *add.* As, *om.* M 84 him[1]] and *add.* LwHu$_2$W wurchepen him] *om.* B him[2]] *om.* LB$_3$PH$_6$Cc and dreden him] *om.* AsM 85 And] H$_7$RLB$_3$SrAPH$_6$Pl, *om.* HBH$_5$AsWsLwHu$_2$ECcMLdTW 86 wil lufen] loouen B$_3$As God] Jesu CcM him] H$_7$RBLB$_3$SrAHu$_2$PH$_6$LdPlT, wurschipen him and dreden him *add.* HH$_5$AsWsLwECcMW a] *om.* Hu$_2$EH$_6$ not . . . man[2]] *om.* CcM not] and *prec.* B God] but *add.* H$_5$Ws in] *corr. fr.* and E 87 or] eiþer T 88 mykel] gretly Hu$_2$ to . . . God] for to louen hym M þe] *om.* LP of] *om.* T 89 gude and gracyouse] *rev.* E gude and] *om.* LB$_3$PH$_6$ 90 and[1]] *om.* LB$_3$P and . . . man (l. 91)] *om.* M and þat is] *om.* Lat. and[2]] H$_7$RLB$_3$SrAPH$_6$CcPl, *om.* HBH$_5$AsWsLwHu$_2$ELdTW 91 þe] a LB$_3$PH$_6$ beholdeth God/in man] *rev.* H$_5$ in] and Cc man] secundum deitatem *add.* Lat. Jesu] God H$_5$Ws 92 manhed/. . ./godhed] *rev.* H$_5$WsH$_6$ oned . . . so (l. 95)] *om.* As `oned . . . godhed (l. 93)´ W$^G$, *om.* HH$_5$WsLwW oned] vnyed E, in o persone *add.* Cc 93 taken . . . is] and M and/in . . . Jesu] H$_7$BSrHu$_2$CcLdT, *rev.* RLB$_3$AEPH$_6$Pl`T^G´, et in persona Jesu Christi Lat. `is´ T^G, *om.* BHu$_2$LdT oned] vnyed E

as þe godhed is more souereyn and more wurthi þan is þe manhed, ryȝt so þe gostly beholdynge of þe godhed in Jesu man is more wurthi, more gostly and more medful þan beholdynge of þe manhed alone, wheþer he beholde þe manhed as dedly or as gloryfyed. And riȝt so be þe same skil, þe lufe þat þe soule felyth in þenkynge and beholdynge of God in man, whan it is graciously schewed, is wurthyere, gostlyere and more medful þan al feruour of deuocyon þat þe soule feleþ by ymagynacyon only of þe manhed, schew it neuer so mikel outwarde. For in reward of þat, þis is bot manly; for oure Lord scheweþ him not in ymagynacion as he is ne þat he is, for þe soule myȝt not þat tyme f. 83^{v} for frelte of fleschlyhed suffren | him so.

Nerþeles vnto swilk soules þat kun not þenken on þe godhed gostly, þat þei schuld not erren in her deuocyon, bot þat þei schuld be conforted and strengthed þurgh sum maner inward beholdynge of Jesu for to forsake synne and þe lufe of þe werd: þerfor oure Lord Jesu tempreþ his vnseable lyȝt of his godhed, and cloþeþ it vndire bodily lyknes of his manhed, and scheweþ it to þe ynnere eye of a soule and fedeþ it with þe lufe of his precyous flesch gostly. Þe whilk lufe is of so grete myȝt þat it sleþ al wikked lufe in þe soule, and strengtheþ it for to suffre bodyly penaunce and oþer bodily disese in tyme of nede for þe lufe of Jesu. And þis is þe schaduynge of oure Lord Jesu ouer a chosen soule, in þe whilk schadwynge þe soule is kept fro brennynge of werdly lufe. For ryȝt as a schadwe is made of a lyȝt and of a body, ryȝt so þis gostly schadwe is made of þe blissed vnseable lyȝt of þe godhed and of þe manhed oned þerto schewed to a deuout soule. Of þe whilk schadwe þe prophet seyþ þus: *Spiritus ante faciem nostram*

94 manhed] alone *add.* M 95 þe^{1}] *om.* Cc gostly] *om.* M wurthi . . . gostly] worthyer . . . ghostlyer W 96 more^{2}] *rep.*, *canc.* H_6 beholdynge] H_7LB_3Sr-LwAHu_2PMPlW, þe *prec.* HRH_5AsWsEH_6CcLdT þe] *om.* LdPl alone] of one As, *om.* M 97 he beholde] he beholdeþ As, þei beholdyn RAPl as^{1} . . . gloryfyed] *om.* M as^{1}] is As as^{2}] elles *prec.* T, *om.* H_5AsWs gloryfyed] et inmortalis *add.* Lat. 98 `þat' Cc  þe$^{3}$] $H_7RLB_3$SrAP$H_6$CcMPl, a $HBH_5$AsWsLw$Hu_2$ELdTW  and] or in Ld  99 God] $H_7$, þe godhed Σ [þe *om.* Ld], de deitate Lat.  in man] Christi Lat.  man] Jesu *prec.* M  whan] what As  `it' B_3Cc graciously] graciouse As is^{2}] it *prec.* As 100 þan] is *add.* M al] H_7, þe Σ, feruor Lat. deuocyon] þe *prec.* As þe soule] soules A 101 schew] sowe As, he *add.* H_5Ws so] fer neuer so *add.* H_5Ws, fer ne so As 102 `þat' $H^{c}$  þis is] nys As  oure] gode *add.* $Hu_2$  him not] *rev.* $H_5$Ws  103 in] þe *add.* Pl  for . . . so (l. 104)] *om.* Lat.  not] *om.* As  104 frelte] þe *prec.* M  of] $H_7RLB_3$SrAEP$H_6$CcMPl, þe *add.* $HBH_5$AsWsLw$Hu_2$LdTW  `fleschlyhed' W^{G}, flesshede BLwW him] H_7RLB_3SrAPH_6CcPl, it LwMW, *om.* HBH_5AsWsHu_2ELdT 105 Nerþeles] Therfore M vnto] to ALdT on] H_7LB_3SrEPH_6CcMPlT, of $HRBH_5$AsWsLwAHu_2LdW þe godhed] Jesu God M þe] *om.* Pl 106 gostly] *om.* B_3 `not' Cc her] *om.* T þat^{2}] *om.* Sr 107 strengthed] restreyned As þurgh]

riȝt as þe godhed is more souereyn and more wurþi þan is þe manhede, riȝt so þe gostly biholdynge of þe godhed in Ihesu man is more worþi, more gostly and more medful þan þe beholdynge of þe manhode alone, wheþer he behold þe manhed as dedly or as glorified.
104r And riȝt so bi þe same skil, | þe luf þat a soule feliþ in þinkynge and beholdynge of þe godhede in man, when it is graciously schewd, is worþier, gostlier, and more medful þen þe feruour of deuocioun þat þe soule feliþ bi ymaginacioun only of þe manhede, schew it neuer so mikel outward. For in rewarde of `þat´, þis is bot manly; for oure Lorde schewiþ him not in ymaginacioun as he is ne þat he is, for þe soule miȝt not þat tyme for freelte of þe fleschlied suffren so.

Nerþeles vnto swilk soules þat can not þinken of þe godhed gostly, þat þei schuld not erren in here deuocioun, bot þat þei schuld be conforted and strengþed þurgh sum maner inward beholdynge of Ihesu for to forsake synne and þe luf of þe werld: þerfore oure Lorde Ihesu tempreþ his vnseable liȝt of his godhed, and cloþiþ it vndir bodily liknes of his manhed, and schewiþ it to þe inner eiȝe of a soule and fediþ it with þe luf of his precious flesche gostly. Þe whilk luf is of so grete miȝt þat it sleep al wikked luf in þe soule, and strengþiþ it for to suffre bodily penance and oþer bodily disese in tyme of nede for luf of Ihesu. And þis is þe schadwynge of oure Lord Ihesu ouer a chosen soule, in þe whilk schadwynge þe soule is kept fro brennynge of werdly luf. For riȝt as a schadwe is made of a liȝt and of a body, riȝt so þis gostly schadwe is made of þe blessed vnseable liȝt of þe godhed and of þe manhede oned þerto schewd to a deuoute soule. Of þe whilk schadwe þe prophet seiþ þus: *Spiritus ante faciem nostram Christus*

in H_5Ws, be MT inward] rewarde As 108 Jesu] hym M, eius Lat. þe[1]] false *add.* Hu_2, *om.* W þerfor] and *prec.* As, *om.* M Jesu] *om.* Ld, Jesus Christus Lat. 109 vnseable] inuisible A cloþeþ] cloþid LB_3PCc, closeþ Pl vndire] colour of *add.* Hu_2 bodily] his *add.* M 110 it] hym M to] vnto AsW, into M ynnere] *om.* M a] H_7HRBH_5AsWsLwAHu_2ECcMLlTW, þe LB_3SrPH_6Pl and] as a man þat M 111 flesch] flesshely Ws gostly] *om.* M is . . . lufe (l. 112)] *om.* As is] *om.* H_5 `of´ Pl 112 myȝt] light *prec.*, *canc.* Sr in þe soule] *om.* BLdT and] *om.* As strengtheþ] strengþe R$H_5$LwW, strengthed $LB_3$P, makiþ it strong $H_6$ 113 disese] disesis CcT 114 þe] $H_7$AsMLd, *om.* Σ Jesu] Dei Lat. `is´ Cc schaduynge] schewyng As of[2]] *rep.* H_6 oure Lord/Jesu] *rev.* T Jesu] *om.* As ouer] of Pl a . . . soule] alle chosen soulys As 115 brennynge of] *om.* A 116 werdly] þe *add.* As a[2]] *om.* Cc of[2]] *om.* LB_3PH_6 117 þis] þe As shadwe] humanitatis Christi *add.* Lat. is] *om.* As of[1]] a liȝt þat is of *add.* As blissed vnseable] vnseable gostely Ld vnseable] inuisible A 118 oned] vnyed E þerto] and is *add.* LB_3PH_6, and *add.* As schewed . . . soule] that is gostly shewed þerto *add.*, *rep.*, *canc.* M schewed to a] *rep.* Ld schewed] schewith A to] vnto BHu_2T 119 schadwe] schadewede H_5, schadewynge As þus] Tren. 4° *add.* BLHu_2EPLdT nostram] vestram AsSrLd, `est´ *add.* Cc

Christus Dominus, sub vmbra eius viuemus inter gentes. Oure Lord Crist befor oure face is a spirit, vndir his schadue we schul lyfen amonge folkes. Þat is, oure Lord Jesu in his godhed is a spirit þat may not be seen of vs lyfend in flesch as he is in his blissed lyght. Þerfor we schul lyfen vndire þe schadwe of his blissed manhed as longe as we are here. Bot þogh þis be soth, þat þis lufe in ymagynacion be gode, nerþeles a soule schuld desyren for to hafe gostly lufe in vnderstondynge of þe godhed; for þat is þe ende and þe ful blis of þe soule, and alle oþer bodily beholdynges are bot menes ledende a soule to it.

Lo, þus kenned oure Lord Mary Magdeleyn, þat schuld be contemplatyfe, whan he seyd to hire þus: *Noli me tangere, nondum enim ascendi ad Patrem meum*. Touche me not, I am not ȝit steyed vp to my Fadre. Þat is for to seyn, Mary Magdaleyn lufed brennendly oure Lord Jesu befor þe tyme of his f. 84r | passion, bot hire lufe was mikel bodily, and lytel gostly. Sche trowed wele þat he was God, bot sche lufed him litel as God, for sche cowthe not þan; and þerfore sche suffred al here affeccyon and here þoght fallen in him as he was in forme of man. And oure Lord blamed hire not þan, bot preysed it mykel. Bot aftere, whan he was rysen fro ded and appered to here, sche wuld ha wurchiped him with swilk maner of lufe as sche did before; and þan oure Lord forbede hire and seyd þus: Touche me noȝt; þat is, sette not þe restynge ne þe lufe of þin hert in þat forme of man þat þou sest with þi fleschly eyghe only, for to resten þerin, for in þat forme I am not styed vp to my Fadere; þat is, I am not euen to my Fadere, for in forme of man I am lesse þan he. Touche me not so, bot

120 `sub´ Ws, *om*. H°H5As Oure] That is *prec*. EH$_6$ 121 is] as LwW his] þe Ld we schul] *rev*. A 122 folkes] H$_7$HBH$_5$LB$_3$AsSrWsHu$_2$EPH$_6$LdPl, folke RLwACcMTW Jesu] God *add*. M, Jesus Christus Lat. in his godhed/is a spirit] *rev*. M 123 vs] none þat is H$_5$Ws, his As schul] ssolde B 124 lyfen vndire] vndirstondyn Cc lyfen] be lyuyng Pl þe] his AM schadwe . . . manhed] umbra et protectione humanitatis sue, et numquam dimittere fidem dileccionm ec cogitacionem assiduum de eadem Lat. blissed] H$_7$H$_5$LB$_3$SrWsEPH$_6$Cc, *om*. HRBAsLwAHu$_2$MLdPlTW, *om*. Lat. 125 ymagynacion] of þe manhod *add*. CcM nerþeles] cum hac tamen et vltra hanc Lat. 126 for to hafe] *om*. As gostly] more *prec*. M in] and T 127 godhed] of Jesu, if he [hit M] myth come therto *add*. CcM þe[1]] *om*. As ende and þe] *om*. B ende] ful *prec*. As þe[2]] *om*. R þe[3]] a EM oþer] *om*. LwW 128 beholdynges] byhyoldynge As menes] menynge and As to it] þerto Sr to] vnto AsT it] I . . . fleschly (*lines* 153–5 *occur at this point in* Σ; *variants will be listed below*) 129 Lo] H$_7$, *om*. Σ kenned] H$_7$HRLSrLwAPPl`W^{G}´, tauȝte B$_3$AsWsHu$_2$EH$_6$CcMLdTW, techide H$_5$, lernede B þat] sche RAs 130 to hire] H$_7$LB$_3$SrAPH$_6$M, *om*. HRBH$_5$AsWsLwAHu$_2$ECcLdPlTW, sibi Lat. þus] Io. 20° *add*. BLHu$_2$EP, Io. 28 *add*. Ld, Ioh. 10 *add*. W nondum] non M 131 enim] *om*. LdPlT Touche] þat is *prec*. E am] man As ȝit] *om*. RA 132 for] *om*. LwW brennendly] well W 133 þe . . . of] *om*. Cc þe] H$_7$H$_5$LB$_3$AsSrWsAEPH$_6$MPlW, *om*. HRBLwHu$_2$LdT hire] þe M 134 and] H$_7$LB$_3$AsSrPH$_6$CcMW, *om*. HRBH$_5$WsLw-

104v *Dominus, sub vmbra* | *eius viuemus inter gentes.* Oure Lord Crist bifore oure face is a spirit; vndir his shadwe we schal lif amonge folkes. Þat is, oure Lord Ihesu in his godhed is a spirit þat may not be seen of vs lifande in flesche as he is in his blissid liȝt. Þerfore we schal lifen vnder þe schadwe of his manhede as longe as we are here. Bot þawȝ þis be soþ, þat þis luf in ymaginacioun be gode, nerþeles a soule schuld desiren for to hafe gostly luf in vndirstandynge of þe godhede; for þat is þe ende and þe ful blis of þe soule, and alle oþer bodyly biholdynges are bot menes ledend a soule to it. I sey not þat we sul departe God ⌜fro⌝ man, \`but we schul loue Ihesu, God and man´, God in man and man in God, gostly not fleschly.

Þus kenned oure Lord Marye Magdalen, þat schuld be contemplatif, whan he seide þus: *Noli me tangere, nondum enim ascendi ad þatrem meum.* Touche me not, I am not ȝit stied vp to my Fader. Þat is for to seyn, Marye Magdaleyn lufed brennandely oure Lord Ihesu befor tyme of his passioun, bot here luf was mikel bodily, litel gostly. Sche trowed wel þat he was God, bot sche lufed him litil as God, for sche couþe not þan; and þerfore sche suffred al here affeccioun and al here þoȝt fallen in him as he was in forme of man. And oure Lord blamed hire not þan, bot preisid it mikil. Bot aftir, whan he was risen fro ded and appered to hire, sche wold haue wurschipid him with swilk maner luf as sche did before; and þan oure Lord forbede hire and seid þus: Touche me not, þat is, sette not þe reste ne þe luf of þine hert in þat forme of man þat þu seest with þi flescly eiȝe only, for
105r to reste þerin, for in | þat forme I am not stied vp to my Fadir; þat is, I am not euen to þe Fader, for in forme of man I am lesse þan he.

AHu$_2$ELdPlT, et Lat. trowed] leuede BLd, beleued T bot] *om.* Lw 135 him] *om.* Lw litel] but *prec.* Ld as God] *om.* As cowthe] H$_7$HH$_5$WsLwAHu$_2$LdPlW, coude RLB$_3$AsSrEPH$_6$CcMT, nesciuit Lat. not] as *add.* T þan] þat tyme A sche] he As, *om.* B, Christus Lat. 136 al] *om.* Ld and] H$_7$RLB$_3$AsSrAPH6CcMPl, al *add.* HBH$_5$WsLwHu$_2$ELdTW, et Lat. fallen] feld As him] bodily *add.* M 137 þan] *om.* As it] hire SrELdPlT 138 Bot] For R, *om.* As aftere] afterward Hu$_2$Ld and] he *add.* LB$_3$PH$_6$ to here] *om.* Ld 139 him] here *add.* As of] H$_7$LB$_3$SrPH$_6$CcPl, *om.* HRBH$_5$AsWsLwAHu$_2$EMLdTW lufe] *om.* As 140 before] tofore H$_6$, aforn Cc þus] *om.* M 141 þe^1] þyn AsLwLdW restynge . . . lufe] loue . . . reste T restynge] H$_7$RLB$_3$SrAPH$_6$CcMPl, reste HBH$_5$AsWsLwHu$_2$ELdTW þe^2] þyne As, *om.* Ld hert] so as þou dedest *add.* M in þat forme] *rep.* A 142 þi] *om.* Ld fleschly] bodily M eyghe] eiȝen As resten] refresshen As 143 forme] of man *add.*, *canc.* Pl am (*bis*)] haue Ld vp] *om.* M þat^2 . . . Fadere (l. 144)] *om.* AH$_6$ my^1] H$_7$AsAM, þe HRBH$_5$LB$_3$SrWsLwHu$_2$EPH$_6$CcLdPlTW, Patri Lat. 144 forme] þe *prec.* AsT, þat *prec.* W lesse] *om.* As he] *om.* As Touche] þerfor he seid *add.* Cc me not] þou nouȝt me As bot] fidem tuam *add.* Lat.]

sett þi þoght and þi lufe into þat forme in þe whilk I am euen to þe Fadere, þat is þe forme of þe godhed, and lufe me, know me, and wurchip me as a God and man godly, not as a man manly. So schalt þou touche me; for syþen I am boþe God and man, and al þe cause why I schal be wurchipped and lufed is for I am God and for I toke þe kynd of man. And þerfor make me a God in þin herte and in þi lufe, and wurchip me in þin vnderstondynge as Jesu God and man, souereyn sothfastnes and as souereyn godenes and blissed lyfe, for þat am I. I sey not þat we schuld departen God fro man in Jesu, bot we schul lufe Jesu boþe God and man, God in man and man in God, gostly not fleschly.

Þus kend oure Lord hire as I vnderstonde, and also al oþer soules þat are disposed to contemplacyon and able þerto, þat þei schuld don so. Nerþeles oþer soules þat are not sotil in kynde ne are not ȝit made gostly þurgh grace, it is gode to hem þat þei kep forth here owen werkynge in ymaginacion with manly affeccions vntil mor grace come frely to hem. It is not siker to a man for to lefen a gode vtterly vntil he se and fele a bettre. Vpon þe same wyse it may be seyd of oþer maner
f. 84^{v} felynges þat are lyke to bodily: as herynge of delytable | songe, or felynge of confortable hete in þe body, or seenge of lyȝt, or swetnes of bodily sauour. Þese are not gostly felynges, for gostly felynges are felt in þe myȝtes of þe soule, principally in vnderstondynge and in lufe and lytel in ymaginacion. Bot þese felynges are in ymaginacyon, and

145 lufe] be mene of þat forme in which I am lesse þan my Fader *add.* M into] in E, to LwW in] into Sr þe^{1}] H$_7$RLB$_3$AsSrAPH$_6$CcPlT, *om.* HBH$_5$WsLwHu$_2$EMLdW euen] euere Sr þe^{2}] mi A 146 þe^{2}] *om.* As me^{1}] H$_7$HRBH$_5$AsSrWsLwAH$_6$CcPlTW, and *add.* `L′B$_3$Hu$_2$EPMLd me^{2}] *om.* A 147 a^{1}] H$_7$LB$_3$SrEPH$_6$CcM, *om.* HRBH$_5$AsWsLwAHu$_2$LdPlTW and] in M godly . . . man^{2}] *om.* As godly] gostli M, be gostly sith *add.* CcM, *om.* Lat. a^{2}] H$_7$HSrLwMPlW, *om.* RBH$_5$LB$_3$AsWsAHu$_2$EPH$_6$CcLdT manly] be [þe M] bodily sith *add.* CcM, *om.* Lat. 148 þou] nout *add.* CcM syþen] þat *add.* E boþe] *om.* H$_6$ 149 wurchipped and lufed] H$_7$RLB$_3$SrPH$_6$CcMPl, *rev.* HBH$_5$AsWsLwAHu$_2$ELdTW þe] *rep.* B 150 me] *om.* M a] *om.* Pl þin] gostli *add.* M 151 Jesu . . . man] *om.* M and] H$_7$RLB$_3$AsSrWsLwHu$_2$EPH$_6$MPlW, in HBH$_5$ACcLdT, in Lat. 152 as] H$_7$LB$_3$SrPH$_6$CcM, *om.* HRBH$_5$AsWsLwAHu$_2$ELdPlTW souereyn . . . and^{2}] *om.* T and^{2} . . . lyfe] oned to man M lyfe] lawe As 153 þat^{1}] totum istud Lat. am I] *rev.* H$_6$MTW, I am I Lw I sey . . . fleschly (l. 155)] *see above*, l. 128 it. þat^{2}] *om.* R we schuld] þu schalt AM schuld] H$_7$LB$_3$AHu$_2$PH$_6$CcMLdPlTW, sul HRBH$_5$AsSrWsLwE, refuse the manhede of Jesu and *add.* `Lw′CcMW fro . . . man$^{2}$ (l. 154)] *om.* As ⌜fro⌝H$^{c}$, and H$_5$AsWs in . . . man$^{1}$ (l. 154)] *canc.* Lw in . . . man$^{2}$]. *om.* H$^{\circ}$ in Jesu] H$_7$RBLB$_3$SrAHu$_2$EPH$_6$CcLdPlT, *om.* HH$_5$WsLwACcMW, in Domino Jesu Christo Lat. bot . . . man$^{2}$ (l. 154)] `but . . . man′ H^{c} 154 we . . . fleschly (l. 155)] þou shalt in Jesu man beholde, drede, wondir and loue gostly þe godhede, and so shalt þou without departyng loue God in man, and both God and man. `Lw′MW schul] schulde SrPl, in al oure herte *add.* H$_5$Ws Jesu . . . man^{2}] *om.* H$_5$WsLwW

Touche me not so, bot sett þi þoȝt and þi luf into þat forme in whilk I am euen to þe Fader, þat is þe forme of þe godhed, and lufe me, knowe me, and worschip me as God and man godly, not as man manly. So schalt þu touche me; for siþen I am boþ God and man, and alle þe cause whi I schal be lufed and worsciped is for I am God and for I toke þe kynde of man. And þerfore make me a God in þin herte and in þi luf, and worschip me in þin vndirstandynge as Ihesu God in man, souereyn soþfastnes and souereyn godnes and blissid lif, for þat am I. And þus kenned oure Lord hire as I vndirstande, and also al oþer soules þat are disposid to contemplacioun and able þerto, þat þei schuld do so.

Nerþeles oþer soules þat are not sotil in kynde ne are not ȝit made gostly þurgh grace, it is gode to hem þat þei kepe forþ here owne wirkynge in ymaginacioun with manly affeccioun vntil more grace come freely to hem. It is not siker to a man to leuen oo gode vtterly til he see and fele a better. Vpon þe self wise it may be saide of oþer maner felynges þat are like to bodily: as herynge of delitable songe, or felynge of confortable hete in þe body, or seenge of liȝt, or swetnes of bodily sauour. Þese are not gostly felynges, for gostly felynges are felt in þe miȝtes of þe soule, principally in vndirstandynge and lufe and litel \`in´ ymaginacioun. Bot þese felynges are in ymaginacioun, and

boþe] *om.* BHu$_2$LdT, *om.* Lat. God[2] . . . God[3]] *om.* R God[2] . . . man[2]] *om.* Pl and . . . fleschly] *canc.* Lw man[3]] *om.* As 155 gostly not fleschly] *om.* Lat. not] and *prec.* AsAW 156 þus] H$_7$LB$_3$SrPH$_6$CcM, And *prec.* HRBH$_5$AsWsLwAHu$_2$ELdPlTW, Sic Lat. kend] H$_7$HRLSrLwP, taught H$_5$B$_3$AsWsAEH$_6$CcMLdTW, teched Hu$_2$, lernede B hire] Mariam Magdalenam Lat. al] *om.* Cc 157 able] yabled As don so] *rev.* R 158 sotil . . . not] *om.* Hu2 \`in . . . þurgh (l. 159)´ *d.h.* Ld kynde] nor be not yet made sotel in kynde *add.* M ne . . . not] *om.* R ne] nor E \`ȝit´ Ld made] *om.* B 159 kep] ȝet *add.* M owen] *om.* B$_3$ 160 affeccions] H$_7$RLB$_3$SrAPH$_6$CcPl, affeccioun HBH$_5$AsWsLwHu$_2$EMLdTW, affeccionibus Lat. vntil] til H$_5$WsAT, vnto B$_3$AsMW, vnto þe tyme þat Hu$_2$ 161 to[1]] *om.* A a[1] . . . gode] men þat louen one God As for] H$_7$RBLB$_3$SrAHu$_2$PH$_6$CcMLdPl, *om.* HH$_5$WsLwTW gode] werk *add.* LB$_3$EPH$_6$\`T^{G}W^G´, thynge *add.* LwCcTW, dede of deuocion H$_5$Ws, donum bonum Lat. vtterly] *om.* H$_5$Ws vntil] H$_7$RLB$_3$SrPH$_6$Cc, til HRBH$_5$AsWsLwAMLdPlTW, vnto B$_3$E, to Hu$_2$ 162 and fele] *om.* Lat. fele] se Cc Vpon] On M, In Ld, himselfe on *add.* As same] H$_7$BH$_5$LB$_3$SrWsAHu$_2$EPCcT, self HRAsLwMLdPlW it] *om.* Ld oþer] an *prec.*, *canc.* Cc maner] *rep.* A 163 bodily] þe body As, þing *add.* A, þinges *add.* LB$_3$EPH$_6$, felynges *add.* Wc of] a *add.* H$_6$ delytable] H$_7$HRH$_5$LB$_3$AsSrWsAEPH$_6$CcMPl, delectable BLwHu$_2$LdTW songe] songis Ld 164 of[1]] or R confortable] *om.* Pl or[1]] *om.* LwW or[2]] of *add.* As 165 þese] Those R, þoo Pl felynges[1]] felyng Cc for . . . felynges (l. 168)] *om.* As 166 in[1]] off Ld myȝtes] miȝt M soule] and *add.* H$_6$ in[3]] H$_7$RLB$_3$AsSrAPH$_6$CcPl, *om.* HBH$_5$WsLwHu$_2$EMLdTW 167 lytel/in] *rev.* Cc lytel] a *prec.* H$_6$ \`in[1]´ H$^c$, *om.* H$^\circ$H$_5$WsLd \`But . . . þerfor´ (l. 168)] Hu$_2$ þese] those R are] felt in the myȝtes of the body [body *corr. fr.* sowle Lw] *add.* LwW in[2]] *om.* Sr ymagynacion] ymaginaciouns H$_5$Ws, ymaginacione sensuum corporalium Lat.

þerfor þei are not gostly felynges, bot whan þei arn best and most trewe ȝit are þei bot owtward toknes of þe inly grace þat is felt in þe myȝtes of þe soule. Þis may openly be proued be Holy Writte seyend þus: *Aparuerunt apostolis dispertite lingue tanquam ignis, seditque supra singulos eorum Spiritus Sanctus*. Þe Holy Gost apered to þe apostles in þe day of Pentecost in liknes of brennend tonges and enflawmed alle here hertes and satte vpon ilk of hem. Now soþ it is, þe Holy Gost, þat is God in himself vnseable, was not þat fyre ne þo tunges þat were seen, ne þat brennynge þat was felt bodily, bot he was vnseably felt in þe myȝtes of here soules. For he lyȝtned here reson and kyndled here affeccyon þurgh his blissed presence, so clerly and so brennendly þat þei hadden sodeynly þe gostly knowyng of sothfastnes and þe perfeccyon of lufe, as oure Lord behyȝt hem, seyend þus: *Spiritus Sanctus docebit vos omnem veritatem*. Þe Holy Gost schal teche ȝou al sothfastnes. Þan was þat fyre and þat brennynge noȝt ellys bot a bodily tokne outward schewed in witnessynge of þat grace þat was inwardly felt. And as it was in hem, so it is in oþer soules þat are visited and lyȝtned withinne of þe Holy Gost, and han with þat swilk outward felynge in confort and witnessynge of þe inward grace. Bot þat grace is not as I hope in al soules þat are perfyte, bot þer oure Lorde wylle. Oþer inperfyte soules þat han swilk felynges outwarde and han not ȝit resceyfed þe inward grace, it is not gud to hem for to resten in swilk felynges to mykel, bot in as mikel as þei helpen þe soule to more stabelnes of þoght in God and to more lufe. For sum moun be trewe and sum moun be feyned, as I hafe seyde before.

168 felynges] felyng CcM 169 þe[1]] *om.* LB$_3$PH$_6$M inly] only As, inward M 170 openly be] H$_7$RSrAH$_6$CcMPl, *rev.* HBH$_5$LB$_3$AsWsLwHu$_2$EPLdTWWc proued . . . Writte] weten As 171 þus] Act. 2° *add.* BLHu$_2$EPLdTW supra] super LB$_3$PH$_6$ 172 ⌜Sanctus⌝ L, þat is *add.* BE to þe apostles/in . . . Pentecost (l. 173)] *rev.* Ld to] vnto T 173 \`day´ As \`of´ L in] H$_7$RLB$_3$AsSrAPH$_6$CcMPl, þe *add.* HBH$_5$WsLwHu$_2$ELdTW liknes] lignes M \`of´ L tonges] *om.* M alle] H$_7$RL\`B$_3$´SrAPH$_6$CcMPl, *om.* HBH$_5$AsWsLwHu$_2$ELdTWWc 174 \`here´ B$_3$ satte] sette As ilk] ilkon M, eueryche E Now] *om.* T þe . . . Gost/þat] *rev.* T 175 is] *om.* H$_6$ in] H$_7$HRBH$_5$SrWsLwAHu$_2$MLd\`Pl´TW, *om.* LB$_3$AsEPH$_6$Cc, in Lat. vnseable] vnvisyble B, inuisible A, and *add.* T þo] H$_7$HRBH$_5$SrWsAHu$_2$ECcLdPlT, þe LB$_3$AsLwPH$_6$MWWc þat] þe LB$_3$PH$_6$Pl 176 was[2]] bodili *add.*, *canc.* L vnseably] vnseable AsM, inuisibelli A in þe myȝtes] *om.* Lat. 177 liȝtned] lyȝtyde H$_5$Ws, lyȝtyng Lw here reson] to hem þere here resons M kyndled] kyndelyng Lw, tendede BLd, tend AT 178 affeccyon] affeccions M 179 sodeynly þe gostly] sodeyn M þe[1]] þis Pl 180 of lufe] *om.* Cc as] and þat Sr oure Lord/behyȝt hem] *rev.* R Lorde] *om.* B hem] to *prec.* R þus] Io. 16° *add.* LHu$_2$EPLdT, Io. 6° *add.* B, Io. x *add.* W 181 þe] H$_7$LB$_3$SrPCcM, þat is *add.*

þerfore þei are not gostly felynges, bot whan þei are best and most trewe ȝit are þei bot outward toknes of þe inly grace þat is felt in þe
5v miȝtes | of þe soule. Þis may be openly proued be Holy Writ seiend þus: *Apparuerunt apostolis disper`t´ite lingue tanquam ignis, seditque supra singulos eorum Spiritus Sanctus*. Þe Holy Gost appered to þe aposteles in þe day of Pentecost in þe liknes of brennande tonges, and enflaumed her hertes and sat vpon ilke of hem. Now soþ it is, þe Holy Gost, þat is God in himself vnseable, was not þat fire ne þo tunges þat were seen, ne þat brennynge þat was felt bodily, bot he was vnseably felt in þe miȝtes of her soules. For he liȝtend here resoun and kyndeled here affeccioun þurgh his blissed presence, so clerly and so brennandely þat þei haden sodeynly þe gostly knowynge of soþfastnes and þe perfeccioun of luf, as oure Lorde behiȝt hem, seiande þus: *Spiritus Sanctus docebit vos omnem veritatem*. Þat is: þe Holy Gost schal teche ȝow al soþfastnes. Þan was þat fire and þat brennynge not elles bot a bodily tokne outwarde, schewd in witnesynge of þat grace þat was inwardly felt. And as it was in hem, so is it in oþer soules þat are visited and liȝtned withinne of þe Holy Gost, and han with þat swilk outwarde felynge in conforte and witnesynge of þe grace inwarde. Bot þat grace is not as I hope in alle soules þat are perfit, bot þere oure Lorde wil. Oþere inperfite soules þat han swilk felynges outwarde and han not ȝit resceifed þe inward grace, it is not good to hem for to resten in swilk felynges to mikel, bot in as mikel as þei helpen þe soule to more stabilnes of þoȝt in God and to more luf. For summe moun be trew and summe mowne be feyned, as I hafe saide bifore.

HRBH$_5$AsWsLwAHu$_2$EH$_6$LdPlTWWc ȝou al] þow Hu$_2$ 182 sothfastnes] and al trowthe *add.* Cc þat^{2}] the Cc 183 in^{1}] *om.* ELd witnessynge] witnesse CcT was . . . felt] senciebant Lat. 184 And] *om.* Lw it is] H$_7$RLB$_3$AsSrHu$_2$PH$_6$CcLd, *rev.* HBH$_5$WsLwAEMPlTW is] was As 185 of] with As han/with þat] *rev.* H$_6$ with þat] þerwyþ LdT 186 outward] inwarde Pl felynge] felyngis LB$_3$PLdTWs, sensaciones Lat. in] and RSr confort] comfortynge As and] in *add.* As witnessynge] witnesse T, swetnesse Cc inward grace] H$_7$LB$_3$SrEPH$_6$CcM, *rev.* HRBH$_5$AsWsLwAHu$_2$LdPlTWWc 187 is not/as I hope] *rev.* M is] nys As hope] trowe BH$_5$Ws, suppose Hu$_2$ þer] weere Ld, wher þat T 188 wylle] wold Cc inperfyte soules] *rev.* LB$_3$PH$_6$ felynges] felyng Cc 189 and] an M þe] *om.* LwW it] *om.* Hu$_2$ `not´ Cc  to$^{1}$] for M, *om.* Ld  for] H$_7$HRBH$_5$LAsSrAHu$_2$EPCcMLdPl, *om.* B$_3$WsLwH$_6$TW  190 felynges] felynge M  to mykel] outwarde LwW  in as] for `as´ Cc 191 to^{1} . . . and] *om.* Lw to^{1}] in As more] *om.* Ld stabelnes of þoght in God/. . ./lufe] *rev.* W of] in T in] to H$_6$ God] Jesu M, *om.* As to^{2}] into T 192 moun^{1}] men moten As moun^{2}] men moste As seyde before] forseyd As before] her *prec.* Pl

f. 85r How þis maner of spekynge, reformynge of a soule in felynge, | and in what wyse it is reformed, is founded in Seyn Poules wordes. Capitulum xxxi[m]

Now I hafe seyd to þe a lytel of reformynge in feyth, and also I hafe touched þe a lytel of þe forthgoynge fro þat reformynge to þe heyghere reformynge þat is in felynge. Not in þat entent as I wold be þese wordes setten Goddys werkynge vndyr a laghe of my spekynge, as for to seyn þu[s] werkeþ God in a soule and non oþer wyse. Nay, I mene not so. Bot I sey after my symple felynge þat oure Lord Jesu werkeþ þus in sum creatures, as I hope. And I hope wel þat he werkeþ oþerwyse also þat passeþ my wytte and my felynge. Nerþeles, where he werke þus or oþerwyse by sundry menes, in lengere tyme or in schorter tyme, with mikel trauelle or litel trauelle, if al come to on ende, þat is, to perfyte lufe of him, þan is it gode inogh. For if he wil ȝifen a soule on o day þe ful grace of contemplacyon and withouten ony trauelle, as he wele may, as gud is it to þat soule as if he had ben examyned, pyned, and mortifyed, and purifyed twenti wynter tyme. And þerfore vpon þis maner wyse take þou my seynge as I hafe seyd, and namly as I thenk for to seyn. For now by þe grace of oure Lord Jesu schal I speke a lytel as me þenkeþ more openly of reformynge in felynge, what it is and how it is made, and whilk are gostly felynges þat a soule resceyfeþ.

Nerþeles, first, þat þou take not þis maner of spekynge of reformynge of a soule in felynge as feynenge or fantasye, þerfor I

Chapter 31 *title*: H$_7$RLB$_3$SrAEPH$_6$MLdTW How a soule is reformyd in felyng, what it is and how it is made, and which ben gostly þingis þat a soule receyueþ H Of þe refourmynge in felynge, what it is and whiche ben þe gostly felynges þat a soule resceyueþ, and how it nys nouȝt worldely but spiritualy. As On what manere a man shal haue þe knowynge of his owne soule, and how a man shal sette his þouȝte and his loue in Jesu God and man, o person. Pl [*cf. above, Chapter 30 title*] *om.* BH$_5$WsLwHu$_2$Cc 1 How] Off H$_6$ reformynge] H$_7$LB$_3$SrAEPM, of *prec.* RCcLdPlTW, of þe *prec.* H$_6$, de Lat. of a soule/in felynge] *rev.* ALdTW felynge] H$_7$RLB$_3$SrPH$_6$M, schal be take *add.* AELdTW, sensacione Lat. 2 in what wyse] *om.* M in[1]] on ALdTW is[2]] it *prec.* H$_6$, and how hit *prec.* AELdTW founded] H$_7$M, founden RLB$_3$SrPH$_6$, founde ALdTW, growndid E, fundatur Lat. 4 I hafe[1]] *rev.* Cc to þe/a lytel] *rev.* M of] in M, þe *add.* Sr, þyn *add.* As 5 touched] seyd and *prec.* As þe/a lytel] *rev.* T þe[1]] H$_7$RLB$_3$SrAPMPl, to þe HBH$_5$AsWsLwHu$_2$EH$_6$CcLdTW, *om.* Lat. to þe heyghere] *om.* A 6 reformynge] *canc.* A in þat] in þe Ld, be þe M as] þat H$_5$WsLwW 7 þese] þoo Pl, At M werkynge] H$_7$LB$_3$SrEPH$_6$CcMW, werkes HRBH$_5$AsWsLwAHu$_2$LdPlT, operacionem Lat. 8 as] and As þus] -s *canc.* H$_7$ God] Jesu M a] *om.* As and] in *add.* AsSr non] not T 9 mene] ne *prec.* B Bot] for *add.* Ld I sey] *om.* As þat] I hope *add.* M 10 ⌜Jesu . . . sum⌝ L Jesu] *om.* MW in sum creatures/as I hope] *rev.* Cc as I hope] *om.* M hope

[CHAPTER 31]

Now I hafe seide to þe a litel of reformynge in faiþ, and also I hafe 6r touched to þe a litel of þe forþgoynge | fro þat reformynge to þe hiȝere reformynge þat is in felynge. Not in þat entent as I wolde bi þese wordes setten Goddes werkes vndir a lawe of my spekynge, as for to seien þus wirkiþ God in a soule and non oþer wise. Nay, I mene not so. Bot I saie after my symple felynge þat oure Lorde Ihesu wirkiþ þus in sum creatures, as I hope. And I hope wel þat he wirkiþ oþerwise also þat passiþ my wit and my felynge. Nerþeles, wheþer he wirke þus or oþerwise by sundry menes, in lengre tyme or schorter tyme, with mikel traueil or litel traueil, if al come to on ende, þat is to þe perfit luf of him, þan is it good inowȝ. For if he wil gif o soule on o day þe ful grace of contemplacioun and withouten any traueil, as he wel may, as gode is þat to þat soule as if he had ben examined, pyned, mortified and purified, twenty wynter tyme. And þerfore vpon þis maner wise take þu my seiynge as I haue seide, and namely as I þenke for to seien. For now bi þe grace of oure Lord Ihesu schal I speke a litel as me þenkiþ more openly of reformynge in felynge, what it is and how it is made, and whilke are gostly felynges þat a soule resceifiþ.

Nerþeles, first, þat þu take not þis maner of spekynge of reformynge of a soule in felynge as feynynge or fantasie, þerfore I

(*bis*)] trowe A hope wel] suppose B hope[2]] also *add.* Ld wel] *om.* CcT 11 also] wel *add.* B, be oþer menes *add.* M wyttte and my] *om.* Lat. and my] in Ld 12 where] H_7L, wheþer Σ, siue Lat. werke] worchith T \`þus´ Cc sundry] diuers AHu_2PlT menes] mekenesse As in] and R 13 lengere] longe Ld or . . . tyme] *om.* Ws or[1]] oþere As in] H_7LB_3SrP, *om.* HRBH_5AsWsLwAHu_2EH_6CcMLdPlTW schorter] schort LB_3PLd or[2] . . . trauelle] *om.* T or[2]] oþere As trauelle[2]] *om.* Cc, *om.* Lat. 14 if] þat *add.* T to[2]] sey *add.* A, *om.* T perfyte] H_7RLB_3SrAEPH_6CcMLdPl, þe *prec.* HBH_5AsWsLwHu_2TW of him] *om.* M is it] *rev.* LdW gode] all *prec.* T 15 \`he wil ȝifen´ Sr wil] wolde Pl a . . . on] in T on] opon A \`of contemplacyon´ Pl 16 and] *om.* H_6 as[2]] also B 17 is it] H_7Sr, *rev.* LB_3EPH_6Cc, is þat HRBH_5As-WsLwAHu_2MLdPlTW þat] þe AHu_2CcM \`as´ L if] þow B he] it $B_3$ examyned] and *add.* A and[1]] $H_7$L$B_3$SrP$H_6$Cc, *om.* HRB$H_5$AsWsLwA$Hu_2$EMLdPlTW, *om.* Lat. and[2]] an M 18 twenti] a *prec.* Sr, in *prec.* As, \`be´ *prec.* Cc wynter tyme] ȝer AE \`tyme´ $W^G$, long $H_6$, *om.* LwW vpon] on WsE, in A maner] on one *add.* As, of *add.* E wyse] *om.* SrM 19 \`þou´ W^G, in LwW, *om.* As for[1]] *om.* LwW 20 schal I] *rev.* H_6 \`schal´ Pl, *om.* As speke] *om.* B 21 more] þe *prec.* As reformynge] reformacyon Cc, þe *prec.* Ld, of a soule *add.* T in felynge] *om.* R made] *om.* A 22 þat] þe wheche M 23 first] *om.* M þou] I LwW 24 as] *rep.*, *canc.* Cc, *om.* M feynenge] feyned E or] oþer As fantasye] fantesing Cc þerfor/I schal] *rev.* Hu_2

schal grounden it in Seynt Poulys wordes where he seyth þus: *Nolite conf[o]rmari huic seculo, sed renouamini in nouitate sensus vestri*. Þat is: 3e þat are þurgh grace reformed in feith, conforme 3ow not henforward to maners of þe werd, in pride, in coueytyse, and oþer synnes, bot be 3e reformed in newhed of felynge. Lo, here þou maight se þat Seyn Poule spekeþ of reformynge in felynge, and what þat new felynge is he expouneþ in anoþer place þus: *Vt impleamini in agnicione* f. 85[v] | *voluntatis eius, in omni intellectu et sapiencia spirituali*. Þat is: We preye God þat 3e moun be fulfilled in knowynge of Goddis wille, in al vndirstondynge and in al maner gostly wysdom. Þis is reformynge in felynge. For þou schalt vnderstondyn þat þe soule haþ two maner of felynges: one withouten of þe fyfe bodily wittes, anoþer withinne of þe gostly wyttes þe whilk are properly þe my3tes of þe soule: mende, reson and wille. Whan þese my3tes are þurgh grace fulfilled in al vnderstondynge of þe wil of God and in gostly wysdom, þan haþ þe soule new gracyous felynges. Þat þis is soth, he scheweþ in anoþer place þus: *Renouamini spiritu mentes vestre, et induite nouum hominem qui secundum Deum creatus est in iusticia, sanctitate et veritate*. Be 3e renewed in þe spirit of 3oure soule; þat is, 3e schul be reformed not in bodily felynge ne in ymaginacion, bot in þe ouer partye of 3oure reson. And cloþe 3ou in a new man þat is schapen aftere God in ry3twysnes, holynes and sothfastnes. Þat is, 3oure reson, þat is properly þe ymage of God, þurgh grace of þe Holy Gost schal be cloþed in a newe ly3t of sothfastnes, holynes and ry3twysnes, and þan is it reformed in felynge. For whan þe soule hath perfyte knowynge of God, þan is it reformed. Þus seyth Seyn Poule: *Expoliantes veterem*

25 \`it´ Cc   Poulys] Poul HT   þus] Ro. 12° *add.* BLHu$_{2}$EPTW, Jo. 12 *add.* Ld   26 conformari] confirmari H$_{7}$ vestri] Christi M   þat is] to seye þat *add.* As, *om.* Cc   27 þurgh grace/reformed] *rev.* BAs   3ow not] *om.* Ws   28 henforward] a3en Cc, *om.* As   to] H$_{7}$RLB$_{3}$SrAPH$_{6}$Pl, in M, þe *add.* HBH$_{5}$WsLwHu$_{2}$ECcLdTW, haue þe *add.* As   maners] maner Ld   þe] this Cc   in[1]] as *prec.* As   in[2]] and M, *om.* As, *om.* Lat.   and] H$_{7}$, in *add.* Σ   29 be 3e] *rev.* As   in . . . felynge] in nouitate sensus vestri seu sensacionis vestre Lat.   in . . . of] newynge As   in newhed] and newed M   newhed] newynge H$_{5}$Ws   of] H$_{7}$HRBH$_{5}$SrWsLwAHu$_{2}$CcLdPlTW, 3oure *add.* LB$_{3}$EPH$_{6}$M\`W[G]´, þe *add.* As    felynge] felingus A    þou mai3gh] *rev.* Hu$_{2}$, mi3te yow M, may 3e Cc    maight] may CcPl    30 \`spekeþ´ Pl, seiþ As   31 expouneþ] expungnyth Cc   anoþer] manere of *add.* As   þus] Col. 1° *add.* BLHu$_{2}$EPLdTW, *om.* AsPl   in[2]] *om.* Cc   32 in] *om.* E   et] in E   33 3e] we H$_{5}$AsWs   34 maner gostly] *rev.*, *marked for trsp.* L   maner] of *add.* CcPl, *om.* Lat.   gostly wysdom] *rev.* A   \`þis . . . wysdom. (l. 39)´ H[c], *om.* H°H$_{5}$AsWs    þis] þat LB$_{3}$Hu$_{2}$PH$_{6}$    is] in *add.* \`L´B$_{3}$P   35 For . . . felynges] *om.* Cc   of] *om.* A   36 felynges] felyng H$_{6}$T   one] \`is´ *add.* Cc    of[1]] *om.* LwH[c]    bodily] *om.* T    wittes] and *add.* ECc    anoþer] \`is´ *add.* Cc   37 þe[2]] *om.* A

schal grounde it in Seynt Poul wurdes where he seiþ þus: *Nolite conformari huic seculo, sed reformamini in nouitate sensus vestri*. Þat is: Ȝe þat are þurgh grace reformed in feiþ, conforme ȝow not henforwarde to þe maners of þe werld, in pride, in coueitise, and in oþer synnes,
106^v bot be ȝe reformed in newed | of felynge. Loo, here þu maiȝt see þat Seynt Poul spekiþ of reformynge in felynge, and what þat newe felynge is he exponiþ in anoþer place þus: *Vt impleamini in agnicione voluntatis eius, in omni intellectu et sapientia spirituali*. Þat is: We preie God þat ȝe may be fulfilled in knowynge of Goddis wille, in alle vndirstandynge and in al maner gostly wisdom. ʻThis is reformyng in felinge. For þou shalt vndirstond þat þe soule haþ two maner of felinges: one withouten [of] þe fyue bodili wittes, anoþer wiþinne of þe gostly wittes þe which arne properly þe miȝtes of þe soule, mynde, resoun, and wille. When þese myȝtes arne þurȝ grace fulfillid in al vndirstondyng of þe wille of God and gostly wisdam', þan haþ þe soule new graciouse felynges. Þat þis is soþ, he schewiþ in anoþer place þus: *Renouamini spiritu mentis vestre, et induite nouum hominem, qui secundum Deum creatus est in iusticia, sanctitate et veritate*. Be ȝe renewed in þe spirit of ȝoure soule; þat is, ȝe schul be reformed not in bodily felynge ne in ymaginacioun, bot in þe ouer party of ȝour resoun. And cloþe ȝow in a new `man´ þat is schapen aftir God in riȝtwisnes, [holynes and soþfastnes]. `Þat is, ȝour resoun, þat is properli þe image of God þurȝ grace of þe Holi Gost, shal be cloþed in a new liȝt of soþfastnes, holynes and riȝtwisnes´, and þan is it reformid in felynge. For whan þe soule haþe perfit knowynge of God, þan is it reformed. Þus seiþ Seint Poul: *Expoliantes veterem*

soule] As *add.* H$_6$ mende] and *add.* Lw 38 þese . . . are/þurgh grace] *rev.* LB$_3$P þese] þose RPl are/þurgh grace] *rev.* E 39 of^2] in T God] Jesu M in] *om.* LwH^{c}W þe soule] þe H$_5$, ȝee Ws 40 `þis´ Cc 41 þus] Eph. 6° *add.* BLHu$_2$EPLdTW et . . . hominem] *om.* H$_6$ induite] vos *add.* T 42 `est´ Cc, *om.* B iusticia] et *add.* A, *om.* Cc et veritate] veritatis A et] in *add.* LB$_3$P veritate] That is *add.* E ȝe] now *add.* `L´B$_3$P 43 `þe´ As, *om.* W ȝoure] þi M, oure Ld ȝe] þat *prec.* BHu$_2$Ld be] `nout´ *add.* Cc reformed not] *rev.* As not] *om.* Cc 44 þe] *om.* Sr ouer] othir Cc ȝoure] *om.* Cc 45 `And . . . man´ T^G `man´ *interl.* H schapen] formid A God] Jesu M 46 holynes . . . ryȝtwysnes (l. 48)] *om.* H°H$_5$AsWs `holynes and sothfastnes´ T^G, *om.* T and] in *add.* A `þat$^1$ . . . ryȝtwysnes (l. 48)´ H$^c$ þat$^1$] This M 47 þe$^1$ . . . it (l. 49)] *om.* M `God´ Sr Gost] þat *add.* H$_6$ 48 sothfastnes/. . ./ryȝtwysnes] *rev.* A and^2] *om.* Sr 49 is it] *rev.* AsLwCcTW `For . . . perfyte´ T$^G$, *om.* T perfyte] perfitly felyng and Ld 50 God] Jesu Cc, Jesu wiþ loue M `þan is it reformed´ T^G, *om.* T is it] *rev.* CcLdW reformed] in feling *add.* A þus] þys Ld, also *add.* M seyth/Seyn Poule] *rev.* Hu$_2$, Col. 3° *add.* BLHu$_2$EPLdW

hominem cum actibus suis, et induite nouum, qui renouatur in agnicione Dei, secundum ymaginem eius qui creauit eum. Spoyle ȝoureself of þe old man with alle his dedys; þat is, caste fro ȝou þe luste of þe werd, with al werdly maners. And cloþe ȝou in a newe man; þat is, ȝe schul be renewed in þe knowynge of God aftere þe lyknes of him þat made ȝou.

By þese wordes maight þou vnderstonden þat Seyn Poule wolde f. 86r han mennes soules reformed in perfyte knowynge of God, for þat is | þe new felenge þat he spekeþ of generally. And þerfor vpon his wurd I schal seyn more pleynly of þis reformynge, as God ȝifeþ me grace. For þer is two maner knowynges of God. On is had principally in ymaginacion, and lytel [in] vnderstondynge. Þis knowynge is in chosen soules begynnend and profitend in grace, þat knowen God and lufen him al manly not gostly, with manly affeccyons and with bodily lyknes, as I hafe before seyd. Þis knowynge is gode, and it is lykned to mylke be þe whilk þei are tenderly norisched as children, til þei ben able for to comen to þe fadres bord and taken of his hand hol brede. Anoþer knowynge is principally felt in vnderstondynge, whan it is conforted and illumyned be þe Holy Gost, and lytel in ymaginacion. For þe vnderstondynge is lady, and ymaginacion is a mayden seruend to þe vnderstondynge whan nede is. Þis knowynge is hol brede, mete for perfyte soules, and it is reformynge in felynge.

51 et] H_7Hu_2, *om.* Σ nouum] hominem add. AHu_2 52 eum] in iusticia et veritate *add.* M, þat is *add.* E ȝoureself] $H_7HRBH_5SrWsLwHu_2ECcPlTW$, ȝou silf $LB_3AsAPMLd$, ȝou H_6 of] and M 53 with . . . werd] *om.* Ld luste] H_7, lufe Σ 54 al] his *add.* E maners] and condicions *add.* Hu_2 newe] meke *add.* T be] *om.* As 55 renewed] reulid R, rennled Pl God] Jesu M \`þe^2' Pl 56 By] But T maight þou] *rev.* AsLwCcW maight] $H_7LB_3AsSrAEPH_6CcM$, may $HRBH_5WsLwHu_2LdPlTW$ 57 perfyte] partie LB_3P knowynge] dileccione et cognitione Lat. of God] *om.* As God] Jesu M, Jesu Christi Lat. 58 his] þis SrMLd wurd] wordis LwW, now *add.* As I schal] *rev.* E 59 schal] wolde M pleynly] $H_7RBLB_3SrAHu_2EPH_6CcMLdPlT$, openly HH_5WsLwW, plane Lat. as] ȝif As ȝifeþ] wolde ȝefe As 60 is^1] be M, sunt Lat. maner] $H_7HRBH_5AsSrWsLwAHu_2PlTW$, of *add.* LB_3EPH_6CcMLd, of þe As knowynges] H_7M, knowynge $HRBH_5LB_3AsSrWsLwAHu_2EPH_6CcLdPlTW$, cogniciones Lat. God] Jesu M is^2] his *add.*, *canc.* L had principally] *rev.* H_6 had] *om.* Cc 61 ymaginacion] þe *prec.* As in^1] *om.* H_7 þis

hominem cum actibus suis; induite nouum, qui renouatur in agnicione Dei, secundum ymaginem eius qui creauit eum. Spoile ȝourself of þe olde man with alle his dedis; þat is, kaste fro ȝow þe luf of þe werld with alle werdly maners. And cloþe ȝow in a new man; þat is, ȝe schul be renewed in þe knowynge of God aftir þe liknes of him þat made ȝow.

Bi þese wordes may þu vndirstanden þat Seint Poul wold han mennes soules reformed in perfite knowynge of God, for þat is þe newe felynge þat he spekiþ of generally. And þerfor vpon his worde I
107r schal seien more | openly of þis reformynge, as God ȝifiþ me grace. For þer is two maner knowynge of God. On is had principally in ymaginacioun, and litel in vndirstondynge. Þis knowynge is in chosen soules bigynnande and profitande in grace, þat knowen God and lufen him al manly not gostly, with manly affeccionns and with bodily liknes, as I hafe bifore saide. Þis knowynge is good, and it is likned to milk bi þe whilk þei are tendrely norisched as children, vntil þai ben able for to comen to þe faders borde and taken [of] his hande hool brede. Anoþer knowynge is principally feled in vndirstandynge, whan it is conforted and illumined bi þe Holy Gost, and litel in ymaginacioun. For þe vndirstandynge is ladi, and þe ymaginacioun is as [mayden] seruende to þe vndirstandynge when nede is. Þis knowynge is hol brede, mete for perfite soules, and it is reformynge in felynge.

knowynge] *rep.* A   62 in grace] *om.* H$_6$ God] Jesu M   63 al . . . gostly] *om.* Lat. gostly] godly Cc   with[1]] but *prec.* H$_6$ 64 before seyd] *rev.* H$_6$ it] *om.* M   65 til] H$_7$H$_5$LB$_3$SrWsAPH$_6$CcMLdT, vntil HRBLwHu$_2$W, vnto AsEPl   66 for] *om.* As and . . . brede] *om.* Cc   of] on H   hol] holy B   67 Anoþer] And þat oþer LB$_3$EPH$_6$, And oþere As   knowynge] cognicio Jesu Lat.   is] þys *add.* Ld   principally felt] *rev.* AE felt] felynge As   whan . . . Gost/and . . . ymaginacion (l. 69)] *rev.* Cc   whan . . . Gost (l. 68)] *om.* LwW   68 illumyned] enlumyned As, lyȝtnyd LdT   lytel] a *prec.* Hu$_2$ in] *om.* Ld   69 ymaginacion[1]] And þat is *add.* Cc   For . . . ymaginacion[2])] *om.* As   lady] þe *prec.* R   ymaginacion[2]] H$_7$LB$_3$SrPH$_6$CcMT, þe *prec.* HRBH$_5$WsLwAHu$_2$ELdPlW   a] H$_7$RLB$_3$SrAHu$_2$PH$_6$CcMPlT, as HBLd, as a H$_5$AsWsLwW, *om.* E   70 mayden] maynden H, maide T   to] vnto As   þe] *om.* T   `þis´ W^G, *om.* LwW   71 hol] holy B, oold LB$_3$PH$_6$ mete] et solidus cibus Lat.   perfyte] chosene B   it] *om.* Pl   reformynge] reformid RAs

How grace openeth þe ynnere eygh of a soule into gostly beholdynge of Jesu, and how þer is þre maner of knowynges of Jesu by example of þre men stondend in þe sunne, a blynd, and an eye-spered, and a forth-lokende. Capitulum xxxii[m]

A soule þat is called fro þe lufe of þe werd and aftere þat is ryȝted and assayed, mortifyed and purifyed, as I hafe before seid, oure Lord Jesu of his mercyful goodnesse reformeþ it in felynge whan he voucheþ-saufe. He opneþ þe ynnere eye of þe soule whan he lyȝtneþ þe reson þurgh touchynge and schynynge of his blissed lyȝt for to seen him and knowen him; not al fully at ones, bot lytel and litil be dyuers tymes, as þe soule may suffre him. He seeþ him not what he is, for þat may no creature don in heuene ne in erthe; ne he seeþ him not as he is, for þat syȝt is only in þe blisse of heuene. Bot he seeþ him þat he is: an vnchaungeable beynge, a souereyn myȝt, souereyn sothfastnes, and souereyn goodnes, a blissed lyfe, and an endles blisse. Þis seeþ þe
f. 86v soule, and mikel more þat comeþ | withalle; not blyndly and vnsauourly, as doth a clerk þat seeþ him by clergy only þurgh myght of his naked reson, bot he seeþ him in vnderstondynge þat is conforted and lyȝtned by þe ȝifte of þe Holy Gost, with a wonderful reuerence and a priuey brennend lufe, with gostly sauour and heuenly delyte, more clerly and more fully þan it may be writen or seyd.

Chapter 32 *title*: H$_7$RLB$_3$SrAEPH$_6$M`T^{G}W$^{G\prime}$ How God openyþ þe ynner ȝye off þe soule for [*om.* T] to se hym, not alle at onys but by diuers tymys and of þre maner [of] [*om.* Ld] refourmyng off a soule by ensampul. LdTW How a soule ykleped fro þe world in goodnesse and refourmed be oure Lord þurgh touchynge and shewynge of his blessed liȝt þurgh his blyssed ȝiftis of brennynge loue shal be raueshyd into clennesse and perfite vnderstondyng. As How þis maner of spekynge, 'reformynge of a soule in felynge,' in what wise hit is reformede, is founded in Seynt Poulis wordis. Pl [*cf. above, Chapter 31 title*] Qualiter gracia aperit interiorem oculum anime in spiritualem consideracionem Jesu Christi; et quomodo tria sunt genera cognicionum Jesu Christi, per exemplum trium hominum in sole stancium: hominis ceci, hominis habentis oculos clausos, et hominis apertis oculis aspicientis. Lat. *om.* HBH$_5$WsLwHu$_2$Cc 1 a] þe RAM into . . . is (l. 2)] for to se him, noȝt al at onus, but bi diuers times, and of A 2 is] aren M maner] maners M of] R knowynges . . . Jesu] reforming of soule A knowynges] H$_7$, knowynge RLB$_3$Sr-EPH$_6$M`W$^{G\prime}$, cognicionum Lat. 3 by] an *add.* M of . . . forth-lokend] *om.* A a] H$_7$RSr, on LB$_3$AEPH$_6$M 4 and] H$_7$RSr, *om.* LB$_3$AEPH$_6$M eye-spered] H$_7$RSr, oþer haþ his iȝen sperid LB$_3$AEPH$_6$`W$^{G\prime}$, oþer wiþ on eiȝe spered M a] H$_7$RSr, on M, þe þridde LB$_3$AEPH$_6$ 5 is[1]] *om.* As called] cleped AsH$_6$LdT þe[1]] H$_7$H$_5$LB$_3$AsWs-AEPH$_6$CcMPlTW, *om.* HRBSrLwHu$_2$Ld þe[2]] *om.* W werd] wo- *prec., canc.* Sr is[2]] H$_7$RAsSrLwHu$_2$CcMPlW, it *prec.* HBH$_5$LB$_3$WsAPH$_6$LdT 6 `and purifyed´ Pl before seid] *rev.* H$_6$T oure . . . Jesu] Dominus noster Jesus Christus Lat. Lord] blissed *prec.* Hu$_2$ 7 reformeþ] reformed As it] *om.* Ld whan he voucheþ-saufe] on þis maner wise M 8 reson] of þe soule *add.* A 9 touchynge and] *om.* Lat. for to

[CHAPTER 32]

A soule þat is callid fro luf of þe werld and after þat it is riȝted and assaiede, mortified and purified, as I hafe bifore saide, oure Lord Ihesu of his merciful goodnes reformiþ it in felynge when he vouchiþsaufe. He opneþ þe innere iȝe of þe soule when he liȝtneþ þe resoun þurgh touchyng and schynynge of his blissed liȝt for to seen him and knowen him; not alle fully at ones, bot litel and litel bi diuers tymes, as þe soule may suffren him. He seeþ him not what he is, for þat may no creature done in heuen ne in erþe; nor he seeþ him not ⌜as⌝ he is, for þat siȝt is oonly in þe blis of heuen. Bot he seeþ him þat he is: an vnchaungeable beynge, a souereyn miȝt, souereyn soþfastnes, souereyn goodnes, a blissid lif, an endeles blis. Þis seeþ þe soule, and mikel more þat comiþ withal; not blyndely and nakedly and
107[v] vnsauourly, as doþ a clerke | þat seeþ him bi his clergi only þurgh miȝt of his naked resoun, bot he seeþ him in vndirstandynge þat he is confortid and liȝtned bi þe gifte of þe Holy Gost, with a wondirful reuerence and a priue brennande lufe, and with gostly sauour and heuenly delite, more clerly and more fully þen it may be wryten or seide.

seen] ad diligendum Lat.   10 knowen] for to *prec.* H_5SrWs, to *prec.* As   him] as he voucheþ sauf for to shewen hym *add.* M   not . . . him[2] (l. 11] *om.* Lat.   not] how A   al] as Cc   11 him[2]] Jesu nout only as man be ymaginacyon, but he seth hym [as *add.* M] God in man CcM, þat is *add.* RA, þat he is *add.* Pl   not] fully *add.* M   what] as T   for . . . is (l. 12)] *om.* As   12 in heuene ne] *om.* H_6M   in[2]] on M   he[1] . . . not] *om.* M   he[1]] *om.* T   ⌜as⌝ H[c], what H_5WsWc   13 is only] *rev.* As   only] kept *add.* M   him] *om.* H_6 an] *om.* Pl   14 vnchaungeable] *corr. fr.* vnseable Ld   beynge] and *add.* M   myȝt] and *add.* As   souereyn[2]] a *prec.* AH_6Ld   and] H_7RLB_3SrLwAPCcMPl, a AsEH_6Ld, *om.* HBH_5WsLw-Hu_2TW   15 goodnes] good Cc   a] and Lw, and *prec.* As   lyfe] loue As   and] H_7RH_5LB_3AsSrWsAEPH_6CcMPlT, *om.* HBLwHu_2LdW   an] *om.* As   16 soule] of Jesu *add.* M withalle] þerwith ALdT, and *add.* M   blyndly] blyndynge As, nakedly and *prec.* Wc   and[2]] H_7RLB_3SrAPH_6CcMPl, nakedly and *add.* HBH_5WsLwHu_2ELdTW, nakedly and nouȝt *add.* As, et Lat.   17 vnsauourly] sauourly LB_3P, vnsauourably R   a] þe As   þat . . . him] *om.* M   him] *om.* Cc   \`by´ L, with B   clergy] H_7RLB_3SrAEPH_6Cc, his *prec.* HBH_5AsWsLwHu_2MLdPlTW, scienciam suam Lat.   18 myght] light T   he] þat oþir LB_3EPH_6, the soule Wc   him in] be Cc, God Wc   him] *om.* Ws vnderstondynge] naked *add.*, *canc.* H   þat] H_7RLB_3AsSrLwAEPH_6PlW, he *add.*, *canc.* H, he *add.* BH_5WsHu_2CcMLdT, qui Lat.   19 lyȝtned] lyȝt Ld, lyghted W   and] *om.* As   with] H_7LB_3SrPH_6Cc, and *prec.* HRBH_5AsWsLwAHu_2EMLdPlTWWc, cum Lat.   20 and[2]] a *add.* E   21 clerly] certeynly As   it] *om.* LB_3P   writen or seyd] *rev.* B_3

þis syght, þogh it be bot schortly and litel, is so wurthi and so myȝtty þat it dragweþ and rauisceth al þe affeccyons of þe soule þerto fro beholdynge and þe mynde of al erthly thynges, for to reste þerin euermore if þat it myght. And of þis maner syȝt and knowenge, þe soule groundeþ alle his inward werkynge in al þe affeccyons; for þan it dredeþ God in man as sothfastnes, wondreþ him as myȝt, lufeþ him as gudnes. þis syȝt and þis knowynge of Jesu, with þe blissed lufe þat comeþ out of it, may be called reformynge of a soule in feith and in felynge þat I speke of. It is in feith for it is mirk ȝet, as in rewarde of þat ful knowynge þat schal ben in heuene. For þan schal we seen him not only þat he is, bot as he is, as Seyn John seyth: *Tunc videbimus eum sicuti est*. þat is: þan schul we seen him as he is. Nerþeles it is in felynge also, as in rewarde of þat blynde knowynge þat a soule haþ stondende only in feith. For þis soule knoweþ sumwhat of þe kynde of Jesu God þurgh þis gracyous syȝt, bot þat oþer knoweþ it not, bot only troweþ it; þis is soth.

Nerþeles þat þou mogwe þe better conceyfe þat I mene, I schal schew þese þre maner reformynge of a soule be example of þre men stondende in lyȝt of þe sunne. Of þe whilk þre, one is blynde, anoþer may seen bot ⌜he⌝ haþ his eyen spered, þe þred loketh forth ful-syȝt. þe blynd man haþ no maner knowynge þat he is in þe sunne, bot he troweþ it if a trew man telle it him, and he betokneþ a soule þat is only reformed in feith þat troweþ in God as Holy Kyrke techeþ and wote not what. þis sufficeþ as for saluacyon. þat oþer man seeþ a lyȝt of þe

22 syght] whanne it is gracyous *add.* CcM [whanne it *canc.* Cc] bot] *om.* LB$_3$SrPH$_6$ schortly] shorte T`W^{G}′ is] it is Hu$_2$CcLd wurþi/. . ./miȝtty] *rev.* T 23 affeccyons] H$_7$BA, affeccioun Σ, affeccionem Lat. þerto/fro . . . thynges (l. 24)] H$_7$LB$_3$SrPH$_6$Cc, *rev.* HRBH$_5$AsWsLwAHu$_2$ELdPlTW [and þereto As] 24 fro . . . thynges] *om.* M beholdynge] þe *prec.* AsCc and] *om.* LdT þe] *om.* Cc thynges] H$_7$RAs, þinge HBH$_5$LB$_3$SrWsLwAHu$_2$EPH$_6$CcMLdPlTW, terrenorum Lat. þerin] þere As 25 þat] H$_7$RLB$_3$SrAEPH$_6$CcPl, *om.* HBH$_5$AsWsLwHu$_2$MLdTW maner] of *add.* LwW knowenge] cognicionis Jesu Christi Lat. þe . . . knowynge (l. 28)] *om.* As 26 his] hir Hu$_2$ inward werkynge] *rev.* LwW in] and M 27 dredeþ] rediþ E God] Jesu M in man] *om.* Lat. sothfastnes] and *add.* `Cc′Wc wondreþ] in *add.* Lw, of *add.* Cc myȝt] and BH$_5$Ws`Cc′ as^{3}] of hys Lw 28 and] in R þis^{2}] goodnesse and *add.* Lw, goodnes and this *add.* W þe] þat A lufe] *om.* Pl 29 of it] þerof Sr of^{1}] ȝif As called] cleped AsH$_6$LdT reformynge] þe *prec.* LB$_3$PH$_6$Cc, in *prec.* As a] *om.* Ld feith/. . ./felynge] *rev.* LwW in^{2}] *om.* Cc 30 þat . . . feith] *om.* M speke] spak Cc It^{1}] *om.* Pl in^{1} . . . mirk] soþe As mirk] H$_7$HRLAsSrPCcMPl, derk BH$_5$B$_3$WsLw-AHu$_2$EH$_6$LdTW rewarde] þe *prec.* H$_7$ 31 ful] *om.* A knowynge] of Jesu wyth the blessed loue that comyth oute of it *add.* LwW ben] of hym *add.* M For] *om.* T 32 not only] *om.* T bot] and T, euen LB$_3$PH$_6$ seyth] 1^{a} Io. 3° *add.* BLHu$_2$EPLd, 1 Io. 4 *add.* TW eum] euen L, *om.* B$_3$P 33 sicuti] H$_7$HRBH$_5$WsLwAHu$_2$EPCc-MLdT`W^{G}′, sicut LB$_3$AsSrH$_6$PlW þat is] *om.* M þan . . . we] alle we shulle As, whan

þis si3t, þou3 it be bot schortly and litel, is so wurþi and so mi3ty þat it drawiþ and rauischiþ al þe affeccioun of þe soule fro beholdynge and þe mynde of al erþly þinge þerto, for to reste þerin euermore if it mi3t. And of þis maner si3t and knowynge, þe soule groundiþ al his inwarde wirkynge in alle þe affeccions; for þan it drediþ God in man as soþfastnes, wondreþ him as mi3t, lufiþ him as goodnes. þis si3t and þis knowynge of Ihesu, with þe blissed lufe þat comiþ out of it, may be called reformynge of a soule in faiþ and in felynge þat I speke of. It is in faiþ, for it is mirke 3it as in rewarde of þat ful knowynge þat schal be in heuene. For þan schal we seen him not only þat he is, bot as he is, as Seynt Johan seiþ: *Tunc videbimus eum sicuti est*. þat is: þan schul we see him as he is. Nerþeles it is in felynge also, as in rewarde of þat blynde knowynge þat a soule haþ stondende only in feiþ. For þis soule knowiþ sumwhat of þe kynde of Ihesu God þurgh þis gracious si3t, bot þat oþer knowiþ not, bot only trowith it is soþ.

Nerþeles þat þu may þe better conceife what I mene, I schal schew þese þre maner reformynge of a soule bi example of þre men standende in li3t of þe sunne. Of þe whilk þre, on is blynde, anoþer may see bot he haþ his ei3en stopped, þe þridde lokiþ forþ ful-si3t. þe
08r blynde man haþ | no maner knowynge þat he is in þe sunne, bot he troweþ it if a trewe man telle him, and he bitokneþ a soule þat is only reformid in feiþ þat trowith in God as Holy Kirke techeþ and wot not what. þis sufficiþ as for saluacioun. þat oþer man seeþ a li3t of þe

we schul Ld   it] *canc.* Ld   is] it *add.* Ld   in] *om.* Sr   34 as] *om.* Cc   þat[1]] *rep*, *canc.* L, þe SrCc   35 stondende] stondyn RB, stondeþ As, þat stondeþ M, que . . . stat Lat.   þis] þe B   þe] very *add.* W   36 God] *om.* AsCcM   þis] hys LwHu$_2$LdW   þat] *om.* As   knoweþ] he *prec.* As   it] H$_7$LB$_3$SrEPH$_6$CcM, *om.* HRBH$_5$AsWsLwAHu$_2$LdPlTW, sic Lat.   not] *om.* M   37 troweþ] leeueþ B, bileuith AT   it . . . soth] *om.* M   it] *om.* H$_5$AsWsLd   þis] þat As, þat it H$_5$SrWs, þatt þys Ld, *om.* HLwW, istud Lat.   38 mogwe/þe better] *rev.* W   mogwe] maist AsE, mi3t ALd, mightest T   þe better/conceyfe] *rev.* T   þe] *om.* As   þat] H$_7$RLB$_3$SrAPH$_6$CcMPl, what HBH$_5$AsWsLwHu$_2$ELdTW   39 þese] H$_7$HBH$_5$SrWsLwHu$_2$TW, þose R, þis CcM, þee LB$_3$AsAEPH$_6$Pl, *om.* Ld   þre maner] *rev.*, *marked for trsp.* Cc   þre] *om.* M   maner] maneres Pl, of *add.* AsAE   reformynge] reformyngis AsHu$_2$H$_6$CcLd   example] an *prec.* As   40 ly3t of] *om.* M   ly3t] H$_7$HRBH$_5$LAsSrWsAHu$_2$PMLdT, the *prec.* B$_3$LwEH$_6$Cc`Pl´W   sunne] out *add.*, *canc.* Cc   blynde] blyng Cc   anoþer] þe þoþere As, and *prec.* LB$_3$AsPH$_6$   41 bot] *om.* As   he . . . eyen] his ei3e is M   ⌜he⌝ *over a longer erasure* H$_7$, `he´ Pl   spered] H$_7$RLB$_3$SrHu$_2$PH$_6$CcMPl`W[G]´, stopped HH$_5$AsWsLwEW, yclosid BA, schytt LdT, and *add.* AsCc   loketh forth] may se Ld   loketh] lokid R   forth] wyþ LdT, with *add.* AsAH$_6$CcM`W[G]´   42 no] non As   maner] more A, of *add.* AsECcT   43 troweþ] leeueþ BM   it] H$_7$RAsSrAMPlT, to it Cc, *om.* HBH$_5$LB$_3$WsLwHu$_2$EPH$_6$LdW, sic Lat.   him] *om.* As   he] *om.* H$_6$ only reformed] *rev.* As   44 troweþ] leeueþ BM, beleuyþ LdT   God] Jesu M, Jesum Christum Lat.   ⌜as⌝ L   techeþ] vs *add.* M   45 `not´ L   what] quid hoc est Lat.   man] om. LB$_3$PH$_6$ a] *rep.* Lw, *om.* H$_6$

sunne, bot he seeþ it not clerly whate it is, ne as it is, for þe lyd of his
f. 87[r] eye letteþ him þat he may not. Bot he seeþ þurgh | þe lyd of his eye a glemerynge of grete lyȝt, and he betokneþ a soule þat is reformed in feith and in felynge and so is contemplatyf. For he seeþ sumwhat of þe godhed of Jesu þurgh grace, not clerly ne fully, for þe lyd, þat is his bodily kende, is ȝit a wal atwix his kende and þe kende of Jesu God and letteþ him fro þe clere syȝt of him. Bot he seeþ þurgh þis wal, after þat grace toucheþ him more or lesse, þat Jesu is God and þat Jesu is souereyn gudnes and souereyn beenge and a blissed lyf, and þat al oþer gudnes comeþ of him. Þis seeþ þe soule be grace, not ageynstondend þe bodily kend; and þe more clene and sotyl þat þe soule is made, þe more `it´ is departed fro fleschlyhed, þe scharpere syȝt it haþ and þe myghtyere lufe of þe godhed of Jesu. Þis syȝt is so myghty þat þogh no man lyfende wold trow in Jesu ne lufen him, he wuld neuer trowe þe lesse ne lufe him þe lesse, for he seþ it so sothfastly þurgh grace þat he may not vntrowe it. Þe þred man, þat hath ful syȝt of þe sunne—he troweþ it not for he seeþ it fully—betokneþ a ful blissed soule þat withouten any wal of body or of synne seeþ openly þe face of Jesu in þe blisse of heuene. Þer is no feith, and þerfor he is fully reformed in felynge.

Þere is no state abofe þis seconde reformynge þat a soule may come to here in þis lyf, for þis is þe state of perfeccyon in þe weye to heueneward. Nerþeles, al þe soules þat arn in þis state are not alle ilyke ferforth. For sum han it litel and schortly and seldom; and sum

46 it] him A ne . . . is[2]] *om.* SrLwW lyd . . . eye] lidde`s´ . . . iȝe`n´ L, lides . . . iȝen B_3EP lyd] lyth Cc his] þe As 47 letteþ] letten B_3E may not] H_7RLB_3SrAPH_6Pl, see *add.* HBH_5AsWsLwHu_2ECcMW, se it *add.* LdT, non potest Lat. Bot] ȝif *add.* As seeþ] see As þurgh] be Cc lyd . . . eye] lidde`s´ . . . iȝe`n´ L, lides . . . iȝen B_3EP lyd] lyth Cc his] þe AT 48 glemerynge] a maner of shynyng *add.* Hu_2, splendorem tenuem Lat. grete] a *prec.* LB_3WsPCc lyȝt] that ther is a liȝt *add.* M he] þat RAPl, it As, om. B_3 49 in] into Sr so] *om.* Pl is] it *prec.* Sr, he *prec.* MT, he *add.* `Lw´W 50 of Jesu] *om.* RAPlWc, Jesu Christi Lat. not . . . fully] *om.* Pl ne] nouȝt *add.* As lyd þat is] lyth of Cc lyd] liddes L$B_3$EP, iȝe *prec.* E$H_6$`W[G]´ his] *om.* As 51 kende] as *add.* As atwix] H_7HLSrLwP, atwen H_6, bytwexte RBB_3AsHu_2ELdPlW, bitwene H_5WsACcM Jesu God] H_7HBH_5WsLwHu_2TW, Jesu LB_3SrPH_6CcMLd, God RAEPl, Jesu þat is God As, deitatis Christi Jesu Lat. 52 him[1]] *om.* Cc of him] of it RAPl, of Jesu M, of God Wc, *om.* LwW þis] ys Lw 53 þat[1]] the LwPlCc or] oþer A Jesu . . . is (l. 54)] is Jesu and þat is God a M Jesu is] þer is a RAPl and[1]] *om.* H_5Ws þat[3]] *om.* E 54 Jesu is] þer is a RAPl and[1]] *rep.* R, a *add.* RAMPl a . . . þat] *om.* RAPl a] *om.* LdT þat al] *rev.* W 55 oþer] *om.* H_6 comeþ] fro him and *add.* H_5Ws, est Lat. þis] Thus W 56 ageynstondend] withstondyng Cc þe bodily] ⌜alle þe bo⌝dili L, al þe bodili B_3P, þat bodily Sr clene . . . is[2] (l. 57)] *om.* As clene and sotyl] *rev.* T clene and] cler SrLd, *om.* RAPl þat] *om.* BH_5WsM 57 soule] bodi M is[1]] it Cc made] *om.*

sunne, bot he seeþ it not clerly what it is, ne as it is, for þe lid of his eiȝe lettiþ him þat he may not see. Bot he seeþ þurgh þe lid of his eiȝe a glymerynge of grete liȝte, and he bitokneþ a soule þat is reformid in feiþ and in felynge and so is contemplatif. For he seeþ sumwhat of þe godhed of Ihesu þurgh grace, not clerly ne fully, for þe lid, þat is his bodily kynde, is ȝit a wal atwix his kynde and þe kynde of Ihesu God and lettiþ him fro þe cler siȝt of him. Bot he seeþ þurgh þis wal, after þat grace touchiþ him more or lesse, þat Ihesu is God and þat Ihesu is souereyn godnes and souereyn beenge and a blessed life, and þat al oþer godnes comiþ of him. Þis seeþ þe soule bi grace, not ageyn-stondende þe bodily kynde; and þe more clene and sotil þat þe soule is made, and þe more it is departid fro flesclied, þe scharpere siȝt it haþ and þe miȝtier lufe of þe godhed of Ihesu. Þis siȝt is so miȝti þat þawȝ none oþer man lifende wolde trowe in Ihesu nor lufe him, he wold neuer trowe þe lesse ne lufe him þe lesse, for he seeþ it so soþfastly þat he may not vntrowe it. Þe þridde man, þat haþ ful siȝt of þe sunne, he troweþ it not for he seeþ it fully, and he bitokneþ a ful blissude soule þat wiþouten ony wal of body or of synne seeþ openly þe face of Ihesu in þe blis of heuene. Þer is no feiþ, and þerfore he is fully reformed in felynge.

Þer is no state aboue þe secunde reformynge þat a soule may come to here in þis life, for þis is þe state \`of´ perfeccioun ⌜and⌝ þe wey to
8^v heuen | warde. Nerþeles alle þe soules þat are in þis state are not alle ilike fer forþ. For summe haue it litel, schortly and seldom; and

RAMPl, *om.* Lat. þe more] H_7LB$_3$PH$_6$M, and *add.* HRBH$_5$SrWsLwAHu$_2$ECcLdPlTW, a carnalitateque remocior Lat. more] þat *add.* ECc it is] *om.* A \`it´ *above line* H_7, þatt *prec.* Ld, *om.* Lat. fro] þe *add.* R fleschlyhed] fleschlinesse AE, flesshely lustes T, þorwe grace *add.* M 58 syȝt] light T myghtyere] nogher M of Jesu] *om.* RAPl 59 þat] *om.* T þogh] *om.* As no] H_7RLB$_3$SrAPH$_6$CcMPl, none oþer HBH$_5$AsWsLw-Hu$_2$ELdTW, nullus alius Lat. trow] byleeue BALdT, and beleue *add.* Wc Jesu] God RAPl ne] noþer B lufen] levyn Cc 60 wuld] scholde H_6 neuer trowe] *rev.* LB$_3$PH$_6$ trowe] byleeue BALdT, nor bileue *add.* Hu$_2$, or beleue *add.* Wc, him *add.* B_3 ne . . . lesse] *om.* A him] *om.* RMPl, neuere *add.*, *canc.* L \`so´ $W^G$, *om.* W  61 \`þurgh grace´ W^G, *om.* AsWWc vntrowe] but trowen Sr, or mistrowe *add.* T, vnleeue B, vnbeleue Wc 62 ful] þe *prec.* As he troweþ] wheche leueþ M troweþ] leeueþ B 63 betokneþ] H_7LB$_3$SrPCcM, and he *prec.* HBH$_5$AsWsLwHu$_2$EH$_6$LdTW, and þat *prec.* RAPl, et talis designat Lat. ful] *om.* As any] oþer *add.* M of[2]] *om.* LB$_3$AsP 64 Jesu] þe godhede RAPl, Jesu Christi Lat. þer] þat B \`is´ Cc  no] hole As, *om.* $B_3$  65 fully] ful E  66 state] estate M  þis] $H_7$RSrAH$_6$CcMPl, þe HBH$_5$⌜L⌝B$_3$AsWsLw-Hu$_2$EPLdTW, ista Lat.  67 state] astate M  \`of´ *interl.* H in[2]] and Lw⌜H^c⌝W þe[2]] þis A 68 al] *om.* T þe] þo As, *om.* RCcPl state] astate M 69 ilyke] lyke W ferforth] forward B, proficiunt in eodem Lat. sum[1]] men *add.* A it] *om.* M litel] a *prec.* Hu$_2$ seldom] after þe mesure of grace *add.* M

lengere, clerere and oftenere; and sum han it clerest and lengest, aftere þe aboundaunce of grace; and ȝit al þese han þe ȝifte of contemplacyon. For þe soule haþ not perfyte syȝt of Jesu al at ones, bot first a lytel, and after þat [it] profyteþ and comeþ to more felynge; and as longe as it is in þis lyfe it may wexen more in þe knowynge and in þis lufe of Jesu. And sothly I wote not what were more leefe to swilk a soule þat haþ a lytel felt of it, þan vtterly, alle oþer þynges lefte and sette at noȝt, only tente þerto, for to hafe clerer syȝt and clennere lufe of Jesu in whom is al þe blissed Trinete.

þis maner of knowynge of Jesu, as I vnderstonde, is þe openynge of
f. 87v heuene | to þe eye of a clene soule, of þe whilk holy men speken of in here wrytynge. Not as sum men wenen, þat þe openynge of heuene is if a soule myght sen by ymaginacion þurgh þe skyes abofen þe firmament, how oure Lord Jesu sitteþ in his mageste in a bodily lyȝt as mikel as an hundreþ sunnes. [Nay] it is not so, ne þogh he se neuer so heyghe on þat maner, sothly he seeþ not þe gostly heuene. þe heyghere he styeth abofen þe sunne by swilk ymaginacion for to se Jesu God, þe lowere he falleþ beneþen þe sunne. Nerþeles þis maner syȝt is sufferable to symple soules, þat kun no better seken him þat is vnseable.

70 clerere] clerlier R, clere Hu_2 and[1]] *om.* RCc oftenere] H_7HLAsSrLwAHu_2PH_6W, often R, oftere B$H_5$$B_3$WsEMLdPlT, *om.* Cc it] best *add.* LwW clerest/. . ./lengest] *rev.* As and[2]] *om.* HH_5As, *om.* Lat. 71 aboundaunce H_7SrWsAHu_2CcMT, abundynge HRBH_5-LB_3AsLwEPH_6LdPlW, habundanciam Lat. þese] þose R, þoo Pl þe[2]] *om.* As of[2]] grace and *add.* Cc 72 For . . . ones] *om.* Ld ⌜haþ . . . Jesu⌝ L no`t´ $B_3$, noo LwAEWc, non As perfyte] perfitly þe R syȝt] loue M Jesu] God RAPl 73 lytel] and a lytel *add.* LwW þat . . . and[2]] it RAPl `it´ L, *om.* $H_7$$B_3SrH_6$Ld and comeþ] þe more and comynge As felynge] sensacionem seu cognicionem Lat. 74 ⌜is . . . lyfe⌝ L `þis[1]´ H^c, *om.* H°BH_5AsWs lyfe] love As, *om.* M þe] H_7RLB_3SrAPH_6CcMPl, *om.* HBH_5AsWsLwHu_2ELdTWWc and] *om.* As þis[2]] H_7HBLB_3SrLwHu_2EPH_6CcMLdTW, þe RH_5AsWsAPl, *om.* Wc 75 Jesu] God RAPl, Domini Jesu Christi Lat. wote] ne *prec.* H_5, not BAs not] nere B, neuer M leefe] leuer Hu_2, loue M, lykyng Wc, *om.* A 76 haþ] *om.* A a lytel/felt] H_7RLB_3Sr-APCcMPl, *rev.* HBH_5AsWsLwHu_2EH_6LdTWWc felt] feelyng RM, felith A, sensit vel gustauit Lat. vtterly/alle . . . þynges] *rev.* Hu_2 vtterly] *om.* M alle] and *prec.* As þynges] þing Sr 77 sette] hem *add.* LB_3P only tente] H_7RLB_3SrAPH_6MPl, *rev.* HBH_5AsWs-LwHu_2ECcLdTW, and take heed only Hu_2, and attende only Wc only] and *prec.*

summe lengere, clerere and oftner; and summe han it clerist [and] lengest, aftir þe abundynge of grace; and ȝit alle þese han þe ȝifte of contemplacioun. For þe soule haþ not perfit siȝt of Ihesu al at ones, bot first a litel, and aftir þat it profiteþ and comiþ to more felynge; and as longe as it is in `þis´ lif it may wexen more in knowynge and in þis luf of Ihesu. And soþly I wote not what were more lefe to swilk a soule þat haþ felt a litel of it, þan vtterly, alle oþer þinges left and set at noȝt, tent only þerto, for to hafe clerer siȝt and clenner luf of Ihesu in whome is alle þe blissid Trinite.

þis maner knowynge of Ihesu, as I vndirstande, is þe openynge of heuene to þe iȝe of a clene soule, of þe whilk holy men `speken´ of in here writynge. Not as summe wenen, þat þe openynge of heuen is as if a soule miȝt seen by ymaginacioun þurȝ þe skies abouen þe firmament, how oure Lorde Ihesu sittiþ in his maieste in a bodily liȝt as mikel as an hundred sunnes. Nay it is not so, ne þawȝ he see neuer so `h´eiȝe on þat maner, soþly he seþ not þe gostly heuen. þe hiȝere he stieþ aboue þe sunne for to see Ihesu God so bi swilk ymaginacioun, þe lowere he falliþ bineþ þe sunne. Nerþeles þis maner siȝt is suffrable to symple soules, þat kunne no bettere seke him þat is vnseable.

LB_3PH_6Cc, but *prec.* As clerer] clere BMWc, clenner T 78 Jesu . . . al] *om.* RAPl al] *om.* M blissed] holi M 79 of[1]] $H_7RLB_3SrAEPH_6CcT$, *om.* $HBH_5AsWsLwHu_2MLdPlW$ `of[2]´ R Jesu] God RAPl as I vnderstonde/is] *rev.* As þe] *om.* T 80 to þe eye of/a clene soule] *rev.* $H_5$ clene] clere T of þe whilk] whereof $H_5Ws$ speken of] *om.* As `speken´ *interl.* H of[3]] $H_7HRBLB_3AsSrLwHu_2EPPlTW$, *om.* H_5WsAH_6CcMLd 81 men] H_7H_5Ws, *om.* Σ þe[1]] *om.* M 82 if] $H_7RLB_3SrAPH_6CcMPl$, *om.* $HBH_5WsLwHu_2ELdTW$, as ȝeve þat As, si Lat. `sen´ Pl skyes] skye E, cloudus A `abofen´ A, et *prec.* Lat. 83 Jesu] *om.* RAPl sitteþ] sittyng M bodily] *om.* RAMPl 84 mikel as] *om.* Ws Nay] þat H_7 ne] *om.* AT se] sawe As 85 on] in AMLd þe[1]] *om.* T 86 he] þat *prec.* Sr styeth] seeth RAPl þe] cloudus and þe *add.* A by . . . ymaginacion/for . . . God] $H_7RLB_3SrAPH_6CcMPl$, *rev.* $HBH_5AsWsLwHu_2ELdTW$, per talem ymaginacionem ad videndum Jesum verum Deum Lat. ymaginacion] ymaginaciouns H_5WsPl 87 Jesu] *om.* RAPl God] *om.* CcM þe[1]] so *prec.* AsECcM beneþen] to *add.* As þis maner] þe As, of *add.* E 88 symple] synful *prec.* As þat kun] the whiche cunnyn no ferther ner Cc no] not Ws better seken] melius inquirere vel perfeccius Lat. seken] to *add.* Cc 89 vnseable] inuisible A

How Jesu is heuene to þe soule, and how a soule schal seke Jesu abofe itself and within itself, and why Jesu is called fyre and lyght. Capitulum xxxiii^m

What is heuene to a resonable soule? Sothly, not ellys bot Jesu God. For if þat be heuene only þat is abofen a þinge, þan is God only heuene to mans soule. For he is only abofe þe kynde of a soule. Þan if a soule þurgh grace may han knowynge of þat blissed kend of Jesu, sothly he seeþ heuene, for he seeþ God.

Þerfore þer are many men þat erren in vnderstondynge of sum wordes þat are seid of God, for þei vnderstonden hem not gostly. Holy wryteng seith þat a soule þat wil fynd God schal liften vpward þe ynnere eye and seke God abofen itself. Þan sum men þat wulde don after þis seyenge vnderstonde þis word abofe hemself as for heyghere settynge in stede and for wurthines of place, as on element or o planet is abofe anoþer in settynge and in wurthines of bodily place. Bot it is not so gostly. For a soule is abofe alle bodily þynge, not by settyng of stede, bot by sotylte and wurthynes of kende. Ryȝt so on þe self wyse, God is abofe alle bodily and gostly creatures, not by settynge of stede bot þurgh sotylte and wurthines of his vnchaungeable blissed kende. And þerfor he þat wil wysly seke God and fynde
f. 88r him, he schal not rennen out | with his þoght as if he wold clymbe abofen þe sunne & [persen] þe firmamente, and ymagynen þe mageste as it were a lyȝt of an hundreþ sunnes; bot he schal raþer dragwe doun þe sunne and alle þe firmamente, and forgeten it and casten it beneþen

Chapter 33 *title*: $H_7RLB_3SrAEPH_6MLdPlTW$ [Pl *below, at Chapter 34*] How grace openeþ þe [miȝte *canc.*] inner eye of þe soule into goostly beholdyng of Jesu. Pl [*cf. above, Chapter 32 title*] *om.* $HBH_5WsLwHu_2Cc$ 1 How . . . soule[1]] What heuene is As þe] a R `and[1] . . . itself[2] (l. 2)´ $T^GW^G$, *om.* ALdTW schal . . . lyght (l. 3)] may haue þe blyssed knowynge of Jesu As Jesu[2]] *rep.*, *canc.* L, God Pl 2 `why Jesu´ T^GW^G, *rev.*, *marked for trsp.* Pl, why he ATW, wyche Ld called] clepid H_6LdW `and lyght´ $T^GW^G$, *om.* ALdTW 4 ellys] *om.* RAPl God] *om.* RAPl, verus Deus Lat. 5 þat] he *add.* AsT`W^G´, *om.* Cc only[1]] soule As a] $H_7BH_5LB_3SrWsHu_2PMLdPl$, al $HRAsLwAEH_6CcTW$, aliqua Lat. God] Jesu *prec.* M 6 heuene] *om.* B to mans soule] *om.* A mans] a *prec.* AsPl For . . . soule] *om.* E soule] anime racionalis Lat. 7 þurgh grace/may] H_7, *rev.* Σ may] *om.* T knowynge] þe *prec.* As þat] þe SrWc of Jesu] *om.* RAPl Jesu] illius . . . scilicet deitatis Jesu Christi Lat. 8 heuene . . . seeþ] *rep.* P God] Jesu M 9 þerfore] *rep.* Ld erren] ben A, are Pl, *canc.* As 10 God] Jesu M hem not] *rev.* M 11 wryteng] $H_7HBLB_3AsSrLwAHu_2PH_6CcMW$, writte RWsELdPlT`$W^G$´, wrytis H_5, scriptura Lat. a] mannys *add.* Sr wil] wolde ELdPl fynd] resceyue As God] Jesu M liften] rere Ld vpward] vp $H_5SrWsCc$ 12 God] hit M itself] the self Cc men] $H_7HRBH_5WsLwAHu_2ECcMLdPlTW$, *om.* $LB_3AsSrPH_6$ 13 vnderstonde] vnderstondynge As hemself] itself $AsHu_2$ 14 heyghere] his ȝere As, þe *prec.* Ld for] $H_7RLB_3AsSrAEPH_6CcMPl$, *om.* $HBH_5WsLwHu_2LdTW$, quantum ad Lat.

[CHAPTER 33]

What is heuen to a resonable soule? Soþly not elles bot Ihesu God. For if þat be heuen only þat is aboue al þinge, þan is God only heuen
9r to mannes soule. For | he is only abofe þe kynde of a soule. Þan if a soule may þurghe grace haue knowynge of þat blissid kynde of Ihesu, soþly he seeþ heuen, for he seeþ God.

Þerfor þer are mony men þat erren in vndirstandynge of summe wordes þat are seide of God, for þei vndirstanden hem not gostly. Holy writynge seiþ þat a soule þat wil fynde God schal liften vpwarde þe innere eȝe and seke God abofe itself. Þan summe men þat wolde don aftir þis seynge vndirstonden þis word 'abofe' hemself as for hieȝere settynge in stede and wurþines of place, as on elemente and on planet is abofe anoþer in settynge and worþines of a bodily place. Bot it is not so gostly. For a `soule is´ [a]boue al bodily þinge, not bi settynge of stede bot bi sotelte and worþines `of kynde´. Riȝt so on þe selfe wise, God is aboue al bodily and gostly creatures, not bi settynge of stede bot þurghe sotelte and worþines of his vnchaungeable blissid kynde. And þerfore he þat wil wisely seke God and fynden him, he schal not renne out wiþ his þoȝt as he wolde clymbe abouen þe sunne and persen þe firmament, and ymagynen þe maieste as it were a liȝt of an hundred sunnes; bot he schal raþer drawe downe þe sunne and al þe firmament, and forgeten it and kesten it bineþ him þer he is, and

wurthines] worþiere LB$_3$P of] a *add.* As place] bodily *add.* A of . . . wurthines (l. 15) *om.* A as] and T 15 or o planet] *om.* Ld or] H$_7$LB$_3$SrLwAEPH$_6$CcMPlW [*corr. fr.* and Lw], and HBH$_5$AsWsHu$_2$LdT, *om.* R, vel Lat. `o´ W$^G$, *om.* LwW planet] place AsSr settynge] syttyng CcM in$^2$] H$_7$RBLB$_3$AsSrAEPH$_6$CcMLdPlT, *om.* HH$_5$WsLw-Hu$_2$W of] H$_7$RBLB$_3$SrAEPH$_6$CcMLdPlT, a *add.* HH$_5$AsWsLwHu$_2$W bodily place] kynde T bodily] worldly As 16 not] no B$_3$ a . . . abofe] a `soule is´ boue H^c; a boue H° alle] H$_7$HBH$_5$AsWsLwHu$_2$ECcMLdTW, a RLB$_3$SrAPH$_6$Pl, omnem Lat. þynge] þingis AsCcM not] *om.* As 17 settyng] syttyng CcM stede] a *prec.* As bot] boþe As `of kende´ H^c, *om.* H°H$_5$AsWs on] H$_7$HRBH$_5$AsWsLwAHu$_2$ECcMPlTW, in LB$_3$SrPH$_6$Ld 18 þe self] þysylff Ld self] same WsAHu$_2$T God] Jesu M abofe] bodely T bodily and gostly/creatures] *rev.* A 19 settynge] syttyng M þurgh] bi A vnchaungeable] and *add.* ACc 20 seke] felyn SrM God] Jesu M 21 out] extra se Lat. if] H$_7$RLB$_3$SrEPH$_6$CcPl, þoȝ AsT, *om.* HBH$_5$AsWsLwHu$_2$MLdW, quasi Lat. 22 persen] HBLB$_3$SrWsHu$_2$PH$_6$, perschen H$_5$, perchen As, peryȝhe, *corr. fr.* perche Ld, perishe ET, parten R⌜Lw⌝ACcMPlW, pursew H$_7$, penetrare Lat. mageste] diuinam maiestatem Lat. 23 as . . . sunnes] velud lucem corpoream luce solis in centuplo maiorem Lat. `were´ Cc a liȝt] *om.* LwW a] þe B$_3$M `bot´ W^G, *om.* W doun] adoun M 24 forgeten] for to geten As and^3] for to *add.* As

him þere he is, and setten al þis and al bodily þyng also at noȝt, and þenken þan if he kan gostly boþe of himself and of God also. And if he do þus, þan seeþ þe soule abofe itselfe and þan seeþ it heuene.

Vpon þis self maner schal þis wurde withinne ben vnderstonden. It is commonly seyd þat a soule schal seken oure Lord withinne al þynge and withinne itself. Soth it is þat oure Lord is withinne al creatures, not on þat maner as a kernel is hyd withinne þe schelle of an notte or as a lytel bodily þyng is hid and holden withinnen anoþer mykel. Bot he is withinnen al creatures as holdend and kepend hem in here beenge, þurgh sotylte and þurgh myght of his owen blissed kende and clennes vnseable. For ryȝt as a þynge þat is most precyous and most clene is leyd ynnerest, ryȝt so be þat lyknes is it seyd þat þe kend of God, þat is most precyouse, and most clene, and most gostly, ferthest fro bodilyhed, is hid withinnen al þynges. And þerfor he þat wil seke God withinnen, he schal forȝete first al bodily þyng, for alle þat is withouten, and his owen body; and he schal forgete þe þenkynge of his owen soule, and þenken on þat vnmade kende þat is Jesu, þat made him, quykneth him, holdeþ him, and gyfeþ him reson and mende and lufe, þe whilk is withinnen him þurgh his priuey myȝt and souereyn sotylte. Vpon þis maner schal þe soule—whan grace toucheþ it, ellys it wil bot lytel avayle—seke Jesu and fynde him withinne itself and withinne alle creatures, as me þenkeþ.

Also it is seyd in Holy Writte þat God is lyȝt. So seyþ Seyn Ion:

25 þere] þeras LB$_3$SrEPM and[2] . . . also/at noȝt] *rev.* Pl þyng] þyngis AsMLd also/at noȝt] R also] *canc.* As, *om.* H$_6$Cc 26 þenken þan] *rev.* H$_6$ þan] hem As, *om.* Sr boþe of himself] body and soule As boþe] *om.* H$_5$Ws God] Jesu M 27 seeþ] setteþ he As, he *add.* T itselfe] H$_7$HRBH$_5$SrWsLwAHu$_2$MLdPlTW, himself LB$_3$AsEPH$_6$, the self Cc \`and´ W^G, *om.* LwW seeþ it] *rev.* H$_6$ it] he AsMT, into *add.* LwW [*canc.* W^G] 28 Vpon . . . itself (l. 30)/Soth . . . creatures] *rev.* As Vpon] On WsACcM þis self] þis same WsT, þe same H$_6$Cc self . . . þis[2]] same As self maner] maner wise Hu$_2$ withinne/ben vnderstonden] *rev.* Cc It] and *prec.* Pl 29 commonly] comely Ld seyd] *om.* As seken . . . withinne] ⌜see oure Lord wiþynne⌝ [⌜-ynne⌝ *canc.*] L seken] H$_7$HRBH$_5$SrWsLwAHu$_2$CcMLdPlTW, see ⌜L⌝B$_3$AsEPH$_6$, querere Lat. withinne] wiþ ⌜L⌝B$_3$ [⌜-ynne⌝ *canc.* L] 30 itself] the self Cc, But *add.* As \`is[2]´ Cc al] erþly *add.* As creatures] creature\`s´ H, but *add.* E 31 on] in AsAM, þat *add*, *canc.* H, *om.* Pl as] þat *prec.* Pl, that LwW \`a´ Pl, þe As hyd] *om.* Cc with\`inne´ L an] H$_7$, þe Cc, a Σ or] ouþer AsA, for M, elles *add.* T 32 as] *om.* B$_3$Cc a] *om.* H$_6$ bodily] *om.* M hid and holden] H$_7$RLB$_3$SrAPH$_6$CcPl, hadde and holden E, holden HBH$_5$AsWsLwHu$_2$MLdW, hidde T, continetur Lat. anoþer mykel] a gretter thyng Cc mykel] H$_7$HRBLB$_3$SrLwHu$_2$PH$_6$CcLdPlW, more AE\`W^G´, gretter H$_6$, þyng *add.* H$_5$As-WsEMT, maiorem Lat. 34 þurgh] *om.* LwEMW owen] *om.* LB$_3$SrPH$_6$ blissed] gostly *add.* B 35 as] ȝe seen *add.* As þat is] *om.* As precyous] preciousest As 36 clene] clennest As is[1]] *om.* As ynnerest] neþerist RPl, neþermost A, most inner As, in-muste T is it] H$_7$BHu$_2$Pl, *rev.* HBH$_5$LB$_3$AsSrWsLwAEPH$_6$CcMLdTW þat] *om.*

setten al þis and al bodily þinge also at noȝt, and þenke þan if he kan gostly boþ of himself and of God also. And if he do þus, þan seeþ þe soule aboue itself and þan seeþ it heuen.

Vpon þis self maner schal þis wurde 'withinne' be vndirstande. It is comunly seide þat a soule schal see oure Lorde withinne al þinge and withinne itself. Soþ it is þat oure Lorde is withinne alle creature`s´,
9v bot not on | þat manere as a kirnel is hid withinne þe schelle of a nut or as a litel bodily þinge is holden within anoþer mikel. But he is within alle creatures as holdend and kepende hem in her beenge, þurȝ sotilte and þurghe miȝt of his owne blessed kende and klennes vnseable. For riȝt as a þinge þat is most precious and most clene is leid innerest, riȝt so bi þat liknes it is seid þat þe kende of God, þat is most precious, most clene and most gostly, ferrest fro bodilichede, is hid within alle þinges. And þerfor he þat wil seke God within, he schal forget first alle bodily þinge, for al þat is withouten, and his owne body; and he schal forgete þenkynge of his owne soule, and þenken on þat vnmade kynde, þat is Ihesu, þat made him, qwikneþ him, holdiþ him, and gifiþ him resoun and mende and lufe, þe whilk is within him þurgh his miȝt and souereyn sotilte. Vpon þis maner schal þe soule `do´ when grace touchiþ it, elles it wil bot litel `availe to´ seken Ihesu and fynd`e´n him within it and within alle creatures, as me þinkeþ.

Also it is seide in Holy Writ þat God is liȝt. So seiþ Seint Johan:

LB_3SrP 37 God] Jesu M `is[I]´ Cc and[I]] $H_7$RBL$B_3$SrAP$H_6$MPl, *om.* H$H_5$AsWs-LwH$u_2$ECcLdTW, et Lat. most gostly] `mostely´ Pl gostly] goodly LwCcW ferthest] H_7RH_5LB_3SrWsLwPH_6CcMPl, ferrest HBAHu_2ELdW, fertheriste T, First As 38 bodilyhed] þe moste bodily As And þerfor] *rep.*, *canc.* E 39 forȝete first] *rev.* H_6 forȝete] gorgete W al] wordilly thynges and *add.* M þyng] thynggis LwCcMLdW 40 and[I] . . . and[2]] *om.* A and[I]] *om.* Hu_2 and[2]] *om.* RAPl þe] H_7RLB_3SrAEPH_6CcPl, *om.* HBH_5AsWsLwHu_2MLdTW þenkynge] cogitacionem seu ymaginacionem Lat. of] on As 41 þenken] to *prec.* As on] vpon As, of Pl þat[I]] the LwW vnmade kende] mankynde and of kynde As þat is Jesu] *om.* RAMPl 42 him[I]] and *add.* As, *om.* Lw quykneth] quikyþ H_5Ws, quikned RAsCc him[2]] and *add.* LB_3PH_6M him[4]] *om.* Cc and[2]] *om.* CcM 43 þe] *om.* As withinnen] with As priuey] H_7RLB_3SrAEPH_6CcMPl`$T^G$$W^G$´, *om.* HB$H_5$AsWsLwH$u_2$LdTW, occultam Lat. 44 Vpon] On Ws soule] $H_7$$H^{\circ}$RBAsAH$u_2$$H_6$MPlT, do *add.* `L´B_3SrLw`$H^c$´EPLdW, worche *add.* $H_5$Ws, *add.* felyn Cc, faciet Lat. 45 it[I]] hym L$B_3$P$H_6$Cc ellys] or *prec.* Lw`H^c´TW it wil] *rev.* M wil bot] well T wil] hyl As, ben *add.* Cc lytel] a *prec.* B_3Hu_2 avayle] H_7RAH_6MPl, `availe to´ $H^c$, to *add.* L$B_3$AsSrLwEPCcLdTW, *om.* $H^{\circ}$$H_5$AsWs seke] felyn $H_5$Ws Jesu] God RAPl fynde] to *prec.* Lw$H^c$EW him] *om.* M 46 itself] $H_7$RL$B_3$SrLwAEP$H_6$MPlW, `-self´ H^c, the self Cc, it H°BH_5Ws-Hu_2LdT, þat As and withinne] *rep.*, *canc.* Sr 47 Writte] I Io. I *add.* Ld þat . . . Ion] *om.* M Ion] I° Io. I. *add.* BLHu_2EPW, I[a] Ioh. *add.* T

Deus lux est. þat is: God is lyȝt. þis lyȝt schal not ben vnderstonden as for bodily lyȝt, bot it is vnderstonden þus: God is lyȝt: þat is, God is f. 88[v] trewth and sothfastnes, | for sothfastnes is gostly liȝt. þan he þat most gracyously knoweþ sothfastnes, best seeþ God. And nerþeles it is lykned to bodily lyȝt, for þis skille. Ryȝt as þe sunne scheweþ to þe bodily eye itself and al bodily þyng be it, ryȝt so sothfastnes, þat is God, scheweþ to þe reson of þe soule itself first, and by itself al oþer gostly þynges þat nedeþ to ben knowen of a soule. þus seyth þe prophete: *Domine, in lumine tuo videbimus lumen*. Lord, we schul seen þy lyȝt be þi lyȝt; þat is, We schul seen þe þat art sothfastnes by þiself.

On þe selfe wyse it is seyd þat God is fyre: *Deus noster ignis consumens est*. þat is: Oure Lord is fyre wastende; þat is for to seyn, God is not fyre elementare þat heteth a body and brenneþ it, bot God is lufe and charite. For as fyre wasteþ al bodily þinge þat may be wasted, ryȝt so þe lufe of God wasteþ and brenneþ alle synne out of þe soule and makeþ it clene, as fyre makeþ clene al maner metalle. þese wurdes, and alle oþer þat are spoken of oure Lord in holy wrytenge by bodily lyknes, must nedes ben vnderstonden gostly, elles þer is no sauour in hem. Nerþeles þe cause why swilk maner wurdes are seyd of oure Lord in Holy Writte is þis. For we are so fleschly þat we kun not speken of God ne vnderstonden of him bot if we by swilk wurdes first ben entred in. Nerþeles whan þe ynner eye is opned þurgh grace for to han a lytel syȝt of Jesu, þan schal þe soule turne lyȝtly inogw al swilk wurdes of bodily þynges into gostly vnderstondynge.

þis gostly opnynge of þe ynnere eye into knowynge of þe godhed I calle reformynge in feith and in felyng. For þan þe soule sumwhat

48 þat is] *om*. H_5Ws þis] þe LB_3PH_6, þat As schal] ne *prec*. As not/ben vnderstonden] *rev*. E not] *om*. RAPl vnderstonden] thus *add*. Cc as . . . vnderstonden (l. 49)] *om*. RAPl 49 lyȝt] *om*. As is[1]] shall be M vnderstonden þus] *rev*. Cc þat . . . is[3]] *om*. M 50 trewth] trewe R sothfastnes[2]] softfastnesse L, goddys liȝt As liȝt] *om*. As þan] *om*. RAPl þat] *om*. Ws most gracyously/knoweþ] *rev*. E 51 gracyously] graciouse As God] g- *prec*., *canc*. Sr, Jesu M And] *om*. Cc 52 to[1]] þe *add*. AsW for] be As skille] resoun Hu_2 sunne] shyneþ and *add*. Pl þe[2]] *om*. B 53 eye] be *add*. Sr itself] the self Cc, riȝt so *prec*. As and . . . itself[2] (l. 54)] *om*. As al] a B_3 þyng] thyngis CcM be it] briȝt LB_3P so] *om*. H_5 54 God] Jesu M itself[1]] the self Cc first] *om*. M itself[2]] the self Cc oþer] *om*. M 55 þynges] H_7AsCcLdPlT, þinge HBH_5LB_3SrWsLwAHu_2EPH_6MW, omnia alia spiritualia Lat. nedeþ] neden AsPl ben knowen] the knowynge W a] the Cc 56 prophete] Ps. 35° *add*. BLHu_2EPLdTW lumen] þat is *add*. AsE 57 þy . . . seen] *om*. RAPl þy] H_7HBH_5SrWsLwHu_2CcMLdTW, þe As, *om*. LB_3EPH_6 be þi lyȝt] *om*. Sr sothfastnes] soþfast B 58 selfe] $H_7HRH_5LB_3$AsSrLwPCcLdPlTW, same WsAHu_2EH_6M seyd] seen Pl God] oure Lord *prec*. Hu_2 fyre] Heb. 12° *add*. BLHu_2EPLdTW Deus] iuxta illud Scripture *prec*. Lat. 59 consumens est] *rev*. A est] *om*. As is[1]] for to sey *add*. H_6 Lord] *om*. Cc þat[2] . . . seyn] *om*. H_6 is] more *add*.

Deus lux est. Þat is: God is liȝt. Þis liȝt schal not ben vndirstanden as for bodily liȝt, bot it is vndirstandid þus: God is liȝt; þat is, God is trewþ and soþfastnes, for soþfastnes is gostly liȝt. Þan he þat most graciously knowiþ soþfastnes, best seeþ God. And nerþeles it is likned to bodily liȝt, for þis skil. Riȝt as þe sunne schewþ to þe bodily eiȝe itself and al bodily þinge bi it, riȝt so soþfastnes, þat is God, schewiþ to þe resoun of þe soule itself first, and by itself al oþere gostly þinge
10r þat nediþ to be knowen of a soule. Þus seiþ þe prophet: *Domine, in lu* | *mine tuo videbimus lumen*. Lord, we schul see þi liȝt bi þi liȝt; þat is, we schul see þe þat art soþfastnes bi þiself.

On þe self wise it is seide þat God is fire: *Deus noster ignis consumens est*. Þat is: Oure Lord is fir wastende; þat is for to seie, God is not fire elementare þat hetiþ a body and brenneþ it, bot God is luf and charite. For as fiire wasteþ al bodily þinge þat may be wasted, riȝt so þe luf of God brenniþ and wastiþ al synne out of þe soule and makiþ it clene, as fire makiþ clene al maner metal. Þese wordes, and al oþer þat are spoken of oure Lorde in holy writynge bi bodily liknes, moste nedis ben vndirstonden gostly, elles þer is no ⌜sauour⌝ in hem. Nerþeles þe cause whi swilke maner wordes are seid of oure Lorde in Holy Writt is þis. For we are so flescly þat we kun not speken of God ne vndirstonden of him bot if we bi swilke wordes first ben entrid in. Nerþeles when þe inner eiȝe is opned þurȝ grace for to hafe a litel siȝt of Ihesu, þan schal þe soule turne liȝtly inowȝ alle swilke wordes of bodily þinges into gostly vndirstondynge.

Þis gostly opnynge of þe inner iȝe into knowynge of þe godhed I calle reformynge in feiþ and in felynge. For þan þe soule sumwhat

As for] *om*. H_5Ws 60 not fyre] *rev*. M elementare] elemental Sr, lumentarye As þat] þe A God[2]] Jesu M 61 al bodily þinge þat] omnia corporalia que . . . possunt Lat. al] a Sr \`þinge´ Cc 62 God] Jesu M wasteþ and brenneþ] $H_7$RL$B_3$SrAP$H_6$CcMPl, *rev*. HB$H_5$AsWsLw$Hu_2$ELdTW synne] synnes M 63 \`makeþ[1] . . . fyre´ Pl make\`þ´[1] L it] *om*. Sr as . . . clene] *om*. Sr clene al maner] *om*. M al maner] omnia genera Lat. maner] of *add*. AsPl 64 Lord] God *add*. M wrytenge] wrytt LwA$H_6$CcW 65 bodily lyknes] similitudines corporales Lat. must] bihouith A nedes] nede Ws, nedeþ B, nede\`þ´ Pl, *om*. T, to *add*. M elles] For *prec*. H_5Ws, or *prec*. CcM is no] nys none As 66 ⌜sauour⌝ H, trowþe H_5Ws, resoun As, sapor vel delectacio spiritualis Lat. in] of M why] þat *add*. H_5Ws maner] of *add*. As of] *om*. As 67 in Holy Writte] *om*. A ⌜þat . . . God⌝ L 68 speken] *om*. LB_3P God] Jesu M vnderstonden] haue vndirstondyng Hu_2 of] *om*. Pl we] he Hu_2 by . . . first/ben] *rev*. M by . . . wurdes/first] *rev*. Sr first ben] *rev*. EH_6 69 \`ben´ Pl in] *om*. As whan] þat *add*. As \`grace´ Cc 70 Jesu] God RAPl, Domino Jesu Christo Lat. 72 ynnere] eye [*space*] A into knowynge] in tokenynge As I calle] ycleped As 73 calle] clepe H_6LdT in[1]] into Lw and in] of As in[2]] om. LwH_6W sumwhat feleþ] *rev*. RLdT sumwhat] somdell M feleþ in vnderstondynge of þat þing þat it had before only in naked trowynge. And þat is þe bigynnynge of contemplacion, of þe whilk Seyn Poule seyth þus: *Non contemplantibus nobis que videntur, sed que non videntur; quia que videntur, temporalia sunt, que autem non videntur, eterna sunt*. Þat is: Oure contemplacion is not in þinges þat are seen, bot it is in þinges vnseable; for þinges þat are seen are passend, bot f. 89r þinges vnseable are aylastend. To þe whilk | sy3t euerilk a soule schuld desyre for to come, boþe here in partye and in þe blisse of heuene fully. For in þat sy3t and in þat knowynge of Jesu is fully þe blisse of a resonable soule and endles lyf. Þus seyþ oure Lord: *Hec est autem vita eterna: vt cognoscant te verum Deum et quem misisti Jesum Christum*. Þat is: Fader, þis is endles lyf: þat þi chosen soules knowe þe [and] þi Sone Jesu Crist whom þou hast sent, on sothfast God.

O[f] two maner of lufe, formed and vnformed, what it meneþ, and how we arn beholden for to lufe Jesu mykel for oure makynge, bot mykel more for oure byeng, bot most for oure ful safeng, whan he gyfeþ þe Holy Gost to vs and makeþ vs saf þurgh lufe. Capitulum xxxiiii[m]

Bot now wondres þou, syn þis knowynge of God is þe blis and ende of a soule, why þan hafe I seid þe here before þat þe soule schuld not elles coueyte bot only þe lufe of God. I spake noþinge of þis sy3t, þat a soule schuld coueyte þis. Vnto þis I may seyn þus: þat þe sy3t of Jesu

74 in[1]] of þe R þat[1]] þe Pl, *om.* Sr it] is RMLdT, I Pl had] *om.* M only] H$_7$RLB$_3$SrAEPH$_6$CcMPl, *om.* HBH$_5$AsWsLwHu$_2$LdTW, solam Lat. 75 trowynge] byleeue BLdT, *corr. fr.* knowynge B$_3$ þe[1]] *om.* LB$_3$PH$_6$ 76 þus] 2[a] ad Cor. 4° *add.* BLHu$_2$EPLdTW Non] in *add.* B, enim *add.* T `nobis´ Sr, in rebus M, *corr. to* vobis Ld sed . . . videntur[2] (l. 77)] *om.* AsA videntur[1]] vident E 77 sunt] *om.* Sr 78 Oure] *om.* M contemplacion is] contemplacions are Pl in] of H5Ws 79 it is] *om.* RACc seen] seable E passend] temperal and *prec.* B 80 þinges vnseable] H$_7$RLB$_3$SrAPH$_6$CcPl, *rev.* HBH$_5$AsWsLwHu$_2$EMLdTW vnseable] invisible B aylastend] H$_7$HRBH$_5$LWsPCcM, euerlastinge B$_3$AsLwAHu$_2$EH$_6$PlW, alwey lastynge SrLdT To] Onto Cc, vnto M euerilk a] H$_7$HR, euerych B, euery H$_5$LB$_3$AsSrWsLwAHu$_2$EPH$_6$CcMPlTW, eche Ld soule] wi3t As 81 schuld] sch- *prec.*, *canc.* Sr come] H$_7$RLB$_3$SrWsAPH$_6$CcMPl, to *add.* HBH$_5$AsLwHu$_2$ELdTW 82 fully] al *prec.* Cc, plenarie et perfecte Lat. in[2]] *om.* M Jesu] God RAPl 83 þus . . . Lord] H$_7$RLB$_3$Sr`Lw´AEPH$_6$CcMPlTW, For oure Lord saiþ hymself in þe Gospel Hu$_2$, *om.* HBH$_5$AsWsLd, vnde Deus dicit Lat. Hec] Io. 17° *prec.* BLHu$_2$EPLdT, Joh. vii *prec.* W 84 autem] *om.* MLdT cognoscant te] cognoscatis M verum] H$_7$RLB$_3$SrAPH$_6$CcLdPlTW, vnum HBH$_5$AsWsLwHu$_2$EM, verum Lat. `quem´ Cc Jesum Christum] *rev.*, *marked for trsp.* Cc 85 þis] þatt Ld is] *om.* RA þi] þe AsCc 86 and] in H$_7$, et Lat. Jesu Crist] H$_7$RLB$_3$SrAPH$_6$CcMPl, *om.* HBH$_5$AsWsLwHu$_2$ELdTW, Jesum Christum Lat. sent] *om.* As on] as Cc, *om.* RAH$_6$Pl God] Jesu Crist *add.* E

feliþ in vndirstandynge of þat þinge þat it had bifore in nakid
trowynge. And þat is þe bigynnynge of contemplacioun, of þe
whilk Seynt Poul seiþ þus: *Non contemplantibus nobis que videntur,*
sed que non videntur; quia que videntur, temporalia sunt, que autem non
videntur, eterna sunt. Þat is: Oure contemplacioun is not in þinges þat
are seen, bot it is in þinges vnseable; for þinges þat are seen are
10v passende, bot vnseable þinges are aylastende. To þe | whilk siȝt
euerilk a soule schuld desire for to come to, boþe here in party and in
þe blis of heuen fully. For in þat siȝt and in þat knowynge of Ihesu is
fully þe blis of a resonable soule and endles lif: *Hec est autem vita*
eterna: vt cognoscant te vnum Deum et quem misisti Ihesum Christum. Þat
is: Fader, þis is endeles life: þat þi chosen soules knowe þe and þi
Sone whom þu hast sent, on soþfast God.

[CHAPTER 34]

But now wondrest þu, siþen þis knowynge of God is þe blis and þe ende of a soule, whi þan haue I seid here bifore þat a soule schuld noȝt elles coueite bot only þe luf of God. I spake noþinge of þis siȝt, þat a soule schuld coueit þis. Vnto þis I may say þus: þat þe siȝt of Ihesu is

Chapter 34 *title*: H$_7$RLB$_3$SrAEPH$_6$MLdTW `How þou maist see þat loue formed is not cause whi a soule comeþ to þe gostly siȝt of Jesu, but loue vnformed, þat is God himself, is cause of al þis knowyng´. *in plummet, over erasure* H[c] þat parfite loue and gostly vnderstandynge of a perfite soule þe wiche is made brennyng and feruent by þe grace of þe Holy Gost lyfteþ vp a soule in steringe to þe perfeccioun of perfite felynge As How Jesu is heuen to þe soule and how a soule shal seche God aboue hitselfe and wiþinne hitselfe, and whi Jesu is called fire and liȝt. Pl [*cf. above, Chapter 33 Title*] *om.* BH$_5$WsLwHu$_2$Cc 1 Of[1]] On H$_7$, In Sr maner] maners RLdT of[2]] loues: of *add.* E, *om.* H$_6$ lufe[1]] loues M and vnformed/what it meneþ] *rev.* LB$_3$P vnformed] vnreformed Sr, loue *prec.* E what] and *prec.* E it meneþ] þei menen E 2 beholden] holde TW for[1]] *om.* H$_6$TW `Jesu´ L mykel] *om.* M 3 mykel] *om.* A byeng] ayen-bieng TW bot[2]] and AMLdTW most] alther *prec.* RLATW 4 `whan . . . saf´ W[G], *om.* ALdTW gyfeþ] vs *add.* M to vs] *om.* M 5 þurgh] by `W[G]´E `lufe´ W[G], þat he loueth vs *add.* RA, of Jesu *add.*, *canc.* L, þatt he louyd us Ld, yeftes of his loue TW, dileccionem Lat. 6 syn] for as mych as Hu$_2$ of[1]] *rep.*, *canc.* L God] Jesu CcM blis] blissedhede As ende] H$_7$BHu$_2$H$_6$, þe *add.* HH$_5$`L´B$_3$AsSr-WsLwAEPCcMLdPlTW 7 a] þe E hafe I] *rev.* Pl seid] yseyd As þe[1]] H$_7$Sr, *om.* Σ before] tofore A þe[2]] H$_7$RLB$_3$SrAPH$_6$CcMPl, a HBH$_5$AsWsLwHu$_2$ELdTW schuld] schal LB$_3$PH$_6$Ld not elles] noþyng M 8 only] all *prec.* As, *om.* ALd God] Jesu CcM I] and *prec.* H$_5$Ws, bot *prec.* LB$_3$EPH$_6$ syȝt] loue nor liȝt M, visione seu cognicione Lat. 9 þis[1]] þus ALdT Vnto] As to H$_5$Ws, To LdT I may] *rev.* W þe] þis A syȝt] visio seu cognicio Lat. of Jesu] *om.* RAPl is ful blis of a soule, and þat is not only for þe syȝt, bot it is also for þe blissed lufe þat comeþ out of þe syȝt. Nerþeles for lufe comeþ out of knowenge and not knowenge of lufe, þerfor it is seid þat in knowynge and in syȝt principally of God with lufe is þe blis of a soule, and þe more he is knowen þe better he is lufed. Bot for as mikel as to þis knowynge, or to þis lufe þat comeþ of it, may not þe soule come withouten lufe, þerfor seyd I þat þou schuldest only coueyte lufe. For lufe is cause why a soule comeþ to þis syght and to þis knowynge; and þat lufe is not þe lufe þat a soule hath in itself to God. Bot þe lufe þat oure Lord haþ to a synful soule þat kan ryȝt not lufen him is cause whi þis soule comeþ to þis knowynge and to þis lufe þat comeþ out of it. And on what maner þat is I schal telle þe more openly.

Holy wryters seyn, and sothfast it is, þat þer is two maner of gostly lufe. On is called vnformed, anoþer is called formed. Lufe vnformed is God himself, þe þred persone in þe Trinite, þat is þe Holy Gost. f. 89^{v} He is lufe vnformed and vnmade, as Seyn Ion seith þus: | *Deus dileccio est*. God is lufe, þat is þe Holy Gost. Lufe formed is þe affeccyon of a soule, made by þe Holy Gost of þe syȝt and of þe knowynge of sothfastnes, þat is God, only sterid and sette in him. Þis lufe is called formed, for it is made by þe Holy Gost. Þis lufe is not God in himself, for it is made; bot it is þe lufe of þe soule, felt in þe syȝt of Jesu and stered to him only. Now may þou se þat lufe formed is not cause why a soule comeþ to gostly syȝt of Jesu; as sum men wuld þenken þat þei wlde lufe God so brennendly, as it were be þere owen myght, þat þei were wurthi for to hafe þe gostly knowynge of him. Nay, it is not so. Bot lufe vnformed, þat is God himself, is cause of alle þis knowynge.

10 ful] þe *prec.* As   of] to Ld   þat] *om.* Pl   `not´ W^G, *om.* W   is^{3}] al *add.*, *canc.* L   þe^{2}] H$_7$RLB$_3$SrAPH$_6$CcMPl, þat HBH$_5$AsWsLwHu$_2$ELdTW   11 syȝt] visione seu cognicione Lat.   12 and] *om.* RAPl   of] H$_7$RLB$_3$SrAPMPl, fro Wc, out *prec.* HBH$_5$AsWsLwHu$_2$EH$_6$LdPlTW   in . . . and] *om.* LB$_3$P   13 God] Jesu M   with] whiche As, when Pl   14 more] þat *add.* ET   he is^{1}] *rev.* As   he is^{2}] H$_7$BLB$_3$SrHu$_2$EPH$_6$CcLdPlTW, *rev.* HRH$_5$AsWsLwAM   to] *om.* M   15 ⸢or⸣ L   þis] þe M   comeþ] procedit et causatur Lat.   of it] þeroffe M   16 lufe^{2}] alia dileccione Lat.   `only´ $W^G$, *om.* LwW   17 why] þat *add.* H$_5$Wc   `þis^{1} . . . to^{1}´ W^G, *om.* W   and^{1}] to *add.*, *canc.* L   18 is . . . lufe^{2}] *om.* As   þe^{1}] þat M   lufe^{2}] same *prec.* RAPl   in] *om.* M   itself] himself As, the self Cc   God] Jesu CcM   19 oure Lord] God LB$_3$PH$_6$, he As, a soule M, Deus Lat.   oure] blissed *add.* Hu$_2$ haþ] to þis is *add.* As   synful] symple LB$_3$P   lufen] but *add.* Pl   is] and a As   cause] þe *prec.* TWc   20 þis^{1}] a As, þe M, þat a Wc   þis^{2}] þat M   `out´ W^G, *om.* LB$_3$LwPW   21 on] in Ld, *om.* As   þat] þis B$_3$, for Wc, it *add.* T   ⸢openly⸣ L, propreli B$_3$ 22 wryters seyn] Writ seiþ H$_6$ wryters] writyngus A   seyn] and seyn *add.*, *canc.* L   ⸢þat . . . maneres⸣ L   is^{2}] aren M   maner] maneres ⸢L⸣B$_3$P   23 lufe] loues M   called (*bis*)] cleped AsH$_6$LdT   vnformed^{1}/. . ./formed] *rev.* LwCcMW   vnformed^{1}] loue and *add.* Wc, non formata seu facta Lat.   anoþer] and oþer R, and *prec.* Ld

ful blis of a soule, and þat is not only for þe siȝt, bot it is also for þe blissed lufe þat comiþ out of þat siȝt. Nerþeles for lufe comiþ oute of knowynge and not knowynge oute of luf, þerfore it is seid þat in knowynge and in siȝt principally of God with lufe is þe blis of a soule, and þe more he is knowen þe better is he lufed. Bot for as mikel as to þis knowynge, or to þis luf þat comiþ of it, may not þe soule come withoute luf, þerfore seide I þat þu schuldest only coueite luf. For lufe is cause whi a soule comiþ to þis siȝt and to þis knowynge; and þat lufe is not þe lufe þat a soule haþ in itself to God. Bot þe luf þat oure Lorde haþ to a synful soule þat kan riȝt not lufen him is cause whi þis soule comiþ to þis knowynge and to þis lufe þat comiþ out of it. And on what maner þat is I schal telle þe more openly.

Holy wryters seyn, and soþ it is, þat þer is two maner of gostly lufe.
111r On is called vnformed, anoþer is callid formed. Lufe | vnformed is God himself, þe þridde persoun in þe Trinite, þat is þe Holi Gost. He is lufe vnformed and vnmade, as Seynt Ion seiþ þus: *Deus dileccio est*: God is lufe, þat is þe Holy Gost. Lufe formed is þe affeccioun of þe soule, made bi þe Holy Gost of þe siȝt and þe knowynge of soþfastnes, þat is God, only stirid and sett in him. Þis luf is callid formed, for it is made bi þe Holy Gost. Þis luf is not God in himself, for it is made; bot it is þe luf of þe soule, felt of þe siȝt of Ihesu and sterid to him only. Now may þu see þat lufe formed is not cause whi a soule comiþ to þe gostly siȝt of Ihesu; as summe men wolde þenken þat þei wolde luf God so brennandely, as it were bi þeire owne miȝt, þat þei were worþi for to haue þe gostly knowynge of him. Nay, it is not so. Bot luf vnformed, þat is God himself, is cause of al þis knowynge. For a

`is²´ Sr formed] loue *add.* AWc, facta seu formata Lat. Lufe vnformed] *rev.* A, and vnmade *add.*, *canc.* E 24 is¹] cleped *add.* As God] Jesu M in] of LdT þe²] H_7HRBH$_5$AsSrWsLwAELdPlTW, *om.* LB$_3$Hu$_2$PH$_6$CcMWc 25 and vnmade] *om.* As þus] H_7HRH$_5$B$_3$AsSrWsLwAHu$_2$H$_6$CcMPl, I° Io. 4° *add.* BLHu$_2$EPLdTW, *om.* LwEH$_6$CcPlTW Deus] *rep.*, *canc.* A 26 est] þat is *add.* E Gost] is *add.* As formed] þat *add.* Pl a] H_7RLB$_3$AsAPCcMPl, þe HBH$_5$SrWsLwHu$_2$EH$_6$LdTW 27 of²] H_7RBSrLwECcLdPlW, *om.* HH$_5$LB$_3$AsWsAHu$_2$PH$_6$MT þe³] *om.* Hu$_2$ of³] þe *add.* As 28 sothfastnes . . . God] Jesu M in] on Ld called] ycleped As, cleped H$_6$LdT 29 formed] *om.* As is²] nys As ⌜God . . . made (l. 30)⌝ L God] Jesu M, *om.* B$_3$ 30 made] facta . . . seu creata Lat. bot it is] be As it²] þis H$_6$, *om.* H$_5$Ld þe¹] *om.* RMPl þe soule] God As in] H_7, of Σ, ex Lat. Jesu] God RAPl `and´ L 31 stered] steriþ B$_3$ Now may þou] þu maiste Ld 32 gostly] H_7RBLB$_3$-SrAHu$_2$PH$_6$MLdPl, þe *prec.* HH$_5$WsLwECcTW, a *prec.* As Jesu] God RAPl as] and LwW wuld] schuld Sr 33 God] Jesu M 34 ⌜for . . . knowynge⌝ L for] *om.* M gostly] *om.* B$_3$ him] God RAPl, Jesu M so] soþ As 35 God] Jesu M alle þis] *rev.*, *marked for trsp.* B$_3$ alle] *om.* As

For a blynd wrecched soule is so ferre fro þe clere knowyng and þe blissed felynge of his lufe þurgh synne and frelte of þe bodily kende, þat it myȝt neuer come to it ne were þe endles mykelnes of þe lufe of God. Bot þan, bycause þat he loueþ vs so mykel, þerfore he ȝifeþ vs his lufe, þat is þe Holy Gost. He is boþe þe ȝifere and þe ȝifte, and makeþ vs þan by þat ȝifte for to knowen him and lufen him. Loo, þis is þe lufe þat I spake of, þat þou schuldest only coueyten and desyren þis vnformed lufe þat is þe Holy Gost. For sothly, a lesse þinge or a lesse ȝifte þan he is may not auaylen vs for to brynge vs to þe blissed syȝt of Jesu.

And þerfore we schul fully desyren and asken of Jesu only þis ȝifte of lufe, þat he wuld for þe mykelnes of his blissed lufe touchen oure hertys with his vnseable lyȝt to þe knowynge of him and departen with vs of his blissed lufe, þat as he lufeþ vs þat we myghten lufen him aȝen. Þus seyth Seyn Jon: *Nos diligamus Deum, quoniam ipse prior dilexit nos*. Þat is: Lufe we now God, for he first lufed vs. He lufed vs mikel whan he made vs to his lyknes, bot he lufed vs more whan he boght vs with his precyous blode, þurgh wilful takynge of ded in his manhed, fro þe powere of þe fend and fro þe pyne of helle. Bot he lufeþ vs most whan he ȝifeþ vs þe ȝifte of þe Holy Gost, þat is lufe, by
f. 90r þe | whilk we knowen him and lufen him, and arn made syker þat we arn his soules chosen to saluacion. For þis lufe are we more bounden to him þan for ony oþer lufe þat euer schewed he for vs, eyþer in oure makynge or in oure byenge. For þogh he had made vs and boght vs, bot if he saf vs withalle, what profyte is it ellys to vs oure makenge or oure byenge? Sothly ryȝt none.

36 þe[1]] þis T, blynde knowynge þat is to sey fro þe *add*. As, *om*. Ld and] of Cc þe[2]] clere *add*. M 37 þe] *om*. T 38 myȝt] may B to it] þerto SrM were] H_7RBLB_3SrAHu_2EPH_6CcMLdPlT, it *add*. HH_5AsWsLwW mykelnes] mekenesse LB_3PH_6, meknes mechelnes H_5Lw þe lufe of God] godly loue Ld, Goddis loue T 39 God] Jesu M þat] he *prec*. H_6, vs *add*., *canc*. L, *om*. LwTW vs[1]] *om*. A 40 lufe] Sone Sr, to vs *add*. A He . . . ȝifte] *om*. M boþe] *om*. LwW þe[2]] *om*. Pl ȝifere/. . ./ȝifte] *rev*. LB_3P 41 makeþ vs þan] þanne makiþ `he´ vs $H_6$ vs . . . ȝifte] *om*. M him[1]] $H_7$RL$B_3$SrAP$H_6$CcMPl, *om*. HB$H_5$AsWsLw$Hu_2$ELdTW lufen] to *prec*. AsE him[2]] He is boþe þe geuer and þe gifte and make vs þanne be þat gifte for to knowe hym and loue hym *add*. M 42 spake] sp- *prec*., *canc*. Sr 43 `þis . . . desyren (l. 46)´ Pl þis] is *add*. M sothly] soþe As a[1]] *om*. Pl þinge . . . lesse] *om*. Ld 44 þan he is] *om*. Hu_2 is] þere *add*. As auaylen . . . to[1]] *om*. T auaylen] ablen R vs[1]] *om*. Ld vs[2]] *om*. Ld 45 of] *om*. As Jesu] God RAPl, Domini nostri Jesu Christi Lat. 46 we schul] H_7H_5Ws, *rev*. HRBLB_3AsLwAHu_2EPH_6MLdPlT, shuld we SrCcW fully desyren] *rev*. Pl fully] *om*. AsCc asken . . . only] only aske Pl of Jesu] *om*. RAMPl only/þis . . . lufe] *rev*. E 47 he] we As þe] *om*. H_6 mykelnes] excellence A his] þis As, loue *add*., *canc*. L blissed lufe] loue so blessed LwW blissed] *om*. Hu_2Wc oure] hure M 48 his] *om*. As vnseable] inuisibel A 49 `blissed´ W^G, *om*. LwW lufe] towchyn

blynde wrecched soule is so fer fro þe cleer knowynge and þe blissed felynge of his lufe þurȝ synne and freelte of þe bodily kynde, þat it miȝt neuer come to it ne were it þe endeles mikelnes of þe lufe of God. Bot þan, bicause þat he lufiþ vs so mikel, þerfore he gifiþ vs his lufe, þat is þe Holi Goste. He is boþ þe gifer and þe gifte, and makiþ vs þan bi þat gifte for to knowen and lufen him. Loo, þis is þe luf þat I spake of, þat þu schudest only coueiten and desiren þis vnformede luf þat is þe Holi Gost. For soþly, a lesse þinge or a lesse gifte þan he is may not auailen vs for to bryngen vs to þe blissed siȝt of Ihesu.

And þerfore schul we fully desiren and asken of Ihesu only þis gift of lufe, þat he wulde for þe mikelnes of his blissed luf touchen oure
11v hertes with his vnseable liȝt to þe knowynge of hym | and departen with vs of his blissid luf, þat as he lufiþ vs þat we miȝten loue him ageyn. Þus seiþ Seynt Jon: *Nos diligamus Deum, quoniam ipse prior dilexit nos*. Þat is, Loue we God now, for he first loued vs. `He loued vs´ mikel whan he made vs to his liknes, bot he loued vs more when he boȝt vs with his precious blode, þurȝ wilful takynge of ded in his manhed, fro þe power of þe fende and fro þe pyne of helle. Bot he lufiþ vs most when he gifiþ vs þe gifte of þe Holy Gost, þat is luf, bi þe whilk we knowen him and louen him, and are made siker þat we are his sones chosen to saluacioun. For þis lufe are we more bounden to him þan for ony oþer luf þat euer schewd he for vs, eiþer in oure makynge or in oure be`i´ynge. For þawȝ he had made vs and bouȝt vs, bot if he safe vs withal, what prophet is it elles to vs oure makynge or oure byinge? Soþly, riȝt none.

oure hertys *add.*, *canc.* Cc lufeþ vs] *om.* As þat²] *om.* B$_3$MLd him] *om.* As 50 Jon] Poule Pl, Iª Io. 4° BLHu$_2$EPLdW Deum] Dominum Ld quoniam] quia AT ipse] *om.* T 51 Lufe . . . God] lett vs nowe loue God Ld we now] *om.* AsCc now God] H$_7$RBLB$_3$SrAHu$_2$PH$_6$MPl, *rev.* HH$_5$WsLwETWWc first lufed vs] *rev.* Ld `He lufed vs´ H^c, *om.* H°As 52 mikel] *om.* A 53 boght] bo- *prec.*, *canc.* Sr of] *om.* Cc 54 fro] for A powere] dower Pl 55 lufeþ] H$_7$HBLB$_3$SrLwAHu$_2$EPH$_6$MPlTW, loued RH$_5$AsWsCcLdWc [*corr. fr.* louyþ ⌜Ld⌝], diligit Lat. vs most] *rev.* LB$_3$P ȝifeþ] ȝaf H$_5$AsWs, gaft Cc vs²] to *prec.* AsCc þe²] *om.* LP 56 knowen/. . ./lufen] *rev.* H$_5$Ws knowen him and] *om.* E and lufen him] *rep.*, *canc.* Sr 57 arn] made *add.* M soules chosen] chosyn childryn Cc soules] H$_7$As, chylder Wc, sones Σ, filii Lat. are we] *rev.* Ld more/bounden to him] *rev.* Ld more/bounden] *rev.* T `more´ H$_6$ `bounden/to him´ W^G, *rev.* LwW 58 ⌜þan⌝ L þat euer] *om.* Pl euer] ere- *add.*, *canc.* Sr schewed/he] H$_7$HRBH$_5$AsSrWsLwAHu$_2$W, *rev.* LB$_3$EPH$_6$CcMLdPlT`W^G´ for] to H$_6$T, elles to M eyþer] *om.* B$_3$ oure . . . or] his manhede As oure] *om.* MPl 59 or] eiþer Ld oure] *om.* MPl byenge] begynnynge As, enbyynge Ld, ayenbyenge TW For þogh] *rep.*, *canc.* L þogh] *om.* Ws had] *om.* Cc vs¹] *om.* Hu$_2$ 60 if] *om.* Hu$_2$LdT saf] sauede H$_5$WsM, hadde saue T withalle] also B, þerwith ALdT profyte is] profited As, profitith TW is it ellys] were it H$_6$ or] *om.* Ld 61 byenge] aȝenbeying CcLdT none] *corr. fr.* nought Ws, nouȝt AsHu$_2$TW, nichil Lat

þerfore þe most tokne of lufe schewed to vs, as me þenkeþ, is þis: þat he ȝifeþ himself in his godhed to oure soules. He ȝaf himself first in his manhed to vs for oure raunson, whan he offred himself to þe Fader of heuene vpon þe awtere of þe cros. þis was a fayre ȝifte and a grete tokne of lufe. Bot whan he ȝifeþ himself in his godhed gostly to oure soules for oure saluacion, and makeþ vs for to knowen him and lufen him, þan lufeþ he vs fully. For þan gyfeþ [he] himself to vs; and more myght he not ȝifen vs, ne lesse myght not sufficen to vs. And for þis skille is it seyd þat þe ryȝtynge of a synful soule þurgh forȝifnes of synnes is aretted and appropred princypally to þe werkynge of þe Holy Gost. For þe Holy Gost is lufe, and in þe ryȝtynge of a soule oure Lord Jesu scheweþ to þe soule most of his lufe, for he doth away al synne and oneþ it to him. And þat is þe best þinge þat he may don to a soule, and þerfore is it appropred to þe Holy Gost.

þe makynge of a soule is appropred to þe Fader, as for souereyn myght and powere þat he schewed in makynge of it. þe byenge is aretted and apropred to þe Sone, as for þe souereyn witte and wisdom þat he schewed in his manhed, for he ouerkam þe fend princypally þurgh wysdom and not þurgh strengthe. Bot þe ryȝtynge and þe ful safenge of a soule by forȝifnes of synnes is appropred to þe þred persone, þat is þe Holy Gost. For þerin scheweþ Jesu most lufe vnto mans soule, and for þat þinge schal he most souereynly be lufed aȝen of vs. His makynge is common to vs and to alle vnresonable creatures, for as he made vs of noȝt so made he hem; and þerfore is þis werk
f. 90v grettest of myȝt, bot it is not most [of] lufe. Also þe byenge is | common to vs and to alle resonable soules, as to Jewes and to

62 tokne] tokening A of lufe/schewed to vs] *rev.* T schewed to vs/as me þenkeþ] *rev.* B_3 þenkeþ] `it′ *add.* R 63 ȝifeþ] ȝyue Pl his] *om.* As soules] liknes Hu_2 He] *rep.* M ȝaf] ȝeuith RM first/in his manhede] LB_3AP first] whan he *add.* Lw 64 in his manhede/to vs] *rev.* H_6Wc to vs for] was imade to Lw 65 þe[1]] same maner *add.*, *canc.* L awtere of þe] *om.* M of] on As fayre] ryghte *prec.* W 66 grete] ryght *prec.* W lufe] þe most þat miȝt be schewid in manhode *add.* RAMPl whan] what tyme W ȝifeþ] ȝaf As 68 lufen] lo-| *prec.* L, to *prec.* E, for to *prec.* W þan . . . and] *om.* RAMPl ȝyfeþ he] *rev.* SrWc he[2]] *om.* H_7 himself] fully *add.* As 69 more] *rep.* A myght he] *rev.* H_5Ws myght[1]] may H_6 ȝifen] to *add.* As, vnto *add.* Wc ne] þen R, and A, nor Pl myght[2]] he *add.* Hu_2H_6 sufficen/to vs] *rev.* T `to′ E, *om.* ACcLd 70 skille] reson $Hu_2$ is it] $H_7$RBAMPl, *rev.* H$H_5$L$B_3$AsSrWsLw$Hu_2$EP$H_6$CcLdTW it] þatt Ld ryȝtynge] ryȝtnynge B `synful′ T[G], *om.* BCcLdT, peccatricis Lat. of synnes] *om.* Sr 71 aretted and] *om.* T, *om.* Lat. princypally . . . appropred (l. 75)] *om.* M 72 For] in *add.* As `in′ E þe] *om.* RT ryȝtynge] ryȝtnynge B 73 Jesu] God Wc, *om.* RAPl scheweþ] *rep.*, *canc.* L to þe soule/most . . . lufe] *rev.* Wc to þe soule/most] *rev.* T þe] H_7RLB_3SrAEPCcPl, a HBH_5AsWsLwHu_2H_6LdTW away/al synne] *rev.* A 74 And[2]] *om.* RAPl 75 is it] H_7HBHu_2, *rev.* RH_5LB_3AsSrWsLwA-

þerfore þe most token of lufe schewd to vs, as me þinkiþ, is þis: þat he gifiþ himself in his godhed to oure soules. He gaf himself first in his manhede to vs for oure raunsoun, when he offred himself to þe Fader of Heuen vpon þe auter of þe cros. Þis was a faire gift and a grete tokne of lufe. Bot when he gifiþ himself in his godhed gostly to oure soules for oure saluacioun, and makiþ vs for to knowe him and lufe him, þan lufiþ he vs fully. For þan gifiþ he himself to vs; and more miȝt he not gifen vs, ne lesse miȝt not suffice to vs. And for þis skil it is seide þat þe riȝtynge of a synful soule þurȝ forgifnes of synnes is
112^{r} arettid and apropred principally to þe wirkynge of þe Holy Gost. | For þe Holy Gost is luf, and in þe riȝtynge of a soule oure Lorde Ihesu schewiþ to a soule most of his luf, for he doþ awey alle synne and oniþ it to him. And þat is þe best þinge þat he may don to a soule, and þerfore is it apropred to þe Holi Gost.

Þe makynge of a soule is apropred to þe Fader, as for þe souereyn miȝt and power þat he schewiþ in makynge of it. Þe byenge is aretted and apropred to þe Sone, as for þe souereyn wit and wisdom þat he schewyd in his manhed, for he ouerkam þe fende principally þurowȝ wisdom and not þurȝ strengþ. Bot þe riȝtynge and þe ful sauynge of a soule bi forgifnes of synnes is apropred to þe þridde persone, þat is þe Holy Gost. For þerin schewiþ Ihesu most lufe vnto mannes soule, and for þat þinge schal he most be lufed ageyn of vs. His makynge is comune to vs and to al vnresonable creatures, for as he made vs of noȝt so made he hem; and þerfor is þis werk gretteste of miȝt, bot not most of luf. Also þe byenge is comune to vs and to alle resonable soules, as

EPH_6CcMLdPlTW appropred] to þe Fader as for þe souereyn miȝt *add.*, *canc.* H Holy . . . þe^{1} (l. 78)] *om.* A 76 a] the LwW souereyn] H_7RLB_3SrAPH_6CcMPl, þe *prec.* HBH_5AsWsLwHu_2ELdTW 77 myght/. . ./powere] *rev.* T schewed] H_7RBSr-ACcMPl, scheweþ HH_5LB_3AsWsLwHu_2EPH_6LdTW, ostendit Lat. þe] by *prec.* Lw byenge] aȝenbyng LdT, of it *add.* W 78 and apropred] *om.* LwTW apropred] proprede H_5 as] and Cc for þe] *om.* H_5AsWs for] to A 79 þat . . . wysdom (l. 80)] *om.* Hu_2 schewed] *corr. fr.* schewþe Ld, ostendit Lat. þe fend/princypally] *rev.* AsE 80 þe^{1}] ful *add.* Cc ryȝtynge] ryȝtnynge B, riȝtwisnes Pl 81 a] *om.* As þred . . . þe (l. 82)] *om.* CcWc, *om.* Lat. 82 þerin] moste *add.* As scheweþ Jesu] *rev.* E Jesu] God RAMPlWc, Dominus noster Jesus Lat. vnto] into H_5Ws, to RALdT 83 mans] a *prec.* LB_3PM \`most/. . . be´ $W^G$, *rev.* W souereynly] $H_7$RBL$B_3$SrA-$Hu_2$P$H_6$CcMLdPlT\`W^G´, *om.* HH_5AsWsLwEW be lufed] belovyd AsLw aȝen/of vs] *rev.* LwW aȝen] *om.* As 84 His] þe *corr.* Ld vnresonable] resonable Cc, bestys and *add.* Ld 85 as] vs M made he] H_7HRBH_5AsSrWsLwAHu_2PCcPlTW, *rev.* LB_3EH_6MLd hem] helle Ld and . . . lufe (l. 86)] *om.* H_5Ws is þis] he is Sr 86 \`it is´ $T^G$$W^G$, *om.* AsTW it] *om.* Sr \`not´ Pl ⌜most . . . lufe⌝ L of] *om.* H_7B_3APl, *canc.* L, in Lat. byenge] deyinge As, begynnyng Ld 87 and to] *om.* As to^{4}] *om.* H_5WsLwTW

Saracenys and to fals cristen men. For he dyed for al soules ilyk, and boght hem if þei willen han þe profyte of it; and also it suffyceþ for þe byenge of alle, þogh it so be þat alle han it not. And þis werkyng was most of wisdom, and not most of lufe. Bot þe ryȝtynge and þe halwynge of oure soules þurgh þe ȝifte of þe Holy Gost, þat is only þe werkynge of lufe; and þat is not common, bot it is a speciale ȝifte only to chosen soules. And sothly þat is þe werkynge of most lufe to vs þat arn his chosen children.

þis is þe lufe of God þat I spake of, whilk þou schuldest coueyten and desyren, for þis lufe is God himself and þe Holy Gost. þis lufe vnformed, whan it is ȝifen to vs, it werkeþ in oure soules al þat gode is and al þat longeþ to gudnes. þis lufe lufeþ vs or þan we lufen him, for it clenseth vs first of oure synnes, and makeþ vs for to lufen him, and makeþ oure wil stronge for to ageynstonden alle synnes; and it stereþ vs for to assayen oureself þurgh dyuers excercyse boþe bodily and gostly in alle vertus. It stereþ vs also for to forsake þe lufe and þe lykynge of þe werd; it sleþ in vs alle wykked sterenges of synne and fleschly affeccions and werdly dredys; it kepit vs fro alle maliciouse temptacyons of þe fende; and it dryfeth vs oute fro besynes and vanites of þe werd and fro conuersacion of werdly lufers. Al þis doth þe lufe of God vnformed whan he ȝifeþ himself to vs. We don ryȝt not bot suffren him and assente to him; for þat is þe most þat we done, þat we assenten wilfully to his gracyouse werkynge in vs. And ȝit is þat wil not of vs bot of his makynge, so þat me þenkeþ he doth in vs alle þat is wele don, and ȝit we seen it not. And not only doth he þus, bot aftere

88 and . . . men] *om.* Lat. for^2] *rep., canc.* L al] *om.* As 89 willen] wolden BH$_6$ profyte] perfyte loue W of it] þerof LB$_3$PH$_6$Cc, of liȝt Pl it^2] *om.* M suffyceþ] H$_7$LB$_3$AsSrEPH$_6$PlTW, sufficed HRBH$_5$WsLwAHu$_2$CcMLd, sufficiens fuit Lat. 90 for] to Ws byenge] begynnyng Ld it^1 . . . þat] *om.* RAMPl so be] *rev.* AsLwETW werkyng] H$_7$LB$_3$SrPH$_6$M, werk HBH$_5$AsWsLwHu$_2$ECcLdTW, *om.* RAMPl, operacio Lat. 91 was] \`is´ Pl and$^1$] H$_7$\`W^G´, *om.* Σ not . . . lufe] *om.* Lat, et non maxime amoris H$_{8G}$ not] *om.* As 92 halwynge] ⌜sauyng⌝ H$_6$ oure soules] a soule A þat] it T 93 and] *om.* RAMPl \`not´ P, ȝit *add.* As \`a´ W^G, *om.* H$_5$WsLwEW \`ȝifte´ H^c, *om.* H$^\circ$H$_5$AsWs 94 chosen] the *prec.* Cc soules] *corr. fr.* chyldryne Ld þat^1] it Ld þe] H$_7$RLB$_3$AsSrAHu$_2$EPH$_6$CcMLdPl, *om.* HH$_5$WsLwTW werkynge of/most] H$_7$RLB$_3$SrAEPH$_6$MPl, *rev.* HBH$_5$WsLwHu$_2$LdTW, opus maxime dileccionis Lat. 95 his] *om.* As 96 of God] *om.* Lat. spake] speke LB$_3$PH$_6$, dixi Lat. whilk] þe *prec.* LdT schuldest] H$_7$HRBH$_5$AsSrWsLwAHu$_2$CcLdPlTW, schalt LB$_3$EPH$_6$M 97 and desyren] *om.* A is] of Sr and] *om.* CcWc \`lufe´ Pl, is *add.* As 98 to] vnto As soules] H$_7$RLB$_3$SrAEPH$_6$CcMPl, soule HBH$_5$AsWsLwHu$_2$LdTW, animabus Lat. al] And *prec.* As 99 lufe] *om.* As, scilicet Spiritus Sanctus *add.* Lat. þan] H$_7$RLB$_3$SrEPH$_6$CcMPl, þat HH$_5$AsWsLwW, *om.* BAHu$_2$LdT for . . . him (l. 100)] *om.* T 100 clenseth] causeþ As first . . . vs] *om.* As vs^1] first *add.* H$_5$WsM ⌜for . . . him⌝ L and^2 . . . synnes (l. 101)] *om.* RAMPl and^2] it *add.* Cc 101 ageynstonden]

to Iewes and to Saracens and to fals cristen men. For he dyed for alle soules ilike, and bouȝte hem if þei wilen haue þe profit of it; and also it sufficed for þe byenge of alle, þawȝ it so be þat alle han it not. And þis werk was most of wisdom, not most of lufe. Bot þe riȝtynge and þe halowynge of oure soules þurȝ þe gift of þe Holy Gost, þat is only þe wirkynge of lufe; and þat is not comune, bot it is a special `gifte´ only to chosen soules. And soþly þat is most wirkynge of lufe to vs þat arn his chosen children.

þis is þe luf of God þat I spake of, whilk þou schuldest coueiten and desiren, for þis luf is God himselfe and þe Holy Gost. þis luf
f. 12v vnformed, | when it is gifen to vs, it wirkiþ in oure soule al þat good is and al þat longiþ to godnes. þis lufe lufiþ vs er þat we lufe him, for it clensiþ vs first of oure synnes, and makiþ vs for to luf him, and makiþ oure wil stronge for to ageynstonde alle synnes; and it stiriþ for to assaien ⌜oure⌝selfe þurȝ diuers exercises boþe bodily and gostly in alle vertues. It stiriþ vs also for to forsaken þe luf and þe likynge of þe werld; it sleeþ in vs alle wicked stirynges of synn and flescly affeccions and werdly dredis; it kepiþ vs fro malicious temptacions of þe fende; and it drifiþ vs out fro bisynes and vanitee of þe werdle and fro conuersacioun of werldly lufers. Al þis doþ þe luf of God vnformed, when he gifiþ himself to vs. We don riȝt noȝt bot suffren him and assentyn to him; for þat is þe most þat we don, þat we assente wilfully to his gracious wirkynge in vs. And ȝit is þat wil not of vs bot of his makynge, so þat me þinkiþ þat he doþ in vs al þat is wel don and ȝit we seen it not. And not only doþ he þus, bot aftir þis lufe doþ more.

withstonde As   alle . . . þurgh (l. 102)] *om.* As   it] *om.* RLwAPlTW   102 vs] H_7RLB_3SrLw`$H^c$´AEP$H_6$CcMPlTW, *om.* H°B$H_5$WsH$u_2$Ld, nos Lat.   ⌜oure⌝self $H^c$, vs self B$H_5$H$u_2$Ld   exercyse] $H_7$AsLwAW, exercyses Σ, exercicia Lat.   103 in . . . vertus] *om.* RAMPl   in] and As   It . . . werd (l. 104)] *om.* $B_3$Wc   It[1]] and A   `stereþ´ T^G, strengthith T   `lufe . . . of[2] (l. 104)´ *om.* LwW, `in latino: þe lufe . . . werd´ W^G, 104 þe] *om.* T   alle] werkes *add.*, *canc.* L   wykked] fleschly W`T^G´   synne] synnes LB_3P 105 fleschly] worldly T   and werdly dredys] timorisque mundani Lat.   dredys] drede Pl it] and Cc, it spekeþ for vs *prec.* As   vs] also *add.* Hu_2 alle] *om.* HLwHu_2W, omnibus Lat. 106 it] *om.* AW   oute] LB_3SrEP   besynes . . . vanites] þe *prec.* (*bis*) B   and vanites/of þe werd (l. 107)] *rev.* R   and[2]] from. *add.* LB_3EPH_6 107 vanites] H_7RSrACcMPl, vanitee HBH_5LB_3WsLwHu_2EPH_6LdTW, vanitatibus Lat.   fro] *om.* H_6 conuersacion] conuersaciouns As   lufers] loues A   108 to] vnto As   vs] and *add.* H_6, and opnyth þe sith of oure soule into Jesu *add.* Cc   109 suffren him and] *om.* As   most] þyng *add.* H_5Ws   done] may *prec.* A   110 þat wil/not] H_7HRBH_5SrWsACcMLdPl, *rev.* LB_3-LwHu_2EPH_6TWWc   111 not] *om.* As   ⌜of[2] . . . ma⌝kynge] L   makynge] operacione et gracia Lat.   þat[1]] *om.* Cc   me] we Ld   þenkeþ] H_7LB_3SrAPH_6CcMLd, þat *add.* HRBH_5AsWsLwHu_2EPlTW   in vs] *om.* B   is wele don] we A   112 don] *om.* Lw we seen] *rev.* W, cognoscimus vel videmus Lat.

þis lufe doth more. For he opneth þe eye of þe soule and scheweþ to þe soule þe sy3t of Jesu wonderfully and þe knowynge of him, as þe soule may suffre it þus bi lytel and bi lytel; and be þat sy3t he rauyscheþ al þe affeccyon of þe soule to him.

And þan bygynneþ þe soule for to knowen him gostly and brennendly for to lufen him. þan seeþ þe soule sumwhat of þe f. 91r kende | of þe blissed godhede of Jesu, how þat he is alle and þat he werkeþ alle, and þat al gode dedis þat arn done and gode thoghtes arn only of him. For he is al souereyn my3th and al souereyn sothfastnesse and al souereyn godenesse; and þerfore euerylk gode dede is done only of him and by him, and he schal only han þe worchip and þe thank for al gode dedis, and noþyng bot he. For þogh wrecched men stele his worchipe fro him here for a whyle, neuerþeles atte þe laste ende schal sothfastnes schew wele þat Jesus dide alle and man dide ryght not of himself. And þan schul ⌜theues⌝ of Goddis gude þat are not acorded with him here in þis lyfe for her trespas be demed to þe dede, and Jesu schal fully be worcheped and thanked of al blissed creatures for his gracyous werkynge.

þis lufe is not elles bot Jesu himself, þat for lufe werkeþ al þis in mannis soule and reformeth it in felynge to his lyknesse, as I haue before sayde and sumwhat as I schal seyn. þis lufe bryngeth into þe soule þe fulhede of al vertus, and makeþ hem al clene and trewe, softe and esy, and turneth hem al into lufe and lykyng; and on what maner wyse he doth þat, I schal telle þe a lytel afterward. þis lufe dragweth þe soule fro fleschlyhede into gostlynes, fro erthly felynge into heuenly sauoure, and fro veyn beholdynge of werldly thynges into contemplacion of gostly creatures and of Goddis priuetes.

113 þis] *om.* As   doth] he *prec.* Hu$_2$, he *add.* CcLdT, he *add.*, *canc.* Lw, no *add.*, *canc.* L   of þe] `þe´ of Cc   to þe soule] yt CcWc   114 Jesu wonderfully] hymselue RAMPl   115 `suffre´ Sr   þus] *om.* Ld   bi^2] H$_7$HRBH$_5$LB$_3$WsLwHu$_2$PH$_6$MPlTW, *om.* AsSrAECcLd   he] *om.* As   116 þe^1] *om.* As   affeccyon] affeccions APl   þe^2] a Hu$_2$ 117 for] *om.* H$_5$AsWs   118 lufen] leuen R, *corr. fr.* leue A   sumwhat] *om.* A   þe^2] *om.* As   119 kende of þe] *om.* RAMPlT   of Jesu] *om.* RAMPlWc   Jesu] oure Lord *prec.* Hu$_2$ how þat] H$_7$HBH$_5$AsSrWsLwHu$_2$ECcLdTW, hou LB$_3$PH$_6$, þat RAMPl   he^1] it B$_3$ and . . . alle (l. 120)] *om.* T   and] *om.* As   þat^2] H$_7$HRBH$_5$SrWsLwAHu$_2$CcLdPlTW, than M, *om.* LB$_3$AsEPH$_6$ he^2] *om.* LwH$_6$ 120 alle] *om.* As   þat^1] *om.* T   dedis] ben *add.* Ld, is *add.* Hu$_2$ and^2] þe *add.* As, al the *add.* Cc   121 only] holi As   my3th/. . ./sothfastnesse] *rev.* Sr   and] *om.* H$_6$ al^2] *om.* As   122 and^1] *om.* M   gode dede] dede þat is good Hu$_2$ dede] deded Ld   123 only^1] H$_7$RLB$_3$SrAEPH$_6$CcMPl, *om.* HBH$_5$AsWsLwHu$_2$LdTW, solummodo Lat.   schal only] *rev.* A   only^2] ony Cc, *om.* TWc   124 thank] þong B   and . . . he] *om.* Lat.   noþyng] none Hu$_2$Wc, no man Cc   For] But Sr wrecched] wykkede B   men] man Lw, peccatores Lat.   125 fro him] H$_7$RBLB$_3$SrAHu$_2$EPH$_6$CcMLdPlT, *om.* HBH$_5$AsWsLwW, ab eo Lat.   for] *om.* Sr   neuerþeles] 3it *add.* A   atte þe] atte L   126 schew wele] *rev.* H$_6$ wele] *om.* B

For he opneþ þe eiȝe of þe soule and schewiþ to þe soule þe siȝt of Ihesu wundirfully and þe knowynge of him, as þe soule may suffre it þus bi litel and bi litel; and bi þat siȝt he rauischiþ alle þe affeccioun of þe soule to him.

And þan bigynniþ þe soule for to knowen him gostly and brennandly for to lufen him. þan seeþ þe soule sumwhat of þe kynde of þe blissed godhed of Ihesu, how þat he is al and þat he wirkiþ al, and þat alle gode dedis þat are done and gode þouȝtes arn only of him. For he is alle souereyn miȝt and alle souereyn soþfastnes and alle souereyn godnes; and þerfore euerilk gode dede is don of him and bi him, and he schal only han þe wurschip and þe þanke for alle
13^r gode dedis, and noþinge | bot he. For þawȝ wrecched men stele his wurschip here for a while, nerþeles at þe last ende schal soþfastnes schewen wel þat Ihesu did al and man did riȝt noȝt of himself. And þan schal þefes of Goddis gode þat are not acorded with him here in þis `liif´ for ⌜here⌝ trespas be demyd to þe dede, and Ihesu schal be fully worsciped and þankid of alle blessid creatures for his gracious wirkynge.

? þis luf is not elles bot Ihesu himself, þat for lufe wirkiþ al þis in a mannes soule and reformiþ it in felynge to his liknes, as I hafe bifore seide and sumwhat als I schal seien. þis luf bryngiþ into þe soule þe fulhed of alle vertues, and makiþ `hem´ alle clene and trewe, soft and esy, and turneþ hem alle into luf and into likynge; and on what maner wise he doþ þat, I schal telle þe a litel aftirwarde. þis luf draweþ þe soule fro fleschlied into gostlynes, fro erþly felynge into heuenly sauour, and fro veyn biholdynge of werldly þinges into contemplacioun of gostly creatures and of Goddis pryuetes.

Jesus] loue RAMPl and] þat *add.* `L´$B_3$EP$H_6$  dide$^2$] *om.* As  127 schul] þese *add.* As, the *add.* Cc  theues] ȝeues Pl  Goddis] *om.* Lat.  gude] god[-is *canc.*] $H_5$, goodis $B_3$Ws$H_6$, bona Lat.  128 in þis lyfe] *om.* $H_6$  lyfe] `liif´ *corr. fr.* luf H^c, loue H_5 her] ⌜here⌝ H^c, his BH_5 demed] deuydid M to] vnto T þe] *om.* LwW 129 Jesu] loue RAPl, Lucifer M fully be] H_7RLB_3SrAEPH_6CcMPl, *rev.* HBH_5AsWsLwHu_2LdTW thanked] laudabitur Lat. blissed] *om.* As 130 gracyous] *om.* W 131 Jesu] God RAMPl in] a *add.* HBH_5AsWs 132 it] *om.* As 133 before sayde] *rev.* Cc as] ellys B, also LdT, *om.* As þe] a B_3 134 fulhede] fulheded R, fulnes Ws `hem´ H^c, hym LwPlW, *om.* H°AsCc al^2] *om.* Pl and^2] faier *add.* Ld trewe] and *add.* Cc 135 hem al] *rev.* Pl hem] it Hu_2, hym *corr. fr.* hem Lw, hym W into] to M and^2] H_7RLB_3SrAEPCcMPl, into *add.* HBH_5AsWsLw$Hu_2$$H_6$LdTW on] in T, *om.* M 136 þat] *om.* As a lytel] H_7HBH_5LB_3AsWsLwHu_2EPCcLdW, *om.* RSrAH_6MPlT, modicum Lat. afterward] here *prec.* As þis] þy As 137 þe] *rep.*, *canc.* H fro^1 . . . sauour (l. 138)/and/fro . . . priuytees (l. 139)] *rev.* W, `alius est ordo apud latinum´ W^G fro^1 . . . sauour (l. 138)] *om.* Lw 138 heuenly] gostli E and] *om.* W veyn] veynly Cc 139 of^1] *rep.*, *canc.* H creatures] creature BH_5Ws

How some soules lufen Jesu by bodily feruours and by þer owne manly affeccions þat are stered by grace and by resone, and sum lufe Jesu more restfully by gostly affeccyons only stered inward þurgh speciale grace of þe Holy Gost. Capitulum xxxv[m]

T[h]an may I seyn þat he þat hath most of þis lufe her in þis lyf most pleseth God, and most clere syght schal haue of him in þe blisse of heuene, for he hath þe most ȝifte of lufe here in erthe.

þis luf may not ben had by a mannes owne trauelle, as sum men wenen. It is frely had of þe gracious ȝifte of Jesu after mykel bodily and gostly trauelle goende before. For þer arne sum lufers of God þat maken hemself for to lufe God as it were by here owne myght; for þey f. 91v | strynen hemself þurgh grete violence, and panten so strongly þat þey bresten al into bodily feruours as if þei wolden drawe doun God fro heuene to hem, and þey sayn in here hertes and with her mouth: A, Lord, I lufe þe, and I wil lufe þe. I wold for þi lufe suffren ded. And in þis maner werkynge þey felen grete feruour and mikel grace. And soth it is, as me thenkeþ: þis werkyng is gode and medful, if it be wele tempered with mekenes and with discrecion. Bot neuerþeles þese men lufen not, ne han not þe ȝifte of lufe on þat maner as I speke of, ne þey asken it not so. For a soule þat hath þe ȝifte of lufe þurgh gracious beholdynge of Jesu as I mene, or ellis if he haue it not ȝit bot wold hafe it, it is not besy for to streyne itself ouer his myght, as it were by bodily strengthe for to han it by bodily feruours and so for to felen of þe lufe of Jesu. Bot him thenkeþ þat he is ryȝt noȝt, and þat he kan don ryȝt noȝt of himself, bot as it were a dede þynge, only hanggend and born vp by þe mercy of God. He seeth wele þat Jesus is

Chapter 35 *title*: H_7RLB_3SrAEPH_6MLdPlTW   þat he þat most loueþ and pleseþ God here in þis lyf shal haue most blisse and knowynge in tye comynge, and þat some men trauaylle þereaboute for to hauen þis perfecicoun and ȝit þey hauen it nouȝt. As   *om.* HBH_5WsLwHu_2Cc   1 How] þat *add.* LdTW   soules lufen] soule louith ALdTW `and´ A   2 manly] *om.* LB_3EPH_6 þat . . . Gost (l. 4)] etc. M   by[1]] *rep.* B_3 and[2]] howȝ *add.* EW   3 more] *om.* LdW   4 þurgh] by T, þe *add.* Sr   speciale] specialli Ld, *om.* LB_3EPH_6 grace] and goodnesse *add.* Sr   5 Than] Tan H_7 hath most] *rev.* LwAW   hath] *om.* M   þis[1]] his AsA   her] *om.* LdT   þis[2]] his As   6 pleseth] plese Ld   most] more LdT   him] and most fully loue hym *add.* `Lw´W   7 hath] had RAPl   ȝifte] of God *add.* H_5AsWs   lufe] hym Cc   in] on BHu_2, þis *add.* Pl   8 had] so *add.* RAMPl   a] *om.* B   mannes owne] *rev., marked for trsp.* L   men] *om.* HLwELdW   9 wenen] þat *add.* As, for *add.* H_6 It . . . before (l. 10] *om.* RAMPl   10 before] *om.* Ld   sum] men *add.* Pl   11 hemself] hem Cc   `for[1]´ Sr, *om.* LwATW   þey] to A   12 strynen] ⌜streyn⌝ H[c], stryuyn with Sr, steryn RBAsM   þurgh] by H_5Ws, for to loue God as it were be As   panten] peynen Ld, peynen hem As, labur Hu_2 13 bresten] breken H_5B_3AsWs   al] H_7RLB_3SrAEPH_6CcMPl, *om.* HBH_5AsWsLwHu_2LdTW,

[CHAPTER 35]

Þan may I seien þat he þat haþ most of þis lufe here in þis lif most plesiþ God, and most cleer siȝt schal han of him in þe blis of heuen, for he haþ þe most gift of lufe here in erþe.

Þis luf may not ben had by a mans owne traueil, as summe wenen. It is frely had of þe gracious gift of Ihesu after mikel bodily and gostly traueile goende bifore. For þer are summe louers of God þat maken hemself for to lufe God as it were bi here owne miȝt; for þei ⌜streyn⌝ hemselfyn þurgh grete violence, and panten so strongly þat þei bresten into bodily feruours as þei wolden drawe downe God fro heuen to hem, and þei seien in here hertes and wiþ here mouþ: 'A,
13^{v} Lorde, I lufe þe, and I wil lufe þe. I wolde for | þi luf suffre dede.'
And in þis maner wirkynge þei felen grete feruour and mikel grace. And soþ it is, as me þinkiþ: þis wirkynge is good and medful, if it be wel tempred with meknes and with discrecioun. Bot nerþeles þese men luf not, ne haue not þe gift of luf on þat maner as I speke of, ne þei aske it not so. For a soule þat haþ þe gift of lufe þurȝ gracious biholdynge of Ihesu as I mene, or elles if he hafe it not ȝit bot wolde haue it, he is not bisy for to streyne himself ouer his miȝt, as it were bi bodily strengþe for to han it bi bodily feruours and so for to felen of þe lufe of God. Bot him þinkiþ þat he is riȝt noȝt, and þat he kan do riȝt noȝt of himself, bot as it were a ded þinge, only hangend and born vp bi þe mercy of God. He seeþ wel þat Ihesu is al and doþ al, and þerfor

totaliter Lat. bodily] stronge As as if] H$_7$RLB$_3$SrAEPH$_6$CcMPl, as þouȝ Ld, as HBH$_5$AsWsLwHu$_2$TW, quasi Lt 14 here] *om.* H$_5$WsM 15 and . . . þe^2] *om.* Sr I^2] *om.* Cc 16 maner werkynge] *rev.* M maner] of *add.* LwTW 17 as] *om.* W is^2] and M medful] nedefull M 18 with] *om.* LdT neuerþeles] ȝet RAMPl þese] those RMPl 19 men] louers Hu$_2$ lufen not] *om.* Pl lufen] ne *prec.* As ne han not] *om.* LB$_3$P `þe´ Pl on . . . lufe (l. 20)] *om.* Sr as] þat H$_5$WsM speke] spake REMT, iam loquor Lat. of] *om.* B$_3$ 20 asken it] askid M it not] *rev.* H$_5$Ws it] *om.* Ld lufe] Goddis *prec.* A, of Jesu *add.* T þurgh . . . Jesu (l. 21)] *om.* RAMPl 21 Jesu] him T, God Wc bot] and RAMPl 22 wold] he *prec.* CcWc it^2] H$_7$Sr, he HBH$_5$LB$_3$AsWsLwAHu$_2$EPH$_6$CcLdTW, he Wc, *om.* RAMPl for] *om.* Ld itself] H$_7$RLB$_3$SrPMPl, himself HBH$_5$AsWsLwAHu$_2$EH$_6$CcLdTW 23 by^1] *om.* LB$_3$P it by] *om.* RAMPl 24 of^1] *om.* LdW þe lufe of] *rep.* Ws Jesu] H$_7$LB$_3$SrEPH$_6$Cc, God HRBH$_5$AsWsLwAHu$_2$MLdPlTWWc, Jesu Christi Lat. þat^1] þe B and . . . noȝt (l. 25)] *om.* As 25 kan don] kan, doþ H$_5$ riȝt] *om.* H$_5$Ws himself] nerhand *add.* RMPl, wel ney *add.* A 26 hanggend] hoonged Hu$_2$ born vp by] burnyng vpon Ld by] on Cc mercy] omnipotentem misericordiam Lat. Jesus] God RAMPlWc, Christ *add.* H$_6$

al and doth al, and þerfor askeþ he not ellis bot þe ȝifte of his lufe. For siþen þe soule seeth þat his owne lufe is noght, þerfor it wold han his loue, for þat is inogwe. Þerfor preyeth he, and þat desyreth he, þat þe lufe of God wold towchen him with his blissed lyght þat he myght seen a lytel of him by schewyng of his gracious presence. For þan schuld he lufen him, and so by þis way cometh þe ȝifte of lufe, þat is God, into a soule.

Þe more þat þe soule noȝteth itself þurgh grace, by syght of þis sothfastnesse sum tyme withouten ony feruour schewed owtward, ant þe lesse it thenketh it lufeth or seeth God, þe nerrere neghtheth it to perceyfe þe ȝifte of þe blissed lufe. For þan is lufe mayster and werkeþ in þe soule and maketh it for to forȝeten itself and for to seen and byholden only how lufe doth. And þan is þe soule more suffrende þan f. 92r doende, and þat is clene lufe. Þus Seynt Poule mened whan | he seyd þus: *Quicumque Spiritu Dei aguntur, hii sunt filii Dei*. Þese al þat are wroght with þe Spirit of God are Goddis sones; þat is, þese soules þat arn made so mek and so buxum to God þat þey werken not of hemself, bot suffren þe Holy Gost ay steren hem and werken in hem þe felyngges of lufe, with a ful swete acorde to his sterynge, þese are specially Goddes sones, most lyke vnto him.

Oþer soules þat kunnen not luf þus, bot trauellen hemself by here owne affeccyons, and steren hemself þurgh thenkynge of God and bodily exercyse for to drawen owte of hemself by maystrie þe felynge of lufe by feruours and oþer bodily sygnes, lufe not so gostly. Þey

27 and[2] . . . noght (l. 28)] *om.* T þerfor . . . noght (l. 28)] *om.* As askeþ he] *rev.* H$_6$, ab eo *add.* Lat. not] no B$_3$ his] *om.* LwW 28 siþen] H$_7$RLB$_3$SrAEPH$_6$CcMPl, þat *add.* HBH$_5$WsLwLdW, as mych þat Hu$_2$ soule] soules B$_3$ is] nys B his loue] þe loue of God RAMPl `his[2]´ Cc 29 þat[1]] *om.* Cc he[2]] *om.* Cc 30 lyght] syȝte Ld 31 seen/a lytel] *rev.* Cc seen] him *add.*, *canc.* B$_3$ a lytel] *om.* As by . . . him (l. 32)] *om.* A by . . . presence] *om.* RAsMPl schewyng of] H$_7$LB$_3$EPH$_6$Cc, *om.* HBH$_5$WsLwHu$_2$LdTW, manifestacionem Lat. his] hy Ld 32 so] *om.* H$_6$ 33 soule] and *add.* AsWc 34 þe[2]] H$_7$HRBLB$_3$AsSrLwAEPH$_6$MPl, a H$_5$WsHu$_2$CcLdTW noȝteth] noteþ As, neȝeþ Pl, lakyth Cc itself] H$_7$HRH$_5$LB$_3$AsSrWsLwHu$_2$EPH$_6$MW, himself BACcLdPlT þis] his As, *om.* LdWc 35 withouten] by þowte B schewed owtward] H$_7$LB$_3$SrEPH$_6$Cc, *rev.* HBH$_5$AsWsLwHu$_2$LdTWWc, schewed RAPl, schewith M 36 lesse] þat *add.* W thenketh] H$_7$RLB$_3$SrAPH$_6$MPl, þat *add.* HBH$_5$AsWsLwHu$_2$ECcLdTW lufeth] God *add.* Ld `or seeth´ Pl, *om.* Wc nerrere] neer B$_3$, more neer H$_6$ neghtheth it] H$_7$RLB$_3$SrAPMPl, *rev.* HBH$_5$AsWsLwHu$_2$H$_6$CcLdTW, he nyȝiþ it E neghtheth] neyssheþ B to] H$_7$RLB$_3$SrLwAPH$_6$CcMPlW, for to HBH$_5$AsWsHu$_2$ELdTWc 37 þe[2]] þis Sr 38 `it´ T[G], *om.* AsAT for to] to Cc, *om.* LwW forȝeten] gette Hu$_2$ itself] hymself BLB$_3$P and[2] . . . only (l. 39)] *om.* As for[2]] *om.* Cc 39 byholden] to *prec.* E how] as As `þan´ Cc 40 þat] þis Hu$_2$ clene] clere T, vera . . . et sincera Lat. Seynt Poule/mened] *rev.* H$_6$ mened] meneþ AsCc seyd] seyth

askiþ he noȝt elles bot þe gifte of his lufe. For siþen þat þe soule seeþ þat his owne luf is noȝt, þerfore it wolde han his loue, for þat is inowȝ. þerfore preieþ he, and þat desiriþ he, þat þe luf of God wolde touchen him with his blissed liȝt þat he miȝt seen a litel of him bi his graciouse presence. For þan schuld he lufen him, and so bi þis wey comiþ þe gifte of luf þat is God into a soule.

þe more þat þe soule noȝtiþ itself þurȝ grace, bi siȝt of þis soþfastnes summe tyme withoute ony feruour outwarde schewyd, and þe lesse it þenkiþ þat it lufiþ or seeþ God, þe nerrer it neiȝeþ for to perceif þe gifte of þe blissed lufe. For þan is lufe maister and wirkiþ in þe soule, and makiþ it for to forgetyn itself and for to seen and beholden only how luf doþ. And þan is þe soule more suffrande þan doande, and þat is clene lufe. þus Seint Poul mened when he seide
14^{r} þus: | *Quicunque Spiritu Dei aguntur, hii filii Dei sunt*: Alle þese þat are wroȝt wiþ þe spirit of God are Goddes sones; þat is, þese soules þat are made so meke and so buxom to God þat þei wirken not of hemself, bot suffren þe Holy Gost stiren hem and wirken in hem þe felynges of luf, with a ful swete acorde to his stirynges, þese are specially Goddis sones, most like vnto him.

Oþer soules þat kun not lufe þus, bot traueilen hemself bi here owne affeccions, and steren hemself þurgh þinkynge of God and bodily exercice for to drawen out of hemself by maistrie þe felynge of luf bi feruours and oþer bodily signes, luf not [so] gostly. þei don wel

CcLd 41 þus] Ro. 8° *add.* BLHu$_2$EPLdTW Quicumque . . . Dei^2] *om.* M sunt/filii Dei] H$_7$RLB$_3$SrAEPH$_6$MPl, *rev.* HBH$_5$AsWsLwHu$_2$LdTWWc, sunt filii Cc, *rev.* Lat. Dei^2] þat is *add.* E þese al] H$_7$, *rev.* Σ þese] those M, tho CcPl 42 wroght] lad Ld þe] *om.* As sones] *om.* As þese] those RM, þoo Pl, *om.* LwLdTW soules] homines Lat. 43 so^2] *om.* H$_6$ \`of′ E, wiþ LB$_3$P 44 þe$^1$ . . . felyngges (l. 45)] *om.* Cc þe$^1$ . . . Gost/ay] *rev.* E ay] H$_7$RLPM, euere B$_3$AEH$_6$Pl, alwey Sr, *om.* HBH$_5$AsWsLwHu$_2$LdTWWc, semper Lat. steren] to *prec.* EWc werken] to *prec.* E \`in hem′ W^G, *rev.* W þe^2] *om.* LB$_3$PH$_6$ 45 felyngges] felyng LdT a] *om.* H$_6$ ful] *om.* W acorde] corde W, concordia volluntatis sue Lat. sterynge] H$_7$RLB$_3$SrAEPH$_6$CcMPl, stirynges HBH$_5$AsWsLwHu$_2$LdTWWc, instinctum Lat. þese] þose RM 46 specially] special LB$_3$PH$_6$Wc, principaly Sr, moste *prec.* Ld most] muche T vnto] to LwAW 47 by . . . hemself/þurgh . . . God (l. 48)] *rev.* RAMPl by] with B 48 owne] *om.* Cc affeccyons] affliccions W steren] streyn Ws þurgh] her owne *add.* LwW thenkynge] þenkekyng Ld and^2] by RAMPl, with *add.* As 49 for] *om.* H$_6$ to] *rep.*, *canc.* L hemself] hem LB$_3$PH$_6$ by] þe *add.*, *canc.* L felynge] felyngis Hu$_2$ 50 by] *om.* LB$_3$PH$_6$ sygnes] syngnys Sr, *corr. fr.* synnys Ld, As *skips from here to Chapter 36/37* þat lufe] of loue H$_5$AsWs, þei *prec.* Sr not] *om.* As so] *canc.* H, \`so′ W^G, *om.* RH$_5$WsAMPlW done wele and medefully, by so þat þei wille knowen mekely þat here werkyng is not kendly þe gracious feleng of lufe bot it is manly, don be a soule atte þe biddynge of resone. And neuerþeles þurgh [þe] godenesse of God, bycause þat þe soule doth þat in it is, þese manly affeccyons of þe soule stered into God by mans werkyng are turned into gostly affeccyons, and are made medful as if þey had ben don gostly in þe first bygynnynge. And þis is a grete curtaysye of oure Lord schewed vnto meke soules, þat turneth al þese manly affeccyons of kendly lufe into þe affeccyon and into þe mede of his owne lufe, as if he had wroght hem alle fully by himself. And so þese affeccyons so turned moun ben called affeccyons of gostly lufe þurgh purchace, noȝt þurgh kendly brynggynge forth of þe Holy Gost.

I sey not þat a soule may werken swylk manly affeccyons only of itself withouten grace, for I wote wele þat Seynt Poule seyth þat we moun right noȝt don ne thenken þat gode is of owreself withouten grace: *Non enim quod sumus sufficientes cogitare aliquid ex nobis, quasi ex nobis; sed sufficiencia nostra ex Deo est*. Þat is: We þat lufen God wenen not þat we sufficen for to lufen or to thenken gode of oureself only, bot oure suffiscenge is of God. For God werkeþ in vs alle, boþe gode wille

f. 92v and gode werk, as Seynt Poule seyth: *Deus est qui operatur | in nobis eciam velle et perficere pro bona voluntate*. Þat is: It is God þat werketh in vs boþe wil and fulfillyng of gode wil. Bot I sey þat swilk affeccyons arn of God, made by þe mene of a soule after þe general grace þat he ȝifeth to alle his chosen soules, not of speciale grace made gostly by towchynge of his gracious presence, as he werketh in his parfyte

51 by] $H_7BLB_3SrHu_2PH_6LdPl$, ⌜be⌝ H^c, be LwCc, be it T, yf W [`it be´ *add.* $W^G$], if it be RAEM, *om.* $H_5AsWs$, si tamen Lat. knowen mekely] *rev.* M 52 is[1]] nys As kendly þe] *rev.* LwW þe] ne RM it] *om.* E manly . . . soule] *om.* Cc manly don] $H_7RLB_3APH_6MPl$, *rev.* Sr, a manly doynge $HBH_5AsWsLwHu_2ET$, manly doynge W [`a´ *prec.* W^G], off manly doyng Ld, humaniter fit Lat. 53 ⌜biddynge⌝ L, begynnyng T þurgh] þouȝ Ld þe[2]] *om.* H_7 54 bycause] by þe cause As þat[1]] at R, *om.* H_6 `þe´ *canc.* L, *om.* P þat[2]] *rep.* $BHu_2LdT$ it] hym Cc þese] those RM, þoo Cc 55 stered] sterith M into] in As 56 made] *om.* W if] þouȝ LdT 57 first bygynnynge] *rev.* E `first´ B_3Pl grete] gre A, bigynnynge *add.*, *canc.* L curtaysye] and gentilnes *add.* Hu_2 of . . . Lord/schewed] *rev.* H_6 58 vnto] $H_7RLB_3EPH_6CcMPl$, into Sr, to $HBH_5AsWsLwAHu_2LdTW$ meke soules] many soules As, a meke soule LB_3EP, anime vere humili Lat. turneth] turnyn Cc 59 of[1]] to H_5AsWs into[1] . . . lufe] *om.* T þe[1]] $H_7HBH_5WsLwAHu_2ECcMLdPlTW$, *om.* $RLB_3AsSrPH_6$ þe[2]] *om.* R lufe[2]] blissed *prec.* Hu_2 60 hem] þan As himself] hemself B þese] those RMPl affeccyons] manly *prec.* LwW so] þus T, to kyndely loue As 61 moun] man M called] cleped AsH_6LdT affeccyons] affectioun B 62 þurgh] bi Pl brynggynge forth] *rev.*, *marked for trsp.* L brynggynge] *corr. fr.* brynyng Ld forth] but þurgh þe ȝifte As 63 soule] man As werken] wirkyng M `affeccyons´ Pl of] be Cc 64 itself]

and medfully, ⌜be⌝ so þat þei wil knowen mekely þat here wirkynge is not kyndely þe gracious felynge of lufe bot it is a manly doynge bi a soule at þe biddynge of resoun. And nerþeles þurgh þe godnes of God, bicause þat þe soule doþ þat in it is, þese manly affeccions of þe soule stirid into God bi mannes wirkynge are turned into gostly affeccions, and are made medful as if þei had be done gostly in þe first bigynnynge. And þis is a grete curtesie of oure Lord, schewd to meke soules, þat turneþ alle þese manly affecciouns of kyndely luf into þe affeccioun and into þe mede of his owne luf, as if he had wroȝt hem alle fully bi himself. And so þese affeccions so turned moun be callid affecciouns of gostly lufe þurgh purchase, not þurȝ kyndely bryngynge forþ of þe Holy Gost.

I sey not þat a soule may wirken swilke manly affecciouns only of itself withouten grace, for I wote wel þat Seynt Poul seiþ þat we moun riȝt noȝt don ne þinken þat good is of oureself withouten grace: *Non*
14v *enim quod sumus sufficientes cogitare aliquid ex nobis, quasi ex nobis;* | *sed sufficiencia nostra ex Deo est*. Þat is: We þat luf God wenen not þat we sufficen for to lufen or for to þenken good of oureself only, bot oure sufficynge is of God. For God wirkiþ in vs al, boþe goode wil and goode werk, as Seynt Poul seiþ: *Deus est qui operatur in nobis et velle et perficere pro bona voluntate*. Þat is: It is God þat wirkiþ in vs good ‵wille′ and fulfillynge of gode wil. Bot I sey þat swilke affecciouns arne gode, made by þe mene of a soule aftir þe general grace þat he gifiþ to alle his chosen soules, not of special grace made gostly bi touchynge of his graciouse presence, as he wirkiþ in his perfit lufers, as I hafe bifore

hymself B, the self Cc for . . . grace (l. 66)] *om*. As þat[1]] *om*. E 65 owreself] vs self B, ‵vs′ self Ld, oure [Lorde *canc*.] self Pl withouten] by þowten B grace] 2 Cor. 3° *add*. LHu$_2$EPLdTW, 1 Cor. 3° B, ubi sic habetur *add*. Lat. 66 enim] *om*. LB$_3$EPH$_6$, *om*. Lat. quod] *om*. LdT, *om*. Lat. quasi ex nobis] H$_7$HRBH$_5$AsSrWsAHu$_2$CcMLdPlTW, *om*. LB$_3$LwEPH$_6$ 67 nostra] vestra As þat[2]] *om*. A lufen] God *add*. Pl 68 or to[2]] H$_7$RSrCcPl, or for to HBH$_5$LwAHu$_2$ELdTW, of for to sufficen for to As, and LB$_3$PH$_6$M, ne Ws gode] on him Pl oureself] vs self BLd only] bi our sufficience *add*. A 69 suffiscenge] H$_7$HRH$_5$AsSrWsLwAHu$_2$MLdPlW, sufficience BLB$_3$EPH$_6$T, sufficiens only Cc vs] *om*. W alle] *om*. T wille/. . ./werk] *rev*. LwW 70 werk] wyrchynge B seyth] Phi. 2° *add*. BLHu$_2$EPLdTW est] *om*. M 71 eciam] H$_7$Pl, et Σ, et Lat. et] *om*. Hu$_2$ perficere] proficere Pl It is/God] *rev*. E It is] H$_7$HRBH$_5$SrWsLwAECcMLdPlTW, *om*. LB$_3$AsHu$_2$PH$_6$ 72 boþe] H$_7$RLB$_3$SrAEPH$_6$CcMPl, good HBH$_5$AsWsLwHu$_2$LdTW, et Lat. ‵wille′ H[c], *om*. H°As fulfillyng] fillynge LB$_3$PH$_6$ 73 of God] H$_7$RLB$_3$SrAEPH$_6$CcMPl, ‵of′ good Lw, gode HBH$_5$AsWsHu$_2$LdTW, ex Deo Lat. mene] wyll and *prec*. LwW a] such *prec*. B$_3$ he] oure Lord Hu$_2$ 74 his] þese As, *om*. MW speciale] a *prec*. Cc by] the *add*. Cc, *om*. M 75 his[1]] þis As he werketh] we werchen As his[2]] here As

lufers, as I hafe before seyd. For `in´ inperfyte lufers of God lufe werketh al ferly by þe affeccyons of man; bot in perfyte lufers lufe werketh neerly by his owne gostly affeccyons, and sleth for þe tyme in a soule al oþer affeccyons, boþe fleschly, kendly and manly. And þat is proprely þe werkynge of lufe by himself. Þis lufe may ben had a litel in party here in a clene soule þurgh gostly syght of Jesu, bot in þe blisse of heuene it is fulfilled by clere syght of him in his godhed; for þer schal non affeccyon be felt in a soule, bot al godly and gostly.

Þat þe ȝifte of lufe among alle þe ȝiftes of Jesu is wurthiest and most profytable, and how Jesu doth al þat þat is wele done in his chosen only for lufe, and how lufe maketh þe vsynge of al vertus and al gode dedes lyght and esy. Capitulum xxxvi^{m}

Aske þou þan of God noþyng bote þis ȝifte of lufe, þat is þe Holy Gost. For among al þe ȝiftes þat oure Lord ȝifeth is þer none so gode ne so profytable, so wurthy ne so excellent, as þis is. For þere is no ȝifte of God þat is boþe þe ȝifere and þe ȝifte bot þis ȝifte of lufe, and þerfore it is þe best and þe wurthiest. Þe ȝifte of prophecye, þe ȝifte of myracles werkynge, þe ȝifte of grete kunnynge and counseylyng, and þe ȝifte of grete fastynge or of grete penaunce doyngge, or any oþer swilke, are grete ȝiftes of þe Holy Gost; but þey are noȝt þe Holy Gost, for a reproued soule and a dampnable myght haue alle þese ȝiftes as fully as a chosen soule.

And þerfore alle þes maner ȝiftes are not mikel to ben desyred, ne

76 hafe] *om.* W before seyd] *rev.* LwW For . . . ferly] but H_6 `in´ *interl.* $H_7$ inperfyte] $H_7$SrAPl, vnperfit H B$H_5$AsWsLwHu$_2$EPCcMLdTW, `vn´perfite L, perfite B_3 of God] *om.* LwW 77 ⌜al⌝ L, `al´ $T^G W^G$, as T, *om.* LwW ferly] freely B, fer`s´ly L, fersly A, fersly *corr. fr.* freesly Ld, libere Lat. affeccyons] afecciooun B perfyte] inperfite AsE 78 neerly] nyȝe Hu$_2$, ⌜veri⌝li L, verili B_3AsEPH_6, intimius Lat. his] þe A gostly] *rep.* B_3, *om.* As for þe tyme/in a soule] H_7RLB_3SrAEPH_6CcMPl, *rev.* HBH_5AsWsLwHu$_2$LdTW tyme . . . al] *om.* B 79 fleschly] and *add.* LB_3AsEP manly] namely As 80 þe . . . lufe^{1}] loue werchynge As `by´ Pl himself] itselfe of loue As `þis´ W^G, Thus LwW a] in *prec.* LwW 81 gostly H_7RLB_3SrAPH_6CcMPl, þe *prec.* HBH_5AsWsLwHu$_2$ELdTW Jesu] God RAMPl, Domini Jesu Lat. 82 heuene] as *add.* As it is] *rev.* T fulfilled] impletur et perficitur Lat. of him] H_7BSrHu$_2$$H_6$CcLdT`$W^G$´, of Jesu ⌜L⌝$B_3$EP, *om.* H$H_5$AsWsLwW, ipsius Lat. him in his] þe RAMPl him in] ⌜Jesu in⌝ L 83 non affeccyon/be] *rev.* As non] nout Cc felt] left L$B_3$P$H_6$, sencietur Lat. `al´ $W^G T^G$, *om.* LwTW godly and gostly] spiritualis Lat. godly] bodily Ld gostly] etc. *add.* Lw

Chapter 36 *title*: H_7RLB_3SrAEPH_6MLdPlTW þat þere is non ȝifte of God so profitable as is þe ȝift of loue, þe wiche is þe Holi Gost; and how man shuld aske it and nouȝt ellys but perfeccioun and lastyng þere-ynne. As *om.* HBH_5WsLwHu$_2$Cc 1 þe^{1}] oþer T 2 how] þat *add.* Ld þat þat] H_7Sr, þat Σ is] to doone *add.*, *canc.* L wele] *om.* M in . . . esy

seid. For in vnperfit lufers of God luf wirkiþ al ferly bi þe affeccions of man; bote in perfit lufers lufe wirkiþ nerly bi his owne gostly affecciouns, and sleþ in a soule for þe tyme al oþer affecciouns, boþe flescly, kyndely and manly. And þat is proprely þe wirkynge of lufe bi himself. Þis luf may ben had a litel in partie here in a clene soule þurȝ þe gostly siȝt of Ihesu, bot in þe blis of heuen it is fulfillid bi cler siȝt in his godhed; for þer schal none affeccioun be felid in a soule, bot al godly and gostly.

[CHAPTER 36]

Aske þou þan of God noþinge bot þis gifte of lufe, þat is þe Holy Gost. For amonge alle þe giftes þat oure Lorde gifiþ is þer none so gode ne so profitable, so worþi ne so excellent, as þis is. For þer is no gifte of God þat is boþ þe gifer and þe gifte bot þis gift of luf, and þerfore is it þe best and þe worþiest. Þe gifte of prophecie, þe gifte of miracles wirkynge, þe gifte of grete knowynge and conseilynge, and
15r þe gifte of grete fastynge or of grete penaunce doynge, | or ony oþer swilk, are grete giftes of þe Holy Gost; bot þei arne not þe Holy Goste, for a reproued and a dampnable miȝt han alle þose giftes as wel as a chosen soule.

And þerfor alle þese maner giftes are not gretly for to desiren, ne

(l. 4)] *om.* M   3 chosen] louers TW, soulis *add.* EPl   lufe[2]] he Pl   5 of God/noþyng] *rev.* T   of God] *om.* Hu_2 lufe] God As   6 is þer] H_7HRBAsWsAHu_2CcMLdPlT, *rev.* LB_3SrLwEPH_6W   7 profytable] ne *add.* As   so[2]] *om.* LB_3AsP   8 þat is] *rep.* B_3 þat] but it As   boþe] eke As   þe[1]] *om.* LB_3PH_6 ȝifere/. . ./ȝifte] *rev.* LB_3APH_6 þis] allone *add.* T   of] is As   and þerfore] *rep.* A   and] *om.* Cc   9 it is] *rev.* HBCcPl   þe[1]] *om.* Sr   wurthiest] ȝifte *add.* H_5Ws   prophecye] and *add.* Cc   ȝifte[2]] yeftes W   10 myracles] myracle As   werkynge] doynge Pl   þe . . . fastynge (l. 11] *om.* T   grete] the *prec.* LwW, *om.* RM   kunnynge and counseylyng] *rev.* H_6 kunnynge] H_7RLB_3SrAEPH_6CcMPl, knowynge HBH_5AsWsLwHu_2LdW   and[1]] of *add.* Cc   11 fastynge] fastyngis B   or[1]] and RM   or any] and alle Cc   oþer swilke] *rev.* Cc   12 swilke] whiche Pl   ȝiftes] and alle swiche other *add.*, *canc.* Cc   but . . . Gost] *om.* Sr   13 soule/and a dampnable] *rev.* H_5AsWs   soule] *om.* HLw   a[2]] *om.* Lw   þese] þose HRM, þoo Pl   14 fully as] hath LwW   fully] H_7RLB_3SrAEPH_6CcMPl, wel HBH_5WsHu_2LdT, *om.* LwW, plene Lat.   as[2]] *om.* Lw   a chosen soule] chosen soulis Hu_2 soule] may *add.* RAMPl   15 þes . . . ȝiftes] *om.* RM   þes] þoo Pl   maner] H_7HBSrLwAHu_2CcPlTW, of *add.* H_5LB_3AsWsEPH_6Ld   mikel . . . ne] *om.* A   mikel/. . ./gretly] H_7RLB_3SrAEPH_6CcMPl, *rev.* HBH_5AsWsLwHu_2LdTW   to] H_7RLB_3SrAEPH_6CcMPl, for *prec.* HBH_5AsWsLwHu_2LdTW   ben desyred] H_7RLB_3SrAEPH_6CcMPl *corr. fr.* desiren Hu_2, desiren, HBH_5AsWsLwLdTW, desideranda Lat.   ne] neyþer H_5

gretly for to chargen. Bot þe 3ifte of lufe is þe Holy Gost, God f. 93[r] himself, and him may no soule hafe and be dampned with him. | For þat 3ifte only saueth it fro dampnacyon and makeþ it Goddis sone, pertinere of heuenly heritage. And þat lufe, as I haue befor seyd, is not þe affeccyon of lufe þat is formed in a soule, bot it is þe Holy Gost himself, þat is lufe vnformed þat saueth a soule. For he 3ifeth himself to a soule first or þe soule lufe him, and he formeth affeccyon in þe soule and makeþ þe soule for to lufen him only for himself. And not only þat, bot also by þis 3ifte þe soule lufeth itself, and alle his euen-cristen as þe self, only for God; and þis is þe 3ifte of lufe þat makeþ schedyng atwyx a chosen soule and a reproued. And þis 3ifte makeþ ful pes atwix God and a soule and oneth al blissed creatures holly in God. For it makeþ Jesu to lufen vs, and vs him also, and ilk of vs for to lufen oþer in him.

Coueyt þis 3ifte [of] lufe principally, as I haue seyd. For if he wil of his grace 3if it on þat maner wyse, it schal open and lyghten þe reson of þi soule for to seen sothfastnesse, þat is Jesu, and gostly thynges. And it schal steren þin affeccyon holly and fulli for to lufen him, and it schal werken in þi soule only þat he wil, and þou schalt beholden him reuerently with softenesse of lufe and seen how he doth. Þus biddeth he by his prophete þat we schulden done, seyend þus: *Vacate, et videte quoniam ego sum Deus*. Cese 3e and seth þat I am God. Þat is, 3e þat are reformed in felyng and han 3oure inner eye opned into þe syght of gostly thynges, cese 3e sumtyme of owtward werkynge, and seeth þat I

16 is] of As   God himself] *rev.* H_5 God] and As, *om.* T   17 with him] $H_7BH_5LB_3AsSrWsHu_2PH_6Cc$, with⌜al⌝ H^c, withal RLwCcMTW, þerwyþe Ld, *om.* A, cum hoc Lat.   18 þat] þe B_3E only/saueth it] *rev.* LwTW   only saueth] As   it[1]] hym B, *om.* As   it[2]] to *add.* As, *om.* Ws   sone] *om.* A   19 pertinere] $H_7H_5LB_3SrWsEPH_6CcM$, percener HRAsALwPlW, perceuer Hu_2, takere B, participem Lat.   þat] *om.* Sr   befor] toforn As   is . . . it (l. 20)] *om.* Lat.   20 þe[1]] *om.* Lw   of] þe *add.* E lufe] þat I haue before seide *add.* E   in] *om.* As   soule] for he yeuyþ hym self to a soule first *add.* Hu_2 `bot . . . soule (l. 21)´ R   21 þat[1]] *om.* As   a] þe E   22 to a soule/first] *rev.* T   lufe] $H_7HRH_5AsWsLwAHu_2EH_6MLdPlT$, loueþ $LB_3SrPCcW$, diligat Lat. formeth] formed M   affeccyon] $H_7RLB_3SrEPH_6MPl$, þe *prec.* $HBH_5AsWsLwAHu_2CcLdTW$ 23 and[1] . . . soule] *om.* As   soule] oonli *add.* LB_3EP only] *om.* R   24 þis 3ifte] þese 3iftes As   itself] the self Cc   and . . . þe self] *om.* As   25 þe self] H_7, itself $HH_5SrWsLwHu_2LdTW$, himself $RBLB_3AEPH_6CcMPl$, seipsam Lat.   þis] þat As   is] *rep., canc.* H   makeþ] makid M   26 schedyng] chedyng Pl, chydynge As, schewynge H_5Ws, disseueraunce B, departyng Hu_2Cc, diuidit Lat.   atwyx] $H_7HRLSrLwPW$, bytwexte $H_5B_3AsWsHu_2EMLdPl$, by twene BAH_6CcT a chosen soule] H_7, chosen soules $HRBH_5LB_3AsSrWsLwAHu_2LEPH_6CcMLdPlTW$, electos Lat.   chosen] þe *prec.* E   a[1] . . . And] *om.* As   a[2]] H_7, þe $RH_5LB_3SrWsEPH_6MPl$, *om.* $HBLwHu_2LdTW$, reprobis Lat.   þis 3ifte] *om.* A   3ifte] *om.* LB_3P 27 atwix] $H_7HRLSrLwPW$, bytwyxte $BB_3AsEMLdPl$, bytwene $H_5WsAHu_2H_6CcT$ oneth] al euen As   holly]

mikel for to chargen. Bot þe gift of lufe is þe Holy Gost, God himself, and him may no soule haf and be dampned with⌜al⌝. For þat gifte only safiþ it fro damnacioun, and makiþ it Goddis sone, percener of heuenly heritage. And þat luf, as I hafe bifore seid, is not þe affeccioun of luf þat is formed in a soule, bot it is þe Holy Gost himselfe, þat is luf vnformed þat saufiþ a soule. For he gifiþ himself to a soule first er þe soule luf him, and he formiþ þe affeccioun in þe soule and makiþ þe soule for to lufen him only for himself. And not only þat, bot also bi þis gift þe soule lufiþ itself and alle his euene-cristen as itself, only for God; and þis is þe gifte of lufe þat makiþ schedynge atwix chosen soules and reprofed. And þis gifte makiþ ful pees atwix God and a soule and oniþ alle blissed creatures holly in God. For it makiþ Ihesu for to lufen vs, and vs him also, and ilke of vs for to lufe oþer in him.

Coueite þis gifte of luf principally, as I hafe seide. For if he wil of his grace gife it on þat maner wise, it schal opnen and liȝtnen þe resoun of þi soule `for to sene soþfastnes, þat is God and gostly þinges. And it shal stire þi affeccion holli and fulli for to loue him, and it shal werken in þi soule´ only as he wil, and þu schalt biholde Ihesu reuerently with softnes of lufe and seen how he dooþ. þus biddiþ he by his prophete þat we schulde done, seyende þus: *Vacate, et videte quoniam ego sum Deus*: Cese ȝe and seeþ þat I am God. þat is, ȝe þat
15^{v} are reformed in felynge and han ȝour inner iȝe opned into | siȝt of
gostly þinges, cese ȝe sumtyme of outwarde wirkynge, and seeþ þat I

H_7HRLB_3APH_6CcMLdPl, holy BLwHu_2TW, hole H_5As, hool Ws, only Ld, al *prec.* RM, totaliter Lat. in] to ACc 28 Jesu] God RMPl, him A to^{1}] H_7RLB_3SrAPCcMPl, for to HBH_5AsWsLwHu_2EH_6LdTW vs^{2}] *om.* As ilk] euerych BLwHu_2PlTW 29 him] also *add.* E 30 ȝifte . . . principally] loue ȝifte of principalte As of] and H_7, dileccionis Lat. lufe] of God *add.* RAMPl 31 it^{1}] the *add.* LwW and lyghten] *om.* Cc 32 þi] þe Pl `for . . . soule (l. 34)´ H^{c}, om. H$^{\circ}$$H_5$AsWs for . . . holly (l. 33)] *rep.* LwW Jesu] H_7BLB_3SrHu_2EPH_6CcLdPlT, God RLw⌜H^{c}⌝AMPlW [*bis* LwW], Jesus Lat. 33 it] that M affeccyon] *corr. fr.* affeccions L, affecciouns EPM holly] holy T, hooli E, hooly . . . holy W, hooly [*bis*] Lw (*in repeated phrase*) `and^{1} . . . him´ (l. 34) L 34 þat] H_7, as Σ, iuxta voluntatem Lat. and] as As beholden] holdyn Cc him] H_7RLB_3SrAEPH_6CcMPl, Jesu HBH_5AsWsLwHu_2LdTW, eum Lat. 35 softenesse] H_7HBH_5LB_3AsWsLwHu_2PH_6TW, soþefastnes RSrAECcMLdPl, sobrietate Lat. and seen] *om.* RAMPl doth] and *add.* As þus] þis LB_3EPH_6 36 by his prophete/ þat . . . done] *rev.* H_6 his] þe RAsM schulden] schul H_5Ws þus] Ps. 45° *add.* LHu_2EPLdT, Ps. 4° *add.* B 37 Deus] etc. *add.* Ld, þat is *add.* BHu_2ECc `Cese ȝe´ T$^{G}$, Takeþ heede BT seth] ȝee *add.* WsLdT `þat is´ As. As *skips from here to Chapter 37/19* him[self] ȝe þat] *rev.* Hu_2 38 inner] om. WsH_6 ⌜eye opned⌝ L þe] H_7RH_5AsWsCc, þat *prec.* APl, *om.* HBLB_3SrLwHu_2EPH_6MLdW syght of] *om.* T of] *om.* SrLd 39 owtward werkynge] *rev.*, *marked for trsp.* Sr werkynge] worchinges T, also *add.* M, and of ȝoure owen manly wirkyng also *add.* RAPl þat] *om.* Lw

am God. þat is, seeth only how I Jesu, God and man, do; behold ȝe me, for I do al. I am lufe, and for lufe I do alle þat I do and ȝe don noght. And þat þis is sothe I schal wele schewen ȝow, for þer is no gode dede don in ȝow ne gode thoght felt in ȝow bot if it be don þurgh me, þat is þurgh myght, wisdom and lufe, myghtyly, wittyly and louely; ellis it is no gode dede. Bot now is þis sothe þat I Jesu am boþe myght, wisdom and blissed loue, and ȝe noght, for I am God. þan mowe ȝe wele seen þat I only do al ȝoure gode dedys, and ȝoure gode
f. 93v thoghtes and gode lufes | in ȝow, and ȝe don riȝt noght. And ȝit neuerþeles are þese gode dedis called ȝoure, not for ȝe werken hem principally bot for I ȝif hem to ȝow for lufe þat `I´ haue to ȝow. And þerfore, sithen I þat am Jesu and for lufe do al þis, cese ȝe þan of beholdyng of ȝoureself and sette ȝoureself at noght, and lokeþ on me and seeth þat I am God, for I do al þis. þis is sumqwat of þe meneng of þe vers of Dauid before sayde.

Se þan and behold what lufe werkeþ in a chosen soule þat he reformeth in felynge to his lyknes, whan reson is lyghtnede a litel in þe gostly knowynge of Jesu and to þe felyng of his lufe. þan bryngeth lufe into þe soule þe fulhed of vertus, and turneth hem alle into lykyng and softnes, as it were withouten werkyng of þe soule. For þe soule stryueth not mykel for þe getyng of hem as it dide byfore, bot it hath hem esyly and feleth hem restfully, only þurgh þe ȝifte of lufe þat is þe Holi Gost. And þat is a wel grete conforte to þe soule and a gladnesse vnspekable, whan it feleth sodeynly—and wote neuer

40 God] for I do al I *add.*, *canc.* H, into syȝt *add.*, *canc.* Lw þat . . . do] and man, so As Jesu . . . man] *om.* RAMPl and man] *om.* LB$_3$P 41 al] for *add.* Sr I[2] . . . alle] *om.* H$_5$Ws þat] euer *add.* A and[2] . . . noght] *om.* Lat. don noght] *rev.*, *marked for trsp.* Pl 42 noght] no þyngis Ld, no þinge T And[2]] *om.* LB$_3$PH$_6$ wele/schewen ȝow] *rev.* T wele] H$_7$RBAHu$_2$MLdPlT, *om.* HH$_5$LB$_3$AsSrWsLwEPH$_6$CcW *om.* Lat. þer] þe B$_3$ no] non As 43 dede] *om.* A don[1]] þow it fel As in[1]] by LwW ne . . . ȝow[2]] *om.* RAMPl ne] non *add.* As, neyþer no H$_5$, nor no Ws thoght] dede As if] *om.* T it] *om.* B$_3$ don] felt Hu$_2$ 44 me . . . þurgh] *om.* As myght] H$_7$RLB$_3$SrAEPH$_6$CcMPlT, my *prec.* AsA, and *add.* HBH$_5$AsWsLwHu$_2$LdW, potenciam Lat. and[1]] blissed *add.* As lufe . . . and[1] (l. 46)] *om.* RAMPl myghtyly] þat is *prec.* LB$_3$EPH$_6$, seu potenter Lat. wittyly] and *prec.* As 45 louely] loue As it is] *rev.* HH$_5$Ws `no´ L, not HAs Bot] *om.* LB$_3$PH$_6$ is þis] it is Hu$_2$Ld þis] H$_7$, it Σ I Jesu] *rev.* As 46 myght] H$_7$LB$_3$EPH$_6$Cc, and *add.* HBH$_5$AsSrWsLwHu$_2$LdTW, potencia Lat. noght] riȝt *prec.* Hu$_2$ God] good Lw 47 wele] *om.* As only] H$_7$RLB$_3$SrAPH$_6$CcMPl, *om.* HBH$_5$AsWsLwHu$_2$ELdTW, *om.* Lat. `and . . . dedis (l. 49)´ H[c] and . . . thoghtes] *om.* Lw ȝoure[2]] H$_7$RLB$_3$SrAEPH$_6$CcM, þourȝe Pl, alle *prec.* BH$_5$AsWsH[c]Hu$_2$Ld, all TW gode[2]] H$_7$RLB$_3$SrAEPH$_6$CcMPl, alle your *prec.* BH$_5$AsWsLwH[c]Hu$_2$LdW, all þe *prec.* T, *om.* Lat. 48 and[1] . . . noght] *om.* Lat. 49 are/þese gode dedis] *rev.* LdT þese] those RM, all *prec.* TW called] ycleped AsH$_6$LdT ȝoure] ȝourys Sr 50 bot] *om.* As lufe] þe *prec.* AsCc `I´ *interl.* H$_7$

am God. þat is, seeþ only how I Ihesu, God and man, do; beholde ȝe me, for I do al. I am lufe, and for lufe I do al þat I do and ȝe do noȝt. And þat þis is soþ I schal schew ȝow, for þer is it no gode dede done in ȝowe ne gode þouȝte felt in ȝow bot if it be done þurȝ me, þat is þurȝ miȝt and wisdom and luf, miȝtily, wittily and lufely; elles is it not gode dede. Bot now is it soþ þat I Ihesu am boþ miȝt and wisdom and blissed luf, and ȝe noȝt, for I am God. þan mowe ȝe wel seen þat I do alle ȝoure gode dedis, `and alle ȝour good þouȝtes, and alle your good loues in yowe, and ȝhe don riȝt noȝt. And ȝet neuerþeles ben þise good dedes′ called ȝoure, not for ȝe wirken hem principally bot for I gife hem to ȝow for luf þat I hafe to ȝow. And þerfor, siþen þat am Ihesu and for lufe do al þis, `cese þan of þe ⟨beholdyng of yourself and⟩ setteþ youreself att noȝt, and lokiþ on me and seeþ þat I am God, for I do alle þis′. þis is sumwhat of þe menynge of þat vers of Dauid bifore seide.

See þan and beholdiþ what lufe wirkiþ in a chosen soule þat he reformiþ in felynge to his liknes, wha`n′ þe resoun is liȝtend a litel to þe gostly knowynge of Ihesu and to þe felynge of his lufe. þan bryngiþ lufe into þe soule þe fulhed of vertues, and turneþ hem alle into softnes and into likynge, as it were withouten wirkynge of þe soule. For þe soule strifiþ not mikel for þe getynge of hem as it did bifore, bot it haþ hem esily and feliþ hem restfully, only þurgh þe gifte of luf þat is þe Holy Gost. And þat is a wel grete conforte and gladnes vnspekable, whan it feliþ sodeynly and wot neuer how þe vertue of

51 sithen I þat] H_7HRBLwMPlW, sithen þat I H_5AsSrWsLdT, syn I LB_3AEPH_6Cc, bicause I Hu_2, ex quo ergo ego Jesus Lat. am . . . lufe] am loue RMPl, am loue and A and] *om.* Cc for . . . do/al] *rev.* As do] dooth LwW `cese . . . þis[1] (l. 53)′ $H^c$ ȝe þan] *rev.* RLwMW ȝe] *om.* $H^c H_5$AsWs, now *add.* $Hu_2$ 52 beholdyng . . . and] *trimmed* H beholdyng] $H_7$RL$B_3$SrAEP$H_6$CcMPl, þe *add.* HB$H_5$AsWsLw$Hu_2$LdTW ȝoureself] ȝow self BLd `and[1] . . . ȝoureself′ Pl 52 sette] ȝe *add.* Ld lokeþ . . . and] *om.* RAMPl lokeþ on me] beholde me stedfastly Hu_2 on] þou As 53 seeth] I am *add.*, *canc.* L meneng of þe] *om.* Pl meneng] and exposicion *add.* T 54 þe] H_7RLB_3AsSrLw-AEPH_6CcMPlW, þat HBH_5WsHu_2LdT of Dauid] *om.* T before sayde] *rev.* Cc before] aboue T sayde] *rep.*, *canc.* H 55 Se] *om.* As and] þerfore As lufe] he *add.* As he reformeth] is refourmed As, reformyd M 56 `in felynge′ Pl, *om.* $H_6$ reson] $H_7$, þe *prec.* Σ a litel] *om.* SrA in[2]] $H_7$, to Σ, ad Lat. 57 Jesu] God RAMPl his] *om.* RAMPl `lufe′ Cc þan] he *add.* As bryngeth lufe] bryngith he RM, he bringeth A, bryngeþ `hit′ Pl 58 soule] and *add.* As þe[2]] *om.* Ws turneth] haþ turned As 59 lykyng and softnes] $H_7$RL$B_3$SrAP$H_6$CcMPl, softnes and into [in T] likynge HB$H_5$AsWsLw$Hu_2$ELdTW, dileccionem Lat. softnes] soþfastnesse CcT 60 not] *om.* E mykel] gretly $Hu_2$ it dide] dyd he Lw 61 `hath′ Sr hem[2]] him As, ben M restfully] restly As þe] *om.* Ws 62 to þe soule] *om.* HH_5WsLwW, anime Lat. a[2]] H_7RBLB_3AsSrAEPH_6CcMLdPlT, *om.* HH_5WsLwHu_2W 63 neuer] not LdT

how—þat þe vertu of mekenes and pacience, sobernesse and sadnesse, chastite and clennes, lufereden to his euen-cristen, and al oþer vertus, þe whilk were sumtyme trauellous, pyneful, and hard to him for to kepen, arn now turnede into softnesse and lykynge and into wonderful lyghtnes, so ferforth þat him þenketh it no maistrie ne hardnes for to kepen ony vertu, bot it is most lykyng to him for to kepen it. And al þis maketh lufe.

Oþer men þat stonden in þe common weye of charite, and are not ȝit so ferforth in grace bot werken vnder þe biddyng of reson, stryuen and fyghten al day ageyns synnes for þe getyng of vertus, and sumtyme þei ben abouen and sumtyme benethen, as wrestelers arn. Þese men don ful wele. Þei han vertus only in reson and in wil, and not in sauour ne in lufe, for þei feghten hemself as it were by her owne myghtes for hem. And þerfore moun þei not han ful rest ne fully þe f. 94r heyghere hand. Neuerþeles þei schul han mikel mede, bot þei | arn not ȝit meke inogw. Þei han not put hemself al fully in Goddis hand, for þei seyge him not ȝit. Bot a soule þat hath gostly syght of Jesu takeþ no grete kepe of stryuenge for vertus. It is not besy abouten hem specially, bot it [setteth] al here besynes for to kepe þat syght and þat behaldynge of Jesu þat it hath, for to hold þe mende stabilly þerto and bynd þe lufe only to it þat it falle not fro it, and forȝeteth al oþer thynges as mikel as it may. And whan it doth þus þan is Jesu sothfastly maystre in þe soule and þe soule is fully buxum to him. And þan feghteth Jesu for þe soule ageyns alle synnes, and vmschadweth it

64 þat] $\mathrm{H_7RBLB_3AsSrAHu_2EPH_6CcMLdPl}$, *om.* $\mathrm{HH_5WsLwTW}$ þe] *om.* $\mathrm{LB_3P}$ and pacience/sobernesse] *rev.* $\mathrm{H_5}$ pacience] of penaunce B sobernesse] $\mathrm{H_7RLB_3SrAHu_2EPH_6CcMPl}$, sobirte $\mathrm{HBH_5AsWsLwLdTW}$ and[2]] softnesse and *add.* As 65 lufereden] loue E, louyng Cc and[2]] to *add.* $\mathrm{H_6}$ al] also RAM 66 þe] to T sumtyme] *om.* $\mathrm{HH_5AsWsLw}$ trauellous . . . hard/to him] $\mathrm{H_7LB_3SrEPH_6CcMW}$, *rev.* $\mathrm{HBH_5WsLwHu_2LdT}$ trauellous] and *add.* Sr to him] *om.* RAMPl 67 now] noȝte M softnesse] sothnesse Cc and[1]] into *add.* As into[2]] a *add.* $\mathrm{H_6}$ 68 þat him] *rep.*, *canc.* L it] is *add.* $\mathrm{H_5Ws}$, *om.* LwAW no[1]] non $\mathrm{H_5Ws}$, *om.* $\mathrm{BHu_2LdT}$ ne] $\mathrm{H_7RLB_3SrAPH_6CcMPl}$, no *add.* $\mathrm{HBH_5WsLwHu_2ELdTW}$, non *add.* As hardnes] hardynesse B 69 ony] euery W lykyng] likned *prec.*, *canc.* H to[1]] vnto $\mathrm{H_5AsWs}$ for . . . it] *om.* As for] *om.* $\mathrm{H_6}$ 70 lufe] and *add.* As 71 þe] *om.* Pl common weye] comonetee LwW `weye´ $\mathrm{H_6}$ and . . . reson (l. 72)] *om.* RAMPl `not´ H^c, *om.* $H^{\circ}\mathrm{H_5}$ 72 werken] werkyng $\mathrm{H_6}$ reson] and *add.* $\mathrm{H_6}$ stryuen] $\mathrm{H_7RLB_3SrAPH_6CcMPl}$, þei *prec.* $\mathrm{HBH_5AsWsLwHu_2ELdTW}$ 73 synnes] synne Sr for] and *prec.* Ws þe getyng] þe geetynggis Lw, to geten $\mathrm{H_5AsWs}$ of] al *add.*, *canc.* Pl 74 þei] *om.* $\mathrm{LB_3EP}$ 75 þese] þose HRLwM wele] wyll Lw han] alle *add.* `L´$\mathrm{B_3EPH_6}$ only] $\mathrm{H_7RLB_3SrAEPH_6CcMPl}$, *om.* $\mathrm{HBH_5AsWsLwHu_2LdTW}$, solum Lat. in[2]] *om.* LwEW wil . . . in[2] (l. 76)] *om.* As and[2]] $\mathrm{H_7Hu_2}$, *om.* Σ 76 feghten] wyth *add.* LwTW as . . . myghtes/for hem (l. 77)] *rev.* Cc 77 myghtes] $\mathrm{H_7RLB_3SrAEPH_6CcMPl}$, miȝt $\mathrm{HBH_5AsWsLwHu_2LdTW}$, viribus Lat. for] to ȝete *add.* $\mathrm{B_3}$ moun]

meknes and pacience, sobirte and sadnes, chastite and clennes, lufered to his euen-cristen. And al oþer vertues, þe whilk were to him 16r traueilous, | peynful and harde for to kepen, are now turned into softnes and likynge and into wundirful liȝtnes, so fer forþ þat him þinkeþ it no meistrie ne no ha`r´dnes for to kepen ony vertue, bot it is most likynge to him for to kepe it. And al þis makiþ lufe.

Oþer men þat stondiþ in þe commine wey of charite, and are `not´ ȝit so fer forþ in grace bot wirken vnder þe biddynge of resoun, þei strifen and feiȝten al day ageyn synnes for þe getynge of vertues, and sumtyme þei ben aboue and sumtyme bineþ as wrestellers arne. Þose men don ful wel. Þei han vertues in resoun and in wil, not in sauour ne in lufe, for þei feȝten hemself as it were bi here owne miȝt fo`r´ hem. And þerfore moun þei not han ful rest ne fully þe `h´eiȝere hande. Nerþeles þei schulen han mikel mede, bot þei are not ȝit meke inowȝ. Þei han not put hemself al fully in Goddis hande, for þei seiȝen him not ȝit.

Bot a soule þat haþ gostly siȝt of Ihesu takiþ no grete kepe of strifynge for vertues. He is not bisy aboute hem specially, bot he settiþ al his bisynes for to kepe þat siȝt and þat biholdynge of Ihesu þat hit haþ, for to halde þe mende stabely þerto and bynde þe luf only to it þat it falle not þerfro, and forgeteþ al oþer þinges as mikel as it may. And whan it doþ þus þan is Ihesu soþfastly maister in þe soule [and þe soule ys fully buxum to hym. And þenne fyȝtteþ Ihesu for þe soule] ageyn alle synnes, and vmschadwþ it with his blissed presence,

ne *prec.* As   not] *om.* As   han] þe *add.* As   ful] *om.* RAMPl   ne fully] and þe fullier As   79 ȝit] it T   not^{2}] ȝit *add.* LB$_3$EPW   al] *om.* AsWs   fully] holy B   80 for] þerfore H$_6$ seyge] saw Hu$_2$ ȝit] *om.* A   hath] þe *add.* HE`W^{G}´, *om.* As   gostly] lyth and gastly Cc   syght] liȝte Pl   Jesu] God RAMPlWc, Jesu Christi Lat.   81 no] non As   grete] *om.* RAMPl   kepe] hede PlWc   stryuenge] stryuyngis Hu$_2$ for] of BH$_5$AsWsLd   vertus] for that tyme *add.* LwTW   It . . . sumtyme (39/127)] *om.* Hu$_2$ It is] ne A   It] H$_7$RLB$_3$SrEPH$_6$MPl, He HBH$_5$AsWsLwCcLdTWWc   is] nys As   82 it] H$_7$RLB$_3$SrEPH$_6$MPl, he HBH$_5$WsLwCcLdTWWc, *om.* As   setteth] seeth H$_7$ here] H$_7$RLB$_3$SrEPH$_6$Pl, his HBH$_5$AsWsLwCcMLdTWWs, myȝt and *add.* H$_6$, suam Lat.   þat^{1}] the Cc   þat^{2}] the Cc, *om.* AsWc   83 Jesu] God RAMPlWc, Jesu Christi Lat.   it hath] *rev.* M   hath] and *add.* AsCc   þe mende . . . þerto] Jesum . . . in memoria Lat.   stabilly] stable AsMWc   84 bynd] to *prec.* AsE   þe] his Cc   to it] therto Cc   þat . . . and] *om.* RM   þat . . . it^{2}] *om.* APl   fro it] H$_7$RLB$_3$SrEPH$_6$Cc, þerfro HBH$_5$AsWsLwLdTWWc   forȝeteth] H$_7$HRBLB$_3$SrAEPH$_6$MLdT, forgete H$_5$WsLwCcPlWWc, for to gete As, obliuiscatur Lat.   oþer] *om.* E   85 it^{1}] he Cc   it^{2}] he Cc   Jesu] loue RAMPl, God Wc   86 in . . . soule (l. 87)] *om.* LwW   and . . . soule (l. 87)] *om.* HH$_5$AsWs   is fully] *om.* A   87 Jesu] *rep.*, *canc.* L, loue RAMPl   vmschadweth] H$_7$HSrLdW, *corr. to* beschadowth Lw, byschadeweþ BAH$_6$T, vmbischadueþ LB$_3$EPPl, al byschadeweþ H$_5$Ws, with schadewith RM, aboute yshadweyd with As, shadewith Cc with his blissed presence, and geteth it al vertus; and þe soule is so conforted and so born vp with þe softe felynge `of lufe´ þat it hath of þe syght of Jesu, þat it feleth no grete desese owtwarde. And þus sleth lufe generally al synnes in a soule and reformeth it in new felynge of vertus.

How loue þurgh a gracious beholdynge of Jesu sleth alle sterynges of pride and makeþ þe soule perfytely meke, for it makeþ þe soule for to lesen sauour and delyte in al erthly worchepe. Capitulum xxxvii^{m}

Neuerþeles how lufe sleth synnes and reformeth vertus in a soule more specially schal I seyn; and first of pride, and of meknes þat is contrarye þerto. Þou schalt vnderstonden þat þer is two maner of meknes. One is had by werkyng of reson; anoþer is felt of þe specyal ȝifte of lufe. Bothe arn of lufe, bot þat on lufe werketh by reson of þe soule, þat oþer werkeþ by himself. Þe first is inperfyte, þat oþer is perfyte.

Þe first meknes a man feleth of ⟨behaldyng⟩ of his owne synnes and of his owne wrecchednes; þurgh whilk beholdynge he þenketh himself vnworthy for to han ony ȝifte of grace or ony mede of God, bot he thenkeþ it inogw þat he wold of his grete mercy graunten him forȝifnes of his synnes. And also he þenkeþ him bycause of his owne synnes þat he is wors þan þe most synner þat lyueth, and þat euerilk man doth bettre þan he. | f. 94^{v} And so by swilk beholdyng kasteth he himself doun in his thoght vnder alle men; and he is besy for to ageynstonden þe steryngges of pride as mykel as he may, boþe bodily pride and gostly, and despyseth himself, so þat he assenteþ not to þe

88 blissed] blysful Cc   geteth] ȝevith Cc   it] to *prec.* T, *om.* R   so] *om.* MLd   89 softe felynge of] siȝt and þe RAMPl   `of lufe´ *interl.* H$_7$ þat] *om.* As   90 þe . . . Jesu] God RAMPl, visione Jesu Christi Lat.   syght] light T   no] non As   desese] of it *add.* As   91 al synnes] synne AsCc   new] þe RAPlW   felynge] felynges LwW, *om.* Cc

Chapter 37 *title*: H$_7$RLB$_3$SrAEPH$_6$MLdPlTW   How loue sleeþ synne and retourneþ vertues, and how he þat is verrey meke þynken hemselfe worst of alle creaturys, and how loue perfit and gracious is nouȝt kendely ȝen but abouen all kynde of þe grace special of God. As   *om.* HBH$_5$WsLwCc   1 loue] sleeþ *add.*, *canc.* B$_3$ þurgh] *om.* W   a] H$_7$LB$_3$SrEPH$_6$M, *om.* RALdPlTW   alle] þe *add.* H$_6$ 2 and . . . worchepe (l. 4)] *om.* M   perfytely . . . soule (l. 3)] *om.* TW   perfytely meke] *rev.* RALdPl   3 `in . . . worchepe´ L   6 schal I seyn] I sey RM   schal I] *rev.* H$_6$ of^2] *om.* As   is] it MW   7 contrarye] vertue *add.* LwW   þerto] *om.* Lw   þou . . . meknes] *om.* Ld   þou] First *prec.* Cc   is] hys LwM   8 by] in A   anoþer] and *prec.* As, And oþer Lw, and þat oþer E   is] *om.* M   felt] and hadde Cc   of^2] bi LB$_3$SrPH$_6$ þe] H$_7$HRBH$_5$AsWsLwACcMLdW, *om.* LB$_3$SrEPH$_6$PlT   9 Bothe] But *prec.* LB$_3$EPH$_6$ `of^2´ B$_3$, *om.* Ld   lufe^2] *om.* Ws   by^1] wyþ B   10 þat] the Cc, and *prec.* AsCc, but *prec.* LwW

and getiþ it alle vertues; and þe soule is so conforted and so born vp with þe softe felynge of luf þat it haþ of þe siȝte of Ihesu, þat it feliþ no grete disese outward. And þus sleeþ lufe generally alle synnes in a soule and reformiþ it in new felynge of vertues.

[CHAPTER 37]

6[v] Nerþeles how lufe sleeþ synnes and reformiþ vertues in | a soule more specially schal I seien; and first of pride, and of meknes þat is contrarie þerto. Þu schalt vndirstanden þat þer is two maner of meknes. On is had bi wirkynge of resoun; anoþer is felt of þe special ȝifte of lufe. Boþe arn of luf, bot þat on lufe wirkiþ bi resoun of þe soule, þat oþer he wirkiþ bi himself. Þe first is inperfit, þat oþer is perfite.

Þe first meknes a man feliþ of beholdynge of his owne synnes and of his owne wrecchednes; þurȝ þe whilk beholdynge he þinkeþ himself vnworþi for to haue ony gifte of grace or ony mede of God, bot him þinkiþ it inowȝ þat he wold of grete mercy graunten him forgifnes of his synnes. And also he þinkiþ him bicause of his owne synnes þat he is wers þan þe most synner þat lifiþ and þat euerilk man doþ better þan he. And so bi swilk biholdynge kesteþ he himself doun in his þoȝt vnder alle men; and he is bisy for to ageynstonden þe stiryngis of pride as mikel as he may, boþe bodily pride and gostly, and despiciþ himself, so þat he assentiþ not to þe felynges of pryde.

werkeþ] H$_7$RLB$_3$AsSrAPH$_6$CcMLdPlT, he *prec.* HBH$_5$WsW`T^{G}´, he *add.* E, dileccio operatur is[1]] *om.* Ws inperfyte] H$_7$HRH$_5$LB$_3$AsSrAEPH$_6$CcMPl, vnperfiȝt BWsLw-LdTW þat] the Cc is[2]] *om.* R 12 meknes] that *add.* W behaldyng] behald-dyng *over line break* H$_7$ 13 owne] *om.* B$_3$ whilk] H$_7$RLB$_3$SrAPH$_6$CcMPl, þe whilk HBH$_5$-AsWsLwELdTW he] him AsLdT, *om.* R 14 himself] hym R for] *om.* T of[1]] H$_7$HRH$_5$AsSrWsLwALdPlTW, or BLB$_3$EPH$_6$CcM, donum gracie Lat. 15 he[1]] H$_7$RLB$_3$SrPMPl, him HBLwAEH$_6$LdTW, it Cc, *om.* H$_5$AsWs it] him Cc his] *om.* HB 16 his] *om.* B And . . . synnes] *om.* RAMPl he] hym H$_6$ owne] *om.* Cc 17 þat] how *prec.* RAMPl wors] *two- or three-word canc.* H þe most] eny E 18 so] *om.* Pl by swilk] in his H$_6$ beholdyng] beholdyngis Sr kasteth he] *rev.* ECc kasteth] *canc.* Lw, thresteþe LwW he] *om.* LB$_3$PH$_6$ 19 himself doun] him As *skips from here to Chapter* 35/50 lufe[2] himself] him Cc, self M in . . . thoght/vnder . . . men] *rev.* E thoght] þouȝtis LB$_3$EPH$_6$ besy] þanne *add.* As `for´ L 20 ageynstonden] vnderstonde As steryngges] stirynge HAs boþe] *om.* M 21 gostly] pryde *add.* As and] For he As despyseth] disposeþ LB$_3$EPH$_6$, despicere Lat. assenteþ] ne *prec.* As

felyngges of pryde. And if his hert be taken sumtyme with it, þat it be diffouled with veyn ioye of wurchepe or of knowynge or of preysynge or of any oþer thyng, as sone as he may perceyfe it he is euel payed with himself; and hath sorwe for it in his hert, and asketh forȝifnes for it of God, and scheweth him to his confessour and accuseth himself mekly and resceyueth his penaunce. Þis is a gode mekenes, bot it is not ȝit perfyte, for it is of soules þat are bygynnende and profytende in grace, caused of þe behaldyng of synnes. Lufe werkeþ þis meknes by reson of þe soule.

Parfyte meknes a soule feleth of þe syght and þe gostly knowenge of Jesu. For whan þe Holy Gost lyghtneth þe reson into þe syght of sothfastnesse, how Jesu is alle and þat he doth al, þe soule hath so grete lufe and so grete ioye in þat gostly syght, for it is so sothfast, þat it forȝeteth itself and fully leneth to Jesu with al þe lufe þat it hath for to beholden him. It takeþ no kepe of þe wurthines of itself ne of synnes before don, bot setteth at noght itself with al þe synnes and alle þe gode dedis þat euer it dide, as if þer were nothyng bot Jesu. Þus meke was Dauid whan he seyd þus: *Et substancia mea tanquam nichilum ante te*. Þat is: Lord Jesu, þe syght of þi blissed vnmade substaunce and þyn endles beeng scheweth wele vnto me þat my substaunce and þe beeng of my soule, þat is chaungeable, is as noght anemptes þe. Also anemptes his euen-cristen, he hath no reward to hem ne demynge of hem, wheþer þey be better or werse þan himself is. For he holdeth himself and alle oþer men as it were euen-lyke noȝt of hemself anemptes God; and þat is soth, for al þe godenes þat is don in himself or in hem is only of God, whom he beholdeth as al. An[d]

22 felyngges] felynge AsCc, stiringus AE hert] soule Ld be] ben H_5 with it] þerewith T it[1]] *om.* As it[2]] he T, *om.* As 23 diffouled] defended As of[1]] or LB_3PH_6Cc, and *add.* Pl wurchepe] worse schippyng As of[2] . . . thyng (l. 24)] *om.* As of[2]] *om.* Cc knowynge] H_7SrPl, kunnynge Σ of[3]] *om.* RECcM 24 of] *om.* Cc as] also A \`is´ Cc payed] apayd As 25 for it/in his hert] *rev.* H_6 his] H_7ECc, *om.* Σ and[2] . . . God] *om.* Ld for it/of God] *rev.* H_6 for it] *om.* Cc for[2]] $H_7RLB_3SrAEPMPl$, of $HBH_5AsWsLwH_6LdW$, of *corr. fr.* for T 26 it[2]] *om.* A accuseth] he *prec.* LB_3EPH_6 himself] him T 27 resceyueth] receyue H_5 a] H_7, *om.* Σ it is not/ȝit] *rev.* H_6 28 ȝit perfyte] *rev.* T perfyte] meknes *add.* LwW \`of´ Sr 29 caused] causynge B, because As synnes] his *prec.* As werkeþ] worscheþ As meknes] nouȝt by hymselue but *add.* RAMPl 30 þe] *om.* Ld 31 Parfyte] But *prec.* Cc meknes] of *add.* A þe[1]] a As and] of A, of *add.* E þe[2]] *om.* RMLd \`knowenge´ Pl 32 Jesu] God RAMPl, Jesu Christi Lat. into þe syght] *rep.* Ws þe[3]] *om.* BT 33 Jesu] God RAMPl is] *corr. fr.* dooþ Ld and] how *add.* As þat he] *om.* Pl þat] *om.* T 34 and] *om.* $HH_5AsWsLw$ \`þat´ $B_3$ syght] knowyng *add.*, *canc.* H so sothfast] soþfastnesse As, et delectabilis Lat. so] *om.* $LB_3PH_6$ 35 \`it[1]´ As, he A itself] hymself B, the self Cc leneth] fallyþ H_5Ws, turneþ As, innititur Lat. Jesu] God RAMPl þe] *om.* M for] *om.* T 36 him] and *add.* Cc kepe] hede A of[1]] to the self and to Cc

And if his herte be takyn sumtyme with it, þat it be defoulid with veyn ioye of worschipe or of kunnynge or of preisynge or of ony oþer þinge, as sone as he may perceife it he is yuel paied with himself, and haþ sorw for it in hert, and askiþ forgifnes of it of God, and schewiþ him to his confessour and accusiþ himself mekely and resceifiþ his penaunce. Þis is good meknes, bot it is not ȝit perfit, for it is of
17r soules þat are bigynnande | and profitande in grace, caused of behaldynge of synnes. Lufe wirkiþ þis meknes bi resoun of þe soule.

Perfit meknes a soule feliþ of þe siȝt and þe gostly knowynge of Ihesu. For whan þe Holy Gost liȝteneþ þe resoun into þe siȝt of soþfastnes, how Ihesu is al and þat he doþ al, þe soule haþ so grete luf, so gret ioy in þat gostly siȝt, for it is so soþfast, þat it forgetiþ itself and fully leneþ to Ihesu with al þe lufe þat it haþ for to beholden him. It takiþ no kepe of vnworþines of itself `ne of synnes bifore done, bot settiþ at noȝt itself´ with al þe synnes and alle þe gode dedis þat euer it did, as if þer ware noþinge bot Ihesu. Þus meke Dauid was whan he seid þus: *Et substancia mea tanquam nichilum ante te*. Þat is: Lord Ihesu, þe siȝt of þi blessed vnmade substaunce and þin eendles beeynge schewiþ wel vnto me þat my substaunce and þe beenge of my soule is as noȝt anentes þe. Also anentes his euen-cristen he haþ no rewarde to hem, ne demynge of hem wheþer þei ben better or wers þan himself is. For he holdiþ himself and alle oþer men as it were euen, ilike noȝt of hemself anenptes God; and þat is soþ, for al þe godnes þat is don in himself or in hem is only of God whom he beholdiþ as al. And þerfore settiþ he alle oþer creatures as noȝt, as he

þe] H$_7$RLB$_3$AsSrAEPH$_6$CcMPl, no LwW, noon T, *om.* HBH$_5$WsLd wurthines] H$_7$H$_5$AsSrWs, vnworþines HRBLB$_3$LwAEPH$_6$CcMLdPlTW, indignitatem Lat. itself] hymself B, the self Cc `ne . . . itself (l. 37)/H$^c$, *om.* H°H$_5$AsWs 37 synnes] þe *prec.* ACc before] aforn Cc setteth] it *add.*, *canc.* L itself] hymself B, the self Cc 38 `þe´ L it] he LB$_3$PH$_6$ dide] but onlych with brennynge loue biholdiþ Jesu *add.* H$_5$Ws if] þou BA Jesu] God RAMPl, Dominus Jesus Christus Lat. 39 was Dauid] H$_7$RLB$_3$AsSrAEPH$_6$CcMPl, *rev.* HBH$_5$WsLwLdTW seyd þus Et] seith Cc þus] Ps. 138° *add.* BEPT, Ps. xxxviii *add.* W 40 nichilum] nichil Ws Lord Jesu] *om.* T Jesu] *om.* RAMPl ⌜þe . . . blissed⌝ L [blessed *marg.*] þe] þi L^c, þyn As blissed] *om.* Ws vnmade] vnseable Pl 41 and] in Cc scheweth] schewid M vnto] to SrAH$_6$LdT my] is þe As 42 þe] *om.* W þat is chaungeable] H$_7$RBLB$_3$Sr-AEPH$_6$CcMLdPlT`W^G´, *om.* HH$_5$AsWsLwW, que mutabilis est Lat. is^2] nys As 43 þe] me Sr Also] And *prec.* As to hem] *om.* T 44 ne] to þe *add.* RAMPl of] *om.* Cc wheþer] whi Pl, þat *add.* LdT himself] hym Cc 45 alle] *om.* RM men . . . were] *om.* As it] þei Sr euen-lyke] H$_7$AsH$_6$Cc, euen, ilike HBH$_5$LB$_3$WsLw-AEPLdPlTW, euen alike RSrM, euene lich H$_6$Cc, equaliter Lat. 46 hemself] hem Cc anemptes] but *add.* As God] Jesu Cc þat^1] *om.* Ld þe] *om.* Sr godenes] goode dedis A is don] sit Lat [fit UpHe] 47 `himself´ W^G, hemselfe W in hem] himselfe As And] An H$_7$

þerfore setteth he al oþer creatures at noȝt as he doth himself. þus meke was þe prophete whan he seyd þus: | f. 95r *Omnes gentes quasi non sunt, sic sunt coram eo, et quasi nichilum et inane ita reputate sunt ei.* Al men are befor oure Lord as noght and as vnnayte, and noght þey are acounted to him. þat is, anemptes þe endles beeng and þe vnchaungable kende of God, mankende is as noght. For of noght it is made and to noȝt it schal turnen, bot if he keped it in þe beeng þat made it of noȝt. þis is sothfastnesse, and þis schuld make a soule meke if it myght se þurgh grace þis sothfastnesse.

þerfore whan lufe opneth þe inner eye of a soule for to seen þis sothfastnesse with oþer circumstances þat come withal, þan bygynneth þe soule for to ben sothfastly meke. For þan by þe syght of God it feleth and seeth itself as it is; and þan forsaketh þe soule þe beholdynge and þe lenyngge to itself, and fully falleth to þe beholdyng of him. And whan it doth so, þan setteth þe soule ryght noȝt of al þe ioye and al þe wurchepe of þis werld; for þe ioye and þe werdly wurchepe is so litel and so noȝt in regarde of þat ioye and þat lufe þat it feleth in þe gostly syght of Jesu and knowynge of sothfastnes, þat þogh he myght han it withouten ony synne he wold noȝt of it. Ne þogh men wold wurchepen him, preysen him, fauour him, and setten him at grete state, it lyketh him right noȝt, ne þogh he had þe cunnyng of al þe seuene artz of clergie, and of alle craftes vnder sunne, or had power for to werken alle maner miracles, he hath no more deynte of al þis ne no more sauour of hem þan for to gnawen vpon a drye stikke. He had wele leuer forȝeten al þis and for to ben alon out

48 setteth he] *rev.* H$_6$ at] as HH$_5$WsLd 49 þus] Ysa. 40° *add.* BLEPLdTW 50 sunt[1]] H$_7$RBH$_5$AsSrCcMPl, sint HLB$_3$WsLwAEPH$_6$LdTW sic sunt] *om.* As sunt[2]] *om.* Sr quasi] ad As et[2]] *om.* As inane] vane Ld, inanes T ita] H$_7$RLB$_3$SrEPH$_6$CcMPl, *om.* HBH$_5$AsWsLwALdTW, *om.* Lat. reputate] reputati LB$_3$AsEPH$_6$ ei] *om.* LB$_3$PH$_6$ Al] þat is *prec.* ECc 51 `as[2]´ B, *om.* AsT  vnnayte] H$_7$HRBPl, vnnouȝt AsM, vnnotefull ⌜Lw⌝W, vnmyȝt B$_3$, in vayne H$_5$SrWsLdT, veyn `L´PLd, emty H$_6$, thow they weryn nout Cc noght[2]] as *prec.* LdT 52 acounted] countede Pl, ycounted T þe[2]] *om.* T 53 God] Jesu H$_5$AsWs as] at Sr it is] *rev.* HBH$_5$Ws 54 to] into into L, into B$_3$EPH$_6$ it schal] H$_7$AECcPl, *rev.* BH$_5$WsLd, it schu⌜lde⌝ L, it schold RB$_3$SrPH$_6$M, ⌜schulde⌝ it H^{c}, schulde it LwTW, conuertetur Lat. if] *om.* BAT he] *rep.*, *canc.* H keped] H$_7$HRBLB$_3$LwPH$_6$CcMLdTW, kep H$_5$AsWsAEPl, helpe Sr made it] God made him As 55 is] a *add.* M `make´ H$_6$  56 se/þurgh grace] *rev.* AEH$_6$  þis] his Ld  sothfastnesse] and þis schulde make *add.*, *canc.* B$_3$  57 þerfore . . . soþfastnesse] *om.* AsMLd  a] H$_7$RLB$_3$SrAEPH$_6$CcPl, þe HBH$_5$WsLwTW  58 circumstances] circumstance MPl  `with´al] H$_6$, þerwith BALdT þan] þat H$_5$ 59 þe soule] homo Lat. for[1]] *om.* T to] seen þe soþfastnesse; þerefore whan þe loue openeþ in þe ynner eiȝe of þe soule for to seen þe soþfastnesse, for to *add.* As by . . . God] *om.* As God] Jesu Cc 60 `it´ feleth] H^{c}, *rev.* H$^{\circ}$BLd [it *seq. canc.* H] for⌜sakeþ þe soule þe⌝ L 61 beholdynge] of himself *add.* A þe[1]] *om.* H$_6$ lenyngge to] lovyng of Cc itself] hymself BB$_3$A, his self Pl, the self Cc

doþ himself. Þus meke was þe prophet whan he saide þus: *Omnes gentes quasi non sint, sic sunt coram eo, et quasi nichilum et inane reputate sunt ei*: Alle men are bifore oure Lord as noȝt and as vnnayt, and noȝt þei are acounted to him. Þat is, anenptes þe endeles beenge and þe vnchaungeable kynde of God, mankynd is as noȝt. For of noȝt is it made and to noȝt ⸢schulde⸣ it turnen, bot if he kepid it in þe beenge þat made it of noȝt. Þis is soþfastnes, and þis schuld make a soule meke if it miȝt seen þurȝ grace þis soþfastnes.

7v Þerfore when lufe opneþ þe inner iȝe of þe soule for to seen þis | soþfastnes with oþer circumstaunces þat comen withal, þan bigynniþ þe soule for to ben soþfastly meke. For þan bi þe siȝt of God \`it´ feliþ and seeþ itself as it is; and þan forsakiþ þe soule þe biholdynge and þe lenynge to itselfe, and fully falliþ to þe biholdynge of him. And whan it doþ so, þan settiþ þe soule noȝt bi alle þe ioye and þe worschep of þe werld; for þe ioye of werdly worschip is so litel and so noȝt in rewarde of þat ioye and þat loue þat it feliþ in þe gostly siȝt of Ihesu and knowynge of soþfastnes, þat þawȝ it miȝt haue it withouten ony synne he wold not of it. Ne þawȝ men wolde worschipen him, preisen him, fauoren him, or setten him at grete state, it likiþ him noȝt, ne þawȝ he had þe connynge of alle þe seuen artes of clergie, and of alle craftes vndir sunne, or had power for to wirken alle maner mirakles, he haþ no more dente of al þis ne no more sauour of hem þan for to gnawen on a drye stikke. He had wel lefer forgetin al þis and for to ben

falleth] falle Pl þe^{2}] *om.* A 62 him] H_7HRBLB_3AsSrAEPH_6MLdPl, Jesu H_5WsLwCc-TW, Dei Lat. þe soule] yt Cc soule] at *add.* T ryght] H_7RLB_3SrAEPH_6CcMPl, *om.* HBH_5AsWsLwLdTW of^{2}] H_7RLB_3SrAEPH_6CcMPl, bi HBH_5AsWsLwLdW, *om.* T 63 ioye] ioyes Pl, gloriam Lat. al] H_7RLB_3SrAEPH_6CcMLdPlT, *om.* HBH_5AsWsLwW þe^{1}] *om.* B wurchepe] worshepes Pl þis] H_7RLB_3SrEPH_6CcMPlT, þe HBH_5As-WsLwALdW for] and As ioye and þe werdly] *om.* As, gloria honoris mundani Lat. and þe] H_7, of þe H_5Ws, of Σ 64 and so] or Cc þat^{1}] þe Pl ioye and] glorie vel Lat. and] of *add.* ET 65 \`feleth´ Pl þe] *om.* $B_3$, hac Lat. syght] loue T 66 he] $H_7$RL$B_3$Sr-AP$H_6$CcMPl, it HB$H_5$AsWsLwLdTW \`han´ Pl ony] *om.* ACc wold] nolde As of it] haue B 67 wold] nouȝt As preysen] ne *prec.* As fauour him] *om.* Lat. fauour] ne *prec.* As, and *prec.* LwW and] H_7RLB_3SrAPH_6CcMPl, or HBH_5AsWsLwELdTW, et Lat. 68 state] estate WsM lyketh] ne *prec.* As right] H_7RLB_3SrAEPH_6CcMPl, *om.* HBH_5AsWsLwLdTW þe] *om.* PlW 69 artz of clergie] artes liberales Lat. and . . . sunne] *om.* Cc and of] with As alle] þe *add.* H_5AsWs craftes] artis Sr sunne] H_7HBH_5LB_3AsSrWsPH_6CcT, þe *prec.* RLwAEMLdPlW 70 for] *om.* AsE alle] oþer *add.* As maner] of *add.* H_5Ws miracles] þynge makeles As 71 þis] þese H_5AsWs, omnibus istis Lat. \`no´ W^G, ne L, *om.* LwW of^{2}] in A for] *om.* W vpon H_7RLB_3Sr-EPH_6MPl, on HBH_5AsWsLwLdTW 72 drye] dedde T wele] ful H_5 forȝeten] for to ȝeten As, for to *prec.* RM þis] these Cc, omnia ista Lat. and . . . werd (l. 73)] *om.* Ld

of þe syght of þe werd, þan for to þenken on hem and be wurcheped of al men. For þe hert of a trew lufer of Jesu is made so mykel and so large þurgh a litel syght of him and a litel felyng of his gostly lufe, þat al þe lykyng and al þe ioye of al erthe may not sufficen for to fille on corner of it. And þan semeth it wele þat þese wrecched werdly lufers þat arn as it were rauyssed in lufe of here owne wurchep, and pursew
f. 95^v after it for to han it with al þe myght and al þe witte | þat þei han, þei han no sauour in þis meknesse, þei are wunder fer þerfro. Bot þe lufer of Jesu hath þis meknes lastendly, and þat not with heuynes and stryfynge for it bot with lykynge and gostly gladnesse; þe whilk gladnes it hath, noȝt for it forsaketh al þe wurchepe of þis werd, for þat were a proude meknes þat langeth to an ypocryte, bot for he hath a syght and a gostly knoweng of sothfastnesse and of wurthinesse of Jesu þurgh þe ȝifte of þe Holi Gost.

þat reuerent syght and þat loueli beholdyng of Jesu conforteth þe soule so wonderfully, and bereth it vp so myghtily and so softely, þat it may not lyken ne fully resten in non erthly ioye, ne it wil not. He maketh no fors wheþer men lakken him or preysen him, [wurchepen him or dispysen him] as for himself: he setteth it not atte hert neyþer for to ben wele payd if men dispysen him, as for more meknes, ne for to ben euel payed þat men schuld wurchepen him or preysen him. He had leuer for to forgeten boþe þat on and þat oþer, and only thenken on Jesu, and gete meknes by þat waye, and þat is mikel þe sykerere weye whoso myght come þerto. þus dide Dauid whan he seyd þus: *Oculi mei semper ad Dominum, quoniam ipse euellet de laqueo pedes meos.* þat is: Myn eyen are ay op⌜o⌝ne Jesu oure Lord, for why he schal kepe

73 syght] solicitudinem Lat. on] of M be] to *prec.* As wurcheped] worchip Cc 74 mykel] meke H_5Ws 75 and] of *add.* E his] *om.* H_6T, *om.* Lat. 76 þe^1] feelynge *add.*, *canc.* L al^2] *om.* M \`al$^3$' Pl, þe *add.* AsE, *om.* RAM  fille] fulfille As$H_6$CcT  77 corner] cornel Cc  \`it^1' L And] *om.* Cc semeth it] *rev.* H_6 þese] þose RM, þo Pl 78 \`as' Pl in] with Sr 79 it^1] *om.* ALdT for . . . it^2] *om.* As with . . . han^2] *om.* Cc with] and *prec.* LB_3P þe^1] þeir Ws myght/. . ./witte] *rev.* T al^2] with B_3, *om.* HH_5AsWs han^1] mai M, for *add.* As þei han (l. 80)] *om.* H_5Ws 80 þis] *om.* Ws meknesse] derkenesse As 81 Jesu] Jesum Christum Lat. þis] is As þat] *om.* Cc with heuynes] *om.* M 82 for] with H_5Ws, with *corr. fr.* for Lw gostly] H_7RLB_3Sr-AEPH_6CcMPl, *om.* HBH_5AsWsLwLdTW, spirituali Lat. \`þe whilk gladnes' H^c, *om.* $H^o$$H_5$Ws 83 gladnes] he *add.* As noȝt] it *add.* H_5Ws it^2] he As al] H_7RLB_3As-SrAEPH_6CcMPl, *om.* HBH_5WsLwLdTW, omnem Lat. þis] H_7RLB_3AsSr-AEPH_6CcMPl, þe HBH_5WsLwLdTW 84 þat] and As for] *om.* M ⌜he hath⌝ L 85 and a] of As a] *om.* Cc of^2] *om.* AsLwTW wurthinesse] þe *prec.* EH_6 86 Jesu] Domini Jesu Lat. þurgh] *om.* Pl þe^1] *om.* LB_3EPH_6 87 þat^1] of *prec.* As þ⌜at⌝^{2} H^c, þe $H^o$$H_5$AsWs loueli] worþi Sr 88 soule] loue W so^1] and As wonderfully] *corr. fr.* wondirly Pl softely] gostly RM, sothly Lw, sothly *add.* W

alone out of þe siȝt of þe werld, þan for to þenken on hem and be wurschiped of alle men. For þe hert of a trewe lufer of Ihesu is made so mikel and so large þurghe a litel siȝt of him and a litel felynge of his gostly lufe, þat alle þe likynge and alle þe ioye of alle erþe may not suffice for to fille a corner of it. And þan semiþ it wel þat þese wrecched werdly lufers þat arn as it were rauisched in luf of here owne worschipe, and pursuen aftir it for to han it with al þe miȝt and þe wit þat þei han, þei han no sauour in þis meknes, þei ere wondre fer þerfro. But þe lufer of Ihesu haþ þis meknes lastendly, and þat not with heuynes and strifynge for it bot with likynge and gladnes; `þe which gladnes´ it haþ, not for it forsakiþ þe worschip of þe werld, for
18^{r} þat | were a proude meknes þat longiþ to an ypocrite, bot for he haþ a siȝt and a gostly knowynge of soþfastnes and of wurþines of Ihesu þurȝ þe gifte of þe Holi Gost.

þat reuerent siȝt and þ⌜at⌝ lufly beholdynge of Ihesu confortiþ þe soule so wundirfully, and beriþ it vp so miȝtily and so softly, þat it may not liken ne fully resten in none erþly ioye, ne it wil not. He makiþ no fors wheþer men lakke him or preise him, worschip him or despice him, as for himself. He settis it not at herte neiþer for to be wel paied if men dispice him, as for more meknes, ne for to be yuel paied þat men schulden worschip him or preise him. He had leuer for to forgete boþe þat on and þat oþer, and only þenken on Ihesu, and gete meknes bi þat wey, and þat is mikel þe sikerer wey whoso miȝt come þerto. þus did Dauid when he seide: *Oculi mei semper ad Dominum, quoniam ipse euellet de laqueo pedes meos*. þat is: Myn eiȝen are ay open to Ihesu oure Lorde, for whi he schal kepe my

89 not] no Ld lyken ne] *om.* Cc non] no E ne^{2} . . . not] *om.* Cc not] for *add.* As He . . . Jesu (l. 95)] *rep., canc.* R, *rep.* [*om. the first iteration of* or^{1} (l. 90) . . . him^{1} (l. 91)] AMPl He maketh] Nec curat homo habens hanc visionem Lat. 90 no] none T lakken . . . him^{2} (l. 91)] *om.* (*bis*) R lakken] blame Ld him^{2}] hem M, *om.* Ld wurchepen . . . him^{2} (l. 91)] *om.* H_7Cc, honorent vel contempnant Lat. wurchepen him] *om.* Sr 91 him^{2}] hem R it] *om.* Ws 92 for] *om.* Lw to] *om.* Ld payd] apayd As if] that Lw dispysen . . . men (l. 93)] *om.* Lw as] *om.* H_5Ws more] *om.* Sr 93 payed] apayed H_5AsWsLd þat] if H_5Ws or preysen him] *om.* Lw 94 leuer] wel *prec.* LB_3EPH_6`W^{G}´ for to] *om.* LB_3PH_6, *om. in first iteration* R forgeten] ȝete As boþe] *om.* A þat^{1}] þan As only thenken] *rev.* A thenken] considerare et cogitare Lat. 95 on] of B Jesu] Domino Jesu Christo Lat. and^{1} . . . þerto (l. 86)] *om.* Lat. gete] for to *prec.* As þat^{2}] þis LB_3EPH_6 `is´ Cc mikel þe] *rev.* T þe] *om.* Ld 96 `who´so] H_6, who W dide] seide T þus] H_7RLB_3SrAEPH_6CcMPl, *om.* HBH_5AsWsLwLdTW, Ps. 24° *add.* BLEPLdTW 98 ay] H_7HRLAPCcM, euere BH_5AsWsLwEH_6PlW, alwei B_3SrLdT opone] RLB_3SrAEPH_6CcMPl, op⌜o⌝ne H_7, open to HBH_5AsWsLwLdTW oure] my ⌜L⌝B_3EP`W^{G}´ he] our Lord Lw kepe] pluke LwW

my fete fro þe snares of synne. For whan he doth so þan forsaketh he vtterly himself and vndercasteth him holly to Jesu. And þan is he in a syker warde, for þe scheld of sothfastnes þat he beholdeþ kepeth him so wele þat he schal not ben hurt þurgh no strenghe of pryde as long as he holdeþ him withinne þe schelde, as þe prophete seyth: *Scuto circumdabit te veritas eius; non timebis a timore nocturno*. Sothfastnes of God schal vmgif þe with a scheld, and þat is if þou, al oþer thynges left, only beholde him. For þan schalt þou noȝt dreden for þe nyghten drede; þat is, þou schalt not dreden þe spyce of pride, wheþer he come by nyght or by day, as þe nexte vers seyth after þus: *A sagitta volante in die*. Pryde cometh by nyght for to assaylen a soule whan it is f. 96r despised and reproued | [of] oþer men, þat it schuld by þat fallen into heuynes and into sorwe. It cometh also as an arwe flyend in þe day, whan a man is wurcheped and preysed of al men, wheþer it be for werdly doyng or for gostly, þat he schulde han veyn ioye in himself and fals gladnes restendly in a passand thynge. Þis is a scharpe arwe and a perilous; it flyeth swyftely, it stryketh softly, bot it woundeth dedly. Bot þe lufer of Jesu, þat stably beholdeþ him by deuout prayers and besily thenk[ynge] on him, is so vmbelapped with þe syker scheld of sothfastnes þat he dredeth not; for þis arw may not entren into þe soule, ne þogh it come it hurteth noght, bot glenteth away and passeth forth.

And þus is þe soule made meke, as I vnderstonde, by þe werkynge of þe Holi Gost þat is þe ȝifte of lufe; for he opneth þe eye of þe soule for to seen and to lufen Jesu, and he kepeth þe soule in þat syght

99 þe] H_7RLB_3SrAEPH_6CcMPl, *om.* HBH_5AsWsLwLdTW snares] gryuus A, or greues *add.* BT synne] H_7RBLB_3SrAEPH_6CcMLdPl, synnes HH_5AsWsLwTW For] *om.* Ws so] *rep.*, *canc.* H forsaketh he] *rev.* As 100 vtterly] witerly Lw vndercasteth . . . holly] holi betakeþ him As vndercasteth] subicit et submittit Lat. to Jesu] *om.* B_3 Jesu] God Cc, Jesu Christo Lat. a] *om.* RM 101 þat] H_7RLB_3Sr-APH_6CcPl, the M, þe whilk HBH_5AsLwELdTW, whiche Ws beholdeþ] H_7RLB_3Sr-AEPH_6CcMPl, holdiþ HBH_5AsWsLwLdTW, considerat Lat. `kepeth´ Sr 102 schal not] ne schal Sr þurgh] þe *prec.*, *canc.* Sr no strenghe] þe farynge As strenghe] H_7Cc, sterynge Σ, motum Lat. 103 holdeþ] beholdiþ HH_5 withinne þe schelde] þereynne þat is þis As þe schelde] þer A þe[1]] H_7RLB_3SrEPH_6CcMPlTW, þat HBH_5WsLwLd as] þat As seyth] Ps. 90° *add.* BLEPLdT, Ps. x. W 104 non . . . nocturno] etc. Ld, *om.* T Sothfastnes] þat is *prec.* H_5WsECc of God] H_7RLB_3SrAEPH_6CcMPl, *om.* HBH_5AsWsLwLdTW, Dei, que est Jesus Christus Lat. 105 vmgif] H_7B_3Sr, vmgo RM, go about AH_6, vmbiclip HLwPW, vm⌜biclippe⌝ L, , al bicleppe BH_5Ws, byclippe T, vnclippe Ld, vmbelappe AsEPl, vyron Cc is] *om.* As þou] leve *add.* Cc oþer] *om.* Cc thynges] *om.* Ld 106 left] leeue RAsM, *om.* Cc only beholde/him] *rev.* Pl only] and As beholde] to be holdyn Cc him] þe in þe loue of drede As For[1]] and Cc schalt þou] *rev.* T þou noȝt] *rev.* HB for[2] . . . dreden (l. 107)] *om.* A for[2]] of As nyghten] H_7, nyȝttende RM, nyȝtynge Pl, nyght SrCc, niȝtes HBH_5LB_3AsWsLwEPH_6LdTW

feet fro snares of synnes. For whan he doþ so þen forsakiþ he vtterly himself and vndirkestiþ him holly to Ihesu. And þan is he in a siker warde, for þe schelde of soþfastnes, þe whilk he holdiþ, kepiþ him so wel þat he schal not ben hirt þurgh no stirynge of pride as longe as he beholdiþ him withinne þat scheld, as þe prophet seiþ: *Scuto circumdabit te veritas eius; non timebis a timore nocturno*: Soþfastnes schal vmbiclip þe with a scheld, and þat is if þu, alle oþer þinges left, only biholde him. For þan schalt not þou drede for þe niȝtes drede, þat is, þu schalt not drede þe spirit of pride, wheþer he come bi niȝt or
18^{v} by day, as þe next vers seiþ | aftir þus: *A sagitta volante in die*. Pride comiþ bi niȝt for to assailen a soule, when it is despiced and reprofed of oþer men, þat it schuld bi þat fallen in heuynes and into sorwe. It comiþ also as an harw flyende in þe day, whan a man is worschipid and preised of alle men, wheþer it be for worldly doynge or for gostly, þat he schulde han veyn ioie in himself restendly in a passend þinge. Þis is a scharpe arwe and a perilous; it flieþ swiftly, it strikiþ softly, bot it woundiþ dedly. Bot þe lufer of Ihesu, þat stably biholdiþ him bi deuoute preiers and bisy þinkynge on him, is so vmbilappid with þe siker schelde of soþfastnes þat he drediþ not; for þis arwe may not entren into þe soule, ne þawȝ it come it hirtiþ not, bot glentiþ awey and passiþ forþ.

And þus is þe soule made meke, as I vndirstande, bi þe wirkynge of þe Holy Gost þat is þe gifte of luf; for he opneþ þe iȝe of þe soule for to seen and lufen Ihesu, and he kepiþ þe soule in þat siȝt restfully and

107 spyce] H_7, spiritis As, spirit Σ, spiritum Lat. 108 by^{2}] *om.* R after] *om.* BLB_3PH_6 þus] þis AsLd, *om.* Cc, Ps. 90° *add.* BLPT, Ps. x. *add.* W 109 die] a negocio perambulante in tenebris *add.* A, etc. *add.* AsLdT cometh] *rep.*, *canc.* L soule] sely *prec.* T it] *om.* Cc 110 of] *om.* H_7 fallen] fallynge As into] H_7RLB_3Sr-$AEPH_6CcMPlT$, in $HBH_5AsWsLwLdW$ 111 It cometh/also] *rev.* Cc also] *om.* As in þe day] hit comeþ As in] on LwW 112 is . . . preysed] worschippeþ and pursueþ As 113 for] *om.* RMT 114 and . . . gladnes/restendly] *rev.* LwW and fals gladnes] *om.* HH_5AsWs and] a *add.* H_6 in] and As passand] and weyward *add.* B 115 a] *om.* BA perilous] arwe *add.* LB_3EP it^{1}] and Pl, for *prec.* As swyftely] sodeynly B it^{2}] and *prec.* W stryketh] smyteþ BASrLdT, s- *prec.*, *canc.* Sr bot] *om.* RAMPl 116 dedly] be ware with þat *add.* R, . . . þerof *add.* A, . . . of þat *add.* H_6, . . . be that *add.* M þat] standiþ and *add.* H_6 him] *om.* W by] and with As 117 and] besekeþ him *add.* H_5AsWs besily] $H_7H_5LB_3AsSrWsPH_6CcPl$, bisy HRBLwAEMLdTW thenkynge] þenkinges T, þenken H_7, þenkeþ H_5Ws, he þenkeþ As, cogitacionem Lat. on] of Cc him . . . of (l. 118)] *om.* As so] *om.* A vmbelapped] al bylapped B, vmlappid RM, bilappid AT, wlappid H_6, and kept *add.* Cc 118 sothfastnes] stedefastnesse As dredeth] it *add.* H_5Ws may] ne *prec.* As into] to H_5Ws 119 ne] and Cc \`come it´ L, *om.* B_3 hurteth] it *add.* Ws glenteth] glasiþ H_6, glydith Cc away/. . ./forth] *rev.* Pl 121 þe^{2}] *om.* LB_3PH_6 122 for] as he o- *add.*, *canc.* L eye of þe] *om.* As 123 to^{2}] $H_7RLB_3SrPH_6CcM$, for *prec.* AEPl, *om.* $HBH_5AsWsLwLdTW$ Jesu] vt prius dictum est *add.* Lat. þat] þe AsCc

restfully and sykerly, and he sleth al þe sterynges of pryde wonder priuely and softely—and þe soule wote neuer how—and he also bryngeth in by þat weye sothfastly and louely þe vertu of mekenes. Al þis doth loue, bot not in alle his lufers ilyk ful. For sum han þis grace bot schortly and lytel, as it were ȝit in þe bygynneng of it and a litel assayend toward it, for here conscience is not ȝit fully clensed þurgh grace. And sum han it more fully, for þei han clerer syght of Jesu, and þei fele more of his lufe. And sum han it most fully, for þey haue þe ful ȝifte of contemplacyon. Neuerþeles he þat lest hath on þis maner as I haue sayde, sothly he hath þe ȝifte of parfyte meknes, for he haþe þe ȝifte of perfyte loue.

How lufe sleth alle þe sterynges of yre and enuy softly and reformeth in þe soule þe vertus of pees, of pacyence and of perfyte charite to his euen-cristen, as he dyde specially in þe apostels and in þe martiers. Capitulum xxxviii[m]

Lufe werkeþ wysely and softely in a soule þer he wil, for he sleth myghtily ire and enuye and al passions of angrines and malencoly in it, and bryngeth into a soule vertus of pacience and myldnesse, pesybilte f. 96v and luferede to his euen-cristen. It is ful mykel | maystrie and grete hardnes to a man þat standeth only in þe werkynge of his owne reson for to kepen pacience holly, reste and softnes in herte, and charite anemptis his euene-cristen if þei disesen him vnskilfully and don him wronge, þat he ne schal don sumwhat ageyn to hem þurgh sterynge of ire or of malencolie, eyther in spekynge or in werkyng or in boþe. And

124 restfully] rightfulli M and he sleth] *om.* M and²] *om.* As wonder] wondyrfully Lw, wonderfully and W 125 softely] sothly Cc and² . . . how] *om.* Lat. neuer] not LdT he also] $H_7RLB_3SrAEPH_6CcMPl$, *rev.* $HBH_5AsWsLwLdTW$ 126 bryngeth in/by þat weye] *rev.* H_6 þat] þe H_5AsWs sothfastly . . . vertu] of soþfastnesse and lowenesse þe werk As sothfastly] softli H_6 127 doth] is his As bot] *om.* H_5Ws his] þese Sr, *om.* As ilyk ful] licheful Ld ful] fully Pl, *om.* AsCc sum] men *add.* LB_3EPH_6 þis] *om.* Pl 128 and lytel] a lytil As lytel] lythly Cc ȝit] $H_7RLB_3SrAEPH_6CcMPl$, *om.* $HBH_5AsWsLwLdTW$, adhuc Lat. and²] *om.* M a . . . it (l. 129)] modicam degustacionem Lat. 129 assayend] assaid R it] $H_7RLB_3SrAEPH_6CcMPl$, *om.* $HBH_5AsWsLwLdTW$, illius Lat. here] the LwW ȝit] *om.* Pl fully clensed] $H_7RLB_3SrAEPH_6CcMPl$, *rev.* $HBH_5WsLwLdTW$, clarified fully As þurgh] bi T 130 sum] men *add.* LB_3EPH_6 clerer] cleer RM, claram Lat. 131 his lufe] eius presencia et amore Lat. sum] men *add.* LB_3EPH_6 han it] *om.* M most] more CcM fully] parfitely Cc 132 ful] *om.* H_5AsWs þat] haþ *add.*, *canc.* L lest hath] *rev.* LdT 133 sayde] aforn *prec.* As sothly] I hope *prec.* LwW meknes . . . perfyte (l. 134)] *om.* As 134 ȝifte of/perfyte] *rev.* T

Chapter 38 *title*: $H_7RLB_3SrAEPH_6MLdPlTW$ þat þis loue lost in mannys soule be sterryngys of synne may ben yȝouen aȝein be pacience and full makyng aseeþ þurgh and suffryng and bodily penaunce As *om.* $HBH_5WsLwCc$ 1 sleth] destruit seu occidit Lat. þe] H_7, *om.* Σ yre] wraþthe H_6LdTW softly] *om.* Lat. 2 of³ . . . martiers (l.

sikerly, and he sleeþ alle þe stirynges of pride wundre priuely and softly—and þe soule wote neuer how—and also he bryngiþ in by þat wey soþfastly and lufely þe vertue of meknes. Al þis doþ lufe, bot not in al his lufers ilike fulle. For summe han þis grace bot schortly and litel, as it were in þe bigynnynge of it and a litil assaynge toward, for þeir conscience is not ȝit clensid fully þurȝ grace. And sum han it more fully, for þei han clerer siȝt of Ihesu, and þei fele more of his loue. And summe han it most fully, for þei han þe ful gifte of contemplacioun. Nerþeles he þat lest haþ on þis maner as I hafe seide, soþly he haþe þe gifte of perfit meknes, for he haþe þe gifte of perfite lufe.

[CHAPTER 38]

119r Lufe wirkiþ wisely and softly in a soule þer he wil, for he | sleeþ miȝtily ire and enuye and alle passiouns of angirnes and malencoly in it, and bryngiþ into þe soule vertues of pacience and mildnes, pesibelte and lufreden to his euen-cristen. It is ful harde and a grete maistrie to a man þat stondiþ only in wirkynge of his owne resoun for to kepen pacience, holy rest and softnes in herte, and charite to his euen-cristen if þei disesen him vnskilfully and don him wronge, þat he ne schal sumwhat don ageyn to hem þurghe stirynge of ire or of malencoly, eiþer in spekyngis or in wirkynge or in boþe.

4)] *om.* M of^{3}] H_7RSrAPl, and LB_3EPH_6LdTW, paciencie Lat. and . . . martiers (l. 4)] `and yn martirs´ $T^G W^G$, *om.* ALdTW 3 in þe] H_7SrPl, *om.* Σ 5 wysely] visily Cc and softely/in a soule] *rev.* A and softely] *om.* M softely] sothly Cc, sobrie Lat. þer] where B, what A 6 ire] wreþþe BEH_6 and^{2}] *om.* M passions] passion H_5, pas- *prec.* L angrines] angris SrM, angeris Cc, anguissh As, angustie Lat. 7 a] H_7RLB_3Sr-$AEPH_6$CcMPl, þe HBH_5AsWsLwLdTW and^{2}] mekenes and *add.* Pl, *om.* A myldnesse] and *add.* H_5AsWsCc, humilitatis Lat. 8 luferede] loue E, of lovyng Cc to] of Cc mykel . . . hardnes] $H_7RLB_3SrAEPH_6$CcMPl, harde and a grete maistrie HBH_5As-WsLwLdTW, arduum et difficile Lat. mykel] H_7RSrAH_6CcMPl, grete HBH_5`L´-$B_3$AsWsLwEPLdTW 9 hardnes] difficulte A `a´ Pl `only´ Pl þe] H_7RLB_3Sr-$AEPH_6$CcMPl, *om.* HBH_5AsWsLwLdTW 10 kepen] hem in *add.* As holly] H_7RBAsSrACcMLdPl, holy HH_5WsLwLdTW, ⌜oon⌝ly L, only B_3EPH_6, integre Lat. ⌜r⌝este] L, and *add.* RAPl, and in *add.* As, *om.* M softnes] soberte Ld, sobrietatem Lat. and^{2}] in *add.* As 11 anemptis] $H_7RLB_3SrAEPH_6$CcMPl, to HBH_5AsWsLwLdTW, erga Lat. if] þow B, for As 12 don sumwhat] $H_7RLB_3AsSrAEPH_6$CcMPl, *rev.* HBH_5WsLwLdTW ageyn/to hem] *rev.* As ageyn to] aȝens LB_3EPH_6 to hem] *om.* Sr 13 ire] wreþþe B or^{1}] ouþer A, and H_6 of] *om.* T eyther] ouþir WsA, or BPl, and H_6 spekynge] spekyngis H, verbo Lat. or^{2}] eyþer H_5H_6 in^{3}] *om.* LwW And] *om.* Cc neuerþeles if a man be stered or trubled in himself and be made vnrestful, be so þat it be not to mikel passend ouer þe bondes of reson, and þat he kepe his hand and his tunge and be redy for to forȝife trespasse whan mercy is asked, ȝit þis man hath þe vertu of pacience, þogh it be bot weykly and nakedly, for as mikel as he wold haue it, and trauayleth besily in refreynynge of his vnskilful passions þat he myght haue it, and al[so is] sori þat he hath it not so as he schulde. Bot to a trew lufer of Jesu it is no grete maystrie for to suffren al þis; for whi lufe fyghteth for him, and sleth wonder softely swilk rysynges of wreth and of malencoly, and makeþ his soule so esy, so pesible, so suffrend and so godely þurgh þe gostly syght of Jesu with þe felyng of his blissed lufe, þat þogh he be despised or reproued of oþer men, or take wronge or harme, schame or vylanye, he chargeth it not. He is not mikel stered ageyns hem, for if he were mykel stered he schuld forberen þe confort þat he feleth withinne his soule, bot þat wil he not. He may lyghtlyere forgeten al þe wronge þat is don to him þan anoþer man may forgife it þogh mercy were asked. And so he had wele leuer forgeten þan forgifen it; for him þenkeþ it is so most ese to him.

And lufe doth al þis, for lufe opneth þe eye of þe soule to þe syght of Jesu, and stableth it with þe lykyng of loue þat it feleth by þat syght, and conforteth it so myghtily þat it taketh no kepe what-so men ianglen or done ageyns him—it hangeth nothyng vpon him. Þe most harme þat he myght hauen were a forberyng of a gostly syght of Jesu, and þerfore it is leuer to him for to suffre al oþer harmes þan þat

14 if] H_7, þogh Σ, licet Lat. stered or trubled] *rev* As stered] sterith M or] H_7HBH_5LB_3AsSrAEH_6CcLdPlT, and RWsLwPMW, et Lat. be^{2}] H_7RLB_3Sr-AEPH_6CcMPl, *om.* HBH_5AsWsLwLdTW 15 be^{1}] if it *prec.* RAEMLd`$W^G$´, þan ȝif it *prec.* As, it *add.* T, *om.* B$H_5$WsCc `so´ R it] he RAMLd to mikel] *om.* T to] so H_5AsWs ouer] *om.* RT 16 he] *rep.* M kepe] kepeþ H_5Ws and^{1}] oþer As for] *om.* PlT forȝife] gife M 17 trespasse] H_7RLB_3SrPH_6MPl, þe *prec.* HBH_5AsWs-LwAECcLdTW is asked] hit askeþ Pl is] his M þe] *om.* M 18 bot] *om.* H_6 `weykly´ $W^G$, weyke W, wikidle M, febly B, leþili Ld, lethi T `he´ Pl it^{2}] *om.* Ld and^{2} . . . it (l. 20)] *om.* T 19 in] *om.* Lw refreynynge] reformyng CcPl vnskilful] vnkilful H passions] pacience M 20 and . . . it^{2}] *om.* Cc also is] al H_7 hath it] it | it M so] H_7RLB_3SrEPMPl, as sone H_6, *om.* HBH_5AsWsLwACcLdTW, sicut Lat. `to´ *interl.* H 21 is] nys As `no´ Cc, nouȝt AsAPl grete] *om.* RMLdT al þis] omnia ista Lat. 22 lufe] dileccio Jesu Christi Lat. him] hem B_3 softely] fulli M, sobrie Lat. rysynges] H_7RLB_3SrAPH_6CcM`$T^G$$W^G$´, stiryngis $H_5$AsWsLwELdPlTW, stirynge HB, motus Lat. 23 wreth] wreeche Ws, ire RM of] al L$B_3$EP$H_6$, alle *add.* Cc, *om.* Sr `and^{2}´ L esy] sobriam Lat. so^{2}] and *prec.* LwAW so^{3}] of T 24 godely] H_7HAsWsPl, goodly RBH_5LB_3SrLwAEPH_6CcMTW, goudeli Ld, spiritualem Lat. þe^{1}] *rep.*, *canc.* H syght] liȝt Pl 25 or] H_7RLB_3SrAEPH_6CcPl, and HBH_5AsWsLwMLdTW, vel Lat. 26 take] to be born As wronge] on honde *add.* H_5AsWs harme] H_7HRBAsSrLw-

And nerþeles þawʒ a man be stirid or trubled in himself and made vnrestful, be so þat it be not to mikel passende ouer þe bondes of resoun, and þat he kepe his hande and his tonge and be redy for to forgif þe trespas when mercy is asked, ʒit þis man haþ þe vertue of pacience, þawʒ it be bot weikly and nakedly, for as mikel as he wolde haue it, and traueiliþ bisily in refreynynge of his vn[s]kilful passions þat he miʒte hafe it, and also is sory þat he haþ it not as he schulde. Bot `to´ a trew lufer of Ihesu it is no gret maistrie for to suffren al þis; for whi lufe feʒtiþ for him, and sleeþ wundre softly swilke stirynge of wreþ and of malencolye, and makiþ his soule so esy, so pesible, so suffrende and so godly þurʒ þe gostly siʒt of Ihesu wiþ þe felynge of his blissed luf, þat þawʒ he be despised and reprofed of oþer men, or take wronge or harme, schame or vileyny, he chargiþ it not. He is not mikel stirid ageyns hem, he wil not ben angred ne stired ageyns hem; for if he were mikel stirid he schuld forberen þe conforte þat he feliþ
119v withinne his soule, bot þat | wil he not. He may liʒtlier forgeten alle þe wronge þat is don to him þan anoþer man may forgif it þawʒ mercy were askid. And so he had wel lefer forgetyn it þan forgifen it; for him þinkiþ it so most ese to him.

And lufe doþ al þis, for lufe opneþ þe eiʒe of þe soule to þe siʒt of Ihesu, and stabliþ it with þe likynge of luf þat it feliþ bi þat siʒt, and confortiþ it so miʒtily þat it takiþ no kepe what-so men iangelen or don ageyns him—it hangiþ noþinge vpon him. Þe most harme þat he miʒt han were a forberynge of þat gostly siʒt of Ihesu, and þerfor it is lefer to him for to suffre alle harmes þan þat alone. Al þis may þe soule

AH$_6$CcMLdPlTW, or *add.* H$_5$LB$_3$WsEP, iniuriam Lat. schame] *om.* As it] *om.* Cc is] nys As 27 mikel] mychelis Ld hem] him B$_3$LwH$_6$W for] H$_7$B$_3$SrH$_6$Cc, he wil [nylle As] not ben angred [nor yuel paide *add.* E] ne stired ageyns hem [ageyns hem *om.* As, hym W] *prec.* HBH$_5$`L´AsWsLwAEPMLdPlTW, nec multum vult moueri seu turbari Lat. if . . . stered] þan As stered] *om.* M 28 he feleth] is As withinne] H$_7$HBH$_5$Ws-LwCcLd`Pl´TW, in *add.* RLB$_3$AsSrAEPH$_6$MPl`W$^{G}$´, in . . . intus Lat. 29 not] for *add.* As `to´ T^{G}, *om.* T þan] to *add.* As 30 man] *om.* E may] þat *prec.* As `þogh . . . it$^{1}$ (l. 31)´ T$^{G}$, *om.* T þogh] þurgh As mercy] ʒif it *add.* As, had *add.*, *canc.* M had] were H$_5$AsWs 31 wele] ful LB$_3$P forgeten] H$_7$RLB$_3$SrAPH$_6$CcMPl, for to ʒeten As, it *add.* HBH$_5$AsWsLwELdTW `þan forgifen it´ W^{G}, *om.* LwW forgifen] for to ʒeuen As `is so´ Pl is] H$_7$RLB$_3$AEPH$_6$CcMPl, *om.* HBH$_5$AsSrWsLwLdTW, est Lat. so] *om.* LwW ese] esy MPl, ad quietem Lat. to] vnto Sr 33 to] into WsWc 34 Jesu] Jesu Christi Lat. and] on Cc it^{1}] ipsum hominem Lat. þat] the Cc 35 conforteth] confortid M it^{1}] illum Lat. myghtily] mekel Cc, mekil and so *add.* RM kepe] hede AWc 36 it . . . him] *om.* Cc hangeth] angreþ As vpon] in A þe] But *prec.* As 37 a^{1}] in þe mene while of As, *om.* T a^{2}] H$_7$, þe LB$_3$LwPH$_6$MPlW, þat HRBH$_5$AsSrWsACcLdT, þis E, illius Lat. Jesu] Jesu Christi Lat. 38 for] *om.* LB$_3$PH$_6$T oþer] H$_7$RLB$_3$SrAPH$_6$CcMPl, *om.* HBH$_5$AsWsLwELdTWWc, alia Lat. þat allone] to forgon þat love Cc allone. Alle þis may þe soule wele done and esily, withouten grete f. 97r trubilyng | of þe gostly syght whan desese falleth al withouten-forth and toucheþ not þe body, as is bakbytyng or scornynge or spoylyng of swilk as he hath. Al þis greueth not; bot it goth sumwhat nerre whan þe flesch is touched and he feleth smert, þan is it harder. Nerþeles þogh it be hard and vnpossible to þe frele kende of man for to suffre bodily peyn gladly and paciently, withouten bitter sterynges of ire, angre and malencolye, it is not vnpossible to lufe, þat is þe Holi Gost, for to werk þis in a soule þer he toucheth with his blissed ȝifte of loue.

Bot he ȝifeth a soule þat is in þat plyte myghty felynges of loue, and wonderfully festneth it to Jesu, and departeth þe soule wonder fer fro þe sensualite þurgh his priue myght, and conforteth it so swetely by his blissed presence þat þe soule feleth litel peyn or ellis non of þe sensualite; and þis is a speciale grace ȝifen to þe holy martires. Þis grace had þe apostels, as Holy Writte seyþ þus of hem: *Ibant apostoli gaudentes a conspectu consilii, quoniam digni habiti sunt pro nomine Jesu contumeliam pati*. Þat is: þe apostels ȝeden ioyend fro þe counseyl of þe Jewes whan þey were beten with scourges, and þei were glad þat þei wer wurthi for to suffre ony bodily dessese for þe name of Jesu. Þei were not stered to ire ne to felnes, for to be venged of þe Jewes þat beten hem, as a werdly man wold bene whan he suffreth a lytel harme, be it neuer so litel, of his euen-cristen. Ne þei were not stered to pryde and to heygnes of hemself and to dedyn and to demeng of þe Jewes, as ypocrytes and heretykes are þat wil suffre mykel bodily peyne, and arn redy sumtyme for to suffre þe ded with grete gladnes and myghty wil,

39 þe soule] homo Lat. þe] a LB$_3$EP wele done] *rev.* LB$_3$EPW 40 syght] of Jesu *add.* A 41 toucheþ not] noȝte touched M is] in A, *om.* Pl bakbytyng] bacbytyngis B, bagbytyng H$_5$ or[1]] *om.* Sr 42 hath] yput on him *add.* As greueth] yt *add.* Cc nerre] nere H$_5$Ws 43 he] *om.* M feleth] feel LB$_3$EPH$_6$, it *add.* As`Pl′ is it] H$_7$HRBH$_5$As-SrWsLwAMLdPl, *rev.* LB$_3$EPH$_6$CcTW 44 vnpossible] H$_7$HRBH$_5$AsSrWsLw-AH$_6$CcMPl, impossible LB$_3$EPLdTW, quasi inpossibile Lat. þe] *om.* T for] H$_7$RLB$_3$-SrAEPH$_6$CcMPl, *om.* HBH$_5$AsWsLwLdTW 45 peyn] H$_7$RLB$_3$SrAEPH$_6$CcMPl, penaunce HBH$_5$AsWsLwLdTW, penam Lat. sterynges] steryng CcT ire] wreþþe B, and *add.* MT 46 and] or H$_6$ is[1]] nys As vnpossible] H$_7$HRBH$_5$SrLwAMPl, inpossible LB$_3$WsEPH$_6$CcLdTW, possible As 47 for] *om.* LdT þis] þus E, talem pacienciam Lat. his] H$_7$RBLB$_3$SrAPH$_6$CcMLdPl, þe HH$_5$AsWsLwELdTW of loue] *om.* Pl 48 ȝifeth] H$_7$HRBH$_5$AsSrWsLwACcMLdPlW, to *add.* LB$_3$EPH$_6$T a soule] homini Lat. þat[2]] *om.* Cc myghty . . . of] moche felynge and miȝtty As myghty] myghtily W felynges] felinge T 49 þe soule] H$_7$RLB$_3$SrAEPH$_6$CcPl, his soule M, it HBH$_5$AsWsLwLdTW fer] fare M 50 his] *om.* Pl myght] m- *prec.*, *canc.* Sr and] he *add.* H$_5$Ws 51 ellis] *om.* H$_6$ `non′ L 52 is] was H$_6$ a] þe LB$_3$EPM, *om.* LwW 53 had/þe apostels] *rev.* H$_5$Ws had] `hadden′ *interl.* H^c as] for *prec.* H$_5$Ws `Holy′ *interl.* H^c seyþ] seynge *add.* As, *om.* H$_6$ þus/of hem] H$_7$RLB$_3$AsSrAPH$_6$CcMPl, *rev.*

wel don and esily, withouten grete troblynge of þe gostly siȝt whan disese falliþ al withouteforþ and touchiþ not þe body, as is bakbitynge or scornynge or spoilynge of swilk as he haþ. Al þis grefiþ not; bot it goþ sumwhat nerre whan þe flesch is touchid and he feliþ smert, þan is it harder. Nerþeles þawȝ it be hard and vnpossible to þe freel kynde of man to suffre bodily penaunce gladly and paciently, withouten bittur stirynges of ire, angre and malencoly, it is not vnpossible to lufe, þat is þe Holy Gost, for to wirke þis in a soule þer he touchiþ wiþ þe blissed gifte of luf.

Bot he gifiþ a soule þat is in þat plyȝt miȝty felynges of lufe, and wondirfully festneþ it to Ihesu, and departiþ it wondir ferre fro þe sensualitee þurgh his pryuey miȝt, and confortiþ it so swetly bi his blessid presence þat þe soule feliþ litel peyn or elles none of þe sensualite; and þis is a special grace gifen to þe holy martires. Þis grace `hadden´ þe appostels, as `Holy´ Writ seiþ of hem þus: *Ibant*
20[r] *apostoli gaudentes a conspectu consilii,* | *quoniam digni habiti sunt pro*
nomine Christi contumeliam pati. Þat is: Þe aposteles ȝeden ioiende fro þe conseil of þe Iewes when þai were beten with scorges, and þei were glad þat þei were worþi for to suffre ony bodily dishese for þe luf of Ihesu. Þei were not stirid to ire ne to felnes, to be venged of þe Iewes þat beten hem, as a werdly man ⸢wolde ben⸣ whan he suffriþ a litil harme, be it neuer so litel, of his euen-cristen. Ne þei were not stirid to pride ne to heiȝnes of hemself and to dedeyn and to demynge of þe Iewes, as ypocrytes and heritikes arn þat wilen suffren mikel bodily peyne, and arn sumtyme redy for to suffre dede with grete gladnes

HBH$_5$WsLwELdTW of hem] *om.* As hem] Act. 5° *add.* BLEPLdTW apostoli] *om.* A 54 digni] *om.* B$_3$ Jesu] H$_7$RH$_5$LB$_3$SrWsAPH$_6$CcMPlT`W^{G}´, Christi HBAsLwLdTW, *om.* E, Jesu Lat. 55 ȝeden] wende or ȝeoden B ioyend] *om.* T þe[2]] *om.* Lw 56 þe] *om.* SrLdT 57 bodily dessese] *rev.* AsSr bodily] penaunce gladly and paciently *add.*, *canc.* H name] H$_7$RBLB$_3$SrAEPH$_6$CcMLdPlT, luf HH$_5$AsWsLwW, nomine Lat. Jesu] Jesu Christi Lat. 58 ire] wreþþe B felnes] fersnesse T, or fernesse *add.* Ld, no angrinesse A for] H$_7$RLB$_3$AsSrAEPH$_6$CcMLdPlT, *om.* HBH$_5$WsLwW venged] avenged BW of] on TW 59 hem] him As `a[1]´ L, *om.* M  wolde bene] ⸢wolde ben⸣ H[c], is H$_5$Ws, *om.* As  suffreth] H$_7$HBH$_5$LB$_3$Sr-WsLwEPH$_6$CcLdT`W^{G}´, suffred RAsAMPlW, patitur Lat. 60 be . . . litel/of . . . cristen] *rev.* H$_6$ not] ȝit *add.* Ws, *om.* Cc pryde] noo *prec.* LwW 61 and[1]] H$_7$LB$_3$Sr-APH$_6$Cc, ne HRBH$_5$AsWsLwEMLdPlTW, et Lat. heygnes] heuynes H$_5$WsM, holinesse T hemself . . . and[3]] hem Cc and[2]] ne SrH$_6$, in Pl dedyn and to] *om.* Ld dedyn] þe deþ As 62 are] þanne As, mouentur ad indignacionem Lat. mykel . . . suffre (l. 63)] *om.* M bodily peyne] *rev.* SrLd 63 redy sumtyme] H$_7$RLB$_3$SrAEPH$_6$CcPl, *rev.* HBH$_5$AsWsLwLdTW for] *om.* T þe] H$_7$RSrCcMPl, *om.* HBH$_5$LB$_3$As-WsLwAEPH$_6$LdTW and . . . gladnes (l. 64)] *om.* Sr and] H$_7$Pl, with *add.* Σ, et cum Lat. myghty wil] miȝt As

as it were in þe name of Jesu for lufe of him. Sothly þat gladnes and þat loue þat þei han in suffryng of bodily meschyef is not of þe Holi Gost. It comeþ not fro þe fyre þat brenneth in þe heye autere of heuene, bot it is feyned by þe fend enflawmed of helle, for it is fully f. 97v menged with þe heght of pryde and of presumpcion of hem|self, and despyte and demenge and dedyn of hem þat þus punysscheth hem. And þei wenen ȝit þat al þis is charite and þat þei suffre al þat wronge for þe loue of God, but þei are bygyled by þe mydday fend. A trewe louere of Jesu, whan he suffreþ harm of his euen-cristen, is so strengthed þurgh grace of þe Holy Gost, and is made so meke, so pacient, and so pesible, and þat sothfastly, þat what wronge or harme it be þat he suffre of his euen-cristen, he kepeth ay meknes. He despiseth him not, he demeth him not, bot preyeth for him in his hert and hath of him pite and compassion, mykel more tendrely þan of anoþer man þat neuer dide him harm; and sothly bettre lufe[th] him and more feruently desyreth þe saluacion of his soule, bycause þat he seeth þat he schal haue so mykel gostly profyte þurgh his euel dede, þogh it be ageyns his wille. Bot þis lufe and þis meknes werketh only þe Holy Gost, abouen þe kende of man, in hem þat he maketh trew lufers of Jesu.

How loue sleth coueytyse, liccherie, glotonye, and accidye, and þe fleschly sauour and delyte in alle þe fyue bodily wittes in þe parfyte lufer of Jesu softely and esyly, þurgh a gracyous beholdyngge of him. Capitulum xxxix[m]

Couetyse also \`is′ slayn in a soule be þe werkyng of lufe, for it makeþ

64 Jesu] and A, and *add.* RE for . . . him] *om.* H_5Ws lufe] H_7HRBB$_3$LwACcPlW, þe *prec.* LAsEPH$_6$MLdT Sothly] Trewli H_6 gladnes . . . loue (l. 65)] H_7RLB$_3$-AEPH$_6$CcMPl, *rev.* HBH$_5$AsWsLwLdTW 65 of[1]] þe As meschyef] myscheues Pl, it *add.* Sr is] nys As 66 It] ne *prec.* As \`þe[2]′ Cc 67 feyned] and *add.* As by] of H_6 enflawmed] with þe fir *add.* As is] *om.* B fully] *om.* LB$_3$PCcT 68 þe] *om.* B heght] hiȝest LB$_3$P, hete Ld of[2]] in T, *om.* RM of[3]] in HH$_5$AsWsLd hemself] hymselue RB and[2]] be *add.* As, in *add.* Cc 69 and[1]] *om.* A and dedyn] *om.* Cc dedyn] dedis As hem[1]] hemselfe As 70 And] H_7RLB$_3$SrAEPH$_6$CcMPl, *om.* Σ. HBH$_5$AsWsLwLdTW þei wenen/ȝit] *rev.* H_6 ȝit] *om.* AsLwTW þis] H_7RH$_5$AsWsMW, *om.* HBLB$_3$SrLwAEPH$_6$CcLdPlT þat[1]] *om.* M wronge] H_7RLB$_3$SrAEPH$_6$CcMPl, *om.* HBH$_5$AsWsLwLdTW, iniuriam Lat. 71 but . . . fend] *om.* B_3 but] yhit *add.* T by] H_7RLB$_3$SrAEPH$_6$CcMLdPlT, of HBH$_5$AsWsLwW A] But *prec.* As, Set fidelis dilector Lat. 72 Jesu] Jesu Christi Lat. is] *om.* P 73 þurgh] with T, be *prec.*, *canc.* M grace] þe *prec.* HH$_5$WsEM 74 and[1]] *om.* B_3 so] *om.* HCc and þat sothfastly] *om.* Cc þat[1]] so *add.* ATW, *om.* As \`what′ T 75 it] what *prec.* LP, þat *prec.* B$_3$H$_6$, euere *add.* T suffre] H_7LB$_3$SrAPH$_6$CcPl, suffriþ HRBH$_5$AsWsEMLdPlTW, paciatur Lat. ay] H_7HBH$_5$LWsP, euere B$_3$AsLwAEH$_6$PlW,

and with mi3ty wil, as it were in þe name of Ihesu for lufe of him. Soþly þat loue and þat gladnes þat þei haue in suffrynge of bodily meschef is not of þe Holy Gost. It comiþ not fro þe fir þat brenneþ in þe hei3e auter of heuen, bot it is feyned bi þe feende enflaumed of helle, for it is fully menged with þe hei3eþe of pride and of presumpcioun in hemself, and despite and demynge and dedeyn of hem þat þus punischen hem. Þei wenen 3it þat al is charitee and þat þei suffren al þat for þe luf of God, bot þei are bigilid of þe midday fende. A trewe lufer of Ihesu, when he suffriþ harme of his euen-cristen, is so strengþed þur3 grace of þe Holy Gost, and is made so meke, so pacient and pesible, and þat soþfastly, þat what wronge or harme it be þat he suffriþ of his euen-cristen, he kepiþ ay meknes. He despiciþ him not, he demiþ him not, bot preieþ for him in his hert and haþ of him pite and compassioun, mikel more tenderly þan of anoþer
20v man þat neuer did him harme; | and soþly better lufiþ him and more feruently desiriþ þe saluacioun of his soule, bicause þat he seeþ þat he schal haue so mikel gostly profit of þe yuel dede of þat oþer man, þaw3 it be ageyns his wil. Bot þis lufe and þis meknes wirkiþ only þe Holy Gost, abofe þe kynde of man, in hem þat he makiþ trew lufers of Ihesu.

[CHAPTER 39]

Coueitise also is slayn in a soule bi þe wirkynge of lufe, for it makiþ þe

alwey SrLdT 76 despiseth] disspised M him[1,2]] hem (*bis*) AsA he demeth him not] *om.* T bot] he H_5Ws, he *add.* LwMW him[3]] hem A 77 of] on T, *om.* A him] hem A 78 anoþer] any oþer H_5Ws neuer/dide him] *rev.* Cc lufeth] lufe H_7, he *prec.* As him] hem A 79 desyreth] he *prec.* As of] hem raþer þan of *add.* As his . . . bycause] her soules in A his] of *add.*, *canc.* L 80 seeth] and *add.*, *canc.* L so] nou3t As, *om.* B ⌜profyte . . . it (l. 81)⌝ L þurgh his] H_7RLB_3SrAEPH_6CcMPl, of þe HBH_5As-WsLwLdTW, per eius Lat. dede] H_7RLB_3SrAEPH_6CcMPl, of þat oþer man *add.* HBH_5AsWsLwLdTW 81 `lufe´ H_6 and] in R only/þe . . . Gost (l. 82)] *rev.* RM only] bi *add.* B_3 82 trew] the *prec.* LwW

Chapter 39 *title*: H_7RLB_3SrAEPH_6MLdPlTW How þe louer of Jesu kepeþ no more hem þat he loueþ, and how he dispiseþ alle erþely þyngis and acounteþ it at nou3t. As *om.* HBH_5WsLwCc 1 sleth] slewith $T^G$$W^G$ glotonye] and *prec.* LdTW accidye] slewth AEH_6, sleiþ LdTW and[2]] in R, *om.* LdTW 2 in[1] . . . him (l. 4)] etc. M þe[2]] *om.* ALdPl wittes] and *add.* Sr in[2] . . . Jesu (l. 3)] *om.* TW 3 lufer] loue RLB_3PH_6, dilectore Lat. Jesu] Jesu Christi Lat. softely] soþly Sr a] *om.* Sr 4 him] Jesu TW 5 also/is slayn] *rev.* H_5AsWs is slayn] occiditur . . . et destruitur Lat. `is´ *interl.* H_7 þe] *om.* RM

þe soule so coueytous of gostly gode and to heuenly ricches so ardaunt þat it setteth ryȝt noȝt by alle erthly riches. It hath no more daynte in hafyng of a preciouse stone þan of a calk-stone, ne no more lofe hath he in an hundreþ pound of golde þan in a pounde of lede. It setteth al thyng þat schal perryschen and passen at o prys; no more chargeth þat on þan þat oþer as in lufe. For it seeth wele þat alle þese erthly thynges þat werldly lufers han in so grete prys and lufe so deyntily schal passen away and turne to noght, boþe þe thyng in itself and þe lufe of it.

f. 98^{r} And þerfore he bryngeth it in his thoght bytyme | in þat plyte þat it schal ben after, and so acounteth it at noȝt. And whan werdly lufers stryuen and pleten and feghten for erthly gode, who may ferst haue it, þe lufer of Jesu stryueth with no man, bot kepeþ himself in pees and holdeþ him payed with þat þat he hath, and wil stryfen for no more. For him thenkeþ þat him nedeth no more of al þe rycches in erthe þan a skant bodily sustenaunce, for to saue þe bodily lyfe withalle as long as God wil, and þat may he lightly haue, and þerfore wil he no more han. He is wele at ese whan he hath no more þan skantly him nedeth for þe tyme, þat he may frely be discharged fro besynes abowte þe kepynge and þe dispendyng of it, and fully ȝifen his hert and al his besynes aboute þe sekyng of Jesu, for to fynden him in clennes of spirit. For þat is al his coueytyse; for why, only clene of hert schul seen him. Also fleschly loue of fader and of moder and of oþer werdly

6 þe soule] *om.* B þe] a Sr so] *om.* T gostly] *om.* M ricches] H$_7$HSrLwEH$_6$W, richesse RBH$_5$LB$_3$WsAPCcMLdPlT, richesses As ardaunt] or brennynge *add.* AsT, eþer brennyng *add.* Ld 7 alle] *rep.*, *canc.* B$_3$, *om.* RM riches] H$_7$HRSrLwEH$_6$, rychesse BLB$_3$APCcMLdPlT, þynges and rycchesses H$_5$AsWs, thynges W, diuiciis Lat. in . . . of^{1} (l. 8)] ne trustynge in As in] þe *add.* T 8 o⌜f a^{1}⌝ L of^{2}] H$_7$RSrAEH$_6$CcMPl, in HBH$_5$AsWsLwLdT, on LB$_3$PW, lapidis latericii Lat. a^{2}] *om.* Lw calk-stone] caul stokke LdT no] *om.* TW 9 \`an´ R ⌜a⌝ L, on Cc 10 thyng] þynges] Pl schal] *om.* Cc perryschen and] *om.* A and passen] H$_7$RLB$_3$SrAEPH$_6$CcMPl, *om.* HBH$_5$AsWsLwLdTW, et perituram Lat. o] noo T prys] pryk As no] ne T chargeth] he *prec.* W, he *add.* E\`W^{G}´ 11 þan] þat B, he doth *add.* T þat oþer] anothir Cc lufe] H$_7$As, his *prec.* Σ, quantum ad dileccionem Lat. seeth] H$_7$RBLB$_3$SrAEPH$_6$CcMLdPlT, semiþ HH$_5$AsWsLwW, videt Lat. þese] those RM 12 lufers han in] H$_7$RLB$_3$SrAEPH$_6$CcMPl, men lete HH$_5$AsWsLwLdW, men take B, men setten T prys] H$_7$RLB$_3$SrAEPH$_6$CcMPl, of *add.* HBH$_5$WsLwLdTW 13 schal] scholde W, \`shul´ W$^{G}$ \`þe^{1}´ Pl, *om.* BH$_5$WsLd itself] þe self H$_6$Cc ⌜and^{2} . . . it⌝ L 14 lufe] louere Pl, osye M of it] þerof A 15 in^{1}] into T bytyme] bi tymes T, byfore tyme RAMPl, in tyme Cc in^{2}] H$_7$RLB$_3$SrAPH$_6$CcMPl, into HBH$_5$AsWsLwELdTW 16 so] H$_7$HRBH$_5$AsSrWsLwAMLdW he *add.* LB$_3$EPH$_6$CcPlT acounteth] counteþ Pl at] H$_7$RBLB$_3$SrAEPH$_6$MLdPlT, as HH$_5$AsWsLwCcW, pro nichilo Lat. whan] *om.* Ld werdly] worlde M 17 stryuen . . . pleten . . . feghten] fighten . . . stryuen . . . pleden T pleten . . . feghten] H$_7$RLB$_3$AsSrAEPH$_6$CcMPl, *rev.* HBH$_5$WsLwLdW pleten] H$_7$RH$_5$LB$_3$SrWs-

soule so coueitouse of gostly gode and to heuenly riches so ardaunt þat it settiþ ri3t no3t bi alle erþly riches. It haþ no more deynte in hafynge of a precious stone þan in a kalk stone, ne no more lufe haþ he in an hundred pounde of golde þan in a pounde of lede. It settiþ al þinge þat schal perischen at o pris; no more chargiþ þat on þan þat oþer as in his lufe. For it semiþ wel þat al þese erþly þinges þat werldly men lete so grete pris of and lufe so deyntily schul passe awey and turne to no3t, boþe þe þinge in hitself and þe luf of it.

And þerfor he bryngiþ it in his þo3t bityme into þat plit þat it schal ben aftir, and so acountiþ it as no3t. And when werldly lufers stryfen and fe3ten and pleden for erþly gode, who may first han it, þe lufer of Ihesu strifiþ with no man, bot kepiþ himself in pees and holdiþ him paied with þat þat he haþ, and wil strife for no more. `For him þinkiþ þat him nediþ no more′ of al þe riches in erþe þan a skant bodily sustenaunce, for to saue þe bodily life withal as longe as God wil, and
121[r] þat he may li3tly hafe, and þerfore wil he | no more. He is wel paied whan he haþ no more þan skantly him nediþ for þe tyme, þat he may frely be descharged fro bisynes aboute þe kepynge and þe despendynge of it, and fully gifen his herte and his bisynes aboute þe sekynge of Ihesu, for to fynden him in klennes of spirit. For þat is al his coueitise; for whi, only clene of hert schal see him. Also flescly luf of

EPH$_6$CcMPl, pleden HBAsLwALdTW, placitant Lat. and[2]] or Cc erthly] H$_7$HBH$_5$AsSrWsLwAEH$_6$CcLdPlW, worldly RLB$_3$PMT gode] goodes M, pro terrenis Lat. who] so *add.*, *canc.* H, *add.* BH$_5$WsLdT ferst/haue it] *rev.* As 18 Jesu] Jesu Christi Lat. 19 him] himselfe M payed] appayd As, well apaide T þat þat] H$_7$HRBLB$_3$LwEPH$_6$CcLdPlTW, þat H$_5$AsSrWsAM and] he *add.* LB$_3$EPH$_6$ for no more] vt magis habundet Lat. for] *om.* AsCc 20 `For . . . more′ H[c], *om.* H°H$_5$AsWs þat] H$_7$HRBH$_5$AsSrWsLwAELdPlTW, *om.* LB$_3$PH$_6$CcM `him′ W[G], he LwCcMW rycches] H$_7$HH$_5$LwAH$_6$W, richesse RBAsSrWsCcMLdPlT, richessis LB$_3$EP þan] But desireþ vnneþe to haue As 21 a . . . bodily] his bodely liflode or T a] *om.* A sustenaunce] *corr. fr.* substaunce Pl for . . . may (l. 22)] þe while he leueþ here on erþe and þat he hopeþ he As saue] haue B withalle] þerwith B 22 may he] H$_7$RBLB$_3$SrAEPCcMLdPlT, *rev.* HH$_5$AsWsLwH$_6$W wil he] *rev.* Cc, he nyl As 23 han] H$_7$RLB$_3$SrAEPH$_6$CcMPl, *om.* HBH$_5$AsWsLwLdTW, habere Lat. `He . . . more′ W[G] He] and As at ese] H$_7$RLB$_3$SrAEPH$_6$CcPl, ese M, at ease [*gl.* paied] W[G], paied HBH$_5$WsLwLdT, appayd As no] vnneþes *prec.* As skantly] þat *add.* Pl, *om.* As him] he As 24 for . . . besynes] whiles he is As frely be] *rev.* LB$_3$P, be H$_6$ þe[2]] *om.* MLdT 25 of it] þerof A 3ifen] 3ifeþ B$_3$Cc his[1]] *om.* M al] H$_7$RLB$_3$SrAEPH$_6$CcMPl, *om.* HBH$_5$WsLwLdTW, totam Lat. 26 þe sekyng] to 3ete þe loue As for . . . him] as to leue As 27 why] þe *add.*, *canc.* T only] *rep.*, *canc.* R, with *add.* Cc, *om.* As clene] þe *prec.* WsLd schul] he wold Cc 28 him] God E`W[G]′ Also] And Pl fader . . . oþer] *om.* Sr and[1]] *om.* RAMPl of[2]] *om.* LwCcTW and of oþer] or to ony RAMPl of[3]] *om.* LwW oþer] alle *prec.* As werdly] desires and of *add.* As, thynges or *add.* M frendes hangeth noȝt vpon him; it is euene kyt fro his herte with þe swerd of gostly loue, þat he hath no more affeccyon to fader ne to moder or to ony werdly frende þan he hath to anoþer man, bot if he se and fele in hem more grace and more vertu þan in oþer men. Owttaken þis, þat him were lefer þat his fader and his moder hadden þe selfe grace [þat] sum oþer men han; bot neuerþeles if þei ben not so, þan lufeth he oþer better þan hem, and þat is charite. And so sleth þe loue of Jesu þe coueytyse of þe werd, and bryngeth into þe soule pouerte in spiryt.

And þat doth loue not only in hem þat han right noȝt of werdly gode, bot also in sum creatures þat arn in grete werdly state and han dispendyng of erthly rycches. Loue sleth in summe of hem coueytyse so ferforth þat þei han no lykyng ne sauour in þe hauynge of hem, more þan in a stre. Ne þogh þei ben lost for defaute of hem þat schuld f. 98v kepen hem, þei setten | noȝt þerby; for why, þe herte of Goddis lufer is þurgh þe ȝifte of þe Holi Gost taken so fully with þe syght and þe loue of anoþer thyng þat is so precious and so wurthy þat it wil resceyuen non oþer lufe restendly þat is contrarye þerto.

And not only doth lufe þis, bot also it sleth þe lykyng of liccherye and alle oþer bodily vnclennes, and bryngeth into þe soule verrey chastite, and turneth it into lykyng. For þe soule feleth so grete delyte in þe syght of Jesu þat it lyketh for to be chaste, and it is no grete hardnes to it for to kepe chastite, for it is so most ese and most reste. And vpon þat selfe wyse þe ȝifte of lufe sleth fleschly lustes of glotonye and makeþ þe soule sobre and temperaunt, and bereth it vp

29 frendes] also ne *add.* As vpon] up LB$_3$PH$_6$, in A it is euene] for þei ben As kyt] k- *prec.*, *canc.* Sr, knyt Pl 30 fader] þe *prec.* As ne to] H$_7$RLB$_3$SrEPH$_6$CcM, ne B, or HH$_5$WsLwALdPlTW, and As 31 moder] þe *prec.* As or] nor B, ne RAsM to[1]] *om.* T ony werdly frende] alle oþere erþely þyngis As ony] oþer *add.* H$_5$Ws, aliquem alium Lat. to[2]] vnto Sr, of As anoþer] any oþere As if he] it M se and fele] *rev.* Sr 32 and . . . hem] in him or fele H$_5$AsWsT and[1]] H$_7$RLB$_3$SrAEPH$_6$CcMPl, or HBH$_5$AsWsLwLdTW, vel Lat. and[2]] H$_7$RLB$_3$SrAPH$_6$CcMPl, or HBH$_5$AsWsLwELdTW, et Lat. more[2]] *om.* As oþer men] H$_7$HLB$_3$SrLwEPH$_6$LdW, any oþer man RAs, anoþer man H$_5$WsCcMPlT, anoþur A, aliis hominibus Lat. 33 `þat . . . lefer´ W[G], *canc.* Lw, *om.* W him were] H$_7$RLB$_3$SrAEPH$_6$CcMPl, he had HBH$_5$AsWsLdT, he had *canc.* Lw and] *corr. fr.* or Pl 34 þe selfe] *om.* Pl selfe] same WsH$_6$T þat] þan H$_7$, oþer *add.*, *canc.* H sum . . . þan[1] (l. 35)] he hath thanne anothir. And ellys Cc sum] sumtyme Sr 35 þei ben] it be As lufeth he] *rev.* AsCc lufeth] loue H$_5$ oþer . . . hem] anothir man as wel as hym Cc oþer] H$_7$RLB$_3$SrAPH$_6$MPl, men *add.* HBH$_5$AsWsLwELdTW, alios Lat. and] *om.* W 36 sleth/þe . . . Jesu] *rev.* H$_6$ þe[1] . . . werd] God þe loue of him as of þis worldis loue As þe[1] . . . Jesu] H$_7$RLB$_3$SrAEPH$_6$CcMPl, Goddis lufe HBH$_5$WsLwLdTW, dileccio Jesu Lat. þe[2]] H$_7$, *om.* Σ coueytyse] and þe love *add.* Cc `þe[2]´ H$_6$, þis T 37 in] of BAH$_6$LdT 38 `þat[1]´ Cc, *om.* M in] on B hem] him H$_5$AsWs, hymselue RAMPl han/right noȝt] *rev.* H$_5$Ws han] hath

fader and of moder and of oþer werdly frendes hangiþ not vpon him; it is euen kut fro his herte with þe swerde of gostly lufe, þat he haþ no more affeccioun to fader or moddir or to ony werldly frende þan he haþ to anoþer man, bot if he see or fele in hem more grace or more vertue þan in oþer men. Outakyn þis, þat he had lefer þat his fadir and his modir hadden þe self grace þat summe oþer men han; bot nerþeles if þei be not so, þan lufiþ he oþer men better þan hem, and þat is charitee. And so sleþ Goddis lufe coueitise of þe werlde, and bryngiþ into þe soule pouerte in spirit.

And þat doþ luf not only in hem þat han riȝt noȝt of werdly gode, bot also in summe creatures þat arn in grete werdly state and haue dispendynge of erþly riches. Luf sleeþ in summe of hem coueitise, so fer forþ þat þei han no more likynge ne sauour in hafynge of hem þan in a stree. Ne þawȝ þai ben loste for defaute of hem þat schuld kepen hem, þei sette not þerby; for whi, þe herte of Goddis lufer is þurȝ þe gifte of þe Holy Goste taken so fully with þe siȝt and þe lufe of anoþer þinge þat is so precious and so wurþi þat it wil resceife none oþer lufe restendly þat is contrarye þerto.

And not only doþ lufe þis, bot also it sleþ þe likynge of leccherye
21v and al oþer bodily vnclennesse, and bryngiþ into þe soule | verrey chastite, and turniþ it into likynge. For þe soule feliþ so grete delite in þe siȝt of Ihesu þat it likiþ for to ben chaste, and it is no grete hardnes to it for to kepe chastite, for it is so most esy and most rest. And vpon þe self wise þe gifte of lufe sleeþ fleschly lustes of glotonye and makiþ þe soule sobre and temperaunt, and beriþ it vp so miȝtily þat it may

RH_5AsWsPl werdly] þe *prec.* H_5AsWs 39 gode] goudis Ld state] H_7HRBH_5Ws-LwAH_6CcLdPlTW, estate LB_3AsSrEPM 40 of] in Cc erthly] werdly H_5AsWsCcT, *om.* E rycches] H_7HSrEH_6TW, richesse RBH_5LB_3WsLwAPCcMPl, richessis AsLd 41 lykyng . . . hem/more (l. 42)] H_7RLB_3SrAPH_6CcMPl, *rev.* HBH_5AsWsLwELdTW ne] no *add.* SrLwPl hem] `no more´ *add.* Lw, `more´ *add.* W^G 42 in] of LwW stre] tree M Ne] *om.* Sr defaute] þe *prec.* T 43 þei] *om.* Lw why] *om.* Cc herte] hertis Pl lufer] loueres ACcMPl 44 is] are Pl, *om.* M þe[1]] *om.* LB_3PH_6 ȝifte] grace As and] of LwTW 45 of] and As anoþer thyng] Jesu Cc thyng] that is Jesu and *add* LwTW þat[2]] *om.* M 46 resceyuen non] nout receyven Cc 48 and[1]] of *add.* AsE bodily] *om.* T 49 chastite] charite RMPl turneth] bringith A 50 þe syght of] *om.* Cc Jesu] Jesu Christi Lat. it[2]] *om.* LwW no] not Ld 51 hardnes] liȝtsumness As it for to] *om.* Cc chastite] it chaste AsCc is] haþ Pl so] þe LB_3EPH_6 ese] esy HH_5AsWs, in maxima est quiete Lat. and] so *add.* As most[2]] þe *prec.* LB_3PH_6 reste] to hym *add.* H_6 52 vpon] on Cc þat] H_7, þe Σ selfe] same WsM lufe] the *prec.* Cc fleschly] the *prec.* M, al *prec.* P, *om.* LwW 53 temperaunt] H_7HBH_5SrWsLwCcLdW, temperande RMPl, temperat LB_3AEPH_6T, in good temperure As vp] *om.* A

so myghtyly þat it may not resten in lykyng of mete and drynke, bot it takeþ mete and drynk what it be þat lest aggreueth þe bodily compleccyon, if he may lyghtly hafe it, not for lufe of itself bot for lufe of God in þis maner wyse: þe lufer of Jesu seeth wele þat him nedeth for to kepen his bodyly lyfe with mete and drynke, as long as God wil suffre hem for to be togedre. Þan schal þis be þe discrecyon of þe lufer of Jesu, as I vnderstonde, þat hath felyng and werkyng in loue: þat vpon what maner þat he may most kepen his grace hole, and lest be letted fro þe werkyng in it þurgh takyng of bodily sustenaunce, so schal he do. Þat maner of mete þat lest letteth and lest trubleth þe herte and may kepe þe body in strengthe—be it flesch, be it fysch, be it bot brede and ale—þat I trowe þe soule cheseth for to hafe if it may esily come þerby. For al þe besynes of þe soule is for to þenken on Jesu with reuerent lufe and withouten lettyng of ony thynge if þat it myght. And þerfore syþen þat it behoueth sumwhat be letted and hyndred, þe lesse þat it is letted and hyndred by mete or drynk or by any oþer thyng þe lefere it is. It had lefer taken and vsen þe best mete and most of pris þat is vnder sunne, if it lesse letted þe kepyng of his
f. 99r hert, þan for to taken bot brede and water | if þat letted him more, for he hath non reward for to geten him grete mede for þe pyne of fastynge and be put þerby fro softnes in hert. Bot al his besynes is for to kepen his herte as stably as he may in þe sight of Jesu and in þe felyng of his loue. And sothly as I trowe, he myght with lesse lykynge vsen þe best mete þat is gode in his owne kynde þan anoþer man þat wercheth al in reson withouten þe speciale ȝifte of lufe schuld moun vsen þe werst, owtetake mete þat þurgh crafte of cury is only made for

54 not resten] *rev.* M `drynke´ Cc, drynge H$_5$ 55 aggreueth] H$_7$RLB$_3$SrAEPCcMPl, greueþ HBH$_5$AsWsLwH$_6$LdTW 56 he] it H$_5$SrWs may lyghtly] *rev.* E hafe it] H$_7$RLSrAEPH$_6$CcMPl, haue B$_3$, come þerto HBH$_5$AsLwLdTW, illum . . . habere Lat. lufe] þe *prec.* As, to *prec.* M 57 lufe] H$_7$HRBLB$_3$APH$_6$MLdPlT, þe *prec.* H$_5$AsSrWsLwECcW in] H$_7$A, on HRBH$_5$LB$_3$WsLwEPH$_6$LdTW, and *prec.* AsSrACcMPl wyse] of *prec.* Cc Jesu] H$_7$RLB$_3$SrAEPH$_6$CcMPl, God HBH$_5$AsWsLwLdTW, Jesum Lat. 58 for] *om.* H$_6$ 59 hem] him AsSrCc for] H$_7$RBSrMLdT, *om.* HH$_5$LB$_3$AsWsLwAEPH$_6$CcPlW togedre] here Cc `þis´ T$^G$ þe] *om.* AsLd 60 vnderstonde] haue vnderstondynge As and] in Cc, discrecion and *add.* T in loue] *om.* As 61 loue] the *prec.* LwW [*canc.* W$^G$] vpon] on A þat$^2$] *om.* RAsAMPl most] *om.* T kepen] kepyng M 62 lest] `he´ *add.* Pl letted] lettyg As þe] H$_7$RBLB$_3$SrAEPH$_6$CcMLdPlT, *om.* HH$_5$AsWsLwW in] of Cc 63 do] `with´ *add.* Pl, and takyn *add.* Cc of] *om.* HBH$_5$WsLd letteth] hym *add.* R 64 þe] þi E flesch] or *add.* As be it$^2$] or Pl be$^3$ it] *rep.* M 65 `bot´ W^G, bar A, *om.* LB$_3$LwPW and ale] al H$_5$Ws, take it and all As 66 esily] H$_7$LB$_3$SrEPH$_6$CcM, *om.* HRBH$_5$AsWsLwALdPlTW, *om.* Lat. þerby] þerto B al] *om.* Pl þe^2] a Sr 67 reuerent] of *add.* M and] H$_7$, ay HRH$_5$LWsPH$_6$CcM, euer BB$_3$AsLwAELdPlTW, alwey Sr of . . . myght (l. 68)] if it mighte be of eny oþer þinge T þat] *om.* LB$_3$PH$_6$Cc 68 myght] may Cc

not resten in likynge of mete and drynke, bot it takiþ mete and drynke what it be þat lest grefiþ þe bodily compleccioun, if he may liȝtly come þerto, not for lufe of itself bot for lufe of God. On þis maner wise þe lufer of God seeþ wel þat him nediþ for to kepen his bodily lif with mete and drynke, as longe as God wil suffren hem to ben togidir. Þan schal þis be þe discrecioun of þe lufer of Ihesu, as I vndirstonde, þat haþ felynge and wirkynge in lufe: þat vpon what maner þat he may most kepen his grace hool, and lest be lettid fro wirkynge in it þurȝ takynge of bodily sustenaunce, so schal he do. Þat maner mete þat lest lettiþ and lest trobleþ þe herte and may kepe þe body in strengþe, be it flesche, be it fische, be it bot brede and ale, þat I trowe þe soule chesiþ for to hafe if it may come þerbi. For alle þe bisynes of þe soule is for to þinken on Ihesu with reuerente luf, ay withouten lettynge of ony þinge if þat it miȝt. And þerfor siþen þat it most nedis sumwhat be lettid and hindred, þe lesse it is lettid and hyndred by mete or drynke or ony oþer þinge þe lefer it is. It had leuer vsen þe best mete and most of prise þat is vndir sunne, if it lesse lettid þe kepynge of his
122^{r} herte, þan for to taken | bot brede and water if þat lettid him more, for he haþ no rewarde for to geten him grete mede for þe payne of fastynge and be put þerbi fro softnes in hert. Bot al his bisynes is for to kepen his herte as stably as he may in þe siȝt of Ihesu and in þe felynge of \`his´ luf. And soþly as I trowe, he miȝt with lesse likynge vsen þe beste mete þat is gode in þe owne kynde þan anoþer man þat wirkiþ al in resoun withouten þe special ȝifte of luf schulde mowen vse þe werst, outaken mete þat þurȝ craft of curye is only made for luste: þat

þat] *om.* LwTW   it] y As   behoueth sumwhat] sumwhat must nedis E   behoueth] H$_7$RLB$_3$SrAPH$_6$CcMPl, must nedis HBH$_5$AsWsLwELdTW   sumwhat] *om.* T   be . . . is (l. 69)] him lette and an hundred siþes yletted þus þe bettre and bettre it is to þe soule oþer be any oþer þingis [elle]s but As   be] to *prec.* AE   letted and hyndred . . . hyndred (l. 69)] impediri . . . impeditur Lat.   69 þe . . . hyndred^{2}] *om.* Cc   þat] *om.* HBLwLd   \`it$^{1}$´ Pl, *om.* M   letted and hyndred] *rev.* T, *om.* Sr   letted and] *om.* H$_6$   and] or H$_5$Ws   or$^{1}$] and LB$_3$PH$_6$   drynk] takyng *add.* Cc   by$^{2}$] H$_7$RLB$_3$SrEPH$_6$CcMPl, *om.* HBH$_5$WsLwAELdTW, per Lat.   70 thyng] þe lesse it is hindred *add.* A   þe$^{1}$] \`lesse þe´ *add.* Cc, *om.* T   lefere] better Ld   taken and] H$_7$RLB$_3$SrAEPH$_6$CcMPl, *om.* HBH$_5$AsWsLwLdTW   71 most of pris] drynke As   þat is] *om.* SrLwW   sunne] þe *prec.* LwELdTW   if . . . more (l. 72)] *om.* As   72 bot] *om.* SrAH$_6$ and] or H$_5$ water] *om.* H$_6$Cc   if] *om.* Ws   þat] it ET   letted] lettith M   him more] *om.* Cc   73 non] H$_7$As, no Σ   for^{1}] *om.* LB$_3$PH$_6$Cc   him] hem M   for^{2}] but *add.* As   þe] *om.* H$_6$ 74 and] *om.* As   be put] *rev.* H$_5$ softnes] soþefastnesse As, sobrietate Lat.   in] of Cc   Bot] and As   his] þis Sr, *om.* As   is] moste be As   75 his . . . as^{2}] stablenesse in herte þat As   stably] stable BH$_5$WsT   in^{1} . . . and] *rep.*, *canc.* L   in þe^{1}] haue As   of Jesu] *om.* LdT   and] *om.* As   þe^{2}] *om.* Cc   76 \`his´ H$^{c}$   77 his] H$_7$As, þe Σ   78 in] *om.* Cc   þe] *om.* Ld   79 vsen] *om.* Lw   werst] worse As, mete *add.* Pl   mete] þe *prec.* As   \`of´ Cc   cury] curyosite LwTW   only/made for] *rev.* As

luste: þat maner of mete may he not wele acorden withal. And also on þat oþer syde, if litel mete, as only brede and ale, most kepeth and eseth his herte and kepeth it most in pees, it is þanne most leefe to him for to vsen it so, and namely if he fele bodily strenght only of þe ȝifte of lufe withal.

And ȝit doth loue more, for it sleeth accydy and fleschly ydelnes and makeþ þe soule lyuely and spedy to þe seruice of Jesu; so ferforth þat [it] coueyteth ay to ben occupyed in godenes, namely inward in beholdyng of him, be þe vertu of whilk syght þe soule hath sauour and gostly delyte in preyenge, in thenkeng, and in al oþer maner werkyng þat nedeth for to be don after þe state and þe degre þat he stondeth in asketh—whether he be religious or seculer—withouten heuynes or pynful bitternes.

Also it sleth þe veyn lykyng of þe fyfe bodily wittes. First þe sight of þe eye, þat þe soule hath no lykyng in þe syght of ony erthly thyng; bot it feleth rathere pyne and desese in beholdyng of it, be it neuer so fayre, ne so precious, ne so wonderful. And þerfore as werdly lufers rennen oute sumtyme for to seen new thynges, for to wondren in hem, and so for to feden here herte with þe veyn syght of hem, ryght so a lufer of Jesu is besy for to ronnen away and withdrawen him fro þe syght of swilk maner thyngis, þat þe inner syght be not lettede. For he seeth gostly anoþer maner thyng þat is fayrer and more wonderful, and þat wuld he noȝt forberen. Ryght on þe selfe wyse it is of spekyng and heryng; it is a pyne to þe soule of a lufere of Jesu for to speken or

80 luste] loue H_5Ws, of *add.* As `of′ Sr, *om.* LdT he not] *rev.* BT, not `he′ R not] *om.* M wele acorden withal] be weel acordend R, acorde with wel H_5Ws, wel a corde wiþ LdT wele acorden] *rev.* Sr wele] *om.* ACc withal] with A And] *om.* Sr on] in Ld, *om.* Lw 81 þat] the Cc if] *om.* As litel] symple A, simplex Lat. and[1] . . . most] almost As ale most] almoste M kepeth] H_7, helpeth Σ, iuuet Lat. 82 eseth] ceseth W þanne/most leefe] *rev.* LwW most[2]] þe *prec.* As, *om.* B 83 for] *om.* H_6 vsen] kepe H_6 it] him As and . . . withal (l. 84)] *om.* Lat. he] it H_5WsE fele] fynde MT of] be Cc, on M 84 `of′ T$^G$, *om.* T withal] þerwiþ CcLdT 85 `ȝit′ B, *om.* Ld doth loue] he loueþ it As accydy] slouþe BAEH_6Ld 86 lyuely . . . ay (l. 87)] *om.* LwTW lyuely] besy As, quike E, lyth Cc Jesu] God ACc, Jesu Christi Lat. 87 it] is H_7 ay] euer B_3AsEH_6Pl, alwey SrALd occupyed] accepted As namely] and *prec.* AsLwH_6TW in] þe *add.* T 88 beholdyng of him] consideracionem et visionem Jesu Christi Lat. þe[1]] *om.* Pl whilk] H_7LB_3SrLwPH_6CcMW, such A, þe *prec.* HRBH_5As-WsELdPlT, cuius Lat. syght] H_7RBLB_3SrAEPH_6CcMLdPlT, *om.* HH_5AsWsLwW, visionis Lat. 89 gostly delyte] *rev.* H_5 in[2]] H_7HRBH_5AsSrWsLwACcMLdTW, and LB_3EPH_6Pl thenkeng] thynkyn M in[3]] *om.* M maner] H_7RLB_3AsSrAPH_6CcMLdPl, of *add.* HBLwETW, *om.* H_5Ws werkyng] H_7RLB_3SrAPH_6CcMPl, doynge HBH_5As-WsLwELdTW 90 for] H_7HH_5AsWsLwELdTW, *om.* RBLB_3SrAPH_6CcMPl state] estate AsM and þe] H_7RH_5AsWsAMPl`W^{G}′, and LB_3SrPH_6Cc, or HBELd, of T, *om.*

maner of mete may he not wel acorde withal. And also on þat oþer side, if litel mete, as only brede and ale, most helpiþ and esiþ his hert and kepiþ it most in pees, it is þan most lefe to him for to vsen it so, and namely if he fele bodily strengþe only of þe gifte of luf withal.

And ȝit doþ lufe more, for it sleeþ accidie and fleschly ydelnes and makiþ þe soule lifly and spedy to þe seruice of Ihesu; so fer forþ þat it coueitiþ ay to ben ocupied in godnes, namly inwarde in beholdynge of him, bi þe vertue of þe whilk þe soule haþ sauour and gostly delit in preienge, in þinkynge, and in al oþer maner of doynge þat nediþ for to be done after þe state or degree þat he stondiþ in askiþ wheþer he be religious or seculer, withouten heuynes or peynful bitternes.

Also it sleþ þe veyn likyn`g´ of þe fife bodily wittes. First þe siȝt of þe eiȝe, þat þe soule haþ no likynge in þe siȝt of ony werdly þinge; bot it feliþ raþer peyne and disese in beholdynge of it, be it neuer so faire, neuer so precious, neuer so wundirful. And þerfore as werdly lufers
22v renne out | sumtyme for to see new þinges, for to wundren on hem, and so for to feden here hertes with þe veyn siȝt of hem, riȝt so a lufer of Ihesu is bisy for to rennen awey and withdrawen him fro þe siȝt of swilk maner þinges, þat þe inner siȝt be not letted. For he seeþ gostly anoþer maner þinge þat is fairer and more wundirful, and þat wolde he not forberen. Riȝt on þe self wise is it of spekynge and herynge; it is a peyn to þe soule of a lufer for to spekyn or heren ony þinge þat miȝt

LwW `stondeth´ $W^G$, is LwW 91 asketh . . . seculer] *om.* Lw `asketh´ W^G, *om.* AsW whether . . . seculer/withouten . . . bitternes (l. 92)] *rev.* W religious] re- *prec.*, *canc.* R 93 Also] And *prec.* Pl lykyng] H$_7$`H´RBH$_5$SrWsLwACcLdPlTW, likynges LB$_3$AsEPH$_6$, lekyn M, delectacionem Lat. þe fyfe] þese As `First´ W^G, For W þe sight] *om.* RA 94 þe[1]] *om.* Lw eye] þat is þe siȝt *add.* RM, siȝt *add.* A no] non As lykyng] lekyn M erthly] H$_7$RLB$_3$SrAEPH$_6$CcMPl, werdly HBH$_5$AsWsLwLdTW, siȝt *add.*, *canc.* H, bodely *add.* T 95 feleth rathere] haþ As rathere pyne] *rev.* E rathere] *om.* H$_5$Ws pyne] *corr. fr.* priue M and desese/in . . . it[2]] *rev.* RM beholdyng] þe *prec.* REM 96 ne[1]] H$_7$RLB$_3$SrEPH$_6$CcMPl, neuere HBH$_5$WsLwLdTW, neuere *add.* As, *om.* A ne[2]] H$_7$RLB$_3$SrAEPH$_6$CcMPl, neuere HBH$_5$WsLwLdTW, neuere *add.* As 97 oute] *om.* Cc sumtyme] somtymes T thynges] and *add.* RAMPl in] H$_7$BLB$_3$APH$_6$MLdPlT, on HRH$_5$AsWsLwECcLdW 98 here] hem M herte] H$_7$RLB$_3$SrAPH$_6$MPl, hertes HBH$_5$AsWsLwECcLdTW, corda Lat. with] in A 99 ⌜Jesu . . . ronnen⌝ L Jesu] Jesu Christi Lat. and . . . him] *om.* As withdrawen] to *prec.* E fro] for T 100 maner] of *add.* As, *om.* RM þat . . . thyng (l. 101)] *om.* As he] hit B 101 anoþer] and other M thyng] of thinges M þat is fayrer] *om.* B$_3$ is] *om.* P 102 þat] *om.* BM Ryght . . . heryng (l. 103)] *om.* M on] in Ld selfe] same WsAEH$_6$ it is] H$_7$RLB$_3$As-SrAEPH$_6$CcLdPlT, *rev.* HBH$_5$WsLwW spekyng and heryng] *rev.* E 103 heryng] of *prec.* AsH$_6$ a] þe T of Jesu] H$_7$RLB$_3$SrAEPH$_6$CcMPlTW, of God Wc, *om.* HBH$_5$As-WsLwLd, Jesu Christi Lat.

f. 99^{v} heren ony | thynge þat myght letten þe fredam of his herte fro thenkyng of Jesu. What songe or melodye or mynstralcye owtward þat it be, if it lette þe thoght þat it may not frely and restfully preyen or thenken on Jesu, it lyketh right noȝt; and þe more delytable þat is to oþer men, þe more vnsauourye it is to him. And also for to heren ony maner spekyng of oþer men, bot if it be sumwhat towchend þe werkynge of þe soule in þe lufe of Jesu, it likeþ him ryght noȝt; he is ellys ryȝt sone irk of it. He had wele leuer ben in pees and speke ryȝt noȝt ne heren ryȝt noȝt, þan for to heren þe spekyng or þe techyng of þe grettest clerk of erthe, with al þe resons þat he couthe seyn to to him þurgh mannys witte only, bot if he couthe speke felyngly and steryngly of þe lufe of Jesu. For þat is his crafte principally, and þerfor wuld he not ellys speken, heren ne seen bot þat myght helpen him and forthen him into more knowynge and to bettere felynge of him. Of werdly speche it is no dowte þat he hath no sauour in spekyng ne in heryng of it, ne in werdly talys ne in tydynges, ne in none swilk veyn iangelyng þat longeth not to him. And so it is of smellyng and sauouryng and touchyng: þe more þat þe thoght schulde be distracte and broken fro [gostly] rest by þe vse outher of smellyng or of sauourynge or of any of þe bodily wittes, þe more he fleeth it, and þe lesse þat he feleth of hem þe lefere is him. And if he myght lyfe in þe bodi withouten þe felenge of ony of hem he wold neuer felen hem. For þei truble þe herte ofte-sythes and put it fro rest, and þe moun not ben fully eschewed; bot neuerþeles, þe lufe of Jesu is sumtyme so myghty in a soule þat it ouercometh and sleeth al þat is contrarye to it.

104 heren] for to *prec.* A, to *prec.* M fro thenkyng of] H$_7$RLB$_3$SrAEPH$_6$CcMPl, for to þinken on HBH$_5$AsWsLwLdTW 105 of] on RAWc or^{1}] what *add.* H$_5$AsWsCc or mynstralcye] *om.* Lat. þat] what As, *om.* Wc 106 it^{3}] is Cc, *om.* As or] on T, and Wc, *om.* As 107 Jesu] H$_7$RLB$_3$SrAEPH$_6$CcMPl, him HBH$_5$AsWsLwLdTW, God Wc, Jesu Lat. lyketh] H$_7$LB$_3$PH$_6$T, him *add.* HRBH$_5$AsSrWsLwAEMLdPlW, him yt *add.* Cc, sibi Lat. delytable] delectable BMLdTW þat is] H$_7$, it be Cc, it is Ld, þat it is Σ `to´ Cc 108 heren] of *add.* As 109 maner . . . of] *om.* As maner] of *add.* LwW `spekyng´ H^{c}, þing H$_5$Ws if] H$_7$HRH$_5$SrWsAECcMPl, *om.* BLB$_3$AsLwPH$_6$LdTW þe] and M 110 þe^{1}] H$_7$B, his Σ soule] *om.* Pl him] elles *add.*, *canc.* H ryght noȝt] but litil RAMPl ryght] wel H$_5$, ful Ws is] *rep.*, *canc.* Cc 111 irk] H$_7$HRLSr-CcMPl`W$^{G}$´, wery BH$_5$B$_3$AsWsLwAEH$_6$LdTWWc `of it´ W^{G}, therof LwAW speke/ . . ./heren (l. 112)] H$_7$RLB$_3$SrEPH$_6$CcPl, *rev.* HBAsLwLdTW, loqui vel audire Lat. 112 ne . . . noȝt^{2}] *om.* H$_5$WsAM ne] and RPl or] and AsPl techyng] touchynge B of] on LB$_3$EPT, in ACcPl 113 with . . . him (l. 114)] *om.* Ld þe^{2}] *om.* H$_6$ resons] resoun B `couthe´ W$^{G}$, can W seyn . . . couthe (l. 114)] *om.* Cc 114 witte] wyttes W only] H$_7$RLB$_3$SrAEPH$_6$CcMPl, *om.* HBH$_5$AsWsLwLdTW, solum Lat. bot . . . principally (l. 115)] *om.* Ld `couthe´ W^{G}, can W, oonli *add.*, *canc.* L 115 Jesu] God Wc, Jesu Christi Lat. `his´ R, *om.* As 116 þerfor] *om.* T wuld he not/ellys] *rev.* T ellys speken] *rev.* Lw speken] *om.* LB$_3$PH$_6$ speken heren] *rev.* As `þat´ B$_3$, þat þat H$_5$Ws 117 to]

letten þe fredam of his herte for to þinken on Ihesu. What songe or melody or mynstralcy outward þat it be, if it lette þe þoȝt þat it may not frely and restfully preien or þinken on him, it likiþ him riȝt noȝt; and þe more delitable þat it is to oþer men, þe more vnsauory it is to him. And also for to heren ony manere `speking´ of oþer men, bot if it be sumwhat touchynde þe wirkynge of his soule in þe luf of Ihesu, it likiþ him riȝt noȝt; he is elles riȝt sone irke of it. He had wel leuer ben in pees and here riȝt noȝt ne speke riȝt noȝt, þan for to heren þe spekynge and þe techynge of þe grettest clerke of erþ, with alle þe resouns þat he coude seyen to him þurȝ mannes witte, bot if he coude speken felendly and stirendly of þe luf of Ihesu. For þat is his craft principally, and þerfore wolde he not elles speken, heren ne seen bot þat miȝt helpen him and forþeren him into more knowynge and to
23r better felynge of him. Of werdly speche it | is no doute þat he haþ no sauour in spekynge ne in herynge of it, ne in werdly tales ne in tiþinges, ne in none swilke veyn iangelynge þat longiþ not to him. And so it is of smellynge and sauorynge and touchynge: þe more þat þe þoȝt schulde be distracte and broken fro gostly reste bi þe vse ouþer of smellynge or sauorynge or of ony [oþer] of þe bodily wittes, þe more he fleþ it. Þe lesse þat he feliþ of hem þe lefer is him, and if he miȝt lifen in þe body withouten þe felynge of ony of hem he wolde neuer felen hem. For þei troblen þe herte oft-siþes and putten hit fro reste, and þei moun not ben fully eschwed. Nerþeles þe luf of Ihesu is sumtyme so miȝty in a soule þat it ouercomiþ and sleeþ al þat is contrarie þerto.

into AsCc, *om.* Sr 118 him] Jesu Christi Lat. speche] spekend Cc no[1]] non H$_5$ 119 in[1]] *om.* T in[3]] of H$_6$ tydynges] thynkynges M none] no AET, *om.* As 120 iangelyng] iangelyngis As, ianglis Ld so . . . of] þat is of þe As it is] *rev.* Sr and] of Pl 121 and touchyng] *om.* LwW and] or of ony of þe bodily witte or of RAMPl schulde] *om.* Lw distracte] strauȝte As 122 and] or B fro] for As, of LB$_3$PH$_6$ gostly] bodily H$_7$, spirituali Lat. outher] of oure Lorde As, *om.* H$_5$Ws smellyng/. . ./ sauourynge (l. 123)] *rev.* T or] of Cc, *om.* As of[2]] H$_7$RBLB$_3$AsSrAPH$_6$CcMLdPl, in E, *om.* HH$_5$WsLwTW 123 sauourynge] tasting A of] *om.* Pl any] H$_7$HRLB$_3$SrLw-AEPH$_6$CcMPlW, oþer *add.* BH$_5$AsWsLdT, alicuius Lat. he] it B$_3$ fleeth] feleþ AsM, feleþ of Sr it] *om.* As and] H$_7$RLB$_3$SrAEPH$_6$CcM`Pl´, *om.* HBH$_5$AsWsLwLdTW  þe lesse] *rep.*, *canc.* As  þe[2]] *om.* Lw  124 he] it B$_3$  of hem] it As  of] *om.* T  is him] *rev.* AsA  is] yt it to Cc, his M, to T  him] hem E  if] þat *add.* Sr  125 þe] ony As, *om.* T  `of ony´ Pl, *om.* As 126 þei . . . herte/ofte sythes] *rev.* H$_6$ sythes] tymes SrAEW, tyme H$_6$ it] oute LB$_3$PH$_6$ 127 ben . . . eschewed] thow fully flen hem Cc ben fully] H$_7$HLB$_3$AsLwAPH$_6$Pl, *rev.* RBH$_5$SrWsEMLdTW eschewed] schewid M bot] H$_7$RBLB$_3$SrAEPH$_6$CcMLdPlT, *om.* HH$_5$WsLwTW Jesu] Dei Lat. so] Hu$_2$ *back* 128 `myghty´ Pl  al] þynge *add.* LB$_3$EPH$_6$  is . . . it] contraryeþ it As  to it] H$_7$RBLB$_3$Hu$_2$EPH$_6$CcMLdPlT`W[G]´, þerto HH$_5$SrWsLwAW, for a tyme *add.* `Ws´LwTW [*d.h.*Ws]

What vertus and grace a soule resceyfeth þurgh openyng of þe inner eye into þe gracyous beholdyng of Jesu, and how it may noȝt be geten only þurgh mannys trauelle bot þurgh speciale grace and trauayle also. Capitulum xl^{m}

T[h]us werkeþ lufe outward in a soule, openende þe gostly eye into f. 100^{r} beholdyng of Jesu by inspiracyon of speciale grace, and makeþ it | clene, sotel and able to þe werk of contemplacyon. What þis openyng of þis gostly eye is, þe grettest clerk in erthe couthe neuer ymagenen by his kendly witte ne schewe fully by his tunge. For it may not be geten þurgh study ne by mannys trauelle only, bot pryncipally by grace of þe Holy Gost and with trauelle of man. I drede mykel to speke oght of it, for me þenkeþ I can not; it passeþ myn assay and my lippes are vnclene. Neuerþeles, for I hope þat lufe asketh and lufe byddeth, þerfor I schal seyn a lytel more of it as I hope lufe techeth. Þis opnyng of þe gostly eye is þat lyghtty mirkenes and þat ryght noȝt þat I spake of byfore, and it may be called: purete of spirit and gostly rest, inward stilnes and pees of conscience, heyghnes or depnes of thoght and onlynes of soule, a lyuely felyng of grace and pryuete of herte, þe wakere slepe of þe spouse and a tastyng of heuenly sauour, brennyng in lufe and schynyng in lyght, entre of contemplacyon and reformyng in felynge. Alle þese resons are seyd in holy wrytyng by dyuers men, for ilk of hem spake of it after his felyng in grace, and þogh-alle þei are dyuers in schewyng of wordes, neuerþeles þei are al on in sentence of sothfastnes.

Chapter 40 *title*: H$_7$RLB$_3$SrAEPH$_6$MLdPlTW How þis loue openeþ þe gostly by inspiracioun of grace forto beholde into perfite contemplacioun, and it may nouȝt ben geten but in clennesse and sylence. As *om*. HBH$_5$WsLwHu$_2$Cc 1 grace H$_7$RSrM, graces LB$_3$AEPH$_6$LdPlTW, gracias Lat. þurgh] þe *add*. Ld 2 into . . . also (l. 4)] etc. M 5 Thus] Tus H$_7$ lufe] the *prec*. M outward/in a soule] *rev*., *marked for trsp*. Sr outward] H$_7$H°BH$_5$LB$_3$AsSrWsHu$_2$EPCcLdT, inward H$_6$, *canc*. H, *om*. RLwAMPlW openende þe] openly to þy As 6 makeþ] make As 7 clene] and *add*. BH$_5$WsLd werk] worlde As What] But *prec*. Cc þis . . . eye/is (l. 8)] *rev*. Cc `þ´is] B$_3$ 8 þis] þe HLwATW in] vpon Ld couthe] can W neuer H$_7$, not Σ ymagenen] ymage T 9 his] owne *add*. Hu$_2$ kendly] H$_7$RLB$_3$SrAEPH$_6$CcMPl, *om*. HBH$_5$AsWsLwHu$_2$LdTW, naturale Lat. witte] wittes Pl schewe] scheweþ As 10 þurgh] H$_7$RLB$_3$SrAPH$_6$CcMPl, be HBH$_5$AsWsLwHu$_2$ELdTW ne] *om*. As by^{1}] H$_7$RLB$_3$AsSrAEPH$_6$CcMPl, þurȝ HBH$_5$WsLwHu$_2$LdTW mannys] mennys As by^{2}] H$_7$HBLwHu$_2$CcLdPlTW, þe *add*. RH$_5$AsSrWsAM, þoruȝ LB$_3$EPH$_6$ 11 with] bi Pl trauelle] diligencia hominis et labore Lat. to] H$_7$HBAsLwAHu$_2$CcMLdPlTW, for *prec*. H$_5$LB$_3$SrWsEPH$_6$ 12 oght] *om*. RAsCcM it^{1}] any thyng *add*. RM, de hac apercione [operacione H$_2$H$_8$B$_2$BnR$_2$Up$_2$] Lat. it^{2}] for *prec*. R myn] will and myn *add*. Cc assay] experienciam Lat. 13 for I hope] *om*. T for] *om*. AsLd hope] trowe A þat] H$_7$Cc lufe^{1}] louith T asketh] it *add*. Cc `lufe^{2}´ Cc 14 I schal] *rev*. RPl schal] wyl H$_5$Ws hope] þat *add*. As 15 þis] þe A eye] and it

[CHAPTER 40]

þus wirkiþ lufe [outward] in a soule, opynende þe gostly eiȝe into biholdynge of Ihesu bi inspiracioun of special grace, and makiþ it clene, sotil and able to þe werke of contemplacioun. What þis opnynge of þe gostly eiȝe is, þe grettest clerk in erþ couþe not ymagyn by his witte ne schewe fully bi his tonge. For it may not be geten be studye ne þurȝ mannes traueile only, bot principally bi grace of þe Holy Gost and with trauail of man. I drede mikel to speke ouȝt of it, for me þinkiþ I kan not; it passiþ myn assay and my lippes are vnclene. Nerþeles, for I hope luf askiþ and lufe biddiþ þerfore I schal seyen a litil more of it as I hope lufe techiþ. þis openynge of þe gostly eiȝe is þat liȝty mirknes and riche noȝt þat I spake of bifore, and it may be callid: Purte of spirit and gostly reste, inwarde stilnes and pees of
3v conscience, heiȝenes of þoȝt and onlynes of soule, | a lifly felynge of grace and pryuete of herte, þe waker slepe of þe spouse and tastynge of heuenly sauour, brynnynge in lufe and schynynge in liȝt, entre of contemplacioun and reformynge in felynge. Alle þese resons are saide in holy writynge bi diuers men, for ilke of hem spake of it aftir his felynge in grace, and þawȝ-al þai are diuers in schewynge of wordes, nerþeles þei arne alle in on sentence of soþfastnes.

add. Cc þat[1]] þe ACc ˋlyghttyˊ T^{G}, lyȝtly BHu_2, liȝtsum A, lytil CcT, it liȝtneþ þe As mirkenes] $H_7HRLSrPCcMPlˋT^{G}W^{G}ˊ$ derknesse $BH_5B_3AsWsLwAHu_2EH_6LdTW$ and . . . noȝt] of þe soule *add.* As, *canc.* Cc, *om.* A þat] $H_7RLB_3SrEPH_6MPlˋT^{G}ˊ$, *om.* $HBH_5WsLwHu_2CcLdTW$ ryght] $H_7RMLdPlT$, riche $HBH_5LB_3AsSrWsLwAHu_2$-$EPH_6CcWˋT^{G}ˊ$ 16 spake] haue spoken T byfore] here *prec.* T be] *om.* Cc called] ycleped AsH_6LdT purete . . . felynge (l. 21)] *underlined in* HBH_5 purete] H_7HBLB_3Sr-$LwAHu_2EPH_6CcLdTW$, pouerte RH_5WsMPl, þe porte As, paupertas Lat. of[2]] in H_5Ws 17 and[1]] or As of[1]] $H_7HRBAsAsSrSrLwAHu_2ECcMLdPlTW$, in $H_5LB_3WsPH_6$ or depnes] $H_7RLB_3SrAEPH_6CcMPl$, *om.* $HBH_5AsWsLwHu_2LdTW$, vel profunditas Lat. 18 onlynes] holinesse T, *om.* As of[1]] þe *add.* As felyng] fely As pryuete] a *prec.* AsSr 19 wakere] wake B, man *add.*, *canc.* H, of spryt *add.* Cc spouse] soule LdT a tastyng] doun castynge As a] $H_7RLB_3SrEPH_6CcMPl$, *om.* $HBH_5AsWsLwAHu_2LdTW$ 20 brennyng] bryngynge B and[1]] *om.* LB_3EPH_6 entre] in H_5AsWs and[2]] *om.* Lw 21 reformyng] þe *prec.* H_5Ws, þe fourmynge As þese] those M seyd] *om.* As wrytyng] writingus ACc, writ H_6T by] of H_5AsWs 22 ilk] eueryche BAPlT, euery LwCcW, euery man Hu_2 it] hem LB_3AsPH_6 and] alle- *add.*, *canc.* Cc 23 þogh-alle] H_7HBH_5-$SrWsLwHu_2LdTW$, ȝif alle As, þoȝw RLB_3AEPH_6CcMPl, licet Lat. þei] thise W, alle *add* Cc, *om.* M neuerþeles] ȝet Cc al] *om.* R 24 on in] $H_7RLB_3SrAHu_2EPH_6CcMPlT$, *rev.* $HBH_5AsWsLwLdW$, idem . . . in Lat.

For a soule þat þurgh visityng of grace hath on, hath alle. For why, a syghhende soule to seen þe face of Jesu, whan it is touched þurgh speciale grace of þe Holy Gost, it is sodeynly chaunged and turned fro þe plyte þat it was inne to anoþer maner feleng. It is wonderfully departede and drawen first into itself fro lufe and lykyng of al erthly thynge, so mykel þat it hath lost sauour of þe bodily lyfe and of al þinge þat is, safe only Jesu. And þan is it clene fro al þe felth of synne, so ferforth þat þe mende of it and alle vnordeyned affeccyons to ony creature is sodeynly wesschen and wyped awey, þat þer is no mene lettyng atwix Jesu and þe soule, bot only þe bodily lyfe. And þan is it in gostly reste; for why, alle pynful dowtes and dredis and oþer f. 100v temptacions of gostly enemys are dryfen owt | of þe herte, þat þei truble it noȝt ne synkken not þerin for þe tyme. It is in rest fro þe noye of werdly besynes and pyneful tarying of wikked sterynges, bot it is ful besy in þe fre gostly werkynge of lufe, and þe more it trauayleth so, þe more reste it feleth.

þis restful trauelle is ful fer fro fleschly ydelnes and fro blynd sykernesse. It is ful of gostly werk, bot it is called reste; for grace leseth þe heuy ȝok of fleschly lufe fro þe soule, and makeþ it myghty and fre þurgh þe ȝifte of þe gostly lufe for to werken glad[l]y, sotely and delytabely in al þyng þat grace stereth it for to werken in. And þerfor it is called an holy ydelnes and a reste most besy; and so is it in stillnes fro þe gret cryeng and bestly noyse of fleschly desyres and vnclene thoghtes. þis stilnes makeþ þe inspyracyon of þe Holy Gost in beholdyng of Jesu. For why, his voyce is so swete and so myghty

25 þat] is *add.* As on] he *add.* AE hath alle] *om.* As why] *om.* Cc 26 ˋsyghhendeˊ T^G, seynge As, shinynge T, a desiryng *add.* Hu_2, *om.* Cc soule] desiryng *add.* Cc face] swete blissed *prec.* Hu_2 ⌜þurgh⌝ H^c, with H_5WsT 28 þe] þat B_3Hu_2 plyte] degre Hu_2 it] is T, he B_3 ˋinne . . . first (l. 29)ˊ H^c, *om.* H°H_5AsWs inne to] into SrM, in into ECcLdT ˋvntoˊ W^G maner] of *add.* LwHu_2W wonderfully] wondurly Hu_2T, wondirfull M 29 itself] þe self Cc lufe] þe *prec.* HAsLwW lykyng] lykyngis As, þe *prec.* LwW 30 thynge] thinges CcT, þyngis and As, omnium terrenorum Lat. lost] lefte As sauour] þe *prec.* Lw þe] *om.* H_5AsWsLd bodily] wit *add.*, *canc.* H lyfe] loue As of²] on A 31 þinge] thyngis Cc þat is] *om.* AsH_6 is] ben Cc Jesu] of *prec.* H_5WsHu_2Cc is it] H_7HBH_5SrWsLwAHu_2Pl *rev.* RLB_3AsPˋH_6ˊCcMLdTW al] *om.* H_5Ws þe felth] manere As þe] bodeli M, *om.* ACc of] al manere *add.* H_5Ws 32 and] of *add.* LB_3EPH_6 vnordeyned] H_7HRBH_5AsSrWsLwAMLdPlT, vnordinat LB_3EPH_6CcT, inordinate Hu_2 affeccyons to] H_7RLB_3SrAEPH_6CcMPl, affeccioun of HBH_5AsWsLwHu_2LdTW, affeccio ad Lat. 33 creature . . . mykel (l. 106)] *om.* R. *One folio missing* creature is] creatures aren M is] ˋsoˊ *add.* $T^G W^G$ sodeynly] soþendly Hu_2 and wyped] *om.* H_6 is no] nys non As 34 atwix] H_7HLSrLwEPCc, betwene H_5WsAH_6, bytwyxte BB_3AsHu_2MLdPlTW ˋJesuˊ H_6 þe²] *om.* Sr is it] *rev.* SrAH_6CcW it] ȝite M 35 gostly] bodely Hu_2T why] *om.* CcT alle] H_7HBH_5As-SrWsLwACcMLdTW, þe *add.* LB_3Hu_2EPH_6 pynful] pynes H_5Ws ˋdowtesˊ H^c,

For a soule þat þurȝ visitynge of grace haþ on, haþ al. For whi, a siȝend soule to seen þe face of Ihesu whan it is touchid ⌜þourȝ⌝ special grace of þe Holy Goste, it is sodenly chaunged and turned fro þe pliȝt þat it was ˋin to anoþer maner feling. It is wondirfully departid and drawen first´ into itselfe fro lufe and likynge of al erþly þinge, so mikel þat it haþ lost sauour of þe bodily life and of al þinge þat is, saue only Ihesu. And þan is it clene fro alle þe filþe of syn, so fer forþ þat þe mende of it and al vnordeyned affeccioun of ony creature is sodeynly weschen and wiped awey, þat þer is no mene lettynde atwix Ihesu and þe soule, bot only þe bodily life. And þan is it in gostly reste; for whi, alle pyneful ˋdoutes´ and dredes and al oþer temptaciouns of gostly enmys arn drifen out of þe herte, þat þei troblen not ne synken not þerin for þe tyme. It is in rest fro þe noye of werdly bisynes and peynful [taryinge] of wikked stirynges, bot it is ful bisy in þe fre gostly wirkynge of lufe, and þe more it traueliþ so, þe more rest it feliþ.

þis restful ⌜trauel⌝ is ful fer fro fleschly ydelnes and fro blynde sikernes. It is ful of gostly werk, bot it is called reste; for grace losiþ þe heuy ȝokke of flescly luf fro þe soule, and makiþ it miȝty and free
4r þurghe þe | gifte of þe gostly lufe for to wirken glady, softly and delectably in al þinge þat grace stiriþ it for to wirken in. And þerfor is it called an holy ydelnes and a reste moste besy; and so is it in stilnes fro þe grete cryinge and þe bestly noise of fleschly desires and vnclene þoȝtis. þis stilnes makiþ þe inspiracioun of þe Holy Gost in beholdynge of Ihesu. For whi, his vois is so swete and so miȝty þat

sterynges As, *om.* H_5Ws oþer] H_7LB_3SrAPH_6CcMPl, al *prec.* HBH_5AsWsLw-Hu_2ˋE´LdTW, alie Lat. 36 herte] anima Lat. þei] ne *add.* As 37 truble] troubled T it] H_7LB_3SrEPH_6CcPl, *om.* HBH_5AsWsLwAHu_2MLdPlTW, illam Lat. ne . . . not/þerin] *rev.* As synkken] seken As not] *om.* Cc þerin] þer Pl It] And *prec.* Cc rest] þe *prec.* As fro] as *prec.* T þe] *om.* H_6 noye] noyȝyng H_5Ws, noise Hu_2Cc, *corr. to* noyce Pl, ioye Sr, gaudio Lat. 38 and] fro *add.* E, *om.* LB_3P pyneful] þe *prec.* As tarying] taryingeˋs´ H^c, taryinges LwCcW, caryinge Pl, vexacionis Lat. wikked] þe *prec.* As ˋis´ M 39 more] that *add.* Cc it] ys *add.*, *canc.* Lw 40 it] he W 41 restful] tranquillus et quietus Lat. ⌜trauelle⌝ H^c, felynge H_5Ws, worchynge As and . . . ydelnes (l. 46)] *om.* As and] *om.* LB_3P 42 called] clepid H_6LdT 43 leseth] H_7, vnleseþ Sr, losnyth Cc, losiþ Σ, dissoluit Lat. 44 fre] *om.* A ˋȝifte of´ Pl þe] H_7HH_5WsEPl, holy *add.*, *canc.* HPl, *om.* LB_3AsSrLwAHu_2PH_6CcMLdTW lufe] fro þe soule and makiþ it miȝty *add.*, *canc.* H gladly] gladdy H_7 sotely] H_7, softely Σ, tranquille Lat. 45 in[2]] it Sr 46 it is] *rev.* HBH_5Ld called] clepid H_6LdT is it] H_7HBA-Hu_2MPl, *rev.* H_5LB_3AsSrWsLwEPH_6CcLdTW in] H_7LB_3SrLwAEPH_6CcMPlW, *corr. fr.* inwarde H, inwarde $H^{\circ}BH_5$WsHu_2Ld, moste [in *add.* T^G] inward T, inward *add.* LwW, in Lat. 47 stillnes] fre *add.* A fro] for Hu_2 and[1]] of LwW, fro *add.* Ws bestly] þe *prec.* HH_5WsLwW 48 thoghtes] *om.* As þis] þe B þe[1]] gracious *add.* Hu_2, *om.* W 49 beholdyng] þe *prec.* As Jesu] Domini Jesu Christi Lat.

þat it putteth silence in a soule to iangl[ynge] of alle oþer spekers, for it is a voyce of vertu softly sownyng in a clene soule, of þe whilk þe prophete seyth þus: *Vox Domini in virtute*. þat is: þe voyce of oure Lord Jesu is in vertu. þis voyce is a lyfly worde and a spedy, as þe Apostel seyth: *Viuus est sermo Dei et eficax, et penetrabilior omni gladio ancipiti*. þat is: Qwyk is þe word of Jesu and spedy, more persande þan ony swerd is. þurgh spekyng of þis word is fleschly lufe slayn, and þe soule keped in scilence from al wikked sterynges. Of þis silence it is seyde in þe Apocalyps þus: *Factum est silencium in celo, quasi dimidia hora*. Silence was made in heuene as it were an half houre. Heuene is a clene soule þurgh grace lyfted vp fro erthely lufe vnto heuenly conuersacyon, and so is it in silence; bot for as mikel as þat silence may not lesten hole contynuely for corrupcyon of þe bodily kende, þerfore it is lykned bot to þe tyme of an half houre. A ful schort tyme þe soule þenkeþ þat it is, be it neuer so long, and þerfore it is bot an half houre. And þan hath it pees in conscience; for why, grace putteth owte gnawyng and prikkyng, stryfyng and flytyng of synnes, and
f. 101^r bryngeth in pees and acorde, and makeþ Jesu and a soule | boþe at on in ful acordaunce of wil. þer is non vpbraydyng of synnes ne scharp reprouyng of defautes made þat tyme, for þei are kissed and frendes; al is forȝifen þat was mysdon.

þus feleth þe soule þan with ful meke sykernesse and gostly gladnes, and it conceyueth a ful grete boldenes of saluacyon by þis acorde makyng, for it hereth a pryuey witnessyng in conscience of þe Holy Gost, þat he is chosen sone to þe heuenly heritage. þus Seynt

50 to] fro Pl ianglynge] BLB$_3$SrLwHu$_2$EPH$_6$CcMLdPlTW, ianglend H$_7$, iangelen HH$_5$AsWs, garulacione Lat. alle] *om.* M 51 sownyng] H$_7$ACc, souned HBH$_5$LB$_3$Sr-WsLwHu$_2$EPH$_6$MLdPlTW, sowneþ As, sonans Lat. 52 þus] Ps. 27° *add.* BLEPLdT, Ps. 28 *add.* Hu$_2$ 53 \`in´ T^G, *om.* T þe Apostel] þe Gospel B, Seynt Poul LdT 54 seyth] Hebr. 4° *add.* BLHu$_2$EPLdT Viuus] -rus *add.* H$_5$ Dei] H$_7$AsEH$_6$CcLdPlTW, Domini HBH$_5$LB$_3$SrWsLwAHu$_2$PM, Dei Lat. et eficax] *om.* Lw et^2] H$_7$BCcLdTW, *om.* HH$_5$LB$_3$AsSrWsLwAHu$_2$EPH$_6$MPl, et Lat. 55 ancipiti] H$_7$LB$_3$SrAEPH$_6$Cc, *om.* HBH$_5$AsWsLwHu$_2$MLdPlTW, ancipiti Lat. Qwyk] whiche As Jesu] God A spedy] more *prec.* Pl, and *add.* T persande] perisching H$_5$AsLdW, pershing LwT, perechand Hu$_2$ 56 þis] ⌜h⌝is H^c, his E is^2] al *add.* H$_5$Ws 57 from . . . silence] *om.* As \`it´ is] H^c, *rev.* BHu$_2$ it] *om.* H°H$_5$Ws 58 seyde] spokyn Cc þus] Apoc. 7° *add.* BLHu$_2$EPLd, Apoc. *add.* TW 59 Silence] þat is *prec.* SrECc an half] H$_7$HBH$_5$AsWsLwMLdTW, *rev.* LB$_3$SrAHu$_2$EPH$_6$CcPlT Heuene] Hene As 60 lyfted] rerid LdT vnto] H$_7$, to Σ 61 is it] H$_7$HBWsLwAHu$_2$PlT, *rev.* H$_5$LB$_3$AsSrEPH$_6$CcMLdW, is E þat] þis A, þe Pl, *om.* E 62 lesten] abide Hu$_2$ hole] holy As corrupcyon] þe *prec.* A þe] *om.* LB$_3$PH$_6$M 63 it is] *rev.* MPl bot] *om.* LwH$_6$W an half] H$_7$HBH$_5$AsACcMLdPl, *rev.* LB$_3$SrWsLwHu$_2$EPH$_6$TW schort] sch- *prec.*, *canc.* Sr 64 þe soule/þenkeþ] *rev.* AsPl þe] a Pl it is^1] *rev.* B it is^2] *rev.* Pl is^2] nys As bot] H$_7$H$_5$AsSrWsHu$_2$ECcW, as

it puttiþ silence in a soule to iangelen of alle oþer spekers, for it is a voys of vertue softly souned in a clene soule, of þe whilk þe prophete saiþ þus: *Vox Domini in virtute*. þat is: þe voice of oure Lorde Ihesu is in vertue. þis voys is a lifly worde and a spedy, as þe Apostel seiþ: *Viuus est sermo Domini et eficax, penetrabilior omni gladio*. þat is: Qwike is þe worde of Ihesu and spedy, more persande þen ony swerde is. þurȝ spekynge of [þis] worde is fleschly luf slayn, and þe soule kept in silence fro alle wicked stirynges. Of þis silence `it´ is seyd in þe Apocalips þus: *Factum est silencium in celo, quasi dimidia hora*: Silence was made in heuen as it were an half houre. Heuen is a clene soule þurȝ grace lift vp fro erþly lufe to heuenly conuersacioun, and so is it in silence; bot for as mikel as þat silence may not lesten hole continuely for corupcioun of þe bodily kynde, þerfore it is likned bot to þe tyme of an half oure. A ful schorte tyme þe soule þinkiþ þat
4v it is, be it neuer so longe, and þerfor it is | bot as an halfe oure. And þan haþ it pees in conscience; for whi grace puttiþ out gnawynge and prikkynge, stryfynge and flytynge of synnes, and bryngiþ pees and accorde, and makiþ Ihesu and a soule boþe at one in ful accordance of wille. þer is non ⌜vp⌝braydynge of synnes ne scharpe reprofynge of defautes made þat tyme in a soule, for þei are kissed and frendes; al is forgifen þat was misdone.

þus feliþ þe soule þanne with ful meek sikernes and grete gostly gladnes, and it conceifiþ a ful grete boldnes of saluacioun bi þis acorde makynge, for it heriþ a pryuey witnesynge in conscience of þe Holy Gost, þat he is a chosen sone to heuenly heritage. þus Seint Poul seiþ:

add. HBLB$_3$LwAPH$_6$MLdT, nisi Lat. an half] H$_7$HBH$_5$AsSrWsLwACcMLdPlTW, *rev*. LB$_3$Hu$_2$EPH$_6$ 65 hath it] *rev*. AsH$_6$ conscience] silence T why] *om*. Cc 66 and prikkyng] *rev*. LwW, *om*. Hu$_2$ and[1]] *om*. H$_6$ stryfyng] stering A flytyng] fightyng Sr, chydynge BHu$_2$LdT of synnes] *om*. Cc 67 in] H$_7$LB$_3$SrLw`H^c´AEPH$_6$CcMPlW, *om*. H°BH$_5$AsWsHu$_2$LdT, introducit Lat. and acorde] *om*. As and[1]] *om*. M acorde] accordeþ H$_5$Ws boþe at on] accordyng As boþe at] all T at] *om*. LwAW 68 ful] a *prec*. Pl acordaunce] acordeþ H$_5$Ws, acordyng LdT wil] whiche As is] nys As vpbraydyng] no blamyng no rehersyng *add*. Hu$_2$ ne] and bryngeþ pees and accord, ne þere is non *add*. As 69 made] before *prec*. Hu$_2$, in a soule *add*. Cc þat tyme] H$_7$, in a soule *add*. Σ (*prec*. Cc), in anima *add*. Lat. are] haue W `and´ Cc, made *add*. W  70 al] and *prec*. AsLwH$_6$W  71 ful] *om*. A  meke] mychel AsM  and . . . gladnes] *rep*., *canc*. H  and] H$_7$, grete *add*. Σ, magna *add*. Lat.  72 it] feleþ and *add*. Pl, *om*. W  `a´ Pl 73 for . . . conscience] *om*. As hereth] hath A, bereþ Pl witnessyng] witnesse Cc 74 chosen] H$_7$LB$_3$AsSrAPH$_6$CcMPl, a *prec*. HBH$_5$WsLwHu$_2$ELdTW sone] *om*. As þe] H$_7$SrACcMPlT, *om*. HBH$_5$LB$_3$AsWsLwHu$_2$EPH$_6$LdTW þus] as As Seynt Poule/ seyth] *rev*. H$_6$Cc

Poule seyth: *Ipse Spiritus testimonium perhibet spiritui nostro, quod filii Dei sumus*. Þat is: þe Holy Gost bereth witnsse to oure spirit þat we are Goddis sones. Þat witnessyng of conscience sothfastly feled þurgh grace is þe verrey ioye of þe soule, as þe Apostel seyth: *Gloria mea est testimonium consciencie mee*. Þat is: My ioye is þe witnessyng of my conscience, and þat is whan it witnesseth pees and acorde, trew lufe and frendschip atwix Jesu and a soule. And whan it is in þis pees þan is it in heyghnes or depnes of thoght.

Whan þe soule is bounden with lufe of þe werld, it is þan benethen alle creatures, for ilk a thyng ouergoth it and bereth it doun by maystrye, þat it may not frely seen Jesu ne lufen him. For ryght as þe lufe of þe werd is veyn and fleschly, ryght so þe beholdyng and þe þenkyng and þe vsyng of creatures is fleschly, and þat is a thraldam of þe soule. Bot þan, þurgh opnyng of þe gostly eye in`to´ Jesu, þe lufe is turned and þe soule is reysed vp after here owne kende abouen al creatures; and þan þe beholdyng and þe thenkyng and þe vsynge of hem is gostly, for þe lufe is gostly. Þe soule hath þan ful grete dedeyne for to be buxum to lufe of bodily thyngges, for it is heygh sette abouen hem þurgh grace. It setteth ryght not by al þe werd, for why al schal passen and peryschen. Vnto þis heyghnes of herte, whyles þe soule is keped þerin, come[þ] non errour ne deceyt of þe fende, for Jesu is sothfastly in syght of þe soule þat tyme in alle thyng bynethe him. Of þis speketh þe prophete þus: *Accedat homo ad cor altum et exaltabitur* f. 101^{v} *Deus*. Come man to heygh herte | and God schal ben heyghed. Þat is, a man þat þurgh grace comeþ to heyghnes of thoght schal seen þat Jesu is only heyghed abofen alle creatures and he in him.

75 seyth] Ro. 8 *add*. BLHu$_2$EPLdT Spiritus] *om*. Ld perhibet] peribet Hu$_2$, prohibet Lw quod] H$_7$LB$_3$SrLw⌜H^{c}⌝AEPH$_6$CcMPl, quoniam BH$_5$AsWsHu$_2$LdPlTW, quod Lat. filii Dei/sumus] H$_7$HBH$_5$AsSrWsAHu$_2$CcMLdPlTW, *rev*. LB$_3$LwEPH$_6$, *rev*. Lat. 76 þat] H$_7$, þis Σ 77 witnessyng] witnesse AsT conscience] and *add*. As þurgh] bi T 78 seyth] 2^{a} ad Cor. i$^{\circ}$ add. BLHu$_2$EPLdTW mea] nostra ALd, nostra Lat. est] hec *prec*. AHu$_2$, hic *prec*. Cc 79 mee] nostre ALd, nostre Lat. þat] þis AsM My/ . . ./my] our (*bis*) ALd is] *om*. AsA þe] *om*. Cc witnessyng] H$_7$LB$_3$SrAEPH$_6$MLdPl, witnes HBH$_5$AsWsLwHu$_2$CcTW 80 þat] þis Pl 81 atwix] H$_7$HSrLw, bitwene H$_5$WsAEH$_6$CcT, bytwyx BLB$_3$AsHu$_2$PMLdPlW whan] what Lw, þat *add*. E 82 is it] *rev*. H$_5$WsLdPlT heyghnes] hevynesse Cc or depnes] H$_7$SrCcMPl, *om*. HBH$_5$LB$_3$As-WsLwAHu$_2$EPH$_6$LdTW, vel profunditate Lat. of thoght] *om*. As 83 Whan] For *prec*. As with] bi LB$_3$PH$_6$, the *add*. CcM þe] þis Pl it is/þan] H$_7$LB$_3$SrAEPCcMPl, *rev*. AsT, þan is it HBH$_5$WsLwHu$_2$H$_6$LdTW 84 ilk a] H$_7$HM, iche a H$_5$, eche a LB$_3$AsEPH$_6$, euery SrWsLwAHu$_2$CcLdPlTW it^{2}] *om*. Ld doun] adoun As 85 frely] H$_7$LB$_3$Sr-AEPH$_6$CcMPl, *om*. HBH$_5$AsWsLwHu$_2$LdTW, libere Lat. seen Jesu] *rev*. H$_5$AsWs Jesu] *om*. Lat. him] Dominum Jesum Christum Lat. `as´ As þe] *om*. T 86 ryght . . . fleschly (l. 87)] *om*. M and^{2}] of Sr þe^{3}] H$_7$LB$_3$SrEPH$_6$CcM, *om*. HBH$_5$WsLw-AHu$_2$LdPlTW 87 of^{1}] hem is gostly for þe lufe is gostly *add*., *canc*. H, þe *add*., *canc*. Sr,

Ipse Spiritus testimonium perhibet spiritui nostro, [*quoniam*] *filii Dei sumus*. þat is: þe Holy Gost beriþ witnes to oure spirit þat we arne Goddis sones. þis witnesynge of conscience soþfastly felde þurȝ grace is þe verray ioie of þe soule, as þe Apostel seiþ: *Gloria mea est testimonium consciencie mee*. þat is: My ioye is þe witnes of my conscience, and þat is whan it witnesiþ pees and accorde, trewe lufe and frendschipe atwix Ihesu and a soule. And whan it is in þis pees þan is it in heiȝenes of þouȝt.

When þe soule is bounden with lufe of þe werlde, þen is it bineþ alle creatures, for ilk a þinge ouergoþ it and beriþ it doun by maystrye, þat it may not see Ihesu ne lufen him. For riȝt as þe lufe of þe werlde is veyn and flescly, riȝt so þe biholdynge and þenkynge and þe vsynge of creatures is fleschly, and þat is a þraldom of þe soule. Bot þan, þurȝ
5[r] opnynge of þe gostly eiȝe into Ihesu, þe luf is turned | and þe soule is
reisid vp after his owne kynde abofe alle bodily creatures; and þan þe beholdynge and þenkynge and þe vsynge of hem is gostly, for þe luf is gostly. þe soule haþ þan ful grete dedeyn for to be buxum to luf of bodily þinges, for ⌜it⌝ is heiȝe sette abouen hem þurȝ grace. It settiþ noȝt bi al þe werld, for whi al schal passen and perischen. Vnto þis heiȝenes of herte, whils þe soule is kept þerin, comeþ none errour ne disceite of þe fende, for Ihesu is soþfastly in siȝt of þe soule þat tyme and al þinge byneþ him. Of ⌜þ⌝is spekiþ þe prophet þus: *Accedat homo ad cor altum et exaltabitur Deus*. Come man to heiȝe herte and God schal be heiȝed. þat is, a man þat þurgh grace comiþ to hiȝenes of þoȝt schal seen þat Ihesu only is heiȝed abouen alle creatures and he in him.

all *add*. W is[1] . . . in (43/4)] *om*. Hu_2. *Probably ten fols. missing* a] þe LB_3EP, *om*.H_6 88 þe[1]] soule *add*., *canc*. L, *om*. H_5Ws in`to´] *interl*. $H_7$ 89 here] $H_7$BL$B_3$Sr-AEP$H_6$MLdPlT`W^G´, his HH_5AsWsLwW, the Cc kende] kynke B 90 creatures] H_7Pl, bodily *prec*. Σ, creaturas corporales Lat. and[1]] *om*. Sr þe[2]] H_7H_6T, *om*. Σ þe[3]] H_7HBH_5AsWsLwELdTW, *om*. LB_3SrAPH_6CcMPl 91 for . . . gostly] *om*. H_5AsWs þe lufe is] he loueþ Pl dedeyne] `vn´de⌜ynte⌝ L [quere *marg*.], deynte B_3, vndeynte P, nede As 92 lufe] þe *prec*. Ws bodily] worldly LwW thyngges] þynge As it is] his A ⌜it⌝ H^c, his herte H_5Ws, þis loue As heygh sette] *rev*. Cc 93 hem] hym B setteth] semeþ As ryght] H_7LB_3SrAEPH_6CcMPl, *om*. HBH_5AsWsLwLdTW 94 and] *rep*., *canc*. Sr Vnto] To AH_6 þis] *om*. Sr þe] a B_3 95 comeþ] come H_7, peruenit Lat. non] no E ne deceyt] nede seith M deceyt] deseyd B Jesu] Jesus Christus Lat. 96 in[1]] þe *add*. SrAMPlT syght] þouȝt As in[2]] H_7, and Σ, et Lat. 97 speketh/þe prophete] *rev*. LwW þus] Ps. 63° *add*. BLEPLdW, *om*. Ld `Accedat . . . þus (l. 111)´ T^G, *om*. T ad] *rep*. B et] *om*. LB_3PH_6 98 man] and neyth *add*. Cc þat is] as þoȝ he seide A þat] þis H_6 99 a man/þat] *rev*. LB_3PT^G þat[1]] *om*. As þurgh grace/comeþ . . . thoght] *rev*. M to] the *add*. W, *om*. M schal] he *prec*. As 100 is only] H_7LB_3SrAEPH_6CcMPlT^G, *rev*. HBH_5As-WsLwLdTW only heyghed] *rev*. Pl alle] oþer *add*. As him] hem As

And þan is þe soule alone, mykel straunged fro felawschipe of werdly lufers þogh here body ben in myddys amonge hem, ful fer departed fro fleschly affeccyons of creatures. It chargeth noȝt þogh it neuer se man, ne speke with him, ne hadde confort of him, if it myght ay be so in þat gostly felyng. It feleth so grete homlynes by þe blissed presence of oure Lord Jesu, and so mykel fauour of him, þat it may lyghtely for his lufe forgeten þe fleschly affeccyon and þe fleschly mende of alle creatures. I say not þat it schal not lufen ne þenken of oþer creatures; bot I say þat it schal þenken on hem in tyme, and seen hem and lufen hem gostly and frely, not fleschly ne pynefully as it dide before. Of þis onlynes speketh þe prophete þus: *Ducam eam in solitudinem, et loquar ad cor eius*. I schal leden hire into only stede, and I schal speken to hir herte. Þat is, grace of Jesu ledeth a soule fro noyous compaynye of fleschly desyres into onlynes of thoght, and makeþ it forgete þe lykyng of þe werd, and sowneth by swetnes of his inspyracyon wordis of lufe in eres of þe herte. Only is a soule whan it lufeth Jesu and tenteth fully to him, and hath lost þe sauour and þe confort of þe werd. And þat it myght `þe´ better kepe þis onlynes it fleeth company of al men if it may and seketh onlynes of body, for onlynes of body mykel helpeth to onlynes of soule and to þe fre werkyng of lufe. Þe lesse lettyng þat it hath withouten of veyn karpyng, or withinne of veyn þenkyng, þe more fre it is in gostly beholdyng, and so is it in priuete of herte.

Al withouten is a soule whyles it is ouerleyd and blynded with werdly lufe. It is as common as þe heygh-weye, for ilk a steryng þat cometh of þe flesch or of þe fende synketh in and goth þurgh it. Bot

101 `alone´ $W^G$, aboue LwW, aboue and As straunged] ystrengyd As, strengþid $H_6$M fro] for Ld felawschipe] felschep B, þe *prec.* AsCc 102 here] his CcPl, þe A ben] $H_7$, be Σ, sit Lat. hem] *om.* $B_3$ ful] and *prec.* $H_5$Ws, et . . . totaliter separata Lat. fer] ben þei *add.* AsW`T^G´ 103 It[1] . . . felyng (l. 105)] *om.* A chargeth] chargid CcM 104 se] sai Ld speke] spak Sr him[1]] hem Cc, man AsMPl hadde] haue LwEWT^G him[2]] hem H_5WsCc, man MPl, men As 105 ay be] *rev. rev.* E ay] H_7HH_5LWsPCcMT^G, euere BB_3AsLwEH_6PlW, alwey SrLd be] *rep.* M It] for *prec.* As by] H_7BLB_3AsSrAPH_6CcLd, of Lw⌜H^c⌝EMPlW, in H_5Ws, ex Lat. 106 mykel] R *back* fauour] sauour AsPlW[T^G, *gl.* fervour], `feruoure´ $W^G$ 107 affeccyon] affeccyons AsPl þe fleschly] *om.* Cc, *om.* Lat. 108 alle] oþer As not[1]] *om.* Pl `þat . . . not[2]´ H^c, *om.* H°H_5Ws it] he As ne] or Cc of[2]] on RAECc 109 þat] *om.* E hem] him As 110 hem[1,2]] him (*bis*) As ne pynefully] H_7LB_3SrAEPH_6CcPl`$T^G$´, and pynefully RLw`H^c´MW, *om.* H°H_5WsLdT, vel penaliter Lat. 111 before] and seen hem and lufen *add.*, *canc.* H onlynes] wyldernesse B, mekenesse Ld þus] ysaie *add.* E, Osee 2 *add.* LdTW eam] eum HBAs 112 solitudinem] solitudine W I] þat is *prec.* E hire] him only As only stede] wyldirnesse Cc, wyldernesse or *prec.* B only] an hooli B_3, an *prec.* LEPH_6 113 hir] his

And þan is þe soule alone, mikel straunged fro felaȝschep of werdly lufers þowȝ here body be in middis amonge hem, ful fer departid fro fleschly affeccions of creatures. It chargiþ noȝt þawȝ it neuer see man, ne speke with him, ne had confort of him, if it miȝt ay be so in þat gostly felynge. It feliþ so grete homlynes ⌜of⌝ þe blissed presence of oure Lorde Ihesu, and so mikel sauour of him, þat it may liȝtly for his lufe forgetyn þe fleschly affeccioun and þe fleschly mynde of alle creatures. I sey not ˋþat it shal notˊ lufen ne þinken of oþer creatures. Bot I sey þat it schal þinken on hem in tyme, and seen hem and lufen hem gostly and frely, not fleschly as it did bifore. Of þis onlynes spekes þe prophet þus: *Ducam* [*eam*] *in solitudinem, et loquar ad cor eius*. I schal leden hir into only stede, and I schal speke to hir herte. Þat is, grace of Ihesu lediþ a soule fro noious companye of fleschly 5^{v} desires into onlynes ˋof thoghtˊ, and makiþ | it forgete þe likynge of þe werld, and sowniþ bi swetnes of his inspiracioun wordes of lufe in eres of þe hert. Only is a soule whan it lufiþ Ihesu and tentiþ fully to him, and haþ lost þe sauour and þe confort of þe werld. And þat it miȝt þe better kepe þis onlynes it fleeþ þe companye of alle men if it may and sekiþ onlynes of body, for þat mikel helpiþ to onlynes of soule and to þe free wirkynge of luf. Þe lesse lettyng þat it haþ withouten of veyn iangelynge, or within of veyn þenkynge, þe more free it is in gostly biholdynge, and so is it in pryuete of hert.

Al withouten is a soule whils it is ouerleid and blynded with werdly luf; it is as comune as þe heiȝe-wey. For ilke a stirynge þat comiþ of þe flesche or of þe fende sinkiþ in and goþ þurghe it. Bot þan þurȝ grace

As 114 noyous companye] strepitu societatis Lat. noyous] noyse and evyl Cc onlynes] holynes T ˋof thoghtˊ H^c, or wyldernesse B, *om.* H°H_5WsLd, mentis Lat. 115 forgete] to *prec.* RˋH^{c}ˊEPlˋW^Gˊ, for to *prec.* CcM þe^{1}] love and the *add.* Cc swetnes] þe *prec.* As 116 wordis of lufe] *om.* Cc eres] þe *prec.* ECc Only is/a soule] *rev.* H_6Cc Only] þis *add.* As whan] what T 117 fully] hooly B, *om.* T þe^{1}] *om.* A þe^{2}] *om.* AT 118 ˋþe^{2}ˊ *interl.* H_7, *om.* LwTW þis] his As it . . . onlynes (l. 119)] *om.* SrCc 119 fleeth] sleeþ Ld company] H_7RLB_3AEPH_6MPl, þe *prec.* HBH_5AsWsLw-LdTW and] it *add.* H_5AsWs body] mekil helpeth to flen cumpany of alle men it if may *add.* Cc 120 ⌜onlynes^{1} . . . onlynes^{2}⌝ L onlynes of body] H_7RLB_3SrAEPH_6CcMPl, þat HBH_5AsWsLwLdTW, corporis solitudo Lat. mykel helpeth] *rev.* T soule] þe *prec.* LwW fre] *om.* Cc 121 lufe] godly *prec.* A, soule *prec.* Pl þe] and *prec.* As þat] *om.* LB_3SrPH_6 withouten] H_7HRBH_5AsSrWsLwAECcMPlW, wiþoutforþ LB_3PH_6LdT 122 karpyng] H_7RBLB_3SrAEPH_6CcMPlˋW^Gˊ, iangelynge HH_5AsWsLwW, speche Ld, spekinge T fre] *om.* RAMPl 123 is it] H_7HRLwAW, *rev.* H_5LB_3AsSrWs-EPH_6MLdPlT, is a soule Cc, is B in] *om.* MPl 124 Al] But *prec.* Cc withouten] fore *add.* Ld a] the Cc whyles] whanne Cc, as longe as T 125 as^{1}] the M as^{2}] so M, is *add.* AsCc heygh-weye] ˋcarte wayeˊ W^G ilk a] H_7HRM, eche a H_5LB_3WsLwEPH_6CcTW, eche Ld, euerich B, euery SrAPl 126 or] and M

þan þurgh grace is it drawen in into þe pryue chaumber, into þe syght f. 102r of oure | Lord Jesu, and hereth his pryue counseyls and is wonderly conforted in þe heryng. Of þis spekeþ þe prophete þus: *Secretum meum michi, secretum meum michi*. My pryuete to me, my pryuete to me. þat is, þe lufer of Jesu, þurgh inspiracyon of his grace taken vp fro owtward felyng of werdly lufe and rauysched into pryuete and gostly lufe, ȝeldeth thankyng to him, sayend þus: My priuete to me. þat is, my Lord Jesu in priuete is schewed to me and pryuely hid fro al þe lufers of þe werd, for it is called hid manna, þat may lyghtlyer ben asked þan teld what it is. And þat oure Lord Jesu beheteth to his lufer þus: *Dabo sibi manna absconditum, quod nemo nouit, nisi qui accipit*. þat is: I schal ȝif manna hid þat no man knoweth bot he þat taketh it. þis manna is heuenly mete and aungels fode, as Holy Writte seyth; for aungels are fed fully and filled with clere syght and brennend lufe of oure Lord Jesu, and þat is manna. For we moun asken what it is, bot not wyte what it is. Bot þe lufer of Jesu is not filled ȝit here, bot he is fed by a lytel tastyng of it whyls he is bounden in þe lyf of his body.

þis tastyng of manna is a lyfly felyng of grace, had þurgh openyng of þe gostly eye. And þis grace is not anoþer grace þan a chosen soule feleth in bygynnyng of his conuersion, bot it is þe self and þe same grace, bot it is oþerwyse schewed and feled in a soule. For why, grace wexeth with þe soule and þe soule wexeth with þe grace, and þe more clene þat þe soule is, fer departed fro lufe and lykyng of þe werd, þe more myghty is þe grace, more inward and more gostly schewend þe presence of oure Lord Jesu. So þat þe same grace þat turneth him first

127 þan] *om.* Pl   is it] H_7RLB_3SrEPCcMPl, *rev.* HBH_5AsWsLwAH_6LdTW   drawen] withdrawen LB_3EPH_6 in into] H_7Cc, into HBH_5LB_3AsSrWsLwAEPH_6Cc-LdPlTW, to R, *om.* M, introducitur in Lat.   þe[1]] *om.* LB_3PH_6 ⌜into[2]⌝ H^c, to BH_6CcLdT, of H_5AsWs   128 Jesu] Jesu Christi Lat.   ⌜and hereth . . . counseyls⌝ H^c, *om.* H°H_5Ws   and[1]] he As   hereth] of *add.* BLdT   pryue . . . prophete (l. 129)] louer As   counseyls] counseyle BLd   `and[2] . . . prophete (l. 129)′ H^c, he hetyþ his louer H_5Ws   is] it *prec.* Cc   wonderly] H_7RSrH_6CcMPl, wonderfully BLB_3LwH^cAEPLdTW   129 þe[1]] *om.* BLdT   þus] Ysa. 24° *add.* BLEPLdTW   130 My[1]] þat is *prec.* E   131 þat is] *om.* Cc   þe . . . Jesu] a soule A   lufer] loue R   Jesu] Jesu Christi Lat.   his] Godus A, *om.* AsLwW   taken] is *prec.* AsH_6Cc   132 owtward] þe *prec.* As   pryuete] þe *prec.* LwAsW   and[2]] H_7, of Σ, amoris Lat.   133 lufe] and *add.* AsCc   ȝeldeth] ȝeldyng EM   thankyng] H_7HRBH_5SrWsLwACcMW, þankyngis LB_3AsEPH_6LdT, gracias Lat.   to him/sayend] *rev.* LB_3EPH_6 sayend] and *prec.* LB_3EP, *om.* Lw   134 in] H_7LB_3SrAPH_6CcPl, þi HRBH_5WsLwEMLdTW, be As, in Lat.   þe] *om.* HAsLwLdW   135 called] cleped AsH_6LdT   hid manna] *rev.* T   `hid′ Pl, *om.* AsCc   `lyghtlyer′ E   136 asked] hasched H_5Ws   þan] and RM, be *add.* A   teld] sermonibus enarrari Lat.   oure] *om.* Lw   Jesu] *om.* LdT   lufer] louers RCcM, loues A   137 þus] seying *prec.* WsTW, seyinge *add.* H_5, Apo. 2° *add.* BLEPLdTW   sibi] tibi H_5WsLdT`W$^{G}$′   138 is] þat *add.* As   `I′ Cc   ȝif] to þe *add.* H_5Ws, to him *add.* E   it] *om.* B_3 140 fed fully] H_7, *rev.* Σ   and

it is drawen into þe pryuey chambre ⌜into⌝ þe si3t of oure Lorde Ihesu, ⌜and hereþ his priuy conseilis⌝ `and is wondirfully conforted in heryng. Of þis spekiþ þe prophet´ þus: *Secretum meum mihi, secretum meum mihi*. My pryuete to me, my pryuete to me. Þat is, þe lufer of Ihesu, þurghe inspiracioun of his grace taken vp fro outward felynge of werdly lufe and rauisched into pryuete of gostly lufe, 3eldiþ þankynge to him, seiend þus: My pryuete to me. Þat is, my Lord Ihesu, þi pryuete is schewde to me and pryuely hid fro alle lufers of þe werld, for it is called hid manna, þat may li3tlyer ben askid þen tolde what it is. And þat oure Lorde Ihesu bihetiþ to his lufer þus: *Dabo sibi manna absconditum, quod nemo nouit, nisi qui accipit*. Þat is: I schal gif manna hid þat no man knowiþ bot he þat takiþ it. Þis manna is heuenly mete and aungels fode, as Holy Writ seiþ; for aungels arne
26[r] fully | fed and fillid with clere si3t and brennende lufe of oure Lorde Ihesu, and þat is manna. For we moun aske what it is, bot not wete what it is. Bute þe lufer of Ihesu is not filled 3it here, bot he is fed bi a litil tastynge of it whils he is bounden in þis bodily lif.

Þis tastynge of manna is a lifely felynge of grace, had þur3 opnynge of þe gostly ei3e. And þis grace is not anoþer grace þan a chosen soule feliþ in bigynnynge of his conuers⌜ioun⌝, bot it is þe same and þe selfe grace, bot it is oþerwise felid and schewyd to a soule. For whi, grace wexeþ with þe soule and þe soule wexiþ with grace, and þe more clene þat þe soule is, fer departid fro luf of þe werld, þe more mi3ty is þe grace, more inwarde and more gostly schewend þe presence of oure Lorde Ihesu. So þat þe same grace þat turniþ first hem fro synne, and

filled] *om.* RM with] withe M, þe *add.* H$_5$AsWsE and[2]] of As, in LwW 141 Jesu] Jesu Christi Lat. þat] hec visio seu dileccio Lat. 142 wyte] *rep.*, *canc.* Cc filled 3it] *rev.* H$_6$ filled] fulfyllyde H$_5$Ws here] 3ere Ld 143 by] with B of it] *om.* Pl bounden] *om.* E þe . . . body] H$_7$RLB$_3$SrAPH$_6$CcMPl, þis bodily lif HBH$_5$AsWsLwELdTW, vita sui corporis Lat. his] this RACc 144 of] *rep.* R manna] this *prec.* W a] *om.* Pl þurgh] þe *add.* E, grace *add.*, *canc.* Ld 145 `is´ Pl, nys As, it *prec.* M þan] H$_7$HBLSrLwEPH$_6$CcLdPlT, þat RB$_3$AsAMW, þat *add.* H$_5$Ws, ab alia Lat. 146 bygynnyng] H$_7$HBPl, þe *prec.* Σ his] *om.* B$_3$ conuersion] conuers⌜ioun⌝ H[c], conuersacioun BH$_5$Pl `it´ Sr self/. . ./same] H$_7$, same and self LB$_3$PH$_6$, same T, *rev.* Σ 147 schewed and feled] H$_7$RLB$_3$SrAEPH$_6$CcMPl, *rev.* HBH$_5$AsWsLwLdTW, ostenditur . . . et sentitur Lat. in] H$_7$RLB$_3$SrAEPH$_6$CcMPl, to HBH$_5$AsWsLwLdTW, in Lat. why] *om.* Cc 148 with] in Sr þe[1]] a Pl þe[3]] H$_7$AsM, *om.* Σ 149 þe[1]] *om.* T fer] ferre W, and ferþere RA, and ferre Pl, and the ferther CcM, and *prec.* H$_6$, *om.* H$_5$Ws departed] partid M lufe] þe *prec.* LAsCcW and lykyng] H$_7$RLB$_3$SrAPH$_6$CcMPl, *om.* HBH$_5$AsWsLwELdTW, et delectacione Lat. 150 more myghty] my3tier M more[2]] with As, *om.* Cc more[3]] the *prec.* Cc schewend] in *add.* W 151 þat] *om.* Cc him first] H$_7$RLB$_3$SrAEPH$_6$CcMPl, hem first LdW, first hem HBH$_5$AsWs, hem LwT, primo conuertit hominem Lat.

fro synne, and makeþ him bigynnend and profitend by ȝiftes of vertus and excercyse of gode werkes, and maketh him also perfyte; and þat grace is called a lyfly felyng of grace, for he þat hath it feleth it wele and knoweth wele by experyence þat he is in grace. It is ful lyfely to f. 102^{v} him, for it qwykneth þe soule wonderly and makeþ it so hole þat it | feleth no pyneful disese of þe body, þogh it be feble or sekly; for why, þan is þe body myghtyest, most hole, and most restful, and þe soule also.

Withouten þis grace a soule can not lyuen bot in pyne, for it þenketh þat it myght ay kepe it and nothyng schuld put it away. And neuerþeles ȝit is it not so, for it passeth away ful lyghtly; bot neuerþeles þogh þe souerayne felyng of it passe away and withdrawe, þe relef lefeth stille and kepeth þe soule in sadnes and makeþ it for to desyren þe comyng aȝen. And þis is also a waker slepe of þe spouse, of þe whilk Holi Writte seith þus: *Ego dormio et cor meum vigilat*. I slepe and myn herte waketh. Þat is, I slepe gostly whan þurgh grace þe lufe of þe werd is slayn in me, and wikked sterenges of fleschly desyres are dede so mykel þat vnneþes I fele hem, I am not taryed with hem. Myn herte is made fre, and þan it waketh, for it is scharpe and redy for to luf Jesu and seen him. Þe more I slepe fro outward thynges, þe more waker am I in knowyng of Jesu and of inward thynges; I may not waken to Jesu bot if I slepe to þe werd.

And þerfor þe grace of þe Holi Gost, sperrend þe fleschly eye, doth þe soule slepen fro werdly vanyte, and openend þe gostly eye waken into þe syght of Goddys maieste, hyled vnder clowde of his precyous manhed; as þe Gospel seyth of þe aposteles whan þei were with oure Lord Jesu in his transfyguracion: first þei slepeden and þan, *Euigilantes viderunt maiestatem*: þei wakende seyen his maieste. By

152 makeþ . . . and[2]] maki⌜þ him parfite bygynnyng and⌝ L, maketh hym parfite begynnyng and P him] H$_7$AsAE, hem HRH$_5$LB$_3$SrWsLwPH$_6$CcMLdPlTW, eum Lat. profitend] perfytynge As vertus] vertue W 153 and] H$_7$, *om.* Σ maketh] maken PW him] H$_7$E, hem HRBH$_5$LB$_3$AsSrWsLwAPH$_6$CcMLdPlTW, eum Lat. perfyte/and þat] *rev.* P `perfyte´ L, profite B$_3$, in loue *add.* H$_5$Ws 154 grace] also *add.* `L´B$_3$P, *om.* Lat. called] clepid AsH$_6$LdT, also *add.* E lyfly] presence *add.*, *canc.* H 155 and] þat H$_5$Ws knoweth] it *add.* LB$_3$PH$_6$ wele] *om.* Cc experyence] experiences As 156 qwykneth] aquitith Cc wonderly] H$_7$RLB$_3$APH$_6$CcM, wondirfully HBH$_5$AsSrWsLwELdPlTW it[2]] *om.* Ld so] *om.* SrT hole] fortem . . . et sanam Lat. it[3]] H$_7$HRBH$_5$AsSr-WsLwAMLdTW, he LB$_3$EPH$_6$CcPl 157 or] and HH$_5$WsLwW why] *om.* Cc 158 myghtyest] moste *prec.* T 160 grace] þanne *add.* As a soule] *om.* Pl a] H$_7$, þe Σ 161 ay] H$_7$HH$_5$LWsPCcM, euer BB$_3$AsLwEH$_6$PlW, euermore A, alwey SrLdT And] *om.* CcPl 162 ȝit] *om.* T is it] H$_7$RLB$_3$SrPH$_6$MPl, *rev.* HBH$_5$WsLwAECcLdTW, it nys As passeth away] draweþ away As ful . . . away (l. 163)] *om.* As `ful´ Sr 163 neuerþeles] *om.* Cc of it] *om.* HH$_5$WsLwW, eius Lat. withdrawe] sumwhat *add.* A 164 relef] relees Cc, reliquie Lat. lefeth stille] *om.* As lefeth] dwelleþ Sr for] *om.* T 165 þis] þat B `is´ Pl

makiþ hem bigynnande and profitande bi giftes of vertues and exercice of gode werkis, makiþ hem also perfit; and þat grace is kallid a lifly felynge of grace, for he þat haþ it feliþ it wel and knowiþ wel by experience þat he is in grace. It is ful lifly to him, for it quicneþ þe soule wondirfully and makiþ it so hole þat it feliþ no peynful disese of þe body, þawȝ it be feble and sekely; for whi, þan is þe body miȝtiest, most hooþ and most restful, and þe soule also.

Withouten þis grace þe soule kan not lifen bot in peyn, for it þinkiþ þat it miȝt ay kepe it and noþinge schulde pute it awey. And nerþeles ȝit it is not so, for it passiþ awey ful liȝtly; bot nerþeles þawȝ þe
26v souereyn felynge passe awey and withdrawe, þe reliefe | lefiþ stille, and kepiþ þe soule in sadnes and makiþ it for to desiren þe comynge ageyn. And þis is also þe wakir slepe of þe spouse, of þe whilk Holy Writ seiþ þus: *Ego dormio, et cor meum vigilat*: I slepe and my herte wakiþ. Þat is, I slepe gostly when þurȝ grace þe luf of þe werld is slayn in me, and wicked stirynges of fleschly desires are ded so mikel þat vnneþes I fele hem, I am not taried with hem. Myn herte is made free, and þan it wakiþ, for it is scharpe and redy for to lufe Ihesu and seen him. Þe more I slepe fro outwarde þinges, þe more waker am I in knowynge of Ihesu and inwarde þinges; I may not wake to Ihesu bot if I slepe to þe werld.

And þerfore þe grace of þe Holy Goste, sperende þe fleschly eiȝe, doþ þe soule slepe fro werdly vanytee, and opnende þe gostly eiȝe waken into þe siȝt of Goddis maieste, hiled vndir cloude of his precious manhede; as þe Gospel seiþ of þe apostels when þei were with oure Lorde Ihesu in his transfiguracioun: first þei slepid and þan *Euigilantes viderunt maiestatem*: þei waknend seen his maieste. By

also] *om.* As   a] H$_7$, þe Σ   spouse] soule LdT   166 seith] spekeþ As   þus] Cant. 5° *add.* BLEPLdTW, *om.* RAMPl   I] þat is *prec.* E   168 wikked] *om.* M   sterenges] stiringe LB$_3$P   169 dede] H$_7$SrLwECcTW, ded *corr. fr.* dedid H, dedid H$^{\circ}$RBH$_5$LB$_3$AsWsAPH$_6$MLdPl, mortui Lat.   so] and *prec.* `L´B$_3$AsP   vnneþes I] *rev.* H$_6$   hem$^1$] *om.* Ld   `I am not´ T   `am´ Pl   170 for$^1$] þanne *add.* As   is] mad *add.* H$_5$, ymade *add.* AsWs, *om.* M   for$^2$] *om.* Cc   171 seen him] *rev.* As   seen] for to *prec.* REM, to *prec.* As   172 waker] wakinge T   am I] *rev.* PlW   Jesu] Jesu Christi Lat.   of] H$_7$`H^c´RLB$_3$SrLwAEPH$_6$CcMPlW, in As, *om.* H$^{\circ}$BH$_5$WsLdT   may] am E   173 to] as *prec.* As   174 sperrend] closynge BA, stoppynge As, schettyng H$_6$LdT   doth] makith AM   175 slepen] selpe W, to *prec.* MLdPlT   and] in *add.* As   openend] opned RM, openeþ ECcPl   eye] highe M   waken] wakith H$_5$WsLwW, wakynge AsCcM, waked T, makith hit *prec.* A   176 vnder] H$_7$HRLB$_3$SrWsAEPH$_6$MPl, þe *add.* BAsLwCcLdTW   clowde] cloudes T   precyous] passion *add.*, *canc.* Pl   177 as þe Gospel] þus Holi Writ A   þe^2] H$_7$HBH$_5$AsWsLwAELdPlTW, *om.* RLB$_3$SrPH$_6$CcM   were] *rep.* H$_5$ 178 þei] *om.* Pl   slepeden] slepen B$_3$ and þan] Et TW   þan] þei woken *add.* As, Luc. 9 *add.* T   179 Euigilantes . . . maiestatem] *om.* Ld   Euigilantes] Vigilantes RM   þei] þat is *prec.* E   wakende] H$_7$BH$_5$AsWsCcW, waknend HLwAMLdT, wakynede Pl, þat wakeneden LP, þat wakiden B$_3$EH$_6$ seyen] seynge Pl

slepe of þe apostles is vnderstonden deyeng of werdly lufe by inspiracyon of þe Holy Gost, by here wakyng, contemplacyon of Jesu. þurgh þis slepe þe soule is broght into reste fro dyn of fleschly lust; and þurgh wakyng it is reysed vp into syght of Jesu and of gostly þynges. þe more þat þe eyne are sperred in þis maner slepe fro þe appetyte of erthly thynge, þe scharper is þe inner syght in lufely beholdyng of heuenly fayrehed. þis slepyng and þis wakyng lufe werkeþ þurgh þe lyght of grace in þe soule of þe lufer of Jesu.

How specyale grace in beholdyng of Jesu withdraweth sumtyme f. 103r fro a soule, and | how a man schal haue him in absence and presence of specyal grace. And how a soule schal desyren þat in it is ay þe gracyous presence of Jesu. Capitulum xli[m]

Schew me þan a soule þat þurgh inspiracyon of grace hath openyng of þe gostly eye into beholdyng of Jesu, þat is departed and drawen oute fro lufe of þe werd, so ferforth þat it hath purete and pouerte of spirit, gostly reste, inward silence and pees in conscience, heyghnes of thoght, onlynes and pryuete of herte, waker slepe of þe spouse, þat hath lost lykyng and ioyes of þ⌜is⌝ werd, taken with delyte of heuenly sauour, ay threstende and softly syghende þe blissed presence of Jesu. And I dar hardily pronownce þat þis soule brenneth al in lufe and schyneth in gostly lyght, wurthi for to come to þe name and to þe wurschepe of þe spowse, for it is reformed in felyng, made able and redy to contemplacyon. þese are þe toknes of inspiracyon in openynge of þe gostly eye. For why, whan þe eye is opened þe soule is in ful felynge of alle þese vertus before sayde for þat tyme.

180 slepe] þe *prec.* A   vnderstonden] *om.* LB_3PH_6 by] $H_7RLB_3SrAPH_6CcMPl$, þurgh $HBH_5WsLwELdTW$, þurgh þe As, per Lat.   181 here] *om.* Cc   `wakyng´ $W^G$, waknynge HLw, walkyng W, slomerynge is As   182 into] to Cc   fro dyn] *om.* As   dyn] dyynge B, noyse SrLdTW, *gl. noyse s.h.* Lw, dyynge B   fleschly] þe *prec.* Pl   183 lust] lustys Cc   wakyng] waknynge $HH_5Lw$, walkinge W   syght] $H_7H^{o}RM$, þe *prec.* $BH_5LB_3AsSrWsLwA$`H^{c}´$EPH_6CcLdPlTW$ of[2]] $H_7RLB_3SrAEPH_6CcMPl$, *om.* $HBH_5AsWsLwLdTW$ 184 þynges] þinge As   eyne are] eiȝe is As   sperred] closed BA, yschutte AsH_6LdT maner] wise *add.* As, of *add.* MT   185 erthly] $H_7HRBH_5AsSrWsLwECcMLdPlTW$, worldli LB_3AEPH_6 thynge] `thyngis´ W^G is] in H_6 inner] *om.* As   syght] eye A   in] to A, þe *add.* As   187 Jesu] oure Lorde Jesu BCcLd, Domini Jesu Christi Lat.

Chapter 41 *title*: $H_7RLB_3SrAEPH_6MLdPlTW$ þat a soule þat þurgh þe grace of Jesu haþ openynge of gostly eiȝen departed and withdrawen fro þe worlde and to reste in pees and cylence and oþer vertues haþ and delite of heuene þurgh gostly presence of oure Lord Jesu. As   *om.* $HBH_5WsLwCc$ 1 Jesu] our Lord *prec.* W   2 man] soule TW   schal . . . Jesu[2]] etc. M   him] her TW   absence] þe *prec.* TW   and presence/of . . . grace] *rev.* Ld, in absencia specialis gracie et presencia Lat.   3 presence] in þe *prec.* LdT

slepe of þe apostels is vndirstonden dyenge of werdly lufe þurgh inspiracioun of þe Holy Gost, by here waknynge, contemplacioun of Ihesu. Þurȝ þis slep þe soule is broȝt into reste fro dyn of fleschly luste; and þurgh waknynge it is reisid vp into \`þe´ siȝt of Ihesu and gostly þinges. Þe more þat þe eiȝen are spered in þis maner slepe fro þe appetite of erþli þinge, þe scharper is þe inner siȝt in lufly beholdynge of heuenly fairhed. Þis slepynge and þis wakynge lufe wirkiþ þurȝ þe liȝt of grace in þe soule of þe lufer of Ihesu.

[CHAPTER 41]

27r Schew me þan a soule þat þurȝ inspiracion of grace haþ openynge of þe gostly eiȝe into biholdynge of Ihesu, þat is departid and drawen out fro luf of þe worde, so ferforth þat it hath purte and pouerte of spirit, gostly rest, inward silence and pees in conscience, heiȝenes of þoȝt, onlynes and pryuetee of herte, waker slepe of þe spouse, þat haþ loste lykynge and ioyes of þis werlde, taken wiþ delice of heuenly sauour, ay þristand and softely sikynge þe blessed presence of Ihesu. And I dar hardely pronuncen þat þis soule brennyth al in luf and schynyth in gostely liȝt, wurthi for to come to þe name and to þe wurschip of \`þe´ spouse, for it is reformed in felynge, made able and redy to contemplacioun. Þese are þe toknes of inspiracioun in openynge of \`þe´ gostly eiȝe. For whi, when þe eiȝe is opned þe soule is in ful felynge of alle þese vertues bifore seid for þat tyme.

specyal grace] Jesu TW þat] in *prec.* B_3 4 ay] H_7RLB_3PM, alwey SrALdTW, euere EH_6Pl 5 þan/a soule] *rev.* B openyng of] opnyd Cc 6 þe] *om.* AsE eye] syghte LwW beholdyng] the CcT is] *om.* As 7 lufe] þe *prec.* AsCcTWWc purete . . . spouse (l. 9)] *underlined* HBH_5 purete and pouerte] loue As purete] meknes H_5Ws spirit] þe *prec.* As 8 gostly] and *prec.* As, in *prec.* Cc inward] in word A heyghnes] heuynesse Cc of] in As 9 and] in H_5WsWc waker] and *add.* As spouse] soule Ld 10 lykyng] lykyngis As, the *prec.* Cc ioyes] ioie LB_3EPH_6, gaudium Lat. þ⌜is⌝] *corr. fr.* þe H_7, þe AsLwW delyte] delice HLwW 11 ay] $H_7HRH_5LWsAPM$, ayly Cc, euere $BB_3AsLwEH_6PlTWWc$, alwey SrALd threstende] furstande B, trustyng Sr, restynge As softly] oftly As, soþli LB_3EPH_6, veraciter Lat. syghende] syngyng Sr þe] þat W 12 \`And´ Pl I dar] þan dar I E I] *om.* As pronownce] proneen R, prowen M, puynten As, seyn Cc al . . . schyneth (l. 13)] and liȝteþ As al] *om.* M 13 schyneth] al *add.* Sr lyght] and *add.* As for] *om.* PlT to[3]] *om.* Cc þe[2]] *om.* Pl 14 \`þe´ H^c, *om.* $H^{\circ}H_5Ws$ made able . . . felynge (l. 17)] *om.* Lat. 15 þese] Those R þe] *om.* Cc inspiracyon] þe *prec.* E in] and RM 16 \`þe[1]´ H^c, *om.* $H^{\circ}As$ eye] eiȝen AsWc why] *om.* CcWc in] *om.* H_6 17 þese] those RM sayde] s- *prec.*, *canc.* Sr for . . . tyme] *om.* As þat] þe Pl

Neuerþeles oft-sythes it falleth þat grace withdraweth in partye for corrupcion of mannys frelte and suffreth þe soule falle into itself in fleschlyhede as it was before; and þan is þe soule in sorwe and pyne, for it is blynde and vnsauourye and kan no gode. It is weyk and vnmyghty, encumbred with þe body and with alle þe bodily wittes; it seketh and desireth after þe face of Jesu aȝen, and it may not fynde it. For Holy Writte seyth of oure Lord þus: *Postquam vultum suum absconderit, non est qui contempletur eum*. Þat is: After whan oure Lorde hath hid his face, þer is non þat may beholden him. Whan he scheweth him þe soule may not vnsee him for he is lyght, and whan he hydeth him it may not seen him for þe soule is myrk. His hydyng is bot a sotel assayinge of a soule; his schewyng is wonder mercyful godenes in confort of þe soule.

Haue þou no wonder þogh felyng of grace withdraw sumtyme fro a lufer of Jesu. For Holi Wrytte seyth þe same of þe spowse, þat sche fareth þus: *Quesiui et non inueni illum; vocaui et non respondit michi*. I f. 103^{v} soght and I fonde | not; I called him and he answered not. Þat is, whan I falle doun to my frelte, þan grace withdraweth; for my fallyng is cause þerof and not his fleynge. Bot þan fele I þe pyne of my wrecchednesse in his absence, and þerfore I soght him by sotelte of thoght þer I had him before, and I fonde him not; I called him by grete desyryng of herte and he ȝafe to me no felable answeryng. And þan I cryed with al myn hert: *Reuertere, dilecte mi*. Turne aȝen, þu my loued. And ȝit it semed þat he herd me noȝt. Þe pyneful felyng in myself and þe assaylyng of fleschly lufes and dredis in þis tyme, and

18 oft sythes/it falleth] H$_{7}$RLB$_{3}$SrAEPH$_{6}$CcMPl, *rev.* HBH$_{5}$AsWsLwLdTWWc   oft sythes] som tyme Wc, *om.* H$_{6}$ sythes] time A, tymes TW   for] fro B   19 suffreth] thenne *add.* W   falle] to *prec.* LwCcT, for to *prec.* MW   into itself] *om.* Lat.   itself] the self Cc   20 fleschlyhede] fleschlinesse A   was] were Cc   soule] is *add.* M   sorwe and pyne] *rev.* LwW   pyne] H$_{7}$RLB$_{3}$SrAPH$_{6}$CcMPl, in *prec.* HBH$_{5}$AsWsLwALdTWWc   21 blynde . . . vnsauory] so *prec. bis* T   no] non As   weyk] feble BAWc, liþy LdT   22 encumbred with] encombreþ As   with^{2}] *om.* Cc   þe^{2}] *om.* AsM   wittes] mythes Cc   23 face] H$_{7}$RBLB$_{3}$SrAPH$_{6}$CcMLdPlT, grace HH$_{5}$AsWsLwEWWc, faciem Lat.   24 þus] Job 34° *add.* BLEPLd   25 whan] þat ACc   Lorde] H$_{7}$RACcMPl, Jesu *add.* HBH$_{5}$LB$_{3}$AsSrWsLwEPH$_{6}$LdTW, God *add.* Wc   26 hath] had LB$_{3}$PH$_{6}$ is] nys As   non] no E   him] hem M   Whan] And *prec.* AsWc   27 may] ne *prec.* As   vnsee] see As, sen *corr. fr.* vnsen Cc, vse M   is] his M, þis *add.* H$_{6}$ 28 hydeth] biddeþ Pl   it] he Pl, þe soule T   `not´ H^{c}, *om.* H°B   myrk] H$_{7}$HRLSrPCcMPl, derk BH$_{5}$B$_{3}$AsWsLwAEH$_{6}$LdTW   His] it is As   29 hydyng] abidinge LB$_{3}$EP, it *add.* As   a^{1}] his Cc, *om.* Pl   assayinge] sayinge B$_{3}$ a^{2}] H$_{7}$RLB$_{3}$SrAPH$_{6}$CcMPl, þe HBH$_{5}$AsWsLwELdTWWc   his] it is As   schewyng] it *add.* As   wonder] *corr. fr.* wondirful E, a *prec.* RAMPlTWWc, a *add.* Lw   30 godenes] and goodly As   in] and Ld   31 Haue] ne *prec.* As   `þou´ Pl, ye W, in *add.* H$_{5}$Ws   þogh] H$_{7}$, þe *add.* Σ   felyng of grace] *rev.* As   withdraw] be *prec.* ELw`T´W   a] þe RH$_{5}$Ws   32 lufer] loue Sr   Jesu]

Nerþeles it fallith ofte-siþes þat grace wiþdrawþ in party for corrupcioun of mannys freelte and suffriþ þe soule falle into itself in fleshlied as it was befor; and þen is þe soule in sorw and in peyn, for it is blynde and vnsauory and can no gode. It is weyk and vnmyȝty, encumbred wiþ þe body and wiþ alle þe bodily wittes; it sekiþ and desiriþ after þe grace of Ihesu ageyn, and it may not fynde it. For Holy Writt seith of oure Lorde þus: *Postquam vultum suum absconderit, non est qui contempletur eum.* Þat is: After, when oure Lord Ihesu haþ hid his face, þer is none þat may biholden him. When he shewth him þe soule may not vnsee him for he is liȝt, and whan he hidiþ him it may `not´ see him for þe soule is myrk. His hidyng is but a sotil assaynge of þe soule; his schewynge is wondir merciful goodnes in conforte of þe soule.

27^{v} Haue þu no wondir | þawȝ þe felyng of grace wiþdraw sumtyme fro a lufer of Ihesu. For Holy Writ seiþ þe same of þe spouse, þ⌜at⌝ she farith þus: *Quesiui et non inueni illum; vocaui et non respondit mihi.* I seked and I fonde him not; I called and he answerid not. Þat is, when I falle doun to my freeltee, þan grace wiþdrawþ; for my fallynge is cause þerof and not his fleeng. Bot þan fele I peyne of my wrechednes in his absence, and þerfore I soȝte him [by sotylte of þouȝt þer y hadde hym byfore, and y fond hym noȝt; y callede hym] bi grete desirynge of hert and he gaf to me no felable answerynge. And þan I cried wiþ alle my soule, *Reuertere, dilecte mi.* Turne ageyn, þu my loued. And ȝit it semed as he arde me not. Þe peynful felyng of myself, and þe assailyng of fleshly lufes and dredes in þis tyme, and þe

God Wc, Jesu Christi Lat. For] as As, why *add.* Pl `Holi´ Pl þat sche fareth] *om.* ACcWc þ⌜at⌝ H^{c} 33 þus] Cant. 3° *add.* BLEPLdTW respondit] respondet Lw I] þat is *prec.* E 34 soght] seke H_{5}AsWs fonde] fynde H_{5}AsWsWc not^{1}] H_{7}RLB_{3}Sr-PH_{6}MPl, him not HBH_{5}AsWsLwAECcWWc, not him LdT, illum Lat. called] clepide H_{6}LdT, haue ycleped As him^{1}] H_{7}RLB_{3}SrEPH_{6}CcMPl, *om.* HBH_{5}AsWsLwALdTWWc answered] ansueriþ Ld, me *add.* BH_{5}AsWsE`W^{G}´Wc þat] þis Pl 35 þan] my *add.* H_{6} 36 fleynge] feelinge LB_{3}P, fuga Lat. I] *om.* A þe] H_{7}RLB_{3}SrAEPH_{6}CcMPl, *om.* HBH_{5}AsWsLwLdTW 37 and] *om.* A by . . . him^{3} (l. 38)] H_{7}RBLB_{3}SrAEPH_{6}Cc-MLdPlT, *om.* HH_{5}AsWsLwW 38 had] fond A I^{2} . . . and^{1} (l. 39)] *om.* H_{6} him^{2}] *om.* Lat. not] *om.* M called] clepid LdT 39 desyryng] desir ALdTW, desires Pl `he´ Cc, *om.* B to] *om.* A no] a $H_{5}$AsWs `felable´ W^{G}, feable W answeryng] ansuere ECcT, vnswerynge Pl And^{2}] *om.* T 40 hert] H_{7}RLB_{3}SrAPH_{6}CcMLdPlT, soule HBH_{5}AsWsLwEW, corde Lat. Reuertere] *rep.* Cc dilecte] dilecti Lw mi] Cant. 6° *add.* BLEPLdTW Turne] þat is *prec.* E þu] *om.* A 41 loued] loue A, belouyd As semed] semith M þat] H_{7}RLB_{3}SrAPH_{6}CcMPlT, as HBH_{5}AsWsLwW, as *prec.* ELd `he´ Pl me noȝt] *rev.* T in] H_{7}, of Σ, sensacio mea Lat. 42 þe] *om.* B assaylyng] assaylyngis RB_{3}M, assayinge As fleschly] þe *prec.* AM, my *prec.* CcPl lufes] lustys B, dilectacionum Lat. and^{3}] in *add.* Cc þe wantyng of my gostly strength, is a continuel cryeng of my soule to Jesu; and neuerþeles, oure Lord makeþ straunge a while and cometh not, crye I neuer so fast. For he is syker inogh of his lufer þat he wil not turnen aȝen fully to werdly lufe; he may no sauour haf þerinne and þerfore abydeth he þe lenger.

Bot at þe last whan he wil he cometh aȝen, ful of grace and sothfastnes, and visiteth þe soule þat langwysseth in desyre by syghynges of lufe to his presence, and toucheth it and enoynteth it ful softly with þe oyle of gladnes, and maketh it sodeynly hole from al pyne. And þan cryeth þe soule to Jesu in gostly voyce with a glad herte þus: *Oleum effusum nomen tuum*. Oyle ȝetted is þi name Jesu. Þi name is Jesu, þat is hele. Þan as long as I fele my soule sore and seke for synne, pyned with þe heuy birþen of my body, sory and dredend for perils and wrecchednes of þis lyf, so long Lord Jesu þi name is oyle spared, not oyle ȝoted to me. Bot whan I fele my soule sodeynly touched with þe lyght of þi grace, heled and softed from al filthe of synne, conforted in lufe and in lyght with gostly strengthe and gladnes vnspekable, þan may I sey with lysty lufyng and gostly myrthe to þe: Oyle ȝeten is þi name Jesu to me. For by þe effecte of þi gracyous visityng I fele wele of þi name þe trew expownyng: þu art Jesu hele; for only þi gracyous presence heleth me fro sorwe and fro synne. f. 104r Blissed is þat soule | þat is ay felably fed in felyng of lufe in his presence, or is born vp by brennende desyre to him in his absence. A wyse lufer is he and a wele taght þat sadly and reuerently hath him in his presence, and louely beholdeþ him withouten dissolute lyghtnes, and paciently and esyly bereth him in his absence, withouten venymous despeyre and ouer pyneful bitternes.

43 þe] *om.* H$_6$ wantyng] waytynge As, lackyng LdT a] *om.* Pl 44 Jesu] Dominum Jesum Christum Lat. makeþ] it *add.* RMLdPlT straunge] stronge RH$_6$MLd a while] *canc.* H, *om.* LwW, in hoc tempore Lat. 45 wil] wold LwLd 46 fully/to werdly lufe] H$_7$RLB$_3$SrAEPH$_6$CcMPl, *rev.* HH$_5$AsWsLwLdTW, fully B fully] wilfulli Sr 47 abydeth he] *rev.* LdT abydeth] bidith T 48 at þe] atte As and] H$_7$RLB$_3$SrEPH$_6$CcMPl, of *add.* HBH$_5$AsWsLwAELdTW 49 langwysseth] langureþ Sr in/. . ./by] *rev.* Cc 50 syghynges] siȝyng Ld, sechinge T 51 ful] wel LB$_3$P, *om.* Pl softly] ofte *prec.*, *canc.* L gladnes] g- *prec.*, *canc.* Sr it] *om.* As 52 voyce] wyse Ld 53 þus] Cant. i° *add.* BLEPTW tuum] Can. 1 *add.* Ld Oyle] þat is *prec.* E ȝetted] H$_7$HRSrLwM, ȝet A, ȝoten LB$_3$EPH$_6$`W$^{G}$´, ȝetyn out BWs, ȝettynge out H$_5$, outȝetyd Cc, outȝete LdT, yshedde AsW Jesu . . . is$^1$ (l. 54)] *om.* As Jesu] *om.* LdTW 54 hele] helþe Ld, oyle CcT soule] *om.* M 55 `heuy´ B$_3$ sory] sore M 56 perils] peril T Jesu] *om.* BLdT 57 spared] spareþ As, spred H$_6$, closyd B ȝoted] H$_7$HRBSrLwMPl, ȝet A, ȝoten LB$_3$EPH$_6$, ȝettyde out H$_5$Ws, outȝetun LdT, yshed W, casteþ it As ⌜sodeynly . . . grace (l. 58)⌝ L sodeynly] so *prec.* LB$_3$P 58 lyght of] *om.* B þi] H$_7$RSrACcMPlW, *om.* HBH$_5$LB$_3$AsWsLwEPH$_6$LdT, tue Lat. filthe]

wantyng of my gostly strengþ, is a continuel cryeng of my soule to Ihesu; and nerþeles oure Lord makiþ straunge [a whyle] and comiþ not, cry I neuer so fast. For he is sikir inowȝ of his lufer þat he wil not turn ageyn to wordly luf fully; he may no sauour han þerin and þerfor abidiþ he þe lenger.

Bot at þe last when he wil he comyth ageyn, ful of grace and of soþfastnes, and visiteþ þe soule þat langueshþ in desire bi sikynges of luf to his presence, and touchiþ it and anoyntith it ful softely wiþ þe oyle of gladnes, and makiþ it sodeynly hool fro alle pyne. And þan crieth the soule to Ihesu in gostely voyce with a gladd herte thus: *Oleum effusum nomen tuum*. Oyle ȝotted is þi name Ihesu. Þi name is Ihesu, þat is hele. Þan as longe as I fele my soule sore and seke for
28r synne, pyned wiþ þe heuy birþen of my body, sory and dredende | for periles and wrecchednes of þis life, so longe Lorde Ihesu þi name is oile sparid, not oile ȝottede to me. Bot whan I fele my soule sodeynly touched with þe liȝt of grace, heled and softed fro alle þe filþe of synne, conforted in lufe and in liȝt with gostly strenþe and gladnes vnspekable, þan may I say with lysty louynge and gostly miȝt to þe: Oile ȝotted is þi name Ihesu to me. For bi þe effecte of þi gracious visitynge I fele wel of þi name þe trewe exponynge, þat art Ihesu hele; for oonly þi gracious presence heliþ me fro sorowe and fro synne. Blissed is þat soule þat is ay fed in felynge of luf in his presence, or is borne vp bi desire to him in his absence. A wise lufer is he and a wel taȝt þat sadly and ⸢reuerently⸣ haþ him in his presence, and lufly biholdiþ him withoute dissolute liȝtnes, and paciently and esily beriþ him in his absence withoute venymous despeire and ouer pynful bitternes.

H$_7$RLB$_3$AsSrAPH$_6$CcMPl, þe *prec.* HBH$_5$WsLwELdTW   59 conforted] and *prec.* W   60 may I] *rev.* Cc   lufyng] loue B$_3$, laude Lat.   and] of Pl, with *add.* As   myrthe] H$_7$RSrACcMPlW, miȝt HBH$_5$LB$_3$AsWsLwPH$_6$LdT, *om.* E, iocunditate Lat.   61 ȝeten] H$_7$BLB$_3$EPH$_6$`W^{G}', ȝottid HRSrLwCcMPl, ȝettyde out H$_5$AsWs, outȝotun LdT, yshed W, ycaste A   þe] *om.* M   62 trew expownyng] trouthe expungnyd Cc   þu] H$_7$RBLB$_3$SrAEPMLdPlT, þat HH$_5$WsLwLdW, þat þou AsH$_6$Cc, tu Lat.   Jesu hele] *rev.* LP   hele] helþe LdT, hoole As, *om.* Cc   63 gracious presence] *rev.* HBH$_5$Ld [H *marked for trsp.*]   synne] peccatis Lat.   64 þat] þe LB$_3$EP   ay . . . fed] fedde euere As   ay] H$_7$HRH$_5$WsCcM, euere BAsLwEH$_6$PlW, alwey SrALdT, *om.* LB$_3$P, semper Lat.   felably] H$_7$RLB$_3$SrAEH$_6$CcMPl`W^{G}', *om.* HBH$_5$AsWsLwLdTW, sensibiliter Lat.   65 brennende] H$_7$RLB$_3$SrAEPH$_6$CcMPl, *om.* HBH$_5$AsWsLwLdTW, ardens Lat.   to] vnto As   66 a] H$_7$HRH$_5$AsSrWsLwACcLdPlT, om. LB$_3$EPH$_6$MW   taght] doctus seu instructus Lat.   ⸢reuerently⸣ H   hath] behavith Cc   67 his] *om.* RM   68 him] *om.* Cc   in his absence/withouten . . . bitternes (l. 69)] *rev.* T   withouten] ony *add.* Cc   69 bitternes] amaritudine vel tristicia Lat.

þis chaungeablyte of absence and presence of Jesu þat a soule feleth is not perfeccyon of þe soule, ne it is not ageyns þe grace of perfeccyon or of contemplacyon, bot in so mykel perfeccyon is þe lesse. For þe more lettyng þat þe soule hath of itself fro contynuele felyng of grace, þe lesse is þe grace, and þogh neuerþeles ȝit is þe grace in hitself grace of contemplacyon. þis chaungeabilte of absence and presence falleth as wele in state of perfeccyon as in þe state of bygynnyng, bot in anoþer maner. For ryght as þer is diuersite of felynge in þe presence of grace atwix þese two states, ryght so is þer in þe absence of grace. And þerfore he þat knoweth not þe absence of grace is redy to ben disceyued, and he þat kepeth not þe presence of grace is vnkend to þe visiteng, wheþer he be in þe state of begynners or of perfyte. Neuerþeles þe more stabilnes þat þer is in grace, vnhurt and vnbroken, þe lufelyer is þe soule, more lyke vnto him in whom is no chaungeablite, as þe Apostle seyth. And it is ful semely þat þe soule spouse be lyke to Jesu spouse in maners and in vertus, ful acordende to him in stablenesse of perfyte lufe. Bot þat falleth seldam, now-whare bot in þe speciale spouse.

For he þat perceyueth no chaungeablete in felyng of his grace, bot ay ylyke hole and stable, vnbroken and vnhurt as him þenkeþ, he is oyþer ful perfyte or ellis he is ful blynde. He is ful perfyte þat is sequestred fro al fleschly affeccyons and commoneng of creatures, and al menes are broken away of corrupcion and of synne atwix Jesu and his soule, fully oned to him with softnes of lufe. Bot þis is only grace

70 chaungeablyte] chaungeable Cc   of[2] . . . Neuerþeles (45/5)] *om.* R (*probably six folios missing*)   71 is[1]] nys As, it Ld   perfeccyon[1]] þe *prec.* As   ne] *om.* H$_5$AsWs   72 perfeccyon is] H$_7$RLB$_3$SrLwAEPH$_6$CcMPlW, *rev.* HBH$_5$AsWsLwLdTW, is it As   þe[1]] *om.* Ld   73 lettyng] *om.* Sr   þe] H$_7$ACcMPl, a HH$_5$LB$_3$AsSrWsLw-EPH$_6$LdTW   itself] himselfe AsT, the self Cc   74 þe[1] . . . grace[1]] *om.* LB$_3$P   þogh neuerþeles ȝit] H$_7$LB$_3$EPH$_6$CcMPl, þawȝ `ȝ´it nerþeles H^c, þouȝ ȝet nerþeles BLw, þawȝ it nerþeles H°, neuerþeles it As, ȝit neuerþeles A, þoo Sr, ȝit LdTW, þowȝ þe grace be lytyl bycause of þe lettynge þat þe soule felyþ ofte syþe in hitself, neþeles H$_5$Ws, et tamen non minus Lat.   ȝit] *rep.*, *canc.* Pl   is/þe . . . hitself] *rev.* H$_5$WsCc   hitself] the self Cc grace[3]] þe AsCc   75 þis] is As   chaungeabilte] chaungeablenesse Cc   and] of T 76 as] al B$_3$Lw   state[1]] the *prec.* W   state of perfeccyon . . . bygynnyng] perfectorum . . . incipiencium Lat.   þe] H$_7$LSrEPH$_6$CcMPl, *om.* HBH$_5$B$_3$AsWsLwALdTW   77 þer is diuersite] diuersite is As   þe] *om.* M   78 atwix] H$_7$HLSrLwPCc, atween H$_6$, bytwyxte BB$_3$AsEMLdPlW, bytwene H$_5$WsAT   þese] þe`s´ E, thos M    two] *om.* M    is þer] *rev.* AsSrH$_6$T    þe] *om.* M    of] contemplacioun of As    79 not] *om.* As    grace] he *add.* Cc redy . . . is (l. 80)] *om.* Lw    80 disceyued] resceyued As    `he´ Cc, *om.* M   vnkend] vnknowed Sr   81 visiteng] diuine visitacioni Lat.   þe] *om.* MW   begynners] begynnyngis As, begynnyng Cc   of[2]] þe *add.* As, *om.* LwCcW   perfyte] louers *add.* H$_5$Ws 82 þe] *om.* M   stabilnes] sta- *prec.* M   þer] *om.* A   83 lufelyer] loueare B   more] H$_7$LB$_3$SrPCc, and *prec.* HBH$_5$AsLwEH$_6$MLdPlTW, and þe *prec.* WsA, et similior Lat.

þis chaungabilite of absence and presence of Ihesu þat a soule feliþ is not perfeccioun of þe soule, ne it is not ageyns þe grace of perfeccioun or of contemplacioun, bot in so mikel is perfeccioun þe lesse. For þe more lettynge þat a soule haþ of itself fro continuel felynge of grace, þe lesse is þe grace, and þouȝ `ȝ´it nerþeles is þe grace in itself grace of contemplacioun. þis chaungabilite of absence and presence falliþ as wel in stat of perfeccioun as in state of bigynnynge, bot in anoþer maner. For riȝt as þer is diuersite of felynge in þe presence of grace atwix þese two states, riȝt so is þer in þe absence of grace. And þerfor he þat knowith not þe absence of grace is redy to be desceifid, and he þat kepiþ not þe presence of grace is vnkynde to þe visitynge, wheþer he be in þe state of bigynners or of perfiȝte. Nerþeles þe more stabelnes þat þer is in grace, vnhurt and
28v vnbroken, þe luflier | is þe soule and more like vnto him in whom is no manere chaungabilite, as þe Postel seiþ. And it is ful semely þat þe soule spouse be like to Ihesu spouse in maners and in vertues, ful acordant to him in stabelnes of perfit lufe. But þat falliþ seldom, now`ȝ´here bot in þe special spouse.

For he þat perceifiþ no chaungabilite in felynge of his grace, bot ilike hool and stable, vnbroken and vnhurt as him þinkiþ, he is ouþer ful perfit or ful blynde. He is perfit þat is sequestred fro alle fleschly affeccions and comunynge with of alle creatures, and alle menes are broken awey of corupcioun and of synne atwix Ihesu and his soule, fully oned to him with softnes of luf. Bot þis is only grace aboue mans

lyke] is *add.* As   vnto] to ALdT   84 chaungeablite] H_7W, more *prec.* M, manere *prec.* Σ [maner of H_5AsWs], mutabilitas seu mutacio Lat.   Apostle seyth] apostles say the W   85 soule] *canc. seq.* H_7, *om.* W   spouse] spousesse LdT, to Jesu *add.* Cc   lyke] full *prec.* As   spouse[2]] his *prec.* As   in[2]] *om.* H_6 86 acordende] H_7LB_3SrLwAEPH_6CcW, acordant HBH_5AsWsLwMLdPlT   þat] it LB_3P   87 now-whare] H_7LB_3SrAEPCcPl, now`ȝ´here H[c], now here H°BH_5AsWsLwMLdTW, ellis where H_6, nisi Lat.   þe] *om.* M   spouse] spousesse LdT   88 no] non As, not Ld   his . . . ylyke (l. 89)] ⌜his . . . i⌝like L   89 ay] H_7LPCc, euer B_3EH_6Pl, alwey SrA, al M, *om.* HBH_5AsWsLwLdTW, semper Lat.   ylyke] alyk SrCc   hole and stable] *rev.* LB_3EPH_6 vnbroken] þowȝ it be broken As   and vnhurt] *om.* H_5Ws   90 oyþer] *om.* Cc   ellis he is] H_7LB_3SrAEPH_6CcPl, ellys BLdT, *om.* HH_5AsWsLwMT   he is] *rev.* Pl   ful[2]] ryth Cc   ful[3]] H_7BLB_3SrAEPH_6Cc-MLdPlT`W[G´], *om.* HH_5AsWsLwW   91 sequestred] only *add.* As   commoneng] kunnynge As, comounnyngis Sr, communicacione Lat.   of creatures and] *om.* As   of] with of HBLw [with *canc.* Lw]; wiþ Ld   creatures] H_7LB_3SrAEPH_6CcMPl, alle *prec.* HBH_5WsLwLdTW, creaturarum Lat.   92 al] *om.* M   broken] and *add.* H_6 away] *om.* Pl   synne] synnes T   atwix] H_7HLSrLwEPM, atwyn Cc, bytwexte B$H_5$$B_3$AsWs-MLdPlW, bitwen A$H_6$T   93 oned] ȝouen As   softnes] sothfastnes SrT   Bot . . . kend (l. 94)] *om.* Cc   `is´ L

f. 104^{v} abofe mannes kend. He is ful blynd | þat feyneth him in grace withouten gostly felynge of Goddys inspiracyon, and setteth himself in maner of a stablenesse, as he were ay in felyng and in werkyng of speciale grace, demende þat al is grace þat he doth and feleth withouten and withinnen, þenkend þat what he euer speke or do [is grace], holdende himself vnchaungeable in specyalte of grace. If þer be ony swilk, as I hope þer is none, he is ful blynde in felynge of grace.

Bot þan myght þu seyen þus: þat we schul only lyfen in trowthe and not coueyten gostly felynges ne rewarden hem if þei comen, for þe Apostle seyth: *Justus ex fide viuit*. Þat is: þe ryghtwys man lyfeth in trowthe. Vnto þis I sey þat bodily felynges, be þei neuer so confortable, we schul not coueyten, ne mykel rewarde if þei comen. Bot gostly felynges swilk as I speke of nowe, if þei come in þe maner as I hafe seyd byfore, we schul ay desyren: þat are sleyng of al werdly lufe, opnynge of þe gostly eye, purete of þe spirit, pees in conscience, and al oþer before seyd. We schul coueyten to felen ay þe lyfly inspiracyon of grace made by þe gostly presence of Jesu in oure soule, if þat we myghten, and for to haue him ay in oure syght with reuerence, and ay felen þe swetnes of his lufe by a wonderful homlynesse of his presence. Þis schuld ben oure lyf and oure felynge in grace, after þe mesure of his ȝifte in whom al grace is, to summe more and to sum lesse, for his presence is feled in dyuers maner wyse als he vowcheth safe. And in þis we schul lyfen and werken al þat longeth to vs for to werken, for withouten þis we schul not kun lyfen. For ryght as þe soule is lyf of þe body, ryght so Jesu is lyf of þe soule

94 mannes kend] mankynde T þat] and LB$_{3}$EPH$_{6}$ him in] *rev.* LdT 95 gostly] grace *add.*, *canc.* L Goddys] *om.* As and] þat E 96 maner] H$_{7}$LB$_{3}$AsSrAEPH$_{6}$CcMPl, a *prec.* HBH$_{5}$AsWsLwLdTW. a] H$_{7}$LB$_{3}$SrEPH$_{6}$M, *om.* HBH$_{5}$AsWsLwACcLdPlTW ay] H$_{7}$HH$_{5}$LWsPCcM, euere BB$_{3}$AsLwEH$_{6}$PlW, alwey SrALdT in[3]] þe *add.* Sr, *om.* H$_{6}$ 97 demende . . . grace] *om.* As al] *om.* M he] *om.* M 98 þat] *om.* H$_{5}$AsWs what he euer] H$_{7}$, whateuere he BH$_{6}$, what so euere þat he Sr, what so euer he Σ `he´ Cc speke or do] H$_{7}$, *rev.* Σ [doþ oþer spekeþ A] is grace] *om.* H$_{7}$, est gracia Lat. 99 holdende . . . grace (l. 100)] *om.* As holdende . . . grace[2]] *om.* B$_{3}$ `If . . . grace (l. 100)´ H^{c}, *om.* H°H$_{5}$WsCc 100 is[1]] be LwTW in felynge] *om.* Sr 101 `þan´ H$_{6}$ schul] H$_{7}$, schulde Σ only lyfen] H$_{7}$, *rev.* Σ trowthe] feyþ B, bileue A 102 felynges] þinges Sr hem] *om.* Sr if] þow B 103 seyth] þus *add.* LdT, Hebr. 10 *add.* BLEPLdTW þat is] *om.* T in] be Cc 104 trowthe] feyþ B, bileue A, eþer belyue *add.* Ld Vnto] As to H$_{5}$Ws, To A 105 `not´ Cc, myche *add.* T ne] *om.* As mykel rewarde] *rev.* W rewarde] hem *add.* LB$_{3}$EP if] þowȝ B 106 Bot] with As nowe] riȝt *prec.* As, *om.* LwW þe] þat As maner] name H$_{6}$ 107 as . . . byfore] *om.* As seyd] of *add.* LdT byfore] *om.* Cc schul] scholde W ay] H$_{7}$HBH$_{5}$LWsPCcM, euer B$_{3}$AsLwEH$_{6}$PlW, alwey SrALdT desyren] þo þyngges *add.* H$_{5}$Ws are] alwey Sr sleyng] sleekynge Sr, skelyng M of] H$_{7}$HBAsSrLwAH$_{6}$CcMLdPlTW, *om.* H$_{5}$LB$_{3}$WsEP 108 lufe] openyng of þe gostly luf *add.*, *canc.* H, þe

kynde. He is ful blynde þat feyniþ him in grace withouten gostly felynge of Goddis inspiracioun, and settiþ himself in a maner of stabelnes, as he wer ay in felynge and in wirking of special grace, demande þat al is grace þat he doþ and feliþ withouten and withinnen, þenkand þat what-so-euere he do or speke is grace, holdende himself vnchaungeable in specialte of grace. `If þer be ony sich, as I hope þer is none, he is ful blynde in feling of grace.´

Bot þan miȝt þou seien þus: þat we schulde lifen only in trouþe and not coueiten gostly felynges ne rewarden hem if þei comen, for þe Apostle seiþ: *Justus ex fide viuit*. þat is: þe riȝtwis man lifiþ in trowþ. Vnto þis I sey þat bodily felynges, be þei neuer so confortable, we schul not coueiten, ne mikel rewarden if þei comen. Bot gostly felynges swilk as I speke of nowe, if þei come in þe maner as I hafe seide before, we schul ay desiren: þat arne sleenge of alle werdly luf, opnynge of þe gostly eiȝe, purtee of spirit, pees in conscience, and alle
29r oþer bifore seide. We schul coueiten to | felen ay þe lifly inspiracioun of grace made bi þe gostly presence of Ihesu in oure soule, if þat we miȝten, and for to han him ay in oure siȝt with reuerence, and ay felen þe swetnes of his lufe by a wondirful homlynes of his presence. þis schulde ben oure lif and oure felynge in grace, after þe mesure of his gifte in whom al grace is, to summe more and to summe lesse, for his presence is feled in diuers maner wise as he vouchiþsafe. And in þis we schulde life and wirken þat longiþ to vs so to werken, for withouten þis we schulde not kun lifen. For riȝt as þe soule is þe lif of þe body, riȝt so Ihesu is lyfe of þe soule bi his gracious presence.

whiche ben openynge of þe gostly lufe, openynge of þe gostly *add.* H_5Ws [lufe . . . gostly *canc.* H_5], and *add.* As   purete] pouer As   þe] H_7, *om.* Σ   spirit] and *add.* As   in] of LwW   109 schul] shulde AsW, alwey *add.* T   to felen/ay] *rev.* H_5WsAH_6Pl, *om.* T   ay] H_7HH_5LWsPCcM, euere BAsLwEH_6PlW, alwey SrALd, *om.* B_3 þe lyfly] in loue þurgh As   lyfly] heuenly Pl   110 soule] soulis A, animabus Lat.   111 if . . . myghten] *om.* Lat.   þat] *om.* H_5Ws   haue] *rep.* Ws, louen M   him ay] *rev.* As   ay] H_7HH_5LWsPCcM, euere BB_3AsAEH_6Pl, alwey SrLdT, *om.* LwW   ⌜oure⌝ L, *om.* As   syght] *corr. fr.* desiȝte Pl   112 ay] H_7HH_5LWsPCcM, euere BB_3AsLwEH_6PlW, alwey SrALdT   felen] felynge As, to *prec.* E   þe] þat Pl, *om.* As   lufe] loke As   a] *om.* Pl   113 lyf] loue As   114 grace] and *add.* As   whom] `is´ *add.* Pl   is] *om.* Pl, for *add.* As   115 and] *om.* M   feled] felynge As   in] bi Ld   maner] of *add.* H_5AsWs   116 þis] wise *add.* A   we schul] *rev.* A   schul] $H_7H_5LB_3$AsSrWsAEPH_6CcM, schulde HBLwLdPlTW, debemus Lat.   al] H_7BLB_3Sr-AEPH_6CcMPl, *om.* HH_5AsWsLwLdTW, quicquid Lat.   þat . . . werken (l. 117)] *om.* ALdT   117 for] H_7BLB_3SrEPH_6CcMPl, so HH_5WsLdT, *om.* LwW   þis] grace *add.* As   schul] H_7AsAEMPl, schul`d´ Sr, schulde HBH_5LB_3WsLwPH_6LdTW, nesciemus Lat.   118 lyf[1]] H_7BLB_3SrAEPH_6CcMLdPlT, þe *prec.* HH_5WsLwW, in þe *prec.* As   Jesu is] *rev.* LwW   lyf[2]] loue As, þe *prec.* H_5Ws

by his gracyous presence. And neuerþeles þis maner of felyng, be it neuer so mykel, it is ȝit bot trowthe as in rewarde of þe fulnes þat schal ben of þe self Jesu in þe blisse of heuene.

Lo, þis felyng we schulde desyren, for ilk a soule resonable oweth for to coueyten with al þe myght of it neghhyng to Jesu and onyng to him, þurgh felyng of his gracyous vnseable presence. How þat presence is feled, it may `betere´ be knowen by experyence þan by
f. 105[r] ony wrytyng, for it | is þe lyf and þe lufe, þe myght and þe lyght, þe ioye and þe rest of a chosen soule. And þerfore he þat hath ones sothfastly feled it he may not forberen it withouten pyne; he may not vndesyren it, it is so gode in itself and so confortable. What is more confortable to a soule here þan to be drawen oute þurgh grace fro þe vile noye of þe werdly besynes and fro felth of fleschly desyres and fro veyn affeccyon of alle creatures, into reste and softenes of gostly lufe, priuely perceyuende þe gracyous presence of Jesu, feleabely fed with fauour of his vnseable blissed face? Sothly no thynge—me thenketh—no thyng may make þe soule of a lufer ful myrye bot þe gracyous presence of Jesu as he kan schewen him to a clene soule. He is neuer more heuy ne sory bot þan whan he is with himself in fleschlynes; he is neuer ful glad ne myrye bot whan he is oute of himself fro as he was with Jesu in gostlynes. And ȝit is þat no ful myrthe, for ay þere hangeth an heuy lumpe of bodily corrupcyon on his soule, and bereth it doun and mikel letteth þe gostly gladnes, and þat mote ay be whylis it is in þis lyf.

Bot neuerþeles, for I speke of chaungeablete in grace, how it cometh and goth, þat þou mystake it not þerfore, I mene not of þe

119 of] H$_7$LB$_3$AsSrAEPH$_6$MCcPlT, *om.* HBH$_5$WsLwLdW 120 it is/ȝit] *rev.* Pl is] nys As ⌜ȝit bot⌝ L trowthe] feyþ B, bileue ALd þe fulnes] þe felynge H$_5$Ws, þat HLwW, *om.* As 121 self] same WsT 122 we schulde] H$_7$, *rev.* Σ schulde] schul HBSrLw desyren for] felen in As ilk a] H$_7$HM, eche a LB$_3$AsEP, ech H$_6$Ld, euery BH$_5$SrWsLwACcPl, eueryche T, eueryche a W soule resonable] *rev.* AsLdT oweth] *om.* As 123 for] *om.* Sr myght] H$_7$, miȝtes Σ, viribus Lat. of it] þerof Sr it] his Ld 124 vnseable presence] *rev.* M vnseable] *om.* As 125 `betere´ *interl., d.h.* H$_7$ by[1]] wiþ Pl 126 ony] al As lyf] of þe soule *add.* T lufe] soule B$_3$ myght/. . ./lyght] *rev.* T 127 `a´ Pl hath] H$_7$HBH$_5$LB$_3$AsWsLwEPPlW, *om.* SrAH$_6$CcMLdT ones sothfastly] H$_7$LB$_3$SrLwAEPH$_6$CcMLdPlT, *rev.* HBH$_5$AsWsW 128 feled] feliþ SrCcT forberen . . . not[2]] *om.* M ⌜not[2] . . . gode⌝ L 129 vndesyren] but desire A `it[2]´ *interl.* H itself] his silfe Ld 130 to[2]] for *prec.* As þurgh] with T, *corr. fr.* wiþ B$_3$ fro] of As 131 vile noye of] silence and T vile noye] veyn ioye Sr, disese Cc vile] wondurful AMPl þe] H$_7$H$_5$AsWs, *om.* Σ fro] H$_7$LB$_3$SrAEPH$_6$CcMPl, þe As, *om.* HBH$_5$WsLwLdTW of] *om.* M fleschly] H$_7$BLB$_3$SrAEPH$_6$CcMPlT`W[G]´, þe fleiscli Ld, þe As, *om.* HH$_5$WsLwW, carnalium Lat. 132 affeccyon] , affections LdPlT, occupacioun B and] into *add.* As softenes] soþnes Sr gostly] g- *prec.*, *canc.* Sr 133 fed] For As 134 fauour] sauour E

And neuerþeles þis maner felynge, be it neuer so mikel, it is ȝit bot trouþ as in rewarde of [þe fulnes] þat schal ben of þe self Ihesu in þe blis of heuen.

Loo, þis felynge schul we desiren, for ilk a soule resonable owiþ for to coueite with alle þe miȝtes of it neiȝenge to Ihesu and onynge to him, þurgh felynge of his graciouse vnseable presence. How þat presence is feled, it may better be knowen bi experience þan bi ony writynge, for it is þe lif and þe lufe, þe miȝt and þe liȝt, þe ioie and þe rest of a chosen soule. And þerfore he þat haþ soþfastly ones feled it he may not forberen it withouten pyne; he may not vndesiren it, `it´ is so good in itself and so confortable. What is more confortable to a soule here þan for to be drawe out þurȝ grace fro þe vile noye of wordly bisynes and filþe of desires, and fro veyn affeccioun of alle creatures, into reste and softnes of gostly lufe, pryuely perceifande þe
9v gracious presence of Ihesu, felablely fed with sauour of his vnseable | blissed face? Soþly noþinge, me þinkiþ. Noþinge may make þe soule of a lufer ful merye bot þe gracious presence of Ihesu as he kan schewen him to a clene soule. He is neuer heuy ne sory bot whan he is with himself in fleschlynes; he is neuer ful glad ne mery bot whan he is out of himself f⌜er⌝, as he was with Ihesu in his gostlynes. And ȝit is þat no ful mirþe, for ay þer hongiþ an heuy lumpe of bodily corupcioun on his soule, and beriþ it doune and mikil lettiþ þe gostly gladnes, and þat mot ay be whils it is here in þis life.

Bot nerþeles, for I speke of chaungabilite of grace, how it comiþ and goþ, þat þu mistake it not, þerfore I mene not of þe comune grace

his] graciouse and *add.* T vnseable] inuisible A, vnsemblale and As Sothly] truly Cc 135 no thyng] *om.* As of . . . myrye] to loue As ful] so Cc myrye] of myrthe TW gracyous] fulle myrþe of þe *prec.* As 136 schewen] schewend M him to] *rev.* As him] himself H_6 to] vnto T `soule´ Cc is] nys As 137 more] *om.* As heuy . . . neuer (l. 138)] *om.* Pl heuy ne sory] *rev.* $H_6$ þan] $H_7LB_3$SrEPMPl, *om.* $HBH_5$AsWsLw-$AH_6$CcLdTW 138 ful] so Cc ne] and Cc myrye] ful *prec.* H5WsPl, in ful myrþe As fro] $H_7$MPl, f⌜er⌝ $H^c$, ⌜fer⌝ L, fer[re] EPLw`W^G´ (*canc.* Lw), ffro al fleschlynes H_5Ws, fro þer A, fro þe world so Sr, fro þe world H_6, and Ld, fre B [*also marg. gl. d.h.* H_7, `W^G´], *om.* B_3CcTW, liber Lat. was] whan he was *add.* H_5Ws 139 gostlynes] H_7LB_3AsSr-$AEPH_6$CcMPl, his *prec.* HBH_5WsLwLdTW, spiritualitate Lat. no ful myrthe] not ful merye H_5WsLd no] non As ay] H_7HH_5LWsPCcM, euere BB_3AsLwEH_6PlW, alwey SrALdT 140 lumpe] masse A bodily] bodi Ld 141 doun] *om.* Cc mikel letteth] *rev.* T gostly . . . and] gladnesse of a gostly soule As gostly gladnes] *rev.* H_5Ws mote] schal H_6, it *add.* Sr, nede *add.* A ay] H_7HH_5LWsPCcM, euere BB_3AsLwEH_6PlW, alwey SrALdT. be] *corr. fr.* by Pl, so *add.* As, *om.* Sr 142 is] H_7LB_3SrAPH_6CcMPl, here *add.* HBH_5AsWsLwALdTW, permanet Lat. 143 of . . . mene (l. 144)] *om.* As in] H_7LB_3Sr-PH_6MPl, of HBH_5WsLwAECcLdTW, gracie Lat. 144 and] how it *add.* T mene] it *add.* M not] *om.* Cc þe] *om.* T common grace þat is had and felt in trowthe and in gode wil to God, withouten þe whilk hauyng and lastyng þerin no man may be safe, for it is in þe leste chosen soule þat lyfeth. Bot I mene of a specyale grace felt by inspiracyon of þe Holy Gost, in maner as it is byfore seyd. Þe common grace, þat is charite, lasteth hole what-so-euer a man do, as long as his wil and his entente is trewe to God, þat he wold not synnen dedly, ne þe dede þat he doth willfully is not forbed as for dedly synne, for þis grace is not lost bot þurgh dedly synne. And þan is it dedly synne whan his conscience witnesseth with avisement þat it is dedly synne and ȝit neuerþeles he doth it; or ellys his conscience is so f. 105^{v} blynded þat he holdeþ it no dedly synne þogh he do þat dede | wilfully þe whilk is forbede of God and of Holy Kirke as dedly synne.

Speciale grace, felt þurgh þe vnseable presence of Jesu, þat makeþ a soule a perfyte lufer, lesteth not ay ilyke hole in þe heynes of felyng, bot chaungeabily cometh and goth as I haue seyd. Þus oure Lord seyth: *Spiritus vbi vult spirat, et vocem eius audis, et nescis vnde veniat aut quo vadat*. Þe Holy Gost spyreth where he wille, and þou herest his voyce, bot þu wost not fro whom he cometh or whedere he goth. He cometh priuely sumtyme whan þu art lest ware of him, bot þou schalt wele knowen him or he go, for wonderfully he stereth and myghtyly he turneth þin herte into beholdyng of his godenes, and doth þin herte melten delytabilly as wex aȝens þe fyre into softenes of his lufe; and þis is his voyce þat he sowneth. Bot þan he goth er þu wyte it. For he withdraweth him sumwhat, not al bot fro excesse into soberte; þe heyghnes passeth bot þe substaunce and þe effect of þe grace dwelleth stille. And þat is as long as þe soule of a lufer kepeth

145 had and felt] *rev.* M, feled and hydde As trowthe] feyþ BLdT, bileue A, thouȝte M in^{2}] *om.* M 146 þe] *om.* AsH_6M þerin] þer is As no man may] þere ne mai no man As, may no man M no] *om.* Cc may] þat *prec.* A safe] sauyd LdT 147 lyfeth] is lyuyng E, electa Lat. a] H_7, *om.* Σ 148 felt] lest Sr inspiracyon] þe *prec.* As, inspiracionem specialem Lat. maner] H_7LB_3SrAEPH_6CcMPl, þe *prec.* HBH_5AsWsLwLdTW it is] I haue Pl byfore] afore BAsH_6 149 common] *The second extract in* Td *starts here* þat is] of As lasteth hole] þat is laste wyle As, with a man *add.* Td what-so-euer a man] whateuere a man soo As a man] he Td do] dothe M as] a As 150 his^{1}] he As, þe T his^{2}] *om.* Td God] wythout the whiche hauynge and lastynge *add.* LwW 151 dedly ne þe] *rep.* As þe] synne *add.*, *canc.* Pl doth wilfully] H_7BLB_3AsSrAEPH_6CcMLdPl, *rev.* HH_5WsLwTW forbed] of God *add.* T for] *om.* Td dedly] a *prec.* Sr 152 for . . . synne (l. 152] *om.* A for . . . synne^{2}] *om.* LwMPl grace] *om.* Cc `þurgh´ $W^{G}$, for LdTW dedly] *om.* H$H_5$AsWs is it] $H_7$HB$H_5$AsWsLwMPlT, *rev.* $LB_3$SrAEP$H_6$CcLdW 153 his] *om.* E it] *rep.*, *canc.* L, *om.* M 155 blynded] blynde MPlTd, blyned Ld no] non As þogh] alþawȝ HLwW, and *prec.* BAsLdT þat$^{2}$] þ⸢e⸣ $H^{c}$, þe LwW 156 `and of Holy Kirke´ H^{c}, *om.* H°BH_5WsLdTd, et Ecclesia Lat. of^{2}] *om.* LwTW Kirke] chirge *prec.*, *canc.* Pl synne] and þawȝ he doþ þat dede wilfully þe whilk is forbed *add.*, *canc.* H 157 felt] is y felid T,

þat is had and felt in trowiþ and in gode wil to God, withouten þe whilk hafenge and lastenge þerin no man may be sauf, for it is in þe lest chosen soule þat lifiþ. Bot I mene of special grace felt bi inspiracioun of þe Holy Gost, in þe manere as it is bifore seide. Þe comune grace, þat is charitee, lasteþ hool what-so-euere a man do, as longe as his wil and his entent is trew to God, þat he wulde not synne dedly, ne þe dede þat he wilfully doþ is not forbed as for dedly synne, for þis grace is not lost bot þurghe synne. And þanne is it dedly synne when his conscience witnesseþ with auisement þat it is dedly synne and ȝit nerþeles he doþ it; or elles his conscience is so blynded þat he holdiþ it no dedly synne alþawȝ he do þ⌜e⌝ dede wilfully þe whilk is forbed of God as dedly synne.

Special grace, felt þurȝ þe vnseable presence of Ihesu, þat makiþ a
130^{r} soule a perfit lufer, lasteþ not ay ilike hool in þe heiȝenes of felynge, | bot chaungably comiþ and goþ as I hafe seide bifore. Þus oure Lord seiþ: *Spiritus vbi vult spirat, et vocem eius audis, et nescis vnde veniat aut quo vadat*. Þe Holy Gost spiriþ where he wiþ and þou herest his voice, bot þou wost not when he comiþ ne whider he goþ. He comiþ pryueily sumtyme whan þu art lest war of him, bot þu schalt wel knowen him or he go, for wndirfully he stiriþ and miȝtily he turneþ þin herte into beholdynge of his godnes, and doþ þin herte melte delitably as wex ageyn þe fire into softnes of his lufe; and þis is þe voice þat he souniþ. Bot þan he goþ er þu wite it. For he wiþdrawiþ him sumwhat, not alle bot fro excesse into sobirte; þe heiȝenes passiþ bot þe substance and þe effecte of grace dwelliþ stille. And þat is as longe as þe soule of a lufer kepiþ him clene and falliþ not wilfully to

que sentitur Lat. þe] *om*. PlT vnseable] inuisible A, *om*. Lat. 158 a] *om*. As ay] H$_7$HH$_5$WsCcM, euere BAsLwEPlW, alwey SrALd, alwey euer T, *om*. LB$_3$PH$_6$ 159 chaungeabily] ch- *prec*., *canc*. Sr as . . . seyd] *om*. Td seyd] H$_7$LB$_3$SrAEPCcMPl, bifore *add*. HBH$_5$AsWsLwLdTW, for *add*. H$_6$Td, predixi Lat. oure Lord/seyth] *rev*. H$_6$ 160 seyth] Io. 3° *add*. BLEPLdTW, in Euangelio Lat. et^{2}] H$_7$HBH$_5$WsLwCcMLdTW, sed LB$_3$AsSrAEPH$_6$Pl, set Lat. 161 þe] þat is *prec*. E Gost] he *add*. Td spyreth] enspireþ AsAWc where] whome As herest . . . þu (l. 162)] *om*. A 162 fro whom] H$_7$, fro whennes LB$_3$EPH$_6$T, fro whanne BSrMLd, when HH$_5$AsWsLwACcLdWWc or] H$_7$LB$_3$SrAEPH$_6$MPl, ne HBH$_5$AsWsLwCcLdTWTdWc whedere] wheþer PlW 163 priuely sumtyme] *rev*. T of him] *om*. As. As *inserts* 42/115 and^{1} . . . 43/98 þe^{1} *here* 164 he^{1}] þou W wonderfully] wondirly H$_6$ 165 myghtyly] myȝtfully As he] *om*. W 166 doth] makith AEPlTWTdc delytabilly] delectably BLwTW softenes] soþefastnesse As 167 his^{2}] H$_7$LB$_3$SrAEPH$_6$CcPl, þe HBH$_5$AsWsLwMLdTWWc, eius Lat. er þu] here to As 168 it] *om*. PlTd al] in *prec*. LwW fro] for As excesse] al *prec*., *canc*. L into] in M 169 soberte] sobirnesse CcWc þe^{4}] H$_7$LB$_3$SrAEPH$_6$CcPl, *om*. HBH$_5$AsWsLwMLdTWWc 170 as^{1}] a B$_3$ a] þe H$_5$AsWs, *om*. M kepeth . . . and (l. 171)] *om*. Td him clene and falleth not wilfully to rykleshede or dissolucyon in fleschlynes, ne to outward vanyte, as sumtyme it doth þogh it haue no delyte þerin, for frelte of itself. Of þis chaungeabilte in grace speke I of now.

A commendacyon of preyer offred to Jesu in a soule contemplatif, and how stabelnes in preyer is a syker werk to stonden in, and how ilk felyng of grace in a chosen soule may be sayd Jesu, bote þe more clene þat þe soule is þe wurthier is þe grace. Capitulum xlii^{m}

T[h]e soule of a man whylis it is not towched þurgh special grace is blounte and boystous to gostly werk, and kan not þeron. It may not þerof for weyknes of itself; it is boþe colde and drye, vndeuowte and vnsauourye in itself. Bot þan cometh þe lyght of grace, and þurgh
f. 106^{r} touchynge makeþ it scharpe and sotel, redy and able to gostly werk, | and ȝefeth it a grete fredam and an hole redynesse and wil for to be buxum to alle þe sterynge of grace. For by openyng of þe gostly eye it is applyed al fully to grace, redy for to werken after þe grace stereth. And þan falleth it so sumtyme þat grace stereth þe soule for to preyen; and how þe soule preyeth þan schal I telle þe.

Þe most specyal preyer þat þe soule vseth and hath most confort in I hope is þe Pater noster, or ellis psalmes of þe Sawter; þe Pater noster for lewed, and psalmes and ympnes and oþer seruice of Holy Kyrke for lettred. Þe soule preyeth þan, not in maner as it dyd before, ne in common maner of oþer men by hyghnes of voyce or by renable spekyng oute, bot in ful grete stilnes of voyce and softnes of herte. For

171 falleth] *om.* M wilfully] *two-letter canc. seq.* H to] into H_6, in Td, þe *add.* SrCc, *om.* M rykleshede] rechlesnese AsWc or] of Sr 172 fleschlynes] H_7HH_5As-SrWsLwACcMLdTW, fleschlJeed LB_3EPH_6Pl ne] no Lw, and Td no] non As 173 frelte] fylþe As of] *om.* Ws itself] hymself Sr, the self Cc chaungeabilte] chaungid Cc speke . . . now] have I spokyn inow Cc speke I] I cese M 174 of now] *rev.* Td

Chapter 42 *title*: H_7LB_3SrAEPH_6MLdPlTW 'How a soule þat is not touchid wiþ no goostly grace is blent, boystus, weyke, drye, vndeuoute and vnsauoury in toucheing of anny goostly werke.' *d.h.* H How þe soule of man þe whiche is colde and vndeuout haþ nouȝt þe worchynge of þis grace, and how þe liȝt of grace geten to him aȝein stereþ him. As *om.* BH_5WsLwCcTd 1 A^{1}] *om.* Pl in] H_7LB_3SrEPH_6MPl, of ALdTW, ab Lat. 2 in . . . grace (l. 5)] etc. M 3 ilk] H_7, euery LB_3SrAEPH_6MLdPlTW 4 'clene' W^{G}, clenner TW þat] *om.* LdTW 6 The] Te H_7 'a' Ld, *om.* BLwMW not] *om.* Cc þurgh] H_7LB_3AsSrAEPH_6CcMPl, with HBH_5WsLwLdTWWc, per Lat. 7 blounte] dul A, eþer dulle *add.* Ld gostly werk] gostlynesse As and . . . þeron] *om.* CcWc It] *rep.*, *canc.* Pl, for *prec.* Cc 8 weyknes] febilnesse APlWc, leþynes Ld itself] hymself B, the self Cc 'it . . . itself (l. 9)' T^{G}, *om.* MTWc colde] olde W vndeuowte] *om.* Td 9 itself] the self Cc 10 makeþ it] it is mad AMPl it] *om.* Lw and^{1}] *om.* A redy] *om.* Td 'able' Pl 11 it a]

recleshede, or dissolucioun in fleschlynes, ne to outwarde vanyte, as sumtyme it doþ þawȝ it haue no delite þerin, for frelte of itselfe. Of þis chaungabilite in grace speke I of now.

[CHAPTER 42]

þe soule of a man whils it is not touched with special grace is blont and boistious to gostly werk, and can not þeron. It may not þerof for weiknes of itself; it is boþe colde and drye, vndeuoute and vnsauory in itself. Bot þan comiþ þe liȝt of grace, and þurȝ touchynge makiþ it scharpe and sotil, redy and able to gostly werk, and gifiþ it a gret fredam and an hool redynes in wil for to be buxum to alle þe styrynge of grace. [For by openynge of þe gostly eyȝe hit is applyed fully to grace], redy for to wirken after þat grace stiriþ. And þan falliþ it so sumtyme þat grace stiriþ þe soule for to preien; and how þe soule preieþ þan schall I telle þe.

þe most special preiere þat þe soule vseþ and haþ most confort in I
30v hope is `þe´ paternoster, | or elles psalmes of þe Sauter; þe
paternoster for lewde, and psalmes and ympnes and oþer seruice of Holy Kirke for lettred. þe soule preieþ þan, not in maner as it did bifore, ne in comune maner of men bi heiȝenes of voice or bi renable spekynge out, but in ful grete stilnes of voice and softnes of herte. For

om. Td it] *om.* LB_3P an] *om.* Td and[2]] H_7, in Σ, in Lat. wil] whille M 12 þe[1]] *om.* A sterynge] styryngges H_5SrWsLdPlTd, motibus Lat. For . . . grace[1] (l. 13)/redy . . . stereth] *rev.* TW For . . . grace[1] (l. 13)/redy] *rev.* Lw For . . . grace[1] (l. 13)] *om.* HH_5AsWsWc by] the Cc 13 fully] *om.* Pl `for to wirken . . . soule for (l. 14)´ $T^G W^G$ for] *om.* L$B_3$EP$H_6$ þe] $H_7$M, þat Σ grace[2]] þe *prec.* Td, `þat´ *add.* Lw stereth] þe soule *add.* TWWc 14 And . . . stereth] *canc.* Lw, *om.* AsSr falleth . . . sumtyme] sumtyme it falliþ so H_6 it] *om.* Td for] *om.* AsECc `to . . . how´ (l. 15) Lw 15 schal I] *rev.* $H_5$WsWc 16 þe[2]] a $B_3$ most[2]] þe *prec.* As 17 I hope] *om.* Td hope] trowe BA þe[1] . . . Sawter] *om.* ALd `þe[1]´ H^c, *om.* $H^o H_5$ noster] is *add.* Td 18 lewed] H_7HBAsSrACcMLdPl, þe *prec.* Pl, men *add.* H_5LB_3WsLwEPH_6TW psalmes] þe *prec.* Sr and[2] . . . Kyrke] *om.* Td ympnes] þe *prec.* Sr and[3]] for AsLw seruice] suche As, *om.* Lw 19 lettred] H_7HBAs-SrLwACcMLdPlTW, men *add.* H_5LB_3WsEPH_6, literatis siue clericis Lat. þan not] *rev.* SrH_6CcMTd þan] *om.* As maner] þe *prec.* As, a *prec.* Wc as it dyd] *rep.* A it] he A (*bis*) `ne´ B, *om.* LwW 20 oþer] H_7LB_3SrAEPH_6CcMPl, *om.* HBH_5AsWsLwLdTW, aliorum Lat. voyce] or softenesse *add.* B_3 renable] resonable LdPlWc 21 ful] *om.* PlT softnes] sothnesse Sr

why, his mende is not trubled ne taryed with outward thynges, bot hole gadred samen in itself, and þe soule is sette as it were in gostly presence of Jesu. And þerfore euerylk word and euerylk silable is sowned swetly, sauourly, and delytably, with ful acorde of mouthe and of hert. For why, þe soule is turned þan al into fyre of lufe, and þerfore ilk a worde þat it preyeth pryuely is lyke to a spark spryngand oute of a fyrebronde þat chawfeth al þe myghtes of þe soule and turneth hem into lufe, and ⌜heygh⌝neth hem so confortably þat þe soule listeth ay for to preyen and don non oþer þyng; þe more þat it preyeth, þe bettre it may, þe myghtyer it is. For grace helpeth þe soule wele and maketh al thyng lyght and esy, þat it list ryȝt wele for to psalmen and syngen þe louynges of God with gostly myrthe and heuenly delyte.

þis gostly werk is þe fode of þe soule, and þis preyere is of mykel vertu, for it wasteth and bryngeth to noght al þe temptacyons of þe fend, pryue and apert. It sleth al þe mynde and lykyng of þe werd and of fleschly synnes; it bereth vp þe body and þe soule fro pyneful felyng of wrecchednesse of þis lyf; it kepeth þe soule in felyng of grace
f. 106v and werkyng of lufe; and norischeth it ay ylyke hote and fresche as | stykkes norischen þe fyre; it putteth awey al yrknes and heuynes of hert and holdeth it in myrthe and in gostly gladnes. Of þis preyer spekeþ Dauid þus: *Dirigatur oracio mea sicut incensum in conspectu tuo.* Dressed be my preyer, Lord, as encens in þi syght. For ryght as encens þat is cast in þe fyre maketh swete smelle by þe reke styend vp

22 his] þe Td, is *prec.*, *canc.* E is] nys As ne] and BLdT 23 samen] H_7Pl, togeder HBH_5LB_3AsSrWsLwAEPH_6CcMLdTWTd in itself] *om.* Td itself] hymself Cc and] þerfore *add.* Td is] it Cc as it were] *om.* As in[2]] \`to´ *add.* L, into $B_3$P$H_6$ gostly] $H_7$L$B_3$SrAP$H_6$CcMPl, a *prec.* HB$H_5$AsWsLwLdTW, þe *prec.* E 24 Jesu] God Td word/. . ./silable] *rev.* L$B_3$EP$H_6$Td 25 sowned] shewed Wc, word and a *add.* As swetly sauourly] $H_7$, *rev.* Σ \`swetly´ W^G, swete W sauourly] and *add.* Td ful] *om.* H_5AsWs, \`al´ *prec.* $W^G$ mouthe] m- *prec.*, *canc.* Sr 26 of[1]] *om.* TTd why] *om.* CcWTdc þan] *om.* $H_5$AsWsM al] *om.* BWc into] to L$B_3$EP fyre] þe *prec.*, *canc.* H, þe *prec.* As \`of[2]´ H_6 27 ilk a] H_7HM, eche LB_3PH_6LdT, eche a As, euery BH_5SrWs-LwAECcPlW þat it preyeth] *om.* Td it preyeth] is preid H_6 preyeth pryuely] H_7, *rev.* Σ to] H_7AsSrAH_6CcMPl, vnto HBH_5LB_3WsLwLdW, *om.* T spark] H_7H_5CcMTd, spercle Σ spryngand] þat spryngeþ As 28 fyrebronde] fuyry brond BLd chawfeth] clanseþ LB_3AsPH_6, calefacit Lat. 29 hem[1]] alle *add.* Sr heyghneth] H_7, liȝtneþ Σ [lyȝteþ H_5WsLd, lyȝt B], illuminat Lat. hem[2]] *om.* Cc 30 listeth] likeþ Sr, *om.* B ay] H_7HBH_5LWsPCcM\`$W^G$´, euer $B_3$AsLwE$H_6$PlW, alwey SrALdT for] *om.* $H_5$Ws preyen] ben in preiynge Sr don] $H_7$HBSrLwA$H_6$CcMLdPlTW, to *prec.* $H_5$\`L´B_3AsWsEP non] no E þyng] þynk B þat] H_7, *om.* Σ 31 may] and *add.* B_3 32 wele[1]] so *prec.* Td and[1] . . . wele[2]/for . . . God (l. 33)] *rev.* AMPl and[1]] þat it Td maketh] helpith Cc thyng] þinges Pl, and makith it *add.* Cc þat] *om.* MPl

whi, his mende is not trobled ne taried with outewarde þinges, bot hol gedrid togeder in itself, and þe soule is set as it were in a gostly presence of Ihesu. And þerfor euery worde and euery silable is sowned sauourly, swetly and delitably, with ful acorde of mouþe and of herte. For whi, þe soule is turned þan al into fire of lufe, and þerfore ilk a worde þat it pryuely preieþ is like to a spercle spryngande out of a firebronde, þat chaufiþ alle þe mi3tes of þe soule and turneþ hem into lufe, and li3tneþ hem so confortably þat þe soule list ay for to preien and don non oþer þinge; þe more it preieþ, þe better it may, þe mi3tier it is. For grace helpiþ þe soule wel and makiþ al þinge li3t and esy, þat it list ri3t wel to psalmen and syngen þe louynges of God with gostly mirþe and heuenly delite.

þis gostly werk is fode of þe soule, and þis preier is of mikel vertue, for it wastiþ and bryngiþ to no3t alle temptacions of þe fende, pryuey and apperte. It sleeþ alle þe mende and þe likynge of þe worlde and of fleschly synnes; it beriþ vp þe body and þe soule fro pyneful felynge of wrecchednes of þis lif; it kepiþ þe soule in felynge of grace and wirkynge of luf; and norischiþ it ay ilike hote and fresche as stickes norische þe fire. It puttiþ awey al irkyng and heuynes of hert and
31r holdiþ it in mirþe and in gostly gladnes. Of þis preier | spekiþ Dauid þus: *Dirigatur oratio mea sicut incensum in conspectu tuo*. þat is: Dressed be my preier, Lorde, as encens in þi si3t. For ri3t as encens þat is kast in þe fire makiþ swet smel bi þe reke sti3ende vp to þe eire, ri3t so a

for] H$_7$BLB$_3$SrAEPH$_6$CcMLdPlT, *om.* HH$_5$AsWsLwW 33 to psalmen] seyn Cc syngen] to *prec.* AsE louynges] longynge As, preysinges AH$_6$ God] Jesu Cc with] to make AMPl and[2]] in LwW, so þat þer in hit hath *add.* APl 35 þe[1]] H$_7$LAEPCcMPl, *om.* HBH$_5$B$_3$AsSrWsLwH$_6$LdTW of[1]] for B of mykel] *rev.* A of[2]] a *add.* As 36 þe[1]] H$_7$B, *om.* Σ 37 and[1]] *om.* Ld apert] perte M and[2]] of M lykyng] H$_7$AsSrH$_6$, þe *add.* HBH$_5$LB$_3$WsLwAPCcMLdPlTWTd þe[2]] þis H$_6$ 38 fleschly] the *prec.* Cc synnes] synne As it . . . lyf (l. 39)] *om.* Td 39 felyng of[1]] *om.* T of[1]] and B wrecchednesse] miseriarum Lat. þis] *om.* LB$_3$P felyng of[2]] grace in felyng Cc 40 and[1]] in *add.* ECc it] *om.* LB$_3$AP ay . . . it (l. 42)] *om.* Td ay] H$_7$HBH$_5$LWsPCcM, euer B$_3$AsLwAEH$_6$PlW, alwey SrLdT and[3] . . . norischen (l. 41)] as flesche þat stynkeþ As 41 stykkes] as *prec.* H$_7$ norischen þe] norissheth LwW it] *om.* As awey] *om.* T al] *om.* B yrknes and] *om.* Cc yrknes] H$_7$, yrkyng HLSrLwEPMPlW, werynesse BH$_5$B$_3$WsAH$_6$LdT, grucchynge As and heuynes] *om.* A and] of Sr 42 `in[1]´ H$_6$ myrthe and in] *om.* A myrthe] mighte LwW, potencia Lat. in[2]] H$_7$HBH$_5$AsSrWsLw-AECcLdPlW, *om.* LB$_3$PH$_6$MT gladnes] g- *prec.* Sr Of . . . Jesu (l. 52)] *om.* Td 43 Dauid] Seint *prec.* T þus] Ps. 140° *add.* BLEPT 44 Dressed/be my preyer] H$_7$, *rev.* Cc, þat is *prec.* Σ [*incl.* Cc] my] *om.* As preyer] My power *add.* As Lord] *om.* Cc þi] e3e *add.* Pl For ryght] *om.* As 45 smelle] sauoure M reke] H$_7$HH$_5$LB$_3$Sr-WsLwAEPMW, smoke BAsH$_6$CcLdPlT styend vp] *rev.* Cc styend] rysynge B

to þe [eyre], ryght [so] a psalme, sauourly and softly songen or seyd in a brennend herte, ȝeldeth vp a swete smel to þe face of oure Lord Jesu and to al þe courte of heuene.

`And as´ þar dar no flesch-flye resten vpon þe pottis brynke boylend ouer þe fyre; ryght so may þer no fleschly delyte resten on a clene soule þat is happed and warmed al in fyre of lufe, boylend and plawend psalmes and louynges to Jesu. Þis is verrey preyere. Þis preyer is euermore herde of Jesu; it ȝeldeth graces to Jesu and resceyueth grace aȝen; it makeþ a soule homly and felawly with oure Lord Jesu and with alle þe aungels of heuene. Vse it whoso may, þe werk is gode in itself, and ful gracyous.

And þis maner preyer, þogh-al it be not ful contemplacyon in itself [ne þe werkyng of lufe by itself], neuerþeles it is a party of contemplacyon. For why, it may not be don on þis maner wyse bot in presence of grace þurgh opneng of þe gostly eye; and þerfore a soule þat hath þis fredam and þis gracyous felyng in preyer with gostly sauour and heuenly delyte, hath þe grace of contemplacyon in maner as it is. Þis preyer is a riche offerand filled al in fatnes of deuocyon, resceyued by aungeles and presented to þe face of Jesu. Þe preyer of oþer men þat are besyed in actyf werkes is made of two wordes: for þei oft-sythes formen in here hertes o wurd þurgh þenkyng of werdly besynes, `and´ sownen in her mouthe anoþer word of þe psalme songen or seyd; and neuerþeles if here entent be trew, ȝit is here preyer gode and medeful þogh it lak sauour and swetnes. Bot þis maner preyer offred of a man contemplatyf is made

46 to] into Cc   eyre] eye H$_7$LB$_3$P, aerem Lat.   so] *om.* H$_7$ a psalme] psalmys As   sauourly] sauery Ld   softly] gostly As, swetly Cc, deuote Lat.   or] ben As   49 `And as´ H$_7$, and as Cc, *om.* Σ   no] non B   flesch-flye] fleshle flie MLd, fle HH$_5$AsWs, musca Lat.   vpon] on LwAW   pottis] pyttys As   brynke] side A   boylend] and pleing *add.* E   50 ouer] on LwW   no] non As   fleschly] fleschflie LB$_3$P   on] H$_7$LB$_3$SrAPH$_6$CcMPl, vpon HBH$_5$AsWsLwELdTW   51 happed] H$_7$HAsSrLwAMPlW, lapped BH$_5$LB$_3$Ws-EPH$_6$, wrappid LdT, wappid Cc, cooperta Lat.   warmed al in] wrapped in a clene As   warmed] war and A   fyre of lufe] *rev.* As   fyre] the *prec.* LwW   and plawend] þus synge As, *om.* Lat.   52 plawende] H$_7$H`W$^{G}$´, pleyinge H$_5$LB$_3$SrWsAEPH$_6$CcMPl, rekynge B, seiyng LdT, blowynge LwW   louynges] lovyng Cc, preysingus AH$_6$, long *prec. canc.* E, laudes Lat.   þis$^{1}$ . . . preyere] *om.* LwW   preyere] and *add.* Cc   `þis preyer is´ (l. 53) T^{G}, *om.* T   53 preyer] ys *prec.*, *canc.* Lw, *om.* As   euermore] H$_7$LB$_3$SrAEPH$_6$CcMPl, euer HBH$_5$WsLwLdTW, ay Td, verrely As   Jesu^{1,2}] God (*bis*) Td, Jesu Lat.   it . . . Jesu^{2}] *om.* LB$_3$AsPH$_6$ it] and E   graces] H$_7$Cc, grace HBH$_5$SrWsLwECcMLdPlTW, þanking A, gracias Lat.   54 it] And Cc   55 oure Lord] H$_7$LB$_3$SrAEPH$_6$CcMPl, *om.* HBH$_5$As-WsLwLdTW, Domino nostro Lat.   Jesu] God Td, Jesu Lat.   with] *om.* Cc   alle] *om.* LdT   þe] *om.* LB$_3$PH$_6$ Vse it] vset M   56 gode] ful *prec.* H$_6$ in itself/and ful gracyous] H$_7$LB$_3$SrAEPH$_6$CcMPl, *rev.* HBH$_5$AsWsLdTW   in itself] *om.* Lw   ful]

psalme, sauourly and softly songen or seid in a brennande hert, ȝeldiþ vp a swete smel to þe face of oure Lorde Ihesu and to alle þe court of heuen. Þer dar no [flesc-]fle resten vpon þe pottes brynke boilende ouer þe fire; riȝt so may þer no fleschly delit resten vpon a clene soule þat is happed and warmed al in fire of lufe, boilende and plawende psalmes and louynges to Ihesu. Þis is verrey preier. Þis preier is euer herde of Ihesu; it ȝeldiþ grace to Ihesu and resceifiþ grace ageyn; it makiþ a soule homly and felawly with Ihesu and with al þe aungels of heuen. Vse it whoso may, þe werke is gode and gracious in itself.

Þis maner preier, þawȝ-al it be not ful contemplacioun in itself ne þe wirkynge of lufe bi itself, nerþeles it is a party of contemplacioun. For whi, it may not be don on þis maner wise bot in plente of grace þurȝ opnynge of þe gostly eiȝe; and þerfor a soule þat haþ þis fredam and þis gracious felynge in preier with gostly sauour and heuenly delite, haþ þe grace of contemplacioun in maner as it is. Þis preier is a riche offrande filled al in fatnes of deuocioun, resceifed bi aungels and presented to þe face of Ihesu. Þe preier of oþer men þat are bisyed in actif werkes is made of two wordes: for þei ofte-siþes formen in here hertes on worde þurȝ þinkynge of werdly bisynes, and sownen in her mowþ anoþer word of | þe psalme songen or seid; and not forþi if here entent be trewe, ȝit is here preier gode and medful þawȝ it lacke sauour and swetnes. Bot þis maner offred of a man contemplatif is

H$_7$LB$_3$SrAEPH$_6$CcMPl, *om.* HBH$_5$AsWsLwLdTW 57 And] H$_7$LB$_3$SrAEPH$_6$CcMPl, *om.* HBH$_5$AsWsLwLdTW, Et Lat. þis . . . preyer] *om.* LwTW maner] of *add.* H$_5$Ws, *om.* Ld þogh-`al´] Td, alþowe Ws, And though LwTW, þoȝ A, ȝif al As ful] fully BW, all fully T, *om.* Td contemplacyon] contemplatif Ld itself] the self Cc 58 ne . . . itself] *om.* H$_7$T, nec operacio dileccionis per seipsam *add.* Lat. þe] *om.* LB$_3$PH$_6$ by] in A itself] hymself B, the self Cc neuerþeles] ȝet Cc 59 contemplacyon] in itself *add.*, *canc.* Td For . . . contemplacyon (l. 62)] *om.* Td 60 presence] H$_7$, plente HBH$_5$LB$_3$AsSrWsLwAEPH$_6$CcMLdPlTW, presencia Lat. opneng] þe *prec.* E 61 þis[1]] the M gracyous] *corr. fr.* goostly B$_3$ felyng] *rep.*, *canc.* E in] and Cc preyer] prayenge LwW 62 þe] *om.* LdT 63 offerand] H$_7$H, offrynge BH$_5$LB filled] fulled B, and As in] into Pl 64 resceyued] al *add.* Cc Jesu] Domini Jesu Lat, þurgh *add.* As 65 besyed] by syde B, besye AsLwLdTW is] þat *prec.* As of] H$_7$HRLB$_3$SrLwAEPH$_6$CcMPlTW, in BH$_5$AsWsLd two] *om.* Lat. 66 þei] ben *add.* As sythes] tymys SrAW formen] for men AsM here hertes] *rev.* M o wurd] in outwarde As þurgh] *om.* Ld 67 `and´ *interl.* H$_7$ sownen] sownynge As 68 songen or seyd] synging or seying Cc neuerþeles if] H$_7$LB$_3$SrAEPH$_6$MPl, ȝet if Cc, not forþi if HH$_5$WsLwLdTd, nouȝt for þyn ȝifte As, not for þan if B, not for þat if TW, et tamen si Lat. be] is As 69 ȝit] *om.* Cc is/here preyer] *rev.* Cc here] þis As and[1]] trewe and *add.* As 70 maner] of *add.* Cc `preyer´ W[G], *om.* HH$_5$AsWsW, oracio Lat. offred] offrynge H$_5$AsWs, *om.* W, facta Lat. of] to Ld a] *om.* CcM contemplatyf/is made] *rev.* As

bot of o word. For as it is formed in þe herte, ryght so holly it sowneth in þe mouthe, as it were noȝt bot o thyng þat formeth and sowneth. And sothly no more it is, for þe soule þurgh grace is made hole in
f. 107^r itself, so fer departed fro | fleschlyhede þat `it´ is maister of þe body; and þan is þe body noȝt ellys bot as an instrument and a trompe of þe soule, in þe whilk þe soule bloweth swete notys of gostly lofenges to Jesu.

þis is þe trumpe þat Dauid spekeþ of þus: *Buccinate in neomenia tuba, in insigni die solemnitatis vestre*. Blowe ȝe with a trumpe in þe new mone. þat is, ȝe soules þat are reformed in gostly lyfe þurgh openyng of þe inner eye, blowe ȝe deuoutely sownend psalmes with þe trumpe of ȝoure bodily tonge. And þerfore, syn þis preyere is so plesaunte to Jesu and so profytable to þe soule, þan is it gode to him þat is turned to God—what þat he be—þat wolde plese him and coueyteth for to han sumwhate queynte felyng of grace, for to coueyte þis felynge; þat he myght þurgh grace come to þe lyberte of spirit and offren his preyers and his psalmes to Jesu contynuely, stably, and deuoutely, with hole mende and brennend affeccyon in him, and han it nerhand in custome whan grace wuld stere him þerto.

þis is a siker felyng and a sothfast, if þou may come þerto and beholden it. þe ⌜þ⌝are noȝt neden for to rennen abowte here and þere and aske questyons of ilk gostly man what þu schalt don, how þu schalt lufe Jesu, how þu schalt serue him, and speken of gostly maters þat passen þi knowynge, as parchaunce sum don. þat maner of doynge is not ful profytable, bot if more nede make it. Kepe þe to þi preyeres styfly first wiht trauelle, þat þu myght afterwarde come to

71 bot] nouȝt only As `o´ H as] riȝt *prec.* H$_5$Ws `so´ H$_6$ holly] only H$_6$, *om.* As 72 noȝt] no Ws, *om.* LB$_3$PH$_6$T thyng] þenkyng H$_5$Ws þat] it *add.* H$_5$Ws and] or E`W$^G$´ 74 itself] the self Cc so] and As, *om.* Pl fer] fer`forþ´ L, ferforþ B$_3$P fleshlyhede] H$_7$LB$_3$SrAPH$_6$MLdPlT, þe *prec.* HBH$_5$WsLwECcWTd, þat *prec.* As `it´ *interl.* H$_7$, sche Ld, he T, *om.* As of] ouer LB$_3$PH$_6$ 75 þan] *om.* H$_5$ noȝt ellys] *om.* B$_3$ as] *om.* B$_3$ 76 þe^1] *om.* LB$_3$PH$_6$ of gostly] *om.* Lw lofenges] longyngys As, preysyng H$_6$ 77 Jesu] God MTd, Domini Jesu Christi Lat. 78 þis] That M Dauid] Dauid propheta Lat. spekeþ] spoke LwW, þat *prec.* As of] wher he seiþ *add.* H$_6$, *om.* As þus] Ps. 80° *add.* BLEPLdTW 79 in^1 . . . vestre] *om.* Td in^1] et M, *om.* LEP die] diei H$_6$ vestre] nostre A Blowe] þat is *prec.* H$_5$WsE ȝe] he seyth *add.* Td with] in LB$_3$PCc 80 reformed] renewed Td gostly] þe *prec.* Sr lyfe] *om.* Lw 81 psalmes] þe *prec.* E 82 þerfore] *om.* E syn] H$_7$LB$_3$SrAEPH$_6$CcMPl, for HBLwLdTW, *om.* H$_5$AsWs `so´ W^G, good and *add.* CcPl, *om.* LwW plesaunte] plesande H, plesynge H$_5$WsLdT 83 profytable] profetably Pl is it] *rev.* AsCcTW turned] H$_7$, now *prec.* Cc, new *prec.* Σ, nouiter Lat. 84 þat^1] so AMPlT, so *prec.* H$_6$, *om.* Ws þat^2] *om.* Td wolde] wol CcPl, fayne *add.* As coueyteth] coueite Pl `for´ W$^G$, *om.* LwCcWTd 85 sumwhate] f- *add.*, *canc.* H$_7$ queynte] *om.* Cc of . . . felynge] *om.* AsCc for] *om.* Td felynge] fyrst *add.* Td 86 þurgh grace/come . . . spirit] H$_7$LB$_3$SrLwAEPH$_6$CcMPlW, *rev.* `H^c´BH$_5$WsLdT to]

made bot of `o′ worde. For as it is formed in þe herte, riȝt so holly it sowniþ in þe mouþe, as it were not bot on þinge þat formiþ and sowniþ. And soþly no more it is, for þe soule þurȝ grace is made hol in itself, so fer departid fro þe fleschlied þat it is maistre of þe body; and þan is þe body not elles bot as an instrument and a trumpe of þe soule, in þe whilke þe sowle blowiþ swete notes of gostly louynges to Ihesu.

þis is þe trumpe þat Dauid spekiþ of þus: *Buccinate in neomenia tuba, in insigni die solempnitatis uestre*. Blowe ȝe with a trumpe in þe new mone. þat is, ȝe soules þat are reformed in gostly lif þurȝ opnynge of þe innere eiȝe, blowe ȝe deuoutely sounande psalmes with þe trumpe of ȝour bodily tunge. And þerfor, for þis preiere is so plesande to Ihesu and so profitable to þe soule, þan is it gode to him þat is new turnid to God—what þat he be—þat wolde plese him and coueitiþ for to han sum qweynt felynge of grace, for to coueite þis felynge; þat he miȝte þurȝ grace come to liberte of spirit and offren his preiers and his psalmes to Ihesu continuely, stably, and deuoutly, with hool mende and brennande affeccioun in him, and han it nerhande in custom `when grace wil ster him þerto.

þis is a sikir feling′ and a soþfast, if þu may come þerto and holden it. þe þar not neden for to renne aboute here and here and aske questions of ilk gostly man what þu schalt don, how þu schalt lufe God, and how þu schalt seruen God and speken of gostly materes þat passyn þi knowynge, as perchaunce summe don. þat maner is not ful
32r profitable, bot if more nede make it. Kepe þe to þi | preiers stifly, first with traueile, þat þu miȝt come aftirwarde to þis restful felynge of þis

vnto As   þe] H$_7$LB$_3$AsEPH$_6$Cc, `þis′ H^c, þis LwAMPlW, *om.* H°BH$_5$SrWsLdT   spirit] þurgh *add.*, *canc.* H°   offren] to *prec.* As   his] in *prec.* LB$_3$P   87 preyers] prayere Td   his] *om.* E   Jesu] God Td, Domino Jesu Lat.   stably] and *prec.* LwW, *om.* A   and[2]] *om.* LwTd   88 mende] to God *add.* Td   in him] *om.* Td   in] on B   han] to *prec.* AsE   nerhand] *om.* As   89 `whan . . . felyng (l. 90)′ H^c, *om.* H°H$_5$AsWs   whan] *one-letter canc. seq.* H$_7$ grace] *om.* B$_3$ wuld stere] stireþ LB$_3$P   wuld] wyll LwLdTW   90 a sothfast] soþfastnes H$_5$Ws   a[2]] *om.* AsM   sothfast] stedefast As   þou] he As   may come] *rev.* M   may] maist E, *om.* H$_6$ come] *om* H$_5$ and[2]] to *add.* As   91 beholden] H$_7$, holden Σ   þe] þu H$_5$ ⌜þ⌝are] H$_7$, ⌜þare⌝ L, þar HSrEPH$_6$CcMPl`T$^G$W$^G$′, dar BH$_5$B$_3$WsLwALdTW, ware As   `neden for to′ W^G, neden to H$_5$Ws, *om.* W   for] H$_7$HH$_5$AsWsLwAECcLdTW, *om.* H$_5$LB$_3$WsPH$_6$MLdPl   abowte here] *rev.* As   þere] here HH$_5$ 92 ilk] H$_7$HM, eche H$_5$LB$_3$AsWsPH$_6$Ld, ech a E, euery BSrLwACcTW   schalt] sholde W   don] and *add.* As   93 lufe . . . schalt[2]] *om.* As   Jesu] H$_7$LB$_3$SrAEPH$_6$CcM, God HBH$_5$AsWsLwLdTW, God and Td, him Pl, Jesum Lat.   how þu shalt[2]] *om.* Cc   him] H$_7$LB$_3$SrAEPH$_6$CcMPl, God HBH$_5$AsWsLwLdTWTd, ei Lat.   speken] spekyng M, to *prec.* As   94 passen] passynge H$_5$ þat] And þis As   of doynge] *om.* HH$_5$AsWs   of] *om.* Ld   95 doynge] men *add.*, *canc.* B$_3$ is] nys As   ful] wel Ld   bot] *om.* Ws   `if′ Sr   more] þe *prec.* H$_5$Ws   Kepe] *rep.*, *canc.* Pl   96 þi] *om.* Pl   styfly] stilly H$_5$WsLwTW, *om.* Td   myght] may Cc   afterwarde come] H$_7$, *rev.* Σ   afterwarde] as Td

þis restful felyng of þis gostly preyere, and þat schal teche þe wisdom inowgh sothfastly withouten feynynge or fantasye. And kepe it forth if þu haue it, and lefe it not bote if grace come oþerwyse, and wil refe it fro þe for a tyme and make þe for to werken on anoþer maner, þan may þu lefe it for a tyme and after turne a3en þerto. And he þat hath þis grace in p⌜r⌝eyere asketh not wher vpon he schal sette þe poynt of his thoght in his preyere, wheþer vpon þe wurdis þat he seyth or ellis
f. 107^{v} on God, or on þe name `of´ Jesu, as sum asken, for þe | felyng of grace techeth him wele inow. For why, þe soule is turned al to þe eye and scharply beholdeth þe face of Jesu, and is made ful syker þat þat is Jesu þat it feleth and seeth. I mene not Jesu as he is in himself in fulnes of his blissed godhede; bot I mene Jesu as he wil schewen him to a clene soule holden in body, after þe clennes þat it hath. For wite þou wele þat ilk a felyng of grace is Jesu and may be called Jesu, and after þat þe grace is more or lesse so feleth þe soule and seeth Jesu more or lesse. 3e, þe first felyng of specyale grace in a bygynner, þat is called grace of compunccyon and contricyon for synnes, is verreyly Jesu. For why, he makeþ þat contricyon in a soule by his presence. Bot Jesu is þan ful boystously and roydely feled and seen, ful fer fro his godly sotelte, for þe soule kan no bettre ne may no bettre for vnclennes of itself þanne. Neuerþeles afterward if þe soule profyte and encres in vertus and in clennes, þe same Jesu and non oþer is sen and feled of þe self soule whan it is towched with grace. Bot þat is more gostly, nerre to þe godly kende of Jesu.

97 þis[1]] þe T restful] ri3tfull As þis[2]] þe T, *om.* W þe] *om.* HBLw 98 inowgh] `to þe´ H$^{c}$, to þe LwM forth] for Ld, first Td 99 haue] mi3t A, may Pl and[1] . . . if] to more Td lefe] lese CcM `refe´ W^{G}, bireue T, take E, remeue W 100 for a tyme] *om.* Td and . . . tyme (l. 101)] *om.* ALdT and] wyll *add.* Td `þe´ H$_6$ on] H$_7$HH$_5$SrWsLwAECcMLdPlTW, in BLB$_3$AsPH$_6$, *om.* Td þan . . . þerto (l. 101)] *om.* Td 101 may] mai3t LB$_3$PH$_6$, maiste AsE, m- *prec.*, *canc.* Sr he þat] *rev.* As hath] haue As 102 þis] that M vpon] on Ld 103 in] and As, into M preyere] he askith no3te *add.* M, askeþ not *add.* Pl wheþer] wheth`er´ L, wher Pl `ellis´ Td 104 `of´ *interl.* H$_7$ Jesu] God and *prec.* H$_5$Ws sum] H$_7$HBH$_5$AsSrWsLwACcPlW, men *add.* LB$_3$EPH$_6$MLdT, quidam Lat. 105 techeth] shal teche LdTWc, touchiþ H$_5$AsWs, telliþ E him] H$_7$HBH$_5$AsWsAMLdPlTW, hem LB$_3$SrLwEPH$_6$Cc, illum Lat. wele] *om.* A For why] *om.* Td turned al] *rev.* M al to] H$_7$LB$_3$SrAEPH$_6$CcPl, into HBH$_5$AsWsLwLdTW, all into Td, totaliter . . . ad Lat. þe[2]] H$_7$LB$_3$Sr-Lw`H^{c}´AEPH$_6$CcMPlW, þe gostly T, a gostli Ld, *om.* H°BH$_5$WsCc 106 þe] of H$_5$ Jesu[1]] Domini Jesu Lat. ful] *om.* As þat[1]] in *prec.* H$_6$ þat[2]] H$_7$LB$_3$APH$_6$M, it HBH$_5$AsSrWsLwELdTWWc, he Cc, *om.* Pl, illud Lat. is Jesu þat (l. 107)] *rep.* As 107 Jesu[1]] Dominus Jesus Christus Lat. þat] *om.* Cc it] H$_7$HBH$_5$AsWsLwH$_6$LdPlTW, he `L´B$_3$SrAEPCcMWc feleth] fele W I mene] *om.* Td 108 fulnes of] *om.* Td fulnes] þe *prec.* As I . . . Jesu] *om.* Td 109 a] *om.* As þat it hath] *rep.* M wite . . . þat (l. 110)] *om.* Td 110 þat] H$_7$LB$_3$SrLwAEPH$_6$CcMPlW, *om.* HBH$_5$AsWs-

gostly preier, and þat schal teche wisdam inowȝ soþfastly withouten feynynge or fantasie. And kepe it forþ if þu hafe it, and lefe it not; bot if grace come oþerwise, and wil refe it fro þe for a tyme and make þe for to wirken on anoþer manere, þan may þu lefe it for a tyme and after turne ageyn þerto. And he þat haþ þis grace in preiere askiþ not where vpon he schal set þe poynt of his þoȝt in his preiere, wheþer vpon þe wurdes þat he seiþ, or elles on God, or on þe name of Ihesu, as summe asken, for þe felynge of grace techiþ him wel inowȝ. For whi, þe soule is turnid into eiȝe and scharply biholdiþ þe face of Ihesu, and is made sikir þat it is Ihesu þat it feliþ and seeþ. I mene not Ihesu as he is in himself in fulnes of his blissed godhed; bot I mene Ihesu as he wil schewen him to a clene soule holden in body, aftir þe clennes þat it haþ. For wite þu wel, ilke a felynge of grace is Ihesu and may be callid Ihesu, and after þat þe grace is more or lesse so feliþ þe soule Ihesu more or lesse. Ȝe, þe first felynge of special grace in a bigynner, þat is called grace of conpunccioun and contricioun for his synnes, is verreyly Ihesu. For whi, he makiþ þat contricioun in a soule bi his presence. But Ihesu is þan ful boistiously and rudely felt, ful fer fro his godly sotilte, for þe soule can no bettere ne may no better for vnclennes of itself þan. Nerþeles afterwarde if þe soule profit and encresse in vertues and in clennes, þe same Ihesu and none oþer is seen and feled of þe same soule whan it is touchid with grace. Bot þat is more gostly, nerre to þe godly kynde of Ihesu.

LwLdTW ilk a] H$_7$HM, eeche a LB$_3$P, eche H$_5$WsLd, euery SrACcWc, eueriche T, euerych a BLwPlW of] in B and[1] . . . Jesu] *om.* Td called] cleped AsH$_6$LdT 111 þe] *om.* As or[1]] and Ld so . . . Ȝe (l. 112)] *om.* As so . . . lesse (l. 112)] *om.* Wc and seeth] H$_7$LB$_3$SrAEPH$_6$CcPl, seet M, *om.* HBH$_5$AsWsLwLdTW, *om.* Lat. Jesu/more or lesse] *rev.* LwTW Jesu] *rep.* M 112 more] either *prec.* M Ȝe] *om.* Td specyale grace] *rev.* As specyale] *om.* B in . . . grace (l. 113)] *om.* LB$_3$P bygynner] bigynnynge Pl 113 called] cleped AsLdT, *om.* Td grace of/compunccyon] *rev.* Pl grace] the *prec.* M for] of BTd synnes] H$_7$LB$_3$SrAPH$_6$CcMPl, his *prec.* HBH$_5$AsWsLwELdTW, peccatis Lat. is . . . soule (l. 114)] *om.* M verreyly] very Cc 114 Jesu] ipse Jesu Lat. why] *om.* Td contricyon] þe *prec.* As in] of As soule] is *add.* As 115 ful (*bis*)] *om.* Td boystously] in a soule *add.*, *canc.* Td, As *skips from here to* 43/98 substaunce roydely] ful *prec.* BT feled] felyng Ld and seen] H$_7$LB$_3$SrAEPH$_6$CcMPl, *om.* HBH$_5$AsWsLw-LdTW, ac videtur Lat. 116 his] *om.* AsWcTd godly] H$_7$HBH$_5$AsWsLw-PH$_6$CcLdPl`T$^G$W$^G$´, ghostly SrAEMTW, gudly Td, deitatis Lat. soule] *om.* Ws ne . . . bettre[2]] *om.* LB$_3$PH$_6$WcTd, nec potest melius Lat. for . . . itself/þanne (l. 117)] *rev.* H$_6$ 117 vnclennes] þe *prec.* Cc itself] the self Cc þanne] *om.* AsWc afterward] after `þat´ As if þe soule] *rep.*, *canc.* H `soule´ Cc profyte and encres] profiteþ and encreseþ AsCc 118 oþer] *om.* B$_3$ 119 þe self] a Td with] H$_7$HBH$_5$WsLwELdTW, bi LB$_3$Sr-APH$_6$CcMPlTd, of As þat] it Sr, þis Pl, it *add.* M `is´ Sr 120 nerre] nere H$_5$WsTW, ner M þe] *om.* LB$_3$PH$_6$ godly] goostli P, gudly Td, bodily Ld of Jesu] *om.* Td Jesu] Jesu Christi Lat.

And sothly þat is þe most thyng þat Jesu lufeth in a soule, þat it myght be made gostly and godly in syght and in lufe, lyke to him in grace to þat þat he is by kende, for þat schal be þe ende of alle lufers. Þan may þou be syker þat what tyme þu felest þi soule stered by grace specyally, in þat maner as it is byfore seyd by openynge of þi gostly eye, þat þu seest and felest Jesu. Hold him fast whylis þu myght, and kepe þe in grace, and late him not lyghtly fro þe. Loke after non oþer Jesu bot þat same, by felyng of þat self grace more godly, þat it myght wexen more and more in þe; and drede þe not, þow þat Jesu þat þu felest be not Jesu as he is in his ful godhed, þat þu schuldest þerfore moun ben disceyued if þou lenest to þi felyng. Bot trust þu wele, if þu be a lufer of Jesu, þat þi felyng is trewe, and þat Jesu is trewly feled
f. 108r and seen in þe þurgh | his grace, as þou `mayht´ seen him here. And þerfor, lenne fully to þi felyngge whan it is gracyous and gostly, and kepe it tendrely and haf grete deynte, not of þiself bot of it, þat þu myghtest seen Jesu ay bettre and bettre. For `grace´ schal euene teche þe be itself, if þu wil falle þerto mekely, til þu come to þe ende.

Bot perchaunce now bygynnes þu to wondren whi I sey o tyme þat grace werketh al þis, and anoþer tyme I sey þat lufe werketh, or Jesu werketh, or God werketh. Vnto þis I sey þus, þat whan I sey þat grace werkeþ, I mene lufe, Jesu and God. For al is one, and noȝt bot one: Jesu is lufe, Jesu is grace, Jesu is God; and for he werketh alle in vs by his grace for lufe as God, þerfore may I vsen what word þat I wil of þis foure after my steryng in þis wrytynge.

121 þe] *om.* ELd 122 gostly and godly] H_7LB$_3$SrAEPH$_6$CcPl, *rev.* HBH$_5$AsWs-LwLdTWWc in[1] . . . lufe] *om.* Td in[2]] *om.* Sr lufe lyke] louelynesse As 123 ⌜to⌝ H[c], *om.* H°H$_5$Ws, -cialy in þat maner as it is bifore seide by opnynge of þi gostly eiȝe þu seest and felest Jesu *add.*, *canc.* H þat[2]] *om.* H$_5$WsLd by] in CcTd þe] *om.* Sr 124 may] maiȝt HH$_5$WsWc what] whilke HH$_5$AsWsLdTd tyme] tymis Ld þu] H_7LB$_3$SrAEPH$_6$CcMPlT, þat *prec.* HBH$_5$AsWsLwLdW þi . . . by] *om.* Td 125 it] *om.* E þi] H_7HBH$_5$AsWsLwLdW, þe LB$_3$SrAEPH$_6$CcMPlT, tui Lat. gostly] Holi Goste *prec.* M 126 þat] *om.* Td myght] H_7, may Σ, potes Lat. and[2] . . . grace (l. 127)] *om.* Td 127 after non] þou neuer after As after] *om.* Td 128 bot þat same] þan him. For As þat[1]] H_7HBH$_5$SrWsLwH$_6$CcMLdTW, þe LB$_3$AEPPl þat[2]] H_7HBH$_5$AsSrWsLwACcLdPlTW, þe LB$_3$EPH$_6$M self] same WsH$_6$ godly] gostli AMPl 129 wexen . . . þe[1]] in him wex þe more As more and more/in þe] H_7LB$_3$Sr-AEPH$_6$CcMPl, *rev.* HBH$_5$AsWsLwLdTW þe[1]] þe eye Td, *om.* T þow] þou but As, þerof Td þat[1]] *om.* LwW 130 `be´ L not] *om.* As as he is] *om.* LdT `ful´ Td þat] or ellys As þerfore moun] haue As 131 `moun´ Sr, *om.* TWc if . . . Jesu (l. 132)] but As lenest] H_7CcLd, lenethe M, lenid HBH$_5$SrWsLwAH$_6$PlTWTd, lendist E, loned L [quere: loned or lened *marg.*], loned or lened P [quere *marg.*], lenedest B$_3$, innitaris Lat. þi felyng] the M þu] *om.* Cc 132 feled and seen] *rev.* B 133 in] H_7, of Σ, per Lat. þe] Jesu *prec.*, *canc.* L þurgh . . . grace] *om.* Td his] *om.* As `mayht´ *interl.* H_7, may LwMW, potes Lat. him] *rep.*, *canc.* B$_3$, *om.* A And . . . ende (l. 137)] *om.* Td

32v And soþly þat is þe most þinge þat Ihesu lufiþ in a soule, þat it miȝt be made godly and gostly in siȝt and in lufe, like to him in grace ⌜to⌝ þat þat he is bi kynde, for þat schal be þe ende of alle lufers. Þan maiȝt þu be siker þat whilke tyme þat þu felist þi soule stirid bi grace specially, in þat maner as it is bifore seide bi opnyng of þi gostly eiȝe, þu seest and felist Ihesu. Hold him fast whils þou may, and kepe þe in grace, and lete him not liȝtly fro þe. Loke after none oþer Ihesu bot þat same, bi felynge of þat self grace more godly, þat it miȝt wexen in þe more and more; and drede þe not, þawȝ þat Ihesu þat þou felest be not Ihesu as he is in his ful godhed, þat þu schuldest þerfore moun be desceifid if þu lenid to þi felynge. Bot trost þu wel, if þu be a lufer of Ihesu, þat þi felynge is trewe, and þat Ihesu is trewly felde and seen of þe þurȝ his grace, as þu maiȝt seen him here. And þerfore lene fully to þi felynge whan it is gracious and gostly, and kepe it tenderly and hafe grete deynte, not of þiself bot of it, þat þu miȝt seen and felen Ihesu ay better and better. For grace schal euen teche þe bi itself, if þou wilt falle þerto, til þou come to þe ende.

Bot perchaunce þou bigynnist to wundre whi I sey o tyme þat grace wirkiþ al þis, and anoþer tyme I sey þat ⌜loue⌝ wirkiþ, or Ihesu wirkiþ, or God wirkiþ. Vnto þis I sey þus, þat whan I sey þat grace wirkiþ, I mene lufe, Ihesu and God. For al is on, and not bot on: Ihesu is lufe,
33r Ihesu is grace, Ihesu is God; and for he wirkiþ al in vs | bi his grace for lufe as God, þerfore may I vsen what worde of þese foure þat me list after my sterynge in þis writynge.

134 þi] þe As `and$^{2}$´ Pl 135 haf] *om.* M 136 seen] H$_7$LB$_3$SrAPH$_6$CcMPl, and felen *add.* HBH$_5$AsWsLwELdTW, feele and *prec.* Wc, videre Lat. Jesu] it As ay] H$_7$HBH$_5$LWsPCcM, euere B$_3$AsLwAEH$_6$PlW, alwey SrLdT `grace´ *interl.* H$_7$ euene/teche þe] *rev.* E 137 itself] thy self Cc wil] *om.* A mekely] H$_7$LB$_3$Sr-AEPH$_6$CcMPl`T^{G}W^{G}´, *om.* HBH$_5$AsWsLwLdTW, humiliter Lat. til] to B$_3$ þu come to] *om.* LB$_3$P to] vnto E 138 now] H$_7$Cc, *om.* Σ bygynnes þu] H$_7$, *rev.* Σ wondren] *om.* H$_5$ whi] þat *add.* Cc o] oon M þat] *om.* Pl 139 and . . . werketh^{2}] *om.* H$_6$ and] on *add.* W I sey] *om.* TW I] *om.* Td lufe . . . werketh^{2} (l. 140)] *om.* LwW lufe . . . or] *om.* LdT ⌜lufe⌝ H^{c}, grace BH$_5$As `werketh$^{2}$´ H$_5$, al þis *add.* E or . . . werketh$^{2}$ (l. 140)] *om.* As 140 werketh$^{1}$] al *add.* A werketh$^{2}$] and *add.* As Vnto . . . werketh (142)] *om.* Lw Vnto] As to H$_5$Ws, To A þus] *om.* B$_3$Cc whan I sey] *om.* As þat$^{2}$] LB$_3$PH$_6$ 141 `werkeþ´ Cc I] in As Jesu] in *prec.* As God] in *prec.* As is] are Pl, his M and^{2} . . . one^{2}] *om.* Ld one^{2}] only As, for *add.* H$_6$Cc 142 lufe] but *add.* As grace] and *add.* CcPlTd and] *om.* As for] *om.* Td alle in vs] *om.* A 143 for . . . God] *om.* Lw for lufe] *om.* Td may I vsen] I vse T may I] *rev.* As I^{1}] seyn and *add.* Cc word] *om.* Ld þat I wil/of þis four] H$_7$LB$_3$SrAEPH$_6$CcMPl, of þese foure/þat me list [lust B] HBH$_5$AsWsLwLdTW þat] H$_7$HBH$_5$AsWsLwLdTWTd, *om.* LB$_3$Sr-AEPH$_6$CcMPl þis] þoose Pl 144 foure] þre H$_6$ after my steryng] *om.* Cc `þis´ Td, myn Cc

How a soule þurgh openyng of þe gostly eye resceyueth a gracyous ablenesse for to vnderstonden Holy Wrytte, and how Jesu þat is hid in Holy Writte scheweth him to his loueres. Capitulum xliii[m]

Whan þe soule of a louer feleth Jesu in preyere in maner byfore seyd, and thenketh þat it wold neuer felen oþerwyse, neuerþeles it falleth sumtyme þat grace putteth silence in a soule to vocal preyinge, and stereth þe soule for to seen and felen Jesu in anoþer maner. And þat maner is first for to see Jesu in Holy Writte, for Jesu, þat is al sothfastnes, is hid an [hilid] þerinne, wounden in a softe sendel vnder fayr wordis, þat he may note be knowen ne feled bot of a clene herte. For why, sothfastnes wil not schewe itself to enemys bot to frendis þat lufen it and desyren it with a clene, meke herte. For sothfastnes and mekenes are ful trewe susters, festned togider in lufe and charite; and forthi is þer no laynynge of counseyls atwix hem two. Mekenes presumeth on sothfastnes and nothyng of itself, and sothfastnes trusteth wele on mekenes, and so þei acorden wonderly wele. þan for as mykel as þe soule of a lufer is made meke þorgh inspiracyon of grace by openyng of þe gostly eye, and seeth þat it is noȝt in itself bot
f. 108v only hangeth vpon | þe mercy and þe godenes of Jesu, and lastendly is borne vp by fauour and help of him only, and trewely desyrend his presence, þerfore seeth it Jesu. For it seeth sothfastnes of Holy Writte

Chapter 43 *title*: H$_7$LB$_3$SrAEPH$_6$MLdPlTW `How sofastnes þat is Jesu wol not schewe hym but to frendes þat louen him and desiren him wiþ a meke hert.' *d.h.* H How þe soule of a louer may fele fele Jesu, and how Holy Wryttys sentence is brouȝt vnto his þouȝt be his mynystrys þat ben ankres and besy louers of Jesu. As *om.* HBH$_5$WsLwCcTd 1 openyng] þe *prec.* TW 2 `ablenesse' W$^G$, loue abil ALdTW, humilitatem Lat [habilitatem H$_8$MaUpB$_4$] Holy$^1$ . . . loueres] etc. M 3 him] silfe *add.* LdTW to] vnto Sr 5 `Whan' W^G, Thenne W, But *prec.* Sr maner] H$_7$LB$_3$SrPH$_6$Cc, þe *prec.* HBH$_5$AsWsLwAEMLdPlTWWc byfore] aforn As 6 þat] *om.* Cc it wold] he nolde As wold] may M, miȝte Pl neuer . . . þat (l. 7)] alwey do so ȝit A, ay do so ȝit M, euer do so ȝit Pl, *om.* As neuerþeles] ȝet Cc falleth] befalliþ Ld 7 sumtyme/þat grace] *rev.* As sumtyme þat] H$_7$CcWc, *rev.* Σ sumtyme] *om.* LdT grace] þe *prec.* As putteth] out *add.* As in a soule] H$_7$LB$_3$SrAEPH$_6$CcMPl, *om.* HBH$_5$AsWsLwLdTWTdWc, anime Lat. to] `fro' L, fro B$_3$P vocal] *om.* Td preyinge . . . þe (l. 8)] *rep.* As preyinge] praiere TWc 8 soule] to oþer gostly worke *add.* Td for] H$_7$LB$_3$SrAEPH$_6$CcMPl, *om.* HBH$_5$AsWsLwLdTWWc felen] to *prec.* HBAsLwW anoþer . . . in (l. 9)] *om.* Cc anoþer] oþir LB$_3$EPH$_6$ 9 first] *om.* As for^1] H$_7$LB$_3$SrEPH$_6$CcMPl, *om.* HBH$_5$AsWs-LwALdTW see] and fele A Holy] Hu$_2$ *back* þat is] *om.* Ld þat] *om.* Td al] *om.* H$_6$ 10 sothfastnes] al trouþe *add.* T is] and Ld, *om.* Td hilid] hidil H$_7$, coueryd Hu$_2$Td wounden . . . wordis (l. 11)] *om.* Td wounden] wrappid LdT vnder] of H$_5$Ws 11 fayr] of *add.* A ⌜note . . . feled⌝ L 12 why] *om.* Cc sothfastnes] so⌜þfastnes⌝ L itself] himselfe As, þe self Cc þat] to Pl, *om.* H$_5$ 13 it^1] *om.* LwCcW it^2] *om.* A a]

[CHAPTER 43]

Whanne þe soule of a lufer feliþ Ihesu in preiere in þe maner before seide and þenkiþ þat it wolde neuer felen oþerwise, nerþeles it fallyþ þat sumtyme grace puttiþ sylence to vocal preienge, and steriþ þe soule to seen and to felen Ihesu in anoþer maner. And þat maner is first to seen Ihesu in Holy Writ, for Ihesu, þat is al soþfastnes, is hid and hiled þerin, wounden in a soft sendel vndir faire wurdes, þat he may not be knowen ne felt bot of a clene herte. For whi, soþfastnes wil not schew itself to enemys bot to frendes þat lufen it and desiren it with a meke hert. For soþfastnes and meknes are ful trew sustres, festned togidir in luf and charitee; and forþi is þer no leynynge of conseil atwix hem two. Meknes presumiþ of soþfastnes and noþinge of itself, and soþfastnes troweþ wel on meknes, and so þei acorden wundre wel. Þan for as mikel as a soule of a lufere is made meke þurȝ inspiracioun of grace bi opnynge of þe gostly eiȝe, and seeþ þat it is noȝt of itself bot only hangiþ on þe mercy and godenes of Ihesu, and lastendly is born vp bi fauour and help of him only and trewly desirende þe presence of him, þerfore seeþ it Ihesu. For it seeþ soþfastnes of Holy Wryt wundirly schewde and opend, abofen study

om. B clene] H$_7$LB$_3$SrEPH$_6$CcMPl, *om.* HBH$_5$AsWsLwAHu$_2$LdTWTd, mundo Lat. herte] *The second extract in* Td *ends here* sothfastnes] þat is trouþe *add.* Hu$_2$ 14 ful] *om.* M and^2 . . . two (l. 15)] *om.* Cc and^2] *om.* As 15 forthi] H$_7$HLB$_3$SrAEPMPl, þerfore BH$_5$WsLwHu$_2$H$_6$LdTW, for As is þer] *rev.* SrH$_6$, þer nys As laynynge] leuyng Ws, heling ALd, feynyng Sr, hidyng EH$_6$Pl, `laynyng : hydyng : occultatio´ T$^G$W$^G$, `helyng´ *gl.* Lw, lamentacioun Hu$_2$, occultatio Lat. counseyls] H$_7$LB$_3$SrAEPH$_6$MPl, counseylle HBH$_5$AsWsLwHu$_2$LdTW, consiliorum Lat. atwix] H$_7$HLSrLwAEPH$_6$, bytwexte BB$_3$MLdPlW, bitwene H$_5$WsHu$_2$T, of As 16 on] H$_7$LB$_3$SrAEPH$_6$CcMPl, of HBH$_5$AsWsLwHu$_2$LdTW and^1 . . . and^2] *om.* M nothyng] non þynge As of itself] on þe self Cc itself] hymself B, hirsilfe T 17 trusteth] H$_7$LB$_3$SrAEPH$_6$CcMPl, trusteth trouthe Lw, troweþ HBH$_5$AsWsTW, troweþ or byleueþ B, yifyþ ful trewe credence Hu$_2$, *om.* Ld wele^1] *om.* Hu$_2$ wonderly] H$_7$SrMPl, wundre Σ 18 as^2] that Cc þe] H$_7$H$_5$LB$_3$SrWsAEPH$_6$CcMPl, a HBAsLwHu$_2$LdTW 19 openyng] þe *prec.* As seeth] say As it] *om.* M is] nys As in] H$_7$LB$_3$Sr-APH$_6$CcMPl, of HBH$_5$AsWsLwHu$_2$ELdTWWc, ex Lat. itself] the self Cc 20 hangeth] in God hangyng A vpon] H$_7$, in LwW, on Σ þe^1] his A, *om.* H$_5$Ws and þe] of M `þe$^2$´ L, on *prec.* B, *om.* HH$_5$Ws Jesu] God LB$_3$EP `and^2´ W^G, *om.* LwW lastendly] alwey Hu$_2$ 21 fauour and help] *rev.* A, feruour and hope B him] hem M and^2] þere *add.* As his presence] H$_7$LB$_3$SrAEPH$_6$CcMPl, þe presence of him HBH$_5$As-WsLwHu$_2$LdTWWc 22 it Jesu] *rev.* H$_6$ it^1] he BT For] þat *add.* As sothfastnes] þe *prec.* H$_5$WsWc wonderly schewede and opned, abouen stodye and trauayle and reson of mannys kendly wittis. And þat may wele be called þe felyng and þe perceyfyng of Jesu, for Jesu is welle of wisdom, and by a litel beheldynge of his wisdom into a clene soule he maketh þe soule wys inogw for to vnderstonden al Holy Writte. Not al at ones, in specyale beholdyng, bot þorgh þat grace þe soule resceyueth a newe ablenes and a gracyous habyte for to vnderstonden it specyaly whan it cometh to mende.

þis opnyng and clernes of wytte is made by gostly presence of Jesu. For ryght as þe Gospel seyth of two disciples goend into þe castel of Emaus, brennend in desyre and spekend of Jesu, oure Lord appered presently to hem as a pylgrym and tawght hem þe prophecyes of himself, and as þe Gospel seyth: *Aperuit illis sensum, vt intelligerent scripturas*. He opened to hem clerenes of witte þat þei myght vnderstonden Holy Wrytyng. Ryght so þe gostly presence of Jesu openeth þe wyt of his louere þat brenneth in desir to him, and bringeth to his mynde by mynysterie of aungelis þe wurdis and þe centence of Holi Wriȝt, vnso[ught] and vnavised, on after anoþer, and expounet hem redeli, be þei neuere so hard or so preuy. þe hardere þat þei ben and þe ferþere fro manes resonable vnderstandyng, þe more delitable is þe trewe schewyng of it whan Jesu is mayster. It is expouned and declarid letterly, morally, mystely and [h]euenly, if þe matere suffre it. By þe lettre, þat is lyȝteste and most pleyn, is þe bodely kynde comforted. By moralte of Holy Writ, þe soule is [informed] of vices and of vertus, visely to cun departen þat on fro þat oþer. By mysteyed it is illumyned for to sen þe werkes of God in

23 wonderly] H$_7$HBSrLwCcMLdPlTW, wondirfully H$_5$LB$_3$AsWsAHu$_2$EPH$_6$ schewede] werkynge As opned] opennynge As stodye] with *prec.* As, þe *prec.* EWc trauayle] þe *prec.* E 24 wittis] H$_7$Cc, wit Σ, ingenii Lat. may] *om.* B wele be] *rev.* Pl called] ycleped AsH$_6$LdT þe^2] *om.* T 25 wisdom] resoun and *prec.* T 26 beheldynge] H$_7$, ȝetyng LdT, holdyng Wc, heldynge Σ, effusionem Lat. into] in CcWc þe] a Wc, *om.* Hu$_2$H$_6$ 27 wys . . . for] *om.* As inogw] y`nowȝ´ L vnderstonden] hit þat is in *add.* APl, that is in M ⌜Not⌝ H 28 specyale] a *prec.* Pl ⌜þat grace⌝ L þat] þe Sr þe] a Sr `a newe´ L 29 habyte] habylte As it^1] *om.* Sr 31 þis] *om.* As opnyng] of *add.*, *canc.* E clernes] H$_7$LB$_3$SrAPH$_6$CcMPl, þis *prec.* HBH$_5$AsWsLwHu$_2$ELdTW, claritas Lat. `is´ L, *om.* B$_3$ by] H$_7$B$_3$SrAH$_6$MPl, þe *add.* HBH$_5$`L´AsWsLwHu$_2$PLdTW gostly] graciouse T 32 þe^1] *om.* M into] H$_7$Sr, to Σ 33 Jesu] *om.* LwW Lord] H$_7$E, Jesu *add.* Σ, Jesu our Lorde *add.* LwW 34 presently/to hem] H$_7$SrAH$_6$CcMPl, *rev.* HBH$_5$AsWsLwHu$_2$LdTW as] H$_7$LB$_3$SrLwAPH$_6$CcMPlW, in liknes of HBH$_5$AsWsHu$_2$ELdT`W^G´, velut Lat. and] he *add.* T þe] *om.* H$_6$ prophecyes] prophecye Lw 35 himself] hemselfe AsM seyth] telleþ As, Luc. 24° *add.* BLHu$_2$EPLdTW Aperuit] Apparuit LPH$_6$MPl, Apperuit B$_3$

and trauail and resoun of ma⌜nnus⌝ kyndly wit. And þat may wel be called þe felynge and þe perceifynge of Ihesu, for Ihesu is welle of wisdam, and by a litil heldynge of his wisdam into a clene soule he makiþ þe soule wis inowʒ for to vndirstonden al Holy Wryt. ⌜Not⌝ al
33v at ones, in special biholdynge, but þurʒ þat grace þe soule | resceyuyþ a new abelnes and a gracious habite for to vndirstonden it specially whan it comiþ to mynde.

? þis opnynge and þis clernes of wit is made bi þe gostly presence of Ihesu. For riʒt as þe Gospel seiþ of two disciples goende to þe castel of Emauz, brennande in desire and spekende of Ihesu, oure Lorde Ihesu appered to hem presently in liknes of a pilgrym and taghte hem þe prophecies of himself, and as þe Gospel seiþ: *Aperuit illis sensum, vt intelligerent scripturas*. He opned to hem clernes of wit þat þei miʒten vndirstondyn Holy Writ. Riʒt so þe gostly presence of Ihesu opneþ þe wit of his lufer þat brenniþ in desire to him, and bryngiþ to his mende by ministrynge of aungels þe wordes and þe sentences of Holy Writ, vnsoghte and vnauised, on after anoþer, and expouniþ hem redily, be þei neuer so harde ne so pryuey. þe more harder þat þei ben and þe ferrer fro mans resonable vndirstondynge, þe more delectable is þe trew schewynge of it whan Ihesu is maister. It is expouned and declared letterly, morally, mistily, and heuenly, if þe mater suffre it. By þe letter, þat is liʒtest and most pleyn, is þe bodily kynde conforted. Bi moralte of Holy Writ þe soule is enformed of vices and vertues, wisely to kun departe þe ton fro þe toþer. By mistied it is illumined for to seen þe werkes of God in Holy Kirke, ˋredily for to

36 scripturas] H_7 37 Wrytyng] H_7LwCcMW, Writynges LB_3SrEPH_6, Writ HBH_5-AsWsHu_2LdT, Scripture A 38 þat] it *add.* W in] his As to] vnto As, of Ld 39 mynysterie] H_7SrCcMPl, ministrynge HBH_5AsWsAHu_2LdT, mynystracioun LwW, mysterie LB_3PH_6, ministerium Lat. 40 centence] H_7, sentence B$H_5$$LB_3$AsSrWs-AEP$H_6$CcMPl, sentences HLw$Hu_2$LdTW, sentencias Lat. vnsought and] *om.* A vnsought] vnsoth H_7 41 expounet] H_7, expouniþ Σ, expoungniþ H_6 or] $H_7$$LB_3$Sr-AEP$H_6$CcPl, ne HB$H_5$AsWsLw$Hu_2$LdTW, and M hardere] $H_7$$LB_3$SrLwAP$H_6$Cc-MPlW, more *prec.* HB$H_5$AsWs$Hu_2$ELdT, difficiliores Lat. 42 þat þei ben] *om.* A þe[1]] *om.* LwW ferþere] more *prec.* T manes] mennys LB_3P resonable] wyt and mannys Cc 43 delitable] $H_7$$H_5$$LB_3$AsSrWsAEP$H_6$CcMPl, delectable HBLw$Hu_2$ECc-MLdTW þe] here As of it] þerof Sr, of hem LwW Jesu] Dominus Jesus Lat. 44 expouned] expoungnid H_6 and declarid] *rev.* LB_3, and *canc.* L letterly] litterally LwW heuenly . . . lufely (44/8)] *om.* Hu_2. *Four fols. missing* heuenly] euenly H_7 þe] *om.* As 45 suffre] suffreþ As þe[1]] *om.* LwTW þe[2]] *om.* LwW 47 informed] ⌜enformed⌝ L, conformed Sr, conforted $H_7$$B_3$, informatur Lat. vices/. . ./vertus] *rev.* A of[2]] H_7AH_6CcM, *om.* Σ cun] for to *add.* As þat] *om.* Cc fro] and AMPl 48 mysteyed] þe heuenly As it is] *rev.* MPl it] *om.* As illumyned] liʒtned Ld for to sen] þurgh As þe] *om.* M God] Jesu LwW in] and of Cc

Holy Chirche, redely for to appleyen wurdis of Holy Writ to Crist oure Lord, heued, and to Holy Chirche þat is his mysty body. And þe ferthe, þat is heuenly, longeth only to þe werkynge of lufe, and þat is f. 109^{r} whan al soth|fastnesse in Holi Writ is applyed to lufe; and for þat is most lyke to heuenly felyng, þerfore y calle it heuenly.

Þe lufere of Jesu is his frend nouȝt for he hath deserued it; but for Jesu is ful merciful, goodnesse maketh him his frend by trewe acord, and þerfore, as to a trewe frend þat pleseth him with lufe, nouȝt serueth him by drede as a tharl, schewyth his preuyte. Þus he seyth himself to his appostoles: *Iam vos dixi amicos, quia quecumque audiui a Patre nota feci vobis*. Nowe y seye þat ȝe are frendes, for y make knowen to ȝow alle thynges þat y haue herd of my Fadir. To a clene soule þat hath palet purefied fro filthe of fleschly lust, Holy Writ is lyuely fode and sustenaunce delitable; it sauoureth wonder swetely whan it is wele chewed by gostly vnderstandyng. For whi, þe spirit of lyf is þerin, þat qwykneth alle þe myghtes of þe soule and filleth hem ful with swetnes of heuenly sauour and gostly delyte. Bot sothly him nedeth for to han whyte teeth and scharpe and wele pyked þat schuld byten on þis gostly bred, for fleschly lufers and heretykes moun not touche þe inly floure of it; her teeth are blody and ful of filthe, and þerfore are þei fastende fro felyng of þis brede. By teeth are vnderstonded inly wittes of þe soule, þe whilk in fleschly and in heretykes are blody, ful of synne and of werdly vanite; þei wolden, and þei kun not, come by þe curyouste of her kendly witte to þe sothfast knowyng of Holy Writte. For her witte is corrupte be þe originale synne and actuel also, and is not ȝit heled þurgh grace, and

49 Holy[1]] Writte *add.*, *canc.* Pl `redely . . . Chirche (l. 50)´ H$^{c}$, *om.* H°H$_{5}$AsWsA redely] redy T for] and B appleyen . . . Crist] *trimmed in* H wurdis] H$_{7}$LB$_{3}$SrLwPH$_{6}$CcPl, þe *prec.* BH$^{c}$AEMLdTW 50 Lord] H$_{7}$, *om.* Σ his mysty] mistily his T `his´ Pl, a As mysty] mystik LB$_{3}$APH$_{6}$ And] þat *add.* As 51 ferthe] fir⌜þe⌝ L, feiþ H$_{5}$Ws, quarta expositio Lat. heuenly] celica . . . vel anagogica Lat. longeth . . . heuenly (l. 53)] *om.* H°H$_{5}$AsWs ⌜longeth only⌝ `to . . . felynge (l. 53)´ H^{c} þe] *om.* BLd and . . . lufe (l. 52)] *om.* LdT ⌜and⌝ L is] *om.* LB$_{3}$P 52 in] of E and] *om.* Cc 53 felyng] feelynges M calle] clepe AsLdT 54 for[1]] þat *add.* E hath deserued] deseruith T, desiryd H$_{6}$ ⌜but for Jesu⌝ L for[2]] *om.* B$_{3}$ 55 is ful] H$_{7}$, of his Σ, ex Lat. merciful] mercye ful of As 56 as to] of M, as Sr, *om.* A 57 him] *om.* B a] *om.* B schewyth] H$_{7}$, he *prec.* Σ his] with As preuyte] H$_{7}$LB$_{3}$AsLwAEPH$_{6}$CcMPlW, pryueites HBH$_{5}$WsLdTW, consilia Lat. he seyth] *rev.* E 58 to] of H$_{5}$AsWs appostoles] Io. 15° *add.* BLEPLdTW quecumque] quicumque H$_{6}$ 59 Patre] H$_{7}$H°BLd, `meo´ H$^{c}$, meo Σ Nowe] þat is *add.* E y seye] *rev.* Pl frendes] my *add.* `H^{c}´, my *add.* M 60 knowen to ȝow] yow to knowe T thynges] thyng Cc To] vnto Sr clene] *om.* Lw 61 hath palet] H$_{7}$HBLB$_{3}$AsSrLwEPCcLdTW, is H$_{5}$WsAH$_{6}$MPl, habet palatum Lat. palet] be clene As, þe *prec.* LB$_{3}$P, a *prec.* Cc fleschly] *corr. fr.* fleschlych H$_{7}$ lust] H$_{7}$, lufe Σ 62 swetely] H$_{7}$LB$_{3}$SrLwAEPH$_{6}$CcMPlW, swete HBH$_{5}$AsWsLdT, suauiter Lat. 63 chewed]

⟨applien þe wordes of Holy Writ to Crist⟩ our heued and to Holy Kirke′ þat is his mysty body. And þe ferþ, þat is heuenly, ⌜longeþ only⌝ `to þe werking of loue, and þat is when alle soþfastnes in Holi Writ is applied to luf; and for þat is most like to heuenly felynge,′ þerfor I calle it heuenly.

Þe lufer of Ihesu is his frende, not for he haþ deserued it, bot for Ihesu of his merciful goodnes makiþ him his frende bi trewe acorde; and þerfore, as to a trew frende þat plesyþ him with lufe, not seruiþ
134^r him bi drede as a þral, he schewiþ his pryueites. Þus | he seiþ himself to his apostles: *Iam vos dixi amicos, quia quecunque audiui a Patre `meo′, nota feci vobis*. Now I sey þat ȝe are frendes, for I make knowen to ȝow alle þinges þat I hafe herde of my Fadir. To a clene soule þat haþe palet purified fro filþe of fleschly lufe, Holy Wryt is lifly fode and sustenance delectable; it sauoriþ wondir swete whan it is wel chewed by gostly vndirstondynge. For whi, þe spirit of lif is hid þerin, þat quicneþ alle þe miȝtes of þe soule and fylliþ hem ful with swetnes of heuenly sauour and gostly delyte. Bot soþly him nediþ for to han white teþe and scharpe and wel piked þat schulde biten o⌜n⌝ þis gostly brede, for fleschly lufers and heretikes mowne not touchyn þe inly flour of it; here teeþ are blody and ful of filþe, and þerfore þei are fastende fro felynge of þis bred. Bi teeþ arn vndirstonden þe inly wittes of þe soule, þe whilk in fleschly lufers and heretikes arn blody, ful of synne and of werdly vanytee; þei wolden, and kun not, come bi curiosite of here kyndely witte to soþfast knowynge of Holy Writte. For here wite is corupt bi þe original synne and actuel also, and is not ȝit heled þurȝ grace, and þerfore þei don bot gnawen vpon þe barc

schewede H_5AsPl 64 lyf] loue As is] H_7, hid *add.* Σ, absconditus Lat. qwykneth] quykeþ H_5AsWs hem] him As 65 with] H_7HBH_5AsSrAEPH_6MLdPl, of LB_3WsLwPCcTW and] in Cc him nedeth] it behouith him T 66 nedeth] bihouith As for] *om.* LwTW whyte] stronge T and[2]] on Cc schuld] wel *add.* AMPl 67 byten] bydyn Cc on] o⌜n⌝ H^c, of M þis] his As, þat A not] none As, *om.* M 68 inly] inwarde LwW her teeth are] ben heretykes alle As her] his B and[2]] *om.* LwW 69 þerfore] so H_6 are þei] H_7LB_3SrAEPCcMPl, *rev.* HBH_5AsWsLwEH_6LdTW `are′ Cc felyng] þe *prec.* Pl teeth are] þis brede is to As 70 vnderstonded] H_7, vndirstonden HBH_5LB_3As-SrWsLwAEPH_6CcMPlLdTW inly] H_7LB_3SrLwAPCcMPl, inward H_6, þe *prec.* HBH_5AsWsH_6LdTW wittes] vertues LB_3EPH_6, swetnesse B fleschly] H_7, lufers *add.* Σ, carnalibus dilectoribus Lat. in[2]] H_7LB_3SrLwAEPH_6CcMPlW, *om.* HBH_5As-WsLdTW 71 ful] and *prec.* As of[2]] *om.* AT vanite] vanytees LwH_6W 72 and . . . not/come . . . Writte (l. 73)] *rev.* AMPl þei] H_7LB_3SrLwAEPH_6CcMPlTW, *om.* HBH_5As-WsLd kun] may APl by] to H_5WsCc þe[1]] H_7LB_3Sr`H^c′AEPH_6CcMPl, *om.* H°BH_5As-WsLwLdTW of] be Cc witte . . . sothfast] wyttes soþfastnes and to As þe[2]] H_7LB_3Sr-LwAEPH_6CcMPlW, *om.* HBH_5AsWsLdT 73 sothfast] sothfastnes in LwW þe] H_7HBH_5LB_3SrWsEPH_6MLdPl, *om.* AsLwACcTW 74 is] nys As not ȝit] *rev.* M ȝit] *om.* Cc

þerfor þei don bot gnawen vpon þe bark withouten, karpe þei neuer so mikel þerof; þe inly sauour within þei felen not of. þei are not meke, þei are not clene for to seen it, þei are not frendes to Jesu, and þerfore he scheweth hem not his counseil. þe pryueyte of Holy Writte is closed vnder keye, enseled with a sygnet of Jesu is fynger, þat is þe Holy Gost, and forthi withouten his loue and his leue may no man come in. He hath only þe keye of conynge in his kepyng, as Holy f. 109^{v} Writte seyth, and he is | keye himselfe, and lateth in whom he wil þurgh inspyracyon of his grace and breketh not þe sele. And þat doth Jesu to hys louers, not to al ylyke, bot to hem þat are specially enspyred for to seken þe sothfastnes in Holy Writte, with grete deuocyon in preyeng and with mykel besines in studyen[g] goend before. þese moun comen to þe fyndeng whan oure Lord Jesu wil schew it.

See how grace opneth þe gostly eye and clereth þe witte of þe soule wonderly abofe þe frelte of þe corrupt kend. It ȝefeth þe soule a new ablenes, wheþer it wil reden Holy Writ or heren or þenken it, for to vnderstonden trewly and sauourly þe sothfastnes of it in þe maner before seyd, and for to turne redyly alle resons and wordes þat are bodily seyd into gostly vnderstondyng. And þat is no greete meruayl, for þe same Spirit expowneth it and [declareth] it in a clene soule in confort of it þat first made it; and þat is þe Holy Gost. And þis grace may be and is as wele in a lewed as in a lettred man, as anemptes þe substaunce and þe trewe felynge of sothfastnes and þe gostly sauour of it in generale, þogh þe seen not so many resons of it in specyale, for þat nedeth not. And whan þe soule is þus abled and lyghtned þurgh grace, þan it list for to bene alon summetyme, oute of lettynge and commonynge of al creatures, þat it myght frely assayen his instru-

75 don] ne *prec.* As, not *add.* Ld gnawen] knowen M vpon] H$_7$HBH$_5$SrWsLwAPLdPlW, on AsEH$_6$CcMT bark withouten] rynde wiþoutforþ LdT karpe þei] thow they carpyn Pl karpe] speke H$_5$AsWsH$_6$W 76 þerof] *om.* As þe . . . of] *om.* T þe . . . within/þei . . . not] *rev.* Cc inly] inner T within] *om.* Cc þei felen] H$_7$LB$_3$SrLwEPH$_6$CcMPlW, *rev.* HBH$_5$WsALdT, yknowe þei As þei^{1}] for *prec.* Cc of] *om.* AsACc þei are] For ȝif þei ben As 77 not^{2}] no Sr frendes] frendid Ld 78 hem not] *rev.* T, not to hem Cc hem] *om.* As counseil] þat is *add.* As 79 vnder keye] and As keye] a *prec.* ATW, and *add.* Cc enseled] H$_7$, ⸢se⸣led H^{c}, asseled Sr, seled Σ, sigillatum Lat. Jesu is] H$_7$H$_5$LB$_3$AsAEPH$_6$, Jesus HBAsWsLwCcMLdPlTW, þe fyngyr of Jesu Sr þat . . . Gost] *om.* A 80 forthi] H$_7$HLB$_3$LwEPMLd`Pl´, þerfore BH$_5$SrWsAH$_6$TW, for why As, *om.* Cc loue and his^{2}] *om.* LdT may] ne *prec.* As 81 come in] comyn Cc He] For *prec.* As keye] keyes As 82 and^{2}] H$_7$CcPl, he *add.* Σ lateth in] *rev.* Cc 83 þurgh] by LwW and^{1}] ȝit he ne *add.* As And] *om.* AMPl 84 not] but *prec.* H$_6$ ⸢to al⸣ H^{c} to^{2}] *om.* A ylyke] þylke As bot to hem] *om.* As are specially] *rev.* M are] he E 85 þe] H$_7$BSrAH$_6$CcMLdPlT, *om.* HH$_5$LB$_3$AsWsLwEPW sothfastnes in] softnesse of B

withouten, karpen þei neuer so mikel þerof; þe inly sauour withinne
fele þei noȝt of. Þei ere not meke, þei are not clene for to seen it, þei
are not frendes to Ihesu, and þerfore he schewiþ hem not his conseil.
Þe pryuete of Holy Writte is closed vndir key ⌜se⌝led with a signet of
Ihesus fyngur, þat is þe Holy Gost, and forþi withouten his lufe and
his lefe may no man come in. He haþe only þe keye of kunnynge in his
134v kepinge, | as Holy Writ seiþ, and he is keye himself, and he latiþ in
whom he wil þurȝ inspiracioun of his grace and brekiþ not þe seele.
And þat doþ Ihesu to his lufe`r´s, not ⌜to al⌝ ilike, bot to hem þat are
specially inspired for to seken soþfastnes in Holy Writ, with grete
deuocioun in preyinge and with mikil bisynes in studyynge goynge
bifore. Þese mown come to þe fyndynge whan oure Lorde Ihesu wil
schewe it.

Se now þan how grace opniþ þe gostly `eye´, and cleriþ þe wit of þe soule wondirly aboue þe frelte of corupte kynde. It gifiþ þe soule a new abilnes, wheþer it wil reden Holy Writ or heren or þenken it, for to vndirstanden trewly and sauourly þe soþfastnes of it in þe maner bifore seide, and for to turne redily alle resouns and wordes þat are bodily seide into gostly vndirstandynge. And þat is no grete merueile, for þe same spirit expouniþ it and declariþ it in a clene soule in confort of it þat first made it; and þat is þe Holy Gost. And þis grace may be and is as wel in lewde as in lettred men, as anemptes þe substaunce and þe trewe felynge of soþfastnes and þe gostly sauour in general, þawȝ þei see not so many resouns in special, for þat nediþ not. And whan þe soule is þus abled and liȝtned þurȝ grace, þan it list for to ben alone sumtyme, out of lettynge or comunynge of al creatures, þat it miȝt frely assaien his instrument, þat I calle his

86 and] *om.* AsLdT   in^{2}] as be As, of H_6, and LdT   studyeng] studyens H_7 87 Jesu] God Wc, *om.* LdT   89 See] H_7, A see As, Se now þan Σ, Vide [Vnde Y] ergo nunc Lat.   gostly eye] Holi Gost As   `eye´ $H^c$, *om.* H°$H_5$   90 `wonderly´ Pl   þe^{2}] H_7E, *om.* Σ   91 Writ] write *add.* E   or^{2}] it or to As   it] *om.* A   92 vndirstonden] it *add.* LwTW   sothfastnes] trewþe H_6 93 redyly/alle . . . wordes] *rev.* Pl   redyly alle] *rev.* As   alle] *om.* B_3 94 bodily] *om.* Pl   is] nys As   greete] *om.* E   95 expowneth] expoungniþ H_6 it^{1}] *om.* Cc   declareth] deschargeth H_7, declaret Lat.   97 may be/. . ./is] *rev.* AH_6 may be and] *om.* As   a^{1}] H_7, *om.* Σ, laicis Lat.   lewed/. . ./lettred] *rev.* As   as^{2} . . . man] men as in lettred H_6 a lettred man] H_7, lettred men Σ, litteratis Lat.   lettred] lernyd H_6 þe] grace *add.* As. As *skips back to 41/164 here*   98 þe^{2}] of LB_3P   gostly] *corr. fr.* Holy Gooste Pl   of it] H_7LB_3SrLwAEPH_6CcMPlW, *om.* HBH_5AsWsLdT, eius Lat.   99 not] *om.* B_3 100 þurgh] loue *add.*, *canc.* Pl   101 list] likeþ Sr, listneþ AsM   for] *om.* AsT   to bene alon/summetyme] *rev.* As   lettynge] a *prec.* As   and] H_7, or HBH_5LB_3AsSrWsLw-EPH_6CcLdPlTW, or of AM, et Lat.   102 commonynge] connynge H_5, comyng WsCc   it] he Lw`Pl´W

ment, þat I kalle his reson, in beholdynge of sothfastnes þat is contened in Holy Wrytyng. And þan þer fallen vnto mende wordis and resons and sentence inogwe to occupyen it in ful ordinatly and ful sadly.

And what confort and gostly delyte, sauour and swetnesse, a soule may felen þan in þis gostly werk þurgh dyuers illuminacyons, inly perceyfynges, pryue knowynges, and sodeyn towchynges of þe Holy Gost, by assay þe soule may wyten, and not ellys. And I hope þat he schal not erren, be so þat his teeth, þat are his inly wyttes, be keped whyte and clene fro gostly pryde and fro curyouste of kendly witte. I hope þat Dauid felt ful grete delyte in þis maner werk whan he seyd f. 110^{r} þus: *Quam dulcia faucibus meis eloquia tua,* | *super mel ori meo!* How swete are þi spekynges Lord Jesu to my chekes, ouer hony to my mowthe! Þat is, Lord Jesu, þin holy wordys endyted in Holy Writte, broght to my mende þurgh grace, are swetter to my chekes, þat are þe affeccyons of my soule, þan hony is to my mowth. Sothly þis is a fayre werk and an honeste, withouten pynful trauaile for to seen Jesu þus.

Þis is a maner syght of Jesu, as I seyde before; not as he is, bot cloþed vnder lykenesse of werkes and of wordes, *Per speculum in enigmate*: By a myrroure and be lyknes, as þe Apostel seyth. Jesu is endeles myght, wisdom and godenesse, ryghtwysnesse, sothfastnesse, holynes and mercy. And what þis Jesu is in himself may no soule seen here, bot by effecte of his werkynge he may be seen þurgh þe lyght of grace, as þus: his myght is seen by makyng of alle creatures of noght, his wysdom in ordeynde disposyng of hem, his godenes in safyng of hem, his mercy in forgyffynge of synnes, his holynes in ȝiftes of grace, his ryghtwysnes in hard punyschyng of synne, his sothfastnes in

103 I kalle his] is M   kalle] clepe H$_6$LdT, cleped As   104 Wrytyng] Writ ACcW, Scriptura Lat.   þan] *om.* LB$_3$PH$_6$ [*caret for inclusion, but canc. in marg.* L]   þer] *om.* T   fallen] H$_7$HBH$_5$AsSrWsLwCcLdPlTW, falleþ LB$_3$AEPH$_6$M, occurrunt Lat.   vnto] H$_7$, to Σ, there *prec.* Cc   105 and[1]] *om.* T   and sentence] *om.* M   sentence] H$_7$LB$_3$SrEPCcPl, sentences HBH$_5$AsWsLwAH$_6$LdTW, sentencie Lat.   it] H$_7$LB$_3$SrA⌜H^{c}⌝EPH$_6$CcMPl`W$^{G}$´, him H$_5$WsLwW, *om.* BAsLd   in] inow *add.* A, *om.* LB$_3$PH$_6$Cc `ordinatly´ W^{G}, ordynate W   ful[2]] om. LdT   107 what] þurgh *add.* As   and gostly] *om.* M   and[2]] *om.* LwCc   delyte . . . gostly (l. 108)] *om.* A   sauour] *om.* Lw   108 þan] *om.* As   þis] his LwW   þurgh dyuers] These Lw   dyuers] *om.* As   109 perceyfynges] perceyuynge T   knowynges] knowinge T   towchynges] touchynge T   110 by assay] þat As   not ellys] H$_7$, *rev.* Σ   hope] trowe A   þat] *om.* ELdT   111 erren] *om.* T   be[1]] ȝif hit *prec.* AM, *om.* H$_5$Ws   inly] inwarde LwW   112 witte] and clene. For *add.* As   113 þat] *om.* AsH$_6$ maner] of *add.* H$_5$Ws   werk] *om.* LdT   114 þus] Ps. *add.* B, Ps. 118° *add.* LEPLdTW   How] þat is *prec.* E   115 Lord] our *prec.* H$_6$ ouer . . . mowthe] ⌜or aboue hony to mouþ⌝ L   ouer] or aboue LP, and ouer B$_3$, and aboue EH$_6$, aboue LdT   116 þin] in *prec.* As   endyted] enditeth M   117 my[1]]

resoun, in biholdynge of soþfastnes þat is contened in Holy Wrytynge. And þan þer fallen to mende wordes and resouns and sentences inowe to occupien `it´ in ful ordinatly and ful sadly.

135r And what conforte and gostly delite, sauour and | swetnes, a soule may felen þan in þis gostly werke þurȝ diuers illuminaciouns, inly perceifynges, pryuey knowynges, and sodeyne touchynges of þe Holy Gost, bi assaie þe soule may weten, and elles noȝt. And I hope þat he schal not erren, be so þat his teeþ, þat are his inly wittes, be kepid white and clene fro gostly pryde and fro curiouste of kyndly wite. I hope þat Dauid felt ful grete delyte in þis maner werk whan he seide þus: *Quam dulcia faucibus meis eloquia tua, super mel ori meo!* How swete are þi spekynges Lord Ihesu to my chekes, ouer hony to my mouþ! þat is, Lorde Ihesu, þin holy wordes endited in Holy Writte, broȝt to my mende þurȝ grace, are swetter to my chekes, þat are þe affeccions of my soule, þan hony is to my mouþ. Soþly þis is a faire werke and an honest, withouten pyneful traueil for to seen Ihesu þus.

þis is on maner siȝt of Ihesu, as I seide bifore; not as he is, bot cloþed vndir liknes of werkes and of wurdes, *Per speculum in enigmate*: by a mirour and by a liknes, as þe Apostel seiþ. Ihesu is en`d´les miȝt, wisdom and goodnes, riȝtwisnes, soþfastnes, holynes and mercy. And what þis Ihesu is in himself may no soule seen heere, bot bi effecte of his wirkynge he may be seen þurȝ þe liȝt of grace, as þus: his miȝt is seen by makynge of alle creatures of noȝt, his wisdam in ordinat disposynge of hem, his godnes in sauynge of hem, his mercy in forgifnes of synnes, his holynes in giftes of grace, his riȝtwisnes in harde punischynge of synne, his soþfastnes in trewe rewardynge of

om. M þe] þyn As, *om.* LB$_3$PM 118 þis] ther M 119 and an honeste] *om.* LwW an] *om.* AsSr withouten] by-þouten B pynful] any *prec.* M Jesu þus] *rev.*, *marked for trsp.* L 120 a] H$_7$ALd, oo LB$_3$SrWsLwEH$_6$T, on HBH$_5$AsPMCcPlW maner] of *add.* AsSrLwTW 121 of[2]] *om.* B$_3$ wordes] 1 Cor. 13° *add.* BLEPLdTW Per . . . lyknes (l. 122)/as . . . seyth] *rev.* Cc speculum] etiam *add.* HAs`W[G]´, et *add.* SrLwMPl 122 By] þat is *prec.* E myrroure/. . ./lyknes] *rev.* H$_5$AsWs myrroure] in derknesse *add.*, *canc.* B$_3$ be] *om.* B$_3$AsM lyknes] H$_7$SrCcPl, a *prec.* Σ seyth] he is seyn in *add.* Cc Jesu] *The third extract in* Td *starts here* 123 wisdom] and *prec.* H$_5$AsWs and] in H$_5$As ryghtwysnesse] and *prec.* H$_5$Ws, and *add.* Wc, *om.* As 124 þis] is Jesu [Jesu *canc.*] As, *om.* CcWc may] þere *prec.* As, *one-word canc. prec.* H seen here] seen ne heere Lw`H[c]´EW, hic videre Lat. 125 effecte] affectes H$_5$, affeccioun As, þe *prec.* LB$_3$EPH$_6$Td his] þis As, *om.* T be] *om.* LB$_3$PH$_6$, videri Lat. 126 grace] his *prec.* E as] *om.* H$_5$Ws þus] *om.* Td seen] be seyn *add.*, *canc.* Cc 127 his[1]] of *prec.* As in[1]] bi T, þe *add.* E ordeynde] H$_7$MPl, ordeynyng and SrTd, ordynat Σ hem] him As in[2]] of Cc 128 hem] him As forgyffynge] H$_7$BLB$_3$SrAEPH$_6$CcMLdPlT, forgifnes HH$_5$AsWsLwWWc synnes] his *prec.* As 129 hard] *om.* M of synne] *om.* Td synne] synnys Sr sothfastnes] softnes W

trew⌜e⌝ rewardyng of gode werkys. And al þis is expressed in Holy Writte, and þis seeth a soule in Holy Writte with alle oþer accidence þat fallen þerto. And wyte þu wele þat swilk gracyous knowengys in Holy Writte or in any oþer wrytyng þat is made þurgh grace, are not ellys bot swete lettre-sendyngys made atwix [a] louynge soule and Jesu loued; or ellys if I schal sey sothlyer atwix Jesu þe trewe lufere and soules lufed of him. He hath ful grete tendernes of lufe to alle his chosen children þat are here closed in cley of þis bodily lyfe; and þerfore þogh he be absent fro hem, heygh hid abouen in bosum of þe Fader, fulfilled in delytes of his blissed godhed, neuerþeles he þenkeþ on hem and vysyteth hem ful often þurgh his gracyous gostly presence, and conforteth hem by his lettres of Holy Wrytte, and dryfeth owte of here hertes heuynesse and yrksumnesse, dowtys and dredys, and maketh hem glad and mery in him, trewly trowande to
f. 110v alle his byhetyngys and mekely | abydende in fulfillynge of his wil.

Seynt Poule seyth þus: *Quecumque scripta sunt, ad nostram doctrinam scripta sunt, vt per consolacionem scripturarum spem habeamus.* Al þat is writen, to oure techyng it is writen, þat by confort of wrytynge we myght hafe hope of saluacyon. And þis is anoþer werk of contemplacyon, for to seen Jesu in scripturis after openyng of þe gostly eye. þe clenner þat þe syght is in beholdyng, þe more conforted is þe affeccyon in þe tastyng. A ful lytel sauour felt in a clene soule of Holy Writte, in þis maner before seyde, schul make þe soule setten lytel prys by knowyng of alle þe seuene artys or of al werdly conynges. For

130 trewe] *erasure of three letters' length* H$_7$ rewardyng] reward Cc of gode werkys] *om.* Td And] for *add.* Td þis is] þese arn Sr is . . . þis (l. 131)] *om.* A 131 and . . . Writte^2] *om.* B$_3$SrTTd seeth] seiþ AsCc `with´ Sr oþer accidence] *rev.* E oþer] þe Pl, þe *prec.* Ws accidence] H$_7$Td, accidentes Σ 132 fallen] longen T þerto] H$_7$LB$_3$SrAEPH$_6$CcLdPlT, hereto HBH$_5$AsWsLwMW wyte þu] witten M wele] *om.* Ld þat] all *add.* T knowengys] knowyng Cc 133 any oþer] anoþer H any] or many M, *om.* LwAWWc wrytyng] wriȝtyngis As þurgh] by T 134 lettre-sendyngys] H$_7$BH$_5$SrWsLdPl, letter sendyng M, lett⌜res⌝ sendynges H^c, lettres sendynges LB$_3$PCc, letterus sending AH$_6$WcTd, letteris sende⌜n and⌝ LwW, letters and sendinges T, littere misse Lat. atwix] H$_7$HLSrLwP, bytwexte BB$_3$AsEMLdPlWTd, bitwene H$_5$WsAH$_6$TWc, atwyn Cc a louyng soule] HBH$_5$B$_3$AsWsLwPLdTWWc, louyng soule H$_7$, ⌜a louend⌝ soule L, louynge soules SrAH$_6$CcMPl, animas diligentes Lat. 135 sey] *om.* A sothlyer] soþere Td atwix] H$_7$HLSrLwEP, bytwexte BB$_3$AsMLdPlWTd, bitwene H$_5$WsAT, atwen H$_6$Cc trewe] trewelyer As and] þan As 136 soules lufed of] soule is to As soules] H$_7$CcMPlTd, þe *prec.* Σ of him] *om.* Td `of$^1$´ Ld, to H$_5$Ws him] hem M He] For *prec.* As 137 here] *om.* A ⌜lyfe⌝ H$^c$, loue Pl, body H$_5$Ws, erþe As 138 absent] and *add.* As heygh hid] hiȝed B$_3$Sr hid] *om.* TTd abouen] *om.* B bosum] H$_7$H°BLB$_3$SrAP, `þe´ *prec.* H^c, þe *prec.* H$_5$AsWsLwEH$_6$CcMLdPlTW þe] hys Pl 139 his] H$_7$LB$_3$SrAEPH$_6$CcMPl, þe HBH$_5$AsWsLwLdTWTd, sue Lat. neuerþeles] H$_7$, neuerþeles ȝif LB$_3$SrAEPH$_6$CcPl, neuerþeles ȝit

gode werkes. And al þis is expressed in Holy Writ, and þis seeþ a
135^v soule in Holy Wryt | with alle oþer accidentes þat fallen herto. And wete þou wele þat swilk graciouse knowynges in Holy Writ, or in [any oþer] wrytynge þat is made þurȝ grace, are not elles bot swete lett⌜res⌝ sendynges made atwix a lufende soule and Ihesu lufed; or elles if I schal sey soþlier atwix Ihesu þe trewe lufer and þe soules lufed of him. He haþ ful grete tendrenes of lufe to alle his chosen children þat are here closed in cleiȝe of þis bodily ⌜life⌝; and þerfore þawȝ he be absent fro hem, heiȝe hid abofen in \`þe´ bosum of þe Fader, fulfilled in delices of þe blissed godhed, not forþi he þenkiþ vpon hem and visitiþ hem ful often þurȝ his graciouse gostly presence, and confortiþ hem bi his lettres of Holy Writte, and dryueþ out of here hertes heuynes and irknes, doutes and dredes, and makiþ hem glad and merye in him, trewly trowende to alle his bihetynges and mekly abidende fulfillynge of his wil.

Seynt Poul seid þus: *Quecunque scripta sunt, ad nostram doctrinam scripta sunt, vt per consolacionem scripturarum spem habeamus*. Al þat is wrytyn, to oure techynge it is writen, þat by conforte of writynge we miȝte hafe hope of saluacioun. And þis is anoþer werk of contemplacioun for to seen Ihesu in scriptures after opnynge of þe gostly eiȝe. Þe clenner þe siȝt is in beholdynge, þe more conforted is þe affeccioun in þe tastynge. A ful litel sauour felt in a clene soule of Holy Writ, in þis maner bifore seide, schulde make þe soule settyn litil prys bi knowynge of alle þe seuen artes or of alle werdly kunnynges. For þe

M, not forþi HWsLd, noȝt forþy ȝit Td, not for þan BH$_5$, yet notwythstondyng LwTW, adhuc tamen Lat. 140 on] H$_7$AEH$_6$CcMPl, vpon HBH$_5$AsWsLwLdTW, of LB$_3$P and . . . hem[2]] *om.* M ful often] *om.* Td gracyous . . . presence] grace Td gracyous gostly] *rev.* T gracyous] and *add.* As 141 his] wrytynge or *add.* H$_5$Ws, gracyous *add.* Sr of] *om.* Td 142 yrksumnesse] H$_7$SrCcM, irknes HLP, werynesse BH$_5$B$_3$WsLwH$_6$LdTW, sorynesse As 143 in him] *om.* Td him] hem LB$_3$P trewly trowande] *rev.* As trowande] trystande B, eþer belyuyng *add.* LdT 144 byhetyngys] hytyngis Td, bJestis AE in] H$_7$, and As, þe LB$_3$SrAEPH$_6$CcPl, to þe T, *om.* HBH$_5$WsLwLdWTd wil] *The third extract in* Td *ends here* 145 Seynt] Seying *prec.* Cc seyth þus] *rev.* As, þus seyde H$_5$ seyth] H$_7$LB$_3$AsSrLwEPH$_6$CcMTW, seid HBH$_5$WsALdPl þus] Ro. 15° *add.* BLEPLdTW 146 Al] þat is *prec.* E 147 writen[1]] is *add.* As wrytynge] writinges B$_3$ 148 myght] mai LB$_3$P hafe] *om.* A anoþer] anere As 149 openyng] þe *prec.* Cc eye] and *add.* Sr 150 þe[1]] For *prec.* As þat] H$_7$BLB$_3$SrAEPH$_6$CcMLdPlT, *om.* HH$_5$AsWsLwW þe[2]] his A conforted] comforte AsCc 151 \`in[2]´ Pl clene soule] *rev.*, *marked for trsp.* E clene] sauoure of *add.* As 152 before] aforn As schul] H$_7$, schulde Σ [*corr. fr.* shul Pl], faceret Lat. þe] *corr. fr.* a Pl setten] to *prec.* H$_6$Cc 153 alle] *om.* A þe] *om.* LB$_3$AsP al werdly] a word be As al] the *add.* Cc, the worlde of all *add.* LwW conynges] kunnynge H$_5$AsSrWs

þe ende of his knowynge is saluacyon of a soule in aylastend lyf; and þe ende of oþer as for hemself is bot vanite and passend delyte, bot if þei ben turned þurgh grace to þis ende.

Of þe pryue voyce of Jesu sowned in a soule, whareby it may be knowen, and how alle þe gracyous illuminacyons made in a soule are kalled þe spekyng of Jesu. Capitulum xliiii^m

Lo, þese are fayre new felynggys in a clene soule; and if a soule wer fulfilled in swilk, it myght be seyd, and sothly, þat it were sumwhat reformed in felynge bot not ȝit fully. For why, ȝit Jesu scheweth more and ledeth þe soule inner, and bygynneth to spek more homly and more lufely to a soule, and redy is þe soule þan for to folwen þe sterynge of grace. For þe prophete seyth: *Quocumque ibat Spiritus, illuc gradiebantur et rote sequentes eum*. Whederso ȝede þe Spirit, þider ȝede þe whelys folwend him. By whelys are vnderstonden trewe lufers of Jesu, for þei are rounde in vertus withouten angle of frowardnesse, and lyghtly whyrland þurgh redynes of wil to þe sterynge of grace; for after þat grace stereth and towcheth so þei folwen and so þei werken, as þe prophete seyth. Bot þei haue first a ful syker assay and a trewe knowyng of þe voyce of grace or þei moun do so, þat þei ben not desceyued by þere owne feynynge or by þe mydday fende.

Oure Lord Jesu seyth þus: *Oues mee vocem meam audiunt, et cognosco*
f. 111r *eas et cognoscunt me mee*. My | schepe heren my voyce, and I know hem and þei knowe me. Þe pryue voyce of Jesu is ful trewe and it maketh a soule trewe. Þer is no feynyng in it, ne fantasye, ne pryde, ne ypocrysye, bot softnes, mekenes, pees, loue and charite, and it is ful of lyfe and of grace. And þerfor whan it sowneth in a soule it is of so

154 his] H_7, þis Σ, istius Lat. knowynge] cunnyng CcT saluacyon] satisfaccioun As a] mannes LwTW, *om.* Ld aylastend] H_7HBH_5LWsP, euerlastynge $B_3AsSrLw$-$AEH_6LdPlTW$ 155 oþer] the *prec.* Lw`Hc´M, that *prec.* TW [*canc.* T] hemself] the self Cc passend] H_7ET, a *prec.* Σ 156 turned/þurgh grace] *rev.* E þurgh grace] *om.* Cc þurgh] by BT to] into A þis] his M

Chapter 44 *title*: $H_7LB_3SrAEPH_6MLdPlTW$ `How Jesu scheweþ him and spekeþ more homly and more louely to `a´ soule þat is sumwhat refourmed in feleinge, and he deþ it more ynnermorely to haue knowelech of goostly knoweinge.´ *d.h.* H þat a soule þurgh liȝt of grace may see gostly þingis and fulhed of vertues. As *om.* $HBH_5WsLwCc$ 1 sowned] sownend M, sowning ALdTW, sonante Lat. whareby] where M it] be *add.*, *canc.* L may] schal LdTW 2 and . . . Jesu (l. 3)] *om.* M how] *om.* Pl 3 kalled] clepid ELdT spekyng] H_7AH_6Ld, spekynges $LB_3SrEPPlTW$, locuciones Lat. 4 þese are] þis is A þese] those M fayre new] *rev.* AsT fayre] *om.* LB_3PH_6, pulcre Lat. felynggys] feling A clene soule] soule þat is clene H_6 5 fulfilled] fillid LdT in] wyth LwTW swilk] wilke M and] in As, *om.* H_6T sumwhat reformed] *rev.* LwW, come what refourmynge As 6 not ȝit] *rev.* LB_3EPH_6 ȝit] *om.* Cc fully . . . seyd (l. 67)] *om.* As For why] *rev.* M ȝit²]

ende of þis knowynge is safacioun of a soule in aylastende lif; and þe
36r ende of oþer as | for hemself is bot vanyte and a passende delit, bot if þei be turned þurȝ grace to þis ende.

[CHAPTER 44]

Lo, þese are faire newe felynges in a clene soule; and if a soule were fulfilled in swilke, it miȝt be saide, and soþly, þat it were sumwhat reformed in felynge bot not ȝit fully. For whi, ȝit Ihesu schewiþ more and lediþ þe soule innere, and bygynniþ to speke more homly and more lufly to a soule, and redy is þe soule þan for to folwen þe sterynge of grace. For þe prophet seiþ: *Quocunque ibat Spiritus, illuc gradiebantur et rote sequentes eum.* Whiderso ȝed þe Spirite, þeder ȝeden þe wheles folwende him. Bi wheles are vndirstonden trewe lufers of Ihesu, for þei arne rounde in vertue withouten angel of frowardnes, and liȝtly whirlande þurȝ redynes of wil to þe sterynge of grace; for after þat grace steriþ and techiþ so þei folwen and wirken, as þe prophet seiþ. But þei han first a ful siker assaye and a trewe knowynge of þe voice of grace or þei mown don so, þat þei be not desceifed by ⌜þere⌝ owne feynynge or bi þe midday fende.

Oure Lorde Ihesu seiþ þus of his lufers: *Oues mee vocem meam audiunt, et cognosco eas et cognoscunt me mee.* My schepe heren my voyce, and I knowe hem and þei knowe me. Þe pryuei voice of Ihesu is ful trewe and it makiþ a soule trewe. Þer is no feynynge in it, ne fantasie, ne pryde, ne ypocrisie, bot softnes, meknes, pees, lufe and charite, and it is ful of life and of grace. And þerfore whan it sowniþ in

om. M   7 þe soule/inner] *rev.* A   homly and more] *om.* Sr   and^2] *om.* BLd   8 lufely] Hu$_2$ *back*   for] *om.* LwW   9 sterynge] styrynges BPlT, feelynge LB$_3$PH$_6$, instinctum Lat.   seyth] Eze. i° *add.* BLELdTW   ibat] ibit LB$_3$PH$_6$ illuc] pariter *add.* A, *one-word canc.* H   10 gradiebantur/et rote] *rev.* A   gradiebantur] grediebantur H$_6$ eum] þat is *add.* E   Whederso . . . him (l. 11)] *om.* A   Whederso] Whereso Sr, Whedersoeuere H$_5$Ws   ȝede/þe Spirite] *rev.* SrLdT   11 whelys^2] þe *prec.* CcT   trewe] the *prec.* LwTW   12 Jesu] Jesu Christi Lat.   in vertus] and vertuose T   angle] aungel H$_6$, anger M, cornel Cc, corner LdT, cornerus A   13 whyrland] torninge A, rennyng aboute Hu$_2$ þe] *om.* LB$_3$P   sterynge] stondynge B   14 þat] *corr. fr.* þe Pl   so þei^2] H$_7$LB$_3$SrAEPH$_6$CcMPl, *om.* HBH$_5$WsLwHu$_2$LdTW   15 ful] wel H$_5$ syker] myȝti LB$_3$P, securam Lat.   16 þe . . . of^2] *om.* H$_6$ do so] *rev.* MPl   þat] For *prec.* Cc   17 ⌜þere⌝ H^c feynynge] felinge T   18 Jesu] *om.* Pl   seyth] seyd Cc   þus] H$_7$LB$_3$SrAEPH$_6$CcMPl, of his lufers HBH$_5$WsLwHu$_2$LdTW, in Euangelio Lat.   Oues] Io. 10 *prec.* BLEPLdTW   19 My] þat is *prec.* E   20 is . . . and] valde fidelis est et Lat. [B$_2$R$_2$; *all other Lat. MSS om.*]   and . . . trewe (l. 21)] *om.* Lw   21 trewe] ful *prec.* Ld   \`no´ Cc   feynyng] error A   in it/ne fantasye] *rev.* H$_6$ in it] þerin A   in] on B   ne^1] or A   ne^2] *om.* A   22 softnes] sothnesse Cc, soþfastnesse SrE, sobrietas Lat.   loue] *om.* M   23 lyfe] *om.* Lw, veritatis Lat.   and of] loue and LwW   soule] sodeynly leueþ of honde *add.*, *canc.* Pl   it^2 . . . soule (l. 24)] *om.* Cc   so] H$_7$BLB$_3$SrLwHu$_2$EPH$_6$CcLdPlW, *om.* HH$_5$WsAPlT

grete myght sumtyme, þat þe soule sodeynly leyth of hande alle þat þer is—preyeng, spekyng, redyng or thenkyng, in maner before seyd, and al maner bodily werk—and listneth þerto fully, herend and perceyuend in reste and in lufe þe swete steuene of þis gostly voyce, as it were rauysched fro þe mynde of alle erthly thynges. And þan sumtyme in þis pees scheweth Jesu him, sumtyme as an awghful maystre, and sumtyme as a reuerent fader, and sumtyme as a louely spouse. And it kepeþ a soule in a wonderful reuerence and in a louely beholdyng of him, þat þe soule lyketh wele þan and neuer so wele as þan. For it feleth so grete sykernes and so grete rest in Jesu, and so mikel fauour in his godenesse, þat it wold ay be so and neuer don oþer werk. It thenketh þat it toucheth Jesu, and þurgh vertu of þat vnspekable touchyng it is made stable and hole in itself, reuerently beholdyng only Jesu, as if þer were nothyng bot Jesu o thynge and ⟨it⟩ anoþer, born vp only by þe fauour and þe wonderful godenes of him, o thyng þat it seeth ⌜and feleth⌝.

And þis felyng is ofte-sythes withouten specyale beholdyng of Holy Writte, ne bot with fewe wordes formed in þe hert; not bot þus amonge fallen in swete wordys acordende to þe felyng, oyther lufend or wondrend, or oþerwyse sownend, as þe herte lyketh. Þe soule is ful mykel departed fro lufe or lykyng of `þe´ werld þurgh vertu of þis gracyouse felyng, and also fro mynde of þe werd mykel in þe mene tyme; it taketh non hede þerof, for it hath no tome þerto. Bot þan sumtyme after with þis fallen into a soule dyuers illuminacyons þurgh grace, þe whilk illuminacyons I calle þe spekyngys of Jesu and þe syght of gostly thynges. For wyte þu wele þat alle þe besynes þat Jesu

24 `sodeynly´ L, *om.* B$_3$H$_6$ leyth of hande] kast on side Hu$_2$ leyth] leuith AMPl, it *prec.* Cc þat[2]] euer *add.* H$_6$ 25 spekyng, redyng] *rev.* Sr maner] H$_7$LB$_3$SrAPH$_6$CcMPl, þe *prec.* HBH$_5$WsLwHu$_2$ELdTW 26 werk] werkis H$_6$ `and[2]´ Cc, *om.* M listneth] takiþ heed *add.* Hu$_2$ and[3]] *om.* LB$_3$PM 27 steuene] sownyng Hu$_2$ þis] his H$_7$T, huius Lat. 29 in þis pees/scheweth Jesu him] H$_7$LB$_3$SrAPH$_6$CcMPl, schewiþ Jesu in þis pees himself HBH$_5$WsLwHu$_2$ELdTW, in hac pace ostendit se Jesus Lat. scheweth Jesu] *rev.* H$_6$ 30 awghful] hawtful W, deedfull T, eþer dredful *add.* Ld, a felable *add.* Hu$_2$ and[1]] *om.* Cc a[1]] *om.* Lw 31 louely] loue`li´ L, loue B$_3$ a[1]] H$_7$LwMW, þe HBLB$_3$SrH$_5$Ws-AHu$_2$EPH$_6$CcLdPlT wonderful] wondir Cc in[2]] *om.* Pl 32 louely] lowly Cc 33 grete[1]] moche LB$_3$EP, tantam Lat. grete rest] grest Pl 34 so[1]] *om.* Pl fauour] sauour ELdT in] H$_7$E, of Σ, bonitatis Lat. ay] H$_7$HBLPCcM, euer H$_5$B$_3$WsLwA-Hu$_2$EPlW, alwey SrLdT be] do A 35 þat it toucheth] *om.* Lw vertu of] *om.* LdT 36 vnspekable] vnseable H$_5$Ws stable and hole] H$_7$LB$_3$SrAEPH$_6$CcMPl, *rev.* HBH$_5$Ws-LwHu$_2$LdTW itself] the self Cc 37 beholdyng only] *rev.* Cc as . . . Jesu[2]] *om.* A if] þouȝ B nothyng] noon oþer þyng LdT o thynge] *om.* H$_6$ 38 it] H$_7$LB$_3$SrAPH$_6$CcMPl [H$_7$ *partially erased*], he HBH$_5$WsLwHu$_2$ELdTW anoþer] `it is´ *add. d.h.* H$_7$, þing *add.* ACc only] *om.* LB$_3$PH$_6$Cc, solum Lat. fauour] sauour BLwW þe[2]] *om.* B 39 o thyng

a sowle it is of grete miȝt sumtyme, þat þe soule sodeynly leiþ of
136ᵛ hande al þat þer is—preynge, spekynge, redynge | or þenkynge, in þe maner bifore saide, and alle maner bodily werk—and listneþ þerto fully, herende and perceifende in reste and in lufe þe swete steuen of þis gostly voice, as it were rauisched fro þe mende of alle erþly þinges. And þan sumtyme schewiþ Ihesu in þis pees himself as an a`u´ghful maistur, and sumtyme as a reuerent fader, and sumtyme as a lufly spouse. And it kepiþ þe soule in a wunderful reuerence and in a lufly biholdynge of him, þat þe soule likiþ wel þan and neuer so wel as þan. For it feliþ so grete sikernes and so grete rest in Ihesu, and so mikel fauour of his godnes, þat it wolde ay be so and neuer don oþer werk. It þinkiþ þat it touchiþ Ihesu, and þurȝ vertue of þat vnspekable touchynge it is made hool and stable in itself, reuerently biholdynge only Ihesu, as if þer were noþinge bot Ihesu on þinge and he anoþer, born vp only bi þe fauour and þe wundirful godnes of him, þat is þat þinge þat he seeþ and feliþ.

And þis felynge is oft-siþes withoutyn special beholdynge of Holy Write, ne bot with few wordes `formed in þe hert, noȝt but among fallen in swete wordes´ acordend to þe felynge, ouþer lofende or worschipende or oþerwise sownende, as þe herte likiþ. Þe soule is ful mikel departid fro luf or likynge of þe werld þurȝ vertue of þis gracious felynge, and also fro mende of þe werld mikel in þe mene tyme; it takiþ none hede þerof, for it haþ no thom þerto. Bot þan sumtyme as tyte with þis fallen into a soule diuers illuminaciouns þurȝ grace, þe whilke illuminaciouns I calle þe spekynges of Ihesu and þe siȝt of gostly þinges. For wyte þou wel þat alle þe bisynes þat Ihesu

. . . feleth] *om.* Lat. o thyng] H$_7$LB$_3$SrPCc, of þing H$_6$, þat is þat þinge HBH$_5$Ws-Hu$_2$ELdTW, *om.* LwAMPl it] H$_7$LB$_3$SrAPH$_6$CcMPl, he HBH$_5$WsLwHu$_2$LdTW seeth and feleth] *rev.* LwW ⌜and feleth⌝ *over erasure* H$_7$ 40 ofte-sythes] H$_7$HBH$_5$SrWs-LwHu$_2$CcMLdPlT, ofte tyme LB$_3$EPH$_6$, ofttimes AW 41 ne] and Cc `formed . . . wordys (l. 42)´ H$^c$, *om.* H°H$_5$Ws þe] *om.* A not . . . þus] but if it be that Cc `þus´ Lw, *om.* H^c 42 acordende] acordant A lufend] leuynge H$_5$Ws, laudancia Lat. 43 wondrend] H$_7$LB$_3$SrAPH$_6$CcMPl, worschipende HBH$_5$WsHu$_2$LdT, worschippinge or *prec.* LwEW [or wondering *interl., d.h.* Lw], admirancia Lat. as] *erasure seq.* H$_7$ ful mykel/departed] *rev.* H$_5$Ws ful] *om.* ELdT 44 `þeinterl. H$_7$ vertu] þe *prec.* Hu$_2$ þis] his Ld 45 gracyouse felyng] feling þat is gracios AMPl and also fro] It hath no Cc fro . . . werd/ mykel] *rev.* E mynde] þe *prec.* EH$_6$ mykel] *om.* Cc in] for Cc 46 it] ne *prec.* Cc non] no Hu$_2$H$_6$ tome] H$_7$HBH$_5$LB$_3$SrWsEPCcMPl`W^G´, tyme LwHu$_2$H$_6$TW, leyser A, while Ld þerto] *om.* M 47 after] H$_7$LB$_3$SrAEPH$_6$CcMPl, anon BH$_5$WsLdTW, anon *prec.* Hu$_2$, as tyte HLw`W^G´, aliquando postea Lat. with] *om.* Cc 48 whilk] *om.* Sr illuminacyons] *om.* Cc calle] clepe H$_6$LdT spekyngys] spekinge T

maketh abowte a soule is for to make it a trew perfyte spouse vnto him
f. 111^v in þe heyghnes and þe fulnes of lufe. And for þat may | not be don sodeynly, þerfor Jesu, þat is lufe and of alle lufers þe wysest, assayeth by many wyses and by wonderful menes or it may come abowten; and þerfore þat it myght come to affect of trewe spouseage, he hath swilk gracyous spekyng in lyknes of a wowere to a chosen soule. He scheweth his pryue jewelys, mykel thyng he ȝifeth and more he beheteth, and curteys dalyaunce he schewith; often he visiteth with mykel grace and gostly conforte, as I haue before seyd. Bot how he doth þis in speciale, al fully kan I note telle þe, for it nedeth not. Neuerþeles sumwhat schal I seyn, after þat grace stereth.

Þe drawyng of a soule fully to perfyte lufe is first by þe schewyng of gostly þynges to a clene soule, whan þe gostly eye is opned; not þat a soule schuld rest þerin and make an ende þere, bot by þat ȝit seken him and lufen him only þat is heyghest of al, withouten ony beholdyng of ony oþer þyng þan himself is. Bot what are þese gostly thynges, seyst þu, for I speke ofte of gostly thynges? To þis I answere and seye þat gostly thyng may be seyd alle þe sothfastnes of Holy Writte. And þerfore a soule þat þurgh lyght of grace may seen þe sothfastnes of it, it seeth gostly thynges, as I haue before seyde.

How þurgh gracyous opneng of þe gostly eye a soule is made wys mekely and sothfastly for to seen Holy Kirke as trauaylend and as blissed, and for to seen þe aungels kende reproued for þere malyce. Capitulum xlv^m

Neuerþeles oþer gostly thynges þer ben also, þe whilk þurgh lyght of grace are schewed to þe soule, and are þese: þe kende of alle resonable

50 is] it *prec.* Cc for] *om.* Lw \`a´ Pl perfyte] *om.* LB$_3$PH$_6$, fidelem Lat. 51 and$^1$ . . . al oþer (46/72)] *om.* B$_3$. *Four fols. missing* and$^1$ þe fulnes] *rep.* B, *om.* LPH$_6$, et plenitudine and$^1$] in *add.* E þe] *om.* Pl \`for´ Ld, *om.* W þat] it Cc not] *om.* Pl 52 sodeynly] so *prec.* LwW lufe] verey *prec.* Hu$_2$ þe] *om.* HH$_5$Ws wysest] wysed M 53 wyses] wise Ws, weyes Sr by^2] *om.* H$_5$Ws wonderful] H$_7$LSrAPH$_6$CcMPl, many *prec.* HBH$_5$WsLwHu$_2$ELdTW, mirabilibus Lat. 54 myght] maye M affect] affectis H$_5$, þe *prec.* H$_6$PlW 55 spekyng] H$_7$T, spekynges Σ, locuciones Lat. in lyknes of] in maner of Lw, this maner of W of] H$_7$LSrLwAEPH$_6$CcMPlW, to HBH$_5$WsHu$_2$Ld to] *rep.*, *canc.* H 56 scheweth] summe of *add.* Hu$_2$ pryue] *om.* HH$_5$Ws, secreta Lat. he^2] *om.* LEPH$_6$Pl 57 and] *om.* A curteys] curtasie and Ws dalyaunce] and talkyng *add.* Hu$_2$ often] ofttymes Hu$_2$ 58 \`grace´ Pl haue] *om.* W before seide] said here before Hu$_2$ how he] he hwo W 59 þis/in speciale] *rev.* H$_5$Ws þe] *om.* LPH$_6$ 60 schal I] *rev.* Sr 61 þe^1] *om.* Ld. *The fourth extract in* Td *starts here* fully/to . . . lufe] *rev.* E fully] ful Pl þe^2] *om.* SrCcTd 62 gostly] *om.* Td opned] opene B 63 schuld] schal A rest] duelle T an] H$_7$LSrLwAEPH$_6$CcMPlW, *om.* HBH$_5$WsHu$_2$LdT þere] *om.* Td ȝit] it Lw, to T, \`scholde´ *add.* H, myght Wc, *om.* W 64 only/þat . . . al] H$_7$LSrLwA-

makiþ aboute a soule is for to make it a trew perfite spouse to him in þe heiȝenes and þe fulnes of lufe. And for þat may not be done
137^{v} sodeynly, þerfore Ihesu, þat is lufe and of alle | lufers wisest, assaieþ bi many wises and bi many wndirful menes or it may come aboute; and þerfore þat it miȝt come to effect of trewe spousage, he haþ swilke gracious spekynges in liknes to a wowere to a chosen soule. He schewiþ his iuelis, mikel þinge he gifiþ and more he bihotiþ and curteys dalyaunce he schewiþ; often he visitiþ with mikil grace and gostly conforte, as I hafe bifore seide. Bot how he doþ þis in special, al fully kan I not telle þe, for it nediþ not. Nerþeles sumwhat schal I seyen, after þat grace steriþ.

Þe drawynge of a soule fully to perfite lufe is firste by þe schewynge of gostly þinges to a clene soule, whan þe gostly eiȝe is opned: not þat a soule schulde resten þerin and makyn ende þer, bot bi þat ȝit seken him and lufen him þat is heiȝest of al, only, withouten ony biholdynge of ony oþer þinge þan himself is. Bot what are þese gostly þinges, seist þu, for I speke often of gostly þinges? To þis I answere and seye þat gostly þinge may be seide al þe soþfastnes of Holy Writte. And þerfore a soule þat þurȝ liȝt of grace may seen þe soþfastnes of it, it seeþ gostly þinges, as I hafe bifore seide.

[CHAPTER 45]

Nerþeles oþer gostly þinges þer ben also, þe whilke þurȝ `liȝt of´ grace are schewed to þe soule, and are þese: þe kynde of alle resonable

EPH_6CcMPlW, *rev.* HBH_5WsHu_2LdWc only] namly Td, *om.* T withouten . . . is (l. 65)] *om.* Td ony] *om.* H_6 65 is] his M, *om.* LwW Bot] þan answerst and seyst *add.* Td þese] those M 66 seyst þu] *om.* Td ofte] *rep.*, *canc.* Sr To] vnto Sr I answere] *rev.* Cc 67 thyng] þingis H_6Wc seyd] As *back* sothfastnes] verrey trouþes Hu_{26} 68 lyght] H_7HBH_5AsWsLwHu_2LdTW, þe *prec.* LSrAEPH_6CcMPl 69 it^2] he CcTd before] aforn As, aboue T, *om.* Cc

Chapter 45 *title*: H_7LSrAEPH_6MLdPlTW `How þe synneful man shal ryse out of deedly synne and bysy him for to seche þat þe soule loueþ.´ *d.h.* H þat þere ben oþer gostly þingys yshewed to a deuoute soule as þe Trinyte by reuelaciouns and liȝtes of angres and worchyngis of oþer holy creaturys. As *om.* BH_5WsLwCcTd 1 gracyous] þe *prec.* E, *om.* LPH_6 2 for] *om.* TW seen] þe diuersite of degrees in *add.* ETW as . . . malyce (l. 4)] etc. M 3 and as blissed] *om.* EPTW as] *om.* AEH_6 and^2 . . . malyce (l. 4)] *rep. d.h. in lower marg.* L þe] H_7SrAPl, *om.* LEPH_6MLdTW kende] and first of *add.* ETW ⌜reproued . . . malyce⌝ L for . . . malyce (l. 4)] *om.* ETW 5 Neuerþeles] R *back* oþer] of Ld þurgh] *rep.*, *canc.* Sr `lyght of´ *interl.* H lyght] þe *prec.* Cc 6 þe^1] a CcWc and are þese] *om.* Td þese] those R alle] *om.* As resonable] creatures *add.*, *canc.* Pl

soules and þe gracyous werkyng of oure Lord Jesu in hem; þe kende of aungels, blissed and reproued, and here werkyng; and þe knowyng of þe blissed Trinite after þat grace techeth.

Holy Writte seyth in þe Boke of Songges þus: *Surgam et circuibo ciuitatem, et queram quem diligit anima mea.* I schal rysen and I schal gone abowte þe cyte, and I schal seken him þat my soule loueth. Þat
f. 112r is, | I schal rysen into heyghnes of thoght and gone abowte þe cyte. By this cyte is vnderstonden þe vniuersite of al creatures bodily and gostly, ordeyned and rewled vnder God by lawes of kende, of reson and of grace. I vmgo þis cyte whan I beholde þe kyndes and causes of bodily creatures, þe ȝiftes, graces and blissis of gostly creatures, and in alle þese I seke him þat my soule lufeth. It is fayre lokyng with þe inner eye on Jesu in bodily creatures, for to seen his myght, his wisdom and his godenes in ordenaunce of here kende; bot it is mykel fayrer lokyng on Jesu in gostly creatures. First in resonable soules, boþe of chosen and of reproued, for to seen þe mercyful callynge of him to his chosen: how he turneth hem fro synne by lyght of his grace; how he helpeth hem, techeth hem, he chastiseth hem, he conforteth hem; he ryghteth, he clenseth, he fedeth; how he makeþ hem brennend in lufe and schynend in lyght by plente of his grace. And þis doth he not to o soule only, bot to alle his chosen, after mesure of his grace. Also þe reproued, how ryghtfully he forsakeþ hem—he leueth hem in here synne and doth hem no wrong—how he rewardeth hem in þis werd, suffrend hem for to hafe fulfillyng of here wille, and after þis for to punysche hem endlesly.

7 gracyous] ben þese and þe *add.* As oure Lord Jesu] Jesu Christi Lat. Jesu] God Wc, Crist *add.* B, *om.* Td 8 reproued] yproued As and[2]] in H$_5$WsWc 9 blissed] *om.* Td 10 in . . . Songges/þus] *rev.* H$_6$ Songges] H$_7$RLSrPH$_6$CcMPl, ympnis A, of þe spouse *add.* HBH$_5$AsWsLwHu$_2$ETWTd, of þe spousesse Ld, canticorum Lat. þus] Cant. 3° *add.* BLHu$_2$EPLdTW, of þe spouse *add.* Td, *om.* A 11 I[1]] þat is *prec.* EWc I[2]] *om.* As 12 gone] al *add.* Sr I schal] *om.* Td 13 rysen] aryse As, he seyþ *add.* Td heyghnes] heynest Cc, þe *prec.* Sr of thoght] *om.* HH$_5$AsWs, cogitacionis Lat. 14 this] þe AH$_6$Wc 15 ordeyned and rewled/vnder God (9)] *rev.* H$_5$Ws and rewled/vnder God] *rev.* A lawes] louys As ⌜reson⌝ `and´ L 16 I vmgo] in goynge aboute As vmgo] H$_7$RLAPM, vmbigo H`T[G]W[G]´, go aboute BH$_5$SrWsLwHu$_2$EH$_6$CcLdPlTWTdWc þis] þe A cyte] and *add.* As þe . . . creatures (l. 17)] *om.* M causes] H$_7$RACcM, þe *prec.* HBH$_5$LAsSrWsLwHu$_2$EPH$_6$LdPlTWWc 17 graces] H$_7$RAPH$_6$MPl, þe *prec.* Sr, of *prec.*, *canc.* L, of grace HBH$_5$AsWsLwHu$_2$ECcLdTWWc, gracias Lat. blissis] H$_7$RLAHu$_2$PH$_6$CcMPl þe *prec.* HBH$_5$AsSrWsLwELdTW, þe blysse Wc 18 þese] those R, this M, *om.* LP fayre] a *prec.* T with . . . eye (l. 19)/on Jesu] *rev.* E 19 on] of RAsMPl Jesu] God Td myght] *rep.*, *canc.* Td 20 godenes in ordenaunce] *rev.*, *marked for trsp.* L in] of A here] oþer Td 21 fayrer] fayre Cc lokyng] to loken As Jesu] God Td resonable] þe *prec.* LPH$_6$ 22 of[1]] in Sr, þe H$_6$W, *om.* Lw of[2]] H$_7$RAsSrAECcPl, of þe H$_6$, *om.*

soules, and þe gracious wirkynge of oure Lorde Ihesu in hem; þe kynde of aungels, blissed and reproued, and here wirkynge; and þe knowynge of þe blissed trynite after þat grace techiþ.

Holy Writte seiþ in þe Boke of Songes of þe spouse þus: *Surgam et*
37v *circuibo ciuitatem,* | *et queram quem diligit anima mea.* I schal rise and I schal goo aboute þe cite, and I schal seken him þat my soule lufiþ. Þat is, I schal rise into heiȝenes and gon aboute þe cite. Bi þis cite is vndirstonden þe vniuersite of alle creatures bodily and gostly, ordeynde and rewlid vndir God bi lawes of kynde, of resoun and of grace. I vmbigo þis citee whan I beholde þe kyndes and þe causes of bodily creatures, þe giftes of grace and þe blisses of gostly creatures, and in alle þese I seke him þat my soule lufiþ. It is feire lokynge with þe inner eiȝe on Ihesu in bodily creatures, for to seen his miȝt, his wisdom and his goodnes in ordeynaunce of here kynde; bot it is mikil fairer lokying on Ihesu in gostly creatures. First in resonable soules, boþ of chosen and reproued, for to seen þe merciful callinge of him to his chosen: how he turneþ hem fro synne bi liȝt of his grace; how he helpiþ hem, techiþ hem, chastisiþ hem, confortiþ hem; he riȝtiþ, he clensiþ, he fediþ; howe he makiþ hem brennende in luf and in liȝte bi plente of his grace. And þis doþ he not to on soule only, bot to alle his chosen, after mesure of his grace. Also \`of´ þe reprofed, how riȝtfully he forsakes hem and lefiþ hem in here synne and doþ hem no wronge; how he rewardiþ hem in þis werld, suffrend hem for to haue fulfillynge of here wil, and after þis for to punischen hem endelesly.

HBH$_5$LWsLwHu$_2$PMLdTW reproued] proued As for] *om.* LwW mercyful] merueiles A callynge] clepynge AsH$_6$LdT 23 him] hem A his^1] *om.* W hem] him As, *om.* A his^2] *om.* AM 24 he^1] *om.* H$_5$ hem^1] him As, and *add.* LdT techeth hem] *om.* As techeth] he *prec.* Td he^2] H$_7$RLPCcMPl, and Wc, *om.* HBH$_5$AsSrWsLwAHu$_2$EH$_6$LdTW he^2] H$_7$RLAsSrPH$_6$CcM, and Wc, *om.* HBH$_5$Ws-LwAHu$_2$ELdPlTW hem^3] him As chastiseth hem] chastise him As, chastis Td, and *add.* T he^3] and As 25 ryghteth] H$_7$HBH$_5$SrWsLwHu$_2$TW, hem *add.* RLAEPH$_6$-CcMLdPlTd, him *add.* As he^2] *om.* As clenseth ⌜hem . . . fedeth hem⌝ L clenseth] cloþeþ Pl, hem *add.* ⌜L⌝APCcPlWTdc, him *add.* As he^3] and AsATd fedeth] hem *add.* ⌜L⌝EPCcPl, him and *add.* As \`he$^4$´ Sr hem] him As 26 lufe . . . in$^2$] *om.* LPWc lufe] his *prec.* Td schynend] H$_7$RLSrAPH$_6$CcMPl, *om.* HBH$_5$AsWsLwHu$_2$ELdTWTd, splendentes Lat. in$^2$] *om.* As And . . . grace (l. 28)] *om.* M 27 þis doth] þus E \`þis´ Td, thus LwW doth he] *om.* B to o soule/only] *rev.* As to^1] *rep.*, *canc.* H only] al *prec.* H$_5$Ws alle] *om.* LPH$_6$ after mesure] bi plente LdT after] bi A of] *rep.*, *canc.* L, *om.* Wc 28 grace] mercy B Also] H$_7$, Also alle H$^{\circ}$H$_5$Ws, And of Sr, Also \`of´ H$^{c}$, Also of Σ, \`of´ alle, alle *add.* AsLwEW, *om.*, de Lat. þe] *om.* RWTd ryghtfully] ryȝtwisly H$_5$WsA forsakeþ hem] *rev.* As he^2] H$_7$, and Σ 29 leueth] leue H$_5$, lediþ Hu$_2$ synne] synnes LwHu$_2$W how] and *prec.* As, et Lat. 30 suffrend] suffers Td for] *om.* LwPlTW fulfillyng] the *prec.* LwW 31 þis] lyf *add.* Ws for to punysche] punysche H$_5$, punissheth Ws, ryghtwysly he punysshyth Wc for] *om.* LwW

Lo, þis is a lytel beholdyng of Holy Kyrke whylis it is trauaylend in þis lyfe, for to seen how blak and how fowle it semeth in soules þat are reproued, how fayre and how louely it is in chosen soules. And al þis gostli syght is not ellys bot þe syght of Jesu, not in himself, bot in his mercyful pryuey werkes and in his hard ryghtwys domes, ilk day schewed and renewed to resonable soules. Also ouer þis, for to seen with þe gostly eye þe peynes of reproued in þe ioye and þe blisse of chosen soules, it is ful confortable. For sothfastnes may not be seen in a clene soule withouten grete delyte and wonderful softnes of brennend lufe.

Also þe syght of aungels kende, first of þe dampned and after of þe
f. 112v blissed. It is a ful fayre contemplacyon of þe | fende in a clene soule, whan grace bryngeth þe fende to þe syght of þe soule as a clumsed caytyf, bounden with þe myght of Jesu þat he may not deren. Þan þe soule beholdeth him not bodili bot gostly, seend his kende and his malice, and turneth him vp-so-doun; hospileth him and [rendyth] him al to noȝt; it scorneth him and dispicith him and settith nouȝt be his malice. Þus biddith Holi Writ whan it seyth þus: *Verte impium et non erit*. Turne þe wykkyd, þat is þe fend, vp-so-doun, and he schal be as nouȝt. Mykel wondir hath þe soule þat þe fend hath so mekyl malice and so lytel myȝth. Þer is no creature so vnmyȝthi as he is, and þerfore is it a gret cowardise þat men drede him so muche. He may noþyng don withouten leue of oure Lord Jesu, not so mykel as entren into a swyn, as þe Gospel seyth; my`kil´ lesse may he þan noyȝen ony man.

And þan if oure Lord Jesu ȝeue him leue for to taryen vs, it is ful worthily and ful mercyfully don þat oure Lord Jesu doth. And þerfore

32 `a´ Cc is trauaylend] traueliþ LdT is] in *add.* AW, in chos- *add.*, *canc.* E trauaylend] trauailled As, laborans seu militans Lat. 33 for] *om.* LwW 34 how] and *prec.* AsWc soules] soule As 35 is] nys As not[2]] $H_7HBH_5AsWsLwHu_2ELdTWWc$, ȝit *add.* $LSrAPH_6CcMPl$, non adhuc Lat. his] *om.* LP 36 mercyful pryuey] *rev.* E mercyful] *om.* T his] *om.* B hard] *om.* LwW ryghtwys domes] riȝte wisdome Pl ilk] H_7HRM, ilk a LPTd, euery $BH_5SrWsLwAHu_2ECcLdPlTW$, eche AsH_6 37 schewed] and remembred *add.* LwW to[1]] vnto Sr Also] And *prec.* Ld for] *rep.*, *canc.* H_5, *om.* LwWWc 38 þe[1]] *om.* RM þe[2]] *om.* LPH_6MPl reproued] $H_7HBH_5WsLwHu_2ECc$-LdTW, þe *prec.* $RLAsSrAPH_6MPlWc$ in] H_7, and Σ, et Lat. ioye] ioyes As and] of AsM, *om.* R þe[4]] *om.* Cc blisse] blyssed As 39 seen] but *add.* As 40 softnes] soþefastnesse As, swetnes H_6, sobrietate Lat. of] blessyd *add.* W, blessyd and *add.* Lw 42 þe[2]] $H_7RH_5LSrWsAPH_6CcMPlT$, *om.* $HBLwHu_2LdW$ after] $H_7H°RBH_5SrWsA$-$Hu_2CcLdTW$, sithen M, also As, þat *add.* LLw`$H^c$´$EPH_6M$`Pl´W 43 `a[1]´ Pl ful] *om.* Td fayre] sauory T 44 þe syght of] *om.* Ws þe[1]] *om.* $H_5$ of[1]] to As þe[2]] a Td soule] loue Sr a clumsed] an vnclensed As clumsed] cumbred Sr, wrecchide $H_5WsWc$, *om.* Cc 45 Jesu] God Td deren] ⌜deren⌝`or greue´ L, or greue *add.* P, greue ELdT, hurt

Lo, þis is a litel biholdynge of Holy Kirke whils it is traueilend in þis life, for to seen how blak and how foule it semiþ in soules þat are reprofed, how faire and how lufly it is in chosen soules. And al þis gostly siȝt is not elles bot þe siȝt of Ihesu, not in himself bot in his merciful priuey werkes and in his harde riȝtwise domes, ilke day
38r schewyid and renewde to resonable | soules. Also ouer þis, for to seen with þe gostly eiȝe þe peynes of reprofed and þe ioye and þe blis of chosen soules, it is ful confortable. For soþfastnes may not be seen in a clene soule withouten grete delite and wundirful softnes of brennande lufe.

Also þe siȝt of aungels kynde, first of dampned and after of þe blissid. It is a ful feire contemplacioun of þe fende in a clene soule, when grace bryngiþ þe fende to þe siȝt of þe soule as a clumsed caytyf, bounden with þe miȝt of Ihesu þat he may not deren. Þan þe soule biholdiþ him not bodily bot gostly, seende his kynde and his malice, and turniþ `him´ vp-so-doun; ⌜and spoi⌝leþ him and rendiþ him alto noȝt; it scorniþ him and despisiþ him and settyþ noȝt bi his malice. Þus biddiþ Holy Writt when it seiþ þus: *Verte impium et non erit.* Turne þe wikked, þat is þe fende, vp-so-doun, and he schal ben as noȝt. Mikel wonder haþ þe soule þat þe fende haþ so mikel malice and so litel miȝt. Þer is no creature so vnmiȝty as he is, and þerfore it is a grete cowardise þat men dreden him so mikel. He may noþinge don withouten lefe of oure Lord Ihesu, not so mikel as entren into a swyne, as þe Gospel seiþ; mikil lesse may he þen noyen a man.

And þan if oure Lorde Ihesu gif him lefe for to taryen vs, it is ful wurþily and ful mercifully doon þat oure Lorde Ihesu doþ. And

Hu$_2$, done none harme As, ne dysesen *add.* Cc, nocere Lat. 46 him] *om.* E seend] sendeþ As 47 `him^{1}´ H^c, *om.* H°H$_5$AsWs hospileth] H$_7$H$_5$WsLd, he spoyleþ BCc, ⌜and spoi⌝leþ H^c, and spoyleþ RLwAEMPlTW, and spoilen As, ⌜or spoileþ⌝ L, or spoileþ P, spoileþ SrH$_6$Wc it sporneþ Hu$_2$, confundit Lat. rendyth] rendryth H$_7$, renden As, rentiþ ET, ryues Td, dilaniat Lat. 48 him^1] *om.* RM it] he CcPl, I M, and Wc, *om.* LwTW him^2] *om.* Cc 49 Holi] Kyrk *add., canc.* Td whan . . . þus] *om.* A whan] wher H$_6$ it] he LPCcM þus] Prou. 12° *add.* BLHu$_2$EPLdTW 50 Turne] þat is] *prec.* SrETd þat] whylk Td vp-so-doun] vp and doune Hu$_2$ 51 þe^2] soule *add., canc.* L 52 myȝth] for *add.* AWc is^1] nys As 53 þerfore] forþi Td is it] H$_7$RM, *rev.* HBH$_5$LAs-SrWsLwAHu$_2$EPH$_6$CcLdPlTW is] *om.* Cc a] *om.* LPH$_6$ cowardise] cowardnes MWWc `him´ Sr, hem Lw muche] for *add.* As 54 noþyng] non thyng Sr leue] þe *prec.* As as] to *add.* T 55 my`kil´] *interl., d.h.* H$_7$ may . . . ony] *om.* Td may he/þan] H$_7$HRBLSr-Hu$_2$PCcMLdPlT, *rev.* H$_5$AsWsAEH$_6$, maye he doo thenne to LwW noyȝen] deren RM, or hurte *add.* Hu^2 ony] H$_7$RLSrLwAEPH$_6$CcMPlTW, `eny´ H^c, a H°BH$_5$WsHu$_2$Ld, alicui Lat. 57 Jesu] *om.* TWTdc, Jesus Christus Lat. him] hem W for] *om.* LwW vs] and troble us *add.* LEPH$_6$ 58 ful] *om.* LLwPH$_6$W þat . . . doth] *om.* Td Jesu] God Wc, Jesus Christus Lat. And] *om.* T

welcome be oure Lord Jesu, by himself and by alle his messangers. Þe soule dredyth no more þe blustrend of þe fend þan þe sterynge of a m`o´ws. Wondir wroth is þe fend if he durste seye nay, but his mowth is stoppid by hys owne malyce, his handes arn bounden as a theffe worthi to be demed and hangen in helle, and þan þe soule acuseth him and riȝtfully demeth him after he hath deserued. Wonder not of þis seyng, for Seint Poul mened þe same whan he seyde þus: *Fratres, nescitis quoniam angelos iudicabimus*? Bretheren, wete ȝe nauȝt wel þat we schul deme aungelys, þat arn wickyd spirites þurgh malice þat were made gode aungelys by kynde? as who seyth ȝis. Þis demeng is fygured beforn þe dome in contemplatyf soules, for þei felen a litel tastyng in lyknes of al þat schal be don afterward openly by oure Lord Jesu in sothfastnesse. Schamed and schent is þe fend gretly in himself whan he is þus faren with-al of a clene soule. He wolde fayn fleen awey and he may not, for þe myght of þe heyghest holdith him stille, f. 113r and þat dereth him more þan al þe fir of helle. Wonder | mekely falleth þe soule to Jesu þan with hertly louyngys and thankynge þat he so myghtyly saueth a symple soule fro þe malice of so felle an enemy þurgh his grete mercy.

How by þe self lyght of grace þe blissed aungelys kende may be seen, and how Jesu as man abofe alle creatures, and as God after þat þe soule may seen him here. Capitulum xlvi^{m}

And þan after þis by þe self lyght may þe soule seen gostly þe fayrhed of aungelys: þe wurthines of hem in kende, þe sotelte in substaunce,

59 Jesu] *om.* Td messangers] *The fourth extract in* Td *ends here* þe] þat *prec.* H_6, Than *prec.* Wc 60 dredyth] dreded As more] H_7RAsHu$_2$ECcM þan *add.* HBH_5LSrWsLwAHu$_2$PLdPlTW, plus Lat. blustrend] blasting A, and þe malicious wodenes *add.* Hu$_2$ 61 m`o´ws] *interl. and marg., d.h.* $H_7$  nay] *om.* As  62 is] his LW  by] $H_7$RLSrAP$H_6$CcMPl, with HB$H_5$AsWsLwHu$_2$ELdTW, per Lat.  malyce] and *add.* As  theffe] `that´ is *add.* Cc 63 demed] damed Pl hangen] H_7SrCc, hanged HRBH_5LAsWsLwHu$_2$EPH_6MLdPlTW, hang A þan/þe . . . him] *rev.* RM 64 riȝtfully] rightwisly T demeth] demyd M him] H_7RLSrLw`$H^c$´AEP$H_6$CcMPl`T´W, *om.* H°BH_5AsWsHu$_2$Ld after] þan *prec.* RM, that *add.* LwTW, as Wc deserued] ne *add.* As 65 seyng] dayinge As mened . . . þus] *om.* As mened] menyth CcPl þe . . . þus] so thus saying Cc seyde] seiþ AsMPl þus] 1 Cor. 6° *add.* BLHu$_2$EPLdTW 66 Bretheren] þat is *prec.* E ȝe nauȝt] *rev.* M 68 seyth] sey WsH_6 ȝis] þus H_6, *om.* LP demeng] dome T 70 þat] *rep.* H_5 don] and *add.* `L´P openly/by . . . Jesu] H_7RSrAPH_6CcMPl, *rev.* HBH_5WsLwHu$_2$ELdTW ⌜by . . . Jesu⌝ L by] of LwW 71 in] O peynfull As, *om.* H_5As is] shal ben Cc fend] frend Ld, and fowle rebuked *add.* Hu$_2$ gretly/in himself] *rev.* LPH_6 72 is þus] shal þus ben Cc with-al] H_7RSrMPlT, with HBH_5LAsWsLwAHu$_2$EPH_6CcLdW `of´ Lw, in T, *om.* W 73 þe^1 . . . holdith] he miȝtte of his hiȝenesse holden As heyghest] Holi Gost H_6Pl,

þerfor welcome be oure Lorde Ihesu, bi himselfe and bi al his messangers. þe soule drediþ no more þan þe blustrynge of þe fende þan þe sterynge of a mows. Wnder wroþe is þe fende if he durst say nay, bot his mouþ is stopped with his owne malice, his handes are
138v bounden as a þef worþi to be demyd | and hanged in helle, and þan þe
soule accusiþ hym and riȝtfully demiþ aftir he haþ deseruid. Wonder not of þis seienge, for Seyn Poule mened þe same whan he seide þus: *Fratres, nescitis quoniam angelos iudicabimus?* Breþeren, wite ȝe not wel þat we schal deme aungels, þat are wicked spirites þurȝ malice þat were made gode aungels bi kynde? as who seiþ ȝis. þis demynge is figured before þe dome in contemplatif soules, for þei felyn a litil tastynge in liknes of al þat schal be done afterward bi oure Lord Ihesu openly in soþfastnes. Schamed and schent is þe fende gretly in himself when he is þus faren with of a clene soule. He wolde fayn fleen awey and he may not, for þe miȝt of þe eiȝest holdiþ him stille, and þat deriþ him more þan alle þe fiire of helle. Wndir mekly falliþ þe soule to Ihesu þan, with hertly louynges and þankynges þat he so miȝtily safiþ a simple soule fro alle þe malice of so fel an enmye þurȝ his grete mercy.

[CHAPTER 46]

And þan after þis bi þe self liȝt may þe soule see gostly þe fairhed of aungels: worþines of hem in kynde, þe sotilte in substaunce,

Lorde *add.* T 74 þat] *om.* M dereth] deseeseþ As, greueþ Hu_2ELdTW 75 þe] a good As þan] as As hertly] holy As louyngys] preysyngis H_6, worschepingis LdT and thankynge] *om.* W thankynge] H_7, inly preysyng Cc, þankynges Σ, graciarum accionibus Lat. he] she miȝt As 76 saueth] saue As, sauid Cc symple] *om.* Lw fro . . . malice] *om.* As fro] H_7, alle *add.* Σ [`al´ Pl] þe] *om.* LwW of] þe fende *add.* T so felle an] þe felon Pl felle] foule As 77 his] `grace and his´ *add. interl., d.h.* H_7, grace and his *add.* RAPl mercy] and goodnesse *add.* Cc

Chapter 46 *title*: H_7RLSrAEPH_6MLdPlTW `How a soule þat is ylumined wiþ þe lyȝt of soþefastnes may see goostly þe fayred of aungeles.´ H How also laste [. . .] þe diuersite of aung[els] and þe worchynge of þe Trinyte and oþer þynges. As *om.* BH_5WsLwCc 1 ⌜by . . . of⌝ L self] same LdTW lyght] sight P 2 and . . . here (l. 3)] etc. M how] equaliter Lat. `as[1] . . . God´ $T^G W^G$, [is *add.* W] God and man aboue all creatures TW as[1]] is R, is *prec.* ALd man] a *prec.* Ld, is *add.* E alle] oþer *add.* Ld 3 here] in this liyf *add.* LP [*canc.* L] 4 þan] *The fifth extract in* Td *starts here* after þis] *om.* M þe self] itself H_5AsT, þe same WsAWc `lyght´ *canc.* L, *om.* RP seen gostly] *rev.* Cc seen] be hit selue þe As fayrhed] fairnes WsWc, fader As 5 þe[1]] $H_7$RLSr-Lw`H^c´AEPH_6CcMPlTWWc, *om.* H°BH_5AsWsHu_2Ld `in[1] . . . hem´ (l. 6)] Pl sotelte] $H_7$H°B$H_5$LAsSrWsA$Hu_2$P$H_6$CcLdT, of hem *add.* RLw`H^c´EMPlW, eorum Lat.

þe confermyng of hem in grace in þe fulnesse of endeles blisse; þe sondryhed of orders, þe distinccion of persons; how þey lyfen al in lyght of endles sothfastnesse, and how þei brennen al in lufe of þe Holy Gost after þe wurthines of ordres; how þei seen and lufen and preysen Jesu in blissed rest withouten cessyng. Þer is no syght of body ne figure in ymaginacyon in þis maner werkyng, bot al gostly of gostly creatures.

Þan bygynneth þe soule for to han grete aqweyntaunce of þese blissed spirites and a grete felawschip. Þei are ful tendre and ful besy abowte swilk a soule for to helpe it, þei are meystres for to kenne it, and oft þurgh here gostly presence and touchyng of here lyght þei dryuen out fantoms fro þe soule and mynystren to it al þat it nedeth. Þus Seynt Poule seyd of hem: *Nonne omnes sunt administratorii spiritus, missi propter eos qui hereditatem capiunt salutis?* Wite ȝe not wele þat alle holy spirites are ministres, sent of Jesu for hem þat take þe heritage of hele—þese are chosen soules—as who seyth ȝis. For wite þu wele, þat alle þis gostly werkyng of wordes and of resons broght to þe mende, and swilk fayre lyknes, are made by þe minystrye of aungelis whan þe lyght of grace haboundendly schyneth in a clene soule. It may not be tolde by tonge þe felyng, þe lyghtenynges, þe graces and þe confortes in specyal þat clene soules perceyuen þurgh fauourable felawschepe of blissed aungels. Þe soule is wele at ese with hem for to beholden how þei don þat it wold tente to not ellys.

6 þe[1]] H_7RLAsSrLw`$H^{c}$′AEP$H_6$CcMPlW, *om.* H°B$H_5$WsHu$_2$LdT confermynge] conformynge $H_5$MT in[2] . . . þe[3]] *om.* Td in[2]] $H_7$, and Σ, et Lat. of[2]] hem *add.*, *canc.* T endeles] þe *prec.* T 7 `sondryhed′ T^{G}, sunderhede H_5Lw, in serehed Td, diuersite BWsALdT, departynge AsHu$_2$ orders] sondry *prec.* B þe . . . persons] *om.* Td distinccion] H_7RLSrAPH_6CcMPl, distinccïouns HBH_5AsWsLwHu$_2$ELdTW, distinccionem Lat. lyfen] louen As 8 endles sothfastnesse] *rev.* LwW endles] *om.* RH_5Ws of[2] . . . Gost] H_7RLSrLw`$H^{c}$′AEP$H_6$CcMPlW, *om.* H°B$H_5$AsWsHu$_2$LdTWc, Spiritus Sancti Lat. 9 how . . . cessyng (l. 10)] *om.* Td and lufen] *om.* AsT and[1]] *om.* A 10 withouten] by þowten B no] non As syght . . . ymaginacyon (l. 11)] ymaginacion in syȝt of body in figure Lw 11 ne] of *add.* R`H^{c}′AEPl, no *add.* TW in[1]] of T, þe *add.* As ymaginacyon] ymaginaciouns Pl in[2]] of RM maner] H_7RLSrLw`H^{c}′EPH_6CcMPlW, *om.* H°BH_5AsWsAHu$_2$LdTTd, modo Lat. al] in *add.* As of gostly] *om.* As of] and *prec.* W 13 begynneth] *om.* M for] *om.* AsLwTWWc of] with A þese] his LP, þe SrTW, þis E, thos M, þoo Pl 14 blissed] creatures *add.*, *canc.* L and . . . felawschip] *om.* Td a] *om.* LPH_6 15 for] *om.* LwW helpe] kepe RM þei . . . it] *om.* As for] *om.* LwW kenne] H_7HRH_5LSrWsLwAPM, teche BHu$_2$EH_6CcLdPlTWWc 16 oft] often-tymes Hu$_2$ gostly presence] *rev.* T presence] is *add.* Cc. Hu$_2$ *ends here* lyght] gastly þei *add.* Td þei] H_7H_6Wc, *om.* Σ 17 dryuen] put Wc `fantoms′ $T^{G}W^{G}$, fantasies A$H_6$CcTW, fantho`s′ þys Lw soule] H_7RLSrAPH_6CcMPl, And þei illuminen [liȝtnen LdT] þe soule graciously, þei confort þe soule by

confermynge of hem in grace, and þe fulnes of endles blis; þe sundryhed of ordres, þe distincciouns of persons; how þei lifen al in liȝt of endles soþfastnes, and how þei brennen al in lufe after þe worþines of ordres; how þei seen and lufen and preisen Ihesu in blissed reste withouten cesinge. Þer is no siȝt of body ne figure in ymaginacioun in þis wirkyng, bot al gostly of gostly creatures.

Þan bigynniþ þe soule for to han grete aqweyntaunce of þese blissed spirittes and a grete felawschipe. Þei are ful tendre and ful bisy aboute
39r swilk a soule for to help it, þei are maistres for to | kenne it, and often þurȝ here gostly presence and touchynge of here liȝt drifen out fanthoms fro þe soule. And þei illuminen þe soule graciously, þei confort þe soule by swete wordes sodenly sowned in a clene hert, and if ony disese falle gostly þe seruen þe soule and ministren to it al þat it nediþ. Þus Seynt Poul seid of hem: *Nonne omnes sunt administratorii spiritus, missi propter eos qui hereditatem capiunt salutis?* Wote ȝe not wel þat alle holy spirites are ministres, sent of Ihesu for hem þat takyn þe heritage of helþe—þese are chosen soules—as who seiþ ȝis. For wite þou wel, þat al þis gostly wirkynge of wordes and of resons broȝt to þe mende, and swilk faire liknes, are made bi þe ministerie of aungels when þe liȝt of grace abundantly schyneþ in a clene soule. It may not be tolde by tonge þe felynges, þe liȝtnynges, þe graces and þe confortes in special þat clene soules perceifen þurȝ fauorable felawschipe of blissed aungels. Þe soule is wel at ese with hem for to biholden how þei don þat it wolde tente to noȝt elles.

[with B] swete wordes sodenly sowned in a clene hert, and if ony disese falle gostly þe seruen þe soule *add.* HBH_5AsWsLwELdTW, þei comforte þe saule be any swete wordis sodanly sowned in a clene saule *add.* Td, anima Lat. and . . . ȝis (l. 21)] *om.* Td 18 þus] þis LP, as As Seynt Poule/seyd] *rev.* H_6 seyd] seiþ SrM of] to Cc hem] Heb. 1° *add.* BLEPLdTW administratorii spiritus] ad ministracionem T ⌜spiritus . . . heredita⌝tem (l. 19)] L spiritus] sancti *add.* As, *om.* H_6 19 capiunt] capient T Wite] þat is *prec.* E wele] *om.* Pl þat alle] *rev.* M alle] *om.* As 20 for] to A 21 hele] H_7RSrAH_6MPl, helþe HBH_5LAsWsLwEPCcLdTW þese] Those RM, that Cc chosen soules] þe soules chosen As chosen] *one-letter eras. seq.* H_7, holy *prec.* T who seyth] þoȝ he seid A who] so B seyth] sey WsPl ȝis] þis As 22 þis] þese Pl werkyng] werchynges Pl and] om. Lw resons] and *add.* H_6, to *add.*, *canc.* H þe] þed, -d *canc.* H, *om.* Cc mende] myȝt *prec.*, *canc.* Td, of a soule *add.* A 23 and] alle H_6, of *add.* Td fayre lyknes] faype kyknesse Cc lyknes] liknesses A, similitudines minystrye] mynistring WsWc, mynistryngis Td 24 a clene soule] clene soulis LPH_6 *The fifth extract in* Td *ends here* 25 tolde] cold Lw felyng] H_7AsCc, felynges Σ, sensaciones Lat. þe[2]] and *prec.* RMWc graces] grace MPl 26 clene] þe *prec.* BH_5Ws fauourable] honorable Cc 27 soule] *This folio is damaged in* Lw, *and approximately one-half of the text from here to Chapter* 46/59 honestly *is lacking* wele] so *prec.* LdT hem] him As for] *om.* LwW beholden] holden As how . . . ellys (l. 28)] *om.* As 28 tente] attende Cc, take heed H_6 not] noo thynge LwCcW, nichil Lat.

f. 113^{v} Bot þan with helpe of þe aungels ȝit þe | soule seeth more. For knowyng ryseth abofen þis in a clene soule, and þat is to beholden þe blissed kende of Jesu. Ferst of his glorious manhed, how it is wurthily heyghed abofen aungels kende, and þan after of his blissed godhed, for by knowynge of creatures is knowen þe Creatour. And þan bygynneth þe soule for to perceyuen a lytel of þe pryuetes of þe blissed Trinite. It may wele inogw, for lyght of grace goth before; sche schal not erren as long as sche holdeþ hire with þe lyght. Þan is it opned sothfastly to þe eye of a soule þe onhed in substaunce and distynccyon of persones in þe blissed Trinite, as it may be seen here, and mykel oþer sothfastnesse of þat blissed Trinite pertenent to þis matere, þe whilk is openly declared and schewed by wrytyng of holy doctours of Holy Kirke. And wite þu wele, þat þe same [and] þe self sothfastnes of þe blissed Trinite þat þese holy doctoures, enspired þurgh grace, writen in here bokis in strengthynge of oure trowthe, a clene soule may seen and knowen þurgh þe selfe lyght of grace. I wil not expressen to mykel of þis matere here specyaly, for it nedeth not.

Wonder grete lufe feleth þe soule with heuenly delyte in beholdynge of þis sothfastnes whan it is made þurgh specyale grace, for lufe and lyght go boþe togedre in a clene soule. Þer is no lufe þat ryseth of knowyng and of speciale beholdynge þat may touchen so nere oure Lord Jesu as þis lufe may; for why, þis knowenge is wurthiest and heyghest in itself only of Jesu God and man, if it be specially schewed by þe lyght of grace. And þerfor is þe fyre of lufe flawmend of þis more brennende þan it is of knowyng of ony creature bodily or gostly.

Al þese gracyous knowynges feled in a soule of þe vniuersite of alle

29 helpe] H_7RSrAPCcMPlT, þe *prec.* HBH_5AsWsLwEH_6LdW þe[1]] H_7RLw`H^{c}´AEPlW, *om.* H°BH_5LAsWsPH_6CcMLdTWc aungels] angell W ȝit] *om.* CcWc seeth] seiþ As 30 knowyng] þe *prec.* LEPH_6 ryseth] aryseþ BWc abofen] H_7, al *add.* Σ þis] þese H_5AsWs to beholden] be beholdyng As to] a clene soule *add.*, *canc.* L, for *prec.* RM 31 ⌜kende of Jesu⌝ L of[2]] on H_5 `his´ L it] *rep.* A is] *om.* As wurthily heyghed] *rev.* W wurthily] wondirly Cc 32 aungels] H_7RLSrAPH_6Pl, aungel Cc, al *prec.* HBH_5AsWsLwEMLdTW, angelorum Lat. after] aftirwarde T of] to A, on H_6, *om.* Cc 33 for . . . And] *om.* Cc for] *om.* H_5WsTW is . . . Creatour] *om.* As 34 for] *om.* RAsECcM ⌜perceyuen⌝ H 35 goth] and þerefore *add.* As, here *add.* M before] H_7RLAsSrAPH_6CcMPl, and þerfore *add.* HBH_5WsLwELdTWWc, precedit eam Lat. sche . . . erren (l. 36)] *rep.* Sr sche] hit A, he Cc 36 as long] *rep.* A long . . . hire] sche longeþ here As sche] hit A, he Cc hire] hym Cc, *om.* A with þe] in þat T þe] þat Wc, *om.* M is it] *rev.* T is] *om.* Cc it] *om.* A 37 opned] onlJed W, and *add.* As to] *om.* Cc a] H_7SrCc, þe Σ onhed] onyd Cc, onlJede W 38 distynccyon] distinctiouns H_5LdT, discrecion M of] in BAT as . . . Trinite (l. 39)] *om.* Sr it] H_7RLLw`H$^{c}$´AEP$H_6$CcMPlTW, *om.* H°B$H_5$AsWsLdTWc `may´ Pl here] *om.* B 39 mykel] mekere As ⌜of . . . pertenent⌝ L þat] H_7RAMPl,

Bot þan with þe help of aungels ȝit þe soule seeþ more. For knowynge risiþ abofen al þis in a clene soule, and þat is to beholden þe blissed kynde of Ihesu. First of his glorious manhed, how it is wurþily heiȝed abofe al aungels kynde, and þan after of his blissed godhed, for by knowynge of creatures is knowen þe creatour. And þan bigynniþ þe soule for to ⸢perseyuyn⸣ a litel of þe pryuetes of þe blissed Trinite. It may wel inowȝ, for liȝt of grace goþ bifore, and þerfore sche schal not erren as longe as she holdiþ hir with þe liȝt. Þan is it opned soþfastly to þe eiȝe of þe soule þe onhed in substance and distinccioun
39v of persons in þe blissid Trinitee, | as may be seen here, and mikil oþer soþfastnes of þis blissed Trinite pertinente to þis matere, þe whilk is openly declared and schewde bi writynge of holy doctours of Holy Kirk. And wite þou wel, þat þe same and þe selfe soþfastnes of þe blissed Trinite þat þese holy doctours, inspired þurȝ grace, wryten in here bokes in strengþinge of oure trouþ, a clene soule may seen and knowen þurȝ þe selfe liȝt of grace. I wil not expressen to mikil of þis mater here specially, for it nediþ not.

Wundre gret lufe feliþ þe soule with heuenly delite in beholdynge of þis soþfastnes whan it is made þurȝ special grace, for lufe and liȝt goon togidir in a clene soule. Þer is no lufe þat risiþ of knowynge and of special biholdynge þat may touchen so nere oure Lorde Ihesu as þis lufe may; for whi, þis knowynge is wurþiest and hiȝest in itself only of Ihesu God and man, if it be specialy schewd by þe liȝt of grace. And þerfore is þe fyr of lufe flawmende of þis more brennande þan it is of knowynge of ony creature bodily or gostly.

And alle þese gracious knowynges feled in a soule of þe vniuersite

þis HBH$_5$AsWsELdT, þe ⸢L⸣AsLwPH$_6$CcWWc pertenent] perteyning ATWc 40 declared . . . holy] decla⸢red . . . Hoo⸣li L 41 doctours] and *add.* Sr of] in M, þe *add.* Pl and^2 þe selfe] *om.* T and^2] in H$_7$ þe^1] *om.* Pl 42 of] and B þese] those RM 43 writen] hauen *prec.* As trowthe] feyþ BALdT, soule As 44 and knowen] in knowyng LwW selfe] same WsAT, soule M `of grace′ L 45 specyaly] *om.* LPH$_6$ 46 Wonder] For As, A *prec.* H$_6$ with] gret and *add.* Cc delyte] *om.* A beholdynge] felyng LwW, þe *prec.* T 47 þis] *om.* As þurgh] of As specyale] *om.* H$_6$ 48 go] ygon As boþe] H$_7$RLSrLw`H^{c}′AEPH$_6$CcMPlW, *om.* H°BH$_5$AsWsLdT, simul Lat. no] none As 49 `and′ L, *om.* Lw so nere] sooner TW nere] nyȝe BAH$_6$Ld, hiȝe and so nyȝe As 50 `Jesu′ L, *om.* H$_6$W þis] þe`s′ L ⸢for . . . itself⸣ (l. 51) L why] *om.* ACc and heyghest] *om.* A 51 in] of *prec.* LP itself] the self Cc Jesu God] *rev.* H$_5$ Jesu] and *add.* Ld God] good M 52 fyre of lufe] *rev.* As lufe] þis *prec.* H$_6$ flawmend] flawmed BCc, flaumede in hem Pl, enflawmed As, more *prec.* H$_6$ of þis more] and AH$_6$ of þis] in Cc 53 it is] *rev.* A it] *om.* Cc of^1] in Ws, *om.* H$_5$Ld knowyng of] *om.* Cc knowyng] þe *prec.* H$_6$ `ony′ Pl 54 Al] H$_7$RLSrAPH$_6$CcMPl, And *prec.* HBH$_5$AsWsLwELdTW, Omnes Lat. þese . . . knowynges] þis . . . knowynge LCc þese] those RM

creatures, in maner byfore seyd, and of oure Lord Jesu, maker and kepere of al þis fayre vniuersite, I calle hem fayre wordes and swete f. 114^r spekynges of oure Lord Jesu to a soule þat he wil make | his trewe spouse. He scheweth priuetes and profereth riche giftes of his tresore and arayeth þe soule with [hem] ful honestly. Sche thar not ben aschamed with compaygnye of hire felawes for to apperen afterward to þe face of Jesu spouse. Alle þese louely dalyaunces of pryuey speche atwix Jesu and a soule may be called an hid word, of þe whilk Holy Writte seyth þus: *Porro ad me dictum est verbum absconditum, et venas susurrii eius suscepit auris mea*. Sothly to me is seyd an hid worde, and þe veynes of his rownyngys myn ere hath perceyued. Þe inspiracyon of Jesu is an hid worde for it is pryuey, hid fro al þe lufers of þis werd and schewed to his lufers, þurgh þe whilk a clene soule perceyueth redyly þe veynes of his rownynges, þat are speciale schewyngys of his sothfastnes. For ilk a gracyous knowyng of sothfastnes, felt with inly sauour and gostly delyte, is a pryuey rownynge of Jesu in þe ere of a clene soule. Him nedeth for to haue mykel clennes in soule, in mekenes and in oþer vertus, and to ben halfe defe to noyse of werdly iangelyng, þat schuld wysely parceyuen þese swete gostly rownyngges. Þis is þe voyce of Jesu, of þe whilk Dauid seyth þus: *Vox Domini preparantis ceruos, et reuelabit condensa*. Þe voyce of oure Lord Jesu, graythende hertys; and he schal `schewe þe thykke. Þat is, þe inspiracion of Jesu makith soulis lihte as hertis þat styrten fro þe erthe ouyr boskys and brerys—ouyr al wordly vanyte—and he schewyth to

55 in] *rep*. H_5 byfore] aforn As 56 fayre] *om*. Ws calle] clepe AsH_6 hem . . . be (l. 82)] *om*. A [*folio missing*] hem] hym M and] in LPH_6 57 ⸢spekynges⸣ L, spechys Sr Jesu] Crist *add*. LdT soule] and *add*., *canc*. Cc þat] H_7RLSrPH_6CcMPl, þe whilk HBH_5AsWsLwELdTW make] of *add*. Cc 58 spouse] spousesse LdT priuetes] and sheweth ryche *add*., *canc*. Cc profereth] he *prec*. As his] *om*. LP tresore] tresoures T 59 with hem] RLSrLw`H$^c$´EP$H_6$CcMPlW, with ⸢him⸣ $H_7$, *om*. H°B$H_5$AsWsLdT, cum eis Lat. Sche] that it Cc thar] $H_7$HRSrWsLwMPl, dar B$H_5$LAsEP$H_6$CcLdT, nede W 60 with compaygnye] ⸢with þe company⸣ L with] $H_7$H°RB$H_5$SrWs$H_6$MLdPl, þe *add*. ⸢L⸣AsLw`H^c´EPTW, that *add*. Cc for] *om*. LwW 61 spouse] H_7H°BH_5LWsEPLd, hire *prec*. RSrLwPH_6MPlTW, `here´ *prec*. H^c, his *prec*. As, the *prec*. Cc, Jesu sponsi sui Lat. þese] those RM, þe Sr, this CcW louely] louen As dalyaunces] H_7HBH_5LSrWsEPH_6LdPlT, diliaunce RAsLwCcMW, affabilitas seu familiaritas Lat. of pryuey speche] *om*. Lat. 62 atwix] H_7HRBH_5LSrWsLwLdPlTW, atwyn Cc, betwyxe AsEM, bitwen H_6Pl `a soule´ L a] clene *add*. Pl called] clepid H_6LdT, yclepid As 63 þus] Job 4° *add*. BLEPLdTW est] *om*. Pl 64 eius] *om*. W suscepit] H_7, audiuit Sr, percepit Σ, percepit Lat. Sothly] þat is *prec*. H_5E an hid] and hid a Cc an] and M 65 his] þis As rownyngys] rownynge AsSr ere hath] eeren hauen As 66 priuey] H_7RM, priueli HBH_5AsWsLwEH_6CcLdPlTW, *om*. LP, secrete Lat. þe] *om*. HAsLwW þis] H_7RLEPH_6CcMPl, þe HBH_5AsWsLwLdTW, þe *corr*. *fr*. þis Sr, huius Lat. 67 þurgh þe whilk] wherþorw Sr 68 þe] *om*. LwW

of alle creatures, in maner bifore seide, and of oure Lord Ihesu, maker and keper of alle þis faire vniuersitee, I calle hem faire wordes and swete spekynges of oure Lorde Ihesu to a soule þe whilk he wil make his trew spouse. He schewþ pryueites and profreþ riche giftes of his tresore and araieþ þe soule ful honestly. She þar not be aschamed with companye of her felawes for to apperen afterwarde to þe face of Ihesu \`here′ spouse. Alle þese lufly daliaunces of priuey speche atwix Ihesu
40r and a soule | may be called an hid worde, of þe whilke Holy Writt seiþ þus: *Porro ad me dictum est verbum absconditum, et venas susurrii eius percepit auris mea*. Soþly to me is seide an hid wurde, and þe veynes of his rownynges myn ere haþ perceifed. Þe inspiracioun of Ihesu is an hid wurde, for it is pryueli hid fro alle lufers of þe werld and schewd to his lufers, þurȝ þe whilke a clene soule perceifiþ redily þe veynes of his rownynge, þat are specialy schewynges of his soþfastnes. For ilke a gracious knowynge of soþfastnes, felt with inly sauour and gostly delite, is a priuey rownynge of Ihesu in þe ere of a clene soule. Him bihouiþ for to han mikil klennes in soule, in meknes and in alle oþer vertues, and to ben halfe deefe to noyse of werdly iangelynge, þat schuld wisly perceifen þese swete gostly rownynges. Þis is þe voice of Ihesu.

Explicit hic finis.

rownynges] H_7RLSrEPH_6CcMPi, rownynge HBH_5WsLwLdTW, louynge and rounynge As, susurii Lat.   speciale] H_7AsMPl, special RBLSrPH_6CcLd, specialy HH_5WsLwTW, speciales Lat.   69 For . . . sothfastnes] *om.* Lw   For] or LP   ilk a] H_7HR, ilk M, eche a LPH_6, eche AsLd, euery BH_5SrWsECcPlTW   71 clene] *om.* Lat.   Him . . . soule] *om.* Cc   nedeth] H_7RLAsSrPH_6MPl, bihouiþ HBH_5WsLwELdTW   \`for′ $W^G$, *om.* LwW   \`in soule in′ W^G, and LwW   in[1]] and CcM   soule] a *prec.* As   in[2]] om. LwH_6CcW   72 oþer] H_7, al *prec.* HRBH_5LB_3AsWsLwEPH_6CcMLdPlTW, B_3 *back*, alias Lat.   to[1]] for *prec.* T   halfe] vere Lat.   73 wysely parceyuen] *rev.* B   wysely] *om.* E   parceyuen] perceywyns M   þese swete] þe wisly As   þese] those RM, þe Pl   swet⌜e⌝ H^c, swetly H°Cc   74 rownyngges] rownyng Cc   \`þis′ $W^G$, þat LwW   Jesu] $H^{\circ}$B$H_5$AsWsLdT *originally ended here*. Deo Gracias. *add.* $H_5$Ws, þys is þe Abbaye of þe Holigost þat is founded in a place þat is cleped þe conscience. Explicit Scala Perfeccionis. *add.* As   \`of . . . bok (l. 86)′ H^cT^G, *d.h.* B   ⌜Dauid . . . þus⌝ L   Dauid] *om.* T^G þus] Ps. 28 *add.* BLEPTW   75 preparantis] preparantes LwH_6 condensa] et in templo omnes dicent gloriam. Ad quam nos perducat qui sine fine viuit et regnat. Amen. *add.* Sr   þe . . . bok (l. 86)] *om.* Sr   þe] þat is *prec.* E   oure Lord] *om.* H_6 76 graythende] ordeinyngge B, arayynge LwH_6CcWT^G, \`and makyng′ *add. d.h.* $H_7$   \`schewe . . . bok (l. 86)′ *d.h.* H_7 þe[1]] H_7, *om.* Σ   thykke] thing B   77 Jesu] þat *add.* B, Jesu Christi Lat.   styrten . . . erthe] lepen B   fro þe erthe] on hiȝt H_6 erthe] ⌜herþe⌝ L, herþe B_3P   78 ouyr[1]] of LB_3P   ouyr[2]] H_7, of Σ   \`vanyte′ T^G, vanytees CcT   he] *om.* Cc hem þe thykke, þat arn hys priuytes, þat may not be parceyued but be scharp eye. Þese beholdyngys, sothfastly groundyd in grace and in meknesse, makyn a soule wys and brennyng in desyr to þe face of Jesu. Þese arn goostly thyngys þat I spak of beforn, and þe mow be kallyd newe gracyous felyngys, and I do but touche hem a lytel for wyssyng of þe soule. For a soule þat ys clene, styred be grace to vse of f. 114^{v} thys werkyng, may se | more in an hour of swych goostly mater þan myht ben wryten in a gret bok.'

79 hem] hym M þe . . . hys] *om.* Cc \`þe' Pl arn hys] is Pl priuytes] priuy\`tees' L, priuei B_3 parceyued] perceyueþ H_6 be[2]] H_7RLwH^cEM\`Pl'T^GW, a *add.* B, of a LP, of B_3H_6 80 eye] iȝen H_6, er T^G, *canc.* sothfastly . . . meknesse (l. 81)] *om.* LB_3PH_6 in[2]] *om.* B 82 þese] Those M arn] H_7H_6, þe *add.* Σ spak] speke BPl þe] H_7, þei Σ mow be] arn Cc mow] *om.* LwTW 83 kallyd] cleped BH_6, A *back* newe] *om.* LB_3PH_6 gracyous] *om.* A I] *om.* Cc a] but Cc lytel] at þis tyme *add.* Pl 84 þe] H_7CcT, þi BLB_3LwH^cAPH_6MPlT^GW For a soule] *om.* B clene] *om.* Cc \`vse of' Pl vse] þe *prec.* BT 85 thys] suche ghostly T^G mater] materys Cc 86 wryten] *om.* Cc bok] to whiche brynge þee and me, ȝif it his wil be. Amen. *add.* H_6, Explicit hic finis *add.* HRM, Ecce declaraui tibi seundum scienciam meam simplicem per processum huius libelli qualiter anima humana ad Dei similitudinem reformatur. In prima parte tetigi qualiter quedam anime sunt solum in fide reformate et non in sansacione. Et hoc pertinet ad statum incipiendium. In secunda parte declaraui modicum de progressu illorum qui crescere volunt in gracia seu proficere et peruenire ad reformacionem animarum suarum in sensacione; quales labores et qualia excercicia, quas solicitudines et quali remedia necesse est eos habere contra viles sensaciones peccati in seipsis, contra asperas temptaciones diaboli. Et hoc ad statum pertinet [proficiencium: perfectorum Y]. In tercia parte modicum tetigi quod quando per graciam Spiritus Sancti consciencia mundata est a sensacione peccatorum, et interior oculus anime apertus est, anima reformata est in sensacionem uirtutum, sicut quando anima veraciter sentit humilitatem in corde, perfectam dileccionem et caritatem ad omnes proximos, pacem et pacienciam, castitatem et mundiciam, cum solacio et leticia de illis, et gloria in consciencia. Et hoc pertinet ad statum hominum perfectorum qui per graciam Dei et magnam continuacionem laboris, et per contencionem nocte et die contra peccata vicerunt amaras sensaciones peccatorum, et receperunt per gratiam dileccionis Jesu Christi dulces sensaciones virtutum, et sic in sensacione veraciter reformantur. In quarte parte tetigi de quibusdam animabus que non solum reformantur ad ymaginem Dei in sensacione virtutum, set alcius eciam eleuantur, et ita perfecte reformantur Dei dileccioneque replentur quod senciunt in cordibus suis, et percipiunt secretas inspiraciones Jesu Christi, et spirituales illuminaciones, celestes confortaciones et graciosas cogniciones, mirabiles consideraciones spirituum bonorum, et occultas percepciones celestium gaudiorum. Ad hec gaudia perducat nos saluator noster, Dominus noster Jesus Christus. Amen Prima pars durat usque ad decimum septimum capitulum. Et ibi incipit pars secunda. Tercia pars incipit in principio tricesimi secundi capituli. Et quarta pars incipit in principio capituli quadragesimi primi. Vnde prima pars habet xvi capitula. Secunda pars xv capitula. Tercia pars nouem. Et quarta pars vii. Et sic in toto quadraginta septem capitula. *add* Lat.

APPENDIX

THE TABLE OF CHAPTERS IN H AND B

Scale II MSS HBLSrWsLwEPCcMLdTW have Tables of Chapters either preceding or following the text; of these, HLSrEPMLdTW also have chapter titles in the text. In H, Tables of Chapters of Books I and II of *The Scale of Perfection* were added at the end of the volume in a fifteenth-century hand that does not occur elsewhere in the manuscript. The titles in the Table of Chapters do not agree with the idiosyncratic titles that occur in the text of H, but rather with the titles that occur in the other manuscripts. In B, the Table of Chapters gives a set of chapter titles that is unique except for the fact that the titles in the text of As agree for the latter half of the text—the same portion of text in which As is in agreement with the Carthusian/Brigittine textual group, of which B is a member.

THE TABLE OF CHAPTERS IN LONDON, BRITISH LIBRARY MS HARLEY 6579 (H)

[f. 141^{r}] Here is writen þe Rubrihc of þese ij bokis byfore writen the whiche is namyd the Laddere of Perfeccioun or in Latyn Scala Perfeccionis and after þe ⟨title⟩ of euery chapter þe begyn⟨nyng⟩ of þe same chap⟨ter⟩.

[f. 142^{v}] That a man is þe image of God after þe soule and not after þe body. C^{m} j. For as moche.

Hou it nedid to mankynde þat only þoruȝ þe passioun of Crist shulde be restored and reformyd þat was forshape be þe first synne. C^{m} ij. The riȝtfulnes.

þat Iewis and paynym⟨s⟩ and also fals cristen men beþ not reformed effectuelly þorwȝ þe vertu of þe passioun f⟨or h⟩ere owen defaute. C^{m} iij. Twey maner of men.

Of twey maner reformyngis of þis image, on in fulnes and oon oþer in feiþ. C^{m} iiij. Nou seist þou.

þat reformyng in party is in ij maners, oon in feiþ and anoþer in felyng. C^{m} v. Anoþer reformyng of þis ymage.

þat þoruȝ þe sacrament of baptym þat is groundid in þe passioun of Crist þis image is reformid fro original synne. C^{m} vj. Two maner of synnes.

þat þoruȝ þe sacrament of penaunce þat standiþ in contricion, confession and satisfaccion þis image is reformid fro actuel synne. C^{m} vij. Also what cristen.

Hou in þe sacrament of baptim and of penaunce þoruȝ a priuy vnperseyuable wirkyng of þe Holy Gost þis grace is reformyd þouȝ it be not seyn ne felid. C^{m} viij. But þis reformyng.

þat we shulde beleue stidfastly reformyng of þis grace if oure conscience witnes to vs a ful forsakyng of synne and a trewe turnyng of oure wil to good lyuyng. C^{m} ix. Of þis reformyng.

þat alle þe saulis þat lyuen mekely in þe feiþ of Holy Chirche and haue here feiþ quicned in loue and charite ben reformed be þis sacrament, þouȝ it be so þat þei may not fele þe special yefte of deuocioun or of gostly felyng. C^{m} x. In þis reformyng.

þat soulis reformed neden euere to fiȝte and striue ayens steringis of synne whil þei lyuen here, and hou a soule may wite whanne it assentiþ to steringis and whanne not. C^{m} xj. þis reformyng.

þat þis image is boþe faire and foule whil it is in þis lyfe þouȝ it be reformed, and of diuerste of felyngis priuely had betwen þes soulis þat ben reformed and oþer þat ben not. C^{m} xij. Fayr þanne is.

Of þre maner men of þe whiche summe ben not reformed and summe ben reformed only in feiþ and summe in feiþ and in felyng. C^{m} xiij. By þis þat.

Hou men þat ben in synne forshapen hemself into diuers bestis liknes, and þei ben clepid þe louers of þis world. C^{m} xiiij. A wrecchid man.

Hou loueris of þis world vnablen hem in diuers maners to þe reformyng of here owen soule. C^{m} xv. But nou seyn.

A litil conceil hou loueris of þis world shulde do if þei wolde be reformed in her soule bifore þei parten hens. C^{m} xvj. þese men þouȝ.

þat reformyng [in feiþ / and / in feelyng *rev., marked for trsp.*] may not sodenly be geten but be grace and moche bodily and gostly traueyl in lengþe of tyme. C^{m} xvij. þis reformyng.

þe cause why so fewe soulis in reward of þe multitude of oþere þat comen to þis reformyng in feiþ and in feling. C^{m} xviij. But now seist.

Anoþer cause also of þe same, and hou wilful bodily customys indiscretly rewardid and vsid sumtyme hyndriþ soulis fro feelyng of more grace. C^{m} xix. Anoþer enchesoun.

Hou þat wiþoute moche bodily and gostly besynes and wiþoute moche grace and mekenes soulis moun not be reformed in felyng ne be kept þerinne after þei kome þerto. C^{m} xx. Nou seist þou.

An entre hou a soule shal haue hire in mouyng and werkyng þat wole come to þis reformyng by ensaumple of a pilgrym goyng to Ierusalem, and of twey maner mekenes. C^m^ xxj. Neuerþeles for þou coueytist.

Of tariengis and temptaciounz þat soulis shul fele be here gostly enmyes in here gostly goyng to heuenly Ierusalem and of remedies ayens hem. C^m^ xxij. Now art þou in þe weye.

Of a general remedy ayens wikkid stiringgis and peynful [f. 143^r^] tariengis þat fallen to here hertis of þe fleishe, of þe world and of þe fend. C^m^ xxiij. And after þis.

Of an yuel day and a good nyȝt, what it meniþ and hou þe loue of þe world is likned ⟨to⟩ an yuel day and þe loue of God to a good nyȝt. C^m^ xxiiij. If þou wolt.

Hou þat þe desyr of Ihesu ⟨soþfastly felid⟩ in þis liȝtsom derknes sleeþ alle stiryngis of synne and abliþ þe soule to perceyue gostly lyȝtnynggis fro þe heuenly Ierusalem þat if Ihesu. C^m^ xxv. þanne siþ þis.

Hou a man shal knowe fals imaginacions feyned by þe fend fro þe trewe liȝt of knowyng þat comeþ out of Ihesu and be what toknyngis. C^m^ xxvj. But now be war.

Hou gret profit it is to [þe] soule to be brouȝt þoruȝ grace into liȝtsom derknes and hou a man shal dispose hym if he wole come þerto. C^m^ xxvij. þere ben many.

þat in reformyng of a soule þe werkyng of oure Lord Ihesu is departid into foure `parties´, þat is clepyng, riȝtyng, magnifieng and glorifieng. C^m^ xxviij. Lo I haue.

Hou[1] it falliþ sumtyme þat soules beginnyng and profiting in grace semen to haue more loue as be outward tokenys þan summe hauen þat ben perfit, and yet it is not so in sooþ withinne. C^m^ xxix. But now seist þou.

On what maner a man shal haue knowyng of his owen soule, and hou a man shulde sette his loue in Ihesu God and man, o persone. C^m^ xxx. It nedit to a.

Hou þis maner of spekyng of reformyng in felyng of a soule shal be take and on what wise it is reformid, and hou it is foundid in Seint Poulis woordis. C^m^ xxxj. Nou I haue.

Hou God openyþ þe innere eye of þe soule for to se hym not al at onys but be diuers tymes, and of þre maner reformyng of a soule be ensaumple. C^m^ xxxij. A soule þat is clepid.

[1] Hou] Hout MS

Hou Ihesu is heuene to þe soule and why he is clepid fier. C^{m} xxxiij. What is heuene.

Of two manerz of loue, formed and vnformyd, what it meniþ, and how we ben holde to loue Ihesu moche for oure makyng, but more for oure byeng, but alþer most for oure sauyng þoruȝ þe yefte of his loue. C^{m} xxxiiij. But now wondrist.

Hou þat sum soule loueþ Ihesu be bodily feruoris and by here owen manly affecciouns þat ben stired be grace and be reson, and hou sum loueþ Ihesu more restfully be gostly affeccioun only stirid inward þoruȝ special grace of þe Holy Gost. C^{m} xxxv. Þanne may I sey.

Þat þe yefte of loue among alle þe yeftis of Ihesu is worþiest and most profitable, and hou Ihesu doþ al þat is wel don in his louers onely for loue, and hou loue makiþ þe vsyng of alle vertues and a goode dedis liȝt and esy. C^{m} xxxvj. Axe þou þanne.

Hou loue þoruȝ gracious beholdyng of Ihesu sleþ alle steryngis of pride and makiþ þe soule meke perfiȝtly, for it makiþ þe soule to lese fauour and alle erþely worship. C^{m} xxxvij. Neuerþeles hou loue.

Hou loue sleþ alle stiryngis of wreþþe and enuye softly and refourmeþ in þe soule þe vertues of pes and pacience and of perfit charite to his euen-cristen[2] as he dide specially in þe Aposteles. C^{m} xxxviij. Loue werkiþ.

Hou loue sleþ couetise, lecherie and glotenye, and sleþ þe fleisly sauour and delyt in alle þe fyue bodily wittis softly and esily þorouȝ a gracious beholdyng of Ihesu. C^{m} xxxix. Couetise also.

What vertues and gracis a soule resceyueþ þoruȝ openyng of þe innere eye into þe gracious beholdyng of Ihesu, and hou it may not be get only þoruȝ mannys traueil but þoruȝ special grace and traueil also. C^{m} xl. Þus werkiþ.

Hou special grace in beholdyng of Ihesu wiþdrawiþ sumtyme fro a soule and hou a soule shal haue hire in þe absence and presence of Ihesu, and how a soule shal desire þat in it is alwey þe gracious presence of Ihesu. C^{m} xlj. Shewe me þanne.

A commendacion of prayere offrid to Ihesu of a soule [f. 143^{v}] contemplatif, and hou stabilnes[3] in preiere is a siker werk to stonde inne, and hou euery felyng of grace in a chosyn soule may be seid Ihesu, but þe more clene a soule is þe worþiere is þe grace. C^{m} xlij. The soule of.

Hou a soule þoruȝ openyng ⟨of⟩ þe gostly receyueþ a gracious loue able to

[2] euen-cristen] heuencristen (h *canc.*) MS
[3] stabilnes] *Final -s overwritten* MS

vndirstonde Holy Writ, and hou Ihesu þat is hid in Holy Writ shewiþ hymself to his loueris. C^{m} xliij. Whanne þe soule.

Of þe preuy voice of Ihesu sownyng in a soule wherby it shal be knowe and how alle þe gracious illuminaciouns made in a soule ben clepid þe spekyngis of Ihesu. C^{m} xliij. Lo þese ben fayre.

Hou þoruȝ þe gracious openy[n]g of þe gostly eye a soule is made wise mekely and soþfastly for to sen `þe´ diuersite of degrees in holy chirche as traueyling and for to sen angelis kynde, and first of reprevid. C^{m} xlv. Neuerþeles oþere.

Hou be þe same liȝt of grace þe blissid angelis kynde may be sen, and how Ihesu is as God and man aboue alle creaturis after þe soule may se hym here. C^{m} xlvj. And þanne after.

THE TABLE OF CHAPTERS IN OXFORD, BODLEIAN LIBRARY MS BODLEY 100 (B)

[f. 71^{r}] Ca^{m} 1^{m}. How þys ymage may be reformed to þe ferste lyknesse by grace of hym þat is God.

2^{m}. That jewwes and paynymes haue noȝt þe benefts of þe passion of Cryst.

3^{m}. How þe ymage of God wiche is mannus soule myȝt be restored to his liknesse þe beynge in creature.

4^{m}. How þe reformynge of þis ymage stondeþ in two parties, and how man may haue hit in his lyfe.

5^{m}. How synne of two maners makeþ a soule to lese þe lyknesse and þe schap of God.

6^{m}. How a man ssal gete þe lyknesse of God aȝeyn in his soule lost byfore by hys wykked lyf.

7^{m}. How þis reformynge stondeþ only in feyþ and noȝt in felynge.

8^{m}. How þe ryȝtwyse man and he þat is ryȝtful mad by bapteme lyueþ in hys feyþ.

9^{m}. How stedefast soules leden here lyf and fle al maner of dedly synne.

10^{m}. þat a man or a womman þat is þus reformed most haue myche besynesse to kepe hym clene þerynne.

11^{m}. How mannus soule ys semelich and fayre whan hit is reformed to þe lyknesse, and how foul whan hit is naȝt.

12^{m}. Of two partys withynne a man, þat on is cleped sensualite and þat oþer reson, and how þey ssal be rewled.

13^{m}. How a soule reformed to þe lyknesse of God is þe moste perfyȝt creature þat euere God made, and how he lyynge in þe felþe of synne is lyke to bestis lyknesse onresonable.

14^{m}. How many men vnable þemself bycause þat þey lyen in synne and wol naȝt ryse vp and receyue grace.

15^{m}. How sum men wytynge hemself in dedly synne maken merþe and solace at þey were naȝt þerynne.

16^{m}. That þis reformynge in feyþ may ben had and after gret long traueyle, how it may be comyne to alle chosyne soules.

17^{m}. That [f. 71^{v}] sum men reformed set naȝt here herte to profyte in grace ne to gete hyȝere stat þan þei ben ynne for besynesse of þe world.

18^{m}. How men in here turnynge to God setten hem in diuerse obseruaunce, and how of hem letted þey ben heuy and angry, and how þey ssolde holde þe comyn.

19^{m}. What manere of trauele a man moste vse ȝyf he wol come to þys reformynge.

20^{m}. That a man þat wol go to Jerusalem, þat is þe cite of pees, þe whiche is contemplacion, moste holde hym lowe in meknesse and suffre desese and tribulacion.

21^{m}. How a man þat is in þis weye schal haue enemys to dryue hym out, and how he ssal ouercome hem by knowynge of God and vertue of penaunce.

22^{m}. How þyn enemys seynge þe ynmeueable in þys wey, wolde brynge byfore þe alle þy goode dedys and comende þe of hem, and how þou ssalt putte hem away.

23^{m}. How good and blysful hit is for to be lyȝtned with þe lyȝt of God in þy derknesse and in þy desyre.

24^{m}. How þe fend wol schewe to þe a feyned lyȝt, and how þou ssalt beware of hym and ouercome hym.

25^{m}. How deuowte soules comen into þis derknesse and wot nat what hit is, and how þey ssal knowe hit and feele hit in heere affeccion.

26^{m}. How a soule brouȝt þoruȝ grace into þys derknesse schal afterward be brouȝt to lyȝt of perfyȝt knowynge.

27^{m}. Þat certeyn soules þer ben þe wiche by gret trauayle comen into þys derknesse, and ȝet þey ben naȝt reformed in felynge.

28^{m}. þat a soule moste ferst haue knowynge of hymself and wyþdrawe hym fro þe vsshe of þe bodily wyttys and of his merowere biside hym.

29^{m}. Of þe reformynge in felynge what hit is and wiche ben þe gostly felyngis þerof, and how hit is noȝt wordlche bute spiritualych.

30^{m}. How a soule [f. 72^{r}] clepud from þe world and y-reformed by God þoruȝ schynynge of his lyȝt in techynge schal be rauesshed into perfyȝt vnderstondynge.

31^{m}. What heuene is and how a soule may haue þe knowynge of blessede Jesu.

32^{m}. That perfyȝt loue and gostly vnderstondynge, þe wyche is mad brennynge in a perfyȝt soule by þe grace of þe Holi Goost, lefteþ vp a soule to þe perfeccion of perfyȝt feelynge.

33^{m}. That he þat most loueþ God ssal haue most blysse in tyme comynge, and how sum men trauelen þerabowte and ȝet þey haueþ hit naȝt.

34^{m}. How loue sleeþ synnes and reformeþ vertues, and how he þat is verrey meeke þenkeþ hymself worst of alle creatures, and how loue is noȝt gyue by kynde but aboue kynde by þe grace of God.

35^{m}. That þer is no ȝyft of God so profytable as is þe ȝyft of loue, wich is þe Holi Gost, and how man ssolde aske bit and noȝt ellys but perfection and lastynge þerynne.

36^{m}. That þys loue lost in a mannes soule bycause of synne may be geten aȝeyn by paciense and ful makynge aseth þoruȝ penaunce.

37^{m}. How þe louere of Jesu kepeþ no more þan þat he loueþ, and how he despyseþ alle erþly richesse at nouȝt.

38^{m}. How þys loue openeþ þe gostlych eyȝe into perfyȝt contemplacion, and how hit may noȝt be getyn bute in clennesse and silence.

39^{m}. That a soule þat þoruȝ þe grace of Jesu haþ openynge of gostly eyene wyþdrawyn fro þe wordele to reste and silence haþ delyȝt of heuene þoruȝ gostly presence of Jesu.

[f. 72^{v}] 40^{m}. How þe soule of a louere may feele Jesu and how Holy Wryȝt sentense is brouȝt vnto his þouȝt by hys minystres þat ben ancrys and louers of Jesu.

41^{m}. How þe soule of a man þe wyche ys cold and vndeuoute haþ naȝt þe worchynge of þys grace, and how þe lyȝt of grace getyn to hym aȝeyn styreþ hym.

42^{m}. That a soule þoruȝ lyȝt of grace may seen goostly þynges and fulhede of vertues.

43^{m}. That þer ben oþer gostly vertues and þynges schewed to a deuoute soule as þe Trynyte by reuelacions and syȝttes of angeles and worchynges of oþer hooly creatures.

44^{m}. How also last ys schewed þe diuersite of aungeles and þe worchynge of þe Trynyte and oþere þynges.

Explicit tabula secunde partis huius libelli. Deo gracias.

EXPLANATORY NOTES

Hussey provided his text with separate sets of textual and explanatory notes, based on the text of H. These two sets of notes have been combined, revised, supplemented, and keyed to H_7, the base text of this edition. Many of the explanatory notes that point out sources and parallels to the *Scale* in patristic and medieval monastic and scholastic theological writings, or to Hilton's other works, derive from J. P. H. Clark, 'Notes' and from the notes to the edition of *Walter Hilton's Latin Writings* by J. P. H. Clark and Cheryl Taylor, 2 vols., Analecta Cartusiana, 124 (Salzburg, 1987), which the editors are pleased to recognize here. When multiple editions of sources and parallels are available, citations will be from the first edition of each work listed in the Abbreviations above.

NB. These notes use the sigla **χ** to refer to the manuscripts of the Carthusian/Brigittine textual group collectively, **λ** to refer to the London group, and Σ to refer to all manuscripts not otherwise specified.

TITLE/RUBRIC

Scale II only bears the title *Scale of Perfection* in the **χ** MSS $H_5WsH^cHu_2M$. The fact that *Scale* II has no title in other manuscripts suggests that it may originally not have born a title. The unique *incipit* of *Scale* II in M (which lacks *Scale* I) has the title 'Scole of Perfection' followed by a rubric, 'This book þat folweth . . . ful of perfeccion', that begins an adaptation of the text (which continues into the first sentences of the first chapter) for a more generally religious, and not specifically heremitic, audience.

CHAPTER TITLES

The fact that $HBH_5WsChLwHu_2$ originally had no chapter titles in the text suggests that **χ** originally lacked chapter titles, and that their occurrence in LdTW was a later addition.

CHAPTER I

The idea of the corruption of the image of the Trinity in the fallen human soul, which derives from Augustine's *De Trin.*, and the reformation of the image of God in the contemplative life, recurs throughout chapters 43–5, 53–5, 84–8 and 91 of *Scale* I. The Latin version, 'prius in alio libro', would appear to refer specifically to this. This idea is also the primary theme of

Hilton's Latin letter *De Imag. pec.*, *LW*, i. 69–102. See J. P. H. Clark, 'Image and Likeness in Walter Hilton', *DR* 97 (1979), 204–20.

3 *þou . . . byginnyng* (l. 7). The unique opening of M (which contains *Scale* II only) is apparently intended to adapt it to stand without *Scale* I.

per charite. This is the variant of two of the three earliest manuscripts (H_7H but not R), and is supported by the 'pur charite' of LB_3P as against Σ 'for'. *MED* 'charite' *n.* 4 notes 'for charite' and 'pur charite' as 'common in entreaties and requests', with the variant 'par charite'.

11 1 Cor. 11: 7: 'Vir . . . imago et gloria Dei est.' 'The Apostle', for Hilton as for most medieval writers, means St Paul specifically. Hilton translates this directly as 'Man is þe ymage of God', but adds, 'made to þe ymage and þe likenesse of him', which leads into the next scriptural citation.

14 Gen. 1: 26–7: 'Faciamus hominem ad imaginem et similitudinem nostram . . . Et creavit Deus hominem ad imaginem suam.' Hilton expands slightly to 'schope man in soule'. Scriptural quotations are identified in interlinear additions in B, in the margin in L, Hu_2, P, T and W, and in E and Ld as part of their citation in the text. No other manuscripts identify Hilton's scriptural quotations.

16 *þe ymage and þe likenesse of him*. So RλAsSrACcMPl. This is repetitive, duplicating the phrasing that occurs just two lines above. The H_7 variant probably derives from the eye-skip omisson of the material between the two occurrences of the phrase 'þe ymage'. χ 'his owne ymge and liknes', which may be the result of stylistic smoothing, lacks the repetition that would have occasioned the omission in H_7.

17 *and schal speken of*. This phrase, which is supported by H_7λSrM and the Latin version, 'et de qua adhuc dicere plus', was probably omitted by eye-skip in χCc.

22 *mirknesse*. Here as elsewhere, this form is a probable relict of Hilton's own dialect that was standardized to 'derknesse' in the manuscript tradition as early as the beginning of the fifteenth century.

24 *stonden*. The addition of 'stille' in Lw`H^{c}´ETW is a common by-form of the absolute form in metaphorical use: *MED* 'stonden' *v.* 24(c). See also 'standen stille' at 18/30.

28 *might*. The addition of 'not', primarily in manuscripts of χ and λ, is grammatically redundant ('non' occurs only four words later). Its addition is probably an example of the scribal tendency to clarification of the text; specifically, to make the negation explicit earlier in the sentence.

CHAPTER 2

In this chapter, Hilton sets out the argument for the necessity of the incarnation and death of Christ as an act of atonement to the injured honour of God as developed by Anselm of Canterbury in the *Cur Deus homo*, in *Opera*, ii. 37–133. See R. W. Southern, *Saint Anselm and his Biographer: A Study of Monastic Life and Thought, 1059–c. 1130* (Cambridge, 1963), 77–121.

3 *forsaken*. The Latin version, 'transformata', supports RAsAELdPlTW 'forschapen', over H_7λSr. 'Forschapen' is the more cogent reading, as more appropriate to the present discussion of the deformation of the image of the Trinity in the soul, which was, according to Hilton's Augustinian theology, 'forshapen' in Adam and his descendants. It was not 'humanity' (mankende) that was 'forsaken' by the sin of Adam, but God.

4 *The*. The limner was obviously intended to provide an initial 'þ' here, but provided a 'T' instead; this also occurs at the beginning of Chapters 16, 25, 27, 35, 40, and 42.

11 *amendes*. The cancelled addition of 'were' in L appears to parallel the textual transposition occurring in LwW.

16 *trespast*. The Latin version uses the same perfect form, 'deliquit', both here and in the next line, in parallel with the simple past form, 'trespast', of H_7. In Σ, the first of these two instances uses the perfect tense, 'haþ trespast' which accords better with the simple present-tense forms of the rest of the sentence. The legal terminology of atonement and satisfaction here derives from Anselm.

19 *owe*. The three earliest manuscripts, H_7, H, and R, seem to preserve uniquely a distinction between the indicative for that which the transgressor already owes in any case, and the subjunctive for that which he would not owe were it not for his transgression.

20 *þat*. When 'wherewith' is used as a nominal relative involving an antecedent (*OED* 'wherewith' II.2.b) the consequence is usually expressed with 'to' and the infinitive; here 'wherewith' functions as a conjunction, and requires the relative particle.

21 *awght*. The sense demands the past tense, although the forms 'awght', 'auȝt', 'ouȝt', etc. occurring in most manuscripts can be read as either present or past. The tense is specified only by the variants 'oweth' (RAsPl) and 'owed' (AM). The confusion is due to the ME development of the preterite-present verb 'ought' from the past tense of OE 'aȝan', expanding the semantic field of 'owed' to include that of 'shall'.

22 See Matt. 22: 37.

30 *godhede . . . kynde* (l. 31). The Latin version combines these into 'natura propria deitatis', omitting the intervening material.

33 *nought*. The addition of 'do' uniquely in χ, although supported by the Latin version, 'facere', would appear to be an instance of the scribal tendency to textual explicitness.

34 *touched*. The Latin version expands to 'a viro cognita seu corrupta'. An aspect of the doctrine of the virgin birth of Jesus is the idea that it would be inappropriate for the Son of God to be born of sexual liaison with a man.

36 *God*. The Latin version, 'Spiritus Sancti', supports Σ 'þe Holy Gost', the more cogent reading.

43 *his*. The addition of 'owen' in H_7MT is probably a scribal repetitition of the phrase 'his owen' from the previous line. The added emphasis is unnecessary here.

44 *þe qwhilk kynde*. Presumably an eye-skip omisson in H_7.

45 *þer was . . . Jesu* (l. 47). Hilton here emphacizes that it was because Jesus undertook his sacrifice in his human nature that it was acceptable in recompense for the sin of Adam, something that no other human could do.. The repetition of 'man' is thus probably authorial rather than scribal. The Latin version supports the addition of the name of Christ in λECc, as against H_7HRBH_5AsSrWsChLwAHu_2MLdPlTW, but the expansion of 'Jesus' to 'Jesus Christus' is characteristic of the Latin version.

49 *for loue of sothfastnesse*. The Latin version reads 'pro iusticie dileccione' here, rather than the correct 'veritatis', perhaps under influence of 'pro amore iusticie' ('for loue of ryghtwysnesse') in the next clause.

53 *He . . . bot*. The omission of this phrase in LB_3 (although it is supplied by a correcting hand in L) is possible evidence that B_3 was copied from L before this correction was made. Support for the phrase 'þe loue of' is equally divided among the English manuscripts, but is supported by the Latin version, 'diligere'.

55 *not*. Although omitted by H_7, 'not' is necessary to the sense here.

56 *þan . . . dyen*. LB_3APH_6Ld have here omitted what probably looked like a repetition.

58 *þe best mans dede*. 'Best' could be taken either as modifying 'dede' (in parallel with 'most wurthi'), or 'mans', as the Latin version understands it: 'hominis perfectissimi'. Forms of 'ded(e)' in the English text could be read either as 'deed' or 'death'; the Latin version, 'opus' clearly supports the reading 'deed'.

most. The addition of the definite article in H_7Sr would emphasize the parallelism between 'þe best' and 'þe most'; but if 'þe best' modifies 'man', as has just been suggested, then the phrases are not actually in parallel.

60 *mankynde had founden a man*. The Latin version turns this into a passive construction: 'vnus homo repertus fuit'.

62 *þat . . . ouermore* (l. 63). This phrase is omitted, probably by eye-skip, in HH_5Ws and Cc, but present in the other χ manuscripts.

64 *dyed*. The Latin version, 'moriebatur', supports this reading over RAsAPl 'did'.

66 *reformed . . . heuene* (l. 67). The Latin version distributes these phrases more symetrically: 'ad primam similitudinem reformari et ad celestem gloriam restaurari'.

72 *passion*. The Latin version does not support the χ addition, 'preciouse'.

brynnyng swerd of cherubyn. Gen. 3: 24.

74 *opned*. The Latin version, 'patefacte sunt', supports the past participle here, rather than the adjective 'open'.

75 *euene*. The RAsSr variant 'of heuen' is probably the result of confusion by graphic similarity, reinforced by the common phrase 'king of heaven'. LwH^eE 'of [in E] heuen euen' is possibly the result of a gloss to the same effect.

77 *here . . . reformed* (l. 78). The Latin version supports the Σ variant over the eye-skip omisson in H_7M.

79 *amendis is*. Only LB_3EP read this as plural: 'amendis bee'. *MED* 'amende(s' *n.* notes that both 'amende' and 'amendes' are construed as singular.

CHAPTER 3

7 *Jesu man*. The Latin version, 'Jesus', supports the omission of 'man' in $HH_5WsLwCcTW$, but Hilton is here contrasting the human and divine natures of Christ.

12 *fantum and folie*. The Latin version, 'vanitatem . . . et stulticiam', suggests the phrasing of the following scriptural citation.

13 *Seynt Poule seith*. This, and not the reversed form 'seid Seynt Poule', is Hilton's normal usage.

seith. The Latin version, 'dicit', supports H_7 over Σ in using the present, rather than the past tense. Hilton's verb tense usage in introducing scriptural citations is variable.

14 1 Cor. 1: 23–4.

16 *virtutem*. Although Hilton will translate the remainder of the verse below ('and wysdom'), the phrase 'et Dei sapientiam' here is supported only by

AELdTW among the English manuscripts, with $HBH_5WsChLwHu_2$ compressing the reference to 'etcetera'.

ȝe trowen. The Latin version (and the underlying scriptural verse) support this variant over LB_3EPH_6Cc 'we'.

20 *be þeyre vntrowthe . . . here owen soule* (l. 21). The Latin version, 'per infidelitatem propriam anime sue impediunt reformacionem' transfers 'owen' from modifying 'soule' to 'vntrowthe'.

23 *þe*[3]. The H_7 omission is in error.

24 *or haue*. The Latin version, 'vel habuerit', supports $H_7RLB_3AsPH_6CcM$ (with the variant 'and haue' in Sr) over the $HBH_5WsChLwAHu_2ELdPlTW$ omission.

25–35 Hilton's distinction here between the 'open', 'feeling [affective]' knowledge of the Incarnation by the patriarchs, prophets, and other holy men both before and after the time of Christ, and the 'privy and general' knowledge of 'simple and imperfect souls', may be parallel to the distinction between explicit and implicit faith made by Aquinas in *ST* 2–2, q. 2, a. 6. The Latin version of *Scale* II in fact uses the words 'explicite' and 'implicite'.

25 *ouþer comende or comen*. The Latin version expands these participles into full clauses: 'vel uenturus fuit vel quod iam de facto uenit'.

30 *knewen*. The Latin version, 'cognouerunt', supports the past-tense form here, rather than the present-tense variant of LB_3PM.

priuetes. The plural form of the Latin version, 'sacramenta', supports $H_7RLB_3AsSrAEPH_6CcMPl$ over the singular variant of χ.

32 *han trouthe*. The Latin version, 'fidem habent', supports $H_7HRH_5AsSrWsChLwHu_2MPlTW$ (and the BALd variant 'byleue') over the perfect 'han trowid' of LB_3EPH_6Cc.

36–48 Hilton takes a conservative Augustinian stand here in the late medieval debate on the salvation of righteous non-Christians. See Nicholas Watson, 'Visions of Inclusion: Universal Salvation and Vernacular Theology in Pre-Reformation England', *Journal of Medieval and Early Modern Studies*, 27 (1997), 145–87; Frank Grady, *Representing Righteous Heathens in Late Medieval England* (New York, 2005); Clark, 'Notes', 303–4 n. 8.

37 *greuously*. This adverb is parallel to immediately preceding 'gretly'; the omission of the adverbial suffix in H_7 is an error.

54 *þe articles*. The Latin version, 'alios articulos', here supports $HBH_5WsChLwHu_2CcLdTW$, 'oþer articles', over $H_7RLB_3AsSrAEPH_6MPl$. Because the propositions that Jesus is the Son of God and that his passion suffices for the salvation of humankind are themselves articles of the Christian faith, it is not inappropriate to speak of the 'other' articles here.

But . . . God (l. 57). The omission in HH_5WsT is presumably the result of eye-skip.

56 *here*[2]. The manuscript evidence is divided amongst 'here' (H_7LB_3SrEPH_6Cc), 'þe' (RBAsSrLwH[c]ALdPlW), and no determiner (ChHu_2M), but the parallelism of 'in here sinne and in here fals loue' is a good example of rhetorical repetition of the type favoured by Hilton.

59 *in as mikel . . . had it* (l. 60). The principle behind this argument is that of Luke 12: 48: 'And unto whomsoever much is given, of him much will be required: and to whom they have committed much, of him they will demand the more.'

60 *had it*. The Latin version here, as often, changes pronouns to nouns to add specificity: 'fuissent in fidei articulos informati'.

64 *foule bestes liknes*. In the Latin version, 'turpiter' modifies 'transformata erat', rather than 'similitudinem bestialem'.

66 *reformyng*. H_7RAsSrACcMPl is the more cogent reading here. The phrase 'restoring and reforming' (which echoes the wording of the preceding clause), supported by χE, perhaps overemphasizes the concept of 'restoring', when the main theme of *Scale* II is the reformation of the soul in faith and feeling. λCc 'reforming in faith', which is supported by the Latin version, raises the distinction of the two types of reformation prematurely: this distinction is first introduced in Chapter 5. The threefold distinction made in the present chapter is among those who believe and are saved, those who do not believe, and those who apparently believe, but whose faith is shown to be false by their sinful living.

67 *Soth . . . heuene* (l. 70). This unique H_7 addition, with its digression on the necessity of purgation, either in this life or in Purgatory, is possibly an authorial addition, but it reflects concerns with the theology of penance that are not properly Hilton's subject at this point.

CHAPTER 4

3 The objection, 'Now seist þou . . .', whether addressed to him by a real or a fictional interlocutor, followed by the reply, 'To þis I answere . . .', is common in Hilton (see the openings of Chapters 18 and 20). The insertion of the 'Holy Name' passage into Chapter 44 of *Scale* I is also an example.

8 *þat is in no creature*. In the Latin version, 'creature' is the subject of the sentence: 'nulla creatura . . . est . . . taliter reformata'.

9 *þiself . . . þeself* (l. 12). The Latin version ('te ipsam', 'te ipsa', at this point) addresses the text to a single female recipient throughout.

þe þinkest. The Latin version, 'tu iudicas', supports the variants 'þou þenkist' in H_5LB_3WsAEPH_6', or Pl 'þan þinkest þou' rather than either the

H_7 reading or the alternative 'þe þinke' or 'þe þenkeþ'. The verb 'þenken' was in transition from impersonal to transitive in this period (cf. 'methinks', which remained in use considerably longer than the second- or third-person forms), and the variants here reflect indecision concerning its precise syntactic role.

13 The 'ymage of sinne' figures prominently in *Scale* I, Chapters 53–5, 78, and 84–91. See also Hilton's Latin letter *De Imag. pec.* Bernard McGinn suggests a possible source for the idea of the 'imago peccati' in Ambrose, *Enarratio in Psalmum* 35.8 (*PL* 14: 1002), but notes that Hilton's development of the theme 'seems to be his own creation' (*The Varieties of Vernacular Mysticism, 1350–1550*, The Presence of God: A History of Western Christian Mysticism, 5 (New York, 2012), 628, n. 45). The present chapter marks the end of the excursus on justification with which Hilton began his treatment of the reformation of the image of God in the soul in *Scale* II.

19 *or elles . . . reformed* (l. 20). The Latin version agrees with H_5AsWsChHu_2 in omitting this clause, probably by eye-skip.

28 *endeles goodnes.* The repetition of the definite article in HRBAsSrChLwAHu_2ECcMLdPlTW increases the parallelism of the balanced phrases.

30 *fulfillinge.* W 'full felynge', agrees with the Latin version, 'plenam sensacionem'.

34 Isa. 2: 11.

35 *aylastend.* This form, which occurs in the earliest manuscripts, is probably Hilton's, rather than the alternative 'euerelastynge', which is characteristic of χ generally (except for H) and the later manuscripts.

40 *be.* The textual variants and marginal notes of L and P demonstrate the derivation of P from L. An annotator in L, confused by the scribe's characteristic spelling of the verb 'be' as 'bi', has written in the margin, 'quere: bi or be'. The scribe of P has taken 'bi or be' as an addition to be incorporated into the text (then cancelled 'bi or'), and left 'quere' as a marginal note, with a paraph like those of all of the other marginal notes that he has copied from L.

44–61 This argument derives from Anselm of Canterbury, *De Concordia praescientiae et praedestinationis*, in *Opera*, ii. 243–88, q. 3, c. 9.

49 *anon sodeynli.* The original χ reading seems to have been a form of *OED* 'belive' *adv.* 2a, *MED* 'blive' *adv.* 2, meaning 'immediately', which several scribes did not understand.

51 *þat liued þan þat.* The χ variant attempts to clarify Hilton's syntax by inserting 'ha ben' after 'þan'; the Latin version reduces 'þat liued þan' to the participial phrase 'tunc viuens'.

58 Hebr. 11: 40.

61 *not make a ful end*. The EV of the Wyciffite Bible has 'not be fulfillid'; the LV has 'not be maad perfit'; see *The Holy Bible, Containing the Old and New Testaments, with the Apocryphal Books, in the Earliest English Versions, made from the Latin Vulgate by John Wycliffe and His Followers*, ed. J. Forshall and F. Madden, 4 vols. (Oxford, 1850; repr. New York, 1982)

62 *syn þat a man*. The $HBH_5SrWsChLwHu_2LdTW$ variant 'sen þat man' is more cogent, because Hilton is not speaking of the creation of each individual human here, but of the creation of the human race in Adam.

CHAPTER 5

In the opening of this chapter, Hilton introduces the concept of 'reformation in faith and in feeling' that is fundamental to his conceptualization of the contemplative life. It will remain a major focus throughout *Scale* II. See Sargent, "Walter Hilton's *Scale of Perfection* in Devotional Compilations'. As Hilton describes it, 'feeling' is an affective grace unlike either the sensory gifts that characterize the mystical experiences of Richard Rolle or the imaginative devotion of the Bonaventuran tradition. He will go on in following chapters to employ a number of metaphors to describe this reformation, including those of 'lyȝty mirknes', 'þe openyng of þe gostly eȝe' and 'þe [swete/preve] voyce of Jesu'. He will justify his conceptualization of the reformation in faith and in feeling using a number of Pauline texts (Chapter 31) and show how it corresponds to traditional descriptions of the contemplative life (Chapter 40); and he will describe it through its effects in the later chapters of *Scale* II. In his Latin version, Fishlake translates 'feeling' as 'sensacio', and shows a marked tendency to add devotional emphasis on the humanity and the passion of Christ, in a move that pulls the text in a Bonaventuran direction. J. P. H. Clark interprets 'feeling' as more intellectual than affective, a form of 'interior awareness' or Anselmian 'understanding'; see Clark, 'Notes', 304 n. 15. Similarly, Bernard McGinn describes it as a form of 'awareness' or 'perception'; see *Varieties*, 390.

5 *saufe*. The Latin version scrupulously adds 'post hanc vitam'.

is. The verb is required here; the H_7 omission is an error.

7 *feith*[1]. The addition of 'only' in χECc was probably suggested by the phrase 'in feith only' in the preceding line.

11 *for þow . . . God* (l. 14). The complexity of Hilton's statement of the relationship between salvation by faith and the temptation to sin that still remains in the soul as a result of original sin—that although those who are reformed only in faith will still feel stirrings of sin (a theme that will be developed at considerable length later), they are nonetheless reformed to the image of God and will be saved so long as they do not succumb to temptation—has led to considerable confusion in the textual tradition.

The H_7RAsSrPlCcM variant, with 'he may' preceding the clause 'nought ageynstondene . . . þerto' (including the present tense plural verb form 'ageynstondene' ['withstondyn' Cc]), followed by 'he schal be reformed', is supported by the Latin version, 'licet homo non senciat in se nisi motus peccati et carnalia desideria, et resistere non possit tali sensacioni (seu quoniam sic senciat), si tamen non consenciat tali sensacioni nec in ea delectatur, ad Dei similitudinem per fidem poterit reformi'. The Latin adds a parenthetical alternative phrasing, 'seu quoniam sic senciat'; H_7 omits the necessary 'not' in 'assent þerto'; H_7Cc lack 'he schal be'; and Pl lacks 'be' (is M). In λAE, 'ȝit he may' precedes 'not wiþstondynge . . . þerto' (including the verbal adjective form 'wiþstondynge'), followed by 'be reformed'. In the χA variant 'not agaynstandand . . . þerto' (including the verbal adjective) precedes 'he may be reformid'. The variation is probably the result of the clause 'nought ageynstonden(d/e) . . . þerto' being added in the margin of the archetype, and incorporated variously into the hypearchetypes of the surviving copies. The Latin version also adds the explanatory phrase 'nec in ea delectatur', a variant echoed in Cc: 'ne he hath delectacion there inne'. This is one of several points at which an addition occurs that suggests that Cc (or an ancestor of Cc) may have been compared with the Latin text.

17–18 *begynnynge . . . profytend . . . perfyt*. The classification of *incipientes*, *proficientes*, and *perfecti* as the Latin version translates them, is common in patristic and medieval contemplative literature. Gregory, *Mor. in Job* 24. 11. 28, speaks of *inchoatio*, *mediatas*, and *perfectio*. Hilton here combines 'begynnynge' and 'profytend' souls as types of active men and equates the 'perfyt' with contemplatives. He will later, in Chapters 13 and 30, relate this to his own schematization of those who are not reformed to the image of God, those who are reformed in faith alone, and those who are reformed in faith and in feeling.

17 *actyfe men*. H_7 has muddled this variant.

22 *good*. The addition of 'and' in L, which was then expunged, and the expunction then erased, while B_3 has the addition of 'and' and P lacks it, gives evidence of the derivation of B_3 and P from L in respect to the order of the corrections in it. B_3 (or an intermediate ancestor) appears to have been copied after 'and' had been expunged, and P after the expunction itself had been erased.

24 *to*. Required by the following infinitive: the omission in H_7 is an error.

CHAPTER 6

1 *þe sacrament . . . grounded*. The Latin version, 'uirtutem baptismi que fundatur et constitit', shifts the focus from the grounding of the sacrament of baptism itself in the passion of Christ to the 'virtue'—the efficacy—of the

sacrament. The idea of the 'grounding' of the sacraments in the passion occurs in book 1, chapter 12 of the pseudo-Bonaventuran *Stimulus amoris*: 'Ab hac sacratissima passione omnia sacramenta ecclesiastica trahunt virtutem', although not in the Middle English *Prickynge of Love*. See Falk Eisermann, *Stimulus Amoris: Inhalt, lateinische Überlieferung, deutsche Übersetzungen, Rezeption* (Tübingen, 2001), 30 n. 109.

4 *maner*. The HBE plural form 'maners', is supported by the Latin version, 'genera', although the English text uses a singular verb form. Both 'maner' and 'maners' are capable of being construed as either singular or plural in ME.

sinne. This variant has the support of the two of the three earliest surviving English manuscripts, H_7 and H, as well as BH_5WsChλEA; the variant 'synnes' is supported by RAsSr and the majority of later manuscripts ($LwHu_2$CcMLdPlTW), as well as H^c and the Latin version, 'peccatorum'.

11 *sacrament*. The support of the four earliest surviving manuscripts, H_7H°RB, as well as ChAM, suggests that the omission of the preceding definite article is not a casual error in H_7.

12 *actuel sinne*. RλAsSrAEPl add a preceding definite article, but it is grammatically inappropriate, because actual sin is not a single sin, but a category of sin. The article is probably echoed from the phrase 'þe original sinne' in the previous phrase.

18 *manciples of helle*. Hilton uses the same expression in *Epist. ad Quem.*, *LW*, ii. 267, l. 387: 'ipsa gracie collacio que de mancipio Gehenne facit te filium gracie'. A similar expression, 'and of þe prisoner of helle maketh a percenere of heuenly heritage', occurs below at 8.23.

24 *more*. CcM and the Latin version lack this intensifier.

CHAPTER 7

The defensive nature of this chapter would appear to be in response to Wycliffite criticism of oral confession. See Anne Hudson, *The Premature Reformation: Wycliffite Texts and Lollard History* (Oxford, 1988), 294–301.

3 *actuel sinnes*. The Latin version, 'peccatis actualibus', supports the plural H_7SrM variant over the singular form of Σ.

4 *man or wumman*. The Latin version refers only to the masculine, 'christianus', although the English manuscript tradition is unanimous in referring to both men and women.

8 *in þis*. The scribe of H_7 (or some hypearchetype) may have thought the word 'wil' redundant here because it occurs in the preceding and the following lines.

10 *þis mans soule or wummans*. ACc omit 'or wummans'; the Latin version does not distinguish the reference by gender: 'anima illius'.

15 *He abydeth . . . gifeth he* (l. 19). Hilton's treatment of confession and contrition here ehoes that in *Epist. ad Quem*. See specifically, 'Non expectauit ab illis confescionem criminum per expressionem uocis, sed cordis conuercionem desiderat et expectat. Et ut verius dicam, ipse istam confert et operatur', *LW*, ii. 267, ll. 378–81.

16 *no*. The **χ** variant 'not' is supported by the Latin version, 'Non expectat'.

19 The balance of the Latin version, 'istud querit et petit quia istud ex gracia sua donat et concedit', is achieved at the expense of the arresting brevity of the English.

28 *verrey*. The Latin version, 'veram contricionem', supports the H_7RλAsSrCcMPl variant over the **χ** variant 'vertue of'.

31 Hilton's analogy here is to the legal process by which a patron (usually a judge or a member of the nobility) could apply for a charter of royal pardon to exempt an accused malefactor from trial or punishment for a felony. See Helen Lacey, *The Royal Pardon: Access to Mercy in Fourteenth-Century England* (Woodbridge, 2009). Without the formal proclamation of the charter in court (and in some cases, without actual possession of a copy of the writ), the guilty party might still be apprehended by someone claiming ignorance of the pardon—a not unimaginable occurrence in the reign of Richard II. The English text of the *Scale* suggests that the sinner might need such a charter 'ageyns al his enemys', which conjurs up the image of his being seized off to hell by the ministers of Satan, like the evil summoner in Chaucer's *Friar's Tale*.

38 *only*. The Latin version supports the variant 'by contricion' over the H_7 omission. The scribe of H_7 (or some archetype) may have thought the phrase repetitive here, but the addition is the more cogent variant.

44–50 Concern for scrupulous doubts about confession and forgiveness is a theme that occurs in Hilton's *Epist. ad Quem.*, *LW*, ii. 265–78, ll. 331–621. In restating the idea in terms of the organizing schema of *Scale* II, Hilton adds the observation that the restoration of the soul to grace through penance is an aspect of the reformation of the soul in faith alone, and not of reformation in faith and in feeling.

51–62 Hilton's argument that good spiritual guidance from a confessor might elicit contrition in a hitherto unrepentant sinner is an argument that would have had cogency for some Wycliffite readers. See Hudson, *Premature Reformation*, 429. Hilton uses a similar argument from the imperfection of the Christian Church in his own day in *De Util.*, *LW*, i. 124–9, ll. 100–80, observing that if the faith were as strong in the current age as it was in that of the apostles, there would be no need of religious orders; and in the scholastic *questio*, *De Ador. imag.*, *LW*, i. 187–8, ll. 155–76, that the Church would not need images for inspiration to greater fervour.

56 *schrifte*. The manuscripts of χ consistently use the variant 'confession'.

grace of compunccion. A common concept in the theology of penitence: see Gregory, *Mor. in Job*, 29. 26. 53.

59 *Holi Kirke . . . tyme* (l. 62). Annual confession for all Christians had been prescribed by the Fourth Lateran Council in 1215.

Holi . . . men. H_7 omission, presumably by eye-skip.

63 *Neuerþeles . . . biddyng* (l. 71). Fishlake does not translate this argument, probably feeling that the concession that if men were sufficiently spiritually aware, they would not need the sacrament of confession to arouse them to compunction for sin, and thus that the Church would never have needed to require it, is too close to heretical. It is probable that Hilton's argument, that 'since all men are not so perfect, and perhaps much of the majority of Christian men are imperfect', is ironic, but that Fishlake did not recognize, or did not appreciate, the irony. This passage is also bracketed 'Va . . . cat' in the margin of Ch.

64 *fleyng*. $RBH_5LB_3AsSrH^cAPH_6PlT$ 'felyng' would seem to be an anticipation of the same word later in the sentence, and would also echo the focus of Hilton's argument on the awareness of one's own sinfulness.

65 *is*. The evidence for the variants 'is' and 'hath' is approximately equal, even among the earliest manuscripts: $H_7\lambda$ and probably the original text of H support the former; RAsSr the latter. The antecedent verb in the former case would be 'had ben' in l. 63; in the latter, 'had' in either l. 63 or 64.

71 *þan erreth he gretly*. Hilton appears to be referring specifically here to Wycliffite objections to oral confession. The view was attributed to Wyclif and condemned at the Blackfriars Synod of 1382. Ch has a marginal note at this point, 'Nota contra lollardos'. Hilton never refers to Wyclif or to the Lollards; instead he talks of heresy and heretics.

CHAPTER 8

5 See Hebr. 11: 1.

13–14 *neyþer fele it ne see it*. Hilton uses the same expression to describe faith in *Scale* I, Chapter 21.

21 *þe baptem*. The definite article in H_7 here is unnecessary.

31 *froward*. H_7 'forward', must derive from an accidental scribal metathesis; there is no sense in which a contrary, 'distortam', soul would be 'forward', and 'forward' is not recorded in *MED* as a variant spelling of 'froward'.

34 *percenere*. See *MED* 'parcener' *n.* The common confusion between c/t

and u/n makes it difficult to be sure of the variant of several manuscripts: see below, 36/19. The Latin version, 'heredem', demonstrates the derivation of Hilton's metaphor from the Pauline epistles, especially Rom. 8: 17.

38 *man schuld neuer felen*. The present subjunctive of the Latin version, 'homo . . . senciet', with no reference to 'man's soul', supports H_7RλAsSr-ACcMPl over the χE variants.

48–9 Rom. 8: 1.

CHAPTER 9

3 *to God*. This H_7 reading is redundant, and is probably a confused anticipation of 'to gode lyuynge'.

4 Rom. 1: 17, Hebr. 10: 38. The presence or absence (in χAs) of 'autem' is liable to be because of the various scribes' memory of the scriptural text.

7–8 Rom. 5: 1.

12 *trow . . . chape*. The present indicative forms of the Latin version, 'credit' and 'conformat', support the indicative forms of HRBLB_3AsSrWsLw-AEPH_6CcMLdPlTW (as over H_7H_5) in the former case and RH_5B_3AsWsLwCcMLdPlW (as over H_7HBLSrAEPH_6T) in the latter, although all manuscripts use the subjunctive 'turne' in the next line, while the Latin continues with the indicative 'revertitur'.

15 *bodily lyfe*. The Latin version agrees with M alone in the variant 'body', 'corpore'. The original reading of H was probably χ 'werke'.

17–18 *Karissimi . . . gloria*. 1 John 3: 2: 'Charissimi, nunc filii Dei sumus: et nondum apparuit quid erimus. Scimus quoniam cum apparuerit, similes ei erimus: quoniam videbimus eum sicuti est', conflated with Col. 3: 4: 'Cum Christus apparuerit, vita vestra: tunc et vos apparebitis cum ipso in gloria.' Presumably H_7λLd follow the former text, not the latter, in omitting 'Christus'.

22 *priuey*. The Latin version supports Σ 'al priue' over H_7Ld.

25 *entre*. The Latin version expands this to 'introitum ad hoc sciendum'.

CHAPTER 10

3 *sacrament*. With the exception of Sr, the English manuscripts are uniform in using the singular here, although the Latin version supports the plural. M emphasizes the singular by specifying the sacrament of penance, although Hilton is speaking here of all those who are reformed in faith generally, which is through the sacraments of baptism and penance both.

6 *stedfast*. The $H_7H^{\circ}H_5$WsLB_3SrAPCcPl variant can be taken either adjectivally (taking 'setten' as a copula) or adverbially (*MED* 'stedfast'

adv.); RBAsLw`H^{c}´EH_6MLdPlTW 'stedfastly', which is supported by the Latin version's 'constanter', specifies the adverb.

13 *þei fallen lyghtly . . . vnkunnynge.* Although Hilton is speaking of temptation to the capital sins here (the seven deadly sins), those who succumb 'lightly, as it were through weakness or ignorance' cannot be sinning mortally, because that would require the agreement of the will to an act that is known to be mortally sinful.

16 *forgifnes.* Fishlake does not translate this as 'remissionem' but as 'indulgenciam'—perhaps a mendicant slip.

as . . . reformynge (l. 18). W^{G} supplies the omission in W, but glosses the word 'abide' (the E variant) with the χ variant 'lyuen'.

17 *lesten.* The χ variant 'lifen', which is supported by the Latin version, 'viuant', is probably an echo of the previous line.

18 *or.* The χ variant 'and', which is supported by the Latin version, is theologically less accurate: it is not necessary that those who are reformed in faith persist in that state until death (it is possible that they may sin in the meantime). It would be better if they did persist in that state; but what is necessary for salvation is that they be found in that state in the hour of death.

22 *reformed.* This word is written over the erasure of a shorter word in H, perhaps 'oned' as in T; H_5Ws 'ronnen', is neither shorter nor particularly intelligible.

23 *speciale grace.* Modern theologies distinguish types of grace differently than Hilton does. In the Calvinist tradition, 'common grace' is that by which the sacrifice of Christ offers salvation to the human race as a whole, and 'special grace' ('irresistible' or 'efficacious grace') is that by which the elect are justified by faith. For modern Roman Catholics, 'sanctifying grace' is the grace of salvation offered to the entire human race, but which only the faithful receive through the sacraments; it effects a permanent disposition of the will towards God and is distinguishable from the 'actual grace' that enables individual human beings to perform distinct good acts.

For Hilton, 'reformation in faith' is the result of the common grace of salvation given to humankind by the sacrifice of Christ, with which each faithful Christian cooperates by assenting to let it work in himself (although even that cooperation is itself the result of a 'prevenient' grace). As Hilton points out immediately below, the grace of Christ's sacrifice extends to the entire human race, not just to the saved; but on the other hand, only those who have faith will profit by that grace (cf. Eph. 2: 8: 'For by grace ye are saved through faith, and that not of yourselves, for it is the gift of God'—a text that will underly a good deal of Hilton's later discussion of the agency of spiritual progress). True faith, further, is not merely a matter of assent, but of a habitual intention of the will to avoid sin. Yet this faith does not mean that an individual will no longer feel the unreformed 'image of sin' and the temptation to sin in himself.

'Reformation in faith and feeling', on the other hand, like the various gifts of the Holy Spirit described in 1 Cor. 12: 7–12 (which, e.g., Aquinas, *ST*, 2–2, q. 171, describes as 'gratiae gratis datae'—graces freely given), is the result of the gift of a 'special grace' of affective devotion and 'spiritual savour'. This is the *melos amoris* described by Richard Rolle, at least in those for whom it is truly a spiritual gift and not just a heightened form of the fervour of a contemplative neophite (Hilton never criticizes or condemns Rolle diretly).

For Hilton, as for Augustine, it is equally important to keep in mind that according to the Pauline text underlying the theology of grace, these various graces—these gifts—are the operation of 'one and the same Spirit . . . dividing to every one according as he will'.

24 *in þe rewarde*. The H_7 scribe treats 'rewarde' several times as the concrete noun 'reward', requiring an article, when the more cogent reading of this phrase is the abstract 'in regard of'.

31–2 *on . . . wise, if þou trowe*. H°H_5Ws 'if þow trowe on þe contrarie wise, as if þou trowe' seems to derive from a misunderstood marginal correction intended to transpose the phrases 'on þe contrary wise' and 'if þou trowe' that had been reversed in an exemplar, as in T.

34 *ille*. Although the variant 'euel/euyl' is supported by the majority of manuscripts, and 'euel' is the form used eleven times elsewhere in the H_7 text, as opposed to a total of five times for 'ille', the Northern form 'ille' is supported by the earliest manuscripts here. 'Ille' is a probable relict of Hilton's own dialect that was standardized to 'euel/euyl' throughout the manuscript tradition as early as the beginning of the fifteenth century.

40–1 *In quacumque . . . morietur*. A common maxim that partially conflates Ezek. 18: 21, 'Si autem impius egerit poenitentiam ab omnibus peccatis suis, quae operatus est, et custodierit omnia praecepta mea, et fecerit iudicium et iustitiam, vita vivet et non morietur', and 33: 12 '. . . et impietas impii non nocebit ei, in quacumque die conversus fuerit ab impietate sua', usually referred to the latter locus. See Stanley Chodorow, *Christian Political Theory and Church Politics in the Mid-Twelfth Century: The Ecclesiology of Gratian's "Decretum"* (Berkeley, 1972), 126 n. 20; Alister E. McGrath, *Iustitia Dei: A History of the Christian Doctrine of Justification*, 3rd edn. (Cambridge, 2005), 118 n. 265. Another version of the maxim occurs following Passus VII, line 148 of the C-text of *Piers Plowman*: cf. James W. Marchand, 'An Unidentified Latin Quote in *Piers Plowman*', *Modern Philology*, 88 (1991), 398–400.

48 *he is not reformed to þe liknesse of God*. Hilton's theology of penitence requires 'perfect contrition' for sin: that is, sorrow for the evil of the sin itself and remorse for the offence to God. For Bonaventure, the act of confession may effect 'perfect contrition'; for Aquinas, 'imperfect contrition', or sorrow

for sin because of the threat of eternal punishment, suffices for the sacrament of confession. See Peter Lombard, *Sent.*, 4, d. 16, c. 1; Bonaventure, *In Sent.* IV d. 17, 2, a. 2, q. 2; Aquinas, *ST* Suppl. q. 18, a. 1.

51 *serueth him nought*. This variant is supported by $H_7\chi$ (the LdT variant 'saueth' derives, presumably, from a form without 'of'), and probably the original form of L. The addition of 'of' is supported by RλAsSrECcM (including L as corrected). The Latin version, 'nichil sibi prodest', could support either, in the sense of 'to profit (someone) not at all (with respect to something)'. *MED* 'nought' *pron.* 3 a 'with verbs denoting success', gives 'serven of nought' as meaning 'be useless'.

61–2 *Qui . . . eum*. A reordering of the phrases of Rev. 19: 5: 'Laudem dicite Deo nostro omnes servi eius: et qui timetis eum pusilli et magni.'

62 *grete and smale*. The preponderance of the manuscript evidence (χRAsSrH_6CcPl as over H_7LB_3EP) is for the opposite word order, which is also the order of the scriptural text; but it is in the present order that Hilton will continue in his discussion.

63–4 *profytend . . . perfyte . . . vnperfyte*. Hilton is here making the same distinction as above at 5/17–18 between the 'incipientes', the 'proficientes', and the 'perfecti': those who are progressing spirituality and those who are perfect, as opposed to those who are at the lowest level of spiritual development. The preponderance of the evidence of the English manuscripts, and the Latin version, support this reading over M 'perfite' for 'profitend' and RH_5AsSrWsALd 'profiten' for 'perfyte' (with M 'pertifite').

64 *loue of God*. The manuscript support for the absence or presence of the preceding definite article is approximately equal: H_7RλAsEPl as over χSrACcM.

65–6 *men and wummen, and oþer þat*. The Latin version restricts this to 'hominum qui'.

68 *sacramentys*. The preponderance of the evidence of the early manuscripts (H_7HRBH_5AsWsChLwACcMLdPlTW), as well as the Latin version, 'sacramentis', supports the plural here, over the singular of BH_5λWsChLwW. It is by all the sacraments, and not just one of them, that the 'children' of the Church are metaphorically fed, although to some scribes the image of feeding may have suggested the Eucharist in particular.

fed with melke. A favourite, particularly Pauline antithesis between milk for children (beginners) and 'whole bread' for mature Christians (1 Cor. 3: 1–2; Hebr. 5: 13–14). See Rita Copeland, *Pedagogy, Intellectuals, and Dissent in the Later Middle Ages: Lollardy and Ideas of Learning* (Cambridge, 2001), 72, for the history of this *topos*.

70 *goodnesse*. The λ variant 'mercy' and the addition of 'mercy' in χE are not supported by the remainder of the English manuscript tradition or by the

Latin version; their occurrence in these two groups appears to be the result of convergent variation.

73–4 *speke hemselfe*. In the H_7Rλ AsSrAM variant, which is supported by the Latin version, 'qui loqui nesciunt', 'hemselfe' is emphatic; in χECcPl it is reflexive. The former is more cogent; Hilton's point is that the Church speaks for those who cannot themselves speak, and the idea of speaking 'for hemself' is made redundant by the following 'for here owen nede'.

75 Matt. 15: 22–8.

82 *temptacion*. Although the Latin version, 'temptacionibus', supports the plural, the preponderance of the evidence of the English manuscript tradition is for the singular as over the apparently random agreement of RAsWsH_6CcW.

89–90 *þe preiere and þe trowth*. The manuscript support for the presence or absence of the definite article here is nearly evenly divided, although the support for its omission is drawn almost entirely from χ alone.

CHAPTER II

8 *hem behoueth . . . he wil*. Although the beginning of this sentence is in the singular, as is the following discussion, the majority of the manuscript support is for the plural 'hem behoueth' in the first instance, or the χ variant 'most þei'. Only H_5Ws support 'he' in the both instances, 'moste he . . . he wil'; T supports 'he' in the first instance (corrected to the plural), and H_7CcM in the second. The Latin version is singular in both instances, 'oportet eum . . . velit'. It should be noted that this reading is less probable if the underlying forms are 'him' and Northern 'þem'. It is possible that the original varying use of singular and plural was Hilton's.

10 *so nere*. The original variant of H was probably 'sore', in agreement with H_5PlT.

18 *stryf*. The Latin version, 'contencio', supports H_7RLB_3AsSrLwAEPH_6CcMPlW over BH_5WsChLdT 'Crist' (which was presumably also the original reading of H). 'Crist' is certainly the *lectio difficilior*, with the meaning that the grace of Christ is the ultimate agent of the reformed soul's ability to resist 'pees and fals accord' with the impulse to sin (founded, perhaps, in a moral reading of Matt. 10: 34, 'I come not to bring peace but the sword'). Hilton's emphasis here, however, is on one's own resistance to the tendency to sin, reinforced by the repetition of forms of 'strife' and 'strive', and the intrusive reference to Christ does not seem appropriate to the present argument. The fact that the reading 'Crist' was difficult, perhaps even confusing, to the scribes who did record that variant is further apparent in the fact that three of them go on to record the negative variants 'vnpees' and 'feyned pees'.

breketh. The Latin version expands to 'infringit . . . dissoluit'.

18–19 *pees . . . pees*. The Latin version, 'contencio infringit pacem falsam concordiamque dissoluit. Bonum est quod homo cum omnibus pacem habeat', supports the Σ variant over H_7. H_7 'al þese', is probably the result of a confusion of graphic similars ('pees' and 'þese') compounded by eye-skip. The omission would not have occurred if the underlying text had not read 'pees', rather than 'þese', and the resulting reading in H_7 makes no sense.

21 *of*. The Latin version, 'de', supports the H_7AsSrACc variant over the HRBH_5λWsChAEMLdPlT variant 'ouer' or LwW 'on'.

29 *ferre*. The Latin version, 'libera', supports RBH_5SrWsChALdT 'fre' over H_7λAsLwECcMPlW; 'fre' was presumably the original reading of H, as it is of all χ manuscripts but LwW.

31 *God*. The Latin version, 'Deum', supports H_7RBH_5AsSrWsChLwLdPlTW 'God', which was also the reading of H°. The H^c correction, 'god`e'', agrees with LB_3APH_6CcM 'good'.

35 *Seynt Poule seyth þus*. An omission unique to H_7.

Gal. 5: 17.

40 Rom. 7: 23.

49 Rom. 7: 25.

50 *vero*. The manuscript support for 'vero', H_7λSrECcM plus the Latin version, and the variant 'enim', χRAsAPl, is approximately equal; the modern Vulgate reads 'autem'.

In. Hilton usually, but not always, introduces his translation/explications of Latin scriptural citations with the phrase 'That is'. In the present instance it is supported by χECc, but not H_7RλAsSrAMPl. Only E, the product of meticulous textual cleansing, has 'That is' in all cases.

54 *by felynge of þe vicious sensualite*. The Latin version translates this as 'per appetitum sensualitatis viciose', although Fishlake's usual translation for 'felynge' is 'sensacio'.

56–8 *Non . . . pecatum*. A contracted version of Rom. 7: 15–17: [Quod enim operor, non intelligo:] non enim quod volo bonum, hoc ago: sed quod odi malum, illud facio. Si autem quod nolo, illud facio [consentio legi, quoniam bona est. Nunc autem] iam non ego operor illud, sed quod habitat in me peccatum.' The contraction may derive from manuscript copies of the Bible that Hilton knew, or from his own compression of the sentence.

57 *Sed*[2]. This variant is supported by H_7B_3SrCc and possibly the original text of L, 'Si' by χ`L'PH_6Pl and the Latin version. 'Sed' may be a scribal repetition, either in the text of the Bible that Hilton knew, in his own memory, or in the earliest copies of *Scale* II, of the same word earlier in the

sentence; 'Si', the variant of the modern Vulgate text, could equally be a scribal correction here.

58 *facio*. This variant is supported by H_7λSrCcMPl, 'hoc facio' by χ and the Latin version; 'hoc facio' is the variant of the modern Vulgate text.

iam. This variant (the reading of the modern Vulgate text) is supported by H_7λSrCcM and the Latin version, its omission by χPl.

68 *vnskilful*. H 'vnskil', occurs in *MED* only as a noun, often in the phrase 'with vnskil', meaning 'without regard for principle', 'wrongfully', 'unjustly'.

be so. The variant 'bote so', supported by BH_5WsChLd (and probably H originally) is probably a scribal mistake for the variant 'be it so'. RE 'if it be so', LwH^cW 'if it so be' and T 'be it so' would be variations on the same variant.

70 *reformed in trouthe*. Hilton's phrase is usually 'reformed in feith', but at this point only BALd support that variant; see also 12/6 below.

75 *syght*. λ 'liȝt' is probably the result of confusion of homoeographs.

77 *perceyfeth*. The indicative variant of H_7RPl, as over the subjunctive 'perceyue' of Σ, may be influenced by preceding 'goth'.

91 *þer is þat is siker and certeyn*. The fact that RAs omit 'þat is siker', χ omits 'and certeyn', and the Latin version has only 'securum' suggests that this doublet may have originated in a gloss that was added variously into different manuscripts. The ungrammaticality of RAs, 'þer is and certeyn', on the other hand, suggests its derivation from the deletion the middle words of the phrase—'þat is siker'—because they seemed repetitive. This would mean that the original variant behind RAs (and probably APl as well) was the same as that in H_7B_3LSrEPH_6CcM: 'þer is þat is siker and certeyn', and thus that it is χ that has omitted 'and certeyn', an omission in which the Latin concurs.

97 *synne and wrecchednes*. Support among the English manuscript tradition for the singular form 'synne' (H_7RλAsAECcMPl) is stronger than for the plural (χSr), but only Ld has the plural 'wrechidnessis', while the Latin version, 'peccata et miserias', has the plural in both cases.

98–9 *be not to besy . . . venial*. Hilton also shows a lack of scrupulous concern with whether a sin is mortal or venial in *Scale* I, Chapter 56.

100 *it*. This variant in H_7H_5SrWsCcM provides the verb 'schew' with an extra direct object: the true object is 'swilk sterynges', but the complete sentence, which extends from l. 99 to l. 107, is complex and repetitive.

101 *ilk*. Manuscript support for the variant variants 'ilk' and 'ille' is evenly divided, even among the earliest witnesses, with H_7 and LB_3 reading 'ilk', as over HBRAsSr 'ille' and the Latin version, 'malum'. Other χ manuscripts present complicating synonyms, with H_5Ws reading 'same' (i.e. 'ilk') and

LwW reading 'euery'. Either variant could be defended: 'ilk' as emphatic (but echoing the immediately preceding 'swilk'), and 'ille' as noting that it is specifically the evil stirrings that need to be confessed, because they draw the soul to sin (the statement of which condition could be seen as making 'ille' redundant). Further, either 'ilk' or 'ille' could have given rise to the other by confusion of graphic similars.

bygynneth fasten. *MED* 'biginnen' *v.* 5(b) notes that the infinitive occasionally occurs without preceding 'to'.

105 *and . . . forgyfen*. The omission of this phrase in H_7, and originally in Pl, is probably by eye-skip.

112 *þei*. The Latin version, 'ideo', supports RAsSrLwAECcMPlW 'þerfore þei', over $H_7HBH_5LB_3WsChPH_6LdT$. The preceding phrase the 'for as much as', however, might be thought to render 'þerfore' redundant.

114 *felynge*. The Latin version translates 'sensacionem corporalem'.

115 Matt. 9: 2.

117 *for*. The omission in H_7λMLd is probably by eye-skip. The conjunction is necessary to the introduction of the parenthetical 'for . . . Gost'.

synnes[2]. Manuscript support for the singular and the plural here is evenly divided, with the early manuscripts H_7R, as well as AsAMPlW and the Latin version, supporting the plural, and HBH_5λSrWsChLwECc the singular.

122 *Nisi . . . intelligetis*. This is the form of Isa. 7: 9, not in the Vulgate (which has 'Si non credideritis, non permanebitis'), but in the *Vetus Latina*, whence it was quoted by Augustine, and, on his authority, often cited in the medieval period. Hilton also refers this text to 'the Apostle' in his Latin letters *De Util.* and *Epist. ad Quem.*, *LW*, i. 142, ii. 229.

124 *Trowth . . . after*. See Augustine, *Sermo* 118: 1: 'Præcedit fides, sequitur intellectus.'

127 Matt. 5: 8.

129 *with*[2]. H_7 alone omits this word, which is necessary to the parallelism of the two balanced phrases.

132 Acts 15: 9.

CHAPTER 12

6 *reformed in trouthe*. Hilton's phrase is usually 'reformed in feith', but at this point H_7RλAsSrECcMPl support 'trouthe' and χA 'faiþ'; see also 11/70 above.

7–8 *þis ymage*. The Latin version, 'ymaginis', supports H_7RλAsSr-AECcMPl, without the χ addition of 'foul'.

11 S. of S. 1: 4. Hilton's exposition of these verses parallels that in Bernard, *Serm. super Cant.* 25–7. 'Pellis' means 'skin' or 'hide', and thus by extension 'curtain', as it is translated in modern versions of this scriptural text. The Kedar were pagan desert herdsmen; their tents, 'tabernacula', were traditionally woven of black goat hair. Bernard compares the dark (and metaphorically evil) tents of the Kedar to the fair curtains (thus also 'tents') of Solomon, referring their darkness first to the progress of the beloved from her sinful former life to final perfection. But he then rejects this interpretation and argues that the blackness is in outward appearance only (just as the otside of the tents is discoloured by weather) and the true inward beauty is that of the soul in the eyes of God. Hilton makes use of the same metaphor in *De Imag. pec.*, *LW*, i. 91, ll. 333–39.

12, 14 *pelles . . . skynnes*. Manucript support for the singular or plural form in each of these variants is approximately evenly divided: HRBH$_5$AsWsChLdTW have the singular 'pellis', λSr`Lw´AECcMPl and the Latin version the plural; χAs has the singular 'skynne' and H$_7$RλSrAECcMPl the plural. H$_7$ 'pelle' is an error in any case.

15 *ȝe*. This sentence, the main verb of which is the imperative plural 'wondreth', requires a second-person plural subject. The scribes of H$_7$H$_5$AsCcMLd, or their hypearchetypes, presumably confused by Hilton's tendency to interweave paraphrase and explication into his translation of scriptural texts, seem to have assumed that he was now speaking of 'þe aungels of heuene' in the third person.

20 *vnderstonded*. H$_7$ alone has this weak form of the past participle, here and at 43/70; all other manuscripts use the strong form 'vndirstonden'. *OED* notes that the weak form was 'common from about 1530 to 1585', occurring *inter alia* in the phrase 'understanded of the people' in the Thirty-Nine Articles in *The Book of Common Prayer*.

mirknes. See Bernard, *Serm. super Cant.* 26. 1. 1.

22 *þat*. H$_7$ 'is' is surely erroneous, since what follows is not a past participle, but a finite verb form, and the verb 'is' occurs two words later, at the beginning of the next clause. The scribe of H$_7$ seems to have been misled by the repetition of 'is vnderstonded' and 'is vnderstonden' in the immediately preceding sentence.

pesible. See Bernard, *Serm. super Cant.* 27. 1. 2.

23 *Lord*. Support for this variant, as opposed to 'Lord Jesu', is approximately evenly divided among the English manuscripts, with H$_7$BλSrChCcMLd supporting the former and RAsLwH^{c}AEPlTW the latter. The Latin version reads 'Deus'. This is one of a number of variants that demonstrate a variation between 'Christocentric' and 'non-Christocentric' variants in *Scale* II that parallels that in *Scale* I. See above, pp. cv–cvi, cxxxi.

24 *blissed aungel.* Hilton here draws a parallelism between the dark skins (tents) of the Kedar (fallen souls in whom the devil dwells) and the skin of Solomon (a good angel in whom God dwells); Bernard, citing Ps. 103: 2 ('who stretchest out the heaven like a pavilion'), interprets the skin of Solomon metaphorically as heaven.

25–6 *and . . . skyn.* Among the manuscripts of the Latin version, only B_4H_8Up read 'Et ideo angelus assimilatur pelli' (added at the foot of the page H_8). This is one of the few apparent errors in Y.

31 S. of S. 1: 5a.

34 *werdly.* This is an isolative variant in H_7: the Latin version, 'carnalem', supports the reading of the other English manuscripts, 'fleschly'.

36 *of*[3]. Manuscript support is evenly divided between the H_7χECc variant, in which 'þis ymage', the object of the verbal noun 'berynge', is treated grammatically as objective genitive, 'of þis ymage', and the RλAsSrAMPl variant without 'of', where it is treated as accusative. The Latin version translates the two verbal nouns, 'touchynge' and 'berynge', as nouns: 'tactu et onere ymaginis peccati'.

47 The addition of a chapter break at this point in SrCcM is not necessarily a sign of genetic relationship among these three manuscripts, since it could be the result of conflation or coincident variation. Sr uses the title of Chapter 13 here and omits the usual chapter break there; M inserts a unique chapter title here; and the chapter break here in Cc has no title. It should be noted, however, that CcM share a large enough number of otherwise unique variations to suggest the possibility that a genetic relationship between them underlies the large number of isolative variants found in each. See above, pp. xcviii, ciii-civ, cix, cxxxiii-cxxxiv.

53–4 *and . . . bere.* The Latin version, 'debilis non sufficit se portare', omits the sense of the degree of debility conveyed by the English text: that he is *so weak that* he cannot bear himself.

60 *þurgh grace.* The Latin version, 'per graciam', supports the reading of H_7RλAsSrAECcMPl over the χ omission.

61 *likynges.* The Latin version, 'delectaciones', supports H_7λSrECc 'likynges' over χRBAsAPl 'stirynges'.

62 *for*[1]. The Latin version, 'et', weakens Hilton's expression of consequence to something closer to coincidence.

63 *reste.* The Latin version, 'quietem in eis', supports λE 'reste in hem'.

75 Mark 2: 11. This text is applied similarly in Gregory, *Hom. in Ezech.* 1. 12. 11.

81 *of*[2] . . . *hast* (l. 83). This phrase is not translated in the Latin version, probably as a result of eye-skip in the exemplar.

86 *of*[2]. The Latin version's genitive form, 'peccati', agrees with H_7BλACcMLdW over HRH_5AsSrWsChLwEPlT 'and'.

90 A paraphrase of Eph. 6: 16, 'in omnibus sumentes scutum fidei, in quo possitis omnia tela nequissimi ignea extinguere', with the latter clause of which the Ld reading agrees. The Latin version, 'tela hostis nequissimi ignea', in which 'nequissimi' modifies 'hostis', and 'ignea' 'tela', is closer to the Vulgate than is the citation in the English text. Hilton's immediately following translation, 'þe brennende dartis of þin enemy', omits 'nequissimi'.

CHAPTER 13

Sr has no chapter break at this point.

1 *þre*. The unique H_7 variant, 'þe', is inappropriate since what in fact follows is a list of three categories.

8–22 Hilton's psychology derives primarily from Augustine, as mediated by later medieval writers. See *De Trin.* 12. 3. 3–4. 4, 14. 1. 2–3; *De quant. anim.* 1. 5. 11. For Augustine, wisdom (*sapientia*) and knowledge (*scientia*) are distinct: 'alia sit intellectualis cognitio aeternarum rerum, alia rationalis temporalium' (*De Trin.* 12. 15. 25). Human beings cannot, by their own powers, move from *scientia* to *sapientia*, and the Christian life is a passage through knowledge to wisdom (13. 19. 24). For Aquinas, the higher and lower parts of reason are parts of the same faculty, directed towards different ends: *ST* 1, q. 79, art. 9. In any case, the sensuality (the intellectual faculty comprising the senses and the form of knowledge that arises directly from them) is related to the lower form of knowledge. In chapter 5 of his allegorization of the wives, servants, and children of Jacob, *Benj. Min.*, Richard of St-Victor treats sensuality (Zilpah) as the handmaid of affection (Leah); see the Middle English version, *A Tretyse of þe Stodye of Wysdome þat men clepen Beniamyn*, in *Deonise* 13–14. Aquinas treats of the sensuality and its relation to reason in *ST* 1, q. 81. See also R. Mulligan, '"Ratio Superior and Ratio Inferior": The Historical Background', *New Scholasticism*, 29 (1955), 1–32.

15–18 Augustine compares the higher and lower reason to hubsand and wife, *De Trin.* 12. 3. 7, 12.

15 *over*. The Latin version, 'superiorem partem', supports χRAsSrAEPl, 'ouer party', over H_7λCcM.

maistre and soueraygne. The Latin version, 'magistra', maintains the gender of the antecedent 'pars', although this contradicts Hilton's metaphor of gender roles.

23–38 The concept of the three manners of souls—animal, rational, and perfect—derives from William of St-Thierry's *Lettre d'or* (*Lettre aux frères* *du Mont-Dieu*, ed. Jean Déchanet, OSB, Sources Chrétiennes, 223 (Paris, 1975)), 178–80. For William, the difference between the latter two is: 'Sunt rationales, qui per rationis judicium et naturalis scientiae discretionem, habent et cognitionem boni et appetitum; sed nondum habent affectum. Sunt perfecti, qui spiritu aguntur, qui a Spiritu sancto plenius illuminantur; et quoniam sapit eis bonum cujus trahuntur affectu, sapientes vocantur; quia vero induit eos Spiritus sanctus.' This would appear to be the origin of Hilton's concept of reformation in faith and in feeling: William's 'affectus' is Hilton's 'feeling'. 'Reformation in faith and in feeling' brings about by grace a change in the disposition of the soul according to which the love of God, the acquisition of the virtues, and the avoidance of sin occur freely and easily, without the drudgery required by the acquisition of virtues by the power of reason, guided by faith alone, without the grace of reformation in faith and feeling. Hilton emphasizes in later discussion that the reformation in faith and feeling does not occur without spiritual labour (see Chapters 17, 20–1). Hilton's psychology of the relationship of reason and sensuality, as set out in the present chapter and elsewhere, is quite traditional; accordingly, the sensuality has no part in the higher reformation of the soul, except as it is aligned with reason. It is for this reason that Fishlake's translation of Hilton's 'feeling' as 'sensacio' is inappropriate.

25 *al blynded*. The Latin version, 'totaliter . . . excecata', supports H_7LB_3LwAPLdW over any of the variants that either omit 'al' or reduce the participle 'blynded' to the adjective 'blind'. For a discussion of the incidence and interpretation of the terms 'blind' and 'naked' in Hilton's works and the *Cloud* corpus, see S. S. Hussey, 'Blind Trust, Naked Truth and Bare Necessities: Walter Hilton and the Author of *The Cloud of Unknowing*', in James Hogg (ed.) '*Stand up to Godwards': Essays in Mystical and Monastic Theology in Honour of the Reverend John Clark on his Sixty-Fifth Birthday*, Analecta Cartusiana, 204 (Salzburg, 2002), 1–8.

29 *dedly*. M 'flesshly', agrees with the Latin version, 'carnalibus'.

sterynges. The Latin version, 'motibus', agrees with the plural reading of Σ over the singular of HBChLw. The subsequent plural pronoun 'hem' is also plural.

sensualite. Not necessarily pejorative. The sensuality is what human beings have in common with animals; in Adam and Eve before the fall it was subject to reason, but in the post-lapsarian human condition, as the reason is no longer properly subject to God, so the sensuality is no longer subject to reason.

31 *setteth*. H_7 'sette', which does not agree with the other verbs in the sentence, is surely erroneous.

CHAPTER 14

4 *þe wurthynes . . . God made* (l. 6). See Augustine, *De Quant. anim.* 34. 77.

7 *ful rest.* See William of St-Thierry, *Lettre d'or*, 178, 'non nisi in Deo requiem habet'; Augustine, *Conf.* 1. 1. 1 'inquietum est cor nostrum, donec requiescat in te'.

9–15 The comparison of the eternal joy of heavenly life and the passing pleasures of this world is a commonplace. See the medieval chapter heading of Augustine, *De Civ. Dei* XII. 8: 'De amore peruerso, quo voluntas ab incommutabili bono ad commutabile bonum deficit.'

11–12 *Vnkyndly . . . vnresonabely.* According to Aquinas, *ST* 1, q. 2 a.1, ad 1, all humans have a natural desire for God.

19 *and make . . . þerto* (l. 20). This clause does not occur in the Latin version.

how, be so þey. The evidence of the manuscripts supports H_7λSrCcM and the χRAsAEPl variant 'how it be, so þat' equally; but 'how, be so þei' is the *lectio difficilior*, from which 'how it be, so þat' could be derived as a grammatical simplification.

21 *reuerences.* The Latin version, 'diuiciis vel honoribus', supports H_7 'reuerences'.

28 The representation of the seven deadly sins as beasts is traditional. See the appendix, 'Association of Animals and Sins', in M. W. Bloomfield, *The Seven Deadly Sins: An Introduction to the History of a Religious Concept, with Special Reference to Medieval English Literature* (East Lansing, Mich., 1952), 245–9. James Grenehalgh, in a marginal note in Ch, refers the present passage to Boethius' description of the transformation of Ulysses' sailors into beasts by Circe in the *Odyssey*, in *Consolationis Philosophiæ Libri Quinque*, IV, verse 3.

31 *aȝenstode.* The support for H_7HRH_5AsWsChAMPl and BLB_3LwEPH_6LdTW 'aȝeynstonde' among the English manuscripts is approximately equal, although the earlier manuscripts support the former, as does the imperfect subjunctive form of the Latin version, 'resisteret'.

39 *not trespast.* The placement of the word 'haue' either before or after 'not' in the manuscripts of χ would make it appear that it was added either between the lines or in the margin of the exemplar, leaving uncertainty where it was to be placed.

42 *to renne to Rome.* Hilton uses this metaphor for useless activity in the world several times. See *Scale* I, Chapter 49/1429–30: 'it nedeth not to renne to Rome', *Epist. ad Quem.*, *LW*, ii. 262, l. 275, 'eamus ad curiam Romanam'.

43 *or*[1]. The Latin version 'et' agrees with χ 'and'.

50 *for to restreyn.* The Latin version, 'vel ad refrenandum', supports

HRBH$_5$AsSrWsChLwAEMLdTW, 'ne for to restreyn', over H$_7$λCc. The former reads this phrase as parallel, the latter reads it more cogently as consequent to the preceding phrase.

52–3 *folweth . . . doth.* The H$_7$ variants appear to reflect a recessive Northern present indicative plural ending in '-th' and a reading of 'folweth' as parallel to 'arn' rather than 'fallen'. All other English manuscripts read 'folwe(n)'; the '-th' ending of 'doth' appears to have been understood by the scribes of nearly half the surviving English manuscripts as singular (which would explain the RLB3As`Sr´ChAPCcMLdPl variant 'a swyn'); ETW, on the other hand, correct the verb 'doth' to 'don'.

62 *eyghe.* This form may be either singular or plural in H$_7$, although the preceding verb form 'schal' is usually singular (H$_7$ uses 'schul' for the plural). The singular variant is supported by HRB$_3$AsSrChLwAMPlW and the Latin version 'oculus'; the plural by BH$_5$LWsEPH$_6$CcLdT 'yȝene'.

66 *cursed.* The Latin version translates as 'excommunicati'.

69 Rev. 21: 8. The version of the Vulgate with which Hilton and his scribes were familiar reads 'tumidis', where the modern Vulgate has 'timidis'. The HH$_5$Ws variant 'excecratis' is presumably a spelling for 'execratis'; the erroneous H$_7$RAsAPl variant 'excecatis' (i.e. 'blinded') is not supported by Hilton's immediately following translation, 'cursed'.

73 *poysunners.* The following word in the Latin scriptural text, 'ydolatris' (the Vulgate reading, supported by all manuscripts of *Scale* II) is not translated in H$_7$RB$_3$AsSrAMPl, or originally in L. χ`L´EP add 'worschipers of maumetis'; it is added as a correction in L, and is thus present in P; H$_6$ and Cc have equivalent references to 'idolaters'.

74 *dole.* The Latin version, 'pars illorum', which also occurs in the preceding scriptural text, supports the preceding possessive pronoun in χSrAEH$_6$CcM over the lack of a quantifier in H$_7$RLB$_3$AsAP. The BH$_5$B$_3$SrWsAEH$_6$CcMLdT variant 'part' is probably the result of semantic replacement of the Anglo-Saxon noun with its French equivalent.

CHAPTER 15

6 *but I haue it not. þerfore I am not.* The Latin version, 'set quia talem graciam non habeo, ideo taliter facere non possem', supports the Σ version over the H$_7$T omission of 'for' and the H$_7$ variant 'am' for 'may'. The H$_7$ reading presents a weaker version of the sequence of the argument.

9 *Bot þat auayleþ hem ryght noght; it excuseþ hem not ageyns God* (l. 10). In the English text, the strengthening adverb 'ryght' occurs in the first clause, but in the Latin version, 'Set hoc eis non proficit nec per hoc quoad Deum aliqualiter escusantur', 'aliqualiter' occurs in the second. The conjunction 'ne' at the beginning of the second clause in HBH_5WsH_6TW, 'noþer' Hu_2Ld, 'ner' Ch, is supported by the Latin version.

16 *þei þenke*. $H_7R\lambda AsSrAECcPl$ here read 'þenke' as the transitive verb, 'to exercise the faculty of reason'; χM 'þem þinkeþ'; W 'hem thynken' read it as impersonal, 'to seem'. Support for the transitive and impersonal uses of 'think' varies throughout the manuscripts, and throughout the text.

16–17 *hem behoueth for to*. The correction of L to 'þei moste' (the χ variant)—leaving 'for to' cancelled—must have occurred after the copying of P, as the latter manuscript retains the 'behoves' variant.

20 *peynful*. Manuscript support is approximately equally divided among $H_7\lambda$, the χE variant 'dredful', RAsPl 'ferdful', and SrAM 'ferful'.

27 *assentynge*. This is parallel to the immediately preceding 'fallynge': the H_7 variant 'assenten', which would make it parallel to 'arn', makes nonsense of the remainder of the sentence.

34 *bytyng of conscience*. The Latin translation is 'morsum conscientiae'—the source of the modern English word 'remorse'.

37 *is*. The χ variant here is the subjunctinve 'be' and the Sr variant 'were', but in the following parallel clause, all manuscripts read 'is', except for Sr, which continues with 'were'. The Latin version also uses the indicative.

39 The phrase 'Eat, drink and be merry' is found in Eccl. 8: 15: 'Quod non esset homini bonum sub sole, nisi quod comederet, et biberet, atque gauderet', and in Luke 12: 19: 'requiesce, comede, bibe, epulare'. The usual closing tag in English, 'for tomorrow we shall die' (not present in Hilton) derives from a variant version in Isa. 22: 13: 'Comedamus et bibamus, cras enim moriemur.'

40 *þis*. The Latin version, 'de ista vita', supports χE in adding 'life'.

41 *herte*. The Latin version, 'cordibus', supports the plural 'hertes' of χLB_3AsEPl over the singular of H_7RSrAH_6CcM. The subsequent scriptural citation is singular.

42 Ps. 13: 1, 52: 1.

45 *lyketh . . . synne*. The Latin version, 'iacet in peccato', probably depends on an English exemplar reading 'lyeth in . . . synne', which would echo l. 8 above, 'þei lyen stille in here synne'. No surviving English manuscript preserves this variant.

51 *þer . . . þat²* (l. 52). Supported by the Latin version, 'nulla est vita alia quam ista, vel licet credat quod alia est vita, credit tamen'. The omission of this clause appears to be a case of scribal eye-skip omisson in a sub-hypearchetype of the χ manuscripts $HH_5AsWsLwTW$, or perhaps an omission in the hypearchetype of χ that has been restored in $BChHu_2Ld$.

54 *fele*. The Latin version, 'relinquere', supports RBλAsSr⌜H[c]⌝AELdPl, of which Ws 'fle' would be a scribal variant by confusion of graphic similars. $H_7H_5ChHu_2T$ 'fele', also presumably a case of confusion of homoeographs, is the less cogent reading, because Hilton is not speaking here of the worldly-minded man's 'feeling' of sin within himself, but of his refusal to 'leave' his sin.

56 *oure Lady fast*. A regular fast on Saturday in honour of the Virgin Mary. See for example the reference to a soul in purgatory who tells the narrator of the 'Revelation Showed to a Holy Woman' (dated 1422) that 'there sulde never none fayle of Oure Ladys helpe that comes into purgatorye, that has fastede hir faste byfore'. *Women's Writing in Middle English*, ed. Alexandra Barratt (London, 1992), 171–2. See also Allen's note to *The Book of Margery Kempe*, ed. by Sanford Brown Meech and Hope Emily Allen, EETS OS 212 (1940), 162/11, at 326–7.

seith. The Latin version, 'dicat', supports Σ 'say' over H_7RAsAPl. 'Say' is the more cogent reading because all the other verbs in this sentence are also subjunctive in all manuscripts, with the exception of RAsA 'herith' in the next clause.

58 *he schal neuer gon*. The Latin version expands to 'credit quod nunquam ibit'.

61 *by*. H_7 'vy' is an error.

62 *welth*. The manuscript support for H_7λSrAHu$_2$ECcMPlT and for HRBH$_5$AsWsChLwLdW 'wele' is approximately equal.

Isa. 28: 19.

64 *here*. The Latin version does not support the χ addition, 'ne wil not knowen'.

CHAPTER 16

14 John 1: 5.

16 *myrknes*. The northern dialectal word 'myrknes' (and 'myrk' in the following line), which the Latin version translates as 'tenebre', 'tenebrosa', is apparently characteristic of Hilton's speech; it occurs throughout the text, and is dialectally translated in manuscripts of a more southerly character or later date as 'darkness', 'dark'.

17 *myrknes*. The HSrCh variant 'myrknesses' may be influenced by the plural 'tenebris'/'tenebre' of the immediately preceding scriptural citation.

22 *he is*. Hilton usually uses the neuter pronoun to refer to the soul, but often reverts to the masculine; the feminine pronoun also occasionally occurs as a manuscript variant. The Latin version maintains the use of feminine pronouns and adjectives in referring to 'anima'.

36 *þat*. The variant 'What', which the H corrector shares with RAsLwPlW, converts this relative clause into a parenthetical question. The Latin text in Y reads 'que', referring to antecedent 'vita'; the other Latin manuscripts all read 'quod', referring to antecedent 'filum'.

41 *punyschynges*. The Latin version, 'punicionem', agrees with the singular Σ reading over the plural of H_7Pl.

42 *þei han no*. The Latin version 'carencia' here agrees with χE 'lakkynge of' over H_7RλAsSrACcMPl.

46 *as mikel as is*. 'inasmuch as it is'; the Latin version reads 'in quantum est'.

52 A version of Ezek. 33: 11: 'Nolo mortem impii, sed ut convertatur impius a via sua, et vivat.'

CHAPTER 17

16 *a man þat is broght . . . he þat is broght* (l. 23). The parallelism of H_7RλAsSrAECcMLdPlW is more cogent than HBH_5WsChLwHu_2T, which lacks the relative 'þat' in the first clause.

17 See *The Prickynge of Love*, 122/20, 'for a seke man whenne he resseyuyth a medycyne is not als tite hool'.

34–5 *bot reformynge in felynge . . . may come to*. See the extended ending of the ι version of Hilton's *Mixed Life*, in *English Mystics of the Middle Ages*, ed. Barry Windeatt (Cambridge, 1994; repr. with corr. 1997), 130: 'yit aren we not as tite able and redi for to seke and biholde goostli thinges that are abouen us, until oure soule be maad sotil and til it be maad saad and stablid in vertues bi processe of tyme and encresynge of grace. For, as Seynt Gregor seith, no man sodeynli is maad souereyne in grace, but fro litil he bigynneth, and bi processe wexeth, until he come to the moste.' The reference to Gregory is to *Mor. in Job* 22. 19. 45 and *Hom. in Ezech.* 2. 3. 3.

37 *an heygh leddre*. The only reference—and that in a simile—to a *scale* in a work that bears that name. The metaphor of the ladder of spiritual ascent is traditional, dating back at least to the sixth-century Greek father John Climacus' *Ladder of Divine Ascent* (*Scala paradisi*).

38 *flyen*. The English variant is considerably more emphatic than the Latin version, 'attingere' (and Hu_2 'goyng'); H_5Ws 'styȝen' is an acceptable substitute but possibly derives from confusion of homoeographs, as, more certainly, does BLB_3PH_6MLdTW 'flen', which alters the meaning completely.

42 *whan he . . . lygheþ* (l. 43). 'when Christ, in whom all grace lies, helps a soul'.

43 *speciale help*. Referring to the 'special grace' or 'special gift' of contemplation, which Hilton will discuss from *Scale* II, Chapter 26 onward.

CHAPTER 18

1 *reward*. The H_7 scribe has treated abstract 'regard' as concrete 'reward', with a modifying article. See above, 10/24.

7–8 *and þat is not soth*. The more cogent reading of H_7HRBLB_3AsSrLwA-Hu_2EPH_6CcMPlTW, supported by the Latin version, 'quod non est verum', is that it is not true that the Lord is 'dangerouse', distant and forbidding to his lovers. The phrase 'and þat is not soth' refers to the clause that immediately precedes it. The $H^c$$H_5$WsChLd variant 'and þat it is not soth' ('it' cancelled in H) would apparently mean that it seems to Hilton's interlocutor that reforming in feeling is not true.

11, 20 *herte*. The Latin version 'corda' supports the plural of χM over the singular of H_7RλAsSrAECcPl.

13 *preynge, þenkynge . . . werkynge* (l. 13). The Latin version translates these verbal nouns as abstract nouns: 'orationibus, meditacionibus . . . operacionibus'.

14–17 *hem þenkeþ . . . no more*. Roger Ellis has suggested privately that there are analogues to this in Birgitta of Sweden, *Rev*. Book 3, chapter 28: 'ideo miseri sunt qui sic dicunt, "Sufficit si ero in celo minimus. Noli esse perfectus." O insensata cogito . . .' and Book 4, chapter 62: '"Sufficiat nobis venire ad portam glorie, et si prohibear ab ingressu sufficiat michi residere iuxta portam. Nolo esse perfectus." Hec vox et vita grauis est, quia nemo veniet ad portam glorie nisi perfectus aut perfecte purgatus.'

18 Hilton's *Mixed Life* is sympathetic to a layman of means who wishes to live a life of contemplation, and provides guidance for him in combining it with the active life that his worldly responsibilities require of him; but here he is speaking of those who chose rather to reject the possibility of advancement in the spiritual life.

19 *besynes þat neden*. H_7LB_3AsSrAPPl take 'besynes' as a plural, with a plural verb; R uses a marked plural noun form, 'bysenesses' (as H_7 does five lines below), in agreement with the plural verb; χEH_6CcM read 'besynes' as singular, agreeing with the singular verb form 'nediþ'. The Latin version has a plural noun and an impersonal verb form: 'in . . . solicitudinibus quas oportet fieri'.

21 *fallen out and in*. The Latin version translates 'ab vno proposito in aliud mutantur'.

24 *besynessis*. Only H_7 and the Latin version, 'solicitudinibus' use a marked plural form here. See above, note to 18/19. The Latin version omits the following phrase, 'if þei . . . besynes', presumably by eye-skip either in the English exemplar or in the act of translation.

26 The idea that religion (in the sense of religious orders), and particularly

monasticism, is the most perfect form of Christian life because it is the form most directly aimed towards union with God and allows the fewest distractions from that aim had become a commonplace by the twelfth century. See Bernard McGinn, 'Introduction: The Ordering of Charity', in *The Presence of God: A History of Western Christian Mysticism*, ii: *The Growth of Mysticism: Gregory the Great through the 12th Century* (New York, 1996), 149–57. For the scholastic formulation of the idea, see Aquinas, *ST*, 2[a] 2[æ], q. 186. As Hilton says in *De Util.*, *LW* i, ll. 41–3: 'Cum enim finis humane perfeccionis constat in perfecta dileccione Dei et proximi, ad hunc finem attingendum in iudicio sancte ecclesie non reperitur medium propinquius et congruencius ordine et statu religionis regularis.' At the present point in *Scale* II, however, Hilton goes on to say that progress in the contemplative life is also open to 'oþer men in seculere state'—such as the addressee of his letter on *Mixed Life*—a member of the higher orders of society whose income allows them to be 'fre fro werdly besynes, if þei willen and moun han here nedful sustenaunce withouten grete bodily besynes'. He does, however, name two related intellectual criteria here: that they 'han mikel reson and grete kyndly witte'. Clark and Dorward, in *Scale*, 221, translate this as 'great reasoning power and natural judgement', apparently following the Latin version's translation of 'kyndly witte' as 'iudicium naturale'. It probably means something closer to 'native intelligence'.

30 *þei standen stille as þei weren ydel.* This echoes Hilton's criticism of himself and his interlocutor in *De Imag. pec.*, *LW*, i. 90–1, ll. 319–32, men who had left the active world but yet did nothing useful: 'Quid ergo facimus tu et ego, nostrique similes, homines pigri et inutiles, tota die stantes ociosi?'

38 *if a man.* This reading is supported by a slight preponderance of the surviving English manuscripts, H_7RLB_3AsSrAPCcPl. The Latin version 'sicut de homine . . . extracto' would support χEH_6M 'by a man þat' in repeating the reference to 'a man', but without the relative clause 'þat were . . .'.

41 *schuld.* The χE addition 'sone' may be reflected in the Latin version, 'faciliter'.

44 *ageyn.* The Latin version, 'iterum', here supports $H_7\lambda B_3EPH_6$Cc over χRAsSrAMPl.

45 *þe pitte of synne.* The idea of the 'pit of sin' is traditional, drawing in part on allegorical readings of the 'lacu[s] miseriae' of Ps. 39: 3 and of Jeremiah 38: 6. Clark, 'Notes', 308 n. 86 refers this to Gregory, *Epistola* 7. 37 (*PL* 77: 896). For Hilton's imagery as a structural device, see Hussey, 'From *Scale* I to *Scale* II', in James Hogg (ed.), *The Mystical Tradition and the Carthusians*, iv, Analecta Cartusiana, 130:4 (Salzburg, 1995), 46–67.

46 *he þenkeþ.* The impersonal use of 'think' is here supported only by λACcM.

50 *if he sette . . . for to come . . . and for to trauaile . . . and gif him* (l. 51). The Latin version relates these verbs differently: 'statuat . . . peruenire . . . et . . . laboret . . . assidueque se occupet'.

58 Hilton here echoes the Latin school proverb 'Nemo avarus adhuc inventus est cui quod haberet satis esset'. There are a number of variant versions; *The Castle of Perseverance* has 'Non est in mundo diues qui dicat "habundo"'; *The Macro Plays*, ed. Mark Eccles, EETS OS 262 (1969), 503. See Hans Walther, *Lateinische Sprichwörter und Sentenzen des Mittelalters in alphabetischer Anordnung*, 6 vols. (Göttingen: Vandenhoeck and Ruprecht, 1963–9), no. 17645: 'Divitiis "satis est" non umquam dicet avarus.'

62–6 The Latin version has rewritten the closing sentences of this chapter, perhaps to avoid the comparison of worldly and spiritual covetise: 'Set quo plus habundat plus desiderat, et non cessat ex omnibus viribus laborare vt magis valeat habundare. Multo magis ergo deberet anima electa bona spiritualia desiderare que durant eternaliter et faciunt eam beatam, et ab huiusmodi desiderio non cessare, adquirat quod adquirere valeat.'

63 *for þat is aylastand.* The Latin version, 'que durant eternaliter', supports the relative clause in Σ, 'þat is aylastand', over H_7BChHu_2Ld.

65 *For he . . . haue.* Hilton here reverses the proverb 'Quo plus habundat, eo plus desiderat'.

CHAPTER 19

18 *ferst.* The Latin version has 'in principio' ('in here bygynynge') but, like χA and the original reading of L, lack H_7`L´B_3AsSrEPH_6CcMPl 'ferst'.

19 *menes and weyes.* The teaching that pious practices are means to the spiritual life, and not ends in themselves, is commonplace.

22 *þat.* The Latin version, 'et', agrees here with HAsLwW 'and'.

29 *of.* H, or some exemplar, appears to have misunderstood the use of 'of' here (*OED* XIII.44.c: Indicating that in respect of which a quality is attributed, followed by a verbal noun).

30–1 *þe prentys of it þat is ay ilyke ferforth in lerynge.* The Latin version, 'apprehenticus qui non proficit in adiscendo artem istam set semper permanet in eodem statu', supports the singular here, over the plural of χSrM, 'þe prentises . . . þat arn'.

36–7 *bettre* [*ter*]. The Latin version supplies the noun 'donum' for each of these adjectives.

36 *it.* The Latin version, 'earum', here supports χEM 'hem', which parallels the plural pronoun of the preceding clause, over H_7RB_3AsAPH_6CcPl.

39 *and þat schuld be lettyd because of her wilful custome.* The Latin version, 'cicius quam illud omitti debeat causa consuetudinis voluntarie', obcures Hilton's point here, that willful persistence even in a practice that was once good in itself can be an obstacle to the reception of a greater gift. If the word 'illud' refers jointly to carnality, sensuality, and vain imagination, then the Latin version takes these, not former practices, as the obstacle to progress; if 'illud' refers back to 'donum', the only neuter noun in the preceding phrase (taking 'þat' as demonstrative, rather than relative), then the grammar of the Latin sentence is unclear.

42 *I mene . . . taken* (l. 43). AMPl omit this assurance, perhaps finding it unnecessary to raise the issue of obedience, particularly in a religious setting ('rewle').

44 Ps. 83: 8. The word 'et' preceding 'videbitur' does not occur in either the Latin version or the Vulgate text, but it is translated in Hilton's exposition. This verse is recalled in Bernard, *De Grad. Hum.* 1. 2 and cited in his *Serm. in Quad.* 6. 4 (*PL Serm.* 7.4), a sermon that is an important source for Chapters 21, 22, and 27 below.

46 *Sothly*. The preceding phrase 'þat is', which is supported in this instance by χEH_6CcM, does not precede every translation of a scriptural text in *Scale* II, although it does precede most of them in most manuscripts. Only MS E has 'þat is' at all points. It is not certain that Hilton was uniform in his usage in this regard.

53 *God . . . see*[2]. An eye-skip omisson in H_7. The H variant 'good', which contrdicts the scriptural citation and translation above, is erroneous.

CHAPTER 20

13 *what man or wumman*. The Latin version, 'quod quilibet homo', supports the use of the pronoun 'þat' in χSrACcM, over its lack in H_7λAsEPl. H_6 inserts 'þat' after 'wumman', and H_5 repeats it at the same point. The Latin version also restricts itself to masculine reference.

15, 20 *hem* [*bis*]. The use of singular and plural pronoun forms in this passage is inconsistent in the English manuscript tradition. In the phrase 'hem behoueth', H_7LB_3AsSrChAHu_2PH_6MPl use the plural form and HBH_5LwECcLdTW the singular; in 'him behoueth also', HBH_5SrChLwCcLdTW use the singular form and H_7LB_3AsA-Hu_2EPH_6MPl the plural. The Latin version, 'eum' and a core group of χ manuscripts (HBH_5LwLdTW), plus Cc, use the singular form both times; H_7λAHu_2MPl the plural. SrCh agree using 'hem' the first time and 'him' the second.

18–19 *in þe ferst partye of þis wrytynge*. Chapters 55 to 77 of *Scale* I are occupied with the discussion of the eradication of the seven deadly sins.

Aside from the opening lines, this is the only reference in *Scale* II to the preceding book.

25–6 *in hungre . . . colde*. An echo of 2 Cor. 11: 27.

27 *þis knowest . . . gode lyfynge* (l. 29). This sentence would imply that besides Hilton's *Scale* I, his reader has other spiritual reading available.

29 *mans soule*. The Latin version, 'animam hominis', agrees with the singular variant of H_7RλAsSrAECcMPl over the plural 'mens soules' of χ.

32 *oure Lord Jesu*. This is the first occurrence of the RAsAPl variant 'God' (here with M), where the majority of manuscripts read 'Jesu'. Note also that λELd add 'Crist'.

35 *he is special leche*. On the tradition of Christ the healer, see Rudolph Arbesmann, 'The Concept of "Christus Medicus" in St. Augustine', *Traditio*, 10 (1954), 1–28.

37 *man*. The addition of 'or a woman' in Cc, which belonged to Campsey abbey, may be a sign of adaptation to an audience of women.

38 *kenne*. Although χB_3AsSrAECcPl support the variant 'teche', several of the earliest manuscripts, including H_7, R, and L (with PH_6) support 'kenne'. The substitution of 'teche' is probably an example of semantic standardization.

lerynge. This variant is supported by H_7HRH_5AsCh, the variant 'lernynge' by BH_5LB_3SrLwAHu_2EPH_6CcMLdPlTW. As with 'kenne' above, this is probably an example of semantic standardization: the substitution of 'lerning(e)' for 'lering(e)'.

47 *werke*. The Latin version, 'laborem', here supports H_7RλAsSrAPl in not repeating 'owen', as the χECcM variant does. The addition does produce a closer parallelism between the phrases, as well as improving the cadence of the end of the sentence.

49 *non oþer mede þan him only*. Another echo of William of St-Thierry's description of the spiritual 'perfecti' (see note to 13/28-33 above). The idea is traditional: see Augustine, *De Doct. Christ.* 1. 27. 28.

52–5 For similar treatments of the relationship between human effort and the free gift of grace, see William of St-Thierry's *Lettre d'or*, 344; Richard of St-Victor, *Benj. Min.* 52; *Cloud*, 69.

56 *For he . . . wil*. An echo of John 3: 8.

64 *werkynge*. The Latin version, 'cooperante et laborante', may be a deliberate invocation of the concept of cooperant grace: that is, the grace by which external acts produced by the human will that has been moved by the operant grace of God are themselves produced by God through the medium of the will cooperating with that grace. By grace, the human will

cooperates with grace. Even the cooperation of the human will with grace is thus the result of grace. See, for example, Aquinas, *ST* 1–2, q. 111, art. 2.

71 *ne doth not his besynes*. The Latin version omits this reference to the spiritual labour by which the soul cooperates with grace.

72 *kan not felen of himself sothfastly as he is*. Hilton here expands on the brief discussion of true meekness in *Scale* I, Chapter 68. The Latin version, 'nescit deuote considerare humilitatem Domini nostri Jesu Christi et sentire seipsum miserum esse sicut est veraciter', adds a devotional emphasis on the humility of Christ that is lacking in the English version.

73 *fastynge, wakynge, werynge of þe hayre . . . preyende, wepende, syghende, and þenkende* (l. 76). In the English manuscripts written in scribal dialects that preserve distinct verbal noun and participle endings, the first of these two series are verbal nouns and the second participles (modifying the subject of the sentence, 'he'); in the Latin version, the first are translated as gerunds: 'ieiunando, vigilando, cilicio vtendo', and the second as nouns derived from verbs: 'orationem, ploracionem, et meditacionem, et suspirium'.

75 The outward (or corporal) works of mercy are: feeding the hungry, giving drink to the thirsty, clothing the naked, harbouring the stranger, visiting the sick, ministering to prisoners, and burying the dead.

80–6 The idea of 'poverty of spirit' here is similar to that in Meister Eckhart's famous German sermon 52, on the text 'Beati pauperes spiritu', *Meister Eckhart: Die deutschen und lateinischen Werke*, ed. J. Quint, ii (Stuttgart, 1970), 486–506. See Edmund Colledge and J. C. Marler, '"Poverty of the Will": Ruusbroec, Eckhart and *The Mirror of Simple Souls*', in P. Mommaers and N. de Paepe (eds.), *Jan van Rusbroec: The Sources, Content and Sequels of his Mysticism* (Leuven, 1984), 14–47. The Latin version of *Scale* II revises this passage extensively, adding 'sentire se esse miserum vel' before 'make himself naked', omitting the sentences 'For . . . meke' (ll. 87–90), and adding the scriptural citation at l. 94 below.

83 *noght*. Not the adverb 'not', but the pronoun 'nought'—he cannot feel himself to be what he truly is, which is nothing.

85 *gode*. The Latin version, 'bonis operibus', supports χECcM 'gode dedis' over H$_7$RλAsSrAPl although the concept of deeds is implicit in the following 'doth'.

86 *sothfastnes*. The Latin version gives this a slight devotional emphasis, translating not as 'veritatis' but as 'humilitatis Jesu Christi'.

87 *For . . . is meke* (l. 90). The Latin version lacks these two sentences, perhaps through eye-skip in its English exemplar.

90 Hilton will describe in Chapter 37 how the grace of reformation in faith and in feeling eradicates the sin of pride, which, as he points out here, human effort under the direction of reason can never accomplish.

94 *so*. The Latin version adds at this point 'Dixit Apostolus Sanctus Paulus: Qui se existimat aliquid esse cum nichil sit, ipse se seducit. (Gal. 6: 3). Et certe qui habet huiusmodi humilitatem de qua dixi.'

112–13 *neuer þe more*. The Latin version, 'cicius', supports HH_5LwTW 'neuer þe soner' (Hu_2 'raþir') over H_7RBLB_3AsSrAEPH_6CcMLdPl.

119 *may . . . besynes* (l. 120). This may have been omitted by eye-skip in some sub-hypearchetype of HH_5LwTW, or may have been perceived as redundant.

CHAPTER 21

Title The title of this chapter in H_7 appears to be a scribal contraction, written in a different hand, of the longer title found in RSrAEPH_6MLdPlTW, opening with the same words, 'An entre', which is supported by the Latin version's 'Introduccio'. The title in LB_3AsP offers a different, but equally accurate, summary of the content of the chapter. This title is the first in a series added by a separate correcting hand at the top of the page in H. The disruption in chapter titles at this point is suggestive of a separate unit in the composition of *Scale* II. The extracts from *Scale* II in Ad_1, Ad_2, and Td begin with this section. It should also be noted that the following two chapters, dominated by the metaphor of the journey to Jerusalem, lack Hilton's customary dependence on scriptural citation and exposition as a mode of discourse.

8 The idea of spiritual progress as exile and pilgrimage, particularly to Jerusalem, has scriptural roots in 1 Pet. 2: 11 and Heb. 11: 13–16, and is found in Augustine, *De Doct. Christ.* 1. 4. 10, although it is not developed there as it was in Bernard's *Serm. in Quad.* 6, a text that is a primary source for this and the following chapters of *Scale* II. See Clark, 'Walter Hilton and the Psalm Commentary *Qui habitat*'. It should also be kept in mind that pilgrimage was a common experience, and a common literary trope, in Hilton's day; see Maribel Dietz, *Wandering Monks, Virgins, and Pilgrims* (College Park, Pa., 2005).

10 *for he might not come*. The H_7 variant reads this phrase as parallel to 'for he knew not þe weye', which is redundant. Sr 'for he myghte comyn', is probably an expression of purpose: 'he asked so that he might come'. The Latin version, 'numquid ad illam ciuitatem poterat peruenire' supports HH_5LwAHu_2ELdTW, 'wheþer [wher RBAsSrPl] he miȝte come to þat citee', the more cogent reading. λ 'wheþir [H_6 wher] he myȝte not come' combines elements of both H_7 and χ.

12–13 *peryles are grete of þefes and robbours, and many oþer lettynges þer ben þat fallen to a man in þe goynge*. The Latin version, 'pericula sunt magna, nam latrones et predones et multa alia impedimenta occurrunt homini in eundo', supports λCc, 'peryles are grete, for þefes and robbours and many oþer lettynges þer ben þat fallen to a man in þe goynge.' The H_7 omission of 'and' is in error, since 'þefes and robbours' is the complement of 'peryles are grete of' and 'many oþer lettynges þer ben' is a separate clause. The H_7 scribe appears to have read 'þefes robbours and many oþer lettynges' as a set of parallel nouns without noticing that a grammatical division was necessary somewhere. This complex sentence seems to have confused a number of scribes, starting with the choice to read the word 'peryles' as a plural noun or as an adjective.

19 Reminiscent of the traveller in the parable of the Good Samaritan, Luke 10: 30.

24 *behete*. The Latin version, 'promitto', supports $H_7HBH_5LwHu_2LdT$ over the RλAsSrAEPH_6CcMPlW addition of 'þe'.

30 See Bernard, *Serm. in Quad.* 6. 2 (*PL Serm.* 7: 2); Richard of St-Victor, *De Quatuor gradibus violentae charitatis*; the *Cloud*, chapter 7.

35 *fage*. This rare word, probably the original reading of H, as well as $H_7BH_5LB_3PCcMT$, is the *lectio difficilior*, and is supportd by the Latin version, 'adulari'. To the examples in *MED* 'fagen' *v.* one might add 'fagiars' and 'fagyd' (translating 'laudantes' and adulantes') in *The Fire of Love*, Richard Misyn's 1434 translation of Rolle's *Incendium Amoris*, *The Fire of Love and The Mending of Life or The Rule of Living*, ed. Ralph Harvey, EETS OS 106 (1896), 20, l. 30 and 21, l. 6. The Hu_2 variant 'flater' and Ld 'glose' are synonymous substitutes, but $RAsLwH^cAEH_6PlW$ 'fede' has in its favour only a degree of graphic similarity.

þe with. The transposition of these two words in H_7 is obviously erroneous.

38 *werdly gode*. The Latin version, 'bonis temporalibus', supports the plural λECc variant over the singular of H_7χRAsSrAMPl.

39–40 *I vndertake þi lyfe*. The Latin version, 'manucapio', means literally 'mainprise, go bail for'.

42–3 *syght of pees*. This interpretation is commonplace in Western Christianity at least from the time of Augustine, *Enarr. in Psal.* 64. 3. See the *Cloud*-author's *Discrescyon of Spirites*, in *Deonise*, 85, l. 4; and the Middle English *Pearl*, ll. 951–2.

61 *Jesu*[1]. The Latin version, 'solum Jesu', supports H_7RAsH_6Pl over the addition of 'and' in χLB_3SrEPCcM. The continuation in Td appears to be modelled in part on that in the Latin version.

strenges. Supported by the Latin version, 'corde'. RLB_3PH_6M 'sterynges', fails to follow Hilton's musical metaphor of sympathetic vibration.

66–114 The teaching on the two kinds of humility in the *Cloud*, chapters 13–14, is precisely parallel to Hilton's.

67 *or*[2]. The Latin version, 'et', supports HLwHu$_2$CcLdTW, 'and', over H$_7$RBH$_5$LB$_3$AsSrAEPH$_6$MPl.

71 *in sight . . . beynge* (l. 73). The Latin version recasts this passage to give it a more Christocentric, devotional emphasis: 'considerando benedictam humanitatem Domini nostri Jesu Christi et mirabilem humilitatem bonitatemque eiusdem. Quia per consideracionem humilitatis et caritatis sue.'

72 *þe wunderful godenes*. Td 'þe mekenes and þe charite' appears to reflect the Latin version 'humilitatis et caritatis' (for 'beynge') in the following line.

75 *noȝt in substaunce . . . synne* (76). The Latin version reduces this to 'quasi nichilum', again deflecting Hilton's emphasis on the source of true humility in recognition of the absolute difference between the created soul and Christ the incarnate God, the ideal essence of goodness—an ontological difference that would be the same even if the lover of God were in fact sinless—towards devotion to Christ in his blessed, good, and humble humanity. Hilton stresses, however, that this 'perfect' humility does not do away with 'imperfect' humility based on the recognition of one's own sinfulness, as does the *Cloud*, chapter 14. The Td variant appears to reflect the Latin.

84 *as noȝt to resten in*. The Latin version, 'ad nichil computa quantum ad quietem', supports RλAsSrAECcPl, 'as for to' over the χM variant 'for'. The H$_7$ variant leaves 'noȝt' open to being read either as a pronoun ('nought') or as an adverb ('not').

85 *Keste . . . forgete it*. Echoing Phil. 3: 13.

87 *lefeþ byhynde . . . he hath* (l. 89). Echoing Matt. 19: 27.

93 *wilt lene vpon restendly*. The Latin version translates as 'innitaris vel quiescas'.

104 *clefe sadly þerto*. The Latin version adds 'et constanter ei adhabere et constitue illam vt fundamentum et substanciam omnium orationum atque operacionum tuarum'.

105 *and*[1]. The Latin version, 'ita quod', supports Σ 'þat' in expressing a causal relationship between the two clauses, where the H$_7$ variant expresses consequence at most.

106–7 *spoiled þe and bete þe*. The Latin version, 'spolient . . . verberent', supports Σ 'spoile . . . bete' over H$_7$Pl in using the present subjunctive for both of these verbs.

106 *þe whilk I calle vnclene spyrytis*. See above, 21/12–13.

108 *schortly*. The Latin version, 'veraciter', suggests an exemplar reading 'sothly', although no surviving English manuscript records this variant.

113 *werkys*. The Latin version, 'opera', supports H$_7$RλAsAECcPl over χSrM 'werkyng'.

115–16 *aftere þe degre or state askeþ þat þou standest in*. The omission of this phrase in AMPl suggests a limitation of the openness of Hilton's text to readers of varying social status or religious roles, although it is unclear what audience is addressed thereby. RAsAMPl seem to envisage an audience that is not necessarily religious (i.e. members of religious orders), but may include lay clergy, laity, or anchorites: see below, 21/136, 22/57, 23/53, 27/29, 27/104.

116 *bodily or gostly*. The Latin version, 'siue sit opus corporale siue spirituale', like the previous AMPl variant, suggests an intention to limit the inscribed audience: where Hilton's 'bodily or gostly' describes the 'degre or state' of the reader, Fishlake refers it to the activities ('gostly . . . and bodily also whan þat it nedeþ', as Hilton has already described them) in which the contemplative will engage.

119 *preynge*. The HH_5LwW variant 'prechynge' suggests an exemplar intended for clerical readers. Of the other χ manuscripts, BHu_2LdT read 'preynge', and Ch is lacking; but preaching would not have been an appropriate activity for a Carthusian monk or a Brigittine nun (among whom the χ manuscripts tended to circulate) at any rate.

122 *lesse . . . þenkeþ . . . sauour . . . felest* (l. 123). The Latin version, 'minuatur . . . sapiat . . . sencias', uses the subjunctive here, and continues with a second-person singular jussive subjunctive, 'assumas . . . omittas'. Among the English manuscripts, only H_7Sr have subjunctive 'lesse' and 'sauour/fauour'; all others use the indicative, followed by imperative singular 'take' and 'lefe'. If 'þe þenkeþ' is read as parenthetical, then the indicative mood would be appropriate, but it is not clear that either Hilton or his scribes was particularly scrupulous on this point.

127–8 *and moun wel be chaunged*. The Latin version omits this phrase.

130 The metaphor of sticks and fire, and the related moralization of Lev. 6: 12, 'And the fire on the altar shall always burn, and the priest shall feed it, putting wood on it every day in the morning', probably drawn from Gregory, *Mor. in Job* 25. 7. 16, is a favourite of Hilton's. See *Scale* I, Chapter 32; *Mixed Life*, in *English Mystics*, ed. Windeatt, 119–21; *De Imag. pec.*, 77, ll. 77–81; *De Util.*, 168, ll. 843–45; and below, 42/40–41.

131–2 *flawme and þe hattere is þe*. The Latin version, 'maior est flamma, ignisque callidior', supports $H_7R\lambda AsAECcPl$ over the χSrM omission.

132 *werkynge*. The Latin version, 'operaciones', supports the plural of RAsSrPl.

136 *if . . .laghe* (l. 137). AM omit another reference to the possible non-religious status of the reader. See above, 21/115–16.

140 *Lo*. H_7 'be', makes sense only locally, if the phrase 'be swilk a custom' is separated from the remainder of the sentence.

145 *if a man hafe in custom*. The Latin version, 'si consuetudinem habeas', changes the focus to the second person singular, the 'thou' to whom the text is addressed.

146 *only*. The Latin version, 'solum', supports H_7λSrCcM over the χRAsAPl omission.

CHAPTER 22

Title The H_7λE title is that of chapter 23 in RSrAH_6LdPlTW. The RALdPlTW title of the present chapter is supported by the Latin version; that in Sr is closer to that of H_7λE; and As shares an otherwise unique title, which appears to be little more than an abbreviation of the first sentences of the chapter, with a later corrector of MS H.

4 *is*. The sentence 'how . . . remedye' requires a main verb: H_7 'as', is an error.

8 *to putten . . . lufe of Jesu* (l. 9). The doubling of this phrase in the Latin version, 'expellere a corde tuo illud desiderium quod habes ad dileccionem Jesu Christi, et expellere a mente tua illam fidelem ymaginacionem et illam constantem consideracionem quam habere deberes in Jesu Christo' (with the addition of a reference to 'faithful imagination'), appears to stem from a desire in Fishlake to emphasize the devotional rhetoric of his text.

11 *dredys*. Hilton is here speaking of feelings that arise in the heart, and not of outward 'dedys'; the omission of 'r' in H_7 is an error.

13 *Jesu*. The series of variants in RAsAMPl reading 'God', rather than 'Jesu', begins at this point. These manuscripts are joined by χSr here in the variant 'God', as against H_7λECc. The Latin version has the devotional expansion 'Jesu Christi et deuotam consideracionem humilitatis sue'.

19 *Jesu*. LwW expand to 'oure lorde Jesu', RAsAMPl have the variant 'God', and the Latin version has the devotional expansion 'Jesum Christum et cogitare quantam dileccionem et humilitatem pro me exhibuit et ostendit'.

20 Scrupulosity over imperfect confession as an obstacle to the contemplative life is a matter that Hilton takes up at length in his letter *Epist. ad Quem.*, 265–78, ll. 331–621. William Flete also discusses this as one of the temptations of the contemplative life in chapter 7 of *De Remediis contra temptaciones*; Edmund Colledge and Noel Chadwick, '"Remedies over Temptations": The Third English Version of William Flete', *Archivio italiano per la storia della pietà*, 5 (Rome, 1968), 202–40 at 233, ll. 9–12; *YW*, ii. 116.

22 *þe most*. This variant, with an impersonal meaning equivalent to 'þe most nedes' or 'þe behoueth' (see *MED* 'mōten', *v.* 2, no. 8), is supported by a small number of manuscripts, although including two of the earliest:

H_7HChAPl, as opposed to the active RBH_5λAsSrLwHu_2EMLdPlTW variant 'þou most'.

23 *go home and schryfe þe better*. The Latin version, 'ac melius confiteri', here supports χSr in its lack of any of the variant complements: the redundant 'home and' of H_7, 'first and' of λAsECcMPl, or 'first' of RA.

24 *for þou art schryfen*. The Latin version supports RAsAMPl in omitting this phrase.

36 *what with . . . oþer syde* (l. 37). Hilton explores this idea in *Qui habitat*; *An Exposition of Qui Habitat*, ed. Wallner, 23/17–25/11. See Bernard, *Serm. in Quad*. 6. 2.

38 *do*. The manuscript support for this variant, H_7RλAsSrCcM, as against χAEPl 'make', possibly marks the resistance of a recessive form over standardization.

39 *trauailende*. The Latin version expands to 'laborandum in precibus et bonis operibus et cum firma fide in humilitate Jesu Christi'.

40 *sekenes . . . fantasyes . . . frenesyes*. What Bernard identifies as the 'timor nocturnus' of Ps. 90: 5 (*In Cant*. 33. 6. 11) that can affect beginners in the spiritual life: see Clark, 'Walter Hilton and the Psalm Commentary *Qui habitat*'.

41 *oþer men*. The Latin version, 'alios', could be taken as supporting H_7 over variants with 'some'.

43 *þiself in*. The χ manuscripts HH_5LwHu_2TW and Cc omit the sentence-ending preposition here: HHu_2, 'þi selfyn'; H_5LwCcTW þiself.

44 *ony man*. 'For any man'. In present-day English, the clausal attributive-with-infinitive construction (e.g. 'a hard nut to crack') requires a preposition, usually 'to' or 'for'; in Latin, the subject of the embedded locution ('*he* cracks the nut') is in the dative case. The χCc variant, 'to any man', and the Latin version, 'alicui homini', reflect this requirement; the H_7RλAsSrAEMPl variant, however, demonstrates that the preposition, for Hilton or his scribes, was optional.

50–1 *be at Jerusalem*. The Latin version adds a devotional note, 'et sic per stabilem memoriam Jesu Christi et passionis sue eos a te abicies et depelles'.

54 *forth . . . with*. The Latin version translates as 'desideras'.

57 *and . . . fadere* (l. 58). AMPl omit reference to religious superiors or spiritual advisers. See above, 21/115–16.

59 *be . . . to*. An eye-skip omisson in H_7.

61 *þi*. The H_7RλAsAEPl reading here is redundant (in consideration of the following phrase, 'þat þou dost'), as opposed to the χSrCcM variant 'þe'; the Latin version, 'opera tua, quantumcumque bene fiant', obviates the redundancy.

66 *to yre . . . euen-cristen* (l. 67). The English text posits wrath, melancholy, and ill-will as three possible reactions to one's fellow Christians that may result from the temptation of frustration and malicious criticism. The Latin version describes their relationship differently: 'per malencoliam et malam voluntatem ad iram contra proximos'—that one would be moved by melancholy and ill-will to wrath.

68, 74, 76 *desesys . . . desesis . . . disese.* The Latin version translates all three with the same word, 'molestias . . . molestiis . . . molestiis', keeping the plural reference in all three cases. The English text has the singular in the final case, and $HBH_5SrChLwHu_2MW$ have 'vneses' in the second case.

75–6 *and lefe of þe þenkynge of þat disese.* The Latin version, 'cogitareque quod desistas de talibus molestiis', reverses the relation of 'leave off' and 'thinking'; $RH_5AsSrLwECcW$ omit, and H cancels, 'and' (the more cogent reading, although not necessarily the original). The logical connection of the three parts of this phrase is unclear, and various scribes have resolved it differently.

CHAPTER 23

Title The RASrLdPlTW title is supported by the Latin version. The H_7 title is that of Chapter 24 in $RSrAH_6LdPlTW$; As shares the same title as λE; and H has no title.

7 *and* [*bis*]. The Latin version, 'vel', supports $RAsH_6CcMW$ 'or' over $H_7HBH_5LB_3SrChLwAHu_2EPLdPlT$ 'and' in the first of these parallel phrases, and $HR\lambda AsChLwHu_2ECcMTW$ over $H_7H_5SrALdPl$ in the second. Hilton seems not to have written this as a disjunction, but it was recognized as such by a larger number of scribes in the second instance than in the first—although the two instances are parallel.

11–12 *þi gode dedys and þi vertus.* Pride in one's own spiritual superiority is the 'daemonium meridianum' of Ps. 90: 6 in Bernard's *Serm. in Cant.* 33. 6. 13. See below, 37/111, where it is referred to the 'arwe flyend in þe day' ('sagitta volante in die').

12 *beren vpon þe.* The verbal phrase 'beren upon' ('to accuse') requires a direct object; the omission in H_7 is an error.

26 *and þat is only Jesu.* This phrase, which is omitted by RAsAPl, is supported by the Latin version, which has 'recolligit totam mentem et totum desiderium suum ad amorem Jesu Christi' for 'he dragheþ al his þoght and his ȝernynge vnto o þynge' in the previous line. The longer Christocentric substitution in CcM is the first of several that occur in the next chapters in these manuscripts.

39 *it towcheþ . . . Jesu* (l. 41). The Latin version, 'non cures de illo, non garules cum illo, nec molesteris, ne timeas illum vel delecteris in illo, set celeriter de corde tuo excute, sic dicendo, "Nichil sum, nichil habeo, nichil quero vel desidero nisi dileccionem Domini Jesu Christi."' supports χSr 'charge it not, iangle not þerwiþ, ne angre þe not, drede it not, like it not, bot smyte it oute of þin herte redily; and sei þus: I am notȝ, I haf notȝ, nouȝt I seke ne coueite bot eþ luf of Jesu'. The phrases (1) 'charge it not', (2) 'iangle not þerwiþ, ne angre þe not, drede it not', (3) 'like it not, bot smyte it oute of þin herte redily and sey þus, "I am noȝt, I hafe noȝt"', and (4) 'nouȝt I seke ne coueite bot þe luf of Jesu', appear to have been lacking in the original or in the hypearchetype(s) from which H_7RλAsAPl descend, and to have been added to the underlying text (probably as separate phrases in the margin) and incorporated differently in the various manuscript traditions. χSrCcM have the same order as the Latin version (with omissions in Cc and M). H_7λ omit (1) and all of (2) but the last three words, 'drede it not'. RAsPl have only the first three words of (1), and insert (2) after the opening phrase of (4) 'noȝt I seke'; they then repeat (4) in complete form. A does the same, but inserts (2) between two complete iterations of (4) and repeats (2) again after 'Jesu' at the end of the passage. No version omits this material completely.

42 *strengthe it*. The Latin version, 'robora illud', supports this reading, but not the χ addition of 'and maynteyne it'.

53 *and kepe . . . þi souereyne* (l. 54). The omission of this phrase in RAsAMPl does not seem to be intended to preclude discretion in the ascetic practices of a contemplative (the reader has just been counselled to take rest, food, and drink as much as a pilgrim would in travelling), so much as the advice and direction of spiritual advisers or religious superiors, which might indicate a direction of the text in these manuscripts towards a non-clerical (religious or secular) audience, who would have superiors, but towards an heremitic or lay readership. See above, 21/115–16.

54 *þi*. HLwW 'þe' (corrected by Grenehalgh in W) is erroneous.

55 *slepen*. The Latin version, 'cum aliis loqui temporibus oportunis', seems to derive from an English exemplar reading 'speken', to which Fishlake has added an explanatory phrase.

56 *forþen*. H_7 'forþen', represents *MED* 'forthen', *v.*, rather than Σ 'fortheren'. The phrase echoes Flete, 'and þouȝ it lette hym at oo tyme, it schal supporte hym another tyme'. *De Remediis* chapter 7, ed. Colledge and Chadwick, 233 (*YW*, ii. 117).

CHAPTER 24

1–3 This chapter has two titles in both the English and Latin traditions, and is divided into two chapters in CcM and the Latin version (although not at the same point). The Latin version of the title at this point in H_7λM occurs at the chapter division inserted in the Latin version at 24/57 'þan', below. In RSrALdPlTW, the present chapter has the same title as Chapter 23 in H_7; E has a variant version of this title; and it is the title that occurs at the present point in the Latin version. The RSrALdPlTW title is also that which occurs at the chapter division inserted by M at 24/62 'þis', below; Cc divides the chapter at the same point, but without a new chapter title or number.

5 See Bernard, *De Dilig. Deo* 7. 22: 'Ipse dat occasionem, ipse creat affectionem, desiderium ipse consummat.' The discussion of the action of grace in the soul accords with standard scholastic theology.

6 *þe it*. The manuscript support for this variant (H_7RLB_3AsEPMPl) and its reverse, 'it þe' (HBH_5SrLwALdTW with 'it to þee' H_6), is approximately equal, but the parallelism of the phrases ending in 'þe' has the sound of Hilton; the latter is the more cogent reading.

8 *suffrest . . . assentest*. See Aquinas, *ST* 1–2, q. 111, art. 2, ad 2: 'Deus non sine nobis nos justificat, quia per motum liberi arbitrii, dum justificamur, Dei justitiæ consentimus.'

suffrest. H_7R`H^{c}'RLB_3AsSrAEPH_6CcMPlW, which is supported by the Latin version, 'quod permittis', takes the verb 'suffrest' as parallel to 'dost' and 'assentest'; H°BChLwHu_2LdT 'suffre' takes it as an infinitive complement to the emphatic modal 'dost' (H_5 'suffres' here disagrees with the remainder of χ).

10 *resonable instrument*. Aquinas, *ST* 1–2, q. 68, art. 3 ad 2 points out that a human is not an instrument that is acted upon, but that also acts.

11 *by towchynge of his grace be taken vp*. The similarity of forms of 'by' and 'be', as preposition or verb form, appears to have caused confusion in this passage. The $H_7\lambda$ variant takes 'be taken' as a passive infinitive governed by 'felist'; H_6 adds a preceding 'to'. The χRAsAEMPl variant reads 'taken' as a simple past participle. The Latin version, 'tangi et eleuari', reads the verbal forms of both 'touch' and 'take' as passive infinitives. Sr reads 'touch-' as a passive infinitive in the same way, 'be touched'; Cc reads it as a past participle, 'towchid'. Sr turns the second 'be-' into an intensifying prefix on the past participle 'bytaken'; Cc 'and be[-]taken' should probably be read the same way.

13–14 *for he it is þat desyreþ*. The more cogent reading of Hilton's Augustinian point here is that the very desire to love God is itself the product of 'prevenient' divine grace: it is God that causes the love of God; but his formulation could be taken as quietistic and was flattened into a safe orthodoxy, 'think that you have Jesus, for he it is that you desire', in RAsSrLwAEPlMW and the corrector of H. The H_5 variant retains 'þat desyreþ', but blunts Hilton's point by adding 'þe'. Cc and M present both active and passive senses, adding 'and is desiryd' (Cc) and 'and he it is þat is desired' (M). The Latin version, 'ipse est hoc desiderium', would represent a different, slightly less weakened form of Hilton's statement, 'for he is that desire', a form which is not to be found in any of the surviving English manuscripts.

15 *gostly*[1]. The Latin version agrees with the χ omission.

19 See Ps. 42: 3: 'Emitte lucem tuam et fidelitatem tuam: ipsae me ducant. Adducant me in montem sanctum tuum et in tabernacula tua.' The variant 'veritatem' for 'fidelitatem' also occurs in this Psalm text as it is cited by Bernard in distinguishing the light of the true Noontide from the *dæmonium meridianum* in *Serm. super Cant.* 33. 6. 13.

25 Isa. 26: 8–9.

29 *thenkynges*. The Latin version, 'cogitacionibus', supports this variant. H° 'þinges', with 'kyng' added above the line, appears to be a correction of a simple misreading, but one in that agrees with CcM.

30 *desyreth*. The Latin version, 'desiderasse', agrees with H°BH$_5$LB$_3$ChHu$_2$PH$_6$MLdT 'desyred' or RAsLw`H^c´EW 'hath desired'. The H$_7$SrACcPl variant may reflect the immediately preceding 'seyþ'.

31 *tymeful space*. The Latin version, 'tempus et plenum spacium', probably took '-ful' in its exemplar to be a separate word.

35 *gostly nyȝt*. Neither the definite or indefinite article, inserted here by χLB$_3$EP and RAsSrAH$_6$CcMPl respectively, is appropriate, as Hilton is speaking of 'spiritual night' in general.

42 Gen. 3: 5.

47 *bot . . . day*[2]. The Latin version omits this phrase, perhaps by eye-skip in the exemplar from which it was made.

48 Job 3: 3. The allegorical reading of the day cursed by Job as the false light by which Satan deceived Adam (Gen. 3: 5, cited immediately above) derives from Gregory, *Mor. in Job*, 4. 1. 6. Hilton interprets this text similarly in *De Lecc.*, *LW*, ii. 222, ll. 32–5.

51 *concupyscence*. H$_7$ 'concupysche', is erroneous.

55 *and þerfor . . . aylastende* (l. 56). The Latin version, 'et ideo qui eum diligit est in lumine eternaliter permanente', supports H$_7$HBH$_5$Hu$_2$PCcPl, over the omission in RLB$_3$AsSrLwAEH$_6$MLdTW, which is probably a result of eye-skip.

56 *Qui . . . lumine*. See 1 John 2: 10: 'Qui diligit fratrem suum, in lumine manet.'

57 *þan*. The Latin version inserts an extra chapter division at this point, the title of which is a version of the title of the present chapter in H$_7$λM. See above, Chapter 24 **Title**.

62 *þis*. CcM insert an extra chapter division at this point, to which M gives the title of the present chapter in RSrAH_6LdPlTW. See above, Chapter 24 **Title**.

63 *perfeccion and þe þoght*. MSS H_8UpB_4He of the Latin version read 'affeccionis' and Y reads 'effeccionis', but the Latin has no equivalent for 'and þe þoght'. H_7 is alone in reading 'perfeccion'. χSr have only 'þouȝt'. RλAsAECcMPl 'affeccion and þe þoght' is the more cogent reading.

67 *desyreth*. The Latin version, 'desiderat', supports H_7SrH_6CcPl, which take this verb as parallel to 'setteþ'; the RLB_3AsAPM and HBH_5LwHu_2ELdTW variants, 'desiren' and 'for to desiren' respectively, are complements to 'setteþ', and parallel to 'þenken'.

71 *noþinge logwere or wers þan himself is*. The Latin version, 'rebus transitoriis seu terrenis', changes the emphasis from the moral importance of earthly things relative to that of one's own soul to the transitory, earthly nature of the things themselves—dulling the rhetorical force of Hilton's statement.

73 *a gode nyȝt and a lyȝt mirknes*. The phrase 'gode nyȝt' echoes Gilbert of Hoyland, *In Cant.*, I. 5; the phrase 'lyȝt mirknes' is also used in the *Cloud*-author's *Priv. Couns.* 154, l. 17. These terms and others like them ('ryche noȝt', 'blyndenes') play an important part in the description of the contemplative experience in this section of *Scale* II (see below, ll. 109, 27/85, 138, 171, and 28/70). Clark, '"Lightsome Darkness"', points out that for Hilton, the experience of one's own nothingness is a gift of grace in which the height of contemplation occurs; in the apophatic mysticism of the *Cloud*-corpus, the 'un-knowing' of the nothing that is the closest that the human soul can come to conceiving of God is itself the height of contemplation.

76 *God*. The Latin version, 'Jesu et per deuotas preces ad ipsum fusas', adds a devotional emphasis.

80 Mic. 7: 8.

84 *and . . . þynful* (l. 85). The eye-skip omisson in H_7LwW is presumably coincidental. The *Cloud*, chapter 69, also describes the 'trauayle' and 'pain' of first encountering 'þis nouȝt'; but the travail described there is that of encountering and effacing the memory of sin.

88 *only*. The Latin version, 'nisi de', supports either of the two English variants, 'only of' or 'only on'. The lack of a preposition in H_7 may be the result of eye-skip in a copy with the reading 'on'.

94 *toucheth*. The Latin version, 'tangit eum', supports the addition of 'him' in H_5`L'B_3EPH_6.

Hilton also describes the impossibility of removing sin and temptation from one's heart by one's own effort in *Scale* I, Chapter 90.

97 *abyde grace*. The Latin version expands to 'expecta, occupando te in oracionibus quousque detur gracia'.

99 *to Jesu*. The Latin version expands to 'ab eis ad nudam fidem et ad memoriam Jesu Christi'.

102 *entred in*. The Latin version, 'intrasti hanc obscuritatem', supports the B_3AsSrPM variant 'entred into'.

107 *gadred into itself*. The use of the word 'gadred' to describe the contemplative technique of recollection, probably based on Gregory's *Hom. in Ezech*. 2. 5. 9, is characteristic of Hilton: he uses it also in *Scale* I, Chapters 42 and 52, and below, at 30/10 and 42/23. *MED* does not record it in this technical sense: 'gaderen' *v*. 2 e (b) is closest. The opening of chapter 68 of the *Cloud* (l. 121) seems to refer with ambivalence to Hilton's use of the term in *Scale* I: 'wher anoþer man wolde bid þee gader þi miȝtes holiche wiþ-inne þi-self, and worschip God þere—þof al he sey ful wel and ful trewly, ȝe! and no man trewlier and he be wel conseiuid—ȝit for feerde of disseite and bodely conceyuyng of his wordes, me list not byd þee do so.'

it lysteþ to þenk on ryȝt noȝt. If the additional negative of χSr 'lust not' is not a strengthening of the negative of 'to þenk on ryȝt noȝt' but (as it appears) a double negative, it is a misreading of Hilton's text.

109 *in a gode mirknes*. The Latin version expands 'in bona nocte . . . seu in bona obscuritate'. See ll. 73 above, 27/85, 138, 171, and 28/70 below.

110 *þat a soule . . . erthly thinge. þan . . . clefendly* (l. 114). The Latin version converts the first of these sentences into a temporal clause dependent on the second: 'quod quando anima . . . aliquod terrenum / tunc . . . adhesiue'.

113 *clefynge*. The Latin version, 'eleccione', supports the λE variant 'chesinge'. The variant is presumably a case of confusion of graphic similars: 'le' taken for 'he', and 'f' for staff 's'—which would argue for an 'f'- rather than a 'v'-spelling of 'clefynge' in the exemplar.

116 *erthly þinge*. The Latin version, 'alicuius terreni', supports the χE variant in including the quantifier 'ony'.

120 *For . . . Jesu* (l. 121). If, as seems probable, this phrase has been omitted in H°H_5T by eye-skip, then the original reading of their exemplars must have ended, not with 'God', like RAs`$H^{c'}$APl, but with 'Jesu'.

126 *trewe*. The Latin version, 'lumine vero', supports BLA-Hu_2EPCcMPlTW 'trewe lyȝt'; H_7RSrH_6 support 'trewe' without the repeated head noun; B_3As substitute the noun 'trouþe'. HH_5Lw have 'trew luf' (corrected to 'lyȝt' in Lw); H_5 extends this to 'loue of Jesu'; these latter variants might be the result of a scribal confusion of 'luf' and 'lyȝt'.

138 *And þan . . . cowthe* (l. 145). The Latin version, 'Et si oculus tuus tunc isto modo incipiat respondere, nichil vellem videre; et postea auris, nichil vellem audire; et postea os dicat, nichil vellem gustare, nichil vellem loqui de terrenis; et nasus dicat, nichil vellem odorare; et corpus, nichil vellem tangere; et postea cor tuum dicat, nichil cogitare vellem de terrenis vel operibus corporalibus. nec habere vellem affeccionem carnaliter firmatam in aliqua creatura, set solum in Domino Jesu Christo si scirem', supports HBH_5λSrWsLwHu$_2$ECcMLd, which is the more cogent reading. The parallelism of the phrases describing the responses of the various senses to the question whether they would prefer their own activity (directed to earthly ends) to the love of God has resulted in a number of transpositions and omissions among the various manuscripts. LwW transpose the words of the ear and the mouth; Hu$_2$ omits the first part of the words of the mouth ('sauour'); H_7W omit the second part of the words of the mouth ('speke') and the words of the nose; As omits the words of the body and the words of the heart up to 'þenken ryȝt noȝt'; and RAPl omit the words of the body (RA also omits the following 'and'). It should be noted that the omission in H_7 occurs in the top line of a new folio, and may have been occasioned by a break in the scribe's attention.

142–3 *þin herte seyþ*. H_7 reads 'seyþ' here as indicative—thus parallel to, not consequent upon, 'And þan if þin eyghe bygynne and answere' above. RλSrE 'After, if thy hert seith', repeats the 'if' of the beginning of the sentence, but with the indicative; ACcMPl have 'if', but with the subjunctive. χ reads 'it' instead of 'if', and continues with the subjunctive. The Latin version reads 'et postea cor tuum dicat'.

143 *þinges*. H_7Td are plural here, where the Σ reading is singular; the reading of all English manuscripts in the parallel 'dede' is singular. The Latin version is plural in both, 'de terrenis vel operibus corporalibus'.

CHAPTER 25

8 *vnseable lyght*. The light of God that is so pure that it is unseeable is a common trope in contemplative literature, dating back at least to Gregory, *Mor. in Job* 22. 4. 6.

9–10 See Rom. 13: 12: 'Nox praecessit, dies autem appropinquavit.'

11 Isa. 26: 9. See above, 24/25.

17–18 An expression of the cooperation of the contemplative soul with the gift of grace. The phrase 'vse þe'—'accustom yourself'—may echo Richard of St-Victor's allegorization of Aaron (*Benj. Maj.* 5. 1), who 'had it in keping and in costume to see and fele þe ark when hym list', as translated in the *Cloud*, chapter 73. Hilton will speak of the contemplative's ability to accustom himself to this grace below, 27/20–5.

18–19 *to wonen . . . by . . . to ben homly þerin*. The two infinitives 'to wonen' and 'to ben' are parallel: 'accustom yourself to dwell in this mirkness, and—by attempting often—to become familiar in it'. HBSrLwECc 'be' is to be taken as a spelling for 'by'. The Latin version adds a devotional note:

'exerceas te ad manendum in hac obscuritate (id est ad cogitandum stabiliter de Jesu Christo, de eius caritate, paciencia, humilitate, et passione) et per frequentem experienciam familiaris esse in eadem'. Hilton's 'homly' (translated by Fishlake as 'familiaris') may echo the 'familiaritas' of God and the soul that Richard of St-Victor describes in *Benj. Min.* 11.

21 Isa. 9: 2.

29 *cranes*. The Latin version, 'rimas', supports H_7RLB_3SrAPMPl, the more cogent reading, over **χ**E 'caues' or AsH_6Cc 'creues' (a spelling, presumably, for 'crevise'). This use of the word 'crannies' pre-dates the earliest example in *OED* by fifty years. The term 'rimae contemplationis' is one that Gregory uses, e.g. *Mor. in Job* 5. 29. 52, *Hom. in Ezech.* 2. 5. 16, to describe the 'glimmerings' of contemplative illumination.

33 *fyre*. H_7 'feyþ' is inappropriate.

34 *abofe*. H_7 'aboþe' is nonsense.

37 Ezek. 40. The following exposition derives from Gregory, *Hom. in Ezech.* 2. 5. 1.

40 *rede*. The word used by the scriptural text is 'calamo', which is more appropriately translated as 'reed' than as H⌜L⌝Hu_2P⌜Ld⌝TW^G 'rod' or 'rood' here, and RLwCcPlTW^G below, at 25/50.

48 *lyfe*. The Latin version, 'monte', supports **χ**RBAsECcMPl 'hille'. H_7**λ**SrA 'lyfe' is probably a scribal error involving rationalization ('the life of contemplation'), repetition ('lufe' and 'lyfe'), and the graphic similarity of 'hille' and 'lyfe'. 'Hille' is the more cogent reading: Hilton is thinking here in terms of the allegorization of the text of Ezechiel, in which the city of Jerusalem (allegorically, 'þe perfyte lufe of God') is situated on the 'hille' of contemplation. Zion, originally a fortified hill within Jerusalem, came to signify God's holy place (Ps. 2: 6 and 131: 13, Isa. 46: 13) and was used as a metonym for the city itself (Isa. 1: 27).

52 *touchynge*. The Latin version, 'degustacio', must depend on an English exemplar reading 'tasting', a variant that does not occur in any of the surviving English manuscripts.

CHAPTER 26

4 *mydday fend*. The 'daimonium meridianum' of Ps. 90: 6 (the Psalm 'Qui habitat'). Richard of St-Victor speaks of the devil transforming himself into an angel of light (see 2 Cor. 11: 14) in *Benj. Min.* chapter 81, but Hilton's primary source here is Bernard, *Serm. super Cant.* 33. 5. 9. The present chapter criticizes what Hilton sees as false forms of spiritual insight connected with heresy on the one side (neither the 'Free Spirit' heresy nor Wycliffism is specifically named, although both are possible targets) or with enthusiasm like that of Richard Rolle on the other. Hilton's *Qui habitat*, in *An Exposition*, ed. Wallner, 21, offers a direct parallel to the present passage; parallels to the *Qui habitat* commentary and references to the Psalm text will recur through the remainder of *Scale* II. See Clark, 'Walter Hilton and the Psalm Commentary *Qui habitat*'.

5 *seyþ*. The Latin version, 'videt', supports Σ 'seeþ'—the normal spelling for 'sees'. H_7H_5 'seyþ' is either a variant spelling of this or—if 'says' is what the scribe truly intended—the result of a confusion of graphic similars.

6 *in*. Because 'dysceyuynge' is not the subject of this clause, the H_7 omission of the preceding preposition is in error.

7 *hem þat arn vnwyse*. The Latin version uses the technical term in the discourse of the contemplative life, 'incipientes'.

17 *clere . . . clowdes* (l. 18). The Latin version expands to 'clarum est et valde serenum a nigris nubibus obscuris'.

18 The remainder of this chapter expands upon ideas expressed in Hilton's *Eight Chapters*, chapter 3, in *English Mystics*, ed. Windeatt, 140–2.

22–3 *ne how noȝt þei are in here owen kynde anentys God*. The Latin version omits this phrase, which emphasizes that the human subject is by his very nature nothing in comparison with God, thus focusing the statement rather on the subject's awareness of his sinfulness.

24 *slen*. The Latin version, 'destruere', supports $H_7HRH_5LB_3AsSr$-APH_6CcMPl over $BLwHu_2ELdTW$ 'fleen'. The Latin version also adds a devotional element: 'per memoriam passionis'.

31 *in*. The H_7 variant probably depends on a confusion of the abbreviated form of 'and' for 'in'.

46–56 This discussion of false knowledge is paralleled in Hilton's *Qui habitat*, in *An Exposition*, ed. Wallner, 17–23; the reference to the sun shining out 'bitwene two blake cloudes' is at 22–3.

49 *in*. The same confusion in H_7 as above at 26/31.

alowynge. *MED* records the *adv*. 'aloue', but no *v*. 'a-louen' or 'on-lowen' from which the present form, a verbal noun, would derive. See also Hilton's coinage 'a-doun-castynge' in the parallel discussion at *Qui habitat*, *An Exposition*, ed. Wallner, 23, l. 3. The meaning in either case is 'deprecation' or 'dismissal'.

54 *of*. The H_7 reading 'if' makes sense only locally, 'if a mans owen wytte', ignoring the remainder of the sentence.

58 *þei are so blent with þis feyned ly3t*. See 41/90 below.

59 *and*. The Latin version, 'et', agrees with $H_7LB_3SrLwEPH_6CcMLdTW$ over the HRH_5AsAHu_2Pl omission. The omission misses Hilton's point that those who have this false knowing mistake their own pride and disobedience

to the laws of the Church for perfect meekness and obedience to the law of God. The B variant appears to be an attempt to make sense of the sentence.

61–2 *fredam of spyryt*. This may be a reference to the 'Free Spirit' heresy, which is not known to have had the currency in England that it appears to have had on the European continent, or it may be a reference to an antinomianism that was commonly attributed to late medieval heretical movements more generally. See Robert Lerner, *The Heresy of the Free Spirit in the Later Middle Ages* (Notre Dame, Ind., 1972); J. P. H. Clark, 'Walter Hilton and "Liberty of Spirit"', *DR* 96 (1978), 61–78; but also Kathryn Kerby-Fulton, *Books under Suspicion: Censorship and Tolerance of Revelatory Writing in Late Medieval England* (Notre Dame, Ind., 2006), 260–96. Hilton's parallel discussion in *Qui habitat*, in *An Exposition*, ed. Wallner, 22 describes a more emphatically antinomian position, but does not mention freedom of spirit; that in *Eight Chapters*, in *English Mystics*, ed. Windeatt, 141, does mention 'the spirit of fredom' and the justification of this freedom based on 2 Cor. 3: 17 and Gal. 5: 18.

63 *reynen*. The $H_7BH_5\lambda SrHu_2LdCcMT$ variant, which continues the cloud metaphor, seems more cogent than the RAsLw⌜H^c⌝AEPlW variant 'schewen'. The Latin version, 'seminant', appears to derive from a further variant, 'sewen', which does not occur among the surviving English manuscripts, but is perhaps an error for 'schewen'.

64 *into*. The Latin version, 'totaliter in detraccionem', supports Σ, 'al to', over H_7.

67 See James 3: 14–16: 'Quod si zelum amarum habetis, et contentiones sint in cordibus vestris: nolite gloriari, et mendaces esse adversus veritatem: non est enim ista sapientia desursum descendens: sed terrena, animalis, diabolica. Ubi enim zelus et contentio ibi inconstantia, et omne opus pravum', concatenated with James 1: 17: 'Omne datum optimum, et omne donum perfectum desursum est, descendens a Patre luminum, apud quem non est transmutatio, nec vicissitudinis obumbratio.'

72–3 *be þese toknes*. For the moral discretion of spiritual impulses based on Matt. 7: 16, 'By their fruits you shall know them', see Hilton's *De Lecc.*, *LW*, ii. 231.

78 *blake*. The Latin version, 'atris', supports $H_7\lambda AsSrAECcPl$ over the χM omission.

79 *brennend desyre to Jesu in þis mirknes*. The Latin version omits Hilton's mention of 'mirknes', and adds instead a devotional note: 'et per consideracionem passionis sue'.

81 Ps. 96: 3. Hilton's invocation of this text is similar to that in Bernard, *Serm. super Cant.* 31. 2. 4.

86 *brent in þis fyre of desyre.* Hilton will expand on this metaphor below, 28/40–4.

91 *vnderstondynge.* The Latin version, 'intelligencie', here supports H_7RλAsSrACcMPl over χE, 'gostly knowynge'.

92 Mal. 4: 2.

96 *vndere God.* The Latin version adds imaginative detail: 'sub pedibus Christi'.

97 *reuerent . . . lastendly* (l. 98). The Latin version adds a further devotional emphasis, 'reuerenciam et timorem et spiritualem consideracionem continuam humanitatis sue et humilitatis'.

102 *sunne.* The Latin version adds a devotional emphasis, 'solis Jesu Christi qui in cruce pependit obscurus pro angustia et dolore'. Fishlake's image of Christ, the true sun, obscured by anguish and sorrow, contradicts Hilton's earlier metaphor of the light that appears between two dark, rainy clouds as the false light of the enemy.

105 *in mirknes.* The Latin version again adds a devotional emphasis, 'sub misericordi protectione passionis Jesu Christi'.

110 *mirknes.* The Latin version expands this occurrence of 'mirknes' to 'tenebris huius vitae'.

119 *mirknes.* The Latin version translates this occurrence of 'mirknes' as 'consideracione humilitatis Jesu Christi'.

CHAPTER 27

18 *first . . . hemself.* The Latin version, 'quia est cognicio quam primo habent de seipsis et eleuacio supra seipsas', supports this reading. The eye-skip omisson in H_7 leaves out a necessary part of the sentence.

19 *soth.* The χAsE variant 'soþly', with which the Latin version, 'magis verum', agrees, makes clear that 'soth' is here an adverb.

20–5 See above, 25/17–18.

20 *and*[2]. The Latin version, 'et', supports H_7RλSrAPl over χAsECcM 'or'.

21 *þat.* The omission in H_7 is an error; 'þat' is necessary to the phrase.

24 *sett in þe gate of contemplacyon.* See below, ll. 100–1, 113, 123.

29 *be fre of himself and may.* The omission of this phrase in As may be an indication like 21/115–16 above, of a desire to remove references to differences of religious or lay obedience among the readers.

may go where he wil. The Latin version, 'ire possit quo voluerit', supports H_7RλSrACcMPl over χE, 'may do what he wil'. The 'go where he wil' reading might reflect the kind of criticism that was levelled at Richard Rolle for his changes of hermitage: see Nicholas Watson, *Richard Rolle and the Invention of Authority* (Cambridge, 1991), 47–50.

38–9 *leren for to dyen to þe werd.* The period after the Plague saw the rise of an entire literature on the *disce mori* theme, of which the most salient example is probably the chapter on the *ars moriendi* from Heinrich Seuse's *Horologium Sapientiae*, which was translated into English as chapter 5 of the *Seven Points of True Love and Everlasting Wisdom* (Karl Horstmann, '*Orologium Sapientiae*, or *The Seven Poyntes of Trewe Wisdom* aus MS Douce 114', *Anglia*, 10 [1888], 323–89). This chapter was also translated three times independently in prose, and (partially) in Hoccleve's *Series*; see '*My Compleinte' and Other Poems*, ed. Roger Ellis (Exeter, 2001), 196–233. See Roger Lovatt, 'Henry Suso and the Medieval Mystical Tradition in England', *MMTE* 2 (1982), 47–62.

39–80 This treatment of the deadly sins, of which Bernard's *Serm. in Quad.* 6 is an important source, parallels *Scale* I, Chapters 56–76; the theme will recur below in Chapters 37–9.

40 *wurchipe of þe werd . . . benefyce ne riches* (l. 42). It is possible that there is a personal note in this, reflecting Hilton's rejection of his own worldly career (see above, pp. lxxv-lxxvi).

42 *benefyce.* The Latin version, 'beneficium', supports the singular H_7H_5SrAECcLd variant over the plural 'benefices' of HRBλAsL-wHu_2MPlTW.

44 *afore.* The Latin version, 'pre', supports the H_7 variant (and B_3 'before') over χRLAsSrAEPH_6CcMPl 'abofe'.

He schal coueyten none of al þis. MS Y of the Latin version reads 'Desiderabit homo de omnibus iam dictis', which directly contradicts Hilton's saying. The other Latin manuscripts read 'non' rather than 'homo', where one would expect 'nullum' or 'nihil'. One can only wonder whether Fishlake accidently carried over a word of the original English text, 'non', into his translation.

þis. As the Latin version makes clear, this is to be read as plural.

46 *in herte.* The Latin version, 'in corde', supports H_7RλSr`Lw´AECcMPlW over the HBH_5AsHu_2LdT omission.

47 *forȝeten of þe werd.* The Latin adds 'totaliter'.

48 *þat he suffre not his herte resten / . . . / wenende / . . . / for he forsakeþ / . . . / and þerfor lete wel by himself* (l. 51). H_7H°BL$B_3$$Hu_2$PMLd 'lete' here is parallel with the subjunctive 'suffre', rather than with indicative 'forsakeþ', as the RH_5AsSr `H^c´CcPl variant 'leteþ' would have it (also W 'setteth ', Lw 'leetheth', and E 'demeþ'). The Latin version, 'iudicando', is parallel with 'estimando': 'wenende'. H_6 'to lete' mistakes the subjunctive form for an infinitive, thus parallel to 'resten'. The sense here is *MED* lēten *v.* 14: '~

wel': 'be happy or pleased' (with the same following negative as in 'suffre not' understood)—'that he be not pleased with himself therefore'.

53 *þat he desese no man ne anger hem vnskilfully*. The Latin version of this phrase, 'vt nullum hominem molestet vel ad iram prouocet', supports the singular 'him' of χRAPl over the plural of H_7λCcM. E repeats 'no man'. Hilton may have intended a reflexive reading here: 'that he displease no man, nor anger himself unreasonably'. As reads the phrase both positively and reflexively: 'no man, ne himselfe'.

59 *whan*. The Latin version, 'quando', supports H_7RλAsSrLwAMPlW over HBH_5Hu_2ECcT 'what' or Ld 'whatt so'.

it. The Latin version, 'illam', supports H_7RSrMPl over the χλAsECc omission. HBH_5Hu_2ECcT have already supplied the verb 'ȝif' with a direct object, the preceding 'what' (Ld 'whatt so'); λAsLwAW leave the verb without a direct object.

60 *of*[1]. The Latin version, 'alicuius'. supports the χ addition of 'ony'.

60–61 *erdly* (*bis*). The Latin version, 'terreni' (*bis*), may support H_7, with which M agrees, with the addition of 'fleshly or' in the second instance; $χB_3$AsE have 'werdly' in both instances, which one would expect to see translated as 'secularis'; $RLSrAPH_6$CcPl have 'erdly gode' and 'werdly frende'.

63 *oþer*. The Latin version, 'alias', supports H_7RλSrACcMPl over the χAsE addition of 'al'.

65 This passage echoes the treatment of lechery in *Eight Chapters*, chapter 5, in *English Mystics*, ed. Windeatt, 143–4.

68 *vnclene and grete synne. For it is a grete synne*. The Latin version, 'inmundus. Et graue peccatum est', seems to derive from an English version that omitted 'grete synne. For it' by eye-skip; As similarly omits 'For . . . synne'.

75 This passage echoes the treatment of gluttony in *Scale* I, Chapter 72.

82 *and al oþer . . . may*. H, like H_5As, omits this passage by eye-skip; it was restored by a corrector who apparently compared H to a manuscript like LwW, which omit the words 'al' and 'not' that are characteristic of the other χ manuscripts. The BH_5Hu_2LdT variant with 'not' takes the following clause as subsequent to 'letten him'; the $H_7RLB_3SrLwH^cAEPH_6$CcMPlW reading takes it as subsequent to 'behoueth forsaken'.

85–6 *he þat*. The Latin version, 'vt . . . attingere valeat', supports the purpose clause, 'þat he miȝt' of $HRBH_5$λAsWsLwAECcMLdTW over the restrictive relative clause 'he þat myȝt' come' of H_7SrHu_2. The reading 'he þat' also occurs at l. 88, 'he þat forsakeþ', which might have contributed to scribal confusion at this point.

85 *mirknes of knowwynge*. The Latin version has 'cognicionem humilem'. This might be a deliberate alteration rather than a misreading of 'mirknes' as 'mekenes' (a variant that does not occur among the English manuscripts), especially in the light of 27/138 'gode mirknes'—'bona humilitas'; 27/171 'mirknes'—'humilitate humanitatis Christi'; and 28/70 'mirknes'—'humilitatem vel obscuritatem'. In either case, the exemplar from which the variation derives must have read 'mirknes' like H_7HRLSrPCcMPl, and not 'derknesse' like BH_5B_3LwAHu_2EH_6LdTW. Either Fishlake (or an exemplar of the English manuscript he used) did not understand the word 'mirknes', or he was uncomfortable with Hilton's description of the contemplative experience..

87 Gal. 6: 14, cited in Bernard, *Serm. in Quad.* 6 (7). 3.

90–1 *lufeþ . . . desyreþ . . . pursueþ*. The evidence of the English manuscripts is divided, with HRH_5AsLwAHu_2PlTW omitting 'ne desyreþ it not'. The Latin version, 'et nichil tale mundanum desiderat vel prosequitur', appears to derive from an English text lacking 'lufeþ'.

92 *þe werd he*. The Latin version, 'sibi mundus', supports Σ 'him þe werld' over H_7.

94 *do*. The subjunctive form of the H_7Sr variant (H_6 'ne do') is appropriate for the conditional 'if' statement. The preceding verb form 'sett' is subjunctive, but the remainder of the parallel verbs in this sentence ('haþ', 'setteþ', forȝeteþ') are all indicative in all manuscripts. The RAPL variant 'to do' (Cc 'ne to do') confuses the issue, but may have resulted from an attempt to rationalize the form 'do' as a specification of the way in which the world has no regard for the contemplative. In the Latin version, all the verbs in this series are subjunctive: 'si . . . reputet siue curet . . . faciat . . . tradat'.

98 *vntil*. The Latin version, 'nisi', supports χAsE 'but if'.

100–1 *þe gate to contemplacyon*. See ll. 24 above, 113, 123 below.

104 *as are religyouse and seculers*. RAMPl omit this reference to the state of living of the contemplative. See above, 21/115–16.

106 *hafe*. Cc adds a reference to the state of living of the contemplative, 'to a soule whethir it be seculer or reguler', as does M, 'be hit seculer or religious'.

108 *lufe*. The Latin version, 'amorem', supports H_7M over χRλAsSrECc 'his lufe'; M adds 'of þe world'. The Latin version adds a devotional expansion, 'per diligentem consideracionem Christi et humilitatis sue'.

113 *a þefe and a breker of þe wal*. The Latin version has 'fur, murique confractor'. There is an echo here of John 10: 1: 'He that entreth not by the door into the sheepfold, but climbeth up another way, the same is a thief and a robber.' Hilton uses the same image in *Scale* I, Chapter 91. The contrast is with those who are 'sett in þe gate of contemplacyon', ll. 24, 100–1 above,

123 below. The same metaphor is employed in the *Cloud*-author's *Book of Privy Counselling*, 159–60.

117 Col. 3: 3, cited in Bernard, *Serm. in Quad.* 6 (7). 3.

123 *þis gate*. See ll. 24, 100–1, 113 above.

124–5 Matt. 19: 29. In the modern Vulgate text, 'Et omnis qui reliquerit domum, vel fratres, aut sorores, aut patrem, aut matrem, aut uxorem, aut filios, aut agros propter nomen meum . . .'. See below, 39/28 and *Eight Chapters*, Chapter 1, in *English Mystics*, ed. Windeatt, 137.

129 *þe profyte . . . contemplacyon*. The Latin version omits Hilton's reference to 'mirknes' and substitutes a more devotional aim: 'pacifica confortacio in consciencia quam sentit anima que veraciter humiliatur sub passione Christi'.

136 *þan . . . wil* (l. 137). The scribal revisions to the preceding lines in H (particularly the addition and cancellation of 'he haþ þat most'), and the omission of 'haþ' in H_5, show that a common exemplar of HH_5 probably agreed with $H_7LB_3SrPH_6CcM$ in the present reading rather than with $RBAsLwH^cAHu_2ELdPlTW$, 'þan he þat most coueitiþ of þe werld and haþ alle þe welþe of it vnder his wil haþ'. The variation may have arisen in a scribal attempt to clarify Hilton's complex sentence.

138 *a gode mirknes and a ryche noȝt*. See ll. 24/73 and 109, and 27/85 above, 171 and 28/70 below. The Latin translation, 'humilitas', presumably depended on an English exemplar reading 'mekenes' in error for 'mirknes', like $H_7HRLSrPCcMPl$, rather than 'derknesse' like $BH_5B_3AsLwAHu_2EH_6LdTW$.

140 *niȝt*. The Latin version, 'adnichilacione', supports $H_5\lambda SrM$ 'noȝt'. $H_7H^oBHu_2LdT$ 'niȝt' makes sense as a concrete metaphor for the concept of 'mirknes', which has just been mentioned. The combination of the two terms in $RLwH^cAECcPlW$, 'niȝt or . . . nouȝt', suggests scribal confusion at this point at a very early stage in the transmission of the text.

Ps. 72: 22.

142 *brent*. The Latin version, 'adnichilauit', supports Σ 'broȝt' over H_7LB_3P 'brent'.

146 *fulsumly fele þe lufe of Jesu*. An allusion to the reformation in faith and in feeling that is the focus of *Scale* II.

147 *lufe*. The Latin version adds a devotional expansion, 'et humiliare seipsum continue sub humili humanitate Jesu Christi'.

151–2 Isa. 50: 10.

155 *sadly*. The Latin version, 'firmiter', supports $H_7R\lambda AsSrACcPl$ over the χEM omission.

156 *mekly*. The Latin version, 'humiliter', supports $H_7R\lambda AsSrACcPl$ over the χEM omission.

157 *as it doþ be a man þat had ben*. The Latin version, 'sicut de homine qui diu stetit', supports H_7RλAsSrAECcPl over χM 'as it doþ if a man had ben'.

158 *comeþ*. The verbs of this sentence ('had', 'comeþ', 'schyneþ') are all in the indicative in H_7As and M, as in the Latin version ('stetit', 'intrat', splendet'); the variant 'come', although it is the form presented by the majority of the English manuscripts (χRλSrAECcP, including W 'came'), is the only subjunctive form. The verbs of the following clause in H_7, 'be', 'ware', 'seen', are irregular in form, and are probably scribal slips occasioned by the folio turnover occurring amidst them.

159 *blynde*. The *Cloud* employs a similar metaphor, but to a different end: 'þis nouȝt may betir be felt þen seen; for it is ful blynde and ful derk to hem þat han bot lityl while lokid þer-apon.' For Hilton, the blindness of the soul is the temporary result of his turning from the life of this world: for the *Cloud*-author, the darkness is 'All'.

161 *þat*. The Latin version supports H_7RλSrACcPl over the χAsEM addition of 'euer'.

167–9 Isa. 58: 10–11. In the modern Vulgate text: 'Orietur . . . Dominus semper, et implebit splendoribus animam tuam.'

171 *in þis mirknes*. The Latin version omits Hilton's reference to 'mirknes' and substitutes a more devotional aim: 'in humilitate humanitatis Christi', leaving the explanation of the term 'mirknes' ('tenebras') in the next line without an antecedent.

172–3 *þi myrknes of trauellend desyre and þi blynd trust in God*. See ll. 24/73 and 109, and 27/85 and 138 above, and 28/70 below.

182 *him*. The Latin version adds a devotional expansion: 'et eius benedictam faciem intueri'.

184–5 Isa. 47: 5.

185–7 *Go . . . mirknes*. The Latin version omits.

CHAPTER 28

9–10 Ps. 138: 12.

11 *forsakynge*. The Latin version translates as 'abieccio seu expulsio'.

12 *He formeþ . . . al þis* (l. 14). Hilton here echoes Augustine, *Sermo* 169. 13: 'Qui ergo fecit te sine te, non te justificavit sine te.' For Hilton, this concept is referred specifically to the idea, developed by scholastic theologians, of cooperant grace (see above, note to 20/64).

15–17 Rom. 8: 29–30. In the modern Vulgate text: 'Nam quos praescivit, et praedestinavit conformes fieri imaginis Filii sui, . . . Quos autem praedestinavit, hos et vocavit, et quos vocavit, hos et iustificavit: quos autem iustificavit, illos et glorificavit.' The reference to 'magnificauit' between 'iustificauit' and 'glorificauit' is a common medieval addition.

21 *þogh al.* The second element here should not be understood as a determiner modifying 'þese wurdes', but as part of the conjunction equivalent to PDE 'although'.

24 *Jesu.* The Latin version, 'Deus', supports χRAsSrAPl 'God' over H_7λCc.

35 See *Eight Chapters*, chapter 2, in *English Mystics*, ed. Windeatt, 138–40.

36 *setteþ . . . strekeþ* (l. 37). The Latin version reads these two verbs as infinitives, parallel to the immediately preceding 'go': 'procedere' . . . 'apponere' . . . 'extendere'. Of the English manuscripts, HBAs read 'setten', but none has the infinitive for 'strekeþ'. The majority of the English manuscript tradition reads 'setteþ' and 'strekeþ' as indicative, parallel to the preceding 'bygynneþ'.

synnes. The Latin version, 'peccatis', supports the plural of H_7RλSrACcMPl over the singular of χAsE.

38 *withinne.* The original reading of H agrees with this, but the final '-yn' was cancelled to make the text agree with H_5LwW; the next line has parallel 'withouten' (withoutforth TW).

39 *temptacyons.* The Latin version, 'temptacionibus', supports the plural of H_7RλSrAECcPl over the singular of χAsM.

41 *croked.* The prefix 'in-' in the Latin version, 'incuruatus', is to be taken as an intensifier and not a negation.

werd. The Latin version adds 'et hoc non videt'.

48–57 A similar discussion of the mortification of the soul occurs in Hilton, *Qui habitat*, in *Exposition*, ed. Wallner, i, ll. 3–4. Clark, 'Walter Hilton and the Psalm Commentary *Qui habitat*', 235–6, suggests that both texts derive from Bernard *Qui hab.* 16. 482.

48 *til þat.* H_7, apparently taking 'þat' as the pronoun object of the preposition 'til', rather than as a subordinating particle coordinate with 'til', inserts preceding 'and', as does H_5.

þe rust of vnclennes myȝt be brent out of it. Hilton uses the same expression in *Eight Chapters*, chapter 4, in *English Mystics*, ed. Windeatt, 142: 'this brennand desire wole clense the conscience fro al rust of synne.'

49 *dredys.* The Latin version, 'actus', probably derives from an English exemplar reading 'dedys', a variant not attested by any surviving English manuscript.

50 *for it schal semen.* The corrected reading of H, 'and it shal seme', agrees with W alone.

51 *forsaken of God.* So also in *Scale* I, Chapter 38. According to Clark, 'Notes' 314 n. 185, both reflect Flete, *De Remed.*

60 *were þat*. Perhaps influenced by 'where' in the preceding line, H_7 has confused the graphic similars 'were þat' and, presumably, 'wheþer', for which 'where' is a common contracted form.

66 *profyte of þe soule*. The Latin version adds a devotional expansion: 'ad humiliandum hominem vt cognoscat peccata sua'.

in. H_7 'and' occludes the relationship between 'rest' and 'fleschly felynge'. The scribe mistakes 'and' for 'in' and vice versa several times in *Scale* II; in his own hand, 'in' and the abbreviation for 'and' are remarkably similar, and they may have been so in his exemplar.

68 *gostly lyȝt*. The Latin version adds a devotional expansion: 'per presenciam Jesu Christi'.

69 *mortifyed and broght . . . into þis mirknes* (l. 70). The Latin version reads 'mirknes' here again as 'meeknes': 'mortificata et humiliata et . . . adducta in hanc humilitatem vel obscuritatem'.

70 *þis mirknes*. See above, ll. 24/73 and 109, and 27/85, 138, and 171.

72 *magnyfyenge*. H_7 has mistaken the verbal noun for a present participle.

78 See Ps. 65: 10–12: 'For thou, O God, hast proved us. . . . We have passed through fire and water.' Clark, 'Notes', 314 n. 186, refers this to Flete, *De Remed*.

80–1 *he schal reysen hem vp*. The Latin version, 'eleuabit eas', supports H_7⌜H^c⌝RSrAECcMPl over BH_5AsHu_2LdT 'rysen vp' (which was also the probable original reading of H) or the **λ** variant 'receyue vp hem / hem vp'. The **χ** variation was probably the result of confusion of the weak verb 'raise' and the strong 'rise'.

86 *tribulacyons*. The Latin version, 'tribulacionis', supports the singular **χ**RAsECc variant 'tribulacion' over H_7**λ**SrAMPl.

87 *Puer . . . te*. From the antiphon 'Puer meus noli timere' (both the antiphon and its responsory have 'quia ego sum tecum' after 'timere'). The text is based on Isa. 43: 1–2: 'Et nunc haec dicit Dominus creans te, Iacob, et formans te, Israel: Noli timere, quia redemi te, et vocavi te nomine tuo; meus es tu. Cum transieris per aquas, tecum ero, et flumina non operient te; cum ambulaveris in igne, non combureris, et flamma non ardebit in te.'

CHAPTER 29

9–10 *confortable hete or grete swetnes*. Hilton is here speaking of 'calor' and 'dulcor' or 'melos', two of the three characteristic experiences (together with song—'canor') of the mysticism of Richard Rolle. Because those who have such experiences have not necessarily passed through the 'mirkness' of 'dying to the world' that is the 'gate of contemplation' (see Chapter 23), the spiritual heat and sweetness felt by those who are newly turned to God are not, according to Hilton, to be mistaken for contemplation itself any more than are compunction for sin, fervour in prayer, or devotion in imaginative meditation. All of these, for Hilton, are preliminary.

13 *it semeþ ȝis*. This is not Hilton's response to his interlocutor's question, but an extension of the question; Hilton's response begins at 29/15. The structure of Hilton's argument is that of a scholastic *questio*, in which the statement of the question is immediately followed by a response that is in fact the opposite of the eventual conclusion, and which will then be shown to be false.

by as mykel as. The H_7 variant can be mistaken for the first part of a comparison by degrees: 'by as much as . . . so much', where the second element is lacking. The reading of the other English manuscripts, 'in as mikel as' is clearer.

16 *gostly ymaginacyon . . . gostly felynges* (l. 17). H_7RλSrACcPl support both occurrences of 'gostly' here, χAsEM only the first, and the Latin version, 'spirituales', only the second.

20 *ne þei kan not ȝit þe ȝifte*. The Latin version, 'ille anime que tales habent sensaciones non adhuc reformantur in sensacione perfeccionis', appears to have been based on an English text that lacked this phrase. The Σ variant 'han not' is more cogent than H_7 'kan not'.

21 *in Jesu*. The genitive form of the Latin version, 'Dei', supports the λEM variant 'of' over H_7χRAsSrACcPl 'in'.

22 *felten*. The present tense of the Latin version, 'senciunt', supports HRH_5AsSrLwAECcMLdTW 'felen' over H_7BλHu_2Pl.

24–5 *and syghynge*. The Latin version, 'suspiriis', supports H_7RBλSrHu_2CcMLdPl over the HH_5AsLwETW omission.

25–6 *bodily sterynge*. The Latin version, 'motibus corporalibus', supports RH_5Sr 'steryngis'. With the exception of 'spekynge', 'loqucione', all the nouns in this series are plural in the Latin although, with the exception of the present variant, they are uniformly singular in the English manuscripts.

27 *me þenkyþ*. The Latin version translates this phrase as 'apparet mihi', an impersonal construction, equivalent to 'it seems' rather than 'I think', which is probably Hilton's intention here, since he immediately proceeds to state that he knows the opposite is true.

28 *felynges*. The Latin version, 'sensaciones et feruores', supports Σ 'felynges and feruours' over H_7.

33 *felynge*. The Latin version, 'ostensione', supports the Σ variant 'schewynge' over H_7.

36 *fleschly, festned to here flesch*. The Latin version, 'carni carnaliter coniuncta', takes 'fleschly' as an adverb rather than an adjective, and thus

reads the English as equivalent to 'fastned to their [*or* the] flesh in a fleshly manner'.

41 *with it*. The Latin expansion, 'a tali tactu nec illum ferre potest vel sustinere', duplicates the following phrase: 'And also it is so new and so sodeyn and so vnkowþe þat it may not suffren for to beren it' / 'et similiter tam nouus et subitus et incognitus quod ipsum ferre non sufficit.'

43 Hilton's metaphor here is based on Jesus' saying, 'Neither do they put new wine into old wineskins. Otherwise the wineskins break, and the wine runneth out, and the wineskins perish' (Matt. 9: 17, Mark 2: 22, and Luke 5: 37–8). In Hilton's use of the metaphor, which derives from Gregory, *Mor. in Job* 23. 11. 20, the fermenting process causes the wineskins to swell up and leak, but it does not destroy them.

44 *and resceyfeþ*. The Latin version, 'continens', supports neither H_7Rλ SrACcMPl nor χAsE 'when it resceifiþ'.

45–6 *haþ boyled*. The subjunctive of the Latin version, 'ebullieret', supports HRBH_5AsLwAEMLdTW 'haue boylid' over H_7LB_3SrHu_2PH_6CcPl.

47 *stille and . . . hol*. H_7R 'stille in . . .' would isolate 'hol' as modifying, but following, 'costret', which is syntactically inappropriate. Presumably, this is another case of the confusion of the forms 'in' and 'and': see above, 26/31.

68 *þan . . . þat*. The Latin version multiplies the temporal deixis of this sentence: 'Tunc est verum . . . quando talia confortatiua et feruores que anima sentit dum est in statu . . .'. The intent may have been clarification, but the result is that the sentence lacks a main clause.

71 *þat trauayleþ*. The Latin version, 'laborans', does not agree precisely with any English version, but supports H_7λSrAECcPl over χRBAsM 'traueileþ', which is paralleled by the following 'falliþ' without a coordinating conjunction.

77 *oure Lord, hafend pyte ouer al his creatures*. Ps. 144: 8–9, 'The Lord is gracious and merciful: patient and plenteous in mercy. The Lord is sweet to all: and his tender mercies are over all his works.'

84–97 Chapter 72 of the *Cloud* also observes that the contemplative will come to the perfection of this work only by long and hard travail, but that when they reach that end, 'þei schulen haue it whan þei wile, as ofte as hem likiþ' (128, ll. 1–2).

92 *homlynes with hem*. The Latin version expands this and makes it more explicit: 'familiaritatem cum Dei gracia vel presencia Jesu Christi'.

95 *gostly þynges*. The Latin version expands, 'rerum spiritualium glorieque celestis'.

CHAPTER 30

In this chapter, Hilton expands on his treatment of sensual and imaginative devotion in *Scale* I, Chapter 11.

7–41 Hilton's discussion of the nature of the soul derives from Augustine's dialogue *De Quant. anim.*, esp. chapter 13 (cols. 1047–8), probably mediated by the pseudo-Augustinian *De Spiritu et anima* (*PL* 40, cols. 779–832) and the discussion of the rational man in William of St-Thierry's *Lettre d'or*, 306 ff.

8 *knowynge first.* The Latin version supports χRAsAEMPl over H_7λSrCc in omitting 'first'.

10 *gedred.* See above, 24/107.

16 *in itself . . . felen it* (l. 17). This phrase, which includes the first half of a comparison ('þe more . . . þe ferþer'), is necessary to the sense. The omission in H_7 is probably by eye-skip.

25 *as soþfastnes . . . vertu* (l. 26). An eye-skip omisson in H_7.

30 *in.* H_7 'and', makes no sense here; it probably derives, as elsewhere, from a confusion of the contracted forms of 'in' and 'and'.

34 *þus . . .itself* (l. 36). The omission of this passage in H°H_5As is presumably by eye-skip, and the first half of the passage is omitted in LwW in the same way. In H, the latter half alone is supplied by a corrector, probably working from a copy resembling LwW.

39 *þe vertu . . . han* (l. 40). This is a basic legal principle, first enunciated in the *Institutes* of Ulpian, with which anyone with legal training, like Hilton, would be familiar: 'Justitia est constans et perpetua voluntas jus suum cuique tribuendi.' Hilton's point is that the rational knowledge of what a soul is, or an angel, or God, should be of the same order as this rational knowledge of what justice is.

44 *kynde.* The Latin version, 'cognicio', probably derived from some form of 'ken-' in its English exemplar.

þi soule is bot a myroure. This image derives from the pseudo-Augustinian *De Spiritu et anima*, chapter 52 (*PL* 40: 818), or possibly from Richard of St-Victor, *Benj. Min.*, chapter 72.

47 *þat þou may seen it.* The Latin shifts emphasis slightly: 'vt videre possis in eo teipsam'.

53–7 *For . . . contemplacyon.* This sentence is not translated in the Latin version. It is possible that Fishlake wished to downplay Hilton's rejection of the claim, characteristic of the spirituality of Richard Rolle, that the gifts of fervour and sweetness are marks of true contemplation. Cf. Watson, *Richard Rolle and the Invention of Authority*, 68–9, 113–70. Hilton's view of the secondary nature of these gifts derives from their connection (for him) to imagination, which is usually considered in medieval contemplative literature to be lower than or preparatory to true, intellectual contemplation. Fishlake, on the other hand, seems to be attempting to take every opportunity possible to direct the text more towards imaginative devotion and what Hilton would have thought of as outward, as opposed to inward and spiritual, affect.

58 *þat þe lufe of God is on þre maner wyse.* Descriptions of the types or degrees of love of God are common in late medieval contemplative literature: cf. especially Richard of St-Victor's *De Quatuor Gradibus violentae caritatis*, in *Ives: Épitre à Severin sur la charité, Richard de St-Victor: Les quatres degrés de la violent charité*, ed. Gervais Dumeige (Paris, 1955), or the eighth chapter of Rolle's *Form of Living*, in *English Writings of Richard Rolle, Hermit of Hampole*, ed. Hope Emily Allen (Oxford, 1931), 104–7. Hilton's scheme adds imaginative meditation on the manhood of Christ and 'ghostly sight' of the godhead in the manhood to the overriding theme of *Scale* II: the reformation of the fallen soul to the image of the Trinity in faith alone (which is necessary for salvation) and the reformation of the soul in faith and in feeling. His three types of love of God thus comprise reformation by faith alone, reformation by faith plus imagination of the life and passion of Christ, and affective spiritual realization of the operation of the divinity in the God-man Christ (insofar as that can be achieved in this life), which is reformation in faith and in feeling.

63–4 *in his manhed.* The Latin version, 'et humanitate sua', shows a slight change in emphasis. Where Hilton will go on to contrast imagination of Christ in his manhood with 'ghostly sight' of the godhead in the manhood (a Trinitarian/Christological object of contemplation), Fishlake proposes Christ and his manhood as equal objects of meditation.

65 *and.* The Latin version supports **χ**AsCc over H_7R**λ**SrAEMPl in omititng 'and'.

66 *þe þred lufe is þat þe soule feleth . . . þat is best . . . and þat is perfyte lufe* (l. 68). This sentence comprises three independent clauses in R**λ**SrALwH^{c}EPlW, as in the Latin version, 'Tertia delectio est . . . et hec est . . . et hec dileccio est'. In H°BH_5ACcMLdT the first clause lacks the verb 'is', which reduces the remainder to a relative clause with 'þat' as its subject and 'feleth' as its verb; this in turn renders the second occurrence of 'þat' redundant, since the subject of 'is best' is now 'þe þred lufe' (although LwH^{c}W read 'is þat' both times). The omission of the second occurrence of 'þat' in H_7 (which occurs at a line division) is ungrammatical.

69–88 The best exponent of this kind of imaginative devotion to Christ in Hilton's time is the pseudo-Bonaventuran *Meditationes vitae Christi*, translated into English a few years after the writing of the *Scale* by Nicholas Love as *The Mirror of the Blessed Life of Jesus Christ*.

69 *han . . . fleschly* (l. 71). The Latin version translates only 'þenken on Jesu' and 'lufen' ('cogitant de Jesu Christo et diligunt eum'), omitting Hilton's stress on the limitation of the spiritual gifts of those beginning and progressing in the spiritual life who know only the physical 'conditions and likeness' of Jesus as man, in imagination.

70 *godely*. i.e. 'godly', in his godhead.

73–4 *wurchepyn and lufen him*. The Latin version supports H_7M over $HRBH_5LB_3$AsSrLwAHu_2ECcLdPlTW in not doubling the pronoun.

77 *foot*. The Latin version, 'pedes', supports the plural of χRAsAEMPl over H_7λSrCc.

80–1 *but . . . ben*. The Latin version again omits a clause stressing the limitation of imaginative meditation.

86 *þei beholdyn . . . his passion* (l. 87). The English manuscripts HH_5AsWs-LwECcMW expand 'beholdyn' on the model of the previous sentence to 'beholdyn him, wurschipen him and dreden him'. The Latin version, 'considerant passionem', again omits Hilton's reference to the limitation of imaginative devotion.

92 *oned . . . godhed* (l. 93). The omission of this passage in HH_5WsLwW is probably by eye-skip.

99 *God*. The Latin version, 'de deitate', supports Σ 'þe godhed', over H_7.

102 *for oure Lord . . . so* (l. 104). The Latin version omits Hilton's argument that imagination cannot conceive of the godhead because of the natural limitation of corporality in this life.

105–28 The idea of the manhood of Jesus as an 'overshadowing' by which he 'tempers' his divine protection of the soul is paralleled in Hilton's *Qui habitat*, in *Exposition*, ed. Wallner, 10, l. 15–11, l. 15; 14, l. 1–15, l. 3; see Windeatt, *English Mystics*, 173–75.

119–20 *Spiritus . . . gentes*. The version of Lam. 4: 20 ('Spiritus oris nostri, Christus Dominus, captus est in peccatis nostris, cui diximus: In umbra tua vivemus in gentibus' in the modern Vulgate text) known from the Latin version of Origen's commentary. The text is often cited in this form by Bernard, e.g. *Serm. super Cant.* 31. 3. 8, 48. 3. 6.

124 *vndire þe schadwe of his blissed manhed*. The Latin version adds a devotional expansion, 'sub umbra et proteccione humanitatis sue, et nunquam dimittere fidem, dileccionem, nec cogitacionem assiduam de eadem', which supports HRBAsLwAHu_2MLdPlTW over H_7H_5λSrWsECc in omitting 'blessid'.

128 *to it*. See note to l. 153: 'I sey . . . fleschly' below.

129–55 For medieval contemplative writers, Mary Magdalene was the type of the contemplative life, as her sister Martha was of the active life. Hilton's allegorical treatment of Jesus' words 'Noli me tangere' as referring to carnal and spiritual love of God derives ultimately from Augustine's *Tract. in Ep. Ioan.* 3. 1–2.

130 *to hire*. The Latin version 'sibi' supports H_7λSrAM over the χRAsAECcPl omission.

John 20: 17.

135 *sche*[2]. The Latin version, 'Christus', agrees with the A variant, 'he', which changes the agency of the clause.

148 *for syþen*. This should be read as 'because', and the preceding clause should be read as the result.

151 *and*[2]. The Latin version, 'in', supports the HBH_5ACcLdT variant 'in' over H_7RλAsSrWsLwHu_2EMPlW.

153 *I sey . . . fleschly* (l. 155). This sentence, which appears to be an authorial addition cautioning that the theocentric form of meditation that Hilton has just described does not mean that his reader is being advised to separate the divine from the human nature of Jesus, the God-man, in his meditation, has been incorporated differently into the text in the various manuscripts. Only H_7 places the sentence at its present location; all other mãnuscripts put it at l. 128. In both locations, it immediately precedes the phrase 'þus kend oure Lord . . .', which suggests that it was originally a marginal addition.

The Latin version, 'Non dico quod separare debemus Deum ab homine in Domino Jesu Christo, set diligere debemus Jesum Deum et hominem, Deum in homine hominemque in Deo', supports the H_7λSrE reading. BHu_2LdT omit only the word 'boþe'. H_5Ws and, apparently, the original reading of H omitted 'in Jesu' and 'Jesu boþe God and man', and added 'in al oure herte' after 'schul'; LwCcMW add 'refuse þe manhed of Jesu and' after 'schuld' (in the margin in Lw); LwMW substitute 'þou shalt in Jesu man beholde, drede, wondir and loue gostly þe godhede, and so shalt þou without departyng loue God in man, and both God and man' for 'we schul . . . fleschly'; R omits 'God in man and man in God'; ACcM omit 'in Jesu' (like HH_5Ws); A also omits 'and man in God'; Pl omits 'God in man and man'; and M substitutes its own wording for 'bot we schul . . . fleschly'.

156 *þus*. The Latin version, 'Sic', supports H_7λSrCcM over χRAsAEPl, 'And þus'.

160 *affeccions*. The Latin version, 'affeccionibus', supports the plural of H_7RλSrACcPl over the singular of χAsEM.

163 *herynge . . . sauour* l. 165). Hilton appears to be referring again to Rolle's characteristic experiences of 'calor', 'canor', and 'dulcor' (as well as 'seenge of lyȝt'); Fishlake uses the terms 'auditus cantici', 'sensacio caloris', 'visio luminis', and 'dulcedo corporalis saporis'.

166 *in vnderstondynge and in lufe.* The Latin version gives Hilton's concept a devotional emphasis: 'in intellectu et dileccione Jesu Christi'.

170 *þis . . . Holy Writte.* Hilton's concern here and in the following chapter to ground his theology of the contemplative life in specific citation of Scripture may betray a sensitivity to Wycliffite criticism that 'private religion' (meaning, particularly, the religious orders) does not have any basis in the Gospel, and is in fact based on a fundamentally un-Christian separation of the individual from the community of believers in pursuit of his or her own personal perfection. See Hudson, *The Premature Reformation*, 347–51. Fiona Somerset demonstrates the parallel forms that Wycliffite spirituality might take: 'Wycliffite Spirituality', in Helen Barr and Ann M. Hutchison (eds.), *Text and Controversy from Wyclif to Bale: Essays in Honour of Anne Hudson* (Turnhout, 2005), 375–86, and *Feeling like Saints: Lollard Writings after Wyclif* (Ithaca, NY, 2015).

171–2 Acts 2: 3.

173 *alle here hertes* (l. 174). The Latin version, 'corda', supports χAsE over H_7RλSrACcMPl in omitting 'alle'.

180–1 John 16: 13.

185 *swilk outward felynge* (l. 186). The Latin version, 'tales sensaciones', supports the plural of LB_3PLdTWs 'siche . . . felynges'.

188 *Oþer . . . lufe* (l. 191). The Latin version alters the clauses of this sentence while preserving its logic, by omitting the relative pronoun 'þat' and adding the conjunction 'ideo' before 'non est bonum eis' ('it is not gud to hem').

CHAPTER 31

1 *reformynge.* The Latin version, 'de reformacione', supports the RH_6CcLdPlTW variant 'of reformynge' over H_7LB_3SrAEPM. Hilton is referring specifically to the grounding of the verbal formula ('þis maner of spekynge') in the express words of Scripture, rather than more generally to the theological topic of 'reformynge of a soule in felynge'. The variant 'spekynge of reformynge' presumably arose from a scribal attempt to make local sense grammatically, as did, in another way, the AELdTW addition 'schal be take' after 'felynge'.

12 *where.* This is an accepted spelling for 'wheþer', but one that H_7 does not use elsewhere.

16 *withouten ony trauelle.* Although Hilton describes the 'work' of preparation for reception of the gift of contemplative grace (the 'mikel bodily and gostly besynes' of Chapter 20), this labour can only come into effect through grace (Chapters 20, 40), and in fact grace alone is sufficient (Chapter 35), for the labour is itself a gift of grace.

25–6 Rom. 12: 2. This text is a commonplace in the discourse of the renewal of the image of God in the soul: see Augustine, *De Trin.* 7. 6. 12, 14. 16. 22.

29 *in newhed of felynge.* The Latin version, a combination of repetition and gloss of the scriptural text, 'in nouitate sensus vestri seu sensacionis vestre', supports λEM 'in newehede of ȝoure feelynge'.

31–2 Col. 1: 9.

34 *þis . . . wysdom* (l. 39). H°H_5AsWs omit this, apparently by eye-skip; the H^c correction corresponds to the reading of Lw.

35 *two maner of felynges.* The Latin verson reads 'duplicem . . . sensum seu sensacionem'.

36 *of*[1]. LwH^c omit, apparently understanding 'withouten' here as a preposition, not an adverb: 'one without the five bodily wits', which makes only local sense. The two adverbs, 'withouten' and 'withinne', are parallel.

37–8 *mende, reson and wille.* This trinitarian division of the powers of the soul, *memoria* (the faculty of inherent, eternal knowledge, corresponding to the Father), *intelligentia* (the faculty of reason—the *logos*—corresponding to the Son), and *voluntas* (the faculty of love, correponding to the Spirit), derives from Augustine, *De Trin.* 10. 11. 17–12. 19. The present discussion, which will be expanded upon below at 34/76 draws heavily upon *De Trin.*

41–2 Eph. 4: 23–4. Cited in Augustine, *De Trin.* 12. 7. 12 and 14. 16. 22.

46 *holynes . . . ryȝtwysnes* (l. 48). H°H_5AsWs omit this, apparently by eye-skip; the part supplied by H^c corresponds to the reading of T.

50–2 See Col. 3: 9–10. The phrase 'et induite' in H_7Hu_2 is possibly the result of scribal memory of the scriptural passage, which reads 'et induentes', parallel with 'expoliantes', rather than Hilton's imperative 'induite'. In his following gloss, Hilton uses the imperative for all the verbs here: 'Spoyle ȝoureself . . . caste fro ȝou . . . cloþe ȝou.'

53 *luste.* The Latin version, 'amorem', supports Σ 'lufe'. The H_7 variant may be the result of confusion of graphic similars.

57 *reformed in perfyte knowynge of God.* The Latin version, 'reformari in perfecta dileccione et cognitione Jesu Christi', adds an affective note to Hilton's more abstract formulation.

60 *þer is two maner knowynges.* The number of a head noun modified by 'maner' (or 'maner of') with a plural determiner preceding appears not to be stable in Hilton's usage. Of twenty-four occurrences of 'maner' or 'maner of' throughout the text, eleven modify plural nouns ('felynges', 'ȝiftes', 'knowynges', 'men', 'miracles', 'synnes', 'thynges'), and thirteen singular ('lufe', 'meknes', 'reformyng', 'sinne', 'werkyng', 'wyse'), with varying manuscript support. It is also unclear whether the accompanying verb form (when there is one) is understood as agreeing with the singular 'maner' or the plural head noun: see, for example, 'þer is two maner of reformynge' (4/21), and 'Two maner of sinne maken' (6/4)'.

61 *in*^{1}. The preposition is necessary to the sense here.

63 *al manly not gostly*. The Latin version omits this phrase, which stresses the limitation of meditation on the humanity of Jesus.

65 *mylke . . . children*. For application of the Pauline metaphor of milk for babes to imaginative devotion, see above, 10/68.

66 *of*. H 'on', makes no sense.

69 *þe vnderstondynge is lady*. The metaphor derives from Richard of St-Victor, *Benj. Min.* chapters 4–5. See the Middle English version, *Deonise* 13, ll. 2–4: 'By Bala is vnderstonden ymaginacyon, þe whiche is seruaunt vnto reson as Bala was to Rachel.'

CHAPTER 32

10 *not . . . him*^{2} (l. 11). The Latin version omits, probably by eye-skip.

11 *He seeþ . . . him þat he is* (l. 12). Similarly, Aquinas notes in *Super Boethium de Trinitate*, *Opera Omnia*, 50 (Rome, 1992), q. 1, a.2, ad 1: 'dicendum quod ex hoc quod Deus omnem formam intellectus subterfugit, apparet quod non potest cognosci quid est, sed solum an est'.

13–14 *an vnchaungeable beynge*. The Latin version translates 'essentia'; see Augustine, *De Trin.* 5. 2. 3, 7. 5. 10. Whereas *essentia*, 'being', is an attribute of all created substances, God is being itself (as he is, essentially, all of his attributes: see Augustine, *Civ. Dei* 11. 10. 3: 'quae habet, haec et est, et ea omnia unus est').

16 *blyndly and vnsauourly*. The Latin version, 'obscure et insipide', supports H$_7$RλSrACcMPl over χE 'byndely and nakedly and vnsauourly'.

17 *clergy*. The Latin version, 'scienciam suam', supports χAsMPl, 'his clergi', over H$_7$RλSrAECc.

18–19 *þat is conforted*. The Latin version, 'per intellectum qui confortatur', agrees with H$_7$H^{c}RλAsSrLwAEPlW over H$^\circ$BH$_5$WsHu$_2$CcMLdT, 'þat he is conforted'. Hilton's point is that the understanding, comforted and illuminated by the grace of the Holy Spirit, and not the human reason alone, knows the being of God. It is, in any case, not 'he', the contemplative, that is here being spoken of as comforted and illuminated, but the understanding.

20 *with*. The Latin version, 'cum', supports H$_7$RλSrCc over χRAsAEMPl, 'and with'.

23 *affeccyons*. The Latin version, 'affeccionem', supports the singular of HBH$_5$λSrWsLwAHu$_2$ECcMLdPlTW over the plural of H$_7$BA.

24 *thynges*. The Latin version, 'terrenorum', supports the plural of H$_7$RAs over the singular of HBH$_5$LB$_3$SrWsLwAHu$_2$EPH$_6$CcMLdPlTW.

25 *And of . . . gudnes* (l. 28). The Latin version diminishes Hilton's point that this is a spiritual understanding of Christ, 'God in man', by separating the two aspects, referring to this mode of 'visionis et cognicionis Jesu Christi' at one point in the sentence, and noting that the soul 'timet Deum' at another.

30 1 Cor. 13: 12: 'We see now in a glass, darkly.'

mirk. The Latin version translates this as 'obscura', which will cause confusion when 'blynde' is translated four lines later with the same term.

in rewarde. The H$_7$ scribe has treated abstract 'regard' as concrete 'reward', as in 10/24 above.

32–3 1 John 3: 2.

36 *knoweþ it not, bot only troweþ it; þis is soth* (l. 37). The Latin version, 'non sic cognoscit, set solum credit; istud est verum', supports H$_7$λECcM over HLwW 'knowiþ not, bot only trowith it is soþ', H$_5$Ws 'knowiþ not, bot only trowiþ þat it is soþ', Ld 'knowith nott, butt only troweþe þat þys is soþ', RBAHu$_2$PlT 'knowith nouȝt, but only trowith it. This is soth', or Sr 'knowith it nought, but only troweþ it. Þis is soþ'. The connection of 'þis is soth' to the preceding proposition appears to have caused particular problems for the various scribes.

47 *may not*. The Latin version, 'non potest', agrees with H$_7$RλSrAPl over the χAsECcM addition of 'see'.

57 *þe more*. The Latin version, 'a carnalitateque remocior', agrees with the χRSrAECcPl addition of 'and' over H$_7$λM.

58 *of þe godhed of Jesu*. The Latin version shifts emphasis slightly: 'respectu deitatis Domini Jesu Christi'.

59 *no man*. The Latin version, 'nullus alius homo', agrees with χAsE 'none oþer man' over H$_7$RλSrACcMPl. The Latin version continues to add overdetermining details to this sentence, substituting 'credere . . . Jesum esse Deum' for 'trow in Jesu', 'ille tamen homo qui talem habet visionem' for 'he', and 'hoc credere' for 'trowe'.

63 *betokneþ*. The Latin version, 'et talis designat', agrees with χAsEH$_6$ 'and he bitokneþ', and RAPl 'and þat betoknith', over H$_7$LB$_3$SrPCcM. If 'he troweþ' and 'he betokneþ' are coordinate independent clauses, the conjunction 'and' is required; only if 'he troweþ' is understood as parenthetical can 'and' be omitted.

66 *þis*: The Latin version, 'ista', supports H$_7$RSrAH$_6$CcMPl over χ⌜L⌝B$_3$AsEP ‘þe’. The fact that ‘þis’ is the reading of H_6, while ‘þe’ is written in over erasure in L suggests that the original reading of **λ** may also have been ‘þis’.

67 *in*². The Latin version, ‘in via’, supports **Σ** (including, presumaby, H°) over Lw⌜H^c⌝W ‘and’.

73 *it*. The grammatical subject ‘it’, omitted by $H_7B_3SrH_6Ld$ (and L, originally) must be understood here; presumably the scribes, not noting the remainder of the sentence, took ‘þat’ to be the subject.

73 *felynge*. The Latin version expands to ‘sensacionem seu cognicionem’.

76 *felt*. The Latin version expands to ‘sensit vel gustauit’.

79 *þe openynge . . . here wrytynge* (l. 81). Hilton may be referring here to Richard Rolle’s discussion of contemplation in *Emendatio vitae*, chapter 12: ‘Porro sancti et contemplativi viri revelata facie gloriam Domini speculantur [2 Cor. 3: 18]. Quod fit aut aperto eis sensu, ut intelligant scripturas, aut hostio celi aperto, quod maius est, ut, quasi omnibus obstaculis inter mentem illorum et Deum remotis, purgato cordis oculo celestes cives speculentur.’ *De Emendatione vitae: Eine kritische Ausgabe des lateinischen Textes von Richard Rolle, mit einer Übersetzung ins Deutsche und Untersuchungen zu den lateinischen und englischen Handschriften*, ed. Rüdiger Spahl (Bonn, 2009), 230–2, ll. 65–9.

82 *if a soule myght sen by ymaginacion . . . as mikel as an hundreþ sunnes* (l. 84). Hilton appears to have in mind here the kind of ‘devout imagination’ that is characteristic of the pseudo-Bonaventuran *Meditationes vitae Christi*, as for example in the description of God in heaven sending the archangel Gabriel to announce the Incarnation to Mary: ‘aspice ipsum tanquam magnum dominum, sedentem in solio excelso, vultu benigno, pio et paterno’, or of Christ accepting the commission of the Incarnation, ‘obedientiam et laboriosam legationem suscipiens, Patri se incinavit et recommendavit’. See *Meditationes vitae Christi*, 514b. 15–20, 515b. 13; also *Iohannis de Caulibus Meditationes vitae Christi, olim S. Bonaventuro attributae*, ed. M. Stallings-Taney (Turnhout, 1997), 19, 22: ch. 4, ll. 18–19, 91–2. It is interesting to note that Nicholas Love omitted both of these passages in his translation of this chapter of the *Meditationes* in *The Mirror of the Blessed Life of Jesus Christ*. See Love’s *Mirror*, 23. 8, 27. 26, the notes on these two passages, pp. 354–5, and the discussion on intro 48. A similar observation to Hilton’s is made in chapter 57 of the *Cloud of Unknowing*, which speaks of men that ‘wil make a God as hem lyst, and cloþen hym ful richely in cloþes and set hym in a trone, fer more curiously þan euer was he depeynted in þis erþe’. Cf. *Cloud*, 105, ll. 9–14. Apropos of the last words of the citation from the *Cloud*, we should note that the image of God seated in majesty, surrounded by a sun-like light, is the most common presentation of the divinity in the iconography that Hilton defended in the quodlibetal question

De Ador. imag.; but what is depicted on church walls or in stained-glass windows is not to be taken for the height of contemplation.

84 *Nay*. H_7 'þat' makes no sense here.

86 *styeth*. The Latin version has 'videat', perhaps depending on an exemplar reading 'seeth'.

by swilk ymaginacion or to se Jesu God (l. 87). The Latin version supports H_7RλSrACcMPl over the χAsE transposition.

CHAPTER 33

5 *abofen a þing*. HRAsLwAEH$_6$CcTW 'if þat be heuen only þat is aboue al þinge' expresses an idea similar to that of John 3: 31: 'He that cometh from heaven, is above all.' H_7BH$_5$LB$_3$SrWsHu$_2$PMLdPl 'abofen a þinge', which is supported by the Latin version, 'aliqua', suggests that the definition of heaven, for any thing, is that which is above that thing.

12 *abofe*. *Cloud*, chapter 51 (95, ll. 9–23) similarly notes that 'in mis-conceyuyng of [þis worde IN and þis worde UP] hangeþ moche errour and moche disseite in hem þat purposen hem to be goostly worchers'. This observation is further directed to the expressions 'wiþinne hym-self' and 'abouen him-self'.

15 *or*. The Latin version, 'vel', supports H_7LB$_3$SrLwAEPH$_6$CcMPlW over HBH$_5$AsWsHu$_2$LdT 'and'.

22 *persen*. The Latin version, 'penetrare', supports HBLB$_3$SrWsHu$_2$PH$_6$ over R⌜Lw⌝ACcMPlW 'parten'; the H$_5$AsELdT variants, 'perschen', etc. probably result from confusion of graphic similars. The same is also true of H_7 'pursew', which makes no sense, but may have been suggested by the preceding 'rennen out'. *Cloud*, chapter 57 (105, ll. 9–11) similarly observes: 'þees men willen sumtyme wiþ þe coriouste of here ymaginacion peerce þe planetes, and make an hole in þe firmament to loke in þerate.'

28–46 *withinne*. The Latin version translates the first occurrence of this word correctly as 'intra', but has 'infra' for seven subsequent occurrences. No English manuscript reads 'beneath' at any point; presumably, Fishlake was mislead by the contrasting concern with the word 'above' in the previous paragraph.

29 *seken*. The Latin version, 'querere', supports H_7χRSrACcMPl over ⌜L⌝B$_3$AsEPH$_6$ 'see'.

32 *hid and holden*. The Latin version, 'continetur', supports the HBH$_5$AsWsLwHu$_2$MLdW omission of 'hid and' over H_7RλSrACcPl, the E variant 'hadde and holden', and the T variant 'hidde'.

40 *þenkynge*. The Latin version adds 'seu ymaginacionem'.

43 *priuey*. The Latin version, 'occultam', supports H_7RλSrAECcMPl over the χAs omission.

44 *schal þe soule*. The Latin version, 'faciet anima', supports `L´$B_3$SrLw`H^c´EPLdW 'schal þe soule do', over H_7H°RBAsAHu$_2$$H_6$MPlT. The insertion of two nested parentheses ('whan grace touches it, ellys it wil bot lytel avayle') between the subject 'soule' and the verb 'seke' appears to have confused a number of scribes, with the result that they insert 'do', and make the original main verb, 'seke', into an infinitive ('to seken', 'querere') dependent on the verb 'availe' of the second of the parenthetical conditions. H°H_5AsWs omit 'availe'; the addition of 'worche' following 'soule' in H_5Ws may be a parallel resolution of the same misreading.

48 1 John 1: 5.

54–5 *al oþer gostly þynges þat nedeþ*. The Latin version, 'omnia alia spiritualia que necesse est anima cognoscere', supports H_7AsCcLdPlT over HBH_5λSrWsLwAHu$_2$EMW 'al oþere gostly þinge'. As the Latin verb form 'necesse est' shows, Hilton is using 'nedeþ' impersonally here. The majority of scribes of English manuscripts took the immediately preceding 'þynges' as the grammatical subject, and 'corrected' into the singular. The scribes of As and Pl made the opposite correction, changing 'nedeþ' to 'neden'.

56 Ps. 35: 10. Similarly, the pseudo-Augustinian *De Spiritu et anima*, chapter 12 (*PL* 40: 487) links this and the preceding scriptural quotation to observe, 'sicut solem non videt oculus nisi in lumine solis; sic verum ac divinum lumen non poterit intelligentia videre nisi in ipsius lumine'.

58–9 Hebr. 12: 29, echoing Deut. 4: 24. Hilton also cites this text in *Mixed Life*, in *English Mystics*, ed. Windeatt, 121.

61–3 Hilton uses the same simile in *Scale* I, Chapter 31.

74 *þat it had . . . trowynge* (l. 75). The Latin version, 'de quo prius solam habuit nudam fidem seu credulitatem', supports H_7RλSrAECcMPl over the χAs omission of 'only', and expands on 'trowynge'.

76–8 2 Cor. 4: 18.

83 *þus . . . Lord*. The Latin version, 'vnde Deus dicit', supports H_7RLB_3Sr`Lw´AHu$_2$EPH_6CcMPlTW over the HBH_5AsWsLd omission.

83–4 John 17: 3.

86 *and*. H_7 'in' is another example of this mistranscription.

Jesu Crist. The Latin version, 'Jesum Christum', supports H_7RλSrACcMPl over the χAsE omission.

on sothfast God. The Latin version, 'esse vnum verum Deum', supplies a verb to what reads as an appositive in the English text.

CHAPTER 34

1 *Of.* H_7 'On' makes no sense.

5 *lufe*. Various English scribes appear to have been unsatisfied by the ending of this sentence, and supplied various modifying words and phrases.

6 The end—the goal and purpose—of the intellectual nature of human kind is the knowledge of God. See Aquinas, *ST* 1–2, q. 26, a. 3, citing Augustine, *Conf.* 5. 4. 7: 'Beatus est qui te novit.'

8–11 *syȝt* (*ter*). The Latin version, 'visio(ne) seu cognicio(ne)', appears to be attempting to ensure that the reader does not misunderstand the term 'syȝt' in a physical sense.

10–11 *also for þe blissed lufe*. See Aquinas, *ST* 2–2, q. 180, a. 7, esp. ad 1.

11–16 Aquinas, *ST* 1–2, q. 27, a. 2 argues from Aristotle's *Ethics* that knowledge is the source of love, but (according to the scholastic principle that what is known is known according to the mode of the knower, but what is loved is loved according to the mode of the beloved) that the love of God can arise from the partial knowledge of God possible in this life. Clark, 'Notes', 317 n. 233, notes that the *Cloud*, interpreting the Dyonisian tradition particularly through Thomas Gallus, observes that 'loue may reche to God in þis liif, but not knowing (*Cloud* 33, l. 11)'.

16 *lufe*[1]. The Latin version clarifies how the soule can only come to love by way of love by beginning the discussion of the two kinds of love here, expanding 'lufe' to 'alia dileccione'.

18–31 For the idea that God's charity, like his grace, is prevenient, see *Scale* I, Chapter 68. Clark, 'Notes' 180 n. 286, observes that Hilton follows the Franciscan scholastic tradition, exemplified by Duns Scotus, in teaching that, 'while all grace is charity, not all charity is grace. Grace is the created gift; charity can be both the created gift, and the uncreated Gift, which is God [the Holy Spirit] himself.'

22 The foundational source for the distinction between uncreated love, which is the Holy Spirit, and the created love given to humankind through grace to lead the soul back to God is Augustine, *De Trin.* 15. 17–19. Important further treatments include Bernard, *De Dilig. Deo* 12. 35, William of St-Thierry, *Speculum Fidei* (*PL* 180: 395), *Aenigma Fidei* (*PL* 180: 399), and *Excerpta. super Cantic.* (*PL* 180: 506), Aquinas, *ST* 2–2, q. 23, a. 2. See Karl Rahner, 'Some Implications of the Scholastic Concept of Uncreated Grace', *Theological Investigations*, 1 (London, 1961), 319–46; J. P. H. Clark, 'The Trinitarian Theology of Walter Hilton's *Scale of Perfection. Book II*', in Helen Phillips (ed.), *Langland, the Mystics and the Medieval English Religious Tradition: Essays in Honour of S. S. Hussey* (Cambridge, 1990), 125–40.

25 1 John 4: 8: 'Deus caritas est.'

30 *in*. The Latin version, 'ex', supports the Σ 'of'.

32 *gostly syȝt of Jesu*. The Latin version expands: 'cognicionem vel spiritualem visionem Jesu Christi'.

38 *ne were þe endles mykelnes of þe lufe of God*. The scribes of HH$_5$WsLwW sensed an omission here, and inserted the dummy-subject 'it' after 'were'. The more cogent reading of Σ is an impersonal construction, which the Latin version resolves by paraphrase, 'nisi ex infinita magnitudine dileccionis diuine'.

mykelnes. The insertion of 'mekenesse' preceding 'mykelnes' in H$_5$Lw, and the variant 'mekenesse' instead of 'mykelnes' in λ, suggest that it was a gloss in the exemplars from which these variously descend.

40 *He is . . . ȝifte*. Peter Lombard, *Sent.* 1 d. 18 c. 2, states, 'videtur Spiritus Sanctus dici datum et donum', citing Augustine, *De Trin.* 15. 19: 'Spiritus Sanctus in tantum donum Dei est, in quantum datur eis quibus datur; apud se autem Deus est, etsi nemini datur.'

46–7 *þis ȝifte of lufe*. See Hilton's *Qui habitat*, in *Exposition*, ed. Wallner, 45, l. 14–15: 'And I schal ȝiuen him þe ȝift of loue, þat is, þe holi gost.'

50–1 1 John 4: 19.

51–95 The argument that although the Trinity is love (charity) substantially, charity is particularly the attribute of the Holy Spirit derives from Augustine, *De Trin.* 17. 17.

55 *lufeþ*. The Latin version, 'diligit', supports H$_7$HBλSrLwAHu$_2$EMPlTW over RH$_5$AsWsCc⌜Ld⌝ 'loued'.

57 *soules*. The Latin version, 'filii', supports Σ 'sones'; the H$_7$ variant is probably the result of a confusion of graphic similars.

58 *schewed*. The Latin version expands to 'exhibuit vel ostendit'.

68 *he*. The H$_7$ omission is erroneous: the sentence requires a grammatical subject.

74 *oneþ it to him*. The Latin version expands to 'vnit sibi et coniungit'.

76–82 The appropriation of the three functions of creation, redemption, and salvation to the Father, Son, and Holy Spirit, deriving from Augustine's *De Trin.* 7. 1. 2–4 and 15. 17. 29–31, became commonplace in the medieval period. See Aquinas, *ST* 1, q. 39, a. 8.

77–82 *schewed . . . schewed . . . scheweþ*. The logic of these three parallel verbs seems to require variation in tense: the making of each soul occurred in the past; as did Christ's defeat of Satan, whether Hilton's reference to his victory by wisdom rather than strength refers, as often in medieval theology, to the temptation in the desert or to the crucifixion; but the justification and salvation of the soule is described in the present. The manuscript support for the verb tenses varies: in the first instance, H$_7$RBSrACcMPl use the past tense, while the Latin version supports HH$_5$λAsWsLwHu$_2$ELdTW in using the present. In the second instance, Ld originally used the present tense, but was corrected by the scribe to the preterite; all other English manuscripts use the preterite, while the Latin version uses the present. In the third, all versions agree in using the present tense.

86 *most of lufe*. The preposition of the Latin version, 'maxima in dileccione', differs from that of HRBH$_5$AsSrWsLwHu$_2$EH$_6$CcMLdTW, but does repeat the preposition of the preceding parallel phrase, 'maxima in potencia'. The omission of the preposition in H$_7$B$_3$APl is probably an ellipsis, but the cancellation in L (upon which the omission in B$_3$ probably depends) is intentional.

88 *and to fals cristen men*. The Latin version may have omitted this phrase because it raises the difficult issue of the status with regard to grace of unfaithful Christians.

89 *suffyceþ*. Theologically, the present tense should be required: although the passion took place in the past, its efficacy extends to the present. The Latin version, however, 'sufficiens fuit', supports HRBH$_5$WsLwA-Hu$_2$CcMLd 'sufficed', over H$_7$λAsSrEPlTW.

91 *and not most of lufe*. The Latin version omits this phrase, perhaps taking it as a derogation of the power of love.

94 *werkynge of most lufe*. The Latin version, 'opus maxime dileccionis', supports H$_7$RLB$_3$SrAEPH$_6$MPl over HBH$_5$WsLwHu$_2$LdTW 'most wir-kynge of lufe'.

98 *soules*. The Latin version, 'animabus', supports the plural of H$_7$RλSrAECcMPl over the singular of χAs.

102 *vs*. The Latin version, 'nos', supports H$_7$RLB$_3$SrLw‘H^{c}’AEPH$_6$CcMPlTW over the H$^{\circ}$BH$_5$WsHu$_2$Ld omission.

exercyse. The H$_7$AsLwAW variant must be understood as plural (the form 'exercyses' does not occur in H$_7$).

107–12 The statement of God's agency and human cooperation is congruent with 24/8, 10 and 28/12–14 above. See also Peter Lombard, *Sent*. 2, d. 26, c. 2; d. 27, c. 4.

107 *vanites*. The Latin version, 'vanitatibus', supports the plural of H$_7$RSrACcMPl over the singular of χλE.

111 *makynge*. The Latin version, 'operacione et gracie', is more explicit.

113–14 *scheweþ to þe soule þe syȝt of Jesu*. The Latin version, 'causat in anima visionem Jesu', shifts the sense of the modality of the vision from 'showing to' to 'causing in', although the agent and the goal (uncreated love, and the human soul) remain the same. Something of the same shift may be implied by the Latin version, 'capere', of 'suffre' in the following line.

118 See Hilton's *Qui habitat*, in *Exposition*, ed. Wallner, 26–7; *English Mystics*, ed. Windeatt, 174–5.

121 *myȝth . . . sothfastnesse . . . godenesse* (l. 122). Hilton here (as at 36/44 and 43/123 below) credits to Christ in his relationship to humankind the proper attributes of the three persons of the Trinity because in the operations of God *ad extra*, the agency of the persons is indistinguishable. See Augustine, *De Trin*. 6. 10. 12, Peter Lombard, *Sent*. 1, d. 19, c. 4.

125 *stele his worchipe*. See *Scale* I, Chapter 20.

fro him. The Latin version, 'ab eo', supports H_7RBLB_3SrAHu$_2$EPH_6CcMLdPlT over the HBH_5AsWsLwW omission.

CHAPTER 35

6 *most clere syght . . . heuene* (l. 2). In scholastic theology, which Hilton echoes in *Scale* I, Chapter 61, the blessed in heaven have two kinds of rewards. The first is the essential ('sovereign and principal') reward of bliss itself, which may be greater or lesser according to degree of the love of God in a soul (by the free gift of the Holy Spirit) during this present life (Aquinas, *ST* 2–2, q. 24, a. 3). This is the reward that Hilton is describing at present. A further, 'accidental' ('secondary') reward (the 'aureola', or halo) is given to those whose life is marked by a special dedication to God—traditionally, martyrs, doctors (the great 'teachers' of the Christian church), and virgins. See the continuation of Aquinas's *ST*, *Supplementum* q. 96, a. 1.

9 *It is . . . before* (l. 10). On the relationship of grace and spiritual 'labour', see above, Chapter 20.

10 *sum lufers . . . by here owne myght* (l. 11). See Hilton's *Angels' Song*, in *English Mystics*, ed. Windeatt, 134; also the *Cloud*, chapter 52.

19 *ne han not . . . as I speke of*. The Latin version, 'nec donum dileccionis habent modo quo iam loquor de dileccione', appears to depend on an English exemplar that repeated the phrase 'of lufe'.

21 *or ellis . . . hafe it* (l. 22). The Latin version omits this phrase.

he . . . (l. 22) *it*[2] *. . . itself*. All manuscripts read 'he' in the first instance; H_7Sr read 'it', and HBH_5LB_3AsWsLwAHu$_2$EPH_6CcLdTW 'he' in the second instance (RAMPl omit this word); H_7RLB_3SrPMPl read 'itself' in the third instance (at which point the marginal annotator in L notes, 'quere'), but HBH_5AsWsLwAHu$_2$EH_6CcLdTW 'himself'. As throughout the text, the Latin version uses feminine forms in discussing the soul. Hilton's English text does not use feminine forms (see above, 16/22), but varies in the use of 'he' or 'it' in passages referring to the individual soul; Hilton may not have been entirely consistent grammatically on this point.

24 *Jesu*. The Latin version, 'Jesu Christi', supports H_7λSrECc over χRAsAMPl 'God'.

31 *schewyng of*. The Latin version, 'manifestacionem', supports H_7λECc over the χ omission.

32 *þat is God*. The neuter pronoun of the Latin version, 'quod est Deus', implies that it is 'þe ȝifte' ('donum'), not the 'lufe' ('dileccionis') that is God; Hilton's point is rather that it is this love that is God (for which the Latin would be 'donum amoris, qui est Deus'). See below, 36/17, 61–2.

34 *þe more . . . sothfastnesse*. The Latin version rewrites this in a more devotional direction: 'Quanto anima magis se humiliat sub humanitate Christi, et ad nichilum se redigit per graciam ex consideracione mirabilium et occultorum iudiciorum deitatis sue.' This obscures Hilton's point that what the soul is humbled by is the recognition by that it is God who performs the work of love and contemplation.

þurgh grace. The Latin version substitutes the devotional 'sub humanitate Christi'.

41 Rom. 8: 14. The order of the final words of this text in the modern Vulgate agrees with that of H_7RλSrAEMPl, 'sunt filii Dei' over that of χAs, 'filii Dei sunt', which is supported by Fishlake's Latin version.

þese al. The transposition in H_7 is probably accidental.

42–6 Hilton here underscores the idea of the soul's cooperation with grace. See Aquinas, *ST* 1–2, q. 111, a. 2. See also the *Cloud*, chapter 34.

45 *sterynge*. The Latin version, 'instinctum', supports the singular H_7RλSrAECcMPl variant over the plural of χAs 'stirynges'.

50 *lufe*[1] . . . *þat* (36/37). The displacement of text in As is probably the result of a displaced folio in an exemplar.

51 *by so*. The variation among the English manuscripts here represents variance in understanding of 'by so' as a prepositional phrase (*OED* 'by', *prep*. 23(d), cited thrice from *Piers Plowman*) or 'be so' as a contraction of 'be it so' or 'if it be so'. To this possible source of confusion must be added the scribal variation of spelling between 'be' and 'by'. In H_7, the spelling 'by' is invariably the preposition, but 'be' may be either the verb or the preposition (as it is in the next line). The Latin version, 'si tamen' supports the reading 'if it be'.

52–3 On the acquisition of virtue by the soul itself as directed by reason, see Chapter 13 above, and *Scale* I, Chapter 14.

52 *manly, don*. The Latin version, 'humaniter fit', supports H_7RλSrAMPl over χAsE 'manly doynge'.

53 *þe*[2]. The article is required at this point.

57–62 According to Clark, 'Notes' 319 n. 257, this formulation appears to be original with Hilton.

58 *meke soules*. The Latin version, 'anime vere humili', supports the singular of LB_3EP 'a meke soule', over $H_7R\chi AsSrAH_6CcMPl$.

59 *affeccyon . . . mede*. The Latin version, 'premium dileccionis', alters the parallelism of the English text.

66–7 2 Cor. 3: 5.

70–1 Phil. 2: 13. The modern Vulgate text reads 'vobis' where Hilton has 'nobis'.

71 *eciam*. The reading of the Latin version, 'et', supports Σ and the modern Vulgate text over H_7Pl.

72 *boþe wil and fulfillyng of gode wil*. The Latin version, 'et velle et perficere', supports the repetition of 'wil' in $H_7R\lambda SrAECcMPl$ over χAs.

73 *of God*. The Latin version, 'ex Deo', supports $H_7R\lambda SrAECcMPl$ over χAs 'gode' (of/ good Lw). The lack of the head noun 'God' in the latter variant leaves the subsequent pronouns 'he' and 'his' without a clear antecedent.

74 *not of speciale grace*. Hilton's point here is that the affection that some souls feel by self-induced fervour is accepted and rewarded by God, although this fervour is not produced by the special grace that he spoke of in the previous chapter, but by the common grace by which all Christians are saved. In any case, all is produced by grace. See above, 10/21–5 and below, 41/145.

75 *his parfyte lufers . . . inperfyte lufers of God* (l. 76). The Latin version treats 'perfect' and 'imperfect' here not as adjectives modifying 'lovers', but as adverbs modifying the cognate participles: 'perfecte eum diligentibus . . . diligentibus Deum imperfecte'.

77 *ferly*. Hilton characterizes the fervour that is mediated through the human affections as operating at a distance—'ferly'—whereas the fervour felt by direct action of the Holy Spirit operates without mediation—'neerly'—in perfect contemplatives. The Latin version, 'libere', seems to depend on an exemplar of the English text that had the same variant reading as MS B, 'freely'. In Thomistic terms, the former grace is 'operant' and the latter 'cooperant'.

CHAPTER 36

This chapter, strongly influenced by Augustine, *De Trin*. 15. 17–19, is the culmination of Hliton's spiritual teaching. It sums up what has come before, and what follows are corollaries and examples of the effects of contemplative grace.

9–12 See the lists of the gifts of the Holy Spirit in 1 Cor. 12: 10 (miracles and prophecy) and Isa. 11: 2 (wisdom, understanding, and counsel), to which Hilton adds the practices of fasting and penance.

14 *fully*. The Latin version, 'plene', supports H_7RλSrAECcMPl over χ 'wel'.

17 *and be damned with him*. This, the variant of H_7BH_5λAsSrWsHu$_2$Cc, is the *lectio difficilior*, as opposed to H^{c}RLwCcMTW 'withal' or Ld 'þerwiþe'. Hilton's point is that since divine love, the gift of the Holy Spirit, is the Holy Spirit himself, one cannot have the Holy Spirit and, together with him, be damned. The variant readings weaken this; the Latin version, 'cum hoc', takes 'gift' ('donum') as its antecedent. See above, 35/32, and below, 36/62.

19–20 *is not þe affeccyon of lufe þat is formed in a soule, bot it*. The omission of this phrase in the Latin version may be a case of eye-skip, or it may be the result of the tendency to simplify Hilton's distinction between the special gift of unformed love, which is the Holy Spirit, and the affection of love that arises in the soul from its own efforts, as detailed at the end of the preceding chapter.

30 *of lufe*. The Latin version, 'donum dileccionis', supports Σ over H_7, 'and lufe'. It is clear from the preceding paragraph that the 'gift' is love.

32 *for to . . . soule* (l. 34). The omission in H°H_5AsWs is presumably the result of eye-skip.

Jesu. The Latin version, 'Jesus', supports H_7BλSrHu$_2$ECcLdPlT over RLwH^{c}AMPlW 'God'. 'Jesu' was presumably the original reading of H as well.

34 *him*. The Latin version, 'eum', supports H_7RλSrAECcMPl over χAs 'Jesu'.

35 *softenesse*. The H_7HBH_5λAsWsLwHu$_2$TW variant is more cogent than that of RSrAECcMLdPl, 'soþefastnes' in the sense that the contemplative is not actively working, but observing God's working in the soul. The Latin version, 'sobrietate', may depend on an English exemplar reading 'softenesse', because 'sobrietas' is often Fishlake's translation for 'softenesse' (cf. below, 38/10).

36–7 Ps. 45: 11.

37 *þat is . . . him-* (37/19). For the displacement of text in As see above, 35/50.

41–2 *and ȝe don noght*. The omission of this phrase in the Latin version may be part of Fishlake's tendency to interpret the text as advocating the kind of imaginative devotion, focused on the 'work' undertaken by the contemplative, which Hilton is here describing as secondary to true contemplation. For Fishlake, a stress on the activity of the contemplative may be an attempt to avoid what could be mistaken for quietism in Hilton's treatment of the role of the Holy Spirit in the reformation of the soul (e.g. in the description of those who 'werken vnder þe biddyng of reson, [and] stryuen and fyghten al day ageyns synnes for þe getyng of vertus'), similar to that for which the *Mirouer des simples âmes anienties* of Marguerite Porete was condemned, and attributed to the heresy of the Free Spirit generally.

The heretical belief, which Hilton definitely does not teach, and which Marguerite Porete may not have intended, is that the enlightened soul is so united with God at a 'higher' level that it need not strive to be, nor even care whether it is, virtuous any more. See Michael G. Sargent, 'Marguerite Porete', in Alastair Minnis and Rosalynn Voaden (eds.), *Medieval Holy Women in the Christian Tradition, c. 1100–c.1500* (Turnhout, 2010), 291–309.

42 *wele*. The Latin version supports the $HH_5LB_3AsSrWsLwEPH_6CcW$ omission over $H_7RBAHu_2MLdPlT$.

44 *þurgh myght, wisdom and lufe, myghtyly, wittyly and louely*. The Latin version varies these triads of terms: 'per potenciam, sapienciam, et dileccionem, seu potenter, sapienter, et amabiliter'. The first triad is repeated identically in the next line of both the English and the Latin text. Hilton here again credits the proper attributes of Father, Son, and Holy Spirit to Christ in his relation to humankind. See above, 34/121, below, 43/123.

46 *myght*. The Latin version supports $H_7\lambda ECc$ over the $\chi AsSr$ addition of 'and'.

and ȝe noght. The Latin version, 'et non vos', reads 'noght' as an adverb, not a pronoun: 'and you (are) not might, wisdom, and blessed love', not 'and you (are) nothing'. The English text is capable of either reading.

47 *only*. The Latin version supports χAsE over $H_7R\lambda SrACcMPl$ in omitting this word.

and ȝour . . . gode dedis (l. 49). The omission in H° is presumably the result of eye-skip.

and ȝoure gode thoghtes. The Latin version, 'bonas cogitaciones', supports $H_7RLB_3SrAEPH_6CcMPl$ over $BH_5AsWsH^cHu_2LdTW$, which add 'alle'.

48 *and ȝe don riȝt noght*. The Latin version omits this phrase. Again, Fishlake may be avoiding the imputation of quietism.

51 *sithen I þat am Jesu and for lufe do al þis*. The Latin version, 'ex quo ergo ego Jesus ex amore hec omnia facio', presents a simplification the $\lambda AECc$ variant 'syn I am Jesu and for loue do al þis', leaving out the double predicate 'am . . . and . . . do'. $H_5AsSrWsLdT$ and H_7HBLwW both have a double predicate, but also have intrusive 'þat' either before or after 'I' respectively. The RMPl variant reads 'I þat am loue . . .', and A 'I am loue and . . .': both omit 'Jesu'. Either 'þat' or 'and' is grammatically superfluous, but the original text may have been defective.

56 *in*[2]. The Latin version, 'ad', supports Σ 'to' over H_7.

62 *þat is þe Holi Gost*. The Latin version, 'quod est Spiritus Sanctus', takes 'ȝifte' ('donum'), not 'loue' ('dileccionis') as the antecedent, as in 35/32 above.

63 *whan it feleth . . . þat* (l. 64). The Latin version, 'quando sentit . . . quod', supports H_7RBλAsSrAHu$_2$ECcMLdPl over the HH$_5$WsLwTW omission of 'þat', which reduces the direct object of 'feleth' to the list of specific virtues and reads the further complement, that these virtues are now no longer difficult but easy to achieve, as a separate sentence.

65 *lufereden*. That is, the opposite of hatred. Both words are compounds with 'rede(n)' (counsel) as their second element.

66 *sumtyme trauellous, pyneful, and hard to him for to kepen*. The Latin version shifts the meaning to make the virtues themselves (rather than their keeping) difficult: 'virtutes, que ei quandoque laboriose erant, penales, et graues', although the idea of custody of the virtues does occur twice in the next phrase, 'to kepen ony vertu . . . to kepen it', 'virtutem aliquam custodire . . . custodire virtutes'.

74 *sumtyme þei ben . . . wrestelers arn*. William Flete uses a similar metaphor to describe the fight against temptation: 'now vp, now doun, as wrasteleris ben'. *De Remed.* 25, l. 12.

75 *only*. The Latin version, 'solum', supports H_7RλSrAECcMPl over the χAs omission.

77 *myghtes*. The Latin version, 'viribus', supports the plural of H_7RλSrAECcMPl over the singular of χAs.

80 As William of St-Thierry says in the *Lettre d'or* (364–6): 'Et hoc est destinatum solitarii certaminis, hic finis, hoc praemium, requies laborum, simul et consolatio dolorum. Et ipsa est perfectio et vera hominis sapientia: omnes amplectens in se et continens virtutes, non aliunde mutuatas, sed velut naturaliter insitis sibi, ad similitudinem illam Dei qua est ipse quicquid est.'

82 *it setteth al here besynes for to kepe þat syght*. The Latin version, 'suam', supports χAsCcM 'his' over H_7RλSrEPl. The form 'here' is almost invariably plural, not feminine singular, in this manuscript. Hilton's meaning would be that the soul does not preoccupy itself with the virtues, but makes use of them ('sets all their business') to the end of maintaining the sight of Jesus that it has. The H_7 variant 'seeth' makes no sense, and probably arose from a confusion of graphic similars.

86 *in þe soule and þe soule . . . þe soule* (l. 87). The omissions in LwW and HH$_5$AsWs are presumably the result of eye-skip.

CHAPTER 37

This and the next two chapters treat the destruction of the vices in the soul by contemplative grace, the extirpation of which by means of reason and virtue was the subject of *Scale* I, Chapters 56–76 and 85.

5 The idea that love destroys sin is traditional: see e.g. Gregory, *Mor. in Job* 31. 45. 87, Bonaventure *In Sent.* 3, d. 4, p. 1, a. 2, q. 1.

9 *Bothe . . . þat oþer werkeþ by himself* (l. 10). The Latin version, 'Vtraque humilitas peruenit ex dileccione, set primam humilitatem dileccio operatur per anime racionem; aliam humilitatem per seipsam dileccio operatur', supports HBH$_5$WsEW (which insert 'he' either before or after 'werkeþ' in the second clause) over H$_7$RλAsSrACcMLdPlT. Hilton's point here is that although both forms of humility proceed from divine love, love works the first by means of human reason: we can understand why we should be humble. The second, perfect form of humility, an unmediated gift of grace, operates by itself, for in our experience of the majesty of God we lose all sense of our own worth.

14 *ȝifte of grace.* The Latin version, 'donum gracie', supports H$_7$HRH$_5$AsSrWsLwALdPlTW over BλECcM 'ȝyft or grace'.

15 *he thenkeþ.* As elsewhere, the positive and reflexive usage of 'think' varies. In l.13, only AsLdT read 'him', as opposed to 'he'. In the present case, H$_7$RLB$_3$SrPMPl read 'he', HBLwAEH$_6$LdTW read 'him', and Cc reads 'it'. In the next line, only H$_6$ reads 'hym'.

21 *despyseth.* The Latin version has 'despicere', an infinitive parallel to 'ageynstonden' ('resistere').

22 *his hert . . . with it.* The Latin version, 'tactus fuerit in superbia', with 'he', not 'his hert' as subject, shifts the focus slightly.

25 *his hert.* The Latin version, 'in corde', supports the χRλAsSrAMPl omission of 'his' over H$_7$ECc; 'his hert' may be an echo of the previous clause.

26 *him.* The Latin version, 'illud', shifts the focus slightly.

32–3 *syght of sothfastnesse, how Jesu is alle and þat he doth al.* The Latin version substitutes a devotional passage here: 'visionem Jesu Christi, ad considerandum intime humilitatem humanitatis sue et ad gustandum modicum de bonitate deitatis sue'. To the observation in the next line that this sight is 'so sothfast', Fishlake adds 'et delectabilis'.

36 *wurthines.* The Latin version, 'indignitatem', supports HRBλLwAECcMLdPlTW 'vnworþines' over H$_7$H$_5$AsSrWs. 'Vnworþines' is the more cogent reading because it is immediately connected with 'synnes before don'. For the idea that the soul takes no account of its own worthiness

or unworthiness, nor of sins done before, see also chapters 13 and 16 of the *Cloud* (41, l. 6), 'not lokyng after wheþer he haue ben holy or wrechid'.

ne of . . . itself (l. 37). The omission in H°H_5AsWs is presumably the result of eye-skip.

39–40 Ps. 38: 6. Four of the manuscripts that identify scriptural verses throughout the text have not correctly identified this one: BEPT read 'Psal. 138°'. The first three words of this text do occur at Ps. 138: 15b: 'Et substantia mea in inferioribus terrae.' MSS L and Ld do not identify this text, and only W correctly identifies it as 'Psal. xxxviii'. Clark, 'Notes', 321 n. 276, observes that it is at this point that Hilton comes closest to the teaching of the *Cloud.*

40 *þe syght of þi blissed vnmade substaunce.* The Latin version adds a devotional expansion here, 'consideracio mirabilis humilitatis humanitatis tue et benedicte increate substancie tue', and expands the following phrase, 'endles beeng', into a contrasting 'eterne existencie deitatis tue'.

43 *Also . . . to hem.* The Latin version changes this to 'Habens hanc perfectam humilitatem'.

49–50 Isa. 40: 17.

50 *sunt*[1]. The Latin version, 'non sint' (which is also the reading of the modern Vulgate text), supports HLB_3WsLwAEPH_6LdTW over H_7RBH_5AsSrCcMPl. Although the indicative is grammatically incorrect here, it is the variant of the majority of the earlier manuscripts of the English text. Both this and the next reading may have been corrected by Fishlake and various copyists of the English text out of their own knowledge of the scriptural text or of Latin grammar.

ita. The Latin version supports the χAsA omission, which is also the reading of the modern Vulgate text, over H_7RLB_3SrEPH_6CcMPl.

53 *For of noght . . . turnen* (l. 54). An echo of Gen. 3: 19: 'dust thou art, and unto dust thou shalt return'.

63–4 *ioye and þe werdly wurchepe.* The Latin version, 'gloria honoris mundani', supports Σ 'ioye of werdly worschip' over H_7. The Latin version translates 'ioye' thrice in this passage as 'gloria'.

69 *þe seuene artz of clergie.* That is, the seven liberal arts of Grammar, Rhetoric, Logic, Arithmetic, Geometry, Music, and Astronomy, the standard course of medieval education.

82–3 *þe whilk gladnes.* The omission in H°H_5Ws is presumably the result of eye-skip.

86 *Jesu.* The Latin version adds a devotional expansion, 'id est quia cognoscit mirabilem humilitatem humanitatis Christi et magis mirabilem misericordiam deitatis eius'.

89 *He . . . Jesu* (l. 95). The Latin version, 'Nec curat homo habens hanc visionem vtrum eum homines laudent vel vituperent, honorent vel contempnant, quia quantum ad seipsum nichil de hoc curat, nec eciam placet sibi quod homines eum despiciunt, vt quasi ex hoc videretur magis humilis, nec displicet sibi quod homines honorant vel commendant', supports the χλAsAEMPl reading in its general shape. The variation among RAMPl seems to have arisen from the repetition of this passage in their common exemplar. In R, the second iteration of the passage is marked 'va- . . . -cat'. The phrase 'lakken him or preysen him' is omitted in both iterations. In AMPl, 'lakken him or' is present, but 'dispysen him (l. 91) . . . wurchepen him or (l. 93)' is omitted in the first iteration of the passage, possibly by eye-skip, or as an attempt at correction. The phrase 'wurchepen him or dispysen him (l. 90–1)' is also lacking in H_7Cc, and 'wurchepen him' in Sr, both probably by eye-skip. Hilton's repetitious phrasing at this point seems to have given rise to errors both of expansion and omission; and the phrase 'as for himself' (l. 91) could be understood as being connected to either the preceding or the following sentence, but the Latin connects it causally ('quia') to the latter.

91 *he setteth it not atte hert . . . as for more meknes* (l. 92). Hilton is here criticizing the attitude, crucial to the authorial stance of Richard Rolle (as Watson demonstrates in *Richard Rolle and the Invention of Authority*, 43, 51, 63–4), as well as to fifteenth-century auto-hagiographers generally, that the disapproval of others constitutes a demonstration of one's own superior spiritual status.

95 *and gete . . . þerto* (l. 96). The Latin version omits this.

97 Ps. 24: 15.

98 *opone*. The scribe of H_7 has written the first word of the χ variant, 'open', but corrected this; the following 'to' of the χ variant does not occur in H_7.

101 *sothfastnes*. The Latin version adds a devotional expansion, 'id est preciosa humanitas Jesu Christi'.

beholdeþ. The Latin version, 'considerat', supports H_7RλSrAECcMPl over χAs 'holdiþ'. The variant 'beholdeþ' extends the image of the preceding scriptural citation, 'My eyes are ever toward the Lord'. In the next clause, Hilton will shift to the image of 'holding' the shield of truth, employing a kind of concatenative association by verbal similarity that is common to Latin monastic scriptural exegesis. The variant 'holdiþ' for 'beholdeþ' appears to be an anticipation; HH_5 have 'beholdiþ' instead of 'holdeþ' in the second instance.

102 *strenghe*. The Latin version, 'motum', supports Σ 'stirynge'. H_7Cc 'strenghe' is probably the result of a confusion of graphic similars, suggested by the metaphor of spiritual armour.

103–4 Ps. 90: 5 (the Psalm 'Qui habitat'). The remainder of this chapter parallels what Hilton says in *Qui habitat*, in *Exposition*, ed. Wallner, 13–18; partially excerpted in *English Mystics*, ed. Windeatt, 174–5. See Bernard's commentary on the same text, *Qui hab*. 6. 3 and his use of the image in *In Cant*. 33. 6. 11–12.

104 *Sothfastnes of God*. The Latin version, 'Veritas Dei, que est Jesus Christus', supports H_7RλSrAECcMPl over the χAs omission of 'of God' and adds to that a Christocentric expansion.

107 *spyce*. The Latin version, 'spiritum', supports Σ 'spirit'. The H_7 variant would be an example of *MED* 'spice' *n*.(2).1: 'a type or kind' or something—a species. Examples cited in *MED* refer to 'spice' with reference to pride.

108–9 Ps. 90: 6.

110 *of*. Necessary to the sense, and probably omitted inadvertently by H_7 at the page turnover.

115 See Hilton's *Qui habitat*, in *Exposition*, ed. Wallner, 17, l. 15: 'Hit fleeþ ful swiftliche & entreþ in ful softeliche, but it woundeþ dedliche.'

117 *thenkynge*. The infinitive of H_7, 'thenken', is grammatically inappropriate here.

125 *and þe soule wote neuer how*. The Latin version omits this phrase.

128 *ȝit*. The Latin version, 'adhuc', supports H_7RλSrAECcMPl over the χAs omission.

129 *it*. The Latin version, 'illius', preserves the pronominal reference of H_7RλSrAECcMPl over the χAs omission.

CHAPTER 38

10 *to kepen pacience holly, reste*. The Latin version, 'integre custodire pacienciam, quietem', supports H_7RBAsSrACcMLdPl over both HH_5WsLwLdTW 'for to kepen pacience, holy reste', and λ 'for to kepen pacience oonly, reste'.

softnes. Forms of 'soft-', here and below (l. 22 as well as 'esy' (l. 23), are translated in the Latin version with forms of 'sobrietas'.

13 *spekynge*. The Latin version, 'verbo', supports the singular reading of Σ over H.

20 *also is*. The H_7 variant 'al', an eye-skip omisson, leaves the clause without a verb.

21 *it is no grete maystrie*. Hilton uses the same phrase to describe divine assistance in avoiding sin in *Qui habitat*, in *Exposition*, ed. Wallner, 34, ll. 11–13, 'hit is non hardnes ne maystrie to [the soul] for-to fleo synne whiles þe grace lasteþ'.

22 *rysynges*. The Latin version, 'motus', supports H_5AsWsLwELdPlTW 'stiryngis' (HB 'stirynge') over H_7RλSrACcM.

23 *esy*. Translated in the Latin version here as 'sobriam', but below (31 and 39/51) with forms of 'quies'.

24 *godely*. According to H_7HAsWsPl, Hilton is speaking here of *deificatio*: that by grace the contemplative soul is made God-like. RBH_5λSrLwAECcMLdTW 'goodly' weakens the point. The Latin version, 'spiritualem', appears to be an anticipation of the immediately following 'gostly' (which is translated by the same word).

27 *hem*. The Latin version, 'nec multum vult moueri seu turbari', supports the HBH_5LAsWsLwAEPMLdPlTW addition, 'he wil not ben angred ne stired ageyns hem'. The repetition strengthens the previous sentence rhetorically ('he is not much stirred . . . he wil not be stirred'), but H_7B_3SrH_6Cc may have taken it for dittography—or it may simply be a case of eye-skip omisson.

28 *þat he feleth withinne his soule*. The Latin version adds a devotional expansion: 'ex visione et pacifica presencia Jesu Christi'.

withinne. The Latin version, 'in . . . intus', supports the RλAsSrAEMPl addition of 'in' over the H_7χCc omission.

36 *it hangeth noþyng vpon him*. The Latin version translates this idiomatic English expression as 'nec de hoc aliqualiter molestatur'. The similar phrasing at 39/29, 'hangeth noȝt vpon him', is translated literally, 'non adheret sibi vel pendet'.

37 *a²*. The definite article of λLwMPlW is more cogent than either the demonstratives 'þat' of HRBH_5AsSrWsACcLdT or 'þis' of E, and even more than the indefinite article 'a' in H_7; the Latin version substitutes the possessive pronoun 'illius'.

38 *oþer*. The Latin version, 'alia', supports H_7RλSrACcMPl over the χAsE omission.

42 *bot . . . harder* (l. 43). The Latin version is more explicit: 'si propinquius aliqualiter accedit molestia seu vexacio quando caro tangitur et sentit lesionem, tunc enim difficilius est habere pacienciam'.

52 *þis is a speciale grace . . . martires*. See the pseudo-Augustinian *Sermo de nativitate S. Laurentii* 206, *PL* 39: 2127.

53–5 Acts 5: 41.

57 *name*. The Latin version, 'nomine', supports H_7RBLB_3SrAEPH_6Cc-MLdPlT (which accurately translates the Latin scriptural text) over HH_5AsWsLwW 'luf'.

62 *heretykes . . . lufe of him* (l. 64). Hilton's reference here is probably not to early English Wycliffites, who usually evaded persecution by abjuring their heresy. See Hudson, *The Premature Reformation*, 157–9. On later Wycliffite autohagiography as followers of Christ even unto death, see Somerset, *Feeling like Saints*, 152–9. Further, it should be noted that Hilton died five years before the passage of the statute *De Heretico comburendo*.

67 *feyned . . . enflawmed*. In the Latin version, these are parallel modifiers describing the love and gladness felt by heretics willing to undergo martyrdom: 'similata est a diabolo et inflammata a Gehenna'. In the English text, which lacks 'and' before 'enflawmed' (parallel to 'et inflammata' in the Latin version), the latter modifier may refer rather to 'the fend' than to the false fire of love felt by heretics. Hilton similarly contrasts the true fire of divine love with the false flame kindled by Satan in *De Lecc.*, *LW*, ii. 230–1, ll. 191–217.

70 *þis*. The Latin version, 'totum est caritas', supports the HB λSrLwAECcLdPlT omission of the pronoun over H_7RH_5AsWsMW.

71 *þei are bygyled . . . fend*. An echo of Ps. 90: 6. The theme of the 'daemonium meridianum', and of God's protection of his lovers, paralleled in Hilton's *Qui habitat*, has continued through the text from the opening of Chapter 26.

78 *lufeth*. This verb should be in the indicative mood, parallel to 'despiseth', 'demeth', and 'preyeth' earlier in the same sentence. The H_7 variant 'lufe', notionally a subjunctive verb form, is inappropriate.

CHAPTER 39

10 *and passen*. The Latin version, 'et perituram', supports H_7RλSrAECcMPl over the χAs omission.

11 *lufe*. The Latin version, 'dileccionem', supports H_7As in the omission of the Σ determiner 'his'.

it seeth. The Latin version, 'videt', supports H_7RBλSrAECcMLdPlT over HH_5AsWsLwW 'it semiþ'.

12 *lufers*. The Latin version, 'dilectores', supports H_7Rλ SrAECcMPl over χAs 'men'.

15–16 *in þat plyte þat it schal ben after*. The Latin version makes this more specific: 'qualiter transibunt res huius mundi et peribunt'.

23 *han*. The Latin version, 'habere', supports H_7RλSrAECcMPl over the χAs omission.

The phrasing is similar to that of Hilton's *Bonum est* (84, l. 3) 'For he haþ luitel loue or lykyng in erþly þinges. He wold no more taken of hem þen scantly nedeþ him.'

25 *al.* The Latin version, 'totam', supports H_7RλSrAECcMPl over the χ omission.

27–8 *only clene of hert schul seen him.* Matt. 5: 8.

28–35 Hilton takes a strict stance, derived from Matt. 19: 29, on the balance between the absolute love of God and natural affection for friends and relatives: 'And every one that hath left house or brethren, or sisters, or father, or mother, or wife, or children, or lands for my name's sake, shall receive a hundred-fold, and shall possess life everlasting.' See above, 27/120; *Eight Chapters*, Chapter 1, in *English Mystics*, ed. Windeatt, 137. Bernard takes the same position (although he does not mention parents) in *Serm. super Cant.* 50. 2. 8. Aquinas, *ST* 2–2, q. 26, art. 7–8 argues that one is bound to love those to whom one is connected more than those whom one loves for charity alone.

29 *hangeth noȝt vpon him.* The Latin version doubles this: 'non adheret ibi vel pendet super eum'.

32 *oþer men.* The Latin version, 'aliis hominibus', supports the plural of H_7HλSrLwELdW over the singular variants of RAs, H_5WsCcMPlT, and A.

33 *þat him were lefer.* The Latin version expands and mollifies this: 'quod causa naturalis affeciconis libencius vellet'.

34 *þat sum oþer men han.* H_7 'þan', is ungrammatical, because it sets up a comparison, 'lefer . . . þan', that conflicts with the more immediate 'þe selfe . . . þat'. MSS YB_4H_8UpHe of the Latin version add: 'quam vnus [alius B_4H_8UpHe] homo'.

36 *þe loue of Jesu.* The Latin version, 'dileccio Jesu', supports H_7RλSrAECcMPl over χ 'Goddis lufe'.

38 *not only . . . worldly gode.* That is, this benefit of contemplative grace is not only available to those in poverty (including those in religious orders).

43 *Goddis lufer.* The Latin version reads 'perfecte Deum diligentis'.

46 *resceyuen . . . restendly.* The Latin version reads 'recipere vel admittere'.

51 *ese.* HH_5AsWs appear to have taken this as an adjective, 'easy', although it is parallel to the noun 'reste'.

56 *not for lufe . . . lufe of God* (l. 57). The distinction Hilton makes here depends on that between the use and the enjoyment of a thing in Augustine. See *De Doct. christ.* 1. 4. 4.

itself. The Latin version clarifies: 'illius cibi et potus'.

59 *hem for to be togedre.* The Latin version expands: 'corpus et animam similiter esse seu vniri'.

63 *do.* The Latin version, 'facere et cibum sumere' supports the Cc addition 'and takyn'.

66 *esily*. The Latin version supports the HRBH_5AsWsLwALdPlTW omission over H_7LB_3SrEPH_6CcM.

67 *and*. The Latin version, 'semper de Domino Jesu cogitare cum reuerenti amore, sine impedimento alicuius rei', supports Σ in reading 'ay' rather than 'and', but places the adverb so that it clearly modifies the preceding phrase, and not, as in Σ, 'withouten lettynge'.

73 *grete mede*. The Latin version, 'cibos grossos et rudes', appears to depend on an English exemplar reading 'mete' for 'mede'.

74 *softnes in hert*. The Latin version expands: 'sobrietate cordis et quiete'.

76 *he*. The Latin version expands: 'homo perfecte diligens Deum'.

79 *cury*. The Latin version expands: 'artem et diligenciam cocorum'.

81 *kepeth*. The Latin version, 'iuuet', supports Σ 'helpeth'. The H_7 variant is probably the result of a confusion of graphic similars, and may also anticipate 'kepeth' in the next line.

83 *and . . . withal* (l. 84). The Latin version omits this clause.

93 Hilton has adopted the pattern, common in confessors' manuals, of considering moral progress from the point of view of the seven deadly sins and from that of the five senses. Confessors' manuals add to this the consideration of the commandments.

95–6 *neuer so fayre, ne so precious, ne so wonderful*. The Latin version, 'quantumcumque preciosa sit, mirabilis atque pulcra', supports H_7RλSrAECcMPl over the repetition of 'neuere' in χAs.

98 *herte*. The Latin version, 'corda', supports the plural of χAsECc 'hertes', over the singular of H_7RλSrAMPl.

104 *fredam*. Only manuscripts B_2R_2 of the Latin version read 'libertatem'; Y reads ⌜affectionem⌝, and B_4H_8UpMaBnHeEs 'affectum'.

107 *Jesu*. The Latin version, 'Jesu', supports H_7RλSrAECcMPl over χAs 'him'.

lyketh. The Latin version, 'sibi placet', supports the HRBH_5AsSrWsLwAECcMLdPlW addition of 'him' over H_7λT. The pronoun is present in all manuscripts when the phrase is repeated in a parallel construction two lines later. The variation may have arisen from misunderstanding because of semantic change of 'like' from impersonal to transitive in this period.

þat is. H_7 apparently reads 'þat' pronominally, as the subject of 'is', where Σ read it as a conjunction, introducing 'it is'.

109–10 *bot if it be sumwhat towchend þe werkynge of his soule in þe lufe of Jesu*. The Latin version, 'nisi animam suam aliqualiter excitet ad amorem Dei', simplifies the object of the speech under consideration.

114 *only*. The Latin version, 'solum', supports H_7RλSrAECcMPl over the χAs omission.

115 *principally*. The Latin version expands: 'quam principaliter scire desiderat et adiscere'.

118 *it is no dowte . . . of it* (l. 119). Manuscripts B_2R_2 of the Latin version read 'non est dubium quin in talibus non habet saporem nec in mundanis' here; all others omit the passage, presumably by eye-skip.

121 *þe more*. The Latin version, 'si enim', misses the comparison being set up here. The subsequent 'þe more' (l. 123) and 'þe lesse . . . þe lefere' are translated 'tanto . . . quanto . . . tanto'.

122 *gostly*. H_7 'bodily' has got Hilton's sense precisely backwards.

123 *þe more he fleeth it, and*. Only manuscripts H_8Up of the Latin version read 'tanto amplius se elongat et separet ab ea, et'; all others omit the phrase.

123–4 *þe lesse þat he feleth of hem*. The Latin version shifts the focus here from the contemplative himself to his senses: 'quanto minus sensus in tali vsu occupantur'.

125 *withouten þe felenge of ony of hem*. The Latin version continues in this vein: 'sine huiusmodi vsu sensuum exteriorum'.

126 *þe*[2]. A spelling for 'þei'. The Latin version expands: 'sensaciones illicite per sensus'.

CHAPTER 40

Hilton here identifies the contemplative experience of 'lighty mirkness and rich nought' that he spoke of in chapters 24–7 metaphorically as 'the opening of the ghostly eye'. He goes on, in this and the next chapter, to describe this experience using a number of other metaphors common in the contemplative tradition, which he explicates in turn. Counterbalancing his justification of the concept of 'reformation in faith and in feeling' from the Pauline epistles in Chapter 31, the present discussion offers a justification of his teaching based on the discourse of the contemplative tradition.

1 *grace*. The Latin version, 'gracias', supports the plural of λAELdPlTW 'graces' over H_7RSrM. The text, however, continues to speak only of a single grace.

9 *kendly*. The Latin version, 'naturale', supports H_7RλSrAECcMPl over the χAs omission.

12–13 *my lippes are vnclene*. See Isa. 6: 5: 'I am a man of unclean lips.'

13 *for . . . þerfor* (l. 14). The Latin version omits this phrase.

14 *as I hope lufe techeth*. MSS B_4H_8UpHe of the Latin version read 'estimo quod amor docte quia estimo quod amor illud precepit ac requirit'. Y reads 'prout videtur mihi'. The reason for the omission of Hilton's triple reference to the agency of love as the source of his response to the questions moved by love is unclear.

15 *is þat lyghtty mirkenes and þat riche noȝt þat I spake of byfore* (l. 16). See above, Chapters 24–7, culminating at 27/138–56. Hilton will continue to use the metaphor of the opening of the ghostly eye. The Latin version omits this phrase.

ryght noȝt. HBH$_5$LB$_3$AsSrWsLwAHu$_2$EPH$_6$CcW`T$^{G'}$ 'riche' is more cogent. Hilton has in fact spoken before of the 'riche noght', at 24/115, and often uses the words of the H$_7$RMLdPlT variant here, 'ryght noȝt', to mean 'absolutely nothing', which is inappropriate here.

16–21 *purete of spirit . . . reformyng in felynge.* Each of these terms will be taken up in the course of the following discussion: 'purete of spirit' at 41/7 and again at 41/108, 'gostly rest' at 40/35, 'pees in conscience' at 40/65, 'heyghnes or depnes of thoght' at 40/82, 'heyghnes of herte' at 40/94, 'onlynes of soule' at 40/101, 'priuete of herte' at 40/123, 'lyuely felyng of grace' at 40/144, 'þe wakere slepe of þe spouse' at 40/165 and 41/9, 'a tastyng of heuenly sauour' at 41/10–11, and 'brennyng in lufe and schynyng in lyght' at 41/12–13.

16 *purete of spirit.* The Latin version, 'paupertas spiritus', supports RH$_5$WsMPl 'pouerte', over H$_7$HBλSrLwAHu$_2$ECcLdTW. In the later iteration of this term at 41/7, the phrase is 'purete and pouerte of spirit' ('puritatem et paupertatem spiritus'); at 41/108, it is 'purete of spirit' in English and 'paupertas spiritus' in Latin.

17 *or depnes.* The Latin version, 'vel profunditas', supports H$_7$RλSrAECcMPl over the χAs omission. The same words are also omitted below, at 40/82.

22 *it.* The Latin version specifies 'ista oculi apercione'.

24 *on in.* The Latin version, 'idem sunt in sentencia veritatis', supports H$_7$RλSrAHu$_2$ECcMPlT over HBH$_5$AsWsLwLdW 'in on'.

32 *affeccyons.* The Latin version, 'affeccio ad', supports the singular of χAs over the plural of H$_7$RλSrAECcMPl.

33 *mene lettyng.* The Latin version reads 'medium impediens'.

37 *fro þe noye*: The Latin version reads 'per separacionem a gaudio', perhaps dependent on an English exemplar reading 'ioye' like Sr.

39 *lufe.* The Latin version adds a devotional expansion, 'per assiduam meditacionem de Jesu Christo'.

43 *leseth.* The verb in H$_7$ here is *MED* 'lesen' (*v.* (5.4)), 'to loosen and separate, to remove', not 'lesen' (*v.* (4)), 'to lose'.

þe heuy ȝok of fleschly lufe. For sin as a yoke, see Bernard, *De Dilig. Deo* 13. 36, referring to Ecclus. 40: 1.

44 *sotely*. The Latin version, 'tranquille', supports Σ 'softely' over H$_7$.

46 *holy ydelnes and a reste most besy*. See William of St-Thierry, *Lettre d'or* 300, 'otia negotiosa, quies operosa'.

so is it in stillnes. The Latin version, 'sic est in silencio et tranquillitate', supports H$_7$λSrLwAECcMPlW over H°BH$_5$WsLwHu$_2$LdTW 'so is it inward stilnes'.

49 *his voyce . . . softly sownyng* (l. 51). This is the first occurrence of the theme of the sounding of the sweet voice of Jesus that will recur at 41/167, 44/1, 44/55, 46/56–7, and 46/65–74.

50 *ianglynge*. The syntax of the sentence requires a noun here. The Latin version, 'garulacione', supports the verbal noun of BLB$_3$SrLwHu$_2$EPH$_6$CcMLdPlTW over the present participle of H$_7$, 'ianglend', or the infinitive of HH$_5$AsWs, 'iangelen'.

51 *of vertu*. The Latin version, 'virtute', reads 'vertu' as an ablative of manner, anticipating the ablative of the scriptural text's 'in virtute'.

sownyng. The present participle of the Latin version, 'sonans', supports H$_7$ACc over the past participle of HBH$_5$LB$_3$SrWsLwHu$_2$EPH$_6$MLdPlTW, 'souned', or the present indicative of As, 'sowneþ'.

52 Ps. 28: 4.

54 Hebr. 4: 12. The modern Vulgate text reads 'Dei', not 'Domini'. Cassian makes use of this text similarly in *Collationes* 7. 13 (*PL* 49: 683–5), as does Bernard, *Serm. super Cant.* 74. 2. 6, a sermon with which there are a number of parallels in this section of *Scale* II.

55 *ancipiti*. The Latin version supports H$_7$λSrAECc over the χAsMPl omission.

58 Rev. 8: 1.

59 See Gregory, *Hom. in Ezech.* 2. 2. 14, 'Cœlum quippe est anima justi'; *Mor. in Job* 29. 28. 55, 30. 16. 53.

69 *defautes*. The Latin version adds 'prius commissis'.

made þat tyme. The Latin version, 'illo tempore in anima', supports the Σ addition, 'in a soule' (which precedes 'þat tyme' in Cc) over the H$_7$ omission.

þei. The Latin version specifies 'Jesus et anima'.

70 *al is forȝifen þat was mysdon* (l. 50). The Latin version specifies 'omne delictum remittitur quod prius fuerat perpetratum'.

71 *and gostly gladnes*. The Latin version, 'et magna spirituali iocunditate', supports Σ 'and grete gostly gladnes' over the H$_7$ omission of 'great'.

72 *boldenes of saluacyon*. See 1 John 4: 17, 'that we may have boldness on the day of judgement'. The Latin version, 'fiduciam saluacionis', shows a parallelism with Bernard, *Serm. super Cant.* 7. 3. 3, 'fiducia libertatis', referring to the same text. See also below, 44/33.

74 *is chosen sone.* The Latin version maintains its use of the feminine gender to refer to the soul: 'est electa'.

75–6 Rom. 8: 16. See Bernard, *De Dilig. Deo* 13. 36–14. 37, *Serm. super Cant.* 37. 3. 5, 57. 2. 3–4.

77 *sothfastly feled.* The Latin version adds a subordinating conjunction here, 'dum veraciter sentitur'.

78–9 2 Cor. 1: 12. The modern Vulgate text, like ALd and the Latin version of Hilton, uses the plural 'nostra' and 'nostræ'. See Bernard, *Serm. super Cant.* 25. 4. 7, 63. 2. 3.

82 or *depnes.* The Latin version, 'vel profunditas', supports H_7SrCcMPl over the **χλ**AsAE omission, as above at 40/17.

90 *creatures.* The Latin version, 'creaturas corporales', supports Σ 'bodily creatures' over the H_7Pl omission.

vsynge. See above, note to 39/56–7.

91 *gostly.* The Latin version adds 'non carnalis'.

dedeyne. L appears originally to have confused 'dedeyne' with the graphically similar 'deynte'. This is queried in the margin, and the clarifying prefix 'vn-' was added. B_3 may derive from a copy made before, and P after, this correction was made.

95 *comeþ . . . fende.* In a parallel passage in Hilton's *Qui habitat*, in *Exposition*, ed. Wallner, 38, the protection of the soul from the snares of Satan is said to be accomplished by the ministry of the angels: 'þei defenden a soule miȝtiliche from fendes, And wysliche teche hit þat hit falle not in errours or in heresyes'.

comeþ. H_7 'come', which is either a present subjunctive or a present indicative plural form in the scribal dialect, is ungrammatical in either case.

for Jesu is sothfastly in syght of þe soule þat tyme (l. 96). The Latin version turns this into a subordinate clause and adds a main clause: 'quia Jesus Christus qui veraciter est in aspectu anime illlo tempore custodit illam.

96 *in²*. The Latin version, 'et', supports Σ 'and' over H_7. The Σ variant is the more cogent reading: Hilton's point is not that Jesus is seen at that time 'in' all things that are beneath him, but that the spiritual sight of the soul is focused on Jesus alone, and all else is beneath. The H_7 variant may arise from confusion of the abbreviated forms of 'and' and 'in'.

97 Ps. 63: 7–8. The modern Vulgate text has 'Accedet'. This text is commonly cited in contemplative literature: see Richard of St-Victor, *Benj. Min.* 75, *Benj. Maj.* 4. 7, 5. 4.

102 *here body ben.* H_7 reads 'here body' as plural, although its antecedent is the singular 'soule'.

111–12 Hos. 2: 14. Richard of St-Victor cites this verse in describing the second degree of love of God, *De Quatuor Gradibus violentae caritatis* (*PL* 196: 1218).

120 *onlynes of body.* The repetition of 'corporis solitudo' in the Latin version supports H_7RλSrAECcMPl over χAs 'þat'.

123 *is it.* H_7HRLwAW (including the three earliest surviving manuscripts of the English text) support this reading over the H_5λAsSrWsEMLdPlT inversion.

127 *þan . . . and is wonderly conforted* (l. 129): The Latin version makes this into a temporal comparison: 'quando . . . tunc confortatur mirabiliter'.

in into. The Latin version, 'introducitur in cauernam', supports H_7Cc over χλAsAECc 'into' or R 'to'.

129–30 Isa. 24: 16. At the conclusion of the *Lettre d'or*, written to the Carthusians of Mont-Dieu, William of St-Thierry refers this verse both to their conscience and the cells in which they dwelt.

132 *pryuete and gostly lufe.* The Latin version, 'in secretum amoris spiritualis', supports Σ 'pryuete of', over H_7.

134 *my Lord Jesu in priuete is schewed to me.* The Latin version, 'Dominus meus Jesus mihi ostenditur in secreto', supports H_7λSrACcPl over χREM 'þi priuite'. Theologically, the two statements are nearly equivalent, since, as Hilton has pointed out immediately above, when 'the soul is by grace drawn into the privy chamber of the divine Lover', it is drawn 'into the sight of our Lord Jesus, and it hears his privy counsel'.

137 An abbreviated version of Rev. 2: 17: 'Vincenti dabo manna absconditum, et dabo illi calculum candidum, et in calculo nomen novum scriptum quod nemo scit nisi qui accipit.' This text is cited by Gregory, *Mor. in Job* 19. 2. 4, Richard of St-Victor, *Benj. Min.* 36 and *De Quatuor Gradibus violentae caritatis* (*PL* 196: 25).

139 *heuenly mete and aungels fode.* See Ps. 77: 24–5: 'Et pluit illis manna ad manducandum, et panem caeli dedit eis. Panem angelorum manducavit homo. Cibaria misit eis in abundantia.' By the later medieval period, the concept of the 'panis angelicus' was commonly referred to the Eucharist, as it was in the eponymous Corpus Christi hymn and in Nicholas Love's *Mirror* (152, l. 41–153, l. 1). Hilton, however, is referring to an older, contemplative tradition (see Bernard, *Serm. super Cant.* 35. 4), as he does in *Scale* I, Chapter 79, *De Imag. pec.* 92, ll. 353–5, and *De Lecc.*, 238, ll. 369–71.

141–2 *bot . . . is.* The Latin version adds 'hic perfecte', perhaps anticipating 'ȝit here' in the next line.

142 *not filled ȝit here*. The Latin version expands: 'non adhuc hic saciatur ex hoc manna'.

143 *þe lyf of his body*. The Latin version, 'vita sui corporis', supports H_7λSrMPl over χRAsAECc 'þis bodily lif'.

144 *felyng of grace*. See Hilton's *Qui habitat*, in *Exposition*, ed. Wallner, 34, l. 8. See also William of St-Thierry, *Lettre d'or* 382: 'in ipso lumine veritatis indubitanter videt praevenientem gratiam'.

151 *So . . . in grace* (l. 155). This sentence is in the singular in the Latin version: 'eum' *ter*, which supports H_7RλSrAECcMPl 'him' over χ 'hem' in the first instance, H_7AsAE 'him' over χRλSrCcMPl 'hem' in the second, and H_7E 'him' over χRλAsSrACcMPl 'hem' in the third.

155 *knoweth wele by experyence þat he is in grace*. Similarly Aquinas, *ST* 2–2, q. 45, a. 2, cites the pseudo-Dionysus *De Divinis nominibus* to the effect that by that Wisdom that is the gift of the Holy Spirit, one might be 'non solum discens, sed et patiens divina'.

158 *and þe soule also*. The Latin version omits.

161 *kepe it . . . put it away*. The Latin version clarifies: 'hanc graciam custodire . . . expelleret hanc graciam'.

162 *it passeth away ful lyghtly*. The observation that the contemplative experience is transitory is a commonplace. Gregory, for example, refers to it as 'furtim' in *Hom. in Ezech.* 1. 5. 12, 2. 2. 12, and 2. 5. 17, and 'raptim' in *Mor. in Job* 5. 58, 8. 49–50, 23. 43, and 24. 11. See Cuthbert Butler, *Western Mysticism: The Teaching of SS. Augustine, Gregory, and Bernard on Contemplation and the Contemplative Life*, 2nd edn. (London, 1926), 81. Hilton will continue on this topic in the next chapter.

passeth away. The Latin version expands: 'transit . . . et recedit'.

164 *relef lefeth stille*. The Latin version translates this as plural: 'reliquie . . . manent . . . custodiunt . . . faciunt'.

165 *þis*. The Latin version clarifies: 'hec operacio oculi spiritualis de qua loquor'.

166 S. of S. 5: 2. A commonplace: see Gregory, *Mor. in Job* 5. 31. 54, 23. 20. 38 and the eponymous *incipit* of Rolle's tract (*EW* 60–72; *P&V* 26–33).

169 *dede*. The Latin version has 'mortui'. H°RBH_5LB_3AsWsAPH_6MLdPl 'dedid' is the past participle of *MED* 'dēden' (*v.*).

179 Luke 9: 32. The apostolic vision of the transfiguration of Christ is a common metaphor for the contemplative experience: see Richard of St-Victor, *Benj. Maj.* 5. 2, *Benj. Min.* 77, both of which cite the narrative from Matt. 17: 1–6.

183 *syght*. The lack of the definite article here is supported by the three earliest English manuscripts, H_7H°RM, as opposed to BH_5λAsSrWsLw-A`H^{c}′ECcLdPlTW.

CHAPTER 41

10 *ioyes*. The Latin version, 'gaudium', supports the singular of the λE variant 'ioie'.

11 *softly*. The Latin version, 'veraciter', supports λE 'soþli' over H_7χRSrACcMPl.

14 *reformed in felyng . . . is in ful* (l. 16). Latin MSS $YH_2B_2R_2B_4$HeBn-MaUp_2UtEs read: 'que reformata est pro illo tempore in sensacione virtutum omnium predictarum'; MSS H_8Up read: 'sensibiliter reformatur et reparatur et habilitatur contemplacioni. Hec sunt signa inspiracionis in apercione oculi spiritualis. Quia quando oculus aperitur, tunc est anima in sensacione virtutum omnium predictarum pro illo tempore.' If Y and the other manuscripts represent the exemplar of the Latin version, this original would appear to depend on an English text lacking the phrase 'made able . . . is in ful'. In this case, the omitted material could have been made up in the exemplar of H_8Up by comparison with an Englsh manuscript. Alternatively, H_8Up may be alone in transmitting material coincidently lost by eye-skip in all other Latin manuscripts.

19 Possibly echoing Wisd. 9: 15: 'For the corruptible body is a load upon the soul, and the earthy habitation presseth down the mind that museth upon many things.'

23 *face*. The Latin version, 'faciem', supports H_7RBλSrACcMLdPlT 'face' (which anticipates the following scriptural citation) over HH_5AsWsLwEW 'grace'.

*it*². The Latin version clarifies: 'ipsum Jesum'.

24–5 Job 34: 29, which begins, in the modern Vulgate, 'Ex quo absconderit vultum'.

33 S. of S. 5: 6. The scribal identification of the text in BLEPLdTW would point rather to 3: 1, which lacks the second clause. Hilton's discussion here derives, however, from Bernard's commentary on Cant. 3: 1, *Serm. super Cant.* 74.

34 *I fonde not; I called him*. The H_7RλSrMPl variant understands 'illum' as the object of following 'vocaui' (as the Latin text is punctuated in H_7 and a number of other English manuscipts), rather than of the preceding 'inueni'; χAsA 'I fonde him not; I called' represents the opposite, perhaps corrected to reflect the scriptural text. ECc read 'him' in both places.

36 *cause þerof and not his fleynge*. The Latin version clarifies: 'causa subtraccionis gracie Dei et non fuga ipsius Dei'. Hilton's point depends on the distinction of operant grace, which has its effect immediately, without human cooperation, and cooperant grace, with which the human agent must choose to cooperate (although even the choice to cooperate is itself a gift of grace). See Aquinas, *ST* 1–2, q. 111, a. 2. The gift of contemplation is a form of cooperant grace, and the loss of the feeling of closeness to God is not because God has ceased to offer grace, but because due to human weakness, the contemplative does not receive it.

37 *by sotelte . . . called him* (l. 38). The HH_5AsWsLwW omission is presumably the result of eye-skip.

40 *hert.* The Latin version, 'corde', supports H_7RλSrACcMLdPlT over HBH_5AsWsLwEW 'soule'.

S. of S. 2: 17: 'Revertere: similis esto, dilecte mi, capreae.' The scribal identification of the text in BLEPLdTW would point rather to 6: 12: 'Revertere, revertere, Sulamitis! Revertere, revertere ut intueamur te.' See Bernard, *Serm. super Cant.* 74. 1. 1–4.

41 *felyng in myself.* The Σ reading, that the 'felyng of myself' without the beloved is in itself painful, is more cogent. The Latin version translates with a neutral possessive pronoun: 'penalis sensacio mea'.

48 *ful of grace and sothfastnes*. John 1: 14: 'plenum gratiae et veritatis'.

53 S. of S. 1: 2. Bernard makes meditation on the name of Jesus the focus of *Serm. super Cant.* 15. The theme is particularly prominent in the writings of Richard Rolle: see the Latin *Encomium nominis Jesu* (of which an English version exists, *YW*, i. 186–91); Chapter 9 of *The Form of Living* (*EW* 108; *P&V* 18); the end of the *Commandment* (*EW* 81; *Uncollected Prose and Verse*, 39), and the commentry on the first verses of *Canticles* (Allen, *WA*, 73–6; *Richard Rolle: Biblical Commentaries*, trans. Robert Boenig, Salzburg Studies in English Literature: Elizabethan & Renaissance Studies, 92:13 (Salzburg, 1984), 97–8).

This is the argument of the 'Holy Name passage' added at the end of Chapter 44 in some manuscripts of *Scale* I, responding to his interlocutor's statement that some men have written that whoever cannot be devoted to the name of Jesus will never experience the joys of heaven. William Flete makes the same obervation about the meaning of the name 'Jesus' in Chapter 10 of *De Remed.* 238, ll. 8–13; *YW*, ii. 121.

53, 57, 61 *ȝetted, ȝoted, ȝeten*. The variation of forms ending in '-ed' and '-en' shows development of weak past participial forms of what was originally a strong verb. See *MED* 'yēten' *v.* (3) 1.

58 *þi.* The Latin version, 'tue', supports H_7RSrACcMPlW over the HBH_5λAsWsLwELdT omission.

60 *lufyng*. The Latin version, 'laude', supports a reading meaning 'praising' here, rather than 'loving'. Although the H_7 scribe uses 'luf-', 'lof-', and 'lou-'

for the stem of the noun or verb 'love', he uses 'luf-' only once elsewhere, at 44/42, for the homonym meaning 'praise'.

myrthe. The Latin version, 'iocunditate', supports H_7RSrACcMPlW over HBH_5λAsWsLwLdT 'miȝt'.

62 *þu*. The Latin version, 'tu', supports H_7RBλAsSrAECcMLdPlT over HH_5WsLwLdW 'þat'.

64 *felably*. The Latin version, 'sensabiliter', supports H_7RëSrAECcMPl over the χAs omission.

65 *presence . . . absence*. See Bernard, *Serm. super Cant.* 74. 1. 2: 'Restat igitur ut absentem studiose requirat, revocet abeuntem.'

brennende. The Latin version, 'ardens', supports H_7RλSrAECcMPl over the χAs omission.

70 *chaungeablyte*. The Latin version translates as 'mutabilitas'. This 'vicissitudo' of spiritual experience is the subject of Bernard's *Serm. super Cant.* 74 (see also 17. 1. 1 and 32. 1. 2), of Flete's *De Remed.*, and of *The Chastising of God's Children*.

74 *þogh neuerþeles ȝit*. Hilton emphasizes through a multiplication of adverbial forms the disjunction between two observations: that even though the degree of hindrance that the soul, of itself, feels in the continuity of its experience of grace is a sign of a proportionate decrease in grace, yet nonetheless the grace itself is still contemplative grace. The various variations among χAsSrA represent attempts to simplify or clarify his expression.

79 See Bernard, *Serm. super Cant.* 17. 1: 'Mens ergo quae ignorat abscessum patet seductioni.'

82–4 See James 1: 17: 'Every best gift, and every perfect gift, is form above, coming down from the Father of Lights, with whom there is no change, nor shadow of alteration.'

82 *þe more stabilnes*. See Hilton's *Angels' Song*, 10. *YW*, i. 175.

83 *more lyke*. The Latin version, 'et similior', supports the HBH_5AsWsLw-AEH_6MLdPlTW addition of 'and'.

84 *no chaungeablite*. The Latin version, 'non est mutabilitas seu mutacio', supports H_7W over the Σ addition of 'manere'.

87 *now-whare*. The Latin version, 'nisi', supports H_7λSrH^cAECcPl over χ[H°]AsM 'now here'.

89 *ay*. The Latin version, 'semper', supports H_7λSrAECcPl over the χAs omission.

90, 94 *ful blynde*. On the blindness of spiritual neophytes who are convinced of their own superiority, see above, 26/58.

91 *of*. The double preposition 'with of' of HBLw is ungrammatical, and may have originated as a marginal or interlinear correction, 'of' (as in Σ) for 'with' (as in Ld), in an exemplar, which some scribe or scribes mistook for an addition. Alternatively, 'commoneng with' may have been taken as a compound noun.

creatures. The Latin version, 'creaturarum', supports H_7λSrAECcMPl over the HBH_5WsLwLdTW addition of 'alle'.

and[2]. The Latin version translates this with a causal conjunction: 'ita quod'.

93 *fully oned to him*. The Latin version, 'sic quod anima sua plene vnitur ipsi Jesu', expands this into a full clause.

98 *þenkend þat what he euer speke or do is grace*. The predicate 'is grace' is necessary to this, one of three parallel clauses, 'demende . . . þenkend . . . holdende'. The omission of 'is grace' in H_7 comes at the end of a line, and the next line begins the third clause.

99 *If þer . . . grace* (l. 100). The omission in H°H_5WsCc is presumably the result of eye-skip.

103 Rom. 1: 17, Gal. 3: 11, and Hebr. 10: 38, all echoing Hab. 2: 4.

104 *bodily felynges*. Hilton returns here to a theme raised in *Scale* I, Chapters 10–12, and above, Chapter 29.

108 *purete of þe spirit*. The Latin version, 'paupertas spiritus', may depend on an English exemplar reading 'pouerte', a variant that does not occur among the surviving manuscripts.

109 *al oþer*. The Latin version expands: 'omnes virtutes alie'.

before seyd. See above, 40/15.

110 *soule*. The Latin version, 'animabus', may depend on a plural reading like A 'soulis'.

111 *if þat we myghten*. The Latin version omits.

113 *presence*. The Latin version expands: 'presencie graciose'.

116 *schul*. The Latin version, 'debemus', supports the present subjunctive of H_7H_5λAsSrWsAECcM over HBLwLdPlTW 'schulde'.

117 *for to werken*. The Latin version, 'operari', supports H_7BλSrECcMPl over HH_5WsLdT 'so to werken'.

schul not kun. The Latin version, 'nesciemus', supports the present tense of H_7AsSrAEMPl (including Sr as originally written) over HBH_5λ`Sr´WsLwLdTW 'schuld not kun'.

118 *For . . . soule*[2]. See the pseudo-Augustinian *De Spiritu et anima*: 'Vita corpus anima est, vita anima Deus est' (*PL* 40: 811).

123 *myght*. The Latin version, 'viribus', supports the plural of Σ over H_7.

onyng to him. See 1 Cor. 6: 17: 'But he who is joined to the Lord, is one spirit.'

131 *fleschly*. The Latin version, 'carnalium', supports H_7BλSrAECcMLdPlT over the HH_5AsWsLwW omission.

133 *perceyuende, fed*. The Latin version translates both of these as infinitives, 'percipere', 'pasci', parallel to 'to be drawen oute' ('extrahi') earlier in the sentence.

136 *soule*. The Latin version expands: 'et electe'.

He. The Latin version expands: 'Verus dilector Jesu Christi'.

138 *fro*. 'away'. The Latin version, 'liber', supports B 'fre', which is also added as a marginal gloss in a different hand in H_7. HL, two other of the earliest manuscripts, have both been corrected to 'fer', a variant that also occurs in EPLw, in the latter of which it has been cancelled. H_5WsSrAH_6 all read 'fro' as a preposition, and supply a variety of likely objects. The original reading appears most probably to have been the adverb 'fro' (*MED* 'from' (*adv.*) 1(a) Of place or movement: away), a variant which the majority of the scribes either misunderstood as a preposition and provided with an object, or read as the similarly spelled adverb 'fer'. B_3CcTW omit.

139 *gostlynes*. The Latin version, 'spiritualitate', supports H_7λAsSr-AECcMPl over the χ addition of the modifier 'his'.

ȝit is þat no ful myrthe. The Latin version expands: 'hec leticia non adhuc plena est et perfecta'.

ay þere hangeth an heuy lumpe of bodily corrupcyon on his soule (l. 140). Cf. Wisd. 9: 15; see above, 41/19.

142 *is*. The Latin version, 'permanet', supports H_7λSrACcMPl over the χAsA addition of 'here'.

144 *þerfore, I mene not*. The Latin version understands 'þerfore' as connected to the following clause, which it alters to fit: 'ideo tibi dico quod non intelligo'.

145 *common grace . . . specyale grace* (l. 147). See above, 10/21–5, 35/74.

152 *for . . . synne*[2]. MSS B_4H_8UpHe of the Latin version have 'quia hec gracia non nisi per peccatum mortale', which YH_2MaBnUt omit.

dedly. The Latin version, 'peccatum mortale', supports Σ over the HH_5AsWs omission.

160–1 John 3: 8. See Bernard, *Serm. super Cant.* 17. 1. 1 and 74. 2. 5.

162 *fro whom*. Either the H_7 variant, λET 'fro whennes', or BSrMLd 'fro whanne' is a better translation of the 'vnde' of the scriptural text than HH_5AsWsLwACcLdWWc 'when'.

163 *of him*. The fact that the displacement of text in As (f. 126^r, l. 13 to

f. 128^{v}, l. 8 comprises text from 42/115 to 43/97; f. 128^{v}, l. 9 to f. 130^{v}, l. 28 comprises text from 41/163 to 42/115, followed by text from 43/97 onwards) occurs in mid-line and mid-page suggests that this is the result of an unmarked displacement of folios in its exemplar.

167 *and þis is his voyce þat he sowneth*. This is the second occurrence of the theme of the sounding of the voice of Jesus. See above, 40/49–51, and below, 44/1, 44/55, and 46/56–7.

168 *fro excesse into soberte*. Clark, 'Notes', 325 n. 347, suggests that this is an echo of 2 Cor. 5: 13: 'For whether we be transported in mind, it is to God; or whether we be sober, it is for you.'

CHAPTER 42

In this chapter, Hilton describes the place that the gifts of heat, sweetness, and song occupy in his schema.

8 *colde and drye, vndeuowte and vnsauourye*. Hilton characterizes knowledge without devotion similarly at the end of *Scale* I, Chapter 4.

11 See 24/106–9.

and^{2}. The Latin version, 'in voluntate', supports Σ 'in' over H_7. This is probably another example of the confusion of the forms of 'in' and 'and' in H_7.

12 *For . . . stereth* (l. 13). The Latin version, 'Quia per apercionem oculi spiritualis est ad graciam totaliter applicata, parata operari secundum quod gracia excitat et instigat', supports H_7BλAsSrAECcLdMPl over the HH_5AsWsLwTW variants, all of which appear to arise out of the omission of 'For . . . grace^{I} (l. 6)', replaced (but placed differently) in TW and Lw.

13 *þe*. Both this and Σ 'þat' are to be read here as relative particles, not as quantifiers.

20 *oþer*. The Latin version, 'aliorum', supports H_7λSrAECcMPl over the χAs omission.

renable. The Latin version translates as 'tractam'.

22 *mende*. The Latin version translates as 'memoria'.

23 *gadred samen in itself*. See *Scale* I, Chapters 25 and 87, and 24/107 and 30/10 above.

samen. The H_7Pl variant is here the *lectio difficilior*.

25–6 *ful acorde of mouthe and of hert*. See the *Rule* of St Benedict, chapter 19.

26 *fyre of lufe*. Hilton has here appropriated one of the primary terms of Richard Rolle's description of the mystical experience.

29 *heyghneth*. The corrected form in H_7 does not correspond precisely to any of the possible headwords in *MED*: 'heghen' (*v.*) or 'heightenen' (*v.*), both meaning 'to exalt' or 'to raise', or 'hightenen (*v.*), meaning 'to adorn'. The scribe probably meant something like 'raises' or 'exalts', but the Latin version, 'illuminat' supports Σ 'liȝtneþ', which may have been the original reading of H_7.

40–1 *as stykkes norischen þe fyre*. See above, 21/130.

40 *as*. This word is repeated at the end of the recto and at the beginning of the verso folio in H_7.

42 *myrthe*. The Latin version, 'potencia', appears to depend on an English exemplar reading 'mighte' like LwW.

43 Ps. 140: 2. Hilton uses the same word, 'dressed', as the LV of the Wycliffite bible; the EV has 'reulid'. The use of this text is traditional; see, for example, its citation at the end of the classic discussion of prayer in Cassian's ninth conference: *Collationes* 9. 36 (*PL* 49, 818).

46 *eyre*. H_7 'eye', does not make sense.

ryght so. The word 'so' is necessary here, because this is the latter member of the comparison, 'ryght as . . . ryght so', begun in the preceding line.

49 *And as*. Like the Σ variant, the Latin version, 'Non audet . . .', lacks these transitional words added in the margins of H_7.

flesch-flye. The Latin version translates as 'musca'; the Wycliffite Bible version of Ps. 77: 45 uses 'fleisch flie' to translate 'cynomyia'.

53 *graces*. The Latin version, 'gracias', supports H_7Cc over the singular χλSrEMPl 'grace'. The word here means 'thanks', as opposed to 'grace' (Latin 'graciam') later in the line.

55 *oure Lord Jesu*. The Latin version, 'Domino nostro Jesu', supports H_7λSrAECcMPl over the χAs omission of 'oure Lord'.

56 *þe werk is gode in itself*. The Latin version adds a conjunction to relate this clause to the preceding: 'quia est bona operacio in seipsa'.

57 *And*. The Latin version, 'Et', supports H_7λSrAECcMPl over the χAs omission.

58 *ne . . . itself*. The Latin version, 'nec operacio dileccionis per seipsam', supports Σ over the H_7T omission, which is probably the result of eye-skip.

60 *presence*. The Latin version, 'presencia', supports H_7, the more cogent reading, over Σ 'plente'. It is the presence of grace, not any degree or amount of grace, that brings about this gift.

62–3 *in maner as it is*. The Latin version, 'illo modo', misses Hilton's concession that as pleasurable as this gift is, and as much as it is a gift of grace, it is not in itself contemplation.

63 *a riche offerand filled al in fatnes of deuocyon*. The Latin version reads 'oblacio dives et preciosa repleta pinguedine dileccionis'. Hilton continues here the reference to prayer as a sacrificial offering made begun at 42/42, referring specifically to the 'fatness' of the sacrifice specified in e.g. Lev. 3. 3. See Bernard, *Qui hab.* 9. 2.

64 *resceyued by aungeles.* Hilton mentions the ministry of angels several times in the latter chapters of *Scale* II: see 43/39, 46/23, 29.

65 *is made of two wordes.* The Latin version, 'fit ex verbis', appears to depend on an English exemplar that omitted the word 'two', since the reference to 'o word' ('vnum verbum') remains in the next line. The following reference to 'anoþer word', however, is translated simply as 'verbum', with a corrector's marginal addition, 'quam', in Y.

70 *preyer.* The Latin version, 'oracio', supports Σ over the HH$_5$AsWsW omission.

72 *þat formeth and sowneth.* The Latin version clarifies: 'que format verbum interius et sonat verbum exterius'.

78–9 Ps. 80: 4. See Gilbert of Hoyland's use of this text in his continuation of Bernard's sermons, *In Cant.* 18. 5 (*PL* 184: 92–6).

83 *is turned.* The Latin version, 'nouiter est conuersus', supports Σ 'is new turnid', over H$_7$. Because Hilton's topic here is the prayer of those who are newly turned to contemplation, the specification 'new turnid' is the more cogent reading. The Latin version does not translate the following phrase, 'what þat he be'.

85 *sumwhate queynte.* The scribe of H$_7$ seems to have read 'sum queynte' in his exemplar as a form of 'sumwhat' (presumably a dialectal form with medial '-q-') and recognized but only partially corrected his mistake on beginning the next word, 'felyng'.

96 *wiht.* The only occurrence in H$_7$ of this uncommon spelling for 'with'.

98 *withouten feynynge or fantasye.* See above, 40/95.

105 *him.* The Latin version, 'illum', supports H$_7$HBH$_5$AsWsAMLdPlTW over LB$_3$SrLwEPH$_6$Cc 'hem', which presumably refers back to 'sum [men *add.* LB$_3$EPH$_6$MLdT]'.

þe soule is turned al to þe eye. The Latin version, 'anima totaliter conuersa est ad oculum', supports H$_7$λSrAECcPl over χAs 'þe soule is turnid into eiȝe', literally, although all three forms are equivalent in meaning. Hilton's point is that the intention of the soul does not focus on the object of prayer. In his Augustinian epistemology the soul becomes as it were an eye, perceiving God by the divine light of grace. Note also the spiritual synaesthesia of cognition, sight, and feeling, which will continue throughout this discussion.

111 *feleth þe soule and seeth.* The Latin version, 'anima . . . sentit', supports χAs 'feliþ þe soule' over H_7λSrAECcPl (which may anticipate 'feled and seen' three lines below).

113 *grace of compunccyon*. See above, Chapter 7.

synnes. The Latin version, 'peccatis', supports H_7λSrACcMPl over χAsE 'his synnes'.

115 *boystously*. For the disruption in text in As, see the note to 41/163

feled and seen. The Latin version, 'sentitur ac videtur', supports H_7λSrAECcMPl over χAs 'felt'.

119 *þat*. The Latin version clarifies: 'hec sensacio seu visio'.

122 *in grace . . . by kende* (l. 123). Hilton preserves the distinction that the *deificatio* of the contemplative soul does not make it one with Christ by nature, but subordinately, by grace.

125 *þi*. The Latin version, 'tui', supports H_7HBH_5AsWsLwLdW over λSrAECcMPlT 'þe'.

126 *myght*. The Latin version, 'potes', supports the indicative of Σ 'may' over the subjunctive of H_7.

131 *lenest*. The Latin version, 'innitaris', supports H_7CcLd over the past tense of HBH_5SrWsLwAH_6PlTW 'lenid', B_3 'lenedist', or E 'lendist'. The dependence of P on the corrected text of L is apparent again here, where the text of L reads 'loned', with a marginal annotation, 'quere: loned or lened'; the scribe of P has incorporated the L correction, but only halfway: he has written 'loned or lened' in the text, and 'quere' in the margin.

133 *seen in þe*. The Latin version, 'per', supports Σ 'of' over H_7. Because the text goes on to specify that this vision of Jesus is only 'as þou mayht seen him here', the reading 'feld and seen of þe'—that is, 'by thee'—is more cogent.

136 *seen*. The Latin version, 'videre', supports H_7λSrACcMPl over χAsE 'seen and felen', although the couplet 'felen and seen' has occurred several times in this passage.

137 *mekely*. The Latin version, 'humiliter', supports H_7λSrAECcMPl over the χAs omission.

138–44 Hilton is here recapitulating ideas from Chapter 34, above.

CHAPTER 43

See Michael G. Sargent, 'Walter Hilton on the Gift of Interpretation of Scripture', in *MMTE* viii (Woodbridge, 2013), 51–8.

10 *an hilid*. The contraction of 'and' to 'an' occurs a number of times in the text of H_7; the nonsense spelling 'hidil' for 'hilid' results from confusion of graphic similars.

13 *clene*. The Latin version, 'mundo', supports H_7λSrECcMPl over the χAsA omission. In the double reference, here and two lines above, to a 'clean heart', Hilton is alluding to Matt. 5: 8: 'Blessed are the clean of heart: for they shall see God.'

sothfastnes . . . susters (l. 14). On the relation of truth and humility, see above, 20/87.

24 *wittis*. The genitive singular of the Latin 'ingenii' agrees with Σ 'wit', over the plural of H_7Cc.

25 *Jesu is welle of wisdom*. The image that Hilton is invoking here is the 'fountain sealed up . . . the well of living waters' of S. of S. 4: 12 and 15, to which he also refers in *Scale* I, Chapter 4. See Bernard, *Serm. super Cant*. 3. 1. 1; Hugh of St-Victor, *De Laude charitatis* (*PL* 176: 975).

32 *into*. The Latin version, 'ad', supports Σ 'to', over H_7Sr.

34 *presently*. The Latin version, 'presencialiter', points out that Hilton's meaning here is 'in their physical presence'.

35 Luke 24: 45. This verse describes Jesus's opening of the meaning of the prophecies to his apostles gathered in Jerusalem. His expounding of the Scriptures to the disciples on the way to Emaus and breaking bread with them occurs at Luke 24: 13–31. Note that Hilton translates the word 'sensum' as referring to the intelligence of the disciples, not to the 'sense' of the Scriptures.

40 *centence*. The plural form of the Latin version, 'sentencias', supports HLwHu$_2$LdTW 'sentences' over the singular of H_7BH_5LB_3AsSrW-sAEPH_6CcMPl.

vnsought. H_7 'vnsoth' is probably a spelling error arising from confusion of graphic similars.

41–3 Gregory, *Hom. in Ezech*. 1. 6. 1, 'Scripturae sacrae intelligentia . . . in quibusdam locis obscurioribus tanto maiore dulcedine intenta reficit quanto maiore labore fatigat animum quaesita.'

41 *expounet*. The past tense form of H_7 does not agree with the rest of the sentence.

44 *letterly, morally, mystely and heuenly* . The H_7 variant 'euenly' is an error. The Latin version reads: 'literaliter, moraliter, mistice, et anagogice siue celice'. The fourth manner of reading is also referred to in the next sentence as 'celica . . . vel anagogica'. Hilton is referring to the traditional four senses of scriptural interpretation, the description of which varies among later medieval writers, although its overall shape remains the same. Aquinas, *ST* 1. q. 1. a. 10, lists the senses of Scripture as historical or literal, allegorical, moral, and anagogical. The fullest treatment of the theme is Henri de Lubac, *Medieval Exegesis: The Four Senses of Scripture*, trans. Marc Sebanc and E.

M. Macierowski (Grand Rapids, Mich., 1998–2009; originally published as *Exégèse médiévale: Les quatre sens de l'écriture* (Paris, 1959–69)).

47 *informed.* H_7B_3 'conforted', makes no sense, since Hilton is here distinguishing the various characteristics of the four senses of Scripture: the comfort of human physicality has already been named as the characteristic of the literal sense.

48 *mystyed.* The Latin version clarifies: 'misterium seu misticum intellectum'.

49 *redely . . . Chirche* (l. 50). The omission in H°H_5AsWsA is presumably the result of eye-skip.

50 *oure Lord, heued.* The intrusion of 'Lord' into this phrase in H_7 is probably the result of scribal completion of the phrase 'Crist oure', inattentive to its actual completion in the contrast of 'heued' and 'body' in the text

Holy Chirche þat is his mysty body. The doctrine that all saved souls, whether currently alive or not, constitute a 'mystical body' of which Christ is the head derives from Col. 1: 18, 'he is the head of the body, the church'.

52 *þat.* The Latin version clarifies: 'dileccio'.

53 *y calle it heuenly.* The Latin version expands: 'istam expositionem celicam iudico appellandam'.

54 *but for Jesu is ful merciful, goodnesse maketh him his frend* (l. 55) The Latin version, 'set quia Jesus ex misericordi bonitate sua afficit eum amicum', supports Σ 'bot for Jesu of his merciful goodnes makiþ him his frende' over H_7.

56–7 The contrast between 'filial' and 'servile' love of God is of long standing. Aquinas's discussion in *ST* 2–2, q. 19, a. 2–6 (esp. a. 5) refers to Augustine's *Tract. in Ep. Ioan.*, 9 (*PL* 35: 2049), which makes the distinction between 'amor castus' and 'non castus'. See also Bernard, *De Dilig. Deo* 14.7, and the sermon 'De Timore Dei' among the *Sermones Centum* appended to the works of Hugh of St-Victor in *PL* 175: 413–32 at 428.

57 *schewyth.* H_7 here omits 'he', the grammatical subject of the sentence in Σ, so that 'schewyth' must be read as parallel to 'maketh' above, the subject of which is 'goodnesse'. The number of isolative variants in this passage suggests that the scribe of H_7 was particularly inattentive at this point.

preuyte. The Latin version, 'consilia', supports the plural of HBH_5WsLdTW 'pryueites', over the singular of H_7LB_3AsLwAEPH_6Cc-MPlW.

58–9 John 15: 15.

59 *Patre.* The Latin version (which is identical to the modern Vulgate text) agrees with Σ over the H_7H°BLd omission of 'meo'.

61 *hath palet*. The Latin version, 'habet palatum', supports H_7HBLB_3AsSrLwEPCcLdTW over H_5WsAH_6MPl 'is'. For the derivation of Hilton's extended alimentary metaphor from Gregory's *Mor. in Job* 33. 45. 1, and the further metaphor of the key and the signet, see Sargent, 'Walter Hilton on the Gift of Interpretation of Scripture', 54–8. Robert Stauffer has suggested in private correspondence that the phrase 'I may seie þe wordis of þe prophete: My teeth ben not white to bite of þis breed' in the translator's prologue to the English version of Marguerite Porete's *Mirror of Simple Souls* refers to this locus in Hilton's text, and that the translator, 'M.N.', is thus referring to Hilton as a prophet: see Marilyn Doiron, 'Marguerite Porete: "The Mirror of Simple Souls", a Middle English Translation', *Archivio italiano per la storia della pietà*, 5 (Rome, 1968), 241–355 at 247, l. 20. The reference to Hilton is probable; the description of Hilton as a prophet is not.

lust. This isolative variant in H_7 (Σ read 'lufe') is probably the result of a confusion of graphic similars.

60–81 See Somerset, *Feeling like Saints*, 205–10.

63–4 *þe spirit of lyf*. See below, 44/9–10 and note.

64 *is*. The Latin version, 'absconditus', supports Σ 'is hid', over the H_7 omission.

66 *whyte teeth*. Clark, 'Notes', 326 n. 373, suggests a possible source in Augustine, *De Doct. christ.* 2. 6. 7, referring to S. of S. 4: 2: 'Thy teeth as flocks of sheep, that are shorn, which come up from the washing.'

68 *touche*. The Latin version expands: 'tangere . . . vel gustare'; 'felyng' in the next line is translated 'degustacione'.

70 *vnderstonded*. See above, 12/20, for this weak form of the past participle in H_7.

fleschly. The Latin version, 'carnalibus dilectoribus', supports Σ 'fleschly lufers' over the H_7 omission. Because H_7 has here omitted the head word of the noun phrase, this adjective must be read nominally.

75 *þei . . . gnawen vpon þe bark withouten*. This image also occurs in *Scale* I, Chapters 14 and 20, in *The Cloud of Unknowing*, 107, l. 16, and in the same author's *Pistle of Prayer*, in *Deonise Hid Diuinite*, 57, ll. 23–4.

76 *felen*. The Latin version expands: 'senciunt vel degustant'.

79 *enseled with a sygnet*. See Rev. 5: 1.

Jesu is fynger. For the metaphor of the Holy Spirit as the 'finger of God', see Augustine, *De Trin.* 2. 15. 26, commenting on Exod. 31: 18 (which speaks of the stone tablets 'scriptas digito Dei'), concatenated with Luke 11: 20.

Jesu is. So H_7H_5LB_3AsAEPH_6; HBAsWsLwCcMLdPlTW 'Jesus' represents the earlier Middle English lack of genitive ending on a proper noun borrowed from Latin. Genitive forms like 'Jesu is' gave rise to the sixteenth-

and seventeenth-century misconception that the genitive ending '-s' or '-es' was a contraction of 'his', a misunderstanding that survives in the use of the apostrophe in the modern genitive singular.

81 *þe keye of conynge*. An allusion to Jesus' words to the Pharisees, Luke 11: 52: 'You have taken away the key of knowledge: you yourselves have not entered in, and those that were entering in, you have hindered', concatenated with Rev. 3: 7 (referring to Isa. 22: 22): 'These things saith the Holy One and the true one, he that hath the key of David; he that openeth, and no man shutteth; shutteth, and no man openeth.' The metaphor is used in the opening sentence of Richard of St-Victor's *Benj. Maj*.

87 *fyndeng*. The Latin version expands: 'intelligenciam Scripture'.

89 *See*. The Latin version, 'Vide ergo nunc', supports Σ 'Se now þan'.

95 *declareth*. H_7 'deschargeth' makes no sense here, but presumably resulted from a confusion of graphic similars.

97 *as wele in a lewed as in a lettred man*. The plural of the Latin version, 'in laicis sicut in litteratis', supports Σ over the singular of H_7.

þe. For the disruption in text in As, see the note to 41/163.

99–100 *for þat nedeth not*. The Latin version makes more pointed Hilton's observation that the equality of the laity and educated clergy in their ability to receive the gift of understanding of Scripture is in 'the substance and the true feeling of sothfastness, and the spiritual savour of it in general, although they will not see as many precise ideas in it, for that is not necessary': 'quia hoc non est eis necessarium'—for it is not necessary *to them*. Although Hilton begins with a defence of equality of the spiritual gift of interpretation between the laity and the clergy similar to that which underlies much Wycliffite writing on scriptural interpretation, he ends with the qualification that the educated will see more specifically what the text means.

101 *and*. The Latin version, 'et', supports the isolative variant of H_7 over Σ 'or'.

105 *sentence*. The Latin version, 'sentencie', supports the plural of χAsAH_6 over the singular of H_7LB_3SrEPCcPl.

110 *he*. The Latin version clarifies: 'homo sic se habens'.

114 Ps. 116: 103.

120 *a maner*. H_7 uses the Northern dialectal spelling of the number 'one' here; this is not the indefinite article.

120–1 *not as he is . . . lykenesse of werkes and wordes*. See Hilton's *Qui habitat*, in *Exposition*, ed. Wallner, 49, l. 50; *English Mystics*, ed. Windeatt, 175: 'a luitel I schewe him of me, huled vnder a vayle of feir liknes'.

121 1 Cor. 13: 12.

123 *myght . . . sothfastnes* (l. 129). For the crediting of these attributes of the three persons of the Trinity to Jesus, see above, 34/121 and 36/44.

124–5 *may no soule . . . by effecte of his werkynge.* Hilton expresses the same idea, that God is known indirectly in this world, in *Qui habitat*, in *Exposition*, ed. Wallner, 5, l. 6: 'be þe doynge of þi gracious worchynge . . . I seo þe'.

seen here. The Latin version, 'hic videre', aggrees with this reading. The addition of 'ne' in LwH^{c}ELw changes the meaning of the phrase from 'see here' to 'see nor hear'.

134 *lettre-sendyngys.* The Latin version, 'littere misse', does not agree exactly with any of the English variants, none of which uses a past participle. The scribal confusion evidenced by the large number of variant forms, the majority of which use gerunds or present participles, shows that Hilton's wording was not understood. The *lectio difficilior* is the H_7BH_5SrWsLdPl variant, a compound of noun object and plural verbal noun. See *Augustine*, *Enarr. in Psal.* 64. 2 (*PL* 36: 774).

a louynge soule. The Latin version, 'animas diligentes', supports the plural of $SrAH_6$CcMPl 'louynge soules'. HBH_5B_3AsWsLwPLdTWWc is singular, with the indefinite article: 'a lufende soule'. The original reading of L may have been the same as H_7, 'louynge soule', which lacks a grammatically necessary determiner. H_7CcMPlTd have the plural 'soules lufed of him' in the next line, without the definite article of Σ.

137 *bodily lyfe.* The Latin version expands: 'vite miserie corporalis'.

144 *abydende in fulfillynge of his wil.* The Latin version, 'expectantes implecionem voluntatis sue', supports Σ 'abidende fulfillynge of his wil', according to which the fulfilling of the will of God is that which these souls await. According to the H_7 reading, the object of the waiting is not named, but the waiting itself is the fulfilling of the will of God.

145–6 Rom. 15: 4.

154 *his knowynge.* The Latin version, 'istius cognicionis', supports Σ 'þis knowynge' over H_7. The opposition of 'þis' and 'oþer' makes the Σ reading the more cogent.

155 *oþer.* The Latin version clarifies: 'aliarum scienciarum'.

CHAPTER 44

The discussion of the objects of divine illumination in the contemplative soul in the next three chapters is paralleled in Hilton's *Qui habitat*, in *Exposition*, ed. Wallner, 25–9; *English Mystics*, ed. Windeatt, 174–5.

1 *sowned.* The Latin version, 'sonante', supports the present participle of AMLdTW 'sowning' over the past participle of $H_7LB_3SrEPH_6$Pl (which could derive as a misspelling from a form of the present participle like M 'sownend' in an exemplar or exemplars).

3 *spekyng*. The Latin version, 'locuciones', supports the plural of LB_3SrEPPlTW 'spekynges' over the singular of H_7AH_6Ld.

6 *fully . . . seyd* (l. 67). This unmarked omission in As is probably the result of a disruption in its exemplar similar to that which occurs from 41/163 to 43/97, but in the present case, the displaced material is simply omitted. It may have occupied some of the missing folios that originally followed its atelous text.

9–10 Ezek. 1: 20. Gregory, *Hom. in Ezech.* 1. 7. 11–14 interprets the turning of the wheels of the chariot according to the movement of the 'vitae spiritus' allegorically as referring to spiritual understanding of Scripture.

12 *angle of frowardnesse*. That is, 'angle of deviation' or tangent. The Latin version reads 'angulis tortuosis seu distortis'.

18 *Oure Lord Jesu seyth þus*. χ adds 'of his lufers'; the Latin version adds 'in Euangelio'.

18–19 *Oues . . . mee*. John 10: 27, concatenated with 10: 14.

20 *þe pryue voyce of Jesu*. This is the third occurrence of the theme of the sounding of the voice of Jesus. See above, 40/49–51 and 41/167, and below, 46/55 and 46/56–7.

21 *no feynyng in it, ne fantasye*. See above, 40/95.

23 *lyfe*. The Latin version, 'veritas', may derive from a Latin scribal mistake for 'vita'. No appropriate variation, however, is attested among the surviving manuscripts in either Latin or English.

29–31 See Bernard, *Serm. super Cant.* 83. 4: 'Exigit ergo Deus timeri ut Dominus, honorari ut pater, et ut sponsus amari.'

30 *and*[1] *. . . fader*. MSS YB_4H_8UpHeUtMaBn of the Latin version lack this phrase; B_2R_2 have 'aliquociens ut patrem reuerendum'.

reuerent. The Latin version reads 'reuerendum'. Hilton's meaning here must be 'reverend'.

31 *louely*. The Latin version expands: 'amabilem et dulcem'.

it. The Latin version clarifies: 'hec vox'.

32 *him*. The Latin version clarifies: 'ipsius Jesus'.

33 *grete sykernes*. See above, 40/72.

38–9 *born vp only by þe fauour and þe wonderful godenes of him, o thyng þat it seeth and feleth*. Hilton's point, as Clark and Dorward translate, is 'as if nothing existed but Jesus one thing and himself another, borne up only by the favor and wonderful goodness of Him: that is, of this thing that he sees and feels' (*Scale*, ed. and trans. Clark and Dorward, 297). This seems to require two propositions of which each is preserved in half the manuscripts: 'þat is þat' in χ and 'o thyng þat' in H_7λSrCc. Another hand in H_7 has added 'it is' before 'born', with the effect of turning the present clause into an independent sentence. LwAMPl appear to have omitted the most confusing part of the passage, 'þat is þat o thyng' (which contains what may well have appeared to be a repetition of 'o thyng' from the previous line). The Latin version, 'per fauorem et bonitatem mirabilem eiusdem', omits the problematic ending of the sentence.

41 *formed . . . wordys* (l. 42). The omission of this phrase in $H^{\circ}H_5$Ws is probably the result of eye-skip. The word 'amonge' here is to be read as an adverb; the Latin version has 'interdum'.

þus. The omission of this word from H^c suggests that the correction derives from a manuscript with the same reading at this point as the uncorrected text of Lw.

42 *lufend*. The Latin version, 'laudancia', supports a reading of 'praising' here ('lofend' in the usual form of H_7), rather than 'loving'. See above, 41/60.

43 *wondrend*. The Latin version, 'admirancia', supports H_7λSrACcMPl over HBH_5WsHu_2LdT 'worschipende'; LwEW have 'worschippinge or wonderyng'.

47 *after*. The Latin version, 'aliquando postea', supports H_7λSrAECcMPl over the various χ variants.

53 *wonderful*. The Latin version, 'mirabilibus', supports H_7λSrACcMPl over χE 'many wndirful'.

55 *spekyng*. The Latin version, 'locuciones', supports the plural Σ 'spekynges', over H_7T.

56 *pryue jewelys*. The Latin version, 'iocalia sua secreta', supports Σ over the HH_5Ws omission of 'priuey'.

60 *stereth*. The Latin version expands: 'excitat seu concedit'.

62–3 Hilton makes the same point, that the experience of God's spiritual creatures is not itself the end of contemplation, in *Angels' Song*, in *English Mystics*, ed. Windeatt, 133: 'the soveran and the essencial joy es in luf of God be hymselfe and for hymselfe, and the secundarie es in communyng and behaldyng of angels and gastly creaturs'.

CHAPTER 45

8–9 *and þe knowyng of þe blissed Trinite after þat grace techeth*. The Latin version adds a devotional emphasis, and limits the idea of knowledge of the Trinity: 'et intima consideratio humanitatis Jesu Christi; et postea modica cognicio beatissime Trinitatis secundum quod gracia hominem instruit vel informat'.

10 *Songges*. The Latin version, 'Canticorum', supports H_7RλSrCcMPl over the χAsE addition, 'of þe spouse'.

10–11 S. of S. 3: 2.

13 *of thoght*. The Latin version, 'cogitacionis', supports Σ over the HH_5AsWs omission.

14 Gilbert of Hoyland interprets this text similarly in his continuation of Bernard, *Serm. super Cant.* 4. 3: 'universitas creaturae dici potest non inconvenienter civitas Dei'.

17 *graces*. The Latin version, 'gracias', supports H_7RλSrAMPl over χAsE 'of grace' and Cc 'of gracis' (a reading from which L was corrected).

21 *gostly creatures*. The Latin version adds a devotional expansion: 'Set pulcherimum est aspicere eum in se, primo in benedicta humanitate sua et in sua postea deitate', then repeats the preceding clause, 'Pulcrum est aspicere Jesum in spiritualibus creaturis'.

26 *schynend*. The Latin version, 'splendentes', supports H_7RλSrACcMPl over the χAsE omission.

28 *reproued*. The Latin version clarifies: 'hominibus reprobos, pulcrum est considerare'.

29 *rewardeth . . . suffrend . . . to punysche* (l. 31). The Latin version presents a series of finite verb forms: 'remunerat . . . permittit . . . punit'.

32–41 See Hilton's *Qui habitat*, in *Exposition*, ed. Wallner, 28, l. 13–29, l. 5. Aquinas, *ST* Suppl. q. 104, a. 3, argues that the blessed will see the pains of the damned with joy not because of the pain itself, but because that pain is the result of divine justice.

35 *not*. The Latin version, 'non adhuc', supports λSrACcMPl, 'not ȝit' over H_7χAsE.

38 *in*. H_7 'in' is probably another example of confusion with the contracted form of 'and'.

42–56 The disdain of the contemplative soul for the power of Satan is described in much the same way in Hilton's *Bonum est*, in *Exposition*, ed. Wallner, 80–1. See also the discussion of the breaking of the image of sin in the soul in *Scale* I, Chapter 88, and chapter 13 of the Long Text of the *Revelations* of Julian of Norwich (*A Book of Showings*, ed. Colledge and Walsh, ii. 346–50; *The Writings of Julian of Norwich*, ed. Watson and Jenkins, 169–721).

42 *Also þe syght*. The Latin version clarifies: 'Similiter est de consideracione'.

47 *hospileth*. The H_7H_5WsLd variant is the *lectio difficilior* (*MED* does not record 'huspilen' before 1440 *Promptorium Parvulorum*). Note that H may originally have agreed with H_5Ws in this variant. It is supported by the Latin version, 'confundit', over the other variants, all but one of which use forms of 'spoil'.

47–8 *rendyth him al to noȝt*. The Latin version, 'dilaniat', supports the Σ variant over H_7 'rendryth', which makes little sense here.

49–50 Prov. 12: 7.

54–5 *entren into a swyn, as þe Gospel seyth*. Hilton's reference is to Christ's casting out of the devils (called Legion in the accounts in Mark and Luke) into a herd of swine. See Matt. 8: 28–32, Mark 5: 1–13, Luke 8: 27–33.

55 *ony*. The Latin version, 'alicui', supports H_7RλSrLwAECcMPlTW over the χ variant 'a'.

60 *no more þe blustrend . . . þan þe sterynge*. The Latin version, 'non plus timet flatum . . . quam motum', supports H_7RAsHu$_2$ECcM over the HBH_5λSrWsLwALdlTW doubling of 'þan': 'no more þan . . . þan þe sterynge'.

62–3 See Rev. 20: 2–3: 'And he laid hold on the dragon, the old serpent, which is the devil and Satan, and bound him for a thousand years. And he cast him into the bottomless pit.'

63 *hangen*. The H_7SrCc form, as opposed to χRλAsEMPl 'hanged', shows the use of the strong past participle with transitive meaning.

65–6 1 Cor. 6: 3.

68 *as who seyth ȝis*. The Latin version clarifies: 'vero, eos iudicabimus'.

71 *Schamed and schent*. On the soul's contempt for the devil, see Bernard, *Qui hab*. 13.

72 *þus faren with-al*. The Latin version clarifies: 'tam contempnabiliter tractatur'.

73 *heyghest*. Hussey, 'Latin and English', 475, suggests that H 'eiȝest' should be read as 'most dreadful' (from *MED* 'aue' *n*.).

75 *thankynge*. The plural Latin version 'graciarum accionibus', supports the plural Σ 'þankynges' over H_7.

76 *fro þe malice*. Latin manuscripts YB_2R_2Up$_2$ read 'omnia', but textually displaced: 'a malicia tam crudelis inimici ex sua omnia misericordia infinita' [misericordia *marg*. Y]. Latin manuscripts H_2H_8MaBnUpB_4HeUt agree with H_7 (and Pl before correction) rather than Σ 'fro alle þe malice'.

77 *his*. The Latin version does not support the RAPl addition of 'grace and his', which is added marginally, in a different hand, in H_7.

CHAPTER 46

2 *how Jesu as man . . . and as God.* H$_7$λ support this reading, while R reads 'is' instead of 'as' in the first instance, and ALdET and W insert 'is' before 'as' (T and W insert 'God and' as well). The Latin version is 'et qualiter [equaliter YH$_2$] Jesus in quantum homo est super omnes creaturas et in quantum Deus, prout eum potest anima hic videre'. Grenehalgh renders this ['iuxta lat.'] as 'as man is abofe alle creatures, and as God, aftir þe soule may see hym here'. Hilton's phrasing is elliptical: 'may be seen' should be understood after 'Jesu'. The chapter deals with three things that can be seen by the light of grace: the state of the blessed angels in heaven, the humanity of Christ (which is above all creatures), and the deity of Christ, insofar as it can be perceived in this life.

5 *þe sotelte.* The Latin version, 'subtilitatem eorum', supports RLw`H$^{c\prime}$EMPlW 'þe sotilte of hem', over H$_7$H°BH$_5$λAsSrWsAHu$_2$CcLdT.

6 *in*^{2}. The Latin version, 'et', supports Σ 'and', over H$_7$. This is presumably another case of confusion of the forms of 'in' and 'and' in H$_7$.

7 *sondryhed of orders.* See Bernard, *Serm. super Cant.* 62. 2. 2.

distinccion. The Latin version, 'distinccionem', supports the singular of H$_7$RλSrACcMPl over the plural of χAsE, 'distinccioun s'.

11 *al gostly of gostly creatures.* That is, it is an intellectual, rather than an imaginary or a corporeal, vision. See Augustine, *De Genesi ad litteram* (*PL* 34), 12. 6. 15.

13 On the ministry of the angels, see Hilton's *Qui habitat*, in *Exposition*, ed. Wallner, 36–40; *Angels' Song*, in *English Mystics*, ed. Windeatt, 133.

17 *soule.* The Latin version, 'anima', supports the singular of H$_7$RλSrACcMPl, and agrees in lacking the sentence that follows in χAsE, which appears to be an eye-skip omisson in the one case, or an expansion in the other.

18–19 Hebr. 1: 14. See Bernard, *Serm. super Cant.* 41. 3. 4 and *Qui hab.* 11. 10 on this text.

23 *lyknes.* As the Latin version, 'similitudines', shows, this form is to be read as plural. See *MED* 'līknes(se' *n.*

25 *felyng.* The Latin version, 'sensaciones', supports the plural of Σ over H$_7$AsCc. The series of nouns that follows is all in the plural, and the plural 'felynges' would be the more cogent reading.

29 *For knowyng ryseth abofen þis* (l. 30). On the ascent of knowledge, see Bernard *Serm. super Cant.* 62. 2. 2–63. 3. 4.

31 *manhed.* The Latin version expands, echoing the previous line: 'naturam benedicte humanitatis'.

32 *aungels*. The Latin version, 'angelorum', supports H_7RλSrAPl over the χAsE addition of 'al'.

33 See Aquinas, *Commentum in libros sententiarum Petri Lombardi* 1, d. 3, q. 1, a. 3, in *Opera Omnia* (Paris, 1881), repr. Mediatrix, 2014.

knowynge of creatures. The Latin version simplifies: 'creaturas'.

35 *goth before*. The Latin version, 'precedit eam', supports H_7RλAsSrACcMPl over the χE addition of 'and þerfore'.

38 *here*. The Latin version clarifies: 'pro tempore huius vite'.

41 *and*. H_7 appears here again to have mistaken forms of 'in' and 'and'.

48 *boþe*. The Latin version, 'simul', supports H_7RλSrLwH^cAECcMPlW over the H°BH_5AsWsLdT omission.

53 *þan it is of knowyng*. The Latin version clarifies: 'quam est ignis amoris inflammatus vel perueniens ex cognicione'.

56 *I calle . . . soule*. Another occurrence of the theme of the voice of Jesus. See 40/49–51, 41/167, 44/1, 44/55, and 46/65–74.

hem . . . be (l. 82). A lacks a folio here.

59 *with hem*. The Latin version, 'cum eis', supports RλSrLw`H^c'ECcMPlW over the H°BH_5AsWsLdT omission. The H_7 variant, 'with ⌜him⌝' is erroneous, albeit intentional: the only appropriate complement of the verbal expression 'arayeth . . . with' is the 'riche giftes' to which 'hem' refers.

61 *Jesu spouse*. The Latin version, 'sui', supports RSrLw$H^c H_6$MPlTW 'Jesu hire spouse' over H_7H°BH_5LWsEPLd.

63–4 Job 4: 12. See Gregory, *Mor. in Job* 5. 29. 51.

64–74 This is the final occurrence of the theme of the sounding of the voice of Jesus. See 40/49–51, 41/167, 44/1, 44/55, and 46/56.

64 *suscepit*. The Latin version, 'percepit', supports Σ. The H_7 variant is the reading of the modern text of the Vulgate.

66 *pryuey*. The Latin version, 'secrete', supports χAsECcPl 'priueli' over H_7RM.

68 *rownynges*. The Latin version, 'susurii', supports the singular of χ 'rownynge' over the plural of H_7RλSrECcMPl.

speciale. The Latin version, 'speciales', an adjective modifying 'ostentaciones', supports RBLSrPH_6CcLd 'special'. H_7AsMPl 'speciale' can be read as either an adjective or an adverb; HH_5WsLwTW 'specialy' must be read as an adverb.

72 *oþer*. The Latin version, 'alias', supports H_7 over χRλAsECcMPl 'al oþer'.

74 *þis is þe voyce of Jesu*. This appears to have been the original ending of χ.

74–5 Ps. 28: 9.

75 *condensa*. The Sr addition is the remainder of the Psalm verse.

76 *schewe*. A different hand finishes H_7 from this point.

77 *soulis*. The Latin version clarifies: 'homines illos qui sunt veraciter contemplatiui'.

þat styrten. The Latin version expands: 'et, per beneficium spiritualis dileccionis et celestis confortacionis, facit'.

78 *ouyr al wordly vanyte*. The Latin version expands: 'omnium peccatorum et a mundi vanitate'.

80 *þese . . . Jesu* (l. 82). The Latin version omits.

82 *þese arn*. The Latin version reads: 'Sic sunt ista'.

83 *felyngys*. The Latin version expands: 'sensaciones in anima diligente; non exprimo eos totaliter'.

84 *styred . . . mater* (l. 85). The Latin version clarifies: 'que veraciter mouetur et informatur per graciam Jesu Christi in opere contemplacionis, videre potest et cognoscere maius lumen gracie'.

GLOSSARY

S. S. Hussey produced a Glossary for the edition of *Scale* II based on the spellings of his base manuscript, H. I have expanded and revised it according to the spelling of H_7, the base-text of the present edition. This glossary assumes an elementary level of acquaintance with Middle English. Only spellings and meanings that would not be readily recognized by an educated speaker of present-day English are entered. Words and word forms that are common in present-day English will not be glossed, but uncommon forms and meanings of the same words will be (e.g. the text commonly uses the word 'and', but occasionally the spelling 'an'. Only the latter is glossed here).

Words spelled variously throughout the text are alphabetized according to their most common form. When the letter 'y' is used as a spelling for 'i', it is alphabetized under 'i', when not (as in e.g. 'ay' and 'ypocrite'), it is alphabetized as 'y'. Consonantal 'i' (modern 'j') is alphabetized as 'j', in accordance with modern English spelling, consonantal 'u' is alphabetized as 'v', and vocalic 'v' as 'u'. The letters 'ȝ' and 'þ' are alphabetized following 'g' and 't' respectively. Optional final letters (e.g. 'abofe', 'abofen') are given in parentheses as part of the headword entry. Each item or form in the glossary is referred to the chapter and line where it first occurs, except where the first occurrence is the less common spelling. Usually, the first three occurrences of every word and form are cited, but citations include representation of all variations in spelling or meaning (where more examples are required, more are included). Multiple citations from the same chapter will not repeat the chapter number (e.g. 12/13, 37, not 12/13, 12/37). The order of citation of forms of nouns is all singular forms before plural forms; that of verbs is: infinitive, present tense by person, then number, tense, and mood (present before past; singular before plural; indicative (unremarked) before subjunctive before imperative), then present participle and past participle. A tilde (~) represents the headword in phrases, which follow all other forms, regardless of they include the headword or some other form (particularly of verbs).

ABBREVIATIONS

1 first
2 second
3 third
adj. adjective
adv. adverb
comp. comparative
compl. complement
conj. conjunction
fem. feminine
gen. genitive case
imp. imperative
inf. infinitive
n. noun
obl. oblique case
pa. p. past participle
pa. past tense
perf. perfect tense
pers. person(al)
pl. plural
pr. present tense
pr. p. present participle
prep. preposition
pron. pronoun
refl. reflexive
rel. relative
sing. singular
subj. subjunctive
subs. substantive(ly)
superl. superlative
v. verb
vbl. n. verbal noun

A

abaysssched *pa. p.* disconcerted, discomfited 23/10
abyden *v. inf.* await, remain, experience, survive 5/16, 17/27, 24/60; **abydeth** *3 sg. pr.* 7/15, 41/47; **abydende** *pr. p.* 43/144
abydyng(e) *vbl. n.* delay, hesitation 4/51, 24/132
able *adj.* having a capacity for doing something 17/26, 26/30, 88
able(n) *v. inf.* prepare, enable 15/23, 27/37; **ableth** *3 sg. pr.* 25/2; **able** *3 pl. pr.* 16/29, **abled** *pa. p.* 43/100
ablenes(se) *n.* a capacity for doing something 43/2, 29
abouen *adv.* above, superior 4/32, 14/6, 28/81; **abofe(n)** 27/18, 30/9, 43
aboundaunce *n.* abundance, plenty 32/71
accidence *n.* accidentals, non-essential matters 43/131
accidye *n.* accidia, the deadly sin of sloth 39/1; **accydy** 39/85
acord(e) *n.* consent, heartfelt agreement 9/9, 11/15, 21/62
acordaunce *n.* agreement 40/68
acorden *v. inf.* agree with, reconcile 39/80; **acorden** *3 pl. pr.* 43/17; **acordende** *pr. p.* 41/86, 44/42; **acorded** *3 pa. p.* 34/128
acounteth *v. 3 sg. pr.* rate, regard; **acounted** *pa. p.* 37/52; ; *~ it at no3t* disregards it 39/16
actyf *adj.* relating to the life of action, in contrast to life of contemplation 18/18, 42/65
actuel *adj.* actual sin, freely committed by an individual, as opposed to original sin of Adam and Eve 6/6, 6/12, 7/3
adred *adj.* fearful 12/81, 27/148
aferd *adj.* afraid 22/34
affeccyon *n. sg.* affective capacity, feeling, love 24/144, 26/100, 27/64; **affeccion** 4/31, 11/26, 84 **affeccyons** 24/77, 24/123, 30/73
afore *prep.* in preference to 27/44
after(e) *prep.* following, according to, in pursuit of 1/1, 4/24, 8/52
ageyn *adv.* again, back, in return 1/27, 4/66, 6/10; **a3en** 22/9, 23, 38; **a3eyn** 18/35, 49
ageyn *prep.* against 10/11, 11/107, 21/32; **ageyns** 6/11, 12, 7/31 **ageynes** 2/6, 6/9; **a3ens** 12/83; **a3eyns** 12/82
ageynstonden(e) *v. inf.* withstand, resist 5/13, 8/44, 10/11; **geynstondeþ** *3 sg. pr.* 13/29; **a3enstode** *3 sg. pa.* 14/31; **ageynstondend(e)** *pr. p.* 8/24, 34, 9/10
aggreueth *v. 3 sg. pr.* aggravates, troubles 39/55
aknowe *v. pa. p.* acknowledged, cognizant of 16/24
alday *adv.* continually 18/21, 21/15
alderbest *adj.* best of all 5/23
alyen *n.* foreign person 10/77; **alyens** *pl.* 10/85
alowynge *vbl. n.* deprecation, putting down 26/49
als *conj.* as 2/59, 3/39, 6/22
als swyþe *see* **swyþe**
amende *v. inf.* amend, reform 7/7, 10/45; **amendyn** 16/50
amendes *n. pl.* reparations 2/5, 13, 16; **amendis** 2/31, 39, 62
amys *adv.* wrongly 30/75
amonge *adv.* at the same time, continually 29/79, 44/42
an *conj.* and 11/87, 13/17, 43/10; **ant** 35/35
anemptis *prep.* (*often in the phrase* as ~) in regards to 4/9, 38/11; **anemptes** 11/80, 37/43, 46; **anentys** 26/23
angle *n.* corner 44/12. *See also* **aungel**
angre *n.* anger, wrath 38/46
angre *v. imp. sg.* be or grow angry 22/69; *3 sg. subj.* 27/53, 79; **angred** *pa. part.* 27/55
angri *adj.* angry 15/49
angrines *n.* anger 38/6
anon *adv.* immediately 4/49, 68; **onon** 24/44; **on-one** 16/38
ant *conj. see* **an**
aperen *v. inf.* appear 9/23; **apered** *3 sg. pa.* 30/172
apert *adj.* open, evident 42/37
appetyte *n.* desire, inclination 11/52, 12/10, 40/185
appleyen *v. inf.* apply 43/49; **applye** *v. imp. sg.* 25/17; **applyed** *pa. p.* 42/13, 43/52
applyenge *vbl. n.* applying 21/128
appropred *v. pa. p.* attributed,

appropriate 34/71, 75, 76; **apropred** 34/78
aray *n.* array, attire 27/43
arayeth *v. 3 sg. pr.* adorns 46/59
ardaunt *adj.* ardent, eager 39/6
aretten *v. inf.* attribute, (negatively, to blame) 20/92; **aretted** *pa. p.* 11/63, 34/71, 34/78
aryȝt *adv.* properly 22/21
arn(e) *see* **ben**
arw(e) *n.* arrow 37/111, 114, 118
aschis *n. pl.* asses 14/40
askape *v. 3 sg. pr.* escape 21/108
aske(n) *v. inf.* request, require, demand, plead for 16/50, 56, 24/136; **askest** *2 sg. pr.* 1/3, 4/19, 29/12; **asketh** *3 sg. pr.* 2/4, 7/15, 17; **askeþ** *3 sg. pr.* 20/110, 21/115, 35/27; **asken** *pl. pr.* 35/20, 40/104; **aske** *3 sg. pr. subj.* 27/58; **aske** *imp. sg.* 36/5
askynge *vbl. n.* request, inquiry 10/78
assay *n.* trial, attempt 11/89, 40/12, 43/110
assay(en) *v. inf.* test, attempt, undertake 23/10, 24/134, 34/102; **assayeth** *3 sg. pr.* 44/52 ; **assayend** *pr. p.* 20/25, 37/129; **assayed** *pa. p.* 32/6
assayenge *vbl. n.* testing, investigation, trial 11/81, 25/18; **assaynge** 28/78; **assayinge** 41/29
assaylen *v. inf.* assault, attack 37/109
assaylyng *vbl. n.* assailing 41/42
assent *n.* acquiescence, consent 11/12
assent(en) *v. inf.* assent, consent, express agreement 5/13, 11/24, 34/109; **assentest** *2 sg. pr.* 24/8; **assenteth** *3 sg. pr.* 11/3; **assenteþ** 37/21; **asentid** *3 sg. pa.* 11/90
assentynge *vbl. n.* consent, acquiescenence 11/18, 15/27
as tyte *adv.* immediately 4/42, 48, 10/14; **as tytte** 16/35, 17/18
atte *contraction* at the 9/23
atwix(en) *prep.* between 3/45, 27/66, 32/51; **atwyx** 12/2, 26/15, 36/26
aungel *n.* angel 12/9, 24, 26; **angle** 6/17; **angeles** *pl.* 4/32; **aungels** 12/15, 40/139, 140; **aungelis** 43/39, 46/23; **aungeles** 42/64; **aungelys** 45/67, 68, 46/1
auaylen *v. inf.* avail, be sufficient to 34/44; **auayleþ** *3 sg. pr.* 15/9
auere *n.* possession 14/23, 27/60. *See also* **han**
avisement *n.* forethought 41/153
awghful *adj.* awe inspiring, terrifying 44/30
awght *see* **oweþ**
awtere *n.* altar 34/65
ay *adv.* continually, always 7/57, 11/1, 13
aylastend(e) *pr. p.* everlasting 4/35, 12/65, 14/13; **aylastand** 18/63
aylastendli *adv.* everlastingly 4/7

B

bakbytyng(e) *n.* calumny 26/64, 74, 38/41
baptem *n.* baptism 6/1, 11, 20
baren *v. inf.* strip 20/85
become *v. 3 sg. pa.* became 2/38
bedys *n.* prayers, rosaries 20/100, 21/146
beenge *n.* being, essence 32/54
beeng(e) *vbl. n.* being, 33/34, 37/41, 42
beforegoende *adj.* preceding 26/38
begynnest *v. 2 sg. pres.* begin 22/39; **begyn(ne)** *pl. pres.* 5/24, 15/23; **begynne** *imp. sg.* 21/112; **begynnynge** *pr. p.* beginning; (*used substantively*) beginners, novices in the spiritual life 5/17; **begynnenge** 29/1; **begynnend** 31/62, **bigynnend** 40/152
begynnynge, *vbl. n.* 4/25, 19/32, 28/29; **bigynnynge** 33/75
beheldynge *vbl. n.* sprinkling, imparting 43/26
behete *v. 1 sg. pr.* promise 21/24; **beheteth** *3 sg. pr.* 24/41, 40/136, 44/57; **behyght** *3 sg. pa.* 10/39, 24/41; **behyȝt**; 30/180; **byhyȝt** 28/167
beholden *v. inf.* gaze upon, consider 36/34, 37/36, 41/26; **byholden** 35/39; **beholde** *1 sg. pr.* 45/16; **beholdeth** *3 sg.* 30/91, 37/47, 42/106; **beholdeþ** 37/101, 116, 41/67; **beholdyn** *pl.. pr.* 30/86; **beholde** *sg. pr. subj.* 30/97, 37/106; **beholdeþ** *imp. pl.* 12/32
beholden *adj.*obliged 34/2.
beholdyng(e) *vbl. n.* consideration, meditation 4/11, 12/83, 13/37; **beholdenge** 24/99; **behaldyng(e)** 36/83, 37/29; **beholdyngge** 39/4; **byholdynge** 20/85, 23/23; **beholdyngys** *pl.* 46/80

behouely *adj.* necessary, beneficial 28/45; **behofely** 7/73
behoueth *v. 3 sg. pr.* behoves, is required of 2/17, 18, 11/32; *pl. pr.* 11/8
beyked *v. pa. part.* baked, kiln-fired 28/44
beykynge *vbl. n.* baking, 28/42
ben *v. inf.* be 2/66, 4/23, 66; **art** *2 sg. pr.* are 4/12; **arn(e)** *pr. pl.* are 2/74, 3/34, 49; **ar** 17/13; **ware** *sg. pr. subj.* were 27/159; **ben** *pl. pr. subj.* be 6/18, 10/18, 11/113; **ben** *pa. p.* 1/25, 2/9, 26; ~ *so* (*þat*) provided that 4/40, 11/68, 14/19
benefice *n.* benefit 3/6; **benefyce** 27/42
bere(n) *v. inf.* carry, support, sustain 12/54, 68, 29/35; **bereth** *3 sg. pr.* 11/22, 12/52, 67; **bereþ** 27/72; **beren** *pl. pr.* 28/26; **bare** *sg. pa.* 12/78; **boren** *pa. p.* 28/54; ~ *doun* overcome, depress 27/73, 41/140; ~ *vpon* allege *3 pl. pr.* 23/12
besy *adj.* anxious, busy 7/63, 11/98, 106
besyed *v. pa. p.* occupied 42/65
besyly *adv.* busily, actively 14/79; **besily** 18/34, 51, 37/117; **bisily** 9/13
besynes *n.* occupation, exertion 11/7, 18/19, 26; **besines** 17/6, 24/2, 43/86; **besynessis** *pl.* 18/24
betokeneth *v. 3 sg. pr.* signifies 10/81; **betokeneþ** 25/47; **betokneþ** 12/22, 32/43, 48; **betokneth** 12/34; **betokenes** 21/43
betwix *prep.* between 7/38; **betwixen** 9/9; **bytwyx** 12/41; **bytwix** 24/31, 26/47
biddeþ *v. 3 sg. pr.* states, commands 27/150, 36/35; **biddith** 45/49
biddyng(e) *vbl. n.* command(ment) 2/7, 7/71, 15/25; **byddynge** 9/29, 14/40, 50; **byddynges** *pl.* 11/16
byeng(e) *vbl. n.* redemption 34/3, 59, 61
bygyleth *v. 3 sg. pr.* beguiles, deceives 11/16; **bygyled** *pa. p.* 38/71
byhetyngys *vbl. n. pl.* promises, pledges 43/144. *See also* **behete**
byhyȝt *see* **behete**
bynd *v. inf.* bind, commit, obligate 36/84; **byndeth** *3 sg. pr.* 27/62; **bynden** *3 pl. pr.* 18/27, 19/10; **bynde** *imp. sg.* 21/137; **bounden** *pa. p.* 2/52, 53
bynethe *prep.* beneath 40/96
birthen *n.* burden11/68; **birþen** 41/55
bytyme *adv.* at times 39/15
bytynge *vbl. n.* bite, remorse 12/63, 15/30, 34
blak(e) *adj.* black 4/13, 12/13, 16
blaknes *n.* blackness 12/81
blasfeme *n.* blasphemy 3/11
blynded *v. pa. p.* blinded, deceived 16/21, 27; **blent** 26/58, 27/74; **blended** 28/62
blynd(e) *adj.* blind 14/47, 15/36, 16/17
blyndly *adv.* blindly, without true sight 32/16
blyndenes *n.* 12/86, 16/23; **blyndnes** 16/24
blounte *adj.* blunt, dull 42/7
blustrend *vbl. n.* blustering 45/60
bodily *adj.* physical, carnal 1/13, 4/17, 7/48; **bodili** 7/46, 17/2, 17; **bodyly** 14/7, 27/58, 30/22; **bodely** 43/46
bodilyhed *n.* carnality, corporeality 33/38
boght *pa. p.* redeemed 21/99, 34/53, 59
boyled, boylend *see* **bolneþ**
boystous *adj.* rough, crude 7/46; **boistous** 21/69; ~ *to* inexperienced in 42/7
boystously *adv.* crudely 42/115
bold(e) *adj.* confident, self-assured 11/93, 22/34
boldenes *n.* assurance 40/72
bolneþ *v. 3 sg. pr.* boils up, swells with fermentation 29/32; **boylend** *pr. p.* 42/49, 51; **boyled** *pa. p.* 29/46, 53
bonde *n.* covenant, boundary 7/67; **bondes** *pl.* 38/15
bord *n.* table 31/66
born(e), boren *see* **beren**
boskys *n. pl.* bushes 46/78
bosum *n.* bosom, embrace 3/35, 10/67, 43/138
bounden *see* **bynd**
bowen *v. inf.* bow, bend 16/49
bowynge *vbl. n.* bending 28/43
brede *n.* breadth 25/40, 45
brede *n.* bread 31/67, 39/65, 43/69
breke(n) *v. inf.* break, interrupt 9/28, 14/58, 22/38; **breketh** *3 sg. pr.* 11/18, 43/83; **breken** *pl. pr.* 14/58; **brekend** *pr. p.* 7/5; **breke** *sg. imp.* 24/98
breker *n.* one who breaks something; ~ *of þe wal* a house-breaker, burglar 27/113
brenne(n) *v. inf.* burn 26/84, 101, 102;

brenneþ *3 sg. pr.* 26/80, 33/60, 62, **brenneth** 38/66, 41/12, 43/38; **brennen** *pl. pr.* 30/52, 46/8; **brennend(e)** *pr. p.* 10/83, 12/92, 14/74, **brennyng(e)** 1/19, 4/6, 26/101; **brynnyng** 2/72; **brent** *pa. p.* 17/13, 26/86, 27/142

brennendly *adv.* burningly, passionately 25/35, 30/132, 178

brenstone *n.* brimstone, sulfur 14/75

brerys *n.* briars 46/78

bresten *v. inf.* burst 29/45, 50; **bresteþ** *3 sg. pr.* 29/42, 50; **bresten** *pl. pr.* 35/13

brynge *v. inf.* 22/47, 23/45, 27/20; **bryngeth** *3 sg. pr.* 5/21, 34/133, 36/57, **bryngeþ** 20/65, 68, 24/124; **bringeth** 43/39; **brynge** *pl. pr.* 23/11; **brynge** *sg. imp.* 23/37; **broght** *pa. p.* 10/67, 12/74, 17/16; **broȝt** 17/14, 27/141, 180

bryngere *n.* messenger, bearer 19/46, 48; ~ *of þe laghe* legislator

brynggynge *vbl. n.* bringing 35/62

brynke *n.* brink, edge, rim 18/40, 42, 42/49

bronde *n.* (fire)brand, a burning stick taken out of a fire 6/14; **fyrebronde** 42/28

buxum *adj.* obedient 7/71, 11/16, 13/18

C

caytyf *n.* captive 45/45

calk-stone *n.* chalk-stone 39/8

castel *n.* castle, town 43/32

Cedar *n.* Kedar (*see* Explanatory Note) 12/14, 18, 20

centence *see* **sentence**

cese *v. pl. imp.* cease 36/37, 39, 51

Chanane *n.* Canaan 10/75

chape *see* **schapp, schape**

charge(n) *v. inf.* weigh (mentally), be concerned about 23/8, 24/99, 36/16; **charge** *1 sg. pr.* 21/23; **chargeþ** *3 sg. pr.* 16/25; **chargeth** 38/26, 39/10, 40/103

charite *n.* charity 1/3, 3/51, 10/2

chastiseth *v. 3 sg. pr.* chastises, reproves 45/24

chastysynge *vbl. n.* chastising 15/18

chaunge *v. inf.* change 19/7, **chaunged** *pa. p.* 8/17, 21/128, 40/27

chaungeabily *adv.* changeably, in alternation 41/159

chaungeable *adj.* mutable, inconstant 37/42

chaungeabilte *n.* alternation, inconstancy 41/75, 173; **chaungeablete** 41/88, 143; **chaungeablyte** 41/70

chaungynge *vbl. n.* change, alteration 4/15, 8/7

chawfeth *v. 3 sg. pr.* warms 42/28

chekes *n. pl.* cheeks 43/115, 117

chesen *v. inf.* choose 4/64; **cheseth** *3 sg. pr.* 12/49, 14/14, 39/65, **cheseþ** 15/45; **chese** *pl. pr.* 3/55; **chosen** *pa. p.* chosen, redeemed 3/25, 31, 4/42

chesyng(e) *vbl. n.* choice 4/63, 66

chewed *pa. p.* masticated (mentally), meditated upon 43/63

cyte *n.* city 21/10, 18, 45/12

clefe *v. sg. imp.* adhere 21/104, 27/155; *see also* **klefen**

clefendly *adv.* devotedly 24/114

clefynge *vbl. n.* adherence 24/113

clene *adj.* clean, pure, virginal 2/36, 4/6, 11/8; **clenner(e)** *comp.* more pure 32/77, 43/150

clennes(se) *n.* cleanness, purity 8/15, 10/47, 11/126

clense *v. inf.* cleanse, purify 28/89; **clenseth** *3 sg. pr.* 8/41, 11/133; **clensed** *pa. p.* 11/130, 37/129

clensyng *vbl. n.* cleansing, purification 3/69

clere *adj.* clear, direct 4/6, 11/75, 26/17; **clerer(e)** *comp.* clearer, more direct 32/70, 77, 37/130; **clerest** *superl.* clearest 32/70

clerely *adv.* clearly, directly 30/30; **clerly** 30/178, 32/21, 50

clereth *v. 3 sg. pr.* clears, clarifies 43/89; **clered** *pa. p.* 26/18, 29/47

clergie *n.* scholarship, education 14/20, 37/69; **clergy** 32/17

clerk *n.* scholar 32/17, 39/113, 40/8

clernes *n.* clarity 43/31; **clerenes** 43/36

cley *n.* clay, flesh 43/137

clumsed *pa. p.* benumbed, incapable of speech or movement 45/44

comen *v. inf.* come 17/9, 31/66, 43/87; **cometh** *3 sg. pr.* 7/56, 9/14, 11/124; **comen** *pl. pr.* 4/54, 61, 7/61; **come(n)** *pl. subj.* 41/105, 106; **comende** *pr. p.*

3/25, 11/107; **come(n)** *pa. p.* 1/27, 2/13, 3/25
commine *adj.* common 2/33
commonynge *vbl. n.* fellowship 23/50, 43/102; **commoneng** 41/91
compaygnye *n.* company, companionship 46/60
compleccyon *n.* physical constitution 39/56
compunccion *n.* pain of remorse, guilt 7/56; **compunccyon** 28/32, 29/16, 28; **compunccions** *pl.* 29/7, 64
conceyfe *v. inf.* conceive, understand 32/38; **conceyueth** *3 sg. pr.* 40/72
concupyscence *n.* concupiscence, lust 24/51
conende *pr. p.* knowledgeable 27/48
confermyng *vbl. n.* confirmation, strengthening 46/6
confort *v. inf.* 26/111; **conforteþ** *3 sg. pr.* 29/79; **conforteth** 37/87, 38/35, 50; **conforted** *pa. p.* 30/107, 31/68, 32/19
confortable *adj.* comforting, reassuring 24/85, 25/14, 28/29
confort(e) *n.* comfort, spiritual well-being 28/86, 29/76, 81
connynge *n.* reasoning ability, understanding 10/8, 59; **conynge** 27/42, 43/81; **cunnyng** 37/69; **kunnynge** 36/10; **conynges** *pl.* fields of knowledge 43/153
contre *n.* country, region 25/22
conuersacion *n.* manner of living, behaviour 34/107; **conuersacyon** 40/61
costret *n.* wineskin 29/43, 44, 47
coude *see* **kun**
coueyte(n) *v. inf.* covet, desire (in a positive or a negative sense depending on the object of desire) 18/17, 60, 20/49; **coueytin** 14/9; **coueyte** *1 sg. pr.* 21/23, 57, 60; **coueytest** *2 sg. pr.* 1/3, 21/30, 41; **coueytes** 20/8; **coueytist** 21/3; **coueytez** *3 sg. pr.* 14/10; **coueyteþ** 18/65, 23/27, 27/131; **coueyteth** 39/87, 42/84; **coueyten** *3 pl. pr.* 21/16; **coueyted** *3 pl. pa.* 19/36, 28/80; **coueyte** *sg. subj.* 21/45, 24/137, 27/46; **coueyt** *imp. sg.* 36/30; **coueyted** *pa. p.* 24/29
coueytous *n.* desirous (in a positive or a negative sense depending on the object of desire), greedy 14/54, 73, 39/6
coueytyse *n.* desire (in a positive or a negative sense depending on the object of desire), greed: the sin of avarice 11/72, 13/26, 18/62
couenable *adj.* fitting, appropriate 19/36
counseil *n.* counsel, advice 2/8, 16/1, 22/58; **counseyls** *pl.* 40/128, 43/15
counseil *v. 1 sg. pr.* advise 16/29
counseyl *n.* council 38/55
counseylyng *vbl. n.* counselling, advice 36/10
couthe, cowthe *see* **kun**
crafte *n.* art, skill, métier 14/20, 19/23, 25; **craftes** *pl.* 19/27, 37/69
craftily *adv.* skilfully 21/62
cranes *n.* crannies, gaps 25/29
cun *see* **kun**
cunnyng *see* **connynge**
cury *n.* culinary art 39/79
curyouste *n.* excessive or inappropriate attentiveness 43/72, 112
cursed *pa. p.* damned 14/66, 72
curteys *adj.* generous, courtly 18/4, 44/57
curteysye *n.* generosity, courtliness 7/13; **curtaysye** 35/57

D

dalyaunce *n.* amorous conversation and behaviour 44/57; **dalyaunces** *pl.* 46/61
dampnable *adj.* damnable, deserving of damnation 36/13
dampnacion *n.* damnation 8/43, 11/64; **dampnacyon** 36/18
dampne *v. inf.* damn, condemn 6/7; **dampned** *pa. p.* 2/9, 7/22, 8/51
dar *v. 1 sg. pr.* dare 41/12; **dar** *3 sg. pr.* 42/49; **durste** *v. 3 sg. subj.* 45/61
daunger(e) *n.*; *make* ~ stand or hold oneself aloof 10/77, 84
daungerouse *adj.* aloof 18/7
ded(e) *n.* death 2/39, 49, 51, 53, 59, 68, 3/10; **deth** 4/48, 9/14, 14/61
ded(e) *n.* deed, action 2/21, 25, 58, 8/52; **dedes** *pl.* 3/41
ded *adj.* dead, lifeless 3/54
dedeyne *n.* disdain, scorn 40/91; **dedyn** 26/51, 38/61, 69

dedli *adj.* deadly, mortal 3/51, 7/5, 76; **dedly** 7/11, 37, 8/27
dedlyche *adv.* mortally 11/91
defaded *pa. p.* faded, caused to lose colour 12/33
defaute *n.* fault, lack 3/3, 15/10, 16/10; **defautes** *pl.* 40/69
degre *n.* degree, rank 10/53, 17/8, 18/16
deyen *v. inf.* die 27/115; **dyen** 2/47, 3/51, 56; **dien** 2/54; **dey(e)** *sg. subj.* 10/39, 49
deynge *vbl. n.* death, mortification 27/100; **deyeng** 40/180
deynte *n.* pleasure 37/71, 42/135; **daynte** 39/7
deyntily *adv.* pleasurably 39/12
delyces *n.* joy, pleasures 27/75
delytable *adj.* delightful 27/9, 29/39, 30/163; **delitable** 43/43
delytabely *adv.* delightfully 40/45; **delytably** 42/25; **delytabilly** 41/166
deme(n) *v. inf.* judge, condemn 7/46, 11/96, 45/67; **demeth** *3 sg. pr.* 38/76, 45/64; **demende** *pr. p.* 41/97; **demed** *pa. p.* 22/62, 34/128, 45/63
demynge *vbl. n.* judgement 37/44; **demeng(e)** 38/61, 69, 45/68
departen *v. inf.* depart, divide, separate 8/46, 28/67, 30/153; **departeþ** *3 sg. pr.* 24/33, 28/27; **departeth** 38/49; **departid** *pa. p.* 2/9; **departed(e)** 8/42, 11/30, 40/29; **departyd** 9/14, 16/33
dere *adj.* dear 9/19
deren *v. inf.* harm, injure 8/46, 13/34, 27/178; **dereth** *3 sg. pr.* 45/74
descryued *pa. p.* described 1/5
desert *n.* reward, deserving 10/86; **dissert** 25/54; **desertys** *pl.* 20/55
desese *n.* discomfort, difficulty 21/11, 20, 27/30; **disese** 19/41, 22/76, 29/82; **deseses** *pl.* 20/27; **desesys** 22/68; **desesis** 22/74, **dessese** 38/57; *see also* **disesen** *v.*
despere(n) *v. inf.* despair 11/53, 27/154
despeyre *n.* despair 28/50, 54, 41/69
despysen, despyseth *see* **dispysen**
despyt(e) *n.* spite, scorn 15/48, 20/26, 38/69
desserfen *v. inf.* deserve 20/50
dette *n.* debt 2/22, 51
dettid *v. pa. p.* owed 7/22
diffouled *v. pa. p.* fouled, defiled 4/14, 7/75, 13/26
diffoulynge *vbl. n.* defiling 12/69
dyn(ne) *n.* din, distraction 24/77, 40/182
discretly *adv.* discretely, prudently 13/20
disesen *v. pr. pl.* bring trouble upon 38/11; **desese** *sg. subj.* 27/53; *see also* **desese** *n.*
dispendyng *n.* dispense, spending 39/25, 40
dispysen *v. inf.* despise 37/91; **despyseth** *v. 3 sg. pr.* 37/21; **despiseth** 38/76 **dispicith** 45/48; **despyse** *pl. subj.* 21/32
displesyng *vbl. n.* opposition, displeasure 10/11, 12/57
disposen *v. inf.* dispose 18/29, 20/14, 27/2
disposyng *vbl. n.* disposition 43/127; **disposynges** *pl.* 20/24, 27/103
dissayuable *adj.* deceitful 14/56
disseyued *v. pa. p.* deceived 11/34
dissert *see* **desert**
dissolucyon *n.* dissoluteness 41/171
doghter(e) *n.* daughter 10/76, 27/185, 186; **doghtire** 10/79; **doghters** *pl.* 12/13, 15
doyng(e) *vbl. n.* doing, performing 7/16, 15/18, 18/52; **doyngge** 36/11
dole *n.* share, portion 14/74
dome *n.* judgement 12/40, 44; Last Judgement 45/69; **domes** *pl.* 16/40, 45/36
do(n), don(e) *v. inf.* do, cause, perform 2/22, 26 30/85; **dost** *2 sg. pr.* 21/84, 22/57, 61; **doth** *3 sg. pr.* 11/65, 12/39, 59; cause (someone) to (do something) 22/38, 40/174, 41/166; **doþ** 14/12, 34, 54; **don(e)** *3 pl. pr.* 3/41, 58, 10/23; **doende** *pr. p.* 35/40; **don** *pa. p.* 2/4, 5; ~ *awey* eliminate, remove 24/153, 27/78, 34/73
doun *adv.* down 11/9, 103, 12/58
doun-puttynge *vbl. n.* disdain, abasement 26/48
dowarye *n.* dowry 4/37
dowte *n.* doubt 27/66, 39/118; **doute** 11/78; **doutes** *pl.* 11/112; **dowtes** 22/52, 28/49, 40/35; **dowtys** 27/176, 43/142
drawe(n) *v. inf.* draw, pull, entice, orient (towards) 11/102, 21/112, 35/49; **draghen** 23/31; **dragwe(n)** 24/98, 29/

29, 31; **draweth** *3 sg. pr.* 20/114, 21/121; **draghеþ** 23/24; **dragweþ** 32/23; **dragweth** 34/136; **dragwe** *pl. pr.* 24/92; **drawend** *pr. p.* 19/38; **drawen** *pa. p.* 11/30, 18/38, 45, **draghe** 24/112, **dragwen** 27/8

drawyng *vbl. n.* drawing, attraction 44/61

drede(n) *v. inf.* dread, fear 11/17, 68, 37/106; **drede** *1 sg. pr.* 40/11; **dredeth** *3 sg. pr.* 13/29, 37/118; **dredeþ** 32/27; **dredyth** 45/60; **dreden** *3 pl. pr.* 26/94, 30/73, 84; **drede** 45/53; **drede** *sg. subj.* 28/84; **drede** *sg. imp.* 21/29, 28/84, 88; **dredend** *pr. p.* 41/55; **dred** *pa. p.* 14/30

drede *n.* dread, fear 1/5, 10/47, 48; **dredys** *pl.* 22/53, 27/176, 28/49; **dredis** 40/35, 41/42

dredful *adj.* fearful 11/95; fearsome, frightening 23/31

dressed *pa. p.* addressed 42/44

drye *adj.* arid, unenthusiastic in temperament 7/57, 37/72, 42/8

dryfe *v. inf.* drive 22/9, 28/66; **dryfeþ** *3 sg. pr.* 24/122; **dryfeth** 34/106, 43/142; **dryuen** *3 pl. pr.* 46/17; **dryfen** *pa. p.* 24/111, 40/36

durste *see* **dar**

dwelleth *v. 3 sg. pr.* dwell, remain 24/57, 41/170; **dwel** *3 pl. pr.* 15/22; **dwelle** *sg. subj.* 8/43, 12/38

E

effectuly *adv.* in effect 3/2

eygh(e) *n.* eye 11/129, 14/62, 24/44; **eyge** 21/73, 24/139; **eygne** *pl.* 24/43, 29/51; **eyen** 32/41, 37/98; **eyne** 40/184

eye-spered *pa. p.* with closed eyes 32/4

eld *adj.*old; ~ *Testament*, Old Testament of the Bible 3/26

elementare *adj.* elemental 33/60

elles *adv.* else, otherwise 1/9, 3/29, 4/19; **ellis** 10/21, 19/26, 35/21; **ellys** 19/31, 20/62, 76

encens *n.* incense 42/44, 45

encheson *n.* cause, reason 18/1, 10, 19/1

encres *v. sg. subj.* increase 42/118

endyted *v. pa. p.* written 43/116

enflawmed *v. pa. p.* inflamed, burning 30/173, 38/67

enioyned *v. pa. p.* enjoined, commanded 7/25

enneuy *see* **enuy(e)**

enoynteth *v. 3 sg. pr.* anoint 41/50

enseled *v. pa. p.* sealed 43/79

enspyred *v. pa. p.* inspired 43/85; **enspired** 46/42

entent *n.* intent, intention 1/36, 13/31, 21/58

enteremetynge *vbl. n.* intervention, meddling 26/106

entre *n.* entry, introduction 9/25, 19/35, 21/1

entren *v. inf.* enter 2/74, 16/13, 26/24; **entred** *pa. p.* 24/102, 147, 33/69

enuy(e) *n.* envy 10/10, 11/72, 14/37; **enneuy** 13/26

enuyous *n.* envious 14/36

er *conj.* before 6/18, 41/167

erdli, erdly *see* **erthly**

ere *n.* ear 21/36, 22/55, 46/65; **eres** *pl.* 40/116

erren *v. inf.* err 30/106, 43/111, 46/36; **errest** *2 sg. pr.* 10/34; **erreth** *3 sg. pr.* 7/71; **erren** *3 pl. pr.* 3/37, 33/9

erth(e) *n.* earth 1/24, 7/33, 10/37

erthly *adj.* earthly, secular, material 13/19, 14/23, 43, **erdli** 1/28, 4/11, 8/11; **erthely** 40/60; **erdly** 14/15, 43, 27/57

ese *n.* ease, comfort 23/7, 24/115, 27/139

eseth *v. 3 sg. pr.* comforts, makes easy 39/82; **esed** *pa. p.* 19/11

esy *adj.* quiet, at rest 21/117, 24/84, 105

esyly *adv.* with ease, calmly 24/97, 27/76, 181; **esily** 38/39, 39/66

euel *adj.* evil 10/9, 15/30, 22/66; **iuel** 11/60; **ille** 11/3, 12/45, 68; **ill** 24/47

euel *adv.* evilly, badly 21/19, 37/24, 93; **iuele** 12/45, **ille** 10/34, 15/56

euen(e) *adj.* even, equal, straight 2/75, 28/42, 30/143

euen(e) *adv.* precisely, completely 24/79, 39/29, 42/136

euene *n.* evening 29/82

euen(e)-cristen *n.* fellow Christian(s) 10/7, 57, 20/75

euenhed *n.* equality 28/81

euen-lyke *adv.* equally 37/45

euerylk *adj.* every 1/29, 34/122, 42/24;

euerilk 2/22, 7/60, 15/44; **euerilk a** 4/49, 33/80
excersyse *n.* activity, application 17/41, 27/106, 107; **excersyce** 26/28; **exercyse** 35/49; **excercises** *pl.* 26/88; **exercices** 27/105
expouneþ *v. 3 sg. pr.* expounds, explains 31/31; **expowneth** 44/95; **expounet** 43/41; **expouned** *pa. p.* 43/43
expownyng *vbl. n.* interpretation 41/62

F

fage *v.* cajole, beguile 21/35
fayn *adv.* willingly 11/86, 15/3, 24/86
fayr(e) *adj.* beautiful 12/8, 9, 10; **faire** 1/19, 12/1, 5; **fayrer** *comp.* 39/101, 45/21
fayrhed *n.* beauty 8/18, 16/28, 46/4; **fayrehed** 40/186
fayrnes *n.* beauty 8/32
fallen *v. inf.* fall, occur 11/12, 94, 14/52; **falleth** *3 sg. pr.* 6/17, 7/55; **falleþ** 29/1, 84; **fallen** *3 pl. pr.* 10/13, 11/77, 21/13; ~ *to* agree, acquiesce 1/5, 6/19, 11/12
fallynge *vbl. n.* succumbing 15/26, 20/6
falshed *n.* falsehood 23/17
fantasye *n.* illusion, hallucination 22/52, 31/24, 42/98; **fantasyes** *pl.* 22/40, 26/116
fantum *n.* delusion 3/12; **fantoms** *pl.* 46/17
fareth *v. 3 sg. pr.* go, do 15/47, 18/38, 21/130; **fareþ** 27/157, 29/82; **faren** *pa. p.* 45/72
fast *adv.* strongly, steadily 20/112, 25/28, 29/95
fastende *pr. p.* fasting (unable to taste) 43/69
fatnes *n.* richness, abundance 42/63
feghten *v. inf.* fight 11/1; **feyghteth** *3 sg. pr.* 11/37; **feghteth** 36/87; **feghten** *3 pl. pr.* 36/76, 39/17
feyghtynge *vbl. n.* conflict 20/15
feyneþ *v. 3 sg. pr.* feigns, pretends 26/4, 44; **feyneth** 41/94; **feyned** *pa. p.* 15/28, 26/1, 9
feynyng(e) *vbl. n.* pretence 42/98, 44/17, 21; **feynenge** 31/24
felable *adj.* palpable, capable of being sensed 28/57, 29/32, 41/39
felabyly *adv.* with inward affect 20/84, **felably** 41/64; **feleabely** 41/133
felawes *n. pl.* fellows, companions 46/60
felawly *adj.* companionable 42/54
felawschepe *n.* fellowship 46/26
fele(n) *v. inf.* feel, experience, perceive 6/25, 8/14, 16; **fele** *1 sg. pr.* 11/61, 62; **felest** *2 sg. pr.* 4/12, 14, 8/6; **feles** 12/86; **feleth** *3 sg. pr.* 8/10, 11/22, 12/51; **felen** *pl. pr.* 10/54, 11/111, 15/29; **fele** *sg. subj.* 5/11, 8/13, 12/38; **fele** *sg. imp.* 11/116; **feled** *pa. p.* 7/54, 57, 8/3
felendli *adv.* perceptibly, sensitively 3/32; **felendly** 28/31
felyng(e) *n.* feeling, sensation, affect 4/17, 5/2, 11; **felinge** 5/13, 12/2; **feleng** 17/1; **felynges** *pl.* 5/20; **felyngis** 5/22; *reformynge in* ~ Hilton's term for the affective reformation of the soul in God's image, achieved by an experiential knowledge of God beyond reforming in faith 5/6, 7/45, 8/4
felle *adj.* fierce, cruel 45/76
felnes *n.* fierceness, cruelty 38/58
fend(e) *n.* fiend, devil 2/8, 6/14, 16
fendly *adj.* diabolical 26/72
fer *adv.*far 4/9, 7/57, 16/47 **ferre** 10/29, 11/29, 25/30; **ferþer** 16/5, 18/39, 19/22; **ferther** *comp.* 18/31; **ferþest** *superl.* 21/121 **ferthest** 23/48
fere *n. see* **fyre**
ferforth *adj.* advanced 19/31; **fereforth** 12/40; *as* ~ *as,* to the degree that 21/47; *so* ~ to the degree 2/10, 11/24, 15/33
ferly *adv.* distantly 35/77
ferst *adj.* first 1/18, 20, 27
ferst *adv.* first 7/11, 19/18
ferthe *adj.* fourth 28/75
ficched *pa. p.* fixed, fastened 24/70, 150
figure *n.* mental picture 46/11
fygured *pa. p.* foreshadowed 45/69
fyre *n.* fire 21/131, 132, 25/33; **fere** 14/74
fyrebronde *see* **bronde**
flawme *n.* flame 21/131, 28/88
flawmend *pr. p.* flaming 46/52
fleen *v. inf.* flee 10/6, 58, 45/72; **fleeth** *3 sg. pr.* 13/35, 39/123; **fleth** 12/62; **fle** *sg. pr. subj.* 18/42, 50
fleyng(e) *vbl. n.* flight, escape 7/64, 41/36

flemed *v. pa. p.* put to flight, expelled 1/23
flesch(e) *n.* meat, the physical body (*as opposed to* soul) 8/11, 45, 11/61
flesch-flye *n.* blowfly 42/49
fleschli *adj.* of the flesh, physical (*as opposed to* gostly) 4/15, 5/15, 7/16; **fleschly** 5/12, 8/24, 34; **fleischly** 11/26
fleschlyhed(e) *n.* physicality (*as opposed to* gostlines) 20/109, 114, 30/104; **fleschlihed** 4/16
fleschlynes *n.* physicality (*as opposed to* gostlines) 19/38, 41/137, 172
flytyng(e) *n.* contention, invective 26/70, 40/66
fode *n.* food, nourishment 1/22, 29/70, 79
fole *n.* fool 18/40; **foles** *pl.* 10/34
folie *n.* folly, foolishness 3/12, 19
folwe(n) *v. inf.* follow, pursue 10/12, 11/24, 13/22; **folweth** *3 sg. pr.* 11/85, 12/70, 13/30; **folwen** *pl. pr.* 44/14; **folwe** *sg. subj.* 20/37, 27/27; **folwe** *pl. subj.* 19/41; **folwe** *imp. sg.* 24/16; **folwend(e)** *pr. p.* 7/79, 44/11
folwynge *vbl. n.* following, obeying 26/61
for *conj.* for; ~ *þat* because 2/19, 12/32, 18/30; ~ *to* to, in order to 1/3, 25, 2/8; ~ *why* for which/what reason (either positively or interrogatively) 19/18, 20/19, 29/88
forberen *v. inf.* do without 15/14, 38/28, 39/102
forberyng(e) *vbl. n.* abstaining, suffring loss 24/62, 38/37
force *n.* power; *make no* ~ consider to have no validity 14/19
forfetid *v. pa. p.* forfeited, transgressed 2/7, 7/41; **forfetyd** 7/32, 36
forgon *v. inf.* do without 15/16
formeþ *v. 3 sg. pr.* creates 28/12; **formeth** 36/22; **formed** 3 *sg. pa.* 1/35; **formed** *pa. p.* 34/1, 23, 36/20
formynge *vbl. n.* creation 4/62
forschapen *v. pa. p.* deformed 1/20
forsoth *adv.* forsooth, truly 1/8
forthgoynge *vbl. n.* progress 31/5
forth-lokende *see* **loke**
forþen *v. inf.* assist, promote 23/56
forþenkynge *n.* repentance 7/52
forþi *conj.* therefore 7/58, 24/58
fre(e) *adj.* generous 18/5, 20/56, 108
frele *adj.* frail, weak 11/74
frelte *n.* frailty, weakness 10/13, 22/73, 27/13; **freltes** *pl.* 21/67
frenesye *n.* frenzy, delirium 22/52; **frenesyes** *pl.* 22/40
freten *v. pa. p.* devoured 13/25
fro *conj.* from 1/21, 23, 26
froyte *n.* fruit, result 2/80, 3/55
froward *adj.* contrary, evil 14/46, 15/12, 16/55
frowardnes(se) *n.* perversity, error 16/10, 44/12
ful *adj.* complete 2/11, 4/40, 58
ful *adv.* very 4/9, 10/66, 11/12; completely 4/50, 12/18, 20/94
fulfille *v. inf.* fill completely 27/179, 182; **fulfilled** *pa. p.* 21/82, 31/33, 38
fulfillyng(e) *vbl. n.* completion, perfection 7/29, 14/31; **fulfillinge** 4/30; **fulfyllyng** 8/52
fulhed(e) *n.* fulness, abundance 34/134, 36/58
fulsumly *adv.* abundantly 27/146

G

game *n.* merriment 16/26
gedreþ *v. 3 sg. pr.* (only in the phrase ~ *into itself*) recollect 24/123, **gedred** *pa. p.* 30/10; **gadred** 24/107, 110, 42/23
geynstondeþ *see* **ageynstonden(e)**
generacion *n.* procreation 2/34, 35, 4/47; **generacioun** 2/14
gyf(e) *v. inf.* give 2/17, 19, 15/63; **gif** 20/59; **ȝif** 22/44, 26/76, 27/59; **gyfen** 2/49; **ȝife(n)** 16/45, 18/34, 19/46; **ȝefen** 28/13; **gyfeth** *3 sg. pr.* 7/14, 8/43; **gyfeþ** 20/56, 33/42, 34/4; **gifeth** 7/19; **ȝifeþ** 20/60, 24/6, 31/59; **ȝefeþ** 20/42; **ȝefeth** 42/11, 43/90; **gif** *sg. pres. subj.* 18/51; **gyfe** 20/110; **ȝif** 27/54; **ȝeue** 45/57; **gyfen** *pa. p.* 26/37, 52; **ȝifen** 34/98, 38/52, **ȝefen** 28/13; **ȝofen** 29/19
gyle *n.* guile, deceit 14/56
gilt *n.* guilt, sin 2/39, 79,
gladsum *adj.* cheerful 23/32
glemerynge *n.* glimmering, shining 32/48
glenteth *v. 3 sg. pr.* glances 37/119
glentynges *vbl. n. pl.* glintings, glimmerings 24/148

glyderen *v. 3 pl. pr.* glitter, gleam 25/29
gon *v. inf.* go, walk 7/24, 12/73, 15/58; **goþ** *3 sg. pr.* 27/152; **gon** *pl. pr.* 3/57, 14/45, 29/89; **ȝede** *sg. pa.* 44/10; **ȝeden** *pl. pa.* 38/55; **goend(e)** *pr. p.* 11/132, 21/87, 29/64
gode *adj.* good 2/21, 3/41, 7/8; **gud(e)** 15/13, 30/89, 189
gode *n.* good action or intention 20/85
gode *n.* thing(s), possession(s) 18/58, 21/38, 22/71; **godes** *pl.* 14/55
godenes(se) *n.* goodness 18/4, 20/41, 21/72; **godnes** 21/118; **gudnes** 1/33, 32/28, 54
godhed(e) *n.* divinity 2/30, 4/32
Goddis *n. gen. sg.* God's 2/34, 37, 3/7
godly *adv.* in a manner pertaining to the divine 30/147, 35/83, 42/116
God-ward *adv.* towards God 24/87, 145
goynge *vbl. n.* walking, journey 21/14, 20, 24
Gost *n.* Spirit 5/22, 6/20, 8/2
gostli *adj.* spiritual 1/19, 21, 3/33; **gostly** 8/32, 10/71, 11/120; **goostly** 46/82
gostli *adv.* spiritually 7/36, 17/22; **gostly** 11/117, 12/79, 16/21
gostlines *n.* spirituality 4/16
graythende *pr. p.* making ready 46/76
greuen *v. inf.* grieve, trouble 14/38; **greueth** *3 sg. pr.* 10/14, 22/10, 38/42; **greued** *pa. p.* 11/100
greuous *adj.* grievous, serious 8/46
greuously *adv.* grievously 2/7, 3/37; **greuousely** 10/15
grounde *n.* foundation, basis 2/68, 7/51
grounden *v. inf.* ground, to base 31/25; **groundeþ** *3 sg. pr.* 32/26; **groundede** *pa. p.* 21/49; **groundyd** 46/80
grucche *v. sg. subj.*complain 27/79
grucchynge *vbl. n.* complaining 29/78

Ȝ

ȝa *interj.* yea, truly 14/59, 18/56, 20/61
ȝe *2 pers. pron. pl.* you 3/16, 11/123, 12/13; **ȝou** *obl.* 30/181, 31/45, 53; **ȝoure** *gen.* 27/119, 31/43, 44
ȝede(n) *see* **go**
ȝefe(n), ȝefeþ, ȝefeth *see* **gyfen**
ȝeld(en) *v. inf.* yield, (re)pay 2/46, 30/40; **ȝeldeth** *3 sg. pr.* 40/133, 42/47, 53
ȝere *n. sg.* and *pl.* year 7/60, 19/25, 24/50
ȝerneth *v. 3 sg. pr.* desire 25/35
ȝernynge *vbl. n.* yearning, longing 18/64, 21/124, 23/24
ȝet(e) *adv., conj.* yet 2/57, 7/23, 8/12; **ȝit** 9/21, 14/46, 20/33
ȝetted *v. pa. p.* poured out 41/53; **ȝoted** 41/56; **ȝeten** 41/61
ȝefen, ȝefeþ, ȝif(en), ȝifeþ *see* **gyfe**
ȝifere *n.* giver 34/40, 36/8
ȝifte *n.* gift 10/4, 26/35, 29/20; **ȝiftes** *pl.* 21/37, 36/1, 6
ȝis *interj.* yes, certainly 29/13, 45/68
ȝit *see* **ȝet(e)**
ȝofen *see* **gyf(e)**
ȝok *n.* yoke 40/43
ȝoureself *refl. pron. 2 pers. pl.* yourself 31/52, 36/52

H

habyte *n.* habit, disposition 21/58, 43/29
haboundendly *adv.* abundantly 24/95, 46/24
hafyng *vbl. n.* possession 39/8
halwynge *vbl. n.* sanctification 34/92
ha(n) *v. inf.* have 4/38, 50, 51; **hauen** 38/37; **hafe** 4/65, 11/80, 13/21; **hafe** *1 sg. pr.* 11/41, 13/12, 18/58; **hath** *3 sg. pr.* 4/45, 6/13, 7/4; **haþ** 15/5, 24/28, 90; **han** *pl. pr.* 2/80, 3/6, 9/9; **hadde** *1 sg. pa.* 22/30; **haddest** *2 sg. pa.* 21/76; **hadden** *pl. pa.* 3/29, 59, 39/34; **haue** *sg. subj.* 3/24, 67, 7/34; **hafe** 4/63, 11/98, 131; **hadde** *sg. pa. subj.* 1/24, 40/104; **hafend** *pr. part.* 29/77
hangeth *v. 3 sg. pr.* hang (upon), weigh down 38/36, 39/29, 41/140; **hangen** *pl. pr.* 16/36, 27/84; **hange** *sg. subj.* 23/38; **hanggend** *pr. p.* 35/26; **hangen** *pa. p.* 45/63
happed *v. pa. p.* wrapped 42/51
hardily *adv.* confidently 41/12
heygh(e) *adj.* high 10/30, 12/15, 14/6; **heygher(e)** *comp.* 11/23, 18/12, 21/63; **heyghest** *superl.* 17/38, 19/28, 44/64; **heygest** 17/36
heyghed *v. pa. p.* exalted 40/98, 100, 46/32; **heghed** 4/35
heyghynge *vbl. n.* arrogance 26/48, 51
heyghnes *n.* exaltation (presumption,

when used in a negative sense) 26/59, 40/17, 82; **heygnes** 38/61
heyghneth *v. 3 sg. pr.* raise, exalt 42/29
heyght *n.* height, excellence 24/23, 26/85; **heght** 38/68
heygh-weye *n.* highway 40/125
held(en) *see* **holden**
heldende *pr. p.* pointing, oriented 25/38
hele *n.* health, salvation 10/72, 17/28, 41/54
helen *v. inf.* heal 20/39; **heleth** *3 sg. pr.* 41/63; **heled** *3 sg. pa.* 11/114; **heled** *pa. p.* 17/11, 41/58, 43/74
hem *see* **þei**
hemself(e) *pron. refl. pl.* themselves 3/20, 7/64, 10/74
henforward *adv.* henceforward 31/28
hens *adv.* hence 7/27, 14/80, 16/2; **hennis** 6/8
here *see* **þei**
herebeforn *adv.* before now 4/61
hert(e) *n.* heart, desire 2/23, 7/7, 11/128; **hertis** *pl.* 10/9, 16/16, 46/77; **hertys** 11/133, 16/17, 34/48; **hertes** 14/24, 15/12, 22/2
hertly *adj.* sincere 20/119, 45/75
hertly *adv.* sincerely 16/50, 18/52
heued *n.* head 43/50; ~ *synne* capital or mortal 10/10, 11/72, 20/16
heuen(e) *n.* heaven 1/23, 2/39, 67
heuenli *adj.* pertaining to heaven 1/22, 26; **heuenly** 8/34, 9/7, 12/52; according to the anagogical sense of interpretation of Scripture 43/51
heuenly *adv.* (of scriptural interpretation) anagogically 43/44
heueneward *adv.* toward heaven 32/68
heuy *adj.* heavy, distressing, 15/31; grieved 19/14, 23/5, 24/95
heuynes(se) *n.* difficulty, aggravation 29/78, 37/81, 43/142
hyden *v. inf.* hide 24/68, 26/105, 27/153; **hydest** *2 sg. pr.* 27/170; **hydeth** *3 sg. pr.* 41/28; **hyd** *pa. p.* 22/21, 24/1, 76; **hid** 12/25, 25/12, 27/119
hydyng(e) *vbl. n.* hiding, concealment 24/66, 41/29
hyled *pa. p.* covered 40/176; **hilid** 43/10
hol *n.* whole, entirety 4/29
hol(e) *adj.* whole, unblemished 2/6, 4/26, 5/20
holden *v. inf.* hold, keep, consider 19/9, 21/39, 55; **halden** 18/47; **hold** 21/17; **hold** *1 sg. pr.* 21/118, 27/73; **holdest** *2 sg. pr.* 22/56; **holdeþ** *3 sg. pr.* 16/34, 17/19, 29/81; **holdeth** 37/45, 42/42; **holden** *pl. pr.* 26/58; **hold** 16/7, 26/40; **helden** 3/10, 12; **hold(e)** *sg. subj.* 27/58, 76, 164; **halde** 11/97; **helden** *pl. subj.* 19/34; **hold** *sg. imp.* 21/33, 22/17, 26 **held(e)** 10/35, 21/84, 102; **holdend(e)** *pr. p.* 30/20, 33/33, 41/99; **holden** *pa. p.* 11/6, 30/15, 18
holly *adv.* wholly 21/97, 24/111, 36/27
homly *adj.* familiar, comfortable 25/19, 42/54
homly *adv.* familiarly 44/7
homlynes(se) *n.* familiarity 24/90, 27/65, 41/113
honest(e) *adj.* honourable 27/67, 43/119
honeste *n.* honour 14/49
honestly *adv.* properly 46/59
hope *v. 1 sg. pr.* believe 7/53, 63, 71; **hoped** *3 sg. pa.* 21/9
hospileth *v. 3 sg. pr.* despoils, plunders 45/47
hows *n.* house 27/158, 161

I

ydel *adj.* idle 11/10, 18/30
ydelnes *n.* idleness 20/114, 39/85, 40/41
ilyk(e) *adv.* alike, equally 19/24, 30, 32/69; **ylyke** 41/89, 42/40, 43/84
ilk *adj.* each, every, very 2.74, 11/32, 101; **ilk a** 1/10, 2/76, 77
ille *see* **euel**
ymaginacion *n.* imagination, the faculty that forms mental images from sense perception (see Explanatory Notes 31/32), or the images so produced 11/30, 30/74, 160; **ymaginacyon** 29/16, 30/35, 39; **ymaginacions** *pl.* 19/39; **ynaginacyons** 24/150
in *n.* inn 29/72
inly *adj.* inward 10/20, 17/43, 30/169
inner(e) *adj.* inner, inward, i.e. spiritual 11/129, 24/44, 36/38; **ynner(e)** 30/110, 32/1, 33/69; **ynnerest** *superl.* furthest inward 33/36
innerwarde *adv.* inwards 25/44
inogw *adj.* enough, sufficient 14/42, 33/70, 36/79; **inogh** 7/33, 37, 18/14; **inogwe** 35/29, 43/105; **inow** 3/44, 42/105; **inowgh** 42/98

inperfyte *adj.* imperfect 3/30, 30/188, 35/76
irk(e) *adj.* weary, averse 14/45, 39/111
yrketh *v. 3 sg. pr.* grow weary, feel vexed 12/65
yrknes *n.* weariness 42/41
yrksumnesse *n.* irksomeness, weariness 43/142
iuel(e) *see* **euel(e)**

J

ianglynge *vbl. n.* jangling, chatter 11/26, 23/16, 40/50; **iangelyng** 39/120, 46/73
ianglen *v. pl. pr.* chatter, gossip 38/36
ioyend *pr. p.* rejoicing 38/55
iurne *n.* journey, daily progress 21/112; **iornees** *pl.* 21/55

K

kan *v. 1 sg. pr.* can, be able to do something 4/38, 21/47, 44/59; **kanst** *2 sg. pr.* 21/135; **kan** *3 sg. pr.* 7/46, 11/92, 19/24; **kan** *3 pl. pr.* 20/102, 25/24, 29/20; **cowthe** *3 sg. pa.* 30/135; **cowthe** *sg. subj.* 24/145; **coude** *pl. subj.* 28/80
kare *n.* care, anxiety 16/4
karpe *v. pl. subj.* talk captiously 43/75
karpyng *vbl. n.* talking 40/122
kend *see* **kynde**
kendly *adj.* natural, in accordance with nature 2/14, 4/47, 30/32; **kendli** 2/33
kenne *v. inf.* teach 20/38, 46/15; *1 sg. pr.* 21/26; **kenned** *3 sg. pa.* 30/129
kepe *n.* heed, care 8/16, 17/27, 36/81
kepe(n) *v. inf.* keep, preserve, obey 10/7, 11/8, 18/14; **kepyn** 19/7; **kepeth** *3 sg. pr.* 8/44, 11/84, 37/101; **kepeþ** 28/60, 29/50, 39/18; **kepit** 34/105; **keped** *3 sg. pa.* 3/59; **kepe** *sg. pr. subj.* 21/26, 108, 23/53; **keped** *sg. p. subj.* 37/54; **kepe** *imp. sg.* 23/51; **kepend** *pr. p.* 33/33; **keped** *pa. p.* 40/95, 43/111; **kept** 12/43, 20/3, 21/40
kepyng(e) *vbl. n.* keeping, observance, preservation 3/37, 7/64, 39/25
keste *v. imp. sg.* cast, throw 21/85; **kest** *pa. p.* 14/67
kynd(e) *n.* nature 2/31, 61, 14/35; **kend(e)** 2/41, 8/8, 11/55
Kirk(e) *n.* (*always in the phrase* Holy/Holi ~) the Christian church 3/35, 39, 6/16; **Kyrke** 10/81, 89, 32/44
klefen *v. inf.* split 29/45; **clefen** 29/49
knowe(n) *v. inf.* know, acknowledge 7/70, 14/5, 15/62; **knowest** *2 sg. pr.* know 20/28, 21/111, 22/22; **knoweth** *3 sg. pr.* 13/16, 14/4, 14/10; **knoweþ** 22/46, 25/34; **knowe** *pl. pr.* 9/22, 33/85; **knowen** 31/62; **knowe** *sg. pr. subj.* 16/25, 21/102; **knowen** *pa. p.* 26/45, 55, 75
knowyng(e) *vbl. n.* knowing, knowledge 7/65, 10/54, 66; **knoweng(e)** 32/25, 34/12, 37/31; **knowengys** *pl.* 43/132
kun *v. inf.* know, know how to 22/43, 41/117; **cun** 43/47; **kun** *pl. pr.* 10/73, 30/70, 33/67; **kunnen** 35/47; **couthe** *3 sg. pa.* 39/113, 114, 40/8; **kouþe** *sg. pa. subj.* 21/9; **conende** *pr. p.* 27/48
kunnynge *see* **connynge**

L

laynynge *vbl. n.* concealment 43/15
lakken *v. inf.* disparage 37/90
lakketh *v. 3 sg. pr.* lacks 10/51; **lak** *sg. subj.* 42/69
lakkynge *n.* lack, want 12/56
lakkynge *vbl. n.* disparagement 23/8
langeth *v. 3 sg. pr.* belongs 37/84
langoure *v. inf.* languish 17/28
langwysseth *v. 3 sg. pr.* languishes 41/49
large *adj.* broad, expanded 25/46, 37/75; **larger** *comp.* 10/31
lastend(e) *pr. p.* lasting, continual 20/116, 26/26, 34/125
lastendly *adv.* continually 20/16, 21/58, 26/98
lasteþ *v. 3 sg. pr.* last, continue 11/32, 23/52, 24/40; **lasteth** 41/149
lastyng *vbl. n.* continuation 41/146
lawe *n.* law 2/33, 3/38; **laghe** 11/42, 44, 47; **lawes** *pl.* 10/89, 11/42, 45/15; **laghes** 11/45, 48, 21/50
leche *n.* physician 17/22, 30, 20/35
lede *n.* lead 39/9
lede(n) *v. inf.* lead 10/6, 23/43, 24/17; **ledeth** *3 sg. pr.* 11/43, 49, 40/113; **leden** *pl. pr.* 10/6, 18/18; **ledend(e)** *pr. p.* 19/19, 21/14, 27/102
lefe(n) *v. inf.* leave 15/14, 31, 21/35; **lefeþ** *3 sg. pr.* 21/87, 28/53; **lefe** *pl.*

pr. subj. 19/40; **lefe** *imp. sg.* 21/124, 22/47

lefer(e) *adj. and adv. comp.* more dear, rather, 12/63, 39/70; **leuer** 37/72, 94, 38/31

leyth *v. 3 sg. pr.* lays; **leyd** *pa. p.* 12/54, 73, 21/131; (in the phrase ~ *of hande*) puts aside 44/24

lene *v. inf.* lean, rely 21/93; **lenest** *2 sg. pr.* 42/131; **leneth** *3 sg. pr.* 37/35; **lene** *sg. pr. subj.* 20/77; **lene** *imp. sg.* 27/155; **lenne** 42/134

lenyngge *vbl. n.* reliance 37/61

leren *v. inf.* learn 27/38

lerynge *vbl. n.* learning, instruction 19/31, 20/38, 42

lese(n) *v. inf.* lose 6/4, 18/35, 21/18

leseth *v. 3 sg. pr.* loosens 40/43

lesynges *n. pl.* lies, falsehoods 21/35

lesse *adj.* and *adv. comp.* lesser, smaller 1/30, 18/57, 20/95; **lest(e)** *superl.* 7/60, 10/54, 12/60

lesse *v. sg. subj.* lessen 21/122

lest(en) *v. inf.* last, remain 24/53, 40/62; **lesteth** *3 sg. pr.* 41/158; **lesten** *pl. pr.* 10/17

lete *v. sg. subj.*; (in the phrase ~ *wel by*) release, excuse 27/51

lette(n) *v. inf.* hinder 8/37, 14/32, 21/27; **letteth** *3 sg. pr.* 21/144, 39/63, 41/141; **letteþ** 21/148, 32/47, 52; **letten** *pl. pr.* 20/19, 27/34, 82; **lette** *sg. subj.* 19/41, 23/56, 27/27; **letted(e)** *pa. p.* 22/64, 39/62, 68; **lettid** 16/14; **lettyd** 19/13, 39

letterly *adv.* literally 36/32; according to the literal sense of interpretation of Scripture 43/44

lettyng(e) *n.* hindrance 6/24, 16/23, 21/89; **lettynges** *pl.* 21/13, 23/20, 24

lettre *n.* letter, literal sense 43/45, 134; **lettres** *pl.* 43/141

lettred *pa. p.* literate 42/19, 43/97

leue *n.* leave, permission 43/80, 45/54, 57

leuer *see* **lefer(e)**

lewed *adj.* unlearned 3/34, 42/18, 43/97

lyfly *adj.* living, life-giving 40/53, 144, 154; **lyfely** 40/155; **lyuely** 39/86, 40/18, 43/62

lyghers *n.* liars 14/73

lygheþ *v. 3 sg. pr.* lies 17/43; **ligge** *3 pl. pr.* 3/56

lyght *n.* light, illumination 15/11, 17/14, 24/21; **lyȝt** 24/36, 37, 55; **liȝt** 24/37, 40, 26/4; **lyȝtes** *pl.* 24/36

lyȝt *adj.* light, bright 24/73; **lyȝteste** *superl.* 43/45

lyghten *v. inf.* illuminate 36/31; **lyghtneth** *3 sg. pr.* 37/32; **lyȝtneþ** 32/8; **lyghtned(e)** *pa. p.* 36/56, 43/100; **lyȝtned** 30/177, 185, 32/19

lyghtenynges *vbl. n. pl.* illuminations, gleamings 25/3, 46/25; **lyȝtnynges** 25/29

lyghty *adj.* luminous, full of spiritual light 24/2; **lyghtty** 40/15; **lyȝty** 27/2, 129

lyȝtly *adj.* light, bright 25/1

lyghtly *adv.* lightly, easily 5/9, 7/46, 10/13; **liȝtly** 16/38; **lyȝtly** 24/89, 27/21, 31; **lyghtely** 40/107; **lyghtlyer(e)** *comp.* 38/29, 40/135; **liȝtlyer** 16/36; **lyȝtlyere** 29/66

lyghtnes *n.* lightness, ease 36/68; irreverence 41/67

lymes *n. pl.* limbs 11/43

list *v. 3 sg. pr.* desires 42/32, 43/101; **lysteþ** 24/7; **listeth** 42/30; *hem* ~ (*impersonal*) they wish 27/22

lysty *adj.* joyful 41/60

liter(e) *n.* litter 12/55, 74

lofe *n. see* **lufe**

lofe *v. inf.* praise 10/69; **lufen** *pl. pr.* 23/13: **lufend** *pr. p.* 44/42

lofenges *see* **lufyng**

lofers *n. pl.* lovers 16/1

logwe *adj.* low 20/5; **logwere** *comp.* 24/71, 30/90; **logwest** *superl.* 17/35, 28/21, 30/61; **loghest** 17/37

loke *v. inf.* look, examine, see 26/41; **lokeþ** *v. 3 sg. pr.* 27/132; **loketh** 32/41; **loked** *sg. pa.* 25/41; **loke** *sg. imp.* 9/26, 21/134, 42/127; **lokeþ** *pl. imp.* 36/52 **lokende** *pr. p.* 32/4

lokyng *vbl. n.* looking, seeing; 45/18, 21

longeth *v. 3 sg. pr.* belongs, pertains 4/37, 39/120, 41/117; **longeþ** 34/99; **longen** *pr. pl.* 10/60; **longende** *pr. p.* 24/128

loþe(n) *v. inf.* loathe, hate 12/51, 14/77; **lotheth** *3 sg. pr.* 12/61; **loþen** *pr. pl.* 15/21

loþing *vbl. n.* loathing 7/17

lufe *n.* love 10/46, 51, 57 *and passim, except for* **lofe** 4/11, 17/14, 20/27, 29,

44, 67, 69, 24/74, 39/8; **loue** 1/19, 2/49, 52, 53
lufe(n) *v. inf.* love 3/5, 21/117, 138 *and passim, except for* **lofe** 15/3; **loue(n)** 2/23; **lufeþ** *3 sg. pr.* 24/55, 57, 27/90; **loueth** 12/70, 13/17, 15/45; **loueþ** 34/39; **lufe** *pr. pl.* 26/33; **loue(n)** 3/49, 55, 63, 14/8; **lufed** *pa. sg.* 30/132, 135, 34/51; **louynge** 43/134; **lufed** *pa. p.* 30/149, 34/14, 83; **loued** 41/41, 43/135
lufely *adj.* loving 40/185; **lufelyer** *comp.* 41/83
lufely *adv.* lovingly 44/8
luferede(n) *n.* loving kindness (the opposite of hatred) 36/65, 38/8
lufer(e) *n.* lover 37/74, 80, 43/135; **lufers** *pl.* lovers 26/6, 27/122
lufyng *n.* praise 41/60; **louynges** *pl.* 42/33, 52; **lofenges** 42/76
lufly *adj.* pleasant 21/70; loving 21/76
lust(e) *n.* lust, desire, pleasure 1/22, 8/45, 14/25; **lustes** *pl.* 8/38, 13/23, 14/48

M

magnyfyed *v. 3 sg. pa.* exalted 28/20; **magnifyed** *pa. p.* exalted 28/78
magnyfyenge *vbl. n.* exaltation 28/3, 72, 84
mayden *n.* virgin, maidservant 2/36, 31/70
maysterschipe *n.* mastery, authority, superior force 14/22
maystire *n.* master, teacher 20/37; **mayster** 35/37, 43/43; **maystre** 36/86, 44/30
maystrie *n.* mastery, superior force, accomplishment 11/21, 35/49, 38/8; **maistrie** 14/54; **maystrye** 40/85
makes *v. 2 sg. pr.* make 22/55; **maketh** *v. 3 sg. pr.* 8/33, 12/33, 35/38; **makeþ** 16/26, 18/63, 21/88; **maken** *pl. pr.* 6/4, 16/4, 35/11
makyng(e) *vbl. n.* making, creation 8/40, 26/64, 34/3; **makenge** 34/60
manassynge *vbl. n.* menacing, threatening 22/36
manciples *n. pl.* servants 6/18
maner *n. sg. and pl.* kind(s), type(s) 3/4, 4/1, 21
manhed(e) *n.* humanity, human form 3/9, 30/64, 66
manly *adj.* human, in physically human form 30/71, 74, 102
manly *adv.* as a man 30/147, 31/63
mansleers *n.* murderers 14/72
mater(e) *n.* matter, subject of discussion 27/54, 43/45, 46/40; **maters** *pl.* 42/93
mede *n.* reward, earnings 5/8, 14/44, 20/46
medefully *adv.* deserving reward 35/51
medelure *n.* admixture 4/30
medful *adj.* meritorious 30/96, 100, 35/17; **medeful** 42/69
medycynable *adj.* healing 21/69
medled *pa. p.* mingled 12/7
meke *adj.* meek, humble 12/27, 20/69, 80
mekely *adv.* meekly, humbly 35/51, 42/137, 43/144
meken *v. pl. pr.* humble 10/88, 26/95
mekenes *n.* meekness, humility 16/50, 20/70, 35/18
membris *n.* bodily members 15/50
mende *n.* mind, memory 4/6, 7/61, 21/56; **mynde** 22/69, 24/27, 30/23
mene *v. 1 sg. pr.* mean, intend 1/8, 19/42, 21/66; **meneth** *3 sg. pr.* 23/1; **meneþ** 24/30, 34/1; **mened** *sg. pa.* 8/47, 24/34, 79
mene *n.* mean, middle, intermediary 10/35, 19/36; **menes** *pl.* 19/19, 30/128, 31/12
menged *pa. p.* mixed 38/68
menynge *n.* thought, intention 12/50, 21/57, 103; **meneng** 36/53
merryd *pa. p.* marred, damaged 11/92
meschief *see* **myschief**
messis *n.* masses 15/57
mesure *n.* measure, moderation 17/21, 30, 41/114
metalle *n.* metal 33/63
mete *n.* food 23/52, 27/76, 80; **metys** *pl.* 27/75
meteles *adj.* hungry, without food 29/71
meten *pa. p.* measured 25/39
mydday *n.* noon 27/172
mydday *adj.* noonday 26/4, 26/44, 38/71
myddys *n.* midst, middle 19/17, 25/16; **myddes** 10/35
myȝt *n.* might, power, capacity 27/177, 28/57, 30/21; **myght** 8/29, 24/15;

myȝth 34/121, 45/52; **myghtes** *pl.* 4/17, 30, 18/61; **myȝtes** *pl.* 30/166, 170, 177; **mightes** 1/13, 2/24
myȝty *adj.* mighty 29/44, 49; **myȝthy** 21/118; **myȝtty** 31/23; **myghty** 24/12; **myghtyere** *comp.* 21/133
myghtyly *adv.* mightily, in full force 27/13, 28/35, 36/44
mikel *adj.* great 4/27, 12/42, 18/28; **mykel** 7/62, 11/7, 18/40; **mekel** 17/6; **mekyl** 45/51
mikel *adv. and conj.* much, very 1/3, 30, 2/41; **mykel** 10/59, 16/12, 28/25
mykelnes *n.* greatness, abundance 29/34, 52, 34/38
mylke *n.* milk 31/65
mynde *see* **mende**
mynystren *v. pr. 3 pl.* minister 46/17
mynysterie *n.* ministering 43/39
mirk(e) *adj.* dark 24/125, 25/12, 26/46; **myrk** 16/16, 24/65, 41/28; **myrker** *comp.* 24/75
mirknes(se) *n.* darkness 1/22, 12/20, 24/73; **myrknes** 16/16, 44, 24/81; **mirkenes** 24/94, 103, 26/109; **myrkenes** 24/2, 72
mischef *n.* misfortune, trouble 1/29; **myschief** 16/32; **meschyef** 38/65; **meschef** 12/75; **myschef** 22/41; **meschief** 21/23; **meschefes** *pl.* 21/109, 28/55
mysdon(e) *pa. p.* wrongly done, sinned 9/29, 40/70
mysproud *adj.* arrogant 14/33
mysteyed *n.* the mystical or allegorical sense of interpretation of Scripture 43/48
mystely *adv.* mystically, allegorically 43/44
mystrowend *pa. p.* unbelieving 14/72
mysty *adj.* mystical, spiritual 43/50
myswilled *pa. p.* contrary, unwilling 14/41
morally *adv.* according to the moral sense of interpretation of Scripture 43/44
moralte *n.* the moral sense of Scripture 43/46
mortifyed *pa. p.* slain 27/108, 28/69, 31/17; **mortyfyed** 28/56
mortyfyenge *n.* mortification 29/37
most *v. 2 sg. pres.* must 22/22; **mote** *3 sg. pres.* 41/141; **most** *sg. pa.* 2/35; **mote** *sg. subj.* 2/71, 24/49
moun *v. inf.* may, be able to 2/66, 7/47, 12/92; **mogwe** *2 sg. pr.* 32/38; **mow** *3 sg. pr.* 7/80; **mow(e)** *pl. pr.* 36/47, 46/82; **moun** *pl. pr.* 3/38, 47, 7/77; **mightest** *2 sg. subj.* might 21/4; **myght(e)** *3 sg. subj.* 4/5, 18, 26; **myȝt** 24/124, 27/55, 86; **myghten** *pl. subj.* 16/43, 20/52, 27/21; **myght** 22/13; **mighten** 14/19, 25, 79; **moghte** *pl. subj.* 14/18

N

namely *adv.* especially 17/41, 27/77, 39/83; **namly** 10/33, 73, 11/33
ne *conj.* nor 2/25, 30, 55
neddere *n.* adder 12/63
nede *n.* need 10/74, 13/20
neden *v. inf.* need 42/91; **neden** *pl. pr.* 11/1, 18/19; **nedeth** *3 sg. pr. (refl.)* is necessary to 10/56, 11/13, 17; **neded** *3 sg. pa. (refl.)* 1/30, 2/1; **nedid** 2/27, 32, 4/47
nede *adv.* of necessity 23/36; **nedes** 15/14, 33/65
nedful *adj.* necessary 7/32, 43, 73; **nedeful** 7/66
neyghen *v. inf.* draw near 21/4; **neghes** *2 sg. pr.* 25/28; **neggheth** *3 sg. pr.* 17/15; **negheth** 24/83; **neghtheth** 35/36; **neghen** *pl. pr.* 29/95
neyghynge *vbl. n.* drawing near 24/74; **neyghhyng** 41/123
neiþer *conj.* neither 4/16; **neyþer(e)** 7/73, 8/8, 13; **neþer** 8/16
nere *adv.* near, closely 10/30, 11/10, 17/16; **nerre** *comp.* 22/59, 26/16, 38/42; **nerrere** 35/36
nerhand(e) *adv.* nearly, almost 28/50, 29/72, 42/88
nerre *adj. comp.* nearer 24/75, 78, 25/16; **nest** *superl.* 22/14; **nexte** 17/38, 37/108
neþer *adj.* lower 13/17. *See also* **neiþer**
nerþeles *conj.* nevertheless 22/73, 23/46, 24/84
newhed *n.* newness 31/29
noght *pron.* nought, nothing 15/7, 19/54, 20/36; **noȝt** 21/56, 60, 75; **nouȝt** 45/48; *sette ~ by* consider worthless 15/61
noght *adv.* not 3/67, 13/5, 20/104;

nought 1/1, 13, 2/11; **noȝt** 24/103, 26/23, 30/141; **nouȝt** 43/54, 56, 45/51
noghten *v. inf.* make as nothing 20/84; **noȝteth** *3 sg. pr.* 35/34
noghttynge *vbl. n.* bringing to nought 26/96
noye *n.* trouble, distress 24/1, 40/37, 41/131
noyȝen *v. inf.* harm 45/55
noyous *adj.* harmful, injurious 40/114
noyse *n.* distraction, commotion 24/77, 40/47, 46/72
norysede *pa. p.* nourished, nurtured 3/34
notys *n. pl.* musical notes 42/76

O

o *adj.* one 14/26, 19/54, 20/23; a 43/120
occupien *v. inf.* busy, occupy 22/14; **occupyen** 43/105; **occupieth** *3 sg. pr.* 11/84; **occupyeth** 11/102; **occupyeþ** 24/123; **occupyed** *pa. p.* 23/34, 39/87
ofte-syþes *adv.* oftentimes 7/55; **ofte-sythes** 11/70, 29/85, 39/126
oght *pron.* aught, anything 12/86,14/45, 23/6; **owt** 4/13
oyle *n.* oil 41/51, 53, 56
oneþ *v. 3 sg. pr.* unites 34/74; **oneth** 36/27; **oned** *pa. p.* united 4/32, 30/92, 93
onhed *n.* unity 46/37
onyng *n.* union 41/123
onlynes(se) *n.* solitude 23/50, 40/18, 111
onon, on-one *see* **anon**
open *v. inf.* explain 1/7
or *conj.* before 6/8, 7/16, 26
ordeynd(e) *pa. p.* ordained, commanded 2/54, 7/66, 43/127; **ordeyned** 4/45, 45/15
orders *n. pl.* hierarchies 46/7; **ordres** 46/9
ordinance *n.* rule, precept 7/27; **ordinaunce** 23/54
ordinatly *adv.* according to order, properly 43/105
orison *n.* prayer 15/56; **orisouns** *pl.* 20/99
oslepe *adj.* asleep 16/9
ouer(e) *adj.* upper 13/14, 18, 21; **ouerest** *superl.*17/39
ouercometh *v. 3 sg. pr.* 39/128; **ouerkam** *pa. 3 sg.* 34/79; **ouercomen** *pa. p.* 27/92, 29/72
ouergoth *v. 3 sg. pr.* overruns 40/84
ouerledyng *vbl. n.* oppression 14/54
ouerleyd *pa. p.* overcome, oppressed 11/75, 12/48, 13/26
ouermore *adv.* moreover 2/63, 15/36, 23/29
ouerpassen *v. inf.* surpass, endure 14/20; **ouerpassed** *pa. p.* 11/87
ouertaken *pa. p.* overcome 29/41
out(e) *adv.* out 5/14, 26/2, 109; **owt(e)** 4/13, 14/67, 26/117
owtraious *adj.* outrageous, excessive 14/23; **owtragious** 20/99
outtake *v. 1 sg. pr.* exclude, except 16/47; **outtaken** *pa. p.* 11/19; **owtetake** 39/79; **outtakyn** 8/29; **owttakyn** 14/6; **owttaken** 28/51
owtward *adj.* outward, external, detached 13/9, 20/75, 24/102; **owteward** 29/2
owtward *adv.* externally 27/46, 29/24, 35/35; **outwarde** 7/46; **outewarde** 15/33
ouþer *adv.* either 3/25, 28, 32; **oyþer** 41/90
owen *pron. adj.* own 3/2, 22, 38
oweth *v. 3 sg. pr.* owes 2/18, 22, 41/122; **oweþ** 30/40; **awght** *3 sg. pa.* 2/21, 31, 3/40; **owe** *sg. subj.* 2/19

P

paye(n) *v. inf.* satisfy, (re)pay 2/20, 47, 62; **payed** *sg. pa.* 2/57; **payed** *pa. p.* 11/88, 27/59, 76
payrend *pr. p.* diminishing 18/37
palasie *n.* palsy 11/114; **palasye** 12/72
palet *n.* palate 43/61
paynemys *n. pl.* pagans 3/1, 6, 8
panten *v. pl. pr.* pant 35/12
partie *n.* part, portion 1/4, 5/1; **party(e)** 4/2, 5/3, 7/68, 35/81; **partyes** *pl.* 13/4, 8
passe *n.* step 14/46
passe(n) *v. inf.* pass, pass away, surpass 6/22, 14/76, 16/2; **passeth** *3 sg. pr.* 12/44, 20/54, 37/119; **passeþ** 24/40, 25/10, 53; **passe** *sg. subj.* 6/8, 7/27, 40/163; **passand** *pr. p.* 14/14, 37/114; **passend** 33/79, 38/15, 43/155
peyn(e) *n.* pain, penance, punishment 2/54, 3/59, 6/7; **pyne** 2/31, 14/63, 15/61; **peyns** *pl.* 3/9; **peynes** 3/58, 45/38
peynful *adj.* painful 1/22, 15/20, 31; **pynful** 7/16, 8/38, 9/17

per *prep.* for 1/3
perauenture *adv.* perhaps 3/42, 7/68, 20/98
perceyfe(n) *v. inf.* perceive 25/3, 35/37, 37/24; **perceyuen** 46/26, 34; **perceyfeth** *3 sg. pr.* 11/77; **perceyueth** 41/88, 46/67; **perceyueþ** 23/23; **perceyue** *pl. pr.* 22/51; **perceyue** *sg. subj.* 24/147; **perceyuend(e)** *pr. p.* 41/133, 44/27; **perceyued** *pa. p.* 46/65
perceyfyng *vbl. n.* perception 43/25; **perceyuynges** *pl.* 43/109
percenere *n.* heir, sharer 8/34
perchaunce *adv.* perhaps 16/6, 18/17, 19/12
perfyt(e) *adj.* perfect 5/18, 7/67, 10/64
perysche(n) *v. inf.* perish 21/105, 23/44, 24/53; **peryssche** *sg. subj.* 24/49
persen *v. inf.* pierce 33/22; **persande** *pr. p.* 40/55
pertenent *adj.* appertaining 46/39
pertinere *n.* partner, sharer 36/19
pes *n.* peace 9/7, 9, 36/27; **pees** 11/18, 12/23, 20/20
pesybilte *n.* peacefulness 38/7
pesybily *adv.* peacefully 27/12
pesible *adj.* peaceful 12/22, 23, 38/23
pyked *pa. p.* picked, cleaned 43/66
pyne *see* **peyn(e)**
pynen *v. inf.* pain, torment 20/98; **pyneth** *3 sg. pr.* 10/14; **pyned** *pa. p.* 24/70, 28/56, 59
pyt(te) *n.* pit 14/74, 18/39; **pitte** 16/34, 18/44, 45; **pyttis** *gen. sg.* 18/39; **pittes** 18/47
pyte *n.* pity 29/77; **pite** 38/77
plawend *pr. p.* playing (music) 42/52
plener *adj.* full 7/30
plente *n.* plenty, abundance 7/15, 17/10, 27/31
plesaunce *n.* pleasure 14/43
plese(n) *v. inf.* please 13/31, 24/12, 42/84; **pleseth** *3 sg. pr.* 35/6, 43/56
plesynge *vbl. n.* obsequiousness 22/37, 23/11
pleten *v. pr. pl.* plead, contend 39/17
poynt *n.* point, matter, focus 11/69, 80; *in ~ for to* about to 29/45
preent *v. imp. sg.* imprint 21/103; **prented** *pa. p.* 24/27
preiere *n.* prayer 10/90; **preyere** 20/121, 23/42, 26/107; **preyers** *pl.* 22/56
preyen *v. inf.* pray 32/106, 24/3, 39/106; **preyeth** *3 sg. pr.* 10/71, 35/29, 38/76; **preyend(e)** *pr. p.* 20/24, 76
preyeng(e) *vbl. n.* praying 22/4, 29/25, 39/89
preysen *v. inf.* praise 37/67, 93; **preysen** *pl. pr.* 23/12, 37/90, 46/10; **preysed** *sg. pa.* 30/137; **preysed** *pa. p.* 37/112
preysynge *vbl. n.* praise 14/19, 23/7, 27/41
prentys *n.* apprentice 19/23, 30
preseth *v. 3 sg. pr.* press 11/11; **pressen** *pl. pr.* 24/91
presynge *vbl. n.* 24/101, 148
presently *adv.* in physical presence 43/34
prest *n.* priest 7/30, 73
pris *n.* value, price 39/71; **prisse** 27/95
priuey *adj.* secret, private 8/8, 18, 23; **preuey** 8/1; **priue** 4/16, 22/42, 24/15
priueli *adv.* implicitly, in private, secretly 3/29, 12/2, 25/20;
priuylege *n.* privilege 6/26
pryuete *n.* secret, mystery 40/18, 130, 132; **priuete** 40/123, 133, 134; **preuyte** 43/57; **priuetes** *pl.* 3/30, 34/139, 46/58; **pryuetes** 46/34
proferynges *vbl. n. pl.* offerings, suggestions 24/148, 26/120
profyten *v.* progress, advance 18/12, 20, 31; **profytend** *pr. p.* 10/63, 18/37; **protifend** 31/62, 40/152
profitynge *vbl. n.* progress, advancement 29/69
pronownce *v. inf.* state 41/12
properly *adv.* of its essence 13/16, 31/37, 47
properte *n.* essential characteristic 8/5
psalmen *v. inf.* sing psalms 42/33
purchace *n.* gain, acquisition 10/29, 35/61

Q

queynte *adj.* extraordinary 42/85
qwenchen *v. inf.* quench, extinguish 12/92
qwere *adv.* where 4/24
qwerewith *adv.* wherewith 2/20
qwhat(e) *pron.* what, which 1/8, 2/21; **qwat** 7/4
qwhen *adv.* when 3/68; **qwen** 6/19

qwhi *adv.* why 4/68; **whi** 34/19; **for why** *see* **for**
qwyk *adj.* living 40/55; **quik** 12/25
qwykly *adv.* in a lively manner 28/30
qwykneth *v. 3 sg. pr.* gives life 40/156, 43/64; **quykneth** 33/42; **qwykende** *pr. p.* 30/20; **quikned** *pa. p.* 10/2; **quykned** 10/52
qwhilk(e) *pron.* which 2/44, 3/18, 10/54; **qwilk** 3/51, 66, 4/3; **whilk** 1/4, 3/61, 7/35; **wilk** 1/26, 33, 11/131
qwhom *pron.* whom 1/6

R

ransake *v. imp.* examine with the aim of discovery 9/26
ransakynge *vbl. n.* examining 22/25
rauisceth *3 sg. pr.* ravishes 32/23; **rauyscheþ** 34/116; **rauysched** *pa. p.* 29/26, 40/132, 44/28; **rauyssed** 37/78
ravischynge *vbl. n.* carrying away 11/28
raunson *n.* ransom 34/64
raueyn *n.* ravin, seizure 14/53
receyfe *see* **resceyue**
rede *n.* reed, measuring rod 25/40, 50
reden *v. inf.* read 43/91; **redest** *2 sg. pr.* 20/28
redy *adj.* ready 2/76, 14/42, 52; **redyest** *superl.* 21/6
redyly *adv.* readily, quickly 24/146, 43/93, 46/68; **redily** 23/40, 27/153; **redeli** 43/41; **redely** 43/49
redynesse *n.* readiness 42/11; **redynes** 44/13
redyng(e) *vbl. n.* reading 21/119, 23/50, 44/25
refe *v. inf.* steal 42/99
reformen *v. inf.* re-create, reform 1/32, 2/28, 3/27; **reformeth** *3 sg. pr.* 7/21, 34/132, 36/56; **reformeþ** 28/12, 13, 32/7; **reformyd** *pa. p.* 7/77, 81
reformyng(e) *vbl. n.* re-creation, reformation 1/28, 2/25, 69
refreynynge *vbl. n.* restraining 38/19
rehersen *v. inf.* rehearse, recount 23/21; **reherseþ** *3 sg. pr.* 23/15
reynen *v. inf.* rain 26/62; **reynen** *pl. pr.* 26/63
reyny *adj.* rainy 26/15; **reyne** 26/47
reke *n.* smoke 42/45
reklesnes *n.* heedlessness 11/94
relef *n.* remainder, residue 40/164
religion *n.* religious (e.g. monastic) orders 18/27
religious *adj.* in religious orders 18/26, 39/91
renable *adj.* eloquent, fluent 42/20
rendyth *v. imp. 2 pl.* rend, tear to pieces 45/47
renne(n) *v. inf.* run 14/42, 23/22, 33/21; **ronnen** 39/99; **rennende** *pr. p.* 24/50
reprofynge *vbl. n.* reproving, rebuking 26/65; **reprouyng** 40/69
reproue *v. 1 sg. pr.* reprove, condemn 19/32; **reproue** *pl. imp.* 12/35; **reproued** *pa. p.* 12/21, 28, 36/13
resceyue(n) *v. inf.* receive 2/76, 4/29, 37; **resceyfe** 10/45, 46, 26/91; **resceyueth** *3 sg. pr.* 7/20, 37/27, 42/54; **resceyueþ** 25/9; **resceyfeþ** 28/73, 29/44, 48; **resceyuen** *pl. pr.* 6/20, 16/17; **resceyue** *sg. pr. subj.* 17/17; **receyfe** *sg. imp.* 23/34; **resceyued(e)** *pa. p.* 4/52, 8/22, 27; **resceyfed** 26/34, 30/189
reson *n.* reason, rational faculty, rational argument 4/10, 11/46, 51; **resons** *pl.* 39/113, 40/21, 43/93
resonable *adj.* rational, logical 1/10, 2/59, 4/64
resonably *adv.* rationally 13/30
rest(e) *n.* rest, peace, fulfillment 10/15, 11/108, 12/63
reste(n) *v. inf.* rest, seek fulfillment 12/62, 15/11, 20/76; **resteþ** *3 sg. pr.* 13/28, 34; **reste** *sg. pr. subj.* 20/77; **restende** *pr. p.* 24/129; **rested** *pa. p.* 24/156
restendly *adv.* with a sense of peace and fulfillment 24/103, 37/114, 39/46
restful *adj.* peaceful, fulfilling 24/103, 105, 128
restfully *adv.* with a sense of peace and fulfillment 21/28, 22/13, 35/3
restynge *vbl. n.* rest, fulfillment 24/66, 30/141
reuerences *n. pl.* honours 14/21
reuerencen *v. 3 pl. pr.* honour 30/84
reuerent *adj.* worthy of reverence 37/87, 44/30
reward(e) *n.*, regard 10/24, 14/49, 18/1
rewarde(n) *v. inf.* regard, reward, consider 41/102; **rewardeth** *3 sg. pr.* 45/29; **reward** *sg. subj.* 20/77; **reward** *pl. subj.* 27/47; **rewarded** *pa. p.* 19/2

rewardyng *vbl. n.* rewarding 43/130
rewle *n.* (religious) rule 19/43
rewlen *v. inf.* rule, govern 14/49; **rewlyn** 17/27; **rewlyd** *pa. p.* 13/11; **rewled** 13/13
rewlyng(e) *n.* ruling, governance 13/19, 30
riches(se) *n.* riches, wealth 14/21, 23, 27/42
right *adv.* just, very, precisely 3/25, 16/18, 20; **riȝt** 21/78, 103, 30/40; **ryȝt** 20/109, 24/65, 66
ryȝted *pa. p.* justified, corrected 28/19, 77, 32/5
rightful *adj.* just 2/65
rightfulli *adv.* justly 2/8; **riȝtfully** 45/64
ryghtwys *adj.* righteous, just 9/5, 41/103; **ryȝthwys** 16/40
ryȝtynge *n.* justification, correction 28/84, 34/70, 72
rightwysnes(se) *n.* righteousness, justice 2/10, 3/41; **rightwisnes** 2/53; **ryȝtwysnes** 26/93, 28/36, 30/40
rykles *adj.* heedless 11/10
rykleshede *n.* heedlessness 41/171; *see* **reklesnes**
rysen *v. inf.* rise 10/9, 15/9, 17/18; **ryseth** *3 sg. pr.* 46/30, 48; **rysen** *pl. pr.* 18/53, 22/12, 26/25; **ryse** *sg. imp.* 12/76; **risend** *pr. p.* 8/11
rysyng(e) *vbl. n.* impulse 8/39, 27/18; **rysynges** *pl.* 27/52, 38/22
roydely *adv.* crudely 42/115
ronnen *see* **rennen**
rote *n.* root 11/102
roted *pa. p.* rooted 29/30
rownynge *vbl. n.* whispering 46/70; **rownyngys** *pl.* 46/65, 68; **rownyngges** 46/74
rude *adj.* ignorant, crude 7/45, 30/33

S

sadly *adv.* gravely, seriousy 21/104, 27/155, 41/66
sadnes(se) *n.* gravity 36/64, 40/164
saf(e) *adj.* saved, redeemed 1/33, 10/19, 34/4; **sauf(e)** 3/22, 24, 47
safyng *vbl. n.* redemption 34/4, 43/127; **safenge** 34/81
sagw *see* **sen**
samen *adj.* together 42/23
Saraceyn(e) *n.* Saracen, pagan 6/17, 8/22; **Saraceyns** *pl.* 3/37; **Saracenys** 3/58, 34/88
satisfaccion *n.* satisfaction, recompense 2/11, 7/2, 7/30
saufe(n) *v. inf.* save, redeem 10/50, 21/105, 135; **saf** *sg. subj.* 34/60; **saufe** *pa. p.* 3/22, 24, 38; **safed** 28/55
saule *n.* soul 4/57
sauour(e) *n.* taste, delight 10/20, 23, 21/122
sauour *v. inf.* taste 24/140; **sauoureth** *3 sg. pr.* 43/62; **sauour** *sg. subj.* 21/123
sauouryng(e) *vbl. n.* tasting 39/121, 123
sauourly *adv.* with delight 27/13, 42/25, 46
Sautre *n.* Psalter 19/44; **Sawter** 42/17; **sawters** *pl.* 20/100
scape *v. inf.* escape 21/22
schadwe *n.* shadow 25/22, 24, 30/116; **schadue** 30/121
schadwynge *vbl. n.* overshadowing 30/115; **schaduynge** 30/114
schal *1 sg. pr.* shall 1/7, 17, 35; **schalt** *2 sg. pr.* 8/35, 12/88, 92; **schal** *3 sg. pr.* 2/16, 3/24, 66; **schal** *pl. pr.* 3/21, 5/24, 9/23; **schul** 8/50, 9/1, 10/18; **schulde** *1 sg. subj.*15/5, 22/31; **schuldest** *2 sg. subj.* 21/115, 22/66, 23/14; **schuld(e)** *3 sg. subj.* 1/32, 2/2, 27; **schuld(en)** *pl. subj.* 6/23, 15/13, 16/35
schame *n.* shame 10/47, 12/82, 20/26
schamed *pa. p.* shamed 45/71
schapen *v. pl. pr.* shape, fashion, create 30/72; **schope** *3 sg. pa.* 1/15; **chape** *sg. subj.* 9/12; **schapen** *pa. p.* 7/12, 31/45
schapyng *vbl. n.* shaping, creation 1/18
schapp *n.* shape, image 1/13; **schap** 1/27, 3/65, 6/4
schaply *adj.* beautiful, conformable 12/13; **schapply** 28/18
scharp(e) *adj.* sharp, severe 15/20, 37/114, 40/68; **scharper(e)** *comp.* 32/57, 40/185
scharply *adv.* acutely 42/106
schedyng *n.* separation, difference 36/26
scheld(e) *n.* shield 12/91, 37/101, 103
schent *pa. p.* humiliated 45/71
schewe(n) *v. inf.* show, present 7/24, 30, 9/23; **schew** 20/40, 34/126; **scheweþ** *3 sg. pr.* 26/7, 12, 13; **scheweth** 9/21,

26/6, 37/26; **schewyth** 43/57; **schewith** 44/57; **schew** *sg. subj.* 11/100, 30/101; **schew** *sg. imp.* 41/5; **schewende** *pr. p.* 24/129, 40/150; **schewed(e)** *pa. p.* 26/47, 29/67, 30/99

schewyng(e) *vbl. n.* showing, appearance 29/58, 35/31, 40/23; **schewyngys** *pl.* 46/68

schyne(n) *v. inf.* shine 15/11, 26/101, 103; **schyneth** *3 sg. pr.* 16/12, 41/13, 46/24; **schyneþ** 16/13, 16, 26/9; **schynend(e)** *pr. p.* 25/14, 45/26

schynyng(e) *vbl. n.*. shining, beaming 32/9, 40/20; **schynynges** *pl.* 26/88, 27/180

schort(e) *adj.* short 5/9, 14/77, 21/109; **schorter** *comp.* 20/102, 31/13; **schortest** *sup.* 21/5

schortly *adv.* briefly 21/108, 32/22, 69

schryuen *v. inf.* confess 7/24; **schryfe** 22/23; **schryuen** *pa. p.* 7/61, 10/15, 11/103; **schryfen** 22/24; **schriuen** 9/30

schrifte *n.* confession 7/56, 58, 79; **schryfte** 22/25

sclaundere *n.* slander 3/11; **sclaundre** 3/19; **sklaundre** 19/40, 27/29

seculer *n.* secular (usually but not always referring to a cleric not in religious orders) 39/91; **seculers** *pl.* 26/104

seculere *adj.* not in religious orders 18/28

seek *adj.* sick 12/53, 66; **seke** 41/54

see(n) *v. inf.* see 4/31, 8/3, 16; **sen** 15/40, 32/82, 42/118; **seyen** 40/179; **seest** *2 sg. pr.* 8/5, 21/27, 30/32; **sest** 30/29, 142; **seeth** *3 sg. pr.* 7/20, 15/53, 35/26; **seeþ** 16/20, 20/91, 24/58; **seen** *pl. pr.* 22/33, 23/4, 26/58; **seye** *sg. pa.* 24/46; **seygh** 24/46, 47, 25/37; **sagw** 25/38, 43; **seyge** *pl. pa.* 36/80; **seyen** 40/179; **seend(e)** *pr. p.* 28/45, 45/46

seenge *vbl. n.* seeing 30/164

sey(n) *inf.* say 4/39, 12/27, 52; **seyen** 41/101; **sey(e)** *1 sg. pr.* 4/21, 7/10, 9/15; **seist** *2 sg. pr.* 4/3, 18/4; **saist** 12/87; **seith** *3 sg. pr.* 1/11, 14, 2/23; **seyth** 4/34, 11/35, 49; **sey(n)** *pl. pr.* 3/37, 12/84; **seid(e)** *pa. p.* 1/1, 7/36, 74; **seyd** 8/47, 9/16, 10/78; **sayd(e)** 13/4, 34/133, 36/54; **seyende** *pr. p.* 10/40, 11/56, 20/99

seyenge *vbl. n.* saying, dictum 23/15, 33/13

seke(n) *v.* seek 14/9, 79, 18/12; **sekyn** 19/22; **seke** *1 sg. pr.* 23/40, 45/18; **sekest** *2 sg. pr.* 12/85, 30/16; **seketh** *3 sg. pr.* 14/10, 40/119, 41/23; **sekeþ** 27/131; **seken** *pl. pr.* 14/24, 15/33, 18/31; **seke** *sg. subj.* 30/15; **seke** *sg. imp.* 30/29, 33/45; **sekende** *pr. p.* 21/94

sekenes *n.* sickness 17/12, 17, 20/35; **seknes** 28/56

sekyng *vbl. n.* seeking 39/26

sekly *adj.* sickly 40/157

sele *n.* seal 43/83

self(e) *adj.* same 12/39, 26/52, 29/55

sely *adj.* blessed 28/58

semely *adj.* appropriate 41/84

sendel *n.* silken material 43/10

sensualite *n.* sensuality, faculty of sensation 11/29, 48, 54

sentence *n.* meaning 40/24, 43/105; **centence** 43/40

senteth *v. 3 sg. pr.* assents, agrees 8/47, 12/70; **sente** *pl. subj.* 11/69; **sentid** *3 sg. pa.* 2/8; **sentyd** 11/81; **sentyden** *pl. pa.* 11/73

sere *adj.* separate 14/1, 15/1, 27/102

sessen *v. inf.* cease 18/64; **sesid** *pa. p.* 4/53; **sesseid** 10/77

sette(n), *v. inf.* set, place, establish 20/92, 21/47, 95; **sette** *v. 1 sg. pr.* 21/25; **settest** *2 sg. pr.* 23/6; **setteth** *3 sg. pr.* 17/37, 36/82, 37/37; **setteþ** 19/20, 24/67, 87; **setten** *pl. pr.* 10/6, 14/24, 18/11; **sette** *sg. pa.* 15/61; **sett(e)** *sg. subj.* 18/50, 26/113, 27/31; **sette** *sg. imp.* 23/34; **sett(e)** *pa. p.* 4/11, 63, 27/24

settyng(e) *vbl. n.* placement 33/14, 15, 17

syghende *pr. p.* sighing 20/76, 41/11

syghynge *vbl. n.* sighing 29/25; **syghynges** *pl.* 41/50

syght *n.* sight 4/6, 11/75, 125; **syȝt** 27/68, 121, 164

sykernes(se) *n.* security 7/34, 27/174, 40/42

sikire *adj.* certain 3/40; **siker** 7/49, 11/91, 30/161; **sekyr** 12/50; **syker** 15/40, 16/26, 17/18; **sykerere** *comp.* 37/95

sikirly *adv.* surely 9/31; **sikerly** 21/50; **sykerly** 22/24, 37/124

synketh *v. 3 sg. pr.* sinks 40/126; **synkken** *3 pl. pr.* 40/37
syþen *conj.* since 2/29, 56, 58; **siþen** 5/24, 18/55, 35/28; **sithen** 36/51;
syþes *see* **ofte-syþes**
skant *adj.* scant 39/21
skantly *adv.* barely 39/23
skil(le) *n.* reason 2/14, 4/44, 33/52
skilful *adj.* reasonable 1/32, 7/27, 42
skilfully *adv.* reasonably 22/65, 27/55
sleygh *adj.* clever, prudent 17/41
sleyghly *adv.* slyly, stealthily 24/98
sleyghttes *n.* sleights, tricks 22/15
sleyng *vbl. n.* slaying 41/107
smert *n.* pain 38/43
smytest *v. 2 sg. pr.* strike 21/63; **smyteth** *3 sg. pr.* strikes 15/29; **smyten** *pr. pl.* 24/92; **smyte** *sg. imp.* 23/39; **smyten** *pa. p.* 26/85
sobernesse *n.* moderation 31/48
soberte *n.* moderation 41/169
softed *pa. p.* eased, soothed 41/58
son(e) *adv.* soon 6/14, 14/45, 51; **sonnere** *comp.* 17/31
sondry *adj.* sundry, various 20/41, 42, 21/14; **sondri** 20/42
sondryhed *n.* variety 46/7
sonne *n.* sun 16/13
sores *n. pl.* ills 20/39
sory *adj.* suffering, pained 41/55, 137
soth *n.* truth 24/44
soth(e) *adj.* true 2/5, 45, 15/7; **soþ** 19/26, 30/174
sothli *adv.* truly 3/62, 6/20; **sothly** 7/10, 9/14, 10/16, **soþly** 24/102; **sothlyer** *comp.* 43/135
sothfast *adj.* true 10/37, 21/68
sothfastli *adv.* truly, 7/6; **sothfastly** 8/22, 10/46, 19/29
sothfastnes(se) *n.* truth 2/50, 20/27, 86; **soþfastnes** 30/26
sotely *adv.* subtly 40/44
sotyl *adj.* subtle, characterized by wisdom or perceptivity 19/27, 26/90, 32/56; **sotel** 40/7, 41/29, 42/10; **sotil** 30/158; **sutyl** 19/25
sotylte *n.* subtlety, sagacity 33/17, 19, 34; **sotelte** 41/37, 42/116, 46/5
souereyn(e) *adj.* superior, highest 3/8, 13, 17; **souerayne** 40/163
souereyn(e) *n.* religious superior, ruler 22/58, 23/54; **soueraygne** 13/15
souereynly *adv.* most highly 34/83
souereynte *n.* superiority 14/21
sowneth *v. 3 sg. pr.* sounds, is consonant 40/115, 41/167, 42/71; **sowneþ** 21/64; **sownen** *pl. pr.* 26/64, 42/67; **sownend** *pr. p.* 42/81, 44/43; **sownyng** 40/51; **sowned** *pa. p.* 42/25, 44/1
spare *v. inf.* forbear 22/52
spared *pa. p.* sealed 41/57
spede *v. inf.* succeed, bring to a conclusion 21/54; **spede** *sg. imp.* 23/37
spedful *adj.* helpful, efficacious 7/75, 19/34, 20/9
spedy *adj.* speedy, efficacious 39/86, 40/53, 55
sperrend *pr. p.* closing 40/174; **sperred** *pa. p.* 24/44, 40/184; **spered** 32/41
spyce *n.* species, variety 37/107; **spyces** *pl.* 20/17
spyreth *v. 3 sg. pr.* blows, inspires 41/161
spoyle *v. pl. pr.* destroy, strip 21/31; **spoyle** *sg. imp.* 31/52; **spoiled** *pl. pa.* 21/106; **spoyled** *pa. p.* 21/15
spoylyng *vbl. n.* despoiling 38/41
spotted *v. pa. p.* (spiritually or morally) blemished 4/15
spottes *n.* blemishes 5/16
spouseage *n.* marriage 44/54
spryngen *v. inf.* appear, rise, dawn 25/20, 24, 26/94; **sprygeþ** *3 sg. pr.* 25/10; **spronge** *3 sg. pa.* 25/23; **spryngand** *pr. p.* 42/27; **sprongen** *pa. p.* 25/23
spurged *pa. p.* purified 29/46
stablenes(se) *n.* stability 18/22, 29/93, 41/86; **stabelnes** 30/191, 42/2; **stabilnes** 41/82
stabilly *adv.* stably 36/83
stableth *v. 3 sg. pr.* confirms 38/34
stande(n) *v. inf.* stand, remain, consist 18/15, 36; **stonden** 42/3; **standest** *2 sg. pr.* 21/116; **stondes** *3 sg.* 7/1; **stondeth** 7/44, 78, 8/4; **stondeþ** 16/19, 29/47; **standeth** 38/9; **standeþ** 20/66, 116, 21/78; **stonden** *pl. pr.* 29/14, 36/71; **standen** 18/30, 29/16; **stonde** *sg. subj.* 7/51, 27/164; **standend(e)** *pr. p.* 2/10, 3/21; **stondend(e)** 32/3, 35, 40; **stonden** *pa. p.* 1/24; **standen** 4/26
state *n.* estate, condition 4/25, 10/39, 14/22

stede *n.* position, place 33/14, 17, 40/112
stedfast *adj.* steadfast, firm 10/6, 12/91, 22/3
stedfastly *adv.* steadfastly, firmly 9/1, 12, 10/87
stele *n.* place, rung 17/38
stele *v. inf.* steal 34/125
steryng(e) *vbl. n.* stirring, prompting 8/39, 45, 11/60; **sterynges** *pl.* 5/12, 15, 8/10; **steryngges** 37/20; **steryngis** 8/37; **steringes** 4/15
steryngly *adv.* stirringly 39/115
styeth *v. 3 sg. pr.* ascends 32/86; **styend** *pr. p.* 42/45; **styed** *pa. p.* 30/143
styfly *adv.* steadfastly, resolutely 22/56, 42/96; **stifly** 12/88
stynten *v. inf.* cease 18/61
styntynge *vbl. n.* ceasing 22/57
styred *pa. p.* stirred, prompted 22/66, 46/84; **stired** 11/82
stirte *v. inf.* leap 17/36; **styrten** *pl. pr.* 46/77
stoppe(n) *v. pr. pl.* obstruct 16/10; **stopped** *pa. p.* 14/63, 16/37; **stoppid** 45/62; ~ *owt* excluded 26/117
stoppynge *vbl. n.*; ~ *owt* exclusion 24/73
straunge *adj.* distant, alien; *makeþ* ~ acts distant or without courtesy 41/44
straunged *pa. p.* estranged 40/101
stre *n.* straw 28/71, 39/42
streight *adv.* immediately 6/23
streyne *v. inf.* distrain, force 35/22; **strynen** *pr. pl.* 35/12
streketh *v. 3 sg. pr.* stretches, reaches 28/37
strenght *n.* strength 16/45, 39/83; **strenghe** 37/102
strenges *n. pl.* strings 21/61
strengthe *v. inf.* strengthen 29/70; **strengþes** *3 sg. pr.* 21/120; **strengtheþ** 30/112; **strengthe(n)** *sg. imp.* 23/42, 47; **strengthed** *pa. p.* 22/4, 51, 30/107
strengthyng *vbl. n.* strengthening, confirmation 46/43
stryf *n.* strife 11/18
stryfen *v. inf.* strive, contend 39/19; **stryfeth** *3 sg. pr.* 11/38; **stryfe** *sg. imp.* 21/32, 24/95, 27/79
stryfyng(e) *vbl. n.* contention 26/64, 37/82, 40/66
sufferable *adj.* tolerable 32/88
suffisande *pr. p.* sufficient 3/40
suffiscenge *vbl. n.* sufficiency 35/69
suffre(n) *v. inf.* allow, tolerate, abide 23/7, 26/88; **suffrest** *2 sg. pr.* 24/8; **suffreth** *3 sg. pr.* 5/16, 20/89, 23/22; **suffreþ** 28/46, 64; **suffre** *sg. imp.* 24/97; **suffrend(e)** *pr. p.* 35/39, 38/24, 45/30
sumqwat *pron.* something 2/19, 36/53; **sumwhat** 18/23, 19/15, 25/50
swart *adj.* black 12/32, 33, 35
swartnesse *n.* blackness 12/35
swete *adj.* sweet, pleasant 15/16, 23/30, 29/39; **swetter** *comp.* 43/117
sweten *v. inf.* sweat 20/98
swet(e)ly *adv.* sweetly 27/13, 38/50
swetnes(se) *n.* sweetness 28/31, 29/10, 43/107
swilk *adj.* such 5/16, 11/93, 101; **swilk a** 11/91, 12/55, 21/140; **swylk** 26/74, 35/63; **swylk a** 28/53
swyn *n.* swine 14/47, 52, 45/55
swynken *v. pl. pr.* labour 20/98
swyþe *adv.* truly; *als* ~ immediately 6/22

T

talys *n. pl.* tales 39/119
tary(en) *v. inf.* tarry, delay 21/34, 45/57; **tary(e)** *sg. imp.* 21/28, 22/69, 23/35; **taryed** *pa. p.* 27/132, 28/46, 40/169; **taried** 22/73
taryenge *vbl. n.* tarrying 6/21; **tarying(e)** 22/35, 40/38; **tarienges** *pl.* 22/2
temperaunt *adj.* temperate 39/53
tempreþ *v. 3 sg. pr.* tempers, mixes 30/109; **tempred** *pa. p.* 23/18
tente *v. inf.* attend, pay attention 27/181, 32/77, 46/28; **tenteth** *3 sg. pr.* 40/117; **tente** *sg. imp.* 21/38
thar *v. 3 sg. pr.* needs 46/59
tharl *n.* slave 43/57
theffe, theues *see* **þefe**
thenken *v. inf.* think, meditate, intend 24/3, 35/65, 68; **þenken** 14/75; **thenk** *1 sg. pr.* 31/19; **þinkest** *2 sg. pr.* think 4/9; **thenkeþ** *3 sg. pr.* 37/15; **thenketh** 35/36, 41/134, 43/6; **thenkend** *pr. p.* 20/24; *me, him, it, hem* ~ (*3 sg. pr. impers.*) it seems to me, him, it, them 35/17, 24, 37)
thenkyng(e) *n.* meditation, thought 23/

49, 35/48, 37/117; **thenkeng** 39/89; **thenkynges** *pl.* 24/29
thykke *n.* thicket 46/76
thraldam *n.* slavery, servitude 40/87
threstende *pr. p.* thirsting (for) 41/11
til *prep., conj.* to 10/15, 78, 17/22
tymeful *adj.* temporal 24/31
tyt(t)e *see* **as-tyte**
togedre *adj.* together 30/92, 39/59, 46/48; **togider** 43/14
tokne *n.* token, sign 7/31, 35, 41; **tokenes** *pl.* 26/73, 29/2, 24
tome *n.* time, opportunity 44/46
tome *adj.* empty 21/78
ton *pron.* one; *þe* ~ . . . *þe toþer* the one . . . the other 7/42
tornyng *see* **turnynge**
toþer *see* **ton**
towchen *v. inf.* touch, sense, experience, deal with 35/30; **touche(n)** 30/148, 34/47, 43/68; **towcheþ** *3 sg. pr.* 23/39; **toucheth** 24/94, 38/47, 41/50; **toucheþ** 32/53, 33/45, 38/41; **towcheth** 44/14; **touche** *sg. subj.* 24/146; **touche** *sg. imp.* 30/131, 140, 144; **towchend** *pr. p.* 39/109; **towched** *pa. p.* 42/6, 119
towchynge *vbl. n.* touching 24/11, 29/37, 35/75; **touchyng(e)** 7/6, 12/36, 25/52; **towchynges** pl. 43/109; **touchynges** 29/8
trauaille *n.* travail, travel, trouble 5/10, 17/2, 21/12; **trauail(e)** 11/7, 17/6, 18/13; **trauelle** 20/10, 29/70, 31/13
trauaile(n) *v. inf.* work, toil, trouble 14/17, 18/51, 61; **trauayllen** 14/79; **trauayleþ** *3 sg. pr.* 29/71; **trauaileþ** 25/49, 26/110, 29/75; **trauayleth** 38/19, 40/39; **trauellen** *pl. pr.* 35/47; **trauayle** *sg. subj.* 20/112; **trauellend** *pr. p.* 27/173; **trauailende** 22/39, 24/138; **trauaylend** 45/2, 32; **trauayled** *pa. p.* 10/76, 82, 27/177
trauellous *adj.* laborious 36/66
tresore *n.* treasury 46/58
trew(e) *adj.* true, genuine, right 3/12, 9/2, 20/94
trewly *adv.* truly 8/26, 26/13, 22; **trewely** 43/21
trist *n.* trust, faith 12/27, 27/149, 155
trist *v. 1 sg. pr.* trust 1/6; **trist** *sg. imp.* 27/155
troblen *v. inf.* trouble 24/151; **truble** 39/126; **trubleth** *3 sg. pr.* 11/83, 39/63; **truble** *pl. pr.* 40/37; **trobled** *pa. p.* 24/71; **trubled** 11/71, 75, 38/14
troblynge *vbl. n.* troubling, distress 19/14, 25/32, 27/10; **trubilyng** 38/40
trowe(n) *v. inf.* believe 8/5, 12, 9/1; **trowest** *2 sg. pr.* 4/8; **troweth** *3 sg. pr.* 3/39, 6/22, 8/21; **troweþ** 32/37, 43, 62; **trow(e)** *pl. pr.* 3/5, 19; **trowen** 3/6, 8, 16; **trowe** *sg. subj.* 8/20, 9/12, 10/32; **trow(e)** *sg. imp.* 10/35, 11/104, 115; **trowed** 4/49, 7/47
trowynge *vbl. n.* belief 33/75
trowth(e) *n.* belief, faith 6/19, 10/50, 52; **trowþe** 9/13, 11/132, 12/9; **trouth(e)** 3/24, 27, 32; **trouþe** 3/54, 7/50, 11/136
trumpe *n.* trumpet 42/78, 79, 81
turnynge *n.* conversion 8/14, 29, 9/3; **tornyng** 7/18
twynnynge *n.* disparity 12/42

Þ

þar(e) *see* **þer(e)**
þedir *adv.* thither, in that direction 21/9; **þedere** 21/11
þederward *adv.* in that direction 21/15, 48
þei *3 pl. pron., nom.* they 3/59, 6/23, 26; **þey** 3/6, 22, 38; **þe** 3/53, 6/25, 19/8, 26/31, 39/126, 43/99, 46/82; **hem** *compl.* 3/5, 8/39, 10/7; **here** *gen.* 3/2, 21,38; **þeyre** 3/20, **þer** 3/43, 6/19, 7/61, 16/13
þefe *n.* thief 27/113; **theffe** 45/62; **þefes** *pl.* 21/12, 105; **theues** 34/127
þer(e) *adv.* there, where 1/25, 2/45, 3/23, ; **þar(e)** 21/8, 42/49
þer-vpon *adv.* upon it 15/21
þerby *adv.* by it 16/20, 24/30, 39/43
þerfor(e) *adv.* therefore, for that 1/5, 30, 2/12
þerfro *adv.* from that 4/10, 15/32, 27/112
þerin *adv.* in it 9/26, 10/18, 16/11
þerof adv. from it, of it 10/45, 11/68, 12/50
þerto *adv.* for that purpose, to that, by it 1/33, 2/52, 74
þerwith *adv.* with it, them 11/15, 34, 23/52

þing(e) *n.* thing 2/46, 47, 48; **þinges** *pl.* 4/11, 7/47, 23/23
þinkeþ *see* **thenken**
þis(e) *adj.* and *pron. sg.* this 1/7, 8, 16; **þese** *pl.* 3/20, 36, 50; **þis** 2/13, 5/6
þo *pron.* those 3/62, 7/76, 10/26
þof-al *conj.* although 12/1; **þogh-al(le)** 40/23, 42/57
þogh *conj.* though, although 2/80, 7/28, 51; **þow** 2/18, 42, 3/38
þrede *n.* thread 16/35, 36
þrest *n.* thirst 20/26
þridde *adj.* third 5/23, 28/72; **þred** 30/66, 32/41, 61; **þredde** 5/25
þurgh *prep.* through 1/20, 2/1, 35; **þourgh** 3/2

V (U)

vggen *v. pl. pr.* feel disgust or loathing 15/21
vmbelapped *pa. p.* wrapped around 16/21, 37/117; **vmbylapped** 4/13; **vmbilapped** 16/19
vmbyden *v. inf.* abide, remain 17/20, 20/109
vmgif *v. inf.* encircle, surround 37/105
vmgo *v. 1 sg. pr.* go around 45/16
vmschadweth *v. 3 sg. pr.* shades, overshadows 36/87
vnableþ *v. 3 sg. pr.* 20/114; **vnable(n)** *pl. pr.* 15/1, 10
vnavised *pa. p.* without forethought 43/40
vnavisyly *adv.* without forethought 24/151
vnbuxumnes *n.* disobedience 26/59, 73
vnchaungeable *adj.* unalterable, immutable 21/125, 32/14, 33/19
vnchaungeably *adv.* immutably 21/138
vnconnynge *vbl. n.* ignorance, lack of knowledge 24/104, 27/7; **vnkunnynge** 10/14
vndedly *adv.* immortal 30/27
vndedlynes *n.* immortality 4/37
vndercasteth *v. 3 sg. pr.* makes subject, subordinates 37/100
vndertake *v. inf.* guarantee 21/17, 40
vndesyren *v. inf.* fail to desire 41/129
vndeuowte *adj.* without devotion 42/8
vnese *n.* discomfort 23/7
vnformed *pa. p.* uncreated 34/1, 23, 25
vniuersite *n.* totality 45/14, 46/54, 56
vnkend *adj.* lacking natural gratitude or affection 41/80
vnkyndly *adv.* unnaturally 14/11
vnkowþe *adj.* unfamiliar 29/41
vnkunnynge *see* **vnconnynge**
vnkunnende *pr. p.* unknowing, ignorant 10/82
vnmade *adj.* uncreated 33/41, 34/25, 37/40
vnmyghty *adj.* powerless, feeble 12/56, 41/22; **vnmyȝthy** 45/52
vnnayte *adj.* useless 37/51
vnneþes *adv.* hardly, with difficulty 40/169
vnordeyned *pa. p.* out of order 40/32
vnordinatly *adv.* without order 13/11
vnperceyuable *adj.* imperceptible 8/2, 23
vnperceyuably *adv.* imperceptibly 8/17, 28
vnperfyte *adj.* imperfect 7/68, 10/65
vnpossible *adj.* impossible 38/44, 46
vnresonabely *adv.* unreasonably 14/12, 35
vnresonable *adj.* unreasonable 20/90, 34/84
vnrestful *adj.* disturbed, troubled 27/72, 38/15
vnsauourye *adj.* without pleasurable affect 39/108, 41/21, 42/9
vnsauourly *adv.* without pleasure 32/17
vnschapli *adj.* misshapen, deformed 3/54
vnseable *adj.* invisible 8/32, 25/8, 32/18
vnseably *adv.* invisibly 11/118, 24/15, 30/176
vnsee *v. inf.* not see 41/27
vnskilful *adj.* unreasonable 11/16, 24, 68
vnskilfully *adv.* unreasonably 13/11, 27/54, 38/11
vnspekable *adj.* inexpressible 36/63, 41/60, 44/36
vnstablenes *n.* inconstancy 26/70
vnto *prep.* until 2/17, 3/23, 56
vntrowe *v. 3 sg. pr.* fail to believe 32/61
vntrowth(e) *n.* disbelief, lack of faith 3/20, 21, 6/25
vnwarly *adv.* unawares 11/76, 29/89
vnwarly *adj.* unexpected 18/41
vnwirschepe *n.* insult 2/15
vnwurchipd *pa. p.* unworshipped 14/14
vnwurthi *adj.* unworthy 22/30, 27/114
vpbraydyng *vbl. n.* reproach 12/83, 40/68

vttere *adj.* outward 24/45
vtterwarde *adv.* outwards 25/44

V

veyn *adj.* vain, unprofitable 11/26, 30, 19/38; *in* ~ to no purpose 11/71
veynes *n.* veins 46/65, 68
veyn-glorie *n.* vainglory, inordinate or unwarranted pride 14/16, 26/80
veynly *adv.* inordinately, inappropriately 24/113
venged *pa. p.* avenged 38/58
venials *adj. subs. pl.* venial sins 11/96, 13/35
venym *n.* poison 23/17
venymous *adj.* poisonous 41/69
verrey *adj.* true 7/28, 54, 21/44
vertu(e) *n.* virtue, power 2/72, 3/2, 4; **vertus** *pl.* 13/25, 20/21
vicious(e) *adj.* characterized by vice 9/10, 11/54
visitacyon *n.* appearance, apparition 26/76
vysyte *v. inf.* visit (by divine presence or gift) 21/139; **vysyteþ** *3 sg. pr.* 26/40; **vysyteth** 43/140; **visiteth** 41/49; **visited** *pa. p.* 30/185
visityng *vbl. n.* visitation 40/25, 41/62
vowcheþ-sauf(e) *v. 3 sg. pr.* confers upon, bestows 24/9, 29/80; **voucheþ-saufe** 32/8; **vowcheth-safe** 41/116

W

waken *v. inf.* wake, awaken, remain awake, keep vigil 20/107, 21/147, 40/173; **waketh** *3 sg. pr.* 40/167, 170; **wakende** *pr. p.* 40/179
waker(e) *adj.* wakeful 40/19, 165, 172
wakyng(e) *vbl. n.* waking 15/17, 20/74, 40/181
wal *n.* wall, barrier 27/113, 32/51, 63
wantyng *vbl. n.* lack 41/43
waraunt *n.* warrant, guarantee 7/31, 35, 42
warde *n.* guardianship 37/101
ware *adj.* wary, careful 11/12, 22/7, 41/163
ware *see* **ben**
wasten *v. inf.* consume 26/84; **wasteþ** *3 sg. pr.* 26/79, 33/61, 62; **wasteth** 42/36; **wastende** *pr. p.* 33/59; **wasted** *pa. p.* 33/62
waxen *v. inf.* grow, become 19/51, 22/33; **wexen** 18/66, 22/34, 32/74; **waxeþ** *3 sg. pr.* 14/33
weyk *adj.* weak 12/54, 15/24, 41/21
weyken *v. inf.* weaken 27/177; **weykeþ** *3 sg. pr.* weakens 15/28
weykly *adv.* weakly 38/18
weyknes *n.* weakness 11/9, 16/45, 29,34
wel(e) *adv.* well, properly, certainly, very 2/40, 3/52, 4/9
welth(e) *n.* wealth 15/62, 27/137,
wemme *n.* blemish, stain 2/61
weneth *v. 3 sg. pr.* supposes 15/51; **weneþ** 30/36; **wene(n)** *pl. pr.* 3/39, 10/34, 26/30; **wene** *sg. subj.* 15/52; **wenend(e)** *pr. p.* 11/93, 27/50
werd *n.* world 3/56, 10/47, 82; **werld** 3/23, 6/23, 12/48
werdly *adj.* worldly, temporal, material 5/15, 10/65, 11/103; **werdli** 8/11, 22/10; **werldly** 27/42, 34/138, 39/12
were *n.* confusion 11/78; **weris** *pl.* 11/112
weryed *pa. p.* cursed 24/48, 49, 50
werynes *n.* weariness 29/72
werynge *vbl. n.* wearing 20/74
werk(e) *n.* work, activity11/21, 17/19, 19/16; **wirk** 21/118; **werkes** *pl.* 9/12, 12/39, 13/32; **werkys** 19/50, 20/109, 21/113
werke(n) *v. inf.* work, operate 20/58, 89; **werkyn** 24/8; **werketh** *3 sg. pr.* 14/12; **werkeþ** 20/91, 24/10, 28/14; **wirketh** 8/30, 35/71, 75; **werke** *sg. subj.* 20/61; **werkend** *pr. p.* 20/25
werkyng(e) *vbl. n.* operation, working 2/36, 5/22, 8/18; **wirkyng** 8/23
wesschen *pa. p.* washed 40/33
wexen *see* **waxen**
wey(e) *n.* way, road 3/44, 7/69, 19/17
whare *adv.* where 41/87
whareby *adv.* by which 44/1
whareto *adv.* whereto, for what purpose 20/106, 22/27; **wharto** 20/106
whedre *adv.* whither, to which 21/111; **whedere** 41/162
whederso *adv.* wheresoever 24/16, 44/10
whereso *adv.* wheresoever 26/69, 28/7
wherþurgh *conj.* on account of which 27/43, 54
wheþer *conj.* whether 4/67, 11/78, 81

whi, why *see* **qwhi**
whyl *conj.* while 18/36
whyle *n.* while, time 11/77, 17/20, 27
whyles *adv. and conj.* while 9/20, 11/2, 40/94; **whyls** 12/1, 40/143; **whylis** 41/141, 42/6, 126
whilk, wilk *see* **qwhilk(e)**
whyrland *pr. p.* whirling, turning 44/13
whoso *pron.* whoever 9/12, 20/7, 93
wiht *prep.* with 42/96
wil(l) *n.* will, desire 2/44, 4/63, 9/3; **willes** *pl.* 10/9, 12
wil *v. 1 sg. pr.* desire, wish, intend 1/5, 16/53, 18/57; **wilt** *2 sg. pr.* 1/8, 3/61, 9/24; **wil** *3 sg. pr.* 2/74, 76, 10/44; **wilen** *pr. pl.* 7/70, 15/12, 22/7; **wil** 7/70, 14/45, 15/31; **wold** *1 sg. subj.* 15/3, 19/34, 24/139; **woldest** *2 sg. subj.* 21/37, 96, 23/18; **wold(e)** *3 sg. subj.* 3/9, 21/8, 17; **wolde(n)** *pl. subj.* 3/43, 14/75, 15/16; **wuld** 4/49, 51, 63; **wld(e)** 4/51, 34/33
wyles *n.* wiles, tricks 22/15
wilful *adj.* voluntary 2/49, 19/1, 39
wilfully *adv.* willingly, deliberately 2/57, 5/13, 6/6
wyn *n.* wine 29/44, 45, 46
wynnynge *n.* profit; *of* ~ gainful 19/29
wyssen *v. inf.* guide, teach 26/111
wyssyng *vbl. n.* guidance 46/84
wyte(n) *v. inf.* know 1/8, 3/61, 9/24; **wote** *1 sg. pr.* 28/6, 29/27, 32/75; **wyte** *2 sg. pr.* 41/168; **wote** *3 sg. pr.* 32/44, 36/63, 37/125; **wyten** *pl. pr.* 10/56, 11/73, 15/13; **witen** 27/14, 15, 46/19; **wete** 45/66; **wist(e)** *1 sg. pa.* 27/141, 143; **wyte** *sg. imp.* 24/100, 25/31, 30/53; **wite** 42/109
wyten *v. inf.* accuse, reproach 15/6
wytendly *adv.* knowingly 9/28
withdragwe *v. imp.* depart, withdraw 30/22
withouten-forth *adv.* outside 38/40
with-þi *conj.* on condition 23/8
witte *n.* mind, faculty of thought 11/95, 14/47, 18/29; **wytte** 19/25, 26/54, 31/11; **wyt** 43/38; **wittes** *pl.* senses 24/138, 31/36, 39/2; **wyttes** 13/10, 18/61, 27/11; **wittis** 43/24
wittyly *adv.* wisely 36/44
wld *see* **wil**
wold *see* **wil**
wonder *n.* wonder, marvel 18/5, 25/45, 28/41; **wondre** 11/74, 18/18,
wonder(e) *adv.* wondrously, marvellously 2/7, 15/24, 19/11
wonderli *adv.* wondrously 1/19; **wonderly** 40/128, 156, 43/17
wondren *v. inf.* wonder (at) 39/97, 42/138; **wondres** *2 sg. pr.* 34/6; **wondreþ** *3 sg. pr.* 32/27; **wondreth** *pl. imp.* 12/16; **wondrend** *pr. p.* 44/43
wone(n) *v. inf.* reside, dwell 25/18, 24, 27/148; **woneth** *3 sg. pr.* 12/25; **wonende** *pr. p.* 25/22
wote *see* **wyten**
wowere *n.* wooer, suitor 44/55
wrecchednes(se) *n.* wretchedness, misery 1/24, 11/97, 41/37
wrecched(e) *adj.* miserable 1/23, 7/75, 11/44
wrecchedly *adv.* miserably 4/65, 14/27, 15/22
wreketh *v. 3 sg. pr.* avenges 14/34; **wroken** *pa. p.* 14/33
Wriȝt *n.* Writ, Scripture 43/40
wroth(e) *adj.* wroth, wrathful 14/33, 22/59, 23/5
wurchip(e) *n.* worship, honour 2/51, 3/65, 8/40; **wurschip** 27/94; **wurschepe** 41/14; **wurschipes** 27/89
wurchipe *v. inf.* worship, honour 23/13, 30/81; **wurchiped** *v. pa. p.* worshiped, honoured 27/44, 30/139
wurmod *n.* wormwood 28/71
wurthi *adj.* worthy 2/58, 5/8, 21/83, **wurthy** 14/5, 22/27, 30/68; **wurthyer(e)** *comp.* 30/4, 99; **wurthier** 42/4; **wurthiest** 36/1, 9, 46/50
wurthines(se) 3/65, 14/28; **wurthynes** 14/4, 21/68, 30/31

Y

ypocrysye *n.* hypocrisy 44/22; **ypocrysyes** *pl.* 26/116
ypocryte *n.* hypocrite 37/84; **ypocrytes** *pl.* 38/62

INDEX OF QUOTATIONS AND ALLUSIONS

A. SCRIPTURAL

Hilton quotes the Latin text of Scripture 103 times in *Scale* II, usually providing his own literal translation and an explanatory gloss immediately afterwards. He also alludes to persons and events described in the Bible, such as the prayer of the Canaanite woman for her daughter in Matthew 15: 22–8. Other scriptural texts that are adduced in the Explanatory Notes as underlying Hilton's argument are also listed here. References in the scriptural index are to the first line of the lemma in *Scale* II, cited by chapter and line number.

B. OTHER SOURCES

Hilton does not name any non-scriptural sources in *Scale* II. The following have been adduced as sources or parallels to his thought and expression in the Explanatory Notes. Citations are by the forms of names most commonly used in present-day scholarship in English.